A
DICTIONARY OF
CONTEMPORARY
AMERICAN
USAGE

A
DICTIONARY OF
CONTEMPORARY
AMERICAN
USAGE

by BERGEN EVANS
and CORNELIA EVANS

RANDOM HOUSE · NEW YORK

RN. RA/HE

© Copyright, 1957, by Bergen Evans and Cornelia Evans

All rights reserved under International and Pan-American
Copyright Conventions

Published in New York by Random House, Inc., and
simultaneously in Toronto, Canada by Random House
of Canada Limited.

Library of Congress Catalog Card Number: 57-5379

Fourteenth Printing

PRINTED IN THE UNITED STATES OF AMERICA

PREFACE

When we speak or write we want to be understood and respected. We want to convey our meaning and we want to do it in a way that will command admiration. To accomplish these ends we must know the meanings of words, their specific meanings and their connotations, implications and overtones, and we must know how to combine words effectively into sentences.

A dictionary can help us to understand the meaning of a word. But the only way to understand a word fully is to see it in use in as many contexts as possible. This means that anyone who wants to improve his vocabulary must read a great deal and must make sure that he understands what he reads. There is no short cut to this kind of knowledge. If a man thinks that *noisome* and *noisy* are synonyms, if he uses *focus* and *nexus* interchangeably, if he sees no difference between *refute* and *deny* and if he assumes that *disinterested* means *uninterested,* he will not say what he means. Indeed, he may even say the exact opposite of what he means.

Respectable English is a much simpler matter. It means the kind of English that is used by the most respected people, the sort of English that will make readers or listeners regard you as an educated person.

Doubts about what is respectable English and what is not usually involve questions of grammar. There are some grammatical constructions, such as *that there dog* and *he ain't come yet,* that are perfectly intelligible but are not standard English. Such expressions are used by people who are not interested in "book learning." They are not used by educated people and hence are regarded as "incorrect" and serve as the mark of a class. There is nothing wrong about using them, but in a country such as ours where for a generation almost everybody has had at least a high school education or its equivalent few people are willing to use expressions that are not generally approved as "correct."

A man usually thinks about his work in the language that his co-workers use. Turns of speech that may have been natural to a statistician when he was a boy on a farm simply do not come to his mind when he is talking about statistics. Anybody whose work requires intellectual training—and this includes everybody whose work involves any amount of writing—speaks standard English naturally and inevitably, with possibly a few insignificant variations.

But many people who speak well write ungrammatical sentences. There seems to be some demon that numbs their fingers when they take hold of a pen, a specter called "grammar" which they know they never understood in school and which rises to fill them with paralyzing uncertainty whenever they stop to think.

The only way to exorcise this demon is to state some of the fundamental facts of language. And one of the most fundamental is that language changes constantly. People living in the United States in the middle of the twentieth century do not speak the English of Chaucer or of Shakespeare. They don't even speak the English of

Woodrow Wilson. The meanings of words change and the ways in which words are used in sentences change. *Silly* once meant "holy," *fond* meant "foolish," *beam* meant "tree" and *tree* meant "beam," and so on through many thousands of words. The pronoun *you* could once be used with a singular verb form, as in *Was you ever in Baltimore?* Today we must say *were you.* The word *news* could once be used as a plural, as in *These news were suddenly spread throughout the city.* Today we must treat it as a singular and say *This news was spread.*

Since language changes this much, no one can say how a word "ought" to be used. The best that anyone can do is to say how it *is* being used, and this is what a grammar should tell us. It should give us information on what is currently accepted as good English, bringing together as many details as possible under a few general rules or principles, so that it will be easier for us to remember them.

The older grammars, by some one of which almost every adult today was bewildered in his school days, were very full of the spirit of what "ought" to be done and drew the sanction of their "oughts" from logic rather than from what people actually said. Thus in such a sentence as *There is an apple and a pear in the basket* most school grammars up until a generation ago would have said that one "ought" to use *are* and not *is.* And the schoolchildren (some of whom later became schoolteachers) docilely accepted the pronouncement. However the child would have heard the minister, the doctor, and even the schoolteacher out of school, say *is,* and since he couldn't bring himself to say that the book was wrong in school or these eminent people wrong out of school, he would probably conclude that he didn't "understand" grammar. Unfortunate as that conclusion might have been, it was at least intelligent and preferable to attempting all the rest of his life to speak and write in the unreal manner recommended by the textbook.

The first grammars published in English were not intended to teach English but to get a child ready for the study of Latin. They were simplified Latin grammars with English illustrations. Of course they were incomprehensible, though they probably made Latin easier when the child got to it. Later, when Latin was no longer an important part of education, the schools continued to use books of this kind on the theory that they taught "superior" English, that is, English that resembled Latin.

But the rules of Latin grammar require constructions that are absurd and affected in English, totally unsubstantiated by English usage. And they often condemn constructions that the greatest writers of English use freely. The common man, even the common educated man, has had no desire to be "superior" in some mysterious way and these Latin rules have had very little effect on the way English is actually used by educated adults. But the rules have had this effect, that millions of adults believe that what seems natural to them is probably wrong.

In analyzing the language the old-fashioned textbooks use concepts, or terms, that are valid when applied to Latin but are almost meaningless when applied to an uninflected language such as modern English. The difference between a noun and an adjective, or between an adjective and an adverb, for example, is plain in Latin but not in English. No grammar can explain these differences in English without becoming too involved for an elementary student. Instead of explaining them, therefore, the authors often write as if no explanation were needed, as if the differences were obvious to all but the dullest. And most of us succumb to this. We get tired of feeling stupid and decide, for instance, that an adverb ends in *-ly,* such as *really,* and an adjective doesn't, such as *real.* This leads us to feel uneasy at *Swing low, sweet chariot,* to wonder how road commissioners can be so illiterate as to urge us to *drive slow,* and to get all hot and bothered in fifty useless ways. The child who leaves school knowing that he doesn't know the difference between an adjective and an adverb is unusually strong minded and lucky.

For the last fifty years, however, certain grammarians have been making a scientific study of English. They have been finding out how English is really used by different groups of people, instead of theorizing about how it might be used or dogmatizing about how it ought to be used. The investigations of these men have shown us which grammatical forms are used by educated people and which are not. They make it possible to define and analyze what is standard speech and what is not.

They show us that standard English allows a certain amount of variation. That is, there is often more than one acceptable way of using the same words. The most obvious variations are geographical. Some words are used differently in different parts of the country, but each use is respectable in its own locality. Some variations are peculiar to a trade or profession (such as the medical use of *indicate*). These are as respectable as the group that uses them but they are likely to be unintelligible to the general public. When they are used solely to mark a difference, to give an esoteric flavor, they constitute a jargon.

There are also differences between formal and informal English. Formal English is solemn and precise. It dots all the i's and crosses all the t's. Informal or colloquial English is more sprightly and leaves more to the imagination. Forty years ago it was considered courteous to use formal English in speaking to strangers, implying they were solemn and important people. Today it is considered more flattering to address strangers as if they were one's intimate friends. This is a polite lie, of course; but it is today's good manners. Modern usage encourages informality wherever possible and reserves formality for very few occasions.

This dictionary is intended as a reference book on current English in the United States. It is designed for people who speak standard English but are uncertain about some details. It attempts to list the questions that most people ask, or should ask, about what is now good practice and to give the best answers available. It also contains a full discussion of English grammar, a discussion which does not assume that the student can already read and write Latin.

If any reader wants to make a systematic study of English grammar he should begin with the entry *parts of speech* and follow through all the cross references. Some of these may prove difficult, but no one needs to study it who is not interested. One can use good English without understanding the principles behind it just as one can drive a car without understanding mechanics.

The individual word entries do not assume that the reader is interested in grammatical principles. They assume that he wants the answer to a specific question in the least possible time. The information in them has been drawn chiefly from the *Oxford English Dictionary,* the seven-volume English grammar of Otto Jespersen, and the works of Charles Fries. This has been supplemented by information from *A Dictionary of American English,* edited by Sir William Craigie and James Hulbert, *A Dictionary of Americanisms,* by Mitford M. Mathews, *The American Language,* with its two supplements, by H. L. Mencken, and *The American College Dictionary.* Further information has been drawn from articles appearing in *American Speech* over the past twenty years and from the writings of George O. Curme, John Lesslie Hall, Robert A. Hall, Jr., Sterling A. Leonard, Albert H. Marckwardt, Robert C. Pooley, Thomas Pyles, and others. Some of the statements concerning differences in British and American usage are based on the writings of H. W. Fowler, Eric Partridge, Sir Alan Herbert, Ivor Brown, Sir Ernest Gowers and H. W. Horwill.

The authors want to thank George Ellison, Sarah Bekker, Bernice Levin, Irene Le Compte and James K. Robinson for help in assembling and organizing this material. They also want to thank Esther Sheldon for many helpful comments, Jess Stein and Leonore C. Hauck for the contributions they made in editing this work, and Joseph M. Bernstein for his thoughtful proof-reading.

Throughout the book the authors have tried to present the facts about current usage fairly and accurately. They are aware that there is more than one kind of English. As children, living in the north of England, they spoke a dialect that was in many ways nearer to the English of Chaucer than to that of the *New York Times*. They have, therefore, a personal affection for forms that are older than our current literary forms. As adults they have both had occasion, over many years, to read a great deal of manuscript English, the unedited writings of college students and adults working in various professions. They are therefore familiar with current tendencies in English. They hope that this wide acquaintance with the language has kept them from giving too much weight to their personal preferences. But they have a personal bias, and this should be stated clearly. The authors are prejudiced in favor of literary forms. They prefer the forms used by the great writers of English to forms found only in technical journals. This means that if they list a non-literary form as acceptable there is conclusive evidence that it is accepted. But they may have listed some forms as questionable that are standard in some areas or professions. The reader must decide these things for himself. To anyone who has a serious interest in the language that he hears and uses, the authors would like to say, in the words of Socrates, "Agree with me if I seem to speak the truth."

A
DICTIONARY OF
CONTEMPORARY
AMERICAN
USAGE

To Aunt Cornelia

A

a and **an** are two forms of the same word. The form *an* is used before a vowel sound, as in *an umbrella, an honest man.* The form *a* is used before a consonant sound, as in *a European, a one-horse town, a historical novel, a hotel.* The form *a* should be used before an *h* that is pronounced, as in *history* and *hotel.* Formerly these *h* sounds were not pronounced and *an historical novel, an hotel,* were as natural as *an honorable man, an hour, an heiress.* This is no longer true and these archaic *an*'s, familiar from English literature, should not be repeated in modern writing.

A, an, and *any* are all derived from the same source. *A* (or *an*) is called the indefinite article. Actually, it is used to indicate a definite but unspecified individual, as in *a man in our town, a library book.* In this sense the individual may represent the type, or the entire class, as in *a cat has nine lives.* When we wish to refer indefinitely **to** a single person or thing we say *any,* as in *any man in our town, any library book. A* may also be used to mean *one,* as in *wait a minute* and *in a day or two.* In its first sense, *a* may be used before the word *one,* as in *we did not find a one.* This is acceptable English whenever there is good reason to stress the idea of oneness. But some people consider the construction improper, or unreasonable, and claim that it is better to say *a single one.* It is hard to see why it should be wrong to express the idea of unity twice (*a, one*) and right to do so three times (*a, single, one*).

The word *a* (or *an*) stands before other qualifying words, as in *a very large sum of money,* except words or phrases which indicate an extreme degree of something. These are adverbial phrases and precede the word *a,* as in *so very large a sum of money* and *too small a sum of money.*

abandoned; depraved; vicious. An *abandoned* person—when the word is used with moral implications—is one who has given himself up, without further concern for his reputation or welfare, **to** immoral courses, one hopelessly sunk in wickedness and the indulgence of his appetites (*an abandoned woman, hardened in sin*). It usually suggests a passive acceptance of immorality (*Is he so abandoned as to feel no shame at such an accusation?*). A *depraved* person is one so dis-

torted in character, so vitiated, debased, and corrupt that he seeks out evil (*These dens are the haunts of the worst and most depraved men in the city*). When applied to character, as it often is, it again suggests a wilful corruption, springing from a distorted or perverted nature (*Only a depraved taste could regard these daubs as art*). A *vicious* person is addicted to vice, malignant and aggressive in his wickedness, violent and dangerous (*Drunkenness does not make men vicious, but it shows those who are to be so*).

abbreviations are shortened or contracted forms of words or phrases, used as a symbol of the whole. They are designed for the eye as acronyms are designed for the ear. In written language the abbreviation has always been valuable, for scribes must save time and space whether they write on papyrus, paper or stone. The most famous abbreviation of antiquity, perhaps of all time, was SPQR—*Senatus Populusque Romanus*—the great insigne of Rome.

In general, a reader coming across an abbreviation visualizes or sounds the whole word represented by it, as in *Dr., Co., mfg., cf., pres.* and so on. Many abbreviations, however, have been taken over into speech, probably, as a rule, when the original word or phrase was cumbersome, as in *C.O., DP, IQ, S.R.O., R.S.V.P., G.A.R., D.A.R.,* and the like. This tendency to enunciate the abbreviation, rather than the full word or phrase for which it stands, is increasing. College students talk of *math, lit, poly sci* and *econ* courses without any feeling of being breezy or slangy. What was once the province of vulgar speech and the literary domain of such writers as Ring Lardner and S. J. Perelman now freely serves the popular press where the full forms of *V.I.P., M.C.* (often written *emcee*), *G.I.,* and scores of other abbreviations would now seem very strange.

Some names and terms are so unpronounceable that abbreviations are always used in both writing and speaking. Indeed the original forms, so far as the general public is concerned, are completely unknown: *DDT* for dichlorodiphenyl-trichloroethane, *ACTH* for adrenocorticotropic hormone, *KLM* for the Dutch airline Koninklijke Luchtvaart Maat-schaapij voor Nederland en Kolonien N.V.

Probably the commonest type of abbreviation today, and one that seems to be growing ever more common, consists of the initials of the words of a name or a phrase: *PTA, R.F.D., r.p.m., p.o.w.* The government and the army have contributed many of these new abbreviations. There is no general rule, but there is a tendency, which in time may establish a rule, to omit periods in the names of government agencies but to include them in other cases. This would at least allow us to distinguish *AAA* (Agricultural Adjustment Administration) from *A.A.A.* (American Automobile Association).

Another common form of abbreviation is the shortening of words: *capt., diam., treas.* In many instances the shortened forms have been taken over into the vernacular and occasionally even into standard usage. *Ad,* especially for a short advertisement (as *a want ad*), must now be accepted as standard, as also must *vet* for *veterinary,* though it is still colloquial for *veteran* except in certain combined forms like *Amvets. Co-op* is now so universally employed that it would be pedantic to insist on *co-operative.*

Some abbreviations are formed by contraction: *supt., patd., atty.* or by the retention of only the key consonants: *blvd., hdqrs., tsp.*

Latin phrases are frequently abbreviated, and in the same ways that English words and phrases are abbreviated. Some appear only as initials: *c., e.g. Q.E.D.,* by the way, is always capitalized. Some are shortened: *id., et al., cet. par., aet.* Some are contracted: *cf., pxt. Vox pop* is an example of a shortened Latin phrase that has crept into common English speech. *Ad libitum* ("at pleasure," that is, at the discretion of the performer) was originally primarily applied to music. As an abbreviation—*ad lib.*—it moved over into the drama, took on broader connotations and is now accepted as a noun, verb, or adjective.

Here are some abbreviations which fall outside the ordinary patterns:

G.I.—The initials of a phrase ("government issue") which have taken on a meaning different from the original term but wryly related to it.

A1—Strictly speaking not an abbreviation, since it is not a shortening of anything but simply a symbol.

IOU—A phrase put in terms of initials, although they are not literally the initials of the words they represent. This is one abbreviation which is based on sound rather than on sight.

There is a euphemistic use of abbreviation—in such expressions as *g.d.* and *s.o.b.*—which seeks to make certain phrases not ordinarily used in polite conversation less offensive. To some ears, however, the abbreviation is an added offense, heaping timidity or affected gentility on indecency or profanity.

The ultimate in abbreviation—the abbreviation of an abbreviation—is furnished by CSCN/CHSA which is an abbreviation of COMSUBCOMNELM/COMHEDSUPPACT which is an abbreviation of Commander, Subordinate Command, U. S. Naval Forces Eastern Atlantic and Mediterranean, Commander, Headquarters Support Activities.

abdomen. See **belly.**

aberration means wandering from the usual way or from the normal course. There are various technical uses of the word in biology, optics, and other sciences, but the most common popular use is in the phrase *an aberration of the mind,* where it means a departure from a sound mental state. It does not mean mere absent-mindedness. It should always be used with a qualifying adjective or prepositional phrase descriptive of the nature of the aberration.

abhor. See **hate.**

abide. The past tense is *abided* or *abode.* The participle is also *abided* or *abode.*

Abode is preferred to *abided* when the word means dwelled, as in *he abode in Boston almost all of his life.* When the word is used in its broader meaning *abided* is preferred, as in *he abided by his promise.* But both forms can be used in both senses.

Abide is heavyweight for *remain* or *stay.* It is properly used in the great hymn "Abide With Me." It is no lighter when used in the sense of *live* or *dwell.* In all of these uses it retains an obsolescent, medieval quality.

This very quality, however, gives the note of solemnity that certain occasions deserve. When it means to stand by a person, or one's word, or to await the consequences of some momentous act (*Abide the event. Others abide the question;/Thou art free*), the very quality which makes it improper for lesser uses makes it valuable. Nations *abide* by the terms of a treaty.

The use of the phrase *can't abide* to express dislike (*I can't abide that man!*) is commonly disparaged. But it has force and flavor. Its use to describe situations, or more often persons, that are intolerable and not to be endured strikes the proper note of vehemence that certain old English words and words associated with Scripture convey.

ability; capacity. *Ability* is the power to do, *capacity* is the power to receive. Ability can be acquired; capacity is innate. Ability is improved by exercise; capacity requires no exercise. A pump has an ability to pump a certain amount of fluid. A tank has the capacity to hold a certain amount. A boxer has the ability to hit, the capacity to take punishment.

abject apology. When Milton spoke of the fallen angels rolling in the fires of hell *thick bestrown, abject and lost,* he was using *abject* in its original sense of cast out or rejected. In the hackneyed phrase *an abject apology* it is not the apology that is abject but the one who is making the apology. But since there is something contemptible in one who abases himself too much, a feeling perhaps that he is sacrificing his dignity in the hope of escaping a possible punishment, *abject* in this phrase, as it reflects on the one apologizing, has come to have a connotation of despicable. It is an overworked phrase and should be used sparingly.

abject poverty is poverty so severe or so prolonged that the sufferer from it feels cast out from human society. Here, again, there is a feeling that human dignity has been impaired and there is something slightly despicable in the excess of humility exhibited. *Dire poverty* (from the Latin *dirus*, terrible) is poverty so extreme that it is terrible to behold.

Both phrases have been weakened by repetition and should be used only when they convey the exact meaning that the speaker or writer desires to express.

abjure and **adjure** belong, with *quiddities* and *quillets*, to the solemnity of the legal brief and the juridical charge. *Abjure*, virtually undigested from the Latin *abjurare*, means to solemnly forswear, to renounce, to repudiate. The prefix *ab-* (as in *absent, abdicate*, etc.) negates an oath that has been sworn.

Conversely, the prefix *ad-* affirms the act of swearing (as it affirms ministration in *administration* and monition in *admonition*) in *adjure*, which means to command solemnly, under oath or the threat of a curse.

Neither word is to be used lightly, and it is paramount that their similarity of sound should not confuse their completely opposite meanings.

ablative case. The ablative is a Latin case used principally to show that a noun or pronoun stands in some qualifying relation to the verb. In modern English the ablative relationships are shown principally by prepositions. Old English did not have an ablative and for this reason the word is not used in English grammars as often as the other Latin case names.

ablution; washing. *Ablutions* are performed in a church; *washing* is done in a sink or bathroom. *Ablution* now refers exclusively to the use of water for cleansing in religious rites, the ceremonial bathing of the body or the rinsing of sacred vessels. To describe anyone's washing of his hands and face as *performing his ablutions* is to be ponderously jocular and slightly sacrilegious.

Keats, in the last poem that he wrote, used the word correctly when he spoke of *the moving waters at their priestlike task/ Of pure ablution round earth's human shores.*

abnormal; subnormal; supernormal. *Abnormal*, in the strictest sense, denotes any deviation from the normal. *An abnormally pretty girl* or *an abnormally pleasant day* would certainly be understood. In general, however, the deviation is towards imperfection. *Abnormal driving conditions* will not mean exceptional visibility but, rather, fog, ice, irregular pavement or something of that sort. *Abnormal behavior* may be exceptional, but it is never exemplary. College courses in *Abnormal Psychology* devote little time to the exceptionally brilliant or the unusually happy.

Subnormal denotes things below the average (*Subnormal intelligence is characteristic of morons. Hibernating animals have subnormal temperatures*). A chilly day in Florida or southern California is certain to be described as *subnormal*.

Supernormal is not often used—and just as well, for it is awkward. However, it could be used to describe superior intelligence, superhuman capabilities, and supernatural occurrences. Certain visionaries may be said to have had supernormal powers of sight or hearing. It might be insisted that a fever is a supernormal temperature, but here *abnormal*, with its suggestion of an undesirable deviation, is used.

aboard (on board), **to board** and **boarding** were originally sea terms. In America, where the tradition of the sea and respect for its terms (except in the Navy where the insistent retention of nautical terms in land stations often seems absurd to the landlubber) were not as strong as they were in England, the term was transferred to railroad trains. Where our conductor calls "All aboard!" the English stationmaster says, "Take your seats, please!"

The airplane has taken over many nautical terms, and being welcomed aboard by the stewardess has a mildly adventurous sound without seeming affected. The wings and the motors have to be tersely designated and *port* and *starboard, inboard* and *outboard* seem natural and sensible. (It is a nice illustration of the development of language that although *motor* and *engine* are synonymous in popular usage, an *outboard motor* and an *outboard engine* are wholly different things.)

abode. An *abode* was formerly merely a waiting or an abiding (*Through his body his sword glode,/ Dead he fell, without abode*). Later it came to mean the place in which the abiding was done. Milton calls Paradise *Adam's abode*. The body was often called the abode of the spirit. But to apply the word today to an ordinary house is affectation or heavy jocularity. See **abide**.

abominate. This word may be followed by the *-ing* form of a verb, as in *I abominate dancing*, but not by an infinitive, as in *I abominate to dance*. The construction with the infinitive is not standard.

about. The basic meaning of *about* is around or circling. It may mean physically around, as in *there are spies about* and *he walked about the garden*, or it may mean approximately, as in *there are about a hundred people*. A compound verb including *about* is always weaker or vaguer than the original verb, as *I know him* and *I know about him, I had forgotten that* and *I had forgotten about that*. *About* may be followed by the *-ing* form of a verb, as in *he thought about leaving*, or by an infinitive, as in *he was about to leave*. When followed by an infinitive, *about* means on the point of.

The compound *at about*, as in *he arrived at about 3 o'clock*, is condemned by some grammarians on the grounds that it is redundant. This is not a reasonable claim. *At* is frequently followed by words showing degree, as in *at almost, at nearly, at exactly*, and there is no reason why *about* should not be used in the same way. *About* is used after a great many other prepositions, as in *for about an hour, in about a week, by about Christmas*, and the compound *at about* is sometimes required, as in *they sold at about $3 a share*. It is true that in expressions of time *about* can be used without a preposition, as in *he arrived about 3 o'clock*. But there is no reason why anyone should feel compelled to use it in this way. *At about 3 o'clock* is well established, reputable English.

above is used in written English to mean mentioned earlier, as in *the above examples*. Some grammarians object to *the above examples* on the grounds that *above* is an adverb and should not stand immediately before a noun. Such people have no objection to *the above-mentioned examples* or *the examples above*. And they should not object to *the above examples*. *Above* is accepted as an adjective by the best English scholars and writers. It is used in this way by Franklin, Hawthorne, Scott, Dickens, Thackeray, Quiller-Couch, H. W. Fowler, Bertrand Russell, Gilbert Murray, and by most of the grammarians who condemn it, when they are off their guard.

abrogate; arrogate. To *abrogate* is to annul summarily, to abolish authoritatively or formally (*The power which formed the laws may abrogate them*). The word cannot properly be applied to anything but established custom or usage. When Sir Nathaniel in *Love's Labour's Lost* beseeches Holofernes to *abrogate scurrility*, the use is probably intended to be humorous.

To *arrogate* is to claim presumptuously as a right some dignity or authority to which one is not entitled (*groups which arrogate to themselves the right to use coercion*).

abscissa. The plural is *abscissas* or *abscissae*.

absolute. When used as a grammatical term, *absolute* means grammatically independent. The word is applied to forms of speech that ordinarily are not independent, such as participles, adjectives, transitive verbs, and phrases. The words in small capitals are absolute in: *a* HORSE! *a* HORSE! *my* KINGDOM *for a horse* and THIS SAID, *he formed thee,* ADAM!, *thee,* O MAN! DUST *of the ground!*

Adjectives which name a "complete" quality, such as *perfect,* and *unique,* are sometimes called "absolutes." For a discussion of this, see **comparison of adjectives and adverbs.**

For a discussion of absolute phrases, see **participles.**

absolutely and **positively** are synonyms, containing the same degree of emphasis, interchangeable in any given case, and similarly abused. The meaning of wholly, unconditionally, and completely (*He is absolutely determined to go through with it. He is positively obsessed with the idea of death*) ought not to be degraded into helping to form second-rate superlatives (*absolutely swell, positively magnificent*), or, by themselves, into becoming inflated substitutes for *yes*.

abstract nouns. Some grammarians distinguish between concrete and abstract nouns, defining concrete nouns as those that refer to physical things, such as *house, mud, child,* and abstract nouns as those that refer to qualities which physical things may have but which do not exist by themselves, such as *redness, beauty, childhood*. This distinction raises interesting philosophical questions. How should one classify *heat*? or *the equator*? Fortunately, one does not have to answer these questions in order to use the words correctly because this distinction has no bearing on English grammar. An abstract noun is grammatically like any other noun. See **mass nouns.**

But *abstract* may also mean *more general, less specific*. In this sense *container* is more abstract than *barrel,* and *resources* more abstract than *money*. The more abstract a word is, the more objects it refers to and the less it tells us about them. The more specific a word is, the more information it conveys. It is very easy to use words that are too general. In fact, this is the most obvious characteristic of ineffective writing. A good writer fits his words as closely as possible to his meaning. He will use *container* only if he is talking about several kinds of containers. If he is talking about a barrel, he will call it *a barrel*.

A poor writer who would like to be better should ask himself constantly: Does what I have written cover more ground than I meant to cover? Writing with this question always in mind will do more to develop a respectable style than all the grammar books and vocabulary builders in the world.

abuse; invective; obloquy; scurrility; vituperation. These words convey various degrees of bitterness and roughness in verbal attack.

Abuse and *vituperation* are synonymous and mean coarse and insulting language, used, generally, in some private quarrel or attack. Vituperation has come to have a slight sense of greater fierceness in the reviling. This may be due, as V. H. Collins suggests, to the fact that the five syllables "convey the idea of a torrential flow" or it may be due to an echoic suggestion of *viper* in the sound of the word.

Invective may be vehement and violent and railing, but it may also, differing from *abuse,* be polished. Indeed, when it is *coarse* that adjective is usually employed to mark the fact. Some of the most elegant orations ever delivered have been invectives, though from less able speakers we are likely to have more spite than elegance.

Obloquy is censure or blame, or even abusive language, but it is public and general. It is condemnation by many people rather than an attack by one person (*They held their convictions in spite of obloquy*). Abuse causes anger and resentment; obloquy causes shame and disgrace.

Scurrility is abuse characterized by coarseness and jocularity. It is railing marked by indecency and couched in buffoonery.

The exact meaning of any one of these words is affected, of course, by one's point of view. Emerson probably felt himself abused when Swinburne referred to him as "a gap-toothed and hoary ape . . . coryphæus of [a] Bulgarian tribe of auto-coprophagous baboons," but Swinburne insisted he was merely making a scientifically accurate description. What to the speaker may seem polished *invective* may strike the one spoken of as *vituperation* and even *scurrility*.

abysmal; abyss; abyssal. *Abyss* means a bottomless space. It was *below the thunders of the upper deep/ Far, far beneath in the abysmal sea* that Tennyson's Kraken slept. But science has now taken soundings and, in consequence, *abysmal* and *abyss* are relegated to figurative uses (*Her air of attentiveness conceals an abysmal ignorance*). *Abyss* is allowed in Milton's imaginary landscape of Chaos and other old-fashioned literary imaginings or, with *abysmal*, to describe the geography of the mind (*Despair opened an abyss before his mind's eye*).

Abyssal is a technical term used in descriptions of the ocean floor or of depths below three hundred fathoms. The steep descent from the continental shelf is also called the *abyss*.

Academe. If used seriously, *Academe* refers to Plato's Academy in ancient Athens. As a term for a place of instruction, *Academe* is a pomposity, as in Mary McCarthy's satirical novel of faculty life, *Groves of Academe*. So used, the word is self-destructive and can survive only in cynical uses. The best policy is to use *Academe* with historical accuracy or not at all.

accede. See **allow.**

accelerate and **exhilarate** are like two people who are unrelated but look alike and have become good friends. *Acceleration* means going faster; *exhilaration* means getting gladder (*Much of the exhilaration of driving is due to the acceleration of the car*).

The confusion between going faster and getting happier is one of the fundamental errors of our time and it is not surprising that it has extended to the words. But *exhilaration* is always a mental state, connoting a degree of excitement. *Acceleration* describes matter increasing the rapidity of its motion—though it is possible to conceive of a figurative, mental application of the word, such as *the acceleration of the learning process with practice*.

accent; accentual; accentuate. *Accent* is the characteristic of a vowel or a syllable, having to do with the degree or pattern of stress placed on it. When we say that a foreigner *speaks with an accent* we mean that he knows the words but that his speech is distinguishable because he does not use the same pattern of stresses that native speakers employ.

Like so many useful words, however, *accent* has been engulfed in its figurative extensions. Advertisements, especially of products designed for women, would be lost without the word in their own special application of it. Mascara *accents* the eyebrows, tight skirts *accent* the hips, and so on.

Accentuate is reserved in England, as Fowler notes, for the figurative sense of *accent* and is so used by Americans who find the over-use of *accent* distasteful. Its use should be restricted, however, to the amenities, the trivia, and the esthetics of ordinary life. The prairies do not *accentuate the grandeur of the Rockies*, but it is permissible *to accentuate the color of the floral centerpiece with the whiteness of the table linen*.

Accentual is a technical word, reserved for the description of a rhythm or a pattern of stresses (*The accentual peculiarities of free verse lie in its apparent irregularities*).

accept; except. The essential confusion between *accept* and *except* is one of sound and where there is a doubt which is meant only the context can determine it. *Accept* means to receive willingly (*I accept your offer*). *Except* means to omit or exclude (*Brown was excepted from the list of those to be pardoned*).

acceptance; acceptation. *Acceptance*, a noun, means the act of accepting or of being accepted (*His acceptance of the gift found acceptance with his superiors*).

Acceptation has been restricted to questions of interpretation, principally the interpretation of words (*The original acceptation of "communism" as a political theory differs greatly from its present general acceptation*). More and more, however, *acceptance* tends to take the place of *acceptation* which is now, by some authorities, classified as an archaism.

access; accession. The difference between *access* and *accession* is largely the difference between the act as a possibility and its accomplishment. As Princess, Queen Elizabeth had access to the throne. Her accession followed upon her father's death.

While the opportunity or possibility of entering as it is expressed in *access* (See **access; excess**) remains flexible, *accession* is limited to the idea of entering into a higher rank or a new status, as in the accession of a territory to statehood or of a senator to the presidency.

access; excess. Confusion between *access* and *excess* is chiefly due to the similarity of their sound, but there is a band of meaning in which they overlap.

Access is a noun meaning an approach, a coming into, or the means by which entry is obtained. *Access* to a house is by way of the door. *Access* to a great man requires money or influence.

Excess means going out, the direct opposite of *access*. In the sense of going out of one's mind or beyond one's means, *excess* has come to mean immoderation (*He drinks to excess*); superfluity, in the sense of more than enough, overflowing (*Children are full of excess energy*); the extent to which one thing is more than another (*His appetite is in excess of his capacity*); it has also come to stand in a pejorative sense as a generic term for any immoral, licentious extravagances (Oscar Wilde's epigram: *Nothing succeeds like excess*).

Access is sometimes used for "a coming into" an emotional storm, a sudden outburst of passion (*In an access of rage he stabbed his friend*). Here *excess* might be used, and some English authorities deny the correctness of *access* in this context. But the *Oxford English Dictionary* accepts it. Many distinguished English authors have so used it. And it is certainly sanctioned by American usage.

accessary and **accessory** are linguistic lovers, perpetually exchanging vowels. In American usage *accessary* is recognized only as a noun, but *accessory* is accepted as both noun and adjective. *Accessary* is limited, with us, chiefly to the legal significances of the word, though, even there, *accessory* can be used.

In law an accessary or accessory plays a minor part in a crime. An *accessory before the fact* is one who helped, or at least had knowledge of and did not hinder, the committing of a crime but was not present when the act was done; an *accessory after the fact* knowingly assists or conceals another who has committed a felony.

In common usage *accessory* means something added or attached for convenience or attractiveness and it emphasizes the subordinate nature of the contribution (*The accessory details of the building*). It is an interesting illustration of the confusion latent in the most common words that this word which is in daily use amongst us has different meanings for men and women. To most American women *accessories* means the portable or detachable additions to the costume—hat, bag, earrings, scarf, and so on. To most American men *accessories* means additions to the car—radio, heater, spotlight, and so on.

accident. See **mishap.**

accidents will happen. The suggestion, in many forms, that "time and chance happeneth to all" is common to all languages and where, as in *Ecclesiastes,* it is a sincere comment, the bitter fruit of observation and experience, it can have dignity and force.

But *accidents will happen,* apart from being a cliché, has an exasperating levity to it and a patronizing air of unfeeling consolation—especially if the almost inevitable "in the best-regulated families" is tacked on to it.

All clichés are tedious, but those that are used when real feeling is expected—as in consolation—are dangerous in that their cut-and-dried nature makes one suspect the sincerity of the emotion expressed. This may be unfair, for many worthy people express sincere feelings in clichés and quotations, pathetic in their inarticulateness and more pathetic in the likelihood of being misunderstood.

accommodation; accommodations. With the preposition *to, accommodation* is the act of adapting or being adapted to (*The accommodation of modern furniture to the human figure*).

The use of the word to designate lodgings or food and lodgings is expressed in American usage by the plural, *accommodations,* and in English usage by the singular, *accommodation.* Originally the English used *accommodation.* Othello demanded for his wife *such accommo-dation and besort as levels with her breeding.* Later they used *accommodations.* Defoe, Boswell, and Jane Austen so used it. But they have now reverted to the singular, and the plural in this sense is unknown among them.

In America the plural is now universally used. One wires a hotel for accommodations when only a single room is desired. Pullman accommodations may be a roomette, a bedroom, or several sleeping sections thrown together. Hotels have "Accommodations Desks."

accompanist has supplanted **accompanyist** in general preference as one who accompanies in the musical sense.

according; accordingly. *Accordingly* is the form used alone to qualify a verb, as in *he wrote accordingly.* The form *according* is required before *to,* as in *he wrote according to orders. According* may also be used to qualify a noun, as in *the according hearts of men,* and with *as* to introduce a clause, as in *according as it is understood or not,* but these last constructions are not often heard today.

accountable means responsible, liable. But since only a human agent can be called on to account for his actions (animal trials having ceased in the eighteenth century), the word can only be used to describe human liability (*The dog was responsible for tearing the coat and its owner was held accountable for the damage*).

accredit. See **credit.**

accrue. Although *accrue* has long carried the general sense of to happen or result as a natural growth, to arise in due course, to come or fall as an addition or increment, it is most safely used in a specifically legal context, meaning to become a present and enforceable right or demand (*Interest accrues at the rate of two percent per annum*). It is ostentatious and inaccurate to use *accrue* as a synonym for *result* or *happen* when there are no legal or financial implications, as in *It is unlikely that benefits will accrue from such a belligerent policy.*

accumulative has been replaced in almost all uses by *cumulative,* surviving only in the sense generally expressed by *acquisitive* (*His accumulative instinct led him to buy real estate*).

accusative case. The accusative is a Latin case used principally to mark the object of a verb. In modern English this relationship is shown by position. See **object of a verb** and **objective pronouns.**

accuse. See **charge.**

accustom. This word may be followed by an infinitive, as in *I am not accustomed to lie,* or by the *-ing* form of a verb with the preposition *to,* as in *I am not accustomed to lying.* Both forms are standard.

acid test. Gold, chemically inactive, resists the action of acids that corrode other metals. *The acid test* was, therefore, a test calculated to distinguish gold from other substances such as iron or copper pyrites. As a term for a severe test, *the acid test* has become a cliché.

acknowledge. See **confess.**

acquaint. See **tell.**

acquaintanceship. The suffix -*ship* denotes a state, condition, or quality (as in *friendship* or *scholarship*), an office or profession (as in *professorship*), an art or skill (as in the new humorous word *gamesmanship*), something embodying a quality or state (as in *courtship*), or one entitled to a specified rank (as in his *lordship*).

Since the word *acquaintance* means not only one who is known to a certain degree (*He is an old acquaintance of mine*) but also the state of being acquainted (*The cultured man will have some acquaintance with mathematics*), the adding of the suffix to form *acquaintance-ship* is totally unnecessary. It means nothing that *acquaintance* does not mean and probably came into existence as a false analogy to *friendship, fellowship.*

acquirement and **acquisition** are both nouns that designate things gained by the expenditure of effort or cash. But an *acquirement* is something that has been developed *in* a person— a faculty, a skill, a talent. An *acquisition,* on the other hand, is a material object bought, or obtained by some other means, *by* a person (*Petronius Arbiter's acquirements in taste qualified him to direct Nero's acquisitions of art treasures*).

Acquirement is acceptable in the singular and the plural (*acquirements*), although it is more frequently used in the plural, indicating a diversity of things which collectively make up a talent or faculty.

acronyms are acrostic words formed from the initial letters of other words, or from initial letters or syllables of the successive parts of a compound term, or from initial letters plus final letters of the final part of a compound term.

They serve the same purpose as abbreviations, but are primarily designed for speech and appeal more to the ear than to the eye. They are a form of word play. Some seem to be happy accidents—such as *WRENS,* from Women's Royal Naval Service. Others seem more self-conscious; they were obviously made up first and the compound term then derived from them. *WAVES* certainly seem to be chickens that came before the egg. The acronym suggests the sea effectively but it is hard to imagine that the coiners first thought of the long form, Women Accepted for Voluntary Emergency Service. The name of the Women's Reserve of the United States Coast Guard Reserve, *SPAR,* is among the most ingenious of acronyms. It derives from the Coast Guard motto and its translation, "Semper Paratus— Always Ready," or perhaps simply from the first letter of the first word of the motto and the first three letters of the second word. In the case of *WASP* some liberties had to be taken to make the acronym from the phrase Women's Air Forces Service Pilots.

Among the most unfortunate of acronyms was *CINCUS* (pronounced "sink us") for the Commander in Chief of the United States Navy. In the reorganization of the command of the Navy following Pearl Harbor it was dropped from use.

The acronym seems largely an outgrowth of World War II, though *WRENS* was coined in World War I. Out of the second conflict came such salty acronyms as *SNAFU* and *TARFU,* usually translated as "Situation Normal—All Fouled Up" and "Things Are Really Fouled Up." There were also technical acronyms such as the British *ASDIC* for Anti-Submarine Detection Investigation Committee, and the American *SONAR* for SOund NAvigation Ranging. On both sides of the Atlantic there was *RADAR* for RAdio Detecting And Ranging.

AWOL was an abbreviation in World War I and became an acronym in World War II. That is, in World War I it was pronounced as four letters; in World War II, it was pronounced as a word (ā'wôl). It is still military slang and not accepted as standard English, however.

There seems to be no generally applicable rule as to which abbreviations become acronyms and which do not. Pronounceability of the abbreviation is not the sole deciding factor, else why *NATO,* for instance, but not *OPA*? Some of the older abbreviations, such as *F.O.B.* and *G.A.R.,* are probably too established to be changed. Acronyms represent a new tendency in the language.

Certainly *un*pronounceability or uncertainty regarding pronunciation rules out some abbreviations as acronyms. Thus *Pan-Am* (for Pan-American Airways) is obvious, but *BOAC* (for British Overseas Airway Corporation) is not.

Commercial enterprises and products that have acronyms for names have an important advertising advantage over their less-easily-remembered competitors. *Alcoa* and *Nabisco* are two examples that come immediately to mind.

acropolis. The plural is *acropolises* or *acropoles.*

across; acrost. *Across* is the only acceptable form. Although *acrost* is formed on the same pattern as *amongst* and *whilst,* both of which are acceptable, it has never been literary English.

act; action. The distinction between these two words is difficult to define. Often they are completely synonymous (*His heroic act was long remembered. His heroic action was long remembered*), but there are many places where one would not be substituted for the other (*Rapid action is needed if we are to be saved. It was his act and he must accept the consequences*).

Fowler points out that *action* alone has the collective sense (*We must look to Congress for action in this crisis*) and that where there is doubt *action* tends to displace *act.* (As he says, we would now be inclined to speak not of the *Acts* of the Apostles but of their *Actions*). In the sense where the reference is to the nature of a deed or the characteristic of a deed (*An act of thoughtfulness; the act of a busybody*) *act* is invariably used; but where it is simply a deed or where the meaning expressed in the noun phrase is expressed in an adjective, *action* is preferred (*the act of a careless person; a careless action*).

A deed referred to at the immediate moment of its doing (*in the very act of making off with it*) or contrasted with words or thought (*acts, not words, are what we need*) is likely to be referred to as an *act*, but even here if the sense is collective *action* will probably be used (*speech and action are different things*).

act; play. Used as a verb in the same sense as *play* (*play the fool*), *act* has a serious handicap, that of ambiguity. Its importance as a verb meaning to do, to perform, to execute, and so on, overshadows its theatrical connotations of pretense and dissimulation. The command to *act the man* means something different, and more, than to *play the man*. Therefore where pretense is meant, *play* is preferable.

In slang *act*, as a noun, has come almost entirely to mean pretense (*Oh, he's just putting on an act*). The extension of this usage no doubt reflects the cynicism of the age but it is dangerous and corrosive, for how shall we speak of acts of kindness, of generosity, of courage, and of love?

activate; actuate. To *activate* is to make active (*It was believed that the Sibyl was activated by the Devil*). In physics it means to render radioactive. In the United States Army it means to place a military unit in an active status by assigning to it officers, enlisted men, and all necessary equipment for war strength and training for war service.

To *actuate* is to move mechanical things to action (*The electro-magnet actuated the armature*) or to incite human beings to action by acting upon the will, as motives do (*His motives differed from those by which his predecessor had been actuated. The murderer had not, apparently, been actuated by the desire for money, for over a thousand dollars was found in the dead man's wallet*).

active voice. A verb is said to be in the active voice when it represents its subject as active, that is, as doing, being, or becoming something, as in *he believes the story* and *this is true.* A verb is said to be in the passive voice when it represents its subject as acted upon, or passive, as in *the story is believed.* See **passive voice.**

actress. See **poet; poetess.**

actually; really. *Actually* is an adverb synonymous with *really* used in questions to connote disbelief (*Did you actually see the rope trick?*); in replies to questions in which doubt has been expressed, re-affirming the original assertion (*Yes, I actually saw it!*); and in statements which profess to reveal hitherto concealed truths concerning a matter under discussion (*Actually, it is no great mystery; it's simply a clever deception*).

The last example is a worn-out import from England, a verbal swagger stick used in polite conversation to point up minor revelations (*Jones is a bore, but actually he means well*). The suggestion it carries of superior knowledge on the part of the speaker and the air of condescension that so often accompanies the revelations make it an irritating word. It can become a nuisance, actually. See also **precisely.**

actuate. See **activate.**

adapt; adopt. The confusion between *adapt* and *adopt* may be avoided if one recognizes *apt* in the second syllable of the first word. *Apt* means suited to the purpose. *Adapt* means to make suitable, to adjust to. We say that an object is adapted to its purpose, an animal to its environment. (To adapt an apt proverb: *A bassoon is an ill wind that nobody blows good*).

To *adopt,* on the other hand, is to choose or to make one's own by selection or assent (*American women eagerly adopt the styles which New York dressmakers adapt from French fashions*).

adapted; suitable. *Adapted* is not a synonym for *suitable. Appropriate* or *fitting* would be better for *suitable. Adapted* means that something has been changed to fit and, unless the idea of change or adaptation is in the thought, it would be better to use another word.

addendum. The plural is *addendums* or *addenda.*

addicted; devoted. Although both words mean habitual attachment, *addicted* now means being attached to something which the speaker regards as undesirable (*He is addicted to lying*). Sometimes it is used for humorous effect of things that the ordinary person would not consider undesirable in order to show that the speaker does (*He is addicted to artichokes. He is addicted to good works*).

Devoted means attachment or habitual action, but to good things (*She is devoted to her mother*).

add(ing) insult to injury. The saying is very old. There are several Latin and Greek passages that reflect on the exacerbation that contumely gives to an injury. But the very things that make it a saying—its obviousness, its rhythm, and the balance of the two *in*-'s—make it a cliché, something that slips into the mind easily and is used without further consideration of its appropriateness. If this is exactly what is meant, if it is an insult and not a further injury that has been added, and if this way of saying seems the proper way, despite the fact that it has been expressed this way many millions of times, then say it this way. But it is wiser to avoid the phrase.

addle. An *addle* (or *addled*) egg is a rotten egg and an *addlebrain* or *addlehead* is not only confused, but sterile and stinking. It is not only muddled but muddy. The term is a contemptuous one and not to be used in place of *featherheaded* or *giddy.*

Dizzy, by the way, which is now used widely as a slang term for ludicrously stupid (*a dizzy blond*) originally meant stupid. Slang, which often has a fine feeling for the meaning of words, has brought it full circle.

address; speech; lecture. An *address* is more formal than a *speech* (*the inaugural address*). A *lecture* was originally something which was read. It, too, is formal, though not so formal as an *address,* and it has acquired the connotation of instruction. This latter meaning has given *lecture* the further meaning of a tedious reprimand.

adduce is to bring forward but only in the metaphorical sense of to bring forward in argument, to cite as pertinent or conclusive (*He adduced Joe Louis as proof that a man could be a champion prizefighter and still a modest man*). It is sometimes used erroneously for *deduce* (as in *From that I adduce you agree with me*).

adept. This word is preferably followed by *in* rather than at, as in *adept in getting out of work.*

adequate enough is tautological. Since both words mean the same thing nothing is gained by bringing them together.

adherence; adhesion. In general, *adherence* is figurative, *adhesion* literal. We speak of a person's adherence to a party or a principle and a thing's adhesion to something else. None the less, adhesion to a principle or a party would not be incorrect.

adherent. See **appositive.**

adherent adjectives. See **position of adjectives.**

adieu. The plural is *adieus* or *adieux.*

adjacent; contiguous. Things that are *adjacent* to each other are near to each other (*Austria and Switzerland are adjacent countries*). They may touch each other, but it is not necessary. *Contiguous* means touching, in actual contact. Adjacent houses might have a yard between them; contiguous houses would have a common wall.

However, *contiguous* is sometimes used to mean in close proximity without actually touching and has come to be so used to the extent that this use cannot be considered an error. On the whole, though, *contiguous* suggests that two things are closer than if they were only *adjacent.*

adjectivally is to be preferred to *adjectively.*

adjectives. An adjective is a word that is neither singular nor plural and that is used to qualify a noun, as in *true love, green grass, early bird.* Most adjectives have three forms, known as the positive, the comparative, and the superlative, as in *green, greener, greenest.* See **comparison of adjectives and adverbs.**

In an inflected language such as Latin (but not in English), adjectives have special endings corresponding to various noun endings and these show which noun in the sentence the adjective is qualifying, or belongs with. An adjective-like word that has not been made to "match" some neighboring noun is not attached to any noun and is therefore not an adjective. Any qualifying word that is not an adjective is an adverb. This is all very simple, and with just a little knowledge of an inflected language one can tell an adjective from an adverb without knowing the meaning of the word.

But in English, adjectives look just like adverbs. It is not true that a word is an adverb if it ends in *-ly. Kindly, sickly, deadly,* are normally adjectives. *Early* and *leisurely* are both adjectives and adverbs, and so are *hard, fast, slow.* Perhaps the distinction between adjectives and adverbs should be abandoned in English. But if we are to maintain it with our present definitions of the words, we can only say that a word of this kind is an adjective if it can be used to qualify a noun, and an adverb if it can be used to qualify any of the other parts of speech or the sentence as a whole.

Nouns, and therefore pronouns, can also be used to qualify nouns, as *goose* in *goose feathers.* Such words do not have a comparative and superlative form but neither do all adjectives, and it is sometimes hard to say whether a word in a particular sentence is an adjective or a noun or pronoun being used as an adjective. But this is a question of terminology and does not affect the use of the words. (See **nouns as adjectives.**) Sometimes an adjective is used "absolutely," that is, without naming the noun which it qualifies, as in *the brave deserve the fair,* where the nouns *men* and *women* are understood. Here the adjective is being used as if it were a noun. This sometimes creates a question as to whether the word is to be treated as a singular or as a plural. (An adjective may also become a true noun, as in *the alert sounded.*) See **adjectives as nouns.**

An adjective that is qualifying one noun may also have another noun as its "object." Usually this relationship is shown by the word *of,* as in *fearful of, mindful of, capable of.* Sometimes another preposition is used, as in *impatient with, comparable to, anxious about.* Which preposition is used depends partly on convention and partly on the meaning of the word. (See the individual prepositions.) A few adjectives, such as *like* and *worth,* may be followed immediately by an object without the use of a preposition.

Adjectives can be made from nouns by adding any of a great number of endings, such as *-ish, -like, -ly, -y, -en, -al, -ar, -ory.* Adjectives ending in *-ish* are often derogatory, as *childish* and *womanish,* and other forms, such as *childlike* and *womanly,* are used when speaking with approval. Only a woman can be *mannish.* A man would necessarily be *manly.* The ending *-ish* may also be added to adjectives to mean "approaching" or "like," as in *greenish, oldish, smallish.* The *-y* ending also means "like" and can be used in making adjectives from nouns or from verbs, as in *flowery, creepy, slinky.* The *-en* is used most often with names of materials, such as *golden, leaden, woolen, oaken.* The endings *-al, -ar, -ory,* are used chiefly for more learned words that suggest a Latin origin, such as *autumnal, spectacular, transitory.* There is a strong tendency in current English to drop both the *-en* and the *-al* endings and use the noun form itself as a qualifier, as in *oak table, wool shirt, autumn leaves, coast line.*

Phrases and even full clauses may sometimes stand before a noun as if they were simple adjectives, as in *the man with the I-turn-the-crank-of-the-universe air.* For more commonplace examples of this, see **compound words.** See also **clauses.**

KINDS OF ADJECTIVES

The function of an adjective depends to a great extent upon its position in a sentence. Adjectives are classified according to position as (1) adherent (when they stand before the noun they qualify), (2) appositive (when they follow the noun), (3) predicate (when they follow a verb), and (4) factitive or "objective complement" (when they follow the object of a verb with a special sense). Adjectives are said to be either limiting or descriptive, but this too depends upon their position in the sentence. See **position of adjectives.**

Adjectives may be classified in many ways according to meaning, but only a few of these classifications have any bearing on the use of the words. Adjectives that are made from proper nouns are called proper adjectives and are written with a capital letter. (See **proper nouns.**) The two participles of a verb are usually adjectives, as in *falling rock* and *fallen rock,* and are called verbal adjectives. (See **participles.**) Number words are usually adjectives. These include the cardinal numbers, such as *two, twenty,* and such related words as *dozen, few, many;* and the ordinal numbers, such as *third, fifth,* and such related words as *first, last, other.* (See **number terms.**) A great many pronouns may also be used as adjectives. When used to qualify a noun, the words *this, that, these, those,* are called demonstrative adjectives, and the possessive pronouns, *my, his, their,* and so on, are called possessive adjectives. The articles *a, an, the,* are also adjectives. These last three groups together with the indefinite pronominal adjectives, such as *some, any, each, every,* and the genitive case of nouns, such as *father's,* are sometimes classed together as definitives, because they make the reference as definite or specific as the facts allow. (See **definitive adjectives.**)

Some of these classifications are reflected in the order that is followed when several adjectives qualify the same noun.

ORDER IN A SERIES

A noun may be qualified by more than one adjective. Izaak Walton wrote that he would consider the lilies, and also *those very many other various little living creatures that are fed by the goodness of the God of nature.*

In piling up his adjectives in this way, Walton had no choice about the order in which he must use them. Words such as *very,* which apply to only one word in the series, are adverbs and always stand next to the word they qualify. True adjectives may be joined by *and,* as in *strong and beautiful children,* or they may be set off from one another by commas, as in *strong, happy, beautiful children.* In either case, they are said to be "leveled" and all of them have exactly the same relation to the noun they qualify. Otherwise, in a series of adjectives each word qualifies or limits the meaning of all the words that follow, up to and including the noun. That is, the words which restrict the total meaning most stand first and there is a gradual progression through wider and wider meanings until the noun is reached.

This is so much a part of the natural order in an English sentence that it will ordinarily take care of itself. One does not have to know which kinds of adjectives come first and which second in order to use them properly. But the rules are relatively rigid and can be described in detail.

With certain exceptions which will be mentioned later, the definitive adjectives must stand first. Two words of this kind never qualify the same noun unless they are leveled. Number terms come next, and frequently more than one of them is used. (For the order that must be followed when several words of this class qualify the same noun, see **number terms.**) These are followed by words implying a judgment, such as *beautiful, terrible, expensive, true, different.* There may be several words of this kind. If there are, they are always leveled and it makes no difference what order they are used in. Finally there are the purely descriptive words. Here some variation is allowed, but as a rule the order is size, shape, other characteristics. The other characteristics are usually listed with the most obvious first. Then comes the noun, which may be additionally qualified by a following phrase or clause.

No one is likely to use all the kinds of adjectives there are in the same phrase. But the ones that are used will have to follow this order if the sentence is to lie flat. In the Walton sentence quoted above, the word *various* is likely to jump to the modern ear. He meant by the word "of different kinds" or "to be classified differently." It is therefore a judgment word and belongs where he placed it. But if we hear it as meaning "several" it belongs in place of "very many." If we hear it as "varied" or "having different appearances," it is a general descriptive word and should follow *little.*

The orderly progression of adjectives just described may be disturbed for any of three reasons. (1) Certain words, such as *dear little children* and *nice old lady,* are used together so constantly that they may come to be felt as a single idea and one may hesitate to break into a compound of this sort. As a result, one might say *these curly-headed dear little children* or *that little nice old lady.* (2) The words *all, both,* and the names of some fractions, may stand before a definitive as if they were being used with the word *of,* although the *of* actually is not there, as in *all the day, both the boys, half the price.* (3) Words used to mean "in a high degree" are being used as adverbs. They cannot qualify a noun directly, but they may qualify a definitive adjective and so have the force of qualifying the noun. When they qualify a definitive adjective they stand before it, as in *many a day, what a man, such a storm*. When a word of this kind, or the interrogative adverb *how*, applies to a particular adjective it will bring that adjective forward with it, as in *so rich a man, too rainy a day, how sad a case*. But with these exceptions, the order of adjectives outlined above is always followed.

adjectives as adverbs. Almost any word that can be used to qualify a noun can also be used to qualify some words that are not nouns. There are some words in English, such as *slow, high, even, early*, that can be used with a noun and also with a verb. These words are clearly adverbs as well as adjectives. But there are other adjective-like words which cannot be used to qualify a verb but can be used to qualify the positive form of adjectives, such as *dark, black*, and *bitter*, in *a dark blue dress, a black-eyed child, a bitter cold night*.

There are several things a grammarian might say about this situation. He might say that in English adjectives may qualify adjectives. This represents the facts, but it would require a new definition of an adjective and very few grammarians take such a stand. On the other hand, he might recognize all these words as adverbs, and this is what most grammarians do. But this means that practically all adjectives are also adverbs and the classification ceases to have much value. That is, the fact that a dictionary lists a given word as an adverb tells nothing about whether or not that word can be used to qualify a verb. Some grammarians follow a middle course. They find special explanations for some of these adjective combinations, and those that they can't explain they condemn as an improper use of the word.

An adjective before a color word is always acceptable, as in *a dark blue dress, a greenish yellow car*. Some grammarians say that the color word is here a noun, and therefore properly qualified by an adjective. Others say that the two words, such as *dark blue*, are actually one compound adjective. This difference of opinion may determine whether or not a hyphen is used in such terms. In any case, the adjective before a color word is normal English today. An adverb may also be used here and is sometimes preferred when the adjective form is ambiguous. For example, in *roll on, thou deep and dark blue ocean*, the words *deep* and *dark* may refer to *blue* or they may refer to *ocean*. On the other hand, when the sea is described as *darkly, deeply, beautifully blue*, the adverb forms can only refer to the word *blue*. But these are problems of poetry and exalted prose. In everyday English, *a darkly blue dress* would suggest something mysterious and exotic, certainly nothing as prosaic as a dress that is dark blue.

A combined noun and adjective, such as *warm heart, noble mind, clear sight, empty head*, may be made into an adjective by adding *-ed* to the noun, as in *warm hearted, noble minded, clear sighted, empty headed*. These are usually classed as compound adjectives and are usually hyphenated in deference to this fact. Whether they really are compounds or not is debatable. When the two words are treated as one in making a comparative or superlative form, as in *a warm-hearteder, the empty-headedest*, we clearly have a compound adjective. Forms of this kind do appear but they are rare. We more often treat the first word as an independent adjective (or adverb) and say *a warmer hearted, the emptiest headed*. In this case it is impossible to say that the two words are a compound, and a hyphen is never used when the first element has a comparative or superlative form. The number of words that can be used in this way is almost unlimited. We say *white haired, blue eyed, quick witted, decent sized, good natured*, and so on indefinitely.

The past participle of a verb is sometimes merely a descriptive adjective and when it is, it too may be qualified by an adjective-like word, as in *native born, foreign made, soft spoken, fresh oiled, new laid eggs, new mown hay*. Sometimes the participle keeps its verbal force and in this case a clearly adverbial form is required to qualify it, as in *warmly dressed, well behaved, highly priced, deeply rooted*. Often the speaker may use whichever form suits him best and say *soft spoken* or *softly spoken, high priced* or *highly priced*. But the adverbial form always gives the following word a verb-like feeling. *A beautiful colored object* is an object that has beautiful color. But *a beautifully colored object* is an object that has been colored beautifully.

Adjective forms are also used before adjectives as intensives, as *red* in *red hot* and *stark* in *stark naked*. These words are clearly "adverbs of degree" and cannot be explained away. Faced with such combinations, anyone who has been claiming that there is an innate difference between an adjective and an adverb must either recognize that there is something wrong with his system or conclude that the language itself is wrong. Some have decided that it must be the language.

Constructions of this kind are common in the finest literary English, as in *and it grew wondrous cold* and *St. Agnes' Eve—ah, bitter chill it was!* Some words that were originally adjectives, such as *very* and *pretty*, are used in this way so consistently that no one would think of objecting to them. Others have now disappeared from the language, or at least have a decidedly nineteenth century flavor, as *an uncommon fine fellow, devilish handsome, deuced uncomfortable*. Some are still in use but are not considered standard, as *dreadful sorry, Clementine*. But there are a great many more that are in standard use and pass unnoticed. We may still say *icy cold* and *bitter cold* though we no longer say *it is cruel cold*. We may still use the *-ing* adjectives in this way, as *burning hot, howling drunk.* We may still say *dead tired* and *dead certain.* Some words of this kind are now in use but are under attack, such as *mighty fine, real clever, awful nice, right smart, sure good.* Whether they remain standard English or not will depend on who uses them and who doesn't. There is no question of logic, or of grammatical principles, involved. If the respected members of the community use these words, the words are respectable, and if they do not, the words are not. (See the individual words.)

adjectives as nouns. Nouns may be made from adjectives, or adjectives may be used as if they were nouns. Both kinds of words can be seen in the sentence by Fielding, *we moderns are to the ancients what the poor are to the rich.* The words *moderns* and *ancients* are made from adjectives but they are true nouns, if only because they have been given the ending *s* which does not belong to the adjective. A great many nouns are formed from adjectives in this way, such as *news, slacks, heroics, economics.* In the case of *moderns* and *ancients* the words also have a singular form and the plural form can be used with a numeral, as in *any modern is worth a hundred ancients.* Words that have both a singular and a plural form are nouns. Words that have been formed from adjectives by adding *s* are also nouns, even when they do not have the two forms. Neither of these things is true of the words *rich* and *poor.* They have the simple form of the adjective. And we cannot speak of an individual one or use the words with a number term unless we supply the missing noun *man,* as in *this poor man* and *three rich men.* Adjectives that appear to be nouns because the noun they qualify is not expressed are said to be "adjectives used absolutely." When the meaning of the word depends upon the context, as in *the same, the like, the latter,* some grammarians say that the adjective is being used "pronominally."

As we have seen, a noun can be qualified by an adjective even when the noun is not expressed. The fact that we can use an adjective before a word, as in *the miserable poor, the fortunate rich,* does not prove that the word is a noun. The adjectives, *miserable* and *fortunate,* may apply to an unexpressed noun such as *men.* On the other hand, a noun cannot be qualified by an adverb and an adjective can. The fact that adverbs can be used before such words, as in *the miserably poor, the extremely rich,* shows that they are still felt as adjectives. Sometimes this is the only test of whether or not a word has become a noun.

Most of the adjectives that are used as nouns either (1) name a quality, such as *the small, the pleasant, the new,* and refer to everything that has that quality, or (2) name a group of human beings having a certain characteristic, such as *the wise, the powerful, the unborn.* Adjectives in the first class, that name a quality, are always treated as singulars

although they refer to countless examples of the quality. At one time such words were felt as plurals. Pope said, *be not the first by whom the new are tried.* But today we say *the best is the cheapest in the long run, the unknown is always frightening, the familiar is comfortable.* Words of the second class also name a quality. But they refer to a group of human beings who are identified by this characteristic. They do not refer to the quality itself or to the individuals as instances of the quality. Words of this kind are usually treated as plurals, as in the lament, *the best lack all conviction while the worst are full of passionate intensity* and in *there the wicked cease from troubling and there the weary are at rest.* Burns uses the singular form in *the rigid righteous is a fool,* but this is very rare.

The group that an adjective identifies is not necessarily as broad, or as timeless, as *the rich, the poor, the wicked, the weary.* It may represent an actual, countable, number of people, as it does in *the wounded were removed.* When a word has this limited meaning it may be used with a numeral in speaking of some members of the group, as in *twenty wounded were removed.* When the word is unlimited in its application it can only be used in speaking about the entire group. It cannot be used with a numeral or in speaking of some members of the group. We cannot say *five wise* or *five foolish.*

There are ten adjectives which are also used as nouns to name a nationality group. We speak of *the British, the English, the Irish, the Cornish, the Spanish, the Welsh, the Scotch, the Dutch, the French,* and *the Manx.* (In speaking of other nationality groups we use words which are primarily nouns, such as *the Poles, the Swedes, the Chinese.*) Formerly, the ten adjective-nouns could be qualified by a numeral, as in *twenty thousand Cornish bold,* but this is no longer true. In present-day English these words always represent the entire nation. We may speak of *the Irish* or *the French* but not of *six Irish* or *six French.* In order to speak of the individuals we must introduce a true noun, such as *man, woman, person.*

There are a few adjectives in English that represent a single individual, such as *the accused, the departed, the beloved.* These words do not have plural forms and under some circumstances they may be qualified by adverbs, as in *dearly beloved* and *the lately departed.* This makes them adjectives according to the definitions adopted in this dictionary and an exception to the rule that the English adjective is used to indicate groups and not individuals. Under a different system of definitions these words could be classed as singular nouns. But another system would have other problems and other types of words would have to be listed as exceptions to the rules.

Nouns may be used before other nouns as qualifiers, as *sea* in *sea wall* and *horse* in horse race. In this case one may say that the noun is being used as an adjective or that it is the first element in a compound. Nouns that have been formed from adjectives, such as criminal and juvenile, and adjectives that are being used as nouns, such as the sick, the insane, the condemned, may also be used in this way without losing their noun meanings, as in criminal law, a juvenile court, a sick room, an insane asylum, condemned cells. This is a standard English construction. Occasionally someone notices that the first element in one of these compounds can be read as an adjective. This is all very well as a source of innocent merriment. But anyone who concludes that the compound is a grammatical mistake and solemnly goes about condemning it and those who use it, is being ridiculous. These words are part of the fabric of the language and anyone who hopes to get rid of them will have to remake the language. The -ing form of a verb is often used in this way. These may be true nouns, as in a dining room, a landing field, or they may be an adjective used as a noun, as in a dying wish. In either case, the construction is normal English and needs no apology. See -ing.

adjudicate. See **judge.**

adjure. See **abjure.**

administer. One sense of administer is to give (He administered the medicine which the doctor had prescribed), but the word in this sense is generally restricted to the giving of things which are helpful. It is true that we often hear of a rebuke or even a blow being administered; but unless it is implied that these were salutary corrections (and, of course, most people who bestow rebukes and blows on others think they are salutary), the use, while not incorrect, is not a happy one.

administration; ministry. In America the government in power is called the administration. In England it is called the ministry or simply the Government.

admission; admittance. Much ink has been expended to prove that admittance refers to physical entrance and admission to an entrance into rights and privileges, but with the exception of the sign No Admittance, admittance is rarely seen or heard. Admission serves in all cases (The thief gained admission through a broken window. Admission to the club is eagerly sought).

admit. This word may be followed by the -ing form of a verb, as in he admits having seen us, or by a clause, as in he admits he saw us. It is not followed by an infinitive and constructions such as he admits to have seen us are not standard.

admit; admit of. Admit, to allow to enter (Many colleges will admit only those who have done well in the entrance examinations), to allow as valid (He admits the justness of your claim), to acknowledge or confess, and so on. In contemporary usage admit of is rarely heard, though it is quite proper in the sense of leaving room for (His conduct will not admit of any other construction). See **confess.**

adopt; assume. To adopt is to take to oneself, to make one's own. It is sometimes used as if it meant to feign (He adopted a guise of humility). But this is unfortunate. The word should be assume. To adopt a position or an interpretation would be to take it sincerely as one's own. To assume it is, in this context, merely to pretend that it is one's own. See also **adapt.**

adopted; adoptive. When a child has been taken as one's own by a formal legal act, it is an adopted child. But what are the parents? To say that they are foster parents may not express the exact meaning because foster parents have not necessarily made a legal adoption. In American usage they are commonly called adopted parents, but this is awkward since there is the feeling that they have adopted the child, not the child them. Adoptive (which the British use for the relationship either way) is used by many and seems a happy solution (The adopted child became very fond of her adoptive parents).

adorable. See **amatory.**

adore. See **reverence.**

adumbrate, meaning to foreshadow or to prefigure, is a word too confined to literature to be used in ordinary speech or writing without risking the charge of affectation.

advance; advancement. In the sense of promotion advancement is the word (His being made president of the company was a great advancement for him). In the sense of moving forward or upward, the act of advancing, or progress, advance is proper. The advance of civilization is the forward progress of civilization. The advancement of civilization would be an act whereby the advance would be facilitated.

advanced (in years). See **old.**

advantage. See **possession, vantage.**

advent; arrival. Advent, possibly because of its religious uses (when capitalized it refers to the coming of Christ into the world), marks a high and solemn attitude of mind towards an arrival. We speak of the arrival of a plane or a bus, but (if we are minded to view it solemnly) of the advent of Spring, or the advent of death, and so on.

adventure. See **venture.**

adverbial accusative. Under some circumstances a noun may be used directly as an adverb without first being made part of a prepositional phrase, as years in three years she grew in sun and shower. When such nouns are in the common case, that is, when they are not genitives, the construction is called an adverbial accusative. See **nouns as adverbs.**

adverbial genitive. At one time the genitive form of certain words could be used as an adverb. Most of our adverbs that end in an s (or z) sound, such as nowadays, since, sometimes, upwards, are survivals from this period. The final s in on all fours, at sixes and sevens, and in needs in he needs must, is also a sign of the adverbial genitive. Today there is no feeling that this is a genitive relationship and an apostrophe is never used in words of this kind.

Although the construction is no longer understood, the habit of forming adverbs on the old genitive pattern is not entirely dead. It shows itself in certain final *s*'s and substitute *of* phrases, such as *I work evenings* and *I work of an evening*. (See **genitive case**.) Some grammarians object to these forms on the grounds that the construction ought to be dead. They claim that it is dead in England and that the only acceptable form there is *in the evening*.

But the old genitive is very much alive in the United States. When it leads to an extra *s* on a word that is already an adverb, as in *somewheres*, it is not standard, at least in written material. But the genitive is in good repute and thoroughly acceptable for expressions of repeated time, such as *I like to read of a rainy afternoon* and *Wednesdays I work in the garden*. See also **way** and **nouns as adverbs**.

adverbs. A qualifying word that is not qualifying a noun is an adverb. This means that a great many different kinds of words with different functions in a sentence will all be adverbs.

Adverbs are sometimes defined as qualifying words that indicate time, place, manner, or degree. *When, now, soon,* are adverbs of time, and *where, here, there,* are adverbs of place. *Quickly, suddenly, sweetly,* and *how,* are adverbs of manner. "Degree" is not as clear cut a concept as the others, but *exceedingly, excessively, very,* are ordinarily adverbs of degree. Frequently a word that is an adverb of degree in a particular sentence has other uses in other sentences. For example, *great* is an adverb of degree in *a great many people were there,* but it is an adjective in *he is a great man.* Any qualifying word that indicates time, place, manner, or degree, is being used as an adverb. But there are some words that are unquestionably adverbs and that do not fit easily into any one of these four groups, such as *why, not, only, twice.*

All adverbs, linguistic scholars believe, were originally nouns, pronouns, or adjectives. They are words that were used adverbially so much of the time that they lost all other uses. The word *very* is moving in this direction at present. Originally it was an adjective, as it is in *this very morning,* but it is now used more often as an adverb of degree, as in *he is very tired.* Eventually, it might lose its adjective meaning entirely.

Today we use nouns as adverbs in certain situations. *Sunday* is an adverb of time in *we were there Sunday,* and *air mail* is an adverb of manner in *send it air mail.* (See **nouns as adverbs**.) Adjectives are frequently used as adverbs of degree, as *red* in *a red hot poker* and *bitter* in *a bitter cold night.* (See **adjectives as adverbs**.) We may also form adverbs from nouns by adding *-ways* or *-wise,* as in *endways* and *endwise:* and from adjectives by adding *-ly,* as in *bitterly, artistically, thoughtfully.* For-

merly, adverbs might be formed from adjectives by adding *s,* as in *backwards.*

Groups of words may also function as adverbs, as in *it came at the right time, we were waiting in the garden, he was not in the least worried.* See **clauses**.

KINDS OF ADVERBS

The ideas which are expressed by means of adverbs can be classified approximately under the words time, place, manner, and degree. But in order to discuss how words of this kind are used, we need a different grouping. They can be handled most conveniently if they are divided into five classes: (1) interrogative adverbs, (2) relative adverbs, (3) negative adverbs, (4) adverbs of direction, and (5) descriptive adverbs.

1. The words *when, where, how, why,* are interrogatives when they are used to ask a question, as in *when is he coming back?* These words are also interrogatives when they introduce an indirect, or a "buried," question, as in *he didn't tell me when he would be back.* (It should be noticed that these four words can also be used without any implication of a question, as in *he told me when he was here* and *how he laughed!* When that is the case they are not called interrogatives.)

2. Any adverb that introduces a subordinate clause is a relative adverb. This class includes the words *when, where, how,* and *why* (whether they are being used as interrogatives or not); the word *as;* and some time words, such as *before, after, since.* Relative adverbs serve the purpose of conjunctions.

3. The negative adverbs include the obvious negatives, such as *not* and *never,* and also words which are negative in intention, such as *hardly* and *scarcely.* These words are negative because they are used to mean "almost not," "not quite," "probably not." For example, *little* is a negative adverb in *the world will little note.*

4. Adverbs of direction exist in pairs, such as *up* and *down, in* and *out, over* and *under, back* and *forth.* Words of this kind were originally the second element in a compound verb and are still used in this way a great deal of the time. In *pick up the paper,* we say that *pick up* is a compound verb (similar to *lift*) with a direct object *the paper.* But these detached elements tend to lose their connection with the verb and to be treated as independent words with an "object" of their own. When this happens the word has become a preposition. In *stand by the door,* for example, *stand* is considered the full verb and *by* a preposition introducing an adverbial phrase of place. When no object follows, as in *stand by for half an hour* and *it stands out like a sore thumb,* it is obvious that we have a compound verb. When there is an object, the difference between an adverb and a preposition is not as easy to see. But in *cut off an inch* the last three words do not form a prepositional phrase. Instead, the word *off* is an adverb qualifying *cut,* and *an inch* is the object of

the compound verb *cut off*. This is the proper interpretation whenever it is possible to place the object between the verb and the other word without altering the sense, as in *cut an inch off*. In *step off the rug,* on the other hand, the word *off* is a preposition and has its own object *rug*. This is the proper interpretation when we cannot place the object immediately after the verb and say *step the rug off*.

Compound verbs, such as *pick up* and *cut off* are natural English. They are simple and forceful and are generally preferred to their Latin equivalents. So *give up* is often preferred to *relinquish; give in* to *acquiesce; call out* to *evoke; take up* to *assume; bring in* to *introduce*. The form fits our speech rhythm so well that we often use these extra syllables when they add nothing to the meaning, as in *fill up, eat up, drink down*. The independent element in a compound verb which is not affected by changes in tense is an adverb, although it is not used exactly as other adverbs are.

5. Any adverb that does not belong in one of the preceding groups is to be classed as a descriptive adverb. Adverbs of degree, such as *too, so, very, pretty,* are included in this class. A great many descriptive adverbs are formed from adjectives by adding *-ly,* as in *quickly, slowly, highly, hardly*. Some of these adverbs have two forms: with and without the *-ly,* as in *drive slow, drove slowly; come quick, come quickly*. Descriptive adverbs may also have three forms known as the positive, the comparative, and the superlative. See **comparison of adjectives and adverbs.**

USES OF ADVERBS

1. The principal function of an adverb is to qualify a verb, as in *run quickly, speak louder*. Since the verb is the essential element in a statement and not a detachable part of it, an adverb in this role normally qualifies the entire statement. For example, in *I never saw a purple cow* the word *never* applies to *saw a purple cow* and not to the single word *saw*. Adverbs used in this way are called sentence adverbs. They may stand in any of several positions in a sentence, but each position has its special limitations or special emphasis and as a rule there is very little choice about where a particular adverb should be placed. The most important problems in the use of adverbs have to do with placing sentence adverbs. See **sentence adverbs.**

In some situations an adverb may qualify the verb itself rather than the entire statement. Adverbs of direction are not sentence adverbs. They affect the meaning of the verb itself and cannot be used in the various positions that are characteristic of sentence adverbs. In modern English an adverb of direction that stands before the verb is usually written as a solid compound with it, as in *undertake, overturn, upset*. Occasionally an adverb that is actually the second element, and not the first, is placed before the subject of the verb, as in *up he got* and *down he came*. This word order is so unusual that it is felt as "poetic license." In natural English, an adverb of this kind that is treated as an independent word must follow the verb.

Even then, there is very little choice about where it can be placed. The indirect object of a compound verb must always stand between the two parts of the compound, as *Mother* in *send Mother up some tea* and *her* in *send her up some*. If an indirect object is undesirable in this position for any reason, it must be replaced by a prepositional phrase, as in *send some up to Mother*. (See **indirect object.**) A pronoun usually stands between the two elements even when it is a direct object as in *send it up*. A noun that is the direct object of a compound verb may stand between the two elements or may follow the second, as in *send the box up* and *send up the box*.

People who claim that "a preposition cannot follow its object" sometimes do not recognize the difference between a preposition and the second element in a compound verb. In their anxiety to be correct, they may misplace these adverbs. In a construction of this kind it is always proper for the adverb to follow the object. And if the object is a pronoun, that is the preferred position for the adverb. *Send up it* is not literary English!

Occasionally an adverb belonging to one of the other groups is used to qualify the verb itself rather than the full statement. In this case, the adverb stands immediately before the element in the verb that it qualifies. This is often one of the positions for a sentence adverb. The fact that the adverb is qualifying only one word is shown in speech by a heavy stress on that one word. For example, if a special stress is given to *said* in *I never said he was a fool,* the implication is *I only thought so*. In this case *never* qualifies the isolated word *said*. But this is an unusual construction. In written English the words will be read without stress and the adverb taken as a sentence adverb unless it is made clear that this is not the proper interpretation.

2. An adverb may qualify an adjective. As a rule, an adverb that qualifies an adjective is an adverb of degree, as in *a very red face, a mildly hot day, an astonishingly thin child*. Occasionally it may show manner, as in *a charmingly naive reply, an attractively stout matron*. A predicate adjective or an appositive adjective may sometimes be followed by a qualifying adverb, as in *it is lukewarm only, I am sick almost, a piece of rope longer still*. But the normal position for any adverb except a sentence adverb is immediately before the word it qualifies. In this role it normally qualifies the following word and no others.

Adverbs of degree, however, may qualify the word *a* or *an,* and so have the effect of qualifying the following noun and any intervening adjectives. For example, in *a quite small child, quite* is an adverb of degree qualifying *small*. But in *quite a small child* it qualifies the article and so has the effect of qualifying the phrase *a small child*. An adverb of degree combined with an adjective may function as a compound adverb and qualify *a* or *an* in exactly the same way, as in *so short a time, too low a price, so young and pretty a woman, no more remarkable a man.*

3. Adverbs may also qualify adverbs, and in this way one sometimes gets an accumulation of adverbs, as in *quite hopelessly entangled, not so very well done*. This is very different from an accumulation of adjectives. (See **adjectives.**) In a series of adjectives each word qualifies the noun, as qualified by all the intervening words. But in a series of adverbs each word qualifies only the word that immediately follows it. The relationship is very simple and the position of each word depends entirely on the meaning.

4. Since adverbs qualify adverbs and some adverbs easily turn into prepositions, it is not surprising that an adverb sometimes qualifies a preposition, as *just* in *just across the street* and *nearly* in *nearly through the door*. Here the adverb may be interpreted as qualifying the entire prepositional phrase.

5. Certain adverbs may be treated as if they were nouns, principally adverbs of time and place. They may be qualified by adjectives, as in *this once, every now and then*. They may be the object of a preposition, as in *by now, until then, from there*, or even the object of a verb, as in *leave here, reach there*. This is so far removed from the functions of an adverb that some grammarians say that any word that can be used in this way is a noun, in addition to being an adverb.

adversary. See **antagonist.**

adverse. See **contrary.**

advert; avert. To *advert* means to refer to in the course of a speech or conversation. To *avert* means to turn away or aside (*The auditor adverted to the deficit and the treasurer averted his eyes*). *Avert* also means to prevent (*Many superstitious practices seek to avert evil*).

advertising. From radio, newspaper, billboard, car card, television, from the backs of taxis, the sides of trucks, from skywriting airplanes —from every inch of space that can be painted over, through every moment of the day and night, we are besought, implored, flattered, cajoled, and threatened by advertising. It would be astonishing if the language of this clamorous din did not in some way have a lasting effect on our speech.

In so far as advertising English fulfills one of its two chief functions, letting us know what has been produced, it differs little from any other factual writing. Federal, state, and local laws see to it that there is a reasonable degree of accuracy in describing a product offered for sale. The manufacturer's—or his sales department's—only way around this is to give some common substance or performance an unusual name, so that the public will

think that in this incomprehensible thing they are obtaining mysterious excellence. And so we have *irium* and *gardol* and *Xg4* and *cationic action* which may sell the product but are, fortunately, barred by common sense from entering the language.

It is in its fulfilling of its second and major function, urging us to buy, beseeching us to indulge ourselves, to gratify our whims and vanities, that advertising strains the language. For every product must not only insist that it is the best of its kind but that it is even superior to its own self of six months ago. Superlatives have long since been exhausted and intensives relaxed with overuse and the desperate copy writers have fallen back upon comparisons that do not compare: "Blitz contains 32.5% more cleansing action," "Mopes guarantee 3.1416% more satisfaction." One is not told *than what*. It is simply assumed that the reader is an idiot or is too worn out to care.

The evil effect is actually not very great, for advertising engenders its own anti-toxin, but it must contribute somewhat to the deadening of expression by exaggeration. On the other hand, it is likely to be sensitive to the idiom of spoken English. For, except for one or two products, most things that advertise extensively are dependent upon the mass market and seek to appeal to it in the everyday language of the people. A schoolteacher who said "like" where the grammars recommend "as" might be reprimanded; a copy writer for a cigarette advertisement who used "as" in such a context would be fired.

advice; advise; inform. *Advice* is an opinion, recommended or offered as worthy to be followed. To *advise* is to proffer such an opinion. The first is a noun, the second a verb. (*It is good advice not to advise people too freely*).

The use of *to advise* in business letters (*beg to advise*) meaning to inform is happily falling into disuse. To *inform* is to communicate certain facts, but to *advise* is to suggest that a course of conduct be followed. Since such a suggestion must, of necessity, imply that whatever course of conduct was being followed before the advice was received was either inadequate or wrong, the suggestion is patronizing and may be resented. See also **tell.**

Advise may be followed by an infinitive, as in *I advise him to start at once*, or by the *-ing* form of a verb, as in *I advise his starting at once*. It may also be followed by a *that* clause. But in this case, if *advise* means recommend, the clause verb must be a subjunctive or a subjunctive equivalent, as in *I advise that he go at once*. The infinitive construction is preferred. If *advise* is used to mean merely inform, the clause verb is in the indicative, as in *I advised him I was going.*

advisedly; intentionally. That which is done *advisedly* is done deliberately, after due consideration. That which is done *intentionally* is done by design, with an object, a purpose, an end in view. But human nature being what it is, the two things are far from the same. All first-degree murders are done intentionally; few are done advisedly.

aegis. In Greek mythology the *aegis* is the shield of Zeus. There is only one aegis and in its classical sense the word does not have a plural. Anyone, therefore, who feels the need for a plural should use the English form *aegises,* rather than the pseudo-classical *aeges.*

aerie is the preferred spelling for the nest of a bird of prey, though *aery, eyrie,* and *eyry* are also acceptable.

aesthetics means the philosophy of the beautiful. The adjective *aesthetic,* which is older than the noun *aesthetics,* means responsive to the beautiful. Darwin wrote: *Birds appear to be the most aesthetic of all animals, excepting of course man, and they have nearly the same taste for the beautiful as we have.* Today *aesthetic* may also be used to mean conforming to the principles of aesthetics, and one may hear of *aesthetic wallpaper.* This makes some people wish that we had the second adjective *aesthetical* in common use, in order to distinguish between these very different meanings of the word.

affect; effect. These are totally different words. *Affect* is always a verb (except in a special use in psychology where it denotes a feeling or emotion). It means to act on, to impress, to produce a change in, and it also means to pretend, to feign, to make a show of (*Music affects some people very strongly. She affects great delicacy*). See also **pretend.**

The verb *effect* means to produce as a result, to bring about, to accomplish, to make happen (*He effected his escape by slugging a guard*).

The noun *effect* means result or consequence (*The effect of her scolding was to make the boy angry*); power to produce results (*His pleas were of no effect*); a mental impression produced by painting or a speech or music or some other art or skill (*The decorations made quite an effect*).

Effects, the plural, means personal possessions (*The dead soldier's effects were sent to his family*).

The adjectives stemming from *effect* are often confusing. There are four of them. *Efficacious* means that which produces a desired effect (*The treatment was efficacious and the patient recovered*). *Efficient* means adequate in performance, having and using the requisite knowledge and skill, competent (*The diesel engine is highly efficient. He was an efficient man and soon got the job done*). *Effectual* means adequate, capable of producing the desired effect (*The hydrogen bomb is an effectual weapon only against a few very large cities*). *Ineffectual,* applied to persons, has come to mean vaguely and generally incompetent and useless. *Effective* means producing an intended result (*The tax was effective in limiting incomes*) or it can mean actually in effect (*Prohibition became effective in 1919*).

affection; affectation. In its most general sense, *affection* means settled good will, love, warm attachment (*His affection for his children was touching to see*). *Affectation* means the striving for the appearance of some quality or ability not actually possessed, pretense, artificiality of manner or conduct, an attempt to attract attention by an assumed manner, and so on. (*An affectation of manner can easily alienate affection*).

Formerly the words were interchangeable. Sheridan in *The School for Scandal* speaks of a *gross affection of good manners* and Gibbon refers, with obvious approbation, to a lady's *affectation of the manners, the language, and the literature of France.*

affiliate; affiliation. To *affiliate* is to assume the relation of a child to a parent. This meaning is retained in law where the term means to affix the paternity of a child (*The mother affiliated the child upon Richard Roe*). Branch banks are affiliated with the parent bank and in England (where the word is restricted almost exclusively to this meaning) colleges are affiliated with the university.

In America the term is used loosely for joining, accepting membership in, or even for merely associating or being friendly with (*He affiliated with the Baptist Church. Our nearest neighbors live several miles away, and we don't affiliate with them much*). There is an element of pompousness in these uses, however, and unless a closer relationship than just joining or associating with is meant, it is better to avoid *affiliate.*

affinity. Since *affinity* means an attraction to or a natural liking for, the use of *to* or *for* with it is redundant. *Affinity* is *with* a thing, *between* two things or persons.

affirm. See **declare.**

affix. An *affix,* in grammar, is any meaningful element (prefix, infix, suffix) added to a stem or base, as *-ed* is added to *kill* to make *killed* or *intra-* is prefixed to *mural* to make *intramural.*

afflatus. The plural is *afflatuses* or *afflatus,* not *afflati.*

afflict. See **inflict.**

affluent. See **rich.**

afford may be followed by an infinitive, as in *I can't afford to go every night,* or by the *-ing* form of a verb, as in *I can't afford going every night.* The infinitive is generally preferred.

a fortiori is not the same as *a priori. A priori* is arguing from cause to effect, from a general law to a particular instance (its opposite, *a posteriori,* is arguing back from effects to causes). *A fortiori* is stating a fact which must be even more obviously true if one already accepted is true. Thus if it is accepted that so-and-so drank a gallon of beer, it is an a fortiori fact that he must have drunk two quarts. See also **a priori.**

afraid. This adjective cannot be used immediately before a noun. We may say *the man was afraid* but not *the afraid man.*

Afraid may be followed by a clause, as in *he is afraid he will die,* or by an infinitive, as in *he is afraid to die*. These two constructions do not mean exactly the same thing. *Afraid* may also be followed by the *-ing* form of a verb with the preposition *of,* as in *he is afraid of dying.* This construction may mean just what the clause means, or just what the infinitive means.

African. In England and America an *African* is a Negro, a member of one of the black races inhabiting Africa. An *Afrikaner,* however, in Afrikaans, the language of the Afrikaners, is a white man of Boer descent living in South Africa. The English form of *Afrikaner* is *Afrikander.* A *South African,* in either English or Afrikaans, is a white citizen of any European descent who claims South Africa as his homeland.

Native is the official term for Negro in the Union of South Africa. Most natives call themselves natives, but the educated among them dislike the term and call themselves *Africans.* This is in accord with English and American usage, but it conflicts with Afrikaans in which *Afrikaner* means a white, not a black. In English as used in South Africa no white man is a *native* (even though native) and no black man is a *South African* (even though he and his ancestors have lived in South Africa for many generations). See also **Caucasian, European, mulatto, Negro.**

after. This word may be used as a simple adverb, as in *Jill came tumbling after;* as a preposition with an object, as in *after you, my dear;* or as a conjunction introducing a clause, as in *after you leave.* It is also well established as an adjective, as in *the after life, in after years.* The adjective has a superlative form *aftermost,* which can also be used as a noun.

The basic meaning of *after* is behind or later. This easily becomes following, as in *they throng after him.* From the sense of following, *after* has come to show the aim or object of certain actions, as in *look after the cats* and *strive after success.* This use of *after* is not very widespread; in many cases *for* is preferred.

When *after* is used as a conjunction, the subordinate verb (in the *after* clause) may be in the simple present tense or the simple past tense instead of in the present perfect or past perfect tense. That is, we may say *I will tell them after you leave* instead of *after you have left,* and *I told them after you left* instead of *after you had left.* In Ireland a similar construction is sometimes heard in the principal verb in a sentence, as in *I am after saying* instead of *I have been saying,* but this is not standard English in either the United States or Great Britain.

aftermath. An *aftermath* was a second mowing of a crop of grass from the same land in the same season (*The aftermath seldom or never equals the first herbage*). Except as a deliberate archaism this literal use is now never heard. The word is now used solely in a figurative sense, meaning *results,* and usually unpleasant results of some disastrous occurrence (*the aftermath of war, the aftermath of the storm*). To use it to mean merely anything that follows

is to use it loosely (as in *The ancient football rivalry between Washington State College and the University of Idaho includes a time-honored custom. As an aftermath of each game students from the losing school must walk to the winning campus for appropriate ceremonies*). This whole quotation, by the way, illustrates the pretentiousness and exaggeration so common in sports writing, in which *aftermath* is a favorite word. Since one of the colleges mentioned was founded in 1889 and the other in 1890, "ancient" and "time-honored" are a little strained.

Any careful use of *aftermath* will at least suggest its literal meaning. Pestilence may properly be called the aftermath of war if it is caused by the dislocation during war of peacetime protections against disease, because it is a second, bitter harvest. The San Francisco fire was an aftermath of the earthquake.

after my own heart. The expression *He is a man after my own heart* is a cliché. The careful writer will avoid it. *After* here means like or after the nature of. It is a biblical echo (*who walk not after the flesh, but after the spirit*) and should not be used except when its exact meaning is fully understood.

afterward; afterwards. Both forms are used in the United States, where *afterward* is generally preferred. *Afterwards* is the only form used in England.

again; against. At one time these words were used interchangeably but they now have different meanings and different uses. *Again* now means once more and does not have an object, as in *he ran again.* *Against* means opposed to and always has an object, as in *he ran against a wall.*

Again usually, but not necessarily, follows its verb, as in *he ran again.* When it precedes the verb it may mean "on the other hand" or "speaking again," as in *he fell, but then again he ran.*

agate, meaning a printing type (5½ point) of a size between pearl and nonpareil, is the American term for what in England is called *ruby.*

agendum. An *agendum* is something to be done. The word has two plural forms, *agendums* and *agenda. Agenda* may also be used to mean a list of agendums and it is then treated as a singular, as in *the agenda is being prepared.* In this sense *agenda* has its own plural *agendas,* meaning several such lists, as in *the agendas were compared.*

agent. In various specialized uses the word *agent* has different meanings in America and England. The American *ticket agent* is in England a *booking clerk.* The English *newsagent* is in America a *newsdealer.*

In the early days of the West a *road agent* was a highwayman. It was often shortened to *agent.* The designation was probably originally intended to be humorous and sometimes appeared within quotation marks.

aggravate; annoy; irritate; exasperate; provoke. To *aggravate* means to make heavier. It can be used properly only of the augmentation or intensification of some evil, some sorrow, grievance, or offense (*The failure of his business aggravated Mr. Dombey's grief for the death of his son*). Its common use to mean *annoy* (*Don't aggravate me, child*) and still more common adjectival use (*He's such an aggravating man*) are colloquialisms ("feminine or childish," Fowler sternly calls them) not used in formal speech or writing.

Annoy is simply the French word *ennui* which now means boredom and that is all *annoy* meant at first, though it now expresses a somewhat stronger feeling of discomfort.

To *irritate* is to fret, to chafe, to gall, to excite to impatience or to feelings of anger, though not of any great depth or of any great duration. We speak of a wound as being irritated when through the chafing or rubbing of a coarse bandage it has been superficially inflamed.

Exasperate is a stronger word than *irritate* (though it is sometimes weakened to a mere synonym for *annoy*). The Latin root word *asper* means rough and harsh. A man is exasperated when he has been annoyed or irritated to the point where his self-control is threatened or lost. An exasperated man is a dangerous man.

To *provoke* is to stir up (literally, to call forth) sudden and strong feelings of anger or resentment, usually by some unwarrantable act or wanton annoyance (*The rage which Oswald's impertinence provoked in Lear, already annoyed by the delay of his dinner, was aggravated to fury by Goneril's insolence and the exasperated man rushed wildly from the palace*).

agnostic; atheist; heathen; infidel; pagan. The word *agnostic* was coined in 1869 by Thomas Henry Huxley to describe one who, like himself, felt that the ultimate nature of things, including the existence of a God, is unknown and probably unknowable.

An *atheist* is one who denies the existence of God or of gods (*Socrates was accused of atheism because he did not believe in Zeus*).

An *infidel* is an unbeliever. The word was rather specialized among Christians in former times to apply to Mohammedans and among Mohammedans to Jews and Christians. In recent years there has been a tendency in America to give the word a wider significance and have it apply to agnostics and atheists. Indeed many Americans if they felt that a Mohammedan was a devout believer in his own religion would be reluctant to call him an infidel.

The unconverted of other religions were called *heathens* or *pagans*, both words meaning originally country dwellers, i.e., rustic, backward folk who clung to their own religion after Christianity had been accepted in the cities. Both words, in current usage, tend to be used in slightly comic contexts. *Heathen* is often used jestingly of one who shows gross ignorance of some tenet of his professed faith. *Pagan* is often used to suggest a gay abandon and frank sensuality, such as is imagined at least to have been enjoyed before the dominance of Christian ethics.

agony; agonize. *Agony* is one of the strongest words in English. It means extreme, and generally prolonged, pain and suffering. And *to agonize* means to writhe with such pain (*The agony of the injured man was dreadful to see. He agonized for months over the thought of his son's execution*). To use it—as it is so often used—as a term for mere discomfort (*I was in agony in those new shoes*) doesn't even convey, as it is probably meant to, a feeling of one's suffering because the listener, hearing so violent a word and knowing from the speaker's appearance of health that it can't be justified, at once discounts it. The speaker is usually aware of this and in his turn seeks to bolster the word with extreme emphasis, usually prolonging the sound of the initial *a* into a wail. But it doesn't do much good. *My feet hurt* would most likely be more effective.

agree may be followed by an infinitive, as in *he agreed to go*, or by a clause, as in *he agreed that he would go*. If the *-ing* form of a verb is used we must say *agree on*, as in *he agreed on going*.

agreement: pronouns. See **pronouns.**

agreement: verbs. A verb is said to "agree with" its subject in number and person." Number means the distinction between singular and plural. Person means the distinction between the speaker (called the first person), the person spoken to (called the second person), and the person or thing spoken about (called the third person). English verbs do not show number or person in the past tense. We say *I spoke, he spoke, they spoke*. In the present tense the first and second person in the singular and all three persons in the plural have the same form. We say *I, we, you*, and *they speak*. But the third person singular has a distinctive final *s*, as in *he speaks*. There are a few defective verbs, such as *may, can, might*, which do not show number or person in any tense. The verb *to be* is the only other exception to what has just been said. In the past tense it has two forms, *was* and *were*. In the present tense it has a distinctive first person singular (*am*) as well as a third person singular (*is*) and a general plural form (*are*). (For archaic forms of the verb, see **thee; thou.**) In American English, there is no difference in number or person in the future tense. (In Great Britain *shall* and *will* are used differently in different persons. See **shall; will.**)

NUMBER

Since we can get along with only one form in the past tense, it is obvious that we do not need two forms in the present, but we have two forms and, whether we want to or not, we must decide whether a present tense verb is to be singular or plural. We cannot avoid committing ourselves one way or the other.

The number of an English verb is determined by the actual meaning of the subject or by the grammatical form of the subject element standing closest to the verb. In the King James Bible there is a sentence, *light and understanding and excellent wisdom is found in thee.* Here the singular form *is* may have been used because the writer felt that one thing had been mentioned three times rather than three separate things, or because the word *wisdom* is singular. In a recent translation of the Bible this sentence reads: *light and understanding and excellent wisdom are found in thee.* Here the plural form *are* following the singular form *wisdom* abruptly reminds us that more than one thing is being talked about. The reader who has not realized this must go back and ponder over the meaning of the preceding words.

Usually, as in the last example, a compound subject that involves the word *and* is plural. This is always the case when two distinct things are meant even though only one word is used, and that a singular, as in *the red and the white rose are both beautiful.* When obviously only one thing is meant, as in *the sum and substance is,* a plural verb is ridiculous. Between these extremes is a middle ground where the speaker can decide which form he wants to use, as in *the tumult and the shouting dies.*

A compound subject involving *or* is usually treated as singular if the separate elements are singular and the statement is affirmative, as in *either Dorothy or Andy is at home.* But if the second element is plural, the verb too will be plural, as in *one or two friends are coming.* Constructions in which the first element is plural and the second singular are avoided. In a negative statement, a compound subject involving *or* or *nor* is usually treated as plural, as in *neither Dorothy nor Andy are at home.* (Some grammarians object to this and claim that a singular verb is required in this construction but neither current usage nor literary tradition support their claim.)

A singular subject followed by a parenthetical phrase may be treated as a singular, as in *the island of Australia together with Tasmania constitutes the commonwealth of Australia,* or as a plural, as in *the sheriff with all his men were at the door.* If an affirmative and a negative idea are combined, the verb agrees with the affirmative, as in *justice, not better jobs, is our goal.*

Measures or quantity words that are grammatically singular may be treated as singulars or as plurals, depending on whether the quantity spoken about is thought of as a unit or as a collection of separate items, as in *one half of the country is desert* and *one half of the population are illiterate.* A plural verb is usually preferred in speaking about human beings. Words of this kind that are grammatically plural may also be treated as singulars when what is mentioned is thought of as a unit, as in *ten days is a long time* and *two paces of the vilest earth is room enough.*

Sometimes a subject that would have a singular verb if it and the verb were standing together is given a plural verb because a plural word is standing between them. For example, a singular verb is used in *no one was listening* and *there is a pile of books on the table.* But the verb is made plural in *not one of them were listening* and *a pile of books were on the table.* Although some people protest, there is nothing objectionable about this use of a plural verb. A statement of this kind is actually about a group of people or things, which may be considered as a singular or as a plural. In cases of this kind we usually settle for the form of the word that is standing closest to the verb.

Titles of books which have a plural form, such as *Canterbury Tales* and *Dickens' American Notes,* may be treated as singular or as plural.

Even when the subject of a verb is a single word, the number of the verb will depend upon the meaning rather than the form of the subject. Singular nouns are sometimes used in a plural sense and some nouns which have a plural form are nevertheless singular in meaning. (For special problems of this kind, see **adjectives as nouns, generic nouns, group names, mass nouns, plural nouns, singular nouns,** and the individual words.)

An interrogative pronoun is usually treated as a singular. That is, we may say *who is coming?* and *what is in the box?* regardless of how many people or things are to be expected. *Who* and *which* may also be followed by a plural verb. We may say *who are coming?* and *which are finished?* But a great many people dislike this construction and feel obliged to insert a plural word, as in *who all are coming?, which ones are finished?.* A relative pronoun is singular or plural depending upon its antecedent. That is, we say *the man who was here* and *the men who were here.*

PERSON

All nouns and almost all pronouns are third person and their problems are taken care of under questions of number. The only exceptions are the personal pronouns *I, me, we, us, you,* and interrogatives or relatives representing one of these. The words *me* and *us* cannot be used as the subject of a verb. The word *we* is plural and the word *you* is always treated as a plural. In American English no verb shows person in the plural. This means that questions of person are reduced to the question of what form of the verb should be used with *I* or a word standing for *I.* In all verbs except *to be, I* has the form that is used in the plural. We say *I have, they have, I do, they do.* In the verb *to be, I* has the present tense form *am* and the past tense form *was.*

As a rule, the verb following an interrogative pronoun is in the third person. But when an interrogative *who* or *what* is followed by a form of the verb *to be* and a personal pronoun, the interrogative is felt to be the complement rather than the subject of the verb and the form of the verb is determined by the personal pronoun, as in *who am I?, who is he?, who are you?*. The interrogative *which* may be used in the same way. That is, we might say *which are you?* or *which am I?*, meaning to which group do you belong or do I belong? But *which* may also be felt as the subject of the verb and treated as a third person singular. That is, in looking at a picture of a group of people, we might say *which is you?*

Theoretically, the relative pronouns *who, which,* and *that* require the form of the verb that would be used with the antecedent. That is, one should say *it is silly to ask me who know nothing about it* and *it is silly to ask you who know nothing about it* because one would say *I know, you know*. In practice, a great many people treat the relatives *who, which,* and *that* as third person pronouns which may be singular or plural but which do not carry over any difference in person. That is, many people would say *it is silly to ask me who knows nothing about it*. This is not literary English. But very few people hear it as a grammatical mistake and some feel uncomfortable when the technically correct literary form is used.

An explanatory noun following *I* or *you* does not affect the person of the verb. That is, we say *I, your teacher, am aware* and *you, my teacher, are aware,* and not *is aware*.

When a verb has both an affirmative and a negative subject, it follows the person of the affirmative, as in *I, not you, am to blame* and *you, not I, are to blame*. Theoretically, with any other kind of compound subject the person of the verb is determined by the word standing nearest it, as in *death and I am found eternal* and *neither he nor I am timid*. In practice, most people treat these compound subjects as plural wherever possible. They may be treated as plural when the compound is made with *and*, as in *death and I are found eternal,* or is negative, as in *neither he nor I are timid*.

A compound subject involving *either - - or* is much harder to handle. According to the rules, the last pronoun is the decisive one and we should say *either he or I am responsible* and *either you or I am responsible*. This "correct" form is seldom heard. Some people would use *is* and some people would use *are* in each of these constructions. But most people would avoid the question by saying *either he is responsible or I am*. One grammarian, commenting on this, says, "most people dodge the necessity of making a choice between the two persons as though it were an educational test which they dreaded to meet." But it might be that we dodge it because there is no satisfactory answer. Problems of persons are so rare in English that any construction which calls attention to them seems unnatural.

agree to disagree. The value of antithesis is that it shocks us into attention. Pope's description of a huge, pretentious, but basically commonplace country mansion as a *heap of littleness,* or his statement that Man is *the glory, jest, and riddle of the world* fix themselves in our minds by the striking contrast of the opposing ideas that he brings together. But when repetition has removed the element of surprise, indispensable to the shock, antithesis is likely to be annoying, because it suggests that the speaker thinks he can be clever without making any effort of his own. One can *quote* a brilliant antithesis, since the acknowledgment removes any suggestion that one is claiming the wit as one's own, but one must always bear in mind that a little quoting goes a long way.

Agree to disagree is a cliché, clever when first thought of but long since worn out, along with the patience of those who must hear it.

aid. See **help.**

ailment. See **sickness.**

aim. When *aim* is used in a physical sense, the place is introduced by *at,* as in *aim the gun at the barn door*. In the United States, when *aim* is used in the sense of intend it is followed by an infinitive, as in *I aim to be friendly*. When used in this sense in Great Britain, it is followed by *at* and the *-ing* form of the verb, as in *I aim at being friendly*.

ain't. This word may mean *am not, is not, are not, have not,* or *has not*. It is heard in *I ain't ready, that ain't true, they ain't here, I ain't got it, he ain't got it,* and so on. It is not considered standard in any of these cases, with the possible exception of *am not* used in a question, that is, *ain't I?*

In the United States most people consider *ain't I?* in a class with *he ain't* and the other unacceptable forms. But a few bold spirits insist on using it because the language needs an expression of this sort. *Am I not?* is much too stiff for ordinary conversation and *amn't I?* is practically impossible to say. In England *aren't I?* is considered acceptable spoken English. But in England the *r* in *aren't* is not pronounced. What is actually said is more like *aunt I?* The difference between the English *aren't I?* and the American *ain't I?* is simply the difference that we have in the two pronunciations of *tomato*. However, some Americans who would not say *ain't I?* feel that *aren't I?*, pronounced with its full American *r*, is very respectable. Others consider it affected or "kittenish."

air line. The phrase *air line,* which today in American usage means a company furnishing air transport (usually in scheduled flights), meant up until fifty years ago what we now call a *bee line,* i.e., a straight line, as through the air (*Take any common map . . . and rule an air line across it from Baltimore to St. Louis*). Several railroads incorporated the term into their names to remind the public of the economical directness of their routes. Of these the best known now is the Seaboard Air Line.

airplane is now the universal American spelling and pronunciation. The English still use *aeroplane,* though *airplane* is becoming increasingly common among them.

airship, when used at all, designates what is now more generally called a *dirigible,* a lighter-than-air craft which, in contradistinction to a free-floating *balloon,* may be navigated.

aisle. The English, for the most part, restrict *aisle* to the lateral division of a church separated from the nave by piers or columns or to the passageway between the seats in a church. In America both of these meanings are known and used, but the word is extended to denote any kind of passageway between seats, as in theaters and public conveyances. *Two on the aisle,* which would be incomprehensible to the English, or suggest a marooned couple, means to an American two especially desirable seats in a theater.

alas, poor Yorick! It is sad that "a fellow of infinite jest, of most excellent fancy" should be known to us only through such a thread-bare quotation. Alas, indeed, poor Yorick! There is another line from *Hamlet* that should always be uttered after this one: "What, has this thing appear'd again tonight?" Or, if one perceives that it is about to be spoken, appeal to the speaker's better nature: "Refrain tonight, and that shall lend a kind of easiness to the next abstinence." And if he does forbear: "For this relief, much thanks."

albino. The plural is *albinos,* not *albinoes.* A female albino used to be called an *albiness,* but the word has fallen into disuse. Sex distinctions have nothing to do with albinism.

albumen; albumin. *Albumen* is the white of an egg. *Albumin* is a biochemical term for any of a class of water-soluble proteins. The chemical term is sometimes spelled *albumen,* but the white of an egg is never spelled *albumin.*

alcoholic. See **drunkard.**

alga. The plural is *algae.*

alias means another. The legal term *alias dictus,* of which the common term is an abbreviation, means called at another time or place. Thus *Smith alias Jones* indicates that a man who now calls himself Smith had at some other time or place called himself or had been called Jones.

alibi in law means the defense of having been somewhere else when a crime of which one stands accused was committed (*The fact that he was speaking before a large audience in Boston, three hundred miles away from the scene of the crime, at the time the murder was committed proved a perfect alibi*). By a natural extension it has come to be used in common speech as a synonym for excuse and, as a verb, to offer an excuse. Ring Lardner's Alibi Ike was a baseball player who always had a self-exculpating excuse for anything wrong that he did. When *Life* referred to a certain prizefighter (July 26, 1954) as *an inveterate alibier,* it meant that he could always explain away his failures. When, however, George Orwell (in "England Your England") says that *the wealthy ship-owner or cotton-miller set up for himself an alibi as a country gentleman,* he may mean that the businessman

wished to prove that he could not have been responsible for the crimes of his business, since he was tending his acres, an innocent bucolic, at the time they were committed. Or he may have meant *alias,* that is that the ship-owner or cotton operative wished to go under the then more respectable name of a country gentleman.

Cynicism and the common man's distrust of the law have tinged *alibi* with a suggestion of improbability and even of dishonesty. Purists insist that it should be restricted to its legal meaning, and those who wish to be formally correct will so restrict it. In so doing, however, they will lose the connotation of cunning and dishonesty which distinguishes it from *excuse.*

alight. The past tense is *alighted* or *alit.* The participle is also *alighted* or *alit. Alighted* is the preferred form for the past tense and the participle. *Alit* is archaic.

Alight means to come down deliberately, or with dignity, and we may say *he alighted from the plane.* Things which are not under their own control, such as stones and snow flakes, are said to *light,* and not to *alight,* and we therefore say *he lighted* (or *lit*) *on his head.*

Alight was once also used in the sense of kindle. This usage has completely disappeared except for the adjective *alight,* as in *my candle is alight.*

alike. Thirty or forty years ago some textbooks on English claimed that *alike* could not be used to mean *similarly,* as in *he treats everyone alike.* There is no justification for this claim. *Alike* has been used in this way at least as long as we have had printed books.

alit. See **alight.**

all may be used with a singular noun, as in *all flesh is mortal,* or with a plural noun, as in *all men are brothers.* When used with a singular, *all* means "the whole of it." With a plural, *all* was originally used collectively to mean the entire number taken as a whole or unit, as in *all the angles in a triangle are equal to 180 degrees.* Later, it was also used distributively to mean every one of the individuals referred to, as in *all the angles in a triangle are less than 180 degrees.* Today, *all* with a plural noun usually means "every" but it may also mean "the total." Conceivably, this could create a misunderstanding in some situations.

All is primarily an adjective and qualifies a noun, as in *all things to all men.* It usually precedes its noun, as in *all children believe,* but may also follow it, as in *children all believe.* When it precedes the noun it also precedes all other qualifiers, as in *all these dear little children.*

All is sometimes used as a noun, as in *one who gave all.* It may be used after an objective pronoun, as in *us all,* which is grammatically comparable to *us men;* and either before or after a subjective pronoun. Formerly it frequently came before a subjective pronoun, as in *all we like sheep have gone astray.* This order is still acceptable, but in current English the *all* is more often placed second, as in *we all have strayed.* When used with the pronoun *it*, *all* must be placed second, as in *it all came to nothing.* We can no longer say *all it.* In literary English *all* is not used with *what*, as in *what all did he say?* This is an Americanism. It is acceptable spoken English in the United States but does not often appear in print.

The phrase *all of*, as in *all of us*, is a relatively new construction and fifty years ago was considered rare except with pronouns. It is formed on the pattern of *none of*, *some of*, *any of*, where *of* means belonging to or part of. Some grammarians feel that it is illogical to treat the whole as a part, but it is hard to see why this is any more illogical than treating none as a part. In any case, the grammatical form is now well established and is freely used with nouns as well as pronouns, as in *all of the people.*

In literary English the word *all* does not form a genitive. We do not say *all's opinion* but *the opinion of all* or *everybody's opinion.* This is also true when *all* is combined with a pronoun. *You all's* is heard in the South and is respectable English in some areas. But it is condemned by many Southerners who are nevertheless proud to say *you all.* *We all's*, as in *we all's house*, is not standard anywhere. *All* never qualifies a possessive pronoun. In *it was all our fault*, the *all* attaches itself to *it*; in *all our faults*, it attaches to *faults.* If what is meant is *it was the fault of us all*, the idea cannot be expressed by a genitive or a possessive pronoun.

All may be used as an adverb (qualifying words that are not nouns) whenever the word *entirely* could be substituted, as in *His Royal Highness was all smiles and his consort all diamonds; the heart, all exhausted by doubt;* and the familiar phrases *all powerful, all too soon.* In *they were all dressed up*, the meaning is not "entirely" but "very much." Some grammarians object to this use of *all* but it is accepted spoken English in the United States today. *All but* means "everything short of" and can be used to mean "almost," as in *the all but overpowering urge.*

All the before a comparative form, as in *they laughed all the louder* and *she was all the better for it*, is standard English whenever the comparative itself is justified, as in *they laughed louder, she was better.* This is not the case with *that's all the further it goes* and *is that all the later it is?* Forms like these were used in English literature until about 1600, and they can still be heard in the speech of educated Americans. But they are now considered nonstandard by most grammarians and do not often appear in print. In literary English one says *that's as far as it goes* and *isn't it any later than that?*

Not all is and *all is not* usually mean exactly the same thing. Some grammarians claim that the last part of the line *What though the field be lost? All is not lost!* is a slovenly construc-

tion which, in strict logic, means that none is lost. By the same reasoning, *not all the water in the rough rude sea can wash the balm from an anointed king*, is held to mean, again speaking strictly, merely that some cannot. There is no foundation at all for this distinction. In both cases, regardless of where it appears, *not* negatives the entire sentence. In the strictest logic, both sentences mean: *it is not true that all is lost* or *that all the water can wash* and so on. The sentences as they stand are not ambiguous. If they had been, the critic could not have been so sure that they did not say exactly what they meant. Distinctions such as this, between *all is not* and *not all is*, appeal to a fictitious logic and seem to have been invented for the purpose of proving other people in the wrong. They are not good for much else. Certainly no one should be encouraged to think that *all is not lost* is one way of saying *nothing is lost.* See also **at all** and **still and all.**

all right. The form *alright* sometimes appears in print. It is as justifiable, on theoretical grounds, as *already* and would allow us to make the distinction between *the answers are alright* (satisfactory) and *the answers are all right* (every one of them). But at present most people object to the form *alright* and prefer to see it written as two words.

all things considered. This cautious introduction is better replaced with some specific suggestion or objection.

all things to all men. All men seek in complaisance to adapt their words and often their actions and opinions to suit those whose favor or friendship they desire. In ourselves this is tact or adaptability. In others it is servility, hypocrisy, or downright villainy. The cliché *all things to all men* which commonly describes this tendency has in its ordinary use a derogatory tinge, though St. Paul, from whose writings it is taken (I *Corinthians*, 9:22), makes it a boast.

all to the good. Originally spoken of something not good in itself but which conduced to a whole that was good, *all to the good* is now a hackneyed phrase that has lost all meaning except as an expression of approval at the accretion of something desirable. It has little specific meaning and should be avoided.

allege; assert. To *allege* originally meant to state under oath (*If thou canst ought allege that may be against him, come before the judge*). Then it came to mean to state positively (*Tertullian alleges the contrary*). In current usage it means to state something without adequate proof (*But men in love with their opinions may not only suppose what is in question, but allege wrong matter of fact*).

To *assert* now has the older meaning of to *allege*: to state as true (*She asserted her innocence in the strongest terms. It is not directly asserted, but it seems to be implied*).

It is alleged is sometimes used as a disclaimer of responsibility, but those who so use it should know that its use does not confer immunity from prosecution for libel. The law punishes the *publication* of a libel and publication, in the legal sense, means making public. If you repeat a libel in print, with or without disclaimers, you have published it; you do not have to originate the statement to be liable for it. See also **publish**.

allegory. An *allegory* is a sustained metaphor, a narrative in which the characters and actions are veiled representations of meanings implied but not stated. The best known allegories in English are the parables of the Gospels. The longest and most intricate is Spenser's *The Faerie Queene*. The wittiest is Swift's *A Tale of a Tub*. One of the most successful recent allegories is George Orwell's *Animal Farm*.

The virtue of allegory is that it leads the reader to think for himself, or at least to think that he has thought for himself and so to accept the author's conclusions as his own. The fault of allegory is that its implications may be lost in the story and a false moral deduced instead of the intended one. Thus a child told that the early bird gets the worm may identify himself with the worm and *not* be incited to rise betimes. Then, like all metaphors, allegories easily become ludicrous if one or more of the details is inappropriate.

allergic; antipathetic. An *allergy* is an abnormal sensitivity to certain things, such as dust, molds, pollens, and foods. A generation ago the word was a medical term, almost unknown to the layman. But with the growth of popular interest in allergies, the term *allergic* has come into use among the educated as a humorous term for a violent antipathy. The fact that sufferers from allergies on the ingestion or inhalation of even microscopic quantities of the substance to which they are allergic break out in hives, itch, sneeze, and weep makes the term both strong and ludicrous. *Antipathetic* (though it also means having a constitutional aversion) is too long and too serious, too pompous, for the purposes to which *allergic* is applied. It is still a slang term, but it shows every sign of becoming standard, though with humorous connotations.

alliance. See **liaison**.

alliteration is the repetition of the same sound (vowel or consonant, though the term is usually applied to the repetition of consonants) at the beginning of two or more consecutive or near words or stressed syllables. It was very common in older English poetry (*Then from the moorlands, by misty headlands,/ With God's wrath laden, Grendel came. In the habit of a hermit, unholy of works,/ I went wide in the world, wonders to hear*). It was a part of the highly artificial style called euphuism which Lyly's *Euphues* made a vogue in Elizabethan England ("wherein there is small offence by lightness given to the wise, and less occasion of looseness proffered to the wanton"). The romantic poets revived it and some of the nineteenth century poets carried it almost to

the limits of endurance (*The fair breeze blew, the white foam flew,/ The furrow followed free. The moan of doves in immemorial elms,/ and murmuring of innumerable bees*).

Apt alliteration's artful aid is now rarely invoked. Serious poetry, in its reaction against the stylistic excesses of the poetry of the nineteenth century, shuns it, but popular poetry still uses it (*He hit Tom Hall with a bursting ball/ A hand's breadth over the knee. It takes a heap o'living and some love to make a home*). Serious prose avoids it as strenuously now as it once sought it, but humor employs it and it is useful for emphasis and euphony. Because it is one of the strongest of mnemonic devices, it is used a great deal by advertisers who hope to have their slogans stick in the public mind (*Not a cough in a carload. A treat instead of a treatment*).

Like rhyme, however, of which it is a kind, alliteration can easily be overdone. To contemporary taste, it is one of those things of which "a little more than a little is by much too much." The safe rule is never to use it without a definite purpose and to be sure that the purpose could not be as well served in any other way.

allow. When this word means permit it may be followed by an object and an infinitive, as in *he allows us to smoke*, or, when there is no personal object, by the *-ing* form of a verb, as in *he allows smoking*. When the word means admit it may be followed by a clause, as in *he allowed that we were right*.

allow of; allow for. To *allow of* is to permit (*His weakened condition would not allow of his being questioned by the police*). To *allow for* is to leave a margin of time or space, to make a concession or to bear in mind as an extenuating circumstance (*You can't make it in an hour; you must allow for the detour. He allowed for her great age and was very patient in listening to her complaints*). *Allow for*, like *allow of*, may be followed by the *-ing* form of a verb, as in *allow for his being late*.

allow; permit; consent; let; accede. *Allow* implies the absence of any intent to hinder (*Does your mother allow you to go alone this way?*). *Permit* is often used as a synonym of *allow* but it has a connotation of more formality in the authorization. There must be a permission (*Though some things are commanded us and others forbidden, we are in many others permitted to follow our inclinations*). *Let* is the common everyday word for *allow* and *permit*. If it has a special connotation it is of allowing something to remain as it is or to suffer it to continue or proceed if it is already in motion.

To *consent* is to yield when one has the right to oppose, or at least to refrain voluntarily from opposing (*My poverty, but not my will, consents*). *Accede* is closely synonymous to *consent*, but it often implies a more active agreement, a joining oneself to or sharing in that which is consented to (*There are many who would accede without the faintest re-*

luctance to a barbarous custom, but would be quite incapable of an equally barbarous act which custom had not consecrated).

allspice is the name of a particular spice, pimento, and should not be called *allspices.*

allude; refer. To *allude* is to *refer* casually or indirectly. It calls attention covertly. When a man is alluded to he is not named; it is simply obvious that the remark is applicable to him (*He alludes to enterprises which he cannot reveal but with the hazard of his life*).

To *refer* is to direct attention specifically. One refers to a book by its title and author and to a passage in it by the page. When one seeking employment gives a *reference,* he names a particular person from whom his prospective employer may obtain information about him.

allure; lure; attract; invite; entice. *Allure,* like *attract,* has a neutral connotation. One may be allured or attracted to things harmful or beneficial (*The thirst for glory has allured many a man to his death. The beauty of the day allured the ladies into the garden*). To *lure,* however, to attract as by a falconer's *lure* or decoy, has a suggestion of evil. One is lured to ruin or lured away from one's work (*The proffered toleration was merely a bait to lure the Puritan party to destruction*). So also *entice,* to excite hope or desire by presenting pleasurable motives or ideas, is almost always used in a bad sense. The twisting and squirming of live bait, says gentle, lovable old Isaak Walton, *much enticeth the fish to bite without suspicion.* One is rarely enticed to good.

Invite when applied to persons means to ask them to come, to solicit their company, and carries a suggestion of kindness or courtesy. But when applied to things or conditions, it has an invidious connotation with ironical overtones (*Recklessness invites disaster. Not to resent these insults is to deserve and to invite them*).

Attract, as has been said, is neutral (*His vices have attracted much attention. Adorned she was indeed, and lovely to attract thy love*), but *attractive* is favorable, except in the legal phrase *an attractive nuisance* where the adjective has been tainted by its noun.

allusion; illusion; elusion; delusion. The words *allusion* and *illusion* are often pronounced alike and this has led to confusion. An *allusion* is a passing or casual reference, an incidental mention of something, whether directly or by implication (*These frequent allusions to the details of his private life eventually compelled him to proffer his resignation. The angry flush that at once overspread his face showed that he understood the allusion*). An *illusion* is something that deceives by producing a false impression, a deception, a mockery (*It was only an optical illusion*). An *elusion* is an avoidance of something, an escape (*The planting of flowers on Fanny's grave had been but a species of elusion of the primary grief*). It often has the connotation of a clever escape.

It is a rare word but its adjective, *elusive,* is common and easily confused with *allusive* and *illusive.*

A *delusion* differs from an *illusion* in that it is accepted without question (*some juggler's delusion. The unhappy woman labored under the delusion that her dead son was working in the next room and would appear within a few minutes*). That the sun goes around the earth is accepted today by educated people as an *illusion;* our senses say that it is so, but we know that it is not. Those who accept the appearance of its motion as a reality are *deluded.* Most of us have heard, at one time or another, why the appearance of the sun's motion is *illusory,* but we cannot remember the exact explanation; it has *eluded* our memories.

almighty. See **mighty.**

almighty dollar. When Washington Irving, in 1836, first used this expression to describe "the great object of universal devotion throughout our land," he coined an effective phrase because the word then most commonly associated with *almighty* was "God" and he was saying, in effect, that our commercialism was idolatrous. Few who use it today think of its implied rebuke for false worship. It is thought to describe the power which our wealth exercises in domestic and international affairs. But even in this sense it has been worn out. It is better not to use it at all.

almost ordinarily qualifies a verb, as in *he almost fell,* or an adjective, as in *he was almost certain.* It may also be used to qualify a noun, as in *the almost oblivion* and *in almost terror.* This is an extremely literary construction but it is used by Hawthorne, Coleridge, Thackeray, and others and is recognized by the *Oxford English Dictionary.*

almost and **nearly** both mean within a small degree of or within a short space of, but *almost* designates a smaller degree or a shorter space than *nearly.* A book that is almost completed is nearer its completion than one that is nearly completed.

In America *almost* is used with the negative (*There was almost no snow that winter*). In England *hardly any* or *scarcely any* would be more commonly used. See also **practically.**

alms. Originally this word was a singular, as in *this alms is given for the sick.* This construction may still be used but it has an archaic flavor. Today the word is usually treated as a plural, as in *these alms are given for the sick.* But there is no singular form *an alm* and we cannot speak of *several alms.* The form *alms* is used as the first element in a compound, as in *an alms box.*

alone. See **lonely.**

along; alongst. *Along* is the only acceptable form; *alongst* is not standard now. At one time *alongst* too was standard, as in *he sent his gallies alongst the coast,* but it has not been used in literary English for more than a hundred years.

alpha and omega. See **from A to Z.**

already. See **yet.**

alright. See **all right.**

altercation; fight. An *altercation* is a fierce dispute, a contentious debate (*A judicious reader looks for arguments and loathes altercations*), but it is a verbal encounter. It may easily lead to a *fight*, or physical encounter, but it isn't one. To say *In the altercation noses were bloodied and eyes were blackened* is to misuse the word, though it may be done humorously.

alternatively; alternately. *Alternatively* means the choosing of one or the other of two things or courses (*Alternatively, if you do not choose to fight you may run away*). *Alternately* means the coming of things of two kinds one after the other (*The black and white squares on a checker board are arranged alternately*), or turn and turn about (*We work our shifts alternately*).

alternatives. Some people feel that *alternative* means "one of two" and that it should never be used in any other sense. But a great many more people do use it to mean "one of any number." Gladstone, writing in 1857, said: *My decided preference is for the fourth and last of these alternatives.*

although. See **though.**

altogether; all together. *Altogether* is an adverb meaning wholly, entirely, completely (*He was altogether in the wrong*), or in all (*Altogether there were six of us*) or on the whole (*Altogether, it's just as well you didn't argue with him*).

All together means that the members of a group are or were or will be gathered together in one place (*I have put the bolts all together in the lower drawer. The family will be all together at Thanksgiving for the first time in ten years.*)

aluminum is the American form, *aluminium* the British. Some American chemists use *aluminium* to conform to the analogy of *sodium*, *beryllium*, *potassium*, and so on.

alumnus; alumni; alumna; alumnae. Learning, or the lack of it, was for centuries enshrouded in Latin and everything about a college had to be dignified with a Latin name. In Europe college graduates were known by the degrees they held, but in America a great many people went to college who never got degrees but who—to the delight and amazement of fund-raising officials—were often more vociferous and even more generous in their support of the college than many who had obtained degrees. It was plainly desirable to include them in a group that contained the graduates and to find a solemn name for the lot. The Latin word *alumnus*, foster son, was chosen for the individual and *alumni* for the group. The term had been used in England earlier, but it was and has remained rare there.

Alumnus is a masculine word, but that was all right at first because almost all college students were men, but when women started going to college it was felt that they ought to have a special designation and the feminine form, *alumna*, with the plural *alumnae* was adopted (*She is an alumna of Wilson College, in Chambersburg, Pa. The statistics of the comparative death rates of the alumnae and alumni of Oberlin . . .*). This usage is exclusively American but anyone who wants to use it is correct in doing so. However, the masculine applies to all former students in general (*All alumni are invited and urged to bring their husbands and wives*) and it is not an error to refer to a female graduate as an *alumnus* and to include women with men in the general group of *alumni*. It is an error, however, to use *alumna* as a plural or *alumni* as a singular. If you insist on talking Latin, it is not unreasonable to hold you to at least an elementary knowledge of it.

While some women's colleges may stress their femininity by referring to their Alumnae Guest House or Alumnae Magazine, *alumni* is the usual plural in combinations (*Alumni Day, alumni trustees, alumni banquet*).

When women were first admitted to American colleges there was a great to-do about their degrees. Logicians and feminists agreed that girls could not be *bachelors* of arts or of science and it was proposed, at various times and places, that they should be called *Maids of Philosophy, Laureates of Science,* or *Vestals of Arts.* But, as it so often does in linguistic matters, usage triumphed over logic and every year thousands of young ladies become bachelors of arts and of science without anyone thinking them a whit less feminine for doing so.

always; all ways. *Always* is an adverb meaning all the time, perpetually, uninterruptedly (*I'll be loving you, always. There'll always be an England. The faucet always drips that way; we can't turn it clear off*) or every time, as opposed to *occasionally* or *sometimes* (*He always takes the biggest share. He always leaves the house by six o'clock*).

At one time there was a word *alway*, but this is now archaic and confined to poetry. Both words are used in the King James Bible, and with the same meaning, as in *ye have the poor with you always* and *I am with you alway, even unto the end of the world.*

All ways means all possible ways (*All ways to cure him have been tried*).

am. See **be.**

a.m.; p.m. *A.M.* (also *a.m.* and A.M.), in its commonest meaning is an abbreviation of *ante meridiem,* before noon. *Nine a.m.* is correct. *Nine a.m. in the morning* is redundant. *Nine o'clock a.m.* is overworded. To say *I'll see you in the a.m.* is dreary jocosity.

P.M. (also *p.m.* and P.M.), is an abbreviation of *post meridiem,* after noon. All the above comments on *A.M.* apply also to *P.M.*

Sometimes, in writing the phrase out, *meridian* is written for *meridiem.* This is an understandable blunder, since *meridian* also means midday and *post meridian* means after noon.

But blunder it is, even though it will pass unnoticed by most readers.

amanuensis. The plural is *amanuenses.*

amateur; novice. An *amateur* is one who takes
an interest in something, usually in an art or
sport, for the pure love of it. The *gentlemen
amateurs* in the early days of boxing were not
necessarily practicers of the "manly art" themselves, but its patrons and spectators. Today the
word implies an interest sufficiently strong to
include some participation. There is about it
a faint flavor of bungling and a strong flavor
of enthusiasm. It is often used in condescension
and derogation (*It was not likely that an
amateur . . . should convict these astronomers
of gross ignorance*).

A *novice* is a beginner, whether professional
or amateur. A man may be a novice at his
trade or at a game, if he is only mastering
the rudiments. In ecclesiastical usage *novice*
has the special meaning of one who is on
probation or under training.

Amateur in American usage has a rather
specialized application to sports, where it
means an athlete who has never competed for
money. When such an athlete does receive
money, he is said to have lost his amateur
standing.

amatory; amorous; loving; lovable; adorable.
Amatory and *amorous* have a more frankly
sexual connotation than *loving.* Aphrodisiacs
have been called *amorous medicines, amatory
fascinations,* and *amatories.* An amatory glance
is not the same thing as a loving look. Perhaps it is due to an association of *amorous*
with the French *amour* (everything French is
"sexy" in the popular imagination) or, perhaps, to its frequent riming, in popular song,
with *glamorous* [*q.v.*].

Loving is chaste as an adjective (*I will make
him a true and loving wife*) but concupiscent
as a noun in popular usage (*I need loving,
that's what I need!*).

Lovable is almost entirely divorced from
direct sexual connotation and, synonymous
with *amiable* and *winning,* is reserved for the
elderly, the charming, and the whimsical (*The
humorous pity that is so lovable a quality in
Chaucer*). The amatory synonym, in popular
parlance, is *adorable;* though the sexual meaning is lacking, at least at the conscious level,
when the word is applied to children, especially—as it so often is—to little girls. It may
then be considered as the superlative of *cute.*

Purists who insist that words must mean
"what they say" and refuse to accept the fact
that usage changes their meanings, should ask
themselves whether *adorable* which was applied exclusively to religious meanings so recently that the *Oxford English Dictionary*
recognizes no other applications of it could
now be applied to God, in America, without
moving the devout to uneasiness and the irreverent to levity?

amaze; surprise; astonish; startle; dumbfound.
To be *amazed* is, literally, to be lost in a maze,
to be bewildered, overwhelmed, confused,
stunned. A writer in 1586 said of a woman
that she struck her head so hard against a wall
that *she fell down amazed.* To be *surprised* is
to be come upon unexpectedly, to be taken
unawares (*. . . the surprise and combustion of
Troy*). To be *astonished* is, literally, to be
changed to stone, as if one had seen Medusa.
There is an Elizabethan reference to certain
medicinal waters that have the power to revive
the astonished and benumbed parts of the body
and another to those sick who lie *apoplectical
and astonished.* To be *startled* is to be so taken
by surprise as to make an involuntary start or
sudden movement (*After the first startle she
stood still*). To be *dumbfounded* is to be
stricken dumb with amazement. The word
seems to have been coined as a blend of *dumb*
and *confound.* But the *-found* in *dumbfound*
has no meaning; it is purely fantastic, like the
-muffin in *ragamuffin.*

Words do not, of course, always keep their
literal original meanings, but these particular
words keep enough of theirs to make the
careful writer, one who wishes to express the
exact shade of his meaning, choose among
them and not use them indiscriminately. There
is an apocryphal story told about Dr. Samuel
Johnson, the wit and lexicographer, which,
while it gives an erroneous picture of him,
illustrates the essential difference in meaning
between at least two of these words. The story
is that Johnson's wife came unexpectedly upon
him kissing the maid and exclaimed, "I am
surprised!" "No, Madam," he is reputed to
have answered, "*I* am surprised; *you* are
astonished."

ambiguity. The English language, with its immense vocabulary, its paucity of inflections, its
thousands of homonyms, its flexible grammar
and loose syntax, offers endless danger of (or
opportunity for) ambiguity. Ours is a language
in which almost every statement must be
watched lest it be open to another interpretation than the intended or the seeming one.

Unintentional ambiguity, of course, has
nothing to commend it. It only baffles the
reader or listener and leads to endless confusion and irritation or even disaster. Sometimes the ambiguity resides in a single word.
When we are told, for example, that *Newtonian
science makes us grasp only certain connections in nature,* are we to understand *certain*
as meaning "unquestionable" or "selected"?
More often the ambiguity emerges from a
whole construction. The biggest offender in
this respect in common speech and writing is
the pronoun in indirect discourse. In such a
sentence as "He told his brother that he had
been talking too much," the whole meaning
is dependent upon the antecedent of the second
"he" and the antecedent is not clear. Pronouns,
as a group, are probably responsible for more
unintentional ambiguity than any other part
of speech. Were our pronouns inflected, most
of this would disappear. But since they are

not, one of the cardinal requirements for clarity in English speech is to make sure that the antecedents of all pronouns are clearly perceived.

A great charitable foundation which must solicit millions of dollars from the public in order to carry out its work among those afflicted with infantile paralysis had as its slogan at the time of its drive a few years ago the sentence "You'll never walk alone" under the picture of a child with leg braces and other supports. The meaning was that a child so afflicted need not be in despair; he would always have the foundation beside him in his difficult years ahead. But the sentence could also mean "You will never again walk unaided by braces," a thought, especially when backed by the prestige of the foundation, that must have reduced many sufferers to pitiable despondency, thus doing the very opposite of what it was intended to do.

Other sources of ambiguity are dangling modifiers and participles (*After graduating from high school my father gave me a job selling cars*), misplaced modifiers (*I said when the short subject was over I would leave the theater*) and incomplete comparisons. The assertion *I like Joe as well as Jack* could mean *I like Joe as well as Jack likes Joe* or *I like Joe as well as I like Jack* or *I like Jack and Joe.*

Intentional ambiguity, the deliberate wording of a statement in such a way that two or more meanings may be drawn from it, has its literary and practical uses. Literary ambiguity serves to give extension to meaning, to open up several avenues of thought for the mind to explore, to give overtones to writing in the same way that symbols do. Like symbols, literary ambiguity makes the reader a creative partner of the writer rather than a mere passive receptor.

Practical ambiguity, by blurring meaning, serves diplomacy and humor. In serious use its intent is to evade, to avoid commitment; hence it is often found in political, diplomatic, advertising, professional and official language. It sometimes enables the speaker to speak the truth while allowing the listener to deduce a falsehood. More often it enables the speaker to avoid responsibility for his words by insisting that the meaning accepted was not the one intended.

The master of diplomatic ambiguity, setting a standard that has never been raised (or lowered), was the Oracle at Delphi. Some of its famous utterances—as *Pyrrhus the Romans shall, I say, subdue*—have never been improved on. Either side could take such a prediction as favorable and the oracle could always be wise after the event and side with the winner. Coolidge, up to the point of siding with the winner, was in the Delphic tradition with his *I do not choose to run.*

Every profession has its own clichés of evasion which the layman is expected to take at face value. Such diagnoses as "upper respir-

atory infection" for a cold or "gastro-enteritis" for a stomach ache pacify the patient with polysyllables and leave the doctor uncommitted. A successful Chicago physician used to reassure patients who were worried about their hearts: *Your heart will last as long as you will.* One of the spiritual oracles of our day, in his syndicated column, informed his readers that all nervous troubles "not organic or functional" were due to a lack of faith.

Anyone who has to evaluate another's work or behavior and make a public report of his evaluation—as in work reports, book reviews, students' report cards—must practice ambiguity to a certain extent in order to preserve the peace. To say, for instance, that a child is "not over-aggressive in the group" may avoid an argument with both the principal and the parent.

Ambiguity serves modesty. It serves to avoid a conflict of official position with personal conviction. And it permits ignorance to hide itself in vagueness.

Any pronouncement of policy or procedure that emanates from an official source—governmental or private—is likely to suffer in clarity from having passed through many revising hands. Generally, no one wants or is able to take full or specific responsibility, and no one wants to make it so rigid as to prevent adaptation to circumstances as yet unknown or unforeseen. Typically, the result is qualification piled on qualification, evasion under evasion, and the meaning faint and obscure.

For humor, ambiguity is the favorite resource of the wisecracker. When asked whether she had had anything on when the picture was taken, Miss Monroe replied, "The radio."

ambiguous and **equivocal** both mean having different meanings equally possible, susceptible of a double interpretation. The difference between them is that in *equivocal* the deception possible in the confusion of a double meaning is intentional. In *ambiguous* the deception may or may not be intentional. *Equivocation* is a word of strong condemnation; it means not only a lie but a carefully worded and, at the same time, a cowardly lie.

amend; emend. *Amend* means to alter for the better (*Do thou amend thy face*, Falstaff says to the red-nosed Bardolph, *and I'll amend my life*). Its commonest current usage is a specialized meaning of altering a motion or bill or the Constitution by due legal and parliamentary procedure. Such amendments are presumably alterations for the better but since, in most cases, this presumption is disputed by those who oppose the amendment, the word to many people has come to mean merely to change. Certainly the Eighteenth and the Twenty-first Amendments to the Constitution of the United States cannot both be improvements since one nullifies the other.

Emend was once only another spelling of *amend* but it has become specialized and now means to amend a text by removing errors (*Theobald's substitution of "a' babbled of green fields" for the First Folio's "a Table of greene fields," in Henry V, II. iii. 17-18, is probably the most brilliant emendation in our language).*

amends, meaning reparation for an injury, may be treated as a singular, as in *a full amends was made* and *every possible amends has been made,* or as a plural, as in *these amends were due us but he was in no hurry to make them.* Both of these constructions are standard English. But the word is not a true plural and we cannot speak of *several amends.* A singular form *amend* was once in use, as in *a full amend was made.* This is now obsolete or nonstandard.

America; The United States of America. It does seem a little hard on Canada and all the other countries that compose the Western Hemisphere for the United States of America to be called *America,* as if it were all. But, if it's any comfort to those who resent it, the usage is founded on a lazy disinclination to pronounce the longer name rather than arrogance and it has no official sanction. Dominant countries have always either taken over the name of an entire region or imposed their own names on the regions around them. Nothing can be done about it and it's silly to complain. After all, it can never equal the original injustice of calling two whole continents after Amerigo Vespucci.

amiable; amicable. People are usually spoken of as *amiable;* attitudes, dispositions, arrangements and settlements as *amicable (An amiable man is usually willing to make an amicable settlement).* An amiable person is sweet tempered, kind, gentle, thoughtful of others. He differs from a lovable person in that he does not so much invite as give affection. An amicable settlement usually means no more than a peaceful one: the parties need not be amiably disposed towards each other; it is enough that they are not in open conflict.

amid; amidst. Both forms are acceptable, but both are bookish. In the United States *amid* is considered a little less bookish than *amidst.* In Great Britain it is the other way around and *amidst* is considered the more natural word of the two. See also **among.**

ammunition. See **munitions.**

amoeba. The plural is *amoebas* or *amoebae.*

amok. See **amuck.**

among; amongst. Both forms are acceptable. *Among* is the preferred form in the United States, where *amongst* is often considered "over-refined." But *amongst* is also correct and is the preferred form in England.

Among is related to the word *mingle.* It means, roughly, in the midst of or surrounded by, and implies a group. It therefore cannot be used in speaking of only two objects, as the word *between* can. But nor can it be used in speaking of three or more objects unless these are thought of as a group. *Between* must be used if we want to suggest a relation or a difference between individuals, no matter how many individuals are involved. The *Oxford English Dictionary* says: "*Between* has been from its earliest appearance extended to more than two. . . . It is still the only word available to express the relation of a thing to many surrounding things severally and individually; *among* expressing a relation to them collectively [as a group] and vaguely." That is, we may say *the house stood among the trees* but we cannot define a triangle as *the space lying among three points;* we may say *he sat among the candidates* but we cannot say *he must choose among six candidates.* We speak of *a treaty between three nations* because each nation is bound individually to each of the others. We say *the five diplomats settled the question between them* in order to emphasize the fact that each member of the group agreed individually with each of the others. On the other hand, if we say *the three men had $30 among them,* we are treating the three men as a group and leaving the possibility open that one man had $30 and the other two had nothing at all.

Among cannot be followed by a subjective pronoun or any word or group of words that is obviously singular. However, it is sometimes followed by *each other* or *one another* where literary English requires *themselves* or *ourselves,* as in *they agreed among each other.* This is not at present acceptable in written English.

Although *among* and *amid* are sometimes used interchangeably, *among* is more likely to mean surrounded by or in relation to many things and is followed by a plural word (*among friends*). *Amid,* strictly, describes a middle position between two other things or groups of things and hence is followed by a singular word (*Amid the confusion, he stood calm).*

amoral. See **immoral.**

amorous. See **amatory.**

amount; number. *Amount* means bulk, sum total, aggregate, quantity (*The sheer amount of rubble was appalling. The amount of 2 and 2 is 4. The amount of resistance he met astonished him*). In accounting it has the special meaning of the sum of the principal and interest of a loan (*What is the full amount I owe you?*) which has led to its being used as a synonym for *total.*

Number (in such uses as are likely to be confused with *amount*) applies to separable units (*There were a great number of bricks in the street. There was a vast amount of debris in the street*).

ampersand. The ampersand is the character &. It should be used only in the writing of business addresses which include it (If a firm calls itself *Smith & Jones,* it should be so addressed; if it calls itself *Smith and Jones,* the ampersand should not be used), in formulas, and so on. The ampersand should not be used for *and* in ordinary writing.

ample; enough. That is *enough* which is adequate or sufficient to the need (*There is enough treason there to hang a dozen men*). That which is *ample* is more than enough, enough and to spare (*But Knowledge to their eyes her ample page/Rich with the spoils of time did ne'er unroll*). But since more than enough must include enough, and since what constitutes enough is often disputable and temperaments differ in their estimates, one cannot quarrel with those bold souls who make *enough* synonymous with *ample* or those timid souls who make *ample* synonymous with *enough*. Any qualifying of *ample*, however, such as *barely ample,* is absurd.

Fowler insists that *ample,* when used attributively in the sense of *plenty of,* must be confined to nouns denoting immaterial or abstract things. Careful writers and precise thinkers would do well to heed his delicate and discerning distinctions, but the common man will be safe from all but philosophic grammarians if he merely remembers that *ample is more than enough.*

For all practical purposes *abundance* would be a satisfactory synonym for *ample* and *sufficient* for *enough.*

ample opportunity has become a cliché. Usually *opportunity* or *opportunities* will suffice.

amuck; amok. The Malayans have a special nervous malady that induces, or a special social custom that sanctions, wild fits of murderous frenzy. Those who are subject to these dangerous seizures are said, when the fit is upon them, to be *amoq,* furious. The word came into English in various spellings as early as the 16th century and finally settled down, in the 17th century, as *amuck,* especially in the phrase *to run amuck* which was used to describe someone having an uninhibited tantrum or rushing headlong into some injudicious course of action.

In recent times, when Conrad and Somerset Maugham had made us conscious of Malaya, those in the know preferred the spelling *amok.* There's no law against it, but it's pretentious and invites an embarrassing probe of the user's knowledge of Malayan.

an. See **a.**

anabasis. The plural is *anabases.*

anacoluthon is a term in rhetoric and grammar for a construction involving a break in grammatical sequence. Usually it is the product of ignorance or haste or confusion, but it may be employed as a rhetorical device when the author wants to suggest that the emotion of the speaker is so great that he cannot wait to finish the sentence he began (as in Milton's *If thou beest he—But, O, how fall'n! how changed!*).

A famous example of anacoluthon in the King James Version of Luke 5:14—*And he charged him to tell no man: but go, and shew thyself to the priest*—is rectified in the Revised Standard Version by the insertion of quotation marks: *And he charged him to tell no one; but "go and show yourself to the priest."*

analogous. See **similar.**

analysis. The plural is *analyses.*

analyst; annalist. An *analyst* is one who analyzes (*Mr. Russell Lynes, our analyst of taste*), a chemist or mathematician, or, more recently, a psychoanalyst (*As an analyst Dr. Horney's views were not always strictly Freudian*). An *annalist* is a historian, or one who writes annals, events year by year in chronological order (*The pedantic historian can easily sink into the annalist*).

anaphora is a term in rhetoric for a repetition of the same word or words at the beginning of two or more successive verses, clauses, or sentences. It is a common device in oratory and much used in the Bible (*Where is the wise? where is the scribe? where is the disputer of this world?*) but it should be employed, particularly in political speeches, with great care. One repetition too many and the audience may laugh and there is always the danger that some quick-witted, irreverent wag will shout out a ludicrous answer.

anastrophe is a term in rhetoric or grammar designating a reversal of the usual order of words (*Came the dawn* for *The dawn came*). It was once much employed by poets but is now definitely out of fashion among good writers, though writers of popular romances are addicted to it under the impression, apparently, that it gives their work a fine archaic flavor.

anathema. The plural is *anathemas* or *anathemata,* not *anathemae.*

ancestor; ancestress. Our ancestors include our ancestresses. If we attribute some saying to *our ancestors* or speak poetically of one who *sleeps among his ancestors,* there is no implied differentiation of male from female. An *ancestress* is just as much an *ancestor* as a male forebear. But if for some reason one wishes to indicate that a particular ancestor was a woman, *ancestress* is useful. Thus when Sir Arthur Helps in his *Social Pressure* said that *The ladies of the present day . . . suffer* [tolerate] *much more waste in their households than their ancestresses did,* the word permits him to make it plain that he is referring to extravagance wholly within the province and control of the lady of the house.

ancient. See **old.**

and is a conjunction and is used to connect words or groups of words that are grammatically alike, as *he and I, him and me, coming and going.* The subject of a verb is sometimes made up of words connected by *and.* When these represent more than one person or thing the verb is plural, as in *love and hate are strong.* When they represent the same thing the verb is singular, as in *my friend and advisor is dead.* Between these two examples is a large middle ground where the verb may be singular or plural according to the intention of the speaker, as in *the grouping of the horses, and the beauty, correctness, and energy of their delineation, is remarkable.* See **agreement: verbs.**

In certain constructions, *and* may be used

in place of *to* after *come, go, run,* and *try.* (For a fuller discussion of this, see the individual verbs.) In the United States it is occasionally used in this way with other verbs, as in *be sure and ask, take care and see he gets it, remember and tell me.* These forms are acceptable English in this country.

Good and is sometimes used as an intensifier, as in *I'm good and tired, it's good and cold out.* The construction is condemned by some grammarians but is acceptable spoken English in the United States. *Nice and* is used in much the same way, except that it always implies approval, as in *nice and cold.* This is not similarly condemned because it is always possible to believe that the words are meant separately and independently, and that the speaker might equally well have said *cold and nice.*

And could once be used with the sense of *if,* as in *I'll speak to them and they were Popes.* Today, *and* is only used in this way as a deliberate archaism and when it is, it is usually spelled *an.*

and how! To agree has always been the most obvious way of being agreeable. But the line between affability and servility is fine. The "yes man" is something worse than merely agreeable.

American energy and love of exaggeration demand something more than agreement. The listener must express not only assent to our wisdom but amazement at it. He must seize the speaker's assertion and push it forward, implying that the other is far too modest and reserved in his utterances. And so we hear *You can say that again!* and *And how!*

The fault in the use of such phrases is not grammatical but moral. Those who use them do not need dictionaries so much as clean hands and pure hearts.

and/or. This word form is very popular today. It is seen in the most respectable places and is therefore acceptable current English. But it should be recognized that *and/or* is a legalism, equivalent to *each and every, all and sundry,* that it is commonly used in non-legal English where the simple word *or* would carry exactly the same meaning, and that when it is used in this way it is verbiage and not evidence of the precise thinker.

In most sentences the meaning of two words joined by *or* includes the meaning of those same two words joined by *and.* For example, almost anything we say about *people who read French or German* is also true of *people who read French and German,* since anyone who reads both languages also reads one of them. Similarly, when we say *he does not read French or German* we have also said that *he does not read French and German.* The use of *and/or* in sentences of this kind adds nothing but confusion.

Sometimes the physical facts themselves are exclusive and prevent *or* from carrying the meaning of *and,* as in *up or down, dead or alive.* Sometimes the facts are not exclusive but we want to limit the choice to one. At present we show this by saying "one or the other but not both." It is practically never necessary to point out that *or* includes *and,* but it often is necessary to point out that *or* does not include *and.* We can't accomplish this by using *and/or* in some other situation. Perhaps it would help if we took to writing *students may elect French or/notand German!*

anent. Except in a highly restricted legal sense, *anent* is archaic and had better be left in the oblivion to which time has consigned it. Those who use it as a synonym for *about* or *concerning* (in such sentences as *Anent the real power of the faculty, there can be little doubt; it doesn't exist*) display a stiffness, a self-consciousness, and a pompousness that reflect on the sincerity of what they have to say.

angle is a standard term for point of view in American usage, but it is woefully strained and abused when used, as it so often is in journalism, to mean *interpretation* or even *official position* (as in *O.K., what's the angle? What are we supposed to say?*). Purists, tilting at a geometrical windmill in the hopes of stopping a grammatical error, have complained that you cannot approach anything *from* an angle (as in *Yes, but you've got to approach it from his angle*), that you have to approach *at* an angle. But this is a futile plaint. The term may be killed by its own excesses. Sir Ernest Gowers quotes *a matter of personal angularity* for *point of view.*

Anglo-Indian. See **mulatto.**

angry. See **mad.**

animalculum. The plural is *animalcula. Animalcula* is sometimes treated as a singular and given a new plural form *animalculae.* This won't do. A singular *animalcula* with a regular plural *animalculas* would make good English. But when the word carries the learned ending *ae* it has to be condemned as bad Latin.

annalist. See **analyst.**

annoy. See **aggravate.**

anomalous; irregular; defective. That which is *anomalous* deviates from the ordinary rule, type, or form. It is *irregular* and does not conform to fixed principles or established procedures. An amusing instance of the use of the word, amusing in the extremity of its correctness, was Sir Thomas Browne's statement in his *Pseudodoxia Epidemica* that *Eve anomalously proceeded from Adam.*

To the formalist all irregularity is a fault but there are many, less strict, to whom some anomalies are virtues. But that which is *defective* must in all vocabularies be imperfect. Anomalous vision might mean eyesight of unusual acuity, but defective vision can only mean faulty and imperfect vision.

Anomalous is sometimes confused with *anonymous,* but this is simply a blunder of ignorance, a malapropism so glaring that humanity dictates that one pretend not to have heard it. *Anonymous* means nameless. Of course an anonymous work can be anomalous. The *Tale of a Tub* was.

answer; reply; rejoinder; response; retort; riposte. *Answer* and *reply*, the everyday words, are almost synonymous. A *rejoinder* is an answer to a reply and since tempers are likely to rise when answers begin to be bandied there is in *rejoinder* often the suggestion of incisiveness. *Retort* has a definite connotation of retaliation. It is cutting, severe, witty, a definite counter to a statement or argument.

A *riposte* is a quick thrust in fencing, given after parrying a lunge, and its application to a maneuver in conversation frankly acknowledges the encounter to be a duel. However, the fact that it is not an English word, the fact that it is drawn from a sport (for English-speaking people have not taken dueling seriously for more than a hundred years), and perhaps the fact that most people do not think of conversation as a contest, gives a riposte the meaning of a studiedly clever but not very crushing retort. *Repartee*, also a term from fencing, implies an even lighter answer, though a witty one.

antagonist; opponent; adversary. An *opponent* is one who opposes, who takes the opposite side, usually in a controversy or a debate (*My distinguished opponent, whom I regret to see among his present associates . . .*). An *antagonist*, in the strict sense, is one who opposes in a physical struggle (*He that wrestles with us . . . our antagonist . . .*). It is not always restricted to its strict sense but in extension it carries with it the suggestion of opposition in a hostile spirit, often in a particular contest or struggle (*But at last in Johnson, Macpherson found a formidable antagonist*). The desire of journalists to heighten the drama of everyday events and, especially, to add to the tension and resentment of every disagreement has led to the abuse of *antagonist*. It is too often used as a mere synonym for *opponent*. See also **protagonist.**

Adversary suggests an enemy who fights determinedly and continuously and relentlessly (*Satan, adversary of God and man*).

antagonize; oppose. Though to *antagonize* can mean to *oppose* (*The Democrats are resolved to antagonize this and all other bills . . .*), this meaning is now rare and it has come, particularly in America, to mean to cause to oppose, to arouse hostility in (*The passage of the bill is certain to antagonize the labor unions*). It is something more, too. Those who are antagonized are not only aroused to opposition but are made irritable and resentful. To be so affected is, perhaps, in all but the most philosophic, an inescapable concomitant of being opposed and this suggestion in the word illustrates nicely the manner in which words acquire added shades of meaning.

ante-; anti-. *Ante-* means before, either in place or time. An *antechamber* is a small room that comes before a large one. *Antediluvian* times were times before the Flood and *antebellum*

means before the war. (In American usage *antebellum* means almost exclusively the decades immediately preceding the Civil War and, for some reason, is applied chiefly to the South.)

Anti- means opposed to. An *antitoxin* opposes the effect of a toxin or poison. An *anticlimax* opposes the effect of a climax.

Anticipate is an exception. Here *anti-* equals *ante-*. It is simply an established variant in spelling.

antecedent. When used as a grammatical term *antecedent* means the word or group of words referred to by a pronoun. It does not necessarily come before the pronoun and it may not be mentioned at all. For example, *leaf* is the antecedent of *its* in *the one red leaf, the last of its clan.* But *mastiff* is the antecedent of *her* in *outside her kennel the mastiff old lay fast asleep,* and the antecedent of *what* in *what can ail the mastiff bitch?* is unknown.

Under some circumstances certain pronouns cannot be used without an antecedent which actually precedes them. These words are said to "carry back" or to be "anaphoric." For example, *them, some, any,* are anaphoric when they do not refer to human beings. Anaphoric pronouns must be handled carefully. In a carelessly constructed sentence they sometimes pick up an antecedent that was not intended. In the figure of speech *he put his foot in it,* the pronoun *it* has a general or indefinite reference. But in *everytime he opens his mouth he puts his foot in it,* the *it* suddenly becomes anaphoric and carries back to *mouth.*

A pronoun is said to agree with its antecedent in number. That is, the pronoun should be singular if the antecedent is singular and plural if the antecedent is plural. In English, the number of the pronoun depends on the meaning of the antecedent more than on its strict grammatical form. See **indefinite pronouns** and **agreement: verbs.**

antelope. The plural is *antelopes* or *antelope.*

antenna. The plural is *antennas* or *antennae.* In speaking of radios, *antennas* is the only plural form used. In speaking of insects, either form may be used but *antennae* is generally preferred.

antepenult. The *antepenult* (a shortened form of *antepenultima*) is the last syllable but two in a word, as *syl* in *monosyllable.* See **penult.**

anticipate; expect; hope; await. *Anticipate,* in its strictest sense, meant to seize or take possession of beforehand. (The *Oxford English Dictionary* quotes, under the date of 1623, a soldier who feared that his enemy might *anticipate* the tops of the mountains and hence have him at a disadvantage.) From this sense it was a natural development to conceive of emotions, whether pleasant or unpleasant, being experienced before the event, so that one could, *in anticipation,* foretaste experiences (*Some lives do actually anticipate the happiness of heaven*).

To *expect* means to believe that something will occur. The greatness of Nelson's famous signal, *England expects every man to do his duty,* lay in the calm assurance that the duty would be done. *Expect,* especially when spoken with shrill emphasis by harassed parents or executives uncertain of their authority, meaning require or order (*I expect this to be done by the time I get back!*) is a weak bluster word, for the emphasis belies the assurance which is the word's strength. To *anticipate* means to look forward eagerly to the event, to picture it in the mind's eye, to seize in advance, as it were, the experience to come. So that to make *anticipate* merely a synonym of *expect* is to deprive it of much of its meaning. This has already been done in American usage to such an extent that it can hardly be regarded as a serious fault. But enough of distinct meanings remains for the discriminating writer to prefer one to the other.

To *hope* is to wish that some favorable event will take place, with some expectation that it will. When Swift, in his dreadful last years, on parting from a friend, said quietly *I hope we may never meet again,* the anguish of his pessimism and the depth of his weariness with life were brilliantly expressed by thrusting *hope* with all its common connotations into this unexpected context.

To *await* simply means to be prepared to accept something when it comes (*We await your reply*). One hopes for good. One awaits good or evil.

anticlimax. The word *climax* derives from a Greek word for *ladder.* In rhetoric it signifies a figure in which the meaning rises in a series of images each of which exceeds the one before it in dignity, splendor, or passion. In popular use the word means the last step in a rising series, the point of highest development, though in the eternal search for more superlative superlatives that marks popular speech and writing, *capping the climax* has come to mean much what *climaxing* meant.

An *anticlimax* is that which is opposed (in spirit or by its nature) to a climax. It opposes, that is, the climactic effect which the climax sought to achieve. Since an anticlimax must come after the climax (otherwise the climax would be the climax still, though possibly impaired), it consists of a ludicrous descent when the rhythm or the sense or the development of the action leads the listener or the reader to expect a continued ascent.

Of course, whether something is a climax or an anticlimax depends on the values of the one who judges it. Thus when an enthusiastic Scotch bard apostrophized one Dalhousie, a warrior, as *the great God of War,/ Lieutenant-Colonel to the Earl of Mar,* the order of titles seems to one unfamiliar with the Earl of Mar to be improper. But by standards of Scottish loyalty it may not be. When Hugh Kingsmill, after commenting unfavorably on a poem of Joseph Cottle's, said that *Cottle's other works are three epic poems and a new kind of blacking,* the anticlimax was intentional and meant to drag the luckless bookseller-author down with it. Fowler cites I Kings, 15:23, as an example of anticlimax: *The rest of all the acts of Asa, and all his might, and all that he did, and the cities which he built, are they not written in the book of the chronicles of the Kings of Judah? Nevertheless in the time of his old age he was diseased in his feet.* But Asa's sore feet were a matter of great interest to the various historians of the Old Testament. He is never mentioned without a reference to them. And it may have been that the allusion to them was meant as an anticlimax, a humbling of his greatness.

One of the most-quoted anticlimaxes in English literature is the conclusion of Enoch Arden: *So past the strong heroic soul away./ And when they buried him, the little port/ Had seldom seen a costlier funeral.* Well, the Victorians attached great importance to funeral expenses.

antithesis (the plural is *antitheses*) is a term in rhetoric for setting contrasting phrases opposite to each other for emphasis (as Bacon's *Crafty men contemn studies; simple men admire them; and wise men use them* or Dryden's description of a parsimonious zealot: *Cold was his kitchen, but his head was hot*). The great master of antithesis (as of almost every other rhetorical device) in English is Alexander Pope. And perhaps his most effective use of it is in his description of the affected and effeminate but brilliant and in many ways attractive Lord Hervey: *Amphibious thing! that acting either part,/ The trifling head, or the corrupted heart;/ Fop at the toilet, flatterer at the board,/ Now trips a lady, and now struts a lord./ . . . Beauty that shocks you, parts that none will trust,/ Wit that can creep, and pride that licks the dust.*

The virtuosity of the lines lies in the startling contrasts of the juxtaposed phrases, but their transcendent art lies in the fact that they are used to describe one who (in Pope's estimation) was *himself one vile antithesis.*

antonomasia means a "calling instead." It consists of using an epithet or appellative other than his personal name to identify an individual, or of using a proper name to identify an individual with a certain class of persons.

An example of the first sort of *antonomasia* is the use of a title instead of person's name: "his grace" for a duke; "the reverend" for a clergyman (colloq.); "his nibs" for an important person (slang). There has been quite a vogue for antonomasia of this kind in twentieth century America. Clara Bow was "the It girl," John Barrymore "The Profile," Frank Sinatra "The Voice," Marie McDonald "The Body" and Stan Musial "The Man." In highland Scotland the male head of the house has been "himself" for centuries.

Of the second form, the substitution of a personal name as an epithet, many examples are in current use. F. Scott Fitzgerald recalls a familiar one in *The Great Gatsby* when he has the owl-eyed man describe Gatsby as an impresario because he has real books in his library: *This fella's a regular Belasco.* Even the most illiterate are likely to know that a Jonah brings bad luck, a Scrooge is a tightwad, a Shylock an extortionate usurer, a Solomon a wise man, a Barney Oldfield a fast driver, an Einstein a scientific genius, an Adonis a handsome young man, a Romeo a romantic young lover, a Casanova or a Don Juan a ladykiller, a Mentor a teacher or adviser, a Micawber an incurable optimist, a Hercules a strong man.

Very few women's names have acquired symbolic or generic stature. A Bernhardt, to describe an actress, is one of the very few.

American literature has contributed surprisingly few names to describe a general characteristic. Harriet Beecher Stowe's Uncle Tom is one, though Mrs. Stowe would be aghast to learn that it is now an epithet of contempt. Perhaps the best known is Sinclair Lewis's Babbitt. Faulkner's Snopes, for a rising Southern poor white, and Sartoris, for a declining Southern gentleman, deserve currency.

antonym. An *antonym* is a word opposed in meaning to another. *Good* is the antonym of *bad, hot* of *cold. Antonym* is the antonym of *synonym.*

anxious; eager. One who is *anxious* is full of anxiety, troubled solicitude, uneasiness (*Why didn't you telephone? You knew how anxious, how frantic, I was!*) One who is *eager* is ardently desirous (*I am eager to see the check. He only said it would be "big"*). Originally *eager* meant pungent or sharp (Shakespeare refers to condiments as *eager compounds* that *urge the palate,* and there is the famous reference in *Hamlet* to *a nipping and an eager air* on the icy battlements of Elsinore). An element of this sharpness still remains in the strictly proper use of *eager.* The anxious person is in a state of suspense. The eager person strains in thought toward the coming event. The anxious are fearful, the eager hopeful.

With such fundamental differences in meaning, it would not seem likely that the two words would ever become synonymous or confused. But though *eager* is never used where *anxious* is meant, *anxious* is often used for *eager* (*The child is anxious to go with you*). The use has been protested, but protests are of little avail against usage and usage has a psychological if not a linguistic justification here; for all anxiety is eager for relief and all eagerness, looking forward, has an element of uncertainty, and in all uncertainty there is a measure of anxiety.

any. This word may be used as an adjective qualifying a noun, or as a pronoun standing in place of a noun. When used as a singular it means "one, no matter which." When used as a plural, it means "some, no matter which." As an adjective, it may qualify a singular noun, as in *any child,* or a plural noun, as in *any children.* As a pronoun, it could once be used as a singular, as in *unseen of any.* This is now

archaic. In current English the pronoun *any* is always treated as a plural, as in *if any think they are wise.*

With certain limitations, *any* may also be used as an adverb, to qualify words that are not nouns. In Great Britain *any* is acceptable before a comparative form, as in *any nearer, any less true, any the worse for it;* before *too,* as in *any too much time;* and before *more,* as in *have you any more money* and *he doesn't come here any more.* In the United States *any* may also be used alone with a verb, as in *did you sleep any?* Here the pronoun *any* is being used instead of the adverbial phrase *at all.* This use of *any* is comparable to the use of *everyplace* for *everywhere* and *what time* for *when.* It is acceptable English in the United States.

Any may be used as an adverb in a question, an *if* clause, or a statement that is negative at least by implication, such as *I'm surprised you come here any more.* In literary English it cannot be used in a simple affirmative statement. In some parts of the United States *any* is used in affirmative statements, such as *we go there often any more* (where *any more* means "now"). This is not standard in most parts of the country.

anybody; anyone. These words are singular and take a singular verb, as in *has anybody called?* Since it usually isn't known whether the "anybody" spoken about is a man or a woman, forms of the pronoun *they* are generally preferred to forms of *he* when referring back to *anybody,* as in *if anybody calls tell them I have gone.* This is less true of *anyone.* Forms of *they* are used in speaking of *anyone,* but forms of *he* are also heard frequently.

anyhow; anyhows. The only acceptable form is *anyhow. Anyhows* is not standard.

anyone. See **anybody.**

anyplace. The use of *anyplace* as a substitute for *anywhere,* as in *I could not find it anyplace,* is condemned by many grammarians because the noun *place* is here being used instead of the adverb *where.* This usage is not acceptable in Great Britain but it occurs too often in the United States, in written as well as in spoken English, to be called nonstandard. It is acceptable English in this country.

anytime. In Great Britain the word *anytime* is never used as an adverb, as it is in the sentence *he will see you anytime,* and a preposition is required, as in *he will see you at any time.* But the construction without *at* is standard in the United States and can be heard in the most impressive offices.

anyway; anyways; anywise. Both *-way* forms are standard English in such constructions as *if you are anyway concerned* and *if they are anyways useful.* In the United States *anyway* is preferred to *anyways.* The form *anywise* is also standard English, but it is not often heard in this country.

Some grammarians condemn the use of *anyway* as a connective between sentences, as in *anyway, he didn't come.* Here *anyway* is perhaps short for *anyway you look at it.* The construction is acceptable in spoken English and in written English that hopes to capture the force and charm of speech.

anywhere; anywheres. *Anywhere* is the only acceptable form in written English. In the United States *anywheres* is often heard in the speech of well educated people, but it does not appear in print.

Anywhere is often used with an unnecessary *that,* as in *anywhere that a mule can go.* This construction has been in use for a very short time but it is accepted English in the United States.

apartment. In the United States a suite of rooms is called *an apartment* and treated as a singular, as in *a three-room apartment.* In Great Britain this use of the word is considered archaic; *an apartment* there means one room, and a suite of rooms is treated as a plural and called *apartments.* If treated as a singular it is called *a flat.* What Americans call an *apartment hotel* is known in England as a *block of service flats.*

apex. See **top.** The plural is *apices.*

aphis. The plural is *aphides,* not *aphes.* A new singular, *aphid,* with a regular plural *aphids,* is in use and is generally preferred to the classical *aphis, aphides.*

apiece; a piece. *apiece* means one to each or each by itself, as *Our cakes are a dollar apiece. A piece* is a fragment, as *Our cake is ten cents a piece.*

apocrypha. This word, meaning a collection of writings of doubtful authenticity, was originally plural but is now regularly treated as a singular, as in *the apocrypha is not included.* It has a regular plural, *apocryphas,* meaning more than one such collection.

When the form *apocrypha* was used as a plural, meaning a number of documents, there was a singular form *apocryphon,* meaning one document. This is no longer heard in the United States.

apocryphal means of doubtful authenticity, spurious (*The apocryphal books of the Bible are those not included in the canon*). It is used of anecdotes and legends which cannot be shown to be genuine (*The story of his kissing the maid is apocryphal*).

apologia. The word is a singular, but is sometimes mistaken for a plural. If a plural form is used, it should be *apologias.*

apology; excuse. An *apology* implies that one has been, at least apparently, in the wrong. It is a formal word and expresses the hope of setting things right by explaining the circumstances or by acknowledging a fault and expressing regret for it. There is usually an element of humiliation in having to make an apology.

An *excuse* is a plea in extenuation of a more trivial fault; and where an apology accepts guilt and seeks to make reparation, an excuse seeks, rather, to shift the blame and repudiate guilt.

Since excuses and apologies are often farfetched and do not always seem sincere to the injured, insulted, or inconvenienced person, both *excuse* and *apology* are used facetiously to mean makeshift. When so used they are often preceded by *poor, shabby,* or some other derogatory adjective (*a poor excuse for a house*).

Pardon me is a little stilted when used where *excuse me* would be better. *Excuse me* is simply a polite request to someone to let us pass or to overlook some minor, accidental breach of etiquette. *Pardon me* implies that the other person has power over our fate and has to be besought to forgive us.

a posteriori. See **a priori.**

apostles. See **disciples.**

apostrophe. The apostrophe is used primarily to show that letters have been omitted, as in *we're coming* and *don't hurry.* Contractions such as these represent normal spoken English and there is no reason why they should not be used in writing. In speech we do not say *we are coming* or *do not hurry* unless we want to make the point emphatic, and the practice of not using the contracted form in writing sometimes gives the writing a didactic or quarrelsome tone.

An apostrophe is sometimes used in forming plurals of figures, letters, and words that are not nouns but are being treated as nouns, as in *the 1920's, your p's and q's, the why's and wherefore's.* Many publishers today omit these apostrophes and write *the 1920s, the ps and qs, the whys and wherefores.*

An apostrophe is also used to show the genitive case of nouns, as in *the horse's mouth, a snail's pace, America's heritage.* It is never used with a possessive pronoun. (An apostrophe following a personal pronoun always indicates an omitted letter and usually a contracted *is* or *are. It's* means *it is; who's* means *who is; they're* means *they are;* and *you're* means *you are.*) There is no difference in spoken English between the words *boys, boy's,* and *boys'.* Since we do not need to hear a difference in these words in order to understand what is said, it is obvious that we do not need to see a difference when the words are written. The apostrophe is entirely a printer's problem and has nothing to do with the language itself. It was first used to indicate a genitive singular about 1680, and to indicate a genitive plural about a hundred years later. It is now in the process of disappearing. Bernard Shaw helped to speed this by disregarding apostrophes in his own writing. In using a proper name it is courteous to observe the established form, as in *Teacher's College, the Court of St. James's, Harpers Ferry.* Otherwise, the fewer apostrophes one uses the better. If you use an apostrophe where it does not belong, it shows that you do not know what you are doing. If you omit an apostrophe where one is usually expected, it may only prove that you admire Bernard Shaw.

For the formation of genitive singulars and

plurals, see **genitive case.** For the use of the apostrophe in measure terms, see **measures.**

apostrophe (rhetoric). As a term in rhetoric *apostrophe* designates a digressive address, the interruption of the course of a speech or a piece of writing to address some person or persons, whether present or absent, real or imaginary (*At the close of his argument, he turned to his client in an affecting apostrophe*). By extension it is also applied to any abrupt interjectional speech. Lear, pleading passionately with his daughters that it is not a question of his physical needs, interrupts his argument with an apostrophe to the gods: *But, for true need—/ You heavens, give me that patience, patience I need!/ You see me here, you gods, a poor old man,/ As full of grief as age; wretched in both. . . .*

apotheosis. The plural is *apotheoses.*

apparatus. The plural is *apparatuses* or *apparatus,* not *apparati.*

apparent; obvious; evident; patent. *Obvious* meant, originally, that which stood in the way and was, therefore, unavoidable to view or knowledge. That which is *evident* is that which is made unquestionable by demonstrable facts. A thing or proposition which is *patent* is open to the view or comprehension of all.

The difficulty with *apparent* is that it has two meanings. It can mean capable of being clearly seen or understood and it can mean seeming (as opposed to real): *It is apparent that the apparent honesty of some criminals is their greatest asset.*

An *heir apparent* is one whose right to an inheritance is indefeasible if he survives the ancestor. The plural is *heirs apparent.*

A *patent* is a document conferring certain privileges. The word means that it is open for all to see, a public document, and since all may see it no one can claim that he could not know of its provisions. Yet because patents are taken out to cover the manufacturing rights of proprietary medicines and mechanical devices whose construction before the issuing of the patent was often a closely guarded secret, the word has, in popular usage, the connotation of secrecy, the exact opposite of its standard meaning.

appeal. In American usage *appeal* is intransitive and transitive. (*She appeals to me. The convicted, if dissatisfied with the verdict, can appeal his case to a higher court.*) In British usage the transitive form is obsolete.

appear. This word may be followed by an infinitive, as in *he appeared to leave,* but not by the *-ing* form of a verb. *Appear* may be followed by an adjective describing what appears, as in *he appeared sad,* or by an adverb describing the appearing, as in *he appeared suddenly.*

appendix. The plural is *appendixes* or *appendices.*

apperception. See **perception.**

apple of one's eye (the pupil of the eye) was formerly thought to be a solid, spherical body. The phrase is an echo of the eighth verse of the seventeenth Psalm (*Keep me as the apple of the eye*) which, in turn, is probably an echo of the tenth verse of the thirty-second chapter of *Deuteronomy* (*He led him about, he instructed him, he kept him as the apple of his eye*). As a term for something exceedingly precious and dear it has been worn to meaninglessness by repetition. As an image, in fact, it seems repulsively bloodshot and grotesque.

appointment; assignment; office; post; station. *Appointment* and *assignment* in the sense of a position or a task to be performed are closely synonymous, though Americans are inclined to use *assignment* in many instances where the English use *appointment.* A newspaper reporter's assignment and the daily assignment allotted to a class, together with the assignment of wages in payment of a debt are peculiarly American uses.

An *office,* like a *position,* suggests an employment of some trust and importance. *Office,* with us, is largely confined to a political position. *Post* in the United States means a military or some other public position; in England it is used almost as a synonym for *job. Station* refers to the sphere of duty or occupation (*his station in life*) or to the location of the task (*He was stationed at Albuquerque*).

appositive. A word, or group of words, which follows immediately after another word or group of words and which means the same thing is called an appositive, as *our first President* in *George Washington, our first President, lived in Virginia.* An appositive may be set off by commas. When commas are not used, as in *Peter the Hermit* and *the poet Keats,* the second word or group is sometimes called an adherent. When there is no punctuation, the second part is felt as closer to the first and necessary to it. When commas are used, they sometimes make the second element seem like a parenthetical aside.

appositive adjectives. See **position of adjectives.**

appreciate means to form an estimate of, usually favorable and marked by sensitivity and delicate perceptions in the appreciator. It also means to increase in value (*Gold has appreciated steadily for two hundred years*). In this sense it is the antonym of *depreciate.*

Originally *appreciate,* in the first of the two meanings just given, meant to make an estimate, even an unfavorable one. Burke said. *We must appreciate these dreadful hydras,* and it is to be hoped that college courses in *Musical Appreciation* do not teach their students to approve of every piece they hear. But this meaning is now rare.

The word is used chiefly, in several ways, as an elaborate and slightly grudging means of saying *Thank you* or *I will thank you.* Early visitors to America were struck by the fact that in the West, at least, people were reluctant to say *Thank you,* preferring various circumlocutions such as *Much obliged, Well now, that's mighty good of you,* and *I'll do the same for you some day.* Apparently plain thanks was felt to be undemocratic. Perhaps it was thought to imply an acknowledgment of at least temporary inferiority, an acknowledgment which the frontiersman was in no way and at no time inclined to make.

In its commonest contemporary use, *appreciate* has a vestige of this feeling. *I appreciate what you've done for me* does not directly say *Thanks*. It says, *I have formed a just estimate (with my customary keen insight and delicate perception) of your act and [by implication] I am favorably impressed by it.* Now this is lordly. A king could not be more graciously condescending. But it's a little dishonest (as most circumlocutions are) in that it twists matters in such a way that the recipient of the favor seems to be bestowing it. Of course the ordinary man has very little awareness of all this when he uses the phrase; but he must have some perception of it—he must appreciate it, to some extent—because he so often seeks to bolster the assurance with supporting emphasis (*I certainly appreciate what you've done for me! I sure do appreciate it!*).

Where appreciation is intended, *appreciate* should be used, but when gratitude has to be expressed it is better to swallow one's pride and say *Thank you.*

apprehend; comprehend. As synonyms of *understand* (the only one of their many meanings in which they are likely to be confused), *apprehend* means getting hold of and *comprehend* means embracing fully. What one cannot apprehend one cannot even know about. (*A child does not apprehend danger in an electric wire.*) What one cannot comprehend one is simply unable to understand fully.

Comprehensive means inclusive. *Apprehensive* means perceptive, but apparently, what the perceptive perceive in life is alarming, for it also means anxious, uneasy, and fearful.

apprise; apprize. *Apprise* means to inform or to notify (*He was apprised of the danger. He was apprised of his appointment to the professorship*). It is a rather formal word, often overworked in business correspondence. (See also **tell.**)

Apprize means to put a value upon, to appraise. Actually it is the same word as *appraise*, although it has had a different history. *Apprize* is not used very much, being confined largely to legal matters.

Since *apprise* is sometimes spelled *apprize* and since *apprize* is sometimes spelled *apprise*, any attempt to distinguish between them is absurd. It is simply better—as most people do—to use *appraise* when "to put a value upon," is the meaning.

approach. When used as a noun *approach* is followed by *to*, as in *the approach to the house.* The verb is used without *to*, as in *they approached the house.*

appropriate; expropriate; impropriate. The verb *appropriate* is distinguished from *take* or *give* in that it means to give for a particular person or purpose or to take from a particular person or for a particular purpose. Congress appropriates money because it supplies money only

to meet the purposes of definite bills that have been enacted.

The widespread erroneous use of the word may have had its beginning in the grandiloquent humor of the frontier where a man seeing something that he wanted might say, *I'll just appropriate that,* meaning *I will assign it to my own particular use.*

To *expropriate* is to take, by legal action, land from a private person for the general use. The rare word *impropriate* is limited to ecclesiastical writings. It means the bestowal of church property (as at the time of the dissolution of the monasteries in England) upon private individuals.

approximate. That which is *approximate* is nearly exact; it approaches closely to something or brings it near. *To approximate* is to approach closely.

It is desirable to avoid using the word as if it meant to resemble or to make resemble. That which approximates something comes close to it but does not necessarily appear to be it.

a priori; prima facie. *A priori* means from cause to effect, from a general law to a particular instance, valid independently of observation—as opposed to *a posteriori* (*We cannot a priori determine the value of anything wholly new. We should be guided by observational evidence and not by a priori principles. Knowledge a posteriori is a synonym for . . . knowledge from experience*).

A priori is sometimes misused for *prima facie*, which means at first view, on the first impression, before making an investigation, especially in the phrase *an a priori case.* The two phrases are not the same. The use of technical philosophical terms, especially in a foreign language, lays one open to the accusation of pedantry anyway and to misuse them will quickly get one convicted of both pedantry and ignorance.

apropos. This word is sometimes followed by *to*, but *of* is preferable, as in *this is apropos of what you were saying.*

apt; likely. *Apt* and *likely* are close synonyms, but the careful speaker or writer will make a distinction between them. *Apt*, in its primary sense, means fit or suitable. *Likely* indicates a probability arising from the nature of the situation. Of a witty and cutting reply to some insolent remark it might be said that *It was an apt answer; just the sort of thing that so-and-so would be likely to say.*

When applied to persons, *apt* means inclined or prone; when applied to things, it means habitually liable. *Apt* is often applied to the general situation, *likely* to the specific. We say, *Snow is apt to fall in Chicago in late November.* On a day in late November in Chicago when the weather conditions indicate that there probably will be snow, we say, *It is likely to snow today.*

Apt, when used in the sense of prone or liable, may be followed by an infinitive, as in *he is apt to forget,* but not by the *-ing* form of a verb. When it means capable, it may be followed by *at* and the *-ing* form, as in *he is apt at painting*, but not by an infinitive.

aquarium. The plural is *aquariums* or *aquaria*.

Arab; Arabian; Arabic. *Arab* pertains to the Arabs, *Arabian* to Arabia, and *Arabic* (with the exception of *gum arabic* and the names of certain shrubs) to the languages which have developed out of the language and culture of the Arabians at the time of Mohammed or to the standard literary and classical language established by the Koran.

There is a tendency to call the inhabitants of Arabia *Arabians* to distinguish them from the *Arabs* of North Africa. We call our numerals *arabic* because we acquired them from the Arabs at the great period of their culture.

arbiter; arbitrator. An *arbiter* is one who has power to decide according to his own pleasure. We speak of a *social arbiter*, one whose social preëminence is so widely acknowledged that his word suffices to settle disputes of precedence and custom. Byron spoke of Napoleon as *the arbiter of others' fate,/ A suppliant for his own.*

An *arbiter* differs from a judge in that, once chosen or appointed, his decision in the disputed matter can be purely personal and is not subject to review. He need offer no explanation for it. It is, as we say, arbitrary.

Arbiter and *arbitrator* were formerly synonymous and are still recognized as such by most dictionaries. But the use of the latter term in recent years to designate one assigned to settle labor disputes has led to a change in its meaning. When labor was weak and disorganized an arbitrator might proceed in an arbitrary manner, but now that labor is strong and organized he is expected to be conciliatory and to bring the conflicting parties, as diplomatically as possible, to accept a compromise. So that *arbitrator* now carries—in popular usage—a definite suggestion of tactfulness and patience. The distance the word has moved from *arbiter* in the past generation is made plain by the reflection that an arbitrary man would be most unsuitable today as an arbitrator.

arboretum. The plural is *arboretums* or *arboreta*.

arcanum. The plural is *arcanums* or *arcana*.

archaism. When a word is described as an *archaism* it means that it is old-fashioned and no longer used in general, informal writing.

An obsolete word is one that has fallen completely into disuse. *Swink*, a verb meaning to work hard, is an example. Chaucer uses it consistently (*Let Austin have his swink to him reserved*). But it has not been in use now for centuries and would be meaningless to all but a few scholars.

An archaic word would probably be understood, but it would seem strange. *Forsooth, belike,* and *parlous* are examples. Educated people have encountered most of them in poetry and usually know their meanings; but they would regard their use in ordinary prose or speech as an affectation.

Of course if a skilled writer or speaker chooses to use an archaic word for a distinct purpose—to add a touch of the ridiculous, to indicate affectation in another, or even just to give an archaic flavor—he is free to do so; but he runs the risk of having his subtlety misunderstood and himself scorned.

archives. This word may mean a collection of documents, as in *he rummaged among the archives,* or a building in which such documents are kept, as in *the Archives are on Constitution Avenue.* In either case, the word is treated as a plural.

A singular form *archive* was once in use and could mean one document or one building. This is now obsolete in the United States.

are. See **be.**

arena. The plural is *arenas* or *arenae*.

aren't I?. See **ain't.**

Argentina; Argentine. The country is *Argentina* or, formally, *The Argentine Republic.* An *Argentine* is one of its inhabitants. It is often called *the Argentine,* as the United States is called *the States,* and the term which on its introduction had an air of knowing familiarity about it has increased in popularity to the point where it cannot be regarded as wrong. But those who use it should bear in mind that it is an informal designation.

argot; jargon. An *argot* is a language, usually esoteric, used by a peculiar group, class, or occupation. It was originally thieves' cant, a form of speech which deliberately employed extravagant slang and strange terms in order to conceal its true meaning from outsiders.

Jargon means unintelligible writing or talk. It originally meant a twittering sound and poets have referred to the *sweet jargoning* of birds. Of course argot is jargon to those who do not understand it, but to accuse the special vocabulary of some branch of science or of some sect of being unintelligible is risky since in so doing one lays one's self open to the counter charge of being unintelligent. *Jargon* is a term of contempt and must be used carefully.

arise. The past tense is *arose*. The participle is *arisen*.

arise; rise. *Arise* in the literal sense of getting up from a sitting or lying position (*Arise, and take up thy bed and walk. My lady sweet, arise*) is now rather archaic. We say *rise,* as *Farmers rise early, The sun rises in the east,* and so on.

Arise is used in preference to *rise* in metaphorical senses, when something is coming into being (as *How did this quarrel arise?*) or when something results or proceeds from something else (as *Enmities often arise from jests*).

arm; sleeve. A reference to the *sleeve* of a garment as its *arm* is a natural extension and would be understood by anyone and, surely, it is as much the arm of the garment as the arm of a chair is its arm. None the less it is not accepted in formal usage: A man puts his arm into the sleeve of his coat.

armed to the teeth. This expression would seem to refer to pirates or sailors who in a naval engagement, pistols and knives thrust in their belts, held their cutlasses in their teeth at the moment of boarding, so that they might have their hands free to clutch the rigging or the gunwales. Or at least they are occasionally so depicted in romantic drawings and stories. The excess of ferocity of such overloading with implements of war has about it—at least from the safety of our distance from it—something comic, and the phrase is almost always used now with a humorous intention. Indeed, it strikes us as incongruous to find the phrase used seriously, as in William Cullen Bryant's apostrophe to Freedom: *Armed to the teeth, art thou.*

It has, however, been more than a century now since pirates have boarded ships, with or without cutlasses in their teeth, and the phrase is stale and should be avoided.

arms. When referring to weapons, this is a mass word with plural form. It is followed by a plural verb but cannot be used with a numeral or a numeral word such as *many* or *few.* It has no singular form *an arm.*

This does not apply to the compound *firearms.* This is treated as a regular plural, as in *he had three firearms.* The singular form *a firearm* is rare but can be used.

aroma. An *aroma* was originally a spice. The *Ancren Riwle,* an old English religious work, says that *the three Maries brought aromas for to smear our Lord.* Then it came to mean the odor of spices and then, its current meaning, a spicy odor or bouquet.

Our forefathers, much given to euphemism and jocularity, often used *aroma* facetiously as a synonym for *smell* and, their humorous intention forgotten, some continue to use it in this way seriously, though they still keep enough of the proper meaning to apply it to pleasant smells. But, even so, it is better to restrict it to its specific meaning.

The plural is *aromas* or *aromata,* not *aromae.*

arose. See **arise.**

around; round. In the United States *round* is used to describe an object, as in *this round world,* but otherwise the form *around* is preferred, as in *they flew around the world* and *the earth turns around.* In Great Britain *around* has almost disappeared from speech and *round* is generally preferred, as in *they flew round the world* and *sleeping the clock round.* The British form is unusual in the United States but it is acceptable. It should not be written with an apostrophe, as in *'round.*

In Great Britain *round* always suggests a circle. It means circular or surrounding. In the United States *around* can also be used to mean within a certain area, as in *they traveled around Europe,* and approximately, as in *he is worth around a million.* These uses have been standard in the United States for at least seventy-five years.

arrange. This word may be followed by an infinitive, as in *I arranged to meet him at five.* If the *-ing* form of a verb is used it must be introduced by the preposition *for,* as in *I arranged for meeting him at five. Arrange* may also be followed by a clause, but the clause verb must be a subjunctive or a subjunctive equivalent, as in *I arranged that I should meet him at five.* The infinitive construction is generally preferred.

arrant. See **errant.**

arresting; striking; impressive. *Arresting* is recognized by almost all dictionaries as a synonym for *striking,* in the sense of *impressive.* But the careful writer will, as always, try to select the adjective that gives the exact meaning he wants to express. An arresting occurrence is one that stops and holds the attention. *Impressive* (perhaps merely in its sound, which is a considerable reason) suggests a more massive impact than *striking.*

arrival. See **advent.**

arrive on the scene. It is better just to arrive. The histrionics, obvious in the phrase, have been overworked.

arrogance. See **pride.**

arrogate; arrogant. See **abrogate.**

art; artifice; artful; artificial; arty. The ordinary man mistrusts the skilled man, assuming (probably with full justification) that he will employ his skill unscrupulously to his own advantage. And the man who lacks a skill has a tendency to revenge himself upon anyone who has it by despising him. Hence although *art* keeps its primary meaning of skill or the product of a skill, it has a secondary meaning of wiliness or trickery, and in most of its derivatives the derogatory meaning has come to predominate.

An *artifice* is now almost always a cunning or crafty stratagem. (Both *cunning* and *crafty* were once quite innocent words, meaning simply knowing and able.) It was not always so; formerly God himself was often called *the Great Artificer* of the universe.

Artful is now definitely condemnatory, suggesting one who takes unfair advantage, though it once meant wise or admirably clever. Dickens' *Artful Dodger* seems a more proper expression to us today than Milton's *artful strains.*

Artificial, as opposed to *natural,* has always been condemnatory, though, amusingly, *handmade* (which means the same thing) has come in our machine age to be a term of high approbation with much of the estimation attached to *natural.* See also **synthetic.**

Arty is slang. The suffix expresses contempt. Sometimes the contempt is just for art itself but there is usually at least a pretense that it is for exaggerated or deliberately contrived effects that are more obvious than true skill would have made them.

articles. In English grammar there are two "articles"—the word *a* or *an,* which is called the indefinite article, and the word *the,* which is called the definite article. Articles qualify nouns and are therefore a kind of adjective.

artillery. When referring to men this word usually takes a plural verb, as in *the artillery were* *to the right of us.* When referring to the guns it always takes a singular verb, as in *the artillery was left behind.*

artist; artiste; artisan. An *artist* is anyone who follows any pursuit or employment in which a high degree of skill is obtainable. The modern tendency to restrict the word to those engaged in the fine arts, especially in painting, has led to the introduction, or more accurately the re-introduction, of the French word *artiste* to describe a public performer, such as a dancer or singer.

There are many others, of course, who think they have carried their occupation to the point of its being an art and they—especially in such employments as dressmaking, cooking, and hairdressing that have, in the popular estimation, their best practitioners in France —often refer to themselves or are referred to as *artistes* also. But it is better, and really more complimentary, to call them *artists.*

An *artisan* was originally an artist, one who cultivated an art. But he is now one employed in the industrial arts, a mechanic or handicraftsman.

artless; ignorant. *Artless* used to be used as a close synonym of *ignorant.* Johnson refers to the *artless industry* which many contemptuously assume is all that is needed to write a dictionary. But with the gradual strengthening of the derogatory in so many meanings of *art, artless* has come to mean innocent, ingenuous, unaffected. *The artless prattle of children* conveys the modern meaning. When applied to style, *artless* means simple and sincere.

With the immense increase in the world's knowledge in the past century and the demand for a considerable amount of it in the activities of the commonest person, *ignorant* has been acquiring increasing condemnation. It was once pitying; it is now almost abusive. See also **unsophisticated.**

as is a conjunction. It is used to introduce clauses of various kinds and to make a comparison between things that are claimed to be equal in some respect.

ACCEPTABLE USES

As is primarily an adverbial conjunction. It can be used to introduce almost any kind of adverbial clause, that is, almost any clause that does not qualify a noun or pronoun, or stand in the place of a noun. A single *as* can be used to introduce clauses of manner (*do as I do*), of time (*as I was leaving*), and of cause (*as I was tired, I went to bed*). *As if* always introduces an unreal condition, as in *you look as if you were dead,* and therefore requires a past subjunctive verb form, that is, a past tense verb used with present tense meaning or one of the past subjunctive auxiliaries, such as *should, would, might.* We do not say *you look as if you may be tired.* See **subjunctive mode.**

As may also be used as a relative. That is, it may refer back to and qualify any of the four words, *as, so, the same, such.* (If *the same* or *such* is being used as a pronoun, *as*

is said to be a relative pronoun. Otherwise, it is called a relative adverb.)

A comparison logically involves the form *as - - as,* as in *there are as good fish in the sea as ever came out of it* and *she's as pretty as a picture.* In current English we often drop the first *as,* as in *it is clear as crystal.* In this sense *as* can be said to introduce clauses of degree. Occasionally the second half of a comparison may be dropped because it is obvious, as in *I can see as well from here,* where *as from there* is understood. *As - - as* may also be used in making a concession, as in *as universal a practice as lying is, and as easy a one as it seems, I do not remember to have heard three good lies in all my conversation.* Here too the first *as* may now be dropped, as in *bad as it was, it could have been worse.*

A few phrases involving *as - - as* are peculiar in one way or another. In a clause introduced by *as soon as* a past tense form of the verb may be used instead of a past perfect (completed action) tense. That is, we may say *as soon as he arrived* instead of *as soon as he had arrived.* Similarly, a present tense form is always used instead of a future perfect form. That is, we say *as soon as you arrive* rather than *as soon as you will have arrived. As long as* is sometimes used to mean *since,* as in *as long as you are here, we might as well begin;* and *as much as* is sometimes used to mean *practically,* as in *he as much as told me.* These expressions are both acceptable spoken English, but they are not used in formal writing. *As well as* is ordinarily used after a full statement, as in *Bob was there as well as Frank.* But it is sometimes used to join two words, both of which are the subject of the same verb. In this case, the verb is usually singular but may be plural, as in *Bob as well as Frank was* (or *were*) *there.*

So and *as* come originally from the same word and *so - - as* can often be used in place of *as - - as.* Some grammarians claim that *as - - as* cannot be used in a negative sentence, as in *he is not as serene as his mother,* and that *so - - as* is required here. This is not true. Either form may be used in a sentence of this kind. But *so* is frequently used to mean in an unusually high degree, as in *do you know anyone so capable as Irene?* Here it has the effect of an intensive, as if the voice was being raised. Most good writers and speakers, therefore, prefer *as - - as* in a negative as well as in an affirmative sentence, except when they want this heightened tone.

Grammarians who claim that *so - - as* must be used in a negative statement sometimes explain their position by saying that *as - - as* can be used only in comparisons of equality and that *so - - as* is required in comparisons of inequality. This is confused and confusing. A comparison of inequality requires *than,* as in *less serene than his mother,* and the inequality may be either affirmed or denied.

Similarly, *as - - as* and *so - - as* both express equality, whether it is affirmed or denied.

So - - as may be used with an infinitive to show purpose or result, as in *it was so loud as to be deafening*. Formerly, it could be used to introduce a full clause of purpose or result, as in *this so amazed our men as they forsook their commanders*. This construction is now obsolete. In current English a full clause of this kind must be introduced by *that* and not *as*.

The same may always be followed by *as*. We may say *I read the same books as you* or *I read the same books as you do*. When, as in the first example, no verb follows, the word *that* cannot be used and *as* is required. When, as in the second example, there is a following verb, either *that* or *as* may be used. In current English, *that* is the preferred form, as in *I read the same books that you do*.

Similarly, the word *such* can always be followed by *as*. We may say *on such a night as this* or *opinions should be such as could be discussed pleasantly at dinner, not such as men would fight for*. When, as in the first example, no verb follows, *that* cannot be used and *as* is required. When, as in the second example, *as* is followed by a full clause containing a verb, the word *that* and a personal pronoun may be used instead of *as*, as in *such that they could be discussed* and *such that men would fight for them*. The construction with *as* is preferred.

UNACCEPTABLE USES

As could once be used to introduce a clause which was the object of *say, think, know*, or *see*, as in *I don't say as you are right*. In current English, *that* is required here and the construction with *as* is not generally standard. But a few survivals of the old form, such as *I don't know as I can*, are still used by educated people in the United States and are acceptable spoken English in this country.

In current English, *as* cannot refer back to any word except one of the four mentioned above. It cannot refer to or represent a noun or any pronoun except *the same* or *such*. This was not always true. At one time *as* could refer to *those*, as in *those of the foot soldiers as had not found a place upon the ship*. This construction was used in the United States after it had become obsolete in England, as in the ballad, *those as don't like me can leave me alone*. But it is now nonstandard in both countries. Similarly, *as* can no longer be used to refer to a personal pronoun, as in *let them marry you as don't know you*. It cannot be used to introduce a clause that qualifies a noun. We may say *I know such a man as you describe*, because here *as* refers to *such*. But we cannot say *I know a man as has a horse*, where *as* refers directly to *man*.

SUBJECTIVE OR OBJECTIVE PRONOUN

In literary English, *as* does not affect the case of the following word. That is, a pronoun after *as* in a comparison has the same form that it would have if it were standing alone without the comparison. For example, *he* is used in *such men as he are intolerable* because *he* would be used in *he is intolerable;* and *him* is used in *I cannot tolerate such men as him* because *him* would be used in *I cannot tolerate him*.

Some grammarians say that a subjective pronoun is allowable after *as* whenever it is possible to read "a suppressed verb" into the sentence, as in *I cannot tolerate such men as he* (is). This is theoretically permissible, but people who have learned English from literature rather than from textbooks will usually hear it as a grammatical mistake. In the best modern English a subjective pronoun is not used after *as* unless it is followed by a verb, as in *I work as hard as he does*. If it is impossible to use a following verb, as in *I blame you as much as him*, or if the following verb sounds silly, as in *such men as he is*, an objective pronoun is used instead.

Very often a comparison with *as* involves some form of the verb *to be*. It is still true that the pronoun has the same form that it would have if it were standing alone without the comparison. The question here is, which form of the pronoun is to be used after a linking verb. The formal rules of grammar require a subjective pronoun, as in *is she as tall as I?* But an objective pronoun, as in *is she as tall as me?*, is generally preferred. See **linking verbs**.

As is sometimes used to mean in the capacity of, as in *he appeared on the stage as me*. In this sense, it is followed by an objective, and never by a subjective, pronoun. *He appeared on the stage as I* would be understood to mean *as I did*. See also **because**.

as a matter of fact. A cliché sometimes interjected into the conversation in order to give the interjecter time to think of some way of evading the facts.

ascend up. Despite the fact that the phrase occurs three times in the King James version of the Bible, *ascend up* is redundant. The "up" is implicit in *ascend*.

ascent; ascension. The English use *ascent* where Americans keep the older form *ascension*. An English fair would announce a *balloon ascent*, an American circus a *balloon ascension*. Gibbon speaks of a man's *ascent to one of the most eminent dignities of the republic;* H. F. Pringle, an American historian, speaks of *the ascension to power of Woodrow Wilson*.

When the initial letter is capitalized the word refers exclusively to the bodily passing of Christ from earth to heaven.

ascribe; attribute. To *ascribe* something is to add it (originally in writing) to an account. It now means, generally, to impute, assign, or refer (*The disaster was ascribed to his negligence*). *Attribute* means to consider as belonging of right (*Mercy is attributed to God*).

In grammar an attribute is a word or phrase subordinate to another and serving to limit its meaning. In *the brown cow, brown* limits the meaning of *cow;* it is an attribute of *cow*.

ash; ashes. These words mean exactly the same thing. *Ash* is grammatically singular and *ashes* grammatically plural, but both are mass nouns. *Ashes* does not mean any more of the stuff than *ash* does.

Some grammarians claim that the form *ash* is only used in speaking of ash from tobacco and in compounds such as *bone ash* and *volcanic ash,* and that other substances, such as coal and trash, are always said to leave *ashes.* This distinction is not observed in the United States. We sometimes speak of the *ash* in a furnace and sometimes of cigarette *ashes.*

Only the form *ash* is used as the first element in a compound, as in *ash tray, ash can.*

ask. This word may be followed by an infinitive, as in *I asked him to leave.* It may also be followed by a *that* clause, but the clause verb must be a subjunctive or a subjunctive equivalent, as in *I asked that he leave.* The infinitive construction is generally preferred. *Ask for* followed by an infinitive, as in *I asked for him to leave,* is heard frequently but is considered unacceptable by some people.

When not followed by a verb, *ask* and *ask for* are equally acceptable, as in *ask mercy* and *ask for mercy. Ask for* is generally preferred in this construction. See **inquire.**

asparagus. The plural is *asparaguses* or *asparagi.* The plural form is used only in speaking of the plants. The food is always treated as a singular, as in *this asparagus is good* and *how long did you cook it?*

aspect. See **phase.**

aspiration. See **inspiration.**

aspire may be followed by an infinitive, as in *he aspires to write poetry.* It is also heard with the *-ing* form of a verb, as in *he aspires to writing poetry,* but this is not standard usage.

assay; essay. Both words originally meant the same thing, to test or try. *Essay* got its meaning of a short literary composition by the accident of Montaigne's modestly calling his meditations *essais* or "attempts" at setting down his thoughts. Bacon took over the word from Montaigne and the success of his *Essays* fixed this meaning on the word in English. The older meaning still lingers on. James Russell Lowell speaks of *essaying a task,* but it is close to an archaism now. *Assay* is now confined entirely to the testing of metals.

assembly; assemblage. *Assembly* applies to a company of persons gathered together (*the General Assembly of the United Nations*). An *assemblage* can be of persons or things; when it is applied to persons it suggests a more informal group than an assembly (*an assemblage of bird watchers, an assemblage of wires and switches*). It is a less respectful term.

assert. See **allege; claim; declare.**

asset; assets. *Assets* is a singular noun with a plural form. It comes from the French *assez,* enough, and was originally a law term meaning (property) enough (to satisfy certain claims). *Asset* is a false form, based on the mistaken assumption that *assets* is plural. The

Oxford English Dictionary does not recognize its existence. Fowler regards it with stern disapproval and adjures his readers to shun it. Yet it is a common word in our language now and a useful one. It is an asset to the language. That it is a false singular is of no importance; so is *pea,* a false singular from *pease.* To say of such-and-such a member that he is *an asset to the club* or of another that *his good nature is his chief asset* is to express oneself concisely in terms that are certain to be understood. See also **possession.**

assignation, when used to designate a tryst, carries the suggestion that the meeting is illicit. Houses of prostitution were formerly, especially in America, called *assignation houses* or *houses of assignation* and this probably fixed the meaning, though its over-elegance would, in itself, suggest that there was something inelegant being hidden behind it. The colloquial *date,* which has replaced in common speech almost every other word for an appointment, has, when applied to lovers' meetings, a suggestion of innocence. This may be due to its having been introduced by teen agers.

assignment. See **appointment.**

assist may be followed by the *-ing* form of a verb, introduced by the preposition *in,* as in *he assisted us in screening the applicants.* It is sometimes heard with a *to*-infinitive, as in *he assisted us to screen the applicants,* or with the simple form of a verb, as in *he assisted us screen the applicants,* but these forms are not standard usage. See **help.**

assonance. See **pun.**

as such is often interposed in a sentence with solemn gravity yet in a way that is meaningless. Thus in such sentences as *The threat, as such, may be disregarded* or *The house, as such, adds nothing to the value of the property,* it is hard to see what *as such* adds. If the threat may be disregarded as a threat, it may be disregarded. If the house does not add value to the property as a house, could it possibly add it any other way? In the very rare case where it might be a shrine or a ruin so picturesque that people would pay to see it, it might add to the value of the property. But such a possibility is highly uncommon and *as such* is all too common.

assume. See **adopt.**

assume; presume. In the sense of infer, suppose, or take for granted, *assume* and *presume* are closely synonymous and often interchangeable. The maker of fine discriminations, however, will use *presume* when he wishes to express a strong conviction of likelihood, *assume* when merely advancing an hypothesis. (*I presume he is not guilty* conveys my belief that he is probably innocent. *You may assume whatever you choose* has an element of scorn in it, since *assume* may include any supposition, however wild. One would never, in scorn, say *You may presume whatever you choose.*)

The primary meaning of *assume* is to feign (*He assumed the guise of a fool*). Here *presume* cannot be used as a synonym. And *assume* cannot be used as a synonym of *presume* when *presume* means to use unwarrantable boldness, to thrust oneself forward (*He presumed to walk at the head of the procession*). The presumptuous person always encroaches upon the rights of others but *presume* should not be used when *encroach* should be used. *She presumes upon my patience* is not as acceptable as *She encroaches upon my patience.*

assumption; presumption. A *presumption* is a supposition based on probable evidence; whereas an *assumption* can be made without any evidence at all, merely as the beginning of a chain of reasoning.

When *assumption* is capitalized it refers to the bodily taking up into heaven of the Virgin Mary after her death.

assurance; insurance. *Assurance* is the older term, now almost completely replaced in the United States by *insurance*. In Canada and England *assurance* is still used to some extent and the term is fixed in the names of some large insurance companies there.

assure; ensure; insure. The commonest meaning of *assure* is to tell a person confidently that something exists or will happen, so that he may be encouraged and rely on it with full trust (*I assured him of my undying affection*).

To *ensure* is to make sure or certain (*The very mention of his name will ensure you a respectful hearing. Snow tires will ensure safer driving in winter*).

Insure is a variant spelling of *ensure* which is applied, in its commonest use, to the securing of indemnity in case of loss or death by the payment of stated sums, premiums, at definite intervals or by the payment of a lump sum. (*To be well insured ensures peace of mind and is vastly assuring.*)

asterisks are used primarily in reference work. The main uses are:

1. To mark material for footnotes when so few footnotes are used that numbering is unnecessary. The asterisk goes after the period of the statement to be footnoted, and again at the bottom of the text at the beginning of the footnote.

2. To indicate omission in a quotation, though three dots are used more often. See **ellipsis.**

3. To indicate hesitation or passage of time in narrative writing. See **ellipsis.**

as the crow flies. This cliché for going in a straight line without regard to topographical obstacles had some meaning at its introduction a hundred years or so ago when roads twisted and wound and the slow, low-winging flight of the crow was known to everyone. But it is sometimes affected today, especially in America where four-fifths of the roads west of the Alleghenies go straighter than any crow ever flew and where the methods of flight of various birds are totally unknown to the common man. It lingers on only as a part of

the earthy rusticity which becomes an increasing affectation as our lives become increasingly urbanized.

astonish. See **amaze.**

at. This word is a preposition and requires an object. We may say *what hotel are you staying at?* but not *where are you staying at?* The second sentence is wrong, not because it ends with a preposition, but because the word *where* is an adverb meaning "at which place," and cannot be used as the object of *at.* It would not improve matters in the least to say *at where are you staying?*

The simple tenses of the verb *to be* may be followed by *at* but not by *to.* We say *they were at church,* and *they were to church* is not standard. But the perfect (that is, the completed action) tenses may be followed by either *at* or *to,* as in *they had been at church* and *they had been to church. At* suggests the place while they were there; *to* suggests the journey to and from the place and suggests that they are no longer there.

At and *in* can sometimes be used interchangeably, as in *the meeting was held at the hotel,* and *the meeting was held in the hotel. In* suggests that something was surrounded or contained in a way that *at* does not. *In the theater* suggests the inside of the building; *at the theater* suggests a spectator. As a rule, *in* is preferred in speaking of cities. We may say *he was at the conference,* but we would say *he was in New York.*

When *at* is combined with a verb, it usually means that the action of the verb was attempted rather than accomplished, as in *catch at, strike at, guess at.* For this reason, *curse at* is milder than *curse.*

at all. This phrase can be used in a question, an *if* clause, and a statement that is by implication negative, such as *I'm surprised you came at all.* It could once be used in an affirmative statement and meant "wholly," as in *they were careless at all.* This is no longer possible. The construction is heard in some parts of the United States but is now nonstandard or unintelligible.

at a loose end; at loose ends. To be *at a loose end* generally seems to mean to be without anything planned or without anything to do. Partridge thinks the expression is derived "from a horse whose tether has broken or slipped." But Heywood in his *Proverbs* (1546) gives: *Some loose or od ende will come man, some one daie,* a version which suggests some other origin.

In American English one often hears *at loose ends* and the phrase is meant to convey not only having nothing to do but bewilderment and perplexity. Some think it refers to the loose ends of a tangled skein of yarn and the difficulty of unraveling it.

Whatever its origin and meaning, the phrase is a cliché.

at death's door. Whether one lies *at death's door* or simply is there or has been brought there by disease or villainy, the phrase usually should be avoided. The meaning of the phrase is obvious but as a metaphor it is obscure. Perhaps it owes its existence entirely to its alliteration. At any rate, it is a phrase that may well be left at oblivion's door.

ate. See eat.

atheist. See agnostic.

at long last. That the Duke of Windsor was able to charge these words with such deep feeling at the opening of his abdication radio speech (Dec. 11, 1936) only shows that special circumstances and passionate sincerity can infuse meaning into any phrase, however hackneyed in ordinary use. In the speech of most other men, however, who have not had to endure the prolonged ordeal of his extreme perplexity, the phrase is a cliché and to be avoided. The Duke's very use of it makes it all the more to be avoided since the echo of his use is in our minds and makes its use with lesser provocation all the more empty and stilted.

at one fell swoop. The phrase is taken from Macduff's cry in *Macbeth* (Act IV, Scene 3, l. 218) when he is told that his wife and children have been murdered at Macbeth's command: *Did you say all/ O hell-kite! All?/ What, all my pretty chickens and their dam/ At one fell swoop?*

A kite is a hawk [the toy is named after the hovering bird] that preys on rodents and smaller, weaker birds. The phrase conveys not only Macduff's sense of the suddenness of the murderous descent, of his wife and children's innocence and helplessness against the tyrant's attack, but also of his detestation of Macbeth, for a kite is not one of the nobler falcons.

The word *fell* in the phrase means fierce, savage, cruel, and ruthless. It is akin not to the past of *fall* but to *felon* and has connotations of wickedness and bitter savagery. It is, plainly, exactly the word that Macduff wanted and, fortunately, Shakespeare was right there to supply it for him.

But the phrase is now worn smooth of meaning and feeling. Anyone who uses it deserves to be required to explain publicly just what he thinks it means.

at one's wit's end. The *wit* of this tired phrase is the same as in *scared out of his wits.* It means *mind,* not *repartee.*

atop. In literary English this word is used without an object, as in *from the fluted spine atop.* When an object is required, it is introduced by *of,* as in *the greensward atop of the cliff.* These constructions are over-literary and should be avoided. In the United States, *atop* is used with an object, as if it were a preposition, as in *he stood atop the house.* This is not literary English and not spoken English, but it seems to be well established journalese.

atrocious; bad. The *atrocious* is that which is characterized by savagery of exceptional violence and brutality. It is something extraordinarily wicked, exceptionally cruel.

Plainly this is one of the strongest terms of

disapprobation in the language and, equally plainly, to use it as a mere synonym for *bad* is to weaken it. Those who do so belong for the most part to the fashionable world and perhaps hope to imply, in the excess of the word's opprobrium, the excess of their own sensitiveness and perceptivity. He that finds a pun or a play "atrocious" that another would regard as only "bad" must have an exceptional perception of badness. Or perhaps he's just a fool.

attached hereto; attached together. *Attached hereto* is not only redundant but a little pompous. *Attached* by itself does just as well. *Attached together* is also redundant, since to attach things is to join one to the other.

attain; accomplish. To *attain* is to reach, achieve, or accomplish by continued effort (*He attained success. He attained maturity*). *Attain to* connotes an unusual effort or a lofty accomplishment (*He attained to greatness. He attained to fame*).

To *accomplish* is to carry out, perform, or finish a distinct task (*Mission accomplished. One must accomplish much before one attains success*).

attempt. This word may be followed by an infinitive, as in *he attempted to lie,* or by an *-ing* form, as in *he attempted lying.* The infinitive is more forceful and carries a stronger sense of action than the *-ing.* But the two forms are equally acceptable. See endeavor.

attend. See tend.

at the end of one's tether. As a phrase signifying the extreme limit of one's resources or powers of endurance, the cliché is plainly drawn from the condition of a tethered animal. Dr. Charles Funk believes that there has come into the phrase a secondary, more sinister meaning—that someone has reached the end of the hangman's rope. But whatever it means, it is a worn phrase and should be used with care.

at the first blush. *Blush* in this old and worn phrase means glance. That is the older meaning of the word. We are told in fourteenth-century writings that King Arthur *blushed* on a young knight, that a man in flight *blushed backwards towards the sea,* that a King looking through a window *blushed on* a beautiful damsel, and so on. The meaning now attached to the word, of a sudden reddening of the face through modesty, is a later development. The old meaning stays on in our vocabularies in this one phrase only, like a fossil, and it seems a pity to attempt to dislodge it, but the phrase is a cliché and should be avoided in ordinary speech.

attic. See garret.

attorney; lawyer. An *attorney* is one empowered to act for another. *Power of attorney* can be assigned to anyone; he does not have to be a lawyer. It simply means that he is duly appointed to act for another. A *lawyer* is one who practices law and such a one is best qualified to be an *attorney at law.* In America the term *attorney* is almost synonymous with *lawyer.* In England lawyers are today classified as *barristers* and *solicitors.* A *barrister* is a counselor admitted to plead at the bar in any court. A *solicitor* is a lawyer who advises clients, represents them before the lower courts and prepares cases for the barristers to try in the higher courts. An *attorney* in England is a lawyer considerably beneath a barrister in dignity. For some reason the name became tainted with opprobrium and is rarely used, *solicitor* being preferred. Samuel Johnson's remark, of one who had just left the room, that *he did not care to speak ill of any man behind his back, but he believed the gentleman was an attorney* would strike an American as a gratuitous insult. An English lawyer, on the other hand, would be taken aback at the sign in many American office buildings, even in the courts, *Solicitors not allowed,* for *solicitor* in America does not mean a lawyer at all but one who solicits, usually for charities.

attract. See **allure.**

attributive, as a grammatical term, means expressing an attribute and is applied especially to adjectives and adverbs preceding the words which they modify. Thus *funeral,* most commonly now thought of as a noun, is also an adjective. But it has been used as a noun so long that it can now be used as an adjective only attributively (*funeral director, funeral hymns*). Any noun may be used as an adjective attributively and the custom of so using nouns is growing.

attributive adjectives. See **position of adjectives.**

audience; spectators. Literally an *audience* is composed of those who listen. There is no question that those who attend a concert comprise an audience. But do those who attend a moving picture? Purists have insisted that where looking is the sole or chief activity of those being instructed or amused they should be called *spectators,* and it's no crime to make the distinction. But it is a waste of time and energy to try to make others make it. Those extraordinary people who attended the studios to watch the production of radio shows were called the *studio audience* as those who were listening elsewhere were called the radio audience. Television has taken over the term and an audience they will be, collectively, whether hearing or seeing.

Sports have kept, at least for those attending in person, the homely term *crowd,* though those who watch and listen over television and radio are an *audience.*

auditorium. The plural is *auditoriums* or *auditoria.*

aught; naught. Originally these words meant, respectively, "anything" and "nothing," as in *if aught but death part thee and me* and *she naught esteems my aged eloquence.* In these senses they have a decidedly archaic tone and are not used in natural speech today except in a few set phrases, such as *for aught I care* and *it came to naught.* Our common word *not* is a modern form of *naught.*

Both *aught* and *naught* are used today to mean a cipher, or zero. This is understandable for *naught,* which means "nothing," and the form *aught* is supposed to have grown out of pronouncing *a naught* as *an aught.* Literary people sometimes object to the use of *aught* for zero, because they consider it a corruption. People who work with figures often prefer *aught,* because it seems to them to suggest the symbol O. In the United States today, both forms are acceptable. *Aught* is generally preferred.

Both words, *aught* and *naught,* may be spelled with an *ou* instead of *au,* as in *ought* and *nought.* The *au* forms are preferred in the United States.

aura. The plural is *auras* or *aurae.* The essential thing about an *aura* is that it is an emanation, a "flowing out from." In *the setting sun cast a golden aura upon her head,* the word is misused, being confused, apparently, with *aureole.* If there is a proper *aura of mystery* about a man, it will have to proceed from him, not from what others think about him.

aural; oral. *Aural* means of or pertaining to the ear. An *aural aid* would be a hearing device. *Oral* means of or pertaining to the mouth. It can refer to the mouth as a part of the body, as *oral hygiene* or medicine *taken orally,* or it may refer to spoken words in distinction to written, as *oral testimony.* See also **oral; verbal.**

aurora borealis is singular, though the English name for the phenomenon, *the northern lights,* is, of course, plural.

auspices. A singular form of this word, *auspice,* exists. It is not used as much today as formerly but it is still acceptable English. *Under the auspice of the Student Council* would be unusual but still standard. The plural *auspices* is generally preferred.

authentic and **genuine** are synonymous in many uses, both meaning reliable or trustworthy.

But in specific uses they are different. *Authentic* means not fictitious, corresponding to the known facts. *Genuine* means sincere, not spurious. An authentic historical novel would be one that truthfully portrayed the manners, customs, personages and scenery of the age it was concerned with. A genuine diamond is one that is a true diamond, not a zircon or a cleverly mounted piece of glass. Perhaps the essential difference is that in *authentic* there is a sense of correspondence; in *genuine,* a sense of actual being.

To use *authentic* as meaning good or admirable (*He has an authentic style*) is undesirable.

author; authoress. It has now been almost a century since a literate woman was sufficiently a curiosity to have the fact of her sex noted every time her literary activities were mentioned, and so *authoress* is obsolescent. Fowler thought it "a useful word" and thought the public would "keep it in existence," but no one could have foreseen, fifty years ago, that women were soon to do so much that men had thought they alone could do that to attempt to call attention to it would burden the language. See also **man of letters.**

authoritative; authoritarian. That which is *authoritative* has the sanction or weight of authority; or it has the air of authority; it is peremptory, dictatorial. *Authoritarian* is favoring the principle of subjection to authority, opposing the principle of individual freedom. Or it can be one who so favors or opposes.

auto; automobile. As a noun *auto* is less heard now than it used to be. It has been almost completely replaced by *car.* One hears it in adjectival uses (*the auto industry*) but this is almost shop-talk and in even semi-formal contexts *automobile* is used.

autograph. See **signature.**

automaton. The plural is *automatons* or *automata.*

autumn; autumnal. In the United States *autumn* is formal or poetic for the third season of the year. In England it is the usual word. Of the two adjectival forms, *autumn,* in the general usage, is more informal (*autumn fruits, autumn flowers, autumn days*). *Autumnal* is more formal and poetic, is applied more to figurative extensions, and seems, possibly because of its poetic associations, to suggest the more sombre aspects of autumn (*The tumult of thy mighty harmonies/ Will take from both a deep, autumnal tone*).

auxiliary verbs. English has two simple tenses. One form, such as *he walks,* shows that we are talking about the present; and the other, such as *he walked,* shows that we are talking about what is no longer present. (See **present tense** and **past tense.**) All other distinctions are expressed in verbal phrases. When it suits us we can also turn these simple tenses into phrases by using a form of the verb *do,* as in *he does walk* and *he did walk.*

The last element in a verbal phrase is an infinitive or participial form of a meaningful verb. The preceding elements have no independent meaning but add refinements to the total statement. These preceding elements are called auxiliaries. The first auxiliary always shows tense and person, as in *he has walked, they are walking.* Any intervening elements are infinitive or participial forms of an auxiliary verb, as in *he will have been walking.* Grammatically, the verb forms following an auxiliary are exactly like the object of a transitive verb or the complement of the verb *to be.* (See **participles** and **infinitives.**)

The principal auxiliary verbs are: *be, have, do, will and would, shall and should, can and could, may and might, must.* The verbs *need* and *dare* are also listed as auxiliaries by some grammarians.

The word *ought* and the word *used* function like auxiliary verbs, as in *he ought to know* and *he used to know,* but the fact that they require the preposition *to* after them puts them grammatically in a different class. That is, technically *ought* and *used* are independent verbs and a following verb, such as *know,* is really the object of the preposition *to.* This is not an important difference. Some grammarians treat these words as auxiliaries and some do not. Similarly the verb *let* and the verb *get* in some of its uses serve the purpose of auxiliaries, as in *let's start soon* and *I've got to finish this first.* But they are not always classified as such. (See the individual words.)

avenge; revenge; vengeance; vengeful. *Vengeance* is retributive punishment (*Lord God, to whom vengeance belongeth*) and the verb that goes with it is to *avenge.* We avenge the wrong done another and the suggestion of disinterestedness and wild justice that this conveys has given the word an exalted connotation. We *revenge* ourselves for a wrong done to us and here noun and verb are the same—*revenge.* But since in exacting revenge men make themselves judge and executioner, thus violating a fundamental principle of justice, and since we are inclined to exaggerate the wrongs done to us and to feel that no penalty is too severe for those who have offended us, *revenge* has connotations of violence and cruelty.

The words are often confused because the feelings and the situations are often confused. Men frequently seek revenge under the guise of vengeance and champion another whose wrongs are similar to their own.

Vengeful has very little of the idea of seeking justice in it. It has come to mean vindictive, persistent in seeking revenge.

There is a fine use of the word *revenge* in *King Lear* (Act III, Scene 5) when the haughty and ferocious Duke of Cornwall, hearing that the old Earl of Gloucester has befriended the sick and distracted Lear, says: *I will have my revenge ere I depart his house.* Now no wrong has been done Cornwall. He has nothing whatever to avenge or revenge. He has indicated that Lear is to suffer the consequences of his obstinacy and the value of the word is its revelation of the fact that he chooses to regard an act of kindness towards one who is in his displeasure as a deliberate wrong against *him,* something to be revenged!

avenue; street. An *avenue* was originally the approach to a country seat, bordered with trees planted at regular intervals, and in England it is still felt that a *street* is not an *avenue* unless it is tree-lined.

In America the term is used to describe a major thoroughfare, with or without trees and increasingly without. In many American cities avenues and streets run at right angles to each other; if the streets run east and west, the avenues will run north and south. This has exasperated visiting philologists, but the untutored natives find the practice a convenience and are likely to persist in it.

avenue, explore every. Since an avenue is, strictly, a broad, straight, tree-lined approach to a country house and, by extension, a main thoroughfare of a city, it is hard to conceive of anything less suitable for exploration. Yet avenues are "explored" every day and some of them very strange avenues indeed. Sir Alan Herbert quotes from the preface to a cookbook a statement that, in the interests of advancing our knowledge of nutrition, a trapdoor had been fitted in the stomach of a cow in order that her digestive processes might be observed. The preface assured the reader that *every avenue had been explored.* Well, one may doubt the avenue but certainly not the exploration.

The phrase will be avoided by the sensible because it is absurd and by the sensitive because it is a cliché.

average; common; ordinary; typical; mean. An *average* is an arithmetical mean, a quantity intermediate to a set of quantities. If there are two bushels, one weighing 56 lbs. and one weighing 58 lbs., the average is 57 lbs., though it is to be noted that the average, in this example (as in so many others), is nonexistent. *Common* is that which belongs equally to all or is shared alike, as a common denominator. It marks things which are widespread, familiar, and usual. It is generally synonymous with *ordinary.* *Typical* is that which marks a type. The *mean* is that which is intermediate between extremes.

It should be plain, then, that *average* should not be used as a synonym for *common, ordinary, typical,* or *mean.* One often hears of *the average man,* when *the common* (or *ordinary*) *man* is intended. The *typical Norwegian,* for example, is thought of as blond. But since there are many brunettes in Norway, the *average* would be between light and dark and hence in no way typical.

Since everyone strives to be superior and most forms of courtesy gratify our wish to be thought unusual and excellent, *common* and *ordinary* have acquired a slightly derogatory meaning. Since they are synonyms, it is redundant to use them together, but *common ordinary* is widely used colloquially.

averse; adverse; aversion. Both adjectives *averse* and *adverse* mean opposed. *Adverse winds* or *adverse circumstances* are winds or circumstances opposed to those we would have.

Averse means disinclined or reluctant and this introduction of the idea of feelings is the chief distinction. We claim to be *averse to flattery* and despise barbarians for being *averse to learning. What female heart can gold despise?/What Cat's averse to fish?* asked Gray. An *adverse witness* is *averse* to testifying in our favor.

Averse may be followed by *from* or *to,* with exactly the same meaning, as in *men averse from war* and *men averse to war.* Both forms have a long literary history and both are acceptable today, but *to* is generally preferred. *Aversion* may also be followed by *from,* but this is rarely heard today. It is more often used with *to* or *for.* Both words may be followed by the *-ing* form of a verb introduced by a preposition, as in *averse to fighting, an aversion to fighting. Averse* may also be followed by an infinitive, as in *we are not averse to acknowledge.* The *-ing* form is heard more often.

aviator; aviatress; aviatrix. An *aviator* is one who pilots an airplane. In the early days when a woman's doing it seemed amazing it was thought necessary to emphasize her sex, but *aviatress* and *aviatrix* are falling into disuse and the one word applies to all.

avid, keenly desirous, greedy, intensely eager, is a word more often read than heard. And because of its meaning of *excessive* desire, it is well to use it sparingly. All men desire praise, but only a few are *avid* for it and the word should be reserved for them.

avocation; vocation. In America the older meanings of the words are kept: A man's *vocation* is his ordinary occupation, business, or profession (that particular state or function to which it has pleased God to *call* him). His *avocation* is that which calls him away from his vocation—some minor occupation or hobby.

Colloquially in America and more frequently in England, *avocation* is sometimes used as if it meant *vocation,* but this is wrong.

Vocational has acquired a special meaning in education. *Vocational guidance* means guidance in selecting one's life work. It can, and usually does, mean that a student with the ability and inclination is advised to enter one of the professions. But a *vocational school* means a school, often a high school, that teaches its students "practical" courses—manual training, home economics, stenography, automobile repairing, and the like. A *vocational school* is a trade school, a terminal school. In this sense the word has come a long way from its original meaning of "calling." *Vocation* was at first a calling from God, such as that experienced by the youthful Samuel, and for a long time it was applied only to a religious occupation and was conceived as something wholly apart from ability or inclination. There had to be a definite supernatural summons before one entered the ministry and the word *vocation* (and especially its homely translation "calling") still has this meaning in some of its uses. But it is hard to conceive of any supernatural injunction to repair cars or to fix television sets. See also **calling, business.**

avoid. This word may be followed by the *-ing* form of a verb, as in *he avoided saying.* It could once be followed by an infinitive, as in *he avoided to say,* but this is now obsolete.

avoid like the plague. See **plague.**

avouch; avow; vouch for. To *avouch* is to assert positively, to assume responsibility for, to guarantee (*His death was avouched by three separate messengers*). The word is now falling into disuse and is generally replaced by the phrase *vouch for.*

To *avow* is to declare frankly or openly (*The Senator avowed his devotion to his constituents*).

await. See **anticipate.**

awake; awaken. See **wake.**

award; reward. The verb *award* means to assign or bestow according to adjudged merit. The noun *award* means that which is so assigned or bestowed. In its proper uses it is a lofty and dignified word. When there is not sufficient dignity in the gift or the judges, it is a slightly pompous word better replaced by *gift*.

A *reward* is something given in recompense for service. It is pay, compensation, or retribution and punishment. (*Honor is the reward of virtue*).

aware. See **conscious.**

awful; dreadful. Until recently these words both meant inspiring respectful fear and both are now used to mean very disagreeable, as in *that dreadful cat, that awful child*. Some people object to the second use of these words but it is thoroughly established in American speech today.

Technically, *awful* and *dreadful* are adjectives and qualify nouns. But they are also used as simple intensives before another adjective, as in *it came awful close* and *dreadful sorry, Clementine*. This use of *dreadful* is not standard now, although *dreadfully sorry* is acceptable. But some educated people still use *awful* rather than *awfully* before an adjective. They feel that this is the popular idiom and that, since the purists will not forgive them for using the word as an intensive anyway, there is nothing to be gained by a compromise such as *awfully close*. See **adjectives as adverbs.**

awoke; awaken. See **wake.**

axe to grind, to have an. A cliché and therefore to be avoided and the more to be avoided because, like so many clichés, it doesn't have a clear meaning.

In so far as it has a meaning, it implies a hidden personal interest in a seemingly dis-interested proposal. But just how it came to have even this much meaning is somewhat of a mystery. Some (the *Oxford English Dictionary* among them) attribute the origin of the phrase to a story by Benjamin Franklin, but Franklin's story, of a man who wanted his axe ground until the whole surface was as bright as the edge and agreed to turn the grindstone while the smith so ground it, carries, rather, the moral of "Don't bite off more than you can chew." More reliably the phrase has been traced to Charles Miner's *Who'll Turn the Grindstone?* In this anecdote, first published in 1810, a boy is flattered into turning the grindstone while a stranger sharpens his axe. The boy finds the task much harder than he thought it would be and is dismissed at its conclusion not with thanks but with a threat that he'd better not be late to school. But here, again, there is no suggestion of a *hidden* private interest in an apparently altruistic suggestion. The stranger makes his intention plain from the beginning. If the story has a moral it is, "Don't expect gratitude just because you work hard."

The saying probably lingers on because it isn't understood. It has an earthy, rustic flavor. The user appears to be a son of toil and the soil and the poor listener daren't ask "What does that mean?"

axiom. See **commonplace.**

axis. The plural is *axes*.

ay; aye or **aye; ay.** The two adverbs, one meaning always, continually, at all times (*And aye she sighed*) and the other yes (*Aye, aye, Sir*), are pronounced differently though each is spelled either way. *Aye* meaning "always" is pronounced like the *a* in *race*. *Aye* meaning "yes" is pronounced like the *i* in *mice*.

Aye in the sense of "yes" is also a noun (*The ayes have it*).

B

babe; baby. *Baby* is now the standard word, though it is a diminutive of the former standard word *babe* (*and, behold, the babe wept*—Exodus 2:6) which was itself, probably, a diminutive of an earlier *baban*. When *babe* was the standard word for child, *baby*, its diminutive, often meant a doll. The two words seem continually to be interchanging, as in modern slang.

Babe is still retained to imply innocence, guilelessness, and simplicity (*I know no more than a babe unborn*) and *baby*, as both a noun and a verb, to denote an undesirable infantilism (*He's a big baby. Don't baby him*). See also **infant.**

bacillus. The plural is *bacilli*.

back formation is a term used in grammar to describe the formation of a word from one that looks like its derivative or to describe any word so formed. The verb *to typewrite* was so formed from *typewriter*. *Peddler* is a classic example. Usually in English an agent noun is formed by adding the suffix *-er* (or *-or* or *-ar*) to the verb stem, as *builder* from *build* and *singer* from *sing*. But in the case of *peddler* the noun existed first and the verb *to peddle* was formed from the noun. Sometimes (as in the singular *Chinee*) the irregularity of the word is felt and it is not used seriously, but many others have passed into standard usage (as *pea* from *pease* and *diagnose* from *diagnosis*). It is interesting that among such formations whose irregularity would, he felt, be too obvious for anyone to make serious use of them, Fowler lists *donate,* now a fully accepted word.

back of; in back of. Both of these phrases are standard English in the United States. A survey of American usage made about twenty-five years ago found that *back of* was thoroughly established but that *in back of* was "disputable." Since then, *in back of* has been accepted in the finest circles. It appears in foreign-language dictionaries and vocabulary lists compiled by the most reputable institutions, and in publications of the United States Office of Education. (No one any longer questions the propriety of *in front of*.)

backward; backwards. *Backward* is the only form that can be used to qualify a following noun, as in *a backward glance.* Either form may be used in any other construction, as in *move backwards* and *move backward.* In the United States the form *backward* is generally preferred.

Bacon, the essayist, may be called Francis Bacon, Sir Francis Bacon, Baron Verulam of Verulam, Lord Verulam, Viscount St. Albans, or Lord St. Albans. Few men have had as many legitimate names. It is an error, however, to call him Lord Bacon.

bacteria is a plural form and traditionally requires a plural verb.

In general English *bacteria* is treated as a plural when it refers to a collection of individuals, as in *these bacteria are dead* and *all bacteria are larger than viruses.* But when it refers to a class or a variety, it may also be treated as a singular, as in *this particular bacteria is harmless* and *a new bacteria has appeared.* In this sense, a regular plural in *s* is sometimes heard, as in *not enough is known about the bacterias.* This is acceptable. But a double Latin plural, *bacteriae,* is not.

The Latin singular *bacterium* is very rare. It is not heard in general English and is now too vague a term to be used in the laboratory. A technician who had isolated one of these organisms would call what he had found something more specific than *a bacterium.* The word occurs chiefly when this form of life is being discussed in connection with a virus.

bad. The comparative form is *worse.* The superlative form is *worst.* At one time *bad* also had the forms *badder* and *baddest,* but these are no longer standard.

A few generations ago, the word *bad* was an adjective and could only be used to qualify a noun; the word *badly* was an adverb and was the form required to qualify any word that was not a noun. This means that the form *bad* was required in sentences such as *I felt bad, he looked bad,* and so on, where it refers to, or qualifies, the subject of the verb. On the other hand, the form *badly* was required in sentences such as *it hurt badly,* because here the word refers to or qualifies the verb, that is, it tells *how* it hurt.

But today many people believe that *I felt badly* is a "nicer" expression than *I felt bad.* This technically incorrect form has now become acceptable English. We may say *I felt bad* or *I felt badly.* Having established itself after the verb *feel, badly* has begun to appear after other linking verbs, such as *he looks badly, it smells badly,* where *bad* is the traditionally correct form. *Badly* is not yet as well established after these other verbs as it is after *feel.* It sounds like a grammatical mistake to many people. But it is acceptable to many others and will probably be thoroughly established in time.

As *badly* took over some of the functions of *bad,* the form *bad* began to be used in place of *badly,* as in *it hurt bad.* This construction, once standard English, had been obsolete for several centuries when this revival began. Many people still object to this use of *bad* but it has not been attacked as energetically as the adjective use of *badly* and will probably be standard English in time.

Worse and *less* are the only comparative forms in English that do not end in *r,* and *less* now has the duplicate form *lesser.* The word *worser,* as in *the worser sort, my worser self,* was formerly as acceptable as *lesser* now is, but at present it is out of use and considered unacceptable by many people. The words *worse* and *worst* are both adverbs as well as adjectives.

Only the form *worst* can be used before *of,* regardless of how many things are being talked about, as in *in the collision between the convertible and the truck, the convertible got the worst of it. Worse of* is unidiomatic English, and the fact that only two objects are being compared is irrelevant.

The use of *worst* for *most,* as in *what I need worst is money,* is objectionable to most people.

bad blood between them. To say of those who have long nursed grudges against each other, who have an ingrained dislike and resentment of each other, that there is *bad blood between them* is to employ an anemic cliché.

bade. See **bid.**

bag and baggage. *Baggage* has a specialized meaning, the impedimenta of an army. *With bag and baggage*—with the property of the army as a whole and the properties of the individual soldiers—was sometimes one of the terms of an honorable retreat.

The phrase, meaning "with one's whole belongings, completely," probably remained in popular use because of its alliteration. It is now a cliché with all of its original meaning lost and should be avoided in ordinary speech or writing.

baggage; luggage. *Baggage* used to be the American word, *luggage* the English. But in recent years *luggage* has come into currency in America too. Airplanes and trains have *luggage racks* and what used to be called the *trunk* of an automobile is now often called the *luggage compartment.*

In almost all combinations, however, it remains *baggage: baggage room, baggage agent baggage check, baggage car.* He would be a bold man who, west of the Hudson, dared refer to it as *the luggage van.*

bagpipe. In traditional English, one of these instruments is called *a bagpipe* no matter how many pipes it may have, as in *he played on a bagpipe.* In Scotland, the plural form *bagpipes* is commonly used in referring to one instrument, as in *he played on the bagpipes,* and the plural form may even be treated as a singular, as in *give the lad a bagpipes instead of a rattle.* Either form is acceptable in the United States.

bail; bale. You *bail* out a boat with a *bail* (from Old French *baille* "bucket"). You *bale* hay into a *bale* (from Old High German *balla* "ball").

baker's dozen. There are several explanations of why thirteen should be called *a baker's dozen.* Bakers are said to have been notoriously dishonest (there are a number of proverbs that connect the baker with the pillory) and the extra loaf added to every dozen (called *the vantage loaf* or *inbread*) insured full weight. Or the added loaf in twelve is said to have been the legal profit allowed those who bought at wholesale from the bakery and sold at retail.

Whatever the derivation, the phrase is now a cliché and is generally to be avoided.

balance. When this word refers to a weighing instrument it means the entire instrument and the plural *balances* means more than one of these. At one time this word was confused with the word *scales.* The instrument itself was thought of as a plural, as in *thou art weighed in the balances,* and the singular *balance* was used to mean one of the pans, as in *a pair of balances in his hand.* This usage is based on a misunderstanding of the word *balance.* It can still be heard today, but is no longer acceptable English.

balance; remainder; rest; residue. Though described by the Oxford English Dictionary as "commercial slang" and condemned by Fowler as "a slipshod extension," *balance* is used so widely in America for *remainder* that it must be accepted as standard (*Lee, with the balance of the army, was to hold off McClellan*).

Those who wish to make fine distinctions (though they may not be followed or even understood by the balance of their countrymen) will use *balance* only when they have in mind the difference between two amounts that have to be compared. That is, you may say *I'll pay you the balance when I get my pay check* because, apparently, something has been paid and the amount to be received in the pay check will at least equal what is yet to be paid. Certainly *a bank balance,* though properly a *remainder,* is now standard.

Remainder or *rest* is what is left and either is to be preferred to *balance* in ordinary use. It is better to say *I had the rest of the time to myself* than to say *I had the balance of the time to myself.*

Residue is what remains after some process has taken place (*The residue was a light gray ash*). The *balance* of an army might be that proportion whose preponderant weight decided an up-to-that-time evenly matched engagement. The *remainder* of an army might be any part left after the main sections had been dispersed. The *residue* of an army would be that remaining after an engagement or a disastrous retreat.

baleful and **baneful** both mean destructive, pernicious. *Baleful* can also mean malignant and *baneful* can also mean poisonous but in these two particular meanings the words are not interchangeable. *Baneful* is generally applied to things that cause death, *baleful* to menacing influences.

bambino. The plural is *bambinos* or *bambini.*

ban. The necessity of using short words in headlines and the fact that headlines are coming to be more and more the sole reading matter of millions have made headlines a serious force in the shaping of popular speech. Among the most popular of words in headlines is *ban.* In standard English it means prohibit or interdict. A book is banned if it is prohibited by the authorities. It is so used in the headlines but it is also used to signify almost any kind of disapproval or refusal.

banal. See **commonplace.**

bandit. See **thief; robber; burglar.**

banister; baluster. The word *banister* is simply a corruption of *baluster.* A *baluster* is the upright support, with a curved or molded outline. The balusters together form the *balustrade* which supports the railing and it is *this* that children slide down when they *slide down the banisters.* It is hard to conceive of any purist so pure, however, that he would say *The children slid down the railing supported by the balustrade,* and *banisters* serves for *balusters,* railing and all, in domestic and colloquial use. Of course anyone writing about architecture or ordering specific parts for a staircase would do well to use the terms exactly.

bank on (to rely on) derives not from putting money in a bank and so having it to rely on, but from making bank at a gaming table. *You can bank on that* means "You can be so sure of that that you can wager any sum on it against all comers."

banns. This word, meaning a notice of an intended marriage, is used only in the plural form, as in *the banns were published yesterday.* In order to speak of more than one such notice it is necessary to say *the banns of several couples.*

banquet. See **repast.**

baptismal name. See **first name.**

barbarian; barbaric; barbarous; barbarism; barbarity. A *barbarian* was originally simply a non-Greek. The Greeks couldn't understand the language of the northern nations and didn't think it much worth while to try. To them it sounded as if they were simply saying *bar-bar* over and over again and they called them *barbarians.*

A number of nouns and adjectives stem from this root, each embodying some aspect or quality, or supposed aspect or quality, of uncivilized and unlettered people with rough manners.

Barbarian when used as an adjective simply means of or pertaining to barbarians, without any emotional coloring. *A barbarian custom* is a custom of barbarians.

Barbaric has a favorable connotation and is used of those things among barbarians that civilized men find admirable or at least not repulsive. It alludes to the naïveté of barbarians, their rude vigor, their childlike love of splendor, etc. (*The barbaric dissonances of Tchaikowsky's Marche Slave*).

Barbarous alludes to the cruel and unpleasant things associated with barbarians (*The slaughter of the prisoners was a barbarous act*). It is a word inclined to be overworked since its use is self-laudatory in that it implies that the speaker or writer definitely regards himself as civilized in comparison to those of whom he is speaking.

Barbarism means an uncivilized condition (*They lived in a state of barbarism*) and, by extension from this, uncultivated taste, and a special meaning, an illiterate expression (*"They was" is a barbarism*).

Barbarity means some brutal or inhuman conduct (*The barbarities practiced upon the wounded are too dreadful to describe*). This word, too, is used, by figurative extension, to describe faults in taste or solecisms in grammar, but its violence is likely to engender resentment and the implied cultural superiority of its user is likely to engender scorn.

bard was one of an ancient Celtic order of poets. When Tom Moore in *The Minstrel Boy* referred to the boy as *the warrior bard* he was using the word correctly, but opportunities to so use it are rare and hard to contrive. To use it facetiously as a term for any poet is to indulge in a low grade of frigid jocularity. To call Shakespeare *the Bard of Avon* is to come feebly into the rear of an outworn fashion with a lamentable piece of stilted nonsense.

bare. See **mere.**

barely. See **hardly.**

barker to denote someone who stands before a store or theater urging passers-by to enter (*A good barker is indispensable to a sideshow*) is so universal that its use would be fully understood anywhere in the United States.

barn means different things in England and America. The English restrict it to its original meaning of a storage place for grain. In America it also includes shelters or stalls for animals, especially for cows. We speak of *locking the barn door after the horse has been stolen,* whereas in England the proverb is always *the stable door. Barn* in American usage has a specialized meaning of a storage place for streetcars (*car barn*) and a generalized meaning of a large, bleak room or building (*The house was a perfect barn of a place*).

barracks. At one time a singular form *barrack* was used in speaking of one building, as in *he lived in a barrack,* and the plural *barracks* meant a collection of such buildings. In the United States today one building is usually called *a barracks*. The word may be followed by a plural verb, as in *the barracks are crowded,* or by a singular verb, as in *the barracks is crowded.* The singular form *barrack* is still preferred as the first element in a compound, as in *barrack room* and *barrack yard*.

barracuda. The plural is *barracudas* or *barracuda,* not *barracudae.*

barrage is properly a curtain of shelling, the shells so laid down as to make a given line impassable. Military procedures and the terms that describe them are not always clear to the civilian, however, and the word has come in standard usage to mean an overwhelming quantity (*The speaker was greeted with a barrage of questions*).

bar sinister. The use of the term *bar sinister* (chiefly by romantic novelists—including Sir Walter Scott) to denote illegitimate birth is not only hackneyed and pretentious but erroneous.

The persistence of the error may be due to the connotations of *bar* and *sinister*. They carry, between them, a vague suggestion that illegitimate sons are barred from inheriting and have something evil and sneaking about them. The latter idea is very strong: *bastard* is still the commonest term, in the vernacular, for anyone who has been cruel or underhanded.

The proper term—if any novelist wishes to mend his ways—is *bend. A bar,* in the jargon of heraldry, is "an honorable ordinary, formed (like the fess) by two parallel lines drawn horizontally across the shield, and including not more than its fifth part." A *bend* is "an ordinary formed by two parallel lines drawn from the dexter chief to the sinister base of the shield." It, too, includes no more than a fifth part of the shield, though (if the novelist *really* wants to be recondite) it may contain the third part of the shield "if charged."

It's much simpler to say, "He was a bastard."

bartender. The American *bartender* (colloquially *barkeeper* or *barkeep*) is in England a *barman.* For the English *barmaid* there is no American equivalent, in name or person. American mores have never permitted ladies to dispense alcoholic beverages to the public and American courtesy, prudery, democracy, or just plain love of highfalutin language, has given us a vocabulary deficient in standard terms for female human beings who are not ladies.

basal and **basic** mean fundamental. Their use should be restricted to specialized meanings, and *fundamental,* or even the good, solid *bottom,* used at other times. *Basal,* in common usage, is almost a nonce word, being confined to the physiological *basal metabolism. Basic,* however, is increasingly common (*basic facts, basic ingredients, basic principles*) and will probably oust the older words if, indeed, it has not already done so.

bashful. See **modest.**

Basic English is a scientific selection of English words chosen for maximum efficiency of expression and for ease of learning. Conceived by C. K. Ogden of Cambridge, it was worked out by Ogden and his colleague, I. A. Richards, while they were writing *The Meaning of Meaning* (1923). Ogden has continued to promote it in England at the Orthological Institute, while Richards since the late 1930's has been its sponsor at the Language Research Institute at Harvard.

It is called Basic not only because it operates with the most essential words but also because Ogden conceives of it as an auxiliary international language which can easily be learned by anyone anywhere. Although the name was probably not coined as an acronym, the fly-leaf opposite the title-page is set up thus:

B—British
  A—American
    S—Scientific
      I—International
        C—Commercial

It is English because, according to Ogden, English is of all existing languages the most susceptible of simplification and because English is becoming, more and more, a world-wide second language.

Of the 850 words in Basic over 600 are regularly used by a child of six and the other 250 are common. There are 600 nouns and 150 adjectives. Verbs are minimized and called "operations," of which there are 16. Prepositions (20) are called "directives"; they are essential auxiliaries to the operations. The remaining words also assist to put the nouns and adjectives into operation. With the restriction of the verbs, grammar is greatly simplified.

In addition to the basic 850 there are 100 more general science words, which may be augmented by 50 more in any particular field of science. There are also 250 "word groups" (actually idioms), which must be learned as such.

Basic English is primarily utilitarian. Some translations into Basic (such as "Blood, face-water and eye-water" for "Blood, sweat and tears") seem ludicrous, but any translation can be made to seem ludicrous. The vocabulary is limited and Basic English is, therefore, lacking in nuance. A more serious difficulty, in the light of its avowed purposes, is that for all its simplification there are still a lot of very difficult combinations to master.

Here is an example from Ogden's book of what happens on translating into Basic. The selection is from Franklin D. Roosevelt's speech on the bank closings, on March 12, 1933. The greater length and stylistic awkwardness of the Basic translation is typical.

ORIGINAL

I recognize that the many proclamations from State Capitols and from Washington, the legislation, the Treasury regulations, etc., couched for the most part in banking and legal terms, ought to be explained for the benefit of the average citizen. I owe this in particular because of the fortitude and the good temper with which everybody has accepted the inconvenience and the hardships of the banking holiday.

BASIC

Public orders have been given out in great numbers from State Capitols and from Washington; there have been new laws, Treasury decisions and so on. Most of them have been in the language of banking or of the law, and it is right for their purpose to be made clear in the interests of the common man. There is a special need for me to do this, because of the high hope and good feeling with which everyone has taken the loss of comfort and the troubles caused by the fact that banking business has been stopped for a time.

These limitations are but trifles, however, compared to the immense benefits that would accrue from the adoption of some working basic international language, as a second language, that was simple enough to be easily mastered.

basis. The plural is *bases*. A new singular *base* has developed out of the plural *bases*. The two words *base* and *basis* mean exactly the same thing. In most contexts *base* is the preferred form, but *basis* is still favored in speaking about the grounds for an opinion or judgment.

bastinado. The plural is *bastinadoes*.

bathos; pathos. *Bathos* means a sudden and ludicrous descent from the sublime to the commonplace, from the terrible to the flat, from any intense emotion to vapidity. A classic example is a quatrain from Congressman H. C. Canfield's *Elegy on the Loss of U. S. Submarine S4:*

Entrapt inside a submarine,
With death approaching on the scene,
The crew composed their minds to dice,
More for the pleasure than the vice.

Or a couplet from Grainger's *The Sugar Cane:*

Some of the skilful teach, and some deny,
That yams improve the soil.

Bathos is sometimes used as a synonym for *anticlimax* (q.v.) but there is this difference, that *anticlimax* is often intentional, whereas *bathos* is always inadvertent.

Pathos is the quality or power in speech or music of evoking a feeling of tender pity and sympathetic sadness. Its adjective, *pathetic*, is much used—too much, indeed. *Bathos* and its adjective *bathetic* are rarely used except by literary critics.

battle royal, a general engagement, a fight in which several combatants engage, each against all, is a term from cockfighting. It has become a cliché and should be avoided.

bawling out. A *bawling out* is not merely a scolding, but one delivered in a loud voice and a bullying manner (*She bawled him out in public for forgetting her cigarettes*). It is not used in formal speech or writing.

bay window; bow window. A *bay window* makes a bay out from the room. It may be a bay of any kind—rectangular, polygonal, or curved. A *bow*

Hyde became I, but not by an objective pronoun such as *me.* This is so contrary to the spirit of English that the construction must be avoided. One must either accept the facts of English usage and say *Mr. Hyde became me* or find a substitute expression, such as *Mr. Hyde turned into me.* (See **linking verbs.**) *Become* is sometimes used in the sense of "be becoming to" and in this sense is followed by an objective pronoun, as in *nothing in his life became him like the leaving it.*

Become followed by a past participle, as in *it became known, it became torn,* is equivalent in meaning to a passive verb. But grammatically *became* is still a linking verb and the participle a simple adjective describing the subject.

bed of Procrustes, as a term of disapproval for some forced uniformity, is an esoteric cliché. Procrustes (the name means "The Stretcher") was a legendary robber of Attica who made his guests sleep on an iron bed. If they were longer than the bed, he cut off their feet. If they were shorter than the bed, he stretched them till they fitted it. To those who know the legend, the metaphor is hackneyed. To those who don't— the majority of mankind—it is meaningless. One sometimes suspects that this and similar recondite figures of speech are used only that they may be explained later as a means of calling attention to the author's erudition.

bed of roses. We are never assured that anything is *a bed of roses* but that it is not. As a fact, it is inconceivable. As a figure, it is far fetched and artificial. As an expression, it is worn and flat.

bee in his bonnet. To describe a crank with a fixed idea as someone with *a bee in his bonnet* was once clever. Not only is there the persistent, angry buzzing of the idea, excluding all other considerations, but there is the excited, energetic, erratic behavior of such people, with the possibility that, at any moment, they may be stung and rush wildly or dangerously about.

But the phrase has been in use a long time. Quotations show that it was not a Scotch phrase originally and, except in Scotland, *bonnet* has not been the name for men's headgear for more than two hundred years. And in two or three hundred years of constant use the cleverness wears off a phrase. This one deserves an honorable retirement.

beef. When this word refers to cattle the plural is usually *beeves,* though *beefs* is also acceptable. When the word refers to complaints, the only plural is *beefs.* In the latter sense, whether as a noun or as a verb, *beef* is slang.

been. See **be.**

beet. The plural in America is *beets.* In England this has been superseded by *beetroot.*

beeves. See **beef.**

befall. The past tense is *befell.* The participle is *befallen.*

Though *befall* once meant simply to happen (in the *Towneley Mysteries* a crown *byfals* a man, and Thackeray says that Ethel Newcome's birthday *befell in the Spring*), in modern usage it refers almost exclusively to unfavorable happenings (*Whate'er befall, the disaster which then befell the human race, and it befell that they quarreled*).

before may be used as a simple adverb, as in *I had been there before;* or as a preposition with an object, as in *I left before him;* or as a conjunction introducing a full clause, as in *I left before he arrived.* In a clause introduced by *before,* a past tense form of the verb may be used instead of a past perfect (completed action) tense, as in *I left before he came* and *I left before he had come.* In such a clause a present tense verb form must be used instead of a future perfect form. That is, we say *I will leave before he comes* rather than *I will leave before he will have come.*

beg may be followed by an infinitive, as in *I begged him to leave.* It may also be followed by a *that* clause, but the clause verb must be a subjunctive or a subjunctive equivalent, as in *I begged that he leave.* The infinitive construction is generally preferred. *Beg for* followed by an infinitive, as in *I begged for him to leave,* is heard frequently but is condemned by some people.

When not followed by a verb, *beg* and *beg for* are both standard, as in *beg money* and *beg for money. Beg for* is generally preferred in this construction.

beg the question does not mean, as it is often assumed to mean, to evade giving a direct answer. It means to assume without proof, to take for granted the very conclusion in dispute. Thus he who challenges the doctrine of organic evolution and begins by assuming Special Creation has begged the question.

began. See **begin.**

beget. The past tense is *begot.* The participle is *begotten* or *begot.*

A past tense of this verb, *begat,* is used in the King James Bible but is now obsolete.

In the United States, both forms of the participle may be used, as in *he has begotten* and *he has begot.* The form *has begot* is rare and *begotten* is generally preferred. In Great Britain the form *has begot* is unknown and *begotten* is the only form of the participle used. This is the reverse of British practice in the case of the verb *get,* where *got* is the preferred form and *gotten* is considered archaic.

begin. The past tense is *began.* The participle is *begun.*

A past tense *begun,* as in *he begun to make excuses,* was once literary English but is no longer standard.

Begin may be followed by an infinitive, as in *he began to pace the room,* or by the *-ing* form of a verb, as in *he began pacing the room.* The two constructions are equally acceptable.

begin; commence; start. *Begin* is the everyday working word for entering upon an action, taking the first step, arising, coming into existence (*He began to eat his breakfast. If you begin at this end, it will be easier. That's when the trouble began*). Like most very simple words, it is capable of great dignity (*In the beginning God created the heaven and the earth. Begin, then, Sisters of the Sacred Well*).

Commence is a more formal word, suggesting

usually a more elaborate entry into some action. One commences an action at law or commences a long course of study. *Commence* should not be applied to trivial things (*Commence to eat your breakfast*). When there is any doubt, it is safer to use *begin*.

Start has the sense of a sudden beginning, the actual making of a move and setting the process into motion. One starts a watch after it has stopped and, in a like manner, there is a suggestion of immediate action from a state of rest in the word. One who started to eat his breakfast would be conceived of as going about it with more briskness than one who merely began to eat his breakfast.

beginner. See **neophyte.**

beginning of the end. There is not enough cleverness in the paradox to justify any reprieve for this cliché.

begot; begotten. See **beget.**

begrudge; grudge. *Grudge* as a verb is now almost a rarity. *Begrudge* is stronger—*he begrudged him even the little that he had* seems more forceful than *he grudged him the little that he had*—and since the concept *grudging* doesn't want a weaker word the simpler form has been crowded almost out of use.

beguiling. See **insidious.**

begun. See **begin.**

behold. The past tense is *beheld*. The participle is also *beheld*.

An old participle *beholden* (curiously enough, the same word) survives today, but only as an adjective meaning under obligation, as in *I was beholden to him.*

behoove; behove. *Behoove,* to be needful or proper for or incumbent on (chiefly in impersonal use), is the American form. *Behove* is widely used in England, and is usually given the preference in British dictionaries.

belated. See **late.**

believe. This word may be followed by a clause, as in *I believe they are ripe,* or by an infinitive, as in *I believe them to be ripe.* The clause construction is preferred when the verb *believe* is active, as in the examples just given. When *believe* is passive, only the infinitive construction can be used, as in *they are believed to be ripe.*

believe it or not. As an introductory formula this expression is intended to warrant credence even though that which is about to be related will seem incredible. It is, really, not a fair offer. Anyone who said, *Well, since you say I may believe it or not, I think I will not,* would probably incur the enmity of the speaker. Meanwhile he, by simply using the phrase, has aroused the annoyance of all discriminating listeners.

believe (or can't believe) one's own eyes. Those who protest that they can't believe their own eyes are likely at another time to affirm that *seeing is believing.* Both expressions are clichés and those who use either are not those whose powers of questioning would justify much respect anyway.

belittle; disparage. *Belittle* is a milder word than *disparage. Belittle* simply means to make something seem less (*He belittles everything I do*). It

is generally used figuratively. *Disparage* has the added suggestion of bringing reproach upon the person whose accomplishments or possessions are belittled, or lowering his reputation or dignity (*These disparaging remarks have made him much despised*).

Belittle appears to have originated in the United States, thereby incurring Fowler's disapproval. He proposes a number of words which he thinks better, among them *minimize* and *poohpooh,* but few lexicographers would be inclined to agree with him on this.

bellicose; belligerent; pugnacious; quarrelsome. *Bellicose* means inclined to war, warlike, and should, therefore, properly be restricted to a description of nations or peoples. It has been applied in humorous exaggeration to individuals so often, however, that it is often used seriously as a synonym for *pugnacious* which is the proper adjective for a person who wants to start a fight. The difference between *quarrelsome* and *pugnacious* is that a quarrelsome person confines his aggression to words—unless, of course, he happens to start a quarrel with a pugnacious person!

Belligerent strictly means engaged in warfare (*The belligerent nations refused the offer of arbitration*). Since war, like jealousy, grows by what it feeds on, people at war are usually warlike or *bellicose,* so that it is not astonishing that *belligerent* has come to have the meaning of *bellicose.* There may also be an ellipsis in the use (*His attitude was [that of a] belligerent*).

bellows. When this word means an instrument for blowing air it is usually followed by a plural verb, as in *the bellows are ready.* But it may also be used with a singular verb, as in *the bellows is ready,* and as a true plural, as in *sixty bellows are ready.* These forms are acceptable. But in literary English *a pair of bellows is ready* and *sixty pairs of bellows are ready* would generally be preferred. The double plural *bellowses* is not standard.

belly; abdomen; stomach; tummy; guts. *Belly* is a good, sensible, established, time-honored word for that part of the human body which extends from the breastbone to the pelvis and contains the abdominal viscera. Its dignity could not be better illustrated than in Sir Winston Churchill's proposal that the Allies invade Europe through the Balkans, striking the Nazis in their *soft underbelly.*

Many feel the word to be improper or coarse. This feeling is stronger in England than in America where, in the vernacular and in slang, the word is a part of many effective phrases (*bellyache* for "complain," *bellylaugh, belly dancer,* to do a *belly smacker* in diving, and so on).

Abdomen is the medical term. Its use in anything but clinical conversations or reports is pompous and mealy-mouthed.

Stomach describes a particular organ, a saclike enlargement of the alimentary canal. It is sometimes used of a larger area (as in *stomach ache*) and has figurative applications (*I cannot stomach his insulting behavior*), but the word is not applicable to the entire belly and every reader or hearer knows it. That defeats the purpose of using it, because when a euphemism is obvious then the unpleasantness that it seeks to hide is emphasized rather than minimized.

Tummy is simply disgusting when used by anyone over the age of four. It was hatched in English nurseries and the sole purpose that it serves is to illustrate the futility of attempting through euphemisms to avoid the facts of life. For *tummy* is a euphemism for *stomach* which (in the sense in which *tummy* is used; for even the most delicate never refer to a tummy pump or a tummy ulcer) is already a euphemism. If anything could make the word worse than it already is, it is its coy use in advertisements of ladies' underwear.

Guts, when used literally, describes the entrails. By inescapable association it is a coarse and unpleasant word, but where a coarse and unpleasant word is wanted it is the word to use. For its figurative uses, see **guts.** Its singular form is less offensive than the plural.

belong. In English usage when *belong* is followed by a preposition, it is followed by *to.* American usage, retaining the basic idea of "having a rightful place," permits any preposition that indicates place (*The book belongs in the library. The cups belong on the shelf. The pan belongs under the sink*).

bend. The past tense is *bent.* The participle is also *bent.*

An old participle *bended* survives today but is used only as an adjective, as in *on bended knee.* Even as an adjective, *bent* is used more often than *bended,* as in *a bent wire.*

Bent, meaning "determined," may be followed by an infinitive, as in *he was wholly bent to make his kingdom and his people happy.* But the *-ing* form of a verb with the preposition *on,* as in *he was bent on making them happy,* is generally preferred.

bends. As a name for caisson disease, *the bends* is limited to the United States.

beneath contempt. Since contempt is generally lofty and haughty, the phrase would not seem very effective. Its meaning is probably elliptical: the act or whatever is being spoken of is so base that it is beneath consideration, *even* of contempt. The phrase is usually spoken in a manner that suggests strong contempt and conveys the embarrassing implication that the speaker is actually far more deeply offended than he likes to admit. It is just as well not to use it at all.

benedick; benedict. The bachelor who in Shakespeare's *Much Ado About Nothing* gloried in his unwedded freedom—until he fell in love with Beatrice—was called *Benedick,* and the writer who wishes to show that he is aware of the origin of the term will so spell it. And, of course, any direct reference to the character must be so spelled, and with a capital *B.* But *-ict* and *-ick* are only variant spellings and anyone who in cheerful ignorance or disregard of the etymology chooses to write of *a benedict* has committed no grievous error.

beneficent; benign; benevolent; munificent. A *beneficent* person is one who does good for others.

A *benevolent* person is one of good will who wishes others well (*There are far more of the benevolent than the beneficent in the world*). A *benign* person is one who is kind and gracious, of an even and pleasant disposition.

Munificence is sometimes the consequence of benevolence, but it need not be. It simply means extreme liberality in giving and that is sometimes prompted by vanity. When in Browning's "My Last Duchess" the duke, speaking to the envoy, refers icily to *the Count your master's known munificence* no one assumes that benevolence is involved. *Munificent* is sometimes used as if it meant magnificent or splendid, and, of course, *munificence* can make splendor and magnificence if it chooses, but this use is an error.

The antonyms to *beneficent, benign,* and *benevolent* are *maleficent, malign,* and *malevolent.*

benefit of the doubt. To regard a man as innocent because, despite strong evidence against him, he has not yet been proved guilty is often —all too often—referred to as *giving him the benefit of the doubt.* The phrase is now a cliché and should be avoided in ordinary speech or writing.

bent. See **bend.**

bereave. The past tense is *bereaved* or *bereft.* The participle is also *bereaved* or *bereft.*

Bereaved is used more often than *bereft* in speaking of the loss of a person and *bereft* is more usual in other contexts, as in *the bereaved family, bereft of joy.* This distinction is not rigidly observed and the two forms may be used interchangeably.

bereavement; loss. *Reave* means to tear away forcibly. A man *bereft* of reason is one whose rationality has been rudely taken from him by some violent excess of grief, passion, or misfortune. For the past three centuries it has been used of the loss of immaterial possessions.

Compared to this, *loss,* the mere deprivation of something one once had, seems a mild word, yet in its simplicity there is sometimes a force exceeding that of the emotionally charged *bereavement. Bereavement* is used, particularly, of the loss sustained by the death of someone loved. It seems more stately, more fitted to funereal solemnities. Yet this fact is a little evident and the word is slightly tainted with artificiality: *My loss is greater than I can bear* is moving; *My bereavement is greater than I can bear* would make the discerning listener slightly uncomfortable.

beseech. The past tense is *besought* or *beseeched.* The participle is also *besought* or *beseeched.*

Besought is generally preferred for both the past tense and the participle. *Beseeched* is an old form no longer used in Great Britain but still heard in respectable American speech.

Beseech may be followed by an infinitive, as in *I besought him to tell me the truth.* It could once be followed by a *that* clause, as in *beseeching God that he would give them the victory,* but this construction is now archaic.

beside; besides. At one time these words had the same meaning and could be used interchangeably, but today they mean different things. *Beside* now means "next to" and always has an object, as in *standing beside me*. In some situations, of course, "next to" is not near enough, as in *beside the mark* and *beside himself*. The form *besides* now means "in addition to" and may or may not be followed by an object, as in *three people were there, besides me* and *she is stupid, and ugly besides*. When *besides* is followed by an object, it is called a preposition; when it is not, it is called an adverb.

Besides may be followed by the *-ing* form of a verb, as in *what has he done, besides reading the paper?* The simple form of a verb may also be used after the verb *do*, and is generally preferred in this construction, as in *what has he done besides read the paper?*

besought. See **beseech.**

bespeak. The past tense is *bespoke*. The participle is *bespoken*.

best. See **good.**

bestial. See **brutal.**

bestir is always used reflexively (*If he would bestir himself he would soon finish the job*). Kent's sneer at Oswald, in *King Lear* (*You have so bestirr'd your valor*), would not be used today.

best laid schemes o' mice an' men. Usually distorted to *the best laid plans of mice and men*, Burn's poignant line is usually given with a jocular lilt when some trifle has gone awry. The damage is done and even as a quotation it should now be let alone.

bestride. The past tense is *bestrode* or *bestrid*. The participle is *bestridden* or *bestrid*.

Bestrode is the preferred form for the past tense. *Bestridden* is preferred for the participle, but *bestrid* is also standard in both cases. The participle *had bestrode* is also used in Great Britain.

bet. The past tense is *bet* or *betted*. The participle is also *bet* or *betted*.

In the United States *bet* is preferred for both the past tense and the participle, but *betted* is also heard and is acceptable. Both forms are also heard in Great Britain. It is said that *bet* is used when speaking of a specific event, as in *I bet $500,* and *betted* when speaking in a more general manner, as in *they betted a great deal in those days.*

bête noire. If you must describe some particular bugbear, some object of extreme aversion, in French, the term is *bête noire*, not *bête noir* or *bete noir*.

betimes, before it is too late, soon, early in the morning, and so on (*Up betimes, and after a little at my viol, to my office*—Pepys; *Unless he act betimes, all will be lost*), while standard usage, now smacks of the consciously literary and would be regarded as an affectation.

better. See **good.**

between indicates a relation involving two things, and only two. But it does not follow that we cannot use the word whenever more than two things are mentioned. We say *the difference between the three men* when we are thinking of **each** man compared with each of the others,

separately and individually. But we would say *the three men quarreled among themselves* because we are then thinking of them as a group of three, and not as a series of pairs. For further discussion of the difference between *between* and *among,* see **among.**

Between cannot be followed by a subjective pronoun. Logically, it cannot be followed by a word or group of words that is singular. But it may be followed by *each* or *every* with a singular noun, as in *between each house, between every pause,* where the meaning is "between each one and the adjoining." Some grammarians object to this, but the construction is used by many great writers, including Shakespeare, Pope, Fielding, Goldsmith, Scott, Eliot, Dickens, and is acceptable to most educated people today.

When the two items are mentioned after *between,* they must be joined by *and,* and not to. We say *between the ages of five and twelve,* and not *between the ages five to twelve.*

between the devil and the deep sea (sometimes *the deep blue sea* and sometimes [formerly] *the dead sea*) as a term for being between two difficulties equally dangerous is a proverb of great age and much use. Like many sayings, it may owe its vitality to its alliteration. It is now spoken humorously and deserves to be retired.

between you and I is not standard English, but this particular expression has such a long and honorable history and has been used by so many great writers that it cannot be classed as a mistaken attempt to speak "elegant" English.

betwixt and between. English is rich in pairs of rhythmical, often alliterative, synonyms, joined by *and: kith and kin, safe and sound, might and main.* Often, as in *bag and baggage* (*q.v.*), there is, or once was, a difference in the meaning of the two words. But one suspects that scholarship has sometimes been overzealous—and oversuccessful—in discovering these differences. They probably got fixed in our speech more because of their rhythm and alliteration than because of any combination of fine shades of meaning. Some of them, especially those from the English translations of the Bible, may have been the fruit of the translators' uncertainty in the face of their desire to be exact. Where they were not sure of the meaning of a word, they often used synonymous pairs to be sure of getting the full meaning somewhere between the two meanings (*defender and keeper, meek and lowly, gladden and delight*). Similarly in legal phraseology there are many synonymous repetitions (*metes and bounds, ways and means, will and testament*) which were no doubt intended to make the meaning absolutely clear and—also no doubt —in many instances led to endless quibbling and controversy.

Betwixt and between is such a phrase. It is now a cliché and says nothing that is not said in *between.* It would be wrong, however, to call it an error. In informal speech its rhythm might be just what was needed, or its additional syllables might afford the speaker just the pause or vantage that he wanted. In a formal speech, though, it would seem pompous or wordy, as it would also in formal writing.

bevy. The old names for companies of men or animals were strange and wonderful. As a company of sheep are known as a *flock* and a company of cattle as a *herd*, a company of geese were known as a *gaggle* and a company of pheasants as an *eye*. Companies of roes, quails, larks, maidens and ladies were known as a *bevy*. The term lingers on chiefly in the clichés *a bevy of belles* and *a bevy of beauties*. Since these now have a mincing affectation about them and since the word cannot seriously be applied to any other sort of collection or company, it seems certain to become obsolete.

beware. In present-day English this verb has only an imperative and an infinitive form.

beyond the pale. *Pale,* the dismal region to which we assign those whom we regard as beyond the bounds of moral or social decency—is the word which we know best in its collective *paling*, a fence of stakes or pickets. *Pale*, originally that which was enclosed with pales (*the cathedral pale*), came to mean any territory within a certain limit that was under the protection of the Church or of some kingdom and that enjoyed certain privileges. *The pale* or *the English pale* was the country immediately around Dublin within which the English held sway before Cromwell subdued the entire island.

When first used as a metaphor, it was a brilliant extension, but it is now overused and its literal meaning is almost completely lost.

biannual; biennial. *Biannual* seems to have been a late nineteenth century coinage. It means half-yearly and is unfortunately and often confused with *biennially* which means every two years. It is said that the words were confused in a revision of the constitution of the state of New Jersey with the result that the legislators, who had adopted the revision, found themselves bound to meet every six months instead of every twenty-four, as they had intended.

It is simply better to say "every six months" or "every two years." The words, even when properly used, are cumbrous and have a flavor of documents and fine print.

Biblical English. By Biblical English is usually meant English as used in the so-called Authorized Version of the Bible, published in 1611 by special command of King James I of England. It is this version of the Bible which has given to English speech and writing so many memorable phrases and distinctive rhythms. While later versions or translations often render the Hebrew or Greek originals more accurately, they rarely have a superior power or literary grace.

Compare, for instance, several versions of *Matthew 5:6*—

King James (1611): *Blessed are they which do hunger and thirst after righteousness: for they shall be filled.*

Smith and Goodspeed (1931): *Blessed are those who are hungry and thirsty for uprightness, for they will be satisfied!*

James Moffatt (1935): *Blessed are those who hunger and thirst for goodness: they will be satisfied.*

American Revised Standard Version (1951): *Blessed are those who hunger and thirst for righteousness, for they shall be satisfied.*

It is difficult for the common reader to see in what way these—and countless other—rewordings in the various versions are an improvement. *Uprightness* is far less modern than *righteousness*, and *goodness* has connotations that make it a weak synonym for *righteousness*. The common, simple, everyday word for having eaten enough is to be *full. Satisfied* suggests a desire to add a touch of gentility. Revising is a difficult task and requires many things of the reviser. Some of the most important are enumerated in *Psalms 24:4.*

The language of the King James Version *is* archaic. It was archaic even when it first appeared, for its wording is sometimes that of the Wycliffite versions of the late fourteenth century and often that of the various versions published during the middle fifty years of the sixteenth century—Tyndale's version, Coverdale's version, and the versions known as the Geneva Bible and the Bishops' Bible. The indebtedness to Tyndale's version (1525-1535) is so great that all Protestant versions of the books on which Tyndale worked are more revisions of his version than independent translations. Thus *I Corinthians* 13:1 reads in Tyndale: *Though I speake with the tonges of men and angels and yet had no love I were even as soundynge brasse: and a tynklynge Cymball.* In the King James Version it reads: *Though I speak with the tongues of men and of angels, and have not charity, I am become as sounding brass, or a tinkling cymbal.* The King James Version is the more felicitous, but it is still only a happy revision. In the Revised Standard Version (which states in its preface that one of its aims is "to put the message of the Bible in simple, enduring words") this passage reads: *If I speak in the tongues of men and of angels, but have not love, I am a noisy gong or a clanging cymbal.*

Although the literary quality of the Bible is uneven, certain characteristics of its style may be noted.

1. Throughout, there is an elevation of language. *"I am Alpha and Omega, the beginning and the ending," saith the Lord, which is, and which was, and which is to come, the Almighty.*

2. The use of the word *and* at the beginning of sentences gives a sense of continuity to narratives, but it also conveys a feeling of the endlessness of existence, the rise and fall of life. Of the twenty-five verses of the second chapter of *Second Kings*, only two do not begin with *and.*

3. Repetition of word or meaning is used to heighten effect: *Turn in, my lord, turn in to me. Bless me, even me also, O my father. Thou dost but hate me and lovest me not.*

4. Doublets and triplets contribute to the rhythms and enhance the poetry: *And gladness is taken away, and joy out of the plentiful field; and in the vineyards there shall be no singing, neither shall there be shouting. Let darkness and the shadow of death claim it for their own; let a cloud dwell upon it; let all that maketh black the day terrify it.*

5. The constant use of the question emphasizes the seeking quality in the Bible, the searching for the ways of God and answers to the mystery of life. It also often suggests sadness and plaintiveness: *What is man, that thou art mindful of him? and the son of man, that thou visitest him?* Or it may heighten anger or denunciation: *Wilt thou hunt prey for the lion? or fill the appetite of the young lions, When they couch in their dens, and abide in the covert to lie in wait?*

The imagery of the Bible draws on objects of daily use. Death is the pitcher broken at the fountain, the wheel broken at the cistern, Amos says that the sins of the people of Israel press upon him as a cart is pressed that is full of sheaves. Man is born unto trouble as the sparks fly upwards and his days are swifter than a weaver's shuttle.

The majority, accepted view is that the King James Version has offered a powerful and desirable stimulus to English prose style. And certainly it would be hard to find any English writer of stature whose style is wholly free from the influence of the Bible. Professor John Livingston Lowes, in an essay entitled "The Noblest Monument of English Prose," has spoken brilliantly in support of the majority view. A minority opinion is offered by Somerset Maugham in *The Summing Up* (1938): "To my mind King James's Bible has been a very harmful influence on English prose. I am not so stupid as to deny its great beauty. It is majestical. But the Bible is an oriental book. Its alien imagery has nothing to do with us. Those hyperboles, those luscious metaphors, are foreign to our genius. I cannot but think that not the least of the misfortunes that the Secession from Rome brought upon the spiritual life of our country is that this work for so long a period became the daily, and with many, the only, reading of our people. Those rhythms, that powerful vocabulary, that grandiloquence, became part and parcel of the national sensibility. The plain, honest English speech was overwhelmed with ornament. Blunt Englishmen twisted their tongues to speak like Hebrew prophets . . . Ever since, English prose has had to struggle against the tendency to luxuriance." Maugham goes on to say that English writers have much to learn from Americans, since American writing has escaped the tyranny of the King James Bible and has formed its style on living speech.

bid. The past tense is *bade* or *bid*. The participle is *bidden* or *bid* or *bade*.

In American usage *bid*, as a noun, means not only the offer of the sum that one—especially at an auction—is willing to pay (*His bid was the highest and the vase became his*) but also what in England is called a *tender*, the statement of the price at which one is willing to do a piece of work or supply specified goods (Army Regulations state that *when sealed bids are required, the time of opening them shall be specified*).

By an extension of the first of these meanings *bid* has come in America to mean an attempt to gain some office or power or to fulfill some purpose (*His bid for the Senate was unsuccessful*). In colloquial use it means an invitation (*She hoped for a bid to the Beta formal*).

In the sense of a command or greeting or saying farewell, the preferred form for the past tense of *bid* is *bade* (pronounced *bad*) or *bad* (*He bade him heed his words. We bade them a tearful farewell*), although *bid* may also be used. The preferred form for the past participle is *bidden* but *bid* and *bade* are also used (*He had already bidden the executioner to do his worst when the reprieve arrived. Do as you are bid*). In the sense of command, the active voice is followed by the infinitive without *to* (*I bid him speak*), the passive with *to* (*He was bidden to speak*).

In the sense of offering a sum of money or making any other sort of a tender, *bid* is the past and the past participle (*He bid more than anyone else. I have bid all I can afford*).

biennium. The plural is *bienniums* or *biennia*.

big; great; large. *Great* has come to mean size connected with some emotion about the size. *Big* and *large* refer more directly to mere size and quantity. A great wave would suggest, for example, something more than just a big wave or a large wave. It would suggest the writer's or speaker's awe at the size of the wave.

Great means "a high degree of" when applied to abstract things that vary in degree (*It was great ignorance, Gloucester's eyes being out,/ To let him live*). *Large* was formerly used with such abstractions as charity, tolerance, satisfaction, and so on, but it has now been almost entirely replaced by *great*. *Big* is sometimes used here, but usually with an intent to be humorous and in a slangy way. *Great satisfaction* would be vulgarized into *big kick*.

Where one of a class is singled out for emphasis, as being possessed of the attributes of that class to an unusually high degree, *great* is most likely to be used, though *big*, in American usage, is coming more into popularity. Where the English would be inclined to say *a great fool*, Americans would say *a big fool*. A *great friend* (*He's a great friend of mine*, i.e., an especial friend) would never be replaced by *a big friend*. *A great talker* would mean not only one who talks a lot but one who talks well; whereas *a big talker* (not likely to be heard at all) would have the pejorative suggestion of one whose words were greater than his deeds.

Big is used almost entirely in America now to signify one of importance (*He's a big man in Hadleyburg*) or of high-souled generosity (*A *really big man overlooks these little annoyances*).

Large is limited to physical size and to great scope or range (*a large order, a man of large scope and vision*).

big as life. Sometimes the wit who has described something or someone as *as big as life* will cap his jocularity by adding *and twice as natural.* But he has not really relieved the tedium; the simile is a cliché in either form.

bill, used in America in the sense of a piece of paper, is in England a *note.* We say *a five-dollar bill.* The English say *a five-pound note.* The slip received from the waiter or waitress in a restaurant, stating the amount owed, is becoming increasingly, in America, the *check.* For some reason it is felt to be more genteel.

billet-doux. The plural is *billets-doux.* In the singular, the final *x* is silent. In the plural the added *s* in *billets* is silent and the final *x* in *doux* is pronounced with a *z* sound. As a result, so far as speech goes this word has a regular plural in *s.* The irregularity is entirely a matter of spelling.

billiards, although plural in form, always takes a singular verb, as in *billiards is great fun.* The singular form, *billiard,* is used as the first element in a compound, as in *elliptical billiard balls.*

billingsgate. There seems to be—or to have been—something about dealing in fish that coarsened the vocabulary. One cannot scold more abusively, according to the proverb, than a fishwife. Billings Gate was a famous fishmarket in London, famous for its fish and famous also for its colorfully abusive language. Pepys and Boswell have both left accounts of it so startling that but for their testimony it would scarce be credited.

As a term for abusive language, *billingsgate* would seem literary and a little affected to Americans. We lack traditions in these matters. See **blasphemy; profanity; cursing; swearing; etc.**

billion, in American usage, is a thousand millions. In English usage it is a million millions. The American meaning (which is also that of France and Germany) is made clear in a quotation from the *Congressional Record: Mr. Speaker, I should like to strike the word "billion" out of the English language. . . . I prefer the actual statement of a thousand million.* The British word for a thousand million is *milliard.*

Fifty years ago the difference of meaning attached to the word by the two countries was purely a theoretical matter, but today, when a *billion* seems to be the basic unit of government expenditure, it must cause considerable misunderstanding and our appropriations must seem even more startling to the ordinary Englishman than they do to us.

The word *billion* is used in the same way that *million* is. The singular form is treated as an adjective and used without *of,* as in *three billion years,* except when it refers to part of a specified whole, as in *two billion of these years.* Expressions involving *billion* usually refer to money and are usually treated as singulars, as in *three billion dollars was set aside.* But they may also be treated as plurals, as in *three billion dollars were set aside.*

The plural form *billions* cannot be qualified by a numeral. It is a noun and requires *of* when followed by the name of anything countable, as in *billions of dollars;* the *of* is omitted only before a degree word such as *more, less, too many,* as in *billions more dollars.*

Few usually takes the adjective construction, as in *a few billion dollars;* *many* usually takes the noun construction, as in *many billions of dollars.* But either form may be used with either word.

bimonthly; semimonthly. *Bimonthly* means every two months. It also means twice a month. Ambiguity in a term that measures time is preposterous. The imagination staggers at the thought of the committees that have met in vain, the reports that have not been ready or, being ready, have contained only one-fourth of the expected information—all because of the use of this word. In the interests of punctuality and sanity, it should be abandoned.

Some have tried to solve the problem by using *semimonthly* for "twice a month" and *bimonthly* for "every two months." Aside from the awkwardness of *semimonthly,* this does no good so long as others continue to use the ambiguous *bimonthly.* It's a pity that we have never accepted *fortnightly* (an abbreviation of *fourteen-nightly,* every two weeks) into general use. It is sensible, clear, and "established. To Americans, however, it has a "literary" taint.

bind. The past tense is *bound.* The participle is also *bound.*

And old participle *bounden* survives, as in *our bounden duty,* but it is heard only in ecclesiastical English.

Bind may be followed by an infinitive, as in *I bind myself to keep the peace.* It is not followed by the *-ing* form of a verb. A construction such as *I bind myself to keeping the peace* is not standard English.

birds of a feather. Three hundred years before the beginning of the Christian era, Aristotle listed in his *Rhetoric,* as an instance of an established proverb, *Birds of a feather flock together.* The proverb, for those who need the support of the ages to state the obvious, remains in full vigor. Its initial phrase, however, *birds of a feather,* is now a cliché and should be avoided, though its use is a very mild crime.

biscuit. What the English call a *biscuit,* the Americans call a *cracker* (though one of the largest and best known of the American companies that manufacture crackers calls itself *The National Biscuit Company*). The American *biscuit,* a kind of bread in small, soft cakes, raised with baking powder or soda, or sometimes yeast, is more like the English *scone,* but it is lighter, never sweet, and almost always served hot.

bishopric. See **see.**

bison. The only plural is *bison.*

bite. The past tense is *bit*. The participle is *bitten* or *bit*.

The participles *bitten* and *bit* are equally acceptable in the United States. In Great Britain *had bitten* is preferred and *had bit* is considered unacceptable by many people.

bite off more than one can chew. The warning not to *bite off more than you can chew* is one of those homely bits of superficial wisdom that continue to be repeated out of sheer inertia. This one seems to have originated in America in the late nineteenth century and from the frequent use of *chaw* in the earlier versions probably originated in the custom of letting another man bite off a free *chaw* from a plug of tobacco. It was considered amusing for the biter to take the biggest bite he possibly could (Mark Twain says the invariable counter to the jest was for the donor to look ruefully at what was left of the plug and say sarcastically, "Here, gimme the *chaw,* and you take the *plug*"), and the saying was probably part of the ritual.

It has long ago worn out what little humorous and philosophical value it had and should be abandoned.

bitter end. Scholars have found the origin of this phrase in the *bitter* or turn of the cable or ship's ropes about the *bitts* and explain it to mean being at the end of one's rope. It may be, but since *bitter* is an established word, in the sense of having a harsh or disagreeable taste, and since the termination of some series of calamities or a disastrous course is particularly bitter in the thought that it is now irremediable, and since the phrase is at least as old as the *Book of Proverbs* (*Her end is bitter as wormwood*), the scholars seem all at sea.

Whatever its origin, however, the phrase is now a cliché and generally should be avoided.

black; blacken; denigrate. *Black* is used as a verb in the literal sense of making black (*He blacked his face for the minstrel show. He blacked the blackguard's eye*). All other senses are expressed by *blacken* (*The bones had blackened with age. He never misses an opportunity to blacken his uncle's reputation. The sky was blackening ominously*).

Denigrate is a ponderous synonym for *blacken* in the sole sense of defaming.

Blackfoot. The plural of *the Blackfoot* is *Blackfoot* or *Blackfeet.*

Originally *Blackfoot* was the name of a tribe and was used with a plural verb, as in *the Blackfoot are there.* By extension it was also used as a singular and as a true plural, to mean one or more members of the tribe, as in *a Blackfoot is here* or *many Blackfoot are there.* Today many people say *Blackfoot* when speaking of one member of the tribe and *Blackfeet* when speaking of more than one. Since even one person has two feet, the distinction has nothing to do with physical facts but grows out of a grammatical problem. Apparently people find it difficult to use a plural verb after the word *foot,* or a singular verb after the word *feet.* At present either form for the plural is acceptable.

blame. At one time people who devoted themselves to making English grammar "logical" objected to the expression *I am to blame* on the grounds that what was meant was "I am to be blamed." But *I am to blame,* meaning "I am at fault," is standard English and has been standard for at least five hundred years. It is so well established that the unfamiliar form, *I am to be blamed,* can only be understood as referring to a future event. Logic is not as popular as it once was and this issue seems to have died. But the word *blame* is not to be allowed to rest. Today some people claim that *he blamed it on me* is not good English and that one should always say *he blamed me for it. He blamed it on me* is standard English; that is, it is used by well educated people. It is at least a hundred years old. And it is a very convenient expression. It says simply that he claimed I was responsible for it, and does not imply that he blamed me in the least. He may even have approved of whatever it was. The statement, therefore, is not equivalent to *he blamed me for it.* It would be a pity to lose such a useful expression merely because someone, for no obvious reason, had decided that it was not the standard idiom.

blank; form. *Blank* in the sense of a printed form with spaces to be filled in is one of those words that keeps its older meaning in America while it has been replaced in England by the word *form.* Shakespeare uses it in the American sense —and in an extraordinarily modern context—in *Richard II: And daily new exactions are devis'd,/ As blanks, benevolences, and I wot not what.* But the last recorded instance of this use in England was in 1780.

Form is also used in this sense in America and is gaining on *blank,* but *blank* is still universally used and understood in the United States.

blasphemy; profanity; cursing; swearing; indecency; obscenity; vulgarity. Coarse and violent talk rarely confines itself to one category and the fact that several words are usually applicable to any such outburst may have helped to create a vagueness in the popular conception as to the exact meaning of many of the words used to describe it.

Such talk is often genteelly called *vulgar.* But *vulgar* originally meant simply characteristic of the common people. The vulgar tongues were the common languages as distinguished from Latin and there was even a *vulgar Latin,* the language spoken by the people as opposed to the literary language written by the cultivated. The *Vulgate* simply means the popular edition of the Bible, published, that is, for the populace. With the growth of democracy *vulgar* in the sense of marked by ignorance and want of good breeding is not used as much as it formerly was.

A *fane* is a temple and an act or word is *profane* when it uses sacred things that belong in the temple irreverently. *Profane* also has the innocuous meaning of "secular" (*Professor of Sacred and Profane History*). It is *profanity* to take the name of God "in vain." *Blasphemy* is *profanity,* an impious utterance or action concerning God or sacred things. It was blasphemous in the eyes of many Jews to pronounce one of the four-letter symbols for God rather than using one of the substitute words, to call Him *jaweh* or *jehovah,* that is, instead of *adonai* or *lord.* This is interesting because it shows that one sect's reverence may be another sect's blasphemy.

Cursing and *swearing* are frequently used together, as if they meant the same thing. But they are quite different. A *curse* is the expression of a wish that evil befall another. To *swear* is to make a solemn declaration with an appeal to God or some other supernatural being or object to confirm the declaration, often binding the appeal with an *oath.* An *oath* is a formally affirmed statement which also invokes supernatural sanction and often invites penalties in the event of non-fulfillment or prevarication. Neither is improper unless *profanely* uttered.

Indecency is simply impropriety, an offense against recognized standards of good taste. And since the standards of good taste proscribe profane cursing and swearing, blasphemy, profanity, coarse vulgarity, and obscenity, *indecency* may be properly used to cover them all.

Obscene is a strong word for an impropriety. It refers to those things—particularly those connected with excretion and reproduction—which are highly offensive and disgusting. *Obscenity* is the language relating to these things. *Pornography* is obscene literature or art.

blatant; flagrant. *Blatant* means loud-mouthed, offensive, noisy and, by a natural extension, obtrusive (*A mass of human beings whose want, misery, and filth are patent to the eye and blatant to the ear*). The word was coined by Edmund Spenser to describe, in *The Faerie Queene,* the beast upon which *Envy* and *Detraction* rode.

Flagrant means glaring, notorious, scandalous. The root word has to do with burning and the word means flaming in the sense that flames are widely visible. *Flagrante delicto* means, literally, "while the crime is blazing." Blatancy in one inclined to crime makes flagrancy highly probable.

blaze a trail. A *blaze* was originally a white spot on the forehead of a horse. It was transferred in America to the white mark made on trees, to indicate a path, by chipping off a slice of bark.

To blaze a trail by chipping off pieces of bark from the trees alongside the trail is a perfectly good phrase when used in its literal sense. In figurative uses, however, it is badly worn.

bleed. The past tense is *bled.* The participle is also *bled.*

blend. The past tense is *blended* or *blent.* The participle is also *blended* or *blent.*

Blended is the preferred form for both the past tense and the participle. *Blent* is acceptable but is slightly archaic, or poetic.

bless. The past tense is *blessed* or *blest.* The participle is also *blessed* or *blest.*

Blessed and *blest* are equally acceptable in verb forms. One is not preferred above the other. But *blessed* is the only form used before a noun, as in *this blessed day.* A verb form followed by an adjective form is seen in *then God be blest, it is the blessed sun.* When used alone as if it were a noun, *blest* is preferred to *blessed,* as in *the islands of the blest,* and *the blest in Christ shall gather/ over on the other shore.*

blessing in disguise, as a term for some seeming evil that turned out to be good, is a cliché and should be avoided.

blew. See **blow.**

bliss. See **happiness.**

bloc; block; square. In European usage a political *bloc* is a coalition of factions or parties to achieve some particular measure or purpose. In American politics a *bloc* is a group of legislators, usually of both parties, who vote together for some particular interest (*the farm bloc, the oil bloc*).

Block in English usage, as applied to buildings, consists of a large building divided into separate houses, shops, etc., and this usage is also found in small American towns where a large building whose tenancy is divided among several shops and apartments will be known as so-and-so's *block* (*He rented a store in the Conover block*). The commonest American use of the word, of course, is to describe a portion of a city or town enclosed by four neighboring streets that intersect at right angles. Formerly it was often called a *square,* though this is now largely reserved for an open space in a city. In Philadelphia, however, the older usage persists. *Block* is also used to describe the length of one side of a city *block.*

blond; blonde. *Blond* is the adjective for light-colored hair and skin and the noun for a person having light-colored hair and skin. It may be used of either sex. *Blonde* is used less frequently than it was. When it is used, it can be applied only to women with light hair and skin.

blood-curdling yell. In the old Wild West thrillers, where much had to be made of the war whoop of the Indians, the *blood-curdling yell* was indispensable. By the turn of the century the violence of its exaggeration (and the extermination of the Indians) made it a humorous phrase. But now it is utterly worn out, devoid of thrill or humor, and deserves to be unheard.

bloody but unbowed. "Invictus" (Latin for unconquered), a poem written in a tuberculosis hospital by W. E. Henley and published in 1888, was immensely popular. The second quatrain reads:

> *In the fell clutch of circumstance*
> *I have not winced nor cried aloud.*
> *Under the bludgeonings of chance*
> *My head is bloody, but unbowed.*

The last three words of the last line became a catchphrase which was so overworked by millions who had suffered no particular bludgeoning that it became jocular. A serious use of the phrase is now barred by its jocular use and its jocular use has long since lost its jocularity. It had better be abandoned except in quotations of the full poem—or at least of the quatrain.

bloom; blossom; flower. *Flower* is the good, everyday word (*Full many a flower is born to blush unseen/ And waste its sweetness on the desert air*) and, though somewhat overworked in inspirational and memorial addresses, is the most dignified of the figurative extensions (*The flower of our youth*).

Bloom, whether it be of an actual flowering plant or, figuratively, of youth, or hope, is the flower or the act of flowering, the coming into full beauty or achievement (*Burst to bloom, you proud, white flower,* as an unusually poetic poet apostrophized Chicago). It has, usually, some connotation, too, of the flower's fragility and impermanence.

There is another, specialized, botanical meaning of *bloom:* a whitish powdery deposit or coating on the surface of certain fruits and leaves. This is best known in *the bloom on a peach* and may affect the hackneyed reference to *the bloom of youth* when it is specifically located on the cheeks.

Blossom refers, specifically, to the flower of a fruit-bearing tree. As a verb (*she blossomed out overnight*) it is usually used figuratively to describe a sudden flowering, overpowering in its efflorescence and often carrying a suggestion of the promise of fruit to come.

bloomers. The plural form refers to one garment but is always treated as a plural, as in *these bloomers are small.* In order to use the word with a singular verb or to speak of more than one of these garments, it is necessary to say *this pair of bloomers is small* or *several pairs of bloomers.* A singular form *bloomer* is used as the first element in a compound, as in *bloomer elastic.*

blow. The past tense is *blew.* The participle is *blown.*

A regular past tense and participle, *blowed,* is heard, as in *the wind she blowed a hurricane,* but is generally condemned. It is also heard in the exclamation *I'll be blowed!* Here it would be fatal to try to correct this and say *I'll be blown!*

blow off steam. With the supplanting of steam engines by diesels, the once familiar spectacle of an engine blowing off excess steam has become almost unknown and the figurative use of the phrase *to blow off steam* is rapidly losing the basis of literal meaning which any metaphor must have if it is to stay alive.

blue, as an adjective meaning depressed in spirits, dismal, downhearted, has passed from slang into standard usage (*All alone and feeling blue*).

Blue in the sense of indecent, however, remains slang, though it is interesting to see so staid a work as The (London) *Times Literary Supplement* (Nov. 28, 1952, p. 779) take cognizance of its existence: *Voltaire in his later years retained a repertoire of "blue" stories that he loved to retail.*

The word *blue* occurs in an extraordinary number of slang and colloquial phrases. Eric Partridge, in his *Dictionary of Slang and Unconventional English,* lists over a hundred.

blueprint can be used as a trope for *plan* (*The Mayor's blueprint for the future of the city drew a tremendous ovation from the audience*), but it is well to remember that a blueprint is the final stage in design and should, therefore, be used to designate only a finished and detailed scheme or proposal.

board. There are a number of differences between American and English use of the word *board.* In both countries, for example, it can mean to provide or receive food and lodging but in America this has been extended to include a similar provision for horses and dogs. One sees *boarding stables* and *boarding kennels* widely advertised —the latter of which in particular might strike a visiting Englishman as the announcement of an unusually frank low-grade rooming house.

F.O.B. (*Freight On Board* or *Free On Board*) means in England that at the stipulated price the goods will be loaded on an ocean-going vessel. In America it means that they will be loaded in or on a railroad car. This has at times led to a serious misunderstanding.

The *Board of Trade* is a department of the English government corresponding to the American Department of Commerce. In America a *board of trade* is an unofficial association of business men.

Boardwalk is an American invention, both the thing and the word for it. Ludwig Lewisohn's statement that *The Anglo-American mind hides the edges of the sea of life with a boardwalk of ethical concepts* would be completely incomprehensible to an Englishman.

boat. See **ship.**

boat, be in the same. The use of *we're all in the same boat* to acknowledge a complicity or common danger is a cliché and usually should be avoided.

bodily. See **corporal.**

body. See **corps.**

bogey; bogie; bogy. All three spellings are used interchangeably, though *bogy* (plural *bogies*) is preferred for something that frightens, a specter, and *bogey* for par at golf or for one stroke above par on a hole.

bogus is an Americanism for counterfeit, sham. Mark Twain speaks of one who had appeared at a masquerade *in red cambric and bogus ermine, as some kind of a king.* It is not used in England but has become standard in the United States.

Bogus is frequently replaced by the slang word *phony,* also an American coinage. Whether our richness in such words indicates an unusual amount of fraud and sham among us or an unusually high sense of rectitude that makes us aware of it is a problem more for the social philosopher than for the lexicographer.

bohemian as an adjective, referring to one with artistic tendencies who acts with a disregard for conventional standards of behavior (from the erroneous assumption that gypsies came from Bohemia), has a distinctly literary flavor. As a synonym for *wicked* or *promiscuous* (*her bohemian way of life*), the word is dated, suggesting the stern, mustached father of the eighteen-nineties.

bolt. In American political terminology *bolt* has a special meaning of breaking away from or refusing to support one's party (*Senator Wayne Morse bolted the Republican party*). To say that so-and-so *bolted his ticket* would convey to an American the idea that so-and-so, identified with a definite political party, suddenly refused to permit his name to appear on the list of candidates for election put forward by that party and either went over to the other party or ran for office as an independent. To an Englishman, as Horwill remarks, it would convey the idea that so-and-so had "gulped down a bit of pasteboard without chewing it."

bolt from the blue, as a figurative expression for an unannounced and unexpected blow, has become hackneyed and should be avoided.

B. F. J. Schonland, in his *The Flight of Thunderbolts,* Oxford, 1950, believes that under certain weather conditions people in a deep valley might see lightning and hear thunder from a distant cloud, and the lightning might even strike in the valley, although the sky immediately above was blue.

bona fide, originally adverbial and still so used (*Was the contract made bona fide?*), is usually used adjectivally (*Was it a bona-fide contract?*).

bone. The American slang term *bone up,* for studying hard and fast is, in English slang, to *swot* or to *swot up.* An American *bonehead* is in England, and in America too, a *blockhead.* The American *boner,* slang for a foolish blunder, is in England a *howler.*

bone of contention, as a figure for a cause of discord, is obviously drawn from the dogs and, by overuse, has gone back to them.

book. See **volume.**

bookish is today uncomplimentary. It implies that a man knows books but not life. If the term is applied to his style, it means that it is stilted and pedantic. All of this holds equally for *book-learned.* Dr. Johnson, deep versed in books as he was, made it a point not to "talk from books."

boon companions is restricted now to the forcedly jocular and the studiedly literary, and any term so restricted were well abandoned.

boot; shoe. A *boot* in America is a covering, usually of leather, for the foot and leg, reaching at least to the middle of the calf and often to the knee or higher. Almost all other forms of covering for the feet have come to be called *shoes* in the United States—sometimes *high shoes,* or *low shoes,* or specifically, *sneakers* (rubber and canvas shoes), *moccasins, oxfords,* and so on, but generically, aside from *boots, shoes.*

In England the word *boot* means what in America is designated a *shoe,* or more widely,

a *high shoe,* that is a shoe that comes just above the ankle. In both countries *shoe* is the term for the foot covering usually worn nowadays, ending at or below the ankle.

The term *bootblack,* while still understood in America, has been almost universally replaced by *shoe-shine boy* or *shoe-shine man.*

bore. See **bear.**

bored to death; thrilled. To be *bored to death* or *to tears* or *to extinction* is to be boring, for the term is now a cliché, as dreary as anything it seeks to designate.

It is an interesting reflection on the ways of language that to *thrill* originally meant what to *bore* originally meant: to pierce. And even yet the two words, in their figurative senses, are often applied to the same thing; what one person finds thrilling another finds boring. And *thrilled to death,* like *bored to death,* has become a cliché.

born; borne. See **bear.**

bosom, as an anatomical term, was a nineteenth century elegancy, and while still used, is restricted, with a sort of prurient modesty, to the breasts of a female. In the sense of "intimate" it is still standard in the phrase *a bosom friend* but otherwise would not be understood (as in Regan's statement to Oswald, in *King Lear,* concerning Goneril: *I know you are of her bosom*). The old religious phrase *in Abraham's bosom* lingers on in hymns, sermons, and literature, but few that hear or use it know that it means "in Abraham's embrace."

Shirt bosom was once the regular commercial term (*Shirts made to order, with beautifully embroidered bosoms*—ad in the *New York Times,* 1872) but it has been replaced by *shirt front.* The fronts of dress shirts were called *bosoms* long after the term had been discontinued in relation to everyday shirts, but even that has now been abandoned.

boss; master. *Boss* is an English spelling of the Dutch word *baas,* master (formerly uncle; the Dutch, apparently, having as strong a dislike as we of acknowledging mastership). It is used colloquially throughout America. The word *master,* in this sense, is never heard, possibly because it was used by the slaves. We will speak of mastering a subject or of a master mechanic and, facetiously, of masterminds, but no American would apply the word *master* to anyone for whom he worked. An American worker in a shop has no feeling whatever about the Dutch word. *You'll have to see the boss about that* comes out without a qualm. But he would die a thousand deaths before he would say, *You'll have to see the master about that.* It is inconceivable that an American maid, answering the door, would say that *the master* was not at home.

Save at a few Eastern preparatory schools, where there is often a conscious effort to use English terms, Americans do not refer to teachers as masters. The word is occasionally used in addressing a letter to a boy, but this is now done far less than it used to be.

In U. S. political usage, the term *boss* for one who controls the party organization is standard.

Boston accent. Our grandfathers, particularly those living in and around Boston, were of the opinion that the English spoken in Boston was the "purest" in the whole country. Aside from civic pride and Yankee self-assurance, this may have been based on the distinguished literary figures that flourished there, the proximity of Harvard College, or the assumption that the Cabots, in speaking to God, would naturally employ an impeccable diction.

The idea is not wholly extinct. Miss Theresa A. Dacey, Director of speech improvement for the Boston School Department, was quoted in the Boston *Herald* for March 10, 1948 as saying that "Bostonians speak the purest cultural English of any section of the country" and that their so doing made them objects of undisguised admiration throughout the land. She herself, she recollected, had been "loudly applauded" by a group of New York high-school students for the purity of her diction. She attributed her own and her fellow townsmen's superiority of speech to their "geographic location near the ocean." "The salt in the air," she said, "makes our speech more forceful, gives it more strength."

Waiving such facts as that Bostonians are not alone in living near the ocean, that the effect of salt on the vocal cords is conjectural, that there are several Boston accents and that certain surly folk might be found who refuse to be enraptured by any of them, there still remains room for doubt.

Philologists—at least those who do not live so near Scollay Square as to be prejudiced—maintain that in pronunciation, as in spelling and meaning, usage is the last court of appeal. There is no "correct" or "perfect" pronunciation of any language, in the absolute sense. A language is as it is spoken, and by a happy dispensation most groups are inclined to regard their own twang or drawl or slur as divinely ordained and all deviations from it as deserving of contempt and even death. Were not forty and two thousand Ephraimites slain at the passages of the Jordan because they mispronounced the first syllable of *Shibboleth?* Did not Jack Straw and his following, roaming London during the Peasants' Rebellion, kill any man who pronounced *bread and cheese* otherwise than they did? And did not thousands of Americans vote for Hoover because Al Smith said *raddio?*

Yet a very slight acquaintance with literature suffices to show us that some dreadful mispronunciations (by Boston's standards) have had their day. Shakespeare rhymed *halter* with *daughter* and Pope rhymed *tea* with *obey* and *join* with *line*. Even in Boston *ti* in such words as *attention* and *pronunciation* is pronounced "sh," though it was not always so pronounced. The inhabitants of Baltimore refer to their beloved city as *Bol'm'r* and who shall say that they are wrong? We are amused at Cockney "dropping" of *h*'s and putting them in where

they don't "belong"; but only an illiterate would pronounce the *h* in *heir;* and not aspirating the *h* in *humble, hotel* and *historical* is with some the very touchstone of refinement.

The question of man's "natural" and "proper" speech has long been agitated. It is said that **James I of Scotland** (author of *The Kingis Quair*) sought to settle the matter by having two children reared on an island in the care of a deaf mute—and was vastly pleased when his emissaries reported that the children were speaking Hebrew. He was happy because he was of the opinion that God spoke Hebrew and the children's reported performance showed that Hebrew was our "natural" language.

A similar story is told of various other rulers, among them Psammetichus of Egypt who by the same experiment in the fifth century B.C. (so Herodotus tells us) found the original language to have been Phrygian.

In modern times the problem has not been taken so seriously but there have been several minor conjectures. *De Lawd* in Marc Connelly's *The Green Pastures* spoke with a Negro accent, with the intent of suggesting that the colored folk conceived of God as one of themselves. But this, though dramatically sound, is psychologically questionable. It is more likely that God is always conceived of as belonging to the dominant group. If He no longer speaks in Hebrew or Latin, He at least has a Boston accent.

both may be used as an adjective, as in *both houses are old,* or as a pronoun, as in *both have been remodeled.* When used in these ways, *both* means two and only two. But it can also be used as a conjunction, as in *both Mary and Don.* In this construction *both* may refer to more than two, as in *he prayeth well who loveth well, both man and bird and beast.*

In current English, *both* follows any isolated (that is, any single) pronoun that it qualifies, except a possessive pronoun, as in *we both went* and *we saw them both.* Formerly, it often preceded the pronoun, as in *both they went.* This construction is now obsolete except in the case of *both which,* which is seldom heard any more but is still acceptable English.

As a rule, *both* precedes a single noun that it qualifies, as in *both children laughed.* However, if the noun is also qualified by a definitive adjective, such as *the, these, those,* a possessive pronoun, or another noun in the genitive, *both* may either stand before the definitive adjective or immediately after the noun itself, as in *both the children laughed* or *the children both laughed.* To place *both* between a definitive word and its noun, as in *the both children, his both hands,* is not standard today. When it is placed after the noun, *both* is made emphatic.

When *both* qualifies two words joined by *and,* it ordinarily stands before the first word, even when this is a pronoun, as in *both he and I saw it.* However, when two words joined by *and* are the subject of the same verb, *both* may stand immediately after the second word, as in *men and women both enjoy dancing* and *he and I both enjoy it.* In this position, too, *both* is emphatic. When *both* follows two words joined by *and* that are not the subject of the same verb, as in *it is good for him and me both* and *he can sing and dance both,* it is considered ungrammatical by many people.

Both may always follow a linking verb, as in *the men were both rich;* or an auxiliary verb, as in *the men had both made money.*

Both may be used in a genitive form, as in *both's witnesses.* This construction is archaic in Great Britain but is still in use, and acceptable, in the United States. *Both* may also be used with a possessive pronoun. Formerly, it might follow the pronoun, as in *to their both dishonor.* This word order is now obsolete. It might also precede the pronoun, as in *a plague on both your houses* and *were you both our mothers.* The last example means *the mother of both of us,* and for this reason the noun should, technically, be the singular *mother.* A faulty plural here is condemned by most modern grammarians, but the quotation is from Shakespeare. When used with due regard for number, as in *it is both our fault,* this construction is still considered literary English. When used in speech it almost invariably has a plural noun, as in *it is both our faults.* But the construction is avoided, at least in the United States, and a prepositional phrase, such as *the fault of both of us,* is generally preferred. *Both* followed by a possessive pronoun is still used before the *-ing* form of a verb, as in *both their leaving.* But even here a prepositional phrase, such as *both of them leaving,* seems more natural to most people.

Both of can be used before pronouns, as in *both of them, both of us,* and has been so used since Elizabethan times. Some grammarians trouble themselves about this because *both* here means "all" and the *of* implies "part of." But whether logical or not, this is a standard English idiom. *Both of* before nouns, as in *both of the children,* is still condemned by many grammarians. But it is accepted usage in the United States.

bottleneck. As a word for a place where that which should be flowing freely is choked and its flow retarded, *bottleneck* is a good figure of speech (*The shortage of steel is the real bottleneck that is holding up the promised stream of new cars*). World War II, with its many critical shortages, made the term popular and it became a vogue word and in its overuse the original, literal meaning was often lost sight of, with some ludicrous results. A metaphor does not have to express its original meaning at all times, but if it expresses something incompatible with the original meaning it may reduce a whole passage to absurdity. Lord Conesford, writing to the London *Times,* listed an extraordinary number of such absurdities in the use of this figure. In his collection were *the biggest bottleneck* (which meant the smallest bottleneck), *bottlenecks must be ironed out, the most drastic bottleneck,* a *vicious circle of interdependent bottlenecks* and a *worldwide bottleneck.*

bottom dollar was a common nineteenth century phrase in America for last dollar (*I'm down to my bottom dollar*). It has carried over into the twentieth century, probably because of the preservative power of alliteration, only in the cliché *I'll bet my bottom dollar* or *you can bet your bottom dollar* and should be abandoned.

bought; boughten. See **buy.**

boulevard was, originally, a ring of ramparts around a city. These, planted with trees, became a favorite promenade and the name was, by a natural extension, applied to any broad, main street planted with trees. Professor A. B. Hart, writing in 1903, refers to the growth of *systems of boulevards, broad, winding, and well surfaced, reaching from park to park and often from city to city.* But M. McKernan, in *Life in the U. S.,* misuses the word when he refers to the monotony of *the Kansas-Colorado boulevard.*

bound; bounden. See **bind.**

bourgeois; bourgeoise; bourgeoisie. *Bourgeois* and *bourgeoisie,* two of the milder communist terms of abuse, simply mean "a member of the middle class" and "the middle class," respectively; but since there is no longer an upper class, they also mean a member of the dominant class in a capitalist society and that class as a whole. The words have been used with such persistent malignance that it is astonishing that they are not more tainted than they are, but even so a member of the middle class would not describe himself, except in defiance, as a bourgeois or a member of the bourgeoisie. As a matter of fact, so few Americans think of society in terms of classes that *bourgeois* and *bourgeoisie* are unknown to the masses and sound doctrinaire or pedantic even to the educated.

Bourgeoise is the feminine form of *bourgeois,* though *bourgeois* may be used of either sex.

bourn; bourne. A *bourn* or *bourne* was a boundary. Froissart speaks of the *bounds and bournes* fixed by the treaty of Calais. Cleopatra, in *Antony and Cleopatra,* says, *I'll set a bourn how far to be beloved.* And it was in this sense that Shakespeare used it in Hamlet's famous soliloquy:

> *But that the dread of something after death—*
> *The undiscover'd country, from whose bourn*
> *No traveller returns. . . .*

The use of the word, however, in this context gave it (when it next appeared, for it was not seen again in English print for two hundred years), in figurative and poetic writing—which is all it is used in—the meaning of the limit of a journey, a destination, a goal. And this meaning must now be accepted as standard. That's what poets do to a language!

There's another word *bourn,* meaning stream (Scotch *burn*) or river (*Come o'er the bourn, Bessie, to me*). The two words are etymologically unrelated.

bowels of the earth. Only in the cliché *the bowels of the earth* does modern delicacy permit any extra-clinical use of the once dignified and passionate word *bowels* (*the bowels of pity, in the bowels of Christ, child of my bowels*). However, the phrase is worn out. It has been in constant service since 1593 and should be retired.

bowing and scraping as a contemptuous designation for being excessively courteous, too ceremonious and eager in a demonstration of politeness, is now a cliché and should be avoided. Probably not one user of the phrase out of a hundred knows what the word *scraping* means in this context. It alludes to a particularly elaborate bow (used especially in the *congé*, or leave-taking) in which not only was the head inclined but one knee slightly bent and the foot of the other leg drawn back with a scrape along the ground. It was sometimes called *making a leg* and offered all sorts of opportunities for writhing self-abasement.

bowl; basin. Except in certain technical applications in geology and physical geography (*a river basin*), *basin* in American usage is generally confined to a container used for washing the hands. There is some of the feeling that a *basin* is shallower than a *bowl* and *bowl*, despite its particular use in the phrase *toilet bowl*, is the more dignified of the two words. A special American use of *bowl* is to describe the great amphitheaters or stadiums in which the champion football teams of various sections of the country play each other.

bowls. When referring to the game, the plural word *bowls* takes a singular verb, as in *bowls is good exercise*. When used with a plural verb, *bowls* means the balls, as in *bowls are not always spherical.*

At one time the singular form *bowl* was used as the first element in a compound, as in the following sentence written in 1628: *A Bowl Alley is the place where there are three things thrown away beside Bowls, to wit, time, money, and curses.* This is now archaic and the form *bowling* is preferred, as in *a bowling alley.*

boyish. See **infantile.**

brace. When this word means a pair, or a couple, it has the same form in the singular and the plural, as in *a brace of greyhounds, four or five brace of greyhounds. Brace* cannot stand immediately before a following noun, as a numeral does, but must be joined to it by *of.*

braces. When used to mean an article of clothing, *braces* is the British equivalent of the American *suspenders.* The singular *brace* means one strap and the plural *braces,* more than one strap. For this reason *two braces* means only one pair and it is necessary to say *two pairs* of braces if that is what is meant. See also **suspenders.**

brackets are seldom used except as editorial marks. Their main uses are:

1. To indicate a comment or explanation added by a writer to material he is quoting, as in *"These are the times [the 1770's] that try men's souls."*

2. To indicate action accompanying speech or dialogue, as in *Churchill is half American and all English. [Laughter]*

3. To indicate editorial corrections, omissions or additions, as in *He was born February 2 [actually on the morning of February 3]; You will be pleased [to] hear that we have finished; The President [Lincoln] did not appear concerned.*

4. In mathematical work and formulas, to enclose numbers and symbols which should be treated as a unit, that is, as parentheses around material that already contains parentheses, as in $a[a+b(b-c)]$.

5. As parentheses within parentheses—rarely used, but found in legal documents and reference works, as in (*See Walter Wilson, Bugs is Bugs* [*New York, 1952*], *p. 35.*)

6. In documents, whole portions to be omitted are enclosed in brackets. When more than one paragraph is to be bracketed, each paragraph should start with a bracket, but only the last paragraph should end with a bracket.

brag may be followed by a *that* clause, as in *he brags that he has robbed a bank.* If the *-ing* form of a verb is used it must be introduced by the preposition *of* or *about,* as in *he brags of having robbed a bank.* The construction with *of* is generally preferred.

brain and **brains.** Both forms of this word may be used to mean either the physical organ inside the skull or a man's intellectual capacity. It is often impossible to say which is intended. In many cases the speaker may not feel that there is any difference between the organ and the capacity. The physical organ is obviously what is meant in *a large brain* and *he blew out his brains.* Something more abstract is probably intended in *rack your brain* or *rack your brains.* In both senses, the singular form, *brain,* seems to have a more scientific tone and the plural, *brains,* to be more popular and vivid.

When speaking of more than one individual, *brains* is a true plural and can be used with a numeral, as in *two brains are better than one.*

When speaking of one individual, the plural form *brains* is a mass noun and not a true plural. It is followed by a plural verb but cannot be qualified by a numeral or a word implying number. When not the subject of a verb, it may have singular qualifiers, as in *he hasn't much brains* or *he has very little brains.* Plural constructions, such as *he hasn't many brains,* are intended to be witty.

When the contents of an animal's skull are thought of as food, only the plural form *brains* is used. This too is a mass noun and cannot be used with a numeral. We cook *brains,* not *a brain* or *two or three brains.*

Only the singular form *brain* is used as the first element in a compound, as in *brain size, brain work, brain trust.*

brainy, for *clever,* is an Americanism (*No profession is so singled out by ambitious, brainy young men, as that of the law*) and is dismissed by Fowler with disdain. But it is hard to see why it is any more improper a coinage than *handy,* in analogy with which it was probably made. And, anyway, the argument is academic; the American populace has long ago accepted the word into standard usage.

In America it is spoken in admiration, an adjective of untainted praise, differing from *clever,* which has a light suggestion of shiftiness and unscrupulousness about it, or *intellectual* which has a connotation of self-esteem.

Perhaps the British dislike of *brainy* is, at bottom, a dislike of brains (*If you were a patriot you read Blackwood's Magazine and thanked God you were "not brainy"*—George Orwell, *Such, Such were the Joys,* 1953).

brake; break. *Brake* meaning a place overgrown with bushes or cane (*Down in the canebrake, the other side of the mill*) is still used in Southeastern United States, though not too well known elsewhere. A similar application in England, which seems to have died out in the late nineteenth century, seems to have been limited to a growth of bracken, or heavy ferns, of which, indeed, the word in this sense is an abbreviation.

A car much like an American *station wagon* is in England sometimes called a *shooting brake.*

The uses of *break,* both as a verb and as a noun, are much the same in England and America except for the American colloquial use of *break* to mean opportunity or lucky chance (*Hard work isn't everything; you've got to have the breaks too*) and, sometimes, something very close to forgiveness (*Sometimes a cop will give you a break and tear up the ticket*).

brand. America is a commercial nation, cheerful and unashamed, and our unblushing use of commercial terms in all departments of life has often caused the English acute discomfort. Thus our use of *reckon, figure,* and *calculate,* as synonyms for *think* (as though all thought worthy of the name was confined to casting up an account) and *It doesn't pay* to signify our strongest moral disapproval seem to many Englishmen to betray too engrossing an attention to getting and spending.

Among these words is *brand* when used figuratively as a trademark or brand of goods distinguished by a trademark. They do not mind the literal use (*The ale was of a superior brand. I think you'll like this brand of cheese*) but feel that our metaphorical uses, particularly, often, our humorous uses (*They don't like our brand of humor*), are improper. Thus Partridge feels that Samuel Putnam's statement that Margaret of Navarre *had her own brand of services in her own private chapel* is "highly inappropriate." An American might feel it a little breezy; it would depend on what he happened to think of Margaret of Navarre and her metaphysics.

bran-new; brand-new. *Bran-new* is standard and acceptable, not just a slovenly pronunciation; but *brand-new* is the preferred form.

bravado; bravery. *Bravado* is a boastful, often threatening, display of false courage, an expression of strutting vanity intended to defy and intimidate. *Bravery* is true courage, admirable and praiseworthy (*The man of true bravery is not frightened by a display of bravado*).

breach and **breech,** though pronounced exactly alike, are in no sense synonymous. *Breach* is the act or result of breaking, a rupture, the violation of a law, trust, faith, or promise, and the like. *Breech* is the lower part of the trunk of the body behind or, in ordnance, the mass of metal behind the bore of a cannon or the small arm back of the barrel of a gun or rifle.

breadth; broadness; width; wideness; latitude. The mathematical sense of *breadth* is its basic meaning: the measure of the second principal diameter of a surface or solid, the first being length, and the third (in the case of a solid) thickness. In the sense of freedom from restraint or narrowness (*breadth of mind*) *width,* which is synonymous in the basic meaning, is never used. *Breadth* implies a freedom from restraint of which the speaker or writer approves; *broadness,* when used at all, may imply coarseness, or a freedom from restraint which is not approved. *Width* and *wideness* are both restricted now to definite measurements and used rarely in a figurative sense, though *wideness* used to be (*There's a wideness in God's mercy/Like the wideness of the sea*) and with great dignity.

Latitude when used as a synonym for *breadth,* in the sense of freedom from restriction or liberality, is now confined more to thought than action and expresses something more tolerated than approved (*He has interpreted the rules with considerable latitude*).

break. The past tense is *broke.* The participle is *broken.*

A past tense *brake* is often used in nineteenth century poetry but it has not been standard spoken English for more than three hundred years. In the seventeenth and eighteenth century *broke* was often used for the participle, as in *he had broke the box.* This is archaic today, except in the passive where it now means "without money," as in *he is, was, and always will be broke.* For *a break,* see **brake.**

breakdown in the sense of "analysis" is a technical term taken over from chemistry. It is a vogue word at the moment, much used in place of *classification* (*The breakdown of the votes by counties revealed that the victor's margin was much slimmer than it appeared from the total*). As Sir Ernest Gowers points out, the word can be inept and ludicrous when used of things that can actually and physically be broken down. Thus if one were to speak of *the breakdown of trucks* in the government service one would hardly get a serious hearing for whatever classification one wanted to make. Sir Ernest gives, as one example: *Statistics have been issued of the population of the United States, broken down by age and sex.*

break the ice, as a figure of speech, is still sometimes used in its older sense of making a beginning in an enterprise, though, for the most part, it is fixed in its nineteenth century special application to breaking through the reserve of some cold person (*And your cold people are beyond*

all price,/ When once you've broken their confounded ice). In all of its figurative meanings,
however, the term is now a cliché and to be used
with care.

bred. See **breed.**

breeches. The plural form refers to one garment
but is always treated as a plural, as in *these
breeches are torn.* In order to use the word with
a singular verb or to speak of more than one of
these garments, it is necessary to say *this pair of
breeches is torn* or *several pairs of breeches.*
The form *breeches* is also used as the first element in a compound, as in *his breeches pocket.*
The singular *breech* is now used only for the
rear end of a gun.

breed. The past tense is *bred.* The participle is also
bred.

breezy; fresh; lively. *Breezy,* when applied figuratively to persons, means airy, flippant, and gay.
Lively is more complimentary. A lively mind is
one of quick apprehensions, full of vivid and
rapidly changing images, rapid in its comprehension (*Mercutio had a breezy way, but Hotspur's mind was lively*). *Fresh* in American
usage, when used of a person, means forward or
presumptuous, impertinent, often with a hint of
sexual aggressiveness.

brethren. See **brothers.**

bridesmaid. Traditionally, the form *bride* was
used in this compound, as it still is in the related word *bridegroom.* But the irregular form
bridesmaid has been standard English since the
latter part of the nineteenth century.

brief; short. *Brief* applies to time only and sometimes implies a condensation. *We had only time
for a brief talk* implies not only that the talk
was of short duration but that it was intense
and concentrated. *A short talk* would have
lacked this latter implication. *Short* refers to
either time or space, but when it refers to the
former it suggests a curtailment, often rude or
painful (*He cut him off short*). It sometimes
extends this meaning so far as to mean "lacking"
(as in *short rations, he was short in his accounts*).

In its legal sense, there is a difference between
the American and English usage of *brief.* In
England a *brief* is solely a summary of the facts
of the case prepared by a solicitor for the counsel who is conducting the case. It is a private
document. In America it can be this (*He briefed
him in his arguments*). This is also the *brief* of
briefcase. But it is more often a summary of
arguments filed by counsel in an appellate court,
printed, public, and often voluminous (*I had
the honor to be one of the attorneys in the case,
and filed a brief against the bonds*). See also
outline.

bright and early is a cliché and to people of normal habits of rising, an irritating one. Even its
factual accuracy may be challenged. The airlines report more delays because of fog in their
early morning flights than at any other time of
the day.

bring. The past tense is *brought.* The participle is
also *brought.*

Brung is heard for the past tense and for the

participle, as in *he had brung it,* but this is not
standard English.

Bring may be followed by an infinitive, as in
you will never bring me to admit it, or by the
-ing form of a verb with the preposition *to,* as
in *you will never bring me to admitting it.* The
infinitive construction is preferred.

bring; take; fetch. To *bring* is to cause to come
with oneself. To *take* is to get into one's hands
and to convey away. To *fetch* is to go and bring
something to the speaker (*Take that box and
bring it with you, or if it's too heavy for you
I'll send Joe to fetch it*).

Fetch has a special meaning of to allure
(*What a fetching bonnet!*). When the rascally
duke, in *Huckleberry Finn,* added the line
"Ladies and Children not Admitted" to his advertisement of *The Royal Nonesuch,* he paused
to admire his handiwork: *There,* says he, *if that
line don't fetch them, I don't know Arkansaw!*
Here *fetch* means to allure and to bring in. This
meaning is now a little old-fashioned and rustic,
but still current.

Briton; Britisher. A *Briton* can be either one of
the ancient Celtic inhabitants of England or a
modern inhabitant. *Britisher* was an American
term that had a currency in the United States in
the late eighteenth and nineteenth centuries but
is practically never heard today. The ordinary
American would never use the term *Briton.* He
accords the *Irish* separate recognition, but all
other male inhabitants of the British Isles are
Englishmen to him. If a *Scot* insisted on being
identified as a member of a special nation, his
insistence would be humored, but most Americans wouldn't make the distinction if someone
else did not make it first. An *English woman*
would be used to designate a single English
female, and *English women* would be its plural.
But an *Englishwoman,* as the female of *Englishman,* would not be much used, though it would
be understood. The collective plural *the English*
is used most commonly when generalizing, and
Americans love to generalize about the English
almost as much as the English love to generalize
about Americans.

brittle. See **fragile.**

broad; wide. Everyone is aware that *broad* and
wide are synonymous, but a moment's reflection
calls to mind what seems a bewildering confusion in their idiomatic uses. We speak of
broad shoulders, but of a wide mouth. One
who has traveled far and wide will probably
have a broad outlook. We give a man a broad
hint and a wide berth. The Pilgrims crossed the
broad Atlantic and their descendants the wide
Missouri.

Fowler, in a brilliant analysis of the usage of
these two words, concludes that "*wide* refers to
the distance that separates the limits, and *broad*
to the amplitude of what connects them."

Some things seem to have had *broad,* as a
description of their amplitude, affixed to them
arbitrarily (*broad daylight*); others have a secondary suggestion of generosity or disregard of
the trivial (*a broad outline, a Broad Church-
man*) or of unrestraint (*a broad joke*).

Sometimes the words are interchangeable. There is little or no difference between *a broad grin* and *a wide grin*. A wide discussion, however, is one that covers many topics; a broad discussion, one that does not confine itself within severe limits of propriety or orthodoxy.

When in doubt, consider *wide* the more literal, *broad* the more figurative use.

broadcast. The past tense is *broadcast* or *broadcasted*. The participle is also *broadcast* or *broadcasted*.

Broadcast is the traditional form for the past tense and the participle. But the broadcasters have now made *broadcasted* standard. In substituting a regular verb for an irregular one they have done a service to the language.

broadcloth. In American usage *broadcloth* means a cotton shirting or dress material, usually mercerized. It is what the English call *poplin. Broadcloth* to an Englishman means a napped and calendered woolen cloth, usually black, from which men's coats are made.

broadness. See **breadth.**

broke, broken. See **break.**

bronchia. This word is plural and should not be given an additional plural ending, as in *bronchiae.*

brothers; brethren. *Brothers* is the standard term for sons of the same mother. The singular is used a great deal in America as a semi-facetious form of address (*You said it, brother!*), as an introduction to an informal supplication (*Brother, can you spare a dime?*) and, often, just as an exclamation (*Brother! You should have seen that guy!*). All of these uses are slang.

Brethren, the archaic plural, is rarely used except for members of religious bodies. President Eisenhower, addressing the World Council of Churches Assembly, in Evanston, Illinois, August 19, 1954, besought the delegates to aid the cause of peace *together with your brethren of other faiths.* It was not a term he would have used had he been addressing, say, the Brotherhood of Locomotive Engineers.

The use of the term among lodge members and in rhetorical sermons has caused it to be a humorous word among the irreverent.

brought. See **bring.**

brown as a berry. No one knows a brown berry. Some have suggested that a coffee berry is meant, but Chaucer used the phrase (*His palfrey was as broun as is a berye*) more than two hundred years before coffee had been heard of in England. Anyway, this pointless comparison has been repeated ceaselessly for more than five hundred years and is entitled to at least that long a rest.

brown study. The *brown* in the cliché *a brown study* has an obsolete meaning of gloomy; the *study* has an obsolete meaning of reverie. The whole phrase, *brown study,* however, has now lost even the meaning of a gloomy reverie. It is usually employed to designate an idle or purposeless reverie, a fit of abstraction. The phrase should be avoided.

brunch. See **lunch.**

brung. See **bring.**

brush. Certain uses of *brush,* as a verb and a noun, may be regarded as Americanisms, though some of them were formerly standard in England: a brief, hostile encounter (*He had a brush with the customs men*); lopped or broken branches (*He brought in an armload of brush*); a forceful dash (*There were a good many nags about that could beat him on a brush, but for long drives he had few equals*).

To *brush up* or to *brush up on,* in the figurative sense of to refresh your knowledge of (*He said he had to brush up on his history before the examination. The President said that the House ought to brush up its economics*) must be accepted as standard.

brutal; brutish; brute; beastly; bestial. *Brute,* most commonly used as an adjective in the cliché *brute force,* means having the quality of some nonhuman animal. *Brutish* means gross, carnal, like an animal, lacking in civilized refinement (*When thou didst not, savage,/Know thine own meaning, but wouldst gabble/Like a thing most brutish*). It refers most often, in modern usage, to character.

Brutal, the most commonly used of all these words, means cruel, inhuman, coarse. It is never used without an implication of moral condemnation; whereas *brute,* and sometimes *brutish,* are free from this. *Brute* is usually applied to strength, *brutal* to actions, *brutish* to thoughts or manners.

Bestial, like *brutal,* implies moral condemnation, but it is applied more to lust, uninhibited sexuality, than to ferocity (*The bestial appetites of the brutal invaders*). *Beastly* in standard American usage is a synonym for *bestial.* The English colloquial usage of it to mean nasty or disagreeable (*Let us not be beastly to the Hun*) is not known in America except as a humorous mimicking of English speech.

buck. See **hart.**

bug; bugbear; bugaboo; buggy. *Bug* in American everyday usage means almost any kind of insect (*lightning bug*). In English usage, in this sense, it is restricted to what in America is called a *bedbug* and, for reasons not clear to Americans, is an indecent word. No one in America boasts of having bedbugs, but the bitten traveler would not hesitate to use the word in airing his grievance. But in England, it is not so; it is almost an unmentionable word, possibly because of a klang association (*q.v.*) with *bugger* (*q.v.*).

In America *bug* has come to mean defect or difficulty (*They haven't worked all the bugs out of the new model yet*), an enthusiasm which amounts to a disease (*He's got the tennis bug and is on the courts all day*), and a pyromaniac (*a firebug*). None of these is standard.

Bug in the sense of defect and the *-bug* in *firebug* are probably forms of *bugaboo,* a bogy, some imaginary (or real) thing that causes fear or worry. Americans retain the old form *bugaboo,* while English usage has changed to *bugbear. Bug* is an old form of *bugaboo.* The fifth verse of the ninety-first Psalm in the King James version reads: *Thou shalt not be afraid for the terror by night.* In the Coverdale version (1535) it read: *Thou shalt not need to be afraid for any bugs by night.* An interesting illustration of misunderstandings that lie in wait for the uninstructed reader is found in King Edward's remark, in Shakespeare's *Third Part of King Henry VI,* that *Warwick was a bug that fear'd us all.* To the common reader in America today that line would convey the idea that Warwick was an insect, a crawling creature, who was afraid of everybody. Whereas it means that Warwick was a terror that frightened them all.

Buggy, in *horse and buggy,* may be related to *bug* in its meaning of "bogy." It is not absolutely certain, but it is believed that when these light vehicles were first made they were humorously called *bogies* because they went so fast they were a terror.

bugger in British usage means a sodomite, being the linguistic residue of a piece of medieval religious propaganda to the effect that the Bulgarians, who were heretics, were also sodomites. In England the word is indecent, both as a noun and a verb, though it is used, as many scurrilous terms are, by the lower classes as a term of endearment for children.

In American usage it is a much milder word. Only the educated know of its darker meanings. As a slang term for a fellow, person, or mischievous child it is now falling into disuse. As a verb it is still used widely, in slang, to mean to frustrate or to reduce the confusion (*He came in with his bright ideas again and buggered the works*).

build. The past tense is *built.* The participle is also *built.*

A regular form *builded* was once literary English for both the past tense and the participle, but it is now confined largely to poetry.

building. In American usage *building,* as a term for a block of business offices, always prefixed with *the* (*the Empire State Building, the Chrysler Building*), is used where in England *house* is preferred (*South Africa House, Imperial Chemicals House*). In America, particularly in former days, *house* would mean hotel (*The Palmer House, The Parker House*).

built. See **build.**

bulk, properly magnitude in three dimensions (*A building of great bulk loomed before us*), has, despite the protests of many grammarians, come in standard usage to mean the greater part, the main mass or body (*The bulk of the lumber was stored in an abandoned shed. The bulk of the army was held in reserve*). It still has enough of the sense of three-dimensional mass about it, however, to seem inappropriate if applied to trifling things. *The bulk of the page was devoted to a re-statement of the facts* would seem absurd. And a discriminating speaker or writer would avoid using it as a synonym for *majority. The bulk of the army* suggests a mass. *The bulk of those present voted against the proposal* would not be as good as *the majority of those present.*

bull. The word *bull,* especially when used in combinations, has a number of peculiarly American meanings. As a slang term for boasting, bluffing,

and talking pretentious nonsense it is almost universal in the United States. In college slang *bull session* is a half-contemptuous term for a sophomoric discussion of sex, religion, philosophy, and the mysteries of life in general.

Bulldoze is slang for intimidate. A *bulldozer* used to be one who bulldozed. Now it refers, almost exclusively, to a powerful caterpillar tractor having a vertical blade at the front end for moving earth, stumps, rocks, and so on, or to the operator of such a tractor. Indeed, the verb *to bulldoze* would now mean, to more Americans than not, the use of such a tractor (*The man said he'd be here tomorrow to bulldoze that black dirt around the new house*). The noun is generally listed in the dictionaries as slang and the verb, in this sense, is not listed at all. But in the vast building boom following World War II both words achieved a currency which if continued will compel their acceptance as standard usage.

bull in a china shop. As a simile for destructive blundering, *like a bull in a china shop* must have been amusing when it was first thought of, but it is now wearisome and should be avoided.

It is not even necessarily apt. In 1939 Mr. Fred Waring, in payment of a wager to Mr. Paul Douglas, led a bull into Plummer's China Shop on Fifth Avenue, in New York, after posting bond to cover any damage that might be done. The bull was led up and down the aisles and led out without having done any damage. Mr. Waring himself unfortunately knocked over a small table of china.

bum. In American speech a *bum* is a shiftless or dissolute person, an habitual loafer and tramp. *To bum* is to get for nothing, to borrow with no expectation of returning. *To go on the bum* is to become a tramp and live an idle and dissolute life. As an adjective, *bum* means poor or wretched. The word is never employed formally but it is known and used universally in informal speech. Its American meanings seem to have been influenced by the German *Bumm* and *bummeln.*

In English usage *bum* is an impolite word for the buttocks (*A sorrel gelding with some white hairs on his bum. Many a tatter'd rag hanging over my bum*).

bumblebee is the sole American form. In England it is sometimes called a *humblebee,* not from any humility but because of the humming sound that it makes. The *bum-* of *bumblebee* is from the *booming* sound that it makes, and since the scientific name of the family is *Bombidae, bumblebee* would seem the preference of lay and learned alike.

bumper; fender. A *bumper* in its commonest use in America now signifies a horizontal bar affixed to the front or rear of an automobile to give protection in collisions. In England this is called a *fender;* whereas what the Americans call a *fender* is called a *wing.* Americans and English alike call a piece of timber or a bundle of rope or the like, hung over the side of a vessel to lessen shock or prevent chafing, a *fender.*

The shock absorbers at the end of the line in railroad stations and between railroad cars are called *bumpers* in America, *buffers* in England.

bunch is a connected group or cluster (*A bunch of grapes hung from the vine*). By a natural extension it came to mean a group of similar things (*a bunch of keys*). Its application to human beings (*A bunch of people gathered at the scene of the accident*) is still considered questionable, however; and the use of the word as a synonym for *lot* (*That's a bunch of baloney*) is definitely wrong.

bundle of nerves. The idea that one is nothing but a *bundle of nerves* tied together with ligaments was, at its conception, an amusing and effective piece of humorous exaggeration. It has long since worn out its humor.

burden of proof is the taking over into everyday life of a special legal term *onus probandi* which means the obligation to offer evidence in support of a contention which will convince a judge or jury, with the understanding that if the evidence offered fails to convince, the party will lose the case. In common use it simply means the obligation, in an argument, to make out a case in the affirmative. It is a cliché and should be used carefully.

bureau. The plural is *bureaus* or (less often) *bureaux*.

As a name for a piece of household furniture, a *bureau* in America means a chest of drawers for holding clothing. There is often a mirror attached. In England a *bureau* is a desk or writing table with drawers for papers, an *escritoire*.

-burger. The last two syllables of *hamburger*, ground steak, or a roll or a bun containing ground steak, usually with relish or mustard (and named, presumably, after the city of Hamburg as frankfurters are named after Frankfurt and wieners after Vienna or Wien), have become detached. Almost anything edible that can be ground up and put between the halves of a roll may now be designated a *-burger*: cheeseburgers, nutburgers, pizzaburgers, oliveburgers and turtleburgers are all offered to the passing public. How many of these coinages will remain in the language no one knows. *Cheeseburger,* cheese grilled on top of a meat pattie, is the best established so far.

burglar. See **thief; robber; etc.** And see **steal; purloin; pilfer; etc.**

burglarize seems a clumsy substitute for the ancient and honorable term *to rob*. It is journalistic and, happily, doesn't seem to be making much headway towards standard usage.

burlesque; caricature; parody; travesty; lampoon. A *burlesque* is an artistic composition, especially literary or dramatic, which, for the sake of laughter, vulgarizes lofty material or treats ordinary material with mock dignity (*And the sad truth which hovers o'er my desk/Turns what was once romantic to burlesque.*—Byron).

In America *burlesque* has a special meaning, one probably much better known to the masses than its older meaning: a theatrical entertainment featuring coarse comedy and dancing. Of late years strip tease, an exhibition in which a woman walking to and fro in what is at least intended to be a voluptuous rhythm, slowly divests herself of her clothes, down to a g-string, a small triangle of cloth covering the mons Veneris, has become so indispensable a part of all burlesque shows that *strip tease* and *burlesque* are now almost synonymous.

A *caricature* is a picture, or a description, ludicrously exaggerating the peculiarities or defects of a person or a thing (*The caricatures of Mussolini, whatever their intent, flattered him; for they made him seem more knave than fool*).

A *parody* is a humorous imitation of a serious piece of literature (*Lewis Carroll's "I Met an Aged, Aged Man" is a brilliant parody of Wordsworth's "Resolution and Independence"*). The word is also applied to burlesque imitations of musical compositions.

Travesty is closely synonymous to parody. It is a more serious word, however, implying a deliberate debasing, often intentional, of which the speaker disapproves (*The Russian account of the incident was a travesty*). An unfair or strongly biased court decision is often referred to as *a travesty of justice*.

A *lampoon* is a malicious or virulent satire upon a person. *Parodies, burlesques,* and even *caricatures* can be good natured, but a *lampoon* never is.

burn. The past tense is *burned* or *burnt*. The participle is also *burned* or *burnt*.

In the United States *burned* is the preferred form for the past tense and the participle but *burnt* is also heard, especially when the word is used before a noun, as in *a burnt match*. In Great Britain *burnt* is the preferred form in all uses and *burned* is considered "slightly archaic and somewhat formal."

Burn may be followed by an adjective describing the fire, as in *the fire burned red,* or *it burned bright*. It may also be followed by an adverb describing the process, as in *it burned quickly*.

burn; burn down; burn up. The *down* and *up* of *burn down* and *burn up* are intensives. Either, if applied to a house, would mean total combustion: the house was reduced to the level of the ground, or it went up into the air in the smoke and gases of combustion. *Burn down* is limited to structures and candles; *burn up,* however, can be used of anything when one wishes to convey the idea that the destruction was complete. It is not used of trivial things, though; one *burns* rubbish and *burns up* papers of importance.

burn the candle at both ends. At first a saying concerned with material wastefulness, *burning the candle at both ends* is, today, applied to the wasting of one's physical strength by two courses of action, such as hard work by day and dissipation by night, either one of which would be sufficient to consume the energies of a normal person. It is not always a phrase of condemnation of the person, since it is often used of one who is destroying himself by excessive work or overdevotion to some good cause or high ideal. Perhaps this hackneyed phrase should be used only by the wicked. Certainly, it should be used only after careful consideration.

burn the midnight oil as a term for studying late at night is a cliché and should be avoided.

burning issue has long ago cooled and should be used sparingly.

burnish. See **polish.**

burnt. See **burn.**

burst. The past tense is *burst.* The participle is also *burst.*

Bursted was once literary English but is no longer considered standard.

Bust, meaning "burst," is a deliberate playing with the language. It is therefore slang rather than uneducated English.

Bust is used in the army to mean reduce in rank. In this sense it is not even slang. It is the normal word for that event and is used by all but the most pompous.

bury the hatchet. Frontiersmen and scouts who had lived so intimately among the Indians that they had adopted—or affected to have adopted —the speech and imagery of the noble savages no doubt caused many a gape of astonishment when they first used *bury the hatchet* as a term for making peace. But generations ago the gape became a yawn as the phrase became a cliché. It should be quietly buried in forgetfulness.

bus was printed as *'bus* in America as late as 1923, but all thought of its being a shortening of *omnibus* has vanished as completely as all thought of *omnibus* as a Latin dative plural, meaning "for all," has vanished. *Omnibus,* for a public vehicle, would be understood by anyone in America, but it would be used only by the most old-fashioned.

A peculiarly American use of *bus* is in the phrase *bus boy.* To an Englishman this might suggest a youngster employed in some capacity or other on or around buses. To an American it means a waiter's helper in a restaurant, one who carries out the dirty dishes and does other menial tasks. It, too, derives from *omnibus* and a *bus boy* was once known as an omnibus.

Omnibus has come back into general use in America as a designation for a volume of reprinted works by a single author or a volume of works related in interest or nature or simply a miscellany (*i.e.,* something "for all") and, most recently, as the title of a television show which presents a wide range of entertainment.

business; employment; occupation. An *occupation* is anything which occupies the time. One may speak of an *idle occupation* or *the occupation of an idle hour.* It need not be gainful or even useful. It is used, however, of useful and gainful employment since that also occupies time. *Employment* was used formerly more than now as a synonym for *occupation* but it has come to be restricted to gainful occupation and, in popular usage, to the labor of skilled and unskilled artisans. An educated person would understand the statement that the employment of a doctor's

profession took all his time. But we would not think of a doctor or other professional man *seeking employment. Idle employment* would today seem a paradox.

Business, though originally that which kept a man busy, is now restricted to gainful employment, usually to do with manufacture or the management of buying and selling. See also **avocation, calling, job, profession.**

business; busyness. Since *business* has come to be fixed in a number of specialized meanings— one's occupation or trade, the purchase and sale of goods, volume of trade, one's place of work, movements or gestures by actors on the stage, and so on—a need has been felt for a word to express its original meaning, the state of being busy, and for this the word *busyness* has come into standard use.

business vocabulary. The stilted and stereotyped usages of business English have long been notorious, but happily a new trend has been making itself felt. Many large companies are hiring correspondence experts to give training in business writing. Some have appointed permanent supervisors to oversee communications. Concise, direct language is being recognized as valuable not only for its effectiveness but also for the savings it brings.

The worst type of business vocabulary, obsequious on the one hand (*beg to remain, your esteemed favor to hand*) and pompous on the other (*We will ascertain the facts and advise you accordingly*) is probably a reflection of insecurity in status, left over from the early days of business communications. Until a century ago, it was expected of the tradesman that he would assume a proper humility in his dealings with his customers, and as long as business sought to cater chiefly to the carriage trade there was a social distinction, recognized by both sides, between the shopman and his patrons. An eighteenth-century manual for the ambitious young businessman states that he must be "master of a handsome bow and cringe" in order to ingratiate himself with his customers. The tradesman complied but resented the necessity of doing so and sought to bolster his pride by being lofty and inflated in his dealings with his equals and inferiors. Even today an American is startled and amused at the tone and wording of a communication from an English tailor, "At once crawling on his knees and shaking his fist," Max Beerbohm described it.

A survey conducted by *Fortune* ("The Language of Business," November, 1950) revealed a startling uniformity in the use of words and phrases by business people. Many a meaningless stereotyped phrase has been perpetuated in the symbols of shorthand and carried into the stream of correspondence by products of business schools. Secretaries, as a group, have smaller vocabularies than business men and in the process of dictation the larger vocabulary is confined within the limits of the smaller. It is easier to use words you know the stenographer understands than to interrupt dictation to explain your meaning. And it's safer; strange words increase the chance of dangerous and expensive errors and misunderstandings.

Some of the stereotyped phrases of business correspondence seem to serve as a jumping-off point for an insecure writer, giving him something to brace himself against before he plunges into the unfamiliar specific material of the letter. Others, like *take under consideration, in the process of, company policy* and *at this time,* function as protection from commitment. They are deliberate evasions of coming to the point. This type of phrasing is also characteristic of joint reports and statements of policy and procedure.

Business vocabulary has also absorbed words from a number of related fields, particularly the gobbledegook of government: *expedite, implement, activate, effectuate.* The advertising and sales departments have gone completely overboard at the siren song of the social sciences: *projective techniques, social dynamics, depth interviewing* and, above all, in all of its wonderful combinations, the mighty and magic *psychology.*

The spoken language of business, in contrast to the written, while just as stereotyped, is direct and vigorous, often so terse as to seem to be in code. It is characteristically down-to-earth and is designed to give the impression of enormous executive ability, of a capacity to act. The speaker usually emphasizes his forthrightness; he is not going to pussyfoot, beat around the bush, pull any punches, or use any two-dollar words. None the less if what he has to say deals with policy and he has not yet been informed what policy his superiors have adopted, he will attempt to protect himself by an assurance, usually couched in disarmingly humorous terms, that he is not so presumptuous as to advance an opinion. He is merely *throwing it up for grabs, kicking it around, thinking off the top of his head, sharing his thinking,* etc., etc.

Speeches, as distinguished from conversation, rely heavily on analogy and metaphor. The favorite figures for comparison with the state of business are a highway, a river, a boat, a bridge, a train, an airplane and—far and away the most popular—a football team. The last is so established as to be more commonly spoken of as "the team" and there are few banquets at which the quarterback, the line, the signals, and goals are not referred to. Curiously and conspicuously lacking from these metaphors, however, is any mention of a referee.

bust. See **burst.**

busy. The American *get busy* is the equivalent of the English *stir yourself, look alive.* The American telephone expression *the line is busy* is the equivalent of the English *the number is engaged.*

but. This word sometimes makes a statement negative and sometimes does not. It is sometimes used as a conjunction introducing a clause and sometimes as a preposition with a simple object.

NEGATIVES

One of the principal uses of *but* is to indicate an exception to what is being said, and in this sense it may be part of an affirmative or part of a negative statement, as in *everybody thinks so but you* and *nobody thinks so but you. But* is used in exactly this way in sentences such as *I haven't but a minute to spare* and *I won't be but a minute.* These are not double negatives. What has happened here is that some words, such as "any time," have been dropped from between the verb and *but.* The construction is always understood and is used freely by well educated people. So there is no reason in logic or in practice for objecting to it.

But may also be used to mean "only." At one time the English negative was a simple *ne* or *n'* standing before the verb. One might then say *he n'is but a child,* where *but* means "except." When this lightly pronounced *n* disappeared such statements were still understood and *he is but a child* meant the same thing. Here *but* is carrying the negative idea that was once attached to the verb. This construction is still in use and makes it possible for us to say *I have but a minute.* Undoubtedly, the fact that both constructions are in existence is what leads some people to think that the one using *not* must be a double negative. Actually it is the simpler of the two constructions, closer to the usual meaning of *but,* and the better established. Today, *but* used to mean "only," as in *I have but,* is likely to sound archaic or affected.

But may be used to introduce a parallel and contrasting statement, as in *he went but he did not stay* and *he did not go but he telephoned.* Here *but* is a coordinating conjunction. It means no more than "on the other hand" and can be used in either negative or affirmative statements.

But is often used to introduce a clause that is dependent on a negative statement. In *(there was) not a man but felt the terror in his hair,* the word *but* still means "except" and the sentence can be analyzed as *no man existed except those who felt* and so on. Ordinarily it is said that in this construction *but* represents *that . . . not.* This is a neater way of saying the same thing but may be confusing to people who have difficulty combining negatives. In the sentence just given there is no double negative. But there are too many negatives, and they cancel each other, in *it is not impossible but such a day may come.* Logically, this sentence says that nothing is impossible except that such a day should come. Actually, it is a tortured and twisted statement that fails to make a strong impression.

When we are dealing with verbs that are affirmative in form but negative in meaning, such as *deny, doubt, question,* we have a different situation. Here sentences that, logically speaking, contain too many negatives, such as *I don't doubt but that you are surprised,* are literary English. They are good English because they are found in good literature and when they are heard they recall good literature. Why good writers like this extra negative is more difficult to explain. Apparently they feel that making the affirmative form of a verb of this kind negative is not enough to make its negative meaning affirmative, and that the additional negative in *but* is needed to accomplish this. If these distinctions seem too subtle to be true, one should notice that *it is not unlikely* does not mean *it is likely*. (For *cannot help but,* see **help.** For *I don't know but what,* see **what.**)

SUBJECTIVE AND OBJECTIVE PRONOUNS

When *but* is followed by a simple object, such as a noun or pronoun, it may be considered a preposition. In that case, if the object is a personal pronoun it will have the objective form, as *me* in *no one saw it but me.* On the other hand, *but* may be considered a conjunction. In that case, the object is interpreted as part of a condensed clause, and if it is a personal pronoun it is given the form it would have if the whole clause had been expressed, as in *no one saw it but I* (*saw it*). In current American English *but* is interpreted as a preposition whenever possible, and an objective form of the pronoun is always used unless the word is the subject of a verb that is actually expressed.

Thirty or forty years ago it was customary to say that *but* should always be interpreted as a conjunction. This meant that such unnatural sentences as *they were all there but I* were being recommended. A grammarian writing at that time, after bravely laying down rules and giving examples that must certainly have offended his ear, concludes by advising us not to use the unpleasant word and points out that it can "be replaced by *except* or *save,* thus avoiding any suspicion of impropriety." Unfortunately, the arguments against using *but* as a preposition have also been brought against *except* and *save.* And faced with giving up *but* or the grammar books, most people would give up the grammar books. See also **except.**

butcher, a shortening of *butcher boy,* has a special meaning in the United States of a person who sells candy and magazines on trains (*As he rode toward the Great City he smoked a Baby Mine cigar, purchased of the Butcher*—George Ade). The term is often shortened to *butch* which, possibly because of this association, has become a slang name for any boy whose real name is unknown.

Butcher or *butch* in the sense of a vendor is now old-fashioned and seems to be passing out of use.

butter wouldn't melt in her mouth. *She looks as if butter wouldn't melt in her mouth,* that is, she seems so demure (cold) that even butter wouldn't melt in her mouth; but actually (by inference) she is far from being as demure, cold, or good as she seems.

Heywood listed this as a proverb in 1546 and Swift (by including it in his *Polite Conversations*) classed it as a cliché in 1738. It is still in general use, though most of those who use it would be unable to give a very clear statement of its meaning. It is better avoided.

buxom, when spoken of a woman, means full-bosomed, plump and attractive, radiant in health. The common use of the word as a mere synonym for *fat* fails to exploit its full resources.

buy. The past tense is *bought.* The participle is also *bought.*

The participle *boughten* is not literary English, but was widely used in the United States a few generations ago to mean "not homemade," as in *a boughten dress,* and still has a certain frontier charm. See **purchase.**

buy a pig in a poke. A *poke* is a bag less in size than a *sack.* (A *pocket* is a small *poke.*) A *pig* is, properly, a very young swine. The expression, for buying something unseen or committing oneself to an agreement without making sure of what one is to receive in return, is very old. The *pig* in the poke is the English version of it. All the rest of the European languages have it a *cat.*

The proverb today has a suggestion of that deliberate rusticity which is frequently affected as a mark of distinction from the city dweller. And since no man affects a distinction without implying superiority, such phrases are annoying. This one is still useful, but should be used only after careful consideration.

buy; buyer. *Buy* as a noun, meaning a purchase, especially a bargain (*I got a buy in eggs today. It's not a good buy at that price*), is not standard.

Buyer keeps its standard sense of one who buys from a store or other retail outlet (*Let the buyer beware. This is not a buyer's market*), but a secondary sense of one who buys *for* a store, especially one who buys at wholesale the things that the store sells at retail, is gaining in popularity, so much so that one has to be careful in its use if one is to make one's meaning clear. Certainly in department stores and the retail clothing business, especially in women's wear, this is now the primary meaning of *buyer.* One who buys materials and supplies for a manufacturing concern may be known informally as the buyer, but in his formal title he would probably be the *purchasing agent.* In a department store, however, he would be the *buyer.*

Buyer is always the word when, as in discussions of economics, one wants the opposite of *seller.* And it is retained in popular usage, in preference to *customer* and even *purchaser,* when a single transaction, especially one of some size or importance, is in mind (*He's been trying to find a buyer for that place for twenty years*). See also **patron; customer.**

by may be used as a preposition, that is, with an object, as in *stand by the gate,* or it may be used as an adverb, without an object, as in *stand by.*

The basic meaning of *by* is "near." It is used in this sense in *the road passes by our house.* When it is applied to time, it always means "not later than," as in *I will finish by five o'clock.*

By is also used to show the means or agent of an action, as in *we went by plane* and *it was made by a carpenter.*

Out of these basic meanings have come several others. *By* may show the circumstances surrounding an event, as in *by lamplight, by day.* It may mean "conforming to," as in *by law.* And it is used in expressing measures, as *by the day, by the pound.*

By may also be used to contrast "near" with "actually there." In this sense it has a negative force and may combine with verbs of motion to mean "avoid" or "ignore," as in *death had passed me by.* Sometimes one cannot tell whether *by* is being used in a direct sense or with this negative force, as in *go by Pittsburgh.*

by and large. In the sense of "generally speaking, in every aspect," *by and large* (*By and large the worries of summer residents concerning snakes are far out of proportion to the dangers that exist*) is standard in American usage, though not very often used in England. Apparently it is becoming more common there, for Sir Ernest Gowers states that this "current usage . . . exasperates the sailor" who knows the true meaning of the phrase—"alternately close to the wind and with the wind abeam or aft."

An even stronger reason for avoiding the phrase than the fear of exasperating sailors is that it is often meaningless, used simply as conversational filler.

C

caboose. In America a *caboose* is the last car on a freight train (or, as the English would say, *the brake-van on a goods train*), the car, usually painted red, with a little square lookout on top, whose passing brings a sigh of relief from a line of exasperated automobile drivers queued up at a grade crossing. In England a *caboose* is a galley, a kitchen on the deck of a ship.

cacao; coca; cocoa; coco. *Cacao* is a small evergreen tree, native to tropical America, cultivated for its seeds, from which, roasted, husked, and ground, is made *cocoa. Coca* is applied to two species of shrubs, native in the Andes and cultivated in Java, from the dried leaves of which (chewed by millions of people for their stimulant properties) is made cocaine. *Coco* is a tall, slender tropical palm which produces the coconut.

cache; hide; stash. A *cache* is, in its strictest sense, a secret place of deposit used by explorers. It is a French word and came to us from the French-Canadian woodsmen and explorers. The verb *to cache* means to place in a cache (*We decided to cache our packs and begin our return to the cabin*).

Purists have objected to the use of the word as a synonym for *hide,* but it is a natural extension, especially since hiding is associated with children, misers, and the furtive, and has passed into standard use.

The slang *stash* may be a telescoped form of *to st(ick in a c)ache,* with an echo of *cash* in it.

cactus. The plural is *cactuses* or *cacti.*

cad; cadet; caddie; caddy. Under the harsh custom of primogeniture the lot of the younger son (French *cadet*) was not a happy one. He could get a low rank in the army and be a *cadet.* He could run errands and carry packages, such as a golf bag, and be a *caddie.* But he got no thanks for his labors. His elder brother, lolling genteelly at the 'varsity, suspected him (with full justification, probably) of being resentful, mean, underhand, mendacious, aggressive, and unscrupulous, and despised him as a *cad.*

The English tea *caddy* has no connection with this grim story. It is a variant of *catty,* a transliteration of Malayan *katī,* a weight equal to a little over a pound.

cake (you can't have your cake and eat it too). There would seem to be no better way to have one's cake than to eat it, but *have* in the proverb plainly means to keep. The French version, *You can't have the cloth and the money,* is better. The English version used to be *you can't eat your cake and have it.* That is better but even so Swift listed it as a cliché in 1738. The expression has just the right modicum of obvious wisdom and homely simplicity to appeal to those who find clichés irresistible.

calculate; think. Our fathers were fond of using terms from mathematics as synonyms for *think.* Not that they were especially mathematical. It is probable that they innocently assumed the jargon of the counting house to be the ultimate expression of ratiocination. Mark Twain, in several places, has Huckleberry Finn use *cipher* for *think.*

Of course there is a legitimate use of *calculate* in connection with the expression of an opinion. If a ship's officer says that he calculates the ship is at such and such a position, it is assumed that his statement is the result of calculation. So a man might say that, given this and that circumstance, he calculates to make such and such a profit. But to say *I calculate Aunt Mary won't stay more than two days* is to misuse the word. Concern, however, is not justified, for this sense of the word is passing out of use.

calculus. The plural is *calculi* or *calculuses.* In medicine *calculus* means a small stone. In this sense it usually has the plural form *calculi. Calculus* may also mean some system of calculating or reasoning, and in this sense it is likely to have the plural *calculuses.*

When *calculus* means a particular branch of mathematics developed by Leibnitz and Newton, it is a mass word and does not have a plural. It is often qualified by *the,* as in *a history of the calculus.* This use of the article *the* is obsolete for other branches of mathematics and for the sciences generally. It may have been retained in speaking of the calculus in order to stress the fact that there is only one—no matter what words, such as "differential," "integral," "infinitesimal," may be used to describe it.

calendar; calender; colander. A *calendar* is a tabular arrangement of the days of each month and week in a year. A *calender* is a machine in which cloth, paper, or the like, is smoothed, glazed, etc., by pressing between revolving cylinders. It is also one who does such pressing. John Gilpin's good friend *the calender* was not, as a modern reader might assume, an astrologer but one who operated such a machine or did the sort of work such a machine did. A *colander* is a form of sieve used for draining off liquids, especially in cookery (*The calender marked on his calendar the day when the tinker would return his colander*).

calf. The plural is *calves*. The expression *calves foot jelly* contains an old form of the genitive and is equivalent to *calf's foot jelly*. This is not an instance of a plural noun used as the first element in a compound.

caliber is the diameter of something of circular section, as a bullet, or especially that of the inside of a tube, as the bore of a gun. In ordnance it is the diameter of the bore of a gun taken as a unit in stating its length, as *a fifty caliber 14-inch gun*.

Purists have been unhappy over the figurative extension of the word to mean degree of capacity or ability, personal character, or merit or importance (*A man of his caliber is an asset to the community*). But it is now standard and must be accepted.

calico in the United States means a printed cotton cloth, superior to percale. In Britain it means a white cotton cloth. What is called *calico* in England is called *muslin* in America.

calipers. The singular form *caliper* may be used in speaking of one of these instruments, as in *this caliper is mine,* and the plural form *calipers* in speaking of several instruments, as in *we have three calipers.* The plural form may also be used in speaking of one instrument, as in *these calipers are the ones,* and three instruments may be called *three pairs of calipers.* Both constructions are standard English today. Only the singular form *caliper* is used as the first element in a compound, as in *a caliper-square.*

calix. The plural is *calices.*

call a halt to something, like *to put a stop to* it, implies that the speaker possesses dictatorial powers in the particular situation and has exercised them or is prepared to exercise them vigorously. However, it is worn and hackneyed and should be avoided.

call a spade a spade. There have been a number of objects whose simple designation has been proverbial, among different nations, for plain speaking. The Greeks said *to call a fig a fig and a boat a boat* and regarded such direct talk as characteristic of the uncultivated Macedonians. In English, for centuries, it has been a spade. Why, no one knows.

Amusingly, the phrase is itself a contradiction of what it advocates. No one objects to calling a spade a spade; it is coarser and less inoffensive things that are usually glossed over with euphemisms.

However derived or justified, the phrase is now, except in jest, to be avoided.

calling; vocation. A *calling* was originally a summons from God to enter His service or the inward conviction of such a summons. The child Samuel had a true calling. The word still retains this sense in relation to the ministry where such a summons is felt to be requisite. From this association the word has derived a feeling of dignity, a devotion to some great duty that transcends one's personal material interests (*The conscious warrant of a high calling sustained him through these dreadful years*). It has come to be used, however, more and more (apart from its special use in relation to the ministry) in the mere sense of occupation (*He prostituted himself to the base calling of a hired scribbler*), but it has a slightly archaic and pompous flavor here.

Vocation, which is simply the Latin for *calling,* and would, one assumes, therefore be even more formal, is less formal. The religious connotation does not cling to it and, at least in the United States, it is standard for a man's occupation, business, or profession. It has (except when used as an adjective in such special, almost technical, contexts as *vocational guidance*) a tinge of pomposity. See also **avocation, business, job.**

callus; callous. *Callus* is a noun and means a hard piece of flesh, as in *he has three calluses on his hand.* The only plural is *calluses. Callous* is an adjective and means callus-like or hard, as in *his callous hands, his callous attitude.* The verb, meaning to harden, is formed from the adjective, as in *his hands were calloused by toil.* A verb may also be formed from the noun but this means only to turn into a callus, as in *the spot callused.*

calm before the storm. People speak of *the calm before the storm* as though it were an invariable phenomenon. However, it is not. In its figurative uses, the phrase is a cliché and to be avoided.

calumny. See **libel.**

calves. See **calf.**

calyx. The plural is *calyxes* or *calyces.*

came. See **come.**

campus English. There are, of course, a few hardy campus perennials which are readily comprehensible to the general public, such as *doc, prof, dorm, frat, quad.* But whether there is anything else that may definitely be classified as college slang is open to doubt. It is true that there are feature stories in a number of magazines every year on the current campus expressions, but one suspects that these are whipped up seasonally, by their authors, at the editors' demands, like the stories on Groundhog Day. If the students have the linguistic originality and playfulness attributed to them in these articles, they skilfully conceal it in most of their compositions.

However, like the veiled woman in black who finally appeared in reality to lay a flower on Valentino's grave after the papers had invented her, some collegians seem to feel that a measure of inventiveness is required of them and various colleges claim that certain words have at least a temporary currency among their students.

Some idea of the variations in campus talk may be given by recording some words claimed to have been in use at Princeton in 1941, some North Texas Agricultural College terms in 1948, and some Northwestern University and Wayne University terms in 1955.

To the Princetonian—so the *Princeton Alumni Weekly* of February, 1942, said—a *spook* was a young lady, a *mingle* a game, *red hots* were stags, *hooching* was having a drink, to *float one* was to cash a check and to *soft-sole* was to dance. The Texas terms were less elegant. A *beast* was an unattractive female and a *sad sack* one whose amatory ardors left something to be desired. *Date bait* was an attractive girl, *dream bait* a handsome person of either sex. *Leather express* meant walking. *Office* was the term for a favorite hideout, *rape fluid* for perfume. *Upstream*, used as a verb, designated the unethical practice of thumbing a ride ahead of an already-waiting group of hitchhikers.

At Wayne University, in 1955, *beating the bushes* was looking for a date, a *body snatcher* was one who stole another's date, a *campus roar* was an egotistical professor, one who took all easy (*pipe*) courses was a *plumbing major,* and a *wow* was a worn-out wolf. At Northwestern University, in the same year, a *Mickey Mouse* was a notoriously easy course, a *four-wheel friend* was one devoted to your car, a *clootch* a girl and a *brain* a serious-minded and, possibly, intelligent student.

can. This is the present tense. The past tense is *could.*

He can does not have the *s* ending that we ordinarily expect in the present tense. This is because *can* is an ancient past tense form. But it had come to be felt as a present tense before English became a written language. *Could* is a new past tense form that was created for it. Today, *could* is sometimes used as the past tense of *can,* as in *he could read before he was four years old;* but it has also acquired a present tense meaning, as in *could you help me now?.*

This verb has no imperative, no infinitive, no past participle, and no *-ing* form. Because the words *can* and *could* are grammatically past tense forms, just as the word *went* is, they cannot follow (that is, they cannot be dependent on) another verb. We can no more say *will can, may can, used to could,* than we can say *will went, may went, used to went.* Since we cannot use auxiliaries, such as *do, be, have,* we form negative statements and ask questions in the old direct way that is now obsolete for most verbs, as in *he could not* and *why can't he?.*

Can and *could* themselves are always used as auxiliaries and require another verb to complete their meaning. This may be the simple form of the verb, as in *he can leave,* or *have* and the past participle, as in *he can have left.* In the first case, the statement refers to a present situation. In the second case, it refers to a past event. The complementary verb must be actually stated or easily supplied from the context, as in *can you take this apart?* and *I could yesterday.*

When *could* is used in speaking of the past it means "was able to," as in *I could yesterday,* and is the past indicative form of *can.* When it is used in speaking of the present or the future, as in *could you help me tomorrow,* it is a past subjunctive. In a direct statement *could have* is a past indicative when it means "was able to at that time," and a past subjunctive when it means "it is now possible that at that time. . . ." It may have either meaning in *he could have told her yesterday.* The subjunctive *could* can be used in a conditional clause without the word *if.* In that case, it must stand before the subject, as in *could I find the paper, I would . . .* and *could I have found the paper, I would have. . . .* (See **subjunctive mode.**)

The auxiliary verb *can* has grown out of a verb meaning to know, and is related to such words as *canny* and *cunning.* It has no relation at all to the verb meaning to put up in cans, which is perfectly regular and has the past tense and participle *canned.* Having one simple sound for two such different ideas makes it possible for the farmer's wife to say: *We eat what we can and what we can't we can.*

can; may. Both of these verbs may be used to express possibility, as in *he can come* (or *he could come*) and *he may come* (or *he might come*). But here *can* or *could* means "it is physically possible that" and *may* or *might* means "there is a chance that." *Can* and *may* are never used interchangeably in speaking about a possibility.

But *may* is also used to ask for or grant permission, as in *may I come in?* Some grammarians claim that *can* should never be used in a sentence of this kind, since *can* asks about what is physically possible and not about what is permissible. Actually, this question takes us out of the realm of language and into the intricacies of politeness. *Can* is often used in place of *may* to suggest that the decision is not merely a personal whim but something based on objective facts.

In refusing permission, *you may not* is felt to be disagreeably personal and dictatorial and *you cannot* is almost universally preferred. In discussing a decision, or in arguing about it, *can* is required. We never say *why mayn't I?* or *mayn't I?* but always *why can't I?* or *can't I?,* since we are assuming that something more than a whim is involved. In granting permission *may* is still used occasionally, as in *you may keep it till Friday.* But most people now feel that it is more courteous, less autocratic, to say *you can keep it till Friday.* In asking permission, *may* is generally felt to be more polite than *can,* as in *may I look at it?* but *can* is also used here, as in *can I look at it?* Since the speaker knows very well that he is able to look at it, this use of *can* is simply carrying politeness one step further by refusing to question the other person's good will. In time, this too may be accepted as the more polite form, but that is not yet the case.

candelabrum. The plural is *candelabrums* or *candelabra*. *Candelabra* is also used as a singular with a regular plural *candelabras*. These forms are equally acceptable.

candid. See **frank**.

candidacy; candidature. Americans refer to the state or term of being a candidate as *candidacy* (*During his candidacy he had the support of the labor unions*). The English use *candidature*.

candy; sweets; dessert. In America *candy* is the word for any of a variety of confections made with sugar, syrup, and so on, combined with other ingredients, and for a single piece of such a confection. The plural, *candies*, refers to more than one variety (*Mixed candies*) rather than to more than one piece. When one wishes to speak of more than one piece of candy it has to be expressed as so many *pieces of candy*.

In England *candy* is what used to be called *sugar candy*, crystallized sugar, boiled and evaporated. In America this is often called *rock candy*. There is no plural to the English *candy*.

The English term for *candy* in general is *sweets*. But *the sweet* is their word for what Americans call *dessert*. Sometimes it is called *the sweet course* and the various puddings, ices, and so on, then served would, collectively, be called *sweets*. The English reserve the word *dessert* for fruit (fresh or candied), nuts, and raisins, served as a last course after the *sweet*.

canine. Except in its special zoological meaning of any member of the *Canidae* (dogs, wolves, jackals, hyenas, coyotes, foxes), or as a shortening of *canine tooth, canine* ought to be used with care. It is acceptable as a term for a dog, but if used seriously it is pompous and if used humorously (in mockery of the pompous use) it is threadbare.

cannon. The plural is *cannons* or *cannon*. That is, one may say *only three cannons were left* or *only three cannon were left*.

canon; cañon; canyon; cannon. *Canon* refers to ecclesiastical law, to the sacred books of the Bible, or other sacred books (*canon law; the Epistle to the Hebrews is not a work of St. Paul, but it is preëminently worthy of its honored place in the Canon*), or (chiefly British) is the name of any one of a body of dignitaries or prebendaries attached to a cathedral or a collegiate church (*Sir, it is a great thing to dine with the Canons of Christ-Church*).

Cañon is the Spanish spelling of *canyon,* a deep valley with steep sides, often with a stream flowing through it (*The Grand Canyon of the Colorado is in Arizona*).

A *cannon* is a mounted gun for firing heavy projectiles and other uses extended from this. More and more it is being replaced in usage by *gun*.

The English have a special use of *cannon* as a verb: to make a carom in billiards,

cant derives, ultimately, from *cantare,* to sing. It originally meant the whining, singsong speech of beggars and then the special language or jargon spoken by thieves or gypsies. Linguists use the word in this sense today.

A more popular meaning, however, is an affected or insincere use of religious or pietistic phraseology. It may have been helped to this meaning by the Reverend Andrew Cant (d. 1663), a Presbyterian minister whose sermons were so larded with the jargon of his sect at that time that they were incomprehensible to most men and were delivered in a whining singsong which was then esteemed by many as the height of pulpit eloquence.

From this use it has come to its most common meaning: stock phrases full of pretentious high-mindedness or pseudo-profundity, repeated mechanically because they are fashionable, without being genuine expressions of sentiment. Highly successful books are often no more than tissues of cant, but there is nothing that the good writer abhors more. Johnson's admonition to Boswell, *Clear your mind of cant,* is the beginning of honesty as it is of wisdom.

canvas; canvass. The cloth is *canvas*. The close inspection, scrutiny, soliciting of votes or of orders, is *canvass*.

capacity. See **ability**.

capitalization. Capitals are used for two purposes in writing. The first is to indicate the beginning of a statement. The second is to indicate a particular person, place, or thing as distinct from a general class. Within the first use, the conventions are few and the rules can mostly be predicted by reason. Within the second use, however, the conventions are numerous.

Each publisher has his own rules of capitalization from which he deviates only with reluctance. Each writer will find that his own capitalization habits change with the kind of material he is handling and the audience for whom he is writing—devotion to simplicity and the lower case will have a hard struggle when PTA minutes are to be kept or government letters written. Creative writing can be almost without capitals if the author chooses, though the conventional capital for the first word of the sentence will be appreciated by most readers. Descriptive writing on government, political and religious matters, especially organizational matters, will invariably require a good many capitals. This is partly because a capital has become a mark of respect, and partly because it is needed to prevent the name of a particular thing from being understood as a common noun. Organized bodies often have names which, if not capitalized to show their special meaning, will give a completely different impression—for instance, *Odd Fellow* and *odd fellow*. In general, fewer capitals make for easier reading; however, any time the reader could be confused by its omission, a capital should be used.

CAPITALS USED TO INDICATE A BEGINNING:

1. At the beginning of any sentence.

2. After a colon, but only if a complete

formal statement follows or if a partial statement is to be emphasized, as in *The result was as expected: Two reckless drivers and one dangerous curve could only result in an accident.* and *Verdict: Not guilty.*

3. At the beginning of a complete sentence in parentheses within another sentence, if the writer desires to emphasize the parenthetical matter, as in *There are two possible ways of filing application for fellowships (See our letter of January 1, 1956)*: *First, ...* Generally, however, a sentence of this kind begins with a lower-case letter. (The sentence enclosed does not have a final period.)

4. At the beginning of a direct quotation (and within the quotation, any capitals used in the source quoted), as in *It is in the third act that Portia says "The quality of mercy is not strain'd."* A fragmentary quotation, however, is written with a lower-case letter, as in *He said he "could not support such an action."*

5. At the beginning of every line of poetry (unless the original has used lower-case there). When quoting poetry, capitalize and punctuate exactly as the poet has done.

6. Following a clause introducing an enactment or resolution, as in *Resolved, That ...* and *Be it enacted, That. ...*

CAPITALS USED TO INDICATE AN INDIVIDUAL PERSON OR THING:

1. *Names and Titles of Persons.* A person's name is always capitalized and so is any title preceding his name, as in *John Doe, Mr. John Doe, Admiral John Doe.* However, titles following the name or titles standing alone are not capitalized unless the person referred to will be unmistakably recognized by the title, or the writer wishes to show great respect, as in *the King* and *the President* (of the United States), but *the president of the Krackly Krunch Korporation.*

Hereditary titles are always capitalized, and so are the titles of all heads of nations and their deputies, regardless of whether the title is standing before or after a name or alone, as in *Edward, Prince of Wales* and *he was at that time Prime Minister.*

Governmental, military, judicial, and ecclesiastical titles referring to one specific person may be capitalized. But most publishers capitalize titles of subordinate officials only when the title precedes the name, as in *Judge John Doe, John Doe, judge* and *Doe had then been a judge for ten years.*

Titles of respect, such as *Your Honor, Mr. Chairman,* are always capitalized.

Academic degrees, professorial titles, fellowship titles, and the like, and also their abbreviations, are always capitalized, as in *John Doe, Doctor of Philosophy* and *John Doe, Ph.D.*

A term that is merely descriptive of a position and not an official title should not be capitalized. We would write *John Doe, Professor of Ancient Languages* but *John Doe, Greek professor.*

2. *Names of the Deity.* Names representing the Deity are always capitalized. This is sometimes extended to the personal pronouns *he, him, his,* and, less often, to the relatives *who, whom, whose.* Opinion is divided as to whether the devil should be honored by a capital letter, and some people would therefore write *neither God nor the devil.* However, a personal name, such as *Satan* or *Lucifer,* requires a capital. Gods in which one does not believe are referred to as *gods* and not as *Gods.* Their individual names, however, are capitalized by people interested enough to have made their acquaintance.

3. *Names and Titles of Groups and Group Members.* All names of nations and nationalities are capitalized, whether used as adjectives or as nouns, as in *the Chinese people* and *he is a Chinese.* Governmental bodies and their boards, commissions or committees are capitalized when referred to individually, as in *House of Representatives, United Nations, Ways and Means Committee, Supreme Court.* Words of this kind are not capitalized when used in a general sense. We would write *a Representative should be a representative of his people, a Senate committee, a district court.* Descriptive terms for special types of government organization, such as *empire, monarchy, republic,* are not capitalized.

Names of societies and organizations are capitalized, even when used to identify an individual member. This is often necessary in order to distinguish these names from the same words used in their ordinary sense, as in *the Democratic Party* and *a Democrat* (who may or may not be *a democrat*); *the Lions Club* and *a Lion* (who may be a social *lion,* but not a feline one). Full titles of religious denominations and organized bodies are capitalized, such as *the Methodist Conference.* But we would write *the Methodists will hold a conference.* Names of unions are capitalized, but not the word *union* when it is merely descriptive and not part of the true title, as in *United Steelworkers of America union, the A.F. of L. union.* Names of business firms, manufacturers, and the like are always capitalized, as are copyright and trademark names.

4. *Names of Places.* The words *north, south, east,* and *west,* and their compounds, are not capitalized except when they are part of a recognized name for a particular area, such as *the Deep South, the Middle West, the Far West.* Similarly, words for natural divisions of land and water are not capitalized except when they are part of a recognized title, such as *the Atlantic Ocean, Great Salt Lake, Treasure Island.* Names of streets, avenues, and the like are also capitalized only when part of a proper name, as in *3236 Prospect Street, 19483 Hartwell Avenue, MacArthur Boulevard.* Whenever a common noun forms part of a proper name it should be capitalized, but not otherwise.

5. *Names of Other Physical or Conceptual Things.* Names of famous buildings and of particular rooms in them are capitalized, such as *the White House, the Blue Room, Old Vic, the Washington Cathedral.* The names of the

planets are capitalized, but the words *sun, moon,* and *earth* are written without capitals except when listed with the planets.

Names of the months and of the days of the week are capitalized, but not the names of the seasons. Names of holidays and of religiously significant dates, such as *Labor Day* and *St. Agnes' Eve,* are capitalized, but not other identifying names such as *election day.*

Names of historical significance, such as *Magna Carta, the Dark Ages, Code Napoléon,* are capitalized, as are outstanding sport events, such as *the Kentucky Derby, Sadie Hawkins Day.*

6. *Substitute Names and Personifications.* In general, any words that are used to individualize are given a capital letter. Nicknames, such as *Billy the Kid, Old Hickory,* and popular names of organizations, such as *the GOP, the Quakers,* are always capitalized. A common noun used as a substitute for a proper noun is capitalized, as *the Administration, the Cape* (Cape Cod), *Father.* This applies to the words *the Court* when used to mean the judge of the court, as in *The Court denied the appeal.*

When inanimate objects, geographical divisions, and aspects of nature are spoken of as if they were persons, or are given fanciful titles, the names are capitalized, as in *Old Faithful, Mother Nature, the Bluegrass, the Badlands, the Skull and Crossbones, the Red, White, and Blue.* In this sense the names of the seasons are sometimes capitalized, although they are ordinarily written without a capital.

SPECIAL PROBLEMS

1. Titles of books, songs, lectures, movies, pictures, plays, newspapers, and of sections or subdivisions of written material are capitalized. In these titles the first word and all nouns, pronouns, verbs, adjectives, adverbs, and interjections are given an initial capital. Prepositions and conjunctions are capitalized: (1) when they contain four or more letters, (2) when they are of equal importance with another word in the title which is capitalized, or (3) when they would otherwise be the only lower-case word in the title. Foreign-language titles should be capitalized according to the practice in that language.

2. When a proper noun has lost its original meaning and become a common noun, it should be written without a capital, as in *sandwich, kelly green, bourbon whiskey, madras cloth.* Similarly, adjectives derived from proper nouns are capitalized as long as they retain their original meanings, as in *Elizabethan, Freudian,* but are written without a capital when the original meaning is no longer significant, as in *caesarean.* In scientific classifications, a species derived from the name of the classifier is always put in lower case, as in *Magnolia watsoni.*

3. Single letters used as syllables are always capitalized, as in *X-ray, vitamin B,* the pronoun *I* and the exclamation *O.*

4. When two names or titles have a common element they may be written together as a plural title, as in *First and Elm Streets, Presidents Roosevelt and Truman.*

5. The word *the* may be capitalized in order to adhere to an authorized form, as in *The Hague,* or in order to confer greater honor, as in *The King.* This is unusual, however, and is found only in very formal writing.

6. In expressions of time, it was once customary to capitalize the letters *A.M.* and *P.M.* Today, the lower-case forms *a.m.* and *p.m.* are preferred.

7. A common noun used with a date, number, or letter, as a reference may be capitalized or not according to taste, as in *Article V* or *article V, Chapter 3* or *chapter 3.*

8. Hyphenated words are capitalized as they would be if they were written without a hyphen.

9. When documentary accuracy is required, the capitalization in the original text should be retained.

capitalize. In the literal sense one can *capitalize,* convert into capital, only something that already belongs to him. If one has shares he can capitalize on them by giving them as collateral for a loan or by selling them. If he has a factory he can capitalize a corporation by selling stock. Something of this idea carries over into the metaphorical uses of the word, though it is not always borne in mind. A man may capitalize on his misfortunes, for example, by narrating them over the radio or exhibiting himself on a television show. But the producer and announcer of the show do not capitalize on the misfortunes of others; they exploit them.

caption has given some purists a conniption. In the sense of a heading or title and, even more, the legend under a picture, it is an Americanism. "Rare in British use," grumps Fowler, "& might well be rarer." Partridge thinks it is all right to use it for words above a picture ("as it should be") but feels it is "misused" to mean a legend underneath. But why? It doesn't come from the Latin *caput,* head, anyway; but from *capĕre,* to take. Americans spend a lot of time looking at pictures and they have to have a convenient term for the bit of printing that sometimes goes along with them. *Caption* is now standard usage.

captor; capturer. *Capturer* sounds a little awkward, but it is as correct as *captor* if anyone wants to use it.

carcass. See **corps.**

carcinoma. The plural is *carcinomas* or *carcinomata,* not *carcinomae.*

care. This verb may be followed by an infinitive, as in *I do not care to go.* If the *-ing* form of a verb is used it must be introduced by the preposition *about,* as in *I do not care about going.*

care a rap, not to. A *rap* was a counterfeit farthing. A farthing is worth about half a cent. It seems incredible that anyone would go to the trouble of counterfeiting a coin of so little value —especially when the penalty was death—but it is a measure of the poverty and desperation of the Irish that in the eighteenth century they did. *Copper halfpence or farthings . . . have been for some time very scarce,* Swift wrote in

The Drapier Letters (1724), *and many counterfeits passed about under the name of raps.*

So the phrase once had meaning; if you were not concerned even so much as a rap('s worth), you had little concern indeed. But who knows the meaning now? Or cares a rap for it? It is a cliché, and should be used with care.

carefree; careless. To be *carefree* is to be free of care in an admirable, or at least an enviable, way (*For a carefree vacation, come to Camp Idlewild*). To be *careless* is to be lacking in adequate care, heedless, negligent, unconcerned about things which merit concern (*Careless people are exasperating companions*). The careless are rarely carefree, because their carelessness makes so much trouble for them.

cargo; shipment. Weseen's joke, that goods sent by ship are called a *cargo* and goods sent by car are called a *shipment,* will at least serve to taunt the purists. *Shipment* has the added suggestion of goods that are definitely consigned to someone (*Your shipment has definitely been sent off today. It forms part of the cargo of the steamship Santa Maria*). See also **freight.**

caricature. See **burlesque.**

caries. This is a singular noun, equivalent to *decay,* and not a plural equivalent to *cavities.* We say *caries is preventable,* not *are preventable.*

carom, a term from billiards, a shot in which the ball struck with the cue is made to hit two balls in succession, is in use in America but is no longer used in England where it has been replaced by *cannon.*

carousal; carousel; carrousel. A *carousal,* a noisy or drunken feast, derives from the German phrase *Gar aus!, "completely out,"* a command, equivalent to "Bottoms up!" to drinkers to empty their cups completely in one mighty swill.

A *carrousel,* in America a merry-go-round, in most of Europe a tournament, derives from an Italian word *garosella,* a tournament, diminutive of *garoso,* quarrelsome.

The two words are easily confused because a *carousal* could easily include a ride in a *carrousel* and both make noise which those involved regard as music. Then *carrousel* is often and legitimately spelled *carousel* and *carousal.* In pronunciation, the word for revelry has the accent on the second syllable, the merry-go-round word on the last.

carry. The use of *carry* to mean keep in stock (*The new store will carry a full line of merchandise*), to print or to present (*The newspapers all carried the story on the front page*), and to sustain or to bear a leading part in singing (*He carried the melody*) is peculiarly American. All of these uses are standard.

The American *mail carrier* is the English *postman.* A *carrier* in England is one who conveys parcels, with us the *expressman,* though in legal and business phraseology we use the term *common carrier.*

cart before the horse. Anyone who spoke of some reversal of the usual order of doing things as *putting the cart before the horse* would, if it were the first time the phrase had ever been heard, earn for himself the reputation of an earthy fellow, with a gift for homely metaphor. But since Cicero used the phrase (already a proverb) in 61 B.C., and since horses and carts now play very little part in most Americans' lives, the man who uses the phrase today runs the risk of seeming unoriginal, repetitious, and tedious.

carte blanche (literally a white or blank sheet of paper) is a signed paper left blank for the person to whom it is given to fill in his own conditions. By extension, it means unconditional authority, full power. It is a cliché and, like all foreign phrases introduced unnecessarily into English speech, pretentious.

The plural, if anyone is conceivably interested, is *cartes blanches,* though the man who would use that phrase in English speech has carried affectation almost to splendor.

caryopsis. The plural is *caryopsises* or *caryopsides,* not *caryopses.*

case has so many uses that it is not surprising that it also has abuses.

Etymologically, there are two words. There is the word for a receptacle, from a Norman French word, ultimately from the Latin word *capĕre,* to take hold. From this *case* are derived *casement, case knife,* a tray of wood or metal for holding types for the use of the compositor, the contents of a case (*I'd like a case of soap flakes*), and a hundred extensions and applications of the idea of the container. There is very little confusion in the use of words of this kind.

Then there is the other *case,* meaning originally that which befalls, from the French *cas* and ultimately the Latin *casualis.* And this is the word that has everyone confused, from stenographers to lexicographers. It means an instance of the occurrence of something (*It was a plain case of premeditated murder*), the actual state of things (*That is not the case, and you know it!*), a question or problem of moral conduct (*a case of conscience*), a situation, condition, or plight (*His hat was in a sorry case when he picked it up*), a state of things requiring consideration or decision (*This is a case for the dean*), a statement of facts or reasons (*He made a strong case for his side*), an instance of disease requiring medical attention (*It was apparent the child had a bad case of measles*), and by a natural extension from this, a patient (*The doctor saw his bed cases in the morning*). In law a *case* is a suit or action at law (*The attorney said he would take the case*), or the facts supporting a claim or supporting a defense against a claim (*He had a strong case and the attorney had little concern about the decision*). In grammar *case* denotes a category in the inflection of nouns, pronouns, and adjectives, establishing the relation of these words to other words in the sentence. It also denotes a set of such categories, or the meaning of, or typical of, such a category, or such categories or their meaning collectively. See **case in grammar.**

Then there are idiomatic phrases containing *case. In any case* means under any circumstances, anyhow. *In case* means if. *In case of* means in the event of.

And as if all this weren't enough, there are slang uses, such as *He's a case, he is!* or *They sent Joe up to case the joint first.*

Now where one sound represents two words and each word has a score of meanings and the meanings of one of the words concern categories and abstractions, there is, plainly, danger of confusion. And in this *case* the danger is heightened by the widespread temptation to make the second of the two *cases* a catchall. Despite its score of legitimate uses, *case* is continually being used when it has practically no meaning at all, when the sentence would be just as effective if it were omitted entirely. In such a sentence as *This sort of pacifism has been presented before, in the case of All Quiet on the Western Front,* "the case of" could be omitted. It adds nothing and says nothing. In such a sentence as *In the case of retail selling, there must, of course, be a different sort of advertising,* "the case of" could, and should, be omitted.

Case is not to be avoided, but it is to be used only when needed and when the user is sure that no other word will express his meaning so exactly.

case in grammar. In an inflected language, such as Latin or Old English, nouns, pronouns, and adjectives have special endings, or special forms, which show how these words are related to other words in a sentence. One ending will show that a word is the subject of a verb, another that it is an object, and so on. Latin had six classifications of this kind. In modern English, the relation that one word has to the others is shown chiefly by its position in the sentence. If a child should say, *Him hit she,* we would understand that *him* had done the hitting because that word stands in the proper place for the doer, or agent. But if we depended on case rather than position, we would think that *she* had done the hitting, because that word is in the case used to show the agent.

Old English had almost as many case forms as Latin, but few are left in present-day English. All nouns, and some pronouns, have a genitive case formed with a final *s,* as in *the horse's mouth* and *anybody's guess.* When not in the genitive, such words are said to be in the common case. Except for the genitive, all that has survived from the old case system is six pairs of pronouns, the subjective *I, we, he, she, they, who* and their objective counterparts, *me, us, him, her, them, whom.* These words still follow the old rules to some extent, and there are places where one form must be used and the other must not. The rules are complex and the question of when to use the subjective form and when to use the objective is one of the most difficult problems in English.

Many grammarians use the term *case* to mean the function that a word has in the sentence, or the case that it would have in a completely inflected language. This is useful in studying the history of English and its relation to the other Indo-European languages. But it involves concepts and distinctions that have no meaning for the person who speaks only English. It makes the study of English grammar extremely difficult and takes up time which should be put on the important questions of position and the use of prepositions.

In this book the term *case* is used in the strict sense to mean a special word form, either the genitive or one of the twelve paired pronouns. Other words are considered to have no case, or not to show case.

case; instance; example; illustration. *Case* is a general word, meaning a fact or occurrence or situation that is typical of a class (*His reply was a case of sheer insolence*). An *instance* is a concrete factual case which is adduced to explain a general idea (*General Kutuzov's answer furnished an excellent instance of what I mean by "military intelligence"*). An *example* is one typical case, taken from many similar ones and used to make some principle clear (*The Louisiana Purchase is an example of peaceful acquisition of territory*). An *illustration* (in this sense) is also an example, used to make some principle clear, but it differs from an example in that it may be hypothetical (*Squatters' rights would be an illustration of a legal right based on bad faith*).

casket, originally a small, often ornamented, chest or box used for storing jewels or other precious things, has come in America to mean, primarily, a coffin (*The casket, enveloped in the Confederate flag, was placed in the center of the room*).

But it will not work. Death, the one great fact of life that cannot be vulgarized, glossed over, or concealed in words, will not—so long as men love life—be denied its grimness. Those who bury the dead, whether they disguise themselves in vagueness as undertakers or exalt themselves in technical efficiency as morticians, are still those who bury the dead. *Cemetery* means sleeping place, but no one is comforted thereby. The bruised heart was never yet "pierced through the ear." *Casket* must have seemed a brilliant euphemism to the man who first conceived it, but the solemnity and horror of death has settled on it and tainted it. When American high-school students now come to the casket scene in *The Merchant of Venice* they think of coffins (especially since the golden casket contains "a carrion Death") and either attach an unintended gruesomeness to the scene or giggle, as their natures move them.

cast. The past tense is *cast.* The participle is also *cast.* See **throw.**

cast the first stone. In *John 8:7,* where the challenge *He that is without sin among you, let him first cast a stone at her* first appeared, it had great power. It was then literal. The woman had been taken in adultery and, as the scribes and Pharisees pointed out, the Mosaic law commanded that she should be stoned. But the sin which she had committed was a common one and her indignant accusers, at Christ's statement, slunk away. Outside of this famous passage, however, the phrase has become worn and hackneyed and should be used sparingly.

cast; caste. *Caste* now designates a rigid system of social distinctions. (*He was a high-caste Hindu; the upper caste*). In all other uses the word, as a verb or a noun, is spelled *cast*.

caster; castor. He who or that which *casts* should be a *caster* (*He was an excellent caster with a fly rod. The sculptor who would cast in bronze must have a good caster*). The small wheel on a swivel, set under a piece of furniture, to facilitate moving it, a bottle or cruet for holding a condiment, and a stand containing a set of such bottles are also *casters*, though the swivel, the cruet, and the holder are also called *castors*.

Castor is the name of the beaver, of the secretion of the beaver used in medicine and perfumery, and is the popular name of the oil used as a cathartic and lubricant.

castles in Spain; castles in the air. It is not known why the edifices of fancy should be built in Spain, but they have been for at least seven hundred years. But whether in Spain or merely in the air, the phrase is a cliché, the worse that it affects usually to be a sprightly sally.

Of course even the most worn phrase can be put to original use. When James Boswell said that other people built castles in the air but that he was the first man that ever tried to live in them, the remark was a penetrating piece of self-analysis, wryly humorous and quaintly charming. Bulwer-Lytton's observation that castles in the air are cheap to build but expensive to keep up is profound.

casualty is properly something which happened casually, by chance or accident. It has come to mean something unpleasant, particularly a bodily injury or death. Purists have objected to its transfer from the event to the person suffering the event, but military usage has become standard, and soldiers killed, wounded, or captured as a result of enemy action are now correctly spoken of as casualties and by extension the term includes civilians injured in some disaster (*The tornado took a fearful toll of casualties*). It is not used of one or two persons injured in, say, an automobile accident, though if it were a bus–train collision and the number were great, it might be used.

catachresis is the employment of a word under a false form through misapprehension in regard to its origin. Of course if the false form continues long enough in use among enough people, it will become proper. Thus *causeway* is a corruption of the word *causey* which was the English form of the Norman French *caucie*, a paved road. Since it was a roadway, the last syllable was altered to *way*. Similarly the old French *crevice* became *crayfish* (since it lived in water) and, further, *crawfish* (since it crawled). See also **folk etymology.**

catalysis. The plural is *catalyses*.

catch. The past tense is *caught*. The participle is also *caught*.

Catched is an old form of the verb, used by George Washington and other eighteenth century gentlemen. It is no longer standard.

catch (a disease). See **contract.**

catchup; ketchup; catsup. Any one of the three forms may be used to designate the spiced tomato sauce. The most common now, in general use, is **ketchup.**

catchword. See **slogan.**

category; class. A *class* is a number of persons or things regarded as forming a group through the possession of similar qualities, any division of persons or things according to rank or grade (*Boys of his class usually attend a private preparatory school*). A *category* is a class or division in any general scheme of classification, sometimes scientific but most often philosophical. Though its use as a synonym for *class* is now standard in the United States, the discriminating will always be aware of the difference and reserve *category* for its more particular meaning.

catholic; Roman Catholic. When spelled with a small *c,* the adjective *catholic* means universal in extent, having sympathy with all (*The atom bomb is of catholic concern. She is one of catholic tastes*). When spelled with a capital *C* it is a noun that means one thing to Roman Catholics and another thing to other churches such as the Old Catholics or the Anglo-Catholics. In common American usage, however, regardless of the theological or historical or etymological arguments to the contrary, it refers to Roman Catholics as opposed to Protestants and the adjective with a capital *C* means of or pertaining to Roman Catholics or the Roman Catholic Church.

cattle. In the United States today this word is a true plural, although it has no singular form. We may say *these cattle are thirsty* or *he has ten thousand cattle.*

The word has been used in this way for many centuries but until recently these constructions were considered ungrammatical. In literary English *cattle* was a mass word like *sugar* or *water*. It was possible to speak of *much cattle* but not of *many cattle*. In order to have a singular or a true plural it was necessary to say *one head of cattle* or *three head of cattle*. Today the usual singular is *one animal.*

Caucasian. The use of the word *Caucasian* as a euphemism for white, in its racial sense (*Members of the Caucasian race only served here*), is vulgar, offensive to humanity, language, and ethnology.

caucus. The American word *caucus* has been taken over by the English but, perhaps because of a misunderstanding of the way American political parties work, has been changed in the transfer. In the United States a *caucus* is a meeting of the local members of a political party to nominate candidates, elect delegates to a convention, etc., or of the members of a legislative body who belong to the same party to determine upon action in that body. In England it is a local committee of a political party exercising a certain control over its affairs or actions.

caught. See **catch.**

causative verbs. Many English verbs that name a particular action, such as *he walked* and *he swam across the river,* can also be used to mean "cause something to perform that action," as in *he walked the dog, he swam his horse across the river.* Sometimes we use *cause, make,* or *have* to express this idea, as in *I had him swim across the river.* Sometimes we use the syllable *en* to form verbs meaning "cause to be," as in *blacken* and *enfeeble.* Verbs of this kind are called *causatives.*

At one time English had a great many pairs of verbs, each having a different form, one of which was a causative and one of which was not. Today we are more likely to use one verb in both senses, as is the case with *walk* and *swim.* Some of the old pairs are now felt to be completely unrelated verbs, for example *drench* which was the causative of *drink,* and *fell,* the causative of *fall,* as in *he felled the tree.* Others have survived into the modern period as pairs. Three of these, *lay* and *lie, set* and *sit, raise* and *rise,* are confusing to many people. As a matter of fact, they are no longer the simple pairs they once were. For a discussion of when one of these forms is to be used and when the other, see the causatives **lay, set, raise.** In addition, some irregular verbs, such as *shine, shone,* have parallel regular forms, such as *shine, shined,* that are causatives, as *the light shone on the water* and *he shined the light on the water.* All such verbs are listed in this dictionary. As a rule the usual form of the verb, in this case *shone,* may also be used as a causative, as in *he shone the light on the water.* Some grammarians object to this practice, but it is acceptable to most people.

cause. When used as a verb, this word may be followed by an infinitive, as in *it caused me to go.* It may also be followed by the *-ing* form of a verb, as in *it caused my going,* but the infinitive construction is preferred. Formerly *cause* might be followed by the simple form of a verb, as in *I have caused him kill a virtuous queen.* This is no longer natural English, and a *to-* infinitive is now required here.

cause. See **source.**

cavalry; calvary. It would seem ludicrous to point out that these words have different meanings, were it not that they are frequently confused (*In New York City there is exactly one good cop. . . . He's in Cavalry Cemetery*—facetiously quoted in *The World, The Flesh, and H. Allen Smith,* 1954). *Cavalry* is mounted soldiers collectively. *Calvary* is the place where Jesus Christ was crucified, though the name is sometimes applied to an open-air representation of the Crucifixion.

caviar to the general. Hamlet, speaking to the players at Elsinore, recollects a play that was never acted or, if acted, only once, *for the play . . . pleas'd not the million, 'twas caviar to the general.* That is, it was like caviar (a strange delicacy for which a taste must be acquired), esteemed by epicures but repugnant to the generality, to what is now called "the masses."

This is a cliché of the literary. It is intended, presumably, to show that they know *Hamlet,* that they know the true meaning of a passage which the uneducated would misunderstand, and it implies that they, too, are members of a discriminating minority. Actually, its use marks them as unoriginal and pretentious.

Incidentally, such fragments as we have of the play that Prince Hamlet so esteemed are incredibly bad.

cay. See **quay.**

cease. This word may be followed by an infinitive, as in *he ceased to go there,* or by the *-ing* form of a verb, as in *he ceased going there.* The *-ing* construction is heard more often than the infinitive. See **end** and **stop.**

cedilla. See **diacritical mark.**

ceiling is an overhead interior lining of a room (*The chandelier was suspended from the ceiling*). The word has recently been used metaphorically (perhaps through its aeronautical application where the *ceiling* is the distance between the earth and the base of the lowest cloud bank, or, sometimes, the maximum height to which a specific aircraft can rise) to mean the top limit (*A new ceiling has been fixed on rents*).

In America this metaphorical usage has become so common that it must be accepted as standard. But like all vogue words it is being overworked and like all metaphors is liable to ludicrous application and misuse. Sir Ernest Gowers quotes an official document in which it is said that under certain circumstances a fixed ceiling will be "waived." But you can't waive a ceiling and the term is too near to its literal sense to be so completely detached from it. He quotes another document in which a ceiling on floor space is established in a certain construction project. *Limit* would certainly have been a happier word.

celebrant; celebrator. To celebrate is to make known, to glorify, honor, praise (*For the grave cannot praise thee, death cannot celebrate thee*). A celebrated beauty is one whose beauty has gained wide renown. Among the ways of glorifying is to commemorate, with demonstrations of joy or sorrow or respect. Thus we celebrate birthdays, wedding anniversaries, the Sabbath, and so on. Among the most solemn of glorifications is the performance of religious rites and ceremonies. The Mass is celebrated. Marriages and funerals are celebrated.

Because of the gaiety attendant upon most minor commemorations, *celebrate* has come, in its most common contemporary sense, to mean to be gay and lively and boisterous, often to drink and to revel. One who is so enjoying himself is a *celebrator* or a *celebrater.* *Celebrant* is usually reserved for an officiating priest in the celebration of the Eucharist or a participant in some public religious rite. Such statements as

Thousands of New Year's Eve Celebrants See Wild Drama of Gunfire or *Chief Police Inspector Stephen P. Kennedy put the number of celebrants at 500,000* are at the best ambiguous.

celebrity; celebrated; fame; notoriety; renown.
Celebrity is the state of being publicly known. It is a noisier, more ephemeral state than *fame* which is an enduring *renown,* a favorable estimation that is widespread and lasting (Matthew Arnold said that Spinoza's successors *had celebrity, Spinoza has fame*). The use of *celebrity* to describe a well-known person is standard but greatly overworked. Since *celebrity* is today a marketable commodity, there is a whole industry devoted to manufacturing *celebrities* and the public, though it always pays the passing tribute of a gawk and a gasp, is dimly aware that many of its celebrities are synthetic, and so the word has suffered.

Celebrated, on the other hand, though it has two meanings, "much talked about" (*Lake Michigan is celebrated for its whitefish*) and "famous, in a limited way" (*The celebrated Mrs. Huggins, whose preserves are known throughout the state*), has not suffered the deterioration of *celebrity.*

Renown is close to *fame* (*The inheritors of unfulfilled renown,* Shelley called those men of genius who died before their greatness could be shown), but there is in it a suggestion of more of the present glory than of the lasting esteem. *Renown* is often applied to great military leaders. The Bible speaks of *mighty men which in old time were men of renown.*

Notoriety means the state of being well known. A notorious fact means one that is obvious, publicly known, one of which an ordinary man could not convincingly claim to be ignorant. When applied to persons, *notorious* is always condemnatory. It means that the person is well known for some bad trait or deed (*Mrs. Rudd, the notorious murderess, escaped hanging at Tyburn. To low minds notoriety is as good as glory*).

cement; concrete. *Cement* is often used as a synonym for *concrete* and, when used as it usually is in reference to sidewalks or foundations, this use must be granted at least a colloquial standing. But actually *cement* (usually made by burning a mixture of clay and limestone) is only the binding element in *concrete* which is a mixture of cement, sand, gravel, and crushed rock. (*The road deteriorated rapidly because the contractor had not put enough cement in his concrete mixture.*)

In contemporary American usage *cement,* by a natural extension, has come to mean almost any binding substance which is liquid or semiliquid when applied and hardens to a rocklike consistency.

censor; censure; censer; censorial; censorious. To *censor* is to act as a *censor,* an official who examines books, plays, news reports, motion pictures, radio programs and in wartime even letters for the purpose of suppressing whatever seems objectionable for moral, political, or military reasons (*It is always the simplest cablegrams that the hardened censor suspects most*).

To *censure* is to express disapproval, to blame, to criticize adversely or hostilely (*Lincoln's lenience and humanity were severely censured by many at the time*).

Of, pertaining to, or characteristic of a censor, is *censorial.* To be addicted to censure, to be severely critical or fault-finding, is to be *censorious.*

A *censer* is a container in which incense is burned. The verb is *cense.*

census. The regular plural is *censuses.* The learned plural is *census,* not *censi.*

centenary and **centennial** are both adjectives and nouns meaning a hundredth anniversary or pertaining to a period of a hundred years or recurring once in every hundred years. English usage prefers *centenary* (*The centenary of Darwin's birth was celebrated in 1909*), American usage prefers *centennial* (*Northwestern University celebrated its centennial in 1951*).

center; middle; midst. *Middle* is the everyday working word, to be preferred to *center* except where *center* is specifically the word wanted. *Middle* indicates a point or part equidistant from or intermediate between extremes or limits in space or time (*Keep to the middle of the road. Upon the middle of the night,/Waking she heard the night-fowl crow*). *Center,* a more precise word, is proper in mathematical and metaphorical uses. It is the exact middle. The middle of a room is a vague area equidistant from the walls; the center of a room is an exact point. *Middle* applies only to linear extension—even when linear extension is being used metaphorically (*He's always been a middle-of-the-roader*). *Center* is ordinarily a point within circular, globular, or regular bodies (*The center of the earth*). Even metaphorically, it suggests the core of a sphere. When we say that a man was *the center of attraction,* we imply that others clustered about him. *Center* as a political term, however, is the same as *middle.* When we say that someone is *left of center* we have a linear, not a solid, body in mind.

Midst suggests that a person or thing is closely surrounded or encompassed on all sides, usually by something dense (*In the midst of the storm*), a fact demonstrated by the frequent substitution of *thick* (*He was always in the thick of things*) for *midst.*

cereal is, properly, any gramineous plant yielding an edible farinaceous grain. In English usage the word is confined to technical writings in which various agricultural products are classified. In American usage, however, the word has acquired an additional meaning: a breakfast food made from some cereal. *Eat your cereal, child* would be spoken to a child dawdling over corn flakes but not to one dawdling over stewed corn. A famous brand of rice has on its package, under the heading of *Suggested Uses, As a cereal* and, further down, *As a vegetable.* This really means, "For breakfast, sweetened" and "For lunch or dinner, unsweetened." The problem of rice pudding is met by *In desserts.*

ceremonial; ceremonious. *Ceremonial* means pertaining to, marked by, or of the nature of ceremony (*The centennial was a ceremonial occasion*). It applies only to things. *Ceremonious* can be applied to persons or things. When applied to persons it means overly polite, making too much ceremony for the occasion, punctilious (*I find his ceremoniousness tiring*).

certain. When this word is followed by *of* and the *-ing* form of a verb, it means that the person spoken about has no doubts, as in *he is certain of returning.* When it is followed by an infinitive, it means that there is no doubt about the fact itself, as in *he is certain to return.*

cession; cessation; session. *Cession* is the act of ceding, of yielding. *Cessation* is the act of ceasing. *Session* is the act of sitting together of a body for the transaction of business (*The cession of territories came to a cessation at the next session of Congress*).

chafe and **chaff** are most often confused because not only are their spellings and pronunciations much alike, but the one often leads to the other. A man who is *chaffed* is very likely to *chafe* and one who is *chafed*, if his friends observe it, is likely to be *chaffed.*

To *chafe* is to warm by rubbing or to abrade or to fray by rubbing. Metaphorically, it means to irritate or to annoy (*He's always rubbing the boy the wrong way and the child chafes under it continually*). To *chaff* is to tease, to ridicule, to banter. The origin of the word is uncertain, but it may derive from a joking scattering of chaff (husks) instead of grain to see chickens and birds peck at it in vain. Badinage and banter can be highly exasperating and one man's *chaff* easily becomes another man's *chafe.*

chair is used in America for *chairman* (*The chair sternly rebuked the audience for their laughter*). In England it is always *the chairman.* The chair in which a witness is seated is always known in America as *the chair,* as is also the electric chair. Idiomatically, the witness always "takes" the chair, the condemned criminal "gets" the chair (*When the victim's young wife, disfigured and still on crutches, took the chair, the murderer's lawyer knew, from the expressions on the faces of the jurymen, that his client would get the chair*).

chaise longue (French for an elongated chair) is often folk-etymologized (see **folk etymology)** in popular speech into *chase lounge,* under the impression, no doubt fostered by boudoir comedies, that this is a lounge on which the eternal chase either begins or ends.

challenge. This verb may be followed by an infinitive, as in *I challenge you to tell me,* but not by the *-ing* form of a verb or by a clause.

chamois. The plural is *chamois.* There is no difference in the spelling, but the final *s* is pronounced in the plural and not in the singular.

chance, take a. In American usage a man *takes a chance.* In English usage he *takes his chance.*

The American *chance* means risk (*He took a dreadful chance, flying under the bridge that way*). The English means luck (*These things happen; a chap has to take his chance along with the others*). Of course there are other meanings of the word common to both countries.

change; alter. Although *change* is the simple Saxon word and *alter* the two-syllabled Latin derivative, *change* has acquired so many meanings (to substitute, to give and take reciprocally, to remove and replace, to get smaller money in exchange for, etc.) that where a simple "making different" is to be expressed, the use of *alter* frequently avoids ambiguity. Thus if it is said of someone that he *changed* his costume, we are not certain whether he took off the costume he had on and put on a totally different one or whether he merely made some alteration in the one he had on. If we are told that he *altered* his costume, only the second of these meanings could be understood.

change, when it means interchange, requires a plural object, as in *will you change seats with me?*

change of heart for a change in feelings (usually from bad to good) is a cliché and to be avoided.

chaperon; chaperone. For the person who, for the sake of propriety, attends a young unmarried woman in public or accompanies a party of young unmarried men and women, either *chaperon* or *chaperone* is correct.

character; reputation. *Character* is the aggregate of qualities that distinguishes one person or thing from another. Naturally this aggregate of qualities is the thing most likely to be spoken of when the person or thing is discussed, so that *character* and *reputation,* the estimation in which the person or thing is held by the community or general public, are closely connected and the two words often confused. But a man may have a *reputation* for honesty that is unjustified. He may not have an honest *character* but be a successful hypocrite. See also **personality.**

charge. This verb may be followed by an infinitive, as in *I charge you to tell me.* It could once be followed by a clause with the clause verb a subjunctive, as in *I charge you that you be there,* but this construction is now archaic and the infinitive construction is preferred.

Charge of is an ambiguous phrase. One may say *we left the baby in charge of the nurse* or *we left the nurse in charge of the baby.* Both constructions are in standard use today, and both mean that the nurse has responsibility for the baby. But if the article *the* is used before *charge,* only one sentence order is possible. No one would say *we left the nurse in the charge of the baby.* If there is any possibility of misunderstanding, as there may well be if *Mary is left in charge of John,* the form with *the* should certainly be used.

In English usage a person is *charged with* a fault or crime (*He was charged with aiding and abetting the enemy*). In American usage it is *charged that* a person did this or that (*It was charged that he aided and abetted the enemy*). The former construction is sometimes used in America, but the latter is rarely used in England.

charge; accuse. To *charge* is to make a formal accusation. It is often used of an accusation brought at law (*Charge an honest woman with picking thy pocket?*) or one delivered with the solemnity of an indictment. An *accusation* can be formal, but it can also be informal and even mild (*The younger children accused John of eating more than his share.* Here *charged him with eating more than his share* would be ponderous).

In an impersonal construction only *charge* can be used (*It has been charged that Richard's early associates corrupted his morals*).

chart. See **map.**

charter. See **hire.**

chartered; charted. One sometimes hears or even reads of *unchartered seas.* A *chart* is a map. A *charter* is a document that grants certain rights and privileges.

chateau. The plural is *chateaus* or *chateaux.*

cheap; inexpensive. *Cheap* was originally the process of buying and selling. (From this came *Cheapside,* a part of London in which the shops were congregated, what we would call a shopping center.) As late as 1727, Swift, in his "A Description of a City Shower," wrote: *To shops in crowds the daggled females fly,/Pretend to cheapen goods, but nothing buy.* It is only recently and in a very small part of the world that prices have been fixed. Formerly it was assumed that the purchaser would offer less than what was asked and that the seller would, in time, accept less. Thus *cheapen,* from the buyer's point of view, came to mean to lower the price and from this came all of our favorable meanings of *cheap* (*Eggs are wonderfully cheap now. If you want a cheap vacation, travel on an ocean freighter*). From the seller's point of view, however, it was necessary to lower the quality in order to gain by the transaction even if the price were lowered, and from this come our unfavorable meanings of *cheap:* shoddy, shabby, mean (*It just looks sleazy and cheap. That was a cheap trick to play on a friend*). Some purists have deplored this second use of the word, but surely it is as inherent in its development as the first.

Cheap suggests a low cost. One could say that a diamond necklace was cheap at a hundred thousand dollars. But the word would certainly not be used in its modern sense if one said that it was a cheap necklace. *Inexpensive* is now the commoner word to emphasize lowness of price and suggest that the value is fully equal to the cost.

Cheap has been used as an adverb as long as it has been used as an adjective. *Cheaply* can be used only as an adverb. But *he sold it cheap* is just as good English as *he sold it cheaply.*

check. In the sense of a written order directing a bank to pay money, the English spell the word *cheque,* Americans spell it *check.*

Check, as a verb and a noun, has some uses in America that it does not have in England. A piece of luggage is *checked* in America when it is sent to a destination under the privilege of a passenger ticket. To *check up* or *check up on* is to make an inquiry or investigation for verification. To *check out* is to leave and pay for one's quarters at a hotel ("*I will have to check up on this check before you can check out,*" said the desk clerk).

check; curb; repress; restrain. *Check* implies the sudden arrest of a forward motion (*He checked his horse sharply. The reform movement received a check when the council approved Alderman Smith's resolution*). *Curb* implies the use of a means such as a chain or strap, a frame, or a wall, to guide or control or to force to stay within limits. *Repress* formerly meant only suppress, but now it also implies the prevention of an action or development which might naturally be expected (*A child should not be repressed when he wants to express himself*). *Restrain* implies the use of force to put someone or something under control, and chiefly to hold back (*In his paroxysms two attendants could scarcely restrain him from doing himself harm*).

In New York City *curb* as a verb has acquired —through a combination of a city ordinance, euphemism, and a pun—a special meaning. *Curb your dog,* which is enjoined upon the citizens at almost every lamppost, means not only that the dog must be kept curbed by a leash but that it must be led to the curb (the edge of the sidewalk) to defecate into the gutter. The injunction hidden under the double meaning would not be understood in England where in this meaning the word is spelled *kerb.*

checkers. The game which is America is called *checkers* is in England called *draughts,* where *checker,* spelled *chequer,* is an obsolete name for *chess.*

When used as the name of a game, *checkers* takes a singular verb, as in *checkers is played by two persons.* A single piece is called *a man* and not *a checker.* But the singular form *checker* is preferred as the first element in a compound, as in *checkerboard.*

cheek by jowl. Since the commonest meaning of *jowl* is now a fold of flesh hanging from the jaw, especially of the aged corpulent and the shrunken fat, *cheek by jowl* no longer conveys the sense of jolly intimacy that it did when *jowl* meant cheek. It is not only a cliché but a misleading one and should be avoided.

cheeky. See **impertinent.**

cheerful; cheery. The *cheerful* man feels full of cheer. The *cheery* man acts as if he did and attempts to promote cheer among others. *Cheerfulness* is internal and may not show. *Cheeriness* is external and, sometimes, may show what is not felt. *Cheeriness* of manner has become such an adjunct of salesmanship that the public has become wary of it and the word has acquired a tinge of disrepute (*He was a cheery bird, enough to make the most cheerful man downhearted*).

cherished belief(s). That which we cherish we hold or treat as dear, care for it tenderly, nurture it, and cling fondly to it. This is the manner in which we treat many of our deepest convictions, not accepting or rejecting them dispassionately on the basis of the evidence for or against them. Whoever, then, in the late nineteenth century, thought of this phrase had a vivid conception, and whoever immediately repeated it gained a reputation for such a conception from those who had never heard it before. But now everyone knows it, the original force has worn away with excessive use.

cherub. The plural is *cherubs* or *cherubim* or *cherubims. Cherubim* is the Hebrew plural of *cherub* and, according to some grammarians, the only acceptable plural. In the King James Bible, however, the plural of *cherub* is always *cherubims*. This form is well established in literature, as well as in hymns, and so cannot be called incorrect. The singular form *cherub* inevitably produced an English plural *cherubs,* and this too is standard today. The plural form *cherubims* also produced an English singular, *a cherubim*. This form was in respectable use as late as Dickens but is not considered standard now.

The word *cherub* has almost as many meanings as it has forms. The cherubs of the Old Testament are terrifying symbols of power, more like the winged bulls of Assyria than anything else we know. They are very large and it is said that the Lord God *rode upon a cherub*. Later cherubs were identified as angels of the second rank, excelling in wisdom, which of course is a kind of power. In *Paradise Lost* the word is used with its ancient dignity; for example, Satan, who belonged to the highest rank of angels, disguises himself as *a stripling cherub*. During the Renaissance, cherubs were represented in art as rosy babies. This may have been anti-intellectualism on the part of the artists. They may have refused to believe that heavenly spirits had anything in common with a doctor of philosophy. That the little creatures symbolize wisdom of some kind is shown by the fact that they often have only a head. But as a result of these pictures, many people today feel that a cherub is a baby angel, or perhaps an angelic baby.

When a word has so many apparently different meanings and so many forms, one is tempted to tidy it up by pinning certain meanings to certain forms. Some grammarians have claimed that *cherubim* and *cherubims* are the correct words to use in speaking of the heavenly spirits, and that *cherub* and *cherubs* should be used when speaking figuratively of earthly creatures. Since the singular *cherubim* is no longer in use, this distinction could now be made only in the plural. But the distinction is entirely theoretical. In actual practice the three forms are used interchangeably. All that can be said is that *cherubim,* being a foreign plural, is not used as often in natural speech as *cherubs,* and is therefore pretty much confined to literary English.

Other grammarians feel that *cherubim* should be used as a collective, in speaking of all of them as a whole, and that *cherubs* should be used for the true plural, meaning more than one individual. But this distinction has not been established either, probably because the most familiar use of the word *cherubim* is in the Old Testament descriptions of the Ark of the Covenant, where there are quite clearly two of them and no more.

Cheshire cat, grin like a. Lewis Carroll did not invent the Cheshire cat. When Alice encountered the creature in the Duchess's kitchen its smile was already as mooted an enigma as the Mona Lisa's. One of the sanest conjectures was that some painter of inn signs in Cheshire had depicted his lions rampant with snarls so amiable that they had been taken for smiles. However gay the phrase's origin, its end is dismal. With all humor, absurdity, whimsy, and mystery worn out by repetition, the phrase is entitled, after long service in the cause of the gaiety of nations, to an honorable retirement.

chickenpox. This word is a plural form; the singular would be *pock*. But it is regularly treated as a singular. We say *it is contagious,* not *they are contagious*. The use of the article, as in *the chickenpox,* is old-fashioned or countrified.

The form *chickenpox* is used as the first element in a compound, as in *a chickenpox rash*.

chicory. Horwill points out a pitfall against which the dictionaries offer no definitive protection: what in America is called *chicory* is in England called *endive,* and what in America is called *endive* is in England called *chicory*.

chide. The past tense is *chided* or *chid*. The participle is *chided* or *chid* or *chidden*. In the United States, *chided* is the preferred form for the past tense and the participle. In Great Britain, *chid* is preferred for the past tense and *chid* or *chidden* for the participle.

chief. See **primary; prime; premier, etc.**

chiefly. See **largely.**

child. The plural is *children*. Traditionally, only the singular *child* can be used as the first element in a compound, as in *child prodigies* and *child laborers*. But the plural *children* is being heard more and more in such compounds, as in *children refugees* and *children berry-pickers*. This is technically incorrect, but it is following the established pattern for *man* and *woman* and is acceptable in many places.

Children is a double formation in which a plural ending *en* has been added to an old plural form *childer*. At one time *children* must have sounded as odd to some people as *mices* would sound today. See **infant.**

childish; childlike. See **infantile.**

chilled to the marrow. There is nothing in which the wits strive more for mastery than in describing their woes. And he who most has suffered, as Matthew Arnold observed, "takes dejectedly his seat upon the intellectual throne." Sometime in the nineteenth century a cold but unoriginal wretch must have remarked that he was chilled to the bone. Whereupon a wit stole what little admiration the hackneyed metaphor sought to invoke by declaring that *he* was *chilled to the marrow*. Deeper into the body a chill cannot go. The glory of the ultimate assertion was his and it is to be hoped that he had an appreciative audience to do him honor. But the splendor has long since faded and repetition has blunted rapture. The phrase is now retirable.

Chinese. The singular and the plural are both *Chinese*. At one time this word had a distinct plural, as seen in Milton's lines: *where Chineses drive with sails and wind*. In time this dropped out of the language and the remaining form *Chinese* was used for both singular and plural. Later, this was felt to be a simple plural and attempts were made to form a new singular, such as *a Chinee* and *a Chinaman*. *A Chinee* was never standard English, but *a Chinaman* is accepted in Great Britain today. In the United States the preferred form is *Chinese,* as in *one Chinese* and *two Chinese*.

chip of the old block. *How well dost thou appear to be a chip of the old block?* wrote John Milton in 1642, accepting the English version of the saying. Theocritus (270 B.C.) had it a chip of the old flint, but then he was nearer to the Old Stone Age, where the figure no doubt originated. The saying, calling attention to a likeness between son (occasionally a daughter) and father, usually in a favorable way and jocularly, is a cliché and is to be avoided.

choice. See **nice;** see **option.**

choose. The past tense is *chose*. The participle is *chosen*. The form *choosed* is sometimes heard but is not standard.

Choose may be followed by an infinitive, as in *I do not choose to run*, or by the -*ing* form of a verb, as in *I do not choose running*. The infinitive construction is preferred. *Choose* may also be followed by a *that* clause but the clause verb must be a subjunctive or a subjunctive equivalent, as in *I do not choose that he run*. An infinitive construction, such as *I do not choose to have him run*, is generally preferred.

chord; cord. A combination of three or more tones in harmonic relation is spelled *chord*. So of course is any figurative extension of the idea (*His proposal struck a responsive chord*). The string of a musical instrument and the geometric term for that part of a straight line between two of its intersections with a curve are also spelled *chord*.

A string or small rope composed of several strands twisted or woven together is spelled *cord*, as is any extension of the idea (*an electric cord, a cord cloth*). One hundred and twenty-eight cubic feet of firewood is also spelled *cord*.

In America the spinal *cord* and the vocal *cords* are now so spelled almost always. In England they are sometimes spelled *chord* and *chords*.

chose, chosen. See **choose.**

Christian name. See **first name.**

chronic means habitual, inveterate, constant, having continued a long time (*Being a chronic smoker, he had a chronic cough. Mrs. Jones was*

a chronic invalid and the house was filled with her chronic complaining). *Chronic* should not be used as a mere intensive or a synonym for severe. It is the exact opposite of *acute*.

chrysalis. The plural is *chrysalises* or *chrysalides*, not *chrysales*. A new singular *chrysalid*, with a regular plural *chrysalids*, is also in use. It is not as well established as the similar formation *orchid*, but it is thoroughly acceptable.

cinema. See **motion pictures.**

circle ("social group"). See **clique.**

circumlocution. See **locution.**

circumstances, under the. It is sometimes objected that since *circumstances* are those things or conditions that lie *around* us, we cannot be *under* them. But that is silly. Things can be conceived as enphering us as well as surrounding us on a plane. The weather, as Fowler points out, is certainly a circumstance and we are certainly under it when it is inclement. Many people, especially in England, prefer to say *in the circumstances* and the phrase is correct. But so is *under the circumstances*.

cirrus. The plural is *cirri*.

cite and **quote** are synonymous in one meaning: to repeat a passage from a book or a speech by way of authority. Quoting, strictly, means repeating the actual words and citing means mentioning them, referring to them, or bringing them forward as proof or confirmation. But since the processes are inextricable, usage does not, and cannot, draw a fixed distinction between the two words in this sense.

Each word has other meanings, however, in which they are not synonymous. To *cite* has an old meaning of to rouse to action (*cited to the field of battle*) and a special military meaning of to mention in orders, as for gallantry (*He was cited for bravery under fire*). To *quote* means to enclose words within quotation marks (*He quoted the general directly in his report*)— here *cited* would be incorrect—and to state a price or to state the current price of (*He quoted him ten cents a pound*).

city; town. To say that a *town* is a collection of inhabited houses and that a *city* is a large or important town isn't of much help to someone who is in doubt which to call a specific place. Size is relative and importance is often subjective. In the United States a *city* is an incorporated municipality, usually governed by a mayor and board of aldermen or councilmen. In Canada it is a municipality of high rank and the distinction between it and a *town* is usually based on population. In England a *city* is a borough, usually the seat of a bishop, upon which the dignity of the title of *city* has been conferred by the Crown.

The City in England is that part of London in which the commercial and financial interests are chiefly centered. It corresponds to New York's Wall Street district.

Idiomatically, *city* takes the definite article, *town* does not. We go to town, but to the city. We live in town, but in the city. We get out of town, but out of the city, and so on.

city fathers. To refer to members of the Municipal Council or the Board of Aldermen as *the city fathers* is to strive a little too hard to be elegant. No such filial relation is now felt, if it ever was.

civil. See **polite.**

clad. See **clothe.**

claque. See **clique.**

clarinet is the preferred spelling, though *clarionet* is also correct.

class as a designation of students in a school or college ranked together or graduating the same year (*The Class of 1899*) is standard in American usage but not used in England.

    Class meaning excellence or merit (*That girl's got class!*) is slang. See also **category.**

classic and **classical** are synonymous, but use has accustomed us to one rather than the other in certain contexts. In medicine, for example, it is always *classic* (*a classic case of typhoid*, one which conforms in every way to the standard) when referring to a disease. Certain great works are *classics* in their field, but if their authors were ancient Greeks or Romans, they are *classical* authors. Sports writers label any game between two schools or teams that have played before a *classic* and in this sense the word is sadly overworked.

    In general, *classical* refers to Greek and Latin writers and to the art and culture of ancient Greece and Rome. *Classic* means of the first or highest class or rank, adhering to established standards.

clauses. Any group of words that contains a true verb and its subject (or an imperative) is called a clause, such as *I came* in *tell them I came.*

    If a clause is part of a larger sentence, its relation to the rest of the sentence may be shown in a number of ways. It may be shown by position, as in the example just given where *I came* is standing in the position of the object of the verb *tell.* Or it may be shown by a conjunction. A coordinating conjunction, such as *and* or *but,* shows that the two clauses which it joins have the same function in the sentence, as in *tell them I came and no one answered.* A clause used independently, that is, not as the subject or object of another verb or as a qualifier, is called a principal clause. Such a clause may be joined by a coordinating conjunction, or by mere position in a series, with other independent clauses, as in *I came, I saw, I conquered.* One can then say that the sentence has more than one principal clause. Any other complete statement inside a sentence is a subordinate clause. A subordinating conjunction shows that the clause which it introduces is functioning as a subordinate element in another statement. The subordinate clause may have the function of an adjective, an adverb, or a noun. Subordinate clauses may also show their function by position, or may be introduced by a relative pronoun, an adverb, a participle, or a noun with the force of an adverb. See **conjunctions.**

ADJECTIVE AND ADVERB CLAUSES

    An adjective clause normally follows the word it qualifies. When placed before the word it has a slightly humorous effect and must be hyphenated in order to be understood, as in *with an I-don't-expect-to-be-believed look.* As a rule, an adjective clause is introduced by a relative pronoun and qualifies the antecedent of the pronoun. When the relative pronoun is the subject of the clause verb it must be expressed, as *who* in *the little man who wasn't there;* when it is the object of the clause verb or of a preposition it can usually be omitted, as in *the man I love.* That is, in a qualifying clause the object of the verb or of a preposition does not always have to be expressed. The object usually cannot be omitted when the clause qualifies a proper noun or a common noun that identifies a single individual, as in *my father, whom you met here yesterday, is coming again tomorrow.*

    An adjective clause that is essential to the meaning of the word it qualifies is said to be "defining" or "restrictive," such as *who was here yesterday* in *the man who was here yesterday is coming again tomorrow.* A clause of this kind must not be separated from the word it qualifies by a comma or any other punctuation. An adjective clause that is not defining is said to be "descriptive," such as the clause in *my father, who was here yesterday, is coming again tomorrow.* A descriptive clause gives some additional information that is not essential to the sense of what is being said. It is usually set off by commas. See also **that; which.**

    Any adverbial idea, such as time, place, manner, degree, may be expressed by a clause and the clause may stand in any position appropriate for an adverb. Adverbial clauses may also show the cause, purpose, or result of the action of the principal clause. These are introduced by conjunctions such as *because, since, so.* (See the individual conjunctions.) There are also adverbial clauses of "condition," "concession," and "supposition," which are introduced by such words as *if, unless, although.* In clauses of this kind the verb may have a subjunctive form. See **subjunctive mode.**

    An adjective or an adverbial clause will always qualify the nearest preceding word or group of words that the sense allows. In *they think the men are angry because they are frightened,* the *because* clause is attached to *the men are angry,* regardless of what was intended. If the clause is meant to apply to *they think,* this can be made clear by a comma between *angry* and *because,* which warns the reader that these two words are to be kept apart. Or the clause may be placed first in the sentence. In speech these things are taken care of by pitch and stress. But a writer must examine his sentences carefully to make sure that his clauses qualify the words he intended them to.

NOUN CLAUSES

    A clause may also function as a noun. It may be the subject of a verb, as in *who made it is a mystery;* or it may be the complement of a verb, as in *I would like to know who made it.* When the noun clause is an indirect question it may be introduced by an interrogative pronoun or adverb, or by the conjunction *whether,* as in *I wonder whether he will understand me.* In a clause of this kind the subject stands before the verb as it would in a declarative sentence, and not after the verb as it would in a direct question such as *will he understand me?* This construction is standard, literary English. But sentences such as *I wonder will he understand me* are also heard. Here the interrogative word has been omitted and the clause itself has the word order of a question. This construction is condemned by many grammarians, but it has been widely used since the middle of the nineteenth century and is acceptable to most people today. In the older construction *I wonder whether he will understand me,* the clause should not be separated from the principal verb by a comma and should not be followed by a question mark. In the newer construction the comma and question mark are sometimes used but they are more often omitted, especially in a long or involved sentence such as *if you are asking me will I help you, the answer is no.*

A clause may also be the object of a preposition, as in *his interest in who was coming, she said nothing about when she would return, he brooded over whether he should give up smoking or not.* This construction was almost unknown before the nineteenth century. But it is thoroughly acceptable today, provided the clause begins with *how* or one of the *wh-* words, such as *who, when, whether.* The construction is also heard with the word *if,* as in *what about if I get married,* but this is not at present standard English.

For the case of the pronoun in a subordinate clause, see **who; whom.** For the person, number, and tense of the verb, see **agreement: verbs** and **tense shifts.**

clean bill of health. A bill of health is a certificate as to the health of a ship's company at the time of her clearing of any port. A clean bill of health is an official assurance that no member of the crew is afflicted with any one of certain diseases that would result in the ship's being detained in quarantine in another port. As a way of saying that someone has been proved guiltless of certain charges or is free from the taint of certain imputations, *giving him a clean bill of health* is a cliché.

clean; cleanly; cleanse. As an adjective, *clean* means free from dirt. *Cleanly,* if applied to things, means habitually clean (*It was a cleanly house* would mean that it was a house that was clean all the time). If applied to persons it means always attempting to be and to remain clean (*He was naturally a cleanly man and the dirt of his new surroundings depressed him*). A boy can be clean, at least for a few seconds, without being in any way cleanly. Someone else may have got him clean, but he has no objection to becoming dirty again immediately.

As verbs, *clean* and *cleanse* both mean to make clean. *Cleanse* is used for moral, spiritual, or ceremonial cleaning (*Cleansed of guilt by contrition and atonement, he felt light of heart again*). It may be this connotation of higher things that has led certain manufacturers to prefer *cleanse* to *clean* or *cleanser (kitchen cleanser)* to *cleaner.* Dry cleaners who charge a great deal for their work sometimes attempt to justify the added cost by describing themselves as *cleansers* and their work as *cleansing,* suggesting a delicacy and thoroughness approaching the spiritual. *Cleansing tissues,* for removing cosmetics, have made the word so common that in that context the word seems common and natural and is standard usage.

When *clean* means "entirely," it can be used as an adverb, as in *to make a real portrait of Deity is clean impossible* and *I had clean forgotten.* This use of *clean* is now old-fashioned. The form *cleanly* can also be used as an adverb. It ordinarily means "entirely" or "precisely," as in *cleanly cut.* It may also mean "without dirt," as in *she works cleanly,* but this is rare.

clear; clearly. In current English, *clear* qualifies a noun and *clearly* qualifies a word that is not a noun. In *you make the point clear,* the word *clear* describes the point. In *you make the point clearly,* the word *clearly* describes the making. There is a difference of meaning, or emphasis, here and one should choose the form that says what is intended. Sometimes there is no difference, as in *the moon shone clear* or *clearly,* and then either form can be used.

Clear once meant "entirely," and in this sense could be used to qualify any word that was not a noun, as in *I had clear forgotten* and *that is clear another story.* This use is now considered archaic or uneducated, except before prepositions or adverbs, such as *away, off, out, through, over,* and so on. We must now say *I clearly understood* and *I heard clearly.* But we may say *I read clear through the book, the tide goes clear out, he got clear away.*

cleave. The past tense is *cleft* or *clove* or *cleaved.* The participle is *cleft* or *cloven* or *cleaved.*

When this word means to adhere to, it is a regular verb and only the form *cleaved* is used for the past tense or the participle. There was once a past tense *clave* used in this sense, but this is now obsolete. Occasionally a nineteenth century poet uses *clove* for *clave* but this has to be classed as a mistake.

When the word means to split, any of the forms given above may be used. In the United States, *cleft* is preferred for the past tense and the participle. In Great Britain, the older forms *clove* and *cloven* are preferred. There is a tendency not to use *cleaved* in this sense, but this is not strictly observed.

Two verbs are mixed here. They were once distinct but have come to be alike through changes in pronunciation. The similarity does not cause confusion because the words are used very little. When they are used it is almost always in a set phrase, each of which is a law to itself. For example, we always say *a cloven hoof* but *a cleft palate.*

clench and **clinch** are simply variant pronunciations of the same word. Both mean to grasp, secure, or hold firmly. Yet each word has come to have certain fixed applications in which the other would be inappropriate. Thus we *clench* our fist, a nail, our jaws, a rope, or anything held. But boxers *clinch* when they grasp each other tightly and sailors *clinch* when they fasten by a clinch. We *clinch* an argument or a bargain and a statement that ties up an argumentative opponent is a *clincher*.

While, as has been said, we *clench* a nail, the nail is *clinched*, especially if it is secured by having the point beaten down.

clergy. Originally this word was a group name. It could be used with a singular or a plural verb, as in *the clergy was represented* or *the clergy were represented*. But it meant the class as a whole and could not be treated as a true plural, as in *twenty clergy were present*. This is no longer the case. The plural construction, *twenty clergy,* is standard English today and has been accepted by some grammarians who refuse to accept the similar construction *twenty people*. This new plural, *clergy,* does not have a singular. In speaking of just one member of the clergy we must still use *clergyman*. See also **parson; preacher.**

clever. See **brainy.**

cliché is a French word meaning a stereotype block and is used in English to describe those phrases (there are thousands of them), originally idioms, metaphors, proverbs, or brief quotations, which overuse and, sometimes, changing circumstances have rendered meaningless. Many of them just fill out the vacancies of thought and speech. A man goes to say *far* and he says *far and wide*. Speech is a difficult thing. We spend more time learning to talk than anything else we do. It is an effort, an unceasing effort. There is strong resistance in us to it and the inertia which this resistance sets up is probably the chief cause of our use of clichés.

Many clichés are alliterative, that is, their words begin with the same sound. We do not say we are *cool*, but *cool as a cucumber*. Unless one is *slow but sure,* things go to *rack and ruin* and he may be thrown out *bag and baggage*.

Historical changes have made many clichés utterly meaningless. What does *fell* mean in *one fell swoop?* Or *halcyon* in *halcyon days?* Or *moot* in *moot point?* Yet these and hundreds of other phrases, totally devoid of meaning to those who speak them, are heard every day.

Many clichés were once original and clever, but repetition by millions, possibly billions, of people for hundreds and even thousands of years in some instances, has worn all originality and cleverness away. They were fresh-minted once, but are now battered beyond acceptability. And their use is doubly bad because it characterizes the user as one who thinks he is witty, or would like to be thought witty, and yet is a mere parroter of musty echoes of long-dead wit. His very attempt to sound clever shows him to be dull.

Our speech is probably more crammed with clichés today than ever before. The torrent of printed and recorded matter that is dumped on us every day in newspapers and from radio and television is bound to be repetitious and stereotyped. The brightest day in the world's history

never produced one-millionth, in fresh, original, and honest expression, of the bulk of what cascades over us every day. All this stuff is prepared in furious haste. There is neither time nor energy for care or thought and the inevitable result is a fabric woven of stereotyped phrases. Ninety per cent of what the public reads and hears is expressed in these fossilized fragments and, naturally, ninety per cent of its own expression, apart from the necessities of life, is also expressed in them.

This makes the task of the man who wants to speak and write clearly and honestly a difficult one. He must be on his guard all the time, especially against anything that seems particularly apt. That doesn't mean that he is never to use a current phrase or even a hackneyed one. It may be, for example, that after consideration he really does want to say that the pen is mightier than the sword. And if he does, he'd better say it in the cliché form than in some labored circumlocution. But he mustn't expect to be thought clever for saying it. And, of course, he may deliberately choose to speak in clichés in order that his speech may be common and familiar.

Wits often use clichés as the basis of their wit, relying on the seeming familiarity of the phrase and the expectation of its inevitable conclusion to set the trap for the innocent reader—such as Oscar Wilde's "Punctuality is the thief of time" or Samuel Butler's "It's better to have loved and lost than never to have lost at all"—but that is a wholly different thing.

client; customer. Though, despite the protests of the purists, a *client* and *customer* are listed as synonymous in most dictionaries, the distinction between one who purchases goods from another (*customer*) and one who applies to a lawyer for advice (*client*) is maintained in American usage. The term *client* has spread to those who seek other professional services. Thus advertising agencies have (or hope to have) their *clients* as do many other advisory and consultative enterprises. No doubt in choosing this term they hoped to invest themselves with some of the awe that surrounds the lawyer. Physicians still keep their *patients* (derived from a Latin word meaning one who is suffering).

That *client* and *customer* are not completely synonymous can be shown by the fact that *client* could not be substituted for *customer* in the advertising slogan *The customer is always right*. The advertising agencies would probably be willing to say so, but the lawyers would not.

climate; clime; weather. *Clime* is poetic for a tract or region of the earth (*Now in Injia's sunny clime,/ Where I used to spend my time*) or for *climate* (*This moist and foggy clime*). *Climate* is the composite or generalization of the weather conditions of a region, as temperature, pressure, humidity, precipitation, sunshine, cloudiness, and winds, throughout the year, averaged over a series of years. It has been figuratively extended, in intellectual circles, of recent years to describe the general intellectual atmosphere of a period, and we have such phrases as *the climate of opinion*.

Weather is the state of the atmosphere with respect to wind, temperature, cloudiness, moisture, pressure, etc. *Keep one's weather eye open*, as a term for being on one's guard, is a cliché. It was not Mark Twain but Charles Dudley Warner who first said *Everybody talks about the weather, but nobody does anything about it*. Mr. Warner was witty. Those who repeat his saying are not.

climatic; climactic; climacteric(al). *Climatic* relates to climate (*The climatic changes affected the vegetation*). *Climactic* relates to climax (*The climactic scene had a tremendous impact on the audience*). *Climacteric* (also *climacterical*) pertains to critical periods. There was formerly a theory that there were certain years in which important changes in health and fortune occurred. Of these the sixty-third year was the culmination (nine times seven) and it was called *the grand climacteric*. The word is also used very frequently to describe a period of decrease of reproductive activity in men and women, culminating, in women, in the menopause.

climax in popular usage is the culmination, the highest point (*He was then at the climax of his fortunes*). In rhetoric the word designates a series of related ideas so arranged that each one surpasses the preceding in force or intensity, or (more popularly) the last term or member of such a figure.

Originally a rhetorical climax required that the last important word of one clause be repeated as the first important word in the next (accumulated epanastrophe) but now all that is required is that the intensity of expression or importance of meaning increase with each succeeding member term. Indeed, where there is a series of comments or evaluations it is commonly assumed that they are in a climactic order, so that the order in which they are placed is an indication of the values of the speaker or writer. Thus if it is said of a young lady that she is "young, rich, pretty, and intelligent," it is assumed that the speaker has a different set of values from another who would describe her as "intelligent, pretty, young, and rich."

A fine example of climax, in the older as well as the modern form, is furnished by the third and fourth verses of the fifth chapter of *Romans*: "We glory in tribulations also: knowing that tribulation worketh patience; and patience, experience; and experience, hope; and hope maketh not ashamed." See also **anticlimax**.

climb up; climb down. Since all definitions of *climb* involve the idea of ascent, there are those who insist that *climb up* is redundant and *climb down* a contradiction. But dictionaries follow language; they do not control it. In the word *climb* there is implicit an effort, a strenuous exertion which when exceptionally arduous is expressed in the related word *clamber*. In using *climb up* and *climb down* the common speaker is indicating in which direction this effort is being or is to be applied. So *climb down off your*

high horse is more expressive than *come down off your high horse* in that it recognizes that such a descent may be difficult and undignified.

The common speaker has the age-old support of writers. Thus in *Cursor Mundi* (1300 A.D.) we are told that we *freli may climb up and dun*.

cling. The past tense is *clung*. The participle is also *clung*.

clip means more than to cut; it means to cut off or to cut out, as with shears. We *clip* something out of the paper if we want to save it. The American *clipping bureau* is the English *press-cutting agency*. Hair is *cut* if it is long, *clipped* if it is short. A hedge is invariably *clipped*.

In informal speech *clip* means a rapid pace (*He was coming down the road at a good fast clip when he saw the truck*). This is largely an American use, though it is used in some English dialects. *Clip* in the sense of a sharp blow (*He fetched him a clip on the ear*) is slang.

clipped words. See **abbreviations**.

clippers. An instrument for clipping may be called *a clipper* and three of them may be called *three clippers*. But one instrument may be treated as a plural, as in *are these clippers the ones?*, or referred to as *a pair of clippers*. This is acceptable but not necessary. The singular form *clipper* is preferred as the first element in a compound, as in *a clipper sharpener*.

clique; coterie; claque; set; circle. A *clique* is a small and exclusive group of people, usually of some intellectual pretensions. It is a term of reproach or contempt (the word is simply the French for *click* and alludes derisively to the clicking and clucking sounds of mutual and self-approval made by the members) for those who take unto themselves supreme authority in social or intellectual or artistic matters or who are thought to associate for selfish ends under the guise of some high aspirations or ideals (*Addison had his clique at Button's tavern*).

Coterie also describes an exclusive group, but it is more likely to be in society than in the arts and the term, while often contemptuous, is not always so and is less so than *clique* (*The book was written for an exclusive coterie. He belonged to the most brilliant coteries of the day*).

A *claque* is a set of hired applauders at a theater, or any group of persons ready to applaud for interested motives. It is easily confused with *clique* because the members of a clique so often form a claque to applaud each other. That is one of the chief things that earns them the detestation of outsiders (*The author's friends formed a claque on the opening night to ensure the play's success*).

Set refers to a number of persons of similar background, upbringing, interests, and so on. It often implies wealth or interest in social activities (*the country club set, the Junior League set*) but does not have the derogatory connotations of *clique*. It is a word that has been much expanded by newspapers and is enjoying a—partly humorous—vogue (*the teen-age set, the kindergarten set, the marshmallow set*).

A *circle* is usually thought of as a pleasant

little group meeting chiefly for conversation (*the sewing circle*). It has a small-townish air about it now but nothing derogatory. In the plural it suggests a whole section of society interested in one mode of life, or one occupation (*He moved in the best circles. In jazz circles he is considered a "square"*).

clomb is an old literary form of *climbed*, as in *till clomb above the eastern bar, the hornèd moon* and *the sun clomb Heaven's eastern steep*. It is now rarely seen except in poetry.

Until recently it was heard in many rural areas in the United States. It may have been retained as a sort of opposite to *plumb*, which meant "straight down," (from a plumb line) and by extension "completely" as in plumb tuckered out.

close; closely. Only the form *close* can be used to express "where," as in *stand close, he followed close behind*. The use of *closely* in this way is ungrammatical. *Close* is also the only form that can be used to qualify a noun, as in *a close shave*.

The form *closely* is used to qualify a true verb form, when what is meant is "how," as in *guard it closely* and *follow directions closely*. Either form, *close* or *closely*, can be used in the sense of "how" to qualify a participle, as in *close shaven, close shut*.

close; shut. To *close* is to block an opening (*The peasants soon closed the breach in the dyke*). To *shut* is to close in such a way that nothing can thereafter get in or out (*She shut the door and drew the bolt firmly*). *Close*, which often has a connotation of the use of force (*The mayor pledged himself to close all speakeasies*) is the more general word: an account is closed, an incident, a store, etc. *Shut* is the more homely, more direct, and sometimes the more forceful word. See also **shut**.

close proximity. Since *proximity* means nearness —in place, time, or relation—*close proximity* is redundant. *They lived in close proximity* would be better expressed as either *They lived close to one another* or *They lived in proximity to one another*.

close up and **close down** as emphatic expressions for closing mean much the same, but with nuances of difference. Where that which is *closed down* is something undesirable, such as gambling establishments, the term has a harshness about it and a suggestion of a use of force (*The sheriff's men closed down Steve's Place last night*) that is not as marked in a simple *close*. *Shut down* and *close down* both refer to the stoppage of production in a manufacturing plant but—possibly because of the suggestion of the use of force in *close down*—you *shut down* your own plant, others *close it down*.

clothe. The past tense is *clothed* or *clad*. The participle is also *clothed* or *clad*.

Clad is archaic and, like all archaic words, to be used with circumspection. If a man is *clothed*, we know that he has his clothing on. If he is *clad*, we want to know with what, so that one who is *clad* is always clad in something— righteousness, shining armor, the blue or the gray. *Clad* (perhaps because of the sound association with *glad*) always suggests noble, gay, or lofty things (*with verdure clad*). A day would be *clothed* in mist, *clad* in sunshine. However, both forms are rather bookish.

clothes is a mass noun with a plural form. It is always used with a plural verb, as in *these clothes are new*. But it is not a true plural. It has no singular form and cannot be used with a numeral. That is, we cannot speak of *a clothe* or of *six clothes*. Most words of this kind cannot be qualified by *many* but may be qualified by *much* under some circumstances. *Clothes* is an exception to this rule. We may speak of *many clothes*. We may also speak of *much clothes* or *a good deal of clothes*. Both forms are acceptable. *Much clothes* is the usual construction for words which cannot be used with a numeral, but *many clothes* is heard more often. See **mass nouns**.

clove, cloven. See **cleave**.

clue and **clew** are simply variant spellings of a word that originally meant a ball or skein of thread. Theseus found his way out of the labyrinth after slaying the Minotaur by means of the unwound *clew* that Ariadne had given him. From this and similar legends it came to mean anything that serves to guide or direct in the solution of a problem, but in this meaning it is now almost always spelled *clue*, though *clew* is also correct. *Clew* is the preferred spelling for the nautical sense of the lower corner of a square sail or the after lower corner of a fore-and-aft sail or for the verb meaning to haul the lower corners of a sail up to the yard. The verb is followed by *up* (*We had hardly time to haul down and clew up*, says Richard Dana, describing the sudden onset of a gale, *before it was upon us*.)

clung. See **cling**.

coal oil. See **kerosene**.

the coast is clear to indicate that the way is now open for some sortie or event is a cliché, to be used with care.

coca. See **cacao**.

coccyx. The plural is *coccyxes* or *coccyges*, not *coccyces*.

cock. See **rooster**.

cock of the walk. What is now called a chicken *run* was formerly called a *walk*. Life wasn't so hurried in those days. And it is of this *walk* that the cock in the cliché is master. Few people who use the term could explain it.

cocoa, coco. See **cacao**.

codex. The plural is *codexes* or *codices*.

coeval. See **contemporary**.

cognomen, in its strictest sense, is the third name, the family name or surname of a Roman citizen. Thus *Cicero* was the cognomen of Marcus Tullius Cicero. The term was sometimes applied to an additional name or epithet, as *Africanus* was bestowed on Scipio.

Cognomen is used today to mean either the surname (*The name of Alexander . . . coupled with the gentle cognomen of Partridge*) or the first name (*Priscilla . . . this quaint and prim cognomen*) or a nickname (*Mr. Hunt, better known by the cognomen of Golf-bag Sam).* It is hard to see, however, what advantages it offers over *name.* If used seriously, it seems stilted. If used humorously, it seems ponderous.

cognoscenti. The use of *cognoscenti* for "the knowing ones" shows that the user regards himself as among them, for hardly anyone else could be expected to know the term. It is limited in application to connoisseurs of artistic matters. (*The cognoscenti had hailed his genius long before the masses knew his name*). The singular—though the tribe seems to exist entirely in the plural—is *cognoscente.*

coherence is natural or logical connection, consistency, particularly as applied to thought or language. The word is a figurative extension of *cohesion,* which means a sticking together in a physical sense. It is the quality which gives speech or writing its order and logic. Ideas are presented coherently if they are in an order which makes sense.

Coherence is achieved by the arrangement of words in a sentence, sentences in a paragraph, and paragraphs in a composition so as to bring out properly the relationship of ideas. The essential elements of coherent construction are correct connective words and transitional phrases, precise reference of pronouns, and clear word order.

There must be subjects and predicates in sentences and they should agree in number. Sentences and paragraphs are presented in coherent relationships by means of reference words (*the former, the latter, the last-named*), of repetition of ideas in either the same or different words, of conjunctions (*and, but*), of conjunctive adverbs (*also, however, indeed, as a matter of fact*), and of pronouns.

It is possible to write coherent sentences and coherent paragraphs without achieving a coherent whole. Where such a situation exists, however, it is likely that the speaker is confused in thought or has not been able to come to a definite conclusion in his thought.

cohort was one of the ten divisions in an ancient Roman legion, numbering from 300 to 600 men. In historical writing it still means that. In general use it means any group of warriors or just any group or company.

It is occasionally misapplied to single persons, especially an accomplice or an assistant (*Banting* [*was*] *assisted by his young cohort, Dr. Charles H. Best. The culprit and his three cohorts quickly confessed*). Perhaps this error is based on a false analogy to *co-worker.*

coign of vantage is a projecting corner on a castle or fortification which would make an advantageous observation point. The phrase comes from a minor scene in *Macbeth.* As King Duncan and his party are entering the fatal castle they remark on the pleasantness of its location and the softness of the air. Banquo notes that a great many martlets have made their nests on the castle walls: *No jutty, frieze,/ Buttress, nor coign of vantage,/ but is covered with them.*

Sir Walter Scott picked up the phrase (with acknowledgement) two hundred years later in *The Heart of Midlothian* and, for some reason, it caught on and became a popular phrase and remains an overpopular one, although *vantage* is obsolete and *coign* unknown.

coincident. See **synchronous.**

coiner. See **counterfeiter.**

cold blood. The association of heat with passion is very old and has left its impress on many phrases (*hot-tempered*) as has, also, the belief that the blood is in some way the seat of emotions. In this day of clinical thermometers, plasma, and psychoanalysis most of the old phrases seem ludicrous and have fallen into disuse. *Hot-blooded* (*Why, the hot-blooded France, that dowerless took/ Our youngest born . . .*) is not much heard any more, but *cold-blooded,* describing the deliberate and cruel performance of some unpleasant act, is still common. To act *in cold blood* is tedious through repetition and meaningless to most who use it.

cold light of reason (a little chillier than *the pale cast of thought*) is often the dawn of *the morning after* for those who have *looked on the wine when it was red* or *loved not wisely but too well.* One cliché merely follows another.

cold shoulder. As a term for letting someone know that he is not wanted, *give the cold shoulder* has been so restricted by usage in recent years to the discouragement of amatory advances that the phrase is assumed to describe a female shoulder coldly or disdainfully shrugged or drawn away in distaste. It derives, however, from the custom of offering honored guests hot meat and serving those who had outstayed their welcome with a cold shoulder of mutton. This became proverbial and overuse has made it a cliché. It should be used with care.

collaborate together. Since *collaborate* means to work, one with another, *collaborate together* is redundant.

collation. See **repast.**

collective nouns. Strictly speaking, a collective is a singular noun with a plural meaning. But the term is used loosely by many grammarians and may be applied to almost any noun that is not clearly singular or clearly plural.

There are three ways in which a noun may be singular in one respect and plural in another. These are discussed in this dictionary under the following heads.

1. GROUP NAMES. Some nouns, such as *jury, family, herd,* name a group of separate individuals. When such a group is thought of as a unit, the group name is followed by a singular verb, as in *my family is a large one.* When the group is thought of as a number of individuals, a plural verb is used, as in *my family are early risers.* Words of this kind are sometimes called nouns of multitude. See **group names.**

2. GENERIC NOUNS. A singular noun may be used in speaking of all the individuals of a certain kind, as in *the whale is a mammal* and *man is mortal.* See **generic nouns.**

3. MASS NOUNS. Some nouns, such as *butter, milk, clothes, munitions, riches,* are neither singular nor plural in meaning but name an un-

differentiated whole. Words of this kind that have a singular form are usually followed by a singular verb. Words of this kind that have a plural form are usually followed by a plural verb but are treated in other respects as singulars. See **mass nouns.**

The difference between these three classes of words is not always clear. Mass nouns are used generically more often than not and some generic singulars are indistinguishable from group names. For this reason, many grammarians use the term *collective noun* to mean all three classes. Many others limit the term to what is called in this dictionary *group names.*

Some grammarians include as collectives the name of any whole made up of similar parts, such as *chain, library, forest*. This is a philosophical distinction, not a grammatical one. Words of this kind have no grammatical peculiarities and nothing is gained by putting them in a special class. Some grammarians also list as collectives any noun that has the same form in the singular and the plural, such as *deer* and *grouse*. But words of this kind are true singulars and true plurals. They have no peculiarities beyond the fact that the plural is formed irregularly. In this book a word like *deer* is considered as two forms, one singular and one plural, which happen to be alike.

college. See **university.**

colloquialisms. Colloquial English does not mean English that is not standard. It means the accepted spoken idiom, in contrast to a formal, literary idiom. A grammar published in 1930 lists *do you have swordfish?* as a colloquial construction; the literary form is given as *have you swordfish?* Many of the best contemporary writers and public speakers use colloquial English by preference. They avoid literary forms that could not be used in conversation.

It used to be said that colloquial English was like a good business suit and literary English like formal dress. The analogy still holds. But one should remember that times have changed, that a good business suit is seldom out of place, and that formal dress, where it is not required— at a picnic, for example—may be ridiculous.

collusion; connivance. *Collusion* is secret agreement for fraudulent purpose. It is sometimes confused with *collaboration* but men act in collaboration for good ends, in collusion for bad (*The judge said that the witnesses were in collusion and dismissed the case*).

Connivance implies winking at wrongdoing, assenting to it guiltily, although without taking any active part in it. The word derives from a Latin word meaning to shut the eyes. Men are in collusion. They connive at it.

colon. The colon is used almost exclusively for formal writing. Its main function is to call attention to what follows. It is used:

1. To introduce ideas in a series after an introductory phrase, as in *these are the main exports: metals, primarily iron, copper and tin; grains, primarily wheat; and cotton.*

2. To introduce formally any subject, as in *Mr. Brown moved that the following question*

be referred to the Committee: What are the effects of zoning laws on downtown building activity?*

3. To introduce a quotation of a full sentence or more, as in *in his previous book the author stated: (Quotation follows).*

4. Between clauses when the second summarizes or restates the first, as in *in spite of the politicians, it is the people who will finally decide the issue: they have always been the deciding factor ultimately.*

5. After the salutation in a formal letter, as in *Dear Sir:* (In some European countries an exclamation point is used after the salutation in a formal letter, and a comma in informal letters.)

6. In formal bibliographies, between author and title, between place of publication and publisher, and between volume and page, as in *Keynes, John Maynard: A Treatise on Probability. London: Macmillan and Co., 1921* and *Foreign Affairs 32:353.*

7. To show clock time, as in *4:30 p.m.*

8. To show proportions, as in *The paint should be mixed 1:4.*

Either a capital letter or a lower-case letter may be used after a colon. If a full sentence follows the colon, it generally starts with a capital, as in *The following result was reported: Unanimous agreement was reached by the Council after a very short discussion period.* But we write *the result: unanimous agreement.*

When a colon follows an abbreviation there is no period before the colon, as in *he took the following courses while studying for his M.A: history, psychology, anthropology. . . .*

A dash should not be used after a colon. In informal writing the dash can often take the place of the colon, but the two are no longer used together.

colored. As a euphemism for Negro, *colored* sometimes has an element of condescension. It is not usually intended to be an offensive word, for it carries a plain intention of politeness.

In the Union of South Africa *colored* is the official description of the man with mixed blood. No Bantu is there ever called colored; no man with a dark skin, not a full-blooded Negro, is there ever called a Negro—as he would be in the United States. The white South Africans often use *colored* as a noun, referring to *a Colored*. This is resented by the educated among those so referred to, though they do not feel so strongly when the word is used as an adjective. See **African, Creole, mulatto, Negro.**

colossal. That is properly *colossal* which is like a colossus—of vast size, gigantic, huge, enormous (*He was a man of colossal stature. Wagner's colossal dramas*).

As a mere intensive, however, (*a colossal liar*) with a suggestion of the amusing or absurd (*He was a colossal idiot*) the word is not standard, being a catchword picked up from the Germans among whom, in the nineteen twenties and thirties, *kolossal* superseded almost every other adjective of admiration and wonder.

colossus. The plural is *colossuses* or *colossi.*

combat; contest. A *contest* is a struggle for victory, a competition. It can be amicable and between friends. A *combat* is a fight. It is never amicable. When a sports writer refers to a football game as a *combat* he is, of course, choosing that word to imply that the game will be played with such determination to win on each side that it will have some of the qualities of a combat. But he should call it a *contest.* If it is a *combat,* it should not be allowed.

come. The past tense is *came.* The participle is *come.*

Come used as a past tense, as in *he come home last night,* may be heard today but it has been considered uneducated usage for more than four hundred years.

Come is often followed by a second verb which tells the purpose of the coming. This second verb may be an infinitive, as in *I come to bury Caesar, not to praise him,* or it may be part of a clause, as in *I am come that they might have life.* The form with the clause is now archaic and the infinitive construction is preferred.

Come may be joined to a following verb with *and,* as in *they came and had supper with us* and *they always come and see us when they are in town.* Here the second verb may or may not show the purpose of the coming.

Formerly, *come* might be followed by the simple form of a verb without *to* or *and,* as in *come live with me and be my love.* This construction is still standard in the United States under certain circumstances. It may be used when *come* itself is an imperative, as in *come have supper with us,* or when *come* is dependent on some verb other than *be* or *have.* For example, *come* is dependent on *will* in *will you come have supper,* and on *want* in *I want you to come have supper.* This construction cannot be used when *come* is a simple present tense, as in *I come bury Caesar,* or is compounded with *be* or *have,* as in *he has come bury Caesar.* (To say it technically, the simple form of the verb can be used only when *come* itself is an imperative or an infinitive.) The old forms without *to,* which are acceptable in the United States, are not considered standard now in Great Britain where an *and* is required to weaken the idea of purpose, as in *come and have supper.*

Come may be followed by an adjective. This is especially true when *come* is used as the equivalent of the verb *to be,* as in *it comes natural to me,* or the verb *become,* as in *it came undone.* But it is also true when *come* is used with its regular meaning, as in *come down heavy on the cast iron drill.*

How come is a survival from an older literary form. At one time, the normal way to form a question was to place the verb before its subject, as in *what went ye out into the wilderness to see?* Today we use the verb *do* for this purpose, as in *what did you go to see.* But the old question form may still be used with *how come.* When *come* has a personal subject, the expression is followed by an infinitive, as in *how came you to be there.* When used in the present tense without a subject, the construction is impersonal, meaning *how comes it,* and is followed by a clause, as in *how comes you were there.* Both constructions are standard in the United States today. An impersonal construction without *s,* as in *how come you were there,* does not have the same standing. It is used in speech but not in writing.

come to grief. *Grief,* which is now restricted to meaning mental suffering or distress over affliction or loss, was formerly a much broader term, including physical pain (in his famous catechism on honor Falstaff asks if honor can *take away the grief of a wound*). And it is this, now forgotten, meaning of *grief* that is in the cliché *to come to grief,* to come to disaster—as in *only his glasses came to grief; he revives! what relief!*

come to the end of one's rope (or **tether**). Whether this figure for having exhausted one's resources comes, as some aver, from a grazing horse or, as others say, from the hangman's rope, *to come to the end of one's rope* (or *tether*) is a cliché and should be used sparingly.

comforter. Men seek comfort in different ways. A *comforter* in England is a woolen scarf for wrapping around the neck in cold weather. In America a *comforter* is a quilted bedcover (*She pulled back the comforter and smoothed the blankets*).

comic and **comical** are almost, but not quite, synonymous. Both mean provoking laughter, amusing, funny (though even here *comical* has a slightly different application sometimes, meaning quaint, in a tender way: *such a comical little face*). But *comic* alone, now, means of or pertaining to the nature of comedy; *comical* in that sense is now obsolete. See also **funny.**

comic strips. In an article entitled "Why 100,-000,000 Americans Read Comics," published in 1943 in *The American Scholar,* William Moulton Marston stated that in the "comics" or adventure strip American literature has reached a zenith of popularity never before achieved by any form of reading matter. Eighteen million comic magazines are sold on the newsstands every month and devoured, it is estimated, by 70,000,000 or more readers, at least half of whom are adults. In addition, Moulton goes on to say, approximately one and one-half *billion* copies of four- or five-panel comic strips are circulated every week in the daily newspapers. Of the nation's sizable dailies only two, the *New York Times* and the *Christian Science Monitor,* are without comics. *Life* believes that comic strips comprise "the most significant body of literature in America today," since they are read diligently by over 50% of the nation's adults and perhaps 90% of the children who can read.

The astonishing thing, however, is that despite this enormous number of readers, the comic strips have had very little noticeable effect on our speech and practically none on our writing. H. L. Mencken, with his customary zeal to support what he regarded as the unconventional, declared in his First Supplement to the *American Language*, that the comic-strip artist "had been a very diligent maker of terse and dramatic words." But of the illustrations that he quotes (*zowie, bam, socko, yurp, plop, wow, wam, glug, oof, ulk, whap, bing, flooie* and *grr*) less than half were originated in the comic strips and of those that were originated there, few if any have passed into the language as words. Never has so much balderdash been written so repeatedly for so many with so little lasting effect.

Since comic strips are in the dramatic mode (consisting of speech, actions, and stage directions and noises), there are inevitably a large number of exclamations. For the most part, though, despite the location of an increasing amount of their action in the future, amid interstellar dangers and villains, these exclamations tend to be a little old-fashioned—such as *man!, golly, gosh, oh boy, whee, yipe, Jumpin' Jupiter* and *dagnabit*. One feels that their creators have kept not only the spirit but the dull lexicon of youth.

From all of this some two or three strips must be sharply excepted. The language of *Li'l Abner*, for instance, is a satire on the speech that sentimentality assigns to Southern rustics and the wonderful jargon of *Pogo* reflects not only an acute ear and a whimsical mind but an extraordinarily sensitive awareness of the shaping forces in our speech. And no criticism of the language of the comics can be made more trenchant than that which fills each issue of *Mad Comics*.

comity means courtesy. The Comity of Nations is that courtesy by which nations recognize and give effect within their own territories to the institutions and laws of other nations, or, by extension, the friendly code whereby nations get on together. One sometimes finds the word used as if it meant the French *comité*, party, or even committee.

command. This verb may be followed by an infinitive, as in *I command you to start at once*. It may also be followed by a clause but the clause verb must be a subjunctive or a subjunctive equivalent, as in *I command he go at once*.

commands. See **imperative mode** and **future tense.**

commas, together with colons and semicolons, were once used to show the grammatical relationship between different parts of a sentence. This is no longer true. In the United States today we use a comma to reflect a speech device, which sometimes shows grammatical relationship but sometimes does not. Anyone who learns to hear a comma can use it correctly ever after. The comma break can be identified by comparing the sentence *God rest you, merry gentlemen* with its old form *God rest you merry, gentlemen*. (Here *rest* means keep or cause to remain.) The comma is not a pause, but an abrupt change in pitch.

The most important fact about a comma is that there are places where it must not be used. That is, there are places where a comma alters the meaning of a statement. Max Beerbohm was being witty when he used a comma in writing about *Frank Harris, and many good writers.* There are also a few places where a comma must be used in order to protect the meaning. These significant uses of the comma are discussed below. In addition, there are a good many places where one can use a comma or not as one pleases. The tendency today is to cut these to a minimum. The best overall piece of advice on the use of commas is given by H. W. Fowler: "Any one who finds himself putting down several commas close to one another should reflect that he is making himself disagreeable, and question his conscience, as severely as we ought to do about disagreeable conduct in real life, whether it is necessary."

DOUBLE COMMAS

A pair of commas has very much the function of a parenthesis. Any parenthetical word, phrase, or clause, that is not actually part of the sentence, but more or less of an aside, should be set off by a pair of commas. This includes interrupting words, such as *he said*, exclamations, and the name of a person spoken to. When a parenthetical thought of this kind stands at the beginning or the end of a sentence, the first or the last comma is omitted, as in *She said, "It's late."* and *Are you coming, Dorothy?* Here only one comma appears, but it is functioning as one of a pair.

A word or group of words that repeats the meaning of a preceding word or word group is called an appositive, such as *America* in *this land of ours, America*. Appositives are usually set off by a pair of commas. Sometimes the relation between an appositive and the preceding noun is so close that the two form a unified idea, such as *the river Tiber* and *my brother Dick*. In this case commas are not needed and if they are used have the effect of making the appositive word seem like an explanation or an aside.

An antithetical or contrasting phrase that is not introduced by a conjunction is always enclosed in a pair of commas, as in *it was Stanley, not Jackie, who told me*.

A defining phrase or clause that is essential to the meaning of a preceding word, such as the last three words in *this is the house that Jack built*, must not be set off from the rest of the sentence by a pair of commas. Commas here signify that the words standing between them are not essential. A purely descriptive clause, that is, a clause that is not essential to the meaning, can always be placed between commas. When there is any danger that a descriptive clause will be understood as defining, the commas should be used. But otherwise they do not have to be. A writer who wants to tie the description tightly to the subject may omit the commas, as in *her hair that lay along her back was yellow like ripe corn*.

SINGLE COMMAS

A pair of commas mark an intrusion into a sentence and can occur at any point. The sentence itself stands as if the enclosed words did not exist. But a single comma affects the sentence itself. It is always a signal that the words it stands between are independent of each other.

1. A single comma is often required to prevent misreading. For example, a comma is required in *not long after, he was taken sick* although none is needed in *a week later he was taken sick*. Words such as *only* and *rather* which sometimes qualify a preceding word may need a comma to keep them from qualifying a following word instead, as in *men only, were invited*. A comma may also be needed to keep a qualifying clause from becoming attached to the nearest available word. See **clauses**.

2. A comma should not come between a verb and its object, as it does in *Job cursed, the day that he was born*. See **object of a verb**.

3. A single comma that stands between a verb and its subject is generally considered poor punctuation. But sometimes this cannot be avoided. It cannot be avoided when words such as *only* follow and qualify the subject. And no one should feel that he must place a word of this kind before the subject merely to avoid a punctuation problem. A comma may be required when the subject is a full clause, as in *whatever is, is right*. Very often a single comma separating a subject and a verb can be interpreted as the second in a pair of commas, of which the first has been omitted, as in *the moonlight sparkling on the frosty window, reminded him of the wide fields*. This is considered faulty punctuation, to be corrected by adding a comma after *moonlight* or by removing the comma after *window*. But it is an extremely common error. Most people who write punctuate in just this way and the first comma is added later by an editor or a typist.

4. Commas are used in a series. That is, they are used to set off words or groups of words that have the same function, as in *Mr. Close, Mr. Black, and Mr. Jeter, were there*. The first comma in this series is required but the comma before *and* and the comma that closes the series are optional. People who are interested in punctuation are likely to have very strong feelings about the comma before *and* in a series. But they are evenly divided for and against it. A sensible person will use this comma or not as he pleases, and will refuse to argue the point with anybody.

When more than one adjective qualifies a noun in exactly the same way, they are treated as a series and separated by commas, as in *cheerful, friendly, clever Mildred*. Here the final element in the series is never followed by a comma. See **position of adjectives**.

5. It used to be said that two clauses joined by *and, or, nor, but,* or *for,* required a comma before the conjunction. If the conjunction was not actually used but only "understood," the comma was considered insufficient and a semicolon was required. Today we frequently omit the comma before these conjunctions, and we use a comma rather than a semicolon when there is no conjunction expressed, as in *beautiful is the mother, beautiful is her son*.

6. Any words which come before the subject of a verb may be set off by a comma. If the phrase is short, the comma may be used or omitted. But when a great many words precede the subject, they should be followed by a comma in order to make the subject of the verb stand out clearly. When a clause is actually the complement of some form of the verb *to be*, it too may be preceded by a comma, as in *the truth is, he is lazy*. Technically, this comma separates a verb and its complement. But it is necessary here to separate *he* from the preceding verb so that it is free to unite with the verb that follows.

7. A comma may be used to show that certain words have been omitted, usually words that have already been used earlier in the sentence, as in *one paid for the dinner and the other, for the entertainment*. See **ellipsis**.

TYPOGRAPHICAL USES

The comma has certain uses that have nothing to do with sentence structure.

1. The comma is used to divide large numbers into groups of three figures each, as in *4,910,358*. It is not used in a number which represents a particular year, such as *1956*. Some publishers do not use a comma in any number that has less than five figures and would write *4910*. In some European countries a period is used instead of a comma to group the figures, and a comma is used to represent the decimal point, as in *49.103,58*.

2. A comma is used in dates to separate the day of the month from the year, as in *October 29, 1929*. If a date is incorporated in a sentence, the number of the year is enclosed in a pair of commas, as in *October 29, 1929, was a busy day*. If the number of the year follows immediately after the name of the month, no punctuation is required, as in *October 1929 marked the end of an epoch*.

3. The comma is used to set off parts of an address when these are used in a sentence, as in *Tom is living in Franklin, Warren Co., Ohio, at present*.

4. It is used in bibliographies, indexes, and wherever words or phrases are listed in an inverted order, as in *Butler, Samuel* and *Way of All Flesh, The*.

5. It is used to set off the salutation in an informal letter, as in *Dear Blanche,* and to set off the complimentary close in any letter, whether informal or formal, as in *Your friend,* and *Sincerely yours,*

6. A comma is not used in combination with a dash.

7. If the word immediately before a parenthesis needs to be separated from the rest of the sentence by a comma, the comma is placed after the parenthesis, as in *if Joe is right (and he usually is), we can't finish the work today*.

commence may be followed by the *-ing* form of a verb, as in *he commenced studying law*, or by an infinitive, as in *he commenced to study law*. The *-ing* construction is preferred by some people who feel that *begin* should be used if an infinitive is to follow, as in *he began to study law*. See **begin**.

comment (noun). See **remark**.

commentator. It was probably inevitable that the people who make critical or explanatory remarks about news events over the radio should have chosen to be called *commentators* rather than *commenters*. It is more grandiloquent. A *commenter* (no such word exists in standard usage) would have been one who made comments. A *commentator* is one who makes commentaries and a commentary is an expository treatise consisting of a systematic series of comments. It's a pity the news commentators burdened themselves with such delusions of grandeur, especially since ninety percent of them only read the news anyway. You can hear them stumbling over the hard words.

commit may be followed by an infinitive, as in *I have committed myself to go,* or by the *-ing* form of a verb introduced by the preposition *to,* as in *I have committed myself to going.* Some grammarians object to the use of an infinitive here and claim that only the *-ing* form is acceptable. But both constructions are standard in the United States.

common. See **average; frequent; mutual.**

common; ordinary; vulgar. *Common* means possessed or shared by all alike (*Venus,* says Robert Burton, *was as common as a barber's chair*). When applied to persons it usually has a derogatory connotation of cheapness or inferiority. *Vulgar* means belonging to the people and the meaning attached to it depends on how you view belonging to the common people. The common people themselves (though they probably do not view themselves as such) obviously don't think much of it, since to them *vulgar* means coarse, indecent (*His talk was just vulgar. I was ashamed to be with him*). To a few uncommon intellectuals (who are, no doubt, tired of intellectuals) *vulgar* often means strong in a coarse way (*He had a vulgar virility that offset his coarse greed*). *Ordinary* means what is to be expected in the usual order of things. It is slightly derogatory, but not much; just a tired admission from the sad wisdom of experience that the usual order of things, so far as human beings go, isn't much.

common noun. Any noun that is not a proper noun (that is, any noun that is not the name of a particular person or thing) is a common noun.

common or garden variety. Whoever first took this phrase from a seed catalog (It happened about 1895) and applied it figuratively deserved, and it is to be hoped obtained, applause for a sprightly wit. But it is now a common, or garden, variety of cliché, the bloom withered, the root broken and the stem pawed to a limp shred.

commonplace; banal; hackneyed; stereotyped; trite. *Commonplace* means ordinary and, hence, dull and uninteresting. Before the romantic admiration of the *un*ordinary, commonplace was often used to signify something that was particularly interesting because it had a general or common application. Thus gentlemen of leisure kept *Commonplace Books* in which they copied passages of unusual interest and philosophic breadth that they came across in their reading.

Banal was a French word meaning commonplace. It had originally been a feudal term meaning communal. It was borrowed in the nineteenth century by English literary critics (who, as Fowler growls, had a dozen good words at home to choose from) and carries not only the meaning of *commonplace* but also the contempt for the commonplace felt by such superior people as those who borrowed it. It means inane, insipid, and hollowly pretentious.

A *hackney* was originally "an ambling horse, for ladies to ride on," then a horse for hire, then a horse used in coaches that were for hire (whence our *hack*). These horses were worn out and jaded and by a natural figurative extension the word was used to describe phrases that were worn out and jaded by overuse.

Stereotyped emphasizes the fact that that phrase or idea is the exact response that a certain situation evokes. It is an automatic response, totally devoid of any originality.

Trite derives from a Latin word meaning to rub. But in its current use it is not only something that has been rubbed smooth by use but something which, though originally profound or apt, has lost all freshness through repetition (*He was full of trite sayings*).

commonplace; platitude; triviality; truism; axiom. A *commonplace* is something regularly said on certain occasions (*All men must die*). It may be true or it may be false. It may be useful and sensible. The utterer of a commonplace does not seek the applause that is given to originality but the warmth that comes from the recognition of a common humanity and common experience.

A *platitude* is a dull, trite remark uttered as if it were original and important. The utterer of platitudes expects the admiration accorded to wisdom and gets the contempt reserved for pompous folly.

A *triviality* is some trifling or insignificant remark uttered as if it were just suited to the occasion. It gains the utterer the reputation of being silly.

A *truism* is a self-evident or obvious truth, something which is incontrovertible in itself (Thus *We all ought to do our duty* is a truism because our duty is that which we ought to do). It is something which is indisputably true, needs no proof, and can't be contradicted, yet which is often uttered in a positive, almost aggressive manner, as if the speaker regarded it as a daring proposition and was prepared to defend it against all attack. Such a statement is often followed by a brief silence, not, as the speaker seems to think, of awe at its profundity, but of bewilderment at its being spoken at all.

An *axiom* is an established and universally accepted rule or principle. It is stated, with the full understanding that everyone assents to it, as the beginning of a chain of reasoning.

compact (agreement). See **pact.**

companionable; companionate. *Companionable* means sociable, fitted to be a companion (*He was a companionable fellow, ideal to have along on a camping trip*). *Companionate,* recognized in British dictionaries only as an obsolete word meaning companioned or accompanied, is used in America to mean of, by or like companions, especially in the phrase *companionate marriage*, a form of trial marriage advocated, particularly in the late nineteen-twenties, by certain social reformers (*Since a companionate marriage is to be a childless marriage, it may be questioned how far it will give true marriage a fair trial*).

company. Though *company* as a term for a guest or guests is often classified as questionable by purists, it has been standard English for many centuries (Jeremy Taylor, 1649: *They had more company than wine*. Samuel Johnson, 1775: *Hector had company in his house*). It is standard in current American usage (*We had company and I couldn't get away*) and has been extended in many adjectival uses, such as *company manners* (meaning the more formal deportment appropriate when one has guests).

comparative degree. See **comparison of adjectives and adverbs.**

comparatively; relatively. Since *comparatively* definitely implies a comparison, a careful speaker or writer does not employ it except when he has a fairly definite comparison in mind. That is, he would not say *the weather was comparatively mild* if he only meant that it was fairly mild, though he might say that *after the unseasonable cold of last September, October was comparatively mild*.

Relatively, similarly, has to mean standing in relation to something. This something does not always have to be explicitly stated; it may be implied or generally understood. But it should be there. *Relatively* should not be used as a mild intensive.

compare; contrast. To *compare* things is to bring them together in order to note points of likeness or of difference. In this sense it is followed by *with*. *He compared Washington with Paris* would mean that he considered various aspects of both cities with a view to pointing out wherein they differed and wherein they were alike. To *compare* also means to represent as similar (*Shall I compare thee to a summer's day?*); and in this sense it is followed by *to*. *He compared Washington to Paris* would mean that he found many things in Washington which, when taken together, made him feel that the city of Washington was much like the city of Paris. *Incomparable* has this meaning of *compare*; it does not mean that nothing can be compared *with* the person or object, but that nothing can be compared *to* them. *Incomparable* almost always has a favorable connotation; the comparison cannot be made because the thing alluded to is unique and superior.

To *contrast* is to examine with an eye to differences, or to place things together in such a way that their differences are obvious (*He contrasted the luxury of the aristocrat with the penury of the peasant*).

comparison of adjectives and adverbs. In making a comparison we may say that the things compared are equal in some respect or we may say that they are unequal. In a comparison of equality we use *as* and the simple form of an adjective or adverb. The simple form of an adjective or adverb is called the positive form. In a comparison of inequality we use a modified form of the word. There are two such forms. One is called the comparative and the other, the superlative.

FORMATION

We make the comparative form of an adjective or adverb by adding the syllable *-er* to the positive, and the superlative form by adding the syllable *-est*, as in *green, greener, greenest*. A few words are compared irregularly, such as *good, better, best*, and *bad, worse, worst*. All these have been listed in this dictionary under the positive form.

We may qualify the positive form by *more* or *less* and make what is equivalent to a comparative, or by *most* or *least* and make what is equivalent to a superlative. In order to say that one thing is inferior to others in some respect, we must use the qualified form with *less* or *least*. In saying that something is superior to others we sometimes use the qualified form with *more* or *most* and sometimes the regular inflected form ending in *-er* or *-est*. The inflected form is native English. It is still considered the more natural and more vigorous of the two and is always used in vivid or excited speech. The form with *more* or *most* is due chiefly to French influence and did not come into general use until about four hundred years ago.

The qualified form, with *more* and *most*, is required with (1) adverbs ending in *-ly;* (2) any word that can only be used predicatively, such as *afraid, aware, content;* (3) the word *eager;* (4) words that have an unusual or foreign form, such as *antique, burlesque, bizarre*. Otherwise, either form may be used, as in *louder still and still more loud* and *among all forlornest things, the most forlorn*.

As a rule, the inflected form is preferred for short words, especially those ending in *-d, -t, -r,* or *-y*, such as *loud, soft, clear, happy*. The form using *more* or *most* is preferred for longer words, especially those ending in (1) more than one unstressed syllable, such as *tyrannical;* (2) *-ive* or *-ile*, such as *active* and *hostile;* (3) *-s, -ish,* or *-est*, such as *curious, foolish, honest;* or (4) *-ed* or *-ing*, such as *crooked* and *cunning*. It is also preferred for words that are not often used in comparisons, such as *real, right, just*. But this is a description of what usually happens, not of what must happen. Mark Twain wrote: *the confoundedest, brazenest, ingeniousest piece of fraud*. And words such as *wonderfulest, honestest, crookedest, lovingest, rightest*, are also used occasionally in solemn prose.

When the *more* and *most* forms were less well established than they are now, they were often used with the older inflected forms, as in *the most unkindest cut of all*. This obvious double comparative, or double superlative, is not considered standard now.

MEANING

The comparative and superlative are forms used in comparing individuals in respect to a certain quality The superlative form does not indicate a higher degree of the quality than the comparative, and neither indicates more than is expressed by the positive form. The oldest child in the family may be very young. And we speak of *older men* and *dresses for larger women* in order to avoid the really strong words *old men* and *large women.*

Any quality in respect to which individuals can be compared may logically have a comparative and a superlative form. But it is sometimes claimed that certain adjectives should not be used in making a comparison. A protest of this kind may be based on either of two very different lines of reasoning.

There are certain words in English, such as *perfect, extreme, excellent,* which imply "in the highest degree." These words are sometimes qualified by *more* or *most,* as in *a more perfect example, the most extreme point of view.* Theoretically, such expressions are comparable to *more best, most worst.* But only theoretically. In practice words of this kind, which have a superlative meaning but not an obvious superlative form, have always been used in this way and the construction is standard literary English. Those who object to it do so because they feel that to use *more* or *most* with such words is to debase their meaning.

There are other words, sometimes called *absolutes,* which have no such superlative meaning but which, on the contrary, name characteristics that do not exist in degrees, such as *unique, complete, equal.* It is argued that words of this kind cannot be used in a comparison because, for a thing to possess the quality at all it must possess it completely, and therefore all things that possess the quality possess it equally. This argument disregards the facts of life. In this world we constantly do, and must, compare things in respect to qualities which, as seen from Olympus, they do not possess. We can and do say *this is squarer than that, make them more equal, this is more accurate, this is most singular. Unique* and *complete* are not in a class by themselves, and lists which begin with these words grow rapidly. One grammarian has noticed that *chaste* must be included. But there is no reason to stop there. *True, false, logical, empty,* should also be included. In fact this theory, if it was applied consistently, would make it impossible for us to think about anything but the most obvious facts.

Sometimes the argument against *more unique* or *more complete* is misunderstood and put on the grounds that we cannot have "more" of either of these characteristics than is expressed by the positive form of the word. It is said that *less unique* is permissible, but not *more unique.* This is not true. *Less* implies degrees as much as *more* does. And we can never have "more" of a quality than is expressed by the positive form of the word. Nothing can be smaller than small, older than old, or whiter than white. (We express something approaching this with *more than,* as in *you are more than kind* and *my dear friend, my more than brother.* But here the *more than* is obviously something other than *kind* or *brother,* and the expression means

"words fail me." Certainly no comparison is being made.)

Attacks on grammatical constructions made in the name of logic are usually bad logic. And they are always bad linguistics. The only question that has any bearing on the propriety of a form of speech is: *Is it in reputable use?* And the answer here is that educated people do say *more unique* and *more complete.* If they didn't, these expressions would not be under attack so often. We do not at present say *more previous,* and so it does not occur to anyone to list these words among the things that we ought to avoid.

USES

In Latin the comparative form is used in a comparison involving two things and the superlative in a comparison involving more than two. Some grammarians claim that this ought to be the rule in English too, but the practice of our best writers does not bear them out. Lamb wrote: *of two disputants, the warmest is generally in the wrong.* We all say *put your best foot forward* and *if you tangle with him you'll get the worst of it.* Shakespeare, Addison, Johnson, Goldsmith, Chesterfield, Ruskin, Emerson, Hawthorne, Irving, Scott, Thackeray, all used the superlative in speaking of two only, as do many contemporary writers. In contemporary American English, only the comparative form can be used with *than,* regardless of how many things are being spoken about; and in any other construction, again regardless of the number involved, the superlative is generally preferred.

A comparison made with the comparative form and *than* is said to be *self-exclusive.* That is, the thing compared is put in contrast to the thing or things it is compared with, as in *he is taller than the others.* A comparison made with the superlative, on the other hand, is usually *self-inclusive.* That is, the *of* has almost the force of *among* and the thing compared is seen as part of the group spoken about, as in *he is the tallest of the lot.* This was not always true. Formerly the superlative with *of* could also be used in a contrast, as in *this trade is held the most honorable of all others.* Today we would be more likely to say *more honorable than all others* or *most honorable of all.* But the old construction is still heard occasionally, as in *it was the richest of any university in America.*

The superlative may be used as a pure intensive, with no comparison intended, as in *the rudest remark, a most beautiful woman.* But we more often use a colorful adverb and the positive form of the adjective for this purpose, as in *an extremely rude remark, an astonishingly beautiful woman.* To indicate a moderate degree of some quality we always use the positive form and a belittling qualifier, such as *fairly, rather, somewhat, tolerably.*

The word *the* is sometimes used with a comparative form. If two individuals are being compared, this *the* is a simple adjective, as in *Shelley's intellect was far the keener.* What is meant here is *the keener intellect.* But *the* is often used with a comparative form where this is not the case, as in *he will feel the better for it.*

Here *the* is an adverb of degree and means "that much." In literary English this adverbial *the* is not used unless something else is said somewhere in the context that has a bearing on "that much." For this reason, adverbial *the* is sometimes called a conjunction. The "something else" may refer to the cause of the increase, as *for it* in the example given; or it may refer to the amount. The amount is frequently "none" or "all," as in *none the worse* and *all the better.* Sometimes a double adverbial *the* is used to show that two increases are equal, as in *the more the merrier, the more he gets the more he wants.* A comparative form should not be used with both *the* and *than.* The adjective *the* requires or implies *of,* as in *the keener of the two, the keener man.* Adverbial *the* merely indicates that additional information is available, and is never used in making a comparison. A *the* which serves neither function should not be used, as it is in *if you are not the politer I will slap you.*

Sometimes a comparison of equality, requiring *as . . . as,* and a comparison of inequality, requiring *than,* are combined in the same statement, as in *he had as much or more trouble than I did* and *he had more or at least as much trouble as I did.* In both cases the comparisons have been telescoped. In the first sentence a second *as,* needed for a comparison of equality, has been lost. In the second sentence a *than,* needed for the inequality, is lost. Some grammarians object to telescoped constructions of this kind, but they are acceptable, and customary, English. If one wants to please the grammarians he can avoid the problem by writing, for example, *he had as much trouble as I did, or more.*

There are a number of words in English ending in *-ior,* such as *superior, inferior, posterior, interior, senior,* which are Latin comparatives. In English they are not felt as comparatives and may be qualified by *more* or *less.* But they may also be used alone in making comparisons. When they are, they require the preposition *to* and not the conjunction *than.*

A few words, such as *former, latter, elder, inner, upper,* are English comparative forms that are no longer used in making comparisons. They are now felt as simple adjectives which name a relationship and describe or identify individuals. We may say *the latter period, the elder man,* but we cannot say *this period is latter than, this man is elder than.*

comparisons are odious is a proverb, and no wise man would agree to exclude proverbs from his speech or writing. But he will take care to use them sparingly and only when the occasion calls without doubt for their use. This one is hackneyed—though of course its wisdom is profound and useful. That *comparisons are odorous* is from *Much Ado About Nothing* and no wise man will attempt to cheat Shakespeare of whatever honor there is in its wit.

compasses. In referring to an instrument for drawing circles, the singular form *compass* may be used, as in *fix one foot of the compass here,* and the plural *compasses* in speaking of several such instruments, as in *we have three compasses.* But the plural form is also used in speaking of one instrument, as in *fix one foot of the compasses here,* and three instruments are called *three pairs of compasses.* Both constructions are standard English today. Only the singular form *compass* is used as the first element in a compound, as in *a compass leg.*

compel; impel. *Compel* and *impel* both mean the application of a force, physical or otherwise, to cause something to be done. *Compel* has now more the sense of coercion, of constraining someone to do something which he does not want to do (*The failure of the bank compelled them to retrench severely and to adopt a wholly different way of living*). To *impel* is to urge forward (*The wave behind impelled the wave before*) and in all figurative uses it has the sense of constraining or inciting towards a goal (*A sense of duty impels me to speak in favor of the measure*). Both words may be followed by an infinitive, as in *he compelled her to lead a dreary life,* but not by the *-ing* form of a verb. We cannot say *he compelled her to leading a dreary life.*

compendious means concise, or containing the substance of a subject in brief form (*A dictionary is a compendious work*). It is sometimes misused, perhaps because of the similarity of its sound to *stupendous* and *tremendous,* to mean a large book or treatise. A *compendious* work may be large or small, but its compendiousness has nothing to do with its size.

compendium. The plural is *compendiums* or *compendia.*

compensate; compensation. To *compensate* is to counterbalance, to offset, to make up for. The application of the term to payment for services rendered was originally a stilted piece of elaborate politeness, a way of saying "Of course we wouldn't do anything so vulgar as to *pay* you; we offer this sum merely to offset the loss of your time." It is like calling a fee an honorarium, by which it is implied that the one offering the sum could not hope to pay what the speaker's time and wisdom are really worth and is making merely a token payment. In America the term *compensation* has been used so much for wages or salary that it is now standard in that sense, with none of the connotation of making amends for loss or damage (*The salaries of American judges are rather low in comparison with the compensation offered to judicial officers in Europe*) that it would have in English usage.

competent; competence. To be *competent* is to be properly qualified, to be adequate, to have abilities sufficient to the purpose. In regard to any great or difficult undertaking, it is plainly high praise to be competent; but in critical reviews, particularly of dramatic and musical performances, where superlatives are the rule, the word is almost condemnatory, meaning that the performer had abilities sufficient for the purpose but nothing more (*Smith's performance was competent but the applause of the evening was reserved for Jones*).

Competent may be followed by an infinitive.

as in *he is competent to judge,* or by *in* or *at* and the *-ing* form of a verb, as in *he is competent in judging.* In the first construction *competent* means "qualified." In the second, it means that he does it well.

Competence means adequacy, the quality of being competent. It has come also to have the special meaning of an income sufficient to furnish the necessities of life, without great luxury (*His competence as an artist was not enough to enable him to earn a living but, fortunately for him, he had inherited a competence and so had no great concern about money*).

compilation is a book made up of materials taken from a number of other books. In its central syllable the word is related to *pillage,* though it has been influenced by *pile* (to *pile up*). It is often misused to mean a symposium or a collection.

complacence; complaisance. To be *complacent* is to be pleased, especially with one's self. To be *complaisant* is to be affable, disposed to please others, obliging. The complacent are not always complaisant.

complected was once used to mean *complexioned,* as in *dark-complected Nancy Hanks.* The form is not standard.

complementary. See **supplementary.**

complement; compliment. A *complement* is that which completes or makes entire (*Travel is the complement of schooling*). In military and naval terminology it is the number of men required to fill out a company or man a conveyance (*The addition of the recruits brought the regiment up to its full complement*). It also means either of two parts or things needed to complete each other (*The physical and the spiritual are complements of the complete character*). See also **supplement.**

A *compliment* is an expression of praise (*She paid you a very high compliment*) or a formal act or expression of civility or courtesy (*He sends you his compliments and hopes that you will wait upon him this afternoon*). Except in the phrase *compliments of the season,* this use is now slightly archaic in America.

complement in grammar. The term is used by grammarians to mean any word or group of words that is needed to complete the meaning of a verb. This includes the direct object of a transitive verb. The complement of a linking verb is sometimes called a subjective complement. A noun or pronoun used as the complement of a linking verb, such as *rascal* in *he is a rascal,* may also be called a predicate nominative.

Some verb ideas are not complete without a word which stands after the direct object, such as *ladies* in *they consider themselves ladies* and *trustworthy* in *we found him trustworthy.* Words of this kind are sometimes called an objective complement and sometimes a predicate objective.

complete (verb). See **end.**

complete; entire; whole; total. That is *complete* which has all its parts, is fully developed or perfected. The word is applied to a process or purpose that has been carried to fulfillment. When Hamlet's father's ghost appeared *in complete steel,* it was fully clad in armor, to the last warlike detail.

Entire means whole, with the additional connotation of unbroken unity, of one piece, undivided and continuous (*He read the entire book at one sitting*).

Whole comprises the full quantity, extent, amount, or number, containing all the elements properly belonging, relating to a thing in its entirety (*He told us the whole procedure*).

Total means whole, but it conveys the idea of things added together to make up the whole (*The total of his indebtedness, even after all assets were considered, was immense*). See also **perfect.**

complete verbs. See **intransitive verbs.**

completed action tenses. See **perfect tenses.**

complex. The use of *complex* to mean a fixed idea or obsession (*He's got a perfect complex on the subject!*) is based on a misunderstanding of a technical term. In psychology the word means a group of related ideas, feelings, memories, and impulses which operate together and may be repressed or inhibited together. These groups of thoughts and feelings are not necessarily morbid or abnormal.

complex sentence. A sentence that contains a subordinate clause, such as *she'll be driving six white horses when she comes,* is called a complex sentence. See **sentences.**

compositor. See **typesetter.**

compound sentence. A sentence consisting of two or more simple sentences (*The night is dark and I am far from home*) is called a compound sentence. A sentence made up of two or more independent statements one or more of which is complex is called a *compound-complex sentence.* The independent elements in a compound sentence must be separated by a coordinating conjunction, a comma, or a semicolon. See **sentences.**

compound words. When two nouns stand together, the first may have exactly the force of an adjective and qualify the meaning of the second. This is the case, for example, in *a family affair.* Here *family* is felt as an adjective very much like *private.* That we feel the word in this way is shown by the fact that we can use an adverb before it, just as if it were an adjective, as in *a strictly family affair.* In the case of *sea horse* this is not true. Here the two nouns are felt as a single compound noun representing a single idea. As a rule, when two words are felt as one they are pronounced as one. In *a brown horse,* the word *horse* has its own accent or emphasis. But in *a sea horse* it loses some of this emphasis and is pronounced like the second syllable in a two-syllable word. Similarly, *man* has the emphasis belonging to an independent word in *an English man* but loses it entirely in *an Englishman.* It should also be noticed that an Englishman is a certain kind of man, but a sea horse is not a certain kind of horse.

Each of these factors may be considered in

deciding whether or not two nouns standing to-gether are actually one word. If the compound can be qualified by an adverb, most grammarians would say that the first element is an adjective. If the compound has one major accent, they would say that it is being treated as a single word. If the compound has a meaning different from the meaning of the two words taken separately, they would say that it is a single word.

Nouns are the principal but not the only parts of speech that form compounds. Adjectives may merge with nouns to form nouns. Here, if the two words actually merge the first element ceases to be felt as an adjective and cannot be qualified by an adverb. We may say *a perfectly black bird* but not *a perfectly blackbird*. On this principle *old age* is as much a single word as *blackbird*. We may say *an extremely old man* but we do not say *in extremely old age*. Similarly, different parts of speech may be merged to form adjectives or to form verbs. In each case, the same tests can be applied: how is the compound treated grammatically? how is it pronounced? and what does it mean?

The same principles are considered in deciding whether a compound should be written as one word or as two. But here the problem is additionally complicated by tradition or custom. *Sea horse* and *old age*, for example, should be written as two words simply because they always are written in this way. In general, pronunciation, or the accent that is given to a compound, is considered the most important factor in deciding how a word should be printed. How it is handled grammatically is considered the least important.

SOLID COMPOUNDS

1. A goldfish is not made of gold. A ladybird is not a bird. A butterfly is not made of butter and is not a fly. Words of this kind, that do not mean what the two parts considered separately would mean, are usually printed as solid compounds.

2. Words that have such a strong accent on the first element that the second element tends to disappear are always written as solid compounds, regardless of the meaning of the word. This principle is responsible for considerable confusion and variation in printing styles. Everybody pronounces *postman* as one word and *egg man* as two, and this is reflected in all dictionaries. But whether the man who delivers the milk is a *milkman* or a *milk man* depends on who is speaking. Everybody says *bookkeeper* and *book review*, but *bookcase* and *book end* vary. A writer should not consult a dictionary on questions of this kind but should listen carefully to his own speech. When in doubt, he should separate the words. In this way, at worst he will seem old-fashioned. But if he joins words that other people do not join, he may be unintelligible.

Style books sometimes give a great many rules for compounding, such as the number of syllables in the first word, or the grammatical relation between the words. It may be pointed out that *calfskin* is one word and *alligator skin*

two, or that *brick house* is two words and *brickwork* one. These rules frequently have as many exceptions as examples, and it will be found that in almost every case accent is the determining factor. Where it is not, there is no agreement between one style book and another and it would be better to leave the words separated.

The practice of combining all word pairs that have a single major accent sometimes makes for difficult reading. *Counterattraction* and *counterespionage* undoubtedly have a forward accent, but they are unwieldy words. And the accent in this case is intended to emphasize *counter*, not to submerge it. Both the meaning and the emphasis would be reflected better in *counter attraction*. However, in present practice these and similar combinations are written as one word.

3. Sometimes words that have neither a special meaning nor a one-word accent are joined simply because they are like some other combination that is joined. For example, *cow hand* may be written as one word because *cowboy* is. If this occurs often enough in print the compound will find its way into dictionaries. But if this practice should become the rule it would cover almost all the normal combinations in English, and for this reason particular instances of it should be considered mistakes, no matter where they are found. See also **prefixes** and **suffixes**.

HYPHENATED COMPOUNDS

1. The hyphen is used when two normally distinct functions are united in one person or thing, as in *secretary-treasurer, fighter-bomber, manic-depressive*. Double terms that represent a single office, such as *major general*, are not hyphenated. Compound color terms are sometimes hyphenated and sometimes not. We may write *blue-black* or *blue black*. When nationality names are combined the first word is often modified, as in *Anglo-American, Franco-German*. But the simple forms, *English-American, French-German*, and so forth, are also used today.

2. English has a great many verbs that carry a preposition or adverb with them, such as *flare up, take off, set to*. (See **adverbs**.) These are separate words, but when nouns or adjectives are made from them they are always hyphenated, as in *a flare-up, a lean-to, a go-between, broken-down cars, built-up shoes*. Similar nouns and adjectives are sometimes made from a verb and its object, as in *know-all, do-nothing*.

Words of this kind have the specialized meaning that would justify writing them as one word, but the second element does not lose its individual accent. They are therefore hyphenated. If the second element does lose its accent, the word is written as a solid compound, as in *a setup*. Accordingly *makeup* would be one word, and is so written by some publishers, but others make an exception and keep the hyphen after a silent *e*.

3. A noun with a qualifying word, such as *kind heart, horn rim*, may be made into an adjective by adding -*ed* to the noun, as in *kind-*

hearted, horn-rimmed, saber-toothed. Compounds of this kind are usually hyphenated, on the grounds that they are here being treated as a single word. But if the first element is the comparative or superlative form of an adjective, this interpretation will not hold and the hyphen must be omitted, as in *kinder hearted, kindest hearted.* See **adjectives as adverbs.**

When the past participle of a verb is qualified by a noun or by an adjective-like word, it too is usually hyphenated, as in *air-borne, new-born,* perhaps because these words are so much like the ones just discussed. The adverb *well* is often treated as if it were an adjective and joined to a past participle with a hyphen, as in *well-kept, well-guarded.* The hyphens in these constructions serve no purpose, but it is customary to use them here. Adverbs ending in *-ly* are not treated in this way. They are usually written without the hyphen, as in *newly born, nicely kept.*

4. Fractions and compound numerals such as *two-thirds* and *twenty-three* are usually hyphenated. There is no need for this hyphen either, but it is customary to use one. When one of the terms of a fraction is a compound number, the hyphen which indicates a fraction is dropped, as in *two twenty-thirds, twenty-three thirtieths.*

5. Compounds beginning with *self* are often hyphenated, as in *self-control, self-service, self-support.* Some publishers, however, print these as two words, as in *self support.*

6. When a suffix or prefix is added to an idea that is expressed in two or more words, the whole expression is joined by hyphens. The result is awkward looking, but the expressions themselves are awkward. Example: *Christmas-tree-like, an ex-college-professor.*

7. A hyphen is also used whenever it is needed to prevent ambiguity. This is an important rule. But its application depends on what we consider ambiguous.

Style books often list *walking stick* or *dining room* as a type of word that requires a hyphen. The *-ing* form of a verb may be a noun or it may be an adjective. (See **-ing.**) We have a great many compounds in English in which the first element is an *-ing* noun, such as *sleeping car, drinking glass, landing field, fainting fits, the boiling point.* What is meant in compounds of this sort is *a stick for walking, a room for dining, the point of boiling,* and so on—as practically everybody knows. But it is theoretically possible to read these words as adjectives. Some editors believe that a hyphen should be used here to show that the first element is the noun and not the adjective. That is, the hyphen warns the reader not to suppose that the stick is walking or the room eating dinner. Those with more confidence in the reading public are likely to see no need for this, and may even consider it an affront.

It is hard to find examples of word combinations that are really ambiguous, independent of their position in a sentence. (For this, see **temporary compounds.**) But since *a silver box* some-

times means a box made of silver, the wooden box that holds the table silver should be called *a silver-box,* in any context that is open to both interpretations.

8. The preceding seven rules cover all the "living" uses of the hyphen in America today. But there are some words that have hyphens merely because they always have had them. A writer should be familiar with these, and should write them with their hyphens, but they should not be used as patterns for new expressions.

a. A few technical terms, that are properly one word by special meaning and accent but are not familiar to the general public, are written with a hyphen for easier reading, such as *light-year, east-southeast,* and other complex points of the compass.

b. Certain compounds that involve an apostrophe are hyphenated when used in a figurative sense, such as *bird's-eye, bull's-eye, crow's-feet, mare's-nest.* Because of their special meaning and their accent on the first element, these compounds might be treated as single words, and sometimes are, as in *birdseye, crowsfeet.*

c. There are a number of three-word phrases that are always written with hyphens. These include *four-in-hand, man-of-war, coat-of-arms, forget-me-not* and the names of other flowers, and the *in-law* relationships. *Mother-in-law* does not need hyphens any more than *delegate at large,* which does not have them, but it is always written in this way because it always has been.

d. The word *great,* too, is always hyphenated in family relationships because it always has been. But we now have two forms, *great-aunt* and *grandaunt,* both of which mean exactly the same thing.

e. Words built on a letter of the alphabet, such as *X-ray,* and *U-boat,* are often hyphenated. But there is no need for the hyphen here and it is often omitted in scientific writing, as in *a Y incision* and *the B vitamin.*

f. Some hyphens are simply mistakes. These will appear in the best edited material, but usually they are not copied and die off. Sometimes, however, a mistake is copied so often that it becomes the established practice, as has happened in the case of *court-martial* and *post-mortem.* On theoretical grounds, neither of these words should have a hyphen. But both of them do now have the hyphen.

comprehend. See **apprehend; know.**

comprehensible; comprehensive. *Comprehensible* means capable of being understood (*His books are not comprehensible*). *Comprehensive* means inclusive, of a large scope or mental grasp (*It was a comprehensive scheme and included all points of view*).

A thing is *comprehensible* (or understandable) *by* one's self. It is made *comprehensible to* others.

comprise; constitute; include. To *comprise* is to include, contain, be composed of (*The program comprised twelve events*). To *constitute* is to compose or to form (*Twelve events constitute* *the program*). A body comprises those things of which it is constituted. *Comprise* and *constitute* should not be contused.

It is better to use *comprise* when all of the constituent parts are enumerated or referred to and to use *include* when only some of them are.

conceal. See **hide.**

concealment. See **secretion.**

concede. The use of *concede* in the common phrase *concede the election,* meaning to admit or recognize that the opposing candidate has won, is now standard in American usage. We use *concede* often where the English prefer *admit* or *recognize.*

conceit. See **pride.**

concensus. See **consensus.**

concept; conception. See **idea.**

concern. The phrase *as concerns* is impersonal and means *as it concerns.* The verb is therefore always in the singular. That is, we say *as concerns these men* and not *as concern these men.*

concise. See **succinct.**

conciseness; concision. *Concision* may have been an over-elegant word for *conciseness* fifty years ago but it has since been accepted as standard. Perhaps its concision helped.

conclude; close. When applied to the bringing of a speech to an end, *conclude* is the more formal word and suggests that that which was to be said has been said as planned and brought to a logical finish. Whereas *close* suggests merely that the speaker has ceased speaking (*He concluded by pointing out the dangers of disregarding his advice. He closed his remarks abruptly when the heckling began*).

Purists have objected to the use of *conclude* to mean decide, insisting that it can be used in this sense properly only when the decision reached is the conclusion of a course of reasoning. But the average man assumes, however erroneously, that his decisions *are* conclusions and this meaning, at least in American usage, is now standard (*He concluded he would quit on pay day*). See also **end.**

concomitant means accompanying, concurrent, attending. We speak of *concomitant circumstances* or *concomitant qualities,* meaning circumstances or qualities that go along with whatever we have been discussing.

concord. When used as a grammatical term, *concord* means the agreement between secondary words and the principals they belong to. In some languages concord involves case, gender, person, and number. In English, the rules of concord are very simple. A pronoun, or a pronominal adjective, must have the same number as the noun it belongs with. We say *this hat* and *these shoes* and refer to the hat as *it* and the shoes as *they.* In the case of some words, such as *everybody* and *their,* there is a difference of opinion about how they can be used. All such words have been listed in this dictionary. They should be looked up individually. The only other questions of concord in English have to do with the form of the verb used with certain kinds of subjects. For a discussion of this, see **agreement: verbs.**

concrete. See **cement.**

concreteness has to do with the particular rather than with the general. It puts the abstract in terms of reality by example; it pinpoints the individual entity in a class of things or beings. Concreteness implies a sensory experience of an object, while abstraction implies idea. Thus *daisy* is a concrete instance of the generality *flower, measles* of *illness, etcher* of *artist.* Since most knowledge begins in our grasp of particular details, it is good for a writer to have a sharp eye and ear for the significant concrete term even if he is dealing with ideas.

Concrete terms are not, of course, necessarily better than abstract terms. Which one uses depends on the circumstances. The chief value of concrete words is that they deal with specific things and—if the reader has had an experience of these things—convey one's thought more directly.

concrete nouns. A noun is said to be concrete if it refers to a physical object, or to "something that can be perceived by the senses," such as *mud, water, box.* The term *abstract noun,* on the other hand, may mean any noun that is not concrete, such as *work, language, growth,* but is sometimes restricted to adjective qualities treated as things in themselves, such as *redness, roundness, beauty.* These distinctions are helpful in learning the gender of Latin nouns but in English there is no difference, grammatically, between a concrete and an abstract noun. Many abstract nouns, such as *wisdom,* do not have a plural form, but this is also true of many concrete nouns, such as *mud.* See **abstract nouns.**

condemn; contemn. *Condemn* means to pronounce adverse judgment on, to censure, or to express strong disapproval of (*The judge condemned the criminal to the gallows. He condemned the proceedings in the strongest language*). In American usage *condemn* also means to acquire ownership of for a public purpose, under the right of eminent domain.

Condemn may be followed by an infinitive, as in *he condemned her to lead a dreary life.* It may also be followed by the *-ing* form of a verb with the preposition *to,* as in *he condemned her to leading a dreary life.* The construction with the infinitive is preferred, but both are acceptable.

Contemn is a literary word, not often used. It means to treat disdainfully or scornfully, or to view with contempt. Thus where (in *Deuteronomy* 21:18) the King James version of the Bible speaks of *a stubborn and rebellious son, which will not obey the voice of his father, or the voice of his mother,* the Douay version speaks of *a stubborn and froward son, that . . . contemneth to be obedient.*

condescend may be followed by an infinitive, as in *he condescended to listen to us.* It is sometimes heard with the *-ing* form of a verb with the preposition *to,* as in *he condescended to listening to us,* but this is not standard usage.

conditional clauses. See **subjunctive mode.**

conductive; conducive. *Conductive,* which used to be synonymous with *conducive,* has now become limited to the meaning it has in physics—having the property of conducting or pertaining to the conduction of some form of energy, such as heat or electricity (*Copper and silver are highly conductive metals*).

Conducive (followed by *to,* not by *of*) means contributive or helpful (*Sound sleep is conducive to health. Such remarks are not conducive to good will*).

conductor. In America the official in charge of a railroad train or streetcar is called a *conductor.* When there were two men on the buses, the one who collected the fares was also called a conductor, but now that he has been abolished the one remaining man is called the *driver,* even though he has taken over the duties of the conductor. In England there are bus conductors and tram conductors but not railway conductors. The American conductor's duties in England are divided between the *guard* and the *stationmaster;* his dignity is assumed only by the *stationmaster.*

On a freight train (in England a *goods train*) the American *brakeman* is in England a *guard.* A *guard* in America is a crossing watchman or a gateman.

confess may be followed by a clause, as in *I confess I have heard about it,* or by the *-ing* form of a verb with the preposition *to,* as in *I confess to having heard about it.* It is also frequently used with an infinitive, as in *I confess to have heard about it,* but this is not standard usage.

confess; admit; acknowledge. To *confess* is not only to concede that a fact is true but also to accept, to some extent, a measure of responsibility for its being true. When a man says *I confess I haven't spoken to him,* he acknowledges a certain guilt for not having spoken. To *admit* is to concede, usually under pressure, but, unless a statement of guilt is specifically made, an admission does not necessarily constitute a confession (*He admitted that the charge had been made. He admitted that he was guilty*). In law a confession is always an acknowledgment of guilt.

To *acknowledge* is to recognize or grant the existence of something, but there is in it a suggestion of reluctance. To *acknowledge* a greeting is to receive it coolly and return it with brief formality. To *acknowledge* guilt is to admit it under pressure, usually after a previous denial of it.

confidant; confident. A *confidant* is one to whom secrets are confided. The feminine is *confidante,* though it is acceptable to use *confidant* for either a man or a woman. *Confident* means having a strong belief or full assurance (*He was confident that his confidant would keep his secret*).

confound is, basically, a very strong word. It means to confuse the very elements of, to pour the basic constituents together into a formless mess. When Milton spoke of the fallen Angels as *rolling in the fiery gulf/ Confounded, though immortal,* he wished to convey an idea of complete defeat, of utter destruction this side of annihilation. So that at one time *Confound you* was a stronger imprecation than *Damn you,* though it is now felt to be milder. In the second verse of the British national anthem (*God Save the King*) God is besought to *frustrate the knavish tricks* and to *confound the politics* of Britain's enemies. The latter phrase, in this context, means to reduce to impotent confusion whatever nefarious schemes the enemies may be plotting.

confusion worse confounded is a quotation from the second book of *Paradise Lost* (*ruin upon ruin, rout on rout,/ Confusion worse confounded*—a description of the defeated Angels hurtling downward through Chaos) and meant originally confusion made worse by the commingling of the very elements amid uproar and tumult. As a modern term for utter confusion it has become hackneyed.

confute. See **refute.**

congenial; genial. *Genial* means sympathetic, cheerful, cordial (*His genial disposition made him many friends*). *Congenial* means suited or adapted in spirit, feeling, temper, etc. (*They were congenial and enjoyed each other's company*). Of course genial people are more likely to find congeniality than the sad or surly, for the majority of mankind, however unjustified, is moderately cheerful most of the time. But misery loves company too, and the despondent and resentful and others dominated by unpleasant moods find congeniality in their like.

conjecture. See **guess.**

conjugal. See **matrimonial.**

conjunctions are words that show a grammatical relation between other words or groups of words. This, in turn, may reflect a logical or conceptual relation, but not a physical one. For example, in *Jack and Jill went up the hill,* the conjunction *and* shows that the words *Jack* and *Jill* are together the subject of the verb *went.* If we want to say something about the people rather than about the words we must use a preposition or an adverb, as in *Jack went with Jill* or *Jack and Jill went together.*

The relation between groups of words is sometimes made clear without using a true conjunction. Formerly, the mere fact that a relation existed was shown by juxtaposition, as in *out of sight out of mind* and *stuff a cold starve a fever.* Today we want to be told more about the relation. We may show what the relation is by position, if a clause is standing where only the object of the verb can stand or where only a phrase qualifying a noun can stand. Otherwise, we show the type of relation by the first word in the clause. This may be one of the relative pronouns, *who, which, what, that,* or *as,* or an adverb, such as *when, where, how.* Clauses may also be introduced by participles, such as *supposing, provided, granted.* Sometimes they follow immediately after a noun that is being used as an adverb, such as *minute* in *I remembered the minute I saw him;* or that is part of an adverbial phrase, such as *fear* in *they drove fast for fear they should be late.*

Grammarians make a distinction between

relative pronouns and true conjunctions. In *the man that sells balloons has left*, the first word in the clause, *that*, is the subject of the verb *sells* and represents or means "the man." It is therefore a relative pronoun. But in *I believe that he has left*, the *that* has neither of these functions and merely introduces the clause. In this construction, it is a true conjunction.

An adverb that introduces a clause is classed as a conjunction, although it does not lose any of its adverbial functions. An isolated adverb, such as *before* in *it has happened before*, is a true adverb. If an adverb brings a full clause with it, it has ceased to be an adverb and become a conjunction, as in *it happened before I arrived*. If it forms a phrase with a noun or noun equivalent, it has ceased to be an adverb and become a preposition, as in *it happened before dinner*. See **adverbs.**

The difference between a preposition and a conjunction is sometimes important. A subjective pronoun cannot be used as an object following a preposition. We say *he did it for me* and not *he did it for I*. But a pronoun following a conjunction may be subjective or objective depending upon its function in the sentence. If it is functioning as the subject of a following verb, an objective form cannot be used. For example, the subjective form *I* is required in *he works faster than I do*. When no verb actually follows, there is a difference of opinion as to which form of the pronoun is required. Some grammarians claim that certain words, such as *than*, are always conjunctions and imply a relation to the verb, and that an objective pronoun should not be used where the word is functioning as the subject of a verb. According to these grammarians we are required to say *he works faster than I*, whether the verb follows or not. In practice, we often do say *he works faster than me*. This means that we are treating the word *than* as if it were a preposition rather than a conjunction. The construction is more acceptable for some words than it is for others. (See the individual prepositions or conjunctions.) When a following pronoun is functioning as the object of a verb, a subjective form cannot be used. We say *I know her better than* (I do) *him*. In a case like this there is no need to say whether *than* is being used as a preposition or as a conjunction since we have the same result with either interpretation.

Pronouns, adverbs, and nouns used adverbially may serve as conjunctions. In addition, there are certain words that are used merely as connectives. These pure conjunctions are: *and, or, nor, but, for, than, as, because, if, lest, though* or *although, unless, whether, while,* and *that.*

COORDINATING AND SUBORDINATING
CONJUNCTIONS

Conjunctions are classified as coordinating or subordinating. A coordinating conjunction stands between two elements and indicates that they are grammatically equivalent. The elements may be words, phrases, or clauses. In *he arrived and I left*, the coordinating conjunction *and*

stands between two complete and independent statements, called principal clauses. In *Jack or Jill*, the coordinating conjunction *or* stands between two nouns. A subordinating conjunction always joins two clauses and shows that the one which immediately follows the conjunction is functioning as an element in the other. In *he arrived as I left*, there is only one independent statement, *he arrived*. The subordinating conjunction *as* shows that *I left* is functioning as an adverb of time in the other clause.

The words *and, or,* and *nor,* are always coordinating conjunctions and always stand between similar elements. Nothing as clear cut as this can be said about any of the other conjunctions. *But* is sometimes coordinating and sometimes subordinating. There is a difference of opinion as to whether it may also be used as a preposition. The word *for* is ordinarily a preposition but it is sometimes used as a conjunction. When it is there is a difference of opinion as to whether it is coordinating or subordinating. The words *than* and *as* are usually subordinating but are considered coordinating in certain constructions by some grammarians. (For a further discussion of these problems, see the individual words.) At one time it was customary to use a comma between clauses joined by a coordinating conjunction, but this is no longer required.

The remaining conjunctions are subordinating. Coordination is a much simpler relationship than subordination and the subordinating conjunctions have a variety of functions. (For this, see the individual words.) A subordinating conjunction is always the first word in the subordinate clause but the position of the clause itself in the sentence depends upon its function. (See **clauses.**) As a rule, a clause that is the subject or the object of a verb is not set off from the rest of the sentence by a comma. Adjective and adverb clauses sometimes are and sometimes are not. In general, a clause has the same punctuation that a single word with the same function would have.

Conjunctions are sometimes paired with another word, such as *not only . . . but, either . . . or, if . . . then*. These are called correlative conjunctions. They may be coordinating or subordinating, depending upon the conjunction itself. For a discussion of the word order in clauses of this kind, see **parallel constructions.**

SENTENCE CONJUNCTIONS

Words which indicate that an inference or conclusion is to follow, such as *therefore, consequently, accordingly, then,* are called "conjunctive adverbs" or "illative conjunctions." They are conjunctions in the sense that they show a relation between sentences. But grammatically, they are treated as adverbs. That is, these words do not have a fixed position in relation to the statement they introduce. The clause in which they appear is not, as a rule, joined to another, but is separated by a period or a semicolon. See **sentence adverbs.**

Coordinating conjunctions, such as *and, or, but,* may also be used to show a relation between independent sentences. Actually, this is only a question of punctuation, of where we put a period and a capital letter. A sentence which begins with a coordinating conjunction could have been printed as a continuation of the preceding sentence. In current English we like short sentences, and a long sentence is sometimes easier to read if it is printed as two independent sentences.

connected. See **identified.**

connection. The spelling *connection,* deplored in British style manuals, is standard in America. *Connexion* is now so rare in the United States that it would be regarded as a ludicrous misspelling.

connotation; denotation. To *denote* is to mark, indicate, designate (*The silver bars denoted their wearer to be a captain*). To *connote* is to signify in addition to the primary meaning, to involve as a condition of accompaniment. A word *denotes* the indispensable minimum of definition. A word *connotes* all of the attributes which are not denoted but which are associated with it. Thus the word *pig* denotes a young swine of either sex. It connotes filth and gluttony and high-pitched squealing, the little pig that went to market, the one that built his house of bricks, various characters in literature that have gone by that nickname, and whatever else, in addition to its basic denotation, the word may conjure up in the mind of one who hears or reads it.

connubial. See **matrimonial.**

conscious; aware. To be *conscious* of something is to have an inner realization of it. We are conscious of guilt or innocence, of exhaustion (*He was hardly conscious of his own motives. He was conscious of blushing*), and so on. We are *aware* through our sense perceptions which lead to consciousness (*Half awake, he was aware of a hammering at the door and conscious of a rapidly rising panic fear*).

An act, the motives of which are conscious, is likely to be deliberate or purposive. We are not likely, that is, to blunder into it. But *conscious* should not be used loosely as a synonym for *deliberate.*

consecutive; successive. Both *consecutive* and *successive* apply to things which follow one upon the other. But *successive* refers merely to the position of one thing in relation to another (*Successive disasters reduced him to poverty*); whereas *consecutive* denotes a close and uninterrupted sequence, sometimes with the implication of an established order. *Three successive days* would be any three days in which the last two followed the first and the last followed the second. *Three consecutive days* would be three days in a row, such as January the first, second, and third, or Monday, Tuesday, Wednesday.

consensus. The term for general agreement or concord is *consensus,* not *concensus,* as it is often erroneously spelled, possibly because of some confused notion that there has been a census of ideas and this is its final tabulation.

Consensus of opinion is, strictly, a redundancy, since *consensus* means agreement of opinion, but it is used so often that it must be accepted.

consent (noun). See **permission.**

consent. This verb may be followed by an infinitive, as in *I will not consent to go,* or by the *-ing* form of a verb with the preposition *to,* as in *I will not consent to going.* Both forms are standard. See also **allow.**

consequent; consequential. As adjectives *consequent* and *consequential* both mean following as an effect or result or as a logical conclusion (*The rapid increase of trade and the consequent influx of wealth. These privileges will draw consequential difficulties in their train*). Both words formerly also meant, of persons, important or self-important, those, that is, whose acts or wishes of necessity have consequences. But this meaning is now confined to *consequential* (*Goldsmith was sometimes content to be treated with an easy familiarity, but upon occasions would be consequential and important. He is a consequential man and must be treated with respect*). Indeed, this is now becoming the primary meaning of *consequential* and we encounter it in its other, basic meaning less and less frequently.

conservative. Fowler inveighs against the use of *conservative* as an adjective to mean *moderate* when qualifying a noun such as *figure* or *estimate* as "perhaps the most ridiculous of slipshod extensions." But the processes of language are indifferent to ridicule and have extended meanings in ways far more slipshod than this (as, for instance, in *slipshod extension*). When *conservative* (in its strict meaning of disposed to preserve existing conditions) became opposed in politics to *liberal,* it is not surprising to find it being used as an antonym in other senses. Certainly in American usage *conservative* is now standard in the meaning of *moderate.*

consider is to contemplate, meditate, reflect upon. A considered opinion is one that has been weighed and mulled over. That *consider* should have become, even in standard use, a synonym for *think* is not astonishing, for vanity leads us to regard our most irrational impulses as pondered thoughts and courtesy leads us to at least imply as much for the figmentitious fancies of our friends. But the careful speaker or writer will bear the distinction in mind and not write such sentences as *He considered him an enemy, though he had no grounds for thinking so.*

Consider may be followed by an infinitive, especially a perfect infinitive with *have,* as in *I consider him to have acted disgracefully,* but a *that* clause is generally preferred, as in *I consider that he has acted disgracefully.*

considerable. Traditionally, this word is used only in speaking of immaterial things, such as *considerable trouble, considerable influence.* Its use with material things, as in *considerable money* is not known outside the United States and is questionable here.

In older American speech, though now almost never heard, the adjective *considerable* was used for the adverb *considerably* (*He was considerable tired before he was through*). This usage, from the contexts in which it appears, was plainly regarded as rustic. It was not an Americanism, however, but a survival in America of an older English usage.

consign to oblivion as a term for putting something out of one's mind is a cliché, the worse for being used solely by the affected educated.

consistence and **consistency** are interchangeable in most uses, though *consistency* is always used when "being consistent" (constantly adhering to the same principles) is meant (*A foolish consistency is the hobgoblin of little minds*). *Consistence* usually refers to the state, the degree of density or viscosity (*The mud had the consistence of pitch*), and *consistency* to the quality of uniformity.

consistently; constantly. *Consistently* is sometimes misused for *constantly*. One who *constantly* discusses a certain subject is one who talks about it incessantly, unremittingly, perpetually. One who *consistently* discusses a certain subject is one who at all times in his discussion of it maintains the same attitude towards it.

consistently; persistently. To act *consistently* is to adhere constantly to the same principles, to hold the same course, not to contradict oneself (*He was consistently disagreeable*). To act *persistently* is to be pertinacious, to keep up an unremitting pressure, to endure in the face of opposition (*Desdemona persistently demanded Cassio's reinstatement and thereby worked her ruin*).

consist of; consist in. *Consist of* applies to the component parts of a whole (*A university consists of teachers, administrators, and students*). *Consist in* applies to inherent qualities (*The liberal value of the scientific discipline consists in its fostering of the questioning spirit*).

conspicuous by his absence. When Tacitus in his *Annals* (115 A.D.) remarked that the images of Brutus and Cassius were the more radiant at Junia's funeral because they were not seen at all (*magis praefulgebant quod non videbantur*), he no doubt felt a glow of satisfaction at the brilliance of the oxymoron and inclined his head, one assumes, in acknowledgement of the murmurous plaudits of his admiring friends. It was a good thing, well said, and even Lord John Russell, seventeen hundred years later, deserved applause when, in addressing the Electors of the City of London (April 6, 1859), he observed that a certain provision in Lord Derby's Reform Bill was *conspicuous by its absence.*

But the thing is now a cliché. Its only justification is the surprise of its seeming contradiction and the possibility of surprise has long ago been dissipated by repetition. It remains a cumbrous jocularity, a brazen piece of verbose dullness.

constantly; continually; continuously; perpetually; incessantly. To do something *constantly* is to do it often (*He is constantly tearing up what he has already written and beginning over again*). To do something *continually* is to do it at short intervals (*He is continually reminding me of what I owe him*). *Continuously* means uninterruptedly (*The wind blew continuously for three days*). *Perpetually* properly means continuing or enduring for ever (*The perpetual light of the stars. Graves for a fee will receive perpetual care*),

but it is also, in the exaggeration with which irritation relieves itself, used for *continually,* especially in expression of minor annoyance (*The children are perpetually demanding to go to the zoo again. I have had no leisure; the phone has been ringing perpetually since you left*). *Incessantly* means without ceasing and therefore in its strictest sense is a synonym of *continuously* (*an incessant noise*) but it is used so much for *continually* as well that this meaning must be accepted now as standard.

Of these words, *continuous* and *continuously* also apply to space (*The property line was continuous with the fence*). See **consistently.**

constitute. See **comprise.**

constrain; restrain. To *constrain* a man is to compel him to do something. He may be constrained to appear in court or to make good on some contractual obligation. To *restrain* him is to hold him back from an action, to keep him in check, even by imprisonment.

Constrain may be followed by an infinitive, as in *he constrained them to tell the truth* and *I am constrained to believe him,* but not by the *-ing* form of a verb. We do not say *I am constrained to believing him. Restrain* may be followed by *from* and the *-ing* form of a verb, but not by an infinitive.

constructive; implicit; virtual. One of the meanings of *constructive* is inferential, so construed, deduced by construction. There is a constructive permission to use a private road, for example, if it is not marked as private and is left open. Constructive treason is an act that may be construed as treasonable.

Anything is *implicit* which is implied without being stated. It describes a less formal deduction than that suggested by *constructive.* There is often an *implicit consent* in the lack of an express denial.

That is *virtual* which is such in power, force, or effect, though not actually or expressly such. Thus dictators are the virtual rulers of their countries, though many of them ostensibly hold secondary positions.

constructive criticism. The demand for *constructive* rather than *destructive criticism* (usually with an exaggerated emphasis on the first syllable of each adjective) has become one of the cant phrases of the day. It is true that under the guise of criticism mockery and hatred often vent their spite, and what professes to be a fair and even helpful analysis of a situation or policy is sometimes a malignant attack. But the proper answer to that is to expose the malignance and so point out that it is not criticism at all. Most whining for *constructive* rather than *destructive* criticism is a demand for unqualified praise, an insistence that no opinion is to be expressed or course proposed other than the one supported by the speaker. It is a dreary phrase, avoided by fair-minded men.

consul; counsel; council. The government agent who resides in a foreign state and discharges certain administrative duties is a *consul.* To call him a *counsel* or *council* is a mark of sheer ignorance.

A *consul* was at one time either of the two chief magistrates of the ancient Roman republic. The emperors did not abolish the consulships, but placed themselves in power over the consuls and from that moment the dignity and greatness of the name began to decline until now it stands for merely a minor commercial agent. Almost all titles depreciate in value in time. A *prince* was once the principal man, a *duke* was the leader, a *count* ruled a county, a *marquis* guarded the marches, or borders. The American custom of bestowing many of these titles (especially *Earl* and *Duke*) as first names will no doubt greatly speed the process of devaluation.

consume is to use up, to destroy (*The fire consumed the house*), to eat or drink up (*He consumed a large meal*), to spend money or time wastefully, or to absorb or engross (*Football consumed his energy. The book consumed his time*). The economists have made it a synonym for *use* and in their world it probably must be so accepted as standard, but in ordinary use the careful speaker or writer will reserve it for its special meaning.

contact. In the sense of to get in touch with a person (*I'll contact Jones and get his reaction*) *contact* was once a fighting word. The purists, particularly English purists, made an issue of it. Here was an abomination, an Americanism hideously repugnant. But it was a useful figure (after all, *get in touch with* is also a metaphor and several times as long) and very few business men even knew that the purists existed. Its fault was not so much its impropriety as that it was for a while grossly overworked. It is certainly accepted in spoken English today and will probably become the usual term in written English as well.

The noun *contact,* in the sense of one with whom one is in touch (*The F.B.I. has its contacts in the Communist Party*) is now on the threshold of becoming standard.

contagious; infectious. In medical usage, an *infectious* disease is one communicable by infection, a *contagious* disease one that is spread by physical contact. In popular usage the words are interchangeable, in their metaphorical uses, though *contagious* has come to have a slight connotation of rapidity in spreading (*The laughter was contagious. Mistrust is infectious and once started may weaken an entire nation*).

contain; include. To *contain* is to have within itself. To *include* is to contain as a part or member, or among the parts and members, of a whole. A whole contains its parts and includes any or all of its parts. Thus one might say of a certain package that it contained six reams of paper and that among these six reams were included two of blue paper and one of yellow.

contemplate; meditate; premeditate. In the sense of considering in the mind as something to be done, *contemplate, meditate,* and *premeditate* imply different degrees of intention. One *contemplates* many things that one has no serious purpose of doing, but they still have to be more likely to happen than those things which we merely imagine. One *meditates* more seriously. The word suggests deeper absorption in the possibility, a more searching examination of ways and means (*meditating revenge, under brows of dauntless courage*). Both *contemplate* and *meditate* apply to stages of consideration in which a decision to act or not to act is possible, but *premeditate* is used now exclusively to refer to cogitations preceding something that actually did happen (*His crime was premeditated; he cannot pretend that it was done on thoughtless impulse*). In the law *premeditation* implies sufficient forethought to impute deliberation and intent to commit the act.

contemporary; contemporaneous; coeval. *Contemporary* and *contemporaneous* both refer to things that exist or occur at the same time, but *contemporary* is applied more to people and *contemporaneous* to objects (*Keats was a contemporary of Shelley's. The first volume of Gibbon's* Decline and Fall *and the first volume of Adam Smith's* Wealth of Nations *were contemporaneous*). Where *contemporary* is used without any comparison being made, it refers to the present time (*Contemporary styles in women's clothing permit great freedom of movement*).

Coeval also means existing at the same time, but it implies that the contemporaneousness has gone on for a long time or existed in times of the remote past (*Tyranny is coeval with servility. Rome and Greece were coeval*). Where *coeval* is used of a person, it is usually humorous, implying a contemporaneousness of such duration that it must be measured in terms of history or geology. Lamb says of a superannuated man: *He is forlorn among his coevals; his juniors cannot be his friends.*

Cotemporary and *cotemporaneous,* by the way, are permissible variants, not misspellings. See also **synchronous.**

contemptible; contemptuous. When Pedro, in *Much Ado About Nothing,* says of Benedick that *the man hath a contemptible spirit,* it is apparent from the context that he does not mean that Benedick had a spirit deserving of contempt but one manifesting contempt, a haughty and disdainful spirit. But *contemptible* is no longer synonymous with *contemptuous.* It now means deserving of contempt and *contemptuous* means bestowing of contempt (*It is true that his attitude towards the project is contemptuous, but it must be granted that many of those engaged in it are contemptible*).

content; contented. These adjectives can both follow a linking verb, as in *the man was content* and *the man was contented.* But only the form *contented* can stand before the noun it qualifies. We can say *the contented man* but not *the content man.*

It may be hair-splitting, but in common use *content* suggests more of the meaning of *satisfied* and *contented* more of *pleased in satisfaction.*

content; contents. In current English, the singular word *content* is used in speaking of the significant material contained in a piece of work, and one may say *it has no content*. The plural word *contents* means the topics treated, or more often a list of these topics. When it means a list, it is treated as a singular, as in *is there a contents?* In speaking of a physical container, the plural form *contents* means what is contained in it, and the singular *content* means its capacity. The singular may also be used to mean amount as in *the alcoholic content*. When used with a physical meaning, the plural *contents* requires a plural verb, as in *the contents were surprising*, but it is not a true plural and cannot be used with a numeral.

contentious. See controversial.

contest. In England a *contested election* is one in which there is more than one candidate. In America it is that (*It was a hotly contested election*) but it is also an election in which the validity of the returns is challenged (*Contested elections are determined by Congress*).

In sports, the American *contestant* is the English *competitor*, though the American usage (which is standard in England but simply not employed very much) is coming into use in England more and more.

context means that part of a discourse or writing which precedes and follows a given passage or word, which gives the passage or word its exact meaning. Where a word has many meanings—and some words in English have twenty or thirty meanings and thousands have two or more meanings—it is often only the context that can tell us just which meaning is to be understood.

Out of context, whole passages can be misunderstood. Thus Iago's great speech in *Othello*, beginning

Good name in man and woman, dear my lord,
Is the immediate jewel of their souls

is taught to millions of children as a noble and high-minded utterance. And so, taken by itself, it is. But in the context of the play it is profoundly cynical.

To quote out of context with the deliberate intention of misleading is a moral, not a grammatical, fault. But it is very common, especially in the advertising of books and theatrical performances. Thus a notice before a theater may inform the public, on the authority of a distinguished critic, that this is "Miss W's most brilliant performance." Whereas the critic had written "Miss W's most brilliant performance falls short of most other actresses' mumbling in their sleep."

contiguous. See adjacent.

continually; continuously. See constantly.

continuance; continuation. Though *continuance* and *continuation* are synonymous in meaning the act or fact of continuing, *continuance* means duration or time of continuing (*His continuance in office was made endurable only by the devotion of his friends*). *Continuation* means prolongation, either of time or space. Thus the *continuance* of a house would refer to the time of its continual standing. The *continuation* of a house could refer to an extension, such as a wing, or to the future time in which it would be permitted

to remain standing (*The continuation of its occupancy of this site was debatable*).

Continuance has a special legal meaning in American usage: the adjournment of a step in a proceeding to a future day (*At the attorney's request a continuance was granted*).

continue may be followed by an infinitive, as in *continue to talk*, or by the *-ing* form of a verb, as in *continue talking*. Both forms are acceptable.

Continue may be followed by an adjective describing what continues, as in *he continued silent*. It may also be followed by an adverb describing the continuing, as in *he continued silently*. See also **resume**.

continuing action tenses. See progressive tenses.

contract; catch; get. One of the many meanings of *contract* is to acquire, as by habit or contagion (*He contracted the habit of smoking. He contracted enormous debts*). In reference to the acquirement of a disease, it is a little stilted, though widely used. To *catch* or to *get* a cold is better than to *contract* one, though the rarer diseases or the more common diseases under their rarer names are more fittingly *contracted*. One *contracts* tuberculosis, one *gets* a sty or a boil. A child will probably *get* a light case of measles, but *contract* a severe one.

contradictory; contradictious. Ideas, statements, and terms that are opposed, admitting no middle ground, and mutually exclusive, are *contradictory*. Persons who delight in having ideas and making statements that are contradictory to those expressed by their associates are *contradictious*. They are not, however, often so called. *Quarrelsome, captious, perverse, argumentative, cantankerous* are terms more generally employed to describe such people. *Contrary* is used a great deal colloquially.

contrary; opposite; adverse; reverse. *Opposite* means symmetrical antithesis in position, action or character. It and *contrary, adverse*, and *reverse* refer to two things that differ from each other in such a way as to suggest a relationship. *Contrary*, except when specifically applied to persons, describes something impersonal whose opposition happens to be unfavorable (*a contrary opinion, contrary winds*). *Reverse* describes that which faces or moves in the opposite direction (*a reverse judgment, the reverse of a page*). *Adverse* suggests something hostile in its opposition, being not merely opposite but opposing. *Adverse fortune* is worse than ill fortune in that it implies an active malignance in the bad luck.

contrary-to-fact statements. See subjunctive mode and infinitives.

contrast. See compare.

contribute may sometimes be followed by an infinitive, as in *it contributed to save our lives*. The construction is found in older literature but is rare today. The *-ing* form of a verb with the preposition *to*, as in *it contributed to saving our lives*, is generally preferred.

contrive may be followed by an infinitive, as in *I contrived to meet him*. It may also be followed by a *that* clause. But in this case, the clause verb must be a subjunctive or a subjunctive equiva-

lent, as in *I contrived that I should meet him.*
The infinitive construction is generally preferred.
Contrive is not followed by the *-ing* form of a
verb. We do not say *I contrived meeting him.*

controversial; contentious. That which is subject
to controversy is *controversial.* He who is given
to controversy is *contentious* (*A contentious
man will find every issue controversial*).

conversation. See **dialogue.**

convict. The verb *convict* is sometimes used—
more often in speech than in writing—for *convince* (*No use talking, you can't convict me*).
To *convict* is to prove guilty of an offense, especially after a legal trial. To *convince* is to persuade by argument.

convinced. See **satisfied.**

cookbook. The American *cookbook* is in England
a *cookery book.*

cool as a cucumber. Cucumbers *are* cool. Scientists with thermometers have finally confirmed
what has been known for thousands of years.
But they have come too late to save the hackneyed metaphor *as cool as a cucumber* meaning
self-possessed, unemotional, collected. It is a
cliché and should be used sparingly.

cooperate together. Since *cooperate* means to work
together, *cooperate together* is a tautology.

copula means "connective." Some grammarians
mean by "the copula" only the verb *be.* Others
use the term for any verb that merely links a
subject and a complement, such as *become,
seem, appear.* See **linking verbs.**

copy (noun). See **replica.**

copy (verb). See **recopy.**

copyright; copyrighted. In America a book is *copyright,* in England it is *copyrighted.*

corn means whatever cereal is the chief crop in
the country. In America *corn* means maize, in
England wheat, in Scotland oats. The compounds and derivatives of *corn* in America are
many (*cornfield, corn pone, corn cob, corn
syrup, etc.*). *Corn* is used alone as an abbreviation of *corn whisky* and as a slang term for trite
sentimentality and forced, obvious humor. This
last usage seems to derive from *cornfed* which
a generation ago was a slang term for bucolic
or rustic.

cornerways; cornerwise. Both forms are acceptable.

cornucopia. The plural is *cornucopias,* not *cornucopiae.* The form *cornucopiae* is an old-fashioned English singular, made from a Latin
genitive meaning "horn of plenty." It had a regular English plural *cornucopiaes.* The form
cornucopia is preferred today.

corpora. See **corpus.**

corporal; corporeal; physical; bodily. *Corporal,*
bodily, is now confined almost exclusively in
ordinary speech and writing to the phrase *corporal punishment.* This is sometimes called
corporeal punishment, but that is an error today.
Corporeal and *corporal* used to be synonymous,
but *corporeal* has now become a philosophic
and theological word meaning of the nature of
matter. Theologians speak of *the Corporeal
presence of Christ in the Eucharist.*

Physical indicates the animal or human body

as a material organism (*The physical strength
of men in delirium is not as great as folklore
often represents it*). *Bodily,* which has now replaced *corporal* in all but the one phrase, means
belonging to, or concerned with, the human
body, as distinct from mind or spirit (*Bodily
pain is often overlooked in times of mental
suffering*).

corps. The singular form *corps* means an organized military body (*The Medical Corps, The
Marine Corps*). The plural form, meaning more
than one such body, is also written *corps.*

In the United States a singular verb is ordinarily used in speaking of just one corps, as in
the cadet corps is on its way. But since this
represents a body of men, a plural verb may also
be used in speaking of a single corps, as in *the
cadet corps are on their way.*

corpse; body; carcass; carrion. *Corpse* is a dead
body, usually of a human being. The dead body
of an animal is called a *carcass. Carrion* describes a putrefying carcass. *Body* refers to the
material organism of an individual man or animal, living or dead (*A glow of health suffused
his magnificent body. The body lay where it had
fallen, inert and lifeless*).

corpulent. See **fat.**

corpus. The plural is *corpora,* not *corpi.*

corrective of; corrective for. Though *corrective
of* is preferable (*Greed is not necessarily a corrective of sloth*), *corrective for* is standard in
American usage (*His biting irony was a good
corrective for the lush and sentimental rhetoric
they were addicted to*). The construction is unavoidable as *corrective* comes to be used more
and more as a synonym for *remedy.*

correlative conjunctions. See **parallel constructions.**

correspondence; correspondents. *Correspondence*
is communication by exchange of letters. *Correspondents* are those who exchange *correspondence.*

correspondent; corespondent. A *correspondent* is
one who communicates by letters. A *corespondent* is a joint defendant, especially in a divorce
proceeding, where one charged with adultery is
made a joint defendant. Many an indiscreet *correspondent* has found himself a *corespondent.*

corrugated; coruscated. That which is *corrugated* which
is drawn or bent into folds or alternate furrows
and ridges. A plowed field is corrugated. Sheets
of iron used for facing buildings or for making
drain pipes and culverts are often *corrugated.*

To *coruscate* is to emit vivid flashes of light,
to sparkle or to gleam (*The coruscations of the
tiara were brilliant. His wit fairly coruscated*).

cost. The past tense is *cost.* The participle is also
cost.

cost a pretty penny. To say of something expensive that it *cost a pretty penny* is to be allured
by alliteration into a cliché. It is an affected,
mincing phrase.

costive; costly. Mathews quotes several instances
of the use of *costive* for *costly* (*A scarcity of
ice has been a great hardship heretofore, and to
ship it from Denison made it very costive*). But
since *costive* means constipated and *costly* means

expensive, the confusion could be the result of either ignorance or sly facetiousness (as in another of Mathews' quotations wherein a lady's poodle is referred to as *pretty but costive*).

There is a gag in Hollywood of a famous producer who when told that a certain successful novel would never do for a movie because it was "too caustic" said "Never mind the cost! If it's good, we'll buy it."

costly; dear; expensive. *Expensive* implies a price beyond what a thing is worth and beyond what the purchaser can afford to pay (*Since it got him fired, it turned out to be an expensive indulgence*). *Costly* implies that much was paid or must be paid because of the high value of the object (*a costly jewel*), but it, too, is used, like *expensive*, to imply that too much was paid (*That was a costly joke*). *Dear* in America, in this sense, means high-priced (*It would have been dear at half the price*).

coterie. See **clique.**

couched. The use of *couched* for expressed (*The offer was couched in the most flattering terms*), while not an affectation, is too much a literary word for everyday use.

could. See **can.**

council; counsel. A *council* is a deliberative assembly of persons (*His election to the council assured the citizens of better government*). *Counsel* is advice, opinion (*When we need your counsel, we shall send for you*). The two words are pronounced alike, but it is an illiterate error to confuse them.

The advocate engaged in the direction of a cause in court, or any legal adviser, is *counsel*. When used as such the plural form is *counsel*, as in *the counsel were able to agree*. When the word means advice or opinion, it has the regular plural *counsels*, as in *more moderate counsels prevailed*.

councilor; counselor. A *councilor* is a member of a *council*. A *counselor* is one who gives counsel or advice. Of course a *councilor* could also be a *counselor*.

Counselor has the special meaning, in America, of one in a position of minor authority at a summer camp for boys or girls.

counsel. See **council.**

countenance. See **face.**

counterfeiter; coiner. *Counterfeiter* is the general term in America for one who makes base or imitation coins or paper money. The British term is *coiner* (*My father was I know not where/ When I was stamp'd; some coiner with his tools/ Made me a counterfeit*), though the false coin or bill itself is called a *counterfeit*. The word *coiner* is kept in American usage, at least by those in the government services that deal with counterfeiting, for one who makes counterfeit coins, in distinction to one who makes counterfeit bills, who is a *counterfeiter* ("*Coiners aren't a menace, but they sure are a nuisance*," *Secret Service chief U. E. Baughman summed it up*).

In England and America *coiner* can also mean a minter or stamper of money or one who coins, as of words or phrases (*Hardy was an inveterate coiner of words; he felt that he had a right to make up any word that expressed his meaning*).

counterpart is sometimes used as if it meant opposite; whereas it means duplicate, almost the opposite of *opposite*. Originally a *counterpart* was the opposite part of an indenture and from this has come not only its contemporary meaning of duplicate but its equally valid, though less commonly used, meaning of one of two parts which fit each other or one of two things which are complementary (*The unexpected visitor was the exact counterpart of the photograph he had been shown the night before. Deep-sea valleys . . . are the counterparts of the mountain chains*).

countless, if it is to mean anything, must mean numbers so great that they are incapable of being counted. To use it, then, as a mere synonym for *many* is to defeat emphasis by exaggeration. Thus one often encounters the phrase *countless generations,* but, allowing thirty years to a generation, all the generations within the time of recorded history could be counted in two or three minutes.

coup; coupé. A *coup* is an unexpected and successful stroke, usually a political maneuver or a seizure of political power by a military group. A *coupé* (more often now a *coupe*) is a closed automobile with a body somewhat shorter than that of a sedan of the same line. The *coop* of *hencoop,* whence also the slang word for jail, is an entirely different word, being related to *cup.*

couple. In the United States *couple* is often placed immediately before a noun, as in *a couple dollars, a couple months*. This is following the pattern of *dozen* and may be established in time, but it is not yet standard English. In standard English *couple* must be joined to a following noun by *of,* as in *a couple of chairs*. This *of* is omitted only before degree words such as *more, less, too many,* as in *bring a couple more chairs.*

Couple may be used with either a singular or a plural verb. The plural construction is heard more often than the singular. This is especially true when the word refers to human beings, as in *the couple were dancing.*

Court of St. James (St. James's). From 1697 to 1809 St. James's Palace in London was the royal residence. The palace was so named because its site was once occupied by St. James's hospital for leprous women. The court, to which our ambassadors are still accredited, is, strictly, the *Court of St. James's,* and this spelling may be insisted on by those who want to be letter perfect and historically accurate. The *Court of St. James* is, however, not only a recognized and accepted variant but is preferred by those who feel that the extra *'s* serves no purpose except to display the erudition of those who employ it. The palace, by the way, is always *St. James's Palace.*

courteous. See **polite.**

courtesy. See **curtesy.**

covet means to **desire,** but to desire excessively or wrongfully. This may be due to its use in the tenth commandment. There are also connotations of envy and secrecy in the word. Illicit desires would naturally be kept secret, but this meaning may be strengthened by its similarity in sound to *covert*. But simple desire it is not. We would not think of using it today as it is used in a quotation, dated 1634, in the *Oxford English Dictionary: Boys go up and down with flagons of wine, and fill to those that covet it.* See also **envy.**

cowardly; timid. An act is *cowardly* when it is lacking in normal courage and basely timid (*It was a cowardly thing to leave his post just because he smelled smoke*). An act is *timid* when it shows a lack of boldness or self-confidence. The timid are frightened when there is no real danger (*The child was too timid to ask anyone which bus she should take*). Because men who are cowards when they are in danger are often bullies when they feel secure, and because much has been made of this in popular psychology, many acts are described as cowardly which should be described as arrogant, overbearing, insolent, brutal, tyrannical, or the like. Thus to say *It was a cowardly thing for that big man to hit that defenseless boy* may show a knowledge of the human heart but it shows an ignorance of the English language.

coy. See **modest.**

cracker. See **biscuit.**

craft. When this word means a boat, the standard plural is *craft,* but a regular plural *crafts* is sometimes heard in this sense.

When the word means a skill or trade, the plural is always *crafts.* In this sense, both *craft* and *crafts* are used as the first element in a compound, as in *craftroom* and *craftsroom.* Only the form with *s* is used in *craftsman.*

crave. This word may be followed by an infinitive, as in *I crave to hear his voice.* It may also be followed by a clause with the clause verb a subjunctive or a subjunctive equivalent, as in *I crave that he come.* The infinitive construction is preferred.

crawfish; crayfish. Any of numerous fresh-water decapod crustaceans of the suborder *Macruca* are called *crayfish* by zoologists and the British, but in common American usage they are called *crawfish.* Both, by the way, are folk-etymological corruptions of the old French *crevice.* The *craw-* may have been affected by *crawl.*

The verb to *crawfish,* to crawl or back out of an undertaking, is slang, not standard.

crawl. See **creep.**

credence; credit. *Credence* means belief. To give credence is to believe. (*I could not place much credence in his narrative*). *Credit* also means believe (*I could not credit his narrative*). The *credit* which one has at a store is the amount which the store believes one will pay. But from both of these meanings *credit* branches off into other meanings. *Credit* means financial status, the amount of money at one's disposal in the bank, acknowledgement of merit (*Much credit accrued to him because of his speech before the joint session*), and source of honor (*Dr. Bunche is a credit not only to the Negro race but to the human race*). Thus in the meaning of belief *credence* has the advantage (because it means

only one thing) of being free from any possible ambiguity.

credible; creditable; credulous. *Credible* means believable, worthy of belief or confidence (*His story was credible. I have it on the authority of a credible witness*). *Creditable* means bringing of honor or esteem (*His refusal to accept the bribe was a creditable action*).

The negative of *credible* is *incredible.* The negative of *creditable* is *discreditable.*

Credulous once meant merely inclined to believe. Bishop Hall said (1605) that *a credulous and plain heart* is more acceptable to God than *a curious* [*i.e., inquiring*] *head.* But in general usage today *credulous* means over-inclined to believe, gullible. Buckle refers to *an ignorant and therefore a credulous age.*

credit; accredit. To *credit* is to believe (*I credit your story implicitly*). To *accredit* is to invest with authority (*He was accredited ambassador to Italy*) or to certify as meeting certain official requirements (*The board failed to accredit Podunk Normal College*). *Accredit* also means to ascribe or attribute (*The invention of the submarine was accredited to Fulton. He was accredited with the witticism, whether he actually said it or not*).

Of course where something creditable is ascribed or attributed to someone, where, that is, it may be thought of as being put to the person's credit (*The invention of the submarine is credited to Fulton*) *credit* may be used for *accredit.* But *accredit* may be used for the ascription or attribution of discreditable things; whereas *credit* may not.

creek. In the United States (as also in Canada and Australia) a *creek* is a small stream, as a branch of a river. In English usage it is a narrow recess in the shore of the sea, an inlet or bay. This is the meaning that Chaucer had in mind when he said that his Shipman knew *every cryke in Britaigne and in Spayne.*

Although it would be understood if encountered in reading and although it is incorporated into thousands of place names (meant in the more recent ones to lend an upper-class or romantic air), *brook* is very rarely used in America in ordinary speech.

creep. The past tense is *crept.* The participle is also *crept.* A form *creeped* is heard but is not standard.

creep and **crawl,** as terms for moving along the ground, are frequently interchangeable, but *crawl* suggests a more prostrate motion and it alone has the suggestion of abasement (*He'll come crawling to ask my forgiveness*). *Creep* often has a sinister connotation (*At night when you're asleep/ Into your tent I'll creep. Day by day the Indian tiger/ Louder yelled and nearer crept*), while *crawl* suggests the movement of loathsome rather than of dangerous things (*Yea, slimy things did crawl with legs/ Upon a slimy sea*).

crematorium. The plural is *crematoriums* or *crematoria.*

creole means various things in various places and various punctuations. In the West Indies and

Spanish America it means one born in the region but of European, usually Spanish, ancestry. In Louisiana and elsewhere, when spelled with a capital *C*, it means a person born in the region but of French ancestry. It also means the French language of Louisiana, especially that spoken, or formerly spoken, by white persons in New Orleans. When the initial *C* is not capitalized, it means a person of mixed Creole and Negro ancestry speaking a form of French or Spanish, or a native-born Negro as distinguished from a Negro brought from Africa.

crept. See **creep.**

crevice; crevasse. A *crevice* is a crack forming an opening, a rift, a fissure. A *crevasse* is also a fissure, but a special kind. It is a deep cleft in the ice of a glacier and, in the United States, a breach in an embankment or levee.

crew. See **crow.**

cricket. Only Americans seeking to ape or to ridicule the English ever say *it's not cricket* and they are likely to be bores. We have clichés enough of our own without importing them.

The phrase originated in the fact that cricket, largely an upper-class game, a "gentleman's" game, "is a game full of forlorn hopes and sudden dramatic changes of fortune, and its rules are so ill-defined that their interpretation is partly an ethical business" (George Orwell). Then it values form or style more highly than success. Thus to say that something *is not cricket* doesn't mean that it is dishonest or criminal, but that it simply doesn't measure up to the highest ethical standards.

crime; sin. A *crime* is an act committed or a duty omitted whose commission or omission is injurious to the public welfare and for the commission or omission of which punishment is prescribed by law and imposed in a judicial proceeding. *Sin* is the serious breaking of a moral or divine law. Thus it is a crime, but not a sin, to drive through a red light. It is a sin, but not a crime, to hate your neighbor or to covet his wife. It is a sin to tell a lie, but it is a crime only if you are under oath. Of course many things, such as murder and theft, are both sins and crimes. The words are used interchangeably, lightly and loosely, for emphasis or humor (*It's a crime, the way he makes her work after hours. It's sinful to work on a day like this; we ought to be outdoors*).

crisis. The plural is *crises* or *crisises.*

criterion. The plural is *criterions* or *criteria.*

critical has two meanings. One, inclined to find fault, to judge with severity, involving skilful judgment (*The critical opinions of the play were unanimously favorable. Don't be so critical; you have to make allowances for a beginner. His critical analysis was helpful*) derives from critics and their criticisms. Two, of decisive importance in respect to the outcome, crucial, involving risk, suspense, or peril (*He was taken to the hospital in a critical condition. It was a critical decision in his life*) derives from *crisis.* Since a crisis is often a time or condition of danger, *critical* in this sense means dangerous, but *critical* is, of course, not a synonym for dangerous,

and the careful speaker and writer will use it to mean dangerous only when the danger is one latent in a crisis.

criticism; critique. As a term for a critical examination or review, especially of a literary or artistic work, *critique* is a pretty highfalutin word. Fowler's hope, a generation ago, that the word was dying out, has not been realized. It has a justification in the fact that *criticism* is ambiguous: it may mean a discrimination or discussion of merit, character or quality, or the exercise or application of critical judgment, but it may also mean faultfinding. Among ordinary people, in their ordinary use of the word, that is what it does mean (*I'm doing the best I can and I resent his criticism*). But ordinary people don't know the word *critique* at all. Those who use it, use it almost entirely in works that will be read by those who presumably understand the proper meaning of *criticism. Review* is a good word for a short examination and *study* for a longer one.

In referring to the standard or rules of critical judgment, as in Kant's *Critique of Pure Reason,* the word has a more established validity.

crochet and **crotchet** were once the same word, but their pronunciations are different and one has become specialized and the other has extended its meaning into senses not shared by the first. *Crochet* now refers to a special kind of needlework done with a needle which has a small hook at one end which serves to draw the thread or yarn into intertwined loops. A *crotchet* is a small hook or any one of various devices and instruments with a small hook at one end. In its most commonly used sense it means an odd fancy or whimsical notion—something, that is, that has hooked on to the mind like a burr (*Mr. Dick's crotchet about King Charles's head was one of Dickens's better fancies*). Since people with crotchets are often difficult to deal with, *crotchety* is frequently a synonym for *cantankerous.*

crocodile tears. It was anciently believed, or at least asserted, that the crocodile wept and made mournful noises to attract passers-by that he might devour those whom pity brought within his reach. Moreover, he shed tears as he devoured them. No wonder that these tears became a trope for hypocritical expressions of sympathy and regret. But we no longer believe the fable, and sophistication has long ago exhausted even the quaintness of it. It is now a pure cliché, an allegory best left on the banks of the Nile where Pliny's fancy found it.

cross as a bear. Despite cuddly Christmas presents for children, animated cartoons, and scores of juvenile picture books, a bear, as our ancestors well knew, is not an amiable creature. Directors of zoos regard their bears as more dangerous than the big cats. None the less, the simile, though justified, is hackneyed and should be avoided as a cliché.

cross the Rubicon. The Rubicon was a small stream which in ancient Italy formed the boundary between Italy and the province of Cisalpine Gaul. When, in 49 B.C., Julius Caesar, who had been placed in command of the Gallic legions but had no military authority in Italy itself, crossed this stream at the head of his troops he knew that by so doing he had declared war against Pompey and the Senate. Plutarch tells us that when Caesar came to the river "he communed with himself for a long time in silence. ... But finally, with a sort of passion, ... uttering the phrase with which men usually prelude their plunge into desperate and daring fortunes, 'Let the die be cast,' he hastened to cross the river."

To use *crossing the Rubicon,* then, as a term for taking a step which definitely commits one to an irreversible course of action, is to show oneself acquainted with Plutarch and with the minutiae of Roman history. But after two thousand years and many millions of repetitions, allusions cease to elicit the awestruck or appreciative responses they once brought out. This one is now stale, flat, and unprofitable and should be avoided.

crossways and **crosswise.** Both forms are acceptable.

Crossword-puzzle English. Though the fever of crossword puzzles has abated, the malady lingers on. At the time of the full frenzy there was much discussion of their educational value. Mr. Arthur Maurice, former editor of *Bookman,* claimed that forty dormant words had been edging their way back into controversial currency because of their frequent appearance in crossword puzzles. Among the forty were *mar, cite, abet, sate, ire, goad, emit, leer, aver, foment, eke, pry, elan, carp* (verb), *inert* and *apt.* Certainly all addicts have learned that *em* and *en* are printers' measures, that a period of time may be an *age,* an *eon* or an *era,* and that among real and imaginary animals there are or have been the emu, the ai, the gnu, the yak, the boa, the roc and the asp. But the chief advantage of learning crossword-puzzle words is that it enables one who has learned them to solve other crossword puzzles. There are few other places in the world, for instance, where it is of any value to know that an Anglo-Saxon serf was sometimes called an esne.

Mr. Maurice appended to his essay defending crossword puzzles an imaginary conversation to show how the new words acquired might be used in everyday speech. A short sample will suffice:

Mrs. B.: Are you making that ebon garment for yourself ?

Mrs. A.: Yea. Just a black dress for every day. Henry says I look rather naif in black.

Mrs. B.: Well, perhaps, but it's a bit too anile for me. Give me something in indigo, say, or ecru.

Mrs. A.: Quite right. There is really no neb in such solemn vestments.

Mrs. B.: Stet.

crow. The American phrase for being compelled to make a humiliating retraction or confession of error, *to eat crow,* is expressed in England by the phrase *to eat humble pie.* Both are con-

sidered nauseating dishes, for the *humble* of the English phrase is the *umbles* or unsavory inwards of the deer. See **humble pie.**

A *crow to pick* (the English use the phrase which the Americans use too, *a bone to pick,* means to have an unpleasant matter to discuss with someone.

crow. The past tense is *crowed* or *crew.* The participle is *crowed.*

In the United States *crowed* is the only form commonly used for the past tense but *crew* is still heard in Great Britain. An old participle *crown* is heard in this country, as in *when the cock had crown,* but this is now archaic or countrified.

An interesting illustration of the manner in which usage can become fixed is supplied by *crowed* and *crew.* The educated man would say that a child *crowed* with delight and that so-and-so *crowed* over his enemies in triumph, but he might say that a cock *crew.* If asked to explain his retention of an archaic preterit in this particular application of the verb, he would probably be unable to do so. Yet the usage, in relation to cocks, was established by the fact that in all four of the Gospels, immediately upon Peter's denial of Christ, *the cock crew.*

crowd is a large number of persons gathered closely together. Like *throng,* but unlike *multitude,* it suggests an uncomfortable jostling (*The heat and pressure of the crowd was frightening*). To speak of a group of friends as a *crowd* (*The old crowd was there; we had a wonderful time*) is acceptable spoken English and quite sensible when it is meant to suggest a crowding together. But as a term for a clique (*They're a rotten crowd*—Scott Fitzgerald) it is not standard.

As a verb, *crowd* means to push or press against physically (*They were crowded to the wall and in grave danger*); but there is no reason why, like hundreds of other such verbs, it should not be extended metaphorically (*The new executives soon crowded him out of the company*) so long as the pushing together of a group is meant to be conveyed. To say that one is *crowded for time* is to carry the metaphor to its permissible limits, and to use *crowd* merely as a synonym for pushing (*He was always crowding in where he wasn't wanted*) is wrong.

cruces. See **crux.**

crumble; crumple; rumple. To *crumble* is to break into small fragments or crumbs (*The rock crumbled under his hands and he fell from the cliff*). To *crumple* is to draw or press into irregular folds, or to wrinkle heavily (*Angrily he crumpled the letter and threw it into the wastebasket*). To *rumple* is to *crumple,* but lightly and, usually, playfully (*He affectionately rumpled the child's hair. The coverlets were all rumpled with the horseplay*).

Crumb, the basis of *crumble,* was originally the soft inner part of the loaf, as distinguished from the *crust* (*He that keeps nor crust nor crumb/ Weary of all, shall want some*).

crumby; crummy. *Crumby,* full of crumbs, of the nature of crumbs, friable (though this is usually expressed by *crumbly*), was formerly also spelled *crummy*. The slang *crummy*, mean, shabby (*What a crummy joint!*) seems to stem from an earlier slang meaning *lousy* which, in turn, may have derived from the idea that a louse looked like a crumb.

crux is a cross. The term came to be applied figuratively to anything that torments by its puzzling nature, particularly philosophical and textual difficulties (*The unity of opposites was the crux of ancient thinkers. The consideration of a textual crux sharpens the wits*). In modern usage it has come to be applied almost solely to a vital, basic, or decisive point, especially in the rather tired phrase *the crux of the matter*. It is a word that has been confined, heretofore, to literary problems so that it has distinctly an academic flavor and should be avoided by all who wish to avoid the imputation of pedantry. (The plural is *cruxes* or *cruces*.)

cry; weep. *Cry* is the everyday word. It has in it the suggestion of a passionate, inarticulate but loud lament, an open expression of sorrow. In all meanings of *cry* there is an implication of great noise. *Weep* is a more poetic word (*Weep no more, my lady*). It suggests a quieter expression of grief, though the grief may be as deep (*When that the poor have cried, Caesar hath wept*). *Sobbing* is weeping with a convulsive catching of the breath. A *wail* is a prolonged inarticulate, mournful cry, usually high-pitched (*Then from the jail/ Came the wail/ Of a downhearted frail*). A low-pitched wail would be a *moan*.

cry over spilt milk, no use to. There's no use telling those who think this a fresh and original way of expressing the folly of vain regret that it has been a cliché for a century and a proverb for two centuries before that. But it has.

cry wolf. To say of someone who raises needless alarms that he is *crying wolf* is to employ a cliché. The phrase is a hackneyed reference to Aesop's fable of the shepherd boy who shouted "Wolf! Wolf!" as a joke or just to get attention and then failed to get help when the wolf really came because his cry for help was no longer taken seriously.

cryptic is a mysterious word for mysterious, hidden, secret, occult, and unless one wishes to risk the contempt and resentment which, as well admiration, is sometimes bestowed on those who use strange words, he would do well to use one of the commoner synonyms.

cue; queue. There used to be distinctions between these words. The actor's indication and the rod used in pool and billiards were invariably *cue*. The pigtail and people waiting in line were *queue*, and this spelling still holds for these uses in England. But in America, although it is known that the law-abiding English *queue up* in *queues, cue* is the accepted spelling for all senses, except that *queue* is sometimes used for the pigtail.

cumulus. The plural is *cumuli*.

cups that cheer. Those who refer to alcoholic beverages as *the cups that cheer* are guilty of a number of errors. In the first place, the full phrase, taken from Cowper's *The Task* (1783), is *the cups that cheer but not inebriate*, and it refers to tea. And if, as seems likely, Cowper was echoing a passage from Bishop Berkeley, it referred originally to tar water. Just how an infusion of tar in water cheered him or anyone else, the Bishop did not say; it was probably part of the mystery of his philosophy, Subjective Idealism. The phrase is a cliché, worn out and misunderstood and should be avoided.

curate. See **rector.**

curb; kerb. For the protective margin of the sidewalk, the American spelling is *curb,* the English *kerb.* For *curb* in the sense of *restrain,* see **check.**

curious; inquisitive. *Curious* can mean desirous of knowing or that which makes us desirous of knowing (*Children are very curious, eager to find out anything that they think is being concealed from them by their parents. His behavior seemed curious and occasioned a great deal of speculation in the village*).

In popular usage *curious* in the first of these senses has come to mean almost entirely an eagerness to know something that is not properly one's concern. Like *inquisitive*, with which it is largely synonymous, it implies a prying into other people's affairs. Of the two words, *inquisitive* suggests more action, in the form of asking impertinent questions or investigating in some way. One can be *curious* without doing anything more than wondering (*She was curious about what was going on in her neighbor's house and soon became inquisitive among the children*).

currently. See **presently.**

curriculum. The plural is *curriculums* or *curricula.*

curry favor. To *curry favor,* as an expression for ingratiating oneself with another by flattery or complaisance, is a standard expression not used enough to be condemned as a cliché. But, although its general meaning is plain, it may be doubted if one out of ten thousand who use it have any idea of its specific meaning, and it stands as a striking illustration of the ways of language and the fact that usage can in time make any blunder acceptable.

To *curry* is to groom, as with a currycomb. *Favor* is a corruption of *favel* (until the sixteenth century the saying was *to curry favel*), which is the English form of the Old French *fauvel,* fallow-colored. Fauvel, a fallow horse, was the rascally hero of a romance, the *Roman de Fauvel* (1310). Whether a fallow horse was a symbol of dishonesty before the romance or whether the idea came from the story is not clear, but the thought of currying this cunning rogue as a means of gaining his favor became proverbial, though the rascality of the one curried is not in the modern usage.

curse. The past tense is *cursed* or *curst.* The participle is *cursed.* *Cuss* and *cussed* are often used by educated people as a softened form of *curse.*

cursing. See **blasphemy.**

curtesy; curtsey; curtsy; courtesy. *Curtesy* is a legal term meaning the life tenure formerly enjoyed by a husband in his wife's land inheritance after her death, provided they had issue able to inherit. It is plainly a word that only the historian of land tenure would have much use for today.

Curtsey and *curtsy* are variant spellings of each other and of *courtesy,* which may be used for them. They, however, are fixed in their meaning of one particular act of courtesy, a bow by women in recognition or respect, consisting of bending the knees and lowering the body (*The pretty little Miss dropp'd me a curtsy*).

Courtesy means politeness, excellence of manners (*He was a model of courtesy*). It also means a courteous act or expression or a favor graciously conferred (*He did me a courtesy once and I don't like to be rude to him*). And it can mean consent or indulgence (*By courtesy of the management*).

cuspidor. The substitution of the Portuguese *cuspidor* for the already fairly ornate American *spittoon* must mark a height of vulgar elegance exceeded only by the derivative *cuspidorian* bestowed upon its caretaker.

cuss. See **curse.**

custom; habit; practice. *Custom, habit,* and *practice* all mean an established way of doing things. *Custom,* when applied to a community or to an individual, means a more or less permanent continuance of a social usage (*It is the custom to dye eggs at Easter. Such is the custom of Branksome Hall*). *Habit* applies more to the individual and implies that the same action has been repeated so often that there is a tendency to perform it spontaneously. There can be good habits as well as bad habits, but the word carries a suggestion of the undesirable that is lacking in *custom* (*He has a habit of twitching his left eye, but it is customary among well-bred people not to seem to notice such things*). *Practice* applies to a set of fixed habits or an ordered procedure in conducting activities (*It was his practice to open all of his mail before he read any of it*).

customary. See **usual.**

customer. See **buy; buyer** and **patron.**

customs. When this word means a toll or duty paid on imports, it is now always used in the plural with a plural verb, as in *the customs were paid.* But the word is not a true plural and cannot be used with a numeral. One does not pay *two customs,* although one may pay the customs more than once. Formerly the word was often used in the singular form, with a singular verb, as in *the custom was paid.* This is now obsolete.

The old singular is seen in *custom house,* which is still the literary name for such a building. But we always say *customs officer* and *customs duty,* and the new form *customs house* appears too often to be called anything but standard.

cut. The past tense is *cut.* The participle is also *cut.*

cut a long story short. The phrase *to cut a long story short* has raised false hopes among the victims of the verbose too often to have any validity any more. It is an empty, mocking phrase. The laconic do not need it and the talkative do not mean it. It is a knife turned in the wound of boredom, a warning of continuance when the soul of the listener is crying out for release. If the dictates of humanity do not suffice to suppress it, those of style should.

cut off one's nose to spite one's face. Almost all languages have a proverb or saying about those who do themselves an injury in order to be revenged on an enemy, such as burning their house down to set his on fire; and most of them touch with grim humor on the fact that in the passion of hatred a man will do himself a great damage to do his enemy a small one. But of them all, the English version—*cutting off one's nose to spite one's face*—is the best, the homeliest, the most humorous, and stresses most grimly the immense disproportion between the self-inflicted injury and its reward. Unfortunately, however, the pungent old saying has been weakened by overuse. It has been applied to every trifling inconvenience until hundreds of millions of repetitions, without real appositeness, have robbed it of its force and made it a cliché. It is too good to be abandoned, but it should be allowed to rest.

cute. *Acute* means sharp (*an acute angle*). It was a natural extension to apply it to mental sharpness (*That was an acute observation*). Mental sharpness, even if it were just a bit on the shady side, was much admired by our ancestors and *cute,* meaning shrewd, cunning, crafty was a common word in America a century ago (*Zeke was too cute for them city fellers*). In this sense, however, it is now obsolete, being replaced, to a considerable extent, in slang, by *sharp.*

It is far from obsolete, though, in the sense of pleasing (*a cute kid; a cute hat; a cute idea; gee, honey, you're cute,* and so on to acute nausea) in a pretty, dainty, or droll way. It is interesting that a word meaning crafty, shrewd, penetrating, words that indicate the seeking of one's own interests, should have come to mean attractive or charming, for usually those to whom the earlier meanings apply are unattractive and repellent. Yet the same thing has happened in England with the word *cunning* which is now used almost, though not quite, as much as we use *cute* (*a cunning nipper*). The bridge for the shift of meaning was probably children, in whose attractiveness there is often an element of shrewdness and whose penetrating observations are amusing.

But *cute* as a general term of approval is overworked now to the point of being an abomination.

cyclone; tornado; typhoon; hurricane. A *cyclone* is an atmospheric pressure system characterized by relatively low pressure at its center, and by counterclockwise wind motion in the northern hemisphere and clockwise in the southern. The name is also applied to tropical hurricanes, especially in the Indian Ocean. A *hurricane* is a violent tropical cyclonic storm. It is called a *typhoon* in the western Pacific area, in the China seas, and in India. The term *tornado* is applied to destructive rotary storms in the middle United States, storms which usually appear as a whirling, advancing funnel hanging from a mass of black cloud. It is also applied to violent squalls or whirlwinds of small extent which appear in summer along the west coast of Africa.

cyclops. The plural is *cyclopses* or *cyclopes*. A singular *cyclop,* with a regular plural *cyclops,* has also been in use for several centuries. It is not heard as often as the singular *cyclops,* plural *cyclopses,* but it is thoroughly acceptable.

cynosure. See **nexus.**

D

dabble in the occult. To *dabble* meant, originally, to wet by splashing, to play about in shallow water or mud; hence figuratively, and contemptuously, to be busied, intermittently and in a dilettante way, in some business or pursuit.

What makes *to dabble in the occult* a cliché is the inevitability of the combination. Those who use it would never think of saying *to trifle with the occult* or *to employ oneself intermittently with the occult.* They do not even dabble in the dictionary; invariably and wearyingly, the two words are combined.

daemon; demon. A *daemon* is a subordinate deity in Greek mythology, an intermediary between gods and men. It is often thus distinguished in spelling from *demon,* which is an unclean, evil spirit, a devil.

daily; diurnal. Though *daily* and *diurnal* both mean of or belonging to each day, *diurnal,* referring to the motion of the heavenly bodies and having special applications in botany and the church service, is too heavy a word to be used in complete synonymity with *daily.* The sun makes its diurnal round, but the milkman and the paper boy make their daily round.

dainty. See **nice.**

dam; damn; damned; damnably. A *dam* may be a barrier to obstruct the flow of water, or a body of water obstructed by such a barrier, or a female animal parent (now confined largely to quadrupeds; if applied to a human being done so with derogatory intent). It was formerly the name of a single one of the pieces used in the game of checkers.

Damn, the curse, is pronounced exactly like *dam* and used to be spelled that way. Modern writers, wishing to be toughly realistic and at the same time gently safe, often spell *God damn* as *goddam.* In defense they would probably allege that "That's the way it's pronounced." But *damn* has always been pronounced *dam.* People who say *It's damn cold* or *I'm damn well tired of it all,* distress not only moralists but linguists; for they should say *damned* or *damnably,* according as they wish to suggest that the cold or the general situation has been condemned or is worthy to be condemned. Such people, however, can hardly be held to the niceties of grammar. The purists must get what comfort they can from the thought that at least they no longer use *damnation* as an adverb, as millions of grammatically and morally unprincipled wretches did in the nineteenth century.

damn with faint praise. When Alexander Pope said of "Atticus" (probably Addison) that he would *Damn with faint praise, assent with civil leer,/And, without sneering, teach the rest to sneer* he exposed felicitously the workings of the timid malice that so often underlies a cold virtue. But the felicity of his phrase has been its ruin. A paradox, however brilliant, can astonish us but once and after the billionth repetition there is no more delighted amazement, only weariness.

dandy, in the sense of something fine or first-rate, was formerly a much-overworked word in colloquial American usage. Horwill quotes a man as saying that he had just given his mother-in-law *a dandy funeral.* Its serious use has declined but there has been an ironical revival that has brought it back into general use among the smarter young set. But irony is even more perishable than innocent enthusiasm.

dangling participles. See **participles.**

dare. The past tense is *dared* or *durst.* The participle is *dared.*

This verb was once in a class with *can* and *may* and may still be used just as these verbs are. The word *dare* was an ancient past tense form, meaning "have courage," which had come to be felt as a present tense by the time English became a written language. *Durst* was a new past tense form that had been created for it, which had also come to be felt as a present tense. As a result, neither word had the characteristic *s* ending in the third person singular. Both were followed by the simple form of a verb and not by a *to*-infinitive. One might say *he dare go* or *he durst go.* The verb had no imperative, no infinitive, no past participle, no -*ing* form, and could not follow, or be dependent on, another verb. One could not say *will dare, did dare,* or *used to dare.*

During the last five or six hundred years, the verb has gradually moved out of this class. It has developed full, regular forms with a past tense and participle *dared* and an -*ing* form. It is now possible to say *will dare, did dare, used to dare.* The new verb *dare* has an *s* in the third person singular and is followed by a *to*-infinitive, as in *he dares to go.*

In present day English *durst* is archaic. But

dare may be used with or without an *s* in the third person singular and may be followed by the simple form of a verb or by a *to*-infinitive. It may enter into compounds like any other regular verb or it may be treated as if this was impossible. We may say *I do not dare* and *do you dare?*, or we may use the older forms and say *I dare not* and *dare you?* Some grammarians feel that this is license enough and object when the new forms are used in the old construction, that is, without the *to* of the infinitive, as in *he dares go, he dared go, I don't dare go*. Some also insist that the old forms cannot be used when the word has its relatively new meaning of "challenge," as in *I dare you jump*. But the best writers and speakers have not agreed with them. Combinations of the old and the new forms are used by outstanding writers today, as in *do I dare disturb the universe?* (where the purist requires *dare I disturb* or *do I dare to disturb*).

Now that the verb *dare* has moved out of the class of *can* and *may*, acquiring an *s* in the third person singular and a *to*-infinitive following it, the regular verb *need* seems to be moving in. *Need* often drops its *s* and its *to*, as in *he need not answer*. See **need**.

dash. The dash marks a sharp break in the sentence, an introduction of some surprise element. It is a comfortable punctuation mark since even the most rigorous critic can seldom claim that any particular example of it is a misuse. Its overuse is its greatest danger, and the writer who can't resist dashes may be suspected of un-coordinated thinking.

The primary uses of the dash are:

1. To indicate a sharp break in the sentence, as in *Then he—would you believe it?—ran to the corner grocery.*

2. To show interruption of a sentence or word, especially in dialogue, as in *"But you must have th—"* and *"Well, the only reason I—".*

3. As a replacement for parentheses, especially in informal writing. In this case the dashes are, of course, used in pairs, as in *All those things—the sound of the apples sputtering, the smell of the cinnamon, the glow of the fire—suddenly made him decide to stay.*

4. To summarize, emphasize, or contrast with what has been said earlier in the sentence, as in *A good five-cent cigar—this is what the country needs and wants* and *He could always find a job when he wanted to—he just never wanted to.*

5. After a word or phrase, when followed by several phrases set in separate lines that require this word or phrase to complete their meaning, as in:

I wish they would—
See him nominated.
Get him elected.
Support his policy.

6. To suggest profanity without offending anyone's sensibilities, as in *Why, you—!, You s—!*

It is considered old-fashioned to combine a dash with a comma, a colon, or a semicolon, as in *Dear Sir:—*

dastardly means cowardly, meanly base, and should not be applied to acts, however vicious, in which there is not at least an element of cowardice. Thus the act of the Puerto Rican terrorists who, in November 1950, attempted to assassinate President Truman, though it was shocking, desperate, ferocious, mad, misguided, and murderous, was not, as many papers called it, "dastardly." Whatever else the assassins were, they were not cowards: the attack was made openly in full daylight; they attacked the armed guards directly, with the almost inevitable certainty of being killed themselves.

data. This word is commonly used to mean the information at hand—verbal or statistical reports or laboratory observations. In this sense *data* may be treated as a singular or a plural.

In the social sciences *data* is usually treated as a singular. Specialists in these fields characteristically refer to their data as *it* and talk about *much data* and *very little data*. These are singular constructions. They are perfectly acceptable, provided they are not followed by a plural verb. In the physical sciences *data* is more often treated as a plural. This too is acceptable, provided it is done consistently. But it is not enough to use a plural verb. If *data* is a plural it should be referred to as *they* and not as *it* and should have plural qualifiers such as *these, many, few,* and not singulars such as *this, much, little*.

A singular construction such as *the data is now in, but we have not examined much of it* is perfectly good English. A plural construction such as *the data are now in, but we have not examined many of them* is also acceptable. But mixed forms such as *much of the data are new* and *little data are available* are simply wrong. No one should think that he must treat *data* as a plural merely because Julius Caesar may have done so. Many English singulars have foreign plural forms, such as *stamina*. There are even words with English plural forms, such as *news* and *the United States,* that are nevertheless treated as singulars.

The form *data* may be used as the first element in a compound, as in *data sheets*.

dative case. The dative is a Latin case. It is thought to have originally carried the meaning of "to" or "toward" and was used broadly in classical Latin to show that a noun or pronoun had some intrinsic relation to the verb other than that of nominative or accusative. Most often this was the relation of indirect object. Modern English shows the dative relationships by position or by means of prepositions. See **indirect object** and **objective pronouns.**

davenport. An American who announced casually that he was just going *to lie down on the davenport* would fill an English visitor with consternation or at least curiosity, for *davenport,* which in the United States means a large sofa, often one that can be converted into a bed, means in England a small writing table.

dawn on. To say that something *dawned on* a person, meaning that he began to perceive the import of a remark or an event, is a phrase to be used sparingly.

day before; day after. The omission of the definite article before *day before* or *day after* (*Day after tomorrow is their anniversary*) is accepted usage.

dead as a doornail seems to have been established as a proverbial expression by the time (1350) it first appeared in writing, yet no one knows why a doornail should be deader than any other inanimate thing. It has been conjectured that the particular nail referred to was the one upon which the knocker fell and that its deadness may have been a whimsical assumption from the pounding it received. It has also been conjectured that its deadness may have been suggested by the silence with which such pounding was often received; for until the policed and electrically lighted security of modern times people did not open their doors, especially after dark, merely because someone knocked. This latter guess is supported by the fact that it was sometimes *as dumb as a doornail* or *as deaf as a doornail* or *as dour as a doornail*. But at the best these are only theories. No one has ever found a context that throws any light on the problem. No one really knows what the simile means, and a figure of speech that has been used daily for six hundred years without anyone's knowing what it means must surely be granted to be a cliché.

dead; deadly. *Deadly* means death-dealing, as in *a deadly weapon*. It is an adjective and is used to qualify a noun. *Dead* also qualifies a noun when it is used in its literal sense, as in *a dead horse*. But it may mean deathlike or deathly, and in this sense is used to qualify adjectives, as in *dead white*. We therefore say *I was dead tired* and *the conversation was deadly*.

The adjective *dead* may be used as if it were a noun meaning all people who have died, as the second *dead* in *and dead the dead will stay*. Unlike most adjectives, *dead* may also be used in speaking about a particular group of people, as in *from these honored dead we take increased devotion*. It may also be used with a numeral, as in *there were twenty dead*. At one time *the dead* could be used in speaking of a single individual, as in *blessed is the dead that the rain rains on* and *the dead raising himself the third and last time*. This use of *the dead* as a singular is still heard in some parts of the United States, but it is now rare in literary English.

deadly in the sense of awful or terrible or excessive was once a fairly common colloquialism. Pepys quaintly says that he was compelled on one occasion to sign *a deadly number of pardons* and one of the characters in *She Stoops to Conquer* tells another that he is *a deadly deal wrong*.

deal. The past tense of the verb is *dealt*. The participle is also *dealt*. The noun *deal* means amount and could once be used in just the way we now use *lot*, as in *they talked a deal of nonsense* and *it was a deal of trouble*. It replaced the word *heap*, which had once been used in this way, and is now itself being replaced by *lot*.

In current English *deal* is used in the sense of *lot* only in the expressions *a good deal* and *a great deal*. These phrases require *of* immediately before a noun, as in *a great deal of money*. But they may be used without *of* before degree words such as *more, less, too much, too many*, as in *a great deal more money*. They may also be used to qualify adjectives or adverbs in the comparative, as in *a good deal cheaper, a great deal faster*.

At one time these phrases could be used before plural nouns, as in *a great deal of pieces of timber*. Today, they are only used before mass words. We say *a great deal of china* but *a great many plates*.

dear; dearly. *Dear* is both an adjective and an adverb. It has been used as an adverb from the earliest times, both in the sense of at a high price, as in *By God, he said, that bought me dear*, and in the sense of with deep affection, as in *Rosaline that thou didst love so dear*. The form *dearly* is never used to qualify a noun. See also **costly**.

dear; my dear. Prefixing *my* to the usual *dear* in the salutation of a letter intensifies either the formality or the informality. *My dear son* is more informal than *Dear Son,* (in American usage, not in English) *My dear Mr. Smith* is more formal than *Dear Mr. Smith*.

dearth (scarcity, lack) is in most vocabularies restricted entirely to the phrase *a dearth of information*. It is hardly a cliché, since its meaning is clear to all who use it and it doesn't roll effortlessly off every tongue, but it is worn and should be watched.

deathless. See **undying**.

debar; disbar. To *debar* is to exclude, either literally or figuratively (*He was debarred from the factory grounds. His lameness debarred him from taking part in athletics*). To *disbar* is a technical legal term meaning to expel from the legal profession or from the bar of a particular court (*Disbarment proceedings were instigated at once against the attorneys who had offered the bribe*).

debenture. In England *debenture* is often used for what in the United States is commonly called a *bond*. In America a *debenture* or *debenture bond* is merely a certificate of indebtedness.

decant; descant. To *decant* is to pour off gently, without disturbing the sediment. Wines are decanted from the bottle into a decanter (*Attend him daily as their chief/ Decant his wine and carve his beef*).

A *descant* is a melody or counterpoint accompanying a simple musical theme and usually written above it (*You are too flat,/ And mar the concord, with too harsh a descant*). In part singing it is the soprano (*Children neigh forth the descant. Composed for three voices—descant, tenor, and bass*). It also means to make comments on, to discourse at length and with variety (*To see my shadow in the sun,/ And descant on mine own deformity. Johnson never accustomed himself to descant on the ingratitude of mankind*).

decease. See **die**.

deceit; deception. *Deceit* is the quality of being false (*Deceit lay deep in his nature, hidden under a semblance of hearty frankness*), the act or practice of deceiving or of concealing or perverting the truth with intention to mislead (*Pope's love of deceit seemed to grow with the passing years; he hid himself in ever more subtle mazes of guile*), or that which deceives, a lie, an artifice, or cunning trick (*My lips shall not speak wickedness, nor my tongue utter deceit*).

Deception is properly the act, and not the quality, of deceiving (*This deception shall cost him dear*). It can mean the state of being deceived (*The extent of their deception is fantastic; they are besotted with the charlatan*).

decide may be followed by an infinitive, as in *he decided to go*, or by a clause, as in *he decided he would go*. It may also be followed by the *-ing* form of a verb with the preposition *on*, as in *he decided on going*.

decided; decisive. *Decided* means unquestionable, free from ambiguity (*He showed decided signs of dementia praecox. Anton's weight gave him a decided advantage in the ring over his slighter opponent. He was a decided man: everything was black and white to him; he recognized no doubts or shades of gray*).

Decisive means having the power or quality of determining, putting an end to controversy by swaying the balance definitely and finally in one direction. Decided signs of dementia praecox would be definite, unmistakable signs. Decisive signs would be signs that made it plain that a case about which there had been uncertainty was beyond doubt one of dementia praecox. *Decisive* applies ordinarily to things, events, or decrees. A *decided victory* would be one in which one side triumphed so completely that there could be no question in anyone's mind as to which was the winner. A *decisive victory* would be one that settled a conflict.

Decisive is not usually applied to persons but it may be. When it is, it has the same meaning as *decided*: characterized by, or displaying, decision (*He had a decisive character*). *Decided*, however, cannot be used for *decisive*.

decide; decree; determine; resolve. To *decide* is to make up one's mind, promptly and firmly. To *determine* is to make up one's mind and then doggedly—sometimes obstinately—to stick to the settled purpose. To *resolve* is to settle a disputed or uncertain matter by deliberate choice and will; there is in the word an implication of the expenditure of considerable time and thought in the process of reaching the conclusion. A matter may be decided almost instantaneously but it can be resolved only after cogitation. To *decree* is to ordain or promulgate an edict. A *decree* can be issued only by someone in authority (*The President was determined to end the confusing situation. After talking it over with his advisers he resolved to act. He decided on the proper course and decreed that . . . etc.*).

decimals. See **fractions.**

decimate originally meant to kill one in ten. It was a punishment inflicted on some of the Roman legions for mutiny or cowardice. Those to be killed were chosen by lot. Appius and Antony both decimated mutinous legions and the Earl of Essex decimated some of his regiments in Ireland. The use of the term to mean the slaughter of a great number is general and accepted, but if the number exceed one in ten, then the word instead of conveying horror will, at least to the knowing, understate it. To use *decimate* with any particular percentage or fraction other than one in ten (*More than half the population was decimated by the plague*) is to commit a ludicrous error.

deck of cards. In referring to a *deck of cards* an American is using English which would have been understood by Shakespeare (*But whiles he thought to steal the single Ten,/ The King was slyly finger'd from the Deck*—3 Henry VI) but which would puzzle a modern Englishman who would call it a *pack of cards*. In fact most Englishmen would have been puzzled by the term during the last three hundred years. John Brand in his *Popular Antiquities* wrote in 1777: *In some parts of the North of England a pack of cards is called to this day . . . a deck of cards.* This is but one of many terms which are obsolete in England but still in daily use in America.

declarative sentences. See **sentences.**

declare; affirm; assert; proclaim. To *declare*, to *affirm*, and to *assert*, imply the making known of something, openly and in a formal manner.

To *declare* is to state emphatically, sometimes in the face of actual or expected contradiction. Our Declaration of Independence was a formal announcement which plainly anticipated a contradiction from England. One who declares his innocence does not expect to be believed immediately by all.

To *affirm* is to make a statement supported by one's reputation for knowledge or veracity, or so related to a generally accepted truth that there is little likelihood of its being denied (*The witness affirmed that the accused was a man of the highest integrity. There needs no affirmation of the obvious*).

To *assert* is to state boldly, usually without any other proof than conviction (*Common sense asserts the existence of a reality*).

To *proclaim* is to announce or assert publicly and officiously (*He proclaimed his innocence and challenged his accusers to confront him openly*).

decline may be followed by an infinitive, as in *he declined to go*, or by the *-ing* form of a verb, as in *he declined going*. Both forms are acceptable, but the infinitive construction is preferred.

decorative. See **ornamental.**

decorum; propriety. *Decorum* is propriety of behavior in dress, speech, manners, and so on (*He had a fine sense of decorum and bore himself with grace and ease*). *Propriety* is conformance to established conventions in morals and good taste. *Decorum* suggests dignity and a strong sense of what is becoming. *Propriety* has a wider application than *decorum* and suggests a strict adherence to the rules as rules rather than an innate sense of what is fitting.

decree. See **decide.**

decry; descry. To *decry* is to speak disparagingly of, to belittle, censure or condemn as worthless

(*To decry the previous age is an established procedure in liberal criticism*).

To *descry* is to discover by observation, to make out by looking (*The boy on the mast descried land lying about three leagues off the port bow*).

decumbent. See **recumbent.**

dedicate. A *dedication* was a setting apart and consecrating to a deity. In England the word (except in the sense of ascribing or addressing a book to someone) is never used except when there has been a religious ceremony. But in America the word now often has merely the meaning of *open*. When we are told that a new Stock Exchange Building or a new sausage factory has been dedicated, with the mayor officiating and a party for the employees following the dedication, we are not meant to suppose that thereafter the structure is to be regarded as dedicated.

deduce; infer. *Deduce* and *infer* both mean to come to a conclusion after a process of reasoning from premises or evidence. *Deduce* is the more serious of the two words. An *inference* is something lighter, often arrived at with less sense of responsibility, than a *deduction*. One hears of rash, foolish, false, unjustified, or shallow inferences more often than one hears of deductions of these sorts. *Deduce* is used more than *infer* in scientific and philosophic matters.

deduction. See **induction.**

deem. See **think.**

deer. The plural is usually *deer,* but the regular form *deers* is also heard and is acceptable. Compounds ending in *deer* follow the same pattern, with the exception of *reindeer* which has the regular plural *reindeers* more often than not. See also **elk.**

defamation. See **libel.**

defective; deficient. That is *defective* which has a defect. That is *deficient* which has a deficit. Food would be defective if it were spoiled. It would be deficient if there were not enough of it. It might, of course, be both; and its defectiveness might be the cause of its deficiency. In some things quantity and quality are indistinguishable; a lack of humor, for example, may be either a defect or a deficiency in a man's character.

In dealing with the handicapped, particularly children, the two words have become idiomatically or technically fixed in certain meanings. We speak of the physically defective and the mentally deficient. Even where an arm or a leg was missing, it would be spoken of as a defect not as a deficiency. See also **anomalous.**

defer may be followed by the *-ing* form of a verb, as in *he deferred going,* but not by an infinitive. *He deferred to go* is not standard English.

definite article. See **the.**

definite; definitive. *Definite* means clearly defined or determined, precise, clear in its meaning, exact (*A definite answer must be returned by noon or it will be assumed that he does not wish to negotiate*). *Definitive* means conclusive, having the function of deciding or settling a matter, the fixed and final form. A definite statement is one which is clear. A definitive statement is one from which there can be no appeal. A definite edition is one particular edition. A definitive edition is one that leaves nothing more in the way of editing to be done.

Definite and *definitely* are greatly overworked today and in many instances are nothing more than intensives. In such a sentence as *There was definitely a vague premonition of trouble in the air, definitely* cannot have its proper meaning. And when someone answers, *Yes, definitely,* when asked if he intends to do something, he can only mean certainly or assuredly or indeed, and these are not standard meanings of *definitely.* Whereas were someone to answer *Yes, definitely* when asked if he had marked a road map for another's guidance, and meant thereby that he had marked the map in such a way that the route would be clear, he would have used the word correctly.

definitive adjectives. Certain adjectives ordinarily stand first in a series of adjectives qualifying the same noun. These are called *definitives* because they make the noun idea as definite or specific as the facts allow.

The definitives include: the articles *a, an, the;* the possessives, such as *my, his, whose,* and any noun in the genitive case, such as *father's;* the demonstratives *this, that, these, those;* the relatives and interrogatives *what* and *which;* the indefinites *any, each, every, either, neither, no* or *none, some;* and the words *such* and *enough.*

Two kinds of adjectives may sometimes precede a definitive. (1) The names of some fractions and the words *all* and *both,* which might be treated as nouns and joined to the following words by *of* as in *half of the chocolate cake* and *all of my large books,* may also be used without the *of* as adjectives standing before a definitive, as in *half the chocolate cake, all my large books.* The words *all* and *both,* but not the fractions, may also function as definitives themselves, as in *all men, both men.* (2) An adverb cannot qualify a noun, but it can qualify a definitive which is an adjective, and in this way have the effect of qualifying the noun. Words used to mean "in a high degree" are being used as adverbs and may therefore stand before a definitive, as in *such a sad story* and *what a terrible thing.* When a degree word applies to one adjective in a series, it may bring that word forward with it, as in *so great a man, how sad a tale.* With these two exceptions, the definitives precede all other kinds of adjectives.

defy. This word may be followed by an infinitive, as in *I defy you to tell me,* but not by the *-ing* form of a verb or by a clause.

degenerate. See **deteriorate.**

de gustibus non est disputandum (taste should not be discussed). Modern American taste definitely prefers that we express ourselves in English. When every educated person studied a little Latin, an occasional Latin phrase in one's speech or writing served to mark one as above the herd that knew, at best, only the three R's. But today it serves only to mark one as either a hopeless pedant or an affected ass.

deism; theism. *Deism* is the belief in the existence of a God on the evidence of reason and nature only. It rejects supernatural revelation. *Theism* is the belief in one God as the creator and ruler of the universe, but it does not reject supernatural revelation.

delay. This word may be used with the *-ing* form of a verb, as in *he delayed starting*. It is sometimes used with an infinitive, as in *he delayed to start*, but this is not standard practice.

delectable. See **delightful.**

deliberate falsehood. To refer to some untrue statement as *a deliberate falsehood* is to be at once trite and redundant. The phrase is hackneyed and since a falsehood must be deliberate in the sense of intentional, otherwise it would be simply a mistake, it is redundant.

delicacy; dainty. See **tidbit.**

delightful; delicious; delectable. That is *delightful* which affords delight. That is *delicious* which pleases the senses of taste or smell—though these, especially the sense of taste, are extended figuratively. A delightful meal would be one at which there was pleasant company, in pleasant surroundings and at which, presumably, the food would be delicious. But it is conceivable that delicious food could be served at a meal which was not delightful if the company was unpleasant or the surroundings disagreeable.

Delectable is a poetic form of *delightful*. Bunyan referred to *the Delectable Mountains* in what is perhaps the most famous use of the word. Fowler says that it is now used in England only in an ironical sense but in America, where it is a club-woman gush word, it is used largely as a synonym for *delicious*.

delimit. See **limit.**

delirium. The plural is *deliriums* or *deliria*.

deliver. When this word is used in connection with childbirth, it means "to set free" and not "to hand over." Although it would seem that birth sets the baby free even more than it does the mother, this hasn't been the opinion of people old enough to talk about the matter. In literary English, therefore, it is the mother, and not the child, who is delivered. In the United States one often hears of babies being delivered. This is probably a survival from the stork period when *delivered* had to be understood as handed over.

deliverance; delivery. *Delivery* refers to transfer or conveyance, the utterance of speech, or the act of giving birth (*Its delivery was rapid. His delivery was sonorous and clear. The delivery was normal at term*). *Deliverance* was once synonymous in these meanings, but it is now a legal and ecclesiastical term and means primarily a rescue or release from some undesirable state (*Prayer brings deliverance from guilt*).

delusion. See **allusion.**

delve, in the literal sense of digging with a spade, is known today chiefly in John Ball's fierce rhyme:

> *When Adam dolve and Eve span,*
> *Who was then the gentleman?*

—usually misspoken, for clarity, as "When Adam delved." In the figurative sense of intellectual digging (*Not in the cells where frigid learning delves/ In Aldine folios mouldering on their shelves*) it is slightly pedantic and affected.

demand; claim; require. To *demand* is to ask in a bold, authoritative way (*He demanded immediate admission*). To *claim* is to assert a right to something (*He claimed the respect due his rank and would accept no less*). To *require* is to ask for something as being necessary (*The army requires obedience; it could not function without it*) or to compel (*His lordship required them to be up before daylight and on before him*). See also **inquire.**

demean. There is a verb *demean* which means to conduct or behave oneself (*No man who engaged in the rebellion demeaned himself throughout its course so honorably and so humanely*).

There is also, despite the protests of the purists, another verb *demean* which means to lower in dignity or standing, to debase (*It was, of course, Mrs. Sedley's opinion that her son would demean himself by a marriage with an artist's daughter*). This may have originated in a misconception of the other verb *demean* in certain contexts. It may be modeled from the adjective *mean* as an analogy to *debase,* but the fact remains that it is here. It has been used by some of the best writers and is used by the common speaker far more often than the other verb. Indeed, the common speaker is often astonished to learn (from the purist) that there is another verb. It is now standard usage.

demise is a word of highly special meanings which, in grandiloquence or as a euphemism, is sometimes put to improper uses. Originally it was a law term, signifying the conveyance or transfer of an estate by will or lease. Then it came to refer to the transference of sovereignty on the death or deposition of a sovereign, and here we have such phrases as *death or demise* and *the demise of the crown*. When Edward the Fourth was driven from his throne for a few months this period was called his demise. In most cases, however, the sovereignty has been demised by the death of the sovereign, and so it is a natural extension of the word to speak of a ruler's death as his demise. To speak of an ordinary man's death as his demise, however, is probably erroneous, since no sovereignty is transferred by the act. And it is certainly grandiloquent. One might as well speak of his accession to a job or his abdication on being fired.

demolish. See **destroy.**

demonstrative pronouns and adjectives. Most grammarians mean by *demonstrative pronouns* simply the words *this, that, these,* and *those*. Some grammarians feel that any pronoun which "points out" may be called a demonstrative, such as *the former, the latter, the first, the one, the other, the same*. In either case, these same words can also be used to qualify nouns. When they are, they are called *demonstrative adjectives*. See **this; that.**

demur. See **object.**

den (a room in a house). See **sanctum.**

denigrate. See **black.**

denominate. See **name.**

denotation. See **connotation.**

denote. To *denote* is to be a mark or sign of, to represent by a symbol or to stand as a symbol for. A rapid pulse often denotes a fever. A clinical thermometer shows it. An expensive car may denote its owner to be a man of wealth. His bank account shows it.

dent and **dint** were originally simply variant spellings of the same word, meaning a stroke or blow with a sharp instrument. *Dint* keeps this meaning in figurative uses (*By dint of argument*) but in literal uses both words now mean wholly the consequences of such a stroke or blow. *Dent* is confined exclusively to a literal sense, but *dint* may be used either literally or figuratively. A fender may have a dent or a dint, but a reputation or one's self-esteem can only have a dint.

deny; repudiate. In the sense of declaring to be false, *repudiate* is a stronger word than *deny*, which often has an adverb to give it emphasis. *Repudiate*, of course, has other meanings that *deny* is not synonymous for, such as to cast off or disown (*He repudiated his son*) or to refuse to pay debts because they are disowned (*He repudiated his wife's debts*). See also **refute.**

Deo volente; D.V.; God willing. Though the truly pious are fully aware of the uncertainty of all human plans, they are not as frequently moved as the pharisaical and the superstitious to call public attention to their awareness. The use of the phrase "*D.V.*," the initials of *Deo volente*, or the English form *God willing*, as an interjection after an expressed intention is a verbal counterpart of knocking on wood and has about the same value. As a cliché, it should certainly not be used at all. As a serious expression, one hardly need say, it should be confined to serious occasions. Used, as it is, to suggest that a commercial radio program continues from day to day solely by Divine permission, it fails to convey quite the pious humility that it so ostentatiously intends.

dependant; dependent. Though *dependent* is now standard for all uses, *dependant* for the noun is acceptable.

depleted; reduced. Though one meaning of *deplete* is to reduce the fulness of, *depleted* in common usage means emptied or exhausted, not merely "reduced." *Depletion* almost always suggests an injurious reduction. A garrison, for example, may be *depleted* by sickness; whereas it may be *reduced* by order and for its own advantage.

deplore means to weep for, to bewail, to grieve over, to regret deeply. Yet in the past two or three generations it has been used so much in more-in-sorrow-than-in-anger reproaches that we are a little startled when we come across it in its simple sense. When we read Tennyson in his *Ode on the Death of the Duke of Wellington* asking *Where shall we lay the man whom we deplore?* we are taken aback. One does not, today, allude to deplorable things in a eulogy. Whether the word will purge off this new accretion of meaning or whether high-minded condescension has done its deplorable work remains to be seen. See also **regret.**

depot; station. Those who insist that a distinction must be made between *depot* and *station* may know their etymology but they don't know their railroads. It is true that a *depot* is properly a place of deposit for freight and a *station* the place where a train stops to pick up and deposit passengers. But in all except a very few large cities the *depot* and the *station* were the same building and since freight is a far more important part of the business of most railroads than passengers, the term for the freight warehouse was naturally applied to the whole.

There's more to it than that, though, and a linguistic lesson to boot. *Depot* is, to be sure, a rather highfalutin name, but in the early days railroads were highfalutin things and deserved the best. But *depots*, once rather grand, became shabby, dingy places, gritty, with potbellied stoves, hard benches, fetid air, and long, long, dreary hours of waiting. The glory and elegance went out of the word and it, too, became dingy (*All those loafers always hanging around the depot*) and finally, as often happens to words of unusual elegance, became, as it now is, rustic and provincial. Soon it will become quaint and then charming.

depravation; depravity. *Depravation* is the act of corrupting, *depravity* the state of being corrupted. *Depravity*, of course, encourages *depravation* and *depravation* produces *depravity*.

depraved. See **abandoned.**

deprecate; depreciate. *Deprecate* means to express earnest disapproval of, usually regretfully (*He deprecated the tendency of younger scholars to publish in haste*). To *depreciate* is to belittle, to lessen the value of, to present as of little value (*the depreciation of currency. Goldsmith had an unhappy tendency to depreciate the writings of all other authors of his day*).

derby in America is a stiff felt hat with a rounded crown and a narrow brim, worn chiefly by men. In England it is called a bowler. There is a race called the Derby in both countries. In England it is run annually at Epsom Downs, near London. In America it is run annually at Churchill Downs, Kentucky.

derelict properly means left or abandoned by the owner. Its use in America to mean delinquent or remiss in the performance of a duty (*The committee has been derelict in its duty*—Mark Twain) is a peculiar linguistic phenomenon. It may have originated in sheer ignorance, have been a blunder for *dereliction*. But whatever its origin, it has been in use in the United States for almost a century among the best writers and speakers and is definitely standard. See **flotsam.**

derring do, as a term for heroic deeds and daring, is pseudo-archaic and is usually used in a mildly satiric way.

The history of *derring do*, traced by the *Oxford English Dictionary*, serves to demonstrate, once again, that usage makes anything standard. It all began with Chaucer who said (in 1374) that the knight Troylus was *in no degre secounde,/ In dorrying don that longeth to a knyght*, that is that he was second to no one in "daring to do" whatever it belonged to a knight to do. Fifty-six years later John Lydgate, a minor poet who imitated Chaucer, said that Troylus was a second Hector in manhood, deed, and *dorrying do*. Whether he was just careless and left the final "n" off and didn't bother with an object to the verb, or whether he thought *dorrying don* was some quality of manliness that *longeth to a knyght* will never be known. And things were made worse by the fact that when his book was printed (in 1513 and 1555) "dorrying do" was misprinted as "derrynge do." In this form it was picked up, in 1579, by Edmund Spenser, a great poet and a great pedant, who was looking for archaic words to give a rustic flavor to his poem *The Shepherd's Calendar*. Spenser, in the manner later employed by T. S. Eliot, went out of his way to be obscure and then went further out of his way to add a glossary in the footnotes to enlighten the reader he had bewildered in the text. And in this glossary he defined *derring doe* (whose spelling he had "modernized") as "manhood and chevalrie." He was, apparently, enchanted with the alliteration and incomprehensibility of the term because he used it four other times (once even referring to "Dreadful derring dooers") in his poems.

Sir Walter Scott, a great purveyor of Wardour Street English, found the phrase in Spenser and transferred it to *Ivanhoe,* though he still felt it necessary to gloss it in a note as "desperate courage." From Scott, whose popularity alone was enough to give it currency, it passed to the dime novels, the westerns, and the literary critics.

descant. See **decant.**

describe; narrate. To *describe* is to convey an impression or image in words. A description seeks particularly to reveal the appearance and the nature of things that exist in space (*He described the strange old hotel at which he and his sister had spent their vacation*). To *narrate* is to recount an occurrence, usually by giving the details of an event in the order in which they happened in time (*He narrated the adventures which had befallen them on their vacation*). The two words are easily confused because they refer to processes which are usually mixed. A narrative is more meaningful if the scene in which it took place has been described.

descry; discern; notice; perceive. To *descry* is to catch sight of, especially from a distance (*The English sentinels do keep good watch; if they descry us all our labor's lost*) or to discover from observation (Milton speaks of Galileo looking at the moon through his telescope *To descry new Lands, Rivers or Mountains in her spotty Globe*). It is a literary word today and would seem a little strange or affected in ordinary speech or writing. See also **decry.**

To *discern* is to perceive by the sight or some other sense or by the intellect, to apprehend clearly, or to distinguish differences. *Discern* suggests distinguishing (sometimes with difficulty) a thing for what it really is under confusing or misleading appearances (*But wait, I discern a fault in your argument*).

To *notice* is to become aware of something

which has caught one's attention (*Suddenly I noticed that the man was moving*).

To *perceive*, which is often used as a formal substitute for "see" and "notice," also has the idea of understanding meanings and implications (*After a short while, however, he perceived what they were really up to*).

deserve. The *-ing* form of a verb following *deserve* usually has a passive meaning, as in *he deserves waiting on, he deserves helping.* An infinitive after *deserve* usually has an active meaning, as in *he deserves to wait on us, he deserves to help. Deserve* may also be followed by a clause, as in *he deserves that we should help him,* but this construction is felt to be stiff and an infinitive, such as *he deserves to have us help him,* is generally preferred.

desideratum. The plural is *desideratums* or *desiderata.*

designate is not properly a complete synonym for *describe*. To *designate* is to indicate or show. An officer's insignia designates his rank. To say *I would designate such a remark as pure insolence* is not as correct as to say *I would describe such a remark as pure insolence* or *I would call such a remark,* etc.

desirable; desirous. *Desirable* means worthy to be desired (*a very desirable site for a house*). *Desirous* means having desire, longing, wishful (*We never find ourselves so desirous to finish, as in the latter part of our work*).

desire. This verb may be followed by an infinitive, as in *he desired to tell them,* but not by the *-ing* form of a verb. We do not say *he desired telling them.* The noun *desire* may be followed by an infinitive, as in *the desire to read,* or by the *-ing* form of a verb introduced by *for,* as in *the desire for reading.* The preposition *of* following *desire* shows a genitive, or possessive, relation, as in *the desire of the moth for the star.* Either the verb or the noun may be followed by a clause but the clause verb must be a subjunctive or a subjunctive equivalent, as in *he desired I should tell you* and *the desire that I should tell you.* See **want.**

desperate. See **hopeless.**

dessert. See **candy.**

destroy; demolish; raze. To *destroy* something is to scatter it into useless pieces, to take away its powers and functions so completely that it cannot be restored. It can refer to tangibles or intangibles. It can be sudden and violent or slow and unperceived (*The hurricane destroyed the entire village. In time drink destroyed his will and malnutrition undermined his strength*). *Demolish* applies to organized bodies or structures and implies destruction by the complete separation of parts. A machine is *demolished,* a formal structure of logic is *demolished,* a building is *demolished.* To *raze* is to level down to the ground. It is related to *razor* and means, basically, to scrape. It is applied almost entirely to buildings, though there are some figurative extensions.

deteriorate; degenerate. Both words mean to make or become worse. There is a perfectly good English verb *worsen,* but it might sound strange to most ears now. *Deteriorate* is usually applied to changes for the worse in abstractions (conditions are always deteriorating and so are relations) or in things in whose worsening there is no sense of moral condemnation. The weather deteriorates. So do houses and health. *Degenerate* usually carries a sense of moral condemnation (*Degenerate bastard, I'll not trouble thee*) or implies that in the worsening there has been the loss of some virtuous quality once essential to the person or thing spoken of. Benedict Arnold degenerated from a brave soldier to a buccaneer. Arguments frequently degenerate into squabbles.

determine. See **decide.**

detest. See **hate.**

detract; distract. Both *detract* and *distract* mean to draw away from. But *detract* has come to mean, in most common uses, the taking away from a good reputation, depreciation (*Claudius's drunkenness detracted greatly from his kingly dignity. To listen to detraction is as much an act of detraction as to speak it*). *Distract* has come to mean the drawing of things away from the mind, especially the drawing of attention or fixed purpose away from its aim (*These diversions distract us from our graver purposes*). *Distraction* and *distracted* can mean that the mind has been so far drawn from any settled purpose, or so confused by various drawings away, that it can no longer function in an orderly manner (*The minds of men were too distracted for so deliberate a plan. He ran about like one distracted*).

detritus. The plural is *detrituses* or *detritus,* not *detriti.*

develop. To *develop* (sometimes *develope*) is to unfold, to bring out, to progress from a simple to a more complex form, to advance from a latent to an active stage. That is, in all its meanings there is the implication that there was something there in the first place which has come gradually into existence or operation. Hence to use *develop* as a synonym for *originate* (*Many things wholly new have developed in the past generation. New states that developed after the war*) is to misuse it. A man *catches* a cold if he has been totally free from one. He *develops* a cold if he allows a slight one to become severe.

The use of *develop* to mean to bring to light, or to come to light, to transpire (*A new feature of the shooting developed today, when it was discovered that.... It develops now that he never intended to join us*), now obsolete in England, is standard usage in the United States.

deviate; digress; divagate; diverge; swerve. To *deviate* is to turn aside from the set path in a wandering and often purposeless way (*The rest to some faint meaning make pretence,/ But Shadwell never deviates into sense*). To *digress* is to wander from the main topic, in speech or writing, usually for the purpose of explaining or illustrating (*I have too long digressed, and therefore shall return to my subject*). *Divagate* is a synonym for both *deviate* and *digress,* more inclining to the former, but is so unusual and

literary a word that it could be used only before a select audience if one were to avoid the charge of affectation. Things *diverge* which proceed from a common point in such directions that the distance between them increases (*Two roads diverged in a wood, and I—/ I took the one less traveled by*). It is the opposite of *converge.* To *swerve* is to make a sudden or sharp turn from a line or course (*The car, traveling at great speed, swerved from the road and plunged over the embankment*), though it also often has the meaning of returning to the course as well (*The car swerved around the heavy truck and continued at breakneck speed*).

These meanings all carry over into figurative uses. Thus one who *deviated* from the path of rectitude would be one who wandered from it. One who *diverged* would be one who left it and got farther from it as he continued. One who *swerved* from it would be one who left it with suddenness, under some stress or necessity, and it might mean one who so left it but almost immediately returned to it.

device; devise. *Device* is always a noun. It means an invention or contrivance, a plan, a crafty scheme, or a trick (*What is needed is a device for turning off the alarm before it rings. That's a cunning device, but it won't save him now*). In the plural, *device* has a special meaning of desire or inclination, in the hackneyed phrase "left to his own devices." Presumably the idea arose from the tricks or contrivances which desire would invent.

Devise is used as a noun only in the special legal meanings of a will that disposes of real property, the act of so disposing, or the property so disposed of. As a verb *devise* means to invent or contrive (*He devised a machine that would use the same water over and over. He devised a way of getting out of paying his debts without at the same time losing face in the community*).

devilry; deviltry. *Deviltry* is a variant of *devilry,* the extraneous *t* having been inserted, presumably, to match it with gallantry, peasantry, and the like. Though both words can mean extreme wickedness or cruelty and both can mean hilarity or daring—the impish side of devilish doings—*deviltry* is now used almost exclusively to mean mischievous high spiritedness (*What deviltry are you fellows up to there with those masks and that bucket of paint?*).

devil's advocate. In the Roman Catholic Church, where the term had its origin, *the devil's advocate* is one appointed to present the arguments against a proposed canonization as a saint. He is, indeed, therefore, as Fowler insists, "the blackener of the good" rather than "the whitewasher of the wicked." None the less the general public, lamentably ignorant of holiness in all its ways and forms, uses the phrase to mean the advocate of a bad cause or one who injures a cause by his advocacy of it, and has so used it so long that these meanings must be accepted as standard.

deviser; devisor; divisor. He who devises something, in the sense of inventing it, is its *deviser.* He who devises property to a devisee is a *de-*

visor. That number by which the dividend is divided is the *divisor.*

devote may be followed by the *-ing* form of a verb with the preposition *to,* as in *he devoted himself to earning a living,* but not by an infinitive or a clause.

devoted. See **addicted.**

dexterous; dextrous. Both forms, meaning adroit, are correct. *Dexterous* has the advantage of being more clearly related to dexterity. *Dextrous* has the advantage of being shorter.

diabolical rage differs, apparently, from ordinary rage in the malevolence of its fury and the menace of its hostility. The Devil was thought to be given to special tantrums at the thought of lost bliss and the sight of man's innocence and expectations of felicity to come. But people —at least not many of those who employ five-syllable words—no longer believe in a literal devil who gnashes actual teeth and stamps and screams in ill temper. The term has become a cliché and is generally to be avoided. (So also with **diabolical skill** and **diabolical cunning.**)

diacritical mark is a mark, point, or sign added or attached to a letter or character to distinguish it from another of similar form, to give it a particular phonetic value, to indicate stress, etc.

The chief diacritical marks are the *dieresis* (or *diaeresis*) in English (the sign `··` placed over the second of two adjacent vowels to indicate separate pronunciation, as in *coöperate*), the *tilde* in Spanish [see **tilde**], the *cedilla* in French and Portuguese (a mark placed under *c* before *a, o,* or *u,* as in *façade,* to show it has the sound of *s*), the *umlaut* in German [see **umlaut**] and various accent marks (´, `, ^, ˘, etc.) used to indicate pronunciation and stress.

diagnosis. The plural is *diagnosises* or *diagnoses.*

dialect. See **vernacular.**

dialectal; dialectical. *Dialectal* means of a dialect or characteristic of a dialect (*A dialectal peculiarity of Scotch is the pronunciation as ōō of the sound that appears in English as ou, in house or mouse*).

Dialectical or *dialectic* means of or pertaining to the nature of logical argumentation (*Pure reason is always dialectical. His subtle intellect concerned itself more and more exclusively with the dialectical splitting of dogmatical hairs*). *Dialectical* is often used for *dialectal,* so often that this use is now standard. But *dialectal* cannot be used for *dialectical.*

dialogue; duologue; monologue; soliloquy; conversation; talk. A *dialogue* is a conversation between two or more persons, especially in a play or a novel (*The action was good but the dialogue was forced*). *Duologue* is a conversation between two persons only. The only use it has, and that is rare, is as a special name for a dramatic piece in the form of a dialogue limited to two speakers. A *monologue* is a prolonged talk or discourse by a single speaker, a composition in which a person speaks alone, or a form of dramatic entertainment by a single speaker (*Browning was a master of the dramatic monologue. Bea Lillie's monologues are incompar-*

able). Some insist that a *monologue* cannot be a soliloquy (that is, talking when alone), that it may consist of one person speaking but someone else must be present, as in Browning's famous dramatic monologues. But in America today, it is used a great deal of one person speaking alone, used more that way, indeed, than in its earlier sense, in standard speech and writing. *Conversation* is an exchange of thoughts in spoken words. If more than two persons take part, it may be called a *colloquy* and if it is extraordinarily stuffy and pompous it may be called a *colloquium.* A *conversation* is informal but not quite so familiar as *talk.* When Samuel Johnson, one of the greatest of conversationalists, said *Yes, sir, we had good talk,* he meant that the conversation had been particularly easy and relaxed, lively, interesting, rapid and gay. The spellings *dialog, duolog,* and *monolog* are acceptable.

dialysis. The plural is *dialyses.*

diamond in the rough. To say of someone of sterling worth but uncouth manners or exterior that he is *a diamond in the rough* or a *rough diamond* is to employ a cliché. Do so if you wish, but know that you are doing so.

dice. The singular and the plural are both *dice.* Originally *dice* was the plural of *die,* which meant one of the cubes used in games of chance. In this sense one has very little occasion to use the word in the singular. But when the occasion does arise the form *dice* is now used in place of the old singular *die,* as in *he did not touch a dice. Dice* is also the form used as the first element in a compound, as in *dice playing* and *dice box.* The plural *dices* has been in existence for several centuries but has never become standard.

Today the old singular *die* is used only in the derived sense of a stamp or mold, and in this sense it has a regular plural *dies.* The expression *the die is cast* originally meant *the dice have been thrown.* Most Americans hear this in the new sense of *die,* as if it meant *the mold has been formed.* Either metaphor accounts for the sense of the expression, which is that it is now too late to change one's mind. As a way of saying that a decision has been irrevocably made, *the die is cast* is a cliché.

dickens is employed in many contexts for devil (*What the dickens do you mean? Who the dickens is that? I'll give him the very dickens when I see him*). It is now often thought to be a euphemistic substitution of the last name of the author, Charles Dickens, employed simply for alliteration. This is not so, however. The word was so employed centuries before Charles Dickens was born (*I cannot tell what the dickens his name is*—Shakespeare, *The Merry Wives of Windsor*). It has been suggested that it is a form of *devilkin,* or little devil, but there is no proof.

diction is the element of style which depends on choice of words, as distinguished from sentence structure or arrangement of material. Good diction conveys ideas with clarity and precision of effect, whatever the style may be.

Certain words are associated with particular kinds of diction. *O'er* and *yestereve*, for instance, are poetic terms. *Whereas, aforementioned, party of the first part* and *hereinafter* are legal. The world of sport has its own special vocabulary. But diction cannot always be classified as to type. It is good or bad to the degree that it is appropriate or inappropriate to the subject. Much of the aesthetic quality of style inheres in the diction.

dictum. The plural is *dictums* or *dicta*.

did. See **do.**

die. This verb may be followed by an adjective describing the one who dies, as in *he died happy.* It may also be followed by an adverb describing the dying, as in *he died quickly.*

die a natural death. Our concept of what is natural and what is unnatural has undergone great changes in the past fifty years or so. The phrase is redundant and hackneyed and with the development of new weapons may even become outmoded. In a sense, all deaths are natural or we wouldn't die them.

die; decease; pass away (or **on**); **perish.** *Die* is the grim, everyday word (*Ay, but to die, and go we know not where;/ To lie in cold obstruction and to rot*). It is used of all living things and used figuratively of anything that has displayed an activity that may be likened to life (*When a lovely flame dies. . . . Music, when soft voices die, lingers in the memory*).

Decease is a legal term. It refers only to human beings. Sometimes an individual who is dead will be referred to euphemistically as *the deceased* in a eulogy or a news story, but it is an awkward and not very successful attempt to avoid an unpleasant reality. Those who have died are usually referred to in the plural as *the dead.* Nothing has been able to lessen the dignity and solemnity of the term. To speak of *passing away* or *passing on,* with its implication of a continuation of life elsewhere, is a vulgarity. True faith has never blinked the reality of death.

To *perish* is to become utterly extinct (*shall not perish from the earth*). It is a literary term. When applied to human beings it implies a cruel or unusual death, as by hunger, cold, or neglect (*He perished on the scaffold. Thirty thousand people perished in the Lisbon earthquake*). *Perish the thought* (i.e., don't even think about it any more, let the very thought become extinct) is a cliché.

dieresis. The plural is *diereses.* See **diacritical mark.**

dies. See **dice.**

difference; differentiation. The *difference* between two things is the quality or extent or degree to which they are not the same (*The difference in weight between the two packages was only half an ounce. There is a great difference between dying in hot blood like Romeo and going off like a frog in a frost*). *Differentiation* is the action of distinguishing between two things, the distinguishing of their difference and sometimes the making of differences (*A careful differentiation of their claims showed Anstley's to be the better founded. Long continued isolation*

would often lead to the differentiation of species).

difference; discrepancy; disparity. *Difference* refers to a complete or partial lack of identity (*Though they were brothers, the difference between them was as great as could be. The difference between the two estimates was less than a dollar*). *Discrepancy* usually refers to a difference or inconsistency between things that should agree (*There was always a discrepancy between what he promised and what he did. The discrepancy in his accounts was serious*). *Disparity* implies inequality (*There was a disparity in their height*), often where a greater approximation to equality might reasonably be expected (*The disparity in their accomplishments was puzzling when one reflected that they had the same advantages and opportunities*).

difference and **distinction** may be used interchangeably when they both refer to perceivable dissimilarities (*There is a distinction between a compound and a double fracture* or *There is a difference between a compound and a double fracture*). *Distinction,* however, usually suggests that the perception of the dissimilarity has been the result of analysis and discrimination (*That is a fine distinction to make*). *Difference* refers only to the condition of being dissimilar (*There is a difference there that is surely obvious to all but the wilfully blind*).

When used with the preposition *of* as a term of praise (*a book of distinction*), *distinction* is vague and uncertain. It means rather distinguished than distinct and implies a certain merit of perception in those applying the term. The "Man of Distinction" of the advertisements was meant, apparently, to be both distinguished and discriminating.

different; diverse; various; distinct. *Various* stresses a similarity underlying superficial differences in several kinds of the same general thing. To say that *various accounts of the incident were reported* means that the accounts agreed, at least to the point that it was recognizable that they alluded to the same incident, but differed, or varied, in particulars. The word *different* is applied to either a single thing differing in identity or character from another, or to two or more things differing thus from one another. To say that *different accounts of the incident were reported* would be to imply that the accounts were more divergent than the *various* accounts. They might even disagree in fundamental facts. *Diverse* implies a sharper contrast than *different. Distinct* implies a lack of connection between things which, however, may possibly be alike or similar. *Two distinct accounts of the incident* might agree or disagree in their relation of what had happened, but they would be wholly separate observations.

different from; different than. Walter Page, who was undoubtedly one of the most conservative writers of English in the twentieth century, wrote to his son: *see that you use no word in a different sense than it was used in a hundred years ago.* The great purist did not make a mistake. As he knew very well, *different than* can be found in the writings of Addison, Steele, Defoe, Richardson, Goldsmith, Coleridge, De Quincey, Carlyle, Thackeray, and a great many others. Cardinal Newman wrote: *it has possessed me in a different way than ever before.* John Maynard Keynes, another master of clear and beautiful prose, wrote: *how different things appear in Washington than in London.*

In the examples just given *than* introduces a condensed clause. It could not be replaced by the single word *from* but would require *from that which* or even more words. There is no doubt that the best writers and speakers generally prefer *than* to an elaborate construction such as *from that which.* When what follows is a simple noun or pronoun and not a clause, as in *different from mine, different than mine,* most people prefer *from,* but *than* is also acceptable. In Great Britain the word *to* is often used here, as in *different to mine.* This is comparable to the use of *to* with Latin comparative forms, such as *inferior, anterior, senior,* and is acceptable in Great Britain.

The notion that *from* was the correct word to use after *different,* and that *than* and *to* were incorrect, dates from the eighteenth century. The idea may have been based on nothing more than the fact that the Latin word *differre* means *separate.* In English *than* is the normal word to use in comparing things that are dissimilar. It is true that *than* can only be used with the comparative form of an adjective. It cannot be used with a positive form. We may say *greener than* but not *green than.* And the word *different* looks like a positive form. But the positive form of an adjective cannot be qualified by degree words, such as *much, far, a great deal,* and the word *different* can. We may say *much different* and *far different,* just as we say *much greener* and *far greener. Different* therefore has the standing of a comparative adjective, independently of its use with *than,* and *far different from* may be as disturbing to the speech instinct as *far greener from.*

Different from is established in current English and anyone who likes these words may use them in any construction. But no one has any grounds for condemning others who would rather say *different than,* since this construction is used by some of the most sensitive writers of English and is in keeping with the fundamental structure of the language.

differentiate. See **distinguish.**

diffident. See **modest.**

dig. The past tense is *dug* or *digged.* The participle is also *dug* or *digged.*

Though *digged* is still acceptable as the past tense and participle of *dig* (The man in the parable who had received but one talent *went and digged in the earth, and hid his lord's money*), *dug* has become so much more common that *digged* would seem to many Americans a childish error.

digress. See **deviate.**

dilemma. See **predicament.**

dilettante. The plural is *dilettantes* or *dilettanti.*

diminish; minimize. To *diminish* is to make less; to *minimize* is to make least or reduce to the smallest possible amount or degree. *Minimize* is used, however, to mean belittle (*She always said "Have you a minute to rinse out a few things?" to minimize the effort of doing the laundry*); whereas *diminish* is rarely, if ever, so used. *Diminish* is more likely to be applied to material things (*The pack was diminished by the amount of two pairs of shoes and a tarpaulin*). *Minimize* is more likely to be applied to qualities and abstractions (*It is unwise to minimize the danger; it is great and must be faced*).

dint. See **dent.**

diocese. See **see.**

dip. The past tense is *dipped* or *dipt.* The participle is also *dipped* or *dipt. Dipped* is generally preferred to *dipt.*

diploma. The plural is *diplomas* or *diplomata,* not *diplomae.*

dipper. Though *dipper* as a term for a long-handled ladle or drinking cup had a brief career in England (Mason in his Supplement to Johnson's Dictionary, 1801, mentions it as "a modern invention"), it is now almost exclusively an American word in this sense. It is also used in America, and in America only, as a name for the configuration of stars in Ursa Major called in England "the Plough" or "Charles's Wain" and for a similar configuration in Ursa Minor. These are popularly called *the Big Dipper* and *the Little Dipper* respectively in the United States.

dipt. See **dip.**

direct; directly. *Direct* may be used as an adjective (*He favors the direct approach*) or an adverb (*He flew direct to New York*). Where the meaning is in a direct line of authority or responsibility, *directly* must be used (*He was directly involved*). So also with *exactly, absolutely,* and *precisely* (*The farmhouse was directly in the line of Sherman's fire*).

In the sense of without delay, immediately (*I'll be there directly*), *directly* is an English usage rather than an American. It was so used formerly more in America than it is now, but even then there was the difference that in America it signified "soon" rather than "at once" (*When you say you will do a thing "directly" you mean "immediately"; in the American language—generally speaking—the word signifies "after a little"*—Mark Twain). As a conjunction meaning "as soon as" (*Directly on arriving, he issued orders for the man's arrest*), *directly* is, again, largely an English usage.

For the last hundred years the word *directly* has also been used as a conjunction, that is, to introduce a clause, as in *directly he arrived, I left.* Here the word means "as soon as." The only possible objection to this construction is that it is relatively new. Most conjunctions have developed from adverbs in just this way, and this particular one has been established in English literature by Dickens, Thackeray, and Matthew Arnold.

When *direct* is used as a verb and means order, it may be followed by an infinitive, as in *we directed him to return*. When it means aim at it may be followed by the *-ing* form of a verb with the preposition *to* or *at*, as in *he directed his energies to improving conditions*.

disassemble; dissemble. To *disassemble* is to take apart (*The mechanic disassembled the motor*). To *dissemble* is to give a false semblance to, to conceal the real nature of something (usually one's emotions or motives) under a semblance of something else (*She dissembled her annoyance under a smiling face*).

disaster. See **holocaust; tragedy.**

disbar. See **debar.**

disbeliever. See **agnostic; skeptic.**

discern. See **descry.**

disciples; apostles. A *disciple* is one who is taught. An *apostle* is one who is sent forth to teach others. Since Christ's disciples were also, with one exception, the first apostles of Christianity, there is some natural confusion in the use of the terms. The twelve disciples are: SS. Peter (also called Simon), Andrew, James (the Greater), John, Thomas (also called Didymus), James (the Less), Jude (also called Judas, Thaddeus, and Lebaeus), Philip, Bartholomew (identified with Nathanael), Matthew (also called Levi), Simon (called Zelotes), and Judas Iscariot. The twelve apostles are the same except that Matthias replaces Judas Iscariot. St. Paul is always called an apostle and so are a few others, such as St. Barnabas. The chief missionary to a country is sometimes called its apostle. Thus St. Patrick is often called the apostle of Ireland.

In the Mormon Church an *apostle* is one of the council of twelve officials presiding over the Church and administering its ordinances. *Disciples of Christ*, sometimes called Campbellites, is a Protestant religious body founded in the United States in the nineteenth century.

disclose; expose; reveal; divulge. To *disclose* is to allow to be seen, to make known, to lay open and thereby to invite inspection of, something which had been concealed (*He smiled, and opening out his milk-white palm,/ Disclosed a fruit of pure Hesperian gold. The Gunpowder Plot was disclosed by a letter from one of the conspirators to a friend urging him not to attend Parliament on the fatal day*). See also **discover.**

To *expose* is to exhibit openly, to display to public gaze (*The wind had ripped away the clapboards and exposed the studding*), to so display with a view to unmasking or holding up to ridicule or reproof (*He saw the deception and exposed it*). To *reveal* is to uncover as if by drawing away (*For a moment the mask of benevolence fell and the real man was revealed. Daylight will reveal the disposition of their troops*). To *divulge* is to communicate what was intended to be confidential, secret (*Those apprehended hastened to save themselves by divulging all they knew of Torrio's plans*). It is a word that would probably sound a little affected to

the common ear; *telling* would seem more natural than *divulging*.

disclosure. See **revelation.**

discomfit; discomfort. To *discomfit* is to defeat, to rout utterly (*Thrice hath this Hotspur, Mars in swathing clothes,/ Discomfited great Douglas*), or to throw into confusion or utter dejection, to disconcert (*Dombey was quite discomfited by the question*). To *discomfort* means to disturb the comfort or happiness of, to make uneasy. One might be discomforted by tight shoes or a hard bench or a mosquito in the bedroom, but the word, which is rarely used in its proper sense, is frequently misused for *discomfit* (as in *The Turks, discomforted with the invincible courage of these old soldiers, betook themselves to flight*). Since, of course, he who is discomfited is often discomforted in the process, there are many instances in which one cannot be certain that the wrong word has been used. Thus when Stephen Spender writes, *When I asked myself these questions, I had to admit that what I really wanted was that others should live as I did, not that I should "join the workers": a prospect which discomfited me*, we have no way of knowing whether the prospect utterly routed him or merely made him uneasy. The latter seems more likely and, if so, *discomforted* should have been used.

discover; disclose. In the sense of removing a covering (*If the house be discovered by tempest, the tenant must in convenient time repair it*), *discover* is now obsolete, having been replaced by *uncover*. In the sense of exposing to view, revealing, or showing what was up to that time kept secret (*His refusal to sit at the same table with Carver discovered an unexpected narrowness*) it is rare, having been replaced by *disclose, reveal*, or *expose*. In Elizabethan England to have discovered a plot would have been to have revealed its existence. In modern English it would be to find it out, probably by accident.

discover; invent. *Discover* is used chiefly now to suggest the bringing to light of something which had previously been in existence but had hitherto been unknown (*The discovery of gold in the Klondike.... Columbus's discovery was at first misunderstood*). To *invent* is to make or create something new, especially, in modern usage, something ingeniously devised to perform mechanical operations (*The invention of calculating machines has extended the whole field of conjecture*). Where that which is created is an idea or a system of thought or an abstraction, such as a new way of doing something, it is said to have been *originated*. Idiomatically, however, a lie is always *invented*—perhaps in recognition of the mechanical nature of most prevarications.

discreet; discrete. *Discreet* means wise or judicious in avoiding mistakes, prudent, circumspect, cautious, not rash (*His wife being very reserv'd and discreet in her husband's presence, but in his absence more free and jolly . . .*). *Discrete* means separate, detached from others, distinct by itself (*The grains of sand were clean and discrete, not stuck together in wetness*).

Discrete is pretty much a literary and philosophical word, unknown to the common speaker and writer, and stands as a temptation to the learned to use it that they may explain it is not *discreet*. This is a temptation, needless to say, to be resisted. The negatives of both words are formed by prefixing *in-*.

discrepancy. See **difference.**

discriminate. See **distinguish.**

disease. See **sickness.**

disenfranchise. Though *disenfranchise* is a legitimate word, *disfranchise* is to be preferred. Since, however, the franchise and its recision are matters dear to politicians, to whom also are dear extra syllables and orotund phrases, *disenfranchise* is gaining in favor over its simpler synonym.

disgruntled. See **unsatisfied.**

disinterested; uninterested. Though *disinterested* was formerly a synonym for *uninterested*, it is not now so used. To be *uninterested* in something is to be unconcerned about it, indifferent, showing no feeling of interest (*I told him of our plans, but he seemed uninterested*). *Disinterested* suggests impartiality, freedom from any self-interest or the seeking of personal advantage (*His disinterested kindness to us in our days of misfortune can never be forgotten*).

dislike. This word may be followed by the *-ing* form of a verb, as in *he dislikes working*. It may also be followed by an infinitive, as in *he dislikes to work,* but the *-ing* construction is generally preferred. (See also **hate.**)

disorganized. See **unorganized.**

disparity. See **difference.**

dispatch. See **forward.**

disperse; disburse. To *disperse* is to scatter abroad. To *disburse* is to pay out money (*The young man soon dispersed what his father had so painfully acquired and so grudgingly disbursed*).

displace; misplace. To *displace* is to put out of the usual or proper place. It is confined now, chiefly, to the idea of moving from its proper place something solid and comparatively immovable and moving it in such a way that its displacement is likely to be permanent (*The impact displaced the foundations of the house*). It is also used to mean to take the place of, to replace (*Juliet soon displaced Rosaline in Romeo's affections*).

To *misplace* is to put some object, usually a portable one, in a wrong place so that it is difficult to find (*He has misplaced his glasses and is in a tizzy*).

disposal; disposition. Though *disposal* and *disposition* are sometimes used interchangeably in the sense of arrangement, American usage tends to use *disposal* more for getting rid of, as by gift, sale, or throwing away (*The disposal of the things not sold at the bazaar presented the ladies with quite a problem*). *Disposition* has more to do with arranging and ordering, especially in conformity with a preconceived plan. We speak of the disposition of troops in the field, the disposition of houses and shops in a model city. In general, *disposition* is related to *dispose, disposal* to *dispose of.*

dispose. This word may be followed by an infinitive, as in *this disposed him to take offense,* but not by the *-ing* form of a verb. We do not say *this disposed him to taking offense.*

One *disposes of* something when he deals with it definitely, gets rid of it. One may dispose of an unwanted coat, for example, by burning it, giving it away, or selling it. But *dispose of* is not a synonym for sell and to use it as such (as in *Have you disposed of all your bread today, or have you any loaves left?* when asked in a bakery) is an attempt to be genteel, to avoid commercial language as something low and unfitted to the transaction. So when someone says, *I will dispose of it for a trifle,* he wishes to imply that the exchange he is suggesting is of such advantage to the other party that it cannot possibly be considered an ordinary commercial transaction. Sometimes, of course, this may be the proper wording; the transaction may be far from an ordinary commercial one. But when it is an ordinary commercial transaction ordinary commercial language is more fitting and *sell* is the better word. Then *dispose of,* having many possible meanings, is more likely to be ambiguous.

disqualified. See **unqualified.**

disquisition. See **inquisition.**

dissatisfied. See **unsatisfied.**

dissemble and **dissimulate,** to disguise or conceal under a false appearance, are synonymous and any insistence that there is a distinction between them is unwarranted.

dissenter; dissentient. *Dissenter* is the common and *dissentient* the uncommon word in America for one who dissents (*Don't mind his not agreeing; he likes to be a dissenter*). In English usage *dissenter,* sometimes capitalized, has the special meaning of one who dissents from the service and worship of the Church of England (*Dr. Arnold drew up a disquieting scheme for allowing Dissenters into the Church, though it is true that he did not go quite so far as to contemplate the admission of Unitarians*). *Dissenters* in England are now thought of entirely as Protestants, though formerly the term included Roman Catholics.

dissimulate; simulate. One *dissimulates* to conceal under a feigned semblance something that one has or is. One *simulates* that which one is not or has not, pretending to be or to have it. See also **dissemble.**

dissociate; disassociate. *Dissociate* is the preferred form, though *disassociate* is not incorrect (*Such things are done only by men dissociated from the interests of party*).

distinct; distinctive. That is *distinct* which is clear in its identity, unmistakably itself, plain, definite, easily perceived. If a man has a distinct utterance, he speaks clearly and with precision. *Distinctive* means that which distinguishes something from other things of the same general kind, that highly characteristic of the speaker. It is conceivable that a man's way of speaking might be *distinctive* because it was not *distinct.* See also **different.**

distinction. See **difference.**

distinctive; distinguished. *Distinctive* means characteristic, peculiar, idiosyncratic. *Distinguished,* though it can be used and occasionally is used to mean conspicuous or marked, usually means noted, eminent, famous, having an air of distinction. The two words are not to be confused. Many are distinctive but few are distinguished.

distinguish; discriminate; differentiate. To *distinguish* is to recognize those features of a thing that establish its separate identity (*It is not hard to distinguish a hawk from a crow*). To *discriminate* is to perceive fine distinctions between things, to determine wherein these differences consist and to estimate their significance (*A tea taster can discriminate as many as twenty brands of tea, each from the other*). The commonest use of the word today is in reference to making adverse distinction with regard to certain people and, especially, to unfair treatment on the sole basis of such distinctions (*There shall be no discrimination because of race, creed, color, or country of origin*). Although *discrimination* could be in someone's favor, it is almost always conceived of as in someone's disfavor; and although special treatment on the basis of certain distinctions might be justified, the word now refers almost entirely to some special treatment that is unjustified.

To *differentiate* is to point out exactly and in detail the differences between two things (*It is not always easy to differentiate between shyness and rudeness*).

distract. See **detract.**

ditch (verb). In England to *ditch* means to make ditches or to provide with a ditch (*Her yard was ditched all about with a dry ditch*). This meaning is known in America but not much used. The commoner meaning is "to throw in a ditch" (*The train left the rails and was ditched six miles west of Clinton*) and the commonest of all is the slang use "to get rid of" (*After the holdup the thieves ditched the car in an alley. He ditched her in Albuquerque and went on alone*).

diurnal. See **daily.**

divagate. See **deviate.**

dive. The past tense is *dived* or *dove*. The participle is also *dived* or *dove*. *Dove* is no longer heard in Great Britain but it is still acceptable in the United States, where *dived* strikes many people's ears as "something from the Bible."

diverge. See **deviate.**

divers and **diverse,** though originally the same word, have now, in different spellings, become fixed in different meanings. *Divers* means various, several, sundry (*There are directions to be given to divers workmen before I start*). *Diverse* means unlike, of a different kind or form or character, or of various kinds or forms, multiform (*With habits so diverse, we may well expect corresponding diversity in their forms. The diverse and multiform nature of pleasure . . .*).

Divers is a literary word, with a suggestion of straining to be elegant in its use. Anyone today who would seriously say, with Captain Cook, *fish of divers sorts* would lay himself open to some pleasantries.

diverse. See **different.**

divide. In the United States, Canada, South Africa, and Australia, *divide* as a noun has the special meaning of mountains or high land forming a watershed (*I got a home in Wyomin'/ Far across the Great Divide*). In England as a verb *divide* has the special meaning of voting by separating into two groups (*Mr. B. expressed his intention of dividing the House on the motion*). See also **separate.**

dividend. The extension of *dividend,* the financial return upon an investment in stocks, to figurative uses (*Kindness pays dividends*) probably began as an attempt to seem practical and worldly in dealing with matters that are often thought to be impractical and unworldly. It is much overworked but use has not made it easy; it always sounds a little forced. It's not very appropriate, either: five percent is a pretty good dividend and if that's a good return for a virtuous act one had better either invest one's energies in something more profitable or abandon the hope of profit and allow virtue to be its own reward.

dividers. The measuring or drawing instrument may be called *a divider,* and more than one of them may be called *several dividers.* But one instrument may also be treated as a plural, as in *these dividers are the ones,* or referred to as *a pair of dividers.* This is acceptable but not necessary. The singular form *divider* is preferred as the first element in a compound, as in *a divider point.*

division of words. When it is necessary to break a word at the end of a line, the break should be made between syllables and should be marked by a hyphen, which is attached to the first fragment of the word. Syllables are the sound units that make up a word. If you cannot hear where one syllable ends and another begins, you can look it up in a dictionary. But the rules given below cover most of the problems you will meet. First, some don'ts:

1. Do not divide a proper name.
2. Do not divide abbreviations or letter words, such as A.B., SOS.
3. Do not divide figures, such as *1,386,422.*
4. Do not divide a hyphenated word except at the hyphen.
5. Except in printing, a certain amount of unevenness in the right hand margin is preferable to broken words. Therefore, never separate one or two letters from the rest of the word.
6. Each part of the broken word must be pronounceable. Therefore never break off letters that do not include a sounded vowel, such as *spl-* or *-ble.*
7. Do not break words that have only one real vowel sound in them, such as *people, watched.*
8. Never separate two consonants or two vowels that represent only one sound, such as *th, ch, wh, oi, au.*

If these don'ts are observed, the remaining rules for dividing words are not as difficult as they look:

1. Regardless of how a word is pronounced,

-*ing*, -*ish*, -*ed*, -*er*, -*est*, are usually treated as independent syllables and do not unite with a preceding consonant, as in *tell-ing*, *tall-ish*, *great-est*. There are two exceptions. (1.) If a consonant has been doubled before -*ing*, -*er*, etc., divide between the double letters, as in *run-ning*, *tip-per*. (But do not divide in this way when the word naturally ends with a double letter, as in the examples above, *tell-ing* and *tall-ish*.) (2.) When -*ing*, -*er*, or any of these syllables follows two consonant sounds, the second of which is *l*, divide according to sound, as in *gig-gling*, *tin-gling*, *tick-led*.

,2. When two true vowel sounds come together, divide between the vowels, as in *medi-ate*. But do not divide such words as *appe-ase*, where the *ea* represents one sound.

3. When a single consonant sound stands between two vowels, the consonant remains with the preceding vowel if that is short and has a stress, as in *ráp-idly*, *pród-uct*, *crít-ical*. (The vowel is long in *pró-gram*, *pecú-liar*, *procé-dure*, and it is unstressed in *sépa-rate*, *ómi-nous*, *mécha-nism*.) If you cannot decide how this rule applies in a particular case, and you do not have a dictionary, keep the consonant with the vowel that follows.

4. Except in the three cases discussed above, a syllable always begins with a consonant. Several points follow from this. (1.) The syllables which have an *sh* sound, such as -*cial*, -*tion*, -*ture*, are never broken. Write: *com-mer-cial*, *at-ten-tion*, *ad-ven-ture*. (2.) When two separate consonant sounds come together, divide between them, as in *for-get*. (But do not divide *bet-ween*, because *tw* is one sound.) (3.) You can always divide between double letters, as in *hol-low*, except in the special case of -*ing*, -*ish*, -*er*, -*est*, -*ed*, discussed in rule 1.

divorcé; divorcée; divorcee. A *divorcé* is a divorced man. A *divorcée* is a divorced woman. A *divorcee* is a divorced person of either sex. Divorce has become so common that no one thinks of it any more as something French or feels any need to cloak the mention of it or of the persons affected by it under a foreign term. In common American usage *divorcee* for either a divorced man or a divorced woman is now almost universal.

divulge. See **disclose.**

do. The past tense is *did*. The participle is *done*.

During the nineteenth century it was acceptable English to use the form *don't* in place of *doesn't*, as in *he don't care a straw*. This is no longer considered standard.

Do is a basic verb, meaning to act or to accomplish something. It is the natural verb to use in speaking of an action that has no name, as in *he did a good deed* and *he has done a lot for me*. It is also used as a substitute for a verb that has just been mentioned, as in *I must interrupt you, as you did me*. Today it is often used inside various trade groups in place of a more specific verb which has not been mentioned. For example, doctors speak of doing an examination, musicians of doing a concert, and writers

of doing a book. These expressions are natural English inside the particular group but they are usually objected to by outsiders. The writer who is *doing an article on medicine* may wince when the doctor speaks about *doing a physical examination*.

The words *do*, *does*, and *did*, are also used as auxiliary verbs. English verbs are usually phrases made up of several elements. The only exceptions to this are the simple present tense, such as *he walks*, and the simple past, such as *he walked*. In present-day English there are certain constructions in which the verb must have at least two elements. In order to express the simple present or the simple past in these constructions we use *do* or *does* for the present tense and *did* for the past, followed by the simple form of the meaningful verb, as in *he does walk, he did walk*. It is necessary to have at least two elements to the verb in a question, such as *where did he walk?* and in a negative statement, such as *he did not walk*. We must also have two elements in the verb when a sentence begins with a negative or restrictive adverb, as in *little did he think*. At one time it was possible to say *walked he?, he walked not*, and *little thought he*, but these constructions are now archaic and good contemporary English requires a verbal phrase.

In the United States the only exception to the above rule is *to be*. This verb is never used with the auxiliary *do* except in an imperative. *Do* must be used in a negative imperative, as in *don't be silly*, and may be used in an affirmative, as in *do be quiet*. Otherwise we say *where was he?, he was not here*, and *neither were you*. The verb *to have* is sometimes treated like *to be*, as in *have you a pencil?*, but in the United States it is more likely to be used with the auxiliary, as in *do you have a pencil?*. In Great Britain the auxiliary *do* is not used with *to be* or *to have* (except in an imperative) nor with *used to*. See **used to.**

The same combinations of the verb *to do* and the simple form of the meaningful verb are used to make a simple present or simple past tense statement emphatic, as in *of course I do believe you* and *if I did cry, it would not be from grief*. The word *do* is also used to make an imperative emphatic, as in *do come*. *Do* can be used in this way even when the imperative itself is the verb *do*, as in *do do something about it*.

dock. In its strictest sense a *dock* is the space or waterway between two piers or wharves (*Beyond that lay a wharf and the thick muddy water of a dock*). Only with this sense in mind would *drydock* have any meaning. None the less, by a quite natural extension, the word *dock* has been applied to the pier or wharf (*Jordan . . . had drifted away from the dock when the explosion occurred*) so often that its synonymity for them is accepted as standard in American usage.

docker. See **longshoreman.**

docket. In England *docket* signifies an official memorandum or entry of proceedings in a legal cause, or a register of such entries. In the United

States it signifies a list of causes in court for trial, or the names of the parties who have causes pending (*Court dockets are crowded*). Sports writers, seeking indefatigably to lend an air of freshness to their otherwise monotonous subject, have taken over the word as a term for a list of impending athletic contests (*Three games are on the docket for the Minute Men and Coach Erle Witty's boys*).

doctor. The use of unwarranted titles of respect has long been an element of American humor and even politeness, and *Doc* and *Professor* and *Judge* and *Colonel* are prodigally bestowed amongst us. But *doctor,* in its fulness, is reserved for those who are presumed to have had a doctorate conferred upon them by some institution of higher learning. It may be an obscure and shadowy institution and it may have been conferred for proficiency in some field such as Baby Sitting or the Care of Bunions, which is not admitted to the curriculum of such conservative places as Oxford and Cambridge. But a degree is supposed to have been conferred.

American and English usage of the word differ. The members of the American Medical Association might have to apply sedatives to themselves after reading in a recent authoritative English work that "any member of the medical profession . . . whether he holds the degree of Doctor of Medicine or not" should be "addressed as *doctor*." And an American surgeon would be doubly offended to read in the same work that a surgeon "whether holding a doctor's degree or not, should be addressed as Mr. or Mrs. or Miss." With us no one can be a licensed practitioner unless he holds a doctorate and all surgeons are doctors and, along with other members of their profession, are so addressed.

Dr. is the abbreviation for *doctor.* It may be used before a full name or before a surname only, as in *Dr. Samuel Johnson* and *Dr. Johnson.* In speaking of two men known as *Dr. Johnson* we may say *the Dr. Johnsons.* But if we distinguish two doctors in any way we must make the title plural, as in *Drs. Samuel and William Johnson* and *Drs. Fulton and Price.*

The form *Dr.* should not be used before a name that is followed by letters representing an academic degree, such as *Ph.D.* or *M.D.* The word *doctor* may be used without a proper name as a form of address, as in *do you agree with me, doctor?.* It may also be used in speaking about anyone who has this title, as in *the doctor will see you in a few minutes.*

doe. See **hart.**

does. See **do.**

doff and **don** (coalesced forms of *do off* and *do on*) for "take off" and "put on" have not been in general use for three hundred years. They are now literary and affected.

dogma. The plural is *dogmas* or *dogmata,* not *dogmae.*

dog's life, lead a. Dogs fare ill in proverbs. They are greedy, fierce, filthy, and servile. They defile cisterns, return to their vomit, drive the patient ox from the manger, bark at their own fleas, eat each other, bay the moon, suffer under a bad name, get themselves hanged and beaten, and whine, snarl, cringe, fawn, and slaver in a myriad dangerous and disgusting ways. Dogs are mentioned many times in the Bible, but only with abhorrence. That they licked Lazarus' sores was intended not as an indication of their pity but of his degradation. They fare even worse in Shakespeare than in the Scriptures; their combined servility, ferocity, and filthiness seems to have fascinated the poet with revulsion.

Until fairly recently the dog was a scavenger. His food consisted exclusively of garbage and his residence was the kennel or channel, the loathsome trickle down the center of the street into which refuse was thrown. Great houses, having much garbage, had many dogs, and there was a regular functionary, the dog whipper, to keep them in subjection. Blows and kicks were the rule and for the slightest offense dogs were hanged. Sometimes just for the fun of it.

In such an atmosphere and under such a regime *a dog's life* was, no doubt, a wretched one to lead. *To go to the dogs* was to descend low indeed, and *to die like a dog* to make a miserable end. The sayings might be trite, even then, but at least they had meaning.

But all has changed. No exact date can be set for the metamorphosis of the blatant beast into the lovable pet, but the assertion, in an address to a jury, by Senator George C. Vest, at Warrensburg, Missouri, in 1876, that "a man's best friend's his dog," may definitely be regarded as a milestone on the way. Certainly today, with the veterinarian's bill often exceeding the pediatrician's, with canine psychiatrists, with dog sitters, with vitamin-enriched canned dog food, with quilted coats and fur-lined booties, with rubberfoam mattresses, boarding houses, schools of etiquette and even orphanages, a dog's life can no longer serve as the trope of wretchedness and all phrases that so imply must be discarded as clichés. This does not mean, however, that the dog need be driven utterly from folk sayings. There is a hackneyed term about *living the life of Reilly.* No one knows just who Reilly was or why his existence was thought to be enviable and the phrase has become idle and empty. Let Fido be substituted for Reilly and it will again be filled with meaning.

doldrums may mean a state of depression, or the dumps; the similar state that a ship is in when she can make no headway; or the part of the earth where ships most often got into this condition. Originally, the word meant the nervous state. Later it was applied, either in humor or through misunderstanding, to the areas near the equator. A singular, *doldrum,* is sometimes used, in both senses, but it is very rare.

domestic. Those English visitors who are amused at the American use of *domestic* to mean of or pertaining to our own country, internal, not foreign (*domestic postage, domestic affairs*) have forgotten their own literature. Macbeth lists *malice domestic, foreign levy* among the ills that can no longer touch the dead Duncan, and

Macaulay, in 1849, referred to *The whole domestic and foreign policy of the English government.*

domicile. Though *domicile* does mean *home,* it is better left to the lawyers and the social scientists and, in some special uses, to the zoologists. In everyday use it is pompous if serious, tedious if jocular. See **house; home.**

dominate; domineer. To *dominate* is to rule over, govern, control (*His stepmother dominated him*), or to tower above and so to give control of (*The Rock of Gibraltar dominates the straits*). To *domineer* is to rule despotically, to tyrannize over, to bully (*Oligarchies, wherein a few rich men domineer*). *Domineer* is also used in the sense of commanding by towering above (*The grim castle on its naked rock domineered the town*). Whether to use *dominate* or *domineer* in this sense is dependent upon the degree to which one wishes to stress unfavorable feelings towards the dominance. Of course no one likes to be dominated and *dominate,* sometimes, has unpleasant connotations. *Domineer* always has.

dominoes. When referring to the game, the plural word *dominoes* takes a singular verb, as in *dominoes is fun.* A single piece is *a domino* and *dominoes* used with a plural verb means more than one of these, as in *dominoes are usually black and white.*

Domino may also mean a kind of garment, especially one worn in a masquerade, as in *she wore a pink domino.* This word may have the plural *dominos* or *dominoes.* It is thought that the pieces in the game were called *dominoes* because the backs looked like people in domino cloaks.

donate; give. To *donate* is to make a gift. It is a back formation from *donation* and has long been an object of scorn and ridicule as "a pretentious and magniloquent vulgarism" among English purists. Sir Alan Herbert, who insists that it is merely a snob word, that the rich donate and the poor give, has a great deal of fun translating various well-known passages to include *donate: Donate us this day our daily bread. 'Tis more blessed to donate than to receive. 'Twas all he donated, 'twas all he had to donate.* And certainly it is better to use *give* wherever one can. It is not only simpler; it has more dignity. None the less *donate* is now standard in the United States where even professors of grammar hungrily hope that someone will donate the funds to support a chair in their specialty.

done. See **do.**

do or die. Men have done entirely too much dying in the past generation to be lulled by alliteration into feeling any thrill at the cliché *do or die.* The phrase, chiefly expressed by poets and princes, neither of whom as a class were much given to either doing or dying in the attempt, is now confined almost entirely to ironic uses. When or where the odds against dying were large, it is conceivable that men might have been moved by exhortation and rhetoric to take the chance of dying; where or when the odds in favor of dying are high, the adjuration is likely to prove an incentive to *not do.*

double entendre. There is no use pointing out that *double entendre* does not exist in French or existed only a long time ago and that the proper phrase for a double meaning, one of them usually indelicate, is *double entente.* The proper phrase in English from at least Dryden's time, however erroneous its basis, has been *double entendre* and three hundred years of use will usually make an error standard.

Double meaning is a better phrase, anyway. There is no point nor honesty in pretending that indelicate matters ought to be spoken of in French. In indecency we can hold our own with any nation.

double genitives.

POSSESSIVES

As a rule, a noun in the genitive case or a possessive pronoun can be replaced by an *of* phrase in which *of* is followed by the common form of the noun or the objective form of the pronoun, as in *the sun's heat, the heat of the sun; his picture, a picture of him.* But when the genitive or possessive represents ownership, as in *a child's toy, a dog's bone,* it keeps its form even when it follows the preposition *of,* as in *a toy of the child's, a bone of the dog's.*

This is a curious and interesting construction. It is never misused and no one needs to understand it in order to use it properly. That is fortunate, because it is almost impossible to understand.

Some grammarians say that it is a partitive, that it always implies that there is more of the same, and that in an expression such as *that mother of his* it is derogatory for that reason. But actually this double genitive does not carry a partitive meaning, even where that would be applicable. When we say *he left the party with some of his friends,* we do have a partitive and an implication that there may have been others who did not leave with him. When we say *he left with some friends of his,* the statement merely describes or classifies the people he left with.

This double genitive is essentially a defining or classifying expression. It is used with words such as *a, some, any,* and numerals, which indicate that the following noun is not completely specified. And it is used with one kind of *the* and not with the other. The word *the* usually means "that which is already defined." We are using this *the* in: *There was once a king in Thule, and when the king was old . . . .* But there is another *the* which is simply the sign that a clause is to follow, and which means "more information is coming." We have this *the* in *the man who came to dinner.* The second *the* may be used with the double genitive, as in *the friend of yours who is going abroad told me . . . .* But the first *the,* which says that what follows is already defined, cannot be used in this construction. We cannot say *the friend of yours told me . . . .*

The double genitive is required whenever a

word indicating ownership is placed after *of*. For example, *he found a bone of the dog's* and *he found a bone of the dog* mean different things; and *he found a toy of the child* is meaningless. In fact, a genitive form or a possessive pronoun that does not keep its form after *of* does not represent ownership.

At this point it would seem reasonable to say that the double genitive defines a particular thing by saying to whom it belongs. That is, the genitive relation of ownership is used again in the primary genitive function of a classifying word. (See **genitive case**.) This would be a satisfactory explanation if the double genitive always implied ownership. There is no doubt that ownership after *of* has to be expressed in this way, but it does not follow that everything that is expressed in this way is ownership.

If we assert that the double genitive always implies ownership, some curious things follow. Since we say *a bone of the dog* when we mean a bone from its own body, it would follow that we think the dog is his body and not the owner of it. A human being, on the other hand, must always be spoken of as the owner and not as the body itself, as in *that leg of John's is hurting him again.* But man does not seem to own his appearance, or likeness, since we say *a picture of him.* The expression *this life of mine* would seem to imply that we own our lives; *for the life of me* would not.

There is no doubt that the construction can be used for personal relationships, and without any derogatory implication, as in *a son of his.* What makes *that mother of his* an expression of contempt is the word *that* and not any implications of the partitive genitive. The form is equally contemptuous in situations where the idea of "one of many" is not insulting, as in *that son of yours.* This is so universally true that in suburban English a pleasant word is usually added to counteract the ill effect of *that*, as in *that dear child of yours has ruined my lawn.*

PARTITIVES

The partitive relation is represented in Latin by a genitive. In English it is always represented by a prepositional phrase, which, like other prepositional phrases, can be followed by a genitive *'s*, as in *which of you gentlemen's name is Snodgrass?*. No difficulties arise until the word following *of* is an objective pronoun, as in *one of them, one of us, one of you.* If we followed the pattern of other prepositional phrases we would say *one of them's mother, one of us's mother, one of you's mother.* This is unacceptable with *us* and *you.* The construction is heard with *them* but is condemned by most grammarians. On the other hand, a possessive pronoun is not used here. We do not say *one of their mother* or even *one of their mothers.* Partitive phrases involving a personal pronoun are the only type of expression we have that cannot be handled simply in the genitive, and for this reason people often stumble over them. At present there is nothing to do but recast the sentence and use a second *of* phrase, as in *the mother of one of them.*

double negatives. In English, two negatives in the same sentence generally reinforce one another. *I didn't say nothing* is an emphatic denial and no one who speaks English can misunderstand it. This is the normal way of strengthening a negative in all Teutonic languages, of which ours is one. In the past, double, triple, quadruple negatives were quite acceptable; Sir Launcelot was speaking the purest English when he said, *I never treacherously slew no man.*

Today, this repeated negative is considered a shocking vulgarism. Negative pronouns (such as *no one* and *nothing*), negative adverbs (such as *hardly* and *scarcely*), and negative conjunctions (such as *neither* and *nor*), when used with a negative verb put a man beyond the pale, provided the sentence is short enough. No one who values public opinion can afford to say *I didn't hardly hear you* or *you didn't hear me, neither.*

If the sentence is longer, a supplementary negative added as an afterthought is not felt to be a serious offense. *He couldn't sleep, not even with a sedative* contains a redundant *not*, since what is meant is *he couldn't sleep even with a sedative.* Sentences of this kind are contrary to the theoretical rules of grammar and are avoided by some writers and editors. But they are not the sort of sentence children are drilled in and they are not contrary to the spirit of English. As a result, very few people are offended by them. On the other hand, the sentence *no one thought so, even you* is wrong. Here the phrase after the comma requires a negative and should be *not even you.* (The difference between the two sentences is easier felt than described. In the first, *even with a sedative* is an adverbial phrase; it tells in what way the man could not sleep. In the second, *not even you* is an elaboration of *no one* and becomes the subject of *thought so. Even you thought so* is not what was meant.) The writer who used *even* when he meant *not even* undoubtedly dropped the *not* because he thought it was a double negative. In attempting to show that his English is "purer" than it really is, he has succeeded in showing how worried he is about it. Mistakes of this kind are inevitable when one tries to apply a rule that runs counter to one's speech habits. It is much safer to trust one's ear, and to be satisfied to speak and write the language used by the great majority of educated people.

The person who says *I shouldn't be surprised if it didn't rain* may mean *I expect it to rain.* Here we have a negative in a main clause repeated in a subordinate construction. This type of repetition is required in many languages, and so cannot be called unreasonable. Although it is condemned by some English grammarians, it is used by many of the best writers of English. Jane Austen, for example, writes: *there was none too poor or too remote not to feel an interest*; and Charles Darwin: *it never occurred to me to doubt that your work would not advance our common object.* See also **but**.

Whenever two negatives make an affirmative the double negative is a thoroughly respectable construction, chiefly because it was a standard Latin construction. In Latin, two negatives in the same sentence always amounted to an affirmation and *nobody does not believe* was an emphatic and elegant way of saying *everybody believes.* In English, two negatives make an affirmative when one directly qualifies the other, as in *I am not unhappy.* Even here the words do not completely cancel each other. This double negative expresses rather, the weakest possible positive attitude.

doubletalk. See **persiflage.**

doubtless. See **undoubtedly.**

dove. See **dive.**

dove. See **pigeon.**

dower; dowry. *Dower* is a legal term for the portion of a deceased husband's real property allowed to his widow for her life. A *dowry* is the money, goods, or estate which a woman brings to her husband at marriage. In former times the two words were often used interchangeably but today they are kept to their separate meanings.

down is primarily an adverb meaning toward a lower position, as in *look down*; but it may also be used as an adjective to qualify a noun, as in *a down stroke.* The adjective has a superlative form *downmost* but no comparative. *Down* is sometimes used as a preposition, as in *down the hill,* and sometimes as a verb, as in *he downed them all.*

Down has the same range of meanings that *lower* has. It may mean physically lower, as in *step down,* or it may mean lower in some other sense, as in *mark down the price, run down one's friends, call down the hired help.* It is also used as the opposite of *up,* to mean passing from greater to less energy or from a stronger to a weaker state, as in *quiet down, tone down, soften down.* For differences between *up* and *down,* see **up.**

Down is also used in speaking of geographical directions. In Great Britain it may mean toward the coast, as in *I must down to the seas again;* or it may mean toward a place of less importance. That is, one goes down from London or down from any city to the country. In the United States the first meaning survives in *down East,* meaning the Maine coast, but otherwise is lost. In general, *down* is used in this country to mean "south," or toward the bottom of an ordinary map. People living in Kingston go "down" to New York City.

down at the heel(s), like *out at the elbow,* as a term for being destitute, is no longer descriptive.

downward; downwards. *Downward* is the only form that can be used to qualify a following noun, as in *a downward glance.* Either form may be used in any other construction, as in *he glanced downwards* and *he glanced downward.* In the United States the form *downward* is generally preferred.

dozen. Originally the word *dozen* was always joined to a following noun by *of,* as in *a dozen of eggs.* This construction is not considered standard now except where it has been preserved as an elegance, as in *a dozen of sherry.* In current English, *dozen* is treated as if it were a numeral. It stands immediately before a following noun, as in *a dozen eggs,* except when it refers to a part of some specified group, as in *a dozen of these eggs,* in which case the *of* must be used. Only the singular form *dozen* can be used after a numeral. We say *get three dozen* and not *get three dozens.*

The plural form *dozens* cannot be used after a numeral and cannot be treated as if it were a numeral. It must always be joined to a following noun by *of,* as in *dozens of eggs.* The *of* is not used before degree words, such as *more, less, too many,* and we may speak of *dozens more.* But we do not like to complete this expression by adding another noun. We avoid saying *dozens more eggs.*

Dr. See **doctor.**

draft; draught. Though *draft* and *draught* are merely variant spellings, common usage has fixed them to separate meanings. *Draft* is used for a drawing or design, for the preliminary form of a piece of writing, the act of drawing or pulling or that which is drawn or pulled, the taking of supplies, forces, or money from a given source, the selection of persons for military service, a written order drawing on another person or a bank for money, a drain or demand made on anything. *Draft* and *draught* are used for a current of air. *Draught* is used for a device for regulating the flow of air or gas, the drawing of a liquid from its receptacle (as *Beer on draught*—though in American usage *draft* is rapidly gaining in this sense), drinking, or a drink or potion, a take of fish, the depth a vessel sinks in water, and (in the plural construed as singular) the game of checkers. When used as another name for checkers, however, the word takes a singular verb, as in *draughts is played by two persons.* The preferred name for this game in the United States is *checkers.*

drank. See **drink.**

draw. The past tense is *drew.* The participle is *drawn.*

draw; drag; haul. To *draw* is to move something by a force in the direction from which the force is exerted (*the draw of a magnet; chariots drawn by horses. Drawing her father aside for a moment, she begged him to leave*). To *drag* is to draw with great force some object over a surface upon which it rests, the movement being hindered by friction (*The body had plainly been dragged across the yard to the ditch*). To *haul* is to transport a heavy object slowly with sustained effort. Boats are *hauled* across land. Heavy freight is *hauled.* The slang use of *haul* as a noun (*a rich haul*) implies a heavy take, so heavy that it would be difficult to move.

draw in one's horns. To say of someone who at a threat suddenly abates his truculence that he has *drawn in his horns* is to employ a venerable but not very sound metaphor, since the figure is based on the sudden shrinking into its shell of an alarmed snail, one of the least truculent of creatures and one whose "horns," the delicate antennae or tentacles which bear its eyes, have no menace. The phrase is now a cliché and should be used sparingly.

drawers. When this word means an article of clothing, the plural form refers to one garment but is always treated as a plural, as in *these drawers are warm.* In order to use the word with a singular verb or to speak of more than one such garment, it is necessary to say *this pair of drawers is warm* or *several pairs of drawers.* The form *drawers* is used as the first element in a compound, as in *drawers material.*

drawing pin. See **thumbtack.**

drawn. See **draw.**

draw the line at something, marking it as a limit beyond which one is prepared to fight or to take or accept other drastic action, is a cliché. It seems to be based on the habit of pugnacious frontiersmen, now relegated to boys, of drawing a line in the dirt and defying one's opponent to step across it.

draw the long bow. The long bow, as every boy who has read his Robin Hood stories knows, was a mighty weapon employed in mighty feats by mighty men before villainous saltpeter was digged out of the bowels of the harmless earth to destroy many a good tall fellow so cowardly. Apparently the boasts of old bowmen exceeded credence and their narratives became a term for large exaggeration, a euphemism for boastful lying. But the term is now a cliché. It has been many a century since anyone has been annoyed by the boasting of a longbowman and there is such a richness of contemporary boasting to choose a new figure from that continued use of the old one amounts to neglect of our national resources.

dread may be followed by an infinitive, as in *he dreads to go,* or by the *-ing* form of a verb, as in *he dreads going.* It may also be followed by a clause. Formerly, this was introduced by *lest* and the clause verb was a subjunctive, as in *I dread lest he go.* This is now extremely bookish. A *that* clause with the verb in the indicative, as in *I dread that he will go,* is sometimes heard but an infinitive construction, such as *I dread to see him go* or *I dread to have him go,* is generally preferred.

dreadful. See **awful; horrible.**

dream. The past tense is *dreamed* or *dreamt.* The participle is also *dreamed* or *dreamt.* In the United States *dreamed* is preferred for the past tense and the participle. *Dreamt* is preferred in Great Britain. *Dream* may be followed by a clause, as in *he dreams he is there.* If the *-ing* form of a verb follows *dream* it must be introduced by the preposition *of,* as in *he dreams of being there.*

dregs is a mass word with a plural form. It is regularly used with a plural verb, as in *the dregs are bitter.* But it is not a true plural and we cannot speak of *three or four dregs.* However, a singular form *dreg* exists and may be used to make the absence of dregs, or the smallness, emphatic, as in *leave no dreg* and *if any dreg remain.* We may speak of *many dregs* or of *much dregs.*

dress. The past tense is *dressed* or *drest.* The participle is also *dressed* or *drest.* *Dressed* is the preferred form for the past tense and the participle.

dressed up to the nines. No one is quite sure what the "nines" in *dressed up to the nines* means. It has been suggested that nine being a mystical number it means dressed up to perfection, but that fails to account for the plural, if the word is the plural of the number nine. The phrase sometimes appears as *to the nine.* Burns wrote that a certain action would please him *to the nine* and Charles Reade refers to men or women *being clad in snowy cotton and japanned to the nine.* It has been conjectured that the phrase may derive from *to then eyne, i.e.,* to the eyes, and this would make sense in the common phrase but it would not account for the final *s* there and elsewhere. No context has been found that makes any meaning absolutely clear, and plenty have been found that make any explanation yet advanced untenable. It is one of those phrases to which no specific meaning can be attached, a cliché, to be avoided. *Dressed fit to kill* has a more obvious meaning, but it, too, is hackneyed.

dresser. Though the word *dresser* used to mean in America what it still means in England, a sideboard or set of shelves for dishes and cooking utensils (*The bland illumination filled the entire apartment . . . making the scoured milk pans and the white crockery on the large "dresser" shine*— 1848. *With a nice dinner ready cooked for 'em, and set out in the dresser*—1875), it now means solely a dressing table or bureau (*In this crib there's just a few pieces of furniture which consist of a bed, washstand . . . a dresser and maybe two chairs*—1947).

drest. See **dress.**

drew. See **draw.**

drink. The past tense is *drank.* The participle is *drunk* or *drank.* *Drunk* is the usual participle today, but *drank,* as in *he had drank deep,* is still acceptable in many parts of the United States. This construction was popular with nineteenth century writers, perhaps because *drank* does not suggest too much alcohol as much as *drunk* does. An older participle *drunken* is still in use as an adjective, as in *a drunken sailor,* but we also say *a drunk sailor.*

drive. The past tense is *drove.* The participle is *driven. Drive* may be followed by an infinitive, as in *he drove her to admit it,* or by the *-ing* form of a verb with the preposition *to,* as in *he drove her to admitting it.* The *-ing* construction is generally preferred. Forty years ago many people felt that *drive* could not be used in speaking of an automobile, but this attempt to preserve "pure" English has now been abandoned.

droll. See **funny.**

drop. The past tense is *dropped* or *dropt.* The participle is also *dropped* or *dropt. Dropped* is the preferred form for the past tense and the participle.

drought and **drouth,** pronounced as spelled, are simply variants. *Drouth* is now dialectal in England but is standard in the United States where it is used interchangeably with *drought.*

drove. See **drive.**

drown is a regular verb and the past tense and the participle are *drowned.* In the United States an extra *d* is often heard in this word, as in *he will drownd* and *he was drownded last night.* These were once literary forms but are now considered as uneducated usage, at least when they appear in print.

drug. See **drag.**

drug on the market. What drug? And in what pharmacopoeia to be found? Or is it a drug at all? Is it, perhaps, *dreg,* which is pronounced *drug* in some dialects? Or a *drugget?* Or some confusion of *drag* or *drogue?*

Nobody knows. All the dictionaries can say is what the phrase makes evident: *something which is no longer in demand, something unsaleable.* Dryden said that *virtue shall a drug become.* In a way, it is; and a drag. Sir William Temple said, in 1763, that *horses in Ireland are a drug.* Robinson Crusoe laughed at the coins he found in the wreck: *O Drug! said I aloud, what art thou good for?* The term may have originated in some now-forgotten pun, but however it originated it is now a cliché, an expression that we repeat without knowing exactly what it means. Indeed, it is, perhaps, supreme in its kind, for there is no evidence, from the moment of its first appearance in 1661, that anyone has ever known exactly what it means.

drug store. The nearest thing to a *drug store* that an American will find in England is a *chemist's shop.* They both fill prescriptions and sell medicines, cosmetics, and sick-room supplies; but the soda fountains, lunch counters, magazine racks, and toy and novelty departments that grace and clutter the drug store are unknown in the chemist's shops.

drunk. See **drink.**

drunkard; alcoholic; sot. *Drunkard* is the everyday word, strongly tinged with the disgust, contempt, and amusement that drunkenness inspires in those that have to deal with it (*A Man that is now and then guilty of Intemperance is not to be called a Drunkard*—Steele). *Sot,* originally a fool or an idiot, is an angry word for an habitual drunkard (*bursten-bellied sots . . . this horrid sot . . . who cannot sleep at night till dosed with drink*). *Alcoholic* is the newest and politest term of all, carrying a nobly understanding connotation of psychological and physiological illness. It has replaced *dipsomaniac,* which used to be the understanding word but fell short of perfection because of undignified suggestions in *-maniac.*

There are so many slang terms for drinking, drunkenness, and drunkards that almost any term to be found in a dictionary is comparatively dignified.

drunk; drunken; inebriated; intoxicated. When applied to persons, *drunk* is now the commonest form in America, both predicate and attributive (*After one more drink he was distinctly drunk. The drunk soldier was plainly looking for a*

quarrel). As applied to persons, *drunken* now seems a little archaic and poetic (*What shall we do with a drunken sailor? A drunken man seems to bear a charmed life*), though it is still used to describe states and actions that pertain to, proceed from, or are marked by, intoxication (*This drunken babbling amused some but disgusted most. Weaving through traffic in drunken disregard of all regulations . . .*). (See also **drink.**)

Inebriated is simply a highfalutin word for *drunk.* It is used as a pompous circumlocution or humorously (as in Disraeli's famous reference to Gladstone as *a sophistical rhetorician, inebriated with the exuberance of his own verbosity*).

Intoxicated means poisoned. It was possible formerly to speak of *intoxicated weapons* or of *serpents that intoxicated by their bite;* and the word *toxic,* poisonous, is in everyday use. But *intoxicated,* when used literally, now means to be poisoned by drinking an excess of ethyl alcohol. Used figuratively (*intoxicated with success, intoxicated with happiness*), it means *drunk* but carries less censure than the coarser, downright word. To be *drunk with success* suggests just a shade greater likelihood of doing something offensive or dangerous in one's elation than if one were *intoxicated with success.*

dry goods, textile fabrics and related articles of trade, in distinction from groceries, hardware, and so on, is now an old-fashioned word in America, though still current and standard. There is no equivalent in England. The word embraces what is there called *drapery, mercery,* and *haberdashery.*

dry out. An American, soaked in a downpour, wants to *dry out* his clothes. An Englishman wants to *dry off* his. Perhaps the English climate has made him resign himself to a surface dryness only.

d.t.'s must now be accepted, at least in informal speech and writing, as a standard abbreviation of *delirium tremens.*

dual words. Modern English has only two forms to indicate whether a word is being used in reference to one thing or to more than one: the singular, showing one, and the plural, showing more than one. Some primitive languages have grammatical forms for one, two, three, and more than three things. Old English, like Greek, had forms to indicate one, two, and more than two. There still are in modern English a few words, such as *neither, alternative, both, the latter,* that carry a dual meaning to some extent, that is, that seem to refer to two rather than to more than one.

The tendency in modern English is to free these words from the specific reference to two. *Neither,* for example, was used broadly as early as the seventeenth century, as seen in *neither death, nor life, nor angels, nor principalities, nor powers, nor things present, nor things to come, nor height, nor depth, nor any other creature.* In the nineteenth century, Gladstone felt at liberty to say: *my decided preference is for the fourth and last of these alternatives.* Not all dual words have been used so freely in such high places as *neither* and *alternative,* and anyone writing today is obliged to follow the accepted usage of today. For example, one cannot say *both were there* and be understood to mean *all three were there.* But the distinction between two and more than two is logically out of place in the twentieth century. It belongs to a simpler culture than ours. And no one should try to preserve it, or reinstate it, where custom is allowing it to disappear. For more detailed information, see the individual dual words.

ductus. The plural is *ductuses* or *ductus,* not *ducti.*

dues. The American *dues,* the amount payable to a club to maintain membership, is in England *subscription.*

due to may be used to qualify a noun, as in *a mistake due to carelessness.* This use of *due to* was listed by Dr. Johnson as "proper, but not usual." Since then it has become a familiar form of speech and no one thinks of objecting to it. But the words are also used today to qualify a verb, as in *he failed, due to carelessness.* This construction is relatively new and is condemned by some grammarians.

In both cases the words *due to* are being used as *owing to* might be used. It is claimed that *due to* is acceptable in the first case but not in the second, and that only the form *owing to* may be used with a verb. This distinction cannot be defended on theoretical grounds, since *due to* and *owing to* are grammatically alike. The critics usually content themselves with saying that "*due to* cannot be used to qualify a verb." But it is used to qualify a verb, millions of times every day. And it is used in this way in very respectable places. A tablet in front of the Old State House in Philadelphia reads: *Here the Continental Congress sat from the date it convened, May 10, 1775, until the close of the Revolution, except when, in 1776-77, it sat in Baltimore, and in 1777-78, in Lancaster and York, due to the temporary occupation of Philadelphia by the British army.* (See also **owe.**)

dug. See **dig.**

dull as ditch water. Ditch water today would be unsavory but nothing like the foul mess it was before there was any public sanitation. It seems to have impressed itself, quite understandably, on the senses and vocabularies of our forebears who made it the basis of three unpleasant similes: *as proud* [*digne*] *as ditchwater, as light as ditchwater,* and *as dull as ditchwater.* The first two were presumably ironic, though their exact significance is now puzzling. Perhaps *as proud as ditchwater* may have meant "stinking proud," except for *stinking*'s being a general term of abuse that doesn't make much sense.

The dullness of ditchwater, in the simile that has survived, may have referred to its opacity or its lack of good taste. The latter would apply to uncontaminated standing water. Our ancestors attached considerable importance to the taste of various waters. There is a fine apostrophe in Mark Twain's *Life on the Mississippi* to Mississippi River water as the best of all drinking

waters, being far superior, by virtue of its silt, to the water of the Ohio or the Missouri. But *dull as ditch water* (or its often-heard variant, *dull as dishwater*) is now a sodden simile, pretty much devoid of meaning.

dumb. The American use of *dumb* for stupid (*I can't teach my dog tricks; he's too dumb to learn*) is probably the German *dumm,* rather than a corruption of the old word for speechless, which is retained in standard American usage. *Dumbbell,* a stupid person, is slang.

dumbfound. See **amaze.**

dumbwaiter. In the United States a *dumbwaiter* is a conveyor or framework with shelves drawn up and down in a shaft. It was used more in former days, especially in town houses where the dining room was on the floor above the kitchen. In England a *dumbwaiter* is a small stand, often with revolving shelves, placed near a dining table.

Were servants garrulous, especially while waiting on the table, that so much is made of the silence of things meant to replace them? Cf. *silent butler.*

duologue. See **dialogue.**

durance vile. *Durance* is now archaic for endurance or duration. It survives only in the forcedly jocular cliché *in durance vile,* meaning in forced constraint or prison. Shakespeare, by putting the phrase into Pistol's mouth, implied, as early as 1597, that it was a cliché, bombastic and ludicrous. After almost four hundred years of further use even the humor has worn out.

durst. See **dare.**

Dutch; Dutchman. A *Dutchman* may mean a man from Holland, but in the United States it often means a German, or a German-speaking American. For this reason, *Hollander* is the preferred term in this country for a native of Holland.

In England, since about 1600, the word *Dutch* has been applied only to the language or the people of Holland. But the Dutch word *duitsch* and the German word *deutsch* both mean German, and not *Hollandish.* In many parts of the United States the English word *Dutch* has kept this meaning, especially in areas settled by Germans or Hollanders. The expression *Pennsylvania Dutch* is an example of this American usage.

Many dictionaries label this use of *Dutch* and *Dutchman* as "careless" or incorrect, which it is by British standards. But being correct is small consolation for being misunderstood and the "careful" speaker will bear in mind what his words are likely to mean to his hearers.

The Dutch means the entire people. It is always followed by a plural verb, but it cannot be used with a numeral. We do not speak of *three Dutch,* but of *three Dutchmen.*

Rivalry in trade and jealousy and fear in naval matters bred a resentment of the Dutch in England in the seventeenth century which soon disappeared when England's supremacy was established but which lingers on in the language in a number of phrases such as *Dutch courage* (the courage lent by drunkenness), *Dutch con-*

solation (the assurance that things might have been worse), *Dutch bargain* (not likely to be kept), and other derisive and opprobrious terms. Many of these have been retained in American speech and a number of new ones, mostly humorous and lightly contemptuous, added. Among them are *It beats the Dutch, Well, I'm a Dutchman,* and *Dutch treat* or *going Dutch.* The common term *to talk like a Dutch Uncle,* meaning to talk sternly and to lay down the law, to scold, warn, reprimand, may have hidden in it the fact that the word *boss* is the Dutch *baas* which originally meant uncle. So also with *to cry uncle,* i.e., to admit defeat, to concede that the other man is *baas* or *boss.*

duty. See **service.**

"D.V." See **Deo volente.**

dwarf. The plural is *dwarfs,* never *dwarves.*

dwell. The past tense is *dwelt.* The participle is also *dwelt. Dwelled* is no longer used in standard English, but it was once a literary form, as in *Lot dwelled in the cities of the plain.* See also **reside.**

dyed in the wool. A woolen fabric is *dyed in the wool* if its color was imparted to it while it was yet in the state of unspun wool. Another term for it, now obsolete, was *dyed in grain,* so that in the figurative senses *engrained* and *dyed in the wool* mean the same thing—a conviction or characteristic that is ineradicable because it is in the very basic stuff of its holder's being. This tired phrase is used far more today in America than in England.

dyes. See **dice.**

E

each. At one time *each* and *every* were two forms of the same word and could be used interchangeably to refer to the individual members of a group. Today *every* is used when the members are thought of as a group or whole, and *each* when they are thought of individually. The rule is that "*every* totalizes, and *each* individualizes." *Every* cannot be used in speaking of a group of less than three. *Each* may be used in speaking of only two, but it may also be used in speaking of any larger number.

Each may be used as an adjective, as in *each man.* It may also be used as a pronoun and in this construction may be followed by *of,* as in *each of them.* When used as an adjective, *each* may stand before a singular noun or after a plural noun or pronoun, as in *each man, the men each, they each.* When qualifying a plural noun or pronoun it may also stand after a linking verb or an auxiliary verb, as in *they are each right, they have each decided.*

When *each* is used as an adjective and qualifies a singular noun the combination is always singular, as in *each man carries his own pack.* When *each* qualifies, or refers to, a plural noun or pronoun and precedes the meaningful element in the verb, the combination is plural and is used with a plural verb and plural pronoun, as in *we each have our own opinion* and *they have each done their duty.* The use of a singular pronoun, such as *his,* in a construction of this kind is a grammatical mistake. It is the sort of mistake that would only be made by a person who was over-anxious about his grammar. When *each* follows the meaningful element of the verb, as in *they have tried, each in a different way,* it is independent of the subject, a pronoun and not an adjective.

When functioning as a pronoun, *each* is usually treated as a singular, as in *each carried his own pack,* and some grammarians claim that it must always be treated so. But in literary English there are a number of exceptions to this rule. When *each* refers indefinitely to both men and women the word *their* is sometimes used in place of *his,* as in *each carried their own pack.* (See **they.**) When a plural word stands between the pronoun *each* and its verb, the verb may be singular or plural, as in *each of them is* and *each of them are;* the plural is generally preferred. When *each* refers to more than one singular word joined by *and,* there is more difference of opinion about the number of the verb. H. W. Fowler says that the hymn lines, *soon will you and I be lying, each within our narrow bed,* cannot properly be sung except by married couples. But to most people's taste, calling what is yours and mine *his* is a deeper outrage than calling it *ours,* whether we own it in common or not.

The adjective *each* may qualify a singular noun in the genitive case, as in *each boy's jacket.* But it cannot qualify a plural noun in the genitive or a singular noun that follows a genitive, as in *the boys' each jacket.* The pronoun *each* itself does not have a genitive form. We cannot say *each's.*

In current English the word *each* is often used to mean "each and the next one," as in *between each row.* Some grammarians object to this new meaning, or new use of the word, and say that *between the rows* is required here. But *each* is used in this way by Kipling, Sackville-West, and other modern writers.

Each cannot be used with a negative verb. We may say *each failed* but we cannot say *each did not succeed.* The negative of *each* is *neither, no one* or *not every one.*

each other; one another. These expressions have the same meanings and are used in the same

ways. Either can be used in speaking of only
two or in speaking of a larger number. We may
say *the two men shook hands with one another*
and *the people in the room all knew each other*.
The claim that *one another* should not be used
in speaking of only two and that *each other*
should not be used in speaking of more than
two is an attempt to improve on the language
and not a report of how the words are used or
have been used in the past.

Both expressions have a genitive form, as
each other's, one another's. Both can be used in
any object position, as *they knew one another
and gave each other presents*. But neither expression can be used as the subject of a verb.
We cannot say *we know what each other thinks,
we know how one another is getting along*. In
statements of this kind, the *each* should be
attached to the subject word, as in *we each know
what the other thinks* and *how the other is getting along*.

eager. See **anxious.**

early; soon. *Early* was first an adverb but it developed adjective uses more than seven hundred
years ago. It is now used in both ways, as in
the early bird and *start early*.

That is *early* which comes before the usual
or appointed time. *Soon* means within a short
period after a definite time or event (*He arrived
early and had to wait for the others, but once
the clock had struck they soon appeared*). In
reference to a future event, *early* means in the
near future (*An early date has been set for the
wedding*), *soon* means the same (*They will soon
be married*).

earth; globe; world. *Earth* is the word of commonest use and at the same time, because of its
literary and especially its Biblical associations,
the most dignified (*The earth is the Lord's, and
the fulness thereof. O mother Earth! The earth
abideth for ever*). It is used especially in speaking of a condition of existence contrasted with
that in heaven or in hell (*While we are yet on
earth, let us be mindful, etc. This earthly life*).
Globe was used as a synonym when the roundness of the earth first began to impress itself
upon men's minds (*to circumnavigate the globe.
. . . the great globe itself,/ Yea, all which it inherit, shall dissolve*). It is coming, however, to
be used with increasing frequency to refer to the
inhabitants of the earth and their general activities, though *world* is the commoner of the two
words in such a meaning (*The whole world
hopes for peace*). *This world* serves, like *earth*,
to distinguish the terrestrial state from the celestial or infernal (*We give too much thought to
the things of this world*) and sometimes just
world carries the same meaning (*The world is
too much with us*).

**earthen; earthly; earthy; global; mundane; terres-
trial; worldly.** *Earthen* means composed of
earth, made of baked clay (*an earthen pitcher*).
Earthly means of this earth as opposed to
heaven (*our earthly existence, the earthly paradise, all earthly things above*). *Earthy* means of
the nature of or characteristic of earth as a
material substance (*The cellar was damp and

had an earthy smell*). I Corinthians 15:47 says
that *The first man is of the earth, earthy* and
the latter part of this famous passage has become a cliché meaning, usually, that someone
is broad in his speech.

Global, an adjective so much used now as to
be almost a vogue word, means pertaining to
the whole earth (*Global strategy requires, etc.
. . . Those who are global minded are aware,
etc. . . .*).

Terrestrial is the Latin equivalent of *earthly*.
It applies to the earth as a planet, to it as a place
distinct from heaven (which in smooth parlance
is referred to as *celestial* when opposed to *terrestrial*), and to the land surface of the earth as
opposed to the watery surface (*The terrestrial
area of the earth's surface covers 57,469,928
square miles*).

Worldly is commonly used in a derogatory
sense of being concerned with material, earthly
matters, vanity, social position, and the like, to
the exclusion of spiritual interests or thoughts of
the life to come (*Our sense of the vanity of
worldly honors increases as we grow older*).
Mundane is the Latin equivalent of *worldly*. It
suggests that which is bound to the earth, not
exalted, and therefore commonplace (*Entangled
with the birdlime of fleshly passions and mundane vanity. It was a mundane affair*).

east. The adjective may be *east* or *eastern*. There
is only one comparative form, *more eastern*, and
one superlative form, *easternmost*.

east; orient. In British usage *the east* is a common
term for Asia (*Once did She hold the gorgeous
east in fee*); whereas *the orient* is poetic and
literary. Americans know and use *the east* in this
sense (*the mysterious wisdom of the East*) and
are sufficiently aware of it to feel that *the west*
(which would, for them, be a more accurate
term) would be inappropriate. Then to most
Americans *the East* means the Atlantic seaboard
states, especially the northern ones, and *the West*
means the states from the Rockies to the Pacific.
So that in American usage *the orient* is a practical, everyday word for Eastern Asia (*He was
sent as consul to the Orient*).

easy; easily. *Easy* can always be used to qualify
a noun, as in *a green and easy world*. The form
easily is used only as an adverb and cannot
qualify a noun. *Easy* is sometimes used as an
adverb, as in *take it easy*. This construction is
acceptable spoken English, in the United States
and in Great Britain, but it does not appear in
formal writing. At one time the comparative and
superlative forms of *easy* could also be used as
adverbs, as in *all the easier led away by bad examples*, and *the good man can easiest persuade
himself that God is good*. These constructions
are now condemned in Great Britain. In the
United States they would merely be considered
bookish or affected. See also **facile.**

eat. The past tense is *ate*. The participle is *eaten*.
In Great Britain the past tense is pronounced
et. It is usually spelled *ate*, but the spelling *eat* is
also acceptable there.

Ate used as a participle, as in *had ate*, was
once literary English but is no longer considered

acceptable. Coleridge uses *had eat* (probably pronounced *et*) in *it ate the food it ne'er had eat.* This too was once good English but is no longer used.

eatable; edible. In the sense of something that can be eaten, *eatable* and its Latin form *edible* are synonymous and both are correct. Usage has imposed a faint but unmistakable difference upon them, however, in certain contexts or circumstances. When we say that something **is** *eatable*, we usually mean that it is not very appetizing but is probably not harmful and can be gotten down (*Bread mixed with sea water in time becomes so bitter as not to be eatable*). *Edible*, the more formal word of the two, is generally used in reference to substances which may be eaten with safety but which may be so uncommon or so generally conceived of as one of a number of similar things that may not be eaten that their edibility has to be stressed (*edible berries, edible mollusks*). The fixing of the two words in these meanings (which is not absolute) is fairly recent. But Southey's reference to *the theory of the eatability of cats* would certainly today be *edibility.*

eaten. See **eat.**

eat one's heart out, as a term for silent longing or regret, is a cliché.

eats. Used to mean food, this word is slang.

eaves. This word was originally a singular, but **is** now treated as a plural, as in *the eaves are dripping.* There is no word *an eave* and the singular form with *s* is seen in the compound *eavesdrop*—which once meant the ground over which the eaves dripped and, later (used as a verb) to stand in this space and spy on the people in the house.

echo. The plural is *echoes.*

eclectic is sometimes used as if it meant a discriminating choosing of the best. But its meaning is somewhat broader than that. It means selecting from diverse sources, not following any definite system.

economic; economical. The adjective *economical* is used only in the sense of money-saving. The adjective *economic* may mean money-saving or it may mean belonging to the science of economics. We speak of *an economic attaché* and of *an economic housewife.*

economical; thrifty; frugal; stingy; miserly. *Economical* implies a prudent planning in the disposition of resources so as to avoid unnecessary waste and to effect savings (*The young housewife cannot be too economical if she is to help her husband in his career*). In almost all uses the word has favorable connotations. *Thrifty* is an older, more homely word. It is related to the verb *to thrive,* to grow and flourish, and adds to the sense of saving active industry and management (*Caleb was a thrifty lad and soon was independent*). Too vigorous a concern with one's own welfare, however, has its moral dangers and *thrifty,* especially in ironical uses (for it was for centuries a word extolling one of the greatest of virtues), had some unpleasant connotations (*Disown the debt you cannot pay./*

You'll find it far the thriftiest way). *Frugal* means careful or sparing, opposing luxury. It definitely connotes austerity and sometimes meanness (*The uncovered boards with their frugal strip of carpet. And then there was a corncob that hung upon a string,/ For Father was a frugal man, and would not waste a thing*). With *stingy,* however, saving passes (at least in the estimation of the speaker or writer employing the word) from the admirable or necessary to the unpleasant. Stinginess is frugality with a sting in it. It is penuriousness that hurts, painful niggardliness (*The stingy wretch denied his own children food*). *Miserly* carries stinginess so far that the frugal one himself is now *miser*able. *Miserly* means that one is able to afford things which one denies oneself unnecessarily. Frugality has become avarice.

eczema. The plural is *eczemas* or *eczemata,* not *eczemae.*

edgeways; edgewise. These forms are equally acceptable.

edible. See **eatable.**

edifice; building. Unless the reference is to an unusually large and imposing structure, *edifice* is a pompous word for *building.* In the figurative sense of an elaborate and imposing political or intellectual structure, however, *edifice* is the proper word (*The edifice which Napoleon had so carefully constructed was, at bottom, largely a provision for his relatives*).

edition; impression; printing. An *edition* is one of a number of printings of the same book, newspaper, etc., issued at different times and differing from another by alterations, additions, etc. It is the making of changes that differentiates an edition from an *impression* or *printing,* which is simply one of a number of printings made at different times from the same set of type without alterations.

editor. Because the financial district of London is called "the City," the *city editor* in England means what in America is called *the financial editor.* In America the *city editor* is the man in charge of local news. The English prefer *leader* to *editorial* and *leader writer* to *editorial writer.*

educator (usually "a great educator") is a pompous word. It is interesting to note that it is rarely used of teachers but is reserved for journalistic prose almost exclusively for administrators (*That great educator, Samuel T. Fellenmacher, long head of the Boys Industrial Home*).

effect. See **affect.**

effective; effectual; efficacious; efficient. The word *effective* means that something has the power to produce, or actually does produce, a desired effect (*It was an effective rejoinder and reduced his opponent to silence*). In American usage *effective* has the special meaning of actually in effect. Thus when it is said that a certain law "will become effective" or "became effective" at a certain time, it does not mean, as it would to an Englishman, that at that time the law accomplished its purpose, but only that it will become or did become operative at that time.

Effectual is a word of praise applied to that

which produces the desired effect. An effectual measure or remedy is one that does what was hoped would be done. A law is *effective* when it is in operation, *effectual* if it accomplishes its purpose.

Efficient also means producing the desired effect, but it has the added connotation, in modern usage, of doing so with a high ratio of return for expenditure. It differs from *effectual* in carrying this suggestion and in the fact that it is applied to persons as well as to things (*An efficient secretary is an effectual agent for one who would make his will effective*).

Efficacious suggests the capability of achieving a certain end, a capability often manifested only when actually employed (*an efficacious drug in the cure of these infections*). It, too, is applied only to things, not to persons. See also **affect.**

effeminate. See **female.**

effete is a literary word for exhausted, worn out, applied to something or someone no longer creative (*an effete generation*). Originally it applied to animals and meant that they were no longer capable of producing young. It is not to be confused with *effeminate.*

eft. See **newt.**

egoism; egotism. *Egoism* is the name for the philosophical belief that self-interest is the true end of moral actions. As such, it is opposed to *altruism.* The egoist relates all questions to himself. He may believe, that is, that there is no proof that anything exists but his own mind, that all other people are perhaps figments of his imagination (*Subjective idealism is basically egoism. The mature man, hardened into skeptical egoism, knows no monition but that of his own frigid cautions*).

Egotism, the too frequent use of *I* in conversation, hence boastfulness, too much interest in one's own doings to an exclusion of interest in others, self-conceit, selfishness, is the more common word (*His absorbing egotism was annoying to all who had to associate with him*). *Egoism* and *egotism* do not, necessarily, have to have anything to do with each other. A self-effacing man may be an egoist. An egotist may have no interest in any philosophy whatsoever.

egregious originally meant out of the common, eminent, outstanding, exceptional; but it has become entirely pejorative, meaning now distinguished for some bad quality, flagrant in the extreme (*The man is an egregious ass. His egregious lies are embarrassing to listen to*).

either may be used as an adjective before a singular noun, as in *either one,* or standing alone as a pronoun, as in *either will do,* or together with the word *or* as a conjunction, as in *either Sarah or Babs wrote it.*

Either originally meant "each of two" or "both," as in *the trees on either side of the river.* The word is used in this sense in English literature from King Alfred down to Tennyson, Rossetti, and Stevenson, and including the King James Bible. Another meaning of the word, "one of two, no matter which," is about five hundred years old. In Great Britain, *either* in the original sense of "both" is now said to be archaic or poetic. In the United States it is still natural English. *Either* is used in this country in both senses and both are acceptable.

When *either* means "both" or "each" it is followed by a plural verb, as in *either of them are enough to drive a man to distraction.* Since the word is not used in this way in Great Britain, the plural verb is characteristically American. When what is meant is "only one," the verb is usually singular, as in *either of them is good enough.* But there are exceptions to this. In a negative statement *either* is usually treated as a plural, as in *I do not think either of them are at home.* The pronoun *you* is normally followed by a plural verb form, and we usually say *if either of you are ready.* When words of different number are contrasted, the verb agrees with the nearest word, as in *either he or they are to blame.* When singular pronouns are being contrasted, the strict rules of grammar require the form of the verb that would be appropriate for the last pronoun mentioned, as in *either you or I am to blame.* This is an extremely literary construction. In practice, some people would treat the combined words as *they* and say *are* and some would treat them as *one* and say *is,* but most people would undoubtedly avoid the problem and say *either you are to blame or I am.*

Either may be used with any number of words in a series, as in *either past, present or future.* It could be argued that in a construction of this kind the comma represents the word *or.* But *either* may also be used simply with the meaning of "any one," as in *either of these three.* It has been used in this way for more than three hundred years. The construction is rare, and disapproved by some grammarians; but it is found in the writings of Poe, Emerson, O. W. Holmes, and is recognized as standard by the *Oxford English Dictionary.* Writers who use it apparently feel that *any one* is too indefinite for their purposes.

Either is followed by the word *or,* and never by the word *nor.* In current English, the form *either,* and not the form *neither,* should be used after a verb that has already been made negative by some other word, as in *no one can prevent me, either* and *he never told me either.* This was not always true. Shakespeare writes *no, nor I neither.* The old *neither* can still be heard, but it is now considered archaic.

The pronoun *either* has a genitive form, as in *either's house.* The adjective can be used to qualify a genitive noun, as in *either man's house,* but it cannot follow a genitive noun or any other definitive, as in *the man's either house.* To express this idea we must use the pronoun form and say *either of the man's houses.* See also **double genitives.**

eke out. *Eke* is an Old English word, now archaic, meaning *also* (*The king himself did eat thereof / And eke the court beside*). To *eke out* is, therefore, to add to something in such a way as to make it suffice, or at least to make it do better or last longer than it would without the addition. Thus one may eke out an insufficient income by doing extra work, though the phrase has the definite meaning that that which is added is in itself inferior, inadequate, and hard come by. But to say that someone eked out a miserable existence by doing this or that, where it is merely meant that he so prolonged a miserable existence, is not a correct use of the term.

elapse; lapse. *Elapse* is now solely a verb. It means to pass or slip away and is applied exclusively to time (*Six months had elapsed since she made her resolution*).

Lapse, used as a noun, means a slip or slight error (*a lapse of memory*), a failure or miscarriage through some fault, or slip, or negligence (*a lapse of justice*), a gliding or passing away, as of time (*The lapse of years had wrought many changes*). As a verb it means to pass slowly, silently, or by degrees (*He lapsed into silence. For years the buses no longer ran along Alton Street and in time the franchise lapsed*), to fall or sink to a lower grade or condition, to glide, especially downward (*The sick man lapsed into unconsciousness*).

elder; eldest. See **old.**

elect, when it means choose, and not specifically choose by voting, may be followed by an infinitive, as in *he elected to go himself,* or by the *-ing* form of a verb, as in *he elected going himself.* It may also be followed by a clause with the clause verb a subjunctive or a subjunctive equivalent, as in *he elected I should go.* The infinitive construction is preferred.

-elect. See **suffixes.**

elective. In the terminology of education, Americans employ *elective* where the English use *optional.*

electric; electrical. Though *electric* and *electrical* are synonymous, the former is now by far the more common and in all figurative senses (*The atmosphere of the hall was electric with anticipation*) must be used. *Electrical* is confined now almost entirely to the sense of "concerned with electricity" (*Electrical engineers are much in demand*); whereas *electric* can mean derived from, produced by, pertaining to, or transmitting electricity, or electrifying in the figurative senses of thrilling, exciting, or charged.

electrocute. Fowler's assurance that this "barbarism" jars the nerves of Latinists "much more cruelly than the operation denoted jars those of its victim" must be accepted as a linguist's grim humor. More humorous, though unintended, is his conjecture, in attempting to account for the whole "bad business," that whoever made up the word "took *-cut-* (from *quatere*) instead of the indivisible *secut-* (from *sequi*) for the stem of *execution,* and derived it from *executere.*" The American journalist who invented the term, in 1889, probably never heard of either *quatere* or *sequi.* The process was new. It was about to be applied to one Kemmler, a murderer, and a name was needed for it. *Electrocute,* a portmanteau combination of *electricity* and *execute,* was

imagined and adopted. *Electricute* was tried a few times, but *electrocute* won out and is now standard despite the anguish of Latinists.

It is interesting to think that *electrify,* when applied to persons, means to make unusually alert and lively.

elegant. That is *elegant* which is excellently simple, tastefully fine, or associated with luxury. To use it as a synonym for *pleasing* is vulgar or tediously humorous. Its unsuitableness for such use is apparently felt by many of those who so use it, for they often try to give it a force which it should not have by reinforcing it with "perfectly" (*We had a perfectly elegant time*). However, to say that so-and-so has elegant manners or that this or that object of art or piece of furniture is elegant, rather than merely pleasing, fine, or choice, is to make a significant distinction.

elegy; eulogy. An *elegy* is a mournful, melancholy, or plaintive poem, especially a funeral song or lament for the dead. A *eulogy* is a speech or writing in praise of a person or thing, especially a set oration in honor of a dead person. An elegy often mingles eulogy with its lament and a eulogy in verse might be indistinguishable from an elegy, but there are many contexts in which the two words are not interchangeable. See also **panegyric.**

elemental; elementary. Though *elemental* and *elementary* were once synonymous, they are now differentiated in common usage. *Elemental* is now generally restricted to the four elements, or to the agencies, forces, or phenomena of nature (*elemental fire, the elemental grandeur of the sunset, the elemental fury of the storm*), or to what is primary. *Elementary* is now generally restricted to that which is introductory, or simple (*the elementary schools. Elementary, my dear Watson*).

elevator. Fowler's classification of *elevator* as a "superfluous word," his designation of it as "a cumbrous and needless Americanism," and his stern suggestion that it be at least restricted to "its hardly avoidable commercial sense of grain-hoist," fall on modern ears with all the tinkling quaintness of a harpsichord. It is now standard in American usage, established beyond challenge, too common to be cumbrous. *Lift,* which Fowler would have used in its stead, is, of course, so used in England, but even to traveled Americans it seems comic and to most Americans it would simply be incomprehensible.

elf. The plural is usually *elves,* though *elfs* may also be used.

elicit; extract; extort. To *elicit* information is to draw out, without any suggestion of the use of force, what was latent or implicit. When information is elicited from someone, it is brought out indirectly by questioning. It is possible for information to be elicited from someone without his knowing that he has given it up. To *extract* information is to get it more forcibly and directly, by importuning and threatening (*Third-degree methods may offend the high-minded,* *but they extract the facts the police want*). To *extort* is to get information in much the same manner as to *extract* it, though there is a connotation of more violence and ruthlessness. Illegal demands, such as ransoms in kidnapping cases, are extortions. When information is said to have been extorted, there is a suggestion that there has been strong resistance to giving it up.

elicit; illicit. Nothing but sheer ignorance could confuse *elicit* and *illicit*. *Elicit* is a verb, meaning to draw out (figuratively), to educe, to evoke (*Clever questioning further elicited the fact that he had been at Granston several times before this "first visit"*). *Illicit* is an adjective meaning unlawful (*illicit love*).

elk; deer; wapiti; moose. The animal which in the United States is called the *elk* is the *wapiti,* a species of deer (*Cervus canadensis*) with long, slender antlers. Its equivalent in England, scarcely distinguishable, is the *red deer,* the male of which is the *stag.* By the word *elk* the English designate an animal (*Alces alces*) closely resembling what in America is called a *moose* (*Alces americanus* or the Alaskan variety *Alces gigas*), the male of which has large palmate antlers. And if this is not confusing enough, the word *moose* is sometimes used in England to designate the European elk (*Alces machlis*). Ten minutes spent in trying to unravel this and half a dozen other popular names for birds and mammals will show the layman why scientists use Latin names for species.

ell in common English usage is solely a measure of distance. This meaning is known in America but is now restricted almost entirely to the saying *Give him an inch and he'll take an ell.* An *ell* in America (or an *el*) more generally means the extension of a building, usually at right angles to one end (*Grandfather built the ell after Aunt Susan got married and came to live with him on the farm*). Some believe that this is derived from the fact that the addition and the main building then form a letter L, and so it may be, but Old English uses of the word in this sense, for it was formerly known in England, though it survives only in dialects, suggest that it may have derived from *aisle,* which meant *wing.*

El is used a great deal in America as an abbreviation for *elevated railroad.* This meaning is unknown in England.

ellipse; ellipsis. An *ellipse* is a term used in geometry. It means a plane curve such that the sums of the distances of each point in its periphery from two fixed points, the foci, are equal. It is a conic section formed by the intersection of a right circular cone by a plane which cuts obliquely the axis and the opposite sides of the cone.

Ellipsis is a term used in grammar. It means the omission from a sentence of a word or words that are essential to its grammatical completeness, though not necessarily to the completeness of its sense.

Some authorities would have *elliptic* the adjective for *ellipse* and *elliptical* for *ellipsis,* but in American usage *elliptic* is simply a rare form of *elliptical.*

ellipsis. The plural is *ellipses.*

This term is used by some grammarians to refer to words that do not actually occur in a sentence but which they feel are needed in making a certain kind of grammatical analysis or to explain a grammatical construction. These words are sometimes described as "words which the hearer easily supplies."

There is no doubt that English allows us to omit a great many words that we could have used without changing the meaning in any way. For example, some verb which is known to the hearer has obviously been omitted from the end of the statement *he doesn't want to.* Some grammarians, abusing the privilege of putting words into another person's mouth, recognize no limit to the number of words which they may read into a sentence. It has been claimed that the word *fire!* satisfies a certain definition of a sentence because it represents an ellipsis, which may be (*there is a*) *fire* (*here*) or (*you men*) *fire* (*your guns*). It is sometimes said that a sentence such as *no one saw it but me* is ungrammatical and should be *no one saw it but I* because there is an ellipsis of the word *saw.* The answer to arguments of this kind is to say: "If I had meant *saw,* I would have said *I saw.*" No one should allow himself to be convicted of bad grammar on the basis of words he has not used.

On the other hand, some grammarians seem to think that the composer of a sentence may not omit any word which does not appear elsewhere in the sentence in the same grammatical form. It is claimed that *I was young, they old* is ungrammatical because the word to be supplied is *were* and not *was.* All writers and speakers of English, including these very grammarians themselves, omit words which never will be missed, whether they have already been used in the sentence or not. This is never objectionable unless the sentence becomes misleading, that is, unless the omitted words actually are missed. English that leaves nothing at all to the imagination becomes tiresome, and even insulting.

Speech is highly elliptical. It would scarcely be endurable otherwise. Ellipsis is indispensable to the writer or speaker who wants to be brief and pithy, but it can easily cause confusion and obscurity and must be used with skill.

ellipsis marks have the following uses:

To indicate omissions in a quotation, as in *Give me liberty or . . . death!* If in a longer quotation the ellipsis includes the end of a sentence, the period joins the ellipsis and makes a total of four dots.

To show hesitation or the passage of time in dialogue or narrative, as in *Please, please . . . you mustn't leave* and *The time passed very slowly . . . and Sarah became sleepier and sleepier.*

Ellipses are now shown by three periods. They were once shown by three asterisks, and asterisks are still used in very formal writing, but even here the periods are also acceptable. Some newspapers and magazines use three asterisks in a separate line to show quotation omissions of a paragraph or more in length.

else's, is the standard form for the possessive of a pronoun followed by *else,* as in *somebody else's dog.*

The practice of putting the possessive sign after *else* instead of after the pronoun itself is relatively new and seems to owe its position in literature to Dickens. Other nineteenth century writers, such as Thackeray, Mark Twain, Henry James, wrote *somebody's else.* During the transition from this to the modern form a compromise, *somebody's else's,* was often used.

The old form may still be used with *who* when there is no following noun, but not otherwise. That is, we must now say *who else's signature did you get?,* but we may also say *whose else could I get?*

elucidate. See **explain.**

elude. See **escape.**

elusion; elusive. See **allusion.**

elves. See **elf.**

emanate is to flow from, to proceed from as a source or origin. It is used exclusively of non-material things. Ideas, plans, hopes, fears, and so on, *emanate* from certain persons or conditions; but it would be a mistake to say that a river or a street *emanated.* Since the word means to flow as from a source or point of origin, it is natural to use it as a synonym for *originate,* but unless the sense of flowing out from the point of origination is kept this use is careless and should be avoided. An idea or an attitude may emanate *from* someone; it cannot emanate *with* him.

embargo. The plural is *embargoes.*

emend. See **amend.**

emerge; issue. To *emerge* is to rise or come forth, as from water or some other liquid, especially to come forth into view or notice from concealment. Thus when a question or a problem *emerges* in the course of action or discussion, it arises, unforeseen, out of the situation (*Pegasus emerged from the blood of Medusa. The periscope barely emerged, with a faint feathering of the surface, before the gun was brought to bear upon it. Cromwell, who entered the Civil War as Lieutenant-General of the Horse, emerged absolute ruler of England. On piecing the various pieces of evidence together, the facts gradually emerged*).

To *issue* is also to come forth, but it is used of a number of persons or a mass of matter, or a volume of smoke, coming through an outlet or outlets, and often with the suggestion of a forceful or tumultuous coming forth after having been shut up or enclosed (*The army, breaking through the defile, issued out upon the subjacent plain. The smoke issued from the chimney in rolling clouds*). See also **immerge.**

emigrant; immigrant. An *emigrant* is one who leaves one country to settle in another. An *immigrant* is one who comes into a new country to settle. Thus a man is an *emigrant* from the country of his birth or previous residence, an *immigrant* as he comes into the new country.

eminent. To be *eminent* is to be conspicuous, prominent, exalted in station or public estimation. But since these things are comparative and death is a leveler, no man can be eminent after he is dead. He is then either *famous* or forgotten. Of course *eminent* may be used of a man when the reference is to what he was when he was alive. Strachey's Eminent Victorians were eminent in the Victorian age. At least one of them is now famous. See also **fame, immanent.**

emphasis. The plural is *emphases.*

emphatic tenses. See **do.**

employ is obsolescent for *employment* in England but is still current in the United States in the rather stilted phrase *being in someone's employ.*

As a verb *employ* stresses the service performed, whereas *hire* stresses the wages to be paid for the performance of the service (*She was employed at her needlework. Is not the laborer worthy of his hire?*), though the words are often used interchangeably.

employee. Anyone who is employed is, in the United States, an *employee.* No orthographical distinction is now made between a hired male worker and a hired female worker.

emporium. The plural is *emporiums* or *emporia.* An *emporium* is a place, a town or a city, which is the principal center of trade for a region (*The vast regions of the northwest, for which Chicago is the commercial emporium*). It is used grandiloquently as a term for a large store selling a variety of articles (*When I was working in the paper-box factory I thought I loved a clerk in Kahn's Emporium*). Since the latter meaning has, in common usage, almost entirely replaced the former, anyone who insists on using the word is confronted with the choice of being either grandiloquent or obscure.

empty; vacant. That which is *empty* contains nothing. It is devoid of its usual or appropriate contents. An empty house would be one devoid of furniture. Empty hands carry nothing. An empty mind is free of thought. Though *vacant* is often used interchangeably with *empty,* it is usually applied to that which is temporarily unoccupied. A vacant house could be one from which the family is temporarily absent, though the furnishings remain. A vacant store would be one that is empty at the moment but for which a new tenant is expected or at least hoped. When a position is said to be vacant, it is assumed that it will soon be filled. *Empty* would never be used in such a context. A vacant stare is one devoid of expression; perhaps there is a kind suggestion that the intellectual vacuity back of it is only temporary.

enclose; enclosure. *Enclose* is now preferred to *inclose* and *enclosure* to *inclosure.*

enclosed herewith; under separate cover. *Enclosed herewith* (or *herein*) is a redundancy, since that which is enclosed must of necessity be therewith or therein. The phrase is a piece of outmoded commercial jargon which, fortunately, one doesn't encounter much any more. Some object on the same grounds to *under separate cover*, maintaining that if something is being sent it obviously is not enclosed and hence is being sent separately. But—although the actual wording may seem hackneyed—there is some justification for such a phrase if the object referred to is such that it might conceivably be enclosed in the letter. It's silly to say in a letter, *I'm sending you a crate of oranges under separate cover*, but it may be reassuring to say *I'm sending you the check (or the pamphlet) under separate cover*; though it might be better simply to say *separately*.

enclosed please find. Whether *find* means to come upon by chance or to obtain by search, the combination of request and command in the common phrase *enclosed please find* has an element of absurdity in it. You cannot command anyone to do that which can only happen by chance. It would be more accurate grammatically (and considering the number of things which are said to be enclosed in letters but are not, more accurate factually) to say *enclosed please try to find*. Best of all is not to use the phrase. The proper procedure, now followed more and more, is to state in the body of the letter what is to be enclosed and to have "enclosure" or "encl." typed at the bottom as a directive to the stenographer and an indication to the recipient that the enclosure was at least ordered.

encomium. The plural is *encomiums* or *encomia*.

end may be used as an adjective. When it is, it has no comparative form but it has a superlative form *endmost*.

end; stop; cease; finish; complete; conclude; terminate. English is rich in terms for bringing to a stop. Many can be used interchangeably, yet many are restricted to certain senses, and many have special idiomatic meanings. To list them all and to trace and differentiate their meanings, with illustrations, would take many pages. Only a few may be mentioned here and those briefly, just enough to show the variety of possibilities.

A speaker, for example, might *end, stop,* or *cease* his remarks for a number of reasons. He might have said all he had to say or he might have been interrupted or silenced. If he *finishes, completes,* or *concludes* his remarks, however, he has not been interrupted, since he has been able to put the final touches on his subject, assemble all its component parts, or bring it to its planned end. To *terminate* them could be to bring them to a planned limit or just to stop them (*He terminated his remarks with a flourish* or *At the sight of the dead cat coming through the air, the Senator terminated his remarks abruptly*). In the latter use there is often a touch of jocularity.

endeavor; strive; try; attempt. To *try* is the everyday verb. To see the folly of pompousness one only has to substitute *endeavor, strive,* or *attempt* for *try* in *If at first you don't succeed, try, try, again*. None the less, *endeavor* has its special uses and advantages. To *try* means many things, from straining patience or endurance to

rendering the oil out of something; whereas to *endeavor* means only one thing: to make a continuous effort in the face of difficulties. Then its very ponderousness gives *endeavor* an onomatopoeic advantage in some contexts, for it suggests the strenuous trying, the energetic attempting that the word connotes (*One should know God's word and endeavor to live by it* is far more effective than *and try to live by it* or *and attempt to live by it*).

To *strive* is to exert oneself earnestly, with strenuous effort, towards the accomplishment of something difficult and laborious (*When Ajax strives some rock's vast weight to throw*).

To *atttempt* is more formal than to try and implies the expenditure of somewhat more effort.

As a noun, *try* is used colloquially, and more in England than in America (*I'll have a try at it*). *Endeavor* and *attempt* are the everyday nouns, with *endeavor* being the more common, especially in more general senses (*The endeavor was commendable. A man of high endeavor*). *Attempt* is more likely to be used of a specific try (*His attempt to break the record for the hundred yard dash was bound to fail under such weather conditions*).

ended; ending. That is *ended* which has come to an end at some time in the past (*His advances ended when he found them repulsed*). That is *ending* which is coming to an end or about to end (*We are ending our engagement at the Garrick Theater tomorrow*). All this is quite clear, and those who wish to be unambiguous or unconfused can stick to it. But *ending* may be used, as a historic present, to designate something that is now definitely ended but was not ended at a time in the past (*If you will refer to the inventory for the year ending March 31, 1915, you will find, etc.*).

endemic. See **epidemic.**

endless. See **eternal.**

endless; innumerable. *Endless* mean boundless, infinite, interminable, continuous (as in *endless belt*). To use it for *innumerable*, which means too many to count (*The dishes were just endless; I never saw so many to wash*) is exaggeration. Of course exaggeration has its place in humorous talk and writing, but this particular exaggeration has been made so often that it has lost most of its meaning, a fact made evident by the stress which is so often laid on the word to strengthen it. Then there are instances where the use of *endless* for *innumerable* is ambiguous. When it is said of so-and-so that he told *endless stories*, does it mean that his stories lacked endings, were pointless, or that the list of them lacked ending, that they were too many to count, innumerable?

endorse; indorse. *Endorse,* both in the sense of writing on the back of, approving, supporting, or sustaining is now preferred to *indorse*, although *indorse* is correct and is used more in America than in England.

Endorse was formerly a purely commercial word. Writing in 1883, E. A. Freeman said that thirty-five years before that the application of such a commercial word to agreement or disagreement on philosophical or theological matters would have seemed "irresistibly ludicrous." Now even purists *endorse* each other's protests, policies, and aspirations without a qualm.

endorse on the back. Since the second syllable of *endorse* means back (as in the *dorsal* fin of a fish), to *endorse on the back* is a redundancy. But since *endorse* has the common meaning of write your name on, only scholars are aware that it is a redundancy and the common speaker or writer is justified in using it.

endurance. See **patience.**

endure may be followed by an infinitive, as in *I cannot endure to hear about it,* or by the *-ing* form of a verb, as in *I cannot endure hearing about it.* The two forms are equally acceptable. *Endure* may also be followed by a clause but the clause verb must be a subjunctive or a subjunctive equivalent, as in *I cannot endure you should go.* An infinitive construction, such as *I cannot endure to see you go* or *to have you go,* is generally preferred.

endways; endwise. These forms are equally acceptable.

enema. The plural is *enemas* or *enemata,* not *enemae.*

enemy, when it refers to individuals, is a regular English noun with a regular plural in *s,* as in *my enemy has written a book* and *my enemies have written a book.* But the singular form may also be used as a group name. In this case it may take either a singular or a plural verb, as in *the enemy is retreating* and *the enemy are retreating.* The plural verb is more courteous and is preferred in military English.

enervate. See **innervate.**

engage in. See **indulge in.**

engender was originally to beget (*Then should he take a young wife and a fair/ On which he might engender him an heir*) or to bear (*O Error soon conceived,/ Thou kill'st the mother that engendered thee*). It is now used figuratively to mean to produce or to give rise to. It is, therefore, a synonym for *cause,* but in any careful and discriminating use of it there will have to be the idea of generation, not merely the ground of any action or result. Thus it is correct to say that fear engenders hate or that the clouds engender rain, but it would be incorrect to say that the broken rail engendered the wreck.

engineer. In the United States the term *engineer* is applied to one who manages a locomotive engine. In England such a one is called an engine-driver and *engineer,* in this sense, is restricted to one who manages a marine engine.

England. See **Great Britain.**

enigma. The plural is *enigmas* or *enigmata,* not *enigmae.* See also **riddle.**

enjoin is one of the words in our amazing language which must drive foreigners who are trying to learn it to despair; for it means two directly opposite things: to order a person to do something (*Pythagoras enjoined his scholars to maintain silence during their novitiate*) and to prohibit the doing of something (*We are now asked to enjoin him from infringing a right which does not exist*). In the first of these meanings, *enjoin* has more force than *direct* but less than *command.* The second is chiefly a legal term in England but in America it is standard usage.

Enjoin, in the first sense, may be followed by an infinitive, as in *we enjoined him to return to his duties,* or by a clause with the clause verb a subjunctive or a subjunctive equivalent, as in *we enjoined him that he return to his duties.* The infinitive construction is preferred. In the second sense it is followed by *from* and the *-ing* form of the verb.

enjoy may be followed by the *-ing* form of a verb, as in *I enjoy dancing,* but not by an infinitive. *I enjoy to dance,* for example, is not accepted as standard.

Enjoy means, basically, to experience with joy, to take pleasure in. It is a natural extension to use it to mean to have and use with satisfaction (*The terms upon which the tenancy is enjoyed, etc.*), but if the idea of pleasure in the use is lost sight of and it is used merely in the sense of *have* or even *endure,* it is incorrect and may be ludicrous. To say that so-and-so enjoys good health is sensible because good health is an enjoyable thing. But to say seriously that so-and-so enjoys poor health is absurd; and to say it humorously or ironically is tedious since use and repetition have long ago worn out the freshness of the paradox.

enjoyable. See **immense.**

enlarge. To *enlarge* is to increase in extent, bulk, quantity, scope, or capacity. A photographic negative may be enlarged. A house may be enlarged. A man's interests or his social circle may be enlarged. But his activities must be increased.

enormity; enormousness. *Enormity* now refers entirely to something hugely out of the moral norm (*The enormity of his crimes defies comprehension*). *Enormousness* may be used to suggest the immensity of wickedness (*The enormousness of his crimes, etc.*) but it suggests merely immensity and the wickedness is contained in *crimes.* The word can equally well be applied to virtuous things or acts (*The enormousness of his benefactions, etc.*) and is always used when physical immensity beyond the normal is designated (*Immense as the figures are, the enormousness of the mountains dwarfs them*).

enough may be used as a noun, as in *we have enough,* or as an adjective or adverb. When used as an adjective it may stand before or after the noun it qualifies, as in *enough sugar* and *sugar enough.* When used as an adverb, that is, when qualifying any word except a noun, it must always stand after the word it qualifies, as in *he is tall enough, he worked hard enough. Enough* always follows a noun that is being used in an adjective sense, as in *he is man enough. Enough* cannot follow any of the definitive words, that is, any of the words that make a statement as specific as possible, such as *a, the, this, that, my, his, Dick's.*

Enough may be followed by an infinitive, as in *there is enough to go around* and *there is enough for everybody to have some*. It cannot be followed by a *that* clause. We should not say *the fragments are large enough that their structure can be determined*. This sentence should read *the fragments are large enough for their structure to be determined* or *the fragments are so large that their structure can be determined*. See also **ample**.

enquire; inquire. In American usage *inquire* has almost superseded *enquire,* though, if we may trust Partridge, the situation is reversed in England. See **inquire.**

enquiry; inquiry. In America *inquiry* is now the almost universal spelling. *Enquiry* is recognized as a variant, but it is rarely used. In England however, according to Sir Ernest Gowers, a useful distinction is developing between the two words: an *enquiry* is a question, an *inquiry* is an investigation. One may therefore, he says, make an enquiry concerning an inquiry. See also **query.**

enraged; infuriated; incensed. A man is *enraged* when he has been provoked to violent anger (*Enraged at the deliberate insult, he struck the young man full in the face*). When a man is *infuriated,* his anger has been aroused to the point of frenzy. His rage borders upon or even passes into delirium. Many terms that describe anger (as the common *mad*) stress the similarity or relationship between vindictive resentment and insanity. *Infuriated* is a somewhat stronger word than *enraged* (*Upon receipt of the news he was infuriated and fell upon the messenger with blows and curses*). To be *incensed* is to be inflamed with anger, but the word suggests far more dignity and self control than *enraged* or *infuriated* (*Sir John was incensed at the remark and could maintain even the appearance of composure with the utmost difficulty*). There is also in *incensed,* possibly because of its connotation of restraint, an implication of great provocation and usually of unjust or improper provocation. *Incensed* is used to describe one who is angry when we sympathize with his anger.

ensure; insure. In the sense to make sure, to secure, to make sure or certain to come, *ensure* and *insure* are interchangeable; in the sense to guarantee against risk of loss or harm, *insure* is now the only word and its increasing use in this sense is tending to fix it so that its use in other senses seems improper. See also **assure.**

entail. See **involve.**

enter, when used as a stage direction, is an imperative. It should not be used in a sentence with a singular subject, as in *enter John and walks to the window*. This should read *John enters and walks to the window*.

enthuse. A back formation from *enthusiasm, enthuse,* meaning to become enthusiastic or to move others to enthusiasm (*They enthused immediately upon this subject*—Frank Norris), is colloquial speech in the United States. Its fault —if it has one—is not in its being a back formation but in its being used to mean to get excited

rather than to mean—as it should if it really means to become enthusiastic or to arouse enthusiasm—to get excited because of the absorbing possession of the mind by a certain pursuit or interest.

enthusiastic has to mean more than just *excited*. It is the manifestation of a rapturous intensity of feeling in favor of a person or a principle, proceeding from an overwhelming conviction of the importance of the person or principle (*The enthusiastic eagerness with which he outlined his new system of philosophy. The candidate was greeted with shrill whistles and stampings of feet by his enthusiastic admirers*).

entice. See **allure.**

entire. See **complete.**

entitle may be followed by an infinitive, as in *this entitles you to go*. It is not followed by the *-ing* form of a verb, as in *this entitles you to going*.

entomology; etymology. *Entomology* is the branch of zoology that treats of insects. *Etymology* is the branch of philology that treats of the derivations and histories of words.

entrance and **entry** both mean the act of entering and the place of ingress. Both have special meanings. An actor's appearance upon the stage is an *entrance*. *Entrance* also means the right of entering (as in *entrance examinations* and *He has entrance to the best society*). *Entry* has the special meaning of something recorded in a book or register. In law it means the taking possession of lands or tenements or entering or setting foot on them (*The landlord always retains the right of entry under certain conditions*).

Some authorities make fine distinctions between the two words in the senses in which they are synonymous. They say that where they mean a place of ingress, *entrance* implies only an opening, as a gate or doorway; whereas *entry* implies a passageway. This is more observed in English than in American usage. Where they mean the act of entering, *entrance* connotes the act and *entry* the result of the act, they say. Furthermore, *entrance* suggests the possibility of entering without supervision or permission (*Entrance is by the main door*). These distinctions are not rigid, however, and the common speaker and writer is probably little aware of them.

entreat may be followed by an infinitive, as in *I entreat you to tell me*. It may also be followed by a clause with the clause verb a subjunctive or subjunctive equivalent, as in *entreat her that she ride with me,* but this construction is now archaic and the infinitive is preferred.

entrust. For "to invest with a trust or responsibility, to commit to someone's care, to confide," *entrust* is now preferred to *intrust,* though *intrust* is acceptable.

entry and **entrant** are now used synonymously to designate a competitor in a contest, though *entrant* was formerly felt to be the only correct term.

enure. See **inure.**

envelop; envelope. As a verb, meaning to wrap up as in a covering, *envelop* is now the standard form. As a noun, meaning a cover for a letter or the like, *envelope* is the standard form, though *envelop* is not incorrect.

enviable; envious. That is *enviable* which excites envy or is to be envied (*His position, so secure and honorable, is an enviable one*). He is *envious* who feels envy (*Envious of his friend's success, he cast about for some means to humiliate him*). *Enviable* is a much milder word than *envious*. It is often used as a term of praise. But *envious* suggests one in an unpleasant, ugly, and even dangerous condition.

environs no longer has a singular form. The plural form is used with a plural verb, as in *the environs are attractive,* but it is not a true plural and cannot be used with a word implying number. We cannot speak of *several environs*.

envisage; envision. To *envisage* is to confront, to look in the face, to face (*Let us envisage the facts as they are*), to contemplate or call up a mental picture or image (*The Mayor, speaking before the Council, envisaged the new sewage disposal plant*), or to perceive by intuition (*Nature, to the Buddhist, is envisaged as a nexus of laws*).

To *envision* (of 20th century coinage, by the way) is to see as in a vision (*His blackest hypochondria had never envisioned quite so miserable a catastrophe*) and is properly confined to those ecstatic or alarming foreshadowings that visions are made on. When the mayor envisaged the sewage disposal plant, it is assumed that he saw an actual plant in his mind's eye and with prosaic efficiency communicated to the Council some concept of its mechanism, capacity, structure, and the like. Had he envisioned it, he would have been more poetic, seeing it from afar as a glorious fulfillment, some day to be realized, of the citizens' aspirations.

envy; covet; begrudge. To *envy* is to feel spite and resentment because someone else possesses or has achieved something that one wishes he had himself (*The award has made him envy you, and he is no longer your friend*). The word is used, with a milder connotation, indeed as a sort of strong compliment, in expressions where the context makes it plain that there is no malice or resentment (*How I envy you the hours you spent in his company!*). Used with a negative, it often expresses a mild commiseration (*I do not envy you the responsibilities you have undertaken*).

To *covet* is to desire jealously to possess what belongs to someone else (*Thou shalt not covet thy neighbor's house*). There is a definite connotation of culpability in the desiring it denotes.

To *begrudge* is to be unwilling to allow another to have the possessions or honors or esteem that he is entitled to (*He begrudged him the least comfort in his misery*), or to give, when one must give, reluctantly and with grumbling.

ephemeris. The plural is *ephemerises* or *ephemerides,* not *ephemeres*.

ephemeron. The plural is *ephemerons* or *ephemera*. *Ephemera* is also used as a singular and has the regular plural *ephemeras*. Either of these forms is acceptable today. But a new learned plural *ephemerae* is not. It is not English, and it is not good Latin or Greek.

epic. As a noun *epic* means a narrative, usually in verse, which celebrates the deeds of heroes of history or legend. As an adjective it means something suitable for such a narration, or something of an imposing and heroic character. James Truslow Adams's *The Epic of America* was not inappropriately named, for the history of America is a saga of unparalleled achievement, full of wild poetry, true grandeur, great heroes and heroic deeds. It has the material for twenty epics. But the word is sadly abused in journalism, especially by sports writers whose eternal striving for intensives leads one to suspect, sometimes, that their actual material must be dull and uninspiring. Thus when *Life* (October 18, 1954), refers to a long putt, successfully sunk by Mr. Bobby Jones at Mamaroneck, New York, in 1929, as an "epic" putt, the immense word is ludicrously ill-supported by the achievement to which it is applied. The reader is misled, the language is impaired, and Mr. Jones, whose putt was really a very good putt, is made to seem absurdly pretentious. No one gains.

epical; epochal. *Epical* means of the nature of epic poetry, something worthy to be told in the old epic manner. *Epochal* means of or pertaining to an epoch, a particular period of time marked by some distinctive character. When one speaks of an event as *epochal,* it is generally meant that the event itself was of such tremendous import and so far-reaching in its effects that it serves to mark an epoch.

epicure; epicurean. See **hedonist**.

epidemic; endemic; pandemic. A disease is *epidemic* when it affects a large number of persons at the same time in a locality in which it is not permanently prevalent (*The Spanish Influenza was epidemic in the United States in 1918*). A disease is *endemic* when it is habitually prevalent in a certain locality or habitually peculiar to a certain people (*Sleeping sickness is endemic wherever the tsetse fly is unchecked. Snobbery is endemic to country clubs*). That is *pandemic* which is universal and afflicts all people. (*The fear of the hydrogen bomb is pandemic*).

episode. See **event; happening**.

epistle is a letter, but it is a formal and didactic letter, and to use the word as a synonym for letter (*The unclaimed epistles were pinned on a board in the Post Office*) is pretentious if serious and ponderous if intended to be humorous.

epitaph; epigraph. An *epitaph* is, one might say, a specialized *epigraph*. An *epigraph* is an inscription, especially on a building, a statue or the like. It can be on a tomb. An *epitaph* is a commemorative inscription on a tomb or any brief writing resembling such an inscription.

epithets. An epithet may be a meaningful appellation (*witch-hunter, egghead*) or a descriptive term suggesting the quality of a person or thing (*Richard the lion-hearted, Harry the Horse, rock-bound coast*).

There has come to be a faintly negative connotation to the word *epithet*. It is more commonly associated with unfavorable characterization, with profanity and with name-calling than with favorable characterization or praise. Expressions like *dirty dog, damned liar* and *double-crossing crook* are more likely to come to mind when epithets are mentioned than *wine-dark sea* or *curly-headed baby*.

Epithet is a common weapon in argument, especially in political campaigning, for all the force of connotation can be brought to bear to substitute for or to counteract logic. In fact most political labels carry so much emotion that they have lost their original meaning and are used as opprobrious designations by members of the opposing group: *communist, fascist, Red, capitalist, bourgeois,* etc. In the 1956 presidential campaign the Republicans, insisting on calling their opponents the Democrat Party, to avoid the favorable implications of *democratic,* managed to make even *democrat* seem unpleasant.

equal is sometimes followed by an infinitive, as in *he felt equal to meet them,* but the *-ing* form of the verb is preferred, as in *he felt equal to meeting them.*

equally as. Since *as* implies equation (*He is as tall as you are*), *equally as* (in such sentences as *He was equally as astonished as the others*) is redundant. Fowler sternly calls it "an illiterate tautology," but in the United States it is accepted, and used, by people who certainly are not illiterate.

equilibrium. The plural is *equilibriums* or *equilibria.*

equipment. In the jargon of the airlines *equipment* is used, at least in public dealings with passengers, as a synonym for airplane (*This delay is caused by the late arrival of incoming equipment*). Whether this is thought to be more elegant or whether it corresponds to some classification within the business, it is certainly not standard, though, of course, if it is continued it may become so.

The adjective *mechanical* is used by the airlines in place of such phrases as *mechanical failure* or *mechanical trouble* (*On flight two ninety-eight there's mechanical, but it ought to leave before six o'clock*). This may be the mere adoption of an abbreviated technical expression, but one suspects it is at least in part a euphemistic desire, in dealing with passengers, to avoid anything as disturbing as *mechanical failure* or *mechanical trouble*. And, indeed, these phrases might very well convey a false impression, since the passenger would probably transfer to them his associations with the automobile where *mechanical trouble* usually means a cessation of function or at least a serious impairment of it; whereas on a plane it might signify only what on a car would be called "a need for adjustment" or "regulation." This use of *mechanical* shows a new industry groping for a new word and attempting to divest an old word of its connotations.

equivocal. See **ambiguous.**

errant; arrant. *Errant* means wandering, as a *knight errant* traveling in search of adventure. By a natural extension it came also to mean deviant from rectitude or propriety (*The famous beauty and errant lady, the Duchess of Mazarin*).

Arrant was originally a variant spelling of *errant* (and *errant* is still used for *arrant* sometimes, though never the reverse). It came to be applied especially to vagabonds and other wandering ruffians of whom former times stood in particular fear—arrant rogues, arrant rascals, arrant thieves. From this application the word came to have the force of an opprobrious intensive. That is, the thievery and the roguery and the rascality of these wandering ones (many of them men made desperate by being driven from their farms and villages which were destroyed to make room for grazing lands) was transferred to the adjective *wandering*. So that Swift's allegation that *Every servant is an arrant thief as to victuals and drink* has nothing to do with the servant's being or not being a wanderer. Then it came to mean thorough and unmitigated, and this meaning, with enough of the opprobrious retained to prevent its ever being used in a favorable sense is its current one (*an arrant ass, an arrant fool*).

Errant is now archaic and literary. *Arrant* is fixed in a few opprobrious terms, most of which are clichés. Both words may well be avoided.

erratum. *Errata,* the plural, is also used as a singular to mean a list of errors or corrections and has a regular plural *erratas,* meaning more than one such list. This is an English word and should not be given a Latin plural, as in *erratae.*

error. See **mistake.**

ersatz. See **synthetic.**

eruption; irruption. An *eruption* is a violent bursting out (*The eruption of Vesuvius filled the sky with smoke and flames*). An *irruption* is a violent bursting in (*The Goths . . . making irruptions into Gaul*).

escape; elude; evade. To *escape* can mean to get free from confinement, to regain liberty (*No more dramatic escape from a prison camp has been recorded*). It can also mean to avoid danger, pursuit, observation, or the like, even by sheer luck. A man may escape danger or observation by accident, though there is usually some connotation of intention (*By taking the back way he escaped being seen. He escaped death by the mere chance of stopping to lace his shoe*).

To *elude* is to escape by means of dexterity or artifice (*He eluded pursuit by a series of amazing disguises*). When we say that something eluded our attention, we imply that we almost perceived it, or admit that we should have perceived it. There is a suggestion that the thing itself, by some pixyish sleight or movement, ducked out of sight for a second. There's an element of slyness in it. A fox *eludes* the hounds.

To *evade* is to escape by trickery or cleverness, to get around something that intends to stop us, to avoid doing something or to avoid answering directly. When a man *evades* a question, he does not refuse to answer it. He seems to answer it but actually does not, or he manages to change the subject or pretends to misunderstand the question and gives an irrelevant answer.

escape; escapade. An *escape* is an act of escaping (*The escape was poorly planned and failed*) or the means of escaping (*Our only escape lay directly down the face of the cliff*). An *escapade* was originally an *escape*, but it now means a reckless prank (*Such escapades might have been forgiven a boy, but they were inexcusable in a man of his age*).

esoteric; exoteric. *Esoteric* means understood by or meant for a select few, hence profound, recondite. *Exoteric* means suitable to be communicated to the general public, not pertaining to the inner circle, hence popular, simple, or commonplace. *Exoteric* is a fairly rare word and sometimes used erroneously for *exotic* [q.v.]. The terms *esoteric* and *exoteric* were originally applied to groups of disciples of sages of antiquity. The *esoteric* disciples were the small inner group to whom the master divulged his deeper meanings. The *exoteric* were the larger group of followers, not admitted to intimacy, to whom was divulged only so much as they were thought capable of understanding.

especial; especially. See **special.**

espousal, either in its primary sense of the plighting of a troth, a marriage or an engagement, or in its derivative sense of the advocacy of a cause or the adoption of someone's interests or welfare, is now bookish or archaic.

Esquire, abbreviated as *Esq.,* is a title of courtesy widely used in England and Ireland (though its use is beginning to decline under the feeling that the term is snobbish and now devoid of meaning) but not elsewhere even among English-speaking peoples. Originally it referred to a definite social rank and designated one belonging to the order of English gentry just below a knight, but this significance has been lost and it now has the same meaning as *Mr.* It is used solely in written addresses and when so used it follows the surname, as

> *Richard Roe, Esq.,*
> *Roe Hall*
> *Roehampton*

When *esquire* or its abbreviation is used, no title should be prefixed. That is, *Mr. Richard Roe, Esq.* would be incorrect. But titles may be suffixed. *Richard Roe, Esq., LL.D.,* or

> *Richard Roe, Esq., Professor of Numismatics*
> *Mary Roe College*
> *Roehampton*

would be proper.

essay. See **assay.**

essential; inherent; intrinsic. That is *essential* which is a part of the very being or existence of a thing. Hence that which is essential is necessary if the thing is to maintain its identity. The essential characteristics of a thing are those characteristics which mark its identity, its difference from other things. In popular usage that is *essential* which is indispensable to the functioning of something (*Clean spark plugs are essential to the proper running of the car*).

That is *inherent* which is inborn or fixed from the beginning as a permanent quality or constituent (*Separation of church and state is inherent in our Constitution. Certain properties are inherent in iron*).

Intrinsic means belonging to a thing by its very nature, without regard to external considerations or accidentally added properties (*There is an intrinsic merit in the proposal, despite the opposition it is bound to arouse*). (For *essential* in the sense of that which cannot be dispensed with, see **necessary.**)

essentially; substantially. Setting aside the philosophic meanings of the words, which rarely concern the common man, *essentially* and *substantially* are in most uses interchangeable. It does not matter whether one says that A's story was essentially in agreement with B's or substantially in agreement with it. Yet there are some slight differences, most of them based on the common association of *substance* with *material* in its sense of solid, tangible, and of-this-world as against the ethereal, spiritual, or other-worldly. Thus if it were said of someone that although he had retired from active participation in the management of a business he was still *substantially* the boss, there would be more of a suggestion of his ownership of the business and a feeling that weighty questions must still be referred to him than if it were said that he is still *essentially* the boss. The latter would imply that he was still the boss, but would suggest a more remote, less forcible or immediate control.

Essential and *substantial,* however—such are the ways of language—have clearly different meanings in popular usage. An essential citizen would be one without whom the community would not function. A substantial citizen is one of solid means, respectable and respected, a pillar, but not necessarily an indispensable pillar, of the community.

estimate; estimation. An *estimate* is an approximate judgment or calculation of the value, amount, weight, or the like, of something, especially, in business usage, of what would be charged for certain work to be done (*His estimate of success must be carefully considered, for he is unusually well informed in the matter. The lowest estimate for the concrete work was more than two million*). *Estimation* is, properly, the forming of an estimate (*My estimation of the damages will require some time as its full extent cannot be known until the waters have receded*). *Estimate* and *estimation* are used synonymously so much that the practice must be accepted as standard, but the careful writer will bear the distinction in mind. And he will also bear in mind that as a mere substitute for *opinion* (as *in my estimation*) where no *estimating,* or calculation of value or degree, has taken place, the word is being debased. *Estimation* has also the meaning of *esteem* (as *to hold one in high estimation*), possibly because of the similarity of sound.

eternal; everlasting; endless; incessant; perpetual.
In its religious and other dignified uses, *eternal* means lasting forever, implying not only that that which is spoken of will last for ever but has lasted from eternity up to the time of speaking (*The eternal hills that silent wait* . . .). In less dignified contexts it means constantly recurring to the point of being wearisome (*The eternal racket those kids make is driving me crazy*).

Endless never stops, but goes on continually as if in a circle (*My* . . . *time-bewasted light/ Shall be extinct with age, and endless night*). Indeed, as in *an endless belt,* the word is applied today to a number of devices that move in a circle. It, too, is used in the sense of ceaselessly recurring (*Endless snowstorms prolonged the winter into April*) and, more often than *eternal,* in a pejorative sense (*His endless stories bored everyone in the house*).

Except in some religious contexts (*from everlasting to everlasting*), *everlasting* connotes endurance through all future time from this time forward. It, too, has the dichotomy of expressing awe or rapture in metaphysical contemplations and irritation in mundane (*That everlasting complaining of his!*). Apparently a very little everlastingness in actual matters is hard to take.

Incessant means continuing without interruption (*Incessant application to his studies finally brought the longed-for reward*), and though it can be applied to pleasant things (*incessant delights*) it is so much more frequently applied to unpleasant things that it also has, except where the context makes it otherwise plain, a suggestion of irritation.

Perpetual implies a continued renewing (*The graves will receive perpetual care. The perpetual stream of visitors consumed his strength*).

eternal triangle. In the hackneyed phrase *the eternal triangle,* used to describe lovers or married couples with an intrusive third party, either man or woman, who stirs up jealousy and discontent, the word *eternal* is used in the sense of incessant or recurring. The situation is scarcely more unendurable than the phrase.

eternal verities. As a term for the unchanging truths that presumably lie at the basis of the moral order, *the eternal verities* is a cliché.

ethics and the singular form *ethic* are both used in speaking about a theoretical system of morals, and in this sense both words take a singular verb, as in *his ethics is unique.* In speaking of an actual system of morals that a man lives by, only the form *ethics* is used and only with a plural verb, as in *his ethics are peculiar.* The adjective form is always *ethical,* and not *ethic.*

ethics; morals. *Ethics* and *morals* were once completely synonymous, one being Greek and the other Latin, but in common usage they have come to have distinctions. Fowler trenchantly summarizes the matter by saying that *ethics is the science of morals, and morals are the practice of ethics.* He believes that the impression that ethics is less definitely connected with religion than morals are is "unfounded," and so it may be in philosophy but in the common usage of words it is pretty well established. And more

and more, in the United States at least, *morals* have a sexual connotation. Thus if it were said of one that he was a man *of the highest ethics,* the implication would be that he was strictly honorable in regard to the truth and to financial matters; but if it were said that he was a man *of the highest morals,* the implication would be that he was not guilty of sexual laxity and would not condone it in others.

et seq. This is an abbreviation of the Latin words *et sequentes* or *et sequentia* and means *and the following.*

eulogy. See **elegy.**

euphemism means "speaking fair." It is a term to describe the substitution of a mild, indirect, or vague expression for a harsh, direct, plain, or terrifying one. The use of *euphemisms* (for the term is applied to the words substituted as well as to the process of substituting them) is widespread in every language and is motivated by reverence, kindness, decency, fear, and prudery.

The excretory and reproductive organs and functions of the body are almost always spoken of euphemistically in polite society. So is death. And so are most incurable bodily and mental ills. All of this was once regarded as "genteel" or polite, but there has been a tendency in the past two or three generations, particularly marked among the educated, to speak more plainly. The ribald associations of the Anglo-Saxon words for urinating, defecating, fornicating, and breaking wind will probably prevent their becoming acceptable in everyday uses, but in many other things related to the body the plainness of modern talk would probably be shocking to our grandmothers and grandfathers (though *not* to our great-great grandmothers and grandfathers; there are cycles and fashions in these matters). Thus the word *pregnant* is now acceptable to the politest ears and "in a family way" would seem vulgarly genteel and "with child" quaint.

In regard to death, the speech of the educated today is more direct than that of the uneducated and semi-educated, who still speak of *passing on* for *dying,* refer invariably to the coffin as the *casket* and the funeral as the *service.* The educated, however, in their turn have fears from which they wish to hide in words and have developed, especially in relation to sicknesses, some new euphemisms. Thus the fashionably delicate word for a stroke nowadays is an *accident* and the most elaborate circumlocutions are often devised to avoid mentioning the dreaded name of *cancer.*

The trouble with all euphemisms, of course, is that the unpleasant fact is still there, for all its pleasant name, and will in time infect the euphemism. Thus *cemetery,* now frequently replaced by *memorial park,* was originally a euphemism (it means "sleeping place") for *graveyard,* but the grinning face showed through. So *toilet,* originally merely a dressing room where one made one's toilet, has become a semi-indecent word in the United States and *bathroom,* especially when referred to with any urgency. is becoming one. In England, by the way, where excretory and bathing facilities are often not placed in the same room, an American guest's whispered request, in midday, to be shown to the bathroom sometimes elicits astonishment, astonishment almost as great as that of the guest's when he *is* shown to a bathroom.

The opposite of euphemism is *dysphemism.* If it is plain talk to call a spade a spade and a euphemism to call it a delving instrument, it is a dysphemism to call it a bloody shovel.

euphemism; euphuism. *Euphemism* is the substitution of a fair-sounding word for one that is, for any reason, objectionable. *Euphuism* (a very rare word which no one but the student of Elizabethan literature has any occasion to use) describes the style which John Lyly employed in *Euphues: Or the Anatomy of Wit* (1579) and *Euphues and his England* (1580). It was characterized by alliteration, a long series of antitheses, and elaborate similes based on fabulous natural history. It became a vogue and for a decade or so had many imitators.

euphony is the harmonious arrangement of words, with special reference to pleasing sound, rhythm and appropriateness of meaning. As the word itself implies, it is an aspect of spoken rather than of written language, but its appeal to the mind's ear in prose as well as in poetry is an important element in style. It is euphony, for example, that demands that we say *an apple* instead of the harsh and difficult *a apple.*

A euphonious style is to be achieved in part by the avoidance of unnecessarily harsh sounds (*Who prop, thou ask'st, in these bad days, my mind?*), too many consonants together, combinations of easily confused sounds (*She sells sea shells by the seashore*), and words that rime where rime is not intended (*He was under the dominion of his father's opinion*). Even roughness, however, if it heightens meaning, may be considered euphonious (*What recks it them? What need they? They are sped;/ And, when they list, their lean and flashy songs/ Grate on their scrannel pipes of wretched straw. It is the place of the howling winds, the hurrying of the leaves in old October, the hard clean falling to the earth of acorns*).

Eurasian. See **mulatto.**

European. In America and England a *European* is a native or an inhabitant of Europe. In the Union of South Africa, however, *European* designates one who is white, separating him from all the other native non-whites or non-Europeans as they are there called. Non-whites from other countries are referred to as American non-Europeans or Hawaiian non-Europeans or whatever they may be. A French Negro would be called French non-European and—such are the ways of speech—a Negro from some non-specified country of Europe would be a European non-European.

European plan is an American term for that method of conducting a hotel according to which the fixed charge per day covers only lodging and service. It was formerly much more in use than now (*It was the Alfalfa European Hotel, Al-*

falfa because the name had a pleasing sound; European because no meals were served in the house.—George Ade, 1899). Hotels used to offer their guests either the *European Plan* or the *American Plan,* the fixed charge in the latter covering meals as well as lodging.

The virtual disappearance of the term has a value to the students of language and social history because it reminds them that the disappearance of a word or term may not mean that the thing designated had ceased to exist; it may have become so universal that no distinguishing name was any longer felt to be necessary.

evacuate. Purists have been much agitated at the *evacuation* of wounded soldiers and of civilians from cities during the past two wars, pointing out that the term was properly a medical one, meaning a discharge or ejection through the excretory passages, especially from the bowels. But their exasperation was in part unfounded and in part (one fears) merely a pretext for displaying erudition. The term has been a military term for withdrawing from a town or fortress for almost two hundred and fifty years (*The Army ... would shortly evacuate Savoy*—Steele, 1710) and during the first world war passed into current use through its employment in the newspapers. Strictly it was the place that was evacuated of the troops. But the transference of the word to the troops or the civilians themselves (a transference that took place in non-military uses at least three hundred years ago—almost as long as the word has been used in this sense in English) did no greater violence to the language than had been done before by hundreds of idioms [Actually, we do not wipe a spot off the floor: we wipe the floor and the spot comes off]. In World War II movements of large bodies of children and civilians from the cities, of troops from untenable positions, and wounded from hospitals became common and important in the news. A word was needed and *evacuate* lay to hand with established military associations. It is now standard in this sense, so much so that the man in the street would possibly regard the phrase *evacuate the bowels* as studied, or even unpatriotic. *Evacuate* differs from *empty* in its connotation of some forced or general, usually urgent, movement.

evade may be followed by the *-ing* form of a verb, as in *he evaded telling me.* It cannot be followed by an infinitive, as in *he evaded to tell me.* (See also **escape.**)

eve; evening. Although *eve* may be used as a synonym for *evening,* which means the time about sunset (*The stag at eve had drunk his fill/ But midnight found him drinking still*), it means properly the preceding evening or even entire day. Christmas Eve is December the twenty-fourth; whereas Christmas evening would be late in the day of December twenty-fifth. And the eve of a battle is the period just before, not the night following.

even; evenly. When used as an adjective, *even* means smooth, level, uniform, as in *an even surface, an even share.* When used as an adverb, to qualify any word that is not a noun, it is a peculiar intensive. It says that a particular element in a statement is surprising but nevertheless true, as in *even then* and *he even laughed*. At one time *even* could be used as an adverb in all its senses, but today the form *evenly* is preferred when the adjective meanings of the word are being used adverbially, as in *they shared evenly*.

even tenor of one's way. It was *along the cool, sequestered vale of life* that Thomas Gray's village Hampdens and inglorious Miltons *kept the noiseless tenor of their way*. Transformed to *even tenor* (possibly because a *noiseless tenor* would seem today, when *tenor* in the sense of course or progress is little known, paradoxical, even if desirable) the phrase has become a cliché and should be avoided.

event; episode; incident; occurrence. An *event* is anything that happens (*The minor events of the average day are too slight to deserve notice*). But most commonly it means an important happening (*Coming events cast their shadows before*), especially one that comes out of and is connected with previous happenings (*Political events can affect the prospects of candidates with alarming suddenness*). It also means the outcome or end result of an action (*In the event of his demise, she will inherit.... Whatever the event, you may rely on my friendship*).

An *episode* is one of a progressive series of happenings. It is often distinct from the main course of events, but it arises naturally from them and has an interest and continuity of its own. To use it merely as a synonym for *event* is to debase the language. Cobbett's reference to answering a hundred letters a week *by way of episode* to his other labors would seem a little strange to moderns, though it is proper. The correct use is happily illustrated by Milman's reference to the conquest of Constantinople by the Latins as *that strange and romantic episode in the history of the Crusades*.

An *incident* is a minor event that takes place in connection with a more important event or series of events (*I remember a curious incident that happened during the assault on Guadalcanal*).

An *occurrence* is something, usually of an ordinary nature (*daily occurrences*), that happens, without having any particular connection with or having been caused by antecedent circumstances (*The occurrence of a shower delayed his arrival and so frustrated her plans*). See also **happening**.

eventuate seems to be an American coinage. As a term for happen or come to pass, it seems awkward and ponderous. It is a politician's word and no doubt impresses some of his hearers with a sense of his grandeur; but it makes some others wonder if he is not just reverberating while trying to think of what to say next.

ever means "at any time." It must be used instead of *never* in a negative statement such as *no one ever told me* or as an alternative to a negative, as in *not then or ever*. *Ever* cannot be used as an alternative to an affirmative idea. We must say *seldom or never*, not *seldom or ever*. *If ever*, on the other hand, may be used with either an affirmative or a negative, as in *seldom if ever, not often if ever*. *Ever* could once be used with *or* to mean "before," as in *or ever the silver cord be loosed*, but this construction is now archaic.

The "empty" *ever*, or the use of *ever* as an intensive, dates from the middle of the nineteenth century. This is acceptable as long as the word clearly qualifies a verb, as in *what ever possessed him?* and *Tristram's misfortunes began nine months before ever he came into the world*.

Ever may be combined with relative pronouns to make them indefinite, as in *whoever says that is a fool* and *take whichever you like*. But it should not be combined with an interrogative pronoun as a pure intensive, as in *whoever can it be?*, *whatever did he want?*. This use of the word is heard in Great Britain more often than in the United States, but it is generally condemned in both countries. Some grammarians recommend writing these expressions as two words, as in *who ever can it be?*, *what ever did he want?*, but this does not solve the problem, since the word remains attached to *who* or *what* regardless of how it is printed. The isolated word *ever* is of course standard English when it can be understood as qualifying a verb, as in *who ever thought that?*

In the United States *ever* is used as an intensive after a superlative, as in *the finest ever*. This is acceptable English in this country but in Great Britain is considered an Americanism.

everlasting. See **eternal.**

every means "all, taken separately." But the word *all* may also be used in this sense, as in *all the babies weighed less than ten pounds*. In modern English *all* is more often used in this distributive sense than it is in a collective sense and there is frequently no difference between the words *all* and *every*. It would sometimes be convenient if this were not so, but *all* now has this meaning and no one can say that *every* is the only acceptable word in statements of this kind.

Each also means "all, taken separately." In modern English the principal difference between *every* and *each* is that *every* is used when the members of a group are thought of as a unit, and *each* when they are thought of individually, as in *every boy was there and each did his part*. At one time, *each* was used in speaking about a countable number of individuals and *every* in making a universal statement. This distinction survives today to some extent and may explain the use of *every* rather than *each* in *what every woman knows*, and the first but not the second *every* in *every particle of matter attracts every other particle*. Both distinctions are subtle and neither is strictly observed. Many people who use language sensitively shift from one word to the other simply for variety. Nothing is ever gained by saying *each and every*.

Every is used only as an adjective and only

before a singular noun, as in *every man*. It may be used before a genitive, as in *every man's opinion,* or following a genitive or a possessive pronoun, as in *Dick's every thought, his every whim.* It is unquestionably accepted English to use *every* with the word *between,* as in *between every mouthful,* although some grammarians condemn this. *Every* may be used with *other* to mean "all others," as in *every other person here agrees with me,* or it may be used to mean "every second one," as in *she only comes every other day.* See **other.**

Every is not equivalent to the adverb *ever.* The phrase *ever so often* means "frequently." The phrase *every so often* means "every now and then." Both are standard English when they are used to mean what they do mean.

A noun qualified by *every* is usually followed by a singular verb, as in *every man and woman is aware.* It is also followed by a singular pronoun when there is no question whether it is males or females that are being talked about, as in *every soldier carries his own pack* and *every woman does her own cooking.* But when the reference is to both men and women, or the sex is unknown, a plural pronoun is generally preferred, as in *every member brings their own lunch,* although some grammarians insist on the generic *his.* The plural pronoun is required in speaking of something owned in common, as in *every English man and woman has good reason to be proud of the work done by their forefathers.*

everybody; everyone. These words are usually followed by a singular verb but they are usually referred to by the plural pronoun *they,* rather than the singular pronoun *he.* Cardinal Newman said that a gentleman strives *to make everyone at their ease.* This has been standard English for the word *everybody* for more than four hundred years, and for the word *everyone* for more than two hundred years. A singular pronoun cannot be used when it stands in a coordinate clause, as *he* does in *Everyone clapped and I was glad he did* and *Everyone came but he has gone home.*

every effort is being made. The assurance that *every effort is being made* has become a formula to soothe those whose demands for action must be listened to but need not, or cannot, be satisfied. The fact that it is a cliché, worn smooth by glib repetition, adds to the exasperation of the importunate and in matters of great seriousness —and in any lesser matters the dishonesty of the phrase is apparent—only the stupid, the callous, or the brutal still employ it.

Of course, like other clichés, it has a meaning, and exceptional circumstances and exceptional strength of feeling and depth of sincerity can make that meaning ring true. It is conceivable that someone, somewhere, sometime, somehow could even put conviction back into *Early to bed and early to rise* or *Who steals my purse, steals trash,* but the ordinary man does well to avoid such hackneyed phrases, especially in his moments of sincere feeling, for they will fail him.

everyhow is standard English as used by Hawthorne in *crags, all shattered and tossed about everyhow.* But it is seldom heard and *everyway* is generally preferred.

every mother's son, as a term for every man, is a cliché. It has the tinny ring of a pseudo-profundity, a false earthiness about it.

everyone. See **everybody.**

everyplace. The use of *everyplace* as a substitute for *everywhere,* as in *I looked everyplace,* is condemned by many grammarians because the noun *place* is here being used instead of the adverb *where.* This usage is not acceptable in Great Britain but it occurs too often in the United States, in written as well as in spoken English, to be called anything but standard. It is acceptable English in this country.

everyway. Unlike the similar words, *anyway* and *noway, everyway* does not have the related forms *everyways* and *everywise.* These words simply don't appear. *Every which way* is an Americanism and is considered unacceptable in Great Britain. It is no longer current English in this country. But when it is heard it is considered old-fashioned rather than unacceptable and has a certain rustic charm.

everywhere; everywheres. *Everywhere* is the only acceptable form in written English. In the United States *everywheres* is often heard in the speech of well educated people, but it does not appear in print. *Everywhere* is often used with an unnecessary *that,* as in *everywhere that he has been.* This construction has been in use for a very short time but it is accepted English in the United States.

evidence; testimony; proof. *Evidence* is grounds for belief, that which makes evident, that which tends to prove or disprove something. It may be that which someone says, or it may be derived from documents or inferred from the nature of things (*The witness gave his evidence in a strong, clear voice. The evidence of the fingerprint led the jury to disbelieve his protestation of innocence*).

Testimony is the statement of a witness. In law, of course, the witness is under oath, but the word is used loosely for any declaration relevant to a disputed issue (*The testimony of the arresting officer carried great weight. If you accept the one child's testimony, the other must be lying*). *Testimony* is often used for *evidence,* sometimes carelessly and sometimes with the poetic assumption that "the facts speak for themselves" as in *the mute testimony of the fossils.* But, for the most part, it is better to use *evidence* for the immediate grounds for belief and *testimony* for some person's statement about the facts.

Proof is evidence that is so complete and convincing as to put a conclusion beyond reasonable doubt (*The evidence and the testimony constituted overwhelming proof of his guilt*).

evident. See **apparent.**

evil. The words *worse* and *worst* are said to be the comparative and superlative forms of the adjective *evil.* But we are more likely to use the forms *more evil* and *most evil*. The simple forms in *-er* and *-est* are rare but are also acceptable, as in *the evilest thoughts of the human mind*.

evince; exhibit; manifest. To *evince* originally meant to overcome or subdue (*They will keep their hold until they be evinced or cast out*). Its modern meaning of to show (*He evinced dissatisfaction with your work*) is often an unnecessary and unsuitable elegancy. It should be reserved for such presentations of evidence as make a convincing inference (*The ruins . . . sufficiently evince that anciently there were great buildings in this place*). The word, because it is an elegancy, has, in some contexts, a slight tinge of mockery and gives the "showing" a suggestion of "showing off" (*He evinced great spirit but little skill*).

To *exhibit* is to put something in plain view, usually in a favorable view for particular observation (*He exhibited an unexpected graciousness*). It, too, has the connotation of showing off.

To *manifest* is to make plain to the eye or clear to the understanding. It is a strong word and carries the connotation of conviction. That which is manifest is shown beyond any reasonable doubt (*Caught in a manifest lie, he broke down and confessed all*).

evolute; evolve. *Evolute* exists as a noun in geometry and an adjective in botany, but as a verb, a back formation apparently from *evolution*, it is an ignorant blunder. The verb is *evolve*.

example; instance. An *example* is one of a number of things, or a part of something, taken to show the character of the whole (*No criticism can be instructive which is not full of examples*). It has several other meanings, such as a model to be imitated or a punishment so severe as to serve as a deterrent to others.

An *instance* is an example put forth in proof or illustration. The word does not apply to the objects or incidents directly but only to them as they serve to illustrate some point (*A better instance of his recklessness it would be hard to find*).

The words are fixed in several idiomatic uses. *For instance* and *for example* are interchangeable, but a meritorious person or act serves as a *good example*, not as a *good instance* and a punishment is an *example* not an *instance* in so far as it is intended to deter others. It could, however, be an instance of the judge's severity. In the phrase *wise saws and modern instances*, the word *instances* has become fixed in a context where we would today use *examples*, but we could not now substitute *examples* for *instances* in that phrase. See also **case; ideal.**

example; sample; specimen. In the sense of an individual phenomenon taken as a representative of a type, or of a part as representative of the whole, *example*, *sample*, and *specimen* are synonymous. But there are differences in their meanings and, as with many synonyms, the recognition of these differences and the employment of the proper word to give the exact shade of meaning intended is one of the chief helps to good writing.

An *example* is an object, or an activity, or a condition, or the like, which is assumed to illustrate a certain law or principle or general assertion (*What better example of their perfidy could you want?*). A *sample* (an *example* is merely a sample taken out) usually refers to concrete, tangible things, and means a small portion of a substance, or a single representative of a group or type, which is intended to show what the rest of the substance, or the group, is like (*The man who, having a house to sell, carried about with him a brick as a sample . . .*). *Sample* is largely restricted now to commercial uses and when it is used metaphorically, in place of example, it has a suggestion of contempt or mockery (*There, that's a sample of his kindness for you!*).

Specimen usually suggests that the sample chosen is intended to serve a scientific or technical purpose (*The doctor will require a blood specimen*). It, too, when used more generally, may have an element of contempt or mockery (*What a specimen he is! If you want a real specimen of ingratitude, here's one!*).

exasperate. See **aggravate.**

exceeding; exceedingly. The use of *exceeding* for *exceedingly*, when prefixed to adjectives or adverbs, formerly quite common (*Rejoice and be exceeding glad*), is now an archaism and a stately affectation.

exceedingly; excessive(ly). Until well into the last century *exceedingly* and *excessively* were interchangeable, but since then there has been a differentiation in their meanings. *Exceedingly* now means extremely, very much, to an unusual degree (*I am exceedingly grateful for the many kindnesses you have shown my son*), whereas *excessive* now means exceeding the proper limit or degree, too much, characterized by excess (*The bill was excessive. It is excessively hot for this time of year*).

excellent. See **splendid; superlative.**

excelsior. The solecism in Latin grammar with which the young man in Longfellow's famous poem startled the Alpine village has startled even more several generations of American school-children to whom the word *excelsior* means exclusively soft wood shavings used for stuffing dolls or protecting fragile objects in shipment.

except. See **accept.**

except. When not used as a verb, *except* introduces a contradiction to something that has just been said. It may introduce a full clause beginning with *that*, as in *she knew nothing except that he was there*; a *to*-infinitive, as in *it had no effect except to make him angry*; or the simple form of a verb after some form of *do*, as in *she did nothing except weep*. *Except* cannot be qualified by *not*, when used in this way. In order to deny an exception, the word *excepting* must be used, as in *all were there, not excepting him*.

Formerly, *except* could be used in the sense of "unless," and could introduce a clause without using the word *that*, as in *I will not let thee go except thou bless me.* This construction is now archaic or Biblical.

Often the contrasting word introduced by *except* is a personal pronoun. Some grammarians say that, in current English, an objective form should always be used here, as *me* in *everyone except me ran away.* Others say that *except* is in a class with *but* and that a following pronoun which is placed in contrast to the subject of a verb should be subjective, as the *I* in *everybody is to meet him except I.* In practice, most educated people use an objective form of the pronoun, as in *except me,* in all constructions and a subjective form, such as *except I,* will usually be considered a mistaken effort to be "correct."

except; but; save. *Except, but,* and *save* all indicate something excluded from a general statement. *Except* stresses the excluding (*You may have any one you choose except this one*). *But* simply states the exclusion (*All but one of the survivors were in good health*). *Save,* in this sense, is poetic. (See the individual words.)

exception proves the rule. With what irritating complacency do minor oracles assure us that *the exception proves the rule*—usually as an impudent way of reconciling their own contradictions and inconsistencies.

Were not those who so use the expression armed with triple brass, they might be abashed to know that there are few phrases in the language concerning whose exact meaning there is so much dispute. But amid all the discussion, there is at least this much agreement: it does not mean what it is popularly misused to mean—namely, that the exception *supports* the rule.

Various other explanations have been offered, of which the most generally accepted is that the exception *tests* the rule. *To test* is one meaning of *to prove* (*Prove all things: hold fast that which is good. He saw a gentleman cheapening and proving swords*) and this meaning is retained in a few phrases and names, such as the Aberdeen Proving Ground where new military weapons are tested. But, for the most part, *to prove* today means to demonstrate, to evince, to establish as true.

Of course there is one sense in which an exception does demonstrate the existence of a rule. The very admission that something is exceptional implies a rule or norm, and this may be taken to show that the exception proves there is a rule, but it's fairly far-fetched. And certainly at no time does an exception support, strengthen, or demonstrate the actual working of a rule. If the exception is valid, it shows that the rule cannot be universal and must be accepted as an approximation at the best.

To take exception to something is to make an objection, to demur (*Professor Angstrom took exception to the dean's assertion that the entire faculty desired the proposed change*). *To take exception at* is to be offended (*Some of the more haughty of the aristocracy did take exception at his neglecting to raise his cap to them*).

exceptional; exceptionable. That is *exceptional* which is unusual, extraordinary (*It is an exceptional day on which he does not walk five miles. The founding fathers were exceptional men*). That is *exceptionable* which is objectionable or liable to objection (*No one could take offense at his remarks; there was nothing exceptionable in them. His management of the business has been most exceptionable and cannot be further tolerated!*). See also **unique.**

excess. See **access.**

exclamation points are used to show strong emotion in statements, and to emphasize commands and warnings, as in *"Oh!" he gasped, "It's magnificent!" Look out! Throw me the ball!* They should be reserved for true exclamations and not wasted on sentences where commas would serve as well.

Exclamation points can be used inside or outside of quotation marks, depending upon the meaning of the sentence, as in *He shouted "All aboard!"* and *Fancy him shouting "All aboard"!* If a question ends with an exclamation, the question mark can be omitted following the exclamation point, as in *Who yelled "Fire!".*

exclamations. An *exclamation* is presumably a spontaneous expression of strong emotion. In speech, the fact that a statement is an exclamation is shown by pitch. In writing this is indicated by an exclamation point at the end of the sentence.

A sentence that begins with *how, what,* or *why,* and that has the subject before the verb is an exclamation, as in *how far that little candle throws his beams!, what a surprise this is!, why, you really got here!* But an exclamation may have the form of a declarative sentence, as in *he is here!,* or it may have the form of a question, as in *are you here!* Surprise and questioning are closely related and a true exclamation is likely to take the question form. The pitch leaves no doubt as to what is intended. But some people will always pretend that an exclamation of this kind is a question and then point out that it is a stupid question. This is a harmless way of being unpleasant and should be ignored if possible.

Exclamations are frequently incomplete expressions, such as *if only I had come sooner!* and *that he should be such a fool!* The clause that is needed to complete the thought may remain unexpressed because it is self-evident or because it is too difficult to express and words fail the speaker. When an exclamation contains a verb and no subject, as in *bless his heart!* and *strike me pink!,* it is usually because the subject *God* has been suppressed, either by the speaker or by those who taught him that form of speech.

Whether to use a subjective or an objective pronoun in fragmentary exclamation is a matter of taste. The objective is more usual, but the subjective is also heard, as in *me too!, lucky them!, I dance!, me marry!, not he!, not him!, dear me!.* Some grammarians claim that the pronoun should have the form that it would have if the exclamation was turned into a full declarative sentence. But this is not borne out in speech. The practice of using either form of the pronoun, with a preference for the objective, is very old in English. It is also characteristic of good Latin.

exclusive; select. It is certainly a reflection upon our professions of democracy that the word *exclusive,* in its commonest popular sense, in the United States today means fashionable, high-class, desirable (*She belonged to the most exclusive clubs. Buy a lot in exclusive Mudflat Heights, no down payment!*). It is said that some of the most exclusive New York clubs maintain their right to the adjective by arbitrarily excluding from time to time some of those who are seeking admission, often—just to be democratic—on an eeny-meeny-miny-mo basis.

The word that implies superiority because of the virtues of those included rather than the misfortune of those excluded is *select.* It sometimes requires a little courage to use this word in a democracy, however.

excursus. The plural is *excursuses* or *excursus,* not *excursi.*

excuse. See **apology.**

excuse me; pardon me. *Excuse me* is the proper term by which to ask someone to overlook a minor fault, to allow someone to pass, and so on. *Pardon me* is a stronger term, implying a greater sense of guilt and a desire for forgiveness. Its substitution for *excuse me* is a mark of vulgar gentility.

execrable; inexecrable. *Execrable* means deserving to be execrated, detestable, damnable, abominable (*The treatment of enlisted men on the base was execrable*). *Inexecrable* is an obsolete term which, according to the *Oxford English Dictionary,* is either an intensive for *execrable* (that is, very execrable) or a misprint for *inexorable,* unyielding, not to be moved by prayers or entreaty (In *The Merchant of Venice* we read: *O be thou damn'd, inexecrable dogge*). Since the word is now obsolete, it doesn't much matter which.

executive. In England *executive* as a noun is used solely (or was until recently; the American usage is appearing there) to designate that branch of the government which carries out the laws. In America it means this, but it is also applied to an officer of a business organization, especially to a high officer who has important duties. Already, however, it is being debased or broadened to include many who but two generations ago would have ignominiously been dubbed *clerks.*

An interesting special development of the adjective *executive* in the United States to mean private, in the term *executive session,* is traced by Horwill. When the United States Senate proceeds to deal with executive, as apart from legislative, business—when it considers, that is, nominations for office, the conclusion of treaties, or other executive matters—it goes into executive session, and from such sessions the public and the press are excluded. From this fact the term came to be applied to all private sessions and the original meaning, in this context, seems to have been lost. Horwill quotes a passage from the *Intimate Papers of Colonel House* in which Colonel House refers to a private conversation he had with Woodrow Wilson, when Wilson had "closed his study door so as not to be interrupted," as an *executive session.*

executor has now almost entirely replaced *executer* and *executioner* as the term for one who executes or carries out or accomplishes. *Executioner* has been relegated to its special meaning of one who inflicts capital punishment in pursuance of a legal warrant. *Executor* is thought of chiefly in its legal sense of one named by a decedent in his will to carry out the provisions of the will, but it is also now the term for a general executing agent, *executer* being rarely seen or heard any more.

exegesis. The plural is *exegeses.*

exemplar; exemplary. As a term for a model, or a pattern to be copied, or an example or typical instance, *exemplar* has been replaced almost entirely in popular use by *example.* The word would be understood, but it would be felt to be affectedly literary.

Exemplary, which means worthy of imitation, or serving for a model or pattern or a warning (*His courage made him an exemplary soldier. The penalty was severe but exemplary*) is sometimes used as if it meant excellent. It may mean that, of course, but unless the element of establishing a pattern, a model, or a warning is in the meaning, it should not be employed.

exercise; exorcise. *Exercise* is the use, practice, or performance of something (*The exercise of a virtue strengthens it*), especially of the body (*Daily exercise is recommended as healthful by almost all physicians*). *Exorcise,* a much rarer word, is the expulsion of an evil spirit by adjuration and religious ceremonies.

exercises. The term *exercises* is applied in the United States to numerous formal ceremonies (*The graduation exercises will be in the High School auditorium and will begin promptly at eight*) but in England the term is limited to *religious exercises.*

exert; exercise. Though *exert* and *exercise* are interchangeable in some contexts, *exert* has come to mean the putting forth of more energy in a particular activity as against the idea of a constant and repeated activity in *exercise* (*If you would only exert yourself, you could do it easily. What good is a virtue unexercised?*).

exhausted. See **tired.**

exhausting; exhaustive. *Exhausting* means using up completely, especially the using up of physical energy to the point of fatigue (*It was an exhausting day*). *Exhaustive* means thorough, testing all possibilities (*He made an exhaustive survey. His study of verb endings was exhaustive and exhausting; the subject was thoroughly canvassed and he and everybody who had to listen to him were thoroughly worn out by the time it was done*).

exhibit. See **evince.**

exhilarate. See **accelerate.**

exist; subsist. To *exist* is to be, to have life or animation, to continue to live (*Life could not exist without the sun. The idea that a heretic might have any civil rights simply did not exist*). To *subsist* connotes to exist dependently. One could not say *The idea that a heretic might have any civil rights simply did not subsist,* but one could say *Superstition subsists upon ignorance,* meaning that it maintains or supports itself by this means (*Some animals subsist upon vegetables. From that time on he subsisted on his writings*).

exit is the third person singular present of the Latin verb *exire,* to go out. Its use in stage directions has led to its being employed as a noun meaning a going out or a place of going out. It is sometimes used with ponderous facetiousness as a verb (*Exit Joe Doakes*), even as a plural (*There was a moment's silence, then exit Sam and Edna*). If one must speak Latin, it should be *exeunt* in the plural. Best, except as a stage direction, is not to use it at all.

exoteric. See **esoteric.**

exotic; outlandish; uncouth. *Exotic* means of foreign origin, not native, introduced from abroad but not yet acclimatized. When Murphy in his translation of Tacitus (1793) said that a certain people *invited an exotic king to reign over them,* he simply meant a king from another country. A clear instance of this, the primary meaning of the word, is given in an article in *The National Geographic Magazine* (August 1954). The author had been discussing the sudden appearance of the cattle egret in places where it had not been seen before. *After experiences with such introduced species as the house sparrow and starling,* he says, *we naturally view exotic birds with a jaundiced eye.*

Certainly the sparrow is not generally thought of as an *exotic* bird, for the word in its common use does not mean "introduced from abroad" but suggests the glamorous (see **glamor**) and romantic (see **romantic**) things which the naive associate with "imported." The strange is colorful, rich, attractive, rare and wonderful. It is usually expensive and (perhaps therefore) slightly wicked. And all of these meanings, mingled in varying degrees, are in *exotic* in its popular uses. The dictionaries still give "of foreign origin" the primacy in definition but—at least for American usage—they are behind the times. The word is rarely heard now in that sense. The sentence quoted above from *The National Geographic Magazine* would probably be a little puzzling to the common reader. An American tailor who assured a customer that he had some *fine, new, exotic flannels and worsteds* would, if the customer were a man, probably lose a sale.

That which comes from a foreign land is also, often, repellent in its strangeness, absurd and ridiculous. And these meanings, which were once in *exotic* (*entering the city in that exotick and barbarous garb*) have now been transferred to its homely Anglo-Saxon equivalent, *outlandish.*

Uncouth originally meant unknown. The old proverb *Uncouth unkissed,* which might now serve as an advertisement for a book of etiquette, simply meant that those who were not known would go unwooed. It was an earlier way of saying that full many a flower is born to blush unseen and waste its sweetness on the desert air. But all idea of the unknown has now faded from *uncouth* and only the ideas of strange, rough, and alien remain.

expect may be followed by an infinitive, as in *England expects every man to do his duty,* or by a clause, as in *I expect he will come. Expect* is sometimes used in speaking of a present or past event, as in *I expect you're hungry* and *I expect he was there.* This was once literary English and the word is still used in this way by educated people in the United States. In Great Britain this use is condemned as an Americanism.

expectorate; spit. The practice of euphemism can be dangerous for the unwary and the uninformed. Sometimes in seeking to be refined and elegant they choose a worse word than the one they seek to avoid. *Spit,* for example, is a perfectly good word to describe a natural and often necessary act; whereas *expectorate,* which is sometimes preferred to it by those who think they are being more delicate, is not only ponderous but more unpleasant. For to *spit* is, properly, to eject saliva from the mouth, but to *expectorate* is to bring up and expel phlegm from the lungs by coughing, hawking, or spitting.

Thus a directive of the Breen office, which is concerned with Hollywood's manners as well as its morals but not, apparently, with its sense of style, suggested that directors *Eliminate, wherever it occurs, the action of actually expectorating Spit* (*Time,* Oct. 25, 1954). *Eliminate spitting* would probably have been more accurate and certainly would have been more direct. Anyone *actually expectorating Spit* would be choking and strangling. *Time,* which has its own standards of style, refers to the directive as *blunt.*

expedient. See **politic.**

expensive. See **costly.**

experiment (noun). See **trial.**

expire; terminate. As a transitive verb *expire* means to breathe out (*He expired his last breath just at the turning of the tide*). As an intransitive verb it means to come to an end (*The lease expired in January*). For a transitive verb meaning to bring to an end, *terminate* serves for many of the uses of *expire* (*The landlord says that he will terminate the lease in January*).

explain; elucidate; expound; interpret. To *explain* is used sometimes as if it meant merely to show. It means to make clear or intelligible (*Explaining metaphysics to the nation./ I wish he would explain his explanation*—Byron on Coleridge).

To *elucidate* is to throw light on, usually by illustration or commentary, sometimes by elaborate explanation (*His notes elucidate the text.*

These actions elucidate his policy far better than words). The word is now used in a figurative sense only.

To *expound* is to give a methodical, scholarly explanation. It is used now almost entirely in reference to the Scriptures, to doctrines, to philosophy. It is a grave and ponderous word and therefore lends itself to humor (*For four hours he expounded the text, under thirty-six separate and edifying headings. She . . . quaintly could expound/ The Chicken-feeding power of every crumb she found*).

To *interpret* is to give the meaning of something by paraphrase, translation, or explanation. It is often of a systematic nature and often includes the interpreter's own opinions (*This interpretation of the poem caused considerable consternation among the older professors who had always believed it to be a mere description of a summer's day*).

explicit; express. *Explicit* means that nothing is implied, that everything meant is expressed clearly and unequivocally (*It was explicitly stated that you were in no way obligated to him*). *Express* also means clearly stated rather than implied (*There was an express stipulation to that effect*). But, as Fowler points out, with his incomparable clarity and subtlety, there is a useful distinction between the words: *explicit* means that something has been expressed clearly and in detail, with nothing left to implication; *express* means that and in addition means that it is worded with intention. That which is promised explicitly is unmistakable in its meaning; that which is promised expressly binds the maker of the promise inescapably.

exploit. See **use.**

explore every avenue. See **avenue.**

expose. See **disclose.**

exposé; exposure. The French noun *exposé* means an exposure of something discreditable. The English *exposure* can mean the revealing or uncovering of anything, good or bad (*The exposure of the bone showed the depth of the wound*), that has hitherto been covered or concealed from sight. Since virtues are rarely concealed and vices and crimes almost always are, usage has weighted the word, in its application to human motives and actions, towards the discreditable. It is hard to conceive of any context in which the French form would be essential and it is a safe rule not to use foreign words where they do not serve a purpose that cannot be served by an English word.

expound. See **explain.**

express. See **explicit.**

express (an opinion). See **voice.**

extemporaneous; impromptu; improvised. *Extemporaneous* and *extempory* are adjectives, *extempore* an adjective and an adverb, meaning on the spur of the moment, offhand, without premeditation or preparation. They are applied especially to speeches given from an outline or notes. *Impromptu* applies to a speech or an artistic performance of some kind which one is called upon to give at the moment, without warning (*For an impromptu effort, it was brilliant*). *Improvised* is applied to something composed, or recited, sung, or acted, on a particular occasion and which is, at least in part, made up as the speaker or performer goes along (*The improvised variations on the theme were much admired*). See also **impromptu; temporize.**

extemporize. See **temporize.**

extend. To *extend* is to stretch or draw out and its use is proper any place that this meaning is intended or implied or latent in a metaphor. *To extend a hand in welcome* has a literal meaning which is latent in *extending a welcome*. But what is meant in the common usage of *extending sympathy*? One can conceive, of course, of sympathy being extended to include those often excluded from it, as a philosopher or a sentimentalist might extend his sympathy from the victim to the murderer himself, but in ordinary usage *extend* here means nothing more than *offer* or *send*. This is particularly an American fault: we *extend* thanks, when we only *give* them, and *extend* calls (to fill pulpits) when we only *make* them. Back of many of these uses may be a faint and blurred idea of extending the hand in fellowship or beckoning, but the word is so useful in its proper meaning (*The congregation, on further thought, extended the call to include Dr. Thompson, Dr. Albert's assistant*) that it is too bad to debase it.

extended; extensive. That is *extended* which is stretched out, continued or prolonged, spread out (*Thus Satan . . ./ Prone on the flood, extended long and large,/ Lay floating many a rood*). *Extensive*, when applied to spatial dimensions, means of great extent, wide, broad (*Lord Byron's extensive domains . . .*). When applied to remarks or conversation or discussions, however, *extended* means prolonged and *extensive* means far-reaching, comprehensive, thorough (*His extended remarks grew very tedious. His extensive knowledge makes him a delightful conversationalist*).

extent; extant. *Extent* is a noun meaning the space or degree to which a thing extends. *Extant* is an adjective meaning that something is in existence, not lost or destroyed (*The extent to which Shakespeare's manuscripts were extant at the time of the compiling of the First Folio is a matter of dispute*).

extenuate. To *extenuate* is, properly, to make thin, or to reduce the consistency or density of. It has come to be applied figuratively to faults, in the sense of representing them in as favorable a light as possible by finding excuses for them (*Such cruelty cannot be extenuated by claiming that it was only thoughtlessness. Extenuating circumstances. Speak of me as I am; nothing extenuate,/ Nor set down aught in malice*). One cannot *extenuate* behavior or conduct; it has to be bad behavior and bad conduct. And one cannot use *extenuate* merely to mean making excuses for.

exterior; external. The *exterior* is the outer surface, and *exterior*, as an adjective, refers to that which is outside or on the outside (*The exterior* *surface of the pumpkin is smooth and hard. The exterior decorations of the building were not in keeping with its dignity). External* is the opposite of *internal.* It is the outer part of something, as contrasted with its inner part, not merely the outer surface, and it is that which is apart from something else by being outside of it (*The external structure of the building did not prepare one for the inner arrangement of its space. External influences affect the child far less the first three years of its life than, of course, they will later*).

extort. See **elicit.**

extract. See **elicit.**

extraneous; extrinsic. That is *extraneous* which does not belong to a thing but has been introduced or has come in from the outside. Fossils were once called *extraneous shells* because it was felt that they could not naturally belong in the rocks in which they were found but must have been introduced in some mysterious manner. An *extraneous consideration* is a thought brought into a discussion that has no real place in it, that did not arise in the course of the discussion.

Extrinsic exists now wholly as an antithesis to *intrinsic.* It means something operating or coming from the outside. *Intrinsic merit* is inherent virtue; *extrinsic merit* would be some virtue or evaluation imposed from without, unrelated to an inner merit. The intrinsic value of a certain cancelled stamp might be inestimably small, whatever so little a piece of old paper was worth; but its extrinsic value, if it were a rare item, might be enormous.

eyeglasses. Until recently, the word *eyeglasses* meant spectacles that did not have side pieces going over the ears. In the United States today these things are called *eyeglasses* so long as the frames have a modern design, ear pieces or no ear pieces. The word *spectacles* suggests the very old.

The singular *eyeglass* means one lens and is used in this way when speaking of a scientific instrument, such as a telescope. The pair of lenses ordinarily worn for reading is treated as a plural, as in *these eyeglasses are too strong.* In order to treat this object as a singular or to speak of more than one of them, it is necessary to say *this pair of eyeglasses is too strong* or *three pairs of eyeglasses.*

Theoretically, the singular form *eyeglass* should be used as the first element in a compound, even when referring to reading glasses, as in *an eyeglass case.* But in actual practice, the word is always shortened to *glasses* and this form is used in compounds, as in *my glasses case.*

F

fabrication. See **fiction.**

fabulous, which originally meant told about in fables (*the fabulous voyage of Ulysses*) and known only through myths and legends (*the fabulous Golden Age in Greece*), has come to mean, chiefly, almost incredible (*My dear, she paid a simply fabulous price for it*). As such it it a vogue word, overworked and weakened from overwork, and should be allowed to rest.

face; countenance; physiognomy. The *face* is the front part of the head, from the forehead to the chin, with special reference to its composite features (*But Lancelot mused a little space./ He said, "She hath a lovely face"*). The *countenance* is the face with special reference to its expression (*God made your features, but you made your countenance. His countenance fell at the news*). The verb *to countenance,* meaning to support, to regard with favor (*I beseech you sir,/ To countenance William Visor of Wonscott, against Clement Perkes of the hill*) is derived from turning a favorable countenance upon.

Physiognomy, when used seriously, refers to the face as an index of character (*His physiognomy reflected great benevolence*). However, since many believe that "there is no art to find the mind's construction in the face," it should be used seriously with caution. Facetiously used, it is ponderous and tedious.

face the music, as a term for standing up to trouble, accepting punishment, is a cliché, and, as in many clichés, the figure is not certain. Some think it refers to a singer's facing the orchestra as he or she faces the audience. But this is not entirely satisfactory, since very few performers regard facing the music in this way as trouble or punishment. Some think it has to do with being drummed out of a regiment in disgrace.

facies has the same form in the singular as in the plural and may be used with either a singular or a plural verb.

facile; easy. As a synonym for *easy, facile* has a disparaging sense (*With no facile labor did I gather these materials*). There is a feeling that since "nothing great is lightly won," that which is done *facilely* is not much worth the doing. A *facile pen* is the counterpart of a *glib tongue.*

facility; faculty. A *facility* is something which makes possible the easier performance of an action, freedom from difficulty, ease, opportunities or conditions which make an easier performance possible (*Every facility was placed at* *his disposal. The transportation facilities of the metropolitan area make suburban living pleasant and convenient here).*

A *faculty* (in the sense in which the word is often confused with *facility*) is an ability, natural or acquired, for a particular kind of action (*Boswell's astonishing faculty for making friends*). It also designates one of the mental powers, as memory, reason, and so on (*Although now in his ninety-third year, he had full possession of all his faculties*).

fact. The phrase *the fact that* may be used to introduce a noun clause, especially after a preposition or a verb that cannot take a clause as object, as in *I am impressed by the fact that you were there* and *I don't like the fact that you were there*. This construction is natural enough so long as we are talking about a real event in the past or present. The word *it* performs this same function after many prepositions and a few verbs and is preferred in literary English for statements about a future or imaginary event, as in *I don't like it that you are going away* and *see to it that you are on time.*

The fact that is a favorite expression in scientific writing and is greatly overworked. It is preferred to the literary *it* and is often inserted where *that* is all that is required, as in *he demonstrated the fact that two and two make four* and *he remembered the fact that supper would be late*. Sentences of this kind show that the writer has a scientific respect for facts, even though he cannot identify one.

factious; factitious; fictitious. One is *factious* who is motivated solely by party spirit. He is a member of a *faction* (a small group within a larger group) and creates *faction* (party strife or intrigue). So that which is *factious* is caused by party spirit or strife (*These factious quarrels have almost destroyed the party. The factious dread prosperity, for they live on discontent*).

That is *factitious* which is artificial. It used to have a literal meaning (Boyle spoke of *Beer, Ale, or other factitious drinks*) but it is now restricted to immaterial things (*Luxury creates factitious wants*) and is applied to things that may have their origin in custom or habit but are not natural. It has the meaning also of conventional and it means something not spontaneous, something got up for a particular occasion (*The use of gold and silver is in a great measure factitious. That the applause which greeted the candidate was wholly factitious was shown by the suddenness with which it stopped when the chairman motioned for silence*).

That is *fictitious* which is based on fiction, which is represented as real but is actually imaginary. Thus a *factious* claim would be one advanced solely in the interest of party or one designed to arouse party strife. A *factitious* claim is one that would not have been made but has been created and pushed forward to suit some private end. A *fictitious* claim is either one that has never actually been made or one that has an entirely imaginary basis.

factitive adjectives. See **position of adjectives.**

factor is one of the elements that contribute to bring about a given result (*Certainly his drinking was a factor in his ruin*). Hence to speak of a *contributing factor* is to be redundant. To use *factor* as if it meant simply an occurrence or an event (as in *One of the most pleasant factors of our trip was a visit to the Mammoth Cave*) is incorrect.

faculty. In England the word *faculty,* in its educational sense, retains the old meaning of one of the departments of teaching in a university— the faculty of Medicine, of Law, of Theology, of Arts. In the United States it designates the entire teaching staff of a university and sometimes the administrative staff as well. When used in this sense, the word means the entire group and not an individual member of the group. The plural form *faculties* would imply more than one school. The singular word may be used with a plural verb, as in *the faculty are meeting this afternoon*. But it should not be used with the article *a* or with a numeral as it is in *three faculty were present*. See also **facility.**

faery; fairy. *Fairies* are supernatural beings, generally thought of as diminutive humans, having magical powers which they exercise capriciously (*The fairy footings on the grass*). Their land is *fairyland*. *Faerie* was originally simply a variant spelling of *fairy,* but Spenser, in his *The Faerie Queene,* impressed on it a meaning of a dim, mysterious, romantic, imaginative land, beautiful but with shades of terror and despair, wholly purged of the undignified gamboling and hopping about of the fairies (*None that breatheth living aire does know/ Where is that happy land of Faery*). Keats set the final seal of differentiation on the word in his reference to *magic casements, opening on the foam,/ Of perilous seas, in faery lands forlorn.*

The use of *fairy* as a slang term for a male homosexual is so widespread in America that it is almost impossible to use the word in public with any other meaning.

fail may be followed by an infinitive, as in *he failed to notice it*. It could once be followed by the *-ing* form of a verb, as in *he failed noticing it,* but this construction is now obsolete.

failing. See **fault.**

fair and square is a hearty banality that has stuck like a bur in popular speech because it rimes. It is quite meaningless.

fair; fairly. *Fair* has been an adverb as long as it has been an adjective and can be used to qualify a verb, as in *play fair*. Like many other adverbs, such as *slow* and *hard,* it cannot be used before the verb form. And it cannot be used, as *fairly* can, to mean "almost," as in *he fair jumped. Fairly* is always an adverb and is not used to qualify a noun.

fairly means justly, impartially, clearly, distinctly, handsomely (*He will judge fairly between you. A fairly woven garment*). It also means completely, positively, actually (*His hobby has fairly run away with him*). This use is often employed in exaggeration where the particular emphasis makes it plain that it means "almost as if" rather than actually (*The laughter fairly rocked the building*). At the same time, it can mean moderately, passably, tolerably (*Things are going fairly well with me now. You're fairly safe, if you watch what you're doing*) and there are many written contexts in which one cannot be sure which of the two meanings is intended. There is never any doubt in speaking since the intonation of the voice will always make the meaning clear.

faithfully. See **sincerely.**

faker; fakir. A *faker* is one who fakes, a petty swindler (*Both ladies then came to the conclusion that the fortune teller was a faker*). A *fakir* is a Mohammedan or Hindu religious ascetic or mendicant monk. The two words are often confused, more out of ignorance presumably than skepticism.

fall. The past tense is *fell*. The participle is *fallen*. *Fall* may be followed by the *-ing* form of a verb with the preposition *to,* as in *I fell to eating*. It could once be used in this sense with an infinitive, as in *I fell to eat,* but this construction is now obsolete.

Fall may be followed by an adjective describing what falls, as in *smiling, the boy fell dead*. It may also be followed by an adverb describing the fall, as in *it fell silently*.

fallacy. See **mistake.**

fall between two stools. To say of someone who has failed because he was unable to choose between alternatives that he has *fallen between two stools* is to employ a cliché. The proverb once had considerable force and more robust expression (*Between two stools the ars goeth to the ground*) but it has been exhausted by overuse.

fallen. See **fall.**

fall to with a will, as a term for starting in to eat heartily, is trite.

falsehood. See **lie.**

falseness; falsity. Both *falseness* and *falsity* define a quality of nonconformance with the truth. But they cannot always be used interchangeably. *Falseness* applies to persons and implies an intentional departure from truth or loyalty (*The falseness of the declaration was embarrassingly obvious. The guilt of falseness in their hearts*). *Falsity* is usually applied to reports and documents, doctrines and opinions (*Such reports bear their falsity upon their faces. This doctrine, whose falsity has been a dozen times exposed . . .*). *Falseness* suggests more intentional untruthfulness than does *falsity*.

fame. See **celebrity.**

family is a group name and may be used with a singular verb, as in *the family that has just moved in*. But usually the speaker has in mind the individual members of a family, and in that case a plural verb is required. *My family is all sick* is not standard English because the *all* proves that the speaker is thinking of the individual members, and this in turn requires a plural verb.

famous. See **notable.**

fancy; fantasy; phantasy; imagination. *Fancy* is now confined to light and often playful imaginings (*In the spring a young man's fancy/ Lightly turns to thoughts of love*). A *fancy* waistcoat would be one designed to please a fanciful taste. It would be a little out of the ordinary, but not much.

Though Fowler and Partridge make a distinction between *fantasy* and *phantasy,* assigning to the former the sense of caprice and to the latter the sense of a visionary notion, no such differentiation is maintained by American dictionaries. The two words are regarded as variants, with the preference being given to *fantasy* which is given the meaning of unrestrained or extravagant fancy bordering, sometimes, upon insanity (*These fantasies are often dangerous*). A *fantastic* waistcoat would be one so extravagant in design or material or both as to be ludicrous.

Few words in our language have had their meanings so thoroughly discussed as *imagination*. Generations of Ph.D. candidates have sucked a thin aliment from the problem. And the best one can make of all the discussion is that imagination, as applied to artistic creation, means the blending of memories and experiences in the mind of the artist in such a way as to produce something that has never existed before, yet something that may have in it a vision or interpretation of reality hitherto unperceived (*The lunatic, the lover, and the poet,* [and, one might add, the literary critic when on this subject] / *Are of imagination all compact*).

far. The comparative form is *further* or *farther*. The superlative form is *furthest* or *farthest*. The forms *farther* and *farthest* can only be used in speaking of distance. The forms *further* and *furthest* can be used in this sense and also in the sense of additional, as in *further details* and *further delay*. Some grammarians would like to restrict *further* and *furthest* to figurative senses but this is a hope and not a description of current usage. It seems more likely that *farther* and *farthest* will be dropped from the language and *further* and *furthest* become the only acceptable forms. That has not yet happened, however. And to pronounce the positive form *far* as if it were spelled *fur* is not standard at present.

In Great Britain the word *far* is no longer used to qualify a noun, except in set phrases such as *the far north, a far cry*. This is not true in the United States where *far* is still used as an adjective in natural speech, as in *put it in the far corner* and *open the far window*. For *all the further,* see **all.**

far be it from me, as a rhetorical disclaimer, is not only a cliché but, often, a piece of humbug. It is interesting that Joseph's protestation of innocence in the business of the cup in his brother's sack (*Genesis,* 44:17) which was prefaced in Wycliffe's edition with *Fer be it fro me that I thus do,* was changed in the King James version to read *God forbid that I should do so* and then changed back in the Revised Standard Version to *Far be it from me that I should do so*. Appar ently the latest translators felt a little uneasy at letting Joseph invoke God to support him in a deception, however well intentioned.

far from the madding crowd. One reason that the crowd is madding is that its members are addicted to clichés, of which this (often misquoted as *maddening*) is one.

fascination. To *fascinate* is to hold by enchantment (*The fascination of her charms held him a happy slave*). As a term of exaggerated compliment it is applied to pleasant things and often has no more meaning than *attractive* (*My dear, what a perfectly fascinating bracelet!*). As so often when exaggeration has defeated itself, a last desperate attempt to give the term meaning is made by accenting the word shrilly. When the word is used seriously and literally, it more often applies to unpleasant things, to extreme terror (*Helpless with fear, the rabbit stared, fascinated, at the approaching stoat*).

Something has a fascination *for* one. One is fascinated *by* a person and *with* an inanimate object. *Fascination of* by itself is ambiguous. If one speaks of the *fascination of X by Y*, the meaning is plain. But if one speaks merely of the *fascination of X* it is not always clear whether it means that X was fascinated or fascinating.

fashion; manner. *Fashion* is prevailing custom or style, conventional usage or conformity to it. It was also used formerly to mean manner and method (*He hath importun'd me with love,/ In honourable fashion*) but this use is now obsolescent or out of fashion. *Manner* is now used in reference to individuals and *fashion* reserved for the custom prevailing among people in general (*He had a strange manner of speaking. It was the fashion to prolong the vowels and swallow the consonants*).

fast is as truly an adverb as it is an adjective. The specifically adverbial form *fastly* is now obsolete.

fastidious; finical; squeamish. *Fastidious* means hard to please, excessively critical, over-nice (*The late nineteenth century was in many ways a fastidious age, full of false refinement. I must say he's not at all fastidious about what he piles on his plate*). Though its proper sense is pejorative, it is a point-of-view word; what seems excessively critical to one man may seem justly appraising to another. So that we sometimes find it used in an approving way (*She's very dainty and fastidious*).

Finical or more commonly *finicky* is never used praisingly. There is a connotation of contempt in it. The one who uses the word feels that there is no justification for the finicky one's distaste (*Yet after all that finicky revising there isn't a well-written sentence in the book!*).

Squeamish is the strongest word of the three, for it means one whose repugnance to the improper or the distasteful is great enough to induce nausea. It is still used in its original sense (*The very sight of a safety belt makes me squeamish*) but chiefly employed figuratively (*trifles magnified into importance by a squeam-*

ish conscience. I'll warrant it's some squeamish minx as my wife, that's grown so dainty of late, she finds fault even with a dirty shirt). See also **nice.**

fat; corpulent; stout; plump. *Fat* is the informal, everyday word. It formerly connoted a good deal of jolliness, and still does to some extent, but increasingly it is coming to have unpleasant implications (*Nobody loves a fat man. She's too fat, she's too fat, she's too fat for me*). *Corpulent* suggests fleshly bulk. It's rather a stilted word. Falstaff calls himself *a good portly man i' faith, and a corpulent,* but he is burlesquing the sonorous dignity of Henry IV's speech at the time. *Stout,* now a euphemism for *fat,* especially in reference to ladies and in the garment industry, suggests a heavily built but usually strong and healthy body. It was used much formerly to mean vigorous, brave, undismayed, of great staying power. Keats's tribute to *stout Cortes* would be ludicrous if the modern meaning were read into it. *Plump,* also a euphemism for *fat,* connotes a pleasing roundness, an attractive fulness of flesh.

fatal; fateful. The primary meaning of *fateful* is "involving momentous consequences." The day on which a man began something of great import to him, whether of good or ill, would be a *fateful* day for him. That is *fatal* which causes or initiates death or ruin. A *fatal* day could only be one on which some disaster occurred or had its inception. *Fateful* may mean *fatal; fatal* cannot always be used for *fateful.*

Father Time with his beard, bald head, scythe and hourglass, has been around a long time. He was apparently a venerable personification as long ago as 1594 when Shakespeare alluded to him in *The Comedy of Errors.* The cartoonists cannot let him go, because at the end of every Old and the beginning of every New Year, he is their means of livelihood. But in writing and speaking, where he is a tired cliché, he may be allowed to settle in threadbare dustiness into the oblivion he has so long typified.

fathom. Only the singular form *fathom* can be used as part of a compound adjective qualifying a following noun, as in *a ten fathom cable. A ten fathoms cable* is not standard English. Except in this construction, the plural form *fathoms* is preferred in this country when speaking of more than one.

In English literature the singular form *fathom* is used whenever the word occurs with a numeral, whether it qualifies a following noun or not, as in *full fathom five thy father lies* and *under the keel nine fathom deep.* This is still the usual practice in Great Britain, but not in the United States.

fatigued. See **tired.**

faucet; tap. The American *faucet* is the British *tap.*

fault; failing; foible; weakness; vice. *Fault* is the common, everyday word for a moral shortcoming or imperfection. When applied to animals and inanimate things there is, of course, no implication of moral condemnation; it is there simply an imperfection. But in all applications to human beings (especially in the negative *It's not my fault*) there is an element, weak or strong, of condemnation. When the young man in *Erewhon* who has been condemned to death for having tuberculosis protests that it is not his fault, the judge answers sternly, *Though it is not your fault, yet it is a fault in you.*

Failing, foible, and *weakness* all seek to extenuate or excuse the imperfection alluded to. *Failing* can describe a fairly serious fault (*Drink is his failing. He just can't tell the truth; it's his failing*). *Weakness* suggests a giving way to an improper impulse, self-indulgence; yet it cannot be applied to major faults. A man may be said to have a weakness for liquor or pretty girls, but it would be inappropriate or facetious to refer to a weakness for taking other people's property. *Foible* (which is an obsolete French word for weakness) is the mildest in its implied reproof of all these terms. It suggests that the weakness is light and amusing, crotchety, more an eccentricity than a fault (*He loves to talk about the Civil War; it's his foible*).

Vice is a strong word. It may include sin and may describe a sin apart from him who has committed it (*the vice of swearing*). It is severely condemnatory.

fauna is a singular group name, meaning all the animals of a certain place or time. It is usually followed by a singular verb, but a plural verb is also permissible. The plural, *faunas* or *faunae,* means more than one such group.

favor; prefer. Weseen and Partridge insist that *favor* must not be used as a synonym for *prefer.* But since they grant that *favor* can mean to have a preference for, the distinction is too subtle to concern the common speaker or writer. If it is said that so-and-so favors something, it is not unreasonable to wonder in preference to what and not ungrammatical to satisfy the wonder in a comparison.

faze. See **phase.**

fear may be followed by an infinitive, as in *they fear to go,* or by the *-ing* form of a verb, as in *they fear going,* or by a clause, as in *they fear they will go.* The three forms are equally acceptable. The noun *fear* may be followed by a clause, as in *the fear that they will go,* or by the *-ing* form of a verb introduced by *of,* as in *the fear of going.* The *-ing* form is generally preferred.

fearful; fearsome. *Fearful* and *fearsome* are synonyms, meaning causing fear, but *fearsome* is now slightly archaic and literary. See also **horrible.**

feasible. That is *feasible* which is capable of being done (*His plan is feasible, and I see no reason why it should not be put into operation immediately*). And since whatever is doable is possible, *feasible* can mean possible in one of *possible's* meanings. But many things are possible which are not doable. It is possible, for example, but not feasible that it will rain tomorrow. And the true function of *feasible* (says Fowler) is to pre-

vent ambiguity among the uses of *possible,* by making it clear, where the context may not do so, whether something is doable or just likely to happen. Certainly the use of *feasible* as a mere synonym for *possible* serves no good purpose. To say, *He thought it quite feasible that at some future date we might send rockets to the moon* is pompous or straining too hard to find an unusual word for a usual one. Of course *He thought the sending of a rocket to the moon quite feasible* is a different thing.

feather in one's cap. As a metaphor for a signal accomplishment, something to be proud of, *a feather in one's cap* is now bedraggled and droopy and no feather in anyone's stylistic cap.

feather one's nest. As a term for taking care of one's self, slyly laying by for the future, *to feather one's nest* is strictly for the birds.

feature. The use of *feature* as a verb, meaning to give prominence to or to be prominent in (*The case was featured on every front page. Chaplin featured in "The Gold Rush"*) and as an attributive noun (*He writes feature articles for the Sun-Times*) or just an ordinary noun (*When does the feature go on, please?*), though viewed with alarm by the watchdogs of the language for thirty years has advanced steadily and is now solidly established in American usage. The movies had need for such a word and as they came to play such a large part in our civilization the word, quite naturally, proliferated.

fed. See **feed.**

fee. See **honorarium.**

feed. The past tense is *fed.* The participle is also *fed.*

feel. The past tense is *felt.* The participle is also *felt.* When *feel* means know by touching it may be followed by an object and the simple form of a verb, as in *I felt it break,* or by an object and the *-ing* form of a verb, as in *I felt it breaking.* When used in this sense the word cannot be followed by a *to*-infinitive. When *feel* is followed by a clause, as in *I felt it was broken,* it will be understood to mean believe or have the impression. In this sense *feel* may be followed by a *to*-infinitive, especially in a passive construction, as in *it was felt to be wrong.*

Feel may be followed by an adjective describing the subject of the verb, as in *I felt strong* and *I felt different.* It may also be followed by an adverb describing the action itself, as in *I felt strongly* and *I felt differently.* Sometimes the two forms mean different things and sometimes they do not. According to the traditional rules of grammar, *I felt bad* is the correct form for what people mean when they say *I felt badly.* But *I felt badly* is now also standard English in just this sense. This construction may have originated in the mistaken notion that a verb could not be followed by an adjective. But it has certainly been reinforced by the fact that to many people *bad* means *wicked.* In order to say that they are miserable without saying that they are guilty, they are compelled to use *badly.* There is no doubt that both forms, *feel bad* and *feel badly,* are standard today. To condemn *badly* in the name of grammar is to misunderstand the nature of grammar. Grammatical rules are not something that has been revealed to us, but simply generalizations about the way people use words.

Feel is often used as a synonym for *think* (*I feel you should do it this way*). Much thinking, of course, is inseparable from feeling, in the sense of experiencing emotion, but the word should not be used in this way unless it is intended to convey the idea of strong emotion in the thought or a groping (as one *feels* one's way along in the dark) towards a settled conviction (*I feel that he's wrong, but I would find it hard to give specific reasons for thinking so*). See also **sense.**

feel in one's bones. As a metaphor for premonition, *to feel something in one's bones* is hackneyed. Its origins are uncertain. Perhaps it is connected with the ability which many rheumatics profess to have of being able to tell from twinges in their afflicted joints when there will be a change in the weather.

feet of clay. Nebuchadnezzar dreamt that he saw a great image of which the head was of gold, the breast and arms of silver, the belly and thighs of brass, the legs of iron, and the feet part of iron and part of clay. *Feet of clay* is a reference to this and has become a figure for the weak, human, and unadmirable qualities of some great and admired person. With the decline of knowledge of the Bible among the masses of the people, the figure has little meaning any more.

felicity. See **happiness.**

fell may be the past tense of the verb *fall.* It may also be the present tense of the verb meaning cause to fall, which has the regular past tense and participle *felled.* See **fall.**

felo-de-se. As a synonym for one who commits suicide, *felo-de-se* carries the suggestion of its literal meaning, one who commits a felony in respect to himself. The proper plural, just in case anyone is remotely interested, is *felones-de-se,* though *felos-de-se* is admitted.

felt. See **feel.**

female; feminine; effeminate; womanly. *Female* is the opposite of *male* (*The female of the species is more deadly than the male*). It is the scientific word and the everyday word for a non-male animal, including a human being, and for things pertaining to such an animal (*the female figure, the female organs*).

Feminine means pertaining to a woman. It is the opposite of *masculine* and is rarely used (except in such extensions as *feminine gender* in grammar and *feminine rimes*) to refer to the qualities or adjuncts of any female except the human. It suggests the softer and more delicate qualities of women (*There was something almost feminine in the tender deference with which he appeared to listen*).

Effeminate is a term of contempt, applied to actions or qualities in a man which would be fitting in a woman (*His effeminate giggle infuriated the other men in the bar*). The word

feminine used to be used in this sense but is **not** often so used now.

Womanly suggests the stronger qualities of a woman. It is more homely than *feminine* and has more dignity (*Womanly sobs were heard, and manly cheeks/ Were wet with silent tears*). It also means having the characteristics of a woman as contrasted with those of a girl (*The girl begins to be womanly*). See also **woman.**

fence (on the). To say of someone who is undecided or, more often, is refusing to commit himself to one side or another of a dispute, that he is *on the fence* is to employ a phrase worn out by overuse.

fender. The American automobile *fender* is the British *wing.* The British *fender* is the American *bumper.*

feral. As a word for *wild* (*The dovecote pigeon ... has become feral in several places*—Darwin), *feral* is now solely a literary word. In its literal sense of "animal" it has been applied by some anthropologists to those children who are alleged to have been reared by wolves, bears, baboons, and the like, and if the supply of children or credulity holds out it may become established as a technical term.

ferment; foment. To *ferment* is literally to cause to undergo fermentation and since the process of fermentation gives off gases that cause bubbling and the raising and swelling of such substances as dough and generally indicates intense internal action, to *ferment* is figuratively to seethe with excitement or to cause others to seethe with excitement (*His mind was doubtless fermenting with projects; the Christianity which fermented Europe*).

To *foment* is literally to apply medicated lotions, usually warm (*The leg may be conveniently fomented by putting it in a deep bucket of warm water*). Figuratively to *foment* is to foster, encourage, stimulate, instigate, especially in a bad sense (*The rumor was fomented by those who hoped to profit from the resulting panic. These civil commotions were constantly fomented by the monarchs of Blefuscu*). But since it is often a matter of opinion as to how an agitation was instigated, whether by the introduction of an inner ferment or the application of an outward foment, the two words, in the sense of causing trouble, are synonymous (*He fermented the passions of the vicious* or *He fomented the passions of the vicious*). But neither may be used for the other in its literal sense and even in the figurative uses there are occasions when the careful writer will prefer one to the other.

ferrule; ferule. The metal ring or cap which is put around the end of a post or cane for strength or protection is spelled either *ferrule* or *ferule.* The rod or cane or flat piece of wood formerly used for punishing children by striking them on the hand is spelled *ferule.*

festal; festive. Both *festal* and *festive* refer to a feast or a festival, but *festal* is usually confined to an actual feast or festival. When De Quincey says that *the ball-room wore a festal air* we assume that it was decorated for a feast or festival, but *festive,* although it can refer directly to a feast, can also refer to a general joyousness, a holiday spirit without any particular holiday (*He was in a festive mood*).

fetch. See **bring.**

fever; temperature. The use of *temperature* for *fever* to describe a body temperature above the normal of 98.6° F. (*He has had a temperature for nearly a week*) probably began as a euphemism to avoid the once-frightening *fever,* but it is unfortunate because it adds nothing to make up for its extra syllables and it blurs the proper meaning of *temperature.* It is ironic that *temperature* originally meant to be in temper, to be free from the distemper that a fever indicates.

few may be used to qualify a plural noun, as in *few men believe,* or alone as if it were a noun, as in *few believe.* When *few* is not qualified by a definitive adjective, such as *a, the, this,* it has the force of a negative statement and means not many. When qualified it has the force of an affirmative statement and means a small number, as in *a few men believe* and *a few believe.* In all constructions it is plural and requires a plural verb. When used as a noun, *few* may be qualified by an adjective, as in *an honest few.* At one time the word *good* was used in this way, as in *a good few.* This can still be heard but is now considered old fashioned. *Very* is generally preferred, as in *a very few.* When used in a series of adjectives, *few* is treated as a numeral and placed before descriptive adjectives, as in *a few honest men.*

few and far between. There was a proverb that the visits of angels were *short and far between.* Thomas Campbell in *The Pleasures of Hope,* seduced by alliteration, asked *What though my winged hours of bliss have been/ Like angel visits, few and far between?* Hazlitt in his *Lectures on the English Poets* pointed out (to Campbell's intense irritation) that in altering the expression Campbell had spoiled it, since *few* and *far between* are, in relation to visits, the same thing. None the less, the corrupted "improvement" has taken hold and the sensible original been forgotten.

few; some; several; sundry. *Some* means unspecified but considerable in number, amount, or degree (*They visited us for some weeks. She has some fever. There's some left, enough for a meal*). *Few* means not many (*Few there are who can now remember that day*) but *a few* means more than none (*A few survived to tell the tale*). And, just to confuse matters further, *quite a few* (which ought to mean emphatically only a few) means a fairly large number.

Several means more than two or three but not many (*There are several gentlemen waiting to see you*), but it also means single or particular (*I have called you on three several occasions but never received an answer*) and various (*There are several ways of doing it*).

Sundry is an archaic synonym for *several* (*These benches formed the favorite resting place*

of sundry old men). It continues in general use in the phrase *all and sundry* (everyone collectively and individually) and the word *sundries,* miscellaneous items.

fib. See **lie.**

fiction; fabrication; figment. *Fiction* is something wholly invented, to deceive or to entertain (*He has been playing off a fiction on me. Dramatic fiction copies real life*). A *fabrication* is a statement or series of statements, intended to deceive, in which, to carry more conviction, an element of truth is often interwoven (*What is said to have happened might have been invented, and the occasion and motives for the fabrication may be conceived*). A *figment* is a pure product of the imagination, something, usually, made up to explain, justify, or glorify oneself (*All those noble relatives are figments of his imagination. Whence came this Whiffle and Whimzy within the circumference of thy Figmentitious Fancy?*).

fictional; fictitious; fictive. *Fictitious* now has the meaning, in common use, of counterfeit or false (*That's a fictitious name; you can tell by the sound of it*), though it is still used and understood in the older sense of consisting of fiction, imaginatively produced (*Those fictitious stories that so enchant the mind*). So strongly has the idea of falseness colored the word, however, that many prefer to use *fictional* or *fictive* when referring to fiction (*Is it a fictional book, sir, or a history? What was there in such fictive woes/ To thrill a whole theater?*), though historically *fictive* has had much more of the sense of "untrue" than "of the nature of imaginary narration." See also **factious.**

fiddle; violin. *Fiddles* are still heard in the mountains and at country dances but only *violins* and *viols* at concerts and in orchestras. A fiddler is a merry andrew, to be paid with drinks and patronizing; a violinist is a musician, admired and often richly rewarded. Puritan scorn has enriched the language (though impoverished our stock of harmless gaiety) with many opprobrious terms drawn from playing the fiddle— *fiddling around, to fiddle* (playing aimlessly with the fingers), *fiddlesticks, fiddle-faddle.* Fowler incites us to rebel in the old word's defense. If *fiddle* is now only in familiar or contemptuous use, as the *Oxford English Dictionary* states, he says, it is a matter for regret, and those who defy this canon deserve well of the language. Musicians among themselves refer to their violins as fiddles. But it is a lost cause and only in another land shall we hear again the fiddles tuned to solemn mirth.

fiddle while Rome burns. As a term for being occupied with trifles in the face of a crisis *to fiddle while Rome burns* is one of the most venerable and deeply intrenched of clichés. That it is at variance with the known facts is, of course, irrelevant but it is not uninteresting. The incident upon which the cliché is founded is related by Suetonius who flourished more than fifty years after the event. He says that Nero set fire to the city of Rome to see what Troy looked like when it was in flames and accompanied the conflagration by singing his own composition *The Sack of Ilium* and playing on the lyre. Tacitus who was living at the time of the fire, who knew Nero and who is a far more reliable authority than Suetonius, says that Nero was at his villa at Antium, fifty miles from Rome, when the fire broke out, that he hurried back, took every measure possible to check and control the fire, established shelters and relief measures for the victims, and rebuilt the city after the fire in an intelligent and much improved way.

fiend. *The fiend* is Satan (*because the fiend, our adversary, found him in such thoughts*). *A fiend* is any evil spirit and, by extension, a diabolically cruel or wicked person (*A frightful fiend/ Doth close behind him tread. The man is a perfect fiend*). Colloquially, the term is used in jocular exaggeration of those who cause annoyance or do mischief (*autograph fiends, fresh-air fiends*) and applied to one hopelessly addicted to narcotics (*a dope fiend*).

fight. The past tense is *fought*. The participle is also *fought*. *Fight* once had a past tense *fit* and a participle *fitten* but these have not been standard for a long time. A grammar published in 1765 lists them as "very familiar, or rather low." See **altercation.**

fight tooth and nail. As a term for going at something with ferocious vigor *tooth and nail* has been proverbial for four hundred years and a cliché for about one hundred. It needs a rest.

figment. See **fiction.**

figure (verb). The use of *figure* as a verb to denote computing or expressing in figures or adorning with figures or projecting into figures of speech, and the like, is standard. But to use it to mean to conclude or to judge (*Well, I figured they didn't want me around any more, so I just lit out for home*) or to solve or understand (*He'll soon figure out what they meant*) or to rely on (*You can figure on Bill every time*) is questionable.

figure; number. A *number* is a word or symbol, or a combination of words or symbols, used in counting or to denote a total. A *figure* (in the sense in which it is often confused with a number) is a numerical symbol. A number may be expressed in figures, and an amount or value expressed in numbers may be called a figure (*What's a good round figure as an estimate?*). See **numerals.**

figure of speech. A *figure of speech* or a *trope* is a mode of expression in which words are used out of their literal sense, or out of ordinary locutions, to suggest a picture or an image or to secure some other special effect. Too deliberate and conscious a use of them is now felt to be overly literary. The chief figures of speech (each of which is discussed in a separate entry in its alphabetical order) are: *allegory, anticlimax, antithesis, cliché, climax, euphemism, hyperbole, irony, litotes, meiosis, metaphor, onomatopoeia, oxymoron, personification, synecdoche, syllepsis, zeugma.*

filch. See **steal.**

file; file away. In the sense of arranging papers methodically for preservation and convenient reference, Weseen protests against using *file away*, insisting that it is redundant and that *file* says the same thing. But in popular usage there is a slight difference. *File* alone usually means to arrange methodically for reference and *file away* has more of the meaning of preserving for future reference (*Please file this under the letter N. They don't read these things; they just file them away. You can be sure that remark is filed away in his memory*).

filibuster. In England *filibustering* is confined to its original meaning of buccaneering. In America it is used primarily of one who impedes legislation by irregular or obstructive tactics, usually by making long speeches (*You're filibustering against the wrong bill, Senator*).

filthy lucre. The *filthy lucre* of the Bible is best paraphrased as dishonorable gain. The use of the term to designate money, now chiefly used jocularly, is a cliché.

final completion. Since *completion* means "the state of being completed, conclusion, fulfillment," the phrase *final completion* (*He brought his book to a final completion this summer*) is redundant. It is conceivable, of course, that a man may have announced the completion of something half a dozen times and at last completed it, or circumstances may have compelled him to make new completions, so that a last, irrevocable, unchangeable completion might be called the *final completion,* or the term might be applied ironically. But even under such circumstances it would probably be better to say that he *finally completed* the work.

final; finale. *Final* is chiefly an adjective, meaning the last in place, order, or time (*The chief has the final say. This is your final chance*). As a noun, usually in the plural, it is used in relation to athletic events and college examinations to mean the final event or test (*He failed his finals. Smith was entered in the finals*).

Finale is a noun. It means the conclusion, especially of a musical composition or any performance or course of proceedings (though in reference to the last it is usually used humorously, suggesting that the business has been something in the nature of a stage performance).

finally and **ultimately** are interchangeable in many contexts but not in all. In concluding a speech or a sermon, if one wishes to give his hearers hope, the word is *finally* (*And, finally, my friends, I come to consider, etc., etc., etc., etc.*). In referring to someone else's speech, *finally* could refer to the order (*The defense attorney finally said that . . .*); whereas *ultimately* could only mean after a long time. In philosophy, *ultimate,* through devious turnings of its meaning of "beyond which it is impossible to proceed" can mean original, primary, first (*ultimate causes*).

find. The past tense is *found*. The participle is also *found*. *Find* may be followed by an object and the *-ing* form of a verb, as in *I found my atten-*

tion wandering, or by a clause, as in *I found my attention wandered.* When used in an active form, *find* may be followed by an object and the simple form of a verb, as in *I found my attention wander;* when *find* has a passive form, a *to*-infinitive must be used in place of the simple form of the verb, as in *his attention was found to wander.*

fine. The use of *fine* to mean *well,* as in *he is doing fine* and *it worked fine,* was frowned upon a generation ago. Its status has improved since then but it is not yet literary English. See **nice.**

finesse; fineness. *Fineness* is the quality or state of being fine (*He has a fineness of perception that makes him particularly well qualified to judge such tenuous distinctions*). The use of *fine* to mean excellent or admirable has given *fineness,* in its most common popular use, the meaning of moral superiority (*There is a fineness about him that makes it impossible for him to do anything petty or mean*).

Finesse once meant *fineness* in various of its senses, but is now restricted, in popular usage at least, to delicacy of execution or discrimination (*The finesse of the French language is a source of never-failing delight*) with, in many contexts (in consequence, apparently, of our mistrust of the delicately skillful) a connotation of artifice or cunning (*She was not experienced in the finesse of love. Full of their Finesses, Serve their own Turns in others Businesses*). *Finesse* has a special meaning in card games.

finical; finicky; finicking; finikin. Of the various terms for overfastidiousness—*finical, finicky, finicking,* and *finikin*—*finical* is the earliest. *Finicky* is the commonest American form (*Don't be so finicky. Quit picking at your food. There's nothing wrong with it!*). *Finicking* and *finikin* are used in England but rarely seen or heard in America. Fowler felt that *finicking* (because of a similarity in sound to *niggling* and *fiddling*) best expressed "a hearty British contempt" for fussiness.

The word, whatever form is preferred, seems to have derived from the adjective *fine* which, in turn, is a back formation from the verb *finire,* to finish. See also **fastidious.**

finish may be followed by the *-ing* form of a verb, as in *he finished speaking,* but not by an infinitive or a clause. See also **end.**

finite verbs. Any verb form that is "limited" in the sense that it has a specific tense, person, number, mode, and so on, is called a finite verb. In this dictionary a finite verb is called a true verb. All verb forms are finite except the infinitive, and the *-ing* form and past participle when these are used alone as nouns or adjectives.

fire. The American slang term for peremptory dismissal, to *fire* (possibly originally a pun on *discharge*) is in England *to sack,* or *to get the sack.*

fireworks. The singular form, *a firework,* exists but is seldom heard in the United States. In speaking of just one we are likely to use a more specific name, such as *a roman candle, a pinwheel, a shooting cracker.* But *fireworks* is a true plural. It is always followed by a plural verb, as in *the fireworks were beautiful,* and we may speak of *many fireworks* or *several hundred fireworks.* The form *fireworks* is used as the first element in a compound, as in *a fireworks display.*

first originally meant foremost or earliest, and only later became the ordinal number for *one,* meaning the element that begins a series. The older senses are still in use, especially in the United States where we speak of *the first lady of the land, the first families of Virginia, the first years of life. When they were first married* refers to the early years of their marriage and does not suggest that they were married a number of times.

Whenever *first* stands in the primary position for an adverb, that is, next to or inside the verb form, it has the old meaning of the early period, as in *when you first came in.* When *first* means the beginning of a series, it always stands in a position that is also open to adjectives, as in *when you came in first.* Here it can be argued whether *first* is more closely attached to *came* or to *you.*

When *first* is combined with a cardinal number, it may stand in the position appropriate for *foremost* or *earliest,* as in *the two first years;* or it may stand in the position appropriate for the other ordinals, such as *second* and *third,* as in *the first two years.* Some grammarians claim that the order in *the two first years* is "illogical." That would be hard to prove, since this is the order followed in French (*les deux premiers*) and in German (*die zwei ersten*), and the order seen in *the first two years* did not appear in English until the sixteenth century.

Today, numbers greater than four usually follow *first,* as in *the first hundred years.* But the smaller numbers are frequently placed before *first* when the objects they refer to are thought of individually, as in *the two first chapters were interesting.* Many writers place the cardinal number after *first* only when one group is being compared with another, as in *the first two chapters were more interesting than the second two.*

When *the first thing* is used as an adverb meaning simply *first,* the article *the* may be omitted, as in *do it first thing in the morning.*

first and foremost has everything: it is alliterative, redundant, trite, and it usually doesn't mean much of anything. It's just a way of clearing the throat before you start to talk.

first fine careless rapture. Though the wise thrush may, by singing each song twice over, convince us that he can recapture *the first fine careless rapture,* those who repeat Browning's phrase fail to do so. Our most poetic phrase for glorious originality has become hackneyed, a demonstration of the very lack of that which it celebrates.

firstly has been in the language at least since 1532. Today it is not used as often as the related words *secondly, thirdly,* and so on. Many speakers begin with *first* and then go on with *secondly, thirdly.* But *firstly* is respectable English.

During the nineteenth century *firstly* was condemned as an innovation, although it had been in use for four hundred years. De Quincey wrote: *I detest your ridiculous and most pedantic neologism of firstly.* But many of the best writers of the period, Scott, Gladstone, Byron, Dickens, Thackeray, Kingsley, Carlyle, continued to use it and have handed it down to us as an established element in the language.

first name; baptismal name; Christian name. With an increasing number of non-Christians in the population, *baptismal name* and *Christian name* as a term for one's personal name is being replaced by *first name.* To ask *what is your Christian name?* would seem a little strange now to many Americans.

first saw the light of day. To refer to the place where one was born as the spot where one *first saw the light of day* is to employ an unusually moldy cliché. Those addicted to it should be compelled every birthday to read aloud the third chapter of *Job.*

fish. The plural is *fishes* or *fish.* Until recently the word *fish* was used only as a singular. In the King James Bible, for example, the true plural is always *fishes,* as in *five barley loaves and two small fishes.* But the singular form *fish* was often used to mean all fish, or all of a certain lot, as in *let them have dominion over the fish of the sea* and *the fish that is in the river shall die.* This is a singular noun used generically, or collectively, and not a true plural. In addition, the singular form *fish* may be used as a mass noun when the creatures are thought of as food, as in *boat loads of fish* and *nets full of fish.*

These two uses of the singular undoubtedly gave rise to the feeling that *fish* was a plural form. This has become standard and the form *fish* may now be used as a true plural. That is, we may now say *twenty fishes* or *twenty fish.* This applies equally to compounds such as *three goldfishes* or *three goldfish.* But the movement toward regular plurals is very strong in modern English and the life expectancy of a new irregular plural, such as *fish,* is not very good.

fish to fry. It was Motteux who rendered Rabelais's *Nous aurons bien ici autre chose à faire* as *We have other fish to fry.* The French say *have other dogs to whip.* The frying of fish as a term for having something better to do was definitely established as a proverb in English in the seventeenth century. It is now a cliché.

fissionable, meaning capable of undergoing nuclear fission, has been accepted in America, in the phrase *fissionable material* without any great concern or even awareness that it raised linguistic problems. But the English, if we may judge from letters to the London *Times,* have been much agitated about it. Some feel that while *fissionable* is fashionable only *fissible* is admissible. Others feel that "in the terminology of fissility or fissileness" only *fissive* is admissive. Still others (See *Time,* January 4, 1954) would have it *fissile.* (*The chief advantage is that the critical amount is very much smaller for coal than for any fissile material*—Professor O. R. Frisch, of Cambridge, England).

fistula. The plural is *fistulas* or *fistulae.*

fit. The past tense is *fit* or *fitted.* The participle is also *fit* or *fitted.* In the United States *fit* is used more often than *fitted* for the past tense, as in *it fit last year.* *Fit* is not heard as often for the participle, as in *it had fit the year before,* but is acceptable here. Neither of these constructions is recognized in Great Britain, where *fitted* is always used. *Fitted* is preferred in the United States, for the past tense and for the participle, when the verb means make to fit, as in *his studies had fitted him for the work,* and is required when speaking of clothes, as in *the tailor fitted the coat.* In speaking of clothes *fitted* is also used in the sense of measured, as in *he was fitted for a suit.* *Fit* is also an adjective and when used in this way may be followed by an infinitive, as in *he is fit to work.*

fit as a fiddle. A fiddle has been a symbol of fitness for more than three hundred years, but no one knows why. Perhaps just the gaiety and exuberance connected with its music. The term is now a cliché, retained from deserved oblivion only by inertia and alliteration.

fit for a king. We know what *was* fit for a king. Kings wore ermine and jewelled crowns. They sat in their counting houses counting out their money. They had pipes and bowls and fiddlers three. For lunch they had blackbirds baked in a pie. Their horses and their men (though, of course, they couldn't do everything) marched up the hill and marched down again. But the glory of kings has departed. Except for three or four housebroken survivors, a monarch's life today is not a happy one. What is now fit for a king? Shabby rooms in a hotel on the Riviera, overdue bills, the hissing conspirator, the yawning waiter, the sneering reporter, the gossip columnist, and in the shadow the assassin. *Fit for a king* is now a ghoul's cliché. Let it be mercifully abandoned.

fix. In American usage *fix* is a slatternly verb of all work. It can mean repair, get ready, arrange matters with, cook, comb, concoct (*Fix a tire. Fix yourself up. He's fixed it with the cop. She's fixing supper right now. Wait till I fix my hair. He's really fixing a scheme this time.*)—indeed, almost any action, apparently, that is expected to terminate to the speaker's or listener's pleasure or advantage. We've been using the word this way for a long time; Captain Marryat noticed it as a feature of the American vocabulary when he visited the United States in 1837. So used, it is a sloven's word, avoiding even the faintest exertion towards precision of meaning; but it carries the sloven's rewards of confusion of meaning and eternal exasperation at not being understood.

As a noun the word is used colloquially to mean an unpleasant predicament, some situation from which it is difficult to escape (*I'm in a fix, Jim; you've got to help me out*).

flag (verb). See **wane.**

flagrant. See **blatant.**

flagrante delicto. See **blatant.**

flair was originally a sense of smell, hence a capacity for getting on the trail of something, like a hunting dog (*He has a flair for news. He's one of the best reporters alive*). It is now generally used to mean talent, aptitude, a keen perception (*She has a flair for making costume jewelry*) and even a fondness, though in this last sense, if the word is to mean anything, it ought to convey something more than a mere liking. To say that a woman has a flair for fine clothes suggests that she wears them unusually well, has an instinctive discernment of what sets her off to the best advantage and with unerring taste selects from a mass of things the exact thing for her. The word is a vogue word now, much overused, and sometimes, apparently, confused with *flare*, a sudden burst of flame.

flambeau. The plural is *flambeaus* or *flambeaux*.

flamboyant originally referred to the *shape* of flames, the wavy flamelike tracery of the stonework in the windows of many Gothic cathedrals (*Etchingam church, with its curious flamboyant window. The flamboyant penmanship admired by our ancestors*). It has come, however, to refer to the *color* of flames, flaming rather than flamelike (*the flamboyant colors of autumn*) and from this florid or showy. In this last sense it is slightly derogatory (*The governor's flamboyant rhetoric was often tiresome*).

flammable; inflammable. Some trucks that carry combustible materials are marked *flammable*, others *inflammable* and the knowing will sometimes inform you that the one means combustible and the other explosive, that *inflammable* is intended as a stronger warning. But the Petroleum Institute issues a special dictionary of the terms employed in the industry which says the two words are completely synonymous, thereby agreeing with all other dictionaries. It's just a matter of lack of space or paint, a desire to use bigger letters, a stylistic preference, or a recommendation of the underwriters who found that many people thought that *inflammable* meant *not flammable*.

flash in the pan. The *pan* was that part of a flintlock musket which held the priming, communicating with the charge by means of the touchhole. The pulling of the trigger struck the flint with a steel hammer and produced a spark which ignited the powder in the pan which then exploded the charge. That is, if all went well. But often it didn't. Sometimes (like a cigaret lighter, which works on the same principle) there was no spark. And sometimes only the priming was ignited: it flared up or *flashed* in the pan, but because the main charge was wet or the touchhole stopped up the gun did not go off (*Like false fire in the pan of an uncharged gun, it gives a crack but hurts not. The pistol flashed in the pan, and a spark flew into the cask*). Thus, for our ancestors *a flash in the pan* was a natural figure for an abortive outburst of any kind. With us the phrase has come to be applied more to some momentary success that cannot be repeated, some meteorlike flash of brilliance which compels admiration but does not inspire confidence.

But flintlock guns are now confined to museums, their working understood only by antiquaries, and the famous metaphor, once full of fire and meaning, is now quite cold.

flat; flatly. The form *flat* may be used as an adjective, as in *a flat roof*, or as an adverb, as in *she told him flat*. The adverbial use of *flat* is standard English and has always been standard. *Flatly* is an adverb only and cannot qualify a noun. Like the adverb *flat*, it may mean in a downright manner, as in *she told him flatly that she wouldn't go*. Unlike the adverb *flat*, it may also mean in a dull and spiritless manner, as in *he repeats flatly what other people have said well*.

flat as a pancake is a pretty worn simile for flatness though where, as in something that has been squashed, there is a softness or puffiness in the flatness, it has a suitability.

flat-footed in the sense of taking or showing an uncompromising stand, being firm, explicit (*The others hemmed and hawed but Andy came out flat-footed with it and said he wouldn't have anything to do with the movement*) was once slang but usage has surely made it standard by now.

flatus. The plural is *flatuses* or *flatus*, not *flati*.

flaunt; flout. Flaunt, to parade or display oneself conspicuously or boldly (*The Miss Lambs might now be seen flaunting along the street in French bonnets*) is often confused with *flout*, to treat with disdain or contempt (*Ah, you may flout and turn up your faces. From Fife, great King,/ Where the Norweyan banners flout the sky*). The confusion is not as amazing as some writers profess to find it because the two acts are often related: one who *flaunts* unconventionality or immorality *flouts* the conventions or mores of the community (*Shall she flaunt that brat at the baby show and flout every respectable married woman in town?*).

flautist; flutist. The "proper" word for one who plays a flute is not *flautist*, as the overknowing sometimes insist. *Flautist* is an acceptable word, but it is a fairly recent importation (1860). The more sensible *flutist* had been in use for centuries before the Italianate variant appeared and has remained in use ever since.

flay. To *flay* (participle *flayed;* in older writings often spelled *flea* and *flead*) means to strip the skin off (*With her nails/ She'll flay thy wolfish visage*). Animals are *flayed* for their hides and formerly, as a barbarous punishment, men were *flayed* alive. By extension it came to mean to strip of money or property. By humorous exaggeration it came to mean to criticize or reprove with scathing severity (*He flayed him with scorn, tearing away his pretences of honesty and pitilessly exposing him for the corrupt and cringing thing that he was*). The shortness of the word and the extreme violence of its meaning have made it a favorite word with headline writers whose abuse of it has now devitalized it. *Attorney flays witness* may only mean that the witness was censured or that the attorney doubted the accuracy of his testimony. The word has been so vitiated and overworked in this sense that it is to be avoided in all serious or effective writing.

flee. The past tense is *fled*. The participle is also *fled*. This verb, *flee*, means to run away or escape, as in *like ghosts from an enchanter fleeing*. Poe uses *fly* with this meaning when he says *uh, let us not linger! uh, fly! let us fly! for we must*. In the United States *fly* is no longer used to mean *flee*. But this is still standard practice in Great Britain, where *flee* is felt to be archaic or bookish. In Great Britain *flown*, the participle of the verb *fly*, is also frequently used in place of *fled*, as in *he found that the prisoner had flown*.

flesh and blood. As a term for human nature, *flesh and blood* (*Flesh and blood can't bear it*) is a cliché. Also as a term for a relative (*My own flesh and blood, to turn against me this way!*).

fleshly; fleshy. *Fleshy* now means having much flesh, plump, fat (*There was something repulsive in his moist fleshy hands*), or consisting of or resembling flesh (*These plants have thick fleshy leaves*). *Fleshly* is now restricted to *pertaining to the flesh* in the sense of the bodily, corporeal, physical as opposed to the spiritual. It means carnal, sensual, worldly (*Adultery, fornication, incest, or any other fleshly incontinency. Simplicity and godly sincerity, as opposed to fleshly wisdom*).

flew. See **fly.**

flight. See **trip.**

fling. The past tense is *flung*. The participle is also *flung*.

floor; story. Though *floor* and *story* (often spelled *storey* in England) are both used to designate a horizontal section of a building, *story* is commonly used in reference to height and *floor* in reference to a particular part of a particular building (*His office is on the top floor of a thirty-story building and has a wonderful view of the harbor*).

floorwalker. The American *floorwalker* is in England a *shopwalker*.

flora is a singular group name, meaning all the plants of a certain place or time. It is usually followed by a singular verb, but a plural verb is also permissible. The plural, *floras* or *florae*, means more than one such group.

flotsam and jetsam. As a metaphorical description of the remains of human shipwreck (*Huddled in doorways one sees the flotsam and jetsam of humanity*), *flotsam and jetsam* has been overworked and is a cliché.

In law a distinction was formerly made between these now inseparable terms. A wreck was composed of *flotsam, jetsam, lagan*, and *derelict*. *Flotsam* was that part of the wreckage of the ship and its cargo floating on the surface of the sea. *Jetsam* was that part which had been purposely thrown overboard, jettisoned, either to lighten the ship or to prevent its going down with the ship. Strictly it would have to have been dragged ashore and above the high-water line; otherwise it would be flotsam, which was whatever was found on the shore between high- and low-water lines. *Lagan* was wreckage lying on the bottom of the sea, whether or not marked with a buoy. *Derelict* was the abandoned ship. The goods wherever found were *findals*. These distinctions which are now only of antiquarian

interest were formerly important since they determined who got the spoil. Jetsam went to the lord of the manor, flotsam to the crown. The shipwrecked men were lucky to escape with their lives since if they were dead their clothes and personal belongings might be claimed as either flotsam or jetsam, depending on how far they had been able to crawl before they died—or were killed.

flour; meal. *Meal* is the edible part of any grain (now usually excluding wheat) or pulse ground to a coarse powder and unbolted. In the United States the word particularly designates maize so ground, or cornmeal. *Flour* is bolted meal, meal that is from which the husks have been sifted out after grinding. It is likely to be more finely ground than meal. When used alone the word usually refers to wheat flour. Other flours, such as buckwheat flour or rye flour, are indicated by a qualifying prefix.

flower. See **bloom.**

flown is the participle of the verb *fly*, meaning to move through the air, as in *he had flown from Chicago*. But it is also used in Great Britain as the participle of *flee*, meaning to run away or escape, as in *he saw that the prisoner had flown*. In the United States, this use of *flown* is felt to be literary or archaic.

The verb that describes the movement of a liquid, *flow*, is perfectly regular and has the past tense and the participle *flowed*. Today *flown* is never used in place of the participle *flowed*, although this was once acceptable.

fluctuate; vacillate. Though *fluctuate* and *vacillate* are in many senses synonymous, they differ in that *fluctuate*, to change continually, to vary irregularly, can refer to persons or things (*His income fluctuated between five and ten thousand a year. He was moody, temperamental, fluctuating between hope and despair*) while *vacillate*, to swing unsteadily, is now generally confined to persons or to the moods or conduct of persons. Furthermore, *vacillate* is slightly pejorative; it almost always suggests that the wavering was bad (*He could not decide whether to risk his inheritance by investing it in stocks or to play safe by putting it into government bonds. The fluctuation of the stock market made him vacillate between the two plans*).

flung. See **fling.**

flurry; fluster. A *flurry* is a sudden gust of wind, hence a commotion, sudden excitement, nervous hurry, and attendant confusion (*The sudden flurries of snow-birds,/ Like brown leaves whirling by. His blunder flurried the other actors and put them off their lines*). To *fluster* is to *flurry*, but there is in it a greater sense of confusion, akin to the confusion of too much drink (*He was flustered by her unexpected appearance in the doorway and simply stood there, silly and speechless*).

Flustrate is recognized as a verb, but it is hard to see what it gains over *fluster* and it is often confused with *frustrate*, on analogy to which it was probably formed. A flustrated person (the word is chiefly humorous) is frustrated by his confusion, but a frustrated person may be in

fly   182

full possession of his faculties, calm, and quite clear in his purposes, simply unable to accomplish his ends.

fly. The past tense is *flew*. The participle is *flown*. In the United States these words are used only in speaking of movement through the air, as in *he flew from Chicago,* or of something equally rapid, as in *time flies*. In Great Britain *fly* and *flown* are also used in the sense of escape or run away. (See **flee**.) In the United States there is a regular verb *fly, flied,* used in baseball (*he flied into right field*).

fly off at a tangent, as a term for abruptly leaving one thing to pursue another, is a cliché.

foam; froth. *Foam* and *froth* both mean an aggregation of bubbles and in many contexts may be used interchangeably. A man may *foam* at the mouth or *froth* at the mouth. But *foam* is usually employed when the connotations are pleasant, *froth* when they are unpleasant. Aphrodite arose from the *foam*. A billowing, lacy dress would probably be described as *foamy*. Where the lightness was thought ill of, *froth* would be more likely to be used (*All that frothy talk, what does it mean?*).

fob; foist. A fraudulent imposition is *fobbed off* on the public, or the public is *fobbed off* with such an imposition. But a trick or cheat is *foisted on* the public. The public cannot be *foisted off* with a trick.

focus. The plural is *focuses* or *foci*. See **nexus**.

foible. See **fault**.

foist. See **fob**.

-fold. See **suffixes**.

folio is a sheet of paper folded once to make two leaves (four pages) of a book. The term is also applied to a volume made up of such sheets. Such volumes were likely to be large and in common use the word often means any large, old, leather-bound book. But this is a loose usage. Some quartos (books composed of sheets folded twice into four leaves) are larger than some folios. The essential distinction is not the size but the folding of the sheet.

folk; folks. These words both mean people and both take a plural verb. At one time these words were used just as *people* and *peoples* were. The singular *folk* meant a nation and the plural *folks* meant several nations. The singular could also be used as a group name to mean the masses or the laity. These uses are now obsolete except in poetry. We may speak about *the fairy folk* but we do not speak about *the Iroquois folks*.

In the United States today the singular *folk* is used as the first element in a number of compounds, such as *folklore* and *folk dances*. The plural *folks* is used affectionately in *the young folks* and *the old folks*. These uses are standard throughout the country.

The plural form is also heard in *my folks, poor folks, folks say,* and similar expressions. These are standard English in some areas, principally in the South. In other areas they are acceptable but have a slightly old-fashioned or countrified tone and the more usual word is *people*, as in *my people, poor people, people*

say, and so on. The singular form *folk* when used in this sense carries a distinctly bookish tone.

In some areas, principally the North East, *folks* is used in a special sense, meaning our kind, as in *they are folks*; and *folksy*, which once meant friendly, now means unpretentious. *Folksy* is also used derisively by some of the educated to mean self-consciously unpretentious. These expressions are standard in the areas where they are used.

folk etymology is a term for a change in the form or pronunciation of words in order to make them similar to more familiar words on the basis of a fancied derivation. Thus *Welsh rabbit,* melted cheese on toast, is often called *Welsh rarebit*. The old light, one-horse family carriage was called a *carryall,* a folk etymologizing of its French name *carriole*. The tendency is active in all languages and some of our established words were so formed. Thus *isinglass* is a corruption of an obsolete Dutch word *huysenblas,* a sturgeon's bladder. It is particularly noticeable in geographic names in regions where the original settlers spoke a different language from the one spoken by the present inhabitants. Thus the *Purgatoire,* a river in Colorado, has become, in local pronunciation, the *Picketwire* and Harriet Martineau records that when she visited Illinois in 1834, Joliet had been corrupted to Juliet and that nearby was a hamlet called Romeo.

follow. See **succeed**.

follow in the footsteps of, as a term for emulation, is a worn and wordy cliché. The phrase is elaborated inaptly in Longfellow's

Lives of great men all remind us
We can make our lives sublime,
And, departing, leave behind us,
Footprints on the sands of time;

Footprints, that perhaps another,
Sailing o'er life's solemn main,
A forlorn and shipwrecked brother,
Seeing, shall take heart again.

Aside from the singular *im*permanence of footprints in the sand, the metaphor here calls to mind the most famous of all footprints in sand, that of Man Friday in *Robinson Crusoe*. And one remembers that Crusoe did not "take heart" at the sight of them but was terrified.

follows. *As follows* is an impersonal construction, with an understood subject *it*. The singular form *follows* must always be used. We say *they are as follows* and not *they are as follow*.

fool. The use of *fool* as an adjective (*All boys get these fool notions in their heads at one time or another*), though ignored by some authorities and condemned by others, has enough support in literature (*Ev'n tho' thrice again/ The red fool-fury of the Seine/ Should pile her barricades with dead*—Tennyson) to be acceptable.

foolish; fatuous; silly; stupid. All four words—*foolish; fatuous; silly; stupid*—mean lacking in intelligence and judgment and may be used interchangeably in many contexts. But they have their distinctions, especially when used to describe a person instead of some particular act. *Foolish* implies lack of common sense and, sometimes, a genuine mental weakness (*That was a foolish answer; you must have his help and it will antagonize him. A mild, foolish man, very lovable*). *Fatuous* refers to complacent folly, folly which the foolish person mistakes for wisdom. It suggests pompous emptiness, oracular insipidity (*These fatuous common-places, when one needs specific advice, are infuriating*). *Silly* in Anglo-Saxon meant happy, and the word still has about it a suggestion of that ebullience of gay folly that often marks and attends happiness. It also has about it the disapproval and annoyance at such conspicuous foolishness felt by those who do not share the happiness or approve of the folly (*We were young and very silly. One of the silliest things I ever heard of, to act that way in the bishop's presence!*) *Stupid* implies a natural slowness and deficiency of intellect, a benumbed and dazed state of mind. It is usually an angry and abusive word. It carries with it a suggestion of the brutality that so often goes with obtusity (*The stupid lout just stood there and didn't offer to lift a finger to help. The stupid Huns with their Schrecklichkeit*). A person may be silly without being stupid.

foot. The plural is *feet.* (When this word is being used in the special sense of foot soldiers, it has the unchanged plural *foot,* as in *there were five thousand foot.*)

In literary English, only the singular form *foot* can be used to qualify a following noun, as in *foot warmer, a two-foot ruler, a six-foot-high wall.* The plural form *feet* is sometimes heard in this position, as in *a feet warmer, a two-feet ruler.* This is heard too often to be condemned, but it is not yet literary English and the singular *foot* is preferred.

Formerly, the singular *foot* could always be used after a numeral, whether it qualified a following noun or not, as in *he is six foot underground* and *she is five foot two.* This old use of the singular is still acceptable in the United States, but the plural form *feet* is now preferred when the measurement does not precede the noun, as in *a wall six feet high.*

Foot is also used as the second element in compound adjectives meaning having a certain kind of feet, as in *barefoot boy* and *many a lightfoot lad.* The form *footed* may also be used here and is required when what is being shown is "how many" feet, as in *fourfooted beasts* and *the unfooted sea.*

foot the bill in the sense of "pay the reckoning" (*Order what you want; he'll foot the bill*) is slang in American usage. It is used also, metaphorically, to mean to suffer the consequences.

footless. In English usage *footless* can only mean, literally or metaphorically, having no feet, without footing or basis (*Some footless stockings tied up at the ends, dreamful wastes where footless fancies dwell*). These meanings are recog-

nized in America where it also can mean inapt or futile—possibly through confusion with *bootless* (*The ordering out of the militia was about as footless a procedure as I ever heard tell of*).

footplatemen. The English term *footplatemen* (*The locomotive union has about 70,000 footplatemen and the rival unions about 17,000 footplatemen*) comprises what in America are called locomotive engineers and firemen. The footplate is the platform on which the engineer and firemen of a locomotive engine stand.

for may be used as a preposition requiring an object or as a conjunction introducing a full clause. The basic meaning of *for* is ahead. But the word has a great many uses, some of which overlap and some of which seem to be completely unrelated.

1. Three of these uses only need to be listed, because they are clear cut and present no problems. *For* may be used to show distance, in time or in space, as in *wait for a year* and *walk for a mile.* It may show destination, as in *we set out for* or *we left for Chicago.* And it may mean in favor of, as in *we are all for you* and *we are for truth and justice.*

2. *For* may be used to show that one thing represents, is equivalent to, resembles, or corresponds to, another, as in *he appeared for me, they took me for a fool, they left him for dead,* and *word for word, blow for blow.* In these uses *for* sometimes approaches the meaning of *as.* *For* is used in a related sense to mean adapted to or suitable to, as in *a genius for getting into trouble, an ear for music.* In *the weather is severe for this time of year* and *he is still there, for all I know, for* means in comparison with or as far as. These various uses of the word are hard to define but they all represent a correspondence of one kind or another. They are established in idiomatic English and as a rule do not give any trouble to a native speaker of the language.

3. *For* is used with a great many verbs to show the object of a feeling or an attitude, as in *hope for, strive for, yearn for.* In verbs of forgiving or excusing, what is forgiven is the offense, not the person, and this is often introduced by *for.* This might be expressed by a clause, as in *forgive me that I am late,* but in current English we are more likely to say *forgive me for being late* or *forgive my being late.* Similarly, in *trust Providence for the rest,* the meaning is *trust for the rest to Providence.* In sentences of this kind, the person involved is treated as an indirect object. See **indirect object.**

A noun or adjective that represents a feeling may have its object introduced by *for.* But this is also one of the functions of the genitive case and the word *of* is sometimes used with exactly the same sense. A great many words, such as *thirsty, eager, greedy,* which could once be followed by *of,* are now always used with *for.* Others, such as *love, desire, appreciation, contempt,* may be used with either *of* or *for,* as in *love of money, love for money.* In the case of **a** few words, such as *afraid* and *apprehensive, for* has the special function of showing that the feeling is in the interest of a particular person. We therefore say *I am afraid of fire* and *I am afraid for him*. When this function does not exist and *for* and *of* may be used interchangeably, *for* is generally preferred.

4. *For* is used to show the person whose interests are affected by a given action, or the intended recipient of an action, as in *things worked out badly for all of us* and *we set a trap for them*. In current English there is a strong tendency to use *for* when an action is advantageous, and to use *on* when it is disadvantageous, as in *he lowered the rent for me* and *he raised the rent on me, he closed the door for me* and *he closed the door on me*. This broad use of *on* is not established in literary English but it represents a valuable distinction that may become standard in time.

5. *For* may be used to show purpose, as in *he has gone to the store for groceries,* or cause, as in *he was notorious for covetousness and for parsimony,* or reason, as in *they shouted for joy* and *he couldn't see the woods for the trees.* It may also be used to show a preventive cause or a cause that didn't operate. In this sense it is often equivalent to *in spite of,* as in *the owl, for all his feathers, was a-cold* and *he left, for all I could do to stop him.*

6. At one time *for* could be used before an infinitive, especially when it emphasized the idea of purpose, as in *what went ye out for to see?.* It was sometimes used in this position even when there was no question of purpose, as in *he made the seas for to rage and roar.* In current English *for* cannot stand immediately before an infinitive, and we use *in order* or *so as* to stress the idea of purpose. The old construction can still be heard, as in *I wish for to see him,* but it is no longer standard.

In current English *for* is used to introduce, or to mark, the subject of an infinitive, as in *there was no need for you to leave* and *I am glad for you to have it.* When the infinitive and all the words that go with it are attached to a noun or an adjective, as they are in these examples, this use of *for* is unquestionably literary English. But sometimes they are the object of a verb, as in *the doctor said for him to take a walk.* Twenty or thirty years ago sentences of this kind were not considered standard and a *that*-clause, such as *the doctor said that he should take a walk,* was the only acceptable construction. But the use of the infinitive has increased enormously during the last thirty or forty years. It seems to be replacing the *that*-clauses which require a subjunctive or subjunctive equivalent verb. In the United States *for* is now standard English when it introduces the subject of an infinitive that is being used in place of a *that*-clause. But it is not acceptable when the infinitive is not being used in this way. For example, we do not say *I want that you should come* and therefore *I want for you to come* is also unacceptable.

7. Besides its many uses as a preposition, *for* may also be used as a conjunction. When used as a conjunction it introduces a full clause, as in *forgive me, for I am tired.* Here *for* does not show the object of the feeling or attitude, as it does in *forgive me for being tired.* The conjunction *for* always shows that a following statement is being offered as a reason for something that has just been said. This brings the meaning of *for* very close to the meaning of *because,* and at one time the two words could be used interchangeably, as in *nor for he swelled with ire was she afraid.* This sentence is no longer standard English because it disregards two differences which we now make between the words *because* and *for.*

In the first place, these words now have slightly different meanings. The conjunction *for* introduces a reason, or an explanation for an opinion. The reason given may also be a cause, or an explanation for a fact, as in *it is getting dark for it is going to rain.* But this is not necessarily so. We may also say *it is going to rain for it is getting dark.* Here the *for*-clause gives the reason for the opinion. The word *because,* on the other hand, always introduces a cause. Most people would feel that it was ridiculous to say *it is going to rain because it is getting dark.* Very often the reason we give for an opinion is also intended to be an explanation of the fact, and we may then use either *for* or *because.* In current speech *because* is preferred to *for* whenever both are permissible, perhaps because we feel that facts are more interesting than opinions. For whatever reason, *for* when it is not actually required has an artificial or bookish tone.

In the second place, there is a purely formal difference in the way these words are used. It is sometimes said that *for* is a coordinating conjunction, that is, that it joins two independent statements, and that *because* is a subordinating conjunction and always introduces a subordinate or qualifying statement. Actually no such distinction is felt in current English. There is no difference in emphasis between *we hurried for it was getting dark* and *we hurried because it was getting dark.* In both cases, *we hurried* is felt to be the sole principal clause. A clause introduced by *because,* like a clause introduced by a subordinating conjunction such as *if* or *unless,* may stand before or after the principal statement. We may say *because it was getting dark, we hurried.* The conjunction *for,* on the other hand, like the coordinating conjunction *but,* must always stand between the clauses that it joins. In current English a *for*-clause never precedes the other statement. This limitation makes *for* one of the coordinating conjunctions. But only in a technical sense. So far as the effect of the word goes, *for* has as much subordinating force as the word *because.*

forbade. See **forbid.**

forbear. The past tense is *forbore.* The participle is *forborne. Forbear* may be followed by an infinitive, as in *I forbore to mention it.* If the *-ing* form of a verb is used it must be introduced by *from*, as in *I forbore from mentioning it.* The infinitive is generally preferred.

forbear; forebear. The verb meaning to restrain from, to hold back, to be patient, is *forbear.* The noun meaning ancestor may be either *forebear* or *forbear*, though *forebear* is preferred (*I can't forbear from laughing when he gets to boasting of his forebears*).

forbid. The past tense is *forbade* or *forbid.* The participle is *forbidden* or *forbid.* The form *forbade* is always pronounced *forbad*, and may also be spelled that way. *Forbid* may be followed by an infinitive, as in *he forbade her to speak*, or by the *-ing* form of a verb, as in *he forbade her speaking.* The infinitive is generally preferred.

forbidden fruit. It would seem natural to connect the phrase *forbidden fruit* with the story of Eve's temptation, and this unquestionably has had to do with the phrase's entrenchment in the language. But the Romans and the Greeks both had sayings of much the same kind. This one was proverbial in Chaucer's time and is a cliché in ours.

forbore; forborne. See **forbear.**

force. This verb may be followed by an infinitive, as in *they forced him to go.* If the *-ing* form of a verb is used it must be introduced by the preposition *into*, as in *they forced him into going.* The infinitive construction is preferred.

forceful; forcible. *Forcible* means effected by force or characterized by the use of force or violence (*Finding all doors and windows locked, the police had no choice but to make a forcible entrance*). *Forceful* means full of force. It is used chiefly in such phrases as *a forceful personality* or *a forceful argument.* It may be used as a synonym for *forcible* but such use is now archaic and literary.

forceps is frequently treated as a plural in speaking of one instrument, as in *these forceps are clean.* Three instruments may be called *three forceps* or *three pairs of forceps.* These constructions are standard English today. But *forceps* is actually a Latin singular and a singular construction, such as *a forceps* or *this forceps is clean*, is acceptable but learned. The word has an English plural *forcepses* and a learned plural *forcipes*, neither of which is in common use today. A singular form *forcep* is sometimes heard but is not standard. The form *forceps* is always used as the first element of a compound, as in *a forceps delivery.*

fore. The comparative form is *former.* The superlative form is *foremost* or *first.* The positive form *fore* is not often heard today (except on a golf course). The superlative *foremost* is generally used in its place. The comparative *former* has the meaning in some constructions of standing before something else, principally when used with *the latter.* But it is now more often used to mean preceding in time. It can no longer be used in a comparison with *than.* We say *earlier than* and not *former than.*

The word *first* also retains something of the meaning of *foremost*, but is more often used simply as the ordinal form of the cardinal number *one.* See **first.**

forecast. The past tense is *forecast* or *forecasted.* The participle is also *forecast* or *forecasted.* *Forecast* is the literary form for the past tense and the participle, but *forecasted* is also acceptable in the United States.

forego; forgo. To *forego* is to go before, to precede. To *forgo* is to abstain from (*I must forgo the pleasure of foregoing him into the hall*). *Forgo*, to abstain from, may be spelled *forego*; but *forego*, to precede, may not be spelled *forgo.*

foregone conclusion. Iago, inflaming Othello's mind with jealousy, tells him that he had heard Cassio talking in his sleep and that he had seemed to be making love to Desdemona and warning her to be cautious. Othello cries out in anguish and Iago hastens to insist "this was but his dream." It may have been only a dream, Othello replies, but such a dream *denoted a foregone conclusion.* Scholars have debated the exact meaning of the phrase in this its original context, but it seems fairly obvious: It may have been only a dream, but the very nature of the dream makes it plain that the act of love had definitely been concluded between them some time before. In modern usage the phrase means an inevitable conclusion, an opinion or a decision formed in advance. It is a cliché.

foreign. The use of the word *foreign* to designate a corporation chartered by another state but doing business in the state concerned is a proper legal term and not, as is sometimes assumed, an expression of belligerent provincialism.

foreign plurals. We have in English a great many words that have Latin or Greek plural forms. In most cases, these words also have a regular English plural that has been in existence, side by side with the learned form, sometimes for centuries. There is nothing about the form of these words that makes a classical plural more "natural" than an English one. Other words, of exactly the same types, are used only with English plurals. We can set *cameras* against *formulae*, *circuses* against *alumni*, *museums* against *memoranda*, *complexes* against *indices*, *trellises* against *pelves*, *electrons* and *paragons* against *phenomena* and *criteria.*

It would not be worthwhile to list all the words of this kind that may be used in scientific writing since these include, potentially, more words than exist in Greek or Latin. But several hundred of the most familiar ones can be found in this dictionary. These include all the words in general use for which the foreign plural is the only acceptable form, such as *parentheses.* They also include the words which are most often seen with a wrong plural form. If a learned form is used at all, it must be the right one.

Where two plural forms exist, one should choose the form that is most familiar. This means that a botanist and a physician might make different choices. Faced with choosing *latexes* or *latices* and *fistulas* or *fistulae,* the botanist might choose *latices* and *fistulas,* and the physician, *latexes* and *fistulae.* If the two plural forms are equally familiar, or equally unfamiliar, the English form is safer.

A classical scholar might, perhaps, find it hard to talk about *criterions.* But the number of Americans who know anything about Greek or Latin five years after they have left college is very small. And anyone who uses unfamiliar forms merely because he thinks they add a scholarly tone is likely to prove what an ignoramus he is. Not all words that end in *a* have a plural in *ae,* and not all words that end in *x* have a plural in *ices.* Some words that end in *us* have a plural in *i* and some have a plural in *us.* And some words are learned jokes that have become respectable nouns in English but that cannot possibly be given a plural in Latin. An English plural is safe. It can always be defended. A learned plural is sometimes out of place. And if it is a wrong learned plural, it is very, very wrong.

forensic means pertaining to, or connected with, or used in, courts of law. *Forensic medicine,* for example, is medicine in its relations to law. It also means pertaining to public discussion or debate, in such terms as *forensic eloquence.* But this usage is largely restricted to colleges and universities and has a touch not only of the academic but of the stilted. Sometimes in colleges the word is used as a noun for a debate or *forensic contest.* In the last century written speeches that could be used in debates were called *forensics* at Harvard.

forest. See **wood.**

foreword; preface; introduction. There was a vogue in the nineteenth century for replacing words of Latin origin with Saxon equivalents. Although *preface* had been in use for five centuries, *foreword* was coined to take its place and enjoyed great popularity among those who affected to be unaffected. All sense of its Teutonic strength and simplicity has departed and it is now simply a synonym for the older word. Fowler thought, in 1924, that it was already falling into disuse and allowed himself a paragraph of exultation. But his triumph was premature. The word is still in use, is accepted as standard by all dictionaries, and probably will stay. An *introduction* is likely to be more formal than a *preface* or a *foreword,* or to be more closely connected with what follows.

forget. The past tense is *forgot.* The participle is *forgotten* or *forgot.* In the United States, both forms of the participle are used, as in *I have forgotten* and *I have forgot. Forgotten* is generally preferred. In Great Britain, *forgotten* is the only form of the participle used and *forgot* is considered archaic or poetic. This is the reverse of British practice in the case of the verb *get,* where *got* is the preferred form and *gotten* is considered archaic.

Forget may be followed by an infinitive, as in *I forgot to mail the letter.* If the *-ing* form of a verb is used it must be introduced by the preposition *about,* as in *I forgot about mailing the letter. Forget* may also be followed by a clause, as in *I forgot he had mailed it.* See also **misremember.**

forgetful. See **oblivious.**

forgive. The past tense is *forgave.* The participle is *forgiven. Forgive* may be followed by a *that-*clause, as in *forgive me that I didn't come,* or by the *-ing* form of a verb, as in *forgive my not coming.* But a phrase with the preposition *for,* as in *forgive me for not coming,* is generally preferred.

forgo. See **forego.**

forgot; forgotten. See **forget.**

forlorn hope. *Forlorn* when spoken of persons means abandoned, forsaken, left all alone, desolate (*This is the maiden all forlorn/ Who milked the cow with the crumpled horn*). *Hope* in the phrase *a forlorn hope* originally meant a band of soldiers (*The forlorn hope of each attack consisted of a sergeant and twelve Europeans*—Wellington). The whole thing was actually merely an English spelling of the Dutch *verloren hoop,* "lost heap" or "lost troop," a term applied to soldiers assigned to extremely perilous tasks, meaning, as it were, given up for lost because of the very nature of what they had to do. The French called them *enfants perdus* and the English "forlorn boys."

With the emergence of the meaning of desperate or desolate for *forlorn*—the feeling that would follow upon being abandoned—the Dutch *hoop* was easily folk-etymologized into the English *hope* and the present meaning of the phrase, a vain expectation, an undertaking almost certain to fail, was established. As early as 1641 the phrase was being used in its modern sense, though the old meaning persisted alongside of the new one for two centuries. It is now a cliché.

form. See **blank.**

former. See **fore.**

formula. The plural is *formulas* or *formulae.*

formulate. To *formulate* is to reduce to or express in a formula, and a formula is a set form of words used for stating or declaring something authoritatively or for indicating procedure to be followed. To use *formulate* for *form,* therefore (*to formulate an opinion, to formulate a plan*), is to misuse it, and even when used correctly, except in chemistry or mathematics, it is a fairly pompous word.

fornication is voluntary sexual intercourse on the part of an unmarried person, though the term is used in the Bible as a synonym for *adultery* and sometimes as a synonym for *idolatry.*

forsake. The past tense is *forsook.* The participle is *forsaken.*

forsooth once had almost the solemnity of an oath (*He confirmeth with a double oath, saying forsooth and forsooth*—1547) but it is now used only ironically (*And I, forsooth, am to stay home and wash the dishes while you go to the movies*). Even this use, however, is now felt to be slightly affected.

fort; fortress. In the military sense of an armed place surrounded by defensive works and occupied by troops, *fort* and *fortress* are interchangeable. In common usage *fortress* is applied to larger forts or groups of forts or to the more heavily armed forts (*the great Belgian fortress of Eben Emael*). There is an old joke that *fortress* is feminine and hence harder to silence. The fortified trading posts of the West were invariably called *forts* and the term survives today in many American place names. Of the two words only *fortress* is used metaphorically (*A mighty fortress is our God*).

fortitude. See **patience.**

fortnight, meaning the space of fourteen nights and days, is in everyday use in England but is archaic in the United States where *two weeks* is used instead (*I get a two weeks' vacation early in September*). *Fortnight* is known in America, at least to the educated, but is rarely used.

fortuitous. That is *fortuitous* which is accidental or happens by chance (*This fortuitous encounter was the cause of his death*). Some *fortuitous* events may be favorable but the word is not a synonym for *fortunate* and it is a mistake so to use it.

forum. The plural is *forums* or *fora.*

forward; forwards. *Forward* is the only form that can be used to qualify a following noun, as in *a forward thrust.* It is also the only form used in the two expressions *look forward* and *from that day forward.* It is the preferred form in giving a command, as in *those behind cried "Forward!" and those before cried "Back!"* Either form may be used in any other construction, as in *move forwards* and *move forward.* In the United States the form *forward* is generally preferred.

forward; dispatch; transmit. The use of *forward* and *dispatch* as simple synonyms of *send* has little justification, though it is common in commercial letters (*We regret that a slight delay will be necessary, but assure you that the goods will be forwarded as soon as possible. We have received your order and will dispatch within the week, etc.*). A letter or package is certainly forwarded when it is sent ahead to an address at which the addressee will be and it is forwarded when it is sent on after him to another address. *Transmit* for *send* is labored elegance unless it carries the definite idea of passing something through or over an intermediary. Jones transmits a message or letter from Smith to Robinson. Though hasten is now an archaic meaning of *dispatch,* the idea of haste is still in the word and it means to send off promptly or quickly, with some sense of urgency.

for your information. If that which follows is truly informative, the introductory phrase *for your information* weakens its effect. If it is not, it is simply exasperating. Its use is chiefly ironical. It serves as a polite expression of annoyance at someone else's assertiveness.

In interoffice communication, and such like, it is often used to mean "You don't have to do anything about this; we're merely informing you . . . ." In this use it is an established and acceptable formula, often abbreviated to *FYI.*

fought. See **fight.**

found. See **find.**

fowl. The preferred plural is *fowls.* The singular form *fowl* is often used generically, or collectively, to mean all of them, as in *the fowl of the air.* It may also be used as a mass word meaning this kind of food, as in *they ate fowl all winter.* But only hunters use it as a true plural, as in *several dead fowl.*

fraction. The use of *fraction* to mean a small piece, a remnant (*He will recover only a fraction of the cost*), is over three hundred years old. Shakespeare so uses it. Troilus in *Troilus and Cressida* says bitterly of Cressida that *The fractions of her faith, orts of her love,/ The fragments, scraps, the bits, and greasy relics/ Of her o'ereaten faith, are given to Diomed.* It is true that the mathematical senses of one or more aliquot parts of a unit, the ratio between any two numbers, or a ratio of algebraic quantities analogous to the arithmetical vulgar fraction, are older by several centuries. But three hundred and fifty years of use by the best writers is surely enough to establish a usage as standard. None the less, with the spread of education the mathematical meaning has become the dominant one and those who object to using *fraction* to mean a small part (insisting that since 9/10ths is a fraction, a fraction need not necessarily be a small fragment) have a somewhat better case than they had fifty years ago. But still not a strong enough one, not yet at least, to insist that this common use of the word is an error. Partridge's designation of it as "infelicitous" is about as far as anyone can now go.

fractions. With the exception of *half* and *quarter,* the second term in a fraction is an ordinal number, such as *third, fourth, fifth.* But the fractions are not ordinals. They represent quantities. Unlike the cardinals, they are primarily nouns, but today, especially in scientific work, they are taking on the adjective uses characteristic of cardinals.

Because a fraction is a noun and represents a part of some whole, it is traditionally joined to a following noun by *of* and a definitive adjective (such as *a, the, this, my, all*), as in *one-third of the men, three-fifths of a mile.* In current English this *of* may be dropped, but not the definitive adjective, as in *one-third the men.* This is more likely to occur with simple fractions, such as *one-third,* than with more complicated ones, but we also say *it has nine-tenths the density of water.* When a pronoun follows a fraction, as in *three-fourths of them,* the *of* cannot be dropped.

A generation ago the expression *two miles and a quarter* was considered finer English than *two and a quarter miles,* because in the second form the noun *quarter* is being used as an adjective. Today, the second form is generally preferred. Both are acceptable.

One hyphen is used in a fraction, but not two. We write *one-twentieth* but *one twenty-fourth.* When fractions are expressed in figures, *of* and the definitive adjective are dropped and the following noun is made plural, as in ⅗ *miles.*

Decimals, which are a class of fractions, are always expressed in figures, as in *0.58 grams.*

A fraction may be treated as a singular or a plural, depending on whether it is thought of as a unit or as a certain number of individuals, as in *three-fourths of the surface of the earth is sea* and *three-fourths of the people are illiterate.* In speaking of human beings a plural verb is generally preferred, and we say *one percent are, one in ten are.*

Traditionally, a fraction that ends in *s,* and that is being used to indicate a physical distance, drops the *s* when it stands before another noun, as in *three-eighth inch plate.* It retains the *s* when it is used to measure anything except distance, as in *a two-thirds reduction, a three-fifths majority.* In the United States today these fractions usually retain the *s,* even in distance measurements, and the form without *s* is seldom heard. The word *three-quarters* is an exception to the rule. In literary English and in current speech, it may appear with or without the *s,* as in *a three-quarter majority, a three-quarters inch board.*

Fractions may be used as adverbs of measure, as in *the day is two-thirds gone, he is half dead.* With the exception of *half,* a fraction used in this way must begin with a numeral or the word *a.* We may say *it is one-quarter gone* or *a quarter gone,* but not *it is quarter gone.*

fragile; frail; brittle. That which is *fragile* is easily broken, shattered, or damaged. It must be handled with care to avoid breakage (*These spun glass flowers are extremely fragile*). *Frail* is simply a variant of *fragile* and in many contexts the two words are interchangeable; whatever is fragile is frail. But *frail* has acquired some special meanings of its own; everything that is frail is not necessarily fragile. *Frail,* in particular, applies to health and to immaterial things (*Though still active in his ninetieth year, he was very frail. Alas, her vows proved frail*). *Brittle* applies to anything that breaks readily with a comparatively smooth fracture (*Old bones are brittle*). It usually implies a hard outside finish on delicate material. It has always had metaphorical uses (*One woful day sweeps children, friends and wife/ And all the brittle blessings of my life*) and at the present is almost, in this use, a vogue word (*brittle wit, bright and brittle conversation*).

fragile; frangible. That is *frangible* which is capable of being broken. The word is usually restricted to material objects and literal breakableness. That is *fragile* which is easily broken, delicate, brittle, or frail. It might be said that human bones are frangible but that the bones of the aged are fragile.

frank, candid and **outspoken** imply a freedom from conventional reticence in speech, a blunt boldness, an uninhibited sincerity and plainness in speaking the truth. Virtues, surely, yet virtues that lend themselves so easily and so often as disguises for malice that the world, which doesn't like them very much anyway, reinforces its natural distaste with a justified suspicion. *Frank* is the least tainted of the three. *A frank and open countenance* is wholly laudatory. *A frank statement of the case,* however, is plainly colored by the speaker's agreement with the statement and *a frank criticism* may be a euphemism for a spiteful calumny. *Candid* suggests fairness, openness of mind, sincerity and truthfulness; yet there is often a suggestion of unpleasantness about the exercise of these admirable qualities. They are *outspoken* who express themselves freely, without reserve or concealment, even when it is inappropriate to do so. Such men, like Alceste in Moliere's *The Misanthrope,* displace all mirth and break many a good meeting with admir'd disorder, and while they are praised by the simple, especially those among the simple whose resentments their behavior has gratified, they are disliked by the more sophisticated.

Frankenstein. Properly *Frankenstein* was not the monster in Mary Shelley's book but the creator of the monster, a sensitive, high-minded young student who accidentally stumbled on "the secret of life" and bitterly rued the day he did. And even the monster himself, for all his resentful homicides, was not intended to be wholly repulsive. The novel was written as a Rousseauistic treatise on education; the monster was bad because he was unloved. None the less the term is now established ("almost, but surely not quite, sanctioned by custom," cries Fowler in a plea which he must have felt to be futile) as a name for any monstrous creation, especially one that threatens to destroy its creator (*The Republicans have created this Frankenstein. They must deal with him*). In the novel, by the way, the monster does not kill Frankenstein. Frankenstein dies from exposure while pursuing the fleeing monster across the arctic wastes.

frankly. How our hearts sink at a prefatory *frankly,* for we know some brutality is to follow, and a craven brutality, too, that having by this preface claimed a simple plainness will feel free to recoil in shocked horror, aghast at our brutality or pitying our inability to face the truth, should we reply in kind.

frantic; furious; rabid. To be *frantic* is to be wild with excitement, whether it be of passion, delight, fear, or pain, to be in a state of frenzy, bordering on delirium (*As the night passed and the child could not be found the woman grew frantic and could scarcely be restrained by her neighbors from rushing out into the storm*). *Furious* suggests great violence, the releasing of tremendous (usually malignant) energies (*At the bursting of the oil storage tank the flames surged furiously upwards and engulfed the remainder of the building*). When applied to human beings, it suggests, like *frantic,* a state of violence close to madness, but *furious* suggests a more outward-directed, aggressive violence, anger carried to the extreme (*On receipt of the news he was furious and ordered the hostages to be massacred*). *Rabid* means raving mad, irrational in the extreme, furious, raving, but it is usually applied to the carrying to excess of some one concern (*The rabid isolationists would have had us discontinue even commercial rela-*

tions with all other nations. He was rabid on the subject).

free and easy. As an adjectival phrase meaning unconstrained, unaffected, or careless, *free and easy,* even though it may sometimes be used effectively, is hackneyed.

free for nothing and often *free, gratis, for nothing* are once-humorous tautologies that have long ago lost their humor and should be avoided.

free will; freewill. *Free will* is the term for voluntary decision or for the doctrine that the conduct of human beings is not utterly determined by physical or divine forces (*He did it of his own free will. Nobody forced him to do it*). *Freewill* is the adjective (*a freewill offering*). It also applies to the doctrine of freedom of the will (*The freewill controversy has long been agitated*).

freeze. The past tense is *froze.* The participle is *frozen.*

freight; cargo; shipment. *Freight* means the ordinary conveyance of goods by common carriers, as opposed to express. Or the goods so carried. In English usage *freight* is applied only to goods transported by water. But in American usage, though this meaning would certainly be understood, the term is restricted almost entirely to goods carried on land or in the air (*The amount of freight carried by the railroads and trucks . . . Air freight is becoming increasingly popular*). *Cargo* is the term for goods carried by ship and a *shipment* is a quantity of goods destined for a particular place, no matter how sent (*The Nancy's cargo consisted of potatoes and sugar beets. We are sending you a shipment by air express tomorrow morning*).

frequent; common. *Frequent* now means occurring at short intervals of time (*He made frequent trips to New York that winter*) or of space (*Burr oaks were frequent in the park*). It also means constant or regular (*William Jennings Bryan was a frequent visitor in my grandfather's house*). In the sense of common (in such a sentence as *It is a frequent practice to speak of socialism and communism as if they were the same thing*), however, *frequent* is now quite rare. See also **recurring.**

frequently. See **often.**

fresh. In the sense of forward, impudent, conceitedly intrusive or familiar, *fresh* is purely American slang, probably the German *frech* (impudent, saucy) adapted to English pronunciation. At one time it was so common that it looked as though it were going to become standard but it is now a little outdated and though universally understood in the United States not so often heard. This may have been due to the fact that at its height it acquired so strong a connotation of unwanted sexual advances (*Don't get fresh with me or I'll slap your face*) that it became slightly indelicate. See also **breezy.**

fresh as a daisy is a wilted metaphor.

fret and fume. *Fret* is an intensive form of *eat* (cf. German *fressen*). It means to devour and, applied chiefly to the manner in which animals eat, came also to mean to gnaw. The thought of worry, impatience, and frustration as eating one internally is, apparently, a natural thought. We have not only such poetic thoughts as "eating one's heart out" but the slang term "What's eating you?" or "What's eating on you?" In addition to the idea of chafing (*Falstaff frets like gummed velvet*), there is in the word *fret* a connotation of querulous complaining.

To *fume* is to smoke, and the idea of heat also seems to be naturally associated with chafing, probably as a metaphorical carryover from the physical heat that accompanies physical chafing. And here again the idea is expressed in slang (*Boy, was he burned up when he heard what she'd done! A slow burn*) as well as in standard English, showing that it is still a vital idea.

To *fret and fume,* to gnaw one's own inwards with such fury that they smoke, was once, therefore, a powerful metaphor. But the alliteration that probably suggested the phrase in the first place has kept it, as alliteration often does, in use long after its vigor has been exhausted.

Freudian. See **Rabelaisian.**

Freudian English. The effect of Freud on the English language has been profound, far-reaching and, it would seem, enduring. His impact was first felt shortly after World War I when the avant-garde began using his special nomenclature and such words and terms as *id, libido, superego, subconscious, Oedipus complex* and *inferiority complex* became familiar. As time went on and more people acquired a knowledge of Freud's principles and methods, words like *hallucination, fixation* and *compulsion,* which had formerly been confined to rather restricted and often technical use, found their way into common speech. In a generation there has been such a complete acceptance of these and other psychiatric terms, especially in relation to education, that any suburban PTA meeting would sound to our fathers like a psychiatric clinic.

What is more, many words of general meaning have become so endowed with psychiatric connotations that the newer overtones have supplanted the older ones in many professional and social circles. In such groups words like *anxiety, hostility, dependency, aggressive* and *insecure* are now more often used for their psychological import than for their original meanings.

Along with use has gone misuse. As the terminology seeps down to the less educated, by way of Sunday supplements, digested articles, slick fiction and TV jokes, there is still some cachet to be derived from the use of psychiatric terms. There is always somebody, seemingly, on the next level lower down to be impressed. It is possibly this that has been responsible for the common misuse of *phobia* for *obsession* and *moron* for *psychopath.* In 1951 it was suggested at a meeting of the American Psychiatric Association that *neurosis, psychosis* and *psychoneurosis* be dropped as diagnostic terms because their original meaning [whatever that may have been] had been obscured through excessive and careless use.

Many a psychiatric term has become small change in social conversation: "She can't decide between blue or green for the walls—she's absolutely schizzy about it." Or "I'm feeling good—this is one of my manic days." Or "All his hostilities come out in games."

Comedians and cartoonists have found psychiatry a fertile field. Mother-fixations, obsessions, compulsions and irrational fears have taken the place of the once popular but now strictly forbidden racial jokes. The psychiatrist and his couch are now as solid staples in *The New Yorker* as the bishop and his gaiters formerly were in *Punch*.

friable means easily crumbled or reduced to powder (*Sandstone is friable*). If one had to refer to the suitability of some substance to be fried, the word would be fryable, though the absence of such a word from the dictionaries suggests that there is not much doubt in these matters.

friend. See **personal friend.**

friend in need. Although the proverb *A friend in need is a friend indeed* assumed that exact, jingling form as late as 1772, the idea—that he who befriends us in our hour of need thereby shows himself to be a true friend—is very old, some version of it existing in almost all languages. The saying is slightly ambiguous. To the cynical it could mean *When a friend is in need, then he makes much of his friendship*. But, whatever the interpretation, the phrase has been thoroughly overworked.

frighten; alarm; terrify; scare; intimidate. *Frighten* is the everyday working word. It can mean the arousing of many degrees and kinds of fear (*Don't frighten the children with these silly stories. The hydrogen bomb is a frightening thing*). To *alarm* is to cause a milder degree of fear than to frighten. It is, strictly, merely an alerting at the possibility of danger, but except in the most hardened veterans even that has always its element of fear (*I don't want to alarm you, but it seems to me that, etc. . . .*). *Terrify* is a strong word. It means to create or communicate an intense, overmastering fear (*At the sight of the onrushing train he became terrified and flung himself furiously against the jammed door*). To *scare* is to strike with sudden terror. It was once a serious and even solemn word (*Then thou scarest me with dreams, and terrifiest me through visions*) but overuse has weakened it and humorous use, especially in America (*scared out of his wits, more scared than hurt, scare the pants off*) has removed its dignity. To *scare up*, from frightening game out of cover, has become, in American usage, a term for discovering or bringing to light, usually used humorously (*See if you can scare up a fourth for bridge. If you can scare up some cash we'll join you*). To *intimidate* can mean to frighten, but it's rather formal in that sense; it usually means to deter by threats of violence (*One party is bribed, the other intimidated. The parade, at that particular time, looked suspiciously like intimidation*).

frightened is used in speaking of a particular event, as in *he was frightened by a dog*. In speaking of a chronic condition, we say *afraid*, as in *he is afraid of dogs*. The combination *frightened of* is not standard English.

frock (the origin of the word is unknown) was for centuries applied to a loose outer garment worn by men. Monks wore frocks. Disgraced priests were unfrocked. Peasants wore frocks and smocks and often both. Matthew Arnold refers to *the smock-frocked boors*. Then the term got applied to children's clothes, coveralls of some kind, and finally settled down as a term for a little girl's dress. Or at least one would have thought it had settled there but the dressmakers suddenly took it up about the turn of the century as a chic term, one of those affected simplicities cultivated by expensive shops, for a woman's dress, usually an elegant and expensive dress. Once that was established, however, the term was exploited for the benefit of cheaper dresses. Fowler called it "a nurseryism of the same kind as *nighty & shimmy*" but it did no good. This sense is now standard and, indeed, the first meaning of the word.

from. The basic meaning of *from* is moving away. It can also be used to show cause or motive, as in *to crumble from its own weight*, and *suffering from senile dementia;* the grounds for a judgment, as in *it is clear from the language;* or the distant source of an action, as in *abuse from such men* and *dangerous cuts from a sabre*.

From frequently combines with the words *out, out of, off*, which have similar meanings. These combinations should not be condemned as redundant because the words here strengthen and supplement each other. *From out* is used by almost all the great writers of English. *From out of* is found in the King James Bible and the writings of Bunyan, Thackeray, Wells, Galsworthy, James, Quiller-Couch, and others. *From off* is also standard English but it is now felt to be archaic or poetic. One might say *lift this weight from off my heart,* but under ordinary circumstances we would say *will you take this off my hands*.

Verbs of withholding or hiding are regularly used with *from*, as in *don't conceal it from me*.

Many verbs whose Latin meaning contains the idea of *from*, such as *depart, refrain, expel, dismiss,* are given an additional *from* in current American speech, as in *he was expelled from the university*. When more people read Latin than do today, these verbs were often joined directly to the object, as in *he was expelled the university*. This is still heard in Great Britain, but in the United States it survives only in a few set phrases, such as *to depart this life*.

from A to Z. As a term for thoroughly, from beginning to end, *from A to Z* has become a cliché. The rustic, backwoods form of the phrase, *from A to izzard,* is occasionally heard but it is either humorous or affected. *Izzard* (or *uzzard*) was an old name for *z* or *zed*. Indeed Johnson in his dictionary (1755) referred to it as the "more common" form. *Alpha and Omega,* be-

cause of its Biblical origin and the solemnity of
its use in the Scriptures (Revelation, 1:8), has
more dignity, but it is also used too frequently.

from the cradle to the grave, as a term for all
of life, has become a cliché.

from time immemorial. As a term for that which
has endured from beyond memory or record,
something of great antiquity, *from time immemorial* is hackneyed.

front was originally the forehead (*The very head
and front of my offending. How now, daughter?
What makes that frontlet on? Methinks you are
too much o' late i' th' frown*). To *affront*, by the
way, is to strike on the forehead, to slap the
face, and *effrontery* means being devoid of a
forehead, *i.e.,* having nothing to blush with.

It was a natural extension for *front* to come
to mean the entire face (*Front to front bring
this fiend of Scotland and myself*) and then the
foremost part or surface of anything. It is not
desirable, however, to use it, as it is often used,
to mean the beginning. The front of a book, for
example, is the jacket or cover, not the first
chapter.

frontier. In English usage the word *frontier* means
only that part of a country which borders on
another country (*We were stopped at the
frontier and our luggage was searched*). This is
the primary meaning of the word in America,
but we have another meaning which is almost
as important, namely that part of a country
which forms the border of its settled regions,
outlying settlements (*'Tis wonderful how soon
a piano gets into a log-hut on the frontier*). This
has been extended to include the incompletely
developed regions of a field of knowledge
(*New frontiers of the mind. The frontiers of
physics are now the intellectuals' great hunting
grounds*).

froth. See **foam.**

froze; frozen. See **freeze.**

frugal. See **economical.**

frustrate. See **flurry.**

frustum. The plural is *frustums* or *frusta.*

frying-pan into the fire, out of the. One of the
oldest and most widespread of proverbs, based
on the agonized struggles of a fish being cooked
alive, *out of the frying-pan into the fire* has been
overworked to the point where it must be classed
as a cliché and the thoughtful writer or speaker,
when expressing himself formally, will find some
other way of saying that someone's efforts to
get out of a bad situation have only precipitated
him into a worse one.

fulcrum. The plural is *fulcrums* or *fulcra.*

full; -ful. Almost any container can be used as a
measure of quantity, and this measure can be
expressed in either of two ways. The name of
the container may be followed by the adjective
full, as in *a teaspoon full of water,* or a new
noun may be formed with the suffix *-ful,* as in
a teaspoonful of water. In either case, the plural
is formed by adding *s* to the noun, as *two teaspoons full* or *two teaspoonfuls.*

There is no logical difference between these
two forms. One may drink two glasses full of

milk without dirtying two glasses, just as one may
have another cup of coffee without getting a
second cup. The difference is one of tone or
style. The newer form, with *-ful,* is generally
preferred for familiar measures, such as *teaspoonfuls,* and the older form, with *full,* for less
familiar ones, such as *bins full.* The newer form
has a businesslike, matter-of-fact tone. But the
older form is more vivid and it should always
be used in an exaggeration or a metaphor, as in
he has buckets full of money.

function. To *function* is to perform a function and
a function is an act proper to a person, thing,
or institution. A functionary is an official who
has a specific duty to perform. When we say
*The honors committee could not function if
denied access to the registrar's records,* we are
using the word correctly, because the committee
could not perform its specific duty without these
records. It could *act* without them. It might file
a protest. It might vote its own dissolution. But
in neither of these acts would it be functioning
as the honors committee. Some, to be on the
safe side, insist the word should be restricted to
machinery or to "an organ that works like a
machine" because these things can do only one
thing and that thing is their function. But this
is sacrificing expression on the altar of precision
and grammatical safety and, fortunately, there
isn't the faintest hope or fear that the common
speaker will ever comply.

When used, as a noun, of a social gathering,
function refers to some formal meeting or public
ceremony (*The Governor's ball is the most important function of our social season*). It is misusing the word to apply it to any informal
gathering.

funds are pecuniary resources, money on hand
(*His funds were insufficient to meet his creditors'
demands*). It is pompous to use the word merely
as a synonym for *cash* or *money.*

funeral; funereal. *Funeral* was originally an adjective. But it has been used as a substantive so
long that it can now be used as an adjective
only in the attributive position (*funeral home,
funeral procession*). So much of funerals is
ceremony and business and social that *funereal*
has been set aside by usage to designate the
dismal, melancholy, and mournful aspects of a
funeral (*Though the news was not unexpected,
the company sank into funereal gloom at its
announcement*).

If occasion should arise for an adjective
meaning of or pertaining to a funeral, but not
pertaining to the melancholy and mournful
aspects and not to be used attributively, the
word would be either *funebrial* (or *funebrious*)
or *funerary.*

fungous; fungoid; fungal. *Fungous* means of or
pertaining to, caused by, or of the nature of or
resembling a fungus. *Fungal* is a little-used
synonym. *Fungoid* also means resembling a
fungus or of the nature of a fungus, but it is
largely restricted, as a technical term, to botany
and pathology.

fungus. The plural is *funguses* or *fungi.*

funny; comical; droll; ludicrous; ridiculous; laughable; risible. All of these words mean laughter-provoking, but they indicate different degrees and different kinds of laughter.

Funny is the commonest word, the most general, the most innocent and the mildest (*He's a very funny man. It was so funny we laughed till we were helpless*). In the plural, as a noun, *funnies,* the word is undergoing an interesting change in the United States. Applied to the comic strips which, originally, were or tried to be funny, it got established. But very few comic strips now make any pretense of being funny. They are simply illustrated serial stories of adventure or mishap, many of them gruesome and horrible. But the word sticks and that is the way language grows (*I don't like Jimmy to read all those funnies. They scare the boy to death and he has nightmares*).

Comical keeps a slight suggestion of its derivation from *comedy* in that it is applied almost entirely to something seen (*He had such a comical expression, I had to laugh. He was a comical little kid, the way he used to walk around with that old hat on*). The laughter is described as kindly, but it is a little stronger word than *funny.*

Droll is amusingly queer. It implies something odd or unfamiliar (*a droll fellow, a droll idea*), even slightly absurd, but attractive in its absurdity.

That is *ludicrous* which excites sport, is laughable for its singularity, or adapted to cause sportive laughter or ridicule. It is a stronger word than *funny* or *comical* but not wholly unkind (*It was ludicrous of Shelley to assume that the Irish would welcome him as a deliverer*). It is often applied to people who do absurd things with good motives.

Ridiculous also means exciting to laughter, but the laughter excited by ridicule is contemptuous and derisive. The word is a diminutive; it means "little laughter," snickering, furtive laughter. We may tell *ludicrous* stories about our friends or relatives but ought not, in loyalty, to tell stories that make them seem *ridiculous.*

Laughable plainly means that which elicits laughter and may be applied to any kind of laughter. Usage has tinged it slightly with the idea of derision. If it were used to mean innocent, happy laughter, that fact would have to be made clear in the context.

Risible is a learned word for laughable but since the learned are particularly inclined to derision, it has a somewhat stronger suggestion of contempt, unless the context makes a kindly meaning plain (*The mutual civilities of authors is one of the most risible scenes in the farce of life*).

funny; strange. The use of *funny* for *strange* or *odd* or *peculiar* (*She was very funny about the whole business, seemed to want it done but seemed to not want it done at the same time. You know, it gave me a funny feeling, like being hit in the stomach*) is widespread and not without a charm in the innocent way in which it reveals the simpleton in us that finds the strange laughable.

furious. See **frantic.**

further; furthest. See **far.**

future tense. In American English we can always speak of a future event by using the word *will* followed by the simple form of a verb, as in *he will speak tomorrow.* (In England *shall* is used instead of *will* in some persons and some types of sentences. See **shall; will.**) This combination of verb forms is what we ordinarily mean when we speak of "the future tense." It cannot be used with the auxiliary *do* to make an emphatic statement. We cannot say *he does will speak.* But with this one exception, all the variations found in the present and the past tenses can also be expressed in the future.

To express action completed in the future we use *will* followed by *have* and the past participle of the verb, as in *by then he will have spoken.* This is called the future perfect tense. Both the simple future and the future perfect may be expressed as progressive or continuing action, as in *he will be speaking tomorrow* and *by then he will have been speaking for an hour.* And all four forms may be expressed in the passive voice, as in *it will be discussed tomorrow, by then it will have been discussed, it will be being discussed tomorrow,* and *by then it will have been being discussed for an hour.* The last form, with five elements in the verbal phrase, is an extremely complex construction. It frightens some writers, but it is acceptable English and is often used in speech without attracting attention. See **passive voice.**

The word *will* itself is actually a present tense form and has the past tense *would.* When any of these future tense phrases have to be shifted to a past tense, the *will* is changed to *would,* as in *he promised me he would speak tomorrow* and *I knew that it would be being discussed tomorrow.* See **tense shifts** and **will; would.**

Speaking historically, English, like the other Germanic languages, has only two tense forms, a present and a past. We have several ways of speaking of a future event but they all express the future by means of a present tense verb.

In Old English a simple present tense was often used in speaking of the future. This type of sentence is still popular, especially with verbs of motion, as in *the boat sails next Wednesday, the train leaves in an hour, he arrives tomorrow.* Here the fact that we are speaking about a future event is not shown by the verb itself but by the time words that are used with it, such as *next Wednesday* and *tomorrow.* In current English the progressive form of the present tense is used freely in speaking of the future, with verbs of motion or any other kind of verb, as in *we are seeing them next Wednesday* and *we are eating dinner with my parents tomorrow.* Today a simple present tense form is required in conditional clauses and in temporal clauses that actually refer to the future, as in *if he comes,*

I will tell him and *I will see him when he comes.*

In Old English the verb *will* was also used as an auxiliary to indicate the future, very much as it is in America today. This verb means primarily to desire or to be willing, but it loses this meaning when it is accepted as a conventional sign of the future tense. Later, the verb *shall,* with its past tense *should,* was used as the future auxiliary in literary English. This verb means primarily to be obliged or ought, but it too lost this meaning when it became a mere sign of the future, as in *goodness and mercy shall follow me all the days of my life.* Some of these Middle English *shall*'s and *should*'s are still in use in Great Britain.

In many languages (including Eskimo) the future tense can be used as a courteous substitute for an imperative, as it is in *you will report to the commanding officer at once.* In the **King James Bible** *shall* is the future auxiliary and has exactly the force of our present-day American *will.* The *shall* used in the Biblical commandments had the same tone for the translators of the Bible that the *will* used in military orders has for us today. But it is likely that this use of *shall* was confined to literary English and that for most people in the seventeenth century *will* was the sign of the future and *shall* kept its primary sense of obligation. For those who read very little except the Bible the word became a solemn and awful imperative, an imperative such as only God could use, in spite of the fact that the prophets frequently speak of what the Lord *shall* and shall not do. The words *shall* and *should* have kept a great deal of this meaning in American English. See **shall; should.**

Forms of the verb *to be* followed by a *to-*infinitive, as in *we are to see them tomorrow,* have been used to indicate futurity since about the year 1200. Forms of *to be* followed by *going* and a *to-*infinitive, as in *we are going to see them tomorrow,* first appeared around 1450 and did not become popular until two hundred years later. Today, the older form, without *going,* usually suggests necessity or obligation and is similar in meaning to *shall.* (See also **have.**) The newer form, with *going,* is equivalent to *will.* These verbal phrases can be used in the passive voice, as in *the estate is to be divided* and *the estate is going to be divided.* They are not used in progressive action or completed action tenses, although these are theoretically possible. They cannot be used with the auxiliary verb *do.* But they can be used to express what was future at some time in the past, or futurity in the past, as in *he was to leave* and *he was going to leave.* This is a valuable distinction that cannot be expressed with the auxiliaries *will* or *shall. He would have left* refers to the past, but it can only be used in a contrary to fact statement. In the United States today, *is going to* with its various forms is used more often than *will* in making a statement about the future. And *is to* with its forms is generally preferred to *shall.*

G

gall. In its standard figurative use *gall* means bitterness of spirit or rancor (*Such experiences change the milk of human kindness into gall*). In its slang American use it means impudence or effrontery (*Imagine him having the gall to tell me that he didn't know anything about it!*).

gallon. The standard *gallon* in the United States is the old Winchester or wine-gallon. It contains 231 cubic inches. The British imperial gallon contains 277½ cubic inches. This is the gallon used in Canada.

gallows. This word is both a singular and a plural. We may say *there was a gallows* and *there were many gallows.* The double plural *gallowses* is not standard.

galore is a Gaelic word. In America it is standard use as a humorous word (*Bargains galore!*) but in England, where the Irish influence is not so marked, its use is rarer, something of an affectation.

gamble is slightly pejorative. Though the word means to play a game for stakes. it has the connotation of playing for high stakes, of taking dangerous risks (*a notorious gambler. Any man who cuts out of line on a hill is gambling with his life and the lives of those who are approaching*). People who play bridge for a cent a point or put two dollars on a horse at the racetrack would be annoyed to be told that they were gambling. The milder term is *to play for stakes.*

game. In America all wild animals, including birds and fishes, that are hunted or taken for sport or profit are called *game* (*The streams and forests of the frontier were rich in game*). In England the term is more restricted, being confined to hare, pheasant, partridge, grouse, and moor fowl.

gamesmanship is the art of winning games without actually cheating, and is the most comprehensive of the skills analyzed by Stephen Potter. Its major subsidiaries are lifemanship (an adaptation of the principles of gamesmanship to the smaller world of life) and one-upmanship, the art of being one up on the other fellow by making him feel that something has gone slightly wrong. They all have the same methods in common; and although certain physical gambits, ploys and accessories may be used, the basic strategy is intimidation by conversation.

Gamesmanship encompasses such specialized fields as guestmanship, luncheonship, bridgemanship, losemanship, clothesmanship, clubmanship, etc. Each of these sub-classes has its own peculiar ploys, hampers and blocks, all designed to "break the flow" of the opponent's success.

The use of O.K. words—those currently stylish with Highbrowmen—is of the utmost importance for one-upness. *Mystique* and *classique,* for example, were O.K. in 1951. Mr. Potter promised a monthly list of O.K. words, but this may have been merely a ploy, for no list has appeared. The New Criticism should be able to provide a host of such terms.

There are also O.K. names and subjects, especially useful in writership, but here too it is imperative that they be up-to-date. It is some time now since T. S. Eliot had full O.K. status; Rilke and Kafka were very O.K. 1945-50, but their vogue is fading. But there is always someone new that the opponent has not yet had time to read.

Related to writership is Reviewer's Basic, requiring a special vocabulary but one which is perfectly clear to the cognoscenti. In accord with a fundamental tenet of gamesmanship, attacks are always friendly and begin with faint praise. "I'm afraid . . ." is a good start. Certain words are especially valuable. Thus *catholic* means too wide in treatment to be anything but superficial. *Well-produced* means badly written. *Painstaking* means dull. Any oblique praise can be effective. Chaucer's description of the monk as "A manly man, to been an abbot able" was a masterly piece of early gamesmanship, as was also his praise of the Prioress's French.

Many a reviewer has been able to get one up on a famous writer by condemning him for not having enough of the quality he is distinguished for. Potter gives an example: "The one thing that was lacking, of course, from D. H. Lawrence's novels, was the consciousness of sexual relationship, the male and female element in life." Such an utterance, made in a firm voice and accompanied by a fixed stare, is warranted to shake the stoutest conviction.

Lowbrowmanship is a favorite device of the highbrow. If the opponent has boned up on Masaccio's additions to Masolino's frescoes, express a great interest in Li'l Abner. Though it would perhaps be well, in passing, to refer to Masolino by his real name of Tommaso di Cristoforo Fini just to show that you passed *that* stage long ago. Sometimes three or four words will suffice to get you one up. Potter suggests a splendid ploy: "What, you stayed for the Debussy?"

Well-readship is an area where there can be a good deal of cut-and-thrust. The new-

bookman must be on his toes to counter against the gamesman who has snatched a new book hot from the presses so that he can discuss it on publication day. He has the option of saying either "Let me lend you the American (or English) edition. It's beautifully printed and hasn't got that stupid cut on page 163" or "Good old Pontefract—still churning them out." The former of the two is the better; it suggests not merely that the gamesman has already read the book but that he has collated several editions and is possessed of some particularly fine bit of knowledge that the opponent, in his plodding way, missed.

General conversation offers the gamesman his finest opportunities however. There are many ploys, but two are worth special mention: "languaging up" and "the simple Canterbury block." "Languaging up" consists of confusing, irritating or depressing the opponent by the use of foreign words, fictitious or genuine. And here, again, Chaucer shows the antiquity of the ploy and his own understanding of it when he has the Pardoner say that in his preaching he always brings in a little Latin "to saffron his predication." The Canterbury block is a device for deflating the expert and can best be explained by giving two of Potter's examples. It consists of going the expert one better by adding some little knowing touch to one of his most learned utterances.

> *Expert (who has just come back from a fortnight in Florence): And I was glad to see with my own eyes that this Left-wing Catholicism is definitely on the increase in Tuscany.*
> *The Canterbury: Yes, but not in the South.*

or

> *Expert: There can be no relationship based on a mutual dependency of neutral markets. Otto Hüsch would not have allowed that. He was in Vienna at the time . . .*
> *Lifeman (as if explaining to the rest of the audience): It was Hüsch who prevented the Archbishop from taking office in Sofia.*

Time is deft with this ploy. Mentioning, say, a George X. Marshall in their text, who has just been sentenced for embezzlement or mopery, they will direct the reader, by means of an asterisk and footnote, not to confuse this individual with General George C. Marshall, former Secretary of State, or George Q. Marshall who operates a laundromat in Xochimilco.

gamp. See **gimp.**

gangster. See **thief; robber; burglar.**

gantlet. See **gauntlet.**

gap; gape. A *gap* was originally a breach in a wall or hedge. *To stop two gapps with one bush* was once a proverb, akin to *to kill two birds with one stone.* It also meant an opening in a range of mountains, a use rare in England but common in the United States (*The Delaware Water Gap, The Cumberland Gap. We reached* *the gap, which was like a deep notch cut in the mountain-ridge*). From all of this it is applied to any opening in an otherwise closed row or series (*There was quite a gap where his tooth had been knocked out*). The verb *to gap*, to make a gap in or to be subject to gaps, is rare.

To *gape* is to open the mouth involuntarily, whether from hunger, sleepiness, or absorbed attention (*The mouths of the hungry fledglings gaped frantically, ludicrously. He gaped and scratched his head. "Time to turn in," he said. Fickle changelings and poor discontents,/ Which gape and rub the elbow at the news/ Of hurlyburly innovation*). A *gape* is a breach or rent or the act of gaping. The *gapes* is a disease of poultry characterized by gaping.

garb. The use of *garb* for clothing or *garbed* for clothed is slightly affected. Those who use it are seeking to be elegant or archaic or else, afflicted with a terrible fear that they might have to use *clothing* or *clothed* twice in one sentence or one paragraph, are desperate.

garment for an article of dress is now rhetorical, forcedly elegant. It originally meant an overall outer vestment of some kind (*This city now doth, like a garment, wear/ The beauty of the morning*). Its very elegance and rhetorical nature has made it, in the term *undergarments*, a euphemism in the United States for underwear or underclothing. Even so, it is a little affected.

garnish; garnishee. To *garnish* is to fit out with something which adorns or decorates. Its commonest application is to the decoration of a dish or platter just before it is set on the table (*Garnish with parsley and serve*). It has a number of metaphorical uses (*Vice garnishes her deeds with many a virtuous seeming*).

To *garnishee* is to attach money or property, usually wages, in claim of some debt. The word also applies to the person whose property is so attached. *Garnish* is also used in this sense, but rarely.

garret; attic; loft. A *garret* was originally a turret on top of or projecting from a fortification. Picturesque as these protuberances are, they were apparently squalidly miserable dwelling quarters, for *garret,* of all the words for the topmost story of a house, has a sordid connotation. Perhaps poets made too much of their poverty and of the fact, at the same time, that they lived in garrets. *Attic* to many people has a romantic, nostalgic connotation. They remember the interesting objects stored there, the musty smell, the joys of clandestine rummaging. A *loft* is usually a space open to the rafters of the roof used for storing things, as a hayloft over a barn, or a sail loft.

gas; gasoline. As an abbreviation of *gasoline, gas* is condemned by many authorities. But fifty million motorists are cheerfully unaware of this and would be completely indifferent if they were informed. The purists might as well attempt to chain the wind. The English, by the way, with their *petrol* don't have the problem, though sentries on their linguistic ramparts have re-ported uneasily that *step on the gas* has been heard there. *Gasolene* is an accepted variant spelling, but *gasoline* is preferred.

gauntlet; gantlet. There are two wholly different words spelled *gauntlet*. One, a diminutive of the French *gant*, glove, is the medieval knight's mailed glove which he threw down in challenge (*And casting out, as it were, his gauntlet of defiance*). The word is also applied now to wristlets and to gloves with a cufflike extension to cover the wrist.

The other word *gauntlet* or *gantlet* was earlier *gantlope* (so spelled as late as 1836), deriving from a Swedish word *gatlopp* in which *gat* was a lane or narrow way and *lopp*, a run. It described a military punishment in which the offender had to run between two rows of men who struck at him with switches and even weapons as he ran—*to run the gantlet*.

Though either word may be spelled either way, *gauntlet* is preferred for the glove and *gantlet* for the punishment.

gave. See **give.**

gay Lothario. Occasionally a minor character in literature will become detached from the context in which he or she first appeared and attain an unexpected immortality by being fixed in the language. Yankee Doodle is, in a way, one of these. Mrs. Grundy, a strait-laced and censorious neighbor of whose opinions farmer Ashfield's wife (in Thomas Morton's play *Speed the Plough*, 1798) stood in great awe, has become the type of nosy, middle-class respectability. Lothario, whose name when coupled with "gay" has become a cliché for a light-hearted libertine, was a character in Nicholas Rowe's *The Fair Penitent* (1703). Dame Grundy, by the way, does not even appear on the stage. Fame is capricious even among shadows.

gay nineties. The American term for the last decade of the nineteenth century is the *gay nineties*. In England it is called the *naughty nineties*. Both phrases are tedious clichés.

geese. See **goose.**

gender; sex. Gender is a grammatical device, used in inflected languages, for associating an adjective or a pronoun with the appropriate noun. English shows these relationships by the position of the words in the sentence. It does not have gender, although English grammarians sometimes use the term in connection with words showing sex distinctions (such as the pronouns *he, she,* etc.).

Gender may have been based on physical distinctions originally, but it is hard to say what they were. In some languages round, square, and oblong seem to be basic characteristics. Some languages have more genders than others. French, for example, has two and the Bantu languages have twenty. In any case, gender is not a grammatical reflection of sex. In Old English, which had three genders, *wife* was neuter, *woman* masculine, *moon* masculine, and *sun* feminine.

Sex distinctions, where they exist, are stronger

in English than in languages that have gender. In English *he* and *his* refer to actual males, *she* and *her* to actual females, and *it* and *its* to things without personality. In languages that have gender, the pronouns do not have such a clear reference to sex and the masculine form can be used in speaking indiscriminately of both males and females. According to the theoretical rules of grammar, this is also true in English and the sentence *either the boy or the girl left his book* is technically correct. But in actual practice this construction cannot be used. The pronoun *his* simply will not refer to *girl,* no matter what the rules in the grammar books say.

According to some textbooks this problem can be solved by writing *either the boy or the girl left his or her book.* This is intolerable. In spoken English, the usual solution is to use the plural pronouns *they* and *their,* which do not make a sex distinction, and say *either the boy or the girl left their book.* The wrong number does not seem to disturb us as much as the wrong sex. This solution is unacceptable to some grammarians, who insist that a plural pronoun must not be used in referring to a singular noun. But the construction is now appearing in some of our best literature. Hemingway, for example, writes *why does everybody think they can write?*

Sometimes things or ideas are personified and referred to as *he* or *she.* When this is done, the sex frequently corresponds to the Latin gender of the word. For example, the moon is made feminine and the sun, masculine. This is a purely literary device, a sort of metaphor, and not part of the grammar of the language.

A faint trace of true gender, that is, a distinction which does not reflect sex or imply personification, is sometimes seen in English. In this more or less unconscious classification, *it* seems to refer to what does not interest us greatly. Things that we are interested in take a *he* or a *she.* If the things are inanimate they are referred to (especially by men) as *she,* as, in speaking of a train, *here she comes,* or of a car, *fill her up,* or of any machine, *isn't she a beauty.* When the sex is unknown, interesting animals, such as a runaway horse or a bear one has seen, are usually referred to as *he.* This is a recent development. In Biblical English *she* and not *he* is used in this way. And in current English there are exceptions, of course. Cats are usually *she.* One grammarian explains this by saying: "In speaking of a cat, the use of *he* would invoke a somewhat offensive allusion to sex."

Some English nouns refer to one sex and not to the other, as do *king* and *queen, boy* and *girl.* Some nouns which refer to both sexes can be limited to the female only, by means of a suffix, as in the case of *lion* and *lioness, aviator* and *aviatrix.* At one time these female nouns were very popular, and people talked about poetesses and doctoresses. Today they are out of fashion. In current English the general term is preferred to the sex-limited one and women are called *poets* and *doctors.* Compounds ending in *man*

can be applied to women, as in *Madame Chairman* and *she was a good horseman* or *a good penman.* It is even possible to say *the boats were manned by women.*

genera. See **genus.**

generic nouns. Any noun, except possibly a proper name, can be used in a generic sense to make a statement about a type of thing rather than about some individuals of that type, as in *the leopard shall lie down with the kid.* What is true of the type is true of all the individuals, and this is therefore a statement about all leopards and all kids. *Man is mortal* and *men are mortal* mean the same thing. Both are generic statements because both say something about all men. (The claim that *men perish but man shall endure* is a play on words, and is probably false. The word *men* is here first used generically to mean *all men* and is then put grammatically in contrast to the generic name *man.* From this we are supposed to conclude that the type may be different from the individuals. This is one of countless dilemmas that grow out of the notion that a grammatical distinction is necessarily a logical one.)

Words that are true singulars (not mass nouns) require the article *the* when used generically, as in *the whale is a mammal.* (The singular forms *man* and *woman* are the only exceptions to this.) On the other hand, mass nouns and true plurals do not have an article when used generically, as in *milk is good for you* and *whales are mammals.* When words of this kind are qualified by *the, this, that,* or any definitive adjective, they mean a particular lot and not the type generally, as in *the milk is sour* and *the whales sounded.* (Plural nouns referring to human beings are an exception. *The Germans* and *the chemists* may mean all of them or some of them, depending on the context.)

The use of a singular noun in speaking about a large number of individuals is sometimes confusing. For example, the statement in Exodus 7:18, *the fish that is in the river shall die,* is about all the fishes in the river. But children sometimes suppose that there was only one fish in the Nile at that time. Adults usually understand the plural meaning, but they sometimes conclude that the word itself is a plural. This is a mistake. Although a singular generic noun may refer to a number of individuals, it is a singular and is used with a singular verb, except in the case of certain animal names.

In speaking of animals that are hunted for profit, the singular name may be used generically with a plural verb, as in *the bear are hibernating* and *the sea otter have disappeared.* This does not apply to domestic animals, such as *cows* and *dogs,* or to animals that are a menace and are killed for self-protection, such as *lions* and *weasels.* For these animals we use a singular verb, as in *the dog is a friend to man* and *the lion is dangerous.* When the generic singular is used with a plural verb it is grammatically indistinguishable from a group name. In fact, the species is here being treated as a group. The singular word refers to all of a given kind, collectively. It is not a plural word and cannot be used with a numeral. In standard English we do not speak of *a few otter* or *three bear.*

Hunters sometimes use these singular nouns as if they were plurals. Of course, if enough people do this the singular form finally becomes an accepted plural, as in the case of *fish.* Singulars of this kind, which have become standard plurals, are shown in this book, but no attempt has been made to list all the singulars that may be treated as plurals by sportsmen.

Adjectives can be used with the article *the* as if they were generic nouns when they refer to some quality which things possess, as in *the beautiful is pleasing, the ugly is repellent.* What is meant here is "all that is beautiful" and "all that is ugly." When an adjective is used to identify a class of human beings, it is treated as a group name and used with a plural verb, as in *the English are a nation of shopkeepers.* See **adjectives as nouns.**

generous to a fault. As a term for excessive generosity, liberality carried to such an excess that it may be regarded as a weakness, *generous to a fault* is a cliché. Of the phrase some wag has said "If it's our own, we all are." One of the few virtues of clichés is that they are often useful to wits.

genial. See **congenial.**

genie. See **genius.**

genitive case. The word *genitive* is related to the word *genus* and the primary function of the genitive case is to show that one noun is being used to classify another noun. The genitive is sometimes called the adjective case. All English nouns have a genitive form, such as *life's, people's.* A few pronouns also have a genitive form, such as *nobody's, the other's;* and so do a few adjectives that are being used as nouns, as in *the accused's identity.* These particular pronouns and adjectives are included in everything that is said below about genitive nouns. The possessive pronouns, such as *my, mine, his, hers,* are equivalent to the genitive form of nouns, but in this dictionary they are treated separately and are referred to as possessives. See **possessive pronouns.**

FORMATION

1. If a noun does not itself end in an *s* (or *z*) sound, the genitive is formed by adding *'s.* This is true whether the noun is singular or plural, as in *child's play* and *children's games.*

2. If a plural noun ends in an *s* (or *z*) sound, the genitive is formed by adding only an apostrophe, as in *the boys' dormitory.* An additional *s* (or *z*) sound on a plural noun, as in *the boys's,* is not standard.

3. There is no such uniformity in the case of a singular noun ending in an *s* (or *z*) sound. One may say *Keats' poems* or *Keats's poems.* In older literary English it was not customary to add a genitive *s* to a word already ending in *s.* But thirty or forty years ago this practice was considered archaic for singular nouns and was

confined to classical or religious expressions, such as *Achilles' heel* and *St. Agnes' Eve.* For everyday matters the *'s* was used, even when it brought three *s* (or *z*) sounds together, as in *the hostess's son* and *Charles's senior year.* Today the extra *s* is usually omitted after a proper name, as in *Charles' senior year,* but otherwise retained, as in *the boss's secretary.*

4. The word *sake* is a rule to itself. It may have one *s* sound before it but not two. We may say *for pity's sake, for conscience' sake,* but not *for conscience's sake.* When no genitive *s* is added the apostrophe may be used, as in the examples, or it may be omitted, as in *for appearance sake, for goodness sake.*

SUBSTITUTE FORMS

A genitive can usually be replaced by a prepositional phrase (usually, but not always, with the preposition *of*), and frequently by the simple, uninflected form of the noun, as in *the church roof, the church's roof, the roof of the church.* (See **nouns as adjectives.**) These forms, in the order given, make the qualifying word, *church,* increasingly emphatic. The forms are also increasingly long. The shortest form available is preferred for rapid and concise English; a longer form is used for emphasis or solemnity, as in *the committee report, the committee's report; the man's grave, the tomb of Cyrus.* However, our ear will tolerate more *of*-phrases than it will *'s* genitives and this sometimes determines the choice. Three genitives become ridiculous in *the woman's first husband's only child's godfather,* but six *of*-phrases almost pass unnoticed in *the wife of a son of one of the members of the board of trustees of the university.* Usually we mix these forms.

The genitive always precedes the noun it qualifies and, except in two cases which are discussed below, it precedes all other words qualifying that noun. A prepositional phrase replacing a genitive normally follows the noun, and preferably without any intervening words. An uninflected form must stand immediately before the qualified word. The genitive may also be used independently, without a following noun, as in *the things that are Caesar's* and *we're going to the doctor's.* In this construction the genitive is understood as qualifying a noun that can easily be supplied from the context (such as *things* or *office*). This is sometimes called the absolute genitive or the genitive used absolutely.

MEANINGS AND USES

Textbooks sometimes say that the only living function of the genitive is to represent ownership, and that when it is used for inanimate things (which are normally not owners) a personification is implied. But no ownership is intended in *one's elders, a man's murderer, our son's school,* and no personification in *tomorrow's breakfast, the play's success, the earth's surface, the sun's heat, the nation's economy.* It is a serious mistake to dismiss the genitive as the "possessive" case, because more than half the time it represents some other relation. Unless these relations are understood a speaker does not know when he can substitute a phrase for the genitive or the genitive for a phrase and is tied to stereotyped forms of expression. Three genitive relations are expressed without using a genitive form in Sandburg's description of Chicago: *Hog Butcher for the World, Tool Maker, Stacker of Wheat.*

1. *Classifying or descriptive genitive.* This is the basic genitive function, seen in *the room's furnishings, the airplane's speed, the building's foundations.* In a count of the actual genitive forms appearing in a newspaper this group would not stand highest because it is usually possible to substitute the uninflected form of the noun for the genitive. When there is no reason for emphasizing the descriptive word, the simple uninflected form is preferred, and when there is reason, the *of*-phrase does it better.

Sometimes we have no choice between the genitive and the uninflected form. This may be simply a matter of custom. For example, we may speak of *state rights* or *state's rights,* but *state's prison* is now old-fashioned and countrified. But there are two situations in which the genitive is required and the simple form cannot be used. If a descriptive word is inserted we must use a genitive. We may speak of *New York streets* and *Alaska cities,* but we must say *New York's smaller streets* and *Alaska's southern cities.* And we do not put a word that stands for something that has personality in the completely subordinate position of a simple qualifier; we always give it at least the dignity of a genitive.

What has personality and what does not depends on one's point of view. We are likely to speak of *the dog hair* on the neighbor's rug and *the dog's hair* on our own. When a person becomes a public character he apparently loses his personality. We say *Robinson's bank account* but *the Astor fortune; Mr. Corsen's house* but *the John D. Rockefeller mansion.* Even the same individual may seem more or less human depending on the circumstances. We are likely to speak of *the doctor's advice* and of *the doctor bills.*

2. *Possessive genitive.* This is the genitive that indicates ownership. Obviously, it is only applicable to human beings, and by extension to pets or personified abstractions. Although it accounts for less than half of the genitive forms appearing in print, it is the largest single class. This is because it has no substitute forms. Since the idea of personality is always to the front when we think of ownership, the uninflected form of the word cannot be used here. Nor can we substitute an *of*-phrase. We may use the word *of,* but the genitive keeps its form. That is, *Irene's coat* becomes *a coat of Irene's* and not *a coat of Irene.* For a further discussion of this, see **double genitives.**

3. *Subjective and objective genitive.* Some nouns name an action. With a noun of this kind, either the subject or the object of the action may be expressed as a genitive. For example, the creation of Adam may be spoken of as *God's creation* or *man's creation.* Taken out of con-

text, this genitive is often ambiguous. *The officer's orders* may mean what he has been ordered to do or what he has ordered someone else to do. But in context it is usually clear which is intended.

Both the subject and the object of the action may be named. In that case, since there is only one position for the genitive and they cannot both occupy it at the same time, one of them must be expressed by a prepositional phrase, and both may be. For example, we have a subjective genitive in *mind's control over matter* and an objective in *matter's control by mind.* Here the prepositions *over* and *by* make it clear which is which. An *of*-phrase may replace a subjective genitive, as in *the control of mind over matter,* and it may replace an objective, as in *the control of matter by mind.* It should not do both in the same sentence, as it does in *the gift of a member of a hundred dollars.* An *of*-phrase will be assumed to be objective unless there is some reason for not taking it in that way.

Normally, a word representing something inanimate will be assumed to be an objective genitive, as in *the idea's discovery.* A word representing a human being will be assumed to be subjective, as in *the professor's discovery,* except when the object of the action is more interesting than the agent, and then it will be assumed to be objective, as in *the doctor's rescue, the man's trial, the woman's release.* At one time *the professor's robbery* could be given as an example of this. But in the United States today it is a question whether the robber or the robbed is the more interesting, and this expression would now be ambiguous out of context.

If a subjective or objective genitive does not fit the description just given, it will be ambiguous and should be replaced by a prepositional phrase. This genitive cannot be freely replaced by an uninflected form, although the same relations are expressed by simple word combinations, as the subjective genitive in *night fall* and the objective in *rope walker.*

4. *Genitive of purpose.* This genitive is found in Old English and not in Latin. It is unlike the other genitives in several ways: (1) It cannot be replaced by an *of*-phrase but requires *for.* (2) In the other types of genitive, the genitive noun is singular or plural depending upon its meaning. We say *the child's teacher* or *the children's teacher,* depending on whether we are talking about one child or more than one. In the genitive of purpose the genitive is singular or plural depending on the form of the noun that follows. We say *he is writing a child's book* and *he has written many children's books.* We speak of *a man's college* and *men's colleges, a woman's club* and *women's clubs.* Therefore, if we were being meticulous about the apostrophe, we would write: *he is teaching in a boy's school* and *he has taught in several boys' schools.* (3) This genitive does not stand before the other qualifying words. In the example just given *several* stands before the genitive. In *the child's book that he is writing,* the word *the* refers to

book. In *the child's teacher,* it refers to *child's.* (The simple form of the noun cannot be freely substituted for this genitive, although the same relation exists in many word combinations, such as *fire screen.*)

5. *Measures and other adverbial genitives.* At one time the genitive was used to make adverbs from nouns or adjectives. This genitive survives today in a few set phrases and expressions of measure. See **adverbial genitives** and **measures.**

6. *Survivals.* There are a few genitives in English that are survivals of an old genitive of source, such as *hen's eggs.* These are like the genitive of purpose in that they are attached to the noun and can be preceded by adjectives and definitive words such as *a, the, this,* and other genitives, as in *my six hen's eggs.* Actually they are a kind of compound noun, though they are usually written as two words. They do not justify setting up another class of genitives because this is not a living form. It belongs to a few individual words and cannot be transferred to other words of almost identical meaning. We may speak of *a dozen hen's eggs,* but we cannot speak of *a dozen ostrich's eggs.*

7. *Partitive and appositive genitive.* In Latin, and in some European languages today, the relation of whole to part is shown by a genitive. This is called the partitive genitive. It does not exist in English, but we express the same relation by means of an *of*-phrase, as in *one of us, some of it.* When two nouns, or phrases, stand together and the second merely describes the first, as *president* in *the title president,* the second is called an appositive. In Latin the genitive was sometimes used to indicate this relation and was then called an appositive genitive. The genitive is not used for this purpose in English, but we can use an *of*-phrase to show the same relation, as in *the title of president, the state of Ohio.*

SPECIAL PROBLEMS

1. *Joint possession.* When one thing is owned jointly by more than one person, the genitive *s* may be placed after the last name and not after the preceding ones, as in *Stan, Jeanne, and Ann's home.* But the genitive *s* may also be placed after the preceding names and still indicate joint possession, as in *Stan's, Jeanne's, and Ann's home.* When separate ownership is meant, the genitive *s* always follows each name, as in *Jeanne's and Ann's clothes.*

It would be neater if the middle form described above did not exist, and some grammarians claim that it should not exist, that it is wrong to use two genitive forms to indicate joint possession. But there is no doubt that this form does exist and that it is used by educated people. What keeps it alive is the fact that the personal pronouns have to be used in this way. We cannot say *he, she, and Ann's home* but are compelled to say *his, hers, and Ann's.* And very often we have both nouns and pronouns in the same statement.

2. *Appositives.* When two words or phrases stand together and refer to the same person there may be a question about where to place the genitive *s.* Formerly it was placed after each element, as in *his chaplain's, Mr. Sampson's, careless life.* In contemporary English it is placed after the element that stands immediately before the qualified word and not after the others, as in *by Mahomet my kinsman's sepulcher.* When the genitive is used absolutely and the qualified word does not appear, the genitive *s* may be placed after each element, as in *would you tell us where Gaudy's the grocer's is?,* or only after the final one, as in *she may have a bed at her cousin the saddler's.*

3. *Phrases and clauses.* In English the genitive *s* is not necessarily attached to the noun it actually belongs with. It may follow a prepositional phrase, as in *the king of Spain's daughter.* This peculiar use of the *s* is thoroughly understood and phrases of this kind are almost never ambiguous. But it is possible to construct a sentence in which they are misleading. For example, it is quite true that *the son of Pharaoh's daughter is the daughter of Pharaoh's son.* See also **double genitives.**

Traditionally, a descriptive phrase that contains no preposition and no verb form might stand between a noun and the genitive *s,* as in *Peter the Hermit's teaching,* or it might be placed after the completed genitive construction, as in *it is Othello's pleasure, our noble and valiant general* and *the words were Cicero's, the most eloquent of men.* A full clause qualifying a genitive or possessive form is more difficult to handle. In literary English it never stands before the qualified word but it sometimes follows the completed thought, as in *his words who sent me* and *it is his who finds it.* In longer sentences this construction is a dangerous one because the clause is likely to attach itself to the qualified word rather than to the genitive. Some grammarians say that the construction is always improper. But it has been used successfully by many great writers, including D. G. Rossetti, Browning, Holmes, Thackeray, George Eliot.

In the United States today it is possible in speaking to place a full clause between the *'s* and the word it actually belongs with. It is possible to say *the man you said was coming here from Chicago's son just called.* Fifty years ago this was considered an indecorous way of speaking and only young and foolish people used it. Today it is heard everywhere. There is no literary tradition for it, but there probably will be in time.

genius; talent. A *genius* in its original meaning was an attendant spirit, allotted to every person at birth to watch over him and shape his character and fortunes. It is in this sense that Macbeth uses the word when he says of Banquo *There is none but he/ Whose being I do fear; and under him/ My genius is rebuk'd, as it is said/ Mark Antony's was by Caesar.* Then it came to mean a natural endowment or aptitude, inclination, the sort of thing with which one's genius would endow one or towards which it would guide (*Different men have different geniuses. The squire, whose active genius was al-*

ways at some repair or improvement . . .). In the eighteenth century, when the word had quite a vogue, a man of genius was an ingenious man.

But with the rise of the Romantic Movement, with its exaltation of the abnormal, its fantastic hero worship and its cult of the supernatural, *genius* came to be applied to intellectual powers which seemed almost to proceed from supernatural inspiration or demonic possession and which produced its works in a manner not comprehensible to the ordinary mind. It was at this time that the distinction between *talent* and *genius,* between a special capacity and an exceptional capacity, was drawn with the exaggerated emphasis which still colors the meanings of the words. De Quincey stated the difference with vehement vagueness in a definition that has become classical: *Talent and genius,* he said, *are not merely different, they are in polar opposition to each other. Talent is intellectual power of every kind, which acts and manifests itself . . . through the will and the active forces. Genius . . . is that much rarer species of intellectual power which is derived from the genial nature —from the spirit of suffering and enjoying— from the spirit of pleasure and pain. It is a function of the passive nature.* From this it was only a step to refer to one possessing genius as himself a *genius,* a person set apart from other men by a supra-natural gift.

The word *talent,* an ancient weight of money, attained its present meaning of natural ability or mental endowment through its figurative use in the parable of the talents in Matthew 25: 14-30. It is a very useful word to hold in mind when discussing the "real" meaning of words with purists. Up to and throughout the eighteenth century it was closely synonymous with genius, even including the idea of something divinely entrusted to one. It is interesting that Milton, who became one of the supreme exemplars of *genius* to the romantics, referred to his own powers (in his sonnet on his blindness beginning "When I consider how my light is spent") as *talent.* But the romantic distinction did its work and *talent,* in the modern conception of it, which may be acquired by imitation and training, is now definitely thought of as something infinitely inferior to genius. It is one of the favorite damnings by faint praise in reviews of literary, musical, and artistic performances to say that they *showed talent.*

Genius has two plurals. More than one supranatural ability or more than one person possessing such abilities are *geniuses.* Guardian spirits, attendant spirits—whether good or bad —and more than one jinni or genie, are *genii.*

genteel; gentle; Gentile. The Latin word *gentilis,* from which all three of these words derive, meant of the same clan or tribe or family in the larger sense. *Genteel* once meant well-bred or elegant, showing, that is, the outward signs of belonging to one of the better families, suited to a gentleman, characteristic of the upper classes (*A man might be rich without being genteel. There was nothing vulgar about her; she was genteel and accomplished*). But the

democratic revolution, or perhaps simply the behavior of those who prided themselves on their gentility, has made the word in current usage slightly derogatory, mildly sarcastic (*shabby gentility*), describing rather those who affect the ways and manners of the upper classes than those who actually have them (*So genteel that she always called a leg a limb and a shirt a garment*).

Though *gentle* still keeps some of its older meaning of characteristic of good birth, wellborn, in such terms as *gentlemen* and *gentlefolk,* the meaning is one more recognized than used. It would seem a little affected, archaic, or deliberately literary to employ it in conversation or writing. In current usage it means mild, kind, amiable (*His gentle words soothed the angry boy. My mother's gentle touch delighted everyone. Such gentle humor can never wound*), moderate, or easily handled (*Boil it over a gentle flame. Please chose a gentle horse for me; I am not a good rider*).

Gentile today has the primary meaning, derived from the Bible, of non-Jewish. In medieval Europe it meant heathen. Among the Mormons it has the meaning of non-Mormon. But Kipling's use of the word in the famous passage in *Recessional* (*Such boastings as the Gentiles use,/ Or lesser breeds without the Law*) must be regarded as anomalous. The solemnity of the occasion called in his opinion for Biblical language and it was easy in 1897 to conceive of the English as God's chosen people but *Gentiles* in any accepted sense of the word at that time would have included the English and the lesser breeds.

gentleman; gent; man. A *gentleman* was once a man of a definite social rank, above a yeoman. Shakespeare went to considerable trouble to get his father made a gentleman so that he might be the son of a gentleman. This meaning is now of purely historical interest. In popular usage the term means a man of good breeding, education, and manners. It can also mean a valet (*a gentleman's gentleman*). In polite address (*ladies and gentlemen*) it means a man. Overuse has vulgarized the word (*I'm next in line. I don't believe the gentleman is taking his proper turn*) and *man* remains the more dignified word.

Gent and *gents* as abbreviations are either humorous (*Step right up, gents, and say what you'll have*) or pathetically vulgar (*Tables for ladies and gents*).

gentlewoman. See **woman.**

gentry. When used seriously, this is a group name and may take a singular or a plural verb, as in *the gentry was represented* and *the gentry were represented.* It is not used as a true plural and plural constructions such as *these gentry are ready to leave* are meant to be witty or contemptuous. The word is seldom used seriously in the United States.

genuine. See **authentic.**

genus. The plural is *genera,* and occasionally *genuses,* but never *geni.*

gerrymander is often erroneously written *jerrymander.* The word derives from Elbridge Gerry, one of the signers of the Declaration of Independence, a member of the Continental Congress and later of the Congress of the United States, twice governor of Massachusetts and, at the time of his death, vice-president of the United States. Despite this distinguished and honorable career, his name is fixed in the language through his connivance (in an unsuccessful attempt to get himself elected governor of Massachusetts for a third term) in a scheme to redistribute the electoral districts of the state in such a way that the strength of the party opposing him was concentrated in a few districts. Gilbert Stuart, the painter, seeing a map with the new districts marked on it thought it resembled the body of an animal, added head, claws, and wings and said it would do for a salamander. A gentleman present changed it to *gerrymander,* and the word stuck.

gerunds; gerundives. See -ing.

gesticulation; gesture. A *gesture* is a movement of the body, head, arms, or face, expressive of an idea or emotion (*The gesture of impatience, though slight, was not lost upon the young man who brought his narrative quickly to a close*). A *gesticulation* is the making of a gesture, especially in an animated or excited manner (*Their conversation was carried on with great vivacity and gesticulation*). Gesticulation is the using of gestures; a gesture is a single act of gesticulation.

Gesture has within the past generation acquired the special meaning of an act or proceeding intended for effect, a demonstration (*His offering to remove the hedge if it impeded our view was a neighborly gesture that left us deeply moved*).

get. The past tense is *got.* The participle is *gotten* or *got.* The original meaning of *get* was "seize" or "take hold of." Today the verb is used in the broader sense of "acquire" and may mean acquiring actively or passively, literally or figuratively. Frequently *get* is the simplest, and the best, word to use in expressing these and similar ideas. In this basic sense, it is one of the elemental words of the language.

Get may also be used to mean "arrive at" or "succeed in coming or going," as in *when we get to Seattle* and *we finally got there.* This use of *get* has been literary English for six or seven hundred years and is thoroughly acceptable today.

Get has been used in literary English for four or five hundred years to mean "be able" and "cause." In these senses it is usually followed by an infinitive, as in *did you get to see him?* and *I got him to read it.* In the sense of "cause" it may be followed by an object and a past participle or the -ing form of a verb, as in *we got him discharged* and *he got the machine running.* These forms are all standard English.

Actually the verb *get* has more than seventy distinguishable meanings. Many of these are variations on the sense "acquire." For example, "acquire" may mean "beget," as in *get sons and daughters,* or "capture," as in *the Mounties always get their man,* or "receive," as in *you will get a shock.* In all these senses *get* is unquestionably good English. It is also the idiomatic verb, that is, the preferred verb, in a number of expressions that are hard to classify, such as *I will get supper,* where the word means "prepare," and *how are you getting along?* In general, *get* is a very respectable verb. But it has four uses that are sometimes considered objectionable.

1. *Get* is frequently used like the verb *be* to form a passive, as in *he got hurt.* This construction has been literary English for three or four hundred years but did not become popular until the nineteenth century, at which time it was condemned by many grammarians. In spite of this condemnation, *get* is at present the preferred form for the passive when a speaker wants to emphasize an action, as in *the house will get painted next spring* and *she got married last year.* If *be* or *was* is used instead of *get* or *got* in these sentences, it is impossible to distinguish the action from the resulting state. That is, a house might get painted at Christmas and still be painted in the spring and a woman who was married last year might have gotten married many years before. *Getting* is generally preferred to *being* in progressive tenses where it follows *been* or *be,* as in *the house has been getting painted* or *will be getting painted.* Most people avoid saying *has been being* or *will be being.* *Get* can also be used, where *be* cannot, as a passive following the emphatic *do,* as in *no man wants to be killed, but some do get killed.*

2. *Get* has been used for the last three or four hundred years to mean "become," as in *he gets angry, he got sick.* In these expressions *get* is a linking verb and should be followed by an adjective and not an adverb. The construction is used freely by educated people, at least in speech. But it is condemned by some grammarians, who claim that *become* is required here and that *get* is undignified. As a result, some people who say *get* write *become.* *Get* meaning "come to be" and followed by a past participle or the -ing form of a verb introduced by *to,* as in *we got started* and *I got to thinking,* is a more recent development. These forms are standard English when they are used deliberately to slow down a narrative. But they should be used sparingly. The constant use of this form instead of a direct statement, such as *we started* and *I thought,* is characteristic of careless speech.

The single word *got,* but not the full verb *get,* is sometimes used to make *have* more emphatic. This occurs in two distinct senses:

3. *Get* means "acquire" and what one has just acquired one now possesses. Following this logic, the compound *have got* or *has got* is often used as a simple present tense, equivalent to *have* or *has,* as in *we've got plenty of time* and *the boy's got an apple in his hand.* *Have got* has been used in this way in literary English for more than four hundred years. In 1755 Dr. Johnson entered it in his dictionary without disapproval. It is found in the writings of Scott, Austen, Thackeray, Dickens, Morris, Ruskin,

Carlyle, and most of the great nineteenth century English authors. But it was strongly condemned by nineteenth century grammarians, especially American grammarians, and many people today condemn it. At present, it is more acceptable in Great Britain than it is in the United States. A past tense form meaning simply "had" as in *the boy had got an apple in his hand,* is heard in Great Britain but is almost unknown in this country.

4. The phrase *have got to* or *has got to* is also used as a simple present tense equivalent to *have to* or *has to,* meaning "must." This construction is not more than a hundred years old but it has been used by such public characters as Alice in Wonderland and Franklin Delano Roosevelt. It is thoroughly acceptable in the United States but not in Great Britain. A past tense form, *had got to,* is heard less often but is also acceptable in this country.

When *have got* is used with either of these last two meanings, the *have* is pronounced very lightly and may not be heard. This is acceptable spoken English in the United States. But it is not acceptable written English. The *have* or *'ve* (or *has* or *'s*) must always appear when the words are written down. That is, *we got time* and *we got to go now* may be heard, but they should not be seen.

In Great Britain *got* is the only form of the participle used and the older form *gotten* is considered archaic or Biblical. During the nineteenth century some American dictionaries claimed that *gotten* had also passed out of standard speech in the United States. This must have been based on hope, for it certainly was not based on fact. In the United States *gotten* is still the preferred form of the participle when it is used with *have* to express a completed action, as in *I have just gotten a splinter in my hand.* But only the form *got* is used with *have* as a simple present tense describing a condition or state, as in *I've got an apple in my hand* and *we've got to hurry.* Englishmen use *got* in all constructions and believe that Americans always use *gotten.* As a result, Americans in British novels are likely to say *I've gotten an apple in my hand* and *we've gotten to hurry. Gotten* is never used in these constructions except in British novels.

get; obtain. *Get* implies the coming into possession in any manner (*I got this farm by hard work. You'll get sick. Come and get it*). *Obtain* suggests the putting forth of effort to gain possession and therefore should not be used, although it often is, as a synonym for *get.* One does not *obtain* the measles; they just come. The merciful obtain mercy through the exercise of or as a reward for their own mercifulness. The unmerciful, if they receive mercy, will simply get it, through no effort or merit of their own. See also **secure.**

get up on the wrong side of the bed. To say of someone who is surly and ill-humored in the morning that he *got up on the wrong side of the bed* is to employ a worn and meaningless cliché. It has been a jocular phrase for more than three hundred years now and no one knows which is the right side of the bed or why getting up on (it would be better if it were *from*) a particular side should be conducive to good or ill humor.

gild. The past tense is *gilded* or *gilt.* The participle is also *gilded* or *gilt.* As adjectives, *gilt* is now restricted to the literal meaning (*gilt-edged securities*), whereas *gilded,* while it still has the literal meaning (*the gilded goblet*) or the meaning of anything so colored as to seem gilded (*the little gilded fly*), is used figuratively (*Gilded disasters were called splendid victories*).

gild the lily. As a term for applying unnecessary embellishment, *gilding the lily* is a cliché and, like so many clichés, not only hackneyed but meaningless or confused. Why should a lily be gilded? It is not gold-colored in the first place. The answer lies in the original passage from which the cliché has been drawn. The Earl of Salisbury, in the second scene of the fourth act of Shakespeare's *King John,* is protesting against the king's second coronation:

> *. . . to be possess'd with double pomp,*
> *To guard a title that was rich before,*
> *To gild refined gold, to paint the lily,*
> *To throw a perfume on the violet,*
> *To smooth the ice, or add another hue*
> *Unto the rainbow . . .*
> *Is wasteful and ridiculous excess.*

It is plain that *gild* jumped over from "refined gold" and displaced the more fitting *paint* from in front of "the lily."

gimp; guimpe; gamp. A *gimp* is a flat trimming of silk, wool, or other cord, sometimes stiffened with wire, for garments, curtains, furniture, etc. A *guimpe* is a kind of chemisette or yoke of lace, embroidery, or other material worn with a dress cut out at the neck. A *gamp* (named after Sarah Gamp, a talkative, disreputable nurse in Dickens' *Martin Chuzzlewit* who always carried a large cotton umbrella) is an umbrella, especially one tied untidily. The term is more used in England than in America.

gipsy. See **gypsy.**

giraffe; camel. In South Africa the *giraffe* is called a *camel*—short for *camelopard,* its old name.

gird. The past tense is *girded* or *girt.* The participle is also *girded* or *girt.*

girlish. See **infantile.**

give. The past tense is *gave.* The participle is *given.* When *give* has a personal subject it may be followed by *to believe,* as in *they gave me to believe they were coming,* and by other infinitives, such as *to understand* and *to think,* so long as these mean *to believe.* But the sentence *it gives me to think* is not English. It is a joke and is funny only to high-school students in their first year of French. See also **donate.**

give a wide berth. As a term for avoiding someone, *giving him a wide berth,* a nautical term, is a cliché. It should be used with care.

give the Devil his due. As a term for granting even an enemy his merits, *to give the Devil his due* is a cliché. It was formerly a proverb but has been overworked.

given. See **give.**

given name. See first name.

gladiolus. The plural is *gladiolus* or *gladioli*.

glamour; glamor. *Glamour* is preferred to *glamor* as the word for alluring charm, witchery, fascination, magic and enchantment (*She cast the spell of her glamour over the audience at once*). There is often in the word a sense that the charm is illusory (*How quickly the glamour of the courting days fades when a young couple must live together in a one-room apartment*) and, especially in the United States where the manufacture of female charm is a major industry, often synthetic (*They'll take any tolerable-looking healthy kid and turn her into a glamour girl in a week*). As a synonym for beautiful or lovely, when applied to women, *glamorous* (a common word in popular songs because it rimes with *amorous*) is a copywriter's word, forced and hollow, worn and dishonest.

   Glamour is a Scotch corruption of *grammar*, brought into common English use by Sir Walter Scott. Grammar, than which nothing is less glamorous, meaning originally the study of language which deals with its inflectional forms, became a term for all learning in the days when the study of grammar formed a large part of education. Learning has always been suspect to the unlearned, and under the variation of *gramarye* or *grammarie* grammar became a term for occult learning, magic, or necromancers (*Whate'er he did of gramarye/ was always done maliciously*). And one of the ways necromancers worked was by *casting a glamour* over their victims. Hence our *glamour*.

glance; glimpse. A *glance* is a quick look. A *glimpse* is a momentary sight of. That is a glimpse which one sees in a glance. One has a glimpse of and gets a glance at (*A glance at his face was all that was needed to confirm the bad news. The glimpse of his face, which was all that I could get in so brief a time, confirmed my fears*). A *glimpse* suggests an imperfect view (*I caught a glimpse of the letter as he was folding it, but cannot be sure that it was addressed to the general*).

glean. To *glean* does not mean merely to gather. It means to gather little bits slowly and laboriously. A meaning that has been gleaned, for example, has been hard come by, laboriously collected from a mass of chaff or rubbish over a vast area. The gleaners who come after the reapers get only the spilled grain or occasional stalks that have escaped the sickle. Thus gleaning has also the sense of thorough gathering up of that which others have disregarded. Samuel Johnson uses the word well in *The Vanity of Human Wishes* where, speaking of the dangers attendant upon greatness and the advantages of obscurity, he says:

   Let history tell, where rival kings command,
   And dubious title shakes the madded land,
   When statutes glean the refuse of the sword,
   How much more safe the vassal than the lord.

glee; mirth; hilarity; merriment. *Glee* and *mirth* and, to a lesser extent, *merriment* are all slightly archaic and bookish and unless used with great care seem forced or affected. *Glee* suggests a spontaneous overflow of high spirits or exultation, often expressed in playful or ecstatic gestures. It is used so often in the phrase *childish glee* that any more serious use of it (such as Wordsworth's *holy glee*) would seem inappropriate. It has acquired the special meaning of demonstration of malicious rejoicing over the mishaps of others, especially in the cliché *fiendish glee.*

   Mirth means spontaneous gaiety, but of a more decorous nature than that designated by *glee* (*There was much mirth at this unexpected sally*). *Merriment* denotes fun and a general, innocent good time.

   Hilarity implies noisy and boisterous fun, often exceeding the limits of decorum (*As the evening wore on and the glasses were refilled, the hilarity increased, until angry knockings on the walls reminded us that the neighbors did not approve*).

glimpse. See glance.

global. See earthen.

globe. See earth.

gloomy; pessimistic. *Gloomy* means dark. When applied to persons or, rather, to their dispositions, for it is no longer applied as it used to be to the color of their skins, it means melancholy, depressing, sad (*The expression of these gloomy thoughts soon put an end to what little cheerfulness remained*). *Pessimistic* means characterized by pessimism, the philosophic belief that the world is essentially evil. Since such a belief is conducive to gloom, certainly in those who don't share it, it is a natural development for *pessimistic* to mean *gloomy*. But it is not an absolute synonym. It means gloomy in the extreme, the gloomiest of all possible views. To use it lightly (as in *You're too pessimistic; it isn't going to rain all afternoon*) weakens the word and borders on the pompous.

glorious. That is *glorious* which is delightful in the extreme, whose pleasure is accompanied by exaltation and splendor (*Full many a glorious morning have I seen/ Flatter the mountain tops with sovereign eye*). When used merely as a synonym for *pleasant* or *delightful* it is excessive. This excessiveness suggests that it is forced and the word, already too much for common occasions, is usually buttressed with such ineffectual intensives as *simply* or *perfectly* and the whole phrase uttered with a shrill emphasis that reveals its insincerity.

glottis. The plural is *glottises* or *glottides,* not *glottes.*

glutton. See gourmand.

go. The past tense is *went*. The participle is *gone*. The past tense *went* has been taken over from the verb *wend*, which now has a regular past tense and participle *wended*. One form of the old past tense of *go* survives in the Scottish *gaed*.

   Go is sometimes followed by a second verb that tells the purpose of the going. This may be the simple form of the verb, as in *I had the grace to go hear a sermon* and *go tell Aunt Rhody*. This construction is found frequently in

English literature and is standard in the United States today. But it is no longer standard in Great Britain, where an *and* is required between the two verbs as in *go and call the cattle home*. Neither construction can be used when *go* is a simple present tense or after any form of the verb except *go*. We may say *I will go tell her* but not *I go tell her* or *I went tell her*. These forms require a *to*-infinitive to express purpose.

Went, gone, and the present tense of *go,* followed by *and,* are used before another verb to show indignation or surprise, as in *he went and told her, he has gone and done it again, now he goes and gets married*. This construction is very expressive, but it is not standard. When sentences like this are meant literally (that is, when the person actually moved), they are acceptable. But many people take care to break the pattern in some way, as in *he went and he told her* and *he went quickly and told her*.

The word *going,* combined with some form of the verb *be,* is often used to indicate expectation. This is a favorite way of making a statement about the future. Used in this sense, *going* is always followed by a *to*-infinitive, as in *I'm going to build a castle down in Newport*. Here *go* does not carry any meaning of motion. We may say *I am going to sit still*. When the following infinitive is *to go* it may be omitted, as in *I'm going back and tell her* which means *I am going to go back and tell her*. When *going* and some form of the verb *be* are used to mean motion they are never followed directly by an infinitive. We find some way to avoid this pattern, as in *I'm going now to tell her*.

Go on may mean continue. When it does, it is always followed by the *-ing* form of a verb, as in *go on talking*.

Go may be followed by an adjective describing whatever it is that goes. Sometimes this is because *go* is being used as the equivalent of *be* or *become,* as in *go mad* and *it went hard with him*. But it can also happen when *go* actually carries the meaning of movement, as in *they go around naked*. In this sense *go* may also be followed by an adverb describing the going, as in *they go quietly*.

go in one ear and out the other. The assurance that something that has been said has *gone in one ear and out the other* is often spoken contemptuously by the person to whom the remark was addressed, meaning that he paid no attention to it. But it is a dangerous sneer because it carries the suggestion that there was nothing between the two ears to impede its passage. Even without such a consideration, however, the phrase should be avoided.

go the whole hog. Dr. Charles Earle Funk, in his *A Hog on Ice,* believes that *to go the whole hog,* as an expression for stopping at nothing, carrying through regardless of cost, making every effort, supporting wholeheartedly, may derive from a passage in Cowper's "The Love of the World Reproved; or Hypocrisy Detected." It may also derive, he grants, from the fact that a ten-cent piece was once called a "hog" so that

to go the whole hog was an ironical phrase for the willingness of the parsimonious to spend their money in a cause to which they were devoted. Whatever the origin of the phrase, it is now overworked and to be avoided.

gobbledegook was a term coined by the late Representative Maury Maverick to describe the language, characterized by circumlocution and jargon, of government reports, questionnaires, pronouncements and the like, and especially of inter- and intra-departmental memoranda. He had in mind such phrases as "cause an investigation to be made with a view to ascertaining" for "find out" and "return a considered evaluation" for "give me your opinion."

This sort of writing, which seems to have been begotten upon the legalism of bureaucracy by the inflated vagueness of social science, is not peculiar to America. Every modern country has it and with the increasing part that government plays in the daily life of every individual it is a serious burden. Sir Ernest Gowers, himself a civil servant, speaks in his *Plain Words: Their A B C* of "the sense of despair" produced in the public mind by gobbledegook. The citizen in dealing with officials feels himself utterly lost and helpless in a fog of words. This involved and pompous verbosity, Sir Ernest believes, goes far to defeat the intention of a great deal of social legislation.

Various names have been suggested. Ivor Brown, in England, has offered *barnacular* and *jargantuan* and *pudder* (from the reference in *King Lear* to the gods that keep *this dreadful pudder o'er our heads*), but *gobbledegook* has been accepted in the United States and seems to be on its way to acceptance in England and other parts of the British Empire. It was a happy coinage, combining the self-important, indignant, incomprehensible gobbling of a turkeycock with the idea of a sticky and loathsome muck into which the unhappy listener or reader sinks with a bubbling cry.

George Orwell ("Politics and the English Language") translates a passage from *Ecclesiastes* into gobbledegook:

I returned and saw under the sun, that the race is not to the swift, nor the battle to the strong, neither yet bread to the wise, nor yet riches to men of understanding, nor yet favor to men of skill; but time and chance happeneth to them all

became

Objective consideration of contemporary phenomena compels the conclusion that success or failure in competitive activities exhibits no tendency to be commensurate with innate capacity, but that a considerable element of the unpredictable must be taken into account.

But admirable as the parody is, Orwell's sense of style and the necessity of following the meaning of the original make it far clearer than most gobbledegook. *Time* (May 7, 1947) quotes, from a letter to a veteran who was inquiring about a pension, a more classic specimen: "The non-compensable evaluation heretofore assigned to you for your service-connected disability is confirmed and continued." In other words, he didn't get the pension.

God willing. See **Deo volente.**

golf links; golf course. *Links* was originally a Scottish word for gently undulating sandy ground near the seashore and some of the more rigid purists insist that a *golf links* must be by the sea and a *golf course* inland. But the distinction, however much it may mark one who observes it as knowing in either golf or grammar, is not likely to gain acceptance in America because *golf links* is falling into disuse. It is still known and occasionally used, but it is being replaced by *golf course*, just as the Scottish names for the clubs—*mashie, brassie, niblick,* and the like—have, with the exception of *putter,* been replaced by numbers (*number five iron, number six iron,* and so on).

Links was originally a plural (*The golf links lie so near the mill . . .*) but it may also be construed as singular (*The entire links has been bought and will be cut up into lots*).

gone. See **go.**

good. The comparative form is *better.* The superlative form is *best.* When *good* means holy it is likely to have the comparative form *more good* and the superlative *most good,* as in *the most good, the most charming, the most perfect human creature that ever trod the earth.*

The word *good* is primarily an adjective and is used to qualify nouns. It may follow a linking verb, that is, any verb that is being used to mean "be, become, or appear," as in *it sounds good, it tastes good, it feels good to be alive,* where the word *good* describes the subject of the verb and not the action. (See **linking verbs**.) It cannot be used to actually qualify the verb itself, as it is in *he doesn't hear good.* Sentences of this kind, such as *he writes good, the engine is hitting good,* are not standard. In standard English the word *well* is required here.

Good may be used to qualify another adjective that is standing before a noun, as in *a good long time, a good many men.* The word *very* may also be used here and is preferred by some people. *Very* is now generally preferred before the word *few,* as in *a very few people. Good* is still heard before *few* but this is now considered old fashioned. The words *good and* may be used in place of *very* to qualify an adjective or an adjective-like adverb that follows a verb, as in *I am good and tired, they worked good and hard.* Some grammarians object to this construction but it is accepted spoken English in the United States.

Good may also be used as a noun meaning "what is good," as in *it is for your good.* In *he will do you good* the word *good* is a noun, provided the sentence means "he will do for you something that is good." But if it means "he will do you in thoroughly," then *good* is being used to qualify the verb, and this is not standard English. When *good* means "what is good" it

has only the singular form. But this may be followed by a plural verb when it refers to living creatures, as in *the good are happy.* The plural form *goods* may mean "possessions." When it does it is treated as a plural, as in *these goods are mine.* It may also mean "cloth," and it is then treated as a singular, as in *this goods is mine.* In these senses the plural form is used as the first element in a compound, as in *a dry goods store.*

The words *better* and *best* are adverbs as well as adjectives and can be used in any way that the sense allows.

Had better, or *had best,* means "would find advantageous" and is followed by the simple form of a verb, as *stop* in *you had better stop that foolishness,* and *let* in *you had better let sleeping dogs lie.* This *had* may be pronounced so lightly that it is not heard, as in *we better leave,* but it must always be shown in written English, at least with an apostrophe and *d,* as in *we'd better leave.* In the nineteenth century the form *would better* was sometimes used in place of *had better,* but it never became popular and is now disappearing. *Had better* is always treated as a single idea and should not be broken into by another word. We say *you had better not wait* and not *you hadn't better wait. Had better* can be used in passive constructions, such as *what had better be done* and *sleeping dogs had better be left alone.* Some grammarians object to this because it is not in keeping with the original use of the words. But it is in keeping with modern developments of the passive voice and is thoroughly acceptable English today.

good, bad, and (or **or**) **indifferent.** As an all-inclusive term, that is, *good, bad, and indifferent* (*i.e.,* neutral) is a cliché.

goodly. This word means comely, or admirable in almost any respect. Today it is always used as an adjective qualifying a noun. For a period it was also used as an adverb but this is now obsolete.

Good Samaritan. As a term for anyone distinguished for his charity, *Good Samaritan* is now a cliché. The Good Samaritan is the accepted designation of the "certain Samaritan" who in the parable (Luke 10:30-35) succored the man who had fallen among thieves, but it is interesting that nowhere in the Bible is he called the Good Samaritan.

good will; goodwill. Though the distinction is not rigidly observed, *good will* is usually employed to denote a friendly disposition or benevolence (*He has shown his good will towards me in many ways*) and *goodwill* or *good-will* to denote the asset arising from the reputation of a business and its relations with its customers apart from the value of its stock.

goody. A shortened form of *goodwife, goody* was formerly applied to an elderly woman of humble station (as in Wordsworth's poem "Goody Blake and Harry Gill"). Swinburne's reference to Jane Welsh Carlyle as Carlyle's "Goody" was malicious but clever since Carlyle made so much of his peasant origin. The word is now archaic except at Harvard University where it is applied to the women who look after the students' rooms.

goose. The plural is *geese*. The plural is still *geese* even when the word is qualified in some way, as in *a flock of wild geese*. The singular form *goose* is used as a mass word when speaking of these birds as food, as in *goose is expensive this year*. We may also speak of *hunting wild goose*, but this is not a true plural and *five wild goose* is not standard English. A *mongoose*, of course, is not a *goose*, and this word has a regular plural *mongooses*. The plural of the tailor's *goose* and of the improper gesture is *gooses*.

gopher. In the western United States the word *gopher* designates a number of closely related burrowing rodents, constituting the genera *Geomys, Thomomys,* and allied genera of the family *Geomyidae*. Some of these same animals are also found in southeastern United States, east to Georgia. But here they are called salamanders. In the prairie regions the word *gopher* is applied to numerous small ground squirrels, the spermophiles. Along the Gulf coast a *gopher* is a burrowing land tortoise (*Gopherus polyphemus*) and in the West and Southwest the name is also applied to the gopher snake (*Drymarchon corais couperi*). All of these applications stem from the French *gaufre,* meaning waffle or honeycomb, because each of the creatures honeycombs the ground with its burrowings.

Gordian knot, to cut the. Gordius, king of Phrygia, had connected the pole of a chariot with the yoke by a thong which was tied in an intricate knot. An oracle had declared that whoever untied this knot would become ruler of all Asia. When Alexander the Great came to Gordium and found himself unable to untie the knot, he cut it with one blow of his sword. Hence *to cut the Gordian knot* has become a term for solving a perplexing difficulty by one bold stroke. But the picturesqueness of the phrase or, perhaps, its flattering assumption that all who proceed rashly are Alexanders, has led to its being overworked.

gorilla. See **guerrilla.**

got. See **get.**

gotten. See **get.**

gourmand; gourmet; glutton. *Gourmand* and *gourmet* are both used to designate one who is fond of good eating and prides himself on his knowledge of the delicacies of the table. But *gourmand* is more often used in a disparaging sense for a glutton. The *gourmet* is more a connoisseur, a theoretician; the *gourmand* is more of a doer, a hearty eater of good things. A *glutton* is one who eats to excess and often with little delicacy of choice.

government agencies, abbreviations of titles of. See **abbreviations.**

grab bag. As a term for a receptacle from which one draws without knowing what he is getting, *grab bag* is an Americanism (*There is not a line of this treaty that does not suggest the outworn, discredited grab-bag diplomacy that caused this war*). The English equivalent is *lucky dip.*

graces. The use of the plural form of this word to mean favor, as in *in her good graces,* is a French idiom which has become standard English. At one time the singular was used here, as in *in her good grace,* but this construction is now obsolete.

grade has a number of meanings in America that are not recognized in England. Thus our *grade crossing* is in England called a *level crossing* and the *grade* of our streets is there a *gradient*. Our *grades, grade schools, grade-school pupils* and *grade-school teachers* are unknown in England, where the classes below the high-school level are known as *standards*. The English *grade* eggs and other produce but not examination papers or people.

graduate from. *He graduated from college* is better English than *he was graduated from college*. The first is the form used in most colleges today and was the only form heard in the United States until thirty or forty years ago, as in *Admiral Peary graduated from Bowdoin in 1877.* It is still the only form heard in Great Britain.

Whoever first thought that this expression required a passive form had obviously not thought very much about the English language. We say *the boat upset, the door closed, the hat blew away, the coat caught on a nail, the goods sold quickly,* and so on indefinitely. In each case the verb is understood in a passive sense and we could say *the boat was upset, the door was closed,* and so on. The fact is that English has two ways of expressing a passive idea. One form, *the boat was upset,* always suggests an agent. The other, *the boat upset,* is used when the fact that there was an agent is uninteresting. Most young people, and their families, feel that the college authorities can be forgotten in speaking about the fact of graduation.

One may say *he graduated in 1956*. But if the name of the institution, or some substitute word, is used we must say *from*. *He graduated college* is not standard English and is not improved by being put in the passive, as in *he was graduated college.*

grammar is a systematic description of the ways in which words are used in a particular language. The grammarian groups words that behave similarly into classes and then draws up rules stating how each class of words behaves. What classes are set up and how the rules are phrased is a matter of convenience. A grammarian is free to classify his material in any way that seems reasonable to him. But he is never free to say that certain forms of speech are unacceptable merely because there is no place for them in the system he has designed.

THE CLASSES

Most grammarians are interested in a number of languages. As a rule they set up classes that are useful in handling many languages but that may have very little meaning for a particular language. For example, the distinction between the dative *him* and the accusative *him* is important in the Indo-European languages generally. But in a grammar designed solely to teach English, this distinction does not have to be made. Similarly, there is an etymological or historical difference between the English gerund in *-ing* and the participle in *-ing*. But it is sometimes impossible to say whether a given word is a gerund or a participle; for example, in *journeys end in lovers meeting*. For this reason, some grammarians prefer to handle these forms together under one name, such as "participle" or "*-ing*."

The familiar terms of classical grammar are defined in this dictionary for the convenience of persons who need to use these concepts. But a much simpler classification, based on the structure of present-day English, is employed in all the discussions of usage.

THE RULES

In order to say how words are used, the grammarian must examine large quantities of spoken and written English. He will find some constructions used so consistently that the exceptions have to be classed as errors. But he will also find competing, and even contradictory, constructions, which appear too often to be called mistakes. He must then see whether one of these expressions is used by one kind of person and not by another or in one kind of situation and not in another. If he can find no difference of this sort he accepts the two constructions as interchangeable. In this way he assembles a body of information on how English words are used that may also show differences, such as those between one locality and another, or between spoken and written English, or between literary and illiterate speech. Studies of this kind are called "scientific" or "descriptive" grammars. This is a relatively new approach to the problems of language and the information brought to light in this way is sometimes surprising.

The first English grammarians, writing in the seventeenth and eighteenth centuries, did not attempt to describe the English of their day. On the contrary, they were attempting to "improve" English and they demanded Latin constructions which were not characteristic of English. They objected to the expression *I am mistaken,* because if translated into Latin this would mean *I am misunderstood.* They claimed that *unloose* must mean *tie,* because *un* is a Latin negative. They objected to the "double negative" which was good Old English, and also good Greek, but not good Latin.

These eighteenth century rules of prescriptive grammar have been repeated in school books for two hundred years. They are the rules for a curious, Latinized English that has never been spoken and is seldom used in literature, but that is now highly respected in some places, principally in scientific writing. It should be recognized that these rules were not designed to "preserve" English, or keep it "pure." They were designed to create a language which would be "better" simply because it was more like Latin. Dryden, writing in the seventeenth century, said: "I am often put to a stand in considering whether what I write be the idiom of the tongue or false grammar and nonsense, couched beneath that specious name of Anglicism, and have no other way to clear my doubts but by translating my English into Latin and thereby trying what sense the words will bear in a more stable language." One result of this double translation was that Dryden went through his earlier works and rewrote all the sentences that had originally ended in a preposition or adverb. A generation later, Swift complained that the English of his day "offends against every part of grammar." Certainly this is blaming the foot because it doesn't fit the shoe!

Because some people would like to write the language of the textbooks, the entries in this dictionary not only tell what standing a given construction has in current English but also explain how the rules of the prescriptive grammarian would apply, wherever the rules and standard practice differ. But in such cases the rules are never simple, and the person who has to use this type of English may feel that it would be easier to follow Dryden's example and write in Latin first.

THIS BOOK

The grammar entries in this book are designed for persons who speak standard English but who may be confused about certain isolated points. The entries are arranged so that the answer to a particular problem can be found in the least possible time. But anyone who wishes to make a systematic study of English grammar, using this book, can do so by starting with the entry **parts of speech** and following the references to more and more detailed discussions of each concept.

grand with the meaning of first-rate, splendid, or very good (as in *We had a grand time. The weather was grand all the time. He's a grand fellow; I know you'll like him*) is a much-overworked word. *Grand* properly means imposing in size or appearance, stately, majestic, dignified, that which impresses upon the mind a sense of grandeur (*The view from the north rim of the canyon is awe-inspiring and grand beyond imagination. The coronation was a grand spectacle*). The word has been so debased by exaggeration and overuse, however, that it is often difficult to use it properly. It has become tinny.

grand finale. As a humorous extension into other fields, *grand finale,* drawn from the terminology of concerts, is a cliché.

grandiloquent; magniloquent. To be eloquent is to have the power of fluent, forcible and appropriate speech (*This eloquent little book spoke to men's hearts and moved them to contrition. Burke paid eloquent tribute to the memory of Pitt. His whole attitude was eloquent of discouragement*). *Grandiloquent* and *magniloquent* are both disparaging terms. They suggest pompous and bombastic eloquence, unsuitable lofti ness of utterance (*This miserable mudhole which he grandiloquently calls "the lake." It was absurd to describe so slight a performance in so magniloquent a manner*).

grandiose can be used favorably to designate something which produces an effect of grandeur. Thus Emerson speaks approvingly of Carlyle's *grandiose* style. More often, however, it has a disparaging sense of affected grandeur, pompousness. Augustine Birrell thought Milton *our grandest author*, Gibbon *our most grandiose*. *Grandiose* is confined almost entirely to matters of style.

grateful; gratified. *Grateful* is an adjective meaning warmly appreciative of kindness or benefits (*I am grateful for your assistance at a time when I know you have so much to do*), actuated by or betokening gratitude (*In a delicate and grateful speech he acknowledged his indebtedness to his old master*) or pleasing to the mind and senses (*Then in Oblivion's grateful cup/ I drown the galling sneer. The grateful shade that cools the laborer's brow*). This last sense is restricted to things and is a bookish word. It offers a convenient riming antithesis to *hateful*.

Gratified is the past tense of the verb to *gratify*, to give pleasure by satisfying desires or humoring inclinations (*The old man was gratified beyond words at this unexpected compliment*), to satisfy or indulge (*He gratified his appetite to the full*).

gravamen. See onus.

grave (verb). The past tense is *graved*. The participle is *graven* or *graved*. The participle *graven* is preferred to *graved*, probably because it is familiar to us in *graven images*. But the verb itself is extremely bookish. In everyday English we say *carve*, which is a regular verb with the past tense and the participle *carved*. An old form *carven* was used by nineteenth century poets but has not been normal English for four hundred years. The verb *engrave* is regular and has the past tense and participle *engraved*.

gray; grey. The preferred spelling in America is *gray*, in England *grey*, though both spellings are used in both countries. Some who seek to create distinctions have claimed that *gray* indicates a darker shade than *grey* but their claims have remained unsubstantiated.

Though *grayhound* is often seen, *greyhound* is definitely to be preferred, since the first syllable has no reference to color but is probably the Icelandic *grey*, dog, bitch.

great. See immense, infinite, large.

Great Britain; the United Kingdom; England. Since 1707 the term *Great Britain* has applied politically to England, Scotland, and Wales. *The United Kingdom* consists of Great Britain and Northern Ireland. Up until 1922 it also included Eire. *England*, properly, includes all of Great Britain except Scotland and Wales, but to most Americans *England* means *Great Britain*.

greatly. See materially.

Grecian; Greek. Despite Keats's "Ode on a Grecian Urn" and other poetic uses (*And saw the merry Grecian coaster come,/ Freighted with amber grapes, and Chian wine*), *Grecian* is now limited to the architecture of the ancient Greeks and to the features conventionalized in their statues. All else is now *Greek*.

green-eyed monster. As a term for jealousy, *the green-eyed monster* is now a cliché. It is taken from Shakespeare's *Othello*, from Iago's speech in the third act beginning:

O, beware, my lord, of jealousy!
It is the green-ey'd monster, which doth mock The meat it feeds on.

Scholars have expended much ink and some thought on the passage. Some have insisted that the monster should have been *yellow-ey'd* and that *mock* should be *make*. Others have identified the monster, variously, as a crocodile, a tiger, a cat, a mouse, and a dragonfly. But when the dust of learned controversy has settled, two things are plain: although the general meaning of the passage is clear, its specific meaning remains uncertain; the phrase has been worn out by repetition and should be avoided.

green house; greenhouse. A *green house* is a house that has been painted green or made of green materials. A *greenhouse* is a glasshouse for the cultivation or protection of tender plants (*Behind the green house was a greenhouse*).

grew. See grow.

grievous error. *Grievous* meant pressing heavily upon (*grievous taxes and other burdens*). It was commonly applied to sins of a grave nature, the guilt of which, presumably, pressed heavily upon those who had committed them (*grievous crimes and flagitious facts daily committed*). Then it came to mean atrocious, flagrant. And in this sense transferred to error in the phrase *grievous error* which has now become a cliché.

grill. The use of *grill* to mean a severe and persistent questioning (*Grill him! Beat it out of him! Make him tell you where he's hidden that bloody poker. The police grilled the suspect for twenty-four hours but learned nothing*), a metaphorical extension of *grill* in its sense of broiling on a gridiron, is slang.

grin and bear it. The saying used to be *to grin and abide*. It was so quoted as a proverb in 1802. It changed to *grin and bear it* during the nineteenth century and became a cliché towards the end of the century. One must bear it, but the grin has long since faded.

grind. The past tense is *ground*. The participle is also *ground*.

grisly; grizzly. That is *grisly* which is horrible to behold, gruesome, grim, and ghastly (*Look down and see a grisly sight;/ A vault where the bodies are buried upright!*). That is *grizzly* which is gray or grizzled. The term is used especially of hair and carries a suggestion of roughness as well as grayness (*He had a grizzly, jagged beard of some three weeks growth*). Perhaps by the time one's hair is gray one no longer bothers to keep it as sleek as formerly or perhaps it has grown stiffer with age. The grizzly bear (*Ursus horribilis*), so called from the color of its pelt, probably has a great deal to do with the blending of the two words.

grit (pluck). **See sand.**

grits; groats. In Great Britain *grits* is considered a dialect form of *groats,* but in the United States *grits* is the standard form and *groats* is almost unknown. *Groats* originally meant coarsely ground oats but may now be used also of other grains. In the United States *grits* usually means coarsely ground corn, or maize, but may also be used of other grains. It is a mass word with plural form and is always treated as a plural, as in *these grits are good* and *have some of them.* But it is not a true plural and does not have a singular. We cannot speak of *many grits* or of *a grit.*

grocery. The use of *grocery* to designate a grocery store was until very recently universal in America. It is now being displaced, to a considerable extent, by the names of the great chains of grocery stores, "the A & P," "Kroger's," "National," and so on. And the use of these has led to designating individual, independently owned stores by their specific names. Still, *grocery* is widely used. In England the term is *the grocer's, the greengrocer's,* or *the grocery shop.*

groin; groyne. In America *groin* is the spelling for all uses of the word—anatomical, architectural, and in civil engineering. *Groyn* and *groyne* are recognized, but only as rare variants. In England *groin* is the spelling for the anatomical and architectural senses, but the breakwater is spelled *groyne.*

groom. The use of *groom* for bridegroom (*The groom seemed nervous and kept asking the best man if he was sure that the bride had arrived*) is standard American usage, though in England *bridegroom* is invariably used.

As a verb to *groom* is used in America to mean to prepare a man for a position, especially a political position (*He was being groomed for the presidency*), probably as an extension of the idea of a political contest as a race.

gross. When this word means 144, it is a noun. It cannot stand immediately before another noun, as the word *dozen* can, but must be joined to it by *of. Gross* has the same form in the singular and the plural, as in *a gross of eggs* and *many gross of red buttons.*

ground. See grind.

ground; grounds. These words are used in several senses, all related to the idea of *bottom* or *foundation.* The singular form *ground* is used in speaking of the soil or part of the surface of the earth. The plural form *grounds* is used for decorative ground around a building. It is considered improper, or pretentious, to call farm lands *grounds.* But the plural form may be used for areas that have some other purpose, such as *fishing grounds, burial grounds, picnic grounds.*

When the word means sediment, it is usually plural, as in *coffee grounds.* The singular form is also used in this sense, as in *not a single ground,* but this is very rare.

Either the singular or the plural may be used in speaking of the basis for an opinion or the basis of a science. A man may have *good ground* or *good grounds* for what he thinks.

There is no difference in meaning. But only the singular *ground* can be used to mean a position. In an argument a man holds his *ground,* not his *grounds.*

ground floor, to be let in on. At first thought, *to be let in on the ground floor* is puzzling since, except under unusual circumstances, this is the only floor one could be let in on. As an expression for being granted an interest in some enterprise on the same terms as those accorded the original investors, or being admitted to some enterprise before the general public, it may be, as Partridge suggests, a metaphor from being given an office on the ground floor of a new building. If this is so, it must date back to a time before elevators were in use when being on the ground floor was a decided advantage. The phrase has never been more than a colloquialism and is already jaded.

group names. Some nouns, such as *herd, flock, crowd, jury, family, nation,* are names of groups of living things. They have plural forms, such as *herds, juries, nations,* which mean more than one such group. There is nothing unusual about these plural forms. But words of this kind when used in the singular may be followed by either a singular or a plural verb. When what is said applies to the group as a whole, a singular verb is used, as in *my family is a large one* and *the jury was out for six hours.* When what is being said applies to the individual members of the group, a plural verb is used, as in *my family are early risers* and *the jury were unable to agree.* In most cases, only the speaker knows which form suits his meaning best.

The singular group name with a plural verb is used in England more often than it is in this country. Very few Americans would say *the herd were thirsty.* But this is permissible grammar for anyone who cares to use it. When the group is made up of human beings, the plural verb is usually preferred, even in this country. That is, it is more courteous to say *the staff were willing to work late* than to say *the staff was willing to work late.*

When the name of a group composed of human beings is used with a singular verb, it is referred to as *which;* when used with a plural verb, it is referred to as *who.* Plural qualifiers, such as *these, those, some, many, few,* cannot be used with singular group names. On the other hand, singular qualifiers, such as *this, that, one, any, each,* cannot be used before a plural verb. But the group may be referred to as *it* or *they,* independently of the number of the verb or of a qualifying word, as is done in *when . . . it becomes necessary for one people to dissolve the political bands which have connected them with another.* Here *them* refers to the grammatically singular group *one people.*

Many grammarians who allow both the singular and the plural construction with singular group names warn against using both constructions in the same sentence. This is probably good advice for a poor writer. But the best writers shift their form to fit their meaning. This shifting construction is used by most of the great writers of English and is found in such an impeccable document as the Constitution of the United States. Article I, Section 5, of the Constitution reads: *Each house shall keep a journal of its proceedings, and from time to time publish the same, excepting such parts as may in their judgment require secrecy.* Here *proceedings,* which belongs to the house as a unit, has the singular pronoun *its,* and *judgment,* which belongs only to individual men, has the plural *their.* This is not careless writing. Had the sentence been edited to read *in its judgment,* it would not have been as fine prose as it is.

Although a singular group name may be used with a plural verb, it means the entire group and not some individuals in the group. It is not a plural noun and cannot be used with a numeral. That is, we do not say *three jury were unconvinced.* But occasionally a group name is used in this way so often that it finally becomes an accepted plural. This has happened, for example, with *people* and *clergy.* During the nineteenth century *two people* and *forty clergy* were considered unacceptable expressions, but they are now thoroughly acceptable. Today we have a few words, such as *staff,* which may be in transition from group names to plurals. We sometimes hear *three staff were willing to work late.* This is not yet standard English and is offensive to many people.

All group names that may be used with a numeral are listed in this dictionary as irregular plurals. Nouns that are often used in this way, in violation of our present standards, are also listed. If a group name cannot be found in this book, it is perfectly regular, that is, the singular form may be used with a plural verb but not with a plural qualifier.

Some words that are not actually group names are used in much the same manner. Although we might say of non-human things *fifty percent was destroyed,* in speaking of people we would say *fifty percent were illiterate.* Here *fifty percent* is being treated as if it were a group name. Adjectives used to indicate a class of human beings, and the names of certain animals when used to represent the entire class, are also treated as group names and followed by a plural verb, as in *the wise are happy* and *the sea otter have disappeared.* See **adjectives as nouns** and **generic nouns.**

grouse. The plural is *grouse.*

grow. The past tense is *grew.* The participle is *grown.* A past tense and participle *growed* is heard but is not standard. The arbitrariness of what constitutes standard English is seen very clearly when one compares this verb with *crow.* There the form *crowed* is now standard and *crew, crown* are no longer used.

Grow may be used to mean *become.* In this sense it may be followed by an adjective describing the subject of the verb, as in *he grew bald.* We may even say *it grew smaller.* When used in this sense, *grow* may be followed by an infinitive, as in *I grew to know them better.* It is sometimes heard with the *-ing* form of a verb

and the preposition *to,* as in *I grew to knowing them better,* but this is not standard.

grudge; spite. A *grudge* is a feeling of sullen resentment by one who suffers a real or fancied wrong and seeks retribution (*He bore a grudge against his neighbor for many years because the neighbor once blocked his driveway*). A grudge is usually caused by a trifling wrong. It is not so deep seated or permanent as enmity and is often assuaged when the offender has been "paid back." *Spite* is a sharper, more active resentment, and is as likely to find satisfaction in mortifying the enemy as in injuring him. It can range from malice to pique. One who bears a grudge is likely to have a specific wrong over which he broods; one who harbors spite is likely to be more generally hostile. See also **begrudge; malice.**

Grundy, Mrs. See **gay Lothario.**

guarantee; guaranty. *Guarantee* is correct in all uses, as a noun and as a verb. *Guaranty* may be used for a warrant or pledge or the act of giving security or, as a verb, to guarantee.

From its sense of giving security for the carrying out of assurances, *guarantee* has come to mean making certain (*The United States guarantees the territorial integrity of the Republic of Cuba*) or merely stating an opinion with conviction (*I guarantee he'll agree with us when he hears what we now know*). See also **warrant; warranty.**

guard in America has the special meaning of one who guards prisoners in a penal institution (*During Jim Hall's third term in prison he encountered a guard that was almost as great a beast as he*). In England the term is *warder.*

gubernatorial. The Latin *gubernare* meant to steer a ship. Hence references to functions or attributes of a governor as *gubernatorial* belong to one of the most ancient, worn, and moldy of all metaphors—the ship of state. It is an American word and has a rolling resonance dear to an older generation of political rhetoricians. It is a safe course to avoid it wherever *governor's* or *of the government* can be used instead.

In the days when a father was facetiously referred to as "the governor," *gubernatorial* was sometimes substituted for paternal.

guerrilla; gorilla. *Guerrilla* (also *guerilla*) means irregular warfare (*He organized a series of guerilla raids on and over the border. A sort of guerilla warfare went on constantly between the farmers and the teamsters. The celebrated guerilla leader was, in his way, a gallant man*). English writers insist that the word can be used properly only of the warfare itself and that those who take part in it should be called *guer(r)illeros,* but American usage sanctions *guer(r)illa* for both the warfare and those who wage it (*He put himself at the head of a band of guerillas. Villa's guerrillas did not deserve the name or the treatment of soldiers*).

Whether the slang word for a gangster's slugger is *guerrilla* or *gorilla* is uncertain, since the two words are so often pronounced alike. Some scholars are inclined to think that it is guerrilla, but this is a little fanciful, and if it ever was it has certainly become gorilla, expressing not so much the idea of an irregular warrior as of a powerful brute.

guess; conjecture; surmise. To guess is to form a notion or imperfect opinion without certain knowledge but on the basis of probable indications (By the measure of my grief/ I leave thy greatness to be guessed). In its particular application to the solving of riddles and enigmas, it means to conjecture correctly (Can you guess exactly what I mean?). It is loosely used to mean think, suppose, or imagine and this use, though absurd when applied to a certainty (as in Well, I'm too tired to get up, so I guess I'll just go on sitting), is sanctioned by English writers from Chaucer to Wordsworth. Chaucer says that he guessed he never heard sweeter music than some he alludes to. Shakespeare has Lord Talbot, in First Henry Sixth, say that he guesses it would be better for several scaling parties to assault the walls of Orleans separately. Sheridan uses the word this way and so does Wordsworth. The point has been labored a little because this use is frequently regarded as not standard and among English writers unfamiliar with their own literature and language condemned as an "Americanism." In the United States guess, in this sense, is supposed to prove that one comes from north of the Potomac. But it is heard in many parts of the country, and is standard where it is used.

To conjecture is to conclude or suppose from grounds insufficient to ensure reliability. Conjecture is from a Latin word meaning "to throw together" and there is in the word still a sense of a random throw, an arbitrary choice, guided chiefly by chance, of one opinion from many possible ones (As long as men have liberty to examine and contradict one another, one may partly conjecture, by comparing their words, on which side the truth is like to lie).

Surmise is very close in meaning to conjecture, but it sometimes carries a connotation of suspicion, though not always unfavorable suspicion (My surmise, that he was not really an important military man, proved correct. The neighbors had long surmised that he was much wealthier than his shabby appearance and mean way of living suggested).

guide, philosopher, and friend. First applied by Alexander Pope to Henry St. John, Viscount Bolingbroke, guide, philosopher, and friend has now become a pompous cliché if used seriously and a feeble jest if used facetiously.

guimpe. See **gimp.**

gun. In English usage and in American traditional usage a gun is any portable firearm except a pistol or revolver. In current American usage, however, a gun is often a pistol or revolver or automatic (The bulge in the pocket suggested a gun). An interesting illustration of the manner in which the meaning of a word lies in its connotations is supplied by gunman and rifleman. Though a man's a man and a rifle is a gun, a gunman is a sinister character of the underworld

and a rifleman is a skilled and honorable soldier or an accomplished sportsman.

guts; pluck. Guts is now a coarse word, the mildest of the four-letter words but outside the realm of polite usage. It once had dignity (the Oxford English Dictionary quotes from a 14th century psalter: Clene hert make in me, God, and trewe,/ And right gaste in mi guttes newe) but is now, except when used in its literal sense of intestines, by fishmongers and hunters, used metaphorically for courage and fortitude. Even so, it is felt to be a strong or manly or deliberately rough word and is avoided by the refined. Those who avoid it, however, often use the word pluck (more in use among the English than in America) without knowing that it is an old word for the viscera of an animal.

In American slang guts means impudence more often than courage (He's got his guts, coming in here without knocking), though the two qualities are related. Gut, except when used anatomically to denote the alimentary canal between the pylorus and the anus or, as a verb, to remove the intestines, is a slang word, a facetious back-formation from guts (as in I thought I'd bust a gut laughing at his antics). See also **belly; sand.**

guy. Guy Fawkes was the man employed by the conspirators in the famous English Gunpowder Plot to blow up King James I and all the members of Parliament on November 5, 1605. The plot was discovered and most of those implicated were apprehended and executed. Fawkes became a symbol of hatred and November the fifth is still celebrated in England as Guy Fawkes Day. One of the features of this day is the burning of an effigy, "the guy," a grotesque figure of old clothes stuffed with straw or rags. It is customary for children to drag the guy around with them for several days before the fifth, singing songs and demanding coppers. Hence guy, in England, means anyone so grotesque in appearance that he or she might be compared to one of these effigies.

In American usage the noun guy has no sense of disparagement and may derive from a wholly different word. It simply means man, fellow, chap—indeed any male who may be spoken of without especial respect or reverence. In American usage a regular guy is a complimentary term, implying that the one complimented is one of the people, in no way blighted by any innate or acquired excellences. In England the phrase would mean a veritable freak, an absolute fright, a truly grotesque person.

The verb to guy, however, has the same meaning in the United States that it has in England—to make fun of (His fraternity brothers guyed him unmercifully about his failure to get a date with her). The verb is not used excessively but the noun, though (like the verb) not standard, must be one of the most frequently used words in America. It is a lazy man's word, reducing all adult males to simulacra among whom there is no need to make any distinction. Thomas Wolfe, who gloried in words more than almost any writer of English since the Elizabethan age, uttered a wild cry of anguish, in *Of Time and the River,* at the stupefying use of this "terrible gray abortion of a word" which even then studded the speech of common men "with the numberless monotony of paving brick." "Without it," he wailed, "they would have been completely speechless and would have had to communicate by convulsions of their arms and hands and painful croakings from their tongueless throats—the word fell upon the spirit of the listener with the gray weariness of a cold inces-

sant drizzle, it flowed across the spirit like a river of concrete; hope, joy, the power to feel and think were drowned out under the relentless and pitiless aridity of its flood."

gymnasium. The plural is *gymnasiums* or *gymnasia.*

gypsy; gipsy. The preference in America is for *gypsy.* In England it is for *gipsy.* The word should be capitalized whenever the people or the language is meant (*The old Gypsy uttered the usual gypsy's warning*). The plural is *Gypsies* or *Gipsies.*

H

haberdashery. Among the Canterbury pilgrims there was a haberdasher. Just suddenly, like Venus from the sea foam, he appeared fully formed. But where he came from and whence he got his name, no one knows. Chaucer apparently assumed that the word was well known and does not expatiate upon it. The haberdasher tells no tale and does not appear after a mention in the *Prologue* to *The Canterbury Tales.* Some among the learned have connected the word with the French *avoirdupois.* Others have connected it with *hapertas,* a width of cloth. But no one knows for sure. Even today there is uncertainty. In England a haberdasher sells what in the United States would be called notions—thread, needles, buttons, ribbons, and tape. In America he sells men's furnishings—shirts, collars, ties, hats, gloves, and underwear. *Haberdashery* is what a haberdasher sells and the shop in which he sells it.

habit. See **custom.**

habitable; inhabitable. *Habitable* applies chiefly to buildings or living spaces for human beings (*The house was so overrun with rats as to be no longer habitable*). *Inhabitable* refers to areas or countries in which men or animals can establish settled residence (*Crusoe was relieved to find that the island was inhabitable. All evidence suggests that life as we know it could not inhabit any of the planets except our own*).

The older meaning of *inhabitable,* by the way, was uninhabitable (*Jove has the Realms of Earth in vain / Divided by th' inhabitable Main. The land was inhabitable because of the sterility and barrenness thereof*). This meaning is now obsolete, but it illustrates the pitfalls that await the unwary reader.

habitual. See **usual.**

hackneyed. See **commonplace.**

had. See **have.**

hail; hale. *To hail* is to call or shout from a distance in order to attract attention (*I hailed a taxi and ordered the driver to take me at once to the airport*). *To hale* is to haul, to pull, draw, constrain to go along (*Witnesses to the accident*

hailed a policeman who haled the drunken driver into court*).

To hail from, to come from (*Our passengers hailed from fifteen states*), is standard, though it now has an old-fashioned and slightly rustic flavor.

hale and hearty. *Hale* means healthy, vigorous, robust. By usage it has come to be attached to the old. One never hears a young person, however healthy, spoken of as hale. *Hale and hearty* is one of those alliterative reduplications which so easily become clichés and this one has not escaped the general fate. *Hearty* originally meant courageous and the phrase may once have signified health in mind and body, but all precise meaning has long ago been drained out of it by repetition.

half. The plural is usually *halves,* but *halfs* is also used. *Half* may be treated as a noun or as an adjective or as a compromise between the two. It is a noun when it stands alone, as in *divide it in halves,* and when it is followed by *of* and another noun that is qualified by a definitive adjective (such as *a, the, this, my, some*) as in *half of the world, half of my apple.* It is an adjective when it stands immediately before another noun, as in *a half hour, a half apple.* When used with a pronoun, *half* must always be treated as a noun and followed by *of,* as in *half of us, half of it.* But when used with a noun, this *of* may be dropped, as in *half an apple, half a league onward.* This is an unusual word order, but the construction has been standard English for at least a thousand years. As a rule it makes no difference where the word *half* stands. *Half a league* is *a half league.*

When used as an adjective, *half* may qualify either a singular or a plural noun. Whether a following verb is singular or plural depends upon the noun, as in *half the apples are bad, half the apple is bad.* The singular form *half* standing alone may also be followed by a plural verb when it refers to a number of countable things, as in *half are finished.*

Half may be used as an adverb to qualify a

verb or adjective, as in *he half finished the work*. It is used in this way in expressions of time, such as *at half past five*. We may also say *one half* or *a half* in sentences of this kind, but the qualifying word is not necessary and is usually omitted. *One half* may be written with or without a hyphen. *Two halves* is not a fraction and should not be hyphenated.

half-breed; half-caste. See **mulatto.**

half the battle. Said of something which contributes largely to success, *it is half the battle* is already a cliché, even though the earliest occurrence of the phrase (*Oxford English Dictionary*) is 1849, in Captain Marryat's *Valerie* (*Youth . . . is more than half the battle*).

hallelujah, "praise ye the Lord," is the preferred spelling. But *halleluiah, alleluia, alleluiah,* and *alleluja* are also recognized.

halloo. See **hello.**

halves. See **half.**

hammer and tongs, to go at something. As a term for attacking something, usually a piece of work or an argument, with great force and violence and an attendant clatter, *to go at it hammer and tongs* is now a cliché. A term from the smithy has very little actuality for most English-speaking people now and is bound to be hollow as well as worn out.

hamstring. The past tense is *hamstringed* or *hamstrung*. The participle is also *hamstringed* or *hamstrung*. Theoretically this verb, which means to cut the hamstring, should be formed regularly, with the past tense and participle *hamstringed*. But it has been influenced by the verb *string* and the form *hamstrung* is now generally preferred to *hamstringed*. Both forms are acceptable.

hand in glove. To say of those in intimate association that they are *hand in glove* is to employ a cliché. The older form was *hand and glove* and this makes better sense—i.e., they are as close as *hand and glove*. *Hand in glove* may have been a confusion of *hand and glove* and *hand in hand*. There is a suggestion in *hand in glove* that the intimacy is slightly nefarious, conspiratorial, up to no good.

handicap; hindrance. *Handicap* is a shortening of *hand-in-the-cap*, an old game of wagering and forfeits in which the contestants put their hands in a cap and drew out various amounts of money. The game is described unmistakably in *Piers Plowman* (1362-1399) under the name of *Newe Faire,* though the earliest instance of *handicap* (*Oxford English Dictionary*) is 1653—a salutary warning for those who would construct social history from linguistics or vice versa. From the game it came to mean some extra weight or other condition imposed on a superior in an athletic event to equalize the chances of an inferior, and from that it came to mean any incumbrance or disability that makes success more difficult. Thus it is common today to refer to lame children as handicapped children, though there is no suggestion (unless a pathetic flattery was originally intended) that they are necessarily superior children reduced, by their misfortune, to equality with other children.

A *hindrance* is that which obstructs or pre-

vents action, an incumbrance, a check, a restraint. *Hindered children* would be a more accurate, if less kind, description of those that are lame. To many employments youth, for example, is a hindrance; but it is not a handicap.

handle; manage. To *handle* is primarily, and plainly, to touch or feel with the hands, to manipulate (*The lieutenant handled the detonator gingerly*). Some purists have maintained that this is the full scope of the word, that it should be confined to the act of touching with the hands, but language doesn't accept any such confines and *handle* and *manage* are used interchangeably to mean the control or influence of persons, objects, or operations (*He can handle the most difficult clients* or *He can manage the most difficult clients*). Of course where the meaning is that the hands are used (*His ability to handle the ball soon made him a major-league pitcher*), *handle* is preferable. *Manage* suggests a less purely physical control or direction (*He manages these affairs with great finesse*); and where it means, as it increasingly does, the exercise of managerial functions (*The business is well managed and has shown excellent profits*), *handle* will not serve as a synonym.

handle with kid gloves. As a term for delicate treatment or consideration, *to handle someone with kid gloves* is now a cliché.

hand-me-downs seem originally to have been cheap or ready-made garments, something handed down off the shelf at request instead of being made to measure. The English phrase is *reach-me-downs*. Today, however, in America, the phrase means second-hand clothing, something handed down from the first user.

handwriting on the wall. As a term for a warning of doom, *the handwriting on the wall,* drawn from the apparition at Belshazzar's impious feast, should be used sparingly.

hang. The past tense is *hung* or *hanged*. The participle is also *hung* or *hanged*. At one time these words were used in a slightly different sense. One would say *we hung the picture* but the *picture hanged on the wall*. Today *hanged* is used only to mean killed by hanging. Some grammarians believe that the form *hanged* must always be used when this is what is meant. But the form *hung* is being used more and more in this sense, as in *I have not the least objection in life to a rogue being hung*, and seems to be driving *hanged* from the language.

hang on like grim death is a cliché.

hangar; hanger. A *hangar* is a shed or shelter for aircraft. A *hanger* is that which or one who hangs things, as a *coathanger, pothanger,* or *paperhanger*. It is also the name for a light sabre of the 17th and 18th centuries, often worn at sea. Gulliver had one.

haply; happily. *Haply,* now archaic, means by luck, chance, or accident (*Haply some hoary-headed swain may say,/ "Oft have we seen him . . ."*). *Happily,* once the same word as *haply,* means by good luck, favorable chance, or in a pleasurable manner (*Happily the bullet just missed him. The child sang happily in the swing*).

happen. This verb may be followed by an infini-- tive, as in *we happen to like her,* or by a clause when used impersonally, as in *it happens we like her. Happen* is sometimes used as the equivalent of *perhaps,* as in *happen you'll like her,* but this is not standard now. See **transpire.**

happening; event; episode; incident; occurrence. The use of *happening* as a verbal noun is unexceptionable (*Its happening when it did served to establish the man as a prophet*). But its use as a synonym for event or occurrence (*These are common happenings*) has been strongly condemned. Fowler calls it a "journalistic affectation" and others have echoed his stricture. But it has been so used for four centuries and must be accepted as standard, especially for things that just happen as against more important occurrences which are more likely to be described as *events.*

Events can be happenings of any kind (*All the events that make up an invalid's trivial day*) but the word usually means an important happening, especially one that is connected with and comes out of previous happenings (*The event was eagerly awaited. The publication of a new book by Sinclair Lewis was always an event*). An *episode* is one of a progressive series of happenings, frequently distinct from the main course of events and having a continuity and interest of its own (*Franklin's visit to France was a remarkable episode in a remarkable career*). An *incident* is a minor happening in connection with an event or series of events of greater importance (*There was a delightful incident at Mrs. Preston's Christmas party*). An *occurrence* is simply something that happens, having no connection with or causation by antecedent happenings (*His being ill at the very time Alexander died was an occurrence for which Cesare had made no preparation*).

happily. See **haply.**

happiness; pleasure; felicity; bliss. *Happiness* and *pleasure* both describe satisfaction but they differ in range and duration. *Pleasure* describes a state or feeling of satisfaction, usually of the senses, which is of fairly brief duration (*There is a pleasure in the pathless woods. A witty answer, opportunely given, affords great pleasure*). *Happiness* is a more settled state of contentment, resulting from the attainment of what one considers good. It is a broader term than *pleasure* because it includes not merely satisfaction from sensation but also from ideas of well-being and good fortune (*Life, liberty, and the pursuit of happiness*).

Felicity is a formal word for a state of being happy in a very high degree, intense joy. When the dying Hamlet besought Horatio to go on living, saying *Absent thee from felicity awhile,* the use of the word *felicity* conveyed the Prince's idea of death as an intense pleasure (or, rather, by implication, of life as something intensely repugnant). The choice of this word might be said to be *felicitous,* which also means a happy knack or choice, hitting the bull's eye with more precision than skill alone could ever hope

for. Bacon said that the painter or musician that excelled did so *by a kind of felicity and not by rule.*

Bliss is perfect joy, supreme felicity. It is this that gives Gray's *Where ignorance is bliss, / 'Tis folly to be wise* such force. And since the supremest of all joys, in the Christian conception, was the state experienced in heaven, *bliss* was often used to describe the heavenly state of being (*By the hope I have of heavenly bliss*).

harangue; tirade. A *harangue* is a noisy speech, vulgar and vehement, addressed to a large audience (*These ceaseless harangues were resented by those in the assembly who desired a more temperate and informed discussion of the real issues*). A *tirade* need not be addressed to a number of persons; one auditor will suffice, and while vulgar and vehement public speeches usually are attacks on someone or something, a *harangue* need not be an attack. It could be an exhortation. But a *tirade* is always an outpouring of vituperation or censure (*Her table talk consisted of endless tirades against her husband*).

harass. See **tantalize.**

hard and fast line. As an affirmation of a fixed intention, an unshakable resolve, *to draw a hard and fast line* is now a cliché.

hard; hardly. *Hard* is as truly an adverb as it is an adjective. Sometimes the form *hardly* is used to mean difficult, as in *his hardly earned reputation.* This is permissible, but it is not an improvement on *hard.* In a construction of this kind the word *hard* would be clearer, and more literary.

Hardly means scarcely and has the force of a negative. It should not be used in a negative sentence, such as *I haven't hardly any.* But many people do use it in sentences that aren't so obviously negative, as in *they left without hardly a word.* Technically, this is a double negative and should be *they left without a word* or *they left with hardly a word.* See **double negatives.**

Hardly may be followed by *when,* but not by *than.* One can say *he had hardly arrived when it began to snow,* but not *he had hardly arrived than it began to snow.*

hardly, barely, and **scarcely** all imply that something was accomplished, and is being accomplished, or will be accomplished by a narrow margin. They are sometimes interchangeable, but *hardly* usually serves to mark the difficulty of the accomplishment (*She could hardly keep still until he had finished his sentence. We could hardly get out of the house, the snow was so deep*). *Barely* serves to mark the narrowness of the margin. It says the thing just squeaked by (*He barely made the train. It was moving when he flung himself and his briefcase into the vestibule of the last coach*). *Scarcely* implies a margin so narrow as to be below satisfactory performance (*You would scarcely believe what nonsense he talks. The child can scarcely read a line*).

These words are restrictive in meaning and therefore have the force of a negative. When used with another negative word they may form a double negative.

harmony; melody. Both words refer to musical sound, but they differ in that *harmony* is the blending of simultaneous sounds of different pitch or quality into chords (*"Sweet Adeline" is the most famous product of barbershop harmony*), while *melody* is the rhythmical combination of successive sounds of various pitch, making up the tune or air (*With one finger he picked out the melody on the piano*). See also **melody; tune.**

hart; stag; buck; hind; doe. A *hart* is a male of the deer, commonly the red deer, after its fifth year. A *stag* is an adult male deer. The term is also applied to the males of various other animals. In colloquial American usage it designates a man unaccompanied by a woman at a social gathering or a special party for men unaccompanied by their wives. It also means a swine which has been castrated after the maturation of the sex organs. There is no known etymological connection between these last meanings. A *buck* is a male of the deer, antelope, rabbit, hare, sheep, or goat. It is applied to the males of other animals. A *hind* is the female of the deer, chiefly the red deer, especially in and after the third year. A *doe* is the female of the deer, antelope, goat, rabbit, and certain other animals.

Harvard accent is a cliché of resentment that mingles malice and ignorance in about equal proportions. No college in the country draws its students from as widely divergent regions as does Harvard and upon none would it be harder to fix a peculiarity of speech. When asked to demonstrate what they mean, those who employ the term usually attempt to imitate upper middle-class English speech or the pronunciation of the letter "a" common among the Boston Irish, a group not marked by any affinity for Harvard. See also **Boston accent.**

has. See **have.**

hate; dislike. *Hate* suggests intense aversion, abhorrence (*Gr-r-r—there go, my heart's abhorrence!/ Water your damned flower-pots, do!/ If hate killed men, Brother Lawrence,/ God's blood, would not mine kill you!*). *Dislike* indicates mild aversion (*I dislike having my breakfast interrupted in this way*). The use of *hate* for every small annoyance is puerile. The consistent user should consult either a dictionary or a psychiatrist.

Hate may be followed by an infinitive, as in *I hate to think about it,* or by the *-ing* form of a verb, as in *I hate thinking about it.* These forms are equally acceptable. With *dislike* the *-ing* form is preferred.

hate; abhor; detest; loathe. All of these words suggest strong aversion. *Hate,* the commonest of the four, the everyday, working word, suggests strong aversion (*I hate to see the evening sun go down*) often coupled with enmity and malice (*I hate the Moor;/ And it is thought abroad that 'twixt my sheets/ He has done my office*). *Abhor* expresses a sense of repugnance bordering upon horror (*He so abhorred lying that he could scarcely be persuaded to remain in the same room with anyone whom he suspected of not telling the truth*). *Detest* expresses strong antipathy with a considerable element of disdain (*The man's combination of servility and arrogance, his crawling before his superiors and bullying of all under him, is detestable*). *Loathe* expresses strong dislike and an almost overwhelming disgust (*The greasy, splotched face, the foul breath, the insolent familiarity, with his eternal suggestion that we have some guilty secret in common—Oh, how I loathe the man!*).

haughtiness. See **pride.**

haul. See **draw.**

have. The past tense is *had.* The participle is also *had.* In the present tense the third person singular is *has.* The basic meaning of *have* is possess. Whenever it is followed by a simple object, that is, a noun or pronoun, it has this meaning, as in *they have a new car* and *he hasn't much to say.*

In Great Britain the verb *do* is not ordinarily used with *have* in questions and negative statements as it is with other verbs. That is, *have you* is considered better than *do you have* and *I haven't* than *I don't have.* In the United States both forms are used but the one with *do* is preferred. The word *had* placed before its subject indicates a contrary to fact condition, as in *had I the money, I would . . . .*

There is not much difference between the verb *have,* meaning possess, and the verb *get,* meaning acquire, and the two are often used interchangeably or together for emphasis, as in *I have a cold* and *I have got a cold.* When *have* is used as a full verb the word *got* may be used with it, as in the examples, but cannot be substituted for it. See **get.**

Forms of the verb *have* followed by a past participle of any verb, as in *he has left, they had left,* make the perfect tenses of the second verb. (See **perfect tenses.**) The past perfect tenses made with *had* can be used to indicate that a statement is contrary to fact, as in *had he left earlier, he would have . . .* (See **subjunctive mode.**) The full verb *have* also has perfect tense forms and one can say *he has had supper* or *he had had supper.* But the second element is always the participle *had* and never the simple form *have.* The form *had have* is heard frequently but there is no possible situation in which this is correct English. It is most often used where *would have* or simply *had* is required. (This is discussed more fully under **subjunctive mode.**) The expressions *had rather, had better,* are not the same thing. These are literary English. (See **rather.**)

Have is also used as a causative auxiliary, that is, as an auxiliary verb meaning "cause to." When used in this way in an active construction the form of *have* is followed by an object and the simple form of a verb, as in *I had him come.* The second verb may also have an object, as in *I had him paint the house.* Causative *have* may also be followed by a passive construction. Here the word *be* is understood but never used and the object is followed immediately by a past participle, as in *I had the house painted.* This construction differs from a perfect tense form, such as *I had painted the house,* only in the position of the object. In the perfect tenses the object never stands between the elements of the verbal phrase. (*Get* is also used as a causative. In the passive construction it is used just as *have* is, as in *I got the house painted.* In the active construction it requires a *to*-infinitive, as in *I got him to paint the house.*)

What looks like an infinitive form of this causative *have* is often used without any implication of compulsion on the part of the speaker but almost in the sense of "possess," as in *he would like to have you come* and *it is heaven upon earth to have a man's mind move in charity, rest in providence, and turn upon the poles of truth.* In all of its uses as an auxiliary, *have* keeps a great deal of its primary meaning.

Forms of *have* followed by a *to*-infinitive express necessity or constraint, as in *we have to leave.* Here *have to* is equivalent to *must* and is a much more useful verb. *Must* cannot be used in past or future tense forms and phrases such as *we had to* and *we will have to* are convenient substitutes. In this construction *have* can be used with forms of the verb *do,* as in *we do have to leave* or *we did have to leave.* Or the word *got* may be used to make the statement more emphatic, as in *we've got to leave.* In *you will have to have some one help you,* the first *have* expresses necessity. The second *have* is a causative attached to the verb *help.*

Have is sometimes used simply as a substitute for the passive voice, as in *I had my ankle sprained* and *I had my house broken into.* This is an ambiguous construction because it has exactly the form of the causative *have,* and should be avoided for that reason, at least in writing.

he. See **subjective pronouns** and **his.**

head. When this word is used in counting cattle, the singular form *head* is always used after a numeral, as in *forty head of cattle.* The plural form *heads* is used only when there is no numeral, as in *wealth is reckoned by heads of cattle.* The singular form is, of course, used after the article *a,* as in *not a head of cattle.*

In the United States, the word *cattle* is used as a true plural and no need is felt for the particularizing word *head. Ten thousand cattle straying* is standard English in this country.

head or tail of, not able to make. Sometimes it's *heads or tails,* and sometimes it's *unable to make.* The meaning seems to be that that which does not have a distinguishable head or tail or whose head cannot be distinguished from its tail would be difficult to classify.

The phrase itself, however, is not at all hard to classify. It's a cliché. It's been around for well over two centuries and has been used until all freshness and original meaning have gone out of it and it deserves to be forgotten.

head over heels. The phrase *head over heels* seems to have performed a somersault itself, for things are not topsy-turvy but in their proper order when the head is *over* the heels. Some tenacious purists insist that the phrase is proper-

ly and logically *heels over head,* but, knocking logic heels over head, usage has decreed that it shall be *head over heels.* Moreover, the expression is often used in the United States with no suggestion of somersaulting or cartwheeling, as in *he is head over heels in love* or *he is head over heels in debt.* Admittedly, this makes no sense. But *heels over head* makes no sense either and does not have the advantage of being the familiar idiom. A writer who finds *head over heels* troublesome should keep to literary English and say *extremely* or *very much.*

headlines. That a word is used in a special sense in a headline is no reason for assuming that this sense is standard for that word. Headlines have become a language unto themselves, often incomprehensible until the article itself has been read. Any restraint becomes a BAN. Anyone who is questioned is GRILLED. And all nouns become adjectives to be agglutinated in any sequence. MERCURY PLUMMETS may convey the knowledge that the temperature has fallen, but it isn't standard English. And even a highly literate person would have to be forgiven for not perceiving that ENVOY CHAT DRAWS BAN refers to an eccentric who had been telephoning various ambassadors by long distance and had finally been ordered to stop bothering them.

headquarters. As a rule this word is used with a plural verb, as in *his headquarters are in New York,* but it may also be used with a singular verb, as in *his headquarters is in New York.* There is no singular form *a headquarter.*

healthy; healthful; salutary. Although *healthy* is applied especially to that which possesses health or is characteristic of health (*The children looked wonderfully healthy with their bright eyes and glowing cheeks*), it is also applicable to that which is conducive to health (*Wilhelm found woodchopping a healthy pastime*). *Healthful* used to mean healthy (*Kate was tall and skinny . . . though perfectly healthful*), but this meaning is now rare and the common usage confines the word to that which is conducive to health (*He carefully chose a healthful diet*).

Salutary means conducive to health, especially in aiding recovery from sickness or counteracting some harmful influence (*These mineral waters were thought to be highly salutary for those afflicted with phthisic disorders*). *Salutary* differs from *healthy* and *healthful* in having a wider application. It is applied to anything likely to bring about a better condition, anything wholesome or beneficial (*He had a salutary respect for the old man's temper*). *Healthy* is coming to be used more and more in this sense, often humorously (*He had a healthy respect for the old man's temper. He knew it wouldn't be healthy for him to be found with his hand in the cash register*), but such use is not yet recognized as standard.

heap. Today, this word is standard English only when it means a pile. Four hundred years ago it could be used to mean a multitude, as in *the heaps of people thronging in the hall.* It is still used in a derived sense, as in *he had a heap of trouble,* but this is not now standard. One or two hundred years ago *heap* was replaced by *deal* as the word meaning a large amount. And in current English *deal* is being replaced by *lot.*

hear. The past tense is *heard.* The participle is also *heard.* When *hear* is used in an active form it may be followed by an object and the simple form of a verb, as in *I heard him speak,* or by an object and the *-ing* form of a verb, as in *I heard him speaking.* When *hear* is used in a passive form it may be followed by a *to*-infinitive, as in *he was heard to speak,* or by the *-ing* form of a verb, as in *he was heard speaking.* When *hear* is used in the sense of "hear of" it may be followed by a clause, as in *I heard that he spoke.*

Hear may be followed by an object and a past participle with passive meaning (that is, the *be* of a passive infinitive may be suppressed), as in *I have heard it told that he is a miser.* The *it* may be omitted from a sentence of this kind, as in *I have heard said that he is a miser.* The present tense form *say,* as in *I've heard say he is a miser,* is not the same construction but is an accepted idiom. It has probably been formed from the noun *hearsay.* Both expressions are standard English. *Hear tell* seems to be an effort to introduce variety into this idiom. It is accepted spoken English in the United States but does not now appear in writing. See also **listen.**

heart. The heart is a tough organ but as a term for the seat of the emotions it has been pretty well worn out. As an expression for utter devotion, complete earnestness, absolute sincerity, *heart and soul* is now a cliché. No one with any feeling for freshness in language will refer any more to hearts of gold, or of stone, or of oak. Even if he had to refer literally to something that had an actual heart or center of gold or stone, he would probably use some circumlocution to avoid the hackneyed phrase. For the same reason one no longer speaks or writes of having a heart in the right place or in one's mouth, or of having one's heart bleed for someone. The discriminating will avoid *getting to the heart of the matter.*

heathen. When speaking of men individually, *heathen* is a singular and has a regular plural in *s,* as in *one heathen* and *three heathens.* The singular form may also be used as a group name, meaning all of them, in which case it regularly takes a plural verb, as in *the heathen are hard to persuade.* But this is not a true plural and we do not speak of *three heathen.* See also **agnostic.**

heave. The past tense is *heaved* or *hove.* The participle is also *heaved* or *hove. Heaved* is the preferred form in general English, for the past tense and for the participle, and *hove* is pretty much confined to nautical matters. We say *the ship hove in sight* and *they hove up the anchor,* but other things are usually *heaved.*

heave a sigh of relief. Sighs have been *heaved* out of pensive bosoms so long and so often that the discriminating writer, if he must get a sigh

out of someone will find some other name for the portion of the anatomy from which it comes and some other word for its ejection than *heaved.*

heaven; heavens. These words can be used interchangeably. Some grammarians claim that the plural form *heavens* always means the sky and the singular form *heaven,* the home of the blest. But this distinction is not observed strictly. *Good heavens!* does not refer to the atmosphere, and the New Jerusalem is not intended in *sees in heaven the light of London flaring like a dreary dawn. Heaven* (and sometimes *heavens*) is also used euphemistically as a term for God in various emphatic statements and exclamations (*Heaven only knows. For heaven's sakes*). In this use it is sometimes capitalized, but, usually, those who feel that it ought to be capitalized in this sense recognize it as a piece of profanity and prefer not to use it at all.

heavenly. See **paradise.**

heavy. See **weighty.**

Hebrew; Israelite; Israeli; Jew; Semite. A *Hebrew* is a member of that branch of the Semitic race descended from Abraham, an Israelite, a Jew. *Hebrew* is a Semitic language, the language of the ancient Hebrews, which although not vernacular after 100 B.C., was retained as the scholarly and liturgical language of Jews and is now used as the language of Israelis. When the word is used of a person in the United States today it is usually employed as a euphemism to avoid *Jew* and while the euphemism is, no doubt, well intended, it carries to the sensitive ear the implication that the speaker regards the word he is seeking to avoid as indecent, shameful, embarrassing or dangerous.

An *Israelite* is a descendant of Jacob or Israel. In current American usage the word is confined to Biblical references. An *Israeli* is a native or inhabitant of the state of Israel.

To define the connotations of the word *Jew* would require many harrowing volumes. It is the everyday, working word. It is a word of incomparable dignity and immeasurable scorn and everything in between. It used to be a word of great comic range but that, at least, is fading. Its colloquial uses as an adjective or a verb are all offensive. The guidance to the "correct" use of the noun does not lie in any dictionary but in the heart and mind of the user.

Semite is properly a linguistic term and means a member of a speech family which comprises the Hebrews, Arabs, Assyrians, and others. The noun with its adjective is rarely employed today except by linguists and anthropologists. The compound *anti-Semitism* is, however, widely used as a term for hostility to Jews. The term is no longer accepted openly, as it was in France in the nineteenth century, by those who practice it, but is used almost exclusively by those who disapprove of it. It is a somewhat scholarly word and usually describes those attitudes and degrees of hostility that stop short of the violence to which they incite others. The English term *Jew-baiting* (a closer translation of the German

Judenhetze than *anti-Semitism*) is not much used in America where, happily, the more violent expressions of hostility to Jews are comparatively rare. See also **Yiddish.**

hectic applied originally to the feverish flush characteristic of consumption (*Pale young girls with hectic cheeks*) and although this particular flush is usually a concomitant of weakness and languor the word got connected with the flush of excitement. When Hazlitt said of Shelley that he had *a maggot in his brain, a hectic flutter in his speech,* he may have been alluding to the poet's presumed phthisis but he was probably alluding to his excitable and impetuous nature. Certainly the word has come in contemporary usage to mean, primarily, that which is characterized by great excitement or passion (*The hectic days of the holidays will soon overwhelm us*) and is coming to have—perhaps as a reflection of the increasing average age of the population—more than a tinge of suggestion of the exhaustion that such excitement entails (*We had a hectic day! I'm worn out. It was simply hectic! I just can't stand any more of it*). Many writers have objected strongly to the extension of *hectic*'s meanings beyond flushed or feverish but it has been a natural linguistic process against which it is hard to see how objections may be sustained.

hedonist; epicurean; epicure. A *hedonist* is one who holds that pleasure or happiness is the highest good and since, whatever our practice, the profession of such a doctrine is frowned upon, the word is strongly tinged with disapprobation and *the hedonistic tendencies of the age* are much sermoned against. Although Epicurus taught that the practice of virtue was the highest pleasure, his insistence that the seeking of pleasure was the strongest motive force men have and should be recognized as such has given his philosophy a bad name. During the ages when the ascetic virtues were extolled epicureanism became a synonym for indulgence in sensuous pleasures and the *epicurean* today is one who so indulges. The word is applied especially to one who indulges luxurious tastes in eating and drinking, though *epicure,* curiously enough, is not quite so pejorative as *epicurean.* The primary meaning of *epicure* today is not so much one who indulges as one who cultivates a refined taste.

height is now almost the only form of the word for the state of being high. *Highth* is a recognized variant and *hight* is obsolete. *Heighth* is simply an error for *highth.*

heir; heir apparent; heir presumptive. In the popular conception an *heir,* and especially an *heiress,* is one who expects to inherit—or, as the trustful masses say, "will" inherit. Legally, however, an heir is one who has succeeded to an estate, not one who will inherit but one who has inherited.

An *heir apparent* is one whose right is indefeasible if he survive the ancestor. An *heir presumptive* is less secure. If the ancestor should die immediately, the *heir presumptive* would become the heir, but his right to the inheritance may be defeated by the birth of a nearer relative or some other contingency. In America there is very little use for these terms, at least in common speech; but since there is a suggestion of special knowledge in their use, they must be used correctly.

held. See **hold.**

hello; halloo; hollo; holler. As Fowler says, "the multiplicity of forms is bewildering." In addition to those given there are also *hallo, halloa, hillo, hilloa, hullo,* and *hollow.* All are exclamations to attract attention (or to urge on the dogs in hunting) and all are basically the same word, but usage has restricted certain of them to certain meanings. The common exclamation of greeting is *hello* in America, *hullo* in England. *Hillo* and *halloo* are hunting cries. *Hollow, hollo,* and *holler* designate a cry with a loud voice (*I hollered but he didn't seem to hear me*), the last of the three being commonly regarded as dialectal or nonstandard.

helot. A *helot* was a serf in ancient Sparta, owned by the state but assigned by lot to a certain landowner. The use of the word as a facetious or indignant term for workers (*The helots who toil that others may wallow in idleness*) is affected.

help. In the United States the verb *help* may be followed by the simple form of a verb, such as *peel* in *he helped us peel the onions.* A to-infinitive in this construction, as in *he helped us to peel the onions,* is almost never heard. However, when *helped* is used in a passive form the to-infinitive is generally preferred, as in *we were helped to get out.* In Great Britain the to-infinitive is required in both constructions and the form without *to* is not considered standard.

In the United States *I cannot help but think* is the preferred way of expressing this idea. Grammatically, the construction is as irreproachable as *I cannot choose but think.* But in Great Britain an *-ing* form is required after *help,* as in *I cannot help thinking,* and the form *help but think* is considered unacceptable. British grammarians sometimes claim that the *but* in the American construction constitutes a double negative. They say that *help* here means *avoid* and that the whole expression is equivalent to *I cannot avoid not to think,* which in turn would mean that the speaker was compelled not to think. The answer is that *help* means *avoid* in the British idiom but not in the American. In the American expression *help* retains its basic meaning of *aid* or *further,* and the statement *I cannot help but think* can be properly paraphrased as *I cannot do* (or *further*) *anything except to think,* which of course means that the speaker is compelled to think, as is intended.

help; aid; assist; succor. *Help* is the everyday word for furnishing another with something he needs, especially furthering his efforts or relieving his wants or necessities (*Help me, Cassius, or I sink. God helps them that help themselves. But the jingling of the guinea helps the hurt that Honour feels*). *Aid* and *assist* are more formal

and imply only a furthering or seconding of
another's efforts. *Aid* implies a more active helping than *assist* which suggests not only less help
but also less need for help (*aided and comforted
the enemy; . . . my wife, without whose assistance this book would never have been published*). *Succor* derives from a word meaning to
run under, and there is still in it a sense of
bringing aid, of coming to the relief of. This is
especially so in military contexts where be-
leaguered cities or isolated detachments of
troops are succored or succor is brought to
them. *Succor* is a more emotional word than
help or *assist*. It suggests not only aid but comfort. Except in the military sense, it is, however,
slightly bookish.

help; servant. In the sense of a domestic servant
or a farm laborer, *help* has been used in
America, at least in New England, since earliest
times (*James Penn shall have 20s, to be disposed among such of his servants & helps . . . .
He has always had good help on his farm; he
treats them right. In Indiana and Illinois, where
white servants were employed, they would not
tolerate being called servants. They were known
as "the help"*). It is now applied to hired laborers, especially those whose work does not
require any special skills (*Help wanted. He
laid off half his help*). While *servant*, as applied
to employment in the service of a private individual or organization, is generally regarded as
an undemocratic word, a person in the government can be called a servant without offense
(*a faithful civil servant*).

helping hand. The *helping hand*, especially when
lent, is a cliché.

helpmate; helpmeet. In the second chapter of
Genesis, according to the King James version,
God said that it was not good that Adam should
be alone and that He would *make him an help
meet for him*—that is a helper suitable for him.
Wycliffe had translated the phrase *an helper like
hym* and Coverdale *an helpe, to beare him
company*. The Revised Standard Version has *a
helper fit for him*. In the seventeenth century
help and *meet*, for some reason, were taken to
be one word and since Adam's fit helper turned
out to be Eve, his wife, the new compound was
applied to a wife or husband, usually to a wife
(*A true helpmeet for him, young, beautiful,
rich, and withal virtuous*). In the eighteenth
century *meet* and *mate* were often pronounced
alike (as they are in Ireland today) and the
absurd coinage was soon given a semblance of
sense by being spelled *helpmate*, though the
older spelling persisted alongside the new one
and is still in use even today, especially among
those who like to be quaintly learned. Both
words are a little affected and bookish.

hemlock. In England *hemlock* designates a poisonous umbelliferous herb, *Conicum maculatum*
(*Round about the caldron go;/ In the poison'd
entrails throw, . . ./ Root of hemlock digg'd i'
the dark*). It also designates a poisonous drink
made from this herb (*Socrates drinking the
hemlock,/ And Jesus on the rood*). In the

United States *hemlock* chiefly designates an
evergreen tree of the genus *Tsuga*, the hemlock
spruce (*This is the forest primeval. The murmuring pines and the hemlocks,/ . . ./ Stand
like Druids of old*). The early Americans made
a drink from this spruce which they called hemlock tea. John Galt in his *Lawrie Todd* (1830)
refers to it as "a pleasant and salutary drink."

her; hers. *Her* is one of the objective pronouns.
It is used after a verb or a preposition in place
of the word *she*, as in *have you seen her?* and
did you talk with her? (See **objective pronouns**.)
Her is also used as a possessive in place of the
word *hers*. In this sense, the form *her* is required
when the word qualifies a following noun, as
in *her home, her money*, and the form *hers* is
required in any other construction, as in *have
you seen hers?* and *compare this with hers*. *Hers*
is the form used in a double possessive where
the word is separated from its following noun
by *and*, as in *hers and Sophia's bedroom*. Today,
this construction is generally avoided. We are
more likely to say *her bedroom and Sophia's* or
her own and Sophia's bedroom. Neither word
order shows clearly whether we are talking
about one thing or two, but the old-fashioned
form, *hers and Sophia's*, suggests one thing
possessed in common more strongly than the
forms which use *her*. In current English the
word *hers* is never written with an apostrophe.

here. The adverb *here* cannot qualify a following
noun, as in *this here pencil*, because too many
teacher-hours have been devoted to saying that
it couldn't. If anyone uses this construction we
know at once that either he never went to school
a day in his life, or he is dangerously self-
assertive.

The trouble is not that *here* repeats the idea
of *this*, but that it is an adverb standing in the
adjective position. *This player here* is the purest
English. A few words that are primarily adverbs
have won the right to stand before a noun, as
in *the after life, the above remarks*, but *here* is
not likely to become one of them. See **hither**.

hereabout; hereabouts. These forms are equally
acceptable today, and have been for several
centuries. Some grammarians claim that *hereabouts* ought to be the preferred form, because
the word is used to qualify a verb and *s* is a
formal adverbial ending. But there is no evidence that it actually is preferred.

hern (pronoun) was once acceptable English, but
it has not been used in the literary language for
three hundred years. The only acceptable form
today is *hers*.

hernia. The plural is *hernias* or *herniae*.

hero. The plural is *heroes*.

heroics. This word is always treated as a plural
and is usually meant derisively, as in *these
heroics are wasted on me*. The adjectives *heroic*
and *heroical* do not carry this sense but belong
to the solemn word *hero*. Both forms of the
adjective are acceptable, but *heroic* is heard
more often.

herself. In Ireland this word is sometimes used in
place of the word *her* or *she*, as in *you must ask*

herself and *herself wut tell you.* This was once literary English but is no longer standard in the United States. For the regular uses of *herself,* see **reflexive pronouns.**

hesitate. This word may be followed by an infinitive, as in *he hesitated to tell her.* It is sometimes heard with the *-ing* form of a verb, as in *he hesitated telling her.* This is not standard English.

hew. The past tense is *hewed.* The participle is *hewed* or *hewn. Hewed* is the preferred form for the participle but *hewn* is still acceptable.

hiatus. The plural is *hiatuses* or *hiatus,* not *hiati.*

hiccup; hiccough. The proper word for the characteristic sound caused by a quick, involuntary inspiration's being suddenly checked by a closure of the glottis is *hiccup,* one of the best onomatopoeic words in the language. *Hiccough* is apparently a euphemism or genteelism in spelling. The dictionaries accept it as a permissible variant but, fortunately, it doesn't seem to be gaining much ground. The obsolete spellings of *hickop* and *hicket* were good. It's a pity they've been lost.

hide. The past tense is *hid.* The participle is *hidden* or *hid. Hidden* is the preferred form for the participle. *Hid* is also used, as in *he had hid the package,* but is considered bookish by some people.

hide; conceal; secrete. *Hide* is the everyday working word (*He hid the money under the mattress. She hid her dismay under an assumption of indifference. The stop light was hidden by an intervening pole*). *Conceal* is more formal. A hen would hide her eggs; a man would conceal his motives. *Concealment,* however, has become as much of an everyday word as we have for the act of hiding. *Hiding* is rarely used seriously to describe the act of concealing. To *secrete* means to hide carefully in order to keep secret. It has acquired a faint connotation of furtiveness; a *secretive* person is not merely reticent, there is a suggestion of something slightly dishonest about him. This may be due to a vague confusion with the biological meaning of *secrete* (really a different word), the separating off, or preparation from the blood, as in the secretions of the glands. Thus it may be felt that the secretive man is not merely concealing something, but internally creating something that may help him but harm us. See also **cache.**

hide one's light under a bushel. As a term, usually employed ironically, for concealing one's merits or talents, *to hide one's light under a bushel* (taken from Matthew 5:15) is now a cliché. Except in this phrase *bushel* has not been used for a bushel basket or container for more than two hundred years.

high and dry. To say of something that has been abandoned or someone who has been forgotten or passed over that it or he has been *left high and dry* is a cliché. The figure is of a ship that has been beached.

high; highly. When used in its literal, physical sense *high* is as truly an adverb as it is an adjective. We say *he jumped high* and never *he jumped highly.* When used in a derived sense,

high is an adjective and *highly* an adverb. We say *the table has a high polish* and *it is highly polished.* See also **tall.**

high-toned; stylish. *High-toned* literally applies to sounds that are high in pitch. Though in England the term also means having high or lofty moral principles (*In whose high-toned impartial mind/ Degrees of mortal rank and state/ Seem objects of indifferent weight*—Scott), it is usually employed in this sense in America contemptuously or ironically. Wallace Stevens, for instance, has entitled one of his poems "High-toned old Christian lady." A third sense, the one most frequently intended in America, is stylish, fashionably elegant (*We don't think there is any place in Arizona for high-toned fox hunting* —*Chicago Sun,* Nov. 1, 1946). This sense, however, is still not so stylish as *stylish.*

hilarity. See **glee.**

him. See **objective pronouns** and **his.**

himself. In Ireland and Scotland this word is sometimes used in place of the word *him* or *he* (when applied to the head of the family), as in *I see himself coming* and *himself will soon be here.* This was once literary English but is no longer standard in the United States. For the regular uses of *himself,* see **reflexive pronouns.**

hind. The comparative form is *hinder.* The superlative form is *hindmost* or *hindermost.* See also **hart.**

hinder. The *-ing* form of a verb following *hinder* is usually introduced by *from* or *in,* as in *hinder him from going* and *hinder him in carrying out his plans.* See also **prevent.**

hindrance. See **handicap; obstacle.**

hindsight has such a homely, folksy, Anglo-Saxon ring to it that one would assume that it was the good old word and *retrospection* a stilted latinization dragged in by scholars in recent years. But the contrary is true. *Hindsight* was made up by scholars in the late nineteenth century and *retrospection* is of respectable antiquity, going back to the early seventeenth century. As a contrast to *foresight* (*His hindsight is better than his foresight*), however, especially in such ironical uses as *the wisdom of hindsight,* the word has definitely replaced *retrospection,* but in almost any other sense of looking backwards, *retrospection* is preferable.

hippopotamus. The plural is *hippopotamuses* or *hippopotami.*

hire; rent; charter. *Hire* is the general word, most commonly applied to paying money for labor or services (*He hired twenty machinists. McGill's was not hiring unskilled labor*). In New England *hire* is used in speaking of money borrowed at interest (*They hired the money, didn't they?*) to distinguish it, apparently, from money borrowed at no interest from a friend. The use of *hired man, hired girl,* while retained as a democratic euphemism for servant, seems to have had its origin in the fact that in colonial times there was an important distinction between an indentured servant and a hired servant.

Hire is used also to designate paying for the temporary use of vehicles or buildings (*The school hired an old, dilapidated bus to take the team about the county. Oh, why don't you hire a hall!*), but *rent* is more common in this sense and better. *Rent* is usually applied to paying a set sum once or at regular intervals for the use of a building or personal effects (*We rented the old Coghill property for the winter. You can rent a tuxedo for five dollars*).

Charter used to be confined to paying for the use of a vessel, but it is being used with increasing frequency to designate the hiring of any conveyance for the use of a group (*The garden club found that it was cheaper to charter a bus and much more convenient*). See also **employ**.

hireling. See **venal.**

his. In natural English, the words *he, him,* and *his,* always refer to a male. In theoretical English they can refer to either a male or a female when the sex is unknown. In 1850, this theory was recognized in "An Act for shortening the language used in acts of Parliament" which announced "that in all acts words importing the masculine gender shall be deemed and taken to include females, and the singular to include the plural, and the plural the singular, unless the contrary as to gender and number is expressly provided." But neither this act, nor all the grammar books in the world can alter the fact that, if we are told *somebody telephoned while you were out,* we say *did they leave a message?* In natural English, the words *they, them, their,* are used more often than *he, him, his,* in speaking of an unknown individual who may possibly be a woman. *His* may be used instead of *one's* in referring back to the indefinite pronoun *one,* as in *if one loses his temper.*

hisn. This word was once acceptable English, but it has not been used in the literary language for three hundred years. The only acceptable form today is *his.*

hisself. This word is not standard; the only acceptable form is *himself. Hisself* is made with the possessive pronoun in the same way that *myself* and *yourself* are. It has been in use since the time of King Alfred but has been regarded as bad English for at least five hundred years. A grammarian writing in 1762 thought that *himself* was a corruption and *hisself* the logically correct form. But *hisself* was frowned upon in 1762 as much as it is today. However, when another word *self* stands between the pronoun and the word *self,* the possessive form *his* is required, as in *his own sweet self,* and the objective form *him* is unacceptable.

historic; historical. Though often used interchangeably, *historic* and *historical* have distinguishable senses. *Historic* means well-known or important in history (*The signing of the Declaration of Independence was a historic occasion*). *Historical* means relating to or concerned with history (*The historical King Arthur was a Roman soldier*).

hit. The past tense is *hit.* The participle is also *hit.* Verbs of this kind show us how well we can get along without tense inflections and how much

unnecessary trouble we make for ourselves in preserving such forms as *sing, sang, sung,* and *lie, lay, lain.* This does not mean that any one can take it on himself to disregard the standard forms of speech. But it does suggest that if the rules were relaxed a little, language might do wonders for itself in a few generations and become a much simpler, and more efficient, tool than it now is.

hit below the belt. Originally from boxing, *to hit below the belt* as a term for taking an unfair advantage is now a cliché. It should be used sparingly.

hit the nail on the head. As a term for guessing correctly, stating something accurately, usually with an element of good luck in so doing, *to hit the nail on the head* has been in use for almost four hundred years. It has become a cliché and should be allowed a long rest.

hitch your wagon to a star. Though the idea of the stimulus of an unattainable ideal was in the phrase when Emerson coined it (*Society and Solitude: Civilization*) he had also in mind a more practical interpretation than is now given it. Everything good in man, he had said, depends on what is higher. We can be strong and succeed only if we borrow "the aid of the elements." The strong, downward stroke of an axe is really impelled by the force of gravity, of which the skillful carpenter is taking advantage. Mills on the sea shore which are driven by the tides "engage the assistance of the moon, like a hired hand." And this is wisdom for a man *in every instance of his labor, to hitch his wagon to a star, and see his chore done by the gods themselves.* As a term merely for being nobly ambitious, the admonition *to hitch your wagon to a star* is now a cliché.

hither; here. As an adverb *hither* means to or towards this place. The word is now archaic. *Here* has absorbed the meaning of *hither* (*Come here*) and has retained its basic senses of in this place (*Leave it here*), at this point of time (*Here he paused and waited for the expected applause*), and at this point in a time sequence (*Here is where we came in*).

Hither is one of the few adverbs that have been accepted as adjectives. But it has been accepted, as in *the hither side, the hither shore,* and this use is as respectable as any.

hoard; horde. A *hoard* is an accumulation of something presumably valuable and usually concealed (*A large hoard of coins was discovered beneath the floor boards*). A *hoard of grievances* would differ from an accumulation of grievances in that he who held them would hold them in secret and cherish them. A *horde* was originally a tribe of Asiatic nomads (*They are divided into three hordes, under the government of a khan*). The *Golden Horde,* for instance, was the name of a particular tribe that possessed the khanate of Kiptchak in central Asia in the fourteenth and fifteenth centuries. The word came to be applied to any nomadic group and, usually in an uncomplimentary sense, to a large, unorganized crowd (*The horde* *of Christmas shoppers. A horde of ragged, little boys).*

Hobson's choice, a humorous phrase for no choice at all, is now a cliché in England but not used enough in the United States to be regarded as one here. The phrase derives from Thomas Hobson (about 1544 to 1631), a carrier at Cambridge who rented horses and compelled his customers to take the horse he assigned to them or none at all. It is one of the vagaries of fame that this obscure man should have lent his name to a proverb and been the subject of two poems by John Milton.

hodgepodge; hotchpotch; hotchpot. The original form *hotchpot* is a legal term designating the bringing together of shares or properties in order to divide them equally, especially when they are to be divided among the children of a parent dying without a will (*With regard to lands descending in co-parcenary, that it hath always been, and still is, the common law of England, under the name of hotchpot*— Blackstone). *Hotchpotch,* a British variant of this form, is a general term to describe a heterogeneous mixture, an agglomeration, a jumble, farrago, medley, or gallimaufrey (*That ethnological hotch-potch called the Latin race*). *Hodgepodge* is a variant of *hotchpotch.* Of the two forms it is now the preferred one in America. In its use there is often a suggestion that the jumbling has been clumsy and inept (*The art collection was a hodgepodge of paintings from many periods and in several styles*).

hog. As a standard noun *hog* means a pig, sow, or boar, a domestic swine. In England it has been replaced (except in figurative uses, such as *road hog*) by *pig.* Thus American *hogpen* is English *pigsty.* In colloquial use the word describes a person having the hoggish attributes of selfishness, gluttony, and, less commonly, filthiness (*He was a hog at the table. He was a hog and would always shove out in front and grab what he impudently called "his share"*). In slang usage as a verb, *to hog* is to take something selfishly or to take more than one's share (*So, says I, s'pose somebody has hogged that bag on the sly?. At the movies he was always the one to hog the popcorn*). See also **pig.**

hoi polloi. These Greek words (*hoi,* the; *polloi,* many) signify the masses, the ordinary people. The phrase is often used by those who strain to be erudite to signify the rabble, the lowest class of people. It is condescending, with a touch of the labored jocular. It carries the definite suggestion of "I, who am so steeped in a classical education that I speak Greek as naturally as I do English, etc., etc." Unfortunately, however, many who use the term seem to know no Greek at all, not so much as the definite article, and in their ignorance prefix a superfluous *the* (*I read the News to see what the hoi polloi are doing*). It is a good phrase not to use.

hold. The past tense is *held.* The participle is also *held.* When *hold* is used in the sense of believe, it may be followed by an infinitive, as in *we hold these truths to be self-evident,* or by a clause, as in *we hold that they are self-evident.*

When *hold* is used in the sense of remain, it may be followed by an adjective describing the subject of the verb, as in *the argument holds good.* But when it is used in the sense of keep or grasp, it is qualified by an adverb, as in *the glue holds well.*

holding one's own. As a term for maintaining one's position or condition, *holding one's own* is overworked.

hold-up (rob). See **steal.**

holloa; hollow; holler. See **hello.**

holocaust; disaster. A *holocaust* is a Greek word meaning something which is burnt whole. It was used for a burnt offering and has come to mean, especially in journalistic writing, a great or wholesale destruction of life, especially by burning (*Incendiary bombs led to a holocaust in the slum quarter*). *Holocaust* is often used as a synonym for disaster, but there is a difference: a holocaust may be a disaster, but there are many kinds of disasters which are not holocausts. *Disaster* (which means, literally, a bad configuration of the stars, *i.e.,* just bad luck) designates any unfortunate event, especially a sudden and great misfortune. A *holocaust* may be accidental, but it may also be the result of human intention. A flood, a railway wreck, or the collapse of a building may be a *disaster,* but none of these things is a *holocaust.*

home. Americans frequently use the noun *home* as an adverb showing "place at which," as in *I will stay home Wednesday.* This is standard English in the United States. It is not standard in Great Britain and is condemned by many grammarians who claim that a prepositional phrase with *at* is required, as in *I will stay at home Wednesday.*

The most rigid grammarians allow *home* without a preposition after verbs of motion, as in *I went home* (where it shows "place to which" rather than "place at which"); and after forms of the verb *to be* when motion is implied, as in *I will be home at five* or *he must be home by now.* The famous lines, *home is the sailor, home from the sea, and the hunter home from the hill,* are considered formally correct because it is possible to read motion into *is home* in this case, even though it is an epitaph. But the best will in the world can't read motion into *stay* or *remain.* With these verbs, therefore, some grammarians require an *at.* See also **house.**

homely. The English have retained the word *homely* only in its kinder connotations of domestic, familiar, kindly, plain, unsophisticated (. . . *those plain homely terms that are most obvious and natural. Yet portion of that unknown plain/ Will Hodge forever be;/ His homely Northern breast and brain/ Grow to some Southern tree*). These meanings would be understood in America, but the word is restricted here, especially in its application to people, to the meaning of unattractive. It is usually a euphemism for ugly (*She was the homeliest woman I have ever seen*). The English are often disturbed by this American use. They feel the word has been corrupted. But Shakespeare so used it (*Hath homelie age th'* *alluring beauty took/ From my poor cheek?*) and so did Milton (*It is for homely features to keep home*) and Horace Walpole (*She was extremely deformed and homely*).

homicide; murder; manslaughter. *Homicide,* the killing of one human being by another, includes *murder* and *manslaughter. Murder* is the unlawful killing of another human being with malice aforethought and *manslaughter* is the killing of another human being unlawfully but without malice aforethought.

homonyms. English is rich in *homonyms,* words that are similar in sound and, often, in spelling but different in meaning. Where the words are common and the meanings widely different (as in the bark of a dog and the bark of a tree) there is little danger of confusion, but when vanity and the desire to be thought learned lead a writer or speaker to venture out of his depth, homonyms can cause some preposterous blunders. Thus when a leading newsmagazine which prides itself on omniscience informs its readers that "peasant-born 'Paco' Goya" had "scaled the dizzy dome of St. Peter's in Rome" and carved his initials "on the lantern that had been left there by Michaelangelo," the verb *had been left* suggests that the architectural meaning of *lantern* was not known. And when in a later issue much merriment is made of the fact that President Tyler's wife at her husband's inaugural ball wore "bugles" in her hair, the gaiety implies that the writer of the article was unaware of the fact that one of the meanings of bugle is an elongated glass bead. Here, as elsewhere, modesty is a safeguard against being absurd. Where modesty is lacking, it is well to have a dictionary.

Homonyms, in most instances, derive from different origins—frequently from different languages—and the similarity in sound is accidental. Sometimes they go back to the same source but have altered in spelling and meaning in their individual paths through usage; thus *plain* and *plane* are both from Latin *planus* but *plain* detoured through Old French.

Though homonyms are the cause of a great deal of bad spelling, they are worth the cost because they are also the basis of puns.

homosexual. The first element in *homosexual* is the Greek *homo-* meaning the same, not the Latin *homo,* man. That is, a *homosexual* is one who has sexual feelings, with an impulse towards genital expression, for a person of the same sex. A *homosexual* may be either a man or a woman.

honest; honorable; honesty; honor. An *honest* man is candid, just, fair in his dealings, sincere in his utterances (*After my death I wish no other herald/ . . . To keep mine honor from corruption,/ But such an honest chronicler as Griffith*). The *honorable* man is honest (though his honor may keep him, like Lancelot, falsely true), but honor is a more complex thing than simple honesty. Honesty functions within a system of absolute principles of right; honor functions within a complex system of standards of conduct of what is due to one's self and to

others. It is conceivable that a man might be honest because he felt that honesty is the best policy. The honorable man would probably find such motivation unworthy of himself. To conform to a high standard of honor is far more difficult, in that it is far more complex, than to conform to a high standard of honesty.

When *honor* means privilege, it may be followed by an infinitive, as in *I have the honor to inform you,* provided it is being used with the word *have;* otherwise, it may be followed by *of* and the *-ing* form of a verb, as in *I had the honor of informing him.*

honorable; honorary. That is *honorable* which is worthy of honor. That is *honorary* which is conferred as a mark of honor. The English go in much more than the Americans for honorary secretaryships and the like. For the sake of the dignity conferred by his name, so-and-so will be chosen the *Honorary Secretary* of a society, the actual secretarial duties being performed by a paid secretary. So-and-so is then usually listed on programs and announcements of the society as the *Hon. Sec.* or *Hon. Secretary.* Americans often mistake this for *Honorable,* a title bestowed in America on any public official. In England the title of *Honorable* (also abbreviated to *Hon.*) is confined to certain of the children of peers, maids of honor, judges of the High Court, and members of various Indian and Dominion Councils. *Right Honorable* is reserved for privy councilors, peers below the rank of marquis, certain judges and some lord mayors.

In the United States, the title *honorable* requires the article *the.* It may precede a descriptive phrase, such as *the Honorable Gentleman from Buncombe,* or a full name, as in *the Honorable John Hancock.* But it should not stand immediately before a last name. If the given name or initials are not used some other title, such as *Dr.,* or *Mr.,* must take their place, as in *the Honorable Mr. Hancock.* When the word is abbreviated the article *the* is omitted, as in *Hon. John Hancock.*

Honorable is not used without a proper name as a form of address, or in speaking about a person.

honorarium. The plural is *honorariums* or *honoraria.*

honorarium; fee; wages; pay; salary. In former times it was felt or at least pretended that certain persons were of so exalted a station or possessed of such incomparable skill or knowledge that no adequate compensation could possibly be offered them in return for any services they might perform. A monetary recognition not of the service, but of the honor conferred by their very presence, took the form of an *honorarium* the amount of which—at least in theory—was determined by the donor. Even late into the last century, particularly in England, this applied to unusually great physicians, men who today would be called specialists or consultants. The money (always in gold) was never handed to them directly but discreetly placed on a corner of the mantel and unobtrusively pocketed by the Great One. Today *honorarium* is simply a graceful or embarrassed term for a fee smaller than the speaker would like to accept. It differs from a *fee* in that the amount of a fee is fixed by the one who performs the service, the amount of an *honorarium* by those who receive the service. Physicians now receive *fees. Honorariums* are now given almost exclusively to public speakers who are willing to accept almost anything they can get and grateful for a word which permits them to save face and accept less than they had uneasily demanded.

Wages is used of payment to labor, for services, as by the day or the week. It is the word for regular payment as viewed from the point of view of the payer. The housewife thinks of the cook's *wages.* The economist, identifying himself with the employer, speaks of *wages* as one of the costs of production. From the point of view of the person paid, the common word today is *pay* (*It's good pay for the hours you put in. After all the deductions my week's pay isn't enough for us to live on*).

A *salary* is a fixed compensation paid periodically for regular work or services, especially for work other than that of a manual, mechanical, or menial kind.

A lecturer who is not in a position to demand a definite sum may receive an *honorarium.* Clergymen receive honorariums for performing marriages and officiating at funerals. Almost all professional men now receive *fees,* the amount of which they fix. *Wages* are paid to domestic help and to labor in the abstract. The white-collar class draws its *salary.* The working man gets his *pay.*

honored in the breach. See **more honored in the breach.**

hood. That part of an automobile which in America is called the *hood* is in England called the *bonnet.* That which the English call the *hood* is, in convertibles in America, called the *top.*

hoof. The plural is *hoofs.* The old plural *hooves* is now used only in poetry.

hook or by crook, by, to accomplish something one way or another, by fair means or foul, has lodged in the language, and been there many centuries, probably because of its rime. Its original meaning has long been lost, though some have conjectured it goes back to the custom which permitted peasants to gather as firewood in the lord's woods such dead branches as could be brought down by reaper's hook or shepherd's crook. This, however, fails to account for the "fair means or foul" implicit in the phrase. The chances are that they are simply two things that could be used to snare and draw in something desired and are joined together by the similarity of their sounds.

hop in the senses of catching a train or making a short journey or an airplane's flight or a dance or a dance party is not standard.

hope. This word may be followed by an infinitive, as in *I hope to see him,* or by a clause, as in *I hope I will see him.* In the United States, the clause verb is often in the present tense when what is meant is future, as in *I hope I see him.*

This is standard usage in the United States but is considered an Americanism in Great Britain.

The plural form of the noun, *hopes,* is sometimes used where the singular would seem more appropriate, as in *he was past hopes* and *in hopes of better times.* This has been literary English for three hundred years and more and is still acceptable. See also **anticipate.**

hope against hope. It was Abraham, according to Romans 4:18, *Who against hope believed in hope, that he might become the father of many nations.* Since at the time alluded to Abraham was a hundred years old and Sarah ninety, and since it "had ceased to be" with her, "after the manner of women," his hope was indeed noteworthy. But the phrase has been overworked today.

hopeful. See **optimistic.**

hopeless; desperate. *Hopeless* means without hope and implies abandonment to fate (*After x-rays had shown that the liver was involved, the case was regarded as hopeless. Men have recovered from maladies which seemed hopeless*). Although *desperate* means the state of having given up hope, the word in common usage is not quite as dark as *hopeless.* It conveys, rather, a suggestion of recklessness resulting from a decrease in but not a complete loss of hope. It may apply to either feelings or situations (*As night approached for the second time and no search planes appeared, the men on the raft realized that their situation was desperate but not hopeless. Do not drive men to desperation unless you have the power to crush them, for desperate men are dangerous*).

horde. See **hoard.**

horny-handed son of the soil (or **of toil**). Any reference to a farmer as a *horny-handed son of the soil* or to a laborer as a *horny-handed son of toil* is a dreary cliché. If used, as it now usually is, jocularly, it is a dreary joke.

horrible; awful; dreadful; fearful; terrible; terrific; tremendous. That is *horrible* which inspires horror, a bristling or shuddering fear. That is *awful* which inspires awe, a feeling of deep solemnity and reverence mixed with fear. That is *dreadful* which inspires dread, an oppressive fear of evil to come. That is *fearful* which is either full of fear or capable of instilling fear. That is *terrible* or *terrific* which is terrifying, which moves us, that is, to an unreasoning, overmastering, panic fear. And that is *tremendous* which makes us tremble with dread.

Properly used, these are all strong words, of great dignity and force. *O horrible, most horrible!* cries Hamlet when he learns that his revered father has been murdered by his incestuous brother. Kipling speaks of God's *awful hand,* and Milton of His *dreadful voice.* Blake is amazed at the *fearful symmetry* of the tiger. Death, in *Paradise Lost,* is black . . . *as Night,/ Fierce as ten Furies, terrible as Hell.* Pope in his translation of the *Iliad* speaks of warriors dressing their huge limbs *In arms terrific* and John Evelyn alludes to *the tremendous name of God.*

Hyperbole is deep rooted in our minds, however. The usual narratives of the common man rarely have in them anything to compel attention or elicit admiration and strong words are used to convey weak facts. Every one of these words has been weakened by indiscriminate use until now most of them are, in popular use, mere intensives. This is a normal process of language and, to some extent, must be allowed. If a badly confused situation is said to be *a horrible mess,* the justification for the adjective is hard to challenge because there are wide ranges of sensitiveness and one man shudders at what leaves another unmoved. To a child a building might seem tremendous which to an adult would merely seem large. And so on. There is no absolute guide in words that reflect subjective feelings. The speaker or writer must decide for himself just what degree and kind of fear he wishes to describe.

It is plain, however, that beyond a certain point these words become almost meaningless. To say, *We had a dreadful meal,* unless one had been dining with the Borgias, is to overstate the case—or, more probably, to avoid the effort of selecting from among *nauseous, disgusting, ill-cooked, scant, tasteless,* and so on, a suitable adjective. To say that a pun or a hat is *terrible* is to abdicate all rule over one's vocabulary.

And certainly these words become absurd when they are used, as they seem increasingly to be used, as mere intensives and used before adjectives whose primary meaning contradicts theirs. Such expressions—one hears them a dozen times a day—as "She's awfully nice, really, once you get to know her," "His play's a smash hit, a terrific success," "It was a tremendous pity," "It's dreadfully good of you," etc., may be used as examples. It may be claimed that since usage has made them intensives they must be accepted as intensives, with no more meaning than *very.* But they still retain something of their original meaning and many shades of other meanings that have been acquired and these meanings are likely to intrude and prevent them from being pure intensives or, as above, suggest contradictions of meaning and so create absurdity. See **intensives.**

horse. When used to mean cavalry, this word has the plural *horse,* as in *there were two hundred horse.*

horse of a different color. The origin of the expression *But that's a horse of a different color* (or *of another color*) is uncertain. The earliest known allusion to it occurs in *Twelfth Night* but it is used there in a way that makes it plain that it was already an established saying. Some think it may have had to do with tournaments where the visored knights would be distinguished by the color of their horses. Some think it may have to do with the curious white horses which the Britons or Saxons cut into the chalk downs of Southern England and are kept clear of overgrowth to this day. But all is conjecture. What is sure, however, is that as a term for something of a different nature from what is being considered, the expression is now a cliché, to be used sparingly.

hose. When this word is used to mean a heavy rubber tube, it may have the plural *hoses* or *hose,* as in *three fire hoses* or *three fire hose.* Both forms are acceptable.

When it is used to mean stockings, the only plural is *hose.* In this sense the word originally meant a pair of coverings for the legs and was commonly treated as a plural, as are *trousers, breeches, pants,* and so on. Some of this survives today. We do not ordinarily call a single stocking a *hose* but reserve the word for plural uses such as *buying hose* and *needing hose.*

host; hostess. As the correlative of *guest, host* should be applicable to either a woman or a man who entertains guests in his or her own home or elsewhere. But, despite the insistence of some grammarians, usage has restricted *host* to a man who so entertains. In the biological sense of an animal that supports a parasite, *host* is the term for either male or female. So that if a woman were afflicted with a tapeworm she would be its *host,* but in all more gracious entertainments she is invariably a *hostess.*

Although the primary meaning of *hostess* remains a female host, a woman who entertains guests (*The hostess with the mostes' on the ball. Mrs. Pearl Mesta's career as Washington's Number One Hostess was crowned by her appointment as ambassador to Luxembourg*), a secondary meaning, derived from this one, of a woman employed in a restaurant to seat guests (*The hostess is placed in a difficult position in regard to the other employees who sneer at her ladylike ways and think she has it "pretty soft"*), has become so common that it may very well affect the primary meaning. Some of the airlines officially call the young women who wait on the passengers *hostesses* and the name is often applied, in the papers and by the general public, to all such young women, though many of the lines valiantly struggle to preserve the title of *stewardess.* If the tendency continues—and it seems probable that it will—then a time may come when it will seem improper to refer to someone who has entertained us privately as a *hostess* and a new word will have to be found. Such are the ways of language. One of the oldest meanings of the word, a female innkeeper (*Hostess, my breakfast, come./ O, I could wish this tavern were my drum!*), has fallen into disuse in America, though it is still employed somewhat in England.

hot cakes. See **sell like hot cakes.**

hot water. To be *in hot water* is now a cliché for being in trouble, especially a scrape or some avoidable, not quite criminal but often disgraceful, trouble. It is a very old phrase. A quotation dated 1537 shows that it formerly meant in a ferment or in a condition of discomfort.

house in American usage most commonly denotes an ordinary place of residence (*We sold our house last year*). In the last century many hotels were called Houses—as *Parker House, American House,* and so on. In this use the initial

H was always capitalized. The *Palmer House* would be understood to designate a hotel, the *Palmer house* the residence of a family by the name of Palmer. In English usage *House* designates either a large and unusually splendid residence or an unusually impressive office building, as *Imperial House*. This meaning has been introduced into America with *Lever House* in New York, the office building of Lever Brothers Company. The English term may have been retained to mark the English connections of the firm or merely for its distinction. If it is accepted —if the American people do not insist, that is, on calling it "the Lever Building" despite the company's desire to have it called *Lever House* —the term may spread and be applied to other office buildings. See also **building; residence.**

house; home. Mr. Edgar A. Guest's insistence that *It takes a heap o' livin' and some love to make a home* was, for its time, philologically correct. But usage and the relentless optimism of real-estate dealers has made *home* now practically the equivalent of *house.* The old connotations of family ties and domestic comfort which *home* carried have been obliterated. Whole villages of homes are now mass-produced and any fifty by sixty foot lot will do for a homesite. One may look back longingly to the day when a home was more than a house and there is nothing to stop the discriminatingly sentimental from still preserving the distinction, but it can no longer be insisted on. See also **residence.**

house-cleaning has now a definite idiomatic meaning, the removal of rubbish and dirt from the interior of a house, usually after a considerable period of less thorough cleaning, as in *spring house-cleaning. Cleaning house* would convey much the same meaning and is indeed sometimes used, but *cleaning the house* might suggest cleaning the outside of the house, a suggestion never conveyed by *house-cleaning.*

housewife. An interesting example of the way in which usage establishes meaning is afforded by the fact that *hussy,* or *huzzy,* an ill-behaved girl or a worthless woman, is simply a shortened form of an older pronunciation of *housewife,* a term of sedate dignity.

An even more remarkable development is shown in the words *queen* and *quean.* Both stem from the Anglo-Saxon *cwene,* woman. The king's woman became the Queen. But *quean,* retained now chiefly in the Scottish dialect, means an impudent, bold young woman of the lower classes, often a prostitute (*Draw, Bardolph! Cut me off the villain's head. Throw the quean in the channel. Now Tam, O Tam! had they been queans/ A' plump and strappin' in their teens*). From this word (according to Partridge in his *Dictionary of Slang and Unconventional English*) comes the slang use of *queen* to mean homosexual (*They were sweethearts; sure he's a queen, didn't you know that*—Hemingway). This term is not recognized by any of the standard dictionaries but it is in almost universal use in America.

hove. See **heave.**

how is ordinarily an adverb of manner. When used as an interrogative it always has this meaning and always stands first in the sentence or clause, as in *how could he laugh?*. It may also be used as an adverb of degree. In this sense it also stands first, but the sentence or clause does not have the interrogative word order, as in *how he could laugh! How* may be used as an adverbial conjunction, as in *he told us how to make it.* It may also be used as a pure conjunction, without reference to degree or manner, as in *he told us how he had been left an orphan.* This is standard English. But *as how* used in the same construction, as in *he told us as how he had been left an orphan,* is not standard. (For *how come?,* see **come.**)

however. This word may be used to mean in whatever manner or to whatever extent. It may also be used in the sense of nevertheless. In Great Britain it is sometimes used as an interrogative, with the sense of "how?" as in *however did you guess?*. This is condemned by most British grammarians. *Howsoever* is an archaic form of *however. Howsomever* is a still older form of the same word and is not standard now.

human. The use of *human* or *humans* for human being or human beings is severely condemned by some authorities and censured in varying degrees by most. The condemnations run from "affectation" and "jocularity" to "simply a vulgarism." But it is hard to see why. The word was so used from the sixteenth to the nineteenth centuries (*No man among men, nor humain among the humains*—1533; *Gibbie fell to hugging him* [*the dog*] *as if he had been a human*—1879). The opposition to this use on the ground that *human* is an adjective and not a substantive seems to have developed late in the nineteenth century and to have been one of those schoolmasterish attempts to impose a spurious logic on grammar (like the double negative). But thousands of adjectives are used as nouns every day and made into plurals whenever that seems suitable (*The whites will win unless the blues show more fight than they have shown yet*). A simple word, such as *humans,* is needed to relieve *men* of its double duty of representing all human beings and also the males only. It would have helped the enthusiastic lady who amused Shelley so much by exclaiming: *All, all are men—women and all!*

human and **humane** were once interchangeable variants. Shakespeare refers to a *human statute* where we would say *humane* and Pope's famous line first appeared as *To err is humane, to forgive Divine.* The two words became established in separate meanings, however. *Human* now refers to the good and bad traits of mankind alike (*The sweetest thing that ever grew/ Beside a human door!*) with, perhaps, a little more emphasis on the bad, or at least the weak, than the good (*I'm only human. No, it wasn't noble, but it was the human thing to do. Human frailty, human faults.*). *Humane* is now restricted to the nobler and especially the gentler aspects of man. A *humane* person is one actuated by benevolence and pity, especially—in popular usage

—in his treatment of animals. This specific meaning may have been shaped in part by the Humane Society (*These humane impulses hardly qualified him to be a success in the stockyards*). In former times *humane* also suggested courtesy and refinement and this meaning survives in the term *humane studies* applied to those studies (often called the humanities) which were thought to refine the mind, which concerned themselves with human rather than supernatural matters.

humanist. The *humanists* (sometimes spelled with a capital *H*) were Renaissance scholars who pursued and disseminated the purely human study of the cultures of ancient Greece and Rome. The term is now sometimes applied to classical scholars or to those who are versed in the humanities. But since the study of the cultures of ancient Greece and Rome were thought to weaken one's faith in Christianity, the term came to mean free-thinkers, a meaning strengthened by the adoption of the term by those who, following Comte, have tried to make a religion of humanity and by others who profess to be merely students of human affairs. In all, *humanist* is about as vague and confusing a word as there is and should be avoided except where the context makes the particular meaning clear.

humblebee. See **bumblebee.**

humbleness; humility; humiliation. *Humbleness* is the quality or state of being low in station, meek, unpretentious, modest. *Humility* has the additional suggestion of one's being aware of this lowliness and accepting it as right and proper. We would speak of the humbleness of a man's birth or social position, his humility in cheerfully accepting it. *Humbleness* is not very often used now but in the commercial exploitation of religiosity *humility* has become a vogue word used to such excess that it occasionally borders on the comic.

If *humility* is the cheerful acceptance of humbleness as proper, *humiliation* is the sense of shame at the lowering of one's dignity or prestige, an angry and resentful refusal to accept humbleness as proper or deserved.

humble pie. The learned have insisted that *to eat humble pie,* to humiliate and abase oneself (*To sue for peace when further resistance becomes hopeless is a kind of "humble pie" that fate has condemned all vanquished nations to swallow from time immemorial*) is derived from *umble* or *numble pie,* pie made of the *umbles* or internal organs of the deer. This, they say, was an unsavory dish reserved for menials; hence it would be a humiliation for an upper-class person to eat it. But the use of the term doesn't bear this out. Pepys speaks of a hot umble-pie with apparent approval. Sir Walter Scott calls the umbles "the best," and there is a recipe in the *Babees Book* (c. 1475) for "a dishe of Umbles" under the heading of "For to serve a Lord." The chances are that the phrase is simply a pun, the more likely since *humble* was often pronounced *'umble*. Though the meaning of the phrase may be uncertain, one thing about it is certain: it is overworked.

humor; wit; irony; sarcasm; satire. *Humor* is etymologically akin to *humid.* It was applied to certain bodily fluids—especially the famous four humors, blood, bile, black bile, and phlegm—whose proper proportions kept the body in "temper." Thence it came to mean one's special condition of mind or mood or disposition, a special distinguishing caprice, whim or vagary. In this sense the word was fashionable in Shakespeare's time—as, if we may trust *Every Man in His Humour* and a score of other plays, was the state or condition it designated. And since crotchety, whimsical, odd people are often amusing, *humorous* came to describe those who were ludicrous and those who went out of their way to be ludicrous by exhibiting a facetious turn of mind. However *humor* retained some of its older meaning in such terms as *bad humor, an ill humor, surly humor,* or *a strange humor.* In contemporary usage *humor* covers a great deal that is amusing, but it still has something of its old meaning. It is often whimsical, deliberately incongruous and absurd, extravagant and preposterous. Pudd'nhead Wilson was being humorous when on hearing a dog howl he said that he wished he owned half of that dog because, if he did, he'd shoot his half. Chaucer is a humorous writer and his humor shows in such a statement as that the Prioress spoke French "after the manner of Stratford atte Bowe" and in the Monk's cheerful willingness to "Let Austin have his swink to him reserved."

Wit originally meant knowledge, wisdom, intelligence, judgment, sense, meanings which are retained in such phrases as *at one's wit's end, to live by one's wits, dull witted,* and so on. As a form of humor (in the broadest sense of *humor* as something funny) *wit* is an intellectual matter. It is often spontaneous and consists in discovering analogies between things really unlike and expressing these connections in diverting and amusing ways. Wit startles us. We may smile at humor, but we will either laugh or be angry at a piece of wit. It was witty of Sir Boyle Roche when Curran boasted that he was the guardian of his own honor to congratulate him upon his sinecure. Wit is aggressive and often cruel. The common term *a stroke of wit* is usually justified. He that *maketh others afraid of his wit,* says Bacon, *had need be afraid of others' memory.*

Irony derives from a Greek word meaning a dissembler. The term was first used in reference to Socrates who exposed an opponent's ignorance by pretending to desire instruction or information from him. Today the term means a covert sarcasm, the essential feature of which is the contradiction between the literal and intended meanings of what is said. Thus in *Mac Flecknoe* Dryden never ceases praising his enemy Shadwell, but the praise is all derogatory. He says that Shadwell was *mature in dullness from his tender years* and that while other minor poets to some faint meaning make pretense, *Shadwell never deviates into sense.* The common phrase *the irony of fate* alludes to an apparent mockery of destiny in circumstances in which something turns out the very opposite of what was expected. Thus it is a common irony of fate that rewards and honors passionately desired when we are young are often conferred when we are old and no longer prize them.

Sarcasm derives from a Greek word meaning a tearing of the flesh, or a biting of the lips in rage. It designates a sneer or a taunt uttered in contempt or bitterness. It sometimes employs irony, but when it does so it makes no effort to conceal the real meaning under the apparent one. *Aren't you clever!* spoken tauntingly after someone's blunder or exhibition of ignorance would be a piece of sarcasm. Montesquieu was being sarcastic when he said that *it would not do to suppose that Negroes were men, lest it should turn out that Whites were not.* Sarcasm is usually violent in its aggressiveness, rough and brutal in the extreme, the very opposite of humor.

Satire is the employment of irony, sarcasm, ridicule, and so on, for the purpose of exposing vice, denouncing folly or indecorum. It differs from invective in that it remains humorous. Swift left his fortune to found a lunatic asylum in Ireland,

> *To show* [*he said*] *by one satiric touch*
> *No nation wanted it so much.*

See also **burlesque, jocularity.**

hundred. This word was originally a noun and was followed by *of,* as in *one hundred of leagues.* Today the singular form *hundred* is treated as a cardinal number. That is, it is treated as an adjective and used without *of,* as in *three hundred Spartans,* except when referring to part of a specified group, as in *two hundred of these men.* An expression involving *hundred* is usually treated as a plural, as in *three hundred men were admitted,* but it may also be treated as a singular, as in *two hundred years is a very long time.*

The plural form *hundreds* cannot be qualified by a numeral. It is a noun and requires *of* when followed by the name of anything countable, as in *hundreds of men;* the *of* is omitted only before a degree word such as *more, less, too many,* as in *hundreds more men.*

Few usually takes the adjective construction, as in *a few hundred men; many* usually takes the noun construction, as in *many hundreds of men.* But either form may be used with either word.

hundredweight. This word has a regular plural *hundredweights,* but only the singular form is used with a number word, as in *a few hundredweight of coal.* In Great Britain, a hundredweight is 112 pounds.

hung. See **hang.**

hunt. An Englishman *hunts* foxes, hares, stags and other wild mammals, but he *shoots* game birds. An American *hunts* birds and beasts alike. Except for the very few who engage in fox hunting, no American refers to a hunting expedition as a hunt. One who hunts is in America a hunter, not a huntsman or sports-man. A hunter in England today is likely to be a horse especially trained for hunting (*He rode with dash upon a thoroughbred hunter*), but it was not always so (*The horn of the hunter is heard on the hill*).

hurl; hurdle; hurtle. To *hurl* is to fling violently (*He hurled the book across the room*). To *hurdle* is to leap over a barrier or hurdle or, by extension, to overcome some difficulty that can be conceived of as a hurdle on a racetrack. To *hurtle* is to rush violently, to strike together noisily, to resound noisily, as in collision (*The train hurtled through the station with a great rushing wind that rattled the windows and shook the doors and flung cinders and gravel against the decrepit building*). *Hurtle* is sometimes used to mean *hurl,* especially when the hurling is accompanied by noise, but on the whole the word is bookish and slightly archaic.

hurricane. See **cyclone.**

hurt. The past tense is *hurt.* The participle is also *hurt.*

husky in the sense of burly, sturdy, muscular is an Americanism (*Thirty-eight men he counted, a wild and husky crew*). It is known in England, from American literature and moving pictures, but not used.

hussy; huzzy. See **housewife.**

hydrolysis. The plural is *hydrolyses.*

hymenal; hymeneal; hymenial. *Hymenal* relates to the hymen. *Hymeneal* relates to marriage. *Hymenial* relates to the hymenium, the spore-bearing surface in certain fungi.

hyper-; hypo-. The prefix *hyper-* means over, above, and hence in excess. An organ which is hypertrophied has grown larger than its proper size. One who is hypersensitive is sensitive beyond the normal. A hyperbole is an exaggeration.

The prefix *hypo-* means under. A hypodermic needle goes under the skin or epidermis. A hypocrite was originally a secondary figure on the stage. Hypocrisy may thus derive from the idea of playing a part like an actor. Or it may mean one who conceals an evil intention under a pretense of goodness. Shipley thinks it derives from the fact that the secondary actor served as what in stage parlance today is called "a straight man." That is, he answered back. And we cannot believe that anyone who answers back, who maintains an opinion opposed to our own, is sincere.

hyperbole is the term in rhetoric for obvious exaggeration. There is no intent to deceive. The extravagant language is for emphasis only. Ours is a hyperbolical age. We give *a million thanks* for a trifling favor and are *forever indebted* for something which we have forgotten before we have turned the corner. Such a fashion may sometimes make simple sincerity seem sullen indifference but more often it serves by the force of contrast to give plain speech great weight and effectiveness.

hyphens. Hyphens are sometimes used to indicate stammering, as in *s-s-see,* or spelling out, as in *c-a-n-d-y.* Their more important uses are to join words (see **compound words, temporary compounds, prefixes, suffixes**), or to break a word at the end of a line (see **division of words**).

hypnosis. The plural is *hypnoses.*

hypnotic. A *hypnotic* is an agent that produces sleep. This may be a drug, or in the case of what is commonly thought of as hypnosis, a spell or influence or suggestion. With the increasing use in therapy of hypnotic states induced by suggestion and susceptibility, the adjective will probably continue its trend to mean solely states so induced. But for the present the pharmacopoeias use *hypnotic* to designate a definite class of soporifics and sedatives.

hypocrite is a term of reproach freely bestowed in popular usage upon almost anyone whose actions belie his professions. But the word means one who pretends to be what he knows he is not, who for ulterior motives makes an ostentatious display of virtues which he secretly despises. Such a course of action would require a clarity of purpose, strength of will and histrionic skill so far above those possessed by the ordinary person as to make him who had and could employ them a rare man. It may be doubted if outside of literature there have been many true hypocrites. There have, of course, been millions of muddled people who have failed to perceive the most glaring opposition between their ideals and their actions, and the capacity for combining high principles and low practices seems illimitable. But the intelligence and detachment to be aware of it and the strength of character to exploit it rarely go with the almost blindly stupid selfishness that hypocrisy requires.

hypothesis. The plural is *hypotheses.*

hysterics. This word may be treated as a singular when it is thought of as the name of a disease. But when it refers to the actual physical events it is always treated as a plural, as in *hysterics are painful to watch.* The shorter form of the adjective, *hysteric,* is sometimes used to mean a person who is inclined to hysterics, as in *she always was a hysteric.* In any other use, the longer form *hysterical* is preferred.

I

I. If you are in doubt whether to use *me* or *I,* the chances are that *me* is better. See **subjective pronouns** and **passive voice**.

ibid. This is an abbreviation of the Latin word *ibidem* and means *in the same place.*

-ic; -ical. These are both adjective endings taken over from Greek and Latin. Some adjectives, such as *musical* and *logical,* have only the long form. Some, such as *frantic* and *public,* have only the short form. But a great many have both. In such cases the form in *-ical* is likely to be the older of the two. Occasionally, as in *politic* and *political,* the two forms have different meanings, but as a rule this is not the case.

A grammarian writing in 1765 said, "*-ic* is a foreign, and *-ical* a domestic termination. The former therefore is used upon solemn, the latter upon familiar occasions; as *seraphic* and *seraphical, microscopic* and *microscopical.* When the subject then is naturally solemn, the solemn ending prevails; and where familiar, the familiar." This is no longer the situation. A twentieth century American might say *microscopic* at the breakfast table and give it no thought.

Modern British grammarians say that the form in *-ic* frequently has the restricted meaning of "of the nature of," and the form in *-ical* the wider, or looser, meaning of "practically connected with." They give as examples *a comic song* but *a comical incident, a tragic muse* but *a tragical fate.* In the United States this distinction is recognized only in the case of a few words. In general, the short form in *-ic* is preferred, and the long form in *-ical* leaves many people wondering why the speaker went to the trouble of pronouncing that unnecessary syllable.

-ic; ics. The suffix *-ic* is an adjective ending and is used to form adjectives from nouns, as in *poetic, heroic, metallic.* Adjectives formed in this way may in turn become nouns, as has happened with *classic, cosmetic, lunatic, alcoholic.* Nouns can also be made from adjectives ending in *-ic* by adding *s,* as in *poetics* and *heroics.* The names of most of the sciences were formed in one or the other of these ways.

Names for branches of learning that came into English before 1500 end in *-ic,* as do *music, logic, arithmetic.* Names which came into the language since then end in *ics,* as do *economics, physics, mathematics.* Recently some writers, especially in philosophy, have chosen to use the older ending on the newer words and call their subjects *metaphysic, ethic,* or *dialectic.* There is no difference in meaning between these two forms.

The names of the sciences, or any primarily intellectual subject, are always treated as singulars and are used with a singular verb, as in *his mathematics was inadequate.* Names of practical matters are usually treated as plural, as in *his tactics were admirable.* Frequently the same word may be used in both senses, as in *acoustics deals with problems of sound* and *the acoustics here are bad.*

When words of this kind are used to qualify a following noun they may keep their noun form, as in *a hydraulics engineer,* or they may take either of the adjective forms, as in *an economic attaché, a statistical report.* Sometimes all three forms may be used with the same meaning. We sometimes hear of *a hydraulic engineer* and sometimes of *a hydraulical engineer.* It would be better if the noun form in *-ics* was always used when the science itself is meant, as in *a hydraulics engineer.* This is especially true when the word can be understood in some other way, as *energetic* in *a photochemical reaction may be driven "uphill" in an energetic sense.* The writer meant, "uphill, as the word is understood in the science of energetics." This would have been clearer if the *s* had not been dropped. If the noun form is used for the science itself, the adjective forms could then be applied to whatever comes within the field of that science, such as *a hydraulic press, a ballistic pendulum.* This distinction does not have to be observed in order to write acceptable scientific English today, but if it is observed the words will be understood more easily.

ice. An illustration of idiomatic meanings is furnished by the phrases *to break the ice,* to initiate an action or to penetrate reserve, and *to cut no ice,* a slang phrase widely used in America but unknown in England, meaning to fail to make a favorable impression, or to fail to amount to anything important.

The British sometimes use *an ice* where an American would always say *ice cream.* An *ice* in America is sherbet.

iced tea. These words are usually pronounced as though written *ice tea,* but some people feel that it would be a mistake to write them that way. The form *ice tea* is as justifiable as the form *ice cream,* or *skim milk,* both of which are now standard.

id. This is an abbreviation of the Latin word *idem* and means *the same.*

idea; conception; concept; notion. Anything existing in the mind may be called an *idea* (*I have an idea of what I want to do. That was a great idea. The very idea of such a performance!*). Where an intellectual effort is needed, however, to abstract some quality (such as roundness or redness) from its existence in material objects, the idea that results is called a *concept* (*The concept of time as a dimension is difficult for the lay mind to grasp. The concept of patriotism has been a powerful force in shaping history*). A *conception* is the act of forming abstract ideas, but it has also become in standard usage a synonym for *concept* (*He has a strange conception of honor if he regards such an action as honorable*).

Though *notion* may be a synonym for *idea* (*The notion that the world was round had been conceived centuries before. He had no notion what she intended to do next*), in its commonest usage it suggests a vague or imperfectly conceived idea (*I had no notion such a thing was brewing. I've half a notion to give you the hiding you deserve*).

ideal; example; model. All three of these words refer to something worthy of imitation, a standard to be striven toward. An *ideal* is a standard of perfection either existing merely as an image in the mind (*Absolute honesty is all very well as an ideal, but in practice it might cause a great deal of unnecessary unhappiness*) or based upon a person or conduct (*Abraham Lincoln remains the American ideal in humane statesmanship*).

Example is not necessarily honorific. There are bad as well as good examples (*an example of the best workmanship, an example to be avoided*).

A *model* is primarily a physical shape to be closely copied (*Art students cannot learn portraiture without models. The models for next year's cars are already being constructed*) but it is also a pattern for exact imitation in character or conduct (*American assembly-line techniques have become a model for other nations. The village had always regarded him as a model husband and father*).

identified; connected. *Identified* is often misused, especially in business jargon, as a synonym for *connected* (in such a sentence as *He has been identified with Western Electric for twenty years*). The words, however, are not even loosely synonymous. *Identified* means recognized or established as a particular person or thing (*On the basis of dentures and finger prints the victim of the lodging house fire was identified as Richard Roe*). In the rare instances where a man's fame is so great that it equals or even overshadows that of a company with which he is connected, he and the company might conceivably be *identified* or thought of as one and the same. Thomas A. Edison would be an example. *Connected* means attached to or associated with (*He had been connected with harness-racing scandals* never *He had been identified with harness-racing scandals. Identified,* in this context, is properly used in the statement: *He had been identified as the leader of the harness-racing racket*).

ideology. Sir Alan Herbert is very hard on *ideology.* "A wriggling snob-word," he calls it and says emphatically that "it does *not* mean a given person's principles and beliefs or attitude to life and politics."

But, while it is true that in its strictest sense the word is a philosophic term meaning the science of ideas, most linguists now feel that usage has established it as a standard term for the body of doctrine, myth, and symbols of a social movement, institution, class, or large group, or such a body of doctrine, etc., with reference to some political and cultural plan, together with the means of putting it into operation (*The fascist ideology included the ruthless extermination of all whom the party regarded as unfit*). *Creed* and *faith* have too strong religious connotations to serve as synonyms.

idle. See **lazy.**

idle rich. Originally a term of contempt in nineteenth-century socialism's comparatively polite lexicon of abuse, *the idle rich* was taken over by the populace as a humorous term. But it is now worn out as either an invective or a joke.

i.e., and **e.g.** have distinctly separate meanings. *i.e.,* which is an abbreviation of the Latin *id est* (that is), introduces a definition (*He threatened them with massive retaliation, i.e. the hydrogen bomb*). *e.g.,* which is an abbreviation of the Latin *exempli gratia* (for example), introduces an illustration (*He avoids all frivolous diversions, e.g. dancing*). Though the distinction between the terms may be understood by the writer, it may not be understood by the reader, and even when it is understood by both writer and reader, the terms are still a form of shorthand and not English. It is better to say *for example* and *that is*.

if. This word is a conjunction. Its chief function is to introduce a condition on which the principal statement in the sentence depends, as in *if he falls it will kill him*. *If* may also be used as the equivalent of *though*, as in *if he falls it won't hurt him*. (See **though**.) In either case, the verb in the *if* clause may be a subjunctive or a present or past indicative. (See **subjunctive mode**.) In current English a future tense cannot be used in an *if* clause. The future is implied in *if he asks me*. In *if he will ask me*, the word *will* loses its function of indicating the future and takes on its basic meaning of "be willing to."

When a condition is introduced by *if*, the conclusion may be introduced by *then*, as in *if he said it then it must be true*. As a rule, these sentences are more forceful when *then* is not used. In literary English *if* may be omitted from a conditional clause and the conditional nature of the clause shown by placing *were, had, should,* or *could*, before the subject, as in *were I Brutus, had I but served my God, should he betray me*, and *could I revive within me her symphony and song*.

If is also used to introduce a clause that is merely doubtful or uncertain, as in *she doubts if two and two make four* and *judge, great lords, if I have done amiss*. Clauses that state a condition or have the force of *though* function as adverbs and qualify the principal verb in the sentence. The *if* clauses that merely express uncertainty function as nouns and are usually the object of a verb such as *see, ask, learn, doubt*. The word *whether* is also used to introduce clauses of this kind. Some contemporary grammarians claim that only *whether* can properly be used to introduce a noun clause and that *if* "should be" restricted to adverbial clauses. *If* never has been restricted in this way and is not now. The notion that it should be is very recent. Fifty years ago, grammarians saw nothing wrong in the sentence *I doubt if it is mine*. At that time they were distressed if the word *whether* was used without an expressed alternative. When it occurred in a sentence of this kind, they said it was being used in place of *if*.

if the truth were told or, sometimes, **if the truth were known**, is a formula of introduction to a statement, usually of something contrary to a popularly accepted idea, that has become a cliché. It is better to state whatever fact you have to state and let it carry what conviction it can. A stressing of its truthfulness is as likely to arouse incredulity as to ensure acceptance.

if the worst comes to the worst is a cliché. It is better to say *If it comes to the worst* or *If the worst happens*.

ignominious retreat. All freshness of meaning has long ago been beaten out of *ignominious retreat*.

ignoramus. The plural is *ignoramuses*, never *ignorami*. *Ignoramus* is a Latin verb form meaning *we do not know*. It was once the term used by grand juries in returning what we now call "no bill" or "not a true bill" and meant that they knew of no reason why the defendant should be held for trial. During the seventeenth century grand juries did not always take their responsibilities literally. It is said that "bills preferred to grand juries for high treason duly proved were returned ignoramus." This outraged at least part of the citizenry and the word came to be used as a term of abuse, as in *with nose cock't up and visage like a fury,/ or foreman of an ignoramus jury*. From this, by ways not hard to imagine, the word has come to mean an ignorant person.

ignorant. See **illiterate**.

ilk. The use of *ilk* to mean breed, class, kind, especially in the phrase *of that ilk*, must now be accepted as standard despite the protests of purists for more than fifty years. It originally meant "same." In the old ballad of *King Arthur and the King of Cornwall* we are told that Sir Tristram took powder and mixed it with warm sweet milk and put it in a horn *and swilled it about in that ilk*. Then the word got specialized, particularly in legal documents, to mean "of the same (estate)" when a man's name and the name of his estate were the same. Thus "Macintosh of that ilk" would mean "Macintosh of Macintosh." Through a misunderstanding of this came the modern meaning of "of that sort or kind." But usage has sanctioned this as it has many other mistakes, so that it is now not only an acceptable meaning but the primary meaning.

ill. The comparative form is *worse*. The superlative form is *worst*. (For *worse* and *worst*, see **bad**.) *Ill* is used as an adjective, as in *an ill wind, an ill will,* and also as an adverb, as in *ill blows the wind that profits no body* and *these could ill be spared*. The adverbial form *illy* is also heard, as in *beauty is jealous and illy bears the presence of a rival*. The form *ill* is generally preferred.

Ill may mean hostile, unfavorable, unsatisfactory, as in *ill-intentioned, in an ill moment, ill defined*. In England the word no longer means immoral or blameworthy, but this use survives in Scotland and the United States, as in *ill habits, ill company*.

ill; sick. In England *ill* is the usual word meaning not well. It is ordinarily a predicate adjective and follows the noun it qualifies, as in *a child ill of the smallpox* and *another lying dangerously ill*. The use of *ill* before the noun, as in *a very ill man*, is extremely rare.

In contemporary American usage *ill* and *sick* both mean unwell, in poor health. *Ill* is the more formal word and because of its formality is likely to suggest a more serious indisposition, but this is not absolute. *Sick* in English usage has come to mean nauseated, almost to the point of being an indecent word. An American who announced that he thought he was going to be sick might elicit some sympathy from the assembled company. An Englishman would be more likely to arouse consternation. Here, as with many words, the American usage is the older one, once employed in England but now replaced by the newer or more specialized meaning. When the physician in *Macbeth* tells Macbeth that Lady Macbeth is *not so sick as she is troubled with thick-coming fancies,* the modern English meaning would be ludicrous. Peter's wife's mother lay *sick of a fever.* Ruth, in tears amid the alien corn, was *sick for home.* And so on. Nausea is recognized in America as a form of sickness, especially in such phrases as *a sick headache, sea-sickness,* and *sick at his stomach.* (The form *sick to* is sometimes heard, but *sick at* is preferred.)

illegal; illegitimate; illicit; unlawful. All of these words mean contrary to law, but each has acquired special meanings. *Illegal* is the most sharply restricted of the four, meaning only forbidden by law, contrary to statute (*It is illegal in some states to go fishing on Sunday*). The earliest meaning of *illegitimate* was "not born in wedlock" (*Many of Elizabeth's subjects regarded her as an illegitimate child and hence not lawfully their queen*) and from this it has developed the associated meaning of spurious. It can mean *illegal* and there is an increasing tendency to so use it. *Illicit* expresses more opprobrium than the other words. An illicit love affair is not only an illegal love affair but one of which the speaker or writer disapproves. It is shameful, furtive, dishonest. *Unlawful* can mean contrary to moral standards as well as contrary to law. It is now slightly archaic, its meaning of contrary to law being largely replaced by *illegal* and its meaning of contrary to moral standards being largely replaced by *illicit. Unlawful issue* or *unlawful love* would sound a little strange today. This very fact, however, gives the word certain shades of meaning that are desirable in special contexts. Its overuse by the rhetoricians and moralists of previous generations has given it, for example, a slight flavor of humor in some contexts (*Wi' mair o' horrible and awfu'/ Which even to name wad be unlawfu'*). In others it has an added touch of dignity (*These unlawful aspirations must be repressed*).

illegible; unreadable. That which is *illegible* is hard or impossible to read or decipher. It is used particularly of handwriting. That which is *unreadable* may be so because it is illegible, but more often the word means that it is unsuitable for reading, too dull, awkward, tedious or offensive (*The manuscript was almost illegible and when finally deciphered was unreadable*).

ill-gotten gains. As a term for wealth acquired by evil means, *ill-gotten gains* is a cliché.

illicit. See **illegal; elicit.**

illiterate; ignorant. *Illiterate* is not so general a term as *ignorant.* In its strict sense it means unable to read (*He was illiterate until he was twelve*), but it has come to mean unable to read or write, and, more loosely still, lacking education and even showing a lack of culture (*He loved to be bitter at/ A lady illiterate. Many sensational comic books are written with a vast audience of illiterates in mind*). *Ignorant* means destitute of knowledge, unlearned. It may describe a general condition (*He's just an ignorant lout, what do you expect?*) or refer to a lack of knowledge in regard to some particular subject or fact (*I am ignorant of the cause of their quarrel*). An illiterate person is ignorant, strictly speaking, only in this last sense of lacking knowledge of a particular subject— reading. But in contemporary United States. where free public education is not only available but compulsory, one who is truly illiterate is probably mentally deficient and grossly ignorant and the chances are that *illiterate* will come more and more to mean *ignorant* and *stupid.* It is already being used a great deal to designate one who doesn't know the very basis —the ABC's, as it were—of some specialized field (*He was psychiatrically illiterate. Many of the tycoons are economic illiterates.*)

illness. See **sickness.**

illume; illuminate; illumine. All three of these words mean to light up, to throw light upon, either literally or figuratively, in the sense of explaining an idea to make it clearer. *Illume* is a poetic archaism (*A second sun array'd in flame,/ To burn, to kindle, to illume*) and should be avoided unless the user is a poet nearing his two hundredth birthday. *Illumine* is also strictly for the poets; it went out of fashion with Tennyson (*The long-illumined cities*). *Illuminate,* then, remains the only generally acceptable form.

illusion; illusive; illusory. See **allusion.**

illustration. See **case** and **example.**

imaginary; imaginative. That is *imaginary* which is not real but exists only in the imagination or fancy (*He had suffered all his life from imaginary ailments*). That is *imaginative* which is characterized by or bears evidence of imagination ("*The Rime of the Ancient Mariner*" *is a highly imaginative poem*). An imaginative man would be one who imagines much, a man rich in fancy. An imaginary man would be a nonexistent being conceived of in someone's imagination.

imagination. See **fancy.**

imagination run riot. See **riot.**

imagine. This word may be followed by a clause, as in *I imagine they have finished,* or by the *-ing* form of a verb, as in *imagine finishing so soon.* It may also be followed by an infinitive, as in *I imagine them to have finished,* but the clause construction is generally preferred.

imagine; suppose. Although the primary meaning of *suppose* is to assume that something is true or false for the sake of argument or for the purpose of tracing the consequences, and although the primary meaning of *Imagine* is simply to form a mental image of something not actually present to the senses, the use of *imagine* as a substitute for *suppose* has become so universal (*I imagine five children and four dogs keep you pretty busy*) that it is now standard.

imbue; infuse; instill. The correct use of these three transitive verbs depends upon carefully understood distinctions. *Imbue* means to impregnate or inspire (literally, to saturate), as with feelings or opinions. It is always followed by *with* (*His teachers imbued him with a love of learning*). *Infuse* means to introduce as by pouring. It is always followed by *into* (*His schoolmates tried to infuse a contempt for learning into him*). *Instill* means to infuse slowly or by degrees into the mind or feelings. It, too, is always followed by *into* (*Fear of the father is instilled into most children from their infancy*). *Instil* is a permissible variant spelling, though the preterit and participle remain *instilled* and *instilling*.

imitation. See **synthetic.**

Immaculate Conception. The Dogma of the Immaculate Conception, promulgated by the Roman Catholic Church, teaches that the Virgin Mary was conceived in her mother's womb without the stain of original sin, through the anticipated merits of Jesus Christ. Many Protestants have the mistaken notion that the term applies to Jesus Christ.

immanent; imminent; eminent. *Immanent* is restricted for the most part to theological and psychological writings. It means inherent, remaining within, taking place in the mind of the subject and having no effect outside of it (*God transcends nature and is immanent in nature*). *Imminent* means impending, likely to occur at any moment (*With the paddle gone and the rapids looming directly ahead, death seemed imminent*), projecting, leaning forward, overhanging (*Of hairbreadth scapes i' th' imminent deadly breach*). *Eminent* means high in station or rank, distinguished, prominent or protruding (*His counsel is eminently wise. Our eminent visitor.*)

immaterial. See **unmaterial.**

immature; premature. That is *immature* which is not yet ripe, developed or perfected. That is *premature* which comes into existence too soon, which is mature or ripe before the proper time, or which is overhasty, as in action. *The New Yorker* (Nov. 13, 1954) quotes a solemn newspaper pronouncement that *Six percent of all babies born in the U. S. are immature*. All babies are immature. Six percent are premature.

immeasurable. See **unmeasurable.**

immediately; instantly; instantaneously; directly; right away; straightway; straightaway; presently. Procrastination blunts the force of almost every word that denotes complete absence of delay or lapse of time. *Instantly* still suggests that something happened on the instant (*The light changed to green and instantly the car was*

in motion) and *instantaneously* implies that something happened so soon after something else as to be practically simultaneous (*The post mortem revealed that the passengers had died instantaneously with the explosion*). *Immediately* retains much of this sense, and yet it is possible to say *I'll be there immediately*, although the use of the future tense involves some lapse of time however slight. *Directly*, which originally meant in an undeviating course, is often ambiguous (as in *Tell him to come home directly* or *He spoke directly and to the point*) and therefore to be avoided unless the context makes its meaning unmistakable. When used of time it can mean immediately (*Directly I had finished speaking he began to wave his hand in an effort to gain attention*), but in common use it often implies a delay (*Tell him to wait; I'll be there directly*).

Right away is used more in America than in England (*His face lit up right away. He knew me the minute he saw me*). *Straightway*, which, plainly, like *directly*, originally meant going by an undeviating course, retains a considerable sense of immediacy (*But let the winds of passion swell and straightway men begin to generalize*), but it is now a literary word. *Straightaway* (like *thataway*) is not standard.

Presently, which once meant "at the present moment, at the very time these words are being said" (*The poor woman no sooner looked on the sergeant than she presently recollected him*), has become obsolete in this sense and now conveys an idea of delay rather than of immediacy. The phrase *as we shall presently see* usually introduces a leisurely preamble and rebukes the impatient, implying that in the author's good time whatever he is seeking to convey to us will be made manifest.

immediately; immediately after. The use of *immediately* alone for *immediately after*, in such sentences as *Immediately he sat down there were angry shoutings from the floor* or *The game started immediately the president arrived*, is not the best usage. It is better to use the full phrase.

immense; enjoyable; great. *Immense* and *great* are sometimes used as slang terms to indicate a pleasurable satisfaction more enthusiastic than *enjoyable* seems to convey. *Great* means very enjoyable. *Immense* means exceedingly enjoyable. They are about as precise, however, as the Hollywoodnotes *stupendous, terrific,* and *colossal,* and should be avoided.

immerge; emerge. Though *immerge* and *emerge* have the same basic root, their prefixes give them distinctly different meanings. *Immerge* is most commonly used as a transitive verb meaning to immerse or plunge into a fluid (*He immerged the film in developer*). It is also used intransitively (*The feeding ducks were immerged for over a minute*). *Emerge,* from its basic sense of rise or come forth from, as from water or other liquid (*He emerged from the pool struggling for breath*), has come to mean coming forth into view or notice, as from concealment or obscurity (*The enemy soldiers* *emerged from the hedgerow with their hands above their heads. He soon emerged from the obscurity of local ward politics*).

The best way to avoid any possible confusion between these two words is to use *immerse* in the place of *immerge*.

immigrant. See **emigrant**.

imminent. See **immanent**.

immoral; amoral; unmoral. That is *immoral* which does not conform to the prevailing standard of morality (*"Immoral contracts,"* all *contracts founded upon considerations "contra bonos mores . . ."*). Where conventional morality has been changing, as it has in Europe and America in the past century, *immoral* does not convey a clear meaning unless one knows the code of morality of the person using it. When the poet Shelley refused to live with his wife after he no longer loved her, he was, for example, to some immoral, to others moral. In vulgar usage *immoral* almost always connotes sexual irregularity (*Don't dance or ride with General Bangs,/ A most immoral man*). Samuel Johnson's statement that *A flatterer of vice is an immoral man* might seem unwarranted to many modern readers.

Amoral means apart from moral considerations. The word seems to have been coined by Robert Louis Stevenson who said that there was a great deal in life and letters *which is not immoral, but simply amoral*. A book might be regarded as immoral because it contained certain words whose use was not sanctioned by the prevailing morality, but a dictionary which contained the same words would be amoral. When used of persons, *amoral* usually means someone who does immoral things with no awareness of their immorality because he is not aware of the moral code. *Unmoral* is synonymous with *amoral,* not with *immoral* (*The lower animism is not immoral, it is unmoral*).

immortal. See **undying**.

immunity; impunity. *Immunity* is the state of being immune from or insusceptible to a particular disease (*A successful vaccination confers an immunity from smallpox for many years*), an exemption from any natural or usual liability, obligation, service, or duty (*That particular type of fool seems to enjoy an immunity to shame. Religious pacificism gives an immunity from the draft but intellectual pacifism does not*). *Impunity* is a more limited term meaning exemption from punishment (*You can't go through a stop sign in this town with impunity*) or, in a weaker sense, exemption from unpleasant consequences of some action (*Growing boys seem able to eat almost anything in any quantity with impunity*).

impassive; impassible; impassable. The difference in meaning between *impassive* and *impassible* is slight but important. The difference between these two words and *impassable* is great.

Impassable describes something that cannot be passed over, through, or along (*What roads there were were impassable in winter because of the snow and in spring because of the mud; so the peasants were isolated half of every year*).

Impassive means without emotion, unmoved, calm, and refers primarily to an observed state or condition (*His success as a poker player was assisted by his impassive face*). *Impassible* means noticeably incapable of suffering pain or harm or of experiencing emotion. With *impassible* the emphasis is on insusceptibility, on the cause of the behavior. With *impassive* it is on the behavior itself (*The Pope has been called upon by various newspapers to say whether he would remain impassible to various demands for intervention for the Rosenbergs—Chicago Sun-Times, Feb. 14, 1953*).

impecunious. See **poor**.

impediment. See **obstacle**.

impel; induce; incite; prompt; instigate. To *impel* is to drive or to urge forward. It suggests a good deal of force or urgency and passion (*He was impelled by demonic impulses that swept his reasonings aside*). To *induce* is to lead forward. It is a gentler word than *impel*. It is to lead or move by persuasion or influence (*Such arguments gradually induced him to change his point of view*). To *incite* is to urge on, stimulate, move to action. It is used when non-physical motives are the actuating power and it is usually an urging or stimulating towards something which the one urged himself strongly desires. A man may be impelled by force. He can be incited only by hope or aspiration or desire. *Prompt* is a milder and more general word than *incite* (*I do not know what prompted him to open the letter at that exact moment*). It has the suggestion often of the final nudge towards an action to which the subject was already strongly inclined, a nudge more of circumstances than of any human moving (*He was prompted to the murder by reading in the paper of a man who in similar circumstances had been liberated by his wife's sudden death*). To *instigate* is to goad on, to spur to action, and almost always to bad action (*These suggestions instigated him to commit the horrid crime with which his name is now indissolubly connected*). It also implies that the urging was sly and underhanded. See also **compel**.

imperative; imperious; imperial. These words, though related in meaning, are not interchangeable. *Imperative* means not to be avoided, obligatory (*It is imperative that the pilot remain at the assigned altitude until the control tower gives him permission to descend*). *Imperious* once meant belonging to or befitting an emperor or supreme ruler (*Imperious Caesar, dead and turned to clay,/ Might stop a hole to keep the wind away*), but now it means domineering, dictatorial, overbearing (*Beneath his imperious exterior was a genuine heart of flint*). *Imperial* means of or pertaining to an empire (*The British imperial capital is London*) or of or pertaining to an emperor or empress (*The imperial retinue had sadly dwindled since Henry* *had crossed the Alps with such pomp the year before*).

imperative mode. The imperative is the form of the verb used in commands, requests, and advice. It is not necessarily dictatorial. The difference between an order and a suggestion is shown by the tone of voice or by some other words in the sentence, such as *if you please*. In English, the imperative is the simple form of the verb and ordinarily appears without a subject, as in *go and catch a falling star*. A negative imperative is formed by prefixing *do not* (or *don't*), as in *do not go*.

In contemporary English the imperative is considered a second person form. That is, the subject is said to be an unexpressed *you*. Formerly, if the subject was expressed it followed immediately after the verb, as in *comfort ye my people*. This construction may still be heard, as in *hark you, mind you,* but it now sounds archaic or old-fashioned. Today, if we want to stress the subject of an imperative, we place the pronoun immediately before the verb, as in *you go first*. Some grammarians claim that in sentences such as *somebody lend me a hand,* the imperative is a third person form with the subject *somebody*. Others hold that there is still an unexpressed *you* here, that *somebody* here means *you*. This is a purely theoretical question and makes no difference in practice.

At one time the imperative could be used as a first person plural form. In this case, the word *we* followed the verb, as in *praise we the Virgin all divine* and *don we now our gay apparel*. In modern English we use *let us* or *let's* to indicate this type of imperative, and say *let's put on our best clothes. Let's* may be followed by *you and me,* as in *let's you and me dress up,* but the use of *I* or *us,* as in *let's you and I dress up* and *let's us dress up,* is condemned by some grammarians. See **let.**

An imperative is always the principal verb in a sentence. When a statement such as *leave at once* is repeated in indirect speech, that is, not as a direct quotation, the form of the verb must be changed. After verbs that take an indirect object, such as *command, order, tell,* the imperative may be replaced by an infinitive, as in *he told me to leave at once*. After *say,* which does not take an indirect object, an imperative is traditionally replaced by a subjunctive clause such as *he said I should leave at once* or *he said I was to leave at once*. But in current English *say* is often treated like *tell* and followed by an infinitive, as in *he said to leave at once. For* is sometimes used to indicate the person addressed, as in *he said for me to leave at once*. Thirty years ago these constructions were generally condemned. But they are used today by many well educated people and are probably acceptable English in most parts of the United States. See also **future tense.**

impertinent (pert); impudent; insolent; saucy (sassy); cheeky. The original meaning of *impertinent* was not pertinent to the matter in hand, hence irrelevant. This meaning is still retained in law but is otherwise obsolete. A deliberately introduced irrelevance would be silly and would indicate a lack of proper respect for those whose business was so interrupted. And that—an unseemly intrusion into what does not concern one, or a presumptuous rudeness towards one entitled to deference or respect— is the word's primary meaning today (*He was inclined to regard the expression of any difference of opinion as a piece of impertinence, to be repressed with contempt*). Annoying as impertinence often is, however, there are times when it is amusing and attractive and the diminutive *pert,* especially in colloquial usage, usually expresses an amused admiration (*That was a pert little hat she had on*).

Impudent suggests a shameless impertinence, unblushing effrontery (*The impudence of that young whelp, telling me that when he wanted my advice he'd ask for it!*). *Insolent* means the highest degree of rude presumption, insulting and arrogantly contemptuous behavior (*The recruit was so openly insolent to his superior officers that it was apparent that for some reason he wanted to be court-martialed*). Impertinence is sometimes accidental, the result of folly or ignorance, but the affronts of insolence are deliberate and intended. There is a phrase *studied insolence* which implies that insolence is the product of careful planning and forethought.

Saucy and its American dialect form *sassy* mean salty, full of bite. They are colloquialisms which can mean anything from impertinent to insolent (*The child got sassy and she slapped him*). Like *pert, saucy* can mean piquant and is often used favorably.

Cheeky is also a colloquialism, chiefly British, which means either impudent or insolent. It is a slightly stronger term of opprobrium than *saucy* (*That cheeky remark may cost him his job*).

implement. The primary use of *implement,* as a transitive verb, is to provide with implements (*Whether armed for war or implemented for industry*), though it is not often used in this sense of actual, tangible implements but of the more abstract kind (*The resolution was noble but until it is implemented by specific legislation the voters will probably remain skeptical*). In the sense of filling out or supplementing, it has been severely condemned as either pedantry or barbarous jargon, but usage has made it standard and the worst that can be said for it now is that it is ostentatious and overworked and should be replaced occasionally by the more homely *fulfill* or *carry out*.

implicate. See **involve.**

implicit. See **constructive** and **explicit.**

implore. This word may be followed by an infinitive, as in *I implore you to tell me*. It may also be followed by a clause with the clause verb a subjunctive or subjunctive equivalent, as in *I implored that he tell me,* but the infinitive construction is generally preferred.

imply; infer. The primary meaning of *imply* is to involve as a necessary circumstance. A deed implies a doer. The fact that a man is living implies that he was born. From this it is a natural development for it to mean to indicate or suggest something which is to be inferred without being expressly stated (*It is not directly asserted, but it seems to be implied*). To *infer* is to derive by reasoning from premises, to judge from evidence, or, colloquially, to surmise or guess (*From your silence I infer that you do not approve*). The speaker implies, the hearer infers. Sir Alan Herbert makes the matter clear when he says that inferring is a sort of thinking and implying a sort of saying. He illustrates by saying that *If you see a man staggering along the road you may infer that he is drunk, without saying a word; but if you say "Had one too many?" you do not infer but imply that he is drunk* (*What a Word!* New York, 1936).

None the less *infer* has been used for *imply* for several centuries and by writers of considerable authority (Milton and James Mill among them) and is in such widespread common use that many of the best authorities now bow to usage and accept it as standard. The careful writer, however, will probably want to preserve the distinction, which is a useful one, and will be inclined to regard the common usage here as an accepted laxity rather than an example to be followed.

imply; insinuate. To *imply* is to indicate as something to be inferred (*He did not say in so many words that he was displeased, but he certainly implied it in the tone of his voice*). To *insinuate* is to wind into a meaning like a serpent, to hint, suggest, subtly develop a meaning in the other person's mind, or to establish oneself in his good graces. It is a word of sly and evil connotations; whereas *imply* is an open word. A meaning may be implied rather than spoken directly for bad reasons, but it also may be implied rather than spoken because of diffidence or delicacy or kindness. See also **indicate.**

impolitic; impolitical. That is *impolitic* which is inexpedient, injudicious, unsuitable to the desired end (*It is certainly impolitic to bring up these charges against the man at the very time you need his support*). *Impolitical* is simply an older form of *impolitic,* rendered obsolete by the facts that the newer word is shorter and *political* has come to have a specialized meaning.

important means of much significance, of more than ordinary title to consideration or notice. It is sometimes used as if it meant principal, as in *The important difference between them is that one dress has white buttons and the other gray buttons.* Unless *important* is used here ironically, it is misused.

impossible is enjoying a vogue, not in its primary meaning of unable to be, exist, or happen, but in such senses as unendurable (*He's utterly impossible; I don't see how you manage to stay on speaking terms with him*), incredible (*It's an impossible story*), impracticable (*These impossible suggestions just annoy me; he knows we haven't the necessary money*). These are not corruptions but ellipses, condensations by omission. An impossible person is one with whom it is impossible to get along. An impossible story is one that it is impossible to believe. And so on. Yet the word is being overworked in this manner and it would be better most of the time to use the full phrase.

impostor; imposture. An *impostor* is a person. An *imposture* is an act. An *impostor* is one who imposes fraudulently on others, who practices deception under an assumed character or name (*The military hero turned out to be an impostor who had sat out the war in Mexico*). An *imposture* is the action or practice of imposing fraudulently on others (*His passing himself off as a Russian archduke was one of the more successful impostures of the social season*).

impoverished. See **poor.**

impracticable; impractical; unpractical. The British clearly distinguish between these adjectives by using *impracticable* of things and actions which are not practicable, which are not capable, that is, of being put into practice, or effected, especially with the available means or with reason or prudence (*It was a thoroughly impracticable plan*) and by using *unpractical* of persons who are not practical, who lack, that is, practical usefulness or wisdom (*Because of his unpractical nature, he did not foresee the real difficulties of the situation*). In America *impractical* serves indifferently to mean either *impracticable* or *unpractical,* depending on the context, though *impracticable* is also used as the British use it. Actually, British usage here is a good deal less confusing and therefore is deserving of adoption.

impression. See **edition.**

impromptu; extemporaneous; extempory; extempore. Generally used as an adjective, *impromptu* means offhand, made or done without previous preparation (*At the surprise party in his honor he made a witty impromptu speech*). It is also used as an adverb (*verses written impromptu*) and as a noun (*You won't often hear that clever an impromptu*).

Extemporaneous, as well as its less-used synonyms *extempory* and *extempore,* can mean about the same as *impromptu*—that is, unpremeditated, without preparation or with only partial preparation—but it is applied especially to an unmemorized speech given from an outline or notes (*His vast experience of mountain climbing enabled him to deliver extemporaneous speeches on the subject*). *Extemporaneous* and *extempory* can be used as adjectives only. *Extempore* may be used as an adjective, though it seldom is. It is the only one of the three that can be used as an adverb (*He spoke extempore*—that is, without preparation or notes).

impudent. See **impertinent.**

impunity. See **immunity.**

in. This word may be used with an object as a preposition, or it may be used alone as an adverb or as an adjective.

In is primarily a preposition. It expresses the relation of "contained" or "surrounded by," and implies limitations of space, time, conditions, circumstances. We may say *in the fog, in the evening, in breadth, in my opinion.* The idea of condition or circumstance may be extended to include cause, as in *he acted in anger,* or influence, as in *when in doubt,* or manner, as in *the yellow gods shut up their eyes in scorn.* It may mean merely as regards or in respect to, as in *he was unfortunate in his friends.* It may also indicate the source of pleasant emotions, as in *rejoicing in the truth,* but not of unpleasant ones. We cannot say *suffering in injustice.*

In is closely related to several other prepositions. It may have the sense of *into* when it is used with a verb that carries the idea of motion, as in *come in.* When *in* and *of* compete, *of* has the broad meaning of "pertaining to" and does not show as close, or as internal, a relation as *in. In* differs from *at* in that *at* refers to a particular place without regard to its surroundings. Often it makes no difference which of these words is used. As a rule, we speak of being *in* a city, but we may say *I met her at the station* or *I met her in the station. On* and *in* are not interchangeable. *On* implies the outside and is in contrast to *in.* When streets were narrow lanes filled with overhanging balconies, it was natural to speak of being *in* the street. But in the United States today *on* is the more natural word. We might speak of *fighting in the streets,* where the action seems to be enclosed, but we would always say *I met her on Fifth Avenue* and *we lived on Fifteenth Street. In* can only be used with nouns that are thought of as singular, as in *in the army, in a crowd.* When a group name is thought of as plural, *among* is required, as in *among the people.* (For the use of *the* after *in,* as in *in bed* and *in the bed,* see *the.*)

In is not a conjunction, but it may have as object the word *that,* which in turn may introduce a clause, as in *men differ from brutes in that they can think and speak.* Here *in that* has somewhat the same function as *because.*

The preposition *in* is freely used with verbs of participation, such as *share, join, meddle.* It is also used with certain verbs to show an indirect object, as *trust in.* It may be used adverbially without an object, as in *break in, fence in, fall in with.* It may be used in this way with verbs of motion and with the verb *to be,* as in *when will he be in?.* Sometimes this *in* can be interpreted as a preposition with the object unexpressed. But this is not always true. In the United States, *in* may be attached to a verb that names the beginning of an action in order to show that the action which is beginning is going to go on for a long time, as in *he started in to talk, it set in to rain.* Here *in* is in contrast to *out,* which can be used with the same verbs to show that the action had barely begun, as in *he started out, we set out.*

The simple form *in* is occasionally used as an adjective, as in *the in party said that such a law was unnecessary.* But this is rare in present day English. However, the comparative form *inner* and the superlative forms *innermost* and *inmost*

are in common use. The two superlative forms are equally acceptable. The comparative *inner* is now felt as a simple adjective and is not used in comparisons with *than.*

in apple-pie order. Why the order of an apple pie should be more orderly than that of any other kind of pie is uncertain. As a metaphor for everything being as it should be, *in apple-pie order* is now a cliché. It has the additional disadvantage of being one of those artificially homey phrases that give so much talk a tinny ring of false sincerity.

in back of. See **back of.**

in black and white. As a term for reducing something to writing, especially the terms of an agreement, so that it will be incontrovertibly clear, *to set it down in black and white* is overworked and should be used sparingly.

in spite of the fact that is usually no more than a wordy way of saying *although.*

in the last analysis is a cliché. It sometimes means no more than "finally" and sometimes is no more than a sort of pompous clearing of the throat before the speaker introduces his opinion.

in the last resort. As a term for a final expedient or for the last desperate course of action, *in the last resort* is a cliché. It was originally a translation of a French law term.

in the same boat. As a term for sharing a common predicament and, particularly, for being liable to the same punishment, *in the same boat* is a cliché.

in the street; on the street. The American idiom says that so-and-so lives or does business *on* such-and-such a street. The English idiom says that he lives or does business *in* such-and-such a street. See **in.**

inability; disability. Both of these words suggest a lack of power, capacity, or ability. *Inability* is a want of ability, usually because of an inherent lack of talent or power (*He had a strange inability to make up his mind*). A *disability* is some disqualifying deprivation or loss of power, physical, legal, or otherwise (*His service-connected physical disability entitled him to a full military pension*).

inasmuch as. See **because.**

inapt; unapt; inept. *Inapt* is the common term to mean something which is not apt, fitted or appropriate (*His quotation about the sanctity of marriage was a little inapt when one remembers that this was the bride's third venture into matrimony*). *Unapt* can mean unfitted or unsuited, but it is becoming more fixed in the meanings of unlikely or not disposed (*We are unapt to find the way in the dark. He is unapt to agree with anyone who annoys him*) or not quick to learn (*He was an unapt pupil*). *Inapt* has a secondary meaning of without aptitude or capacity, but the better word for this is *inept* (*It would have been hard to find a more inept swordsman*).

Though these words overlap in some of their meanings, usage seems to be restricting them more and more to their special meanings. Thus the quotation about the sanctity of marriage alluded to in the illustration above was inapt

in so far as it was inapplicable to a third marriage and inept in so far as it was an awkward
thing to have brought up under the circumstances. Only an inept person would have
brought it up. A delicate and perceptive person
would have been unapt to do so.

inaugurate. To *inaugurate* is to install in office
with full inaugural ceremonies. It is a word of
almost ponderous gravity and like all words of
high solemnity may easily become ludicrous if
applied to trivial occasions. The safe rule is to
be sure you want *inaugurate* and not *start* or
begin or *commence*. If you are sure you do, use
it; otherwise stick to the commoner word. See
also **begin.**

incapable; unable. *Incapable* means a settled, inherent lack of ability or power (*He was quite
incapable of commanding troops in combat*).
Unable usually refers to a temporary lack of
ability to do a specific thing (*Because of heavy
snows, he was often unable to drive to work
that winter*).

incensed. See **enraged.**

incentive. See **motive.**

incessant. See **eternal.**

incessantly. See **constantly.**

incident. See **happening** and **event.**

incident; incidental. As an adjective *incident*
means likely or apt to happen (*The confusion
incident to breaking up camp afforded the lurk-
ing Indians an excellent opportunity for a surprise attack*). It also means that which naturally appertains (*The obscurity incident to the
life of a scholar has its compensations*) or that
which is conjoined or attached, especially as
subordinate to a principal thing.

Incidental also means that which is likely to
happen, but it conveys a stronger feeling of the
happening's being fortuitous or in subordinate
conjunction with something else of which it
forms no real part (*Yes, there was some incidental notoriety, but it is unfair to say that his
purpose was to attract attention*); hence purely
casual (*incidental expenses, incidental discomforts*). When *incidental* conveys the idea of
liability, it is followed by *to;* when it conveys
the idea of an incident that merely ensues, it
is followed by *upon.*

Incidentally is used with increasing frequency
by writers and speakers to warn that what is to
follow is an irrelevance or an aside. It can be
ambiguous, since it is not always made clear
whether the stated fact is incidental to some
action alluded to in the sentence or to the sentence as a whole. In the latter sense it can often
be replaced, to the advantage of clarity, by *I
may add* or *I forgot to say that* or some such
phrase. Many times it can be omitted altogether, having no real meaning.

In conformity to its common slurred pronunciation, *incidentally* is often written *incidently.*
This is simply an error. There is no such word
today as *incidently,* although there once was.

incite. This verb may be followed by an infinitive,
as in *incite to riot.* It is sometimes heard with
the *-ing* form of a verb, as in *incite to rioting,*
but this is not standard English. See **impel.**

incline. When used as a verb, this word may be
followed by an infinitive, as in *this inclined her
to leave* and *she was inclined to eat.* It may also
be followed by the *-ing* form of a verb with the
preposition *to,* as in *she was more inclined to
sleeping than to eating.* The noun *inclination*
may be followed by an infinitive, as in *an inclination to eat,* or by the *-ing* form of a verb
with the preposition *for,* as in *an inclination for
eating.*

Inclined in the metaphorical sense of being
favorably disposed to do something must be
confined to people since they alone can have
this sort of inclination. Rather than say of certain trees, for example, that they are *inclined to*
retain their dead leaves well into the spring, it
would be better to say that they *have a tendency to retain* their foliage or simply that they
retain it.

To say of someone accused of some fault
that one is *inclined to give him the benefit of
doubt* is to say that one's opinion is not yet
absolutely settled in condemnation, that one is
disposed, until unquestionable evidence of guilt
has been adduced, towards as favorable an interpretation of the facts as possible. But to say
that one is *inclined to think,* unless one definitely means that one's emotions, attitudes,
knowledge, and so on, are too confused or
uncertain to permit them to be regarded as
thought, is to indulge in unnecessary circumlocution. When Watson once said that he was
"inclined to think" something or other, Holmes
drily urged him to do so. More often than not
the phrase serves as a timid, protective preface
and actually means "I think, but I am prepared
to suppress or amend my opinion should it disagree with yours."

include. See **comprise; contain.**

incognito. There is very little occasion to use the
personal noun, but should it arise, a man is an
incognito and a woman an *incognita* (*The fair
incognita graciously inclined her head*). The
abstract noun is *incognito* only (*She preserved
her incognito*). The original plural of the personal noun was *incogniti,* but its use would seem
an affectation. *Incognitos* is now the accepted
plural of both the personal and the abstract
forms. The adjective and adverb are both *incognito,* no distinction of gender being recognized.

incomparable. See **uncomparable.**

inconceivable. See **unthinkable.**

inconsequent; inconsequential; unimportant. The
primary sense of *inconsequent* is lacking sequence in thought, speech, or action. W. H.
Hudson speaks of the *profound inconsequent
gravity of monkeys and their insane delight in
their own unreasonableness.* That is inconsequent which does not follow from the premises,
as *an inconsequent conclusion.*

Inconsequential once also meant irrelevant
and illogical (*The fiction is unnatural and the
moral inconsequential*), and this meaning is
still recognized as a secondary meaning, but the
word's usual meaning now is "trivial" (*An inconsequential paragraph in his article was seized*

upon as conveying his central doctrine). There is about the word, however, even in this meaning, a suggestion that the triviality is based upon the absurdity or illogicality of the utterance. When the matter is simply of no importance, it is better to use the commoner, unequivocal *unimportant*.

incontinently. The adverb *incontinently* has two different meanings. In one sense it means lacking in restraint, especially sexual restraint (*Queen Isabel . . . living incontinently with Mortimer*). In a second sense, now archaic, it means immediately, at once, straightway (*I will incontinently drown myself*). In neither sense is the word particularly usable. For the first sense some such word as *unrestrainedly* or *unchastely* is to be preferred. For the second, *immediately* or *at once*.

incontrollable; uncontrollable. Though *incontrollable* is still acceptable, its use is increasingly rare. In the United States, as in England, it is being superseded by *uncontrollable*.

incorrect; uncorrected. Though *incorrect* and *incorrectly* are in daily use, *incorrected* is now obsolete. It has been superseded by *uncorrected*.

increase. See **step up.**

incredible; unbelievable. Although *incredible* and *unbelievable* are synonymous in meaning not credible, impossible to believe, *incredible* has been used so much in the weakened sense of something that is difficult to believe, or something which one would never, reasoning from common observation, have thought possible, that this is now its common meaning. Thus when we say of someone that he ran through his inheritance with incredible folly, we do not expect the alleged folly to be rejected as unbelievable. We mean that although such folly would seem impossible, yet it actually happened. *Unbelievable* is sometimes used in this sense, but more often it is qualified with *almost*, showing that the word itself retains its absolute meaning.

incredible; incredulous. That is *incredible* which cannot be believed or seems too extraordinary to be possible. Properly only narratives can be incredible since things, to be things, must exist and hence, if produced or authenticated, must be believed in. However, *incredible* in its weakened sense of so extraordinary as to be almost unbelievable is often applied to things (*He caught the most incredible fish you ever saw. There was an incredible house, built on stilts and painted blue and green*). And since people are among the most extraordinary things on the face of the earth it is often applied, hyperbolically, to people (*He was an incredible man. The whole community was proud of having such a freak in its midst*), sometimes in such paradoxical phrases as *an incredible liar* where it is used to mean not that he was a liar who would not be believed in but so successful a liar that it was hard to believe the degree to which he compelled credulity. Much of the meaning depends on the intonation. To say quietly that someone was *an incredible witness* would probably mean that his testimony failed to carry any conviction, but to stress *incredible* with excited emphasis might mean that the extent to which his testimony compelled conviction was almost unbelievable.

In such a situation there is, of course, infinite possibility for misunderstanding, so that the writer or speaker who wishes to have his meaning clearly understood will avoid the ambiguities which the weakened and hyperbolical uses create by avoiding these uses.

Incredible means unbelievable. *Incredulous* means unbelieving. And since believing or not believing is, so far as we know, solely restricted to human beings, the word must also be so restricted. It is confined to people and to the expressions or gestures by which they indicate their unbelief (*When he told me the same old incredible story, I merely smiled an incredulous smile*).

incubus; succubus. The plurals are *incubuses* or *incubi, succubuses* or *succubi*. In modern usage an *incubus* is an imaginary demon or evil spirit that is supposed to descend upon sleeping persons or, by extension, something that weighs upon or oppresses one like a nightmare. Sometimes a nightmare itself is called an incubus. A *succubus* is, in modern usage, any demon or evil spirit.

In former times, when demonology was a more exact science, an *incubus* was a male demon which haunted the sleep of women and was responsible for their bearing witches, demons, and deformed children. The innocent maiden, however, plagued by his advances, could protect herself with St. Johnswort and vervain and dill. The *succubus* was the female counterpart. The offspring of the union of a man and a succubus was demonic, but the proper prayers, spells, or charms recited by the man upon awakening would prevent its conception. These distinctions no longer hold in standard, common usage, but the learned preserve them and delight in them.

inculcate. To *inculcate* is to impress by repeated statement, to teach persistently and earnestly. It is a transitive verb whose Latin elements mean, literally, to stamp in with the heel. Therefore that which is inculcated must be inculcated *in* or *upon* the subject (*As a teacher he inculcated in his students a love of questioning and a distrust of facile solutions*); the subject is not inculcated *with* that which is inculcated. It is incorrect, for example, to say *His parents inculcated him with frugal habits.* They inculcated frugal habits *in* him.

But even when used correctly *inculcate* is a little pretentious. It is probably better to say *repeatedly impressed on*.

incumbent. See **recumbent.**

indecency. See **blasphemy.**

indefinite article. See **a, an.**

indefinite pronouns and adjectives. Pronouns which refer to certain individuals without specifying which ones, such as *anyone, someone, everybody, each, either, neither, none*, are called indefinite pronouns. When a word of this kind is used to qualify a noun it is called an indefinite adjective.

These words are said to be singular. However, some of them, such as *neither* and *none*, usually take a plural verb, as in *a maid whom there were none to praise*. Others, such as *anyone, everyone, each*, usually take a singular verb, as in *has anyone called?*. But these, too, may be followed by a plural verb, especially when an *of*-phrase stands between the indefinite pronoun and the verb, as in *each of the men were willing to contribute*, although some grammarians insist on a singular verb here too.

After a plural verb has been used, the indefinite word (pronoun or adjective-noun compound) is treated as plural rather than singular. That is, it is referred to by *they, them, their*, rather than by *he, him, his*. But it may also be referred to as *they* even when a singular verb has been used, as in *everyone was here but they have left, every boy and girl invites their own parents, if anyone calls tell them I have gone*. A masculine singular pronoun (*he, him, his*) is impossible after *but*, as in the first illustration; and pedantic, or ridiculous, after *boy and girl*, as in the second. And it is always unidiomatic English in a statement that is actually about an indefinite number of individuals some of whom may be male and some female, although some textbooks require *if anyone calls tell him I have gone*. This use of *they, them, their* in such constructions has been standard English for centuries. The best modern writers, like the great writers of the past, sometimes use the singular *he* and sometimes the plural *they*, depending upon the circumstances rather than on any rule of thumb about the "number" of an indefinite pronoun.

Some grammarians include among the indefinites any word which does not have a specific reference, such as *many, few, all, both, much, other, such*. In this book some of these are treated as number terms and some as individual words with peculiar uses. See **number terms** and the individual words.)

index. The plural is *indexes* or *indices*.

indicate; imply. The transitive verbs *indicate* and *imply* can be interchanged if the user clearly understands the sense he intends. The central meaning of *indicate* is to be a sign of, to betoken, to imply (*Booing indicates disapproval of an umpire's decisions*). But whereas *imply* is one of the central definitions of *indicate*, *indicate* is not the central definition of *imply*. Primarily, *imply* means to involve as a necessary circumstance (*Violence implies danger*); secondarily, with reference to words, it means to signify or to mean (*The word "rush" implies speed*); and only in its third sense, does it mean indicate.

A special medical meaning of *indicate*, to point out a particular remedy or course of treatment as necessary (*Absolute rest was indicated*), has been taken up into general use and is at present something of a vogue word (*Increased taxation was indicated*). See also **imply; infer.**

indicative mode. The ordinary verb forms used in statements or questions about matters of fact are called indicative forms. See **mode.**

indices. See **index.**

indict; indite. These transitive verbs sound alike but have different meanings. *Indict* is a legal term which means to charge with an offense or crime (*What will you do if the grand jury indicts you for perjury? Let anyone who will indict him on the charge of frivolity*). *Indict* is a thoroughly serviceable word with no acceptable substitute. But *indite* is a fancy literary term, meaning to compose or to write or to dictate what someone else is to write down, and almost any substitute for it is preferable. When a modern writer says *indite*, he should smile. The last serious inditing went on in the seventeenth century.

indigent. See **poor.**

indirect discourse. See **tense shift.**

indirect object. The direct object of a verb is a noun or noun equivalent that is essential to the meaning of the verb, as *lie* in *he told a lie*. Without an object of some kind *he told* is a meaningless statement. An indirect object is not essential to the meaning of the verb but shows the person or thing affected by the total action. As a rule an indirect object represents a person, as *me* in *he told me a lie*, but it may also represent a thing, as *it* in *give it some thought*. In Latin this function is shown by a dative case ending, which has the meaning of to or toward. In English the indirect object is sometimes called "the dative of interest or reference," but the function is shown by the position of the word in the sentence.

In a normal English sentence the indirect object stands between the verb and the direct object, as in *give her a book*. If the direct object is moved forward the indirect object remains attached to the verb, as in *what did you give her?*. In a compound verb, it stands between the verb and the adverb, as *them* in *fix them up a box lunch*. See **adverbs.**

The meaning of the indirect object can also be expressed by a prepositional phrase using *to* or *for* (or occasionally *on, in*, or *from*). Some verbs, such as *speak, explain, attribute*, cannot be followed by an indirect object and so require a prepositional phrase to express this relation. A prepositional phrase must also be used with a relative or interrogative pronoun, as in *who did you give the book to?*, since these words always precede the verb and so cannot stand in the indirect object position.

Whether a word is a direct or an indirect object sometimes makes a difference in the meaning of a sentence. When a verb is followed by two noun equivalents, the first may be an indirect object and the second a direct object, or the first may be a direct object and the second an objective complement. (See **object of a verb.**) Both of these constructions are seen in the witticism: *the woman who makes a man a good wife also makes him a good husband*. Here *man* is an indirect object and could be replaced by the phrase *to a man* or *for a man;*

him however is a direct object and could not be rephrased in this way. On the other hand, in *can you spare me a minute?* we may have an indirect object and a direct object, or we may have a direct object followed by an adverb of time. (See **nouns as adverbs**.) This difference is shown in speech by pitch or stress, but in written English there is no way to decide which construction was intended.

In the United States there is no exception to the rule that an indirect object must stand immediately after the verb or be replaced by a prepositional phrase. When a verb is followed by two personal pronouns either form can be used, as in *he gave me it* and *he gave it to me*. In this case, the prepositional phrase is preferred. In Great Britain neither of these constructions is used. The rule there is: when both are personal pronouns, the direct object precedes the indirect, as in *he gave it me*. This construction is impossible to American ears. But it has been standard in England for centuries and is used in the King James Bible (for example, Exodus 23:30). To English ears the American *to*, as in *he gave it to me*, sounds like an affectation, a would-be elegance, to be classed with *it is I*.

Occasionally the only object of a verb is logically an indirect and not a direct object, as in *he told his sister*. In Latin this distinction must be recognized and verbs such as *help, trust, believe, obey, envy, pardon*, require an object with a dative case ending. In English there is no practical difference between the two forms. All that remains of case here is the rule that a subjective pronoun cannot be used immediately after a transitive verb. This is true whether the word represents the indirect or the direct object. We cannot say *I helped they* any more than we can say *I made they*. It is customary in English to call a word of this kind simply *the object* and to distinguish the indirect from the direct only when both are present.

An indirect object may be made the subject of a passive verb. In *they gave him a reward* the direct object of *gave* is *reward* and the normal passive construction would be *a reward was given him*. But in English we may also say *he was given a reward*. This is a very curious construction that is not found in any of the other Indo-European languages.

At one time an indirect object could be placed before the verb, as in *him was given a reward*. An important characteristic of modern English has made this construction impossible today. In present-day English a subjective pronoun is not a form used when the word is the subject of a verb; it is rather a form used when the word stands immediately before a verb. This is why, in spite of the grammarians' protests, we prefer *he is taller than me* or *he is taller than I am* to *he is taller than I*. This feeling for the pronoun made *he was given* a more comfortable phrase than *him was given*, even when the word was an indirect object. This, in turn, led to our modern passive form in which an original indirect object is treated and felt as

the subject of the verb. As late as 1855 the construction was considered ungrammatical but it is now preferred to the older form whenever both forms are possible. That is, most people today if asked to put the sentence *he taught the child music* into a passive form would say *the child was taught music* rather than *music was taught (to) the child*.

indiscreet; indiscrete. These adjectives are pronounced alike but must be distinguished. *Indiscreet* means not discreet, lacking in prudence or sound judgment (*Swift's parents made an indiscreet marriage; he used to say that he felt the effects of it all his life*). *Indiscrete* means not distinctly separate or distinguishable, undifferentiated or homogeneous (*Creation of the world is said to have begun with indiscrete chaos. If he had virtues they were certainly indiscrete from his vices*). *Indiscreet* is a useful word but *indiscrete*, which is easily confused with it and seldom understood in its proper sense, should be avoided.

indispensable. See **necessary**.

indisposition. See **sickness**.

individual; person. *Individual* was originally an adjective, denoting the particular as opposed to the general (*All effective advancement must be by individual, not public, effort*). The individual was the single person in his capacity of one of many. In the nineteenth century, under the influence of that polysyllabic humor which attained its most popular success in the works of Dickens and which loved to make fun of people by exaggerating their dignity, *individual* came to be used a great deal as a noun in place of *person* (*The recalcitrant individual with the glowing proboscis*), and this use, its humor having faded long ago, has become established especially among those addicted to unnecessary syllables. Many speakers and writers use it today with no facetious intent whatever (*an individual of whom this, or any other community, might be justly proud. Who was that individual I saw you with last night?*).

But in the best usage the general word for a single human being is still *person* (*What is a person to do on a desert island?*). If *individual* is to be used as a noun, it should be in order to emphasize the singleness of the person, usually in contrast with some such body as the family, the state, or society in general (*The Club ought not to take a stand on political matters, though the members are free to express themselves, as individuals, in any way they see fit. Even in the best of democracies the rights of the individual are in constant danger of being sacrificed to the will of the society as a whole*). Since it is easier to misuse *individual* than to use it in its proper sense as a noun, it is probably best to think of it in its commoner function as an adjective, where it means single, particular, separate (*Each individual leaf differs in some particular from all the others*).

indolent. See **lazy**.

indoor; indoors. *Indoor* is the preferred form when the word is used to qualify a following noun, as in *an indoor playground. Indoors* is the preferred form when the word is used to qualify anything except a noun, as in *he stayed indoors.* But this distinction is not strictly observed.

indorse. See **endorse.**

indubitably. See **undoubtedly.**

induce. This word may be followed by an infinitive, as in *we induced them to go,* but not by the *-ing* form of a verb or by a clause. See also **impel.**

inducement. See **motive.**

induction; deduction. When these two nouns are used to describe reasoning processes they are often confused. Actually, the processes they describe are of opposite kinds. *Deduction* means applying a general statement or assumption, whether true or false, to a particular case (*My deduction is that since all men die and I am a man I will die*). *Induction* means arriving at a general principle on the basis of probabilities suggested by experiment with and observation of a number of individual cases (*The essence of induction is inferring the general from the particular, the unknown from the known*).

indulge in; engage in. To *indulge in* something suggests an undisciplined satisfaction of improper or harmful desires (*As a sailor he had indulged in all the excesses available to men of that calling*). *Engage* has no such overtone of disapproval. It simply means to occupy oneself, to become involved (*He engaged in business as soon as he had finished college*). One engages in speech but indulges in rhetoric, engages in discussion but indulges in gossip, and so on. The attitude of the speaker towards the activity alluded to is often indicated by the word chosen to describe it and sometimes, for humorous effect, the words may be switched around (*He was for many years engaged in petty larceny. He indulged himself in all manner of charitable activities, especially those concerned with the rehabilitation of fallen women*), but the shock upon which such humorous inversion depends is based on the proper meaning of the word being clear in the reader's mind.

industrial; industrious. *Industrial* means of or pertaining to, or of the nature of, or resulting from, industry or the productive arts (*His father thought that a course in industrial engineering would be a good preparation for him. The industrial world is little concerned with theories that have no immediate application*). *Industrious* means hard-working, diligent (*If you are industrious you can finish the job before dark*).

inebriated. See **drunk.**

ineffable. See **unspeakable.**

ineffective; ineffectual. When applied to persons, usage has established a difference between *ineffective* and *ineffectual.* An ineffective person is an inefficient person, but he may be inefficient in the one situation alone. An ineffectual person is a futile person, powerless, impotent, and inefficient in all situations.

inelastic; unelastic. In England either of these words may be used to signify not elastic, lacking elasticity, unyielding, though *inelastic* is preferred, especially in figurative uses (*He had a maddeningly inelastic mind*). In the United States *inelastic* only is used, in all senses.

inept. See **inapt.**

inexecrable. See **execrable.**

inexpensive. See **cheap.**

inexperienced. See **unsophisticated.**

inexplicable; inexplainable; unexplainable. All three of these adjectives mean not explainable, incapable of being explained or interpreted. *Inexplicable* is the most learned term (*The nature of reality remains an inexplicable mystery*). *Inexplainable* and *unexplainable* have little to choose between them. American usage tends to favor *unexplainable,* but all three words are a little cumbrous and most people wisely avoid them and express the thought in some such phrase as *something I can't understand* or *I can't explain it* or *nobody can explain it.*

infant; child; baby. An *infant,* in the general usage of the word, is a *child* during the earliest period of its life when it is still being carried about, "a babe in arms." *Infant* and *baby* in current American usage are synonymous, though *baby* is the everyday word and *infant* would seem formal or a little archaic. A *child* is a baby or an infant but in general use it applies to persons below the age of puberty and since *baby* is generally used of the very young, a *child* commonly designates someone anywhere between weaning and puberty. In law an *infant* is a minor, a person under twenty-one, and a *child* is any descendant, regardless of age. *Baby* is not recognized in the law as designating a category.

infantile; childish; childlike; puerile; boyish; girlish. All of these words mean characteristic of or befitting the young. But some things that are characteristic of the young are admirable and charming and some are annoying. And what is befitting a child may be contemptible in an adult. Each of the words has acquired a set of connotations that makes it not quite synonymous with any of the others.

Though *infantile* still means that which pertains to an infant (*infantile diseases, the helplessness of the infantile state*), it is most generally used in contempt of adult expressions or actions which are, in the opinion of the speaker or writer, more suitable to a small child than to an adult (*Such endless talk of what he is going to do is infantile and infuriating. Guests are embarrassed to be offered these infantile diversions*).

Childish, like *infantile,* can be used without any implication of disapproval (*His big manly voice,/ Turning again toward childish treble*), but for the most part it is used to designate the improper or silly manifestation in an adult of something which would be proper only in a child (*The unmarried are driven by boredom to childish amusements or vicious delights. To attach importance to a low-numbered license plate is childish. But when I became a man, I put away childish things*).

Childlike is used almost always in a good

sense, connoting the innocence, freshness, and meekness of children. It is a literary word, used chiefly by theologians and others who wish to protect certain important passages in the New Testament from any of the depreciative force that *childish* now carries. And certainly there is a difference, at least in the implication that the words carry, between a childish faith and a childlike faith.

Boyish is now almost always favorable (*boyish charm, boyish ambition, boyish fancies*). An unfavorable attitude towards masculine juvenility will express itself in *puerile* (*That a grown man should descend to such puerile accusations is astonishing*). These meanings are not absolutely hard and fast. *Boyish* could be used unfavorably, but it rarely is any more. And Anthony Wood's assurance that Franciscus Junius *was educated in puerile learning at Leyden* would be understood, after the first amazement, but would seem strange and a little amusing.

Girlish, not having such a synonym as *puellaish* to assume the unpleasant connotations, serves either way, but on the whole it is depreciative. Anything proper to a girl that is unquestionably admirable (as *girlish grace* or *girlish modesty*) is by its nature favorable; but in most other uses there is a faint disparagement (*Of all beyond I was girlishly ignorant. I lost my girlish laughter*). When applied to young men it is definitely depreciative, though *boyish* might be complimentary if applied to a girl.

infectious. See **contagious.**

infer. See **imply, deduce.**

inferno. As a literary euphemism for Hell, *inferno* was introduced about the middle of the nineteenth century. It survives today chiefly in the cliché *a raging inferno,* a worn journalistic term for a bad fire or a bad literary term for the heart, mind, soul, or bosom of one agitated with violent passion.

infertile. See **unfertilized.**

infidel. See **agnostic.**

infinite; great. That is *infinite* to which no bounds can be set. God's mercy is said to be infinite. A young man's aspirations may be infinite because of their very vagueness. Certain mathematical processes and perhaps space itself may with strict propriety be called infinite (*A haze on the far horizon,/ The infinite, tender sky*). Almost all other uses are hyperbolical and *great* or even *very* might be substituted. One cannot eliminate exaggeration from speech and probably should not even try to, but the effective speaker or writer will try to hold it in reserve and at least be aware of it when he is using it. To say *He went to an infinite amount of trouble to find the reference,* for example, is, really, to weaken the intended effect. *He went to great trouble* would probably be more impressive because it is more restrained. Trouble can be as near infinite as almost any human experience, but everyone has had enough trouble to set its bounds beyond anything incurred in looking up a reference.

infinite capacity for taking pains. Miss Jane Ellice Hopkins's preposterously pedestrian and typically Victorian definition of genius as *an infinite capacity for taking pains* has had such a fascination for millions devoid of genius that it has become a cliché.

infinitives. The infinitive is the verb form that simply names the action of the verb, without any other specification such as by whom, when, how, the action occurs. It is called an infinitive because, unlike the other verb forms, it is indefinite in all these respects.

If a verb is transitive and requires an object to complete its meaning, as the verb does in the phrase *he makes music,* the infinitive too will require an object, as in *to make music.* (See **transitive verbs.**) Like the finite verb forms, the infinitive is qualified by an adverb and not by an adjective. But it functions in a sentence as if it were a noun. Historically speaking, the infinitive is a single word, such as *make* or *go.* It may be used as the object of a verb, as in *he must go, he did go,* or as the object of the preposition *to.* In Old English the infinitive was used as the object of the preposition *to* about 25 percent of the time. Today it is used in this way more than 80 percent of the time.

(Some grammarians call the infinitive preceded by *to* "the supine," to distinguish it from the bare infinitive. In this dictionary the true infinitive is called "the simple form of the verb" and the infinitive with *to,* the "*to*-infinitive," or simply "the infinitive.")

In modern English the infinitive without *to* is used after *do, let,* and the regular auxiliary verbs such as *will, can, must* (see **auxiliary verbs**); after *bid, dare, feel, hear, make, need, see,* in the active voice but not in the passive; in certain constructions or with certain senses of the word after *have, help, find, come, go, run, try;* and occasionally after other verbs meaning "see," such as *behold, mark, observe.* The infinitive with *to* is used after the auxiliaries *ought, used,* and in certain senses *be* and *have;* and in all other constructions involving independent verbs. The word *to* may apply to several infinitives in a series, as in *she refused to eat, talk, or move,* or it may represent an infinitive that is easily supplied from the context, as in *he would like to.*

The eighteenth century grammarians, who relied on logic rather than research to solve their problems, had trouble explaining the word *to* before an infinitive. Some said that it was an adverb, some said that it was an auxiliary verb, and some said that it was "an equivocal article." Actually, it is the simple preposition *to,* which means primarily "in the direction of." It was first used with an infinitive to show intention or purpose, as it does in *he was led to believe.* But the construction has spread far beyond this and today the *to* is often no more than "the sign of the infinitive," a prefix which shows that the following word is an infinitive. But grammatically the two words still form a prepositional phrase and are still treated as a prepositional phrase.

(Whether this *to* is explained as a preposition, an auxiliary verb, an adverb, or an "equivocal article," there is no reason why a qualifying word should not stand between it and the infinitive, as in *who dared to nobly stem tyrannic pride.* Whether it should or not is a question of taste, not logic. See **split infinitives.**)

The agent of the action named by an infinitive is called the subject of the infinitive, as *him* in *there is no need for him to come.* Very often, as in the example, the subject is introduced by *for.* This is acceptable under some circumstances and not under others. (See **for.**) As a rule, the subject of an infinitive is the object of a verb or preposition, but it may also be the subject of a passive verb, as *he* in *he was heard to say.* This fact might conceivably affect the case of a personal pronoun following *to be,* but otherwise is of no importance. See **be.**

USES OF THE INFINITIVE

An infinitive phrase may function as an adjective qualifying a noun or pronoun, and when it does, it follows the word it qualifies, as in *the first to come and the last to leave.* It may also function as an adverbial phrase. As a rule, it is an adverb of purpose, as in *she looked down to blush and she looked up to sigh* and *I come to bury Caesar, not to praise him;* but it may show cause, result, necessity, and similar ideas. The infinitive may also be used as a noun. It may be the subject of a verb, or the complement of the verb *to be,* as in *where but to think is to be full of sorrow.* Or it may be the direct object of certain verbs, as in *learn to labor and to wait.*

In many of these uses the infinitive competes with a full clause containing a subjunctive or subjunctive substitute verb. *I do not know what to say* is equivalent to *I do not know what I should say;* and *I am here to see him* is equivalent to *I am here (so) that I may see him.* In contemporary English the infinitive is more common than these subjunctive clauses.

The infinitive also competes with the *-ing* form of the verb. One can say *dogs delight to bark and bite* or *dogs delight in barking and biting.* Frequently the two forms are interchangeable, but not always. Some verbs can take one as object and not the other. The verbs that are most troublesome in this respect have been listed individually in this dictionary. In these entries, the statement that a particular verb cannot be followed by an infinitive means that it cannot take an infinitive as object. It does not mean that the verb cannot be qualified by an adverbial infinitive of purpose.

The infinitive does not express time. The same form is used in speaking of the past, the present, and the future, as in *he liked to skate, he likes to skate, he would like to skate.* The time is shown by the tense of the true verb, such as *like.*

The infinitive *to be* followed by the past participle of a verb, as in *to be seen,* is called the passive infinitive of that verb. This is a relatively new development in English. Until recently the infinitive itself was indifferently active or passive, and it can still be understood in a passive sense, as in *there is a lot to see in Rome.* But the new, distinctly passive form is an advantage when it is necessary to be precise. And it allows us to say such things as *to love and be loved by me.* We can also make a progressive infinitive, as in *to be seeing,* and a progressive passive, as in *to be being seen.* Verbs that are followed by the simple infinitive without *to,* are also followed by the simple form of the passive and progressive infinitives, as in *he may be seen* and *he may be seeing.*

THE PERFECT INFINITIVE

The infinitive *to have* followed by the past participle of a verb, as in *to have seen,* is called the perfect infinitive of that verb. It too can have a passive form, as in *to have been seen,* a progressive form, *to have been seeing,* and a progressive passive, *to have been being seen.* This last form is rare, and some grammarians say that it is never used. But it is a perfectly proper form and is heard occasionally, as in *how would you like to have been being scolded all day?* Again, verbs that are followed by the simple infinitive without *to* also omit the *to* when followed by a perfect infinitive, as in *he may have seen.*

The perfect infinitive sometimes expresses completed action and sometimes indicates that what is said is contrary to fact. It always expresses completed action when it is dependent on a present tense verb, as in *we expect to have left by then,* and may do so when it is dependent on a past subjunctive auxiliary. When it is dependent on a past indicative verb form, it indicates that the action is contrary to fact. Milton writes: *I made him just and right, sufficient to have stood though free to fall.* The perfect form is used with *stood* because actually he did not stand, and the noncommittal form with *fall* because, actually, he fell. The same use of the perfect infinitive is seen in *I thought thy bride bed to have deck't, sweet maid.*

This construction is still used, as in *he expected to have left,* but in contemporary English we more often make a contrary to fact statement by using the auxiliary *had* in the principal verb (that is, by using the past perfect tense), as in *he had expected to leave.* When the two forms are used in the same statement, as in *he had expected to have left,* we have a definitely redundant sentence. The redundancy is not in a class with the double negative, but it offends people who are sensitive to words. The sentence is unliterary, simply because it isn't neat.

A perfect infinitive used after phrases involving *would have, might have,* and so on, is a different matter. These past subjunctive forms are used in the conclusion following a contrary to fact condition, as in *if he had come, I would have been pleased.* The contrary to fact clause may be replaced by a perfect infinitive phrase in just the way that a straightforward subjunctive clause may be replaced by the plain infinitive. In *it would have done you good to have walked in the garden with us,* the words *to have walked* replace *if you had walked.* This is an established literary construction, used by all good writers of English, and should not be confused with sentences such as *he had expected to have left.*

A perfect infinitive is justifiable after some of these verb phrases in other constructions. With the exception of *would* (and in British speech in certain constructions *should*), the subjunctive auxiliaries followed by *have* and a past participle express completed action, which may or may not be contrary to fact. That is, *he could have asked her to send it, he should have asked her to send it,* do not necessarily imply *he did not ask her.* In speech, a special emphasis is put on the first auxiliary to show that such a statement is contrary to fact. After verbs of this kind a perfect infinitive, as in *he could have asked her to have sent it,* is not redundant but precise.

This is not the case with *would have,* which always indicates a contrary to fact statement. Technically, *he would have liked to have left* has the same redundancy as *he had expected to have left.* But practically, there is a difference. On the one hand, the sentence using *would have* suggests the type of sentence in which the infinitive replaces a conditional clause, although that is not actually the case here. On the other hand, if *might have* had been used instead of *would have,* the perfect infinitive would have been appropriate. Theoretically, these facts are irrelevant, but they have an effect on the way the expression sounds. And to most people, *he would have liked to have left* sounds like the natural way to say it.

infinity; infinitude. *Infinity* and *infinitude* are synonymous. Since *infinite,* by definition, is incomprehensible, *infinity,* or the quality or attribute of being infinite, must be even more so, an abstraction of an unintelligibility. Those who deal in such concepts may occasionally, as Fowler drily remarks, find *infinity* tedious. When they do, they can use *infinitude* for variety. Thinkers in limited fields will find the variation needless.

inflammable; inflammatory. That which is *inflammable* is capable of being set on fire, but in popular usage the word is reserved almost exclusively for those substances which catch fire easily and burn with rapidity and violence (*Deposits of gasoline and other inflammable materials must be clearly marked by warning signs*). (See also **flammable.**) When the word is applied figuratively to persons, it means excitable, easily roused to (fiery) passions.

Inflammatory means tending to inflame. Though it would be understood in a literal sense (as in such a statement as *an inflammatory spark* or *the inflammatory torch*), it is no longer so used, being confined to the figurative sense of inflaming or kindling the passions (*These inflammatory speeches fired the mob with murderous fury*). In pathology *inflammatory*

has the special meaning of pertaining to or attended with inflammation (*an inflammatory sore throat*).

inflict; afflict. To *afflict* is to distress with mental or bodily pain, to trouble greatly or grievously (*They were afflicted with plagues. My afflictions are more than I can bear*). To *inflict* is to impose or lay on something unwelcome (*At the captain's command the bosun inflicted a dozen lashes. You have no right to inflict these punitive restrictions upon the child*). An affliction may be inflicted only upon sensitive beings. In such a statement as *The land was afflicted with famine, land* means the living things in the land.

inform. See **advice, tell.**

informant; informer. An *informant* is one who supplies information. An *informer* is also one who supplies information but this meaning has been almost superseded by the specialized meaning of one who makes it his business to bring criminal information concerning others to the police. He differs from a voluntary witness or a citizen doing his duty in that he expects to be paid for the information that he brings and rather specializes in charges of treason. The word was much in use in seventeenth and eighteenth century England when it acquired strong connotations of detestation. It has come into use in America only recently but has rapidly re-acquired much of its former odium.

infrequent; infrequency. See **unfrequent; unfrequented.**

infuriated. See **enraged.**

infuse. See **imbue.**

-ing. The *-ing* form of the verb must be distinguished from ordinary nouns that have the same form. When the Mock Turtle tells Alice that he has studied reeling, writhing, drawling, stretching, and fainting in coils, he is using ordinary nouns because he is talking about courses of study or skills and these are "things," as are concepts, customs, and events. The *-ing* form of the verb never refers to a "thing." It is a way of mentioning the action named by a particular verb, sometimes as a noun, as in *the stretching of the rope,* and sometimes as an adjective, as in *the reeling man.* In what follows we are speaking only about these verb forms and not about similar words which are actually the names of things.

In current English the *-ing* form, if it is not qualified by an adjective (and this includes *a* and *the*) and if it is not followed by *of,* can be used any place in the sentence that the sense permits.

If the *-ing* form follows a personal pronoun and the two words are the object of a verb or of a preposition, the pronoun may have an objective form or a possessive form, as in *do you mind us having secrets?* and *do you mind our having secrets?.* If the two words are standing in a subject position, the pronoun may have a subjective form or a possessive form, as in *you going out is no proof that you are well* and *your going out is no proof.* A noun or any other kind of pronoun followed by an *-ing* form may be in the common case (that is, not in the genitive case), as *anything* in *there's not the least likelihood of anything having happened to them* and *lady* in *is the lady bothering you any reason for you to come bothering me?.*

Some of these constructions are offensive to some people and are condemned by some grammarians, who recommend that the genitive or possessive be used before *-ing* words. But the rules just given describe the way in which most people now use the *-ing* form, and these uses must therefore be recognized as acceptable contemporary English.

Older constructions involving the *-ing* are also heard today. Many people still use nineteenth century forms in which adjective qualifiers, the word *of,* and a genitive case in the preceding word, are required under certain circumstances. (See 1-3 below.) These forms are acceptable in speech and are generally considered more literary than the modern forms. Still older constructions, from the seventeenth and eighteenth century, are also heard but are not considered standard now.

It is possible to describe the modern use of the *-ing* without talking about different kinds of *-ing.* But if anyone wants to use older forms and wants to know which of these are standard and which are not, he will have to recognize certain distinctions. During the nineteenth century it was customary to say that there were three ways of using an *-ing,* or that the *-ing* form had three distinct functions.

1. In one case it had all the characteristics of a noun, as in *the worshiping of idols was forbidden.* This form was referred to as "the verbal noun," but it is now called "the gerund" to distinguish it from true nouns derived from verbs. Grammarians in the first part of the nineteenth century defined this form as the *-ing* preceded by a definitive word, such as *a, the, this, that,* a genitive, or a possessive. This gerund form can be immediately preceded by an adjective but not by an adverb. That is, we can say *the occasional worshiping of idols* but not *the occasionally worshiping of idols.* It cannot be followed immediately by an object but requires the preposition *of.* That is, we cannot say *the worshiping idols was forbidden.* (The word *of* may be omitted when a gerund is preceded by the word *no,* as in *there was no persuading them,* but under no other circumstances.) Only the direct object of the verbal idea can be joined to the gerund by means of *of.* An indirect object requires the preposition *to.* That is, we may say *the giving of candy to children* but we cannot say *the giving of children candy.*

During the nineteenth century the gerund was often required for the subject or the object of a verb, but it was not often used for the object of a preposition, as in *a law against the worshiping of idols,* where a simpler form was possible and preferred.

2. The *-ing* form may have all the characteristics of an adjective. When it does it is called a participle. This form is used in the twentieth century just as it was in the nineteenth. A participle that is an integral part of a sentence must qualify a noun or noun equivalent in just the way an adjective does. It may stand before a noun, as in *a laughing girl,* or it may follow, as in *a girl picking cherries.* A personal pronoun qualified by a participle is subjective or objective depending on its function in the sentence. It is never possessive. This restriction does not apply to nouns or other kinds of pronouns. (An *-ing* form may also be part of a phrase that is grammatically independent of the sentence, as in *generally speaking, girls are a nuisance.* For a discussion of this, see **participles.**) A participle may be qualified by an adverb but not by an adjective (that is, we may say *a girl occasionally picking cherries* but not *a girl occasional picking cherries*); and it may be followed by an object (such as *cherries*) but not by an *of* phrase, unless the verb itself requires *of,* as in *thinking of her.* Earlier, a participle might be followed by *of,* as *picking* in *a dozen of them picking of his bones,* but this is not considered standard now.

3. The third way in which an *-ing* form can be used is seen in *there were laws against worshiping idols.* Here *worshiping* is not an adjective qualifying a noun or pronoun, but it has some of the characteristics of the participial adjective. And it does not have the characteristics required of a gerund. Nineteenth century grammarians called this form of the *-ing* the *gerundive* because it resembled the Latin adjective made from the verbal noun or gerund, and not the simple participle. They defined the gerundive as the *-ing* form of the verb that is used after a preposition. (Today the one word *gerund* is often used for this form as well as for the verbal noun.)

The gerundive could be qualified by an adverb, as in *laws against occasionally worshiping idols,* but it could not be qualified by an adjective, as in *laws against occasional worshiping idols.* A genitive or possessive form is equivalent to an adjective and conservative grammarians claimed that the gerundive could not be preceded by one of these forms. That is, they claimed that one could not say *laws against their worshiping idols.* The gerundive could be followed by a direct object but not by *of.* Formerly it might be followed by *of,* as in *I thank you for receiving of me* and *as to giving of you up.* These old constructions can still be heard today but are no longer considered standard. The gerundive could be followed by an indirect object as well as by a direct, as in *a rule against giving children candy.* (This is also true for the participle.)

These three forms of the *-ing* all occur in: (we will) *silence their mourning with vows of returning, but never intending to visit them more.* There is the gerund *mourning,* which is the object of the verb *silence;* the gerundive *returning*, which is the object of the preposition *of*; and the participle *intending*, which qualifies the pronoun *we*. There is another kind of verbal noun, the infinitive, which can also function as the subject or the object of a verb, and we have this too in *to visit*, which is here the object of the participle *intending*. See **infinitives.**

The Victorian gerundive is treated like a participle but it is essentially a noun and always carries the implication of the verbal noun and not of the adjective. It may be used to qualify a following noun, but when it is it has the force of an abbreviated prepositional phrase, as if a preposition such as *for* had been omitted. *Singing* is a participle in *a singing child* but not in *a singing lesson*. The -ing words are gerundives and not participles in *drinking glasses, walking sticks, growing pains, writing paper*. See **compound words.**

By Victorian standards a gerundive with an object could not be used as the subject or the object of a verb. That is, one could not say *worshiping idols was forbidden* or *the law forbade worshiping idols*. The gerund or some other construction, such as an infinitive or a clause, was required here. In contemporary English, the gerundive is used freely as the subject of a verb, but it is not always acceptable as an object.

By Victorian standards, a noun or pronoun standing immediately before the gerund must be a genitive or possessive. A word standing in this position always represents the subject of the verbal idea expressed in the gerund. A participle, on the other hand, may follow an uninflected noun or a subjective or objective pronoun, but it cannot qualify a preceding genitive or possessive. What form a noun or pronoun standing before a gerundive and representing the subject of the action should have, is a more complicated problem.

During the first half of the nineteenth century, conservative grammarians claimed that a genitive or possessive form could not stand before a gerundive, since an adjective could not stand in this position. Thackeray was reflecting conservative speech when he wrote: *I insist on Miss Sharp appearing*, rather than *Miss Sharp's appearing*. Noah Webster opposed this tradition. He claimed that if the preceding word was the subject of the verbal idea a genitive or possessive form was required.

Modern grammarians settle a question like this by counting instances. An examination of English literature made forty years ago to determine this point shows that from 1400 to 1900 a possessive pronoun was almost always used in preference to an objective pronoun before a gerundive, and that the genitive form of a noun was used approximately half the time. There is no doubt that Webster had a better ear for English than his opponents. By the end of the nineteenth century his teachings had been accepted as standard, and they are what now appear in textbooks.

But in the meantime, the eighteenth and early nineteenth century standards had had their effect. An analysis of the speech of educated Americans made thirty years ago found that the common form of the noun was overwhelmingly preferred to the genitive before a gerundive and that an objective pronoun was used in preference to a possessive pronoun 48 percent of the time. In current English it is more usual to say *on Miss Sharp appearing* than *on Miss Sharp's appearing*. Either form of the pronoun may be used. One may say *I'm surprised at his saying that* or *I'm surprised at him saying that* without intending any difference in meaning or emphasis. A possessive form is often used parallel with a noun in the common case, as in *I can understand an Afghan stealing but I cannot understand his crying*. Of course, if the pronoun itself is the object of a verb or preposition and the -ing a descriptive participle, the pronoun must have the objective form, as in *we saw him running*.

What has been said applies only to an -ing construction that is the object of a verb or preposition. When the -ing is the subject of a verb some people still prefer a noun in the genitive, as in *the children's wanting that surprises me*; but the simple form, as in *the children wanting that surprises me*, is also acceptable and is preferred by many. If the noun itself is the subject of the verb and the -ing a descriptive participle, only the simple form can be used, as in *the children, wanting some candy, came into the room*. In the case of a pronoun, most people prefer a possessive form when the -ing is the subject of a verb, as in *their being my friends makes it worse*; but a subjective form, as in *they being my friends makes it worse*, is used too often by good writers to be called anything but standard. Again, if the pronoun itself is the subject of the verb a subjective form is required, as in *he, being in a hurry, began to run*, but constructions of this kind are not often used.

In the case of pronouns, the situation is complicated by the fact that there are three forms instead of two. A subjective form is often used where the logic of grammar would require an objective or possessive form. When the subjective pronoun is close to the preceding verb or preposition, as in *instead of he converting the Zulus, the Zulu chief converted him*, it is offensive to most educated people, but not to all. When a great many words come between the pronoun and the verb or preposition so that the construction is obscured, the subjective form is acceptable to most people, as the *they* in *without my interfering with their sleep or they with mine* and the *he* in *that would be a motive for her murdering him, not he her*.

An objective pronoun is also heard in a subjective position, as *me* in *me knowing their names surprised them* and *him* in *it's no use him wiring back*. This is in keeping with the tendency in English to use a subjective pronoun immediately before a true verb and an objective form in any other position. Sentences of this kind are acceptable in speech. That is to say, they are seldom noticed by any one except a grammarian. But ordinarily these forms would be changed to possessives before appearing in print.

ingenious; ingenuous. *Ingenious* used to mean possessed of genius (*For epigram few could surpass the learned and ingenious Mr. Thomas Glover*), but it has now been weakened to mean simply clever, especially at contriving or making things (*At the age of ten he had made a most ingenious device whereby his alarm clock, on going off, closed the windows and turned on the heat*). *Ingenuous,* which once meant of free or honorable birth, now means open or frank (*He ingenuously acknowledged the fault and besought the old man's forgiveness*). Cynicism has operated somewhat upon the word and a secondary, though increasingly common, meaning is guileless, innocent, and frank almost to the point of folly (*So ingenuous a revelation of gullibility set the whole table laughing*).

inhabitable. See **habitable.**

inharmonious; unharmonious. As an adjective to describe anything that is discordant or not harmonious, whether it be music or ideas, *inharmonious* is preferred to *unharmonious,* though *unharmonious* is not incorrect.

inherent; innate. That is *inherent* which exists as a permanent and inseparable element, quality, or attribute of something (*There is an inherent baseness in lying that no amount of casuistry can remove*). That is *innate* which is inborn, existing or as if existing in one from birth, or arising from the constitution of the mind rather than acquired from experience (*The moral feelings are not innate but acquired*). See also **essential.**

inhibit; prohibit. *Inhibit* and *prohibit* are in many situations synonymous. Calhoun's insistence that the treaty-making power of the government of the United States is limited *by all the provisions of the Constitution which inhibit certain acts from being done by the government* could just as well have been *prohibit.* None the less, they are not at all times interchangeable and are becoming increasingly less interchangeable as the popular feeling grows that something which is inhibited is restrained or forbidden by some inner feeling or condition and something which is prohibited is restrained or forbidden by some outside authority. A man might be inhibited from smoking by a sense of delicacy or a personal fear of its effect on his health. He would be prohibited from smoking by his doctor's orders, under some circumstances by state fire laws, in airplanes at the take-off by regulations of the Civil Aeronautics Authority, and so on.

inhuman. See **unhuman.**

initiate; initiation. While *initiate* means "begin," the two words are not completely synonymous. An *initiation* may be a formal introduction to certain mysteries. Or it may be an ingenious first act in a new field (*He initiated the present procedures in examining applicants*). One begins a conversation but initiates a series of conferences between persons of great impor-

tance. One takes the initiative *in* doing something not *of* doing it. See also **begin.**

inmates; patients. An *inmate* is, strictly, one who dwells with another or others in the same house. It is still sometimes used, though rarely, in this and the closely associated sense of inhabitant (*The present inmate is a Mr. Murchison*). In current usage *inmates* is used most frequently to designate prisoners in a certain prison or patients in a certain insane asylum (*The inmates sullenly refused to listen to the warden's terms*) or the inhabitants of various institutions such as homes for the aged or the blind. The common application of the word does not seem to rest on any suggestion of criminality or even of social undesirability, though this inference might well be drawn by the sensitive among many of these unfortunates, but on the idea of a more or less permanent dwelling in an institution.

For those who are confined to a hospital for medical or surgical treatment, so long as it is not a hospital restricted solely to mental patients or attached to a penal institution, the term is *patients.* Where an institution for the care of the insane calls itself a hospital its inmates are often called patients. There seems to be an association of the two words.

inmost; innermost. These forms are equally acceptable as superlatives for the idea contained in *in.*

innate; instinct. *Innate* means inborn. *Instinct* when used as an adjective means urged or animated from within, infused with some active principle. *Innate* is followed by *in. Instinct* is followed by *with* (*The urge to self-preservation is innate. There was an innate skepticism in Johnson's mind that warred continually with his deep piety. The buds, instinct with life, lay yet within their sticky teguments*). See also **inherent.**

inner man. The *inner man* which St. Paul prayed might be strengthened by God's spirit was the soul, the inner or spiritual part of man. It was "saving doctrine" which Milton felt *attracts the soul,/ Governs the inner man, the nobler part.* The application of the term to the stomach and of "strengthening" to eating was a flight of mid-nineteenth century humor which has survived its impiety and its humor to become a cliché.

innervate; enervate. To *innervate* is to give nervous energy to, to stimulate through the nerves, or to grow nerves into. The word is restricted to works on anatomy and neurology. To *enervate* is to deprive of nervous strength, to weaken. It is in general use (*enervated by luxury*), but has become specialized, almost to the point of being a cliché, as a term for the enfeebling effect of a hot, moist climate (*The high temperatures of the rain forest are exceedingly enervating to whites*).

innings. In Great Britain this word is a singular as well as a plural and can be used in speaking of just one, as in *the ninth innings.* In the United States the singular form is *inning* and *innings* is used only in speaking of more than one.

innocent as a newborn babe. A baby has long been established as a type of innocence and various wits have labored to heighten the simile. The phrase has appeared at different times over the past four centuries as *innocent as an unborn child, innocent as a newborn babe, innocent as an unchristened babe.* In any form it is now a cliché. W. S. Gilbert gave a humorous freshness to the idea with his *as innocent as a new-laid egg.*

innuendo. The plural is *innuendoes.*

innumerable. See **endless.**

inquire; ask; demand; question. As verbs, these words all imply the seeking of information by one person (or persons) from another (or others). *Ask* is the everyday word (*He asked me what I knew about the incident*), but it is sometimes ambiguous because it has the further meanings of demanding and soliciting (*He asks forty-five dollars for it. I ask you to help me*). *Inquire* is more formal and always implies asking about something specific (*inquire the route, inquire the time of departure*). It has a slight advantage over *ask* because it has a corresponding noun *inquiry* whereas *asking* is limited in its uses and except for the phrase *It's yours—or his—for the asking* has a suggestion of deliberate archaism. To *demand* is to ask for with authority, peremptorily, urgently (*His face grew red with anger and he demanded an answer at once*). To *question* is to ask repeatedly and persistently. Witnesses are questioned in trials and investigations. It carries, also, a connotation of skepticism (*I question the veracity of that statement*).

inquirer; inquisitor. An *inquirer* is simply one who makes an inquiry. An *inquisitor* is a persistent questioner, often inquisitive, eager to know matters which the one questioned may feel he has a right to keep to himself. From association with the Holy Office, better known as the Inquisition, and its chief officer the Grand Inquisitor, the word *inquisitor* has some connotation of one who carries his questioning to a point that is torture to the one being questioned.

inquisition; disquisition. An *inquisition* is an investigation or process of inquiry (*Nor have these mysterious comings and goings escaped the inquisition of the suspicious*). A *disquisition* is a formal discourse or treatise in which a subject is examined and discussed, a dissertation. A disquisition may well embody the results of an inquisition.

inquisitive. See **curious.**

insanitary. See **unsanitary.**

inscrutable. See **mysterious.**

inside of. This phrase ordinarily means "on the inside." It may also mean "in less than," as in *inside of an hour, inside of a mile.* This sense of the word is standard in the United States, but in Great Britain it is considered "colonial."

insidious; invidious; offensive. That is *insidious* which is intended to entrap (*an insidious question*) or is stealthily treacherous or deceitful (*an insidious foe, continually offering terms which he had no intention of abiding by*). The word is often used of a disease which proceeds without any very alarming symptoms to a grave or fatal condition.

That is *invidious* which is prompted by or adapted to excite dislike or ill will, unfairly discriminating. An invidious comparison or invidious praise would be a comparison or praise designed to cast odium rather than actually to compare or praise (*What needs, O monarch, this invidious praise,/ Ourselves to lessen, while our sires you raise?*). *Invidious* used to mean envious and invidious praise would have been praise designed deliberately to excite envy. The sense of envious has now been lost, however, and all that is retained is the ill will that the envy would engender. It differs from *offensive,* however, in that it designates a particular kind of offensiveness, an offensiveness based on unflattering or spiteful comparisons or praise of others. It would simply be *offensive* to compare a man to a pig. It would be *invidious* to compare him to someone who plainly surpassed him in some field of endeavor in which he prided himself on his accomplishments. If the comparison were so worded (as in satire it often is) that it seemed a compliment though it was actually an insult, it would be, as a compliment, *insidious.*

insidious; beguiling. Though *insidious* and *beguiling* both mean treacherous and deceiving, *insidious* designates things which are evilly deceiving and dangerously treacherous while *beguiling* is now largely restricted to things which deceive by pleasing artifice and whose deceptions are not only delightful but involve no great loss or harm to us and sometimes, indeed, do us good (*The child's beguiling ways could always win over her doting grandparents. How often have his affectionate antics beguiled me from melancholy thoughts!*).

insignia. This word has a plural form and may always be used as a plural, as in *all these insignia* and *the insignia are well known.* The Latin singular is *insigne* and some people believe that this is the only correct singular. But the word *insignia* is used as a singular, as well as a plural, in literary English. Hawthorne, for example, wrote *he bore a slender white wand, the dreaded insignia of his office.* In the United States Army *insignia* is used officially as a singular and is given a regular English plural *insignias.*

insinuate. See **imply.**

insipid. See **vapid.**

insolent. See **impertinent.**

insoluble; insolvable; unsolvable. In the senses of incapable of being dissolved and incapable of being explained, *insoluble* is now the standard word, though *insolvable* and *unsolvable* are both admissible variants. *Insolvable* retains one particular, rare meaning: not convertible into cash, as a banknote or bill that cannot be cashed.

inspiration; aspiration. Though the older solemn religious meaning of *inspiration* is understood and still retained in use, the common meaning of the word today is little more than encouragement or hope or that which or he who (or, more often, especially in popular song and story, she who) gives encouragement or hope (*Margie, you've been my inspiration, Margie*). Further weakened, it is used a great deal for a happy thought or unexpected solution to a problem, usually a minor problem (*Hey, I've got an inspiration: there's that fellow visiting Joe—he'll do for a fourth*).

Aspiration remains a more dignified word. It means a lofty and ambitious desire (*The high aspirations and vast yearnings of the young*).

installment plan. The dividing of a debt into equal sums to be paid at fixed successive intervals which is known in America as the *installment plan,* or buying on the installment or selling on the installment plan, is known in England as the *hire purchase plan* or *system.*

instance. See **example; case.**

instant. See **minute.**

instant; ultimo; proximo. While the use of *instant,* abbreviated *inst.,* to mean "of the present month" in referring to dates, as *Yours of the 12th inst. to hand and contents noted,* is quite correct, it has come to be regarded as a piece of business-letter jargon and is now generally avoided. *Your letter of the 12th* will usually do quite as well, though many men prefer, in the interest of strict accuracy, to say *Your letter of May 12,* or whatever month it may be, even though the answer is written in the same month. And though this may seem a little stiff, it is safe.

The same applies, even more strongly, to *ultimo,* abbreviated *ult.,* meaning of the month preceding the present month, and *proximo,* abbreviated *prox.,* meaning in or of the next or coming month.

instanter is a law term for instantly. Outside of legal documents or legal talk it now seems a little forced and affected.

instantly; instantaneously. See **immediately.**

instigate. See **impel.**

instill. See **imbue.**

instinct (adj.). See **innate.**

instinct (noun). See **intuition.**

institute; institution. *Institution* is the general word and covers more meanings. It designates an organization for the promotion of a particular object, usually for some public, educational, or charitable work (*The State Institution for the Blind*), or the building devoted to such work (*Turning the corner, he was confronted with the bleak walls of the Institution*). In sociology an institution is an organized pattern of group behavior, fully accepted by the members of a cultural group (*the institution of slavery*) or any established custom. Colloquially the word is used to designate any familiar practice or object (*Old Sam's drunks were quite an institution in the town*). And, of course, it can mean the act of instituting (*The institution of the new regulations caused a great deal of grumbling among the employees*).

An *institute* may also be an organization for carrying on a particular scientific, educational, or artistic work (*The Institute for Advanced Study*) or the building in which such work is carried on (*The Art Institute*). Like *institution,* it has been used so much as a euphemism for houses of correction, particularly those established for youthful offenders, that in many contexts it has a pejorative connotation (*Root de toot, root de toot,/ We're the girls from the Institute*). It is usually confined to such institutions as have chosen to call themselves institutes and to the buildings that house them. Many universities designate one of their units, usually for advanced study in some special field, an institute (*The Oriental Institute, The Technological Institute*). The word can also mean a short course of studies, established for a particular group and purpose (*The Institute of African Studies*). And it has the special meaning, in the plural, of a collection of principles and precepts (*Calvin's "Institutes" remains one of the world's great demonstrations of logic*).

instructional; instructive. Both *instructional* and *instructive* mean educational, but *instructional* refers more directly to teaching and learning (*Although it is to be hoped that the cruise will be pleasurable, it is intended primarily to be instructional*). *Instructive* refers more directly to the conveying of information but differs slightly from *informative* in that it suggests that the information is conveyed with an instructional purpose (*Once more, Democritus, arise on earth,/ With cheerful wisdom and instructive mirth*). It is this shade of meaning that gives satiric point to Pope's account of the activities of the belles and beaux at Hampton Court in *The Rape of the Lock*:

> *In various talk th' instructive hours they past,*
> *Who gave the ball, or paid the visit last;*
> *One speaks the glory of the British Queen,*
> *And one describes a charming Indian screen;*
> *A third interprets motions, looks, and eyes;*
> *At ev'ry word a reputation dies.*

He had originally written *the cheerful hours* but changed it, in the second edition, to *instructive.* And a happy revision it was, for it suggests, in keeping with the mocking light gravity of the poem, that in Belinda's set a knowledge of these trivia was necessary to one's education as a courtier. The acquirement of gossip was their schooling, indispensable to the business of frivolity.

insufferable. See **unsufferable.**

insurance. See **assurance.**

insure. See **assure; ensure.**

integrate. In mathematics, or anywhere else, *to integrate* means to bring parts together into a whole. It is rarely used in a literal sense (*To say that automobiles were integrated on the assembly line would cause a stare or a laugh*), but it has become a vogue word in educational, advertising, and, especially, psychological circles. Programs are always being integrated, plans are integrated, campaigns are integrated —indeed anything at all that can be combined or joined may be said to be integrated. The diverse or conflicting elements of character or personality are continually being "integrated" by those who approach the problems of the mind or spirit in a brisk, businesslike way. One of the authors of this book saw *Ye must be integrated* scrawled in chalk on the wall of a midwestern theological seminary, one of the more remarkable graffiti of our times. Outside of mathematics, the word needs a rest.

intelligent; intellectual; intelligentsia. *Intelligent* suggests a natural quickness of understanding. The word implies a native capacity independent of education. Indeed, it is often used of animals (*I never had a more intelligent dog*). In addition to such a high degree of understanding, however, *intellectual* implies a capacity and taste for the higher forms of knowledge (*Intellectual pursuits are the solace of advancing years*). An *intellectual* is one who possesses or shows mental capacity of a high degree or (more often) a member of a class or group that professes or is supposed to possess enlightened judgment. Since this implies superiority, it is a term more often applied than claimed and in a democratic society often has slight overtones of contempt. There is no English word to designate the intelligent as a group (the intelligent rarely going in groups and probably too intelligent to permit themselves to be recognized as superior people). *Intelligentsia* first appeared in English during the present century and came from Russia. It is sometimes used seriously, meaning the intellectuals, but more often it is used derisively meaning, as H. G. Wells says, "an irresponsible middle class with ideas." In either case, it is a group name and is regularly used with a plural verb, as in *the intelligentsia were offended*. It is not a true plural and cannot be used with a numeral. We may say *three intellectuals* but we must say *three members of the intelligentsia*.

intelligent; intelligible. To be *intelligent* is to possess good sense and quickness of understanding. An *intelligent* remark is one that shows its utterer to have had these qualities. An *intelligible* remark is one that is clear and can be understood. An intelligent person, if he has anything to say, takes pains to be intelligible to the person to whom he is speaking.

intend. This word may be followed by an infinitive, as in *I intend to go myself,* or by the *-ing* form of a verb, as in *I intend going myself.* Both forms are standard in the United States. *Intend* may also be followed by a clause, but the clause verb must be a subjunctive or a subjunctive equivalent, as in *I intend he go.* An infinitive construction, such as *I intend to let him go* or *to have him go,* is generally preferred.

intended. As short for intended husband or wife, *intended* is colloquial. Fowler calls it "vulgar," the product of an "ill-bred shyness" and wistfully wishes that *betrothed*, a dignified and accurate word, might be "given another chance." But words once out of fashion are rarely given another chance. For some uneasy or evasive reason we feel the relationship is best concealed in the French *fiancé(e)* and *betrothed* has faded

with the attitude it expressed. That words rarely come back is not, however, wholly discouraging; *intended* is also fading from use.

intense; intensive. That is *intense* which exists or occurs in a high or extreme degree (as *the intense brilliance of the sunlight on the snow*) or is acute or vehement (as *intense anxiety* or *an intense gale*). That is *intensive* which is concentrated (as *intensive research, intensive fire*). What is intensive is usually intense, and what is intense may be intensive, but it need not necessarily be so. An intense bombardment would be a severe bombardment. An intensive bombardment, in the strictest sense—as Fowler points out—is one in which "the fire converges upon a much narrower front than that from which it is discharged." In common usage it is one which is directed upon a small section of the city, fortification, encampment or whatever it is that is under bombardment.

Intensive used to be completely synonymous with *intense* (Robert Burton speaks of an *intensive pleasure*), but this use is now obsolete. Of course if the loose use of *intensive* to mean *intense* continues and gains wide enough acceptance, it may be so again. But at the moment it is not.

intensely; very. *Intensely* is often used as a synonym for *very*. In such a sentence as *It was intensely hot* this is admissible, since heat can be intense. In such a sentence as *He was intensely learned* it is confusing and close to meaningless. In such a sentence as *He was intensely rich* it is simply wrong. There must be some element of intensity in the meaning before its use can be justified. If in doubt, use *very*.

intensive pronouns. A pronoun that has no function in a sentence except to emphasize a noun or some other pronoun, such as *himself* in *he himself has said it*, is called an intensive. In current English the *-self* words are used freely in this way.

Formerly, the simple personal pronouns were also used as intensives, as *they* in *thy rod and thy staff they comfort me*. This construction is now considered redundant and is condemned in most textbooks. But it is still literary English. It is used in poetry, as *it in the rain it streams on stone and hillock,* and in prose that has an emotional tone, as *they* in *these men who gave their lives for their country, they did not ask for a cash payment in advance.* But when it occurs in a very simple sentence, such as *my father he says no,* it is generally condemned. Most people today do not use the personal pronouns as intensives. If anyone uses them in this way because he does not know that it's against the rules, his speech is uneducated. But if anyone uses them in this way because he knows that English literature does not support the rules, his speech is "literary." Sometimes one would have to know the speaker in order to classify the sentence. See also **reflexive pronouns.**

intensives. A word that merely makes another word more emphatic is called an intensive, such as *do* in *I do believe you* and *very* in *it is very* *late.* These particular words are conventional intensives and actually make a statement more emphatic. But some words used as intensives may have the opposite effect.

When a certain kind of adverb, such as *fearfully, frightfully, dreadfully,* is used merely to intensify an adjective, it becomes so weak that the entire statement is weakened. *I am sorry* is a stronger statement than *I am dreadfully sorry.* When used properly, these words are among the strongest in the language. Carl Sandburg, describing a fish peddler, says: *his face is that of a man terribly glad to be selling fish.* Here *terribly* keeps its meaning and is very strong. But if the fish peddler himself said: *I am terribly glad to do it,* the statement becomes ridiculously weak. This is because all these words, *terribly, dreadfully,* and so on, mean "inspiring fear or awe" and can only be used properly by an observer who experiences the emotion. A man may say that he feels a terrible joy but he cannot say that he himself is terribly glad. The people around him must be the judge of that. These words, *terribly, dreadfully,* etc., cannot retain their meaning when used as pure intensives. They become mere substitutes for *very,* and the fact that the speaker is not satisfied with *very* but is casting around for a stronger word shows that the emotion is not overwhelming. What he is feeling is obviously less important to him than the effect he wants to make.

Adjectives are frequently used before other adjectives as intensives, that is, as words meaning primarily "in a high degree," as in *icy cold, red hot, dead tired.* In such combinations the first word is functioning as an adverb but that does not make these expressions "ungrammatical." This is a natural English construction that no one thought of questioning until recently. Some combinations of this kind are no longer considered standard, such as *dreadful sorry, powerful glad.* But others, made on exactly the same pattern, are still literary English. Whether one of these expressions is standard or not depends entirely on what sort of people use it. There is nothing wrong in the pattern itself and as a rule nothing is gained by giving the first word a clearly adverbial form. *Deadly tired* and *powerfully glad,* for example, are pathetic attempts to be "correct" and do not improve the original forms, which at least have the advantage of being natural English. See **horrible,** etc.

intent; intention. Though *intent* and *intention* are interchangeable in the meaning of that which is intended, purpose, aim, design, *intent* is now slightly archaic and to most Americans would seem bookish or a little affected. There are occasions, of course, when one wants to be bookish or wants the effect of the less common word. But except on such occasions it should be, of these two words, *intention.*

intentionally. See **advisedly.**

intents and purposes, to all. The full legal phrase used to be *to all intents, constructions, and purposes.* Even simplified, however, it is a wordy way of saying *practically.* It is a hackneyed way, too.

interesting. *Interesting* is one of the most overworked words in the language. It would be a good exercise for the student, every time he finds himself about to write the word, to search his mind to see if there is not some more accurate adjective that could be used in its stead, something that would express the intended meaning more forcefully, with greater freshness. How about *alarming, arresting, attractive, curious, gratifying, pleasing, puzzling, remarkable, striking,* or any one of a hundred other words?

interfere; interference. Sometimes a child that walks awkwardly will strike one ankle bone against the other, often with sufficient force to cause abrasion of the skin and bleeding. Among some old-fashioned people this is called *interfering* and those who hear the word so used for the first time probably assume that is some quaint derivative meaning. But, actually, this is the original meaning (as a term in farriery) and butting in, meddling, intervening, obstructing an opposing player in football, and the jumbling of radio signals are the derivative meanings.

The word *interference* has two meanings in American usage that are not recognized in English usage. It is a technical term in our Patent Office for a proceeding to determine priority (*An application for a patent which, after an interference litigation with Edison, was finally issued to Maxim*). And, as has been indicated above, it is a term in football for interposing between a runner and a tackler to obstruct the tackler (*As any football player knows, to win a game you have to have good interference*).

interject; interpolate. To *interject* is to throw or cast in between. As a procedure in conversation it means to remark parenthetically in an interruption. It may be transitive (*She interjected one of her characteristically absurd remarks*) or intransitive (*She frequently interjected and otherwise made herself a nuisance*). Some writers insist that properly it can only be transitive, but usage simply does not support this.

To *interpolate* is, strictly, to alter a text by the insertion of new matter, especially when the matter is spurious and the insertion done without authorization or with intent to deceive (*These passages have definitely been shown to be interpolations and no reputable scholar has accepted them as genuine for centuries*). It is not always used in the pejorative sense, however; it often means no more than to insert a passage or, in conversation, a comment. When so used it is a milder word than *interject.* It suggests a less rude form of breaking into another's talk, more of an addition to than an interruption of the conversation.

interjections. These are free-floating words, or meaningless syllables, that interrupt the orderly progress of speech. They are accepted as evidence of emotion. An interjection must be set off from the rest of the sentence with commas, unless this is accomplished with an exclamation point. The single letter *O* is always capitalized, but it is not necessary to capitalize longer words such as *oh* and *lo*.

There are fashions in interjections as there are in everything else. *Say!* is an Americanism, *I say!* is British. *La* is now unspeakably old-fashioned, *law* is supposedly dialectal, and *ah* is very genteel. But since these sounds are presumably torn from the speaker without his foreknowledge, any discussion of standards would seem inappropriate. See also **exclamations.**

intermediary; mediator. An *intermediary* is an agent, a go-between, one who is the connecting link between two parties (*He did not buy his stocks directly from the broker but through an intermediary*). A *mediator* is a go-between who serves the special purpose of reconciling, or trying to reconcile, parties at variance (*Charles had hoped that he might be a mediator between his estranged parents but found their hostility to each other increased rather than lessened by his efforts*).

internal revenue. That which in the United States is known as *internal revenue* is in England *inland revenue*. The effect on the taxpayer is much the same.

international languages. Interest in international languages is traceable in large part to the decline of Latin as a medium of scholarship after the rise of nationalism encouraged the use of the vernaculars. A desire for a single vehicle of cultural intercourse between learned groups and knowledge of the languages of Asia and Africa brought back by explorers, merchants and missionaries, spurred the drive to construct an international language. The French philosopher Descartes outlined a plan for a constructed language as early as 1629. Leibnitz, many years later, saw that the basis for such a language could only be established by an analysis of languages then in use. He saw clearly that the two international languages then proposed, by the Scotsman Dalgarno in 1661 and the Briton Wilkins in 1668, would not do because they started with a preconceived system unrelated to any living speech.

The first constructed language actually spoken and written was Volapük ("world speech"), invented in 1880 and received with enthusiasm but nearly dead by 1890. Hard on Volapük came Bopal (1887), Spelin (1888), Mundolingue (1890), Dil (1893), Balta (1893), Veltparl (1896), Idiom Neutral (1903), Ido (1907), Interlingua (1908) and Novial (1928).

Esperanto, the most popular successor to Volapük, was devised by Dr. Ludwig Zamenhof who published in 1887 *Linguo Internacia de la Doktoro Esperanto* ("International Language by Doctor Hopeful"). It is often incorrectly referred to as "the" international language. In 1950 the thirty-fifth annual conference in Paris claimed that one and one-half million people read, spoke and wrote it daily. It has a literature

of about 8,000 books, mostly translations but some originals. Over 1,000 conferences of all kinds have used it for reports and communications.

Interlingua has had two lives. Originally it was the language that developed out of Professor Peano's Latino sine Flexione. The modern Interlingua was started by a group of scholars at an international conference in 1924. It is now being backed by the International Auxiliary Language Association and seems to be gaining ground. In 1954, thirteen journals used Interlingua for summaries of articles (*Science News Letter*, 7/17/54). It is apparently being promoted through sponsorship of scientific organizations. Science Language Association is working for its adoption and some scientific journals occasionally run an article in it.

These, with the exception of Basic English, have been the most serious and successful candidates for acceptance. (See **Basic English.**) As far back as 1817 plans were being advanced for international communication based on ideas rather than on existing languages. Solresol, based on the notes of the scale, was one of the first. Others were Lingualumina, Blaia Zimondal, Zahlensprache, and Ro. These all had the character of codes rather than of linguistic systems and required much memorizing. In the twentieth century similar approaches have produced Antido I and II, Lingvo Kosmopolita, Nov-Esperanto, Latinesce, Nov-Latin, Monario, Europan, Optez, and Romanal, among others.

The English-speaking peoples have not made much contribution to these constructed languages. Their self-satisfaction in language must be exasperating to many who speak other languages, but it is only a matter of degree, for most of the constructed languages are built upon European languages only.

The first significant British contribution to the literature of international languages was C. K. Ogden's *Basic English*, first described in 1929. Ogden has inspired some American competition in Swenson English, Iret and Little English but these have not yet gained any great headway. Basic English is probably the best suited to become an international language. English is already the chief of world tongues. More people speak English today than any other language except Chinese and Chinese is broken into several dialects and confined almost entirely to one continent. There is a great *practical* demand to know English, at least as an auxiliary language and the number of people using English has increased enormously since World War II. Basic English is simply more satisfactory than any of the constructed languages. As H. L. Mencken said, the trouble with the constructed languages is that "the juices of life are simply not in them." They are the work of scholars "drowning in oceans of dead prefixes and suffixes." Whereas Basic springs from a living speech, used by almost

300,000,000 human beings, a speech that forges ahead of all its competitors "simply because it is already spoken by more than half of all the people in the world who may be said, with any plausibility, to be worth knowing."

interpellate; interpolate. To *interpellate* is to interrupt a speech in Parliament or in the Chamber of Deputies to ask a member of the government to explain some official act or policy. It is a rare word, confined now to this special use. To *interpolate* is to alter a text by the insertion of a word or phrase or longer statement. There is usually a suggestion that the inserted matter is spurious and the insertion an act of deceit. The word is also used to mean the interposition of a remark into a conversation. In this sense it has no unfavorable connotation. See also **interject.**

interpret. See **explain.**

interpretative; interpretive. Although the adjective *interpretive* is acceptable for that which serves to interpret or explain, *interpretative* is the preferred form.

interred; interned. That is *interred* which is buried, placed in a tomb, especially with appropriate ceremonies (*The evil that men do lives after them;/ The good is oft interred with their bones*). He is *interned* who is obliged to live within prescribed limits under prohibition to leave them, as a prisoner of war or an enemy alien, or a combatant who has taken refuge in a neutral country. Ships of belligerents are also interned when during wartime they are detained in the port of some neutral country.

Intern is also used as a verb in the United States to mean serving as an intern (or interne), a resident member of the medical staff of a hospital (*After receiving his degree at Northwestern University Medical School, he interned at Christ's Hospital in Cincinnati*).

interregnum. The plural is *interregnums* or *interregna.*

interrogative pronouns and adjectives. The words *who, whose, whom, which,* and *what,* are interrogatives when they are used without an antecedent that precedes them in the sentence. *Who* and *whom* are always pronouns. *Whose, which,* and *what,* may be used as pronouns or as adjectives. Interrogatives always stand before the verb in a simple question, such as *what did he do?,* and in a subordinate clause that carries an indirect question, as in *I don't know what he did.* See **questions.**

(For the person and number of an interrogative pronoun, see **agreement: verbs;** for case, see **who; whom.**)

interrogative sentences. See **questions.**

into. This is a preposition. It represents the relation expressed by *in* with the added implication of motion or direction. *In* also may be used where the idea of motion is involved, as in *he went in the house, he fell in the water.* Some grammarians consider this regrettable and would like to see *in* driven out of these constructions. Some others feel that *in* should be allowed when "the idea of remaining is prominent." Speaking historically, *in* once carried all the meaning of *into,* but this is now decidedly weakened. *Into* suggests motion more emphatically than *in* does, but either preposition can be used.

In is sometimes used as a pure adverb, or as part of a compound verb, as in *they went in.* An expression of this kind may happen to be followed by a prepositional phrase beginning with *to,* as in *they went in to see him, they went in to dinner.* This separate use of *in* and of *to* must not be confused with the single idea *into.* We say *send this in to the secretary* but not *send this into the secretary.*

Into is used freely in a literal sense with verbs of changing, making, moving. It is also used with certain other verbs simply to make the action more penetrating, as in *enter into, examine into. Look at this report* means no more than to read it. But *look into it* means to really learn something about it.

intolerable; intolerant. That is *intolerable* which is unendurable, insufferable, not tolerable (*The heat in the little room exposed all day to the glaring sun was intolerable*). It was formerly used in a loose sense to mean excessive or great (*O monstrous, but one half pennyworth of bread to this intolerable deal of sack?*) but this meaning is now obsolete.

He is *intolerant* who is bigoted, unable or indisposed to endure contrary opinions, especially religious or political opinions (*He was a staunch Republican and intolerant of any expression that seemed to favor the New Deal*). The adjective is often applied to expressions, gestures, or attitudes that reflect the intolerance of those who express or hold them (*Such intolerant phrases may ease the wrath of those who express them but they do not conduce to harmony in mixed groups*). The intolerant are usually intolerable.

intoxicated. See **drunk.**

intransitive verbs. A verb is said to be intransitive if it does not require an object to complete its meaning. Intransitives are sometimes called "complete" verbs. A transitive verb, on the other hand, has an object. The verbs are transitive in *the face that launched a thousand ships and burnt the topless towers of Ilium;* they are intransitive in *now the great winds shoreward blow, now the salt tides seaward flow; now the wild white horses play, champ and chafe and toss in the spray.* (See **object of a verb.**) Linking verbs, such as *is* in *April is the cruelest month,* are considered intransitive. They cannot stand by themselves as other intransitives can, but the words that follow them add something to the meaning of the subject and not to the meaning of the verb. See **linking verbs.**

Many verbs can be used either transitively or intransitively. Most intransitives can be made technically transitive by using an object that simply repeats the meaning of the verb, as in *smile a timid smile, think a bitter thought, live a lonely life.* This device should not be condemned as redundant. It is sometimes a more effective way of qualifying the verb than the usual adverbial construction, such as *smile timidly, think bitterly, live lonelily.* It is found frequently in literature, as in *the latest dream I ever dreamed.*

Some verbs that are usually intransitive, such as *sit* and *walk,* may be used transitively as causative verbs, meaning "cause to do," as *she sat the baby up, he walked his horse.* The intransitive verbs in *The rubbish burns, the boat sinks, the dog starved* are transitive in *burn the rubbish, sink the boat, starve the dog.* The intransitive verb *lie* is sometimes used as a causative, especially in the past tense, as in *she lay the baby down,* but at present this is condemned by most grammarians. See **causative verbs** and **lie.**

Verbs that are usually transitive may also be used intransitively, especially with passive force. For a discussion of this, see **transitive verbs.**

intrigue. Despite the protests of the purists, usage has established *intrigue* in the meaning of to excite the curiosity of, to interest by a puzzling novelty, or even to take the fancy of (*Mr. Johnstone gives a detailed account of their literary background, and intriguing summaries of their work. Her hat intrigued me; I couldn't see how she got it to stay on at that ridiculous angle*). The older meanings of to entangle, to enmesh, to bring or force by underhand machinations linger on but have been almost completely displaced, in popular usage, by the newer meanings which less than fifty years ago Fowler stigmatized as "gallicisms, that have no merit whatever except that of unfamiliarity to the English reader." All of which, of course, does not change the fact that it is a vogue word, greatly overworked by those who like to force dramatic tension into every situation.

intrinsic. See **essential.**

Introduction. See **foreword.**

intrude; obtrude. That is *intruded* which is thrust in. That is *obtruded* which is thrust out or upon something else. We *intrude* upon others' privacy when, uninvited, we come into their rooms. We *obtrude* our opinions upon others when we insist on stating them even though they are unwanted. We *intrude* our opinions into a discussion when they have not been solicited. The last two meanings are plainly inseparable. Whether the opinions have been intruded or obtruded is a matter of argument and point of view; hence under some circumstances the words are interchangeable.

intrust is a variant of *entrust* which is the preferred form.

intuition; instinct. *Intuition* is the direct perception of truths or facts without the intervention of any process of reasoning. It is pure, untaught, noninferential knowledge (*By what intuition he was apprised of our plans I do not know; he certainly could not have learned of them*).

Instinct is an inborn pattern of activity and response common to a given biological stock (*Since the mother abandons the eggs before they are hatched, the young cannot learn from her; their actions must be governed wholly by instinct*). It is used more loosely to designate any innate impulse or natural inclination or natural intuitive power. In these uses *instinct*

and *intuition* are often used interchangeably. If someone says, *I had an instinctive dislike of that man the minute I saw him,* he probably means that he had an *intuitive* dislike, a dislike based on no evidence or process of reasoning but (usually) a dislike which later events proved to have been justified. However, the speaker may have meant that some inborn pattern of activity or response led him to this immediate dislike, as many animals are said to fear their natural enemies on first sight.

An *intuition* produces an opinion or judgment. An *instinct* produces an act or physical response. An *intuition* is an immediate, individual experience, unrelated to anything that has gone before. An *instinct* is a response produced, in some way, by the previous experience of the species. *Intuition* is commonly conceived of as something superior to reason. *Instinct,* ascribed to the lower animals—often in popular zoology as a compensation for their assumed lack of reason—is usually thought of as something inferior to reason. The cliché—both of words and thought—*a woman's intuition* is usually an insult timorously disguised as a compliment. There is a suggestion in it that women's mental processes are above reason; but almost all who use the phrase seriously intend to imply that women lack the power of reasoning and reach their conclusions (which, they admit, are often correct and speedily come to) by some nonhuman means.

inure and **enure** are simply variant spellings. All attempts to make fine distinctions in meaning between them are only baseless ostentation. *Inure* is the preferred form.

invalidated; invalided. A document which has been exposed as spurious or in some other way deprived of its value or authority is *invalidated.* One who has become an invalid or a soldier or sailor who has been retired from active service because of sickness or injury has been *invalided.*

invaluable; priceless. Although the prefix *in-* is usually negative, *invaluable* does not mean "of no value" but "of so great value that no estimate of its value can be conceived." *Invaluateable* would be the proper word, but fortunately it has not been coined. The proper word for "of no value" is *valueless.*

Although the suffix *-less* is negative, *priceless* likewise means a worth so great that no price could be set. In England, especially among the gayer social set, *priceless* has become a vogue word of commendation, especially of wit. It is already so weakened in this sense that it has to be shored up with such vague intensives as *perfectly, absolutely,* and *simply.* America has remained comparatively immune from this visitation. The opposite of *priceless* is *worthless.*

invective. See **abuse.**

invent. See **discover.**

inventory. See **invoice.**

invidious. See **insidious.**

invite. This verb may be followed by an infinitive, as in *we invited them to come,* but not by the *-ing* form of a verb or by a clause. See also **allure.**

invite; invitation. Though damned as incorrect and ill-bred and listed in the dictionaries as slang, *invite* as a synonym for *invitation* has remained impudently in use for three hundred years (*Bishop Cranmer gave him an earnest invite to England*—1659. *Did you get an invite to the Phi Sig dance?*—1957). It is one of those words that may be used with a full assurance that it will be clearly understood but must be used with an awareness that in some quarters it is condemned. If, therefore, you use it in these quarters, you risk condemnation.

invoice; inventory. An *invoice* is a written list of merchandise, with prices, delivered or sent to a buyer (*We trust the shipment reaches you in good condition. The invoice is enclosed*). An *inventory* is a detailed descriptive list of articles, with number, quantity, and value of each (*Every six months he set down an inventory of his stock*). *Taking inventory* is sometimes used metaphorically of taking stock of one's resources. The English term for taking inventory is *stock-taking*. *Invoice* is often misused for *inventory*.

involve; entail; implicate. To *involve* meant originally to envelop or infold by surrounding and it should not be used unless there is some suggestion of including as a necessary circumstance or consequence. To say of someone that he found himself more deeply involved in the consequences of an act than he had intended to be would be to use the word with a proper understanding of its meanings. But to say of a project that *the cost involved has been tremendous* (unless it is definitely meant the cost inextricably connected with a certain policy or action, ensuing upon the decision to put the policy into force or take the action) is to use the word weakly and unnecessarily. Why not simply *The cost has been tremendous*?

To *entail* is to bring on or involve by necessity or consequences (*Moving to New York entailed a change in their whole way of life*). It differs from *involve* in that *involve* often carries a suggestion of trickery in the entanglement with embarrassment to the one involved, consequences not foreseen at the time of the action.

One is often involved in harmless matters and an act may entail good, bad, or indifferent consequences, but one is *implicated* in something discreditable. If a man is involved in a scandal, he may be an innocent victim. If he is implicated there is a suggestion that at least someone thinks him to some extent guilty.

inward; inwards. *Inward* is the only form that can be used to qualify a following noun, as in *that inward eye*. Either form may be used in any other construction, as in *driven inwards* and *driven inward*. The form *inward* is generally preferred in the United States.

ipse dixit. "Unless the witness explains the process of analysis and reasoning by which he reached his conclusion, the jury must take—or refuse to take—the conclusion simply upon his *ipse dixit*." The term is useful, but the colloquial *his say-so* is preferable.

i.q.; I.Q. *i.q.* is an abbreviation of the Latin *idem quod* and means "the same as." When the same letters are capitalized, as in *I.Q.*, they are an abbreviation of the English words *intelligence quotient,* which means the ratio of one particular person's intelligence to the average intelligence of people of his age.

iris. The plural is *irises* or *irides,* not *ires.*

iron curtain. Sir Winston Churchill's statement, at Fulton, Missouri, on March 5, 1946, that *an iron curtain had descended across the continent* of Europe, separating the Soviet sphere from the rest of the Western world, caught the public fancy and passed at once into the language. Like the *Fifth Column* of the Spanish Civil War in 1936, it supplied a dramatic term for something new that had not yet found a name. It was a good metaphor, with all the cold, grim, and menacing connotations of iron and the suggestion, in *curtain,* of shutting out the light.

But the term has become a little too popular —even to the point of impeding and confusing thought in regard to Russia and our relations with her. And like many highly successful and felicitous phrases it has begotten a number of less felicitous imitations, such as the *bamboo curtain* surrounding China or the *nylon curtain* which we have been charged with lowering.

iron hand in a velvet glove. As a term for ruthless severity hypocritically masked in suavity and seeming kindliness, *an iron hand in a velvet glove* is a hackneyed metaphor.

iron out. The metaphorical use of *iron out,* in the sense of removing difficulties or disagreements as an iron smooths out wrinkles (*The Chairman of the Board was confident that these differences of opinion could be ironed out before the next stockholders' meeting*), seems to be confined to American speech and writing. Though many dictionaries do not recognize its existence, it is used and understood everywhere in the United States and is not regarded as slang.

irons in the fire. As a term for having more enterprises than one can well look to, *having too many irons in the fire* is now a cliché. When it was fresh and especially when the sight of a smithy was a part of everyone's daily experience, it was a valuable metaphor. The clangor of the heavier hammers, the rapid ring of the lighter ones, the roar of the bellows, the heat, the flying sparks, the hiss of hot metal being tempered and, above all, the furious urgency engendered by the need to work the metal while it was red hot, and that in the face of considerable danger, all combined to give the figure vitality. But few people today are familiar with a smithy and the metaphor has cooled to the point where it can no longer be worked.

irony. See **humor.**

Iroquois. The singular and the plural are both *Iroquois.* This word was originally a plural but may now be used also as a singular, as in *three Iroquois* and *one Iroquois.*

irregardless. There is no such word as *irregardless.* It is a redundancy, erroneously patterned after irrespective.

irregular. See **anomalous.**

irregular verbs. Practically all English verbs form the past tense and the past participle by adding *-ed* to the simple form of the word, as in *they talk, they talked, they had talked.* Any verb that deviates from this, as in *they speak, they spoke, they had spoken,* is an irregular verb.

In present-day English there are 227 verbs that have at least one irregular form. Some of them change the vowel sound, as in *sink, sank, sunk;* some are completely irregular, as in *be, was, been;* and some are contractions of the regular forms, such as *creep, crept, crept,* and *hear, heard, heard.* Among the irregular verbs there are 72 which also have regular forms, such as *dig, digged* or *dug; spell, spelled* or *spelt.* This means that there are only 156 verbs that cannot be treated as regular, and some of these are archaic and no longer used in natural speech. Estimates of the number of irregular verbs actually in use vary from less than 100 to 150.

Some verbs are used only, or chiefly, in the third person singular, such as *it snows, it sleets.* Potentially, these verbs are regular and can be given other forms when there is occasion for it, as in *thick on Severn snow the leaves.* For this reason they are not counted among the irregular verbs. A few others do not have some of the normal verb forms. For example, *ought* has no *-ing* form, no past participle, and cannot be used as an imperative or an infinitive. But no verb of this kind forms a past tense by adding *-ed,* and therefore all of them come under the original definition of an irregular verb.

All verbs that have any irregular forms are listed in this dictionary. If both a regular and an irregular form are given, either may be used. But where only one form is standard, there is no choice. One cannot say *knowed* for *knew* and, in America at least, one does not say *crew* for *crowed.* There is no logic to this. It is simply a question of usage. But people generally are more insistent, more intolerant, in regard to these verb forms than they are to other parts of grammar, and the use of an out-of-fashion form is always taken as evidence of illiteracy.

irreligious. See **unreligious.**

irreparable loss. Many losses are irreparable but, even so, the phrase has been overworked.

irresponsible; irresponsive. In modern usage *irresponsible* means acting or being without a sense of responsibility (*He's utterly irresponsible; you cannot put him in any position of trust*). *Irresponsive* means unresponding, giving no answer or showing no emotional reaction (*The irresponsive child often offers a more serious problem than his more passionate brother or sister*). The commoner word is *unresponsive.* See also **unresponsible.**

irritate. See **aggravate; tantalize.**

irruption. See **eruption.**

is. See **be.**

ism. Basically, *-ism* is a suffix, forming a noun of action (*heroism, hooliganism, cannibalism, vandalism*). In addition to this it came to indicate the name of a system, whether in practice or theory (*Protestantism, Catholicism, atheism, communism*). From this use it was a natural step to mean a peculiarity (*Americanism, witticism*). When the suffix was detached to become a word in itself, denoting some unspecified system or peculiarity, it connoted scorn and disparagement (*God knows what ism he's embraced now. I can't keep track of 'em*). The favorable word is *theory.*

isotope; isotrope. *Isotope* is a noun, a term applied to any of two or more forms of a chemical element occupying the same place in the periodical table and nearly identical in properties but differing by one or more units in atomic weight. Most of the elements are mixtures of isotopes.

Isotrope is an adjective, a variant of isotopic. In physics it means having the same properties in all directions. In biology it means not having predetermined axes, as certain eggs.

Israelite. See **Hebrew.**

issue. See **emerge.**

issued; supplied. An established meaning of the verb *issue* is the military meaning of be supplied with (*The new arrivals were issued regulation uniforms*). The use of *with* following this use of *issue* (as in *The new arrivals were issued with regulation uniforms*) is redundant and erroneous.

isthmus. The plural is *isthmuses* or *isthmi.*

it. *It* is first of all a pronoun used in speaking about inanimate things or living things that are not thought of as being either male or female, as in *whose baby is it?* When used in this way, *it* is "anaphoric," that is, it must refer to something that has been mentioned previously. It is always singular and refers to something that is expressed by a singular noun.

It is also used with an unspecified reference, as in *it's stuffy in here, it's eleven o'clock,* and various statements about the weather. This is called the "impersonal" *it* and is said to represent "the great neuter of nature."

No one questions either of these uses of *it.* But the word has several other uses which have been challenged. In fact, textbooks sometimes say that these two uses are the only proper ones. This is what is meant by a statement such as: Do not use *it* without a definite antecedent except in impersonal expressions. Anyone who takes a rule like this seriously will find it impossible to write natural English.

It has very important uses as a "dummy" word. It can stand where English sentence order requires the subject of the verb and in this way set the true subject free to stand in some other position. This is especially valuable when the subject is a large group of words, usually an infinitive phrase or a *that* clause, as in *it is surprising to hear you say such things* and *it has been shown that these things always fail.* Here the *it* represents the words beginning with *to* or the words beginning with *that.* This is not a "weak" construction. It is a device for making the true subject more emphatic by allowing *it* to be taken out of its normal position. It may be used for this purpose when the subject is extremely simple, as in *it is the wife who decides.* Here *it* represents merely *the wife.*

It may also be a dummy object. This is useful when the object is long and there is an objective complement which should not stand too far from the verb, as in *we have it in our power to do great harm or great good* and *he took it for granted that I would come.* Here again, *it* represents the words beginning with *to* or *that* and allows us to complete the verbal idea with *in our power* or *for granted* sooner than we otherwise could. Similarly *it* may represent a clause and be the object of a preposition, which could not otherwise have a clause as object, as in, *see to it that the door is locked.*

This is called the "anticipatory" *it,* or the "expletive" *it.* (For the difference between *it* and *there,* see **there.**) Anticipatory *it* is always singular, even when the logical subject is plural, as in *it is the crickets that you hear.* The person and number of the verb in a subordinate clause is more complicated. In *it is not I who is angry* and *it is you who is angry,* the verb *is* is technically correct because the straightforward sentence is *(the one) who is angry is not I* or *is you.* But in current English we are much more likely to make the verb agree with the preceding pronoun and say *it is not I who am angry* and *it is you who are angry.* Since one form is theoretically correct grammar and the other is the usual practice, both forms must be recognized as standard.

It may also be used to represent a complex thought that is perfectly clear from the context but that has not been put into words. This is the "indefinite" or "vague" *it* that the textbooks mean to condemn. But it is an extremely useful device for shortening and simplifying a sentence, as in *it's a long way to Tipperary* and *when the work is slow, it may be nobody's fault.* Here *it* has no antecedent, but since the sentences are perfectly clear it is obvious that no antecedent is required. To avoid constructions of this kind is to have more interest in analyzing language than in using it; or more interest in being "correct" than in being understood.

It is used with prepositions in a number of idiomatic phrases, such as *hard put to it, nothing for it, make a good job of it.* These are all standard English. It is used as an "empty" or meaningless object with certain verbs that do not take an object, such as *bluff it,* and after

certain nouns and adjectives used as if they were verbs, as in *lord it, rough it, brave it.* The same construction is used in many slang expressions, such as *hoof it, leg it, beat it, pub it.*

The word *it* is also used in slang as a noun, meaning something important and nameless, and in this sense is sometimes written with a capital letter, as in *She has It* and *This is It.*

it stands to reason that is one of those exasperating expressions by which we often unwittingly antagonize other people during a discussion. Usually it is meant as no more than a clearing of the throat as a preface to whatever we have to say; but if what we have to say differs from what someone else has just said we have, by this assurance that our opinion is reasonable, implied that his is unreasonable. And people don't like to be told they're unreasonable. They often get quite unreasonable about it.

iterate. See **repeat.**

its. This word is a possessive pronoun and means "pertaining to it." It has no apostrophe and should not be confused with *it's,* which means "it is."

The form *its* is relatively new. That is, it first appeared around the year 1600. It is not found in the King James Bible, where *his* is used instead, as in *if the salt have lost his savor.* Shakespeare uses *its* in only a few places and generally prefers the simple form *it* as a possessive, as in *it lifted up it head.* By the year 1700, *its* was in general use as a possessive standing before a noun, comparable to the words *her* and *their.* But a grammarian writing in 1819 said: "When I see many *its* in a page, I always tremble for the writer."

More recently, *its* has been used alone without a following noun, comparable to the words *hers* and *theirs,* as in *these nations will have attained their maximum development before the rest of the world has attained its.* This construction is technically acceptable today, but it is still extremely rare.

it's not for me to say, if spoken sincerely, would have to be followed by silence. Whereas, as everyone knows, it is usually followed by a flood of self-justification or self-laudation. And since this is intended to persuade or convince it would be more effective if the argument were not immediately preceded by a wornout phrase whose false modesty instigates doubt.

itself. See **reflexive pronouns.**

izzard. See **from A to Z.**

J

jag; load. A *jag* in some English dialects is a load. The word was so used in America a century ago. Thoreau speaks of those whose wealth consisted of nothing more than *a jag of*

driftwood. It then became a slang term for a load of liquor, all that a man could carry (*That moonshine stuff'll really give you a jag*) and, by extension, for any state of intoxication or excitement resembling intoxication (*She has those crying jags about once a month*). These latter meanings are still listed as slang in the dictionaries but the word is so widely used now, especially in the last sense, with no intention of being quaint or original or amusing that it probably ought to be accepted as standard.

Load in this sense, however (*Brother, has he got a load on*), is still slang. As also in the sense of take a good look at (*Get a load of this*) and, in the participle, to be rich (*He's loaded; if that guy dropped a ten dollar bill it wouldn't be worth his time to pick it up*).

jail delivery. In the United States a *jail delivery* is a deliverance of imprisoned persons by force, either a rescue or a breaking out (*A daring attempt at a jail delivery at Pontiac Reformatory was thwarted this morning*). In England the phrase means the clearing of a jail of prisoners by bringing them to trial.

Japanese. The singular and the plural are both *Japanese*. At one time this word had a distinct plural, as seen in the following sentence, written in 1693: *the Japaneses prepare tea quite otherwise than is done in Europe*. This word is now obsolete and the one form *Japanese* is used for both the singular and the plural, as in *one Japanese* and *three Japanese*. The shortened form *Jap* is derogatory and should not be used.

jargon. See **argot; vernacular.**

jeer. As a transitive verb *jeer* is now obsolete in England; the English always *jeer at* someone or something. American usage retains the old transitive form (*They jeered the speaker as soon as he began to talk*) and employs the intransitive as well (*They jeered at Columbus, didn't they?*).

Jehoshaphat. The layman has little occasion to refer to the son of Asa who removed the remnant of the Sodomites but did not take away the high places and whose ships went not to Ophir, but if he must allude to him, the name is *Jehoshaphat* not *Jehosaphat*.

jerrymander. See **gerrymander.**

jetsam. See **flotsam.**

Jew. See **Hebrew.**

Jewess. See **Negress.**

Jew's-harp (Jews' harp); juice harp. For over four hundred years the small lyre-shaped musical instrument with an elastic steel tongue which is held between the jaws and plucked, the tone being changed by varying the position of the mouth, has been connected in English with the Jews. It was called a *Jew's trump* or *Jews' trump* before it was called a *Jew's harp* or *Jews' harp* but no one knows why. The *Oxford English Dictionary* characterizes all attempts to derive the first element from jaws or from the French *jeu* as "baseless and inept." Whether any derogation was originally intended is not known but it is apparently believed that some might now be felt, for the instrument is invariably referred to in radio and television programs as a *juice harp*. Considering the drooling that often accompanies amateur performances on the thing, this is a fairly ingenious emendation, and con-

sidering the fact that it is only on radio and television programs that children hear of the instrument at all any more, the new name is probably better established among the young than the old name and one more word has undergone one more preposterous change.

jimmy; jemmy. The American name for a short crowbar used to effect burglarious entrance is a *jimmy*. The English name is *jemmy*. Both forms are familiar diminutives of James (*Mayor Jimmy Walker. O Jemmy Thomson, Jemmy Thomson, O*). How the name got applied to the instrument nobody knows.

jingo. The plural is *jingoes*.

jinni; jinn. If one *must* employ Arabic in writing an English sentence, the grammar should be correct. The word for those spirits in Mohammedan mythology which are lower than the angels and capable of appearing in human and animal form is in the plural *jinn*, in the singular *jinni*. *How this jinn ever escaped from his bottle* is incorrect. It should have been *How this jinni.* . . .

job; position; situation; place. The standard meaning of *job* is a piece of work, an individual piece of work done in the routine of one's occupation or trade (*How much for the job? We pay by the job. Let's get the job done. Job printing*). In American usage a situation or post of employment is also called a *job* (*Hey mom, I got the job*). In America the word is also applied to an affair, matter, occurrence, or state of affairs (*Well, we've got to make the best of a bad job*). The application of the word to a theft or robbery or any criminal deed (*The gang pulled a job in Madison and were over the Illinois line before daybreak*) is slang.

Position is usually applied to any post of employment above manual labor (*His position in Clark's grocery didn't offer much hope of getting rich quick. This is a good position for the right man. Position wanted. Will travel*). *Place* and *situation* are used mainly today in regard to positions or jobs that are being sought (*situation wanted*). *Place* is now generally restricted to domestic employment, especially of a female (*She had a good place with a Winnetka family for twenty years*).

Job's comforter. Eliphaz the Temanite, Bildad the Shuhite, and Zophar the Naamathite are known now to very few and the term *Job's comforter* for one who under the guise of offering consolation only adds to his victim's distress is now an empty phrase.

John Doe; Richard Roe. *John Doe* is a fictitious personage in legal proceedings, usually the plaintiff. The corresponding fictitious defendant is *Richard Roe*. Their female counterparts are *Jane Doe* and *Mary Roe* who also serve in warrants, when necessary, as John and Richard's respective spouses.

join together. Although *join* means to bring or put together, *join together* is too solidly established as an emphatic phrase (*What therefore God hath joined together, let not man put asunder*) to be forbidden as a redundancy. Purists have tried but usage has been on the other side.

joiner. A *joiner* in England is a carpenter, especially one who does light and delicate work, such as dovetailing, the fitting of jambs and sills (*the workshops of joiners and cabinet-makers*). The word was formerly so used in the United States (*Wanted, a ship joiner, to finish the cabin of a small vessel*—1840) but that meaning is now obsolescent. *Joiner* in current American usage is a colloquial term of good humored contempt for one who makes a practice of joining clubs and lodges and other societies (*The real Joiner loves to sit up on an elevated Throne, wearing a Bib and holding a dinky Gavel*).

jolly; jocose; jocular; jocund; jovial. *Jolly* means full of life and merriment, gaily cheerful, exciting mirth (*For he's a jolly good fellow*). The word is known in America and used, but it is connected so strongly with English speech in the American mind (especially in such uses as *jolly good thing too* or *We'll have to jolly him up a bit; he's rather in the dumps*), and is so invariably employed in waggish burlesques of English speech that a serious use of it would seem slightly affected. *Jolly* is sometimes used colloquially in America to mean banter, make fun of good naturedly.

Jocose and *jocular* both mean sportive, merry, given to joking. Both suggest that the humor involved is a little ponderous and deliberate. One thinks of jocosity as taking place among old men in solid clubrooms. The diminutive in jocular, the "having one's little joke," still colors its meaning faintly. One thinks of jocularity often as a sly joke, the evading of a too direct question by a facetious answer. Both words are somewhat bookish, not in common everyday use.

Jocund is now purely bookish. It seems far too heavy a word for airy mirth or lightness. Milton's *jocund rebecks* would have to be translated into *gay fiddles* today, and Shakespeare's *jocund day* would now be inconceivable *standing tiptoe on the misty mountaintops.*

Jovial does not come to us directly from Jove but from the planet Jupiter which as a natal planet made those born under it joyous and happy. Yet Jove's majesty echoes in it. There is a suggestion of heartiness in the word, of lofty serenity and, sometimes, a touch of godlike condescension. The jovial do not giggle; they chuckle. Joviality is definitely avuncular, not nepotal.

jot or tittle. As an expression of an intransigent or firm refusal to make the slightest change or an insistence that things are going to remain exactly as they are, especially spoken of something set down in writing, *not one jot or tittle will be changed* is a cliché. It is an echo of Matthew 5:18, *One jot or tittle shall in no wise pass from the law,* where *jot* means iota and *tittle* any point (like the dot over an *i*) by which pronunciation is indicated.

journalese. As a term for all newspaper writing, *journalese* is a snob term. There is just as good and effective writing in the best newspapers as in the best books and the faults that are commonly classed as journalese are to be found in all writing.

Nevertheless, the poorer and more sensational papers have these faults to a degree that justifies some name for it. Their writing is frequently trite, oversimplified, distorted, exaggerated, colored for sensational effect and wrenched to meet the space demands of headlines. Their vocabularies are often pretentious and abstract and loaded with violent images which are overworked and soon worn out. A mild example will suffice:

> "*Leaders of South Carolinians for Independent Electors, the group sponsoring the slate, insist their twin objectives are to give segregation South Carolinians a place to go, and make available eight uncommitted electoral votes as the South's bargaining weapon should neither Mr. Eisenhower nor Adlai E. Stevenson win the necessary clear majority of electoral votes from the 47 other states.*"

Aside from the expansiveness of the "should" clause, are the two objectives so similar as to be twins? Wherein does a "clear" majority differ from a majority? And is the cacophonous use of "segregation" as an adjective justified?

Bad newspapers love elaborate words: *obfuscate, plebiscite, inculcate, anomaly, shibboleth, indigenous, cataclysm, aggrandizement, implementation, encroachment, peripheral.* Certain pompous phrases must remain permanently set up in type: *bipartisan foreign policy, act of overt aggression, fusillade of shots, dereliction of duty, titular head of the party, diplomat without portfolio, deficit spending, eschewing presidential ambitions, policy of containment.* But to assume that such inflated terminology is confined to newspapers is to be as ignorant as unjust. It was not some petty, pretentious scribbler who invented *massive retaliation* and *agonizing reappraisal* or spoke of *unleashing* Chiang Kai-shek.

Newspaper writing has to be done under pressure to meet a deadline and such pressure invites the use of clichés. They become a sort of time-and-thought saving code: *legal bombshell, sweeping investigation, innocent bystander, fair sex, kiddies, smoking weapon, ill-gotten gains, minced no words, whirlwind courtship, tongue-lashing.*

Headlines account for the greatest abuse of the meaning of words, but as the meaning becomes established through constant use in headlines, it eventually works its way into news stories. Thus *bid* is made to serve a score of uses in the headlines that are not recognized in the dictionaries. In the headlines all treaties and agreements are *pacts,* all ambassadors *envoys,* all investigations *probes,* all contests for public office *races,* all criticisms *hits* or *raps,* all unsavory agreements *deals,* all increases in pay or charges *hikes,* all requests *pleas.* The reading of headlines is becoming as specialized an activity as the solving of crossword puzzles. Who but the initiate could make sense of SHUNS CHICAGO RETURN GO?

journey. See **trip.**

joy is more than pleasure. It is a keen, lively, ecstatic pleasure (*But there is no joy in Mudville—mighty Casey has struck out*). Hence such phrases as *simple joys* or *quiet joys* must be used with care as they are self-contradictory. Usually *pleasures* is intended. *Delight* is a synonym for *joy*. The phrase *a joy and a delight* is a cliché.

judge. This verb may be followed by a clause, as in *I judge they have finished,* or by an infinitive, as in *I judge them to have finished.* The clause construction is generally preferred.

judge; adjudicate. In addition to its primary meaning of trying a person or case as a judge does, *judge* has the related meanings of forming a critical opinion or an estimate (*I judge it's about a mile further. Their deeds I judge and much condemn,/ Yet when did I make laws for them?*). *Adjudicate* means to award judicially (*The prize was adjudicated to the little man in the bowler hat*) or to sit in judgment, to pronounce judgment on. In this use it is followed by *upon* (*The right to adjudicate upon these pretensions can be claimed only by those who have experienced the same misfortune*). In many contests *judge* and *adjudicate* can be interchanged, but the practice is becoming increasingly common of using *adjudicate* in reference to contests or disputes not in the courts. See also **think.**

judicature; judiciary. As a term for the judicial branch of government, the system of courts of justice in a country, the judges collectively, the British prefer *judicature* and the Americans *judiciary,* though both words are known in both countries and may be used interchangeably.

judicial; judicious. *Judicial* means pertaining to judgment in courts of justice (*judicial proceedings*) or pertaining to courts of law or judges (*judicial functions, judicial chambers*) or proper to the character of a judge (*judicial calm, judicial fairness*). *Judicious* implies the possession and use of discernment and discrimination (*That was a judicious choice*). There are some contexts in which the use of *judicious* may be ambiguous, for a judicial opinion may also be judicious.

junction; juncture. A *junction* is an act of joining (*Soon afterwards Nelson effected a junction with the main body of his fleet*) or a place of joining (*The torn sheet had been so skillfully mended that the junction of its two halves could be perceived only by the most careful scrutiny*).

A *juncture* is also an act of joining (*The juncture of the Ohio and the Mississippi . . .*), though this use is now rare, *junction* being commonly preferred. As a place of joining, it refers to the line or point at which two bodies are joined (*the juncture of the head and neck*). Its commonest meaning, however, is of a point in time which is important because of the concurrence of circumstances (*How remarkable that he should appear at this juncture of events. A critical juncture*). *At this juncture* has come to be used so much for simply *at this moment,*

whether or not the moment is one made significant by the junction of certain events, that a careful writer will avoid it unless the context makes it plain that it is a juncture and not just a moment.

junior. The word *junior* is used much in America, rarely in England. In America it means the third or next to the last year of college or one who is a member of that year (*By his junior year the candidate for the degree must have completed . . .*). It also means of a more recent admission or appointment to an office, especially the United States Senate, where a junior senator is not necessarily younger than his colleague from the same state but more recently elected or appointed.

When an American boy is given his father's name or his grandfather's name he usually appends *junior* to his own name during the lifetime of the older bearer of the name. Miss Amy Vanderbilt in her *Complete Book of Etiquette* says that the word should be in small letters if appended in full but the *J* capitalized if abbreviated and *Mr.* prefixed to the whole (*Mr. William Schwartz, junior* or *Mr. William Schwartz, Jr.*). Where the father himself is already *junior* —where, that is, grandfather, father, and grandson all bear the identical name, and the grandfather and father are still living—the grandson is *third*. On the death of the grandfather, the father would then become *Mr. William Schwartz* and the grandson *William Schwartz, junior,* until he was of age and then *Mr. William Schwartz, junior.* In some places it is customary for a son who has been known as *Mr. William Schwartz, junior,* to retain the *junior* for a year after his father's death.

Though dictionaries do not recognize it, it is well for parents to face the fact that among schoolboys *junior* is a term of good-humored contempt.

It is improper to refer to a girl or young woman as *junior* (as *Miss Helen Smith, Jr.*) even if she does bear the same name as her mother. Of course she could be described as *the junior Miss Smith* to distinguish her from an elder sister, but *younger* would be better. And *Junior Misses* is a definite category in girls' clothing.

junk. In English usage *junk* is still chiefly a nautical word, meaning old, stiff, worn-out, discarded cordage and—by derivation—salt meat (which, apparently, was regarded as having the consistency and appearance of such cordage, and probably its palatability). In America *junk* means any old or discarded material, especially metal, paper, and rags (*They were ashamed because their uncle was in the junk business. There was nothing up there but a lot of old junk. The old mills will simply be dismantled and the machinery sold for junk*). The verb *to junk,* to discard as worthless (*When he got home his ship was a complete wreck. It will be junked*), is wholly American. The word is used as a verb in English, but rarely, and then it means to cut into hunks.

The Chinese ship *junk* is a totally different

word. It is a shortening of the Portuguese form of the Javanese word *jong.*

junket. The sweet custardlike food of flavored milk curded with rennet (*Eat your junket, Deborah!*) was so called because it—or something like it—used to be served on rushes (Italian *giunco,* a rush). Rushes were also spread on the floor or ground at merrymakings and picnics and hence pleasurable entertainments and excursions came to be called junkets. The first meaning is retained in America, though when the *J* is capitalized it is a trademark. The second, however, has undergone a curious, cynical change and in its commonest use in the United States today means a trip taken at public expense by an official or a group of officials ostensibly to obtain information but actually for pleasure (*Several rules committee members have opposed the resolutions on the ground that they would provide "nice junket trips" for committee members*).

just; justly. When these words mean fair or according to justice, the form *just* is an adjective and is used to qualify a noun, and the form *justly* is an adverb and is used to qualify other kinds of words, as in *the just man was justly pardoned.* When the form *just* is used as an adverb and qualifies a word that is not a noun, it means exactly, merely, or very recently, as in *the man has just been pardoned.* The form *justly* is never used to qualify a noun.

juvenile. As an adjective for that which pertains to, is suitable for, or intended for young persons, *juvenile* is neutral in its connotations (*juvenile fiction*), though the frequency of its use in the phrase *juvenile delinquency* may make it in time pejorative. The disparaging adjectives are *childish* and *puerile.* See **infantile.**

K

kangaroo court. As a term for an unauthorized or irregular court, especially for a mock court held by prisoners in jail or an irregularly conducted court in a frontier district, *kangaroo court* is an American term. It is often classified as informal English but it has become so definitely the name for irregular courts conducted in jails by the prisoners themselves that it is hard to see how else one could identify them without resorting to circumlocution.

The origin of the term is unknown. It is, apparently, not Australian but American. Dr. Charles Earle Funk hazards the guess that since the term came into use soon after the gold rush to California, in 1849, the early purpose of such courts may have been to try those who jumped claims.

keep. The past tense is *kept.* The participle is also *kept. Keep* may be followed by the *-ing* form of a verb, as in *keep trying,* but not by an infinitive or a clause. *Keep* may be followed by an adjective describing the subject of the verb, as in *I kept cool,* or by an adverb describing the action itself, as in *it kept well.*

keep a stiff upper lip. As an admonition to be firm in times of stress and trouble, *keep a stiff upper lip* is a cliché. It seems to be an American phrase, coming into use in the 1830's. Like many clichés, its exact meaning is puzzling, since it is not the upper but the lower lip that trembles in weakness and self-pity.

keep a weather eye open. As an admonition to be alert, *keep a weather eye open* is a cliché, a tediously jocular assumption of nautical language.

keep body and soul together. As a term for achieving the bare minimum of subsistence, *to keep body and soul together* or *keeping body and soul together* has been overworked. It has been in constant use for more than two hundred years and should be avoided.

kept. See **keep.**

kerb. See **curb.**

kerosene; paraffin; coal oil. *Kerosene* is, or was until recently, the common American word for heating and illuminating oil distilled from petroleum, bituminous shale, coal, etc. (*She would put kerosene on her fire to make it burn*). The English word for this substance is *paraffin,* a shortening of *paraffin oil* (*He set his face against paraffin and the whole family of oils*); but *paraffin* in the United States means a white or colorless waxy substance, obtained from crude petroleum and used for making candles and forming preservative coatings on paper, homemade preserves, jellies, and so on. This the English call *paraffin wax.* The term *paraffin* is also used in England for medicinal oils taken as laxatives, what in America are called *mineral oils.*

Coal oil is an old-fashioned American term for what is now usually called *kerosene* (*This lamp is especially designed for burning coal oil and similar substances*). But *kerosene* is now generally being displaced by *fuel oil,* very little oil being used any more for lighting but an increasing amount for heating.

ketchup. See **catchup.**

key (island or wharf). See **quay.**

kick. As a noun or a verb meaning a complaint or to complain (*You'll get a kick on that, you wait and see. Aw, they're always kicking about something. Who cares?*), *kick* is accepted spoken English. As a noun meaning a thrill (*I get a* *kick out of just watching that kid*), it is slang. So also is its meaning of stimulation in an alcoholic drink (*That home brew stuff had an awful kick in it*), or, as a verb, to be around (*He's been kicking around here for six months now, don't seem to want to go any place else*), or in the compound, to *kick in,* contribute (*Her lawyer kicked in with the necessary five hundred bucks*). *Kick off,* start (*The drive kicked off with a big rally in the square*), and *kickback,* to pay part of one's wages, fee, or receipts back surreptitiously (*Longshoremen were finding it tougher than ever to get jobs, even through kickbacks of pay, bottles of liquor and cigars*), are slang terms on the way to becoming accepted spoken English.

kill. The use of *kill* to mean to cancel a word, or a paragraph, or item (*Publisher Forsberg decided to kill the editorial page*) is standard in American usage. So also to let an automobile engine go dead (*He killed the engine right on the tracks*).

kill or cure is a cliché, sustained solely by inertia and alliteration.

kill the fatted calf. To *kill the fatted calf* in festal preparation, or the *goose that lays the golden eggs* in greedy folly, or *two birds with one stone* in thrift or efficiency is to be guilty of using very tedious phrases.

kin. Though *kin* is standard in the meaning of one's relatives collectively, kinsfolk, family relation or kinship (*You'll find our kin all through Kentucky. They're kin to us through the Pruitts around Olympian Springs*), it is archaic as a designation of a group of persons descended from a common ancestor (*We're all Adam's kin*) or a single kinsman (*He's no kin of mine*). The word is more widely used in the South, where the older feeling for family relationships is still retained, than in the North. See **kith and kin.**

kind of. The use of singulars and plurals in expressions involving *kind of* is complicated only in the sense that there are several constructions all of which are equally acceptable.

Kind of is singular. Traditionally, it is qualified by a singular, such as *this* and not *these,* and is followed by a singular verb. The noun following *kind of* may be either singular or plural. We may say *this kind of man is dangerous* or *this kind of men is dangerous.* Both constructions are formally correct but the second, with a plural noun before a singular verb, is not heard in the United States. We may also say *these kind of men are dangerous.* This use of a plural qualifier and a plural verb with the singular *kind of* is formally irregular, but it has a long history in literary English. It is used today by educated people and must therefore be recognized as standard English.

Kinds of is a plural and is used only in speaking of more than one kind. It is qualified by a plural, such as *these* and not *this,* and is followed by a plural verb. The noun following *kinds of* may be either singular or plural. We may say *these kinds of tree are easy to grow* or *these kinds of trees are easy to grow.* In the United States a plural noun is generally preferred after *kinds of,* but both forms are standard, literary English.

In every case, a following pronoun is singular if the verb is singular and plural if the verb is plural, as in *this kind of tree is nice if you like it* and *these kind of trees are nice if you like them.*

What has just been said covers everything that anyone needs to know about the use of singulars and plurals with *kind of.* But unfortunately, a great deal of confusion has grown up in recent years over the form *these kind of trees.* Before anyone changes his speech habits in regard to this, he should understand just what it is that is under attack.

About fifty years ago some eminent grammarians commented on the fact that *kind* was used in a way not possible for a word such as *group.* They said that, although grammatically incorrect, this irregular construction was acceptable spoken English, and gave as examples of it: *these kind of men have their uses* and *what kind of trees are those?* If a word like *group* was being used in these sentences we would say: *this group of men has its uses* and *what group of trees is that?* The grammarians were recommending as technically correct *this kind of men has its uses* and *what kind of trees is that?* They had no objection in the world to a plural noun after *kind of.* They themselves, in another context, speak of *a kind of compasses.*

All that can be said about this singular construction with a plural noun is that it is not used in the United States today. We do not use *kind* in exactly the same way that we use *group.* The recommended construction is so alien to our speech habits that American handbooks which condemn *these kind of trees are* do not mention the alternative *this kind of trees is.* They sometimes say that the only acceptable form is *trees of this kind are.* This is absurd. And it becomes even more absurd when applied to *what kind of trees are those?* Sometimes they suggest, or at least students conclude, that one should always say *these kinds of trees.* This is worse yet. *Kinds* should never be used unless more than one kind is meant.

To sum up, if only one kind is meant, *kind* may be used with a singular noun to suggest the type, as in *this kind of tree,* or with a plural noun to suggest the group, as in *these kind of trees* or *this kind of trees.* These kind of trees is idiomatic and literary English. *This kind of trees* is historically justifiable but seldom heard in the United States today.

The phrase *kind of a,* as in *this kind of a man,* is condemned by many grammarians. But it can be heard frequently in the speech of the best-educated people and is found in the works of some of our best writers, including William James.

Kind of is sometimes used to qualify an adjective or a verb, as in *it is kind of silly* and *he kind of hesitated.* This is almost universally condemned. But it too can be heard in the United States in all levels of speech, including the speech of those who condemn it. A sentence such as *I kind of had to leave* undoubtedly creates a bad impression. But this is due more to the speaker's excessive timidity than to his grammar.

kindling wood; matchwood. When an American wishes to say that something has been smashed into minute splinters, he may say that it has been reduced to *kindling wood* (*His calm verdict upon the struggle for the gold standard makes kindling wood of the Republican platform*). An Englishman will say *matchwood* (*Most of the ships that struck were broken up into matchwood*).

kindly; please. The use of *kindly* for *please* in such phrases as *kindly remit* has a touch of unctuousness about it that may defeat its intention of being elegant or ingratiating. The quality of kindness or sympathetic benevolence is not one that can be produced upon demand, especially upon the demand of a creditor. It may be argued that the same holds for pleasure, yet *please remit* is an established formula. So it is, but it is so thoroughly established that in this particular context there is no longer any thought of pleasure, any more than of affection in *Dear Sir.* It is simply a courteous formality and courteous formality is the proper manner in which to ask for something that is owed one. When in a desire to seem less coldly formal one employs words that have unsuitable connotations, one's meaning may be misunderstood. The unusual word may make the demand seem unusual and resentment is quick to seize on trifles to justify itself.

kindred spirits. As a term for those who are alike in natural dispositions and who share the same interests, *kindred spirits* is hackneyed.

King James Version. The version of the Bible, properly known as the Authorized Version, which was prepared at the command of King James I of England and first published in 1611 is often called the *King James Version* (or the *King James' Version*) and often miscalled the *Saint James Version.* The confusion may be abetted by the fact that the British court, to which our ambassador is accredited, is called the *Court of St. James* (which see).

kingly; regal; royal. That which is *kingly* may belong to a king or be fitting for or worthy of a king (*. . . what seemed his head/ The likeness of a kingly crown had on*). *Regal* applies to the office of kingship, to its outward manifestations of majesty and grandeur (*With them comes a third of regal port,/ But faded splendor wan. This exercise of regal authority proved to be immensely popular*). *Royal* is applied especially to what pertains to or is associated with the person of a monarch (*the royal bedchamber, the royal family*) or to that which is ideally like or characteristic of a king, noble, generous, munificent (*What a royal housekeeper his grandfather was, in what magnificent style he kept open house! A royal welcome*).

kith and kin is a cliché, one of those meaningless phrases kept current by alliteration. A fitting punishment for anyone who uses it would be to require him to use the word *kith* at once in some other context. The chances are overwhelming that he couldn't do it. The word meant originally those who are known to us, friends, fellow-countrymen, neighbors, acquaintances. It is related to the old word *couth,* known. In the stable societies of older times all of one's kin were probably kith, though not all who were kith were kin. When Middleton wrote, in 1620, *A maid that's neither kith nor kin to me,* he seems to have had the proper distinction in mind. But for well over a century the two words have been assumed to be synonymous. Burns wrote *My lady's white, my lady's red,/ And kith and kin o' Cassillis' blude,* though one cannot be kith of blood.

klang association is a term applied to the manner in which the meaning of many words is unconsciously affected by our hearing the sound of other words in them. Thus *fakir* (derived from an Arabic word meaning poor) suggests an impostor because it seems to contain *fake* (which is probably derived from a German word *fegen,* to sweep). People expect greyhounds to be gray, though the first syllable has nothing to do with color but is derived from a Norse word for *dog.* In England today *bug* is almost an indecent word and the American's frequent use of it greatly agitates his transatlantic cousin. Since it derives from the same root as *bogey,* it is a harmless word, but the English seem to connect it with *bugger,* sodomite (a corruption of *Bulgarian*); in America, on the other hand, *bugger* seems to have been decontaminated by its klang association with *bug* and mischievous little boys are affectionately called *little buggers* with no moral implication intended.

kneel. The past tense is *knelt* or *kneeled.* The participle is also *knelt* or *kneeled. Knelt* is the preferred form for the past tense and for the participle, but both forms are acceptable.

knees of the gods, on the. To say of something of which the outcome or future is wholly dependent upon chance, or at least of which we no longer have any control, that it is *on the knees of the gods* (or *in the lap of the gods*) is to employ a hackneyed phrase. The term, which is a translation of a phrase that occurs repeatedly in the *Iliad* and the *Odyssey,* originally carried the idea that since the matter had, whether of choice or necessity, been handed to the gods for solution or furtherance, it would be impious of man to attempt to do anything more about it.

knew. See **know.**

knickers; knickerbockers. The plural forms refer to one garment but are always treated as plurals, as in *these knickers are torn.* In order to use the word with a singular verb or to speak of more than one such garment, it is necessary to say *this pair of knickers is torn* or *several pairs of knickers.* The form *knickers* is also used as the first element in a compound, as in *his knickers pocket.*

knife. The plural is *knives*.

knit. The past tense is *knit* or *knitted.* The participle is also *knit* or *knitted*. For a long time *knitted* was used only as an adjective, as in *a knitted coat,* but it is now also used in verb forms. The form *knit* is always used when the word has a figurative sense, as in *she knit her brows,* but we may say *she knit a sweater* or *she knitted a sweater.*

knock has a number of colloquial and slang uses in the United States which are not current in England. Thus the making of harsh or ill-natured criticisms (*Don't knock, boost!*) or, when followed by *about,* to wander aimlessly (*I've knocked about a lot since I quit high school*) or, when followed by *down,* to get money illicitly, usually by embezzling from sums that pass through one's hands (*Those ticket sellers, they really knock down the dough!*).

A striking instance of the idiomatic pitfalls that await the uninstructed is the phrase *knocked up.* The expression is slang in both England and America, but has a totally different meaning in each country. In England the phrase has an old-fashioned meaning of to be awakened by knocking (*I say, if you're leaving early, knock me up, will you?*) and a modern slang meaning of to be tired out. In America it means to make pregnant or to have been made pregnant. A lady who announced in England after a gay evening that she was *completely knocked up* might create a minor ripple of sympathy. The same announcement in America would be sensational.

knot (nautical). A *knot,* as any exasperated seaman is eager to inform any pretentious and ignorant landlubber, is not a measure of distance but a unit of speed of one nautical mile per hour. [The nautical mile is officially fixed in the U. S. at 6,080.20 feet, in Great Britain at 6,080 feet, as against 5,280 feet in both countries for the land mile.] Thus it is wrong to speak of a ship's going so many knots an hour. She simply goes so many knots. Nor does she cover so many knots a day. She goes at so many knots and covers so many miles.

know. The past tense is *knew.* The participle is *known.* When *know* is used in an active form, in speaking of a present or future event it may be followed by a clause, as in *I know she lies,* or by *to be,* as in *I know her to be a liar,* but not by any other infinitive. When speaking of a past event it may be followed by a clause, as in *I know she lied,* or by an infinitive, as in *I have known her to lie.* It may also be followed by the simple form of a verb, as in *I have known her lie,* but the *to*-infinitive is preferred. When *know* is used in a passive form, it is followed by a *to*-infinitive, regardless of the time referred to, as in *she is known to lie* and *she has been known to lie.*

As a word for knowledge, the fact of knowing, *know*—now restricted almost entirely to the phrase *in the know*—is slang. *Know-how,* however, the knowledge of how to do something, faculty, or skill, is now standard in American usage. Some authors have insisted that a distinction must be made between knowing someone and merely having an acquaintance with him, but American usage will not support any such distinction. When someone is asked, *Do you know so-and-so?* he may answer *Only slightly* or *Very well* or make the degree of the acquaintance clear in any way that he chooses, but it does not occur to him that he is being asked if he knows the person in the same sense in which he might be asked if he knows a certain subject. To *know of* someone, however, means to know him only by name or reputation.

know; comprehend; understand. To *know* is to be aware of something as a fact (*I know I'm right. It was apparent that he had known of our plans all along. I know a bank whereon the wild thyme grows*). To *comprehend* is to know something thoroughly and at the same time to perceive its relationship to certain other facts and ideas (*He comprehends the full implication of the figures. A comprehension of the theory would require considerable knowledge of mathematics as well as biology*). To *understand* something is to be fully aware not only of its meaning but of its implications (*I comprehended all that he said, but I failed to understand why he was so upset*). See also **understand, I.**

know enough to come in out of the rain, not to. In a famous book of jests published in the 16th century and attributed to John Scogan, Edward IV's fool, there is a story of a sly fellow who sought to establish himself as a natural idiot by standing under an open downspout during a rainstorm. Apparently the proverb was current even then. By now it is a cliché, a once good, useful phrase worn out by repetition.

know from Adam, not to. As a way of saying that someone is so completely a stranger that even his appearance is unfamiliar, *not to know him from Adam* is a cliché. The original meaning seems to have been: Adam is the prototype of all men; I know that the person alluded to is a man, and I would recognize that much but nothing else. Wits have had great diversion over the possible absence of a navel in Adam as a distinguishing feature.

know the ropes. As a way of saying that someone is thoroughly familiar with a certain situation or procedure, to say that he *knows the ropes* is to employ a cliché.

The origin of the phrase is uncertain. Some say it is from boxing or wrestling, the skillful contestant knowing how best to utilize the protection or impetus of the ropes. But the phrase antedates the use of ropes to mark off the prize ring. It seems most natural that it should have been a nautical phrase, especially from the latter days of sailing vessels when the sails were controlled by a bewildering maze of ropes. But it is interesting that one of the earliest uses of the phrase, exactly where one would expect to find it, in Richard Henry Dana's *Two Years Before the Mast* (1840), argues against this because Dana carefully encloses it within quotation marks (*The captain, who . . . "knew the* ropes," *took the steering oar*) to suggest that he knew that he was using it out of its proper meaning. The oldest uses of the phrase refer to the racetrack, the *ropes* being the reins and those who *knew* them being the most successful jockeys.

known. See **know.**

Kodak; kodak. *Kodak* was a word coined by George Eastman as a trademark for his small box camera. The coinage was too successful; the public soon called many other cameras *kodaks* (*Some of the rest took kodaks with us*) and even used *to kodak* as a verb for to photograph. Competitors have finally managed, however, to make the public aware of brand names for other cameras and *kodak* is not used much any more as a generic term, though *Kodak* remains an Eastman trademark.

kudos. The use of the Greek word *kudos,* meaning praise or renown, for glory, fame, honor, even when restricted to the rather pale and limited glory, fame, and honor of an honorary degree, is an academic affectation. Neither those who confer nor those who receive honorary degrees are so steeped in Greek any more that it comes more naturally to them than English. It was originally a piece of university slang, with a touch of contempt in it (*Lauded in pious Latin to the skies;/ Kudos'd egregiously in heathen Greek*).

L

labor of love. As a term for something which is done solely with the desire to please another, not from hope of gain, *a labor of love* (taken from the Bible) is weakened by overuse.

laconic. See **reticent.**

lady. See **woman.**

ladybug; ladybird. The beetles of the family *Coccinellidae,* known in England as *ladybirds,* are in America most commonly called *ladybugs,* though *ladybird* is known to the educated. They are also sometimes called *lady beetles.*

The first element of the word is a linguistic curiosity, being the ancient uninflected possessive case. It is (*Our*) *lady('s*) *bird* or *bug* or *beetle,* the insect being associated with the Virgin Mary or Heaven in many European languages. For centuries children have besought the creature to fly away home since its house is on fire and its children in various conditions of distress and disaster. *The Oxford Dictionary of Nursery Rimes* says that the meaning of the rime is unknown but that it is "undoubtedly a relic of something once possessed of an awful significance."

laid. See **lay.**

lain. See **lie.**

lama; llama. A *lama* is a priest or monk of the form of Buddhism prevailing in Tibet and Mongolia. A *llama* is a woolly-haired South American ruminant used as a beast of burden and valuable for its fleece.

lament. See **regret.**

lampoon. See **burlesque.**

land flowing with milk and honey. Originally a Biblical term, a poetic epithet for the natural richness of Palestine, *a land flowing with milk and honey* was so overworked by preachers in the nineteenth century that it became a humorous phrase. But repetition has destroyed the humor as it formerly destroyed the solemnity and poetry and the phrase is now merely a husk.

landslide. The sliding down of a mass of soil, detritus, or rock on a steep slope is in the United States called a *landslide* (*Heavy rains often precipitate landslides where the new roads have been cut through the mountains*). In England it is called a *landslip.*

The word is used figuratively in the United States as a political term to describe an election in which a particular candidate or party receives an overwhelming mass or majority of votes (*The presidential election of 1936 was a Democratic landslide*).

language. See **vernacular.**

languor. See **lassitude.**

lap of luxury. As a term for wealth or affluence, *the lap of luxury,* whether one is cradled in it, reared in it, or just living in it, is hackneyed.

lap of the gods. See **knees of the gods.**

lapse. See **elapse.**

larboard. See **port.**

large and **great** are interchangeable in some but not all of their senses. Either may be used to designate dimensions which are unusually extensive. We may speak of a great house or a great body of water or a large house or a large body of water. We may speak of a great number of people or a large number of people.

Large is the less formal term and therefore to be preferred for general use. Only *great* can be used to indicate distinction. A great man or a great painting is something quite different from a large man or a large painting. *Great* also indicates something unusual or considerable in degree (*The birth of the baby brought them great joy*). *Great* is the correct adjective to accompany words like breadth, depth, distance, height, and length. In a large room, the distance from one end to the other is *great.*

largely; chiefly. The adverbs *largely* and *chiefly* suggest different degrees of importance. *Largely* is less emphatic, meaning to a great extent, in great part (*Admiral Collingwood was largely responsible for some of the fleets being wrecked after the victory at Trafalgar*). *Chiefly* means principally, above all (*Nelson was chiefly responsible for the plan of battle*).

large-scale. No one has any quarrel with *large-scale* in its restricted and original sense of drawn to a large scale (*a large-scale map*), but English authors refuse to accept it in the common American use of extensive or of large scope (*The directors decided on a large-scale reorganization of the company*). The term which is used widely in business, especially in relation to reorganizations, promotions, production schedules, advertising campaigns, and other activities where optimism and "vision" are required, seems to mean not that plans and so on will be drawn to a large scale but that in the scale of accomplishment they will be comparatively large.

lark. The word *lark* used alone means in England the skylark (*Alauda arvensis*) and in America the meadow lark (*Sturnella magna* and *Sturnella neglecta* of the family *Icteridae*). The two birds are unlike in appearance, habits, and song and the raptures of the English poets gain a fuller meaning for the American when he first hears the bird that has moved so many of them to ecstasy.

The practice of the early colonists of bestowing the names of English birds on the strange species of the New World, while natural and even touching, has led to considerable confusion. The American robin, for example, is properly a thrush, and the American buzzard is plainly a vulture.

lassitude; languor. As a term for weariness of body or mind, *lassitude* seems to suffer from the very condition it denotes. It is a weak word, slightly affected and bookish. Chapman says of Odysseus, when he collapsed on the bench at Phaeacia after shipwreck and days in the ocean, *the sea had soaked his heart through*. Pope says that the hero lay *lost in lassitude*. This was the passage that moved Keats to his famous sonnet and contemporary taste is definitely with Keats.

Languor and *lassitude* are often interchangeable, but generally *languor* is the milder word of the two, ranging from fatigue (*I nearly sank to the ground through languor and extreme weakness*) through want of energy (*She quickly forgot her languor at the good news. That stick over which his tall person swayed with fashionable languor*) to a tenderness or softness, often amorous (*The lilies and languors of virtue*).

last; latest. These words are both superlative forms of the same word, *late*, but *last* has a much broader meaning than *latest*. In present-day English, only the form *latest* can be used in speaking about lateness. But in other senses the two words may overlap. Both may be used in speaking of the final member in a series of events. But *last* is not restricted to time and may be used in speaking of any things that are in a sequence, as in *the last house on the left*. *Last* is also used in contrast to *next*, to mean the immediately preceding, as in *last summer, last*

Christmas. Where the two words can be used interchangeably, *last* may carry a suggestion of finality that is not in *latest*, as in *I hope his latest book will not be his last*.

Both words may be used as adjectives, as in *the latest train* and *the last train*. Both may be used as adverbs in some constructions, as in *he studied latest* and *he read the paper last*. But *latest* cannot be used as an adverb immediately before a verb. In this position only the form *last* is used and here it does not carry any sense of finality, as in *when I last saw him*.

In current English the adverbial form *lastly* is used only to mark the last point in a discourse.

When *last* is used with a cardinal number, it may either follow or precede the cardinal. Until the seventeenth century it usually followed the cardinal, as in *the two last*. Coleridge wrote, *the fifty or sixty last years of her life*. In current English *last* usually precedes a cardinal, as in *the last two*, except when it is being used in the sense of "the last-mentioned."

In expressions of time, *last* is used without the article *the*, as in *last night, last Tuesday*.

last but not least—one more cliché to which we are led by alliteration's lilt and lure.

last gasp. Whether a man is breathing his *last gasp* or on his *last legs* or collapsing under the weight of or revolting against the imposition of *the last straw*—all the terms are clichés.

late. The comparative forms are *later* and *latter*. The superlative forms are *latest, last, lattermost*.

Late originally meant slow. The earliest meaning of the word that survives today is "behind time," as in *the child was late for school*. In the earliest records *late* also has the meaning of far along in the day or after the usual hour for going to bed, as in *it was already late and we keep late hours*. In both of these senses one can see some relation to the idea of slow. But eventually the idea of far along in the day was extended to far along in any period, as in *the late summer, the late Roman Empire*. Here the idea of slow has been lost. *Late* also acquired the almost unrelated meaning of belonging to the recent past.

Today *late* may be used as an adjective and as an adverb in all four senses. In the first sense of behind time, it is not often used as an adjective qualifying a following noun, but it may be. We may say *the late child*, but as a rule we don't. In the last sense of belonging to the recent past, *late* may be used as an adverb, as in *I sent thee late a rosy wreath*, but this is now considered extremely bookish and the adverb *lately* is preferred. In the other two senses *late* is used freely as an adjective and as an adverb. We speak of *late suppers* and say *they stayed late*. We speak of *the late empire* and say *found as late as Constantine*. The adverb *lately* can be used only in the fourth sense, of recently.

Latter is the older of the two comparative forms. But after *late* had taken on so many senses a new comparative *later* appeared with the limited meaning of after in time. It is both an adjective and an adverb. We may say *at a later time* or *he later told me*. *Latter* now means the part nearer the end, as in *his latter life,* or the more recent. It is no longer used in a comparison with *than.* Its chief function is as a contrast to *former.* The contrast implies that some group has been separated into two parts, but more than two elements may be involved. We may say *the three latter events. Latter* is never used as an adverb. For both meanings of this word we have the distinct adverbial form *latterly.*

Of the superlative forms, *latest* is the superlative of *later.* It appeared when *later* did and means after all others in time. It may be used as an adjective or as an adverb, as in *the latest book* and *he stayed latest.* The word *lattermost* first appeared in the nineteenth century and has never been widely used. It is specifically the superlative of *latter* in its present-day senses and means nearest the end or the most recent. It is used only as an adjective, as in *the lattermost day. Last* is the old superlative of *late.* It is still used in the senses covered by *lattermost* and in some of the senses covered by *latest.* It is both an adjective and an adverb, as in *the last man* and *when last we met.* See **last; latest.**

late; belated. Both *late* and *belated* are adjectives which mean being after the usual or proper time. *Late* is the general term to describe this circumstance without commenting on its desirability or undesirability (*We saw the late edition of the newspaper*). *Belated,* however, connotes an undesirable delay or one that is blamable (*He offered a belated apology for his misconduct*).

late in the day when used literally (*Three o'clock is just too late in the day for lunch*) is a useful, sensible, standard phrase that can never be worn out so long as there is a proper occasion for it. Used metaphorically, however (*1813 was pretty late in the day for Napoleon to be talking about Europe's need for peace*), it is a cliché.

latex. The plural is *latexes* or *latices.*

latitude. See **breadth.**

latter; lattermost. See **late.**

laud. *To laud* for to praise is either a cliché (*lauded to the skies*) or a bookish term that sounds a little affected in ordinary speech.

laudable; laudatory. That is *laudable* which is worthy of being praised (*His desire to pay off his father's debts was laudable*). That is *laudatory* which expresses praise (*He spoke in the most laudatory terms of your loyalty and ability*).

laughable. See **funny.**

laugh in (or **up**) **one's sleeve.** Derisive laughter seems to have been concealed in various ways at various times and places. The French used to laugh in their capes and the Spaniards in their beards. The English took to laughing in their sleeves early in the sixteenth century when sleeves were large and flowing, capable of concealing immense amounts of mirth. But to laugh in one's sleeve today would be awkward and obvious and the phrase is a cliché.

laugh to scorn. Whether one makes one's enemies *laugh on the wrong side of their mouths* or *laughs them to scorn* or *laughs them out of court,* or whether the whole procedure is *no laughing*

matter, and even though one has *the last laugh,* all the terms employed are clichés.

laundry; launder. Articles of clothing to be washed and ironed are *laundry* and the place in which they are washed and ironed is a *laundry.* The verb is *to launder,* not *to laundry.* Clothes are *laundered,* not *laundried.* The process as a whole is *laundering.* It used to be *laundry* (*Chalky water is too fretting as it appeareth in laundry of clothes, which wear out apace if you use such water*—1626), but the adoption of the *-ing* form has simplified at least that much of this so-often-confusing word.

laurel. The word *laurel* in England designates a small lauraceous evergreen tree, *Laurus nobilis,* sometimes called *true laurel.* In America the word is applied to a number of trees and shrubs that in one way or another resemble the true laurel, as *Kalmia latifolia* (*mountain laurel*) or *Rhododendron maximum* (the great rhododendron or *great laurel*). Cecil Sharp (quoted by Horwill) found that the Laurel Country, as it is called, of North Carolina derived its name from the rhododendrons which grow there. There was some *true laurel,* but this was called *ivy,* while the ivy was called *vine.*

lavish; prodigal; profuse. All three of these words mean unstinted, extravagant. They refer to that which exists abundantly and is poured out copiously. One may be extravagant with little; but it takes a great deal to be lavish, prodigal, or profuse.

Profuse is the weakest of the three. It suggests abundance (*profuse strains of unpremeditated art*) but it also suggests exaggeration, over-demonstration of feelings, etc. (*profuse apologies, profuse thanks, profuse protestations of undying affection*). *Lavish* is stronger than *profuse.* It suggests excessive display or generosity on a grand scale (*Such lavish hospitality soon reduced one of the greatest fortunes of the day to no more than a competence*). *Prodigal* suggests wastefulness and improvidence, and again on a large scale. It commonly refers to habits or character and, by inescapable association with the prodigal son of Luke 15:11-32, suggests immorality and ruinous indulgence (*Bankrupt of life, yet Prodigal of ease ... The chariest maid is prodigal enough/ If she unmask her beauty to the moon. These prodigal excesses will furnish material for a thousand sermons that will delight the staid and frugal*).

lawful. See **legal.**

lawyer. See **attorney.**

lay. The past tense is *laid.* The participle is also *laid.* This verb means cause to lie. It therefore implies both an object and an agent. But it does not follow that both have to be mentioned every time the verb is used. According to the strictest rules of English, there are two situations in which one or the other may be omitted.

1. Formerly, the object of *lay* was often a pronoun referring back to the subject of the verb, the agent, as in *now I lay me down to sleep.* As these reflexive pronouns began to be dropped, they were still understood and it was

proper to say *I will lay down for a nap,* meaning *I will lay me down.* Later, grammarians who were more impressed by logic than by facts insisted that since the verb had no object in this construction, it was necessary to use *lie,* as in *I will lie down for a nap.* As so often happens when children are taught grammatical rules that run counter to the established idiom, the result was simply confusion. The children could not say *lie*—because that was not what their respected elders said—and they were afraid to say *lay.* The result was a kind of panic, in which they were sure that whatever they said would be wrong. In current English, *lie* is used more often than *lay* in these constructions where the object would be a reflexive pronoun, and many people consider *lay* undesirable here. But many other people still use *lay.* This may show that the speaker is depending on his grandmother more than on his teachers. Or it may show that his speech habits have been formed by reading English literature.

(In some parts of the United States people speak of *laying up* for a nap, rather than *laying down.* This is not the standard idiom, but it carries a vivid suggestion of old-fashioned high beds. In all parts of the country we say *laid up with a cold* and not *laid down,* regardless of the height of the bed.)

2. When the verb in a sentence is passive the thing acted on becomes the grammatical subject and is always mentioned, but the agent may be ignored. In many English verbs the active form may be used with a passive sense, as in *the door shut, the room filled, the car drives easily.* (See **passive voice** and **transitive verbs.**) This has always been true for *lay.* People have always said *the book is laying on the table* and *let it lay,* just as they say *the water is spilling* and *let it spill.* Some grammarians claim that *lie* is required here, on the grounds that the verb does not have an object. This is an overstatement. *Lie* may be used here, but it is not required.

To sum up. The verb *lay,* with its past tense and participle *laid,* is almost impossible to misuse. It is required in a statement that has both a subject and an object. It is defensible in a statement that has only a subject, provided (1) the understood object is identical with the subject, as in *he lays on the floor,* or (2) the verb is understood in a passive sense, as in *it is laying on the table.* But *lie* may also be used provided the object is not mentioned. We may say *he lies on the floor* and *it is lying on the table.* Both verbs, *lay* and *lie,* are correct so far as theoretical grammar is concerned. The preferred form is the one heard most often in your own community. There is a tendency in present-day English to prefer the verb *lay* in speaking of inanimate objects, and the verb *lie* in speaking of living creatures.

The verb that is apt to be misused is *lie.* Its past tense *lay* and its participle *lain* are often heard with an object, as in *he lay it down* and *he has lain it down.* The strict rules of grammar call for *laid* in these sentences because the object

is mentioned. But some people seem to think that *laid* is wrong under any circumstances. As a result, the technically incorrect forms are used too often to be called unacceptable. That is, they do not suggest a backwoods or uneducated person. But they do suggest a timid person who has tried too hard to please.

English has a number of idioms involving *lay* in which an object is understood but not expressed. For example, *to lay about* means to lay blows about, and *to lay for* originally meant to lay an ambush for. This use of *lay* occurs in many nautical expressions where the course or the ship is understood as object.

The words *lay* and *lie* may also be used as nouns with the same sense they have in the verbs, and either form may be used. *The lie of the land* is a British expression. In the United States the same thing is called *the lay of the land.*

lay it on with a trowel. To say of someone who is flattering another grossly that he is *laying it on with a trowel* was once to employ an effective metaphor. The facts that this is a trade or livelihood for the person doing it and that in the act he is building some edifice of his own, that the material laid on is sloppy and the gesture of laying it on mechanical and habitual, all heighten the effect of the figure. But after three hundred years of steady use and a hundred of overuse, it is worn out.

lay on, Macduff!—usually spoken with a hearty guffaw and immense self-approval by the speaker at the range of his own literary knowledge and the felicity of its application—must be among the most hackneyed of quotations, one whose repetition transgresses boredom into humiliation. *First Henry the Fourth,* I, ii, 101, offers a fitting rejoinder: "O, thou hast damnable iteration."

lay one's cards on the table. As a term for frankly stating one's intentions, admitting one's weaknesses or showing one's resources, *to lay one's cards on the table* is a cliché.

lazy; idle; indolent; slothful. All of these words apply to one who is inactive, but they carry different degrees of moral reproach. *Idle* may imply no reproach at all; one may be relaxing temporarily or inactive through necessity (*In idle moments he rested his eyes. The shutdown at the boxboard plant kept the men idle all the winter*). Or it may be mildly derogatory (*I don't like all those idle boys hanging around the drugstore corner*).

Lazy, though it too can be a neutral word (*Oh, I feel so gloriously lazy. We spent a lazy afternoon on the beach*), is usually derogatory, describing a sluggishness, an aversion to work, especially to continued application (*That lazy, good-for-nothing lout! I've told him a dozen times to put the tools away when he's done. All, with united force, combine to drive/ The lazy drones from the laborious hive*). The verb *to lazy* (*So we would put in the day, lazying around, listening to the stillness*) is usually favorable and at its worst not strongly condemnatory. A special American use of the word *lazy,* with no derogatory implication at all, is its designation of a livestock brand which is placed on its side instead of upright (*Things were pretty quiet at the U Lazy D ranch when Curly dismounted*).

An *indolent* person (the word has the rather charming literal meaning of free from pain) is one who shows a natural disposition to avoid exertion and indulge in ease. Because in our civilization exertion is considered a good thing, the term is derogatory (*An indolent man makes a poor husband*).

Slothful is the most derogatory term of the four. It denotes a reprehensible unwillingness to do such work as one should (*Such a slothful person is bound to be a burden to society*). Sloth is the fourth of the Seven Deadly Sins, more serious than gluttony, avarice, or lechery. Whether we are becoming more energetic or more forbearing, *slothful* is not often used today.

lea; lee; lees. A *lea* is a tract of arable land under grass. Though still used in England in certain dialects and in a great many place names, it is not used at all in the United States, though it is recognized in the older poets (*So might I, standing on this pleasant lea,/ Have glimpses that would make me less forlorn. Now dance the lights on lawn and lea*). From a completely different derivation, *lea* also means a measure of yarn of varying quantity—for wool, usually 80 yards; for cotton and silk, 120 yards; for linen, 300 yards.

A *lee* is a sheltered place out of the wind (*In Iceland a weatherwise soldier takes advantage of every available lee*). The word is perhaps most familiar in the sense, chiefly nautical, of the region or quarter toward which the wind blows. This sense may be used adjectivally (*He headed for the lee shore*). Finally *lee,* derived from a different word, means that which settles from a liquid, especially from wine. It is usually plural and is roughly synonymous with dregs (*In decanting wine one should be careful to disturb the lees as little as possible. I will drink life to the lees*).

lead. The past tense is *led.* The participle is also *led. Lead* may be followed by an infinitive, as in *this led him to believe.* It is also heard with the *-ing* form of a verb and the preposition *to,* as in *this led him to believing.* This construction is not literary English but it is heard too often in the United States to be considered anything but standard.

leading question. A question thought to be unfair (*Have you stopped beating your wife?*) is often miscalled *a leading question.* But a leading question is simply a question so worded as to suggest the proper or desired answer. It is designed not to embarrass the person questioned but to help him. It is unfair only by legal definition; it is the type of question counsel may not ask in examining a witness whom he has called to the stand, since it is, in effect, a form of prompting. But an unfair question, a question so worded that any answer will reflect unfavorably on the person answering is not a *leading question* but a *misleading question.*

leaf. The plural is *leaves.*

lean. The past tense is *leaned* or *leant.* The participle is also *leaned* or *leant. Leaned* is the preferred form for both the past tense and the participle. *Leant* is heard in Great Britain more often than it is in the United States.

leap. The past tense is *leaped* or *leapt.* The participle is also *leaped* or *leapt.* In the United States, *leaped* is the preferred form for the past tense and the participle. Both forms are used in Great Britain, but *leapt* (pronounced *lĕpt*) is preferred.

leaps and bounds. *By leaps and bounds,* as a term for rapid progress, is a cliché. Repetition has drained all the original vigor from it and it should be avoided.

learn. The past tense is *learned* or *learnt.* The participle is also *learned* or *learnt.*

learn; teach. To *learn* is to acquire knowledge. To *teach* is to impart knowledge. The use of *learn* for *teach* (as in *That'll learn you to look where you're going next time*) is not standard and is usually labelled as "vulgar" by the authorities. That is not as severe a condemnation in linguistics as in morals. Indeed, by some linguistic standards it might be regarded as praise. And certainly a usage which has been employed by Wycliffe, Coverdale, Caxton, Spenser, Shakespeare, Fuller, Bunyan, Defoe, Richardson, Coleridge, Disraeli and several million other people during the past six hundred years cannot, by contemporary linguistic standards, be simply dismissed as an error. *And that should learn us,* as Hamlet said, *There's a divinity that shapes our ends, Rough-hew them how we will.*

learnt. See **learn.**

least. See **little.**

leastways; leastwise. *Leastwise* is literary English, but it is seldom heard in the United States. *Leastways* is heard more often but is not standard.

leave (noun). See **permission.**

leave. The past tense is *left.* The participle is also *left.* The primary meaning of *leave* is go away from, but it may also mean abandon or not interfere with and is sometimes used as the equivalent of *let,* as in *you may stay with me as long as you leave me alone.* This is standard English. Any form of the verb *leave,* such as *left,* or *leaving,* may be used in this way, provided it is followed immediately by an object and the word *alone.* In any other construction, *leave* used in the sense of *let* is unacceptable.

Leave may be followed by a *to*-infinitive, as in *I left her to find out for herself,* or by the *-ing* form of a verb introduced by *off,* as in *he left off speaking.* Let, on the other hand, cannot be followed by a *to*-infinitive or an *-ing* form. It must be followed by the simple form of a verb, as in *I let her find out for herself.* In present-day English, *leave* cannot be followed by the simple form of a verb, as it is in *leave me be, leave me do it, leave go of it.* Fifty years ago these forms were acceptable spoken English in the United States and they are found in the writings of Thackeray, the Brontës, R. L. Stevenson. But the construction is now old-fashioned. As a matter of fact, it is heard chiefly in the speech of educated people who consider it amusing to say *leave us go* and *leave us not. Leave alone* is also unacceptable when used in place of the idiomatic *let alone* to mean "not to mention," as in *I couldn't get a girl, leave alone a woman, to help me.*

The word *leave* may be used as a noun to mean departure or leave of absence. In literary English the one form *leave* is used in speaking of one person or of several, as in *they took their leave, they were all given leave.* A plural form *leaves* is sometimes used in the army. (For *I had as leave,* see **lief.**)

leave no stone unturned. When Polycrates asked the Delphian oracle how he should go about finding a treasure presumably buried by Mardonius, one of Xerxes' generals, on the field of Plataea (479 B.C.), the oracle answered, "Move every stone." Since the battle covered a great deal of rocky terrain, the phrase became a proverb for immense and thorough industry. It achieved its present form in English in the early sixteenth century and is now a cliché. Like many clichés, however, it has a certain value, especially for the witty, in the fact that it is a cliché, that one can count on its being known to everyone. Thus when Ogden Nash says that when he throws rocks at seabirds he leaves no tern unstoned, the joke is posited on the cliché.

leave strictly (severely) alone. The injunction to leave something or someone severely or strictly alone must be regarded as a cliché. The meaning seems to be in an ellipsis: leave it alone in strict or severe conformity to the instructions given.

leaves. This is the plural of *leaf.*

leaves much to be desired is a trite and tedious way of saying *unsatisfactory.*

led. See **lead.**

lee. See **lea.**

lees. This word, meaning dregs, once had a singular form, as in *the gross lees settle quickly and also the flying lee in time.* Shakespeare uses the plural form with a singular verb in *the wine of life is drawn and the mere lees is left.* Neither of these constructions is standard today. *Lees* is now treated as a mass word with a plural form. It is always followed by a plural verb, as in *the lees are bitter,* but we do not speak of *a lee* or of *several lees.*

left. See **leave.**

left-handed compliment. Most of the age-old, sinister (*sinister* means left) associations and connotations of left-handedness have disappeared and the phrase *a left-handed compliment,* an ambiguous compliment which on reflection turns out to be an insult, is now a cliché.

left in the lurch. Lurch was a game resembling backgammon, played in the sixteenth century. When one incurred a lurch he had scored nothing or was so far behind his opponent as to be helpless. Hence the figurative meaning of leaving someone in a helpless plight. But all awareness of the original meaning has faded and *to leave someone in the lurch* is now a hackneyed phrase.

There was an older form of the expression, to leave someone *in the lash.* But even linguists have been unable to discover its original meaning.

legal; lawful; licit. That is *legal* which conforms to the prescriptions of authority, especially those of a sovereign or state (*There are many things which are legal which a man of strict honor would not do*). That is *lawful* which is permitted by law or recognized or sanctioned by law (*lawful marriage, lawful heirs*). It is synonymous with *legal* (*legal rights, lawful rights*), though in this sense it is now slightly archaic, but it has more figurative uses than *legal* which is exact and restricted. *Legal* always means in conformity to human law; *lawful* is often used to mean in conformity with moral and religious precepts.

Licit means legal. It is not often used except in the phrase *licit or illicit* in reference to business transactions. See also **illegal.**

legionary; legionnaire. A member of the American Legion, an organization of military veterans, is called a *legionnaire.* A member of the British Legion, the corresponding organization in England, is called a *legionary.* A member of a Roman legion or of the French Foreign Legion is in England called a *legionary* (though some English when referring to the French soldier call him by the French term, *legionnaire,* and Thomas Hardy calls a member of a Roman legion a *legionnaire*). In America, except among the learned who might employ *legionary* to designate a Roman soldier, *legionnaire* is used at all times.

legislator; legislature. A *legislator* is one who gives or makes laws. A *legislature,* made up of legislators, is the legislative, law-making body of a country or state.

legitimate drama (stage, theater). *The Oxford English Dictionary* defines *legitimate drama* as the body of plays, Shakespearian and other, that have a recognized theatrical and literary merit —as opposed, for example, to farce and melodrama. In the United States (where it is often shortened to *legitimate* and in slang *legit*), *legitimate drama* has widened and shifted its sense to mean any drama, including farce and melodrama, produced on the stage—as opposed to that which is presented in motion pictures, on radio or television (*Mrs. Carter, with no legitimate vehicle in sight, has accepted a part in a radio serial. I was in legitimate at the old Alcazar*).

leg to stand on, not a. As a term for having no logical or factual basis, *not a leg to stand on* is a cliché.

leitmotif. See **motive.**

lemma. The plural is *lemmas* or *lemmata,* not *lemmae.*

lend. The past tense is *lent*. The participle is also *lent*.

lend an ear, to. Whether one means simply to listen or to listen with sympathetic interest, *to lend an ear* is a cliché.

lengthways; lengthwise. These forms are equally acceptable.

lengthy; long. *Long* is the everyday serviceable word to describe that which is not short. *Lengthy* is largely restricted to speeches and writings and carries the reproachful suggestion that they are longer than they need be (*The lengthy proceedings had disgusted the nation which had hoped for a speedy decision favorable to the plaintiff*). Before the nineteenth century, by the way, *lengthy* was used only in America and was condemned by many British writers as an Americanism, but by the end of the nineteenth century the British had adopted it.

lent. See **lend.**

less; lesser. These words are both comparative forms of the word *little*. *Lesser* is a double comparative made from the comparative form *less* and is grammatically equivalent to *more smaller*. It first appeared around 1450. By 1600 it was standard English and was used in the King James Bible, as in *the greater light to rule the day and the lesser light to rule the night*. During the eighteenth century Dr. Johnson, and a great many others after him, condemned the form as pleonastic. But it has survived and today is considered a more "literary" word than *less*.

Lesser is now used as the comparative of *little* in the sense of smaller in value or importance, as in *the lesser poets*. It may be used in comparing things that differ only in size, as in *the lesser circle, the lesser distance,* but it cannot be used alone to mean smaller in size as the word *littler* can. We cannot say *the lesser child*. Similarly, it may be used in comparing things that differ only in amount, as in *the lesser sum, the lesser weight,* but it cannot be used to mean smaller in amount. We cannot speak of *lesser money* or *lesser sugar. Lesser* is always an adjective. It may be used before a singular or a plural noun, as in *a lesser man, lesser men,* or without a noun when a comparison is implied, as in *the lesser of the two* and *which is the lesser*. It cannot be used in any other construction.

When *less* is used as an adjective it means smaller in amount and we can speak of *less money, less sugar*. It may be used in this sense to qualify words that themselves show size, value, or importance, as in *less length, less value, less importance,* but in itself it always refers to the amount. *Less* can be used in any way that an adjective can be used. It can be used as a predicate adjective without the article *the,* as in *which is less?* It may be used after a noun, with the force of *minus,* as in *ten less two. Less* may also be used as if it were a noun, as in *the less said the better. The less* may stand before another noun and mean *the less of*. This is not true of *lesser*.

Less may also be used as an adverb and mean to a smaller degree or in a smaller amount. It may qualify a verb, as in *he complains less,* or an adjective, as in *it is less expensive,* or another adverb, as in *he moves less quickly*. It may be used with the word *than,* as in *it is less than I expected* and *he is less a fool than I thought*. The adjective *lesser* cannot be used in any of these ways.

When the word *little* means small in amount it is a singular and qualifies only singular nouns, as in *we had little trouble*. When used with a plural noun it loses this meaning and refers to size or significance, as in *we had little troubles*. Many grammarians claim that *less,* being the comparative of *little* in this sense, cannot be used to qualify a plural noun, as in *less men, less complaints*. They say that the word *fewer* is required here. Some go so far as to say that *less* should never be treated as a plural, even when it is used with *than* and not with a plural noun, as in *less than twenty were invited*. They claim that we must say *less than twenty was* or *fewer than twenty were*. At one time *less* was used freely as a plural. So there is no question here of logic or tradition. It is simply a question of present-day usage. And there is no doubt that *less than* is treated as a plural in standard English today. *Less* before a plural noun, as in *less men,* is not as widely accepted. A great many people object to it. But a great many others, whose education and position cannot be questioned, see nothing wrong in it. In the United States a college president might speak of *less men* or *less courses*.

lessee; lessor. A *lessee* is one to whom a lease is granted. A *lessor* is one who grants a lease (*The lessor often requires a large deposit to prevent the lessee from breaking the lease and moving to less expensive accommodations*).

lest. This is a conjunction and indicates that the following words express something that the speaker does not want to see happen. It may have the force of "in order that – – not," as in *be with us yet, lest we forget*. It may also be used to introduce a clause explaining fear or doubt. In the United States, *lest* is always followed by a subjunctive verb, as in *they were in a panic lest they be overtaken by the police* or *they were in a panic lest the maid leave*. But the word itself is considered bookish and *that* followed by a subjunctive substitute, such as *would* or *should,* is generally preferred.

let. The past tense is *let*. The participle is also *let*. This word, which now means allow, once meant prevent, and still means that in the expression *without let or hindrance*. At one period *let* had both meanings at the same time, which must have been confusing.

When used in its ordinary sense of allow, *let* must be followed by the simple form of a verb, as in *let me go, let me do it. Let* is never followed by a *to*-infinitive, even when it is used as a passive, as in *the grass was let grow* and *I was let know*. As a rule we avoid this passive *let* and find some other word to use, as in *the grass was allowed to grow* and *I was informed*.

Let is used in a number of idiomatic expressions that are difficult to explain but which are nevertheless standard English. *Let alone* may mean "not to mention," as in *he had never owned a white mouse, let alone a white elephant.* When an object stands between *let* and *alone,* as in *let the cat alone,* the compound means "stop annoying." The expression *let go of* is impossible to analyze grammatically, but it is standard English for "take your hand off."

Let is also used to form a peculiar imperative that includes the speaker along with the person addressed, as in *let us be true to one another.* This is sometimes called the first person plural imperative. In spoken English this *let us* is usually contracted to *let's,* as in *let's wash the dishes.* The uncontracted form *let us* is always used when *let* is a regular imperative followed by *us,* that is, when *let us wash the dishes* means "allow us to" and is addressed to somebody not included in the "us." This is a valuable distinction that is made in speech but very often lost in print, largely because of the mistaken notion that contractions are undignified.

When *let* is used as a regular imperative it cannot be followed by a subjective pronoun. That is, we say *let John and me wash the dishes* and not *let John and I wash them.* According to the theoretical rules of grammar, the same thing holds true for the peculiar imperative with *let's.* The contracted *us* is an objective pronoun and presumably should be repeated by the objective *me,* and not the subjective *I,* in a sentence such as *let's you and me wash the dishes.* But in actual practice, the subjective *I,* as in *let's you and I wash the dishes,* is preferred by many people, including some of our best writers. This could be defended, academically, on the grounds that *let's* is here merely a sign of the imperative, that the true imperative is *wash,* and *you and I* its subject. In any case, *let's you and I* is heard too often not to be called standard. *Let's you and me* is preferred by purists, but both forms are acceptable.

Us is sometimes used after *let's,* as in *let's us try it out.* This construction is not often seen in print and is condemned by many grammarians as redundant, although it is hard to see why *us* is any more redundant than *you and me.*

let the cat out of the bag. As a term for disclosing a secret, usually inadvertently, *to let the cat out of the bag* is hackneyed. The origin of the phrase is uncertain. Some think it may refer to revealing the fact that a cat had been substituted for a pig in a sack (*pig in a poke*), but this is not established.

liable. In Great Britain *liable* means subject to or exposed to some undesirable change or action, as in *the adventure is liable to end sadly* and *some of the colors are liable to fade.* Lord Chesterfield wrote in 1749: *You know, I suppose, that liable can never be used in a good sense.* But in older English it was used at least in an indifferent sense and meant subject to any kind of action, good or bad. This usage survives in the United States and an American might say *we are liable to be in Chicago next week* without meaning that that would be a calamity. *Liable* also has the legal meaning of bound by law or legally answerable for.

Americans who see no reason to question their own speech habits often use *liable* in the sense of *likely.* This is true of many public officials and highly respected citizens. Anyone who wants to use the word in this way is in good company. But on the other hand, a great many people know that there is some question about this word, without knowing what the question is. These people are likely to think that *liable* is not standard, even when it is used in the purest British manner. Anyone who wants to avoid giving offense in any quarter will have to avoid the word entirely, except in its purely legal uses.

liaison; alliance. In military terminology *liaison* is the contact maintained between units in order to ensure concerted action. In cookery *liaison* is a thickening for soups, gravies, and so on. In phonetics it means the running together of words in their pronunciation. In personal relationships it describes an illicit intimacy between a man and a woman (*He [Byron] has a permanent sort of liaison with Contessa Guiccioli*). These are the accepted meanings of *liaison.* It should not be used to mean any combination or alliance. An *alliance* is a regularized connection entered into for mutual benefit (*A marriage is an alliance, not a liaison. The alliance between the Western powers and Russia could last only so long as they were threatened by a common enemy*).

libation; drink. A *libation* is a pouring out of wine or other liquid in honor of a deity or the liquid so poured out. The ancient Greeks made libations to their gods as a part of their worship (*Aeschylus's play, The Libation Bearers, begins with libations at the grave of Agamemnon*). The word is not a synonym for *drink* and if so used jocularly is a tedious affectation.

libel; slander; scandal; calumny; defamation. The blanket term to describe the wrong of injuring another's reputation without good reason or justification is *defamation.* *Calumny* is a seldom used term to describe a false and malicious statement designed to injure someone's reputation (*Be thou chaste as ice, as pure as snow, thou shalt not escape calumny*).

In the legal sense, *libel* (from the Latin word meaning a little book) means defamation by written or printed words, pictures, or any form other than spoken words or gestures (*When in Smith's article Jones was alluded to as a petty mobster, Jones sued him for libel*). *Slander* designates defamation by oral utterance (*Had it not been for his senatorial immunity, he would have fallen afoul of the laws of slander*). In popular speech *libel* and *slander* are used synonymously for *defamation,* though *libel* usually implies a somewhat more serious charge. It is best, however, to keep the legal distinction between the two words in mind.

Scandal, in so far as it is synonymous with *libel* and *slander,* means defamatory talk or malicious gossip. But it is a milder word than the others (*He dearly loved a juicy bit of scandal*) and does not carry an implication that the charges are false. *The breath of scandal,* usually used in a disavowal (*The breath of scandal has never touched her name*), is a cliché.

libelant; libelous. *Libelant,* a legal term, is defined differently in England and America. In America it can mean either one who libels, a libeler, or one who institutes suit. In England, says Partridge, only the second sense is acceptable; for the first *libeller* (The English use two *l*'s in all these words) is the only correct form. *Libel(l)ous,* it is agreed on both sides of the Atlantic, is an adjective meaning containing, constituting, or involving a libel, maliciously defamatory (*He wrote a libelous account of the transaction and was promptly sued*).

liberal arts. *Liberal* in the phrases *liberal arts* or *a liberal education* does not have any of the common meanings of *liberal,* such as generous, candid, copious, abundant, bountiful, open-hearted, open-minded, and so on. It means, etymologically, befitting a free man. In practice it means a course of studies comprising the arts, natural sciences, social sciences, and the humanities, which is not designed, as are courses in engineering, business administration, forestry, and so on, to have an immediate utility.

libretto. The plural is *librettos* or *libretti.*

lice. This is the plural of *louse.*

licence; license—both forms are acceptable, but *license* is the preferred spelling for both noun and verb.

licit. See **legal.**

lick into shape. It was believed for millennia that bears brought forth their young as shapeless lumps and gradually licked them into their proper shape. The belief is now known to be erroneous and the phrase is jaded.

lick one's chops. The use of *chops* for *jaws* is now limited, in popular speech, entirely to the phrase *to lick one's chops,* a figure, drawn from a characteristic action of dogs and wolves, denoting eager anticipation of something to be eaten. Except when used literally of a dog or a wolf, the phrase is now a cliché.

lickerish; liquorish. *Lickerish,* a word now dropping out of general use, means eager for choice food, greedy, lustful (*Green peas are ready to satisfy the longing appetite of the lickerish palate. Be not lickerish after fame*). It is related to *lecherous,* not to *lick. Liquorish,* a false variant, narrows the sense to a greed for liquor, imposing in the spelling a limiting folk etymology. But it doesn't matter much. One has to go out of his way to use either word and there are simpler, unambiguous words to convey their meanings.

lie. The past tense is *lay.* The participle is *lain.* Traditionally, this verb can only have a subject and should not be used with an object.

According to the strict rules of grammar, the forms *lie, lying,* and *lain* should never be used with an object, as they are in *I will lie it on the table* and *I have lain it on the table,* and the form *lay* should not be used with an object when

it is a simple past tense, as it is in *I lay it on the table this morning.* When *lay* is not a simple past tense but is used with an auxiliary, it belongs to another verb meaning cause to lie. It is therefore all right to say *I did lay it on the table this morning.* (See **lay.**) As a matter of fact, very few people misuse *lie* or *lying.* But a great many well educated people do use the simple past tense *lay* and the participle *lain* with an object. At present the verbs *lie* and *lay* are hopelessly confused in many people's minds. The confusion is so great and these technically incorrect forms are heard so often, that some grammarians believe they should be recognized as standard English.

An adjective that describes the subject of the verb may stand next to *lie,* as in *he lies sick* and *uneasy lies the head that wears a crown.* An adverb, qualifying the verb, may also stand in the same position, as in *he lies quietly.* The verb *lie* that means "say what is not true" is regular and has the past tense and participle *lied.*

lie low is accepted spoken English for not calling attention to one's self, remaining hidden and inactive, especially in a time of danger. The correct past tense is *lay low* not *laid low. Laid low* is an archaic and slightly bookish phrase for felled or knocked down.

lie; falsehood; fib; untruth; mendacity. *Lie* is the coarse, harsh, direct, everyday word for a statement which distorts or suppresses the truth in order to deceive and *falsehood* the more dignified and less offensive term (*Lies come naturally to him; he has to stop and think when he wants to tell the truth. Such falsehoods are certain to be detected in time and will do much harm to his reputation*). A *fib*—which sounds as though it were a slang word, though actually it is standard, probably a weakening of *fable*—describes a trivial falsehood, often one uttered with good intentions (*He told a little fib about ulcers in order to decline the proffered highball without offending his hostess*). An *untruth* is less reprehensible than a *falsehood.* It describes a statement either intentionally misleading or, more often, made from misunderstanding or ignorance (*Moreover, they have spoken untruths . . . and, to conclude, they are lying knaves. He may not be aware of it, but, none the less, these assertions are untruths and have aroused a great deal of resentment*). *Mendacity,* though not a common word, is still used for the quality of being mendacious, a disposition to lie, or habitual lying (*The brazen mendacity of the assurance took our breath away. He's addicted, as you will find, to a rather colorful mendacity*). As a synonym for a lie, however (*Such mendacities carry no conviction*), it is archaic and its use in this way would seem forced, ostentatious, or pedantic.

lief or **lieve.** This word, with its comparative and superlative forms *liefer* or *liever* and *liefest* or *lievest,* originally meant beloved or precious. It could be used like any other adjective, as in *my liefest lord,* and *children mine, liefe and deare.* It was also used with *had,* where the two words together meant "would hold dear" or "would like," as in *I had as lieve Hellen's golden tongue had commended Troylus.* This construction can still be heard but it now has an archaic tone. In current English *lief* is more often used with *would,* where it means gladly or willingly, as in *I would as lieve stay here.* The comparative form is heard less often but is also acceptable, as in *she would liefer have died.* (In Great Britain this *would* becomes *should* in certain constructions, as in *lief should I rouse at morning.*)

life. The plural is *lives.* The form *life* is used as the first element in a compound, as in *a life-long friend.*

life and soul of the party. Even if applied ironically to an objectionable person, *the life and soul of the party* is a cliché that merely adds to the tedium which the irrepressible one has been engendering.

lifeguard; lifesaver. In American usage a *lifeguard* is an expert swimmer employed on a bathing beach to aid in case of accidents to bathers (*During the two summers he worked as a lifeguard he saved three children from drowning*). In England a *life-guard* is one of a bodyguard of soldiers (the *Life-Guards*) or the entire bodyguard consisting (according to the *Oxford English Dictionary*) of two regiments of cavalry, forming, together with the Royal Horse Guards, the household cavalry. A *lifeguard* in America is also sometimes called a *lifesaver,* though a *lifesaver* need not be a *lifeguard;* he can be anyone who has saved someone from danger of death, especially from drowning. The word is not used much any more in this sense, however, as it has become better known as the trade name of a candy mint made in the form of a lifebelt and in the slang sense as a term for something which opportunely saves one from trouble or embarrassment.

lifelong; livelong. *Lifelong* means lasting or continuing through life (*His lifelong concern about his health may well have made his life less long than it otherwise would have been. They were lifelong friends and endured each other with mild contempt*). *Livelong* (originally *lief long,* dear long) is an intensive of *long,* meaning to the full extent in terms of time (*I've been working on the railroad/ All the livelong day*). It is now seldom used except in bad poetry and the stereotyped phrases *livelong day* and *livelong night,* both of which carry a connotation of tediousness.

light. The past tense is *lighted* or *lit.* The participle is also *lighted* or *lit. Light* may mean kindle or put fire to. A grammar published in 1765 claims that *lit* used in this sense is "very familiar, or rather low." This is no longer true. The forms, *lighted* and *lit,* are equally acceptable today. We may say *she lighted the lamp* or *she lit the lamp.* A participle *litten* is sometimes heard, as in *she has litten the lamp,* but this is not standard.

Light may also mean descend or land. In this sense too, *lighted* and *lit* are equally acceptable. These words are used in speaking of things that come down not under their own control, such as stones, snow flakes, and curses. We may say

one *lit on the roof.* The similar verb *alight* is used in speaking of things that come down deliberately, as in *our friends alighted at the door.* Birds are sometimes said to *light* and sometimes to *alight.* The uncertainty is not in the words, but in what it is the bird is doing.

light as a feather is a simile so worn that the careful writer and speaker will avoid it.

light fantastic. Dr. Johnson once growled that Milton did not write in English but in a language of his own that he made up. And certainly his use of *fantastic* in the famous couplet *Come, and trip it as ye go,/ On the light fantastic toe* to mean "in a manner varied according to your imagination or fantasy" was arbitrary and idiosyncratic. Like many other of his neologisms, however, it was successful, startled the reader into delight and surprised him with a fine excess. But to use this flash of linguistic gaiety, with heavy facetiousness and stale archness, as a cliché for dancing, is lamentable.

light on the subject, to shed. As a term for making something clear or bringing additional information to bear on an obscure or disputed matter, *to shed light on the subject* is weakened by overwork.

lightening; lightning. *Lightning* is a noun meaning a flashing of light, or a sudden illumination of the heavens, caused by the discharge of atmospheric electricity (*Any man with a proper respect for lightning will not touch a wire fence during a rainstorm*). *Lightening* is the gerund or participle of the verb *to lighten* in all of its meanings—to make less heavy, to become less dark, to cheer or gladden, or to flash as or like lightning.

lights. This word may mean the lungs of animals that are used for food. The word *lung* comes from the same source, which meant light in weight. At one time the two words were equivalent, as in *as if his lungs and lites were nigh assunder brast.* Today *lung* is the broader term and has both a singular and a plural form. *Lights* is now used only of animals and only in the plural. It takes a plural verb, but cannot be used with a word implying number.

-like. See **suffixes.**

like. This word is actually used as a noun, a verb, an adjective, an adverb, a preposition, and a conjunction. (For the use of *like* as a conjunction, see **like; as.**)

NOUN

There is one noun form of *like* that is used only in the plural, as in *his likes and dislikes.* There is another form that usually appears in the singular, as in *I never saw his like* or *the like of that.* A plural is also heard here, as in *the likes of you,* but this is not literary English.

VERB

To like, which now means to enjoy or to be pleased with, originally meant to be like or to be suitable for. From this it came to mean to please. Milton says that the angels *color, shape or size assume, as likes them best.* And Rossetti says, *I rode sullenly upon a certain path that liked me not.* The joke often made about some food, that *I like it, but it doesn't like me,* unintentionally combines the present and the earliest meaning of the verb. See also **love.**

Like may be followed by an infinitive, as in *she likes to travel.* It may also be followed by an *-ing* form, as in *she likes traveling.* Some people object to this but it is generally acceptable in the United States. *Like* cannot be followed by a clause. We cannot say *I like that you are here.* In order to say what amounts to the same thing we must insert *it* as the object of *like,* as in *I like it that you are here.* The clause then qualifies the word *it* instead of functioning as the object of *like.*

In literary English *for* is not used after *like* to introduce the subject of an infinitive, as in *he would like for you to come,* and the simpler form, he *would like you to come,* is required. (See **for.**) But *like for* is generally acceptable in the United States. It is standard in the southern states and considered "southern" elsewhere.

In Great Britain the auxiliary *should* (and not *would*) is used with *like* when the subject of the verb is *I* or *we,* as in *I should like to go.* To British ears *I would like* seems to say "I am determined to enjoy." When the subject of the verb is anything except *I, we,* or *you,* the auxiliary *would* (and not *should*) is used, as in *they would like to go.* When the subject of the verb is *you,* the rules are more complicated. See **shall; will.**

In the United States the British *should like* is sometimes heard but *would* is generally preferred, regardless of the subject of the verb. To most Americans, *I should like* seems to say "I know I ought to enjoy."

ADJECTIVE, ADVERB, AND PREPOSITION

When *like* is used as an adjective or an adverb it is followed by an object and this makes it indistinguishable from a preposition. The object may be any noun equivalent, including the *-ing* form of a verb, as in *I felt like laughing.* If the object is a personal pronoun it must have the objective form, as in *like me.* A subjective pronoun following *like,* as in *a girl like I,* is not standard. In current English *like* always means similar to or resembling. It could once be used, as *likely* is, to mean probable, as in *he is like to die* and *there were more like eight of us.* This use is heard today but is old fashioned or questionable.

In older literary English *like* is sometimes used in the comparative or superlative form, as in *liker to a madman* and *likest to a hogshead.* These forms are now archaic and today *like* is always compared by using the words *more* or *most.*

Like is also used as a suffix, as in *owl-like.* (For the use of the hyphen, see **suffixes.**) It should not be used to modify or tone down a full statement. as in *she was out of her mind like* and *he didn't pass his examinations like.*

like; as. When *like* is followed by a full clause instead of a simple noun or noun equivalent object, it is being used as a conjunction, as in *you don't know Nellie like I do* and *wood does not contract like steel does.* This is an estab-

lished function of the word *as.* (See **as.**) Some people believe that it is a grammatical mistake to use *like* in this way. But they are a minority. The second example quoted above is taken from the eleventh edition of the Encyclopaedia Britannica. Keats wrote, *it is astonishing how they raven down scenery like children do sweet meats.* The construction is also found in the writings of Shakespeare, More, Sidney, Dryden, Smollett, Burns, Southey, Coleridge, Shelley, Darwin, Newman, Brontë, Thackeray, Morris, Kipling, Shaw, Wells, Masefield, and Maugham.

During the nineteenth century literary gentlemen felt strongly about this question. Those whose education had been chiefly Greek and Latin said that the use of *like* as a conjunction was a vulgarism. But Furnivall, the foremost English language scholar of the period, defended it. He tells how on one occasion, "having to answer some ignorant in a weekly about the use of *like,* I said to Morris: 'Have you ever used *like* as a conjunction?' 'Certainly I have,' answered Morris, 'constantly.' 'But you know there's a set of prigs who declare it's vulgar and unhistorical.' 'Yes I know. They're a lot of damned fools.' " But Tennyson belonged to the other camp. He told Furnivall: "It's a modern vulgarism that I have seen grow up within the last thirty years; and when Prince Albert used it in my drawing room, I pulled him up for it, in the presence of the Queen, and told him he never ought to use it again." Actually, the Prince was speaking a more classical English than Tennyson realized.

Around 1600 *like* was used with a preposition, usually *to,* whenever a person or thing was being compared, that is, when it qualified a noun or pronoun, as in *like to one more rich in hope* and *like unto whited sepulchres.* It was used with *as* when the comparison involved an action, that is, involved a clause containing a verb, expressed or implied, as in *like as a father pitieth his children,* and the description of the ghost in Hamlet which moved *like as it would speak.*

But about that time the *to* began to be dropped out and its meaning was carried by *like,* which in this way took on the functions of a preposition. This can be seen happening in Hamlet's words: *no more like my father than I to Hercules.* By now this has become standard English and we would normally say *like whitened sepulchres.* But *as* was dropping out of these constructions too, at about the same time. Shakespeare felt that *like* could carry the meaning of *as,* and so function as a conjunction, just as it carried the meaning of *to.* Juliet says, *no man like he doth grieve my heart*—that is, no one grieves her as he does.

The modern purist claims that *like* is correctly used when it functions as a preposition and carries the meaning of *like to,* and incorrectly used when it functions as a conjunction and carries the meaning *like as.* There is no doubt but that *like* is accepted as a conjunction in the United States today and that there is excellent literary tradition for this. There is no reason why anyone should take the trouble to learn when *like* is a conjunction and when it is a preposition, unless he wants to. But if anyone wants to be a purist, he should be a thorough one. He should not himself use *like* as a conjunction in some constructions and condemn other people for using it in this way in other constructions. *Like* is not being used as a preposition unless the single word *to* can be inserted between it and the word immediately following. It is a conjunction in *he takes to it like a duck to water.*

At one time *like* could be used to mean *as if* (just as *as* means *as if* in the statement about the ghost that moved *like* as it would speak). This is acceptable today when the *if* clause is shortened to a few words that do not include a verb, as in *he ran like mad* and *the dress looks like new. Like* is sometimes used in this way before a complete clause, as in *he acts like I was a worm.* Many people who accept *like* in place of *as* do not accept it in place of *as if.* The construction is generally frowned upon, but it is more acceptable in the southern states than it is in other parts of this country.

likely. Today *likely* is used freely to qualify a noun or pronoun, as in *a likely story* and *he is likely to come.* Until recently it could also be used as an adverb, as in *he would likely refuse.* Today this has an old fashioned tone and *likely* is not used as an adverb except when it is qualified by *very* or *most,* as in *he would very likely refuse.* See also **apt.**

limit and **limitation** are synonymous in the senses of a boundary or terminal point, fixed points between which something is confined, or the point at which something is no longer possible or allowed (*This is the limit of my estate. Within these limitations you are free to do as you choose). Limitation has the special meaning of a limiting* condition or circumstance, a restricting handicap or misfortune (*In view of his limitations, his accomplishment was admirable. Deafness is a serious limitation in this job).* In law *limitation* has the special meaning of an assignment, as by statute, of a period of time within which an action may be brought, or the period of time so assigned (*a statute of limitations).*

limit; delimit. To *limit* is to restrict by or as by fixing limits. In this sense it is followed by *to* (*The first four volumes of the study will be limited to Fitz-Greene Halleck's early poems).* It also means to keep within assigned limits (*We must limit expenditures if we expect to show a profit).* In both of these senses the word has been in use for centuries.

To *delimit* is a fairly recent coinage, coming into use after the middle of the last century and being still fairly uncommon. It means to mark or determine the limits of (*The present system of delimiting the towns and preserving the memory of their bounds is archaic),* to demarcate. A delimiting curve is one which separates two regions of the surface upon which it is drawn. To *delimit* does not mean to remove established limits.

limited; small. The use of *limited* should be limited to that which is restricted within limits. It should not, for example, be used as a synonym for *small* (as in *Hurry, I've only a limited amount*

of time or *I have limited resources; these prices are too high for me),* because something may be limited and still be very large.

In England *Limited* designates a company in which the liability of the partners or shareholders is limited to a certain amount (*Hall Brothers, Limited*—abbreviated *Ltd.).* This sense is irrelevant in America where the closest equivalent is *Incorporated.* A special application of *Limited* in the United States is to trains, buses, etc., restricted as to the number or class of passengers, stops, or time occupied in transit (*If you want to save time, take the Twentieth Century Limited).* Unless used as a part of the full name of a special train or bus, the word is not capitalized (*The limited ought to be along any minute now).*

linage; lineage. *Linage* is a two-syllable noun that designates alignment or the number of lines of written or printed matter covered (*They paid the printer on the basis of linage).*

Lineage is a three-syllable word meaning lineal descent from an ancestor, ancestry or extraction, the line of descendants of a particular ancestor (*His pride in his noble lineage was often ludicrous).*

Confusion between the words grows out of the fact that each is a variant spelling of the other, though each retains its own pronunciation in either spelling. To avoid confusion it is best to use (as usage increasingly dictates) *linage* when referring to printing and *lineage* when referring to ancestry or descent.

line. One meaning of *line* is business, profession, trade, sphere of economic activity. It probably developed from the *line* of goods that a salesman carried or sold (*Hardware, that's a good line. He's been in that line of work for thirty years).* The television show *What's My Line* has probably given it the shove, if one were needed, to move it over from slang to standard usage. It is a short and unpretentious word but the slight slanginess that makes it so popular unfits it for more serious uses and *occupation* (*q.v.*) fits into some contexts better.

liniment; lineament. The familiar word in this pair is *liniment,* a liquid preparation for rubbing on or applying to the skin as for sprains and bruises (*Between the halves the coach rubbed liniment on his bad shoulder).* Sometimes *liniment* is mistakenly used for *lineament,* a word which properly means a feature or detail of a face, body, or figure, considered with respect to its outline or contour (*He recognized the bold lineaments of his face).*

linking verbs. Most verbs assert something about their subject, as *he swam, he built a house.* The verb *to be* usually does not do this. It merely connects the subject with some other words, as in *he is honest, he is an honorable man.* This is also true of *seem* and *become,* and about sixty other verbs when they are used to mean be, seem, or become, as in *he remained calm, he appeared anxious, he grew fat.* These are called linking verbs. Their most valuable contribution is in showing time differences, as in *he seems honest* and *he seemed honest,* which cannot be shown in the pidgin English *him honest.* In addition, each verb has its unique meaning and this colors to some extent the relation expressed between the subject and the following words.

ADJECTIVE OR ADVERB

Often, as we see above, a linking verb connects a descriptive word with the subject. This word is an adjective and not an adverb, because it describes the subject and not the verb. For example, *keep* and *stand* are followed by adjectives because they are both being used to mean "be" in *keep cool* and *stand firm*. Many verbs are followed by adjectives because they are being used to mean "become," as in *fall sick, turn sour, wear thin*. A still greater number of verbs are followed by adjectives because they are being used to mean "seem," as *gleamed* in *the steersman's face by his lamp gleamed white;* and *looms* in *a period that looms heroic through the distorting mist of history*. All verbs that refer to some particular sense may be used as substitutes for *seem*, as in *smell sweet, taste good, feel soft, look nice*.

The truly empty verbs, *be, seem, become*, may be qualified by an adverb without changing their meaning. In *Dick is certain*, the adjective *certain* applies to the noun *Dick*. In *Dick is certainly my brother*, the adverb *certainly* applies to the verb *is*. *Is* does not have a different meaning in the two sentences, nor would *seem* or *become*. But any of the other verbs, which are sometimes linking and sometimes not, cease to be linking verbs and take on their full meaning as soon as they are qualified by an adverb. For example, *felt* is a linking verb in *he felt strong* (seemed to himself) but not, in *he felt strongly;* and *worked* is a linking verb in *the hinge worked loose* (became) but not, in *the hinge worked loosely*.

Because the adjective following a linking verb is in a position that ordinarily belongs to an adverb, many people are inclined to use an adverb form, especially after the verbs that mean "seem," as in *it smelled sweetly, it tasted well, it looked nicely*. The same construction in *I feel badly* is now thoroughly established, and other examples are heard too often to be called unacceptable. But they are based on a misunderstanding of grammar. Anyone who would rather use an adverb form after these verbs may do so without being classed as illiterate. But he should not think that he is speaking a superior form of English.

SUBJECTIVE OR OBJECTIVE PRONOUNS

The true linking verbs, *be, seem, become*, and the verb *remain*, sometimes join a noun or pronoun to the subject, as in *he seemed a perfect gentleman* and *he became a colonel*. These nouns and pronouns are called "predicate nominatives" or "subjective complements" because in Latin a word functioning in this way would be in the nominative (or subjective) case. Since English nouns do not have distinctive nominative and accusative cases, it makes no difference what one calls them. But there are six pronouns in English which are nominative (the subjective pronouns, *I, we*, and so on) and six which are accusative (the objective pronouns, *me, us*, and so on), and these create a problem.

The most conspicuous difference between standard English practice and the rules of Latin grammar is in the choice of a pronoun following a linking verb. According to the rules, an objective pronoun cannot be used here because it is not actually the object of a verb. But the tendency in standard English since the sixteenth century has been to disregard the question of what is an object and what is not, and to use the objective form of the pronoun after all verbs. In each of the following sentences the objective pronoun is contrary to the rules, but some of these were written by masters of English and all of them represent standard usage today.

> *In God's name, Janet, is it me thy ghost has come to seek!* (Rossetti)
> *Be thou me, impetuous one!* (Shelley)
> *If it was me, I did it in a dream.* (Keats)
> *It is us, we simple men and women, who must decide.* (Faulkner)
> *It is you who will be blamed for it, not them.*
> *If it had been him, he would have admitted it.*
> *That's her at the door now.*

In natural English a subjective pronoun is used after a linking verb only in the following situations. It is required in a simple identity, such as *I am I* and *he is he*, and before the *-self* words, as in *it was she herself I saw*. A subjective form is frequently used when it is felt as the subject of a following verb that actually has the subject *who*, as in *it was I who said that*. In any other type of sentence, a subjective pronoun after a linking verb sounds like a classroom. A good many Americans use a subjective pronoun in any extremely simple sentence such as *it is I* and *that is he*, but it is never heard in more complicated constructions. Surely, even the most determined purist would refuse to follow the rules and say *in a sense, the books we read become we*.

In writing formal English, "correct" forms that are too much at variance with the spoken language should be avoided. But within the range of forms that are correct and also tolerable, there are three kinds of constructions that are likely to give trouble.

1. When a relative pronoun is the object of a verb it is frequently, and quite properly, omitted. For example, in the sentence *it was this man I saw*, there is an omitted *that* between *man* and *I*. This pronoun is the object of the verb *saw*. When it is omitted, it is very easy to feel that the preceding word is the object of the verb and, if it is a pronoun, to use the objective case, as in *it was him I saw*. This is not bad English, because it is in keeping with good practice. But it is contrary to the rules, which require *he* here, as in *it was he* (that) *I saw*.

2. The form *to be* creates more serious problems. If *to be* is directly attached to the subject of a verb, the formal rules require a following pronoun to be subjective, as in *the man seemed to them to be I*. But *to be* may be attached to the object of the verb, and in that case a following pronoun must be objective, as in *they supposed the man to be me*. To use a subjective form here and say *they supposed the man to be I* is both

"incorrect" and contrary to good usage, and therefore indefensible.

3. The word *being* may also give trouble. If a possessive pronoun or a noun in the genitive case stands before *being,* the rules require a following pronoun to be subjective, as *he* in *think of its being he!* But if the preceding word is not a possessive or a genitive, both the rules and good practice require a following pronoun to be objective, as *him* in *think of it being him!* (For the kinds of pronouns that may be used before an *-ing* verb form, see **ing.**)

When in doubt whether to use a subjective or an objective pronoun, choose the objective form. A wrong subjective pronoun suggests that the writer is straining himself to appear superior to other men, and proves that he does not understand the rules of grammar. A wrong objective pronoun proves nothing more than that he is willing to use the language most of his countrymen use.

links. See **golf links.**

lion's share. As a term for the largest or most important share, usually of the rewards or profits of some undertaking, *the lion's share* is hackneyed.

The phrase derives from either of two versions of a fable by Aesop. In one version a lion, an ass, and a fox hunt together, agreeing to share the spoils. A stag is killed and the ass does the best he can to divide the carcass into three equal portions. Whereupon the lion kills the ass and asks the fox to apportion the proper shares. The crafty and enlightened fox takes a few bites for his share and leaves the rest to the lion. In the other version three other weaker animals join with the lion. When the kill is made the lion divides it into four fairly equal portions, takes the first as his share by virtue of the agreement, the second as his share by virtue of his courage, and the third as his share by virtue of his strength. The fourth share he assigns to his fellow hunters but warns them that they touch it at their peril.

liquefy; liquidate. The sense of *liquefy* is clear enough. It means to make or become liquid (*In great heat the metal will liquefy*). It is *liquidate* that makes trouble. In its primary sense it means to settle or pay a debt or an account (*No effort should be spared to liquidate the National Debt*). It can mean to convert into cash (*He liquidated his assets*) or it can mean to break up, abolish, or do away with. And it is in this last sense, now very much in vogue, that it must be used judiciously because it covers too many meanings. The liquidation of a company and the liquidation of political opponents are actions so diverse that it is putting any word, and especially a word basically metaphorical and hence restricted by the connotations of its literal meaning, to an improper strain to make it describe both. Our language is rich in words expressing various ways of abolishing or doing away with things and it is better to employ whichever of them is closest to your meaning than, for the mere sake of using a word in the vogue, using a word so vague as *liquidate.*

liquid refreshment. Even as a jocularity, making fun presumably of a former elegancy and pretentiousness, *liquid refreshment* is dreary and affected.

liquorish. See **lickerish.**

list. To *list* is to set down together into a list, to make a list of (*The names are to be listed in alphabetical order*). By an understandable extension it is often used to mean to add to a list (*Three new courses are listed in the catalogue*), but mention, include, or add would usually be better. And surely the word has been carried beyond its province when it is used to mean merely to state or to say or to set down (in such a sentence as *She listed her occupation as "Housewife"*).

listen; hear. To *listen* is to pay attention in order to understand the meaning of a sound or sounds (*Listen, my children, and you shall hear/ Of the midnight ride of Paul Revere*). To *hear* is to have a perception of sound by means of the auditory sense (*One could hear the bell buoy out in the harbor*). One can listen without hearing (*I listened carefully but couldn't hear what they were saying*) and hear without listening (*I wasn't listening to what they were saying but I could hear them quarreling*).

Incidentally, one listens *at* something only when one applies his ear to or near the thing in order to hear (*Nelly had listened at many a keyhole*). When one pays attention in order to understand a sound, he listens *to* it (*Listen to the story of a woeful man*).

listen to. These two words may be followed by an object and the *-ing* form of a verb, as in *listen to it singing.* In the United States they may also be followed by an object and the simple form of the verb, as in *listen to it sing.* In Great Britain this is considered an American barbarism, but it is standard usage in this country.

lit. See **light.**

litany; liturgy. A *litany* is a ceremonial form of prayer consisting of a series of invocations or supplications with responses which are the same for a number in succession. *The Litany* is the general supplication of this form in the Anglican *Book of Common Prayer.* A *liturgy* is more extensive than a litany, for it is a form of public worship, a ritual, a particular arrangement of services. It includes prayer and, conceivably, a litany or The Litany. *The Liturgy* is the name for the service of the Eucharist, especially in the Eastern Church, equivalent to the Mass in the Western Church.

literally means in a manner which follows the letter or the exact words (*A figurative phrase if translated literally is almost certain to be ludicrous*), or in a literal or strict matter-of-fact, prosaic sense (*He took the injunction literally and renounced his mother and his brothers*). It has also come to mean actually, in strict accuracy, without exaggeration (*The effect of the bombing was literally devastating. The attack literally decimated the company; one-tenth of the men lay dead*).

Unfortunately this last meaning has led to the

word's being used simply as an intensive, with no regard whatever to any meaning of *literally*, as in such a sentence as *He was literally dumbfounded by the report* where no literal meaning can be attached to *dumbfounded*. The word has become a particular favorite of those who seek to express intense feelings in metaphor, with the paradoxical result that in a great deal of loose, hyperbolic talk *literally* is used to mean the exact opposite of what it properly means. When, for example, on a hot day someone says *I'm literally melting*, he means *I am figuratively melting* and the meaning of *figuratively* here is "not literally." A fish, partly submerged in a chowder, might be said to be *literally stewed to the gills*, but an inebriated man is at best (or worst) only metaphorically stewed to the gills. When we say that we are *literally fed up* with someone, we are either making a confession of cannibalism and gluttony or using *literally* to mean *not literally*. The word should be avoided except in its stricter meanings.

literate; literal. *Literate* means able to read and write, hence educated (*Only through free general education can a literate population be created*). By extension, it has come to suggest literary (*T. S. Eliot is a highly literate man*). *Literal*, as applied to persons, means tending to construe words in their strict sense, unimaginative, matter-of-fact (*He's very literal; if you tell him you are dying with the heat, he'll call an undertaker*). In its general sense, *literal* means following the letter, or exact words, of the original (*Bold as Fitzgerald was, he feared to offend his contemporaries by a literal translation of the entire poem*).

literature. For centuries *literature* has meant writings in which expression and form, in connection with ideas of permanent and universal interest, are characteristic or essential features (*The reading of literature still remains the best form of education*). *Literature* can also mean the entire body of literary writings of a specific language, period, people, or subject (*the literature of England, the literature of the Renaissance, American literature*). In the sciences, where expression and form are not regarded as supremely important, *literature* is often used to mean the entire body of writing relevant to any given subject (*Have you made a thorough search of the literature? I am sure there is an article on that very subject somewhere*) and although this usage is annoying to professors of belles lettres it is probably here to stay.

The use of *literature* to describe any printed matter on any subject (*Please send me descriptive literature concerning your garbage disposal unit. He spent more on campaign literature than his opponent did on the whole campaign*) is usually classed as a misuse. But who is to decide? The authors of advertising folders and campaign biographies may feel that their works have expression and form and are concerned with matters of universal and permanent interest and hence, under the dictionary, entitled to be called *literature*. If enough of them think so and

can persuade enough other people to say so, this meaning may become standard. At the moment it is not.

literatus. The plural is *literati*.

litotes is a figure in rhetoric in which an affirmative is expressed in the negative of its contrary. When St. Paul said that he was *a citizen of no mean city* he meant that he was "a citizen of a great city" and when he said to the Corinthians *I praise you not*, he meant "I blame you." Similarly *not a few* means "many" and *not bad* means "good." Litotes is a form of meiosis or understatement.

little. The comparative forms are *less, lesser, littler*. The superlative forms are *least, littlest*.

When *little* means small in size it is always an adjective and may be used with a singular or a plural noun, as in *a little child* and *little children*. The forms *less, lesser,* and *least* cannot be used with this meaning of *little*. We cannot say *the least child*. It is claimed that in this sense *little* is itself a comparative, as in *the Little Dipper*, and a superlative, as in *the little toe*. But this is very unsatisfactory. During the last century a number of writers have used the forms *littler* and *littlest*. *Littlest*, as in *the littlest child, the littlest fish*, is better established than *littler*, but both can be used when they are needed. And they are sometimes needed. *Small* is a thin, intellectual word and means only what it says. *Little* carries an emotional tone and means that the small size is attractive.

Little may mean small in importance, as in *little people, a little fault*. In this sense too it is always an adjective and may qualify either a singular or a plural noun.

When *little* means small in amount, it may be an adjective, an adverb, or a noun. The adjective is essentially negative and means not large in amount or not much, as in *they gave us little trouble*.

The noun *little* has the same negative meaning when used without a qualifier, as in *little we see in Nature that is ours*. But when it is qualified by a definitive adjective, such as *a, the, my*, the noun is affirmative and means a small amount or some, as in *a little goes a long way*. The form *a little* can be used to mean *a little of* and so function as if it were an adjective with the affirmative meaning, as in *they gave us a little trouble*. When *a little* is made negative, as in *not a little*, it means a good deal, as in *they gave us not a little trouble*. In general, *of* is not used after *little* except when it precedes a definitive adjective, as in *little of the work had been done*. Formerly, *little* was used with *of* in other constructions, as in *little of work had been done*, but this is now considered affected.

The adverb *little* also has the negative sense of not much, as in *the world will little note*. Like *never* and other negative adverbs, its proper position is before the principal verb form. The noun forms, *a little* and *not a little*, may also be used as adverbs and keep their affirmative meanings, as in *comrades, leave me here a little* and *we have been worried not a little*.

When *little* means a small amount or not much, it is always singular. It is used with a singular verb and cannot qualify a plural noun. If we say *they gave us little troubles,* the word *little* inevitably takes on the meaning of small in size or small in importance. To express the idea of small in amount with a plural noun, we must use the word *few.*

Lesser is the comparative form of *little* in the sense of small in value or importance. *Less* is the comparative form in the sense of small in amount. (For the difference in the uses of these two words, see **less; lesser.**)

Least is the superlative form for both *less* and *lesser.* At one time it could also be used in the sense of smallest in size, but this is now extremely rare. It may be used as an adjective, as in *her least whim,* or as an adverb, as in *I am least happy now* and *with what I most enjoy, contented least.* When *the least* qualifies a verb, it means in the least degree. Like the prepositional phrase, it can be used in a conditional clause, a question, or a negative statement, but not in an affirmative statement. We may say *if you are the least worried* or *I am not the least worried,* but we cannot say *I am the least worried.* We may, however, say *I am the least bit worried,* because here *the least* is not an adverb qualifying the verb but an adjective qualifying the noun *bit,* which in turn is functioning as an adverb.

Lesser is a comparative form made from the comparative form *less* and is equivalent to *more smaller.* This does not prevent it from being standard English. On the other hand, the double superlative *the leastest* is not standard. But we may say *the least little* if we like.

little bird told me. As a way of saying I have heard something but will not name my informant, *a little bird told me* is infantile, a sad attempt to appear cute.

liturgy. See **litany.**

live. This verb may be followed by an adjective describing the subject, as in *they lived happy* or *they lived poor.* It may also be followed by an adverb describing the verb, as in *they lived happily* or *they lived poorly.* Sometimes there is no real difference in meaning between the two forms. See also **reside.**

live (adjective). In the meanings of alert and of present interest (*He's a live fellow, that man! It's still a live issue in these parts*), *live* is slang, not standard. The trouble with such uses is that they are too general. Obviously, an alert man must be live, but a live man need not be alert, for alert suggests being live in a certain way— having a ready and prompt attentiveness together with a quick intelligence.

live audience. Since an audience is an assembly of hearers or spectators, *live audience* should logically be a redundancy. And such it certainly would have been up until this generation. But it is an illustration of the strange and rapid ways that words can change their meanings and, at the same time, of the irrelevancy of applying logic to language, that this phrase has a clear and definite meaning to millions of people today and fills a need in their speech. In many radio shows that are heard and even some television shows that are being seen, the audience, whose ecstatic delight with the performance is intended to move the viewers either to join in thoughtlessly or at least to feel that if they don't laugh the fault is theirs, is not there at all. The sounds are dubbed in from recordings made of genuine laughter at more amusing shows.

livelong. See **lifelong.**

lively. See **breezy.**

lives. This is the plural of *life.*

living from hand to mouth. As a term for improvidence or for a complete lack of any store of necessities, *living from hand to mouth* is worn threadbare.

living in clover. As a term for luxurious living or simply good fortune *living in clover* or often, now, merely *in clover* (both shortenings of *living like pigs in clover,* clover being very rich fodder) is a cliché.

Lloyd's is a London insurance underwriting corporation, composed of some three hundred syndicates. It is so called because it was founded in the late seventeenth century at Edward Lloyd's coffeehouse. It is spelled *Lloyd's,* not *Lloyds* or *Lloyds'.*

load. See **jag.**

load down; load up. In the passive, American *load down* equals English *load up* (*He returned from the New York Public Library loaded down with books. The lorries pulled out of Tilbury loaded up with ammunition*). In the active, however, an American uses *load up* (*Load up on that stuff you can grab and let's get out of here*).

loadstone; lodestone. Though either form is correct, *loadstone* is preferred to *lodestone. Lodestar,* however, is preferred to *loadstar.*

loaf. The plural is *loaves.*

loan. The use of *loan* as a verb, as in *he loaned me five dollars,* is condemned in Great Britain as an Americanism. Actually, it is a very respectable verb. It has been in existence for almost eight hundred years and was used in an act of Parliament in 1542. It is thoroughly acceptable in the United States, especially when used by bankers or in speaking about money.

loathe. This word may be followed by the *-ing* form of a verb, as in *I loathe washing dishes,* or by an infinitive, as in *I loathe to wash dishes.* Both forms are acceptable in the United States. See also **hate.**

loaves. This is the plural of *loaf.*

local habitation and a name. Shakespeare, in a glorious passage in *A Midsummer Night's Dream,* says that the poet's imagination *bodies forth the forms of things unknown* and his pen *Turns them to shapes, and gives to airy nothing/ A local habitation and a name.* As a term for anything fixed and definite, the concluding phrase has been reduced to dreary meaninglessness by tedious repetition.

locality; location. A *locality* is a place, spot, or district, with or without reference to things or persons in it, viewed in reference to its geographical situation or its surroundings (*It was a pleasant locality in which to live*). A *location* is a place of settlement or residence (*The doctor's house was in a desirable location, near the center of the town*), or a tract of land of designated situation or limits selected or suitable for a certain purpose (*Myrtle Point is an excellent location for lookout stations*). In the terminology of the motion picture industry a *location* is a place outside the studio, usually out of doors, affording suitable environment for photographing particular scenes or incidents. It is rarely spoken of as *a location* but the actors, camera crews, and so on, are said to be *on location* when shooting scenes in such a spot.

locate. Though decried by English grammarians, *to locate,* in the sense of setting up one's residence, establishing one's place of business (*Where are you folks located now?*), is standard American usage.

locate and **find** are not synonymous. To *locate* something is to discover its place of location by hunting for it (*The mechanic soon located the leak in the gas line. They finally located him in a West Madison Street flophouse*). To *find* something is to meet with it, whether by intention or chance, but without reference to a particular setting (*If I don't locate the book on the fourth floor, I'll assume I can't find it*).

loc. cit. This is an abbreviation of the Latin words *loco citato* and means in the place cited.

lock, stock, and barrel. As a term for the entirety of something, *lock, stock, and barrel,* the component parts of an old-fashioned gun, is worn out.

lock the stable door after the horse is stolen. To speak of a precaution taken too late as *locking the stable door after the horse has been stolen* is to employ a cliché. It is further objectionable in that it has now a false earthiness about it, an assumption of rusticity that carries no conviction.

locus. The plural is *locuses* or *loci.*

locution; circumlocution. A *locution* is a particular form of expression (*The locutions of the mountain folk, such phrases as defining a certain distance as "a whoop and a holler," were strange but usually vigorous and imaginative*). A *circumlocution* is a roundabout way of speaking, the use of too many words. *During the time that,* for instance, is a circumlocution for *while; in this day and age* a circumlocution for *today.* A locution suggests an idiomatic expression and, carefully chosen, locutions may enliven a style. Circumlocutions, on the other hand, are tedious and almost always to be avoided.

lodging; lodgings. Both forms may be used to mean living quarters. There is no difference in meaning. The plural is generally preferred, but the singular is required in the phrase *board and lodging* and may also be used in other contexts, as in *a lodging for the night.*

loft. See **garret.**

lofty. See **tall.**

logic and **grammar.** Maurice Barrès once said that the only difference between a logical argu-

ment and a play on words is that the play on words cannot be translated. This is a fair enough description of what often passes for reasoning. But anyone who insists that grammar and logic are essentially the same ought to accept this gibe as solemn truth.

Logic deals with the rules of valid inference. Grammar deals with the ways in which a given group of people habitually express themselves. There is no reason to think that these would be identical. In the eighteenth century, learned gentlemen talked a great deal about the language spoken in the Garden of Eden, which they called Lingua Adamica, and which, they said, "did not consist merely of conventional signs but expressed rather the very nature and essence of things." If they were right, logic and grammar may have been somewhat similar at that time. But even the eighteenth century grammarians realized that this happy state of affairs had ended with the Tower of Babel.

Any language must be capable of showing logical relationships. But it does not necessarily do so in the most efficient manner. The idea that a grammatical distinction must necessarily reflect a logical one is responsible for much of the bad thinking that has plagued mankind. It is not only the uneducated who fall into this pit. The fact that, in Latin, an adjective is obviously different from a noun, the fact that, grammatically, *nothing* is in a class with *something,* the fact that the copula *is* also means *exist,* confused the best minds of Europe for centuries. On the other hand, the idea that whatever is logical must also be grammatical is responsible for a great deal of bad writing. At its best, it produces an unnatural, and therefore ineffective, prose. This is especially true when the writer is not a logician and feels obliged to change a straightforward statement, such as *everyone does not read the same paper,* into its logically identical but much more obscure form, *not everyone reads the same paper.* At its worst, this theory leads to such grammatical monstrosities as *I won't stay longer than I can't help.*

lone wolf. As a term for one who is highly independent, one who accomplishes his purposes alone, *a lone wolf* is a hackneyed metaphor. It is preëminently an American phrase and is usually restricted to someone whose activities are slightly shady or at least wholly selfish. It seems to be based on the erroneous assumption that wolves normally hunt in packs.

lonely; alone; lonesome. *Lonely* and *alone* both mean a state of solitariness, being without companionship. *Alone* describes the physical fact of isolation. Since most human beings do not like to be alone, it usually carries in its context a suggestion of desolation or dejection (*All alone by the telephone/ All alone, feeling blue*), but it need not; some people like to be alone (*The joy of closing the door behind the last departing guest and knowing that at last one was blessedly alone*). *Lonely* almost always has a suggestion of a dejection of spirits at the thought of aloneness. Even when it is applied to non-human things, there is a projection of the human feeling into the situation (*So lonely 'twas, that God himself/ Scarce seemèd to be there*).

Lonesome and *lonely* are synonyms, but *lonesome* is the more sentimental word of the two (*Lonesome and blue, in spite of all I can do. Look down, look down, that lonesome road/ Before you travel on*). It expresses a slightly greater degree of loneliness (*Like one that on a lonesome road/ Doth walk in fear and dread*) and desolation (*In November days/ When vapors rolling down the valleys made/ A lonely scene more lonesome*).

long. This word is as truly an adverb as it is an adjective. In current English the adverb *long* always refers to time, as in *the world will long remember*. When used as a verb meaning yearn, *long* may be followed by an infinitive, as in *I long to see him;* in any other construction we must use the compound *long for*. See **lengthy**.

long and the short of it. As a term for the essence of some proposition, *the long and the short of it* is a cliché. As a humorous description of a tall person and a short person walking together, it is even more tedious.

long distance is the American term to designate telephone service between distant points (*Spirits of the Greek dead spoke to the living as if over a bad long distance telephone connection*). The equivalent British term is *trunk*.

long-felt want. To say of something needed that there had been *a long-felt want* for it or of something that has been provided that *fills a long-felt want* is to employ an overworked phrase.

longshoreman; docker. The term to describe a man employed on the wharves of a port, as in loading and unloading vessels, is *longshoreman* in America and *docker* in England.

long shot, not by a. The English version of the American *not by a long shot* is *not by a long chalk*, so that it is evident that *shot* and *chalk* are being used in the one sense in which they are synonymous: a tavern reckoning or score.

The phrase is a cliché, its meaning unknown to most who use it, and should be used only with care.

look. When this word means expect it may be followed by an infinitive, as in *I look to hear from you*, but the *-ing* form of a verb with the compound *forward to*, as in *I look forward to hearing from you*, is preferred today.

In the United States *look at* may be followed by an object and the simple form of a verb, as in *look at her strut*. In Great Britain this is considered an American barbarism and the *-ing* form of the verb is required, as in *look at her strutting*. Both forms are acceptable in this country.

When *look* means appear it may be followed by an adjective describing the subject of the verb, as in *it looks good on you, it looks nice on you, he looks angry*. Formerly, an adverb could be used in just this way, as in *how cheerfully my mother looks*. This is no longer standard English. Today, *look* in this sense may be followed by *well*, as in *it looks well on you*, but not by other adverbs, such as *nicely*. (When *look* is

used in the sense of glance it is, of course, followed by an adverb and not an adjective, as in *she looked angrily at him*.)

look daggers. As a term for glaring resentment or resentful glaring or any open expression of hatred in the countenance, *to look daggers* is a cliché.

look; see. *Look* bears to *see* the same relation that *listen* bears to *hear;* in each case the first term suggests preparation for the second. To *look* is to fix the eyes upon something or in some direction in order to *see* (*Look for the silver lining*). It implies a desire to see but not necessarily the fulfillment of that desire (*I am looking, Mother, but I can't see it anywhere*). To *see* is to perceive with the eyes, to view, whether by intention or not (*Once over the pass you will see the town below you*).

lookout; outlook. In the senses of a looking out or a watch kept, *lookout* and *outlook* are interchangeable. *Lookout* is the preferred term, however, to designate the place from which a watch is kept (*A lookout had been erected on top of Bear Mountain*). It is also the term for the observer himself (*The thieves had their lookout at the corner. He spent a year as lookout for the National Park Service*). In slang *lookout* has the sense of the proper object of one's concern (*It's no concern of mine, son; that's your lookout*).

Outlook is the preferred term for the view or prospect seen from a lookout (*The outlook from the ranger's tower consisted of range after range of mist-shrouded mountains*). It is also the proper term for a mental view or attitude (*This warped outlook was certain in time to cause trouble*) or for a prospect of the future (*The financial outlook for the college was not good*).

Lord Bacon. See **Bacon.**

lose. The past tense is *lost*. The participle is also *lost*. See **miss.**

lose the thread of one's discourse is a hackneyed expression. The original suggestion of a clew guiding one out of a labyrinth, with echoes of Ariadne and the dreadful Bull, was good, but all such meaning is now lost and the phrase is empty and tiresome.

lost. See **lose.**

lot; lots. When used to mean merely an indefinitely large amount, these words are both treated as singulars when standing alone, as in *there is a lot here* and *there is lots here*. Both forms are treated as plural when followed by *of* and a plural noun, as in *there are a lot of men* and *there are lots of men*, and as singular when followed by *of* and a word that is singular in meaning, as in *there is a lot of butter* and *there is lots of news*.)

Some people feel that *a lot of* used with a plural verb is questionable, but this has been standard English for 250 years. Others, who would accept this use of *a lot of*, object to *lots* with a singular verb. This has been standard English for about 150 years. Both forms are acceptable in the United States today.

A lot and *lots* may both be used as adverbs,

especially to qualify an adjective or adverb in the comparative, as in *he is working a lot harder, he is working lots harder.*

In all constructions, *lots* is the more emphatic of the two terms, but *a lot* is generally preferred, perhaps for that reason.

loud. This word is as truly an adverb as it is an adjective. Spenser wrote, *a lyonesse that roaring all with rage did lowd requere her children deare.*

loud; showy. Although *loud* properly means striking strongly upon the organs of hearing, as sound or noise, it has assumed, by analogy, the sense of excessively striking to the eye, or offensively showy, making an imposing display, usually in bad taste (*He turned up at the funeral in a loud green pinstripe*). This use is commonly labeled "colloquial" in the dictionaries, meaning that it is used in cultivated speech but not in formal writing. But since there has been a marked tendency for almost two generations now to approximate in writing the easy familiarity of speech the distinction between colloquial and standard has tended to disappear. *Loud* in this sense conveys a striking impression. It is generally accepted and widely used. Its appearance in any piece of writing except, perhaps, a sermon, a legal document, or an epitaph would be accepted today.

loud speaker; loudspeaker. A *loud speaker* is a speaker who speaks loudly. A *loudspeaker* is any one of various amplifying devices by which speech, music, or other sounds can be made audible through a room, hall, or the like (*He is such a loud speaker that even in the municipal auditorium he doesn't need a loudspeaker*).

lour. See **lower.**

louse. The plural is *lice.* The singular *louse* is preferred as the first element in a compound, as in *louse nits* and *lousewort,* but the plural is also heard, and is acceptable, as in *lIce nits* and *licebane.*

lovable. See **amatory.**

love. This verb may be followed by an infinitive, as in *I love to tell this story.* It may also be followed by the *-ing* form of a verb, as in *I love telling this story.* This latter construction is relatively new but it is thoroughly established in the United States.

love; like. *Love* has been used so much to mean to have a strong liking for, to take pleasure in (*She loves to travel—anywhere, it doesn't matter so long as she's moving*), that this sense is accepted as standard. But it is used on such trivial occasions (as in *I'd love to join you for a cup of coffee but I've got to get these reports finished*) that it is often nothing more than an expression of mild inclination. Whether one uses *love* or *like* depends upon the intensity of the emotion one intends to suggest (an adult might say *I like to ride in front; there's more leg room.* Of children, however, whose delight is more intense and not a mere rational preference, it might properly be said *The kids love to ride in front and pretend they're driving*). In general, it is well to avoid using *love* unless the emotion is strong.

love or money. To say that one cannot get something or get something done *for love or money* is to employ one of those phrases that once had vigor but have been worn out by overuse.

loving. See **amatory.**

low. This word has two superlative forms, *lowest* and *lowermost.* The two forms *low* and *lowly* are both adjectives and both adverbs. We may say *the low lands, a lowly captain's daughter,* and *swing low sweet chariot, bow lowly.*

lower; lour. The verb *lower* means to let down from a higher position, to reduce in amount, decrease, diminish. The verb *lower* also means to be dark or threatening, as the sky or the weather, to frown, scowl, or look sullen, and sometimes, though not often now in America, it is spelled *lour.*

The two verbs are wholly different words springing from wholly different roots, but in their meanings there are an astonishing number of opportunities for ambiguity. When the clouds lower, in the sense of threatening rain, they usually lower in the sense of coming down nearer to the earth. When a countenance lowers, in the sense of becoming sullen and threatening, the brows are lowered or drawn down nearer the eyes. Fowler felt that the distinction should be preserved in the spellings, *lower* for letting down and *lour* for being sullen, but this does not hold in standard American usage where *lower* is used for both meanings, though with a different pronunciation, and *lour* is recognized only as a permissible variant spelling for the second meaning.

ludicrous. See **funny.**

luggage. See **baggage.**

lumber. The word *lumber* derives from the *Lombards* (which, in turn, derives from *Langobardi,* long beards) who, as money lenders and pawnbrokers, accumulated stores of cumbrous and discarded household articles. This is still the primary meaning of *lumber* in England, where a lumber room is a place where such things are stored. In America this meaning is recognized (*We've got to clear all that lumber out of the attic; there just isn't room for anything to be put up there*) but the primary meaning of the word in the United States and Canada is timber sawed or split into planks, beams, joists, boards and the like (*See if you can get me some two-by-fours at the lumber yard, Jim*).

The origin of the American meaning is not absolutely certain. One would assume that in a rapidly expanding country where so much building was of wood it was because sawed timbers were stored in the lumber room, but *A Dictionary of American English* says that the specific American meaning "undoubtedly arose from the fact that ship masts, sawed timber, barrel staves, etc., as important but bulky commodities, once blocked or lumbered up roads, streets, and harbors of various towns." The assertion is supported by a number of convincing quotations.

lunch and **luncheon** both mean a light meal between breakfast and dinner or, more loosely, any light meal. Of the two *lunch* is the more casual, *luncheon* more formal (*They dropped in* for lunch one day. The annual luncheon was held at the Brown Hotel. The restaurant offered a very good three-course luncheon for a dollar).

Brunch, a portmanteau combination of breakfast and lunch, is now accepted as standard for a mid-morning meal that serves both as breakfast and lunch but, whether the artificiality of the coinage is too obvious, whether it is used too exclusively by ladies' clubs, or whether the meal it describes is too uncommon, the word, somehow, seems slightly affected. The common man would be appalled to hear it used seriously in his company.

lure. See **allure.**

lustful and **lusty** both convey a sense of vitality, but lustful is restricted to a vitality of sexual desire. It means full of or imbued with lust and is not in most polite circles regarded as a complimentary term (Lustful Tarquin was the ignoblest Roman of them all). Lusty, however, suggests vitality of physical condition. One who is lusty is full of or characterized by healthy vigor and a delight in his own being. The term has favorable connotations for most people, especially pediatricians, poets like Browning and Whitman, and physical education instructors (Those lusty lads who work all day/ And dance all through the night). The adverb of lustful is lustfully, of lusty is lustily.

luxuriant and **luxurious** both derive from luxury, but after a long history in which they have frequently mingled they have achieved separate meanings. Luxuriant now means abundant or exuberant in growth (He parted the luxuriant jungle foliage for a glimpse of the sea. Leonardo's luxuriant genius, efflorescing in painting, sculpture, mechanics, and the arts of war). Luxurious means characterized by luxury, ministering to or conducing to luxury (After a month in the trenches the simple life of the village seemed luxurious). The words are most commonly confused in their adverbs luxuriantly and luxuriously.

lyceum. The plural is lyceums or lycea.

lyric and **lyrical** are both adjectives that can be used of poetry having the form and musical quality of a song, or of one who writes such poetry, or of something sung to the lyre. This last was the original sense. However, lyric is now the established form for most uses (lyric poetry, lyric poets, the lyric muse). It classifies definitely while lyrical describes vaguely (He was positively lyrical in your praises) or survives only in certain titles (The Lyrical Ballads).

The use of the noun lyric for the words of a song (It's got a swell tune but the lyric's no good) is slang.

lyricist; lyrist. A lyrist is one who plays on the lyre or a lyric poet. In England lyricist is sometimes used to refer to the poet; in the United States it is mainly used to refer to the author of the lyrics for a musical comedy.

M

mackerel. The plural is mackerel or mackerels.

mad; angry. Though mad in its basic sense means disordered in intellect, insane, or, in special reference to dogs, afflicted with rabies (Mad as a March hare. The dog, to gain some private ends,/ Went mad, and bit the man), its familiar sense, "moved by anger," has been in use so long and so universally that it would unquestionably be accepted as standard had not purist teachers made it the special target of their disapprobation. They have done their job so well, however, that although it is used a million times every day in our speech (I'm so mad I could spit) and is lodged in a score of phrases (mad as a wet hen), it is not often encountered in formal writing. Angry is the formal word. And since the stigma has been put on mad, one uses it in writing at his peril.

mad as a March hare, mad as a hatter. The wild frolicking of the buck hare in March, its breeding season, has made the creature a trope of giddy recklessness and lunacy for centuries. The hatter is a more recent comparison, though the phrase as mad as a hatter antedates Alice in Wonderland by almost thirty years. Some say the phrase is a corruption of as mad as an adder.

Others believe that it grew out of an occupational disease of hatters, characterized by jerky, involuntary movements, brought on by their handling of mercurial compounds.

Both phrases are more used in England than in America. Both are hackneyed.

Madagascan; Malagasy. Madagascar, the French colonial island in the Indian Ocean off the southeast coast of Africa, has the noun and adjective Madagascan; but the more specific term Malagasy is also used as a noun and adjective to describe a native of Madagascar or the Austronesian language of Madagascar.

madam; madame; ma'am. Madam, as a polite form of address, was used originally to a woman of rank or authority. It is a fine thing, Chaucer says, speaking of an alderman's wife, "to be called ma dame" and to take precedence of others in church. Today it is addressed to any woman and is to be preferred to lady as a form of address (see **woman**). A madam or the madam, and sometimes just madam if the context makes the meaning plain, is the woman in charge of a brothel (Sal, of "My Gal, Sal" was the madam of a sporting house in Evansville, Indiana).

Madame, the conventional French title of respect, originally addressed to a woman of rank, is used distinctively to or of a married woman, either separately or prefixed to her name. The plural is *mesdames.* The abbreviation of the singular is *Mme.,* of the plural, *Mmes.*

Ma'am, as a pronunciation of *madam,* has been relegated in England as a form of address "to the speech of servants or other persons of markedly inferior position" (*Oxford English Dictionary*). In America, outside of the large cities, it is still in use, especially in the South, though it is beginning to sound a little rustic or quaint. In English usage, paradoxically, by the way, it is still the correct, formal term to use in addressing the Queen or a royal princess—perhaps to show that all are but as "servants or other persons of markedly inferior position" in comparison, but more likely out of the conservatism of extreme formality. See also **Mrs.** and **woman.**

madding; maddening. *Madding,* going mad, acting as if mad, frenzied, is known today only in Gray's *Far from the madding crowd's ignoble strife,* and even that, nine times out of ten, is misquoted as *Far from the maddening crowd.* This makes sense to the common man and affords the uncommon man an opportunity to show his superior knowledge. Some who are ostentatious of fine distinctions insist that *mad* is to go mad and *madden* is to drive mad, but the distinction cannot be preserved, for both forms have been used with both meanings (*The devil has madded their minds. Fire in each eye, and papers in each hand,/ They rave, recite, and madden round the land*).

made. See **make.**

mademoiselle. The plural is *mesdemoiselles.*

mad man; madman. A *mad man* may be an angry man or an insane man. A *madman* is invariably an insane man.

maestro. The plural is *maestros* or *maestri.*

magic; magical. Of the two adjectives, *magical* is the more versatile, since it can be used to describe attributes or characteristics (*a magical transformation*) and to stand predicatively (*The reaction was magical*). *Magic,* on the other hand, is now used chiefly to identify (*magic lantern, Magic Flute*).

Magna Charta is, strictly speaking, the "great charter" of English liberties forced from King John by the English barons at Runnymede on June 15, 1215. It has come to mean, in addition, any fundamental constitution or law guaranteeing rights. Partridge declares to British users that for *Magna Charta* should be substituted either the Latin *Magna Carta* or the English *The Great Charter,* since "*Charta* is neither Latin nor English." And indeed it is not, but it has become good standard American and, outside of classrooms, standard English usage too. *Magna Carta* is an acceptable variant spelling.

magniloquent. See **grandiloquent.**

magnitude, of the first. The brightness of the stars is expressed by astronomers according to an arbitrary numerical system, stars of the first five magnitudes being visible to the unaided eye. The use of the word *star* to designate a prominent actor or singer led to the adoption of the astronomical term to distinguish the highest degree of preëminence, but it is now worn out.

magnum opus for one's great work, especially a literary or artistic work (*One man's magnum opus is often another man's magnum opium*), is forced and affected. If a man hasn't the courage to call it his *great work,* let him not try to get the advantages of both vanity and modesty by hiding in Latin.

Mahomet will go to the mountain. In the Middle Ages, when the Mohammedans constituted a very real threat to Europe, Mahomet, under the name of Mahound, was thought to be a demon, worshipped as a god by his misguided followers. In later centuries, when the threat had abated, he was regarded as an impostor and the success of his teachings (which it would have been the grossest impiety to have even thought of investigating) attributed to his boldness and impudence. This last quality was exemplified in the apocryphal story of his summoning the hill and, when it ignored the summons, saying *If the hill will not come to Mahomet, Mahomet will go to the hill,* a story, by the way, which cannot be traced in English beyond the 1612 edition of Bacon's essays. In the passage of time *mountain* has been substituted for *hill,* probably for the sake of alliteration, and the saying and its various parts have been repeated so often that any reference to it is not a mark of wit but of dullness.

maid of honor; maid of honour. *Maid of honor* is a term used in the United States to describe the chief unmarried attendant of a bride. It is also used to denote an attendant, usually unmarried, of the various beauty queens, regional queens who preside at various festivals, and so on. *Maid of honour* is the British spelling and it is used exclusively of a lady in attendance upon the Queen when she appears in public.

mail or **post** may be used as a noun to describe the system of transmission of letters and packages which is a department of the federal government, the delivery of such letters and packages, and the letters and packages delivered. Either word may be used as an adjective to designate the box in which the letters and packages are placed and the man and the vehicle which delivers them. In America the noun *mail* is preferred in nearly all instances except *parcel post.* The plural is sometimes used to designate the entire matter in transit (*The mail must go through. The protection of the mails was assigned to the United States Army*). In America the adjective *mail* is preferred in almost all instances except *Post Office. Postman* would be understood (*The postman always rings twice. Postman's knock*) and is used to designate the man who delivers the mail by some people in eastern cities, but *mailman* is almost universal. The verb *mail* is far more common in the United States than *post,* though *post a letter* is by no means rare.

The British prefer *post* as a noun and a verb, though they use the adjective *mail* in certain set expressions such as *mail-trains, mail-bags, mail-vans.*

mailed fist. As a term for military force, especially its display with intent to intimidate, *the mailed fist* is a journalistic cliché.

maintain. See **assert, claim.**

major, as an adjective, is, strictly speaking, the comparative of Latin *magnus, great.* It means greater, as in size, amount, extent, importance, rank (*The major emphasis in the new cars seems to be on speed rather than on safety*). The word is used a great deal and often indiscriminately. The major difficulty may prove to be the main or principal difficulty. A major campaign speech may be more precisely an important campaign speech, though, of course, it may be *major* in the sense of being more important than other speeches.

major general; the Major General. The form chosen depends on the purpose the words serve. *Major general* is the military term for an officer ranking next below a lieutenant general and the next above a brigadier general. If a particular major general is being referred to, the correct form is *the Major General.* If the term is used as an adjective to characterize an officer by rank, it is capitalized (*Major General Thomas Fairfax*). In England whenever a military officer has a title, the military title precedes the social title (*Major General Sir Reginald Pinney*).

major portion is a vague and pretentious term for *greater part.*

majority can only properly mean the greater part when it is applied to the greater part of a number of things. One may refer to the majority of mankind or the majority of the members of a club or the majority of those who prefer cigarets to cigars, and so on, but to say that *the majority of the valley was flooded* is not the best usage. It would be better to say *The greater part of the valley was flooded.* Strictly speaking, *majority* ought not to be used when *most* serves as well. *Majority* is better reserved for the occasion when a majority and a minority are in mind.

majority; plurality. In relation to an election or to jury returns, a *majority* is a number of voters or votes in agreement constituting more than half the total number (*He barely got a majority; the vote was seven to five*) or the excess whereby the greater number, as of votes, surpasses the remainder (*He won by a majority of two: the vote was seven to five*). A *plurality* may, but does not necessarily, mean a number constituting more than half the total. The usual sense of the term is to describe the excess of votes, when there are three or more candidates, received by the leading candidate over the next candidate (*Since Smith got eight votes, Jones six, and Brown four, Smith had a plurality of two but fell short by two of having a majority*).

make. The past tense is *made.* The participle is also *made.*

Make may be followed by an object and the simple form of a verb, as in *what makes the wind blow?* It could once be followed by an object and a *to*-infinitive, as in *I had killed the bird that made the wind to blow.* This construction is now obsolete when *make* has an active form. When *make* has a passive form the *to*-infinitive is required, as in *the wind was made to blow. Make* may also be followed by an object and a past participle with passive meaning (that is, the *be* of a passive infinitive is usually suppressed), as in *I made it known.*

Make could once be followed by an adjective, but this construction is now obsolete except for a few set phrases, such as *make bold, make merry, make free.*

make; earn. *Earn* means to gain by labor or service (*He earns more delivering milk than he ever did teaching school*) or to merit compensation (*They paid me more than I really earned*). *Make* as a synonym for *earn* (*Even after ten years they are only making forty dollars a week*) has been stoutly opposed by the purists but it is now so common that it must be accepted as standard.

make a clean breast of it. As a term for making a confession, especially one that relieves anxiety and pent-up feelings of guilt, to *make a clean breast of it* is overworked.

make a virtue of necessity. It was St. Jerome who put the idea of gaining merit by accepting gracefully that which one is compelled to do anyway into its present proverbial form of *making a virtue of necessity.* It was definitely a saying and close to a cliché when Chaucer used it eleven hundred years later. By now it is hackneyed and needs a rest.

make bricks without straw. When Moses asked Pharaoh to let the Children of Israel go three days' journey into the desert to sacrifice unto the Lord, the wicked king not only refused but said if the Hebrews had that much time on their hands he would see if he couldn't find more work for them, just to keep them busy, and ordered his taskmasters to give them no more straw with which to make their daily tale of bricks but to compel them to go and gather the necessary straw for themselves. Thus the bricks were not made without straw but the gathering of the straw from the stubble fields was laid on the people as an added burden, the same number of bricks was demanded from them, and they were beaten for failing to meet the demand. Thus the modern use of the phrase *to be compelled to make bricks without straw* as an image meaning to be required to execute some task without being given the necessary tools or materials distorts the actual situation described in the fifth chapter of Exodus. Far worse, it is worn out with overuse.

make hay while the sun shines. As a metaphor for acting while circumstances are favorable, seizing the propitious moment, making the most of opportunities, *make hay while the sun shines* is a faded one.

make no bones about. As a term for not raising objections or not making a fuss or not being very scrupulous, *to make no bones about* is one of those phrases that after four or five hundred years of constant use has lost all sense of its original meaning. It is not known for sure just what it did mean (it sometimes appears as *make no bones of* and sometimes *make no bones in*), but it seems to refer to someone who was too eager to swallow his soup to make any objection to whatever bones might be in it or to permit them to be an obstacle to the swallowing of it.

make one's blood boil. As a term for indicating great indignation, to say of something that it *makes one's blood boil* is to employ a cliché. Whatever force the exaggeration may once have had, it has long ago weakened to meaninglessness through repetition.

make the best of a bad bargain. As a term for accepting a misfortune resignedly or exploiting an unfavorable situation resourcefully, *making the best of a bad bargain* is hackneyed. Boswell spoke the expression with disdain a hundred and sixty years **ago.**

malady. See **sickness.**

malapropism is the misapplication of a word, such as *surface* for *service* or *contagious* for *contiguous*. It is worse than a mispronunciation because a mispronunciation, unless the result of affectation, is simply honest ignorance; whereas malapropisms are likely to occur in the speech of those who, ambitious to use fine language but not industrious enough to consult a dictionary, soar above their abilities and display, in the malapropism, not only their ignorance but their vanity as well.

Malapropism (from French *mal à propos,* inappropriate) derives from Mrs. Malaprop, an affected, talkative woman in Sheridan's *The Rivals* (1775). Of her many misapplications of words the most famous is her reference to "an allegory on the banks of the Nile." It is an instance of the capriciousness of fame that the word should be *malapropism* instead of *quicklyism,* for Shakespeare's Mistress Quickly (*Henry IV,* Parts 1 and 2) does the same thing, often more amusingly. Her assurance (in *Henry V*) that the dead Falstaff is "in Arthur's Bosom" is finer than anything Mrs. Malaprop ever blundered into.

male; masculine; manly; virile; mannish. *Male* always refers to sex, whether of human beings, animals, or plants (*There is no more mercy in him than there is milk in a male tiger*). There are a few extensions of the word as special applications in machinery, gems, and so on, but they are not common and belong in specialized vocabularies. *Masculine* applies to qualities that properly characterize men as contrasted to women (*He had a masculine love of horseplay*). If applied to a woman, it suggests something incongruous with her femininity (*Large shoulders gave her a masculine appearance*) or conveys a compliment (*She had a logical, masculine mind*). *Manly* and *virile* refer to typical qualities in a man that are to be admired. *Manly* implies possession of the noblest and most worthy qualities a man can have, as opposed to servility, insincerity, underhandedness, and the like (*He answered*

his inquisitors in a manly fashion. He bade me act a manly part, though I had ne'er a farthing O,/For without an honest manly heart, no man was worth regarding O*). *Virile* is an even stronger word than *manly.* It formerly emphasized the obvious maleness of one able to procreate but it now implies the vigor, health, and force of mature manhood (*Charlemagne was a virile monarch*). *Mannish* though its central meaning is "characteristic of or natural to a man," is more often used in the senses of "resembling a man" or "imitating a man." It is a term of contempt for affectedly masculine qualities (*Her mannish clothes and hair style hid her natural feminine grace*).

malice; malignity; malevolence; rancor. *Malice* is that ill will or spite which arouses the desire to inflict injury or suffering on another (*And malice in all critics reigns so high,/ That for small errors they whole plays decry*). *Malignity* is intense malice, hatred and the desire to injure so fierce as to dominate the whole mind and bring it to the borders of sanity (*The political reigns of terror have been reigns of madness and malignity,—a total perversion of opinion*). *Malevolence* means literally a wish of evil towards someone and it still has something in it more of the wish than of the act which the wish may instigate. It is a smoldering ill will (*The magic power of the witch lay in the force of her malevolence; her wishing ill could project harm upon the victim, make him liable to natural accidents and the prey of casual misfortunes*).

Rancor is bitter, rankling resentment, inveterate spitefulness and ill will. The word is akin to *rancid;* it is hatred so prolonged and intense that it has, as it were, turned the possessor's nature rancid (*Such rancor is not to be placated; it will find justification for its resentment*).

malignant fate, especially when it pursues someone or "dogs his steps" or "relentlessly dogs his steps," is a cliché.

mall; the Mall; pall-mall; Pall Mall. Though *mall* in its original sense is now obsolete, we know its diminutive *mallet* and its cognate *maul.* *Pall-mall* was a game, something between croquet and golf, played in England up until the eighteenth century. Its "fairways" consisted of long avenues and the word *mall* came to mean a shaded walk, usually public. *The Mall* is a fashionable promenade in St. James's Park, London. It is so called because it was originally a pall-mall alley. *Pall Mall,* the former site of another of these alleys, is now a street in London famous for its clubs.

mamma, a word used by children to signify mother, is the result of reduplication of *ma,* a syllable common in natural infantile utterance. In French the word is *maman,* in Latin *mamma,* in Greek *mámmé,* in Russian and Lithuanian *mama.* In English, *mama* is a variant spelling of the word in this sense. Americans tend to accent the first syllable, the English the second syllable. In comparative anatomy *mamma* has the specialized meaning of the organ, characteristic of mammals, which in the female secretes milk.

The plural of the word for mother is *mammas* (*The children with their mammas in the park*). The plural of the anatomical word is *mammae*.

mammoth, strictly speaking, designates a large, extinct species of elephant, the northern woolly mammoth, which resembled the present Indian elephant but had a hairy coat and long, curved tusks. More broadly, it designates any of various related extinct species of elephant.

By extension *mammoth* has come to be used as an adjective for anything huge or gigantic (*Plans for the production of a mammoth amusement park, dwarfing all others, etc.*). Some grammarians, especially English authors, have objected strenuously to the use of *mammoth* as an adjective, but Americans, whose way of life makes much greater demands for superlatives, have accepted it as standard (*Mammoth sale opens this morning. The mammoth parade began at Third and Main and extended beyond Twelfth Street*). This adjectival use of *mammoth* has been taken up even by the august *National Geographic Magazine* which (in July, 1947) turned it back into a noun (*Electric-drive mammoths are now being turned out by assembly-line methods*).

man. The plural is *men*. Nouns ending in *-man* have plurals ending in *-men* whenever the first part of the noun is itself a meaningful English word, as in *Englishman, juryman, chessman*. When the first part of a noun ending in *-man* is not a true English word, the whole has a regular plural in *s*, as in *Germans, Romans, Ottomans*; the only exception is *women*.

Compounds that have *man* as a qualifying element, and that actually refer to certain classes of men, have the form *men* in the plural, as in *menservants, men friends, men dancers*. This is contrary to the usual practice in English, according to which the first element in a compound is singular even when the whole is plural, as in *maidservants, boy friends, girl dancers*. When a compound that has *man* as a qualifying element means something other than a class of men, it follows the general rule and keeps the singular *man* in the plural, as in *man-hours* and *manholes*.

When the first element of a compound is not a qualifier but the object of the second element, only the singular form *man* may be used, as in *man-eaters* and *man haters*.

When *man* is the second element in a compound meaning a certain kind of man, a preceding noun usually has a final *s*, as in *sportsman, statesman, craftsman*.

The words *man* and *men*, when used generically, may be ambiguous. Either word may be used to mean the human race, as in *man is born unto trouble as the sparks fly upward* and *the best laid schemes of mice and men*. But they may also be used to mean the males only, as in *man is destined to be a prey to woman* and *men were deceivers ever*. The singular *man* is used more often to mean the race, and the plural *men*, to mean the males. But this rule is not followed consistently. When the context does not show that only the male is meant, it will generally be assumed that *men* includes *women*, regardless of what the author may have had in mind, as when Milton undertook *to justify the ways of God to men*. See **gentleman.**

man after my own heart. It was David whom God chose when *He sought him a man after his own heart* to replace the errant Saul. But all remembrance of this, with its sadness and solemnity, has faded from the phrase which is now merely a cliché for anyone who happens to agree with us.

man in the street. Whether one describes the ordinary man as *the man in the street* or the extraordinary man as a *man of parts* or an imaginary adversary, wholly unreal, as a *man of straw* or a wealthy man as a *man of substance* or a military leader who acquires such influence over the people as to threaten the existence of the government as a *man on horseback,* one is employing a cliché. They are all hackneyed phrases, faded and worn, devoid of any clear and vigorous meaning.

man of letters; author; writer. Partridge says that in England an *author* is a writer of fiction, a *writer* is a writer of fiction, history, biography and belles lettres, a *man of letters* is a writer of any or all of these or of poetry or works of scholarship. He feels that *man of letters* should be avoided as pretentious. *Author,* he thinks, has a dusty connotation, turning up chiefly in legal and official and semi-official documents, club titles, income-tax forms, and the like. Of the three terms, he feels *writer* to be the least invidious and hence the most generally useful.

In America *man of letters* is seldom used. It would be understood but would seem stiff and pompous. *Author* designates one who writes a novel, poem, or essay (a more inclusive term than in Britain), the composer of a literary work as distinguished from a compiler, translator, editor, or copyist. *Writer* has a more general meaning and, as in England, is the most used of the terms. It describes one who expresses ideas in writing, one engaged in literary work, one who writes, one whose occupation is writing. In the movies, radio, and television, *writer* means one who prepares the script. It is a regular title and one, by the way, which is not very high in the vast hierarchy of production. An *author* would be thought of as the man who wrote the story upon which the movie or script is based, a *writer* the man who adapted it for movie or television use. Distinguished authors have often worked as writers in Hollywood.

manage. See **handle.**

mandatary; mandatory. *Mandatary* is a noun. It describes a person or nation holding a mandate (*The congressman regards himself as mandatary of his constituents. On the award of the League of Nations, the Union of South Africa became mandatary over the former German colony*).

Mandatory may be used as an adjective or as a noun. It means pertaining to, of the nature of, or containing a mandate. In America it is often used to mean obligatory or compulsory (*The invitation was actually mandatory; the cadet was not permitted to decline it*). This use would be understood in England but is rarely employed there. *Mandatory* has a legal meaning of permitting no option (*There was a mandatory clause in the contract*). And it may mean having received a mandate (*The Union of South Africa became a mandatory power after World War I*).

As a noun *mandatory* is an acceptable variant of *mandatary,* though it is convenient to retain the distinction between the two words and to use *mandatory* as an adjective only.

maneuver. See **trick.**

manifest. See **evince.**

manifesto. The plural is *manifestoes.*

manifold; multifarious; multiform; multiple. *Manifold* means of many kinds, numerous and varied (*His manifold duties included coaching tennis, leading the choir, teaching Latin and English, and supervising the study hall*). *Multifarious* means having many different parts, elements, forms; and whereas *manifold* stresses the combination of diverse elements, *multifarious* stresses their diversity (*that multifarious thing called a state*). *Multiform* means having many forms, of many different forms or kinds (*The danger, though multiform, is not critical*). *Multiple* means consisting of or involving many individuals, parts, elements, relations (*The problem has multiple solutions. The multiple images of a series of mirrors*).

manly; mannish. See **male.**

manner; manners. When *manner* means a way of doing something, it is a singular noun and has a regular plural *manners,* as in *he paints in many different manners.* But when the word means politeness, only the plural form can be used. The word in this sense is treated as a plural, as in *your manners are improving,* but it is felt as a singular and cannot be used with a word implying number. See also **fashion.**

manner born, to the. Horatio, a visitor to Elsinore, walking with his old college friend, Prince Hamlet, on the platform before the castle at midnight, hears a flourish of trumpets, a roll of drums, and a discharge of ordnance. He asks what this means. Hamlet says that the king is having a drinking party and that each time his majesty drains a flagon of wine the feat is hailed with this uproar. Horatio asks if this is an old Danish custom. Hamlet says, *Ay, marry, it is;/ But to my mind, though I am native here/ And to the manner born, it is a custom/ More honored in the breach than the observance.*

It would seem redundant to stress the fact that he is referring to a habit, practice, custom, were it not that wiseacres insist that the phrase is *to the manor born,* that is, to high estate, to the aristocracy. This is absurd for several reasons. One is that the original context of the phrase, given above, doesn't support it. Another is that while a seeming pauper who had come down in the world might boast that he had been born to the manor (though it would be an awkward way of putting it, and except for the corruption of this passage appears nowhere in English), it would be a ridiculous thing for Hamlet to say; for though no doubt he had been born to many manors he had been born to the crown, to the kingdom.

manner of. This expression is somewhat bookish today and is not often used in natural speech. When used, it follows the pattern of *kind of* and not *kinds of.* If it is followed by a singular noun the whole construction is treated as a singular, as in *what manner of man is this?* If it is followed by a plural noun it takes a plural verb and a plural pronoun, as in *what manner of men are these?* Since *manner,* as used in this expression, is historically both a singular and a plural, it is technically correct in either construction and so not open to the attacks sometimes made against *kind of.*

manner of means. *By no manner of means* is an elaboration of *by no means* which is an elaboration of *not.* Each elaboration intends to be more emphatic and intense than the phrase or word it seeks to improve on and once they become, as they have, clichés, they are less emphatic and less intense. *No* and *not* remain effective negatives.

manslaughter. See **homicide.**

mantis. The plural is *mantises* or *mantes.*

mantle and **mantel** were originally simply variant spellings but they have become fixed in different meanings. A *mantle* is a sleeveless cloak and by extension a number of things that cover, envelop, or conceal like a cloak. The verb *mantle* means to cover with or as with a mantle (*The mourning-stole no longer / Mantled her form*). The word used to apply to garments worn by men and by women but for several generations now it has been largely restricted to women's garments.

Mantel is a noun, meaning the more or less ornamental structure above and about a fireplace, usually having a shelf or projecting ledge. It is also used as short for *mantelpiece,* the shelf itself.

manuscript; typescript. In the strict sense a *manuscript* is something written by hand (*His manuscript consisted of ten neatly penned pages*). The word is used loosely, however, to designate an author's copy of his work, whether written by hand or typewritten, which is used as the basis for typesetting (*The manuscript was so full of stenographic errors that the publisher had to send it back to the author*). Some authorities have objected to this extension of *manuscript,* insisting that a typewritten work should be called a *typescript,* but contemporary American usage has accepted the extension of manuscript as standard.

Manuscript is abbreviated *MS.* or *ms.* with the plural *MSS. or mss.*

many. The comparative form is *more.* The superlative form is *most.*

Many is primarily an adjective meaning a large number, and is used principally before a plural noun, as in *many men, many minds.* It may follow the noun, as in *she had children many,* but this is no longer natural English. The adjective *many* may be separated from its noun by *are* or *were,* as in *many are the hearts that are weary tonight.* It is sometimes used in this way with a singular noun, as in *many is the time I have said* and *many is the man who has thought.* This construction is now considered old fashioned in the United States and not accepted as standard in Great Britain. But *many* may still be used before the article *a* in a singular construction, as in *many a man has thought* and *I was many a weary month in finishing it.*

Many may also be used as if it were a noun and is then always a plural, as in *many are strong and rich and would be just* and *the many who know him say.* Formerly, this plural *many* could be preceded by the article *a,* as in *a many of them were there.* The plural word *few* is still treated in this way, but *a many* is now regarded as unacceptable except in the two expressions, *a good many* and *a great many.* There is no difference in meaning between the noun construction *many of* and the adjective *many,* but the construction with *of* is now used only before a pronoun or a definitive adjective, as in *many of these, many of the books.* We do not say *many of books.*

map; chart. A *map* is a representation of the surface of the earth or a section of it or of some other area (*Utopia will not be found on any map*). To say of some community that has suffered a disaster that it has been *wiped off the map* is to employ a hackneyed metaphor.

A *chart* may be an outline map with symbols conveying information superimposed on it, a map designed especially for navigators on water or in the air (*Without up-to-date hydrographic charts, wartime convoy escorts could never have operated*). The word *chart* is also used for a diagram or a table giving information in an orderly form.

marbles. When referring to the game, the plural word *marbles* takes a singular verb, as in *marbles is sometimes played on the sidewalk.* One piece is called *a marble* and *marbles* used with a plural verb means several of these, as in *marbles are round.* Only the singular form *marble* is used as the first element in a compound, as in *marble playing.*

When the word means the material used in building, it is a singular mass noun and the plural *marbles* means different kinds of marble.

The fragments from the frieze and pediment of the Parthenon in the British Museum are known as the *Elgin Marbles.* This term for a collection of sculptured pieces is now archaic except in museum terminology.

mare's nest. Since horses do not climb trees and lay eggs, he who discovers a *mare's nest* is a credulous simpleton who thinks he has found something wonderful but can only have done something silly. Two hundred years ago the finding of a mare's nest had already passed from a good, strong humorous phrase through a proverbial expression into a cliché. It is not much used now but when it is, it is frequently misused, as if it meant a mere false alarm or much ado about nothing.

marionette. See **puppet.**

marital. See **matrimonial.**

mark. The term *easy mark,* for one easily swindled or imposed upon, is an American slang term for which the British equivalent is *gull.*

mark of the beast. As a term for an indication in someone of something common to those of whom we disapprove, *the mark of the beast* is hackneyed. It is an echo of the twentieth verse of the nineteenth chapter of Revelation where the beast is the great whore of Babylon. The term appealed strongly to evangelical preachers, who used it so much in their denunciations that it became a term of jest among the wits and in time worn out by repetition.

mark time. To say of soldiers who lift their feet as though marching but set them down in the same place, so that they do not move forward, that they are *marking time* is to employ a figure of speech. But this particular figure of speech became connected so inseparably and so exclusively to this action that all sense of its being a figure of speech disappeared and it became the ordinary, prosaic name for it. From the action it was taken up again, however, as a new metaphor for any action which fills the time but does not lead to progress (*These sales are just marking time, holding a place in the market until we get ready to expand*) and this use is now so worn by repetition that it is better avoided.

market and **mart** are both acceptable in the United States as names for a trading center. *Mart,* which derives from the Dutch spoken variant of *markt,* market, is archaic in England, Partridge says, and rather literary. But in the United States it flourishes. It may have been used at first to give a touch of distinction, but there are now so many motor marts and furniture marts that it is accepted as standard. When capitalized, *mart* refers to a particular building, as Chicago's Merchandise Mart and Furniture Mart.

marriage. See **wedding.**

martyr; victim. The word *martyr* derives from a Greek word meaning a witness. A martyr was one who witnessed to his faith in his religion by being willing to die rather than to renounce his beliefs (*Stephen was the first Christian martyr*), or one who is put to death or endures great suffering on behalf of any belief, principle, or cause (*He was a martyr in the cause of constitutional liberties*), or, quite loosely, one undergoing severe or constant suffering. In this usage the suffering has to be severe, the illness grave, and the endurance of its pains dignified. One who died of cancer, for instance, after long suffering, might be spoken of as a martyr to the disease. But one who suffers from colds in the head, however unpleasant the affliction may be, cannot be called a martyr.

A *victim* differs from a martyr in that the martyr actively accepts his infliction, while the victim is the passive recipient of his. A *victim* is a sufferer from any destructive, injurious, or adverse action or agency (*Juvenile delinquents are often victims of their environment*), a dupe (*He was the victim of card-sharpers*), a person or animal sacrificed, or regarded as sacrificed, in any undertaking (*He was a victim of the Dieppe raid*), or a living creature sacrificed in religious rites (*the victim led lowing to the altar*).

marvel; miracle. A *marvel* is something to wonder at, a prodigy, something astonishing (*It was a marvel that any of the passengers escaped. Both engines were on fire when the wheels touched the runway*). A *miracle* is a marvel, but it is more; it is something which has an effect in the physical world which surpasses all known or human powers and is, therefore, ascribed to supernatural agency (*Christ's first miracle was changing water into wine*). People who jump off Brooklyn Bridge and survive, or go over Niagara Falls in barrels, perform marvels but not miracles; while far less spectacular natural happenings, such as the provision by certain female insects for the young which they will never live to know, may be described as miracles. Whether a given event is properly a miracle or a marvel is disputable; the employment of one word instead of another is often dependent upon the attitude of mind of the speaker. But there is no doubt that a continuous use of *miracle* to describe any coincidence or amazing happening is vulgar.

masculine. See **male.**

mass. One sense of *mass* is the main body, bulk, or greater part of anything. The word thus becomes an equivalent of *majority* (*In 1944 the mass of American military strength was in Europe*). This use, though occasionally decried, is now standard.

massacre and **slaughter,** whether as nouns or transitive verbs, imply violent and bloody methods of killing. *Massacre* designates the unnecessary, indiscriminate killing of a number of human beings, as in barbarous warfare or persecution, or for revenge or plunder (*It was assumed that the settlers were massacred by the Indians; no trace of them was ever found*). *Massacre* may not be used to describe the killing of one person. *Slaughter,* like *butcher,* is a term usually applied to the killing of animals and gains some of its violent horror when applied to human beings from that fact. An individual may be slaughtered (*Priam was slaughtered as he clung to the altar*) and so may great numbers of people. *Massacre* carries a suggestion that the victims were innocent and helpless or unresisting; whereas soldiers may be slaughtered in battle if the carnage is sufficiently widespread and fierce.

masseur and **masseuse** are both borrowed from the French but now fully naturalized in our language and therefore not to be italicized in writing. A *masseur* is a man who practices massage, a *masseuse* is a woman.

mass nouns. A singular noun is used to refer to one thing and a plural noun to refer to more than one, as *boy* and *boys, book* and *books*. But some nouns, such as *butter, sunlight, Latin, oxygen,* are neither singular nor plural in meaning. They do not refer to precise countable things but to something formless and uncountable. Words of this kind are called *mass nouns*. In contrast, words that refer to countables are called *unit*

nouns. Names of abstractions, such as *beauty, justice, childhood, arithmetic, logic,* are mass nouns, but so are the names of such concrete things as *gunpowder, lettuce, mud, dust,* and *ammunition.*

Most mass nouns, like the examples given so far, are grammatical singulars. These are always treated as singulars. They are used with a singular verb and can be qualified by *the, this,* or *that*. But they do not form plurals and they cannot be qualified by the article *a*. Also, unlike singulars, they can be used without any qualifiers. We can say *sunlight is good for you,* although we cannot say *book is good.*

When a word that is ordinarily a mass noun, such as *fur, space, injustice,* is qualified by *a,* as in *a fur, a space, an injustice,* it is being used in a slightly different sense. In this new sense it is a unit noun, it refers to a countable thing, and can have a plural form, such as *furs, spaces, injustices*. Similarly, a word that is ordinarily a unit noun can be used without *a* as a mass noun. *Lamb* is a unit noun in *there is a little lamb in the meadow* and a mass noun in *there is a little lamb in the icebox*. In the first sentence *a* qualifies *lamb* and makes it a unit noun. In the second sentence *a* qualifies *little* and *lamb* is unqualified. Expressions like this, with more than one meaning, are very common in English. But they are not ambiguous in context—that is, they are not misunderstood—and are not noticed unless one is bored and looking for trouble.

Not all mass nouns are grammatical singulars. Some nouns, such as *munitions, news, measles, riches, savings, morals,* are plural in form but do not refer to countable things. These require special attention. They are mass nouns, not true plurals.

Words of this kind do not have a corresponding singular form and cannot be used with a numeral, which would suggest several singulars. As a rule, these words cannot be used with any qualifier that suggests countables, such as *many, several, few*. That is, in speaking of a savings account we cannot say *how many savings has he?* When such words are not the subject of a verb, they can be qualified by words used with singular mass nouns, such as *much* and *little*. We may say *how much savings has he?* or *he has very little savings*. In these respects, plural mass nouns are being treated as if they were singular mass nouns. In the case of some words, such as *news, hydraulics,* and *economics,* mass nouns with plural form are treated in every respect like singular mass nouns. That is, they are also followed by a singular verb, qualified by *this* and *that,* and referred to by *it,* as in *this news is good; where did you hear it?* But more often mass nouns with a plural form keep some of their plural characteristics. That is, they are followed by a plural verb, qualified by *these* and *those,* and referred to by *they* or *them,* as in *these savings are all I have; I would hate to lose them.*

Many plural mass nouns are like *savings* and *morals.* They are related to unit nouns that have a singular and a plural form but a slightly different meaning. That is, *a saving* means an economy, and in this sense we may speak of *many savings*. But when *savings* means money that has been put aside, it is a mass word and we speak of *much savings*. Similarly, *a moral* is an edifying generalization and we may speak of *many morals*. But *morals,* meaning moral habits or principles, is now a mass noun and we cannot say *he hasn't many morals.* Usually, though not always, a plural noun that does not have a singular form with exactly the same sense is a mass noun and cannot be treated as a true plural.

A few mass nouns, such as *ash* and *ashes, sand* and *sands,* have both a singular and a plural form. This is very convenient, grammatically, since such words can be used in any kind of construction we like. But it should be noticed that there is not the usual difference in meaning between the singular and the plural form. The plural form does not mean more of the substance than the singular does.

Names of foods are usually mass nouns. The names of meats—fish, flesh, or fowl—have the singular form, as in *we ate cod all winter* or *we ate goose every Sunday.* The names of grains—*wheat, barley, rice,* and so on—are also treated as singulars. The only exceptions are *oats* and *grits,* which are treated grammatically as if they were names of vegetables. The names of most vegetables and fruits, when the plant is ready to eat, may be treated as true plurals, as in *there are a few beans left but not many peas,* or as mass words with plural form, as in *there is a little beans left but not much peas.* There are a few exceptions. *Potato* is sometimes, and *cabbage* is always, treated as a singular mass noun, as in *a little potato but not much cabbage. Lettuce* is a singular mass noun, even before the plant reaches the table.

master. See **boss.**

matchwood. See **kindling wood.**

materialize, as a transitive verb, means to give material form to, to make physically perceptible (*The medium materialized the apparition by means of magical words*). Used intransitively, to *materialize* means to assume material or bodily form, to come into perceptible existence (*Mephistopheles materialized as a black poodle*). Used loosely as a synonym for *appear* or *come into existence,* especially when used of things that do not have a physical being anyway (as in *There was a good deal of grumbling but the mutiny never materialized*), it is incorrect and often borders on the silly, as in *Time*'s assurance (November 22, 1954) that despite the promises in various headlines of startling disclosures in a famous murder trial *no new angles materialized.*

materially; greatly. *Materially* means substantially, to an important degree, considerably (*He contributed materially to the success of the undertaking*). Where something material, such as money or equipment, is contributed to a cause or enterprise of some kind, the word has a slightly different meaning (*Though he insisted that he was unfit to advise us, he assisted materially with money and ammunition*), and in such fairly rare

instances there is no doubt that it is the proper word. But much of the time *greatly* would be a better word. It is more common, less pretentious, and less likely to be ambiguous.

matins. In speaking of the church service, only the plural form *matins* is used and this is now regularly followed by a plural verb, as in *the matins were sung.* The singular form *matin* is used only in an extended or figurative sense, as in *the lark's shrill matin.* Both forms are found in compounds, as in *matin time* and *matins book.*

There is not as much variation in the use of the word *matins* as there is in the use of the word *vespers.* Perhaps this is because the great lay public hears vespers while matins are chiefly attended by the clergy, who are more conservative in their use of words.

matrimonial; marital; nuptial; conjugal; connubial. All of these words mean of or pertaining to the married state, but there are some differences in their meanings that have to be observed and others that the careful speaker or writer will want to observe.

Nuptial refers to the wedding or to events immediately succeeding the wedding (*the nuptial day, the nuptial feast*) that are related to it. In describing the marriage itself the word, used as a noun, is always used in the plural (*Their nuptials were solemnized amid a blaze of beauty*). Save for certain legal and quasi-legal uses (*the nuptial contract, pre-nuptial experiences*), *nuptial* is forced and stilted. It is dear to the pens of tired society editors.

Matrimonial is now the most common term for anything concerned with the marriage relation (*matrimonial problems, matrimonial difficulties*). *Marital* comes next, with the attraction of being a shorter word (*Marital troubles often have in them something comic; the couple have made their bed and must lie on it*), but it has, in addition to its general meaning, a specific meaning of pertaining to a husband (*A husband may exercise his marital authority so far as to give his wife moderate correction*).

Conjugal and *connubial* are used interchangeably, though both are a little ponderous and are employed, chiefly, in heavy-handed jocosity. *Conjugal* relates, strictly, to the married persons (*Their conjugal affection was touching to behold*), *connubial* to the married state (*connubial rites, connubial bliss*).

matrix. The plural is *matrixes* or *matrices.*

matter. For *matter* used as a verb, as in *nothing matters,* see **mind.**

matter; material; stuff. *Matter* and *material* both refer to that of which physical objects are composed. *Matter,* as distinct from mind and spirit, is by far the broader term. It applies to anything perceived or known to be occupying space (*The molecular theory of matter . . . supposes that all visible forms of matter are collocations of simpler and smaller portions. All we know about matter is that it is the hypothetical substance of physical phenomena*). *Material* usually means some definite kind, quality, or quantity of matter, especially as intended for use (*It was hard to* get building material during the war. The top of the table was covered with some hard, smooth material painted to resemble marble).

Stuff has much the same meanings as *material*. When used to refer to material objects, it is a loose term (*The building was made of some funny white stuff. Any sort of stuff will do to fill in the holes*). When used abstractly, it is literary and poetical (*The stuff of life to knit me/ Blew hither; here am I*).

matter, the. The use of the phrase *the matter* to mean trouble or difficulty, especially in the question *What's the matter?* is standard usage. It has been so employed for five hundred years and more. Horwill seems to feel that it is an Americanism, and certainly we use the phrase freely to mean "what is the objection to?" or "what can be alleged against?" this or that proposal or course of action, but it was so used in England from at least the fifteenth century on (Falstaff: *How now? Whose mare's dead? What's the matter?*) and if it has fallen into disuse in England in the past few decades (for it was certainly in use at the end of the nineteenth century), it is a change there rather than in the United States.

maunder; meander. To *maunder* is to whine or grumble in an incoherent way, to mutter or talk idly and disconnectedly. Burton in *The Anatomy of Melancholy* characterizes a demented man as *maundering, gazing, listening, affrighted with every small object.* Carlyle speaks of one who was always *mumbling and maundering the merest commonplaces.*

To *meander* is to proceed by a winding course, to wander (*Five miles meandering with a mazy motion/ Through wood and dale the sacred river ran. He was just meanderin' down the pike with nothing special in mind*). Indeed, the word is derived from the name of a Greek river which wound a great deal in its course. But one can meander in speech as well as in walking or flowing and the question of at what point divagation ceases to be meandering and becomes maundering must be decided by the individual observer or listener. Meandering can often be brilliant; maundering is stupid. But whether a digression, especially an aimless and wandering one, is to be described as brilliant or stupid often depends on the charity and sympathy of the listener.

mausoleum. The plural is *mausoleums* or *mausolea.*

maximum. The plural is *maximums* or *maxima.*

may. This is the present tense. The past tense is *might.*

He may does not have the *s* ending we ordinarily expect in a present tense verb. This is because *may* is an ancient past tense form. But it had come to be felt as a present tense by the time English became a written language. *Might* is a new past tense form that was created for it, but which has also come to be felt as a present tense. Today *may* and *might* are treated as subjunctive tenses. They represent different degrees of probability rather than a difference in time. The present subjunctive form *may* represents an event as possible while the past subjunctive form *might* represents it as possible but not

likely, as in *he may come* and *he might come.* In asking permission, *might* is more diffident than *may*, as in *might I come in?*, since it politely suggests that the speaker does not expect to get what he is asking for and so won't be surprised by a refusal. See **subjunctive mode.**

The verb *may* has no imperative, no infinitive, no past participle, and no *-ing* form. Because the words *may* and *might* are grammatically past tense forms, just as the word *went* is, they cannot follow (that is, they cannot be dependent on) another verb. We can no more say *will may, did may, used to might,* than we can say *will went, did went, used to went.* Since we cannot use auxiliaries, such as *do, be, have,* we form negative statements and ask questions in the old direct way that is now obsolete for most verbs, as in *he may not come* and *may I come?*

May and *might* themselves are always used as auxiliaries and require another verb to complete their meaning. This may be the simple form of the verb, as in *I might say,* or *have* and the past participle, as in *I might have said.* In the first case, the statement refers indefinitely to the present or the future. In the second case, it refers to a past event. The complementary verb must be actually stated or easily supplied from the context, as in *do you think you might see him?* and *I may.*

Can frequently is, and sometimes should be, used in place of *may.* For a discussion of this, see **can; may.**

maybe has been so long "as natural as *perhaps,* or more so," in American speech that Fowler's characterization of it as "stylishly archaic" sounds very strange. He admits that it was once normal English, but insists that it became rustic and provincial and is now something of an affectation. So it may be in England, or may have been a generation ago when Fowler first wrote, but in the United States it has always been acceptable.

me. In natural, well-bred English, *me* and not *I* is the form of the pronoun used after any verb, even the verb *to be.* When Mayor Cermak of Chicago was shot by a bullet intended for Franklin Roosevelt, he said: "I'm glad it was me instead of you." A local newspaper thought they could improve the dying man's words and quoted him as saying, "I'm glad it was I." See **objective pronouns.**

meal. See **flour.** See also **repast.**

mean. The past tense is *meant.* The participle is also *meant.*

When this word means intend it may be followed by an infinitive, as in *I mean to wait.* When it means signify it may be followed by the *-ing* form of a verb, as in *this means waiting.*

mean. See **average.**

meander. See **maunder.**

meaningful verb. This expression is used in this book to mean the element in a verbal phrase that supplies the meaning to the phrase, as *eaten* in *the turkey will have been eaten by now.* It is sometimes called the notional verb, in contrast to the others in the phrase, which are auxiliaries.

means. When this word means something that enables one to accomplish his purpose, it can be used as a true singular or as a true plural. We may say *every means has been tried, all means have been tried, one means is still open to us, several means are still open to us.*

When the word means wealth, it is always followed by a plural verb, as in *his means have increased*, never *his means has increased*. But it is here a mass word and not a true plural. We can speak of *great means* or of *no great means*, but not of *many means* or *few means*. When the word is not followed by a verb, it may be treated as a singular and we may speak of *much means* or *little means*.

The singular form *mean* is now used only for something that is in the middle, such as *a geometric mean*, and in this sense the word has a regular plural *means*, as in *insert three geometric means*.

meant. See **mean**.

mean time; meantime. *Mean time*, more properly called *mean solar time*, is time measured by the hour angle of the mean sun. The mean sun is an imaginary and fictitious sun moving uniformly in the celestial equator and taking the same time to make its annual circuit as the true sun does in the ecliptic (*If a navigator does not have the mean time, he cannot determine his position by means of his sextant*).

Spelled as one word and used as a noun, *meantime* means the intervening time (*There must have been little meantime between the lighting of the fuse and the explosion*). Such usage is exceedingly rare and would seem forced and affected. The most common use of the single word is in an adverbial phrase meaning "in the intervening time, during the interval" (*In the meantime, in between time,/ Ain't we got fun?*).

meanwhile is a noun. It may be used in a prepositional phrase, as in *it had grown dark in the meanwhile*, or alone as an adverb, as in *it had grown dark meanwhile*. Both constructions are standard English. In Great Britain this word is often written as two, that is, as *mean while*, but in the United States the solid compound is preferred.

measles. This word has a plural form and may be treated as a plural, as in *measles are contagious* and *he caught them from me*. But it is more often treated as a singular, as in *measles is contagious*, and *he caught it from me*. Both constructions are acceptable. The singular form *measle* is not used in connection with this disease and an individual spot is called a *macule*.

The plural form *measles* is used as the first element in a compound when referring to the disease that occurs in human beings, as in *a measles epidemic*. The singular form *measle* may be used in speaking of certain other diseases that occur in animals, as in *a measle epidemic*.

measures

DISTANCE

The names for units of distance, such as *inch, foot, fathom, mile*, are nouns. When used without a numeral before another noun these words have a genitive form, as in *a mile's walk, a foot's*

depth. When used with a numeral before another noun, the measure term is treated as the first element in a compound and the simple form of the word, that is, the singular form, is used, as in *a three-mile walk, a five-foot pole*. This is true even when an adjective stands between the measure term and the noun, as in *a three-mile-long walk* and *a five-foot-high wall*. But when the measure term is not followed by a noun, the plural form should be used in speaking of more than one, as in *a walk, three miles long* and *a wall, five feet high*.

At one time, these measure terms always had the singular form when used with a numeral, regardless of whether or not they qualified a following noun. This was standard English for measures of distance as late as the eighteenth century and Defoe wrote, *ten mile out of London*. The construction is not standard now, except for *foot* and *fathom*. *Fathom* is still used in this way in Great Britain but is rarely heard in the United States. *Foot* is still used in this way in the United States, as in *he is five foot ten*. But *feet* is also heard here. Both forms are acceptable.

The use of the plural form before a following noun, as in *a three-miles walk*, a *five-feet wall*, is not literary English. But it is heard too often in the United States not to be called standard here.

Measurements are often given in a form such as *it was three feet long by two feet wide*. Here the preposition *by* has an adjective, *wide*, for its object. This is curious, grammatically, but it is the standard way of expressing measures of this kind. In *he stood at two yards distant* and *the wall had risen to ten feet high*, we again have a preposition, *at* or *to*, with an adjective, *distant* or *high*, as its object. These constructions, but not the construction involving *by*, are condemned by some grammarians. So far as theoretical grammar goes, there is no difference between the first sentence and the last two, and no one should feel obliged to avoid these constructions if they seem natural to him.

TIME

The names of units of time, such as *hour, week, month, year*, are also nouns. When used without a numeral before another noun, they too have a genitive form, as in *an hour's walk, a year's delay*. When they are used with a numeral before another noun, no *s* is required. *A half-hour walk, a two-hour walk*, is literary English. But, unlike the units of distance, units of time frequently have a final *s* when standing in this position. If the numeral is *one*, or less than one, the *s* is considered a genitive singular and the expression is written *a one-hour's walk, a half-hour's walk*. When the numeral is larger than *one*, there is no agreement as to whether the *s* represents a genitive singular, a genitive plural, or a simple plural, and the words may be written in any of these ways, as in *a two-hour's walk, a two-hours' walk, a two-hours walk*. All three forms are used by reputable publishers but the last, without the apostrophe, is generally preferred.

An adjective may stand between the time

word and the noun it qualifies, as in *a year-old child*. In this case, the form without *s* is generally preferred, as in *a two-year-old child*. A plural form is sometimes heard here, as in *a two-years-old child*. This is not literary English but it is acceptable in the United States. No apostrophe should be used here.

When a time word is not followed by a noun, the plural form must be used in speaking of more than one, as in *a child two years old* and *he has been away two years*. In the case of time words, the use of the singular form in constructions of this kind has not been standard for four or five centuries. It occurs in some of Shakespeare's plays but only "in the language of low persons."

The adjective *old* is often used in literary English as the object of a preposition, as in *a child of a year old, at ten months old*. This construction is condemned by some grammarians, but it is a standard English idiom.

QUANTITY

Names for measures of quantity, such as *ton, gallon, teaspoon,* are also nouns and are usually joined to other nouns by *of*, as in *a ton of bricks, a smidgin of salt*. The singular form, but not the plural, may be used as the first element in a compound, as in *a five-ton truck, a ten-gallon hat*. In any other construction, measures of capacity require the plural form when speaking of more than one, as in *ten gallons of gas*. But measures of weight can always be used in the singular with a numeral, as in *three ton of coal*. In the United States the plural form is more usual, as in *three tons of coal*. But the singular form is preferred in Great Britain and is acceptable in this country.

See the individual words and **full; -ful**. For the use of the *a* in *five dollars a visit, ten cents a ton*, see **nouns as adverbs**.

meat. A peculiarly American use of the word *meat* is to attach it to the name of the animal whose flesh is being considered as food. *Crab meat*, for example, is standard (*Crab meat is a delicacy of which one easily tires. She was very fond of crab-meat salad*). *Turkey meat* is, perhaps, questionable and *hog meat* is definitely regional, its use being confined, for the most part, to the mountainous regions of southeastern United States. *Horse meat* (or more often *horsemeat*), designating in some contexts, formerly more common than now, what is fed to horses, now generally means the edible flesh of the horse. In this one instance the usage is accepted in England.

meat and drink in the metaphorical sense of spiritual sustenance (*Such praise was meat and drink to him*) is a cliché, to be avoided.

Mecca is a city in Saudi Arabia. It was the birthplace of Mohammed and is the spiritual center of Islam to which every devout Mohammedan hopes some day to make a pilgrimage. Hence it has come to mean a place which constitutes a center or goal for many people, but even in this extended sense it is better to confine it to a place to which people wish to go for some high or solemn purpose or which represents to them

deep aspirations. It is all right to say *Paris is the Mecca of most sophisticated young American artists*. It is journalese to say *Miami Beach is the midwinter Mecca of well-heeled New Yorkers* or *Palm Springs is the Mecca of the elite of Hollywood and all who want to be seen in public with them*. And like all metaphors it cannot be used in any sense that conflicts ludicrously with its original sense. The writer who said that *Rome is the Mecca of all good Catholics* may have meant well but his statement would seem offensive to millions of Roman Catholics.

mechanical. See **equipment**.

Medes and the Persians, laws of. As a term for something fixed and unalterable, *the laws of the Medes and the Persians* is hackneyed. Its use in English is due to its being referred to in two separate passages in the Old Testament (Esther 1:19 and Daniel 6:8) though very few who employ the cliché have any longer a knowledge of that fact.

media in the sense of all of the means by which products may be advertised—newspapers and magazines, radio, television, billboards, etc. (*B. T. Babbitt Co., making a major switch in media strategy, has scheduled an intensive newspaper campaign this fall for its new household cleaner, Bab-O with Bleach*) is a jargon word that will probably have to be accepted as standard in time. Some word is necessary in the advertising world to describe collectively all of the ways of advertising and this quite natural extension of *medium* in its meaning of an agency or instrument is too firmly established now to be easily dislodged. See also **medium**.

mediocre means middling, neither good nor bad, ordinary, average, commonplace. In a democracy such words ought to be regarded as commendatory but they are not. Every man likes to regard himself as superior to others and a word which says one is like most other men is regarded as derogatory. *Mediocre* in common usage certainly carries a pejorative implication. It does not mean bad, but it definitely means poor, feeble, and inferior. *Very mediocre*, though often heard, is not standard. You cannot apply an intensive to the ordinary or average. Of course those who do apply it no longer think of the word as meaning average but poor and hence feel their intensive is justified. But until this sense of *mediocre* is accepted as standard—as in time it well may be—the use of an intensive is improper.

meditate. See **contemplate**.

medium. The plural is *mediums* or *media*. The Latin plural is used correctly in the rather ponderous expression *media of mass communication*. This is sometimes shortened to *mass media*. The new form is then frequently treated as a singular and given a new plural, *mass medias*. Other Latin plurals, such as *agenda* and *candelabra,* have become English singulars in this way and that of itself would not be enough to condemn the new term. This is particularly true since the form *medium* is regularly used in connection with supernatural matters. The real difficulty with *mass medias* is that *mass* has here lost all connection with *communication* and is in danger of taking on the derogatory implication of the masses versus the discriminating few. For this reason it is safer to shorten the expression still further and speak of *medias*.

meet. The past tense is *met*. The participle is also *met*.

meet with an untimely end. To say of one who died before, in the natural order of things, he might have been expected to die, especially of one who died by violence, that he *met with an untimely end* is to use a cliché.

meiosis is a term in rhetoric for understatement. It is the opposite of hyperbole or, more accurately, a form of hyperbole which gets its effects by diminishing rather than enlarging the truth. See **litotes**.

meliorist. See **optimist**.

melody; tune. A *tune* is a *melody*, but a *melody* need not be a *tune*. That is, in addition to tunes there are such things as plainsongs (the unisonous vocal music used in the Christian church from the earliest times) which may be classified as melodies. A tune is a succession of musical sounds forming an air or melody, with or without the harmony accompanying it. Tunes tend to be short and catchy, like nursery rhymes (*But the only tune that he could play/ Was "Over the Hills and Far Away." That's the tune the old cow died on*). *Melody* describes likewise the succession of single tones in musical composition but, unlike the *tune*, a *melody* may go on for a long time (*The song is ended, but the melody lingers on*). *Melodious* and *tuneful*, however, are synonymous. See also **harmony**.

memorandum. The plural is *memorandums* or *memoranda*. Many educated people use the form *memoranda* as a singular, with a regular plural *memorandas*. These forms are therefore acceptable English. But they are offensive to some people. Of the three plurals, *memorandums* probably rouses less antagonism than *memoranda* or *memorandas*.

men. See **man**.

mendacity; mendicity. *Mendacity* is untruthfulness (*the ineradicable tendency of the human mind to mendacity*) or an untruth (*Father, I will not tell a mendacity;/ It is beyond my capacity*). See also **lie**.

Mendicity is the practice of begging or the condition of life of a beggar (*In the case of professional authors, mendicity often trails mendacity along with it*). Though it is an old word, having been in use in English for six hundred years or more, it is still rare and even the most fluent author would not be likely to have occasion to use it.

menial meant originally a household servant, usually employed by contract or a binding stipulation that required him to continue the service for a definite period of time. The word designated one of a body of household servants and it is this that makes any use of it today an affected elegancy, for no one has a body of household servants any more.

As an adjective, *menial* is, and for centuries has been, a term of disparagement and contempt,

synonymous with servile (*The necessity of performing these menial tasks was galling to his pride*).

mentality; mind. *Mentality* means mental capacity, intellectual endowment, degree of intellectual power (*He had the mentality of a child*). It has become a vogue word for *mind* in recent years (*Use your mentality/ Wake up to reality*), and there are many contexts in which either word may be used, for *mind* cannot be defined precisely. But when in doubt it is better to use *mind*.

mention may be followed by the *-ing* form of a verb, as in *I mentioned having gone there*. It is sometimes heard with an infinitive, as in *I mentioned to have gone there*, but this is not standard English.

mentor is a wise and trusted counselor. Mentor was the friend to whom Odysseus, when departing for Troy, gave the charge of his household. In America *mentor* is currently sportswriter's jargon for an athletic coach, especially a football coach. There is a grim appropriateness in the application, though not probably the one intended by the sportswriters; for the demands imposed on coaches, wise and otherwise, by greedy players, ravening alumni, envious faculty members, and harassed administrators, are as onerous as those imposed on the old Ithacan by Penelope's disorderly suitors.

mercenary. See **venal**.

mere; bare. *Mere* means nothing more nor better than what is specified, a scant sufficiency (*He wrested a mere livelihood from the poor land*), pure and simple, nothing but (*Such a suggestion is mere idiocy*). It is often inserted as an intensive (*The book is mere trash; it is ridiculous to hail it as a masterpiece*) where the sentence would be more forceful without it.

Bare, in the sense in which it is synonymous with *mere*, means without other things, no more than. In designating a minimum of sufficiency, the words are often interchangeable, but there is usually a subtle difference in their implications. *Bare* is positive. It means that something is adequate by itself, that there is a chance, etc. (*The bare mention of his name brought the delegates to their feet in a tumultuous demonstration*). *Mere* is negative. It seems to suggest a deficiency. The effects that it attends are more likely to be unpleasant (*mere folly. This is mere conjecture, not an established fact. The mere mention of his name seemed to plunge the delegates into despair*). See also **pure**.

meretricious does not merely mean bad or false or deceptive. It is derived from a Latin word for "prostitute" and it means alluring to a bad end by false attractions, not merely tawdry and showy but tawdry and showy covering up of something base or evil. It is a word of strong condemnation, with moral disapproval underlying aesthetic disapproval. In most uses it is stilted, but there are occasions when it is the word wanted. *False honors*, for example, would simply imply that honors had been conferred where they were not merited. *Meretricious honors* would imply that the honors were the reward of evildoing or used to conceal evildoing.

meridian; meridiem. See **a.m.**

merriment. See **glee.**

Merry England is a cliché. When applied to a place or country, *merry* originally meant pleasant or delightful in aspect. A thirteenth century translation of Genesis refers to the Garden of Eden as *that merry place*. When applied to persons, *merry* means animatedly joyous, hilarious, and this meaning has been substituted in the phrase *Merry England* for the older meaning.

mesdames. This is the plural of *madame*.

mess as a noun quite properly describes a dirty or untidy condition, a state of disorder (*The whole barracks was in a mess*), or a state of embarrassing confusion (*He left his financial affairs in a mess*). But the word is greatly overused. There is often a more precise and vivid equivalent. As a term for a person who is confused or disorganized, it is definitely not standard. As a term for a person who is so covered with mud or so disarranged in appearance that his identity is lost in the messiness of his appearance, so that he is part of a mess, it is an exaggeration, apparently acceptable in speaking to children.

messieurs. This is the plural of *monsieur*.

met. See **meet.**

metal; mettle. From its primary sense of describing any of a class of elementary substances, such as gold, silver, copper, etc., all of which are crystalline when solid and many of which are characterized by opacity, ductility, conductivity, and a peculiar luster when freshly fractured, *metal* has come to mean any formative material, including the characteristic disposition or temper (*Sir, I am made/ Of the selfsame metal that my sister is, / And prize me at her worth*). However, for this last meaning, with its derivative meanings of courage and spirit, the variant spelling *mettle* has become the established form (*The gruelling campaign tested his mettle*). It is always a word of praise, meaning an ardent or fiery spirit, high courage and enthusiasm (*The winged courser, like a generous horse,/ Shows most true mettle when you check his course*). To put a man on his mettle is to put his energy or courage to the test.

metamorphosis. The plural is *metamorphoses*.

metaphor. A *metaphor* is a figure of speech in which a term or phrase is applied to something to which it is not literally applicable in order to suggest a resemblance (*moonlight sleeping on a bank. And tear our pleasures with rough strife/ Through the iron gates of life. Man is the shuttle, to whose winding quest/ And passage through these looms/ God has ordered motion, but ordained no rest*). It may consist, as the examples show, of a single word or an elaborated idea. The virtue of metaphor is that it permits us to say a great deal in few words. Furthermore it sets up in the mind of the reader or listener a creative process that makes him amplify the idea and come to feel that it is his own and hence to accept it.

Metaphors do not suggest merely resemblances. They evoke concomitant images and often call up emotions that strengthen or enlarge upon the intended meaning. Thus when Macbeth says that he has *supped* full with horrors, the very homeliness of the metaphor (to which many eighteenth century critics objected as being undignified, "unworthy" of poetry) heightens the effect; it is as if Macbeth had come to accept horror as his everyday food. And so when Hamlet, considering the effect of his "mousetrap" on his uncle's conscience, says:

> *If his occulted guilt*
> *Do not itself unkennel in one speech,*
> *It is a damned ghost that we have seen,*
> *And my imaginations are as foul*
> *As Vulcan's stithy*

he has employed two good metaphors. His uncle's guilt has been likened to a skulking dog and his own mind to a stithy or an anvil. The latter is particularly good because it suggests not only the dirt, the foulness of his imaginations, but the ceaseless, metallic hammering of them in his brain.

A metaphor is effective if it conveys the desired comparison. It is good insofar as the details and associative comparisons of the primary comparison enhance the desired effect and bad insofar as they call up opposing or incongruous suggestions. (See **allegory, mixed metaphor, simile and metaphor,** and such individual entries as **lay it on with a trowel, literally, ceiling, bottleneck,** and so on.)

metathesis. The plural is *metatheses*.

metempsychosis. The plural is *metempsychoses*.

meteorologist is one proficient in the science of the atmosphere and its phenomena, especially as they relate to the weather. One who studied meteors would be an astronomer.

method; methodology. *Method* is the orderly regulation of procedure in order to carry out a definite purpose. *Methodology* is a branch of logic that seeks to show how the abstract principles of a science may be used to gain knowledge. A method may thus be a specific application of methodology, but method and methodology are no more the same thing than a blow is a club. The use of *methodology* for *method* is common among social scientists, many of whom seem to have a great love of redundant syllables.

meticulous; scrupulous; punctilious. *Meticulous* is derived from a Latin word meaning fearful or timid and kept this meaning in English up until the end of the seventeenth century. In 1535 a Scotch chronicler wrote *If thou be meticulous and dare not see blood drawn. . . .* By the beginning of the nineteenth century, however, it had become fixed as the designation of a particular manifestation of timidity: solicitude about minute details, minute and finical carefulness (*He was meticulous about the appearance of his men, insisting that the very bows of their shoelaces should be of even length*). It has now become a vogue word ("What strange charm," Fowler demands, "makes this wicked word irresistible . . .?") and is used on all occasions to denote an exacting attention to detail.

Scrupulous and *punctilious* are really more suitable words unless one wishes to suggest that the attention to detail is motivated by timidity. A punctilious man is one who is attentive to nice points, especially in conduct, ceremony or proceeding, observing the forms of politeness and correct social usage with great exactness (*The marshal of the faculties insisted on punctilious consideration of academic standing in assigning the various professors to their place in the commencement procession*). A scrupulous man is one who is cautious for fear of erring, attaching great weight in his uneasiness to minute considerations, precise, rigorous (*He was scrupulously honest, returning on one occasion to an astonished host a paper napkin which had been inadvertently packed among his things*).

metonymy is the rhetorical figure which expresses the name of a thing in terms of another which is a part of it or is associated with it. The use of the part for the whole used to be differentiated as synecdoche, but the distinction scarcely exists any more.

This figure of speech may take the form of an effect for a cause or a cause for an effect, as in *The pen is mightier than the sword* where *pen* stands for that which has been written by the pen. The commonest form of metonymy is the sign for the thing signified, as *a good table* for satisfying fare, *the chair* for the presiding officer sitting in the chair, *Shakespeare* for Shakespeare's works, *the press* for newspapers, *Washington* for the federal government, *the scepter* for sovereignty or *the bottle* for strong drink.

metropolis. The plural is *metropolises* or *metropoles*.

mettle. See **metal.**

meum et tuum or, more often, *meum and tuum,* literally "mine and thine," is now a cliché when used as a general term for private property or for the distinction between what is one's own and what belongs to others.

mews. From meaning cages for hawks, this word came to mean a group of stables. In the United States it usually means stables that have been made over into elegant living quarters. The word is ordinarily a singular but it may also be used as a plural, as in *the mews of London.* A double plural *mewses* occurs in an act of Parliament of 1797 and so has at least that much standing.

miasma. The plural is *miasmas* or *miasmata,* not *miasmae.*

mice. See **mouse.**

middle; midst. See **center.**

Middle West; Middle Western; Midwest; Midwestern. *Middle West* is the preferred term to describe that region of the United States which is bounded on the east by the Allegheny Mountains, on the west by the Rocky Mountains, and on the south by the Ohio River and the southern boundaries of Missouri and Kansas. The preference is not overwhelming, however, and many, especially among the younger contemporary writers, seem to prefer *Midwest.* As adjectives, usage seems to favor *Midwest* and *Midwestern* over *Middle West* and *Middle Western.* The average inhabitant of this region is far more likely to call himself a *Midwesterner* than a *Middle Westerner.*

midst. A generation ago many grammarians condemned the expression *in our midst,* on the grounds that there was no "true possession" here. They held that the only acceptable form was *in the midst of us.* The expression *in our midst* had been standard English since the time of Chaucer and there was no justification for limiting the genitive, or the possessive pronouns, to instances of "possession." But the word *midst* does not seem to have survived the battle. In current English we say *middle* for things that actually have a middle, and *among* for collections that do not.

midsummer madness, a quotation from *Twelfth Night* (III, iv, 61), as a term for the height of folly, is worn out.

might. See **may.**

might and main, with all one's. *Might* and *main* may once have had distinct meanings, such as skill and strength, but all memory of any such distinction has been forgotten and the phrase continues in use chiefly through inertia and the fatal fascination of alliteration.

mighty; almighty. The word *mighty* was once very popular as an intensive, as in *mighty glad to see you* and *mighty good of you to come.* It was thoroughly respectable and much more forceful than the little word *very.* Although it is not heard as frequently today, it has an old-fashioned rather than a nonstandard tone. Some younger people use it half humorously, in imitation of their grandparents.

Almighty was once also used as an intensive in this country, as in *almighty smart, almighty quick.* But this word was always questionable. It was used by strong men but not by ladies. Perhaps nobody was quite sure whether it was taking the name of God in vain or not.

mile. Only the singular form *mile* should be used as part of a compound adjective qualifying a following noun, as in *a ten-mile walk.* The form with *s* is sometimes heard here, as in *a ten-miles walk,* but this is not literary English.

Except in this one position, the singular *mile* should not be used in speaking of more than one mile. It sometimes is used in place of *miles* after a numeral, as in *we live ten mile from here.* This construction was literary English two hundred years ago, but it is not now standard.

militate. See **mitigate.**

milk of human kindness. Lady Macbeth feared that Macbeth was *too full of the milk of human kindness* to catch the nearest way to the crown by murdering his liege lord and benefactor. Her term for humanity or pity, unsurpassed in its original context, is now hackneyed.

mill. In both England and America *mill,* as a transitive verb, has a meaning consistent with its primary meaning as a noun; that is, it means to grind, work, treat, or shape in or with a mill (*In Minneapolis wheat from the prairie states is* milled). In America only, mill is also used intransitively to mean to move confusedly in a circle, as a herd of cattle (She sat on, watching the other miners' wives mill and chafe against the barriers. The crowd was milling in the street, but it seemed good natured and the police were having no difficulty controlling it).

millenary; millinery. Millenary, as an adjective, means consisting of or pertaining to a thousand, especially a thousand years, or pertaining to the millennium. As a noun it means an aggregate of a thousand, a millennium, or a millenarian (a believer in the millennium). Millinery, a much commoner word, is a noun designating articles made or sold by milliners, as hats and accessories, or the trade of a milliner.

millennium. The plural is millenniums or millennia.

million was originally a noun and was followed by of, as in a million of thanks. Today the singular form million is treated as a cardinal number. That is, it is an adjective and used without of, as in fifty million Frenchmen, except when it refers to part of a specified group, as in two million of these men. An expression involving million is usually treated as a plural, as in three million pencils were sold, but it may also be treated as a singular, especially when referring to money, as in three million dollars was set aside.

The plural form millions cannot be qualified by a numeral. It is a noun and requires of when followed by the name of anything countable, as in millions of dollars; the of is omitted only before a degree word such as more, less, too many, as in millions more dollars.

Few usually takes the adjective construction, as in a few million dollars; many usually takes the noun construction, as in many millions of dollars. But either form may be used with either word.

mince matters. One of the earlier meanings of mince, now obsolete, was to nullify some statement, usually a condemnatory one, by cutting it up with petty exceptions. Hence not to mince matters was to refuse to do this, to come to the unpleasant point directly without dwelling on extenuations (These were hard sayings, but men did not mince matters in those days). The phrase is now timeworn.

mind. When this is a verb meaning care about, it may be followed by the -ing form of a verb, as in she doesn't mind being late, but not by an infinitive. We do not say she doesn't mind to be late. Mind in this sense is often followed by a that clause, as in she doesn't mind that she is late. This construction is condemned by some grammarians who claim that an it, or the fact, is necessary, as in she doesn't mind it that she's late, but the sentence without it is acceptable in the United States.

At one time matter was used as a verb in just the way we now use mind, as in he mattered not whether he went and if it had not been out of doors, I had not mattered it so much. Today this verb matter is used only in an impersonal construction, as in it doesn't matter and a personal subject always requires mind, as in I don't mind.

When mind means remember it is followed by an infinitive, as in I mind to have seen him once, but this use of the word is now archaic or dialectal. When mind means obey, it is not followed by a verb form.

mind. See mentality.

mind to, have a. The use of mind in the sense of inclination, wish, desire, intention (Compound for sins they are inclin'd to,/ By damning those they have no mind to), is now archaic except in the phrases I've a mind to, I've a great mind to, or I've half a mind to and these are clichés. All have the nature of threats, though the last is usually an admission that the threat will not be carried out.

mind your P's and Q's, as an admonition to be careful, especially in matters of social deportment, is a cliché.

In regard to its original meaning there has been much conjecture, with no really satisfying explanation. Some believe that it was a warning of schoolteachers to those learning to write the alphabet or of master printers to their apprentices in setting type. Some think it has to do with pints and quarts in the alehouse reckoning. Some think it was an injunction of French dancing masters to their charges, to mind their feet (pieds) and pigtails or wigs (queues). And some would have solicitous wives beseeching their husbands, especially if they were seamen who often tarred their pigtails (queues), not to soil their peajackets. The interpretation of linguistic obscurities, as Chaucer once drily remarked, "is a glorious art, certeyn."

mine. See my.

miniature, as an adjective, should be restricted to mean on a very small scale (miniature golf course) or in a greatly reduced form (When what to my wondering eyes should appear,/ But a miniature sleigh, and eight tiny reindeer). It should not be used loosely as a mere synonym for small (as in She had to put up with a miniature kitchen and scarcely any closet space at all).

minimize. See diminish.

minimum. The plural is minimums or minima.

minions of the law, as a term for members of the police force, is a dreary cliché. Minion means darling. Drake was spoken of as the Sea's minion and St. John as Christ's minion. Macaulay said that Pitt was the minion, the child, the spoiled child of the House of Commons. In applying the term to the police there may have been a feeling that in any dispute between a citizen and a policeman the courts would show favoritism to the police. Or—and more likely since the term carries a tinge of contempt—it may have been adopted because of the resemblance in sound between minion and menial.

minister. See pastor.

minority. In its commonest sense, minority is a number forming less than half the whole (Since the Liberal got 25 votes and the Conservative 40, the former's supporters were obviously a minority). Minority may also be used to indicate the extent to which one group is exceeded by another (They were consoled that their minority was only 2). Minority serves also to describe a smaller party or group opposed to a majority, as in voting or other action (*The three dissenting Justices brought in a minority report*). Finally, *minority* describes the state or period of being a minor or under legal age (*Richard, in the minority of the princes, assumed the regency*).

minute; second; moment; instant. The distinction between these four words for indicating very brief periods of time is worth making even though it is frequently ignored in everyday speech. A *minute* is the sixtieth part of an hour and a *second* is the sixtieth part of a minute. The word *second* derives from the fact that the period of time is the result of the second sexagesimal division of the hour. A *moment,* unlike a minute or a second, is not mechanically measurable but is simply a very short, but indefinite, period of time. *Instant,* like *moment,* is not measurable. It describes not a period in time but a point in time now present, or present in reference to some action (the dying Edmund, in *King Lear,* hearing of the deaths of Regan and Goneril, says: *I was contracted to them both: all three/ Now marry in an instant*). In speech all four words are used interchangeably in the sense of *moment* (*Don't wait! I'll catch up with you in a moment* [or *minute* or *instant* or *second*]).

minutia. The plural is *minutias* or *minutiae.*

mirabile dictu for "strange to say" or "marvellous to relate" is a cliché. It was already a worn phrase in the time of Cicero and Vergil.

miracle. See **marvel.**

mirth. See **glee.**

miscarriage of justice. To refer to some decision or sentence that does not happen to please us as *a miscarriage of justice* or, more often and worse, *a grave miscarriage of justice* is to employ a phrase worn out by overuse.

miserly. See **economical.**

mishap; accident. Although the primary meaning of *accident* is now an undesirable or unfortunate happening, the word still retains its earlier meaning of something that happens unexpectedly, without design, by chance (*I was there by accident*). *Mishap* describes an unfortunate accident (*It was a mishap that the letter should have been delivered to that particular wrong address*) but usually something less serious than an *accident.*

Accident, within the past thirty years in America, has come to mean automobile accident. If it is said that so-and-so was *killed in an accident,* it would now be assumed that it was an automobile accident unless otherwise specified.

misplace. See **displace.**

misremember; forget. As a synonym for *forget, misremember* is dialectal (*Ah misremembered to get d' cawn pone*). Its standard meaning is to remember incorrectly (*He misremembered and brought jam instead of jelly*).

Miss. This word used as a title before a woman's name is not an abbreviation and should not be followed by a period. It is a shortened form of the word *mistress* and in current English implies that the woman is unmarried.

In speaking of two women known as *Miss Bonn* we say *the Miss Bonns.* If the women are distinguished by their given names, the word *Miss* must be made plural, as in *the Misses Susie and Laura Bonn.* In the United States the plural *Misses* is seldom used before a single name, as in *the Misses Bonn,* and many people consider this form affected.

The word *Miss* should not be used before a name that is followed by letters representing an academic degree, such as *B.A.* or *M.A.*

In Great Britain the word *Miss* is no longer used as a form of address but this is still acceptable in the United States. In some parts of this country children address their teachers as *Miss.* When the word is used by adults alone without a proper name, it implies that the person spoken to is young. It may be used by saleswomen as a form of flattery. When used by the village elders it is a mild rebuke, or a reminder of the inferior status of the young. *Miss* could once be used without a name in speaking about a young woman, as in *with a boarding school miss for a wife,* but this is no longer standard.

miss and **lose** can both mean to be unsuccessful, to fail to accomplish something (*By not being there he missed his chance. By not being there he lost his chance*). In modern usage, however, *lose* is the stronger word, suggesting a failure that is permanent rather than one of only transitory significance (*If you miss this opportunity, you may lose the chance of the appointment*).

mistake. The past tense is *mistook.* The participle is *mistaken.*

When this verb has an object, it may be used in an active form, as in *I mistook your meaning.* When it does not have an object it is always used in a passive form with active meaning, as in *I was mistaken* and *unless we are mistaken.* An active form here, such as *I mistook* or *unless we mistake,* is unidiomatic and ludicrous. It suggests that the speaker is unfamiliar with modern English usage or that he has appointed himself to remake the language.

mistake; error; fallacy. *Mistake* and *error* are frequently (and pardonably) interchanged, though they are different in emphasis. A *mistake* is an error in action, opinion or judgment caused by bad judgment or a disregard of rule or principle (*He made a mistake in taking mathematics at all*). An *error* is an unintentional wandering or deviation from accuracy or right conduct (*He made an error in multiplication which ended the usefulness of his navigational plot*). A *fallacy* is a deceptive, misleading, or false deduction or belief (*It is a fallacy to hold that since all horses are quadrupeds all quadrupeds are horses. It is a fallacy to think that because every fallacy involves a mistake or an error, all mistakes and errors are fallacies*).

mistaken; misunderstood. *I was mistaken* means "I made a mistake," "I was in the wrong," "I was in error." The proper phrase for "I was improperly interpreted" is *I was misunderstood.* Some grammarians have maintained that the participial adjective *mistaken* must mean *misunderstood* in the sense of being taken amiss or miss taken. But one will avoid ambiguity and confusion if he confines *mistaken* to "wrongly conceived or done," and he will be following the best usage.

mistreat; maltreat. To *mistreat* is to treat badly or wrongly. The word suggests a deviation from some accepted norm of treatment and a deviation always towards the bad. To *maltreat,* to abuse, to handle roughly or cruelly, is to mistreat in a special way. The words are often used interchangeably (Horwill believes that Americans prefer *mistreat* and English *maltreat*) but *maltreat* is usually restricted to the rougher forms of mistreating. A doctor who was a cruel man, a bad husband, and an incompetent physician might maltreat his dog, mistreat his wife, and treat his patients improperly. *Mistreatment* used to cover what is now called *malpractice.* Bulwer-Lytton speaks (1862) of certain unhappy patients who died *from being mistreated for consumption.* Today we would say *from being improperly treated* or *from being given an improper treatment.* If we said that a doctor mistreated his patients, we would most likely be understood to mean that he was rough with them or discourteous or charged them excessive fees.

mitigate; militate. To *mitigate* is to make milder or more endurable, to assuage, moderate, or alleviate something unpleasant (*The smile that accompanied it mitigated the severity of the lecture. Her gentle stroking seemed to mitigate the pain*). To *militate* is to operate against or in favor of something, to have effect or influence on, favorably or unfavorably (*These arguments militate strongly against the fulfillment of his hopes. His frank confession certainly militates in his favor*). The word is more often used in negative than in positive contexts.

Mitigate is sometimes used for *militate* (as in *I do not think these accusations ought to mitigate against him*). This is simply an error.

mixed metaphor. A metaphor is said to be a *mixed metaphor* when its several parts cancel each other out or call up incongruous images and thoughts. There is nothing wrong in merely mixing a metaphor, in combining, that is, in one comparison elements from several different things that have a likeness. The mind is fully capable of perceiving the common element in the comparison. The fault in what is usually recognized as a mixed metaphor is that the mixture is bad. The effect of a metaphor has been compared to that of a stone dropped into a large body of water. As the first splash of the stone sets up an ever widening series of concentric circles, so the primary comparison of the metaphor sets up a series of associative comparisons, widening out into other aspects and qualities of the things compared. And if any of these are grossly inapplicable to the primary comparison the effect may be ludicrous, and what was intended to arouse the reader or listener to a fuller comprehension of the idea may divert him to laughter or direct him to a conclusion wholly different from the one hoped for.

To take an everyday example, consider the appropriateness of the name *Old Ivory* as applied to a shade of household enamel that has a color approximately the same as that of old ivory. It's a good name not merely because it conveys an accurate idea of its color but because old ivory has other qualities that are desirable in an enamel. It is hard and smooth, for of course the ordinary person has never seen a piece of old ivory except in polished objects of art. And this, too, has its effect, for Old Ivory brings up associations of luxury and wealth and beauty. These things, of course, are not produced by an enamel, however well made or applied, but they are part of the dreams that lead us to decorate our houses and repaint old furniture. Now *Pale Custard* would convey an idea of the color just as well. But it would be a singularly *in*appropriate name for an enamel because people don't want to spread custard on their walls and furniture, and the associative ideas of mess and stickiness are the very things one does *not* want in an enamel. Furthermore there is nothing dignified or splendid about custard. There is no use saying that the name is intended only to suggest the color, that the can contains neither ivory nor custard and the purchaser knows it. The mind cannot be restricted to only one part of a thing in a comparison.

Mixing a metaphor is no indication of illiteracy. The greatest writers have done it. Thus Addison, in his poem *Letter from Italy,* says that, fired with excitement at the mention of a certain name,

I bridle in my struggling Muse with pain,
That longs to launch into a nobler strain.

Of which Dr. Johnson remarked: "To *bridle* a goddess is no very delicate idea; but why must she be bridled? Because she longs to *launch;* an act which was never hindered by a bridle: and whither will she launch? into a *nobler strain.* She is in the first line a horse, in the second a boat; and the care of the poet is to keep his horse or his boat from *singing.*" Nor is Addison alone in such blunders. Congreve, in what he thought to be a very fine passage, refers to Melancholy as sitting on *an ancient sigh.* Tennyson's description of the new moon as *like the paring of a lady's fingernail* doesn't seem as poetic to the modern reader as it did to the author. Nor does Dryden's conception of the serous matter exuded by the pustules of smallpox as the disease's tears of repentance for "the fault . . . it did commit." Longfellow's famous assurance that lives of great men all remind us we can make our lives sublime and, departing, leave behind us *footprints on the sands of time* seems unfortunate to the modern reader because his image makes human example and fame not permanent but ephemeral. Instead of being moved to high endeavor, one wonders whether it is worth making much of an effort when all remembrance of us will be swept away by the next tide in the affairs of men. And in addition it is a faintly ludicrous image in that it calls up thoughts of Robinson Crusoe and Man Friday.

The following half dozen or so mixed metaphors, all taken from actual publications or public speeches in which they were presented seriously, may be instructive as well as amusing:

> Crime has within it the cancer which may well be the thin entering wedge leading to the destruction of society if it be not always kept on the shortest possible leash.

> When you boil it right down to brass tacks....

> The Council was still putting its house in order and he was anxious that they should not change horses crossing the stream, while there was so much spadework to be done.

> When you are in a fight, you can't be too particular about whom you get in bed with.

> However, as far as the main plum was concerned, Hitler was shutting the stable door after the horse had escaped.

> The admiral warned the Japanese people that what they are now hearing is only the distant rumbling of the handwriting on the wall.

> This interpretation of Hamlet's madness adds meat to the very foundations of the play.

> There is not an iota of truth in such a thing. It is a deliberate attempt by the Democrats to throw a dust cloud when they know their ship is sinking.

Occasionally an author uses a bad metaphor on purpose. So P. G. Wodehouse's *The raspberry was not actually present, but he seemed to hear the beating of its wings* or Ring Lardner's *He give her a look that you could have poured on a waffle* or Samuel Butler's *And like a lobster boiled, the morn/ From black to red began to turn.* But these are rather good jokes than bad metaphors.

mixer for one who is sociable and mixes easily with other people at social gatherings is a slang term. (*He was a good mixer. He just naturally loved cocktail parties, community picnics, and other neighborly get-togethers*).

mob is a disorderly or riotous assemblage of persons. An abbreviation of *mobile vulgus* (the movable—that is, excitable—common people), the word was for a long time slang but is now standard. It is wrong, however, to use it of any large gathering (as in *The mob was peaceable and hot and happy and fanned itself and perspired and lay apathetic on the beaches and the grassy hummocks*). To be a mob the crowd must be excited, disorderly, and dangerous.

mode or **mood.** In many languages, a verb has different forms depending on the speaker's attitude toward what is said. These are called *modes* or *moods*. English has three modes, the indicative, the subjunctive, and the imperative. The indicative is the form used in speaking about actual events or facts and is by far the most common of the three. In this book, statements about a verb always refer to the indicative form unless one of the other modes is specifically mentioned. The subjunctive is the mode used in speaking about ideas or thoughts in contrast to facts. (See **subjunctive mode.**) The imperative

is the mode used in expressing one's will, as in commands and requests. (See **imperative mode.**)

model. See **ideal.**

moderate and **modest** are synonymous in the meaning of not excessive, extreme, or intense; or of medium quantity, extent, and so on. There would be little to choose between moderate talent, say, and modest talent. In regard to prices and especially fees, however, *moderate* has the suggestion of reasonable, within due limits, not exorbitant, while *modest* suggests something quite low. A moderate demand is a fair and reasonable demand. A modest demand is a demand far less than might have been reasonably made. A *moderate* allowance would be sufficient to meet all normal expenses, as much as most other boys got; a *modest* allowance would be smaller than the average, one that required care and a little self-denial to make do.

Modest has the special application to persons of showing a humble estimate of one's own merits, being free from vanity or boastfulness. *Moderate* has the special application to persons of being reasonable, fair-minded, temperate, not excessive in speech or demands.

There is a tendency to qualify both words with adverbs of superlative force (*a very modest demand, all things considered; He has taken an extremely moderate attitude and is to be commended*). Since their meaning is "between extremes," such a qualification is illogical, but it is understandable when *modest* is thought of as meaning humble or small and *moderate* as meaning conciliatory. The tendency is so strong that the qualification probably has to be accepted as idiomatic.

modern; modernistic. Although *modern* and *modernistic* are given as synonyms in most dictionaries, it is always better to employ *modern* when the meaning is simply of or pertaining to present or recent time, not antiquated or obsolete. *Modernistic* is ponderous if only *modern* is meant and in addition it has special meanings which may produce ambiguity or convey an idea different from the one intended. It can, for instance, mean of or pertaining to modernism, a movement in the Roman Catholic Church condemned by Pope Pius in 1907. And in design it can refer to a short-lived exaggerated style that was popular in the Twenties and Thirties but is now out of fashion.

modest; diffident; shy; bashful; shamefaced; coy. One is *modest* who is free from vanity or egotism, free from ostentation or showy extravagance, with a humble estimate of his own merits. One is *diffident* who lacks confidence in his own abilities, mistrusts himself (*Distress makes the humble heart diffident*). One is *shy* who shrinks from asserting himself, is sensitively timid, has a dislike, almost amounting to panic, of being conspicuous or being compelled to make any public appearance. A modest man is not necessarily diffident. He may have a humble estimation of his own merits but be quite willing to undertake anything that he thinks lies within his powers. Nor are the shy necessarily modest. A man may shrink from asserting himself or from being conspicuous and yet entertain an exaggerated conception of his own abilities and worth.

One is *bashful* who is modest to excess, who is easily put to confusion (*Come, you pernicious ass, you bashful fool, must you be blushing?*). *Shamefaced* (a corruption of *shamefast*) is a synonym for *bashful. Coy,* which until very recently meant only modest, shy, or bashful, now is used almost entirely to mean affectedly shy, displaying a modest backwardness in order to be enticed.

molasses has a plural form and is used with a plural verb in parts of western United States. In the eastern states and in England it is treated as a singular. In either case it is a mass noun and cannot be used with words implying number.

mold is now the standard American spelling for all three words—a hollow matrix for giving a particular shape to something in a molten or plastic state, a growth of minute fungi forming on vegetable or animal matter, and loose, friable earth. *Mould* is recognized as a variant spelling for each of the words and is the preferred spelling in England. The three words, by the way, have no etymological connections.

molten is an old participle corresponding to *melted.* It is no longer used in verb forms but survives as an adjective. We always say *melted* when we are speaking about things that melt easily, such as butter or snow, but we sometimes say *molten* in speaking about things that are more difficult to liquefy, such as gold or glass. Even here we are likely to say *melted* when we are being businesslike. *Lava* is always *molten,* never *melted,* perhaps because we never have any occasion to talk about *lava* in a businesslike way.

moment. See **minute.**

momentary; momentous. That is *momentary* which lasts but a moment or occurs at any moment (*There was a momentary thrill of exultation at the news, but it faded when he thought of his mother. He lived in momentary expectation of death*). That is *momentous* which is of great importance or consequence, fraught with serious and far-reaching consequences (*Henry knew that his resolve to break with the church was a momentous decision*).

momentary aberration, as a term for a temporary fit of inattention or forgetfulness, a sudden violent and irrational state wholly uncharacteristic, is a cliché.

momentum. The plural is *momentums* or *momenta.*

monastic and **monkish** both mean of or pertaining to or characteristic of monks, but *monkish* is almost always depreciatory (*monastic vows, the monastic life, monkish and crabbed learning*). *Monastic* also means of or pertaining to monasteries (*monastic architecture*).

money. This is a mass word and in its ordinary sense does not have a plural. In literary English the plural form *moneys* is considered unacceptable and is used in place of *money* only when a writer wants to suggest Shylock.

The plural form may properly be used in speaking of different coinages or issues, as in *the moneys of several countries.* It is sometimes used in financial reports to mean different sums of money. Here it has a pseudo-archaic flavor. The romantic effect is sometimes heightened by the obsolete spelling *monies.*

monkey plays a larger part in the American vocabulary than in the British. *Monkey with,* to meddle with, or play with idly, is in widespread colloquial use in America but unknown in England. *Monkeyshine,* a mischievous or clownish trick, is American slang. In British slang *monkey* means five hundred pounds.

monologue. See **dialogue.**

monopoly. In American usage it is standard to speak of a monopoly *on* something (*The Government is granting General Motors virtually a monopoly on certain classes of military vehicles*). In British usage, it is a monopoly *of.*

monsieur. The plural is *messieurs.*

Monsignor. The plural is *Monsignors or Monsignori.*

monstrous. Though *monstrous* is a synonym for *huge* (*What a monstrous liar he is, to tell us these fantastic stories!*), the word is not properly restricted to size alone. There must be a suggestion of the unnatural, frightful, hideous, or wondrous in the great size or bigness it designates. To say *That was a monstrous sum of money to spend in less than two years* implies that the speaker is not only impressed but also shocked by the bigness of the amount spent.

mood. See **mode.**

moonlight and **moonlit** both mean illuminated by the light of the moon. *Moonlit* is the more poetic and less used of the two. One might refer to a moonlit scene or a moonlit night but where the adjective is at all established in a phrase, as *Moonlight Cruise, Moonlight Sonata,* it is *moonlight.* The noun is always *moonlight.*

moose. The plural is *moose.* See **elk.**

moot point. In Saxon times a *moot* was an assembly of the people, especially an assembly that served as a court. There were folk moots and hall moots and burg moots and hundred moots and many other kinds of moots. But, except for historical references, this meaning faded away in the thirteenth century. In the sixteenth century, however, the word was adopted at the Inns of Court, the great law colleges in London, as a term for the discussion of a hypothetical case by students, just for the fun or practice of it. Hence *moot* came to have its modern meaning of subject to argument or discussion. As a term for a debatable point, and as a way of saying that there is evidence or there are valid arguments against some dogmatic statement that has just been made, *a moot point* is now hackneyed.

moral; morale; morals. *Moral* is an adjective meaning pertaining to or concerned with right conduct or the distinction between right and wrong (*It is not merely a matter of expediency; there is a moral issue here*).

Morale, a noun, was borrowed from the French during World War I. It means the mental condition in respect to confidence and cheerfulness (*Despite these dreadful sufferings, the morale of the soldiers remained high. Unless there could be some assurance of increased pay, faculty morale, already low, would collapse*).

The lesson to be learned from a story or an event is a *moral,* and in this sense the word has both a singular and a plural form. But only the plural form can be used to mean a standard of conduct. (See also **ethics.**) In this sense the word is treated as a plural, as in *his morals are questionable,* but it is not a true plural and cannot be used with a word implying number.

moral victory. As a consolatory phrase for a defeat which the defeated or his friends feel to have been an ethical victory or at least to have afforded an opportunity for displaying the righteousness of his cause, *a moral victory* is a cliché.

moratorium. The plural is *moratoriums* or *moratoria.*

more. This is the comparative form of the words *much* and *many.*

The adjective *more* first meant "a greater amount of," and in this sense it is always treated as a singular, as in *more sugar* and *there is more in the kitchen.* But in the last two or three hundred years *more* has also come to mean "a greater number of," and in this sense is treated as a plural, as in *more chairs* and *there are more in the dining room.* In both senses, *more* may be used as if it were a noun, as in the examples just given. *More* may also be used as an adverb meaning "to a greater extent." It may qualify a verb, as in *he is sleeping more,* or a phrase, as in *more at a loss.* But its principal function as an adverb is to qualify adjectives and adverbs, making what is equivalent to a comparative form, as in *more happy, more unusual, more quickly.* See **comparison of adjectives and adverbs.**

The word *more* may be qualified by a measure term which tells how much more, as *a lot* in *a lot more work, a lot more men.* These words are often nouns, as the word *lot* is, and would ordinarily require the word *of* before another noun, as in *a lot of work, a lot of men.* The word *of* disappears when the word *more* is used, because the measure term is then no longer standing in a noun relation to the following noun but is functioning as an adverb of degree and qualifies the adjective *more.*

In *more writers than one have said,* the adjective *more* qualifies the plural noun *writers,* which is the subject of the plural verb *have.* But in *more than one writer has said,* the phrase *more than* is a compound adverb qualifying the adjective *one.* The subject of the sentence is the singular noun *writer,* which requires the singular verb *has.* This is one of the rare exceptions to the rule that the number of an English verb is determined by the meaning of the subject rather than by its grammatical form.

more honored in the breach than the observance. There was formerly a custom (still preserved on formal occasions in at least one of the Oxford colleges) of sounding trumpets when some special toast was to be drunk at a banquet. In those nations that prized heavy drinking as a virtue,

carousing was accompanied with a great deal of noise. The usurper Claudius, in *Hamlet,* is a heavy drinker and *his* drinkings, since he is the king, are signalized not only by the sound of trumpets but by the roll of drums (as the wine went down) and even the discharge of ordnance (as it was seen that his majesty had drained his flagon to the bottom). Hamlet and Horatio, waiting on the icy battlements of Elsinore for the appearance of the ghost, hear the tumultuous uproar of the royal wassailing in the banquet hall below and Horatio, astonished, asks what it means. Hamlet, who hates his uncle and loathes him for his drunkenness, explains what is going on. Horatio asks if it is a custom. Hamlet says that it is and adds that although he was born there and is used to it it is, in his opinion, *a custom / More honour'd in the breach than the observance* since such swinish goings on have gained the whole Danish nation the reputation of drunkards and soiled the glory of their true achievements.

What Hamlet is saying, then, as the context makes plain, is that although old customs should be honored by being observed, this particular custom is so dishonorable that it would be more honorable not to observe it than to observe it. Had he only used "honorable" instead of "honour'd" here, he would have saved a great deal of ink and argument.

A paradox confusedly worded has an immense appeal. It seems oracular, cryptic, darkly wise. This phrase has been worn to shreds by generations of the sententious.

more in sorrow than (in) anger. It was Hamlet's father's ghost that, magnanimous under the circumstances, showed *a countenance more in sorrow than in anger.* The phrase is now used almost entirely ironically by the wits and is stilted and hackneyed.

more than meets the eye. As a way of saying that there is more in some situation than is immediately apparent, *there is more to it than meets the eye* is a cliché.

more the merrier. As a term of welcome to an extra, often an unexpected, guest, or just as an addition to the general gaiety, *the more the merrier* is hackneyed. In this particular instance that fact might be an incentive rather than a deterrent to its use, since in the early forcing stages of conviviality one seeks not to distinguish himself but to submerge himself in the group, to show that "the *gang's* all here," not a collection of precise-speaking individuals.

The full form of the proverb is *The more the merrier; the fewer the better fare.*

Mormons. Although the members of the church founded by Joseph Smith in 1830 accept the appellation of *Mormons,* they are, properly, members of the *Church of Jesus Christ of Latter-day Saints,* and as such their organization should be described in all formal writing.

moron was originally a term coined by psychologists to designate a person of arrested intelligence, judged incapable of mental development beyond the stage of an eight- to twelve-year-old child. It is used loosely in popular speech to mean a stupid person (*Any moron would know enough not to give his right name*) and has become a term in the more sensational newspapers for a sex pervert (*Moron strikes again. Removing shrubbery and lagoons will not improve the morals of a moron*). This last use is not standard and should be discouraged if only because it helps to obscure a serious social problem.

Morpheus, in the arms of. To refer to being asleep as being *in the arms of Morpheus* is to employ a strained and tedious expression. It is a pedantic observation, though the affectation of the usual reference to Morpheus justifies it, but Morpheus was not the god of sleep. He was the shaper of dreams. His father, Hypnos, was the god of sleep.

mortal. In addition to its standard meanings of liable to death or pertaining to man as subject to death or pertaining to death or to this world, *mortal* has a number of meanings in America, none of which are found in literary English. It means long and wearisome (*She held me there three mortal hours, going into the details of her various ailments*), great (*He was in a mortal hurry*), and possible or conceivable (*The thing was of no mortal use*). The last of these is probably an extension of its standard meaning of "related to this world in which all living things are mortal." That is, "It is of no use in this world."

Moses, as meek as. We don't hear *As meek as Moses* as much as we used to, but the conservative force of alliteration still keeps it alive.

The phrase is a cliché and seemingly a contradiction. We are assured in Numbers 12:3 that *the man Moses was very meek, above all the men which were upon the face of the earth.* But his actions hardly bear this out. He killed the Egyptian taskmaster, he destroyed Pharaoh's host, he smashed the tablets of the Ten Commandments, he literally forced the golden calf down the throats of the backsliders, he instigated the slaying of about three thousand Israelites as a disciplinary measure and smote the rock which God had commanded him merely to speak to.

All of this may indicate a vigor of character inseparable from his powers of leadership but it doesn't accord with any known definition of meekness. The commentators have striven manfully with the passage, though their task has been the more difficult in that until quite recently it was assumed that Moses himself had written it and it is hard to reconcile the possession of meekness with so unequivocal a declaration of it. The Bishops and Clergy of the Anglican Church (in 1888) saw in Moses' account of his own humility "the simplicity of one who bears witness of himself" and felt that his engaging frankness in the matter "especially manifested ... the direction of the Holy Spirit." Weedon felt that since this particular virtue of the prophet's might otherwise have escaped our attention we had cause to be grateful to him for setting false modesty aside and pointing it out to us. The Cambridge Bible sought to resolve the

difficulty by suggesting that *meek* was here to be understood in the sense of "pious," though they admitted that the suggestion offered "serious difficulty," not the least of which was that no dictionary recognized any such sense.

Then in 1941, speaking before the annual meeting of the Oriental Society, Professor O. R. Sellers, Professor of Old Testament at the Presbyterian Theological Seminary in Chicago, pointed out that *meek* was a mistranslation of the Hebrew word that would be better rendered as *vexed, put out,* or *irritable.*

most; mostly. *Most* is the superlative form of the words *much* and *many.*

The adjective *most* may mean greatest in amount and qualify a singular noun, as in *the most power.* It may also mean greatest in number or nearly all and qualify a plural noun, as in *most men.* It may be used in both senses as if it were a noun, as in *the most he could give was ten dollars* and *most of his friends are away.* In England the article *the* is no longer used before *most* when it has a plural sense and the use of *the* in a construction of this kind is considered a Scotch idiom. In the United States *the* is not used when *most* means nearly all but it is still used when *most* means the greatest number, as in *the most were on my side.*

The suffix *-most* is added to certain nouns and adjectives to form superlative adjectives indicating position, as in *topmost, bottommost, furthermost, innermost.*

Most is also used as an adverb and means to the greatest extent or in the highest degree, as in *he works most.* It may be used before an adjective or adverb to make what is equivalent to a superlative form, as in *most extraordinary, most quickly.* (See **comparison of adjectives and adverbs.**) It may also be used in this position as a pure intensive, or a stronger form of *very,* as in *it was most convincing* and *a most wholesome meal.* It always has this intensive force when it follows the article *a* rather than the article *the.*

In standard English *most* is not used freely as an adverb with the meaning of nearly or almost. It cannot be used in this sense to qualify a verb, as in *he most won,* or before the article *the,* as in *he is most the richest man I know.* But it is used in this sense to qualify the adjective-pronouns *all, everyone, everybody, anyone, anybody,* and the one adverb *always,* as in *most anyone would say* and *we most always go shopping on Saturday.* Some grammarians claim that *most* used in the sense of *almost* is always unacceptable. But there is no doubt that these forms are acceptable spoken English in the United States. They are heard everywhere. And there is no theoretical, or grammatical, reason why *most* should not be used in this way.

The adverb *mostly* could once be used interchangeably with the adverb *most.* The two words may still be used in the same positions but they now mean different things. *Mostly* means in the main or on the whole, as in *their homes are mostly shabby.* The adverb *most,* on the other hand, means in the highest degree or extremely, as in *their homes are most shabby.*

motion pictures; moving pictures; movies; cinema. *Motion picture* has completely triumphed over *moving picture* for all dignified uses (*The Motion Picture Industry, the educational value of motion pictures*). *Movie* and *movies* are universally used in the United States colloquially for a single motion picture or a number of them or the industry as a whole (*There's a good movie on at the Teatro. I don't see many movies. She went out to Hollywood and tried to get into the movies*). *Cinema* in British usage designates the building in which motion pictures are exhibited. In America it is a highbrow word for motion pictures collectively, especially when considered from an artistic point of view. The very people who speak of *the art of the cinema* would, however, probably refer to *the social effect of motion pictures.*

motive; motif; leitmotif. A *motive* is an incentive, something that prompts a person to act (*Vanity is the motive of many acts that seem motiveless*), or the goal or object of a person's actions (*His motive was revenge*). A *motif* is a subject or theme for development or treatment in art, literature, or music (*The motif of Lycidas may be said to be the fear of unfulfillment*), or a distinctive figure in a design, as of wallpaper (*The motif was a cluster of blue roses on a pink trellis*). A motif may thus be a motive. It may be that which motivates the work of art. But no other motive is a motif. A *leitmotif* (sometimes spelled *leitmotiv,* since it was originally a German word as *motif* was French), or *leading motif,* to translate it from German into English by way of French, is a motif or theme associated throughout a musical drama with a particular person, situation, or idea.

motive; inducement; incentive. A *motive* is something that prompts a person to act in a certain way, that determines volition (*The desire to be accepted as a member of the group is said to be a strong motive in human behavior*). It is applied chiefly to an inner urge that moves or prompts to action (*The biographer is on dangerous ground when he seeks to establish motives; the acts he knows, the reasons for them are often obscure*).

An *inducement* is not an inner urge and it is not usually a goal. It is, rather, used as a term for the opportunities which are offered by the acceptance of certain conditions (*The chance to be near his parents was an added inducement to accepting the assignment*). An inducement may be offered by one person to another or it may simply be an element in the situation.

An *incentive* was formerly anything that inspired or stimulated the emotions or imagination (*Incentive comes from the soul's self*) but today it is applied chiefly to something offered as a reward, particularly to stimulate competitive effort (*The incentive of the bonus can hardly be exaggerated*).

motto. See **slogan.**

mould. See **mold.**

mountain out of a molehill. Almost every language has some proverbial expression for magnifying difficulties or grievances out of all proportion to their actual significance or making much ado about nothing. The Babylonian Talmud speaks of enlarging *Yod* (the smallest letter in the Hebrew alphabet) into a city. The Greeks, the French, and others call it making an elephant out of a fly. Alliteration fixed the phrase in English as *making a mountain out of a molehill.* It was proverbial for centuries but has been so hackneyed for at least the past hundred years that it must now be classed as a cliché.

mouse. The plural is *mice.* The singular *mouse* is the preferred form for the first element of a compound, as in *mouse tracks,* but the plural, as in *mice tracks,* is often heard and is also acceptable.

moustache. See **whiskers.**

move; motive; motivate. One of the established meanings of the verb *to move* is to cause to act or operate (*And all the woe that moved him so/ That he gave that bitter cry . . . He was moved partly by charity and partly by a shrewd desire to save himself some money later on*). The use of *motive* as a verb, meaning to provide with a motive, was attempted (Emerson so used it) but it never became very popular. *Motivate,* however, the most recent enlargement, has become so popular within two or three generations of the time of its first introduction that it must be accepted as standard. But it is hard to see what advantage it has over *move.*

move heaven and earth. As a figure for making every effort, doing everything in one's power to accomplish some desired end, *to move heaven and earth* is a cliché. It should be used sparingly.

mow. The past tense is *mowed.* The participle is *mowed* or *mown.*

Mr. is an abbreviation for *mister.* The word is used only before a name and is always abbreviated.

The plural of *Mr.* is *Messrs.* In speaking of more than one man known as *Mr. Lohr,* we say *the Mr. Lohrs.* But when we combine different names we must use the plural form *Messrs.,* as in *Messrs. Tavenner, Humphries, and Newcomb.*

Mr. should not be used after any other title than *honorable* or *reverend* and should not be used before a name that is followed by letters representing an academic degree, such as *B.A., M.A.*

Mister used without a proper name as a form of address is now extremely informal. The more acceptable word is *sir. Mister* is never used without a name in speaking about a man. If we do not know his name, we call him "the man."

Mrs. is an abbreviation for *mistress.* In current English it is used before the name of a married woman. Only the abbreviation is used. The word is never spelled out.

There is no plural for *Mrs.* We may say *the two Mrs. Bonns,* but if we want to distinguish the women we must repeat the *Mrs.,* as in *Mrs. Philip and Mrs. Jerry Bonn.*

The form *Mrs.* should not be used with any

other title, except possibly *honorable* or *reverend*, and should not be used before a name that is followed by letters representing an academic degree, such as *B.A.* or *M.A.*

The word *Mrs.* or *missus* is never used without a proper name as a form of address. It is sometimes used in speaking about the woman of the house, as in *the missus says,* but this is usually intended as humor. When it is not, it is dialectal. *Madam* may be used in place of a woman's name in speaking to her. But it should not be used without a name in speaking about her, as in *madam said.* And it should not be used to avoid saying *you,* as in *does madam wish.* In some department stores this construction is supposed to give a European or cosmopolitan air, but it is inferior English.

A woman whose name one does not know may be referred to as *the woman* or *the lady.* Both words are acceptable, but well educated people usually prefer *woman.* See also **madam; madame; ma'am.**

much. The comparative form is *more.* The superlative form is *most.*

The word *much* may be used as an adjective, an adverb, or a noun. The adjective means a great amount of. It can be used only with a singular noun and only before the noun it qualifies, as in *there is much beast and some devil in man.* *Much* may also be used as a noun, as in *much is forgiven* and *this is not much.* The noun *much* is always singular. It is never qualified by the article *a* but it may be qualified by other definitive adjectives, as in *this much is certain,* and *we have each given our little or our much.*

The adverb *much* means greatly or to a great extent. It is used freely to qualify verbs, as in *he does not talk much, she complains much about her health.* Until recently *much* was used to qualify the past participle of a verb used as an adjective after some form of the verb *to be,* as in *he was much pleased, he was much amused,* but today *very* is generally preferred in these constructions. (For a fuller discussion of this, see **very.**) *Much* may also be used to qualify a prepositional phrase, as in *much at his ease, much on his own.*

Much is now limited in the kinds of adjectives and adverbs it can qualify. It can always be used with a word in the comparative form, as in *it is much clearer, he reads much faster.* It is used with the positive form of an adjective or adverb that is already qualified by some word implying degrees, as in *much too fast.* But it cannot be used with the simple positive form of these words. We can no longer say *much fast* or *much unkind.* At one time such combinations were normal English but *much* has here been replaced by *very.* Words such as *inferior, superior, anterior,* which are actually comparatives but do not have the English comparative form, may be used with either *much* or *very.* The word *like* may also be used with either word. We may say *he is much like his father* or *he is very like his father.* Some people who would use *very like* in an affirmative statement feel that *much like* is

required in a negative, as in *he is not much like his father.* But a great many more also use *very* in a negative statement. *Much* may qualify the article *the,* as in *much the same,* and in this way may precede the superlative form of an adjective or adverb, as in *much the fastest.* It may also qualify the article *a,* as in *she was very much a lady.*

The combination *much of* may occur in several different constructions. In *there is not much of it,* the word *much* is a noun meaning a great amount and is being used in a normal noun construction. In *they were much of an age,* the word *much* is an adverb meaning to a great extent and qualifies the prepositional phrase *of an age.* In *he was not much of a scholar,* the word cannot be interpreted in either of these ways. Here the two words *much of* are being used as a single adverb meaning *much.* Some grammarians say that this is not literary English and that we should say *not much a scholar.* But in the United States *much of* is preferred to *much* in a negative statement of this kind.

much in evidence is a wordy way of saying *evident* or *conspicuous.*

muchly is an unnecessary adverbial form. It is permissible English but never means anything that would not be better expressed by *much.*

much obliged. See **oblige.**

mucilage is the American word for any of various preparations for causing adhesion, particularly of paper. In England the word is *gum.*

mulatto. The plural is *mulattoes.*

mulatto; half-breed; etc. A *mulatto* is the offspring of parents of whom one is white and the other a Negro. *Half-breed* is reserved in America for the offspring of a white person and an American Indian. A *quadroon* is a person who is one-fourth Negro, the offspring of a mulatto and a white. An *octoroon* is a person having one-eighth Negro blood, the offspring of a quadroon and a white. All of these terms are now offensive. The last two are rarely encountered any more.

A *half-caste* is a person of mixed European and Hindu or Mohammedan parentage. The word is disparaging. *Eurasian,* a word for one of mixed European and Asiatic parentage, was coined to take its place and it does have more dignity than *half-breed* or *half-caste,* but contempt will always show through and *Eurasian* is now also felt to be derogatory. *Anglo-Indian* was substituted by some as a further euphemism, but it is ambiguous since this term is (or was) applied formerly to an Englishman who had spent most of his life in India.

All racial designations illustrate the difficulty underlying euphemism: contempt or disdain or dislike cannot be made acceptable to its victims by a mere change of words. See also **creole** and **African.**

mulct is properly a fine (*The state now receives those mulcts which formerly accrued to the sovereign*) and *to mulct* means to levy a fine. Since most people who are fined feel that they have been unfairly dealt with, the word has come to mean to deprive of by trickery (*He was soon mulcted of his inheritance*). Purists have objected to this meaning, but it is a natural development and, in American usage at least, is now standard.

mull. In British usage *to mull* is to make a mess of something, especially in athletics (*Bronson mulled a catch and Ipswich scored*).

In American usage *to mull over* is to ruminate, especially in an ineffective way (*I like a little privacy and mulling things over by myself*). The phrase is usually classified as questionable English but it is now so well established as to be standard.

mumps. This word has a plural form and may be treated as a plural, as in *mumps are contagious* and *he caught them from me*. But it is more often treated as a singular, as in *mumps is contagious* and *he caught it from me*. Both constructions are acceptable. The form *mumps* is used as the first element in a compound, as in *a mumps serum*.

mundane. See **earthen**.

munitions; ammunition. In the seventeenth century these words meant the same thing and *ammunition* was simply a mistaken pronunciation of *munition*. Today the two words are slightly different in meaning and in grammatical form. *Ammunition* now means whatever is needed to discharge firearms, including the projectiles and *munitions* means these together with other materials of war. Both are mass words. *Ammunition* does not have a plural form and we speak of *an ammunition dump*. *Munitions*, on the other hand, is now used only in the plural form and we speak of *a munitions plant*. But we cannot use the word with a numeral or speak of *many munitions*.

mural survives in British usage only as an adjective (*mural tablets, mural decorations*). It was formerly a noun in England, meaning a wall; but this meaning has been obsolete for four hundred years. The adjectival use is common in America but the word has been newly re-created as a noun meaning a mural painting (*He did that fine set of murals in the college library. He painted historical murals for the Minnesota and Wisconsin capitols*).

murder. See **homicide**.

mushroom. As a verb, *to mushroom* means only to spread out as in the shape of a mushroom. It was formerly applied only to bullets but has been extended recently to describe the characteristic cloud above an atomic explosion. In American usage the verb means this but it also describes a rapid growth or spread, often of short duration, not in the shape but in the manner of mushrooms (*The flames mushroomed from the shaft on all floors above. The town mushroomed out in every direction, overrunning a score of prairie villages*).

musical; musicale. *Musical* is an adjective, meaning of or pertaining to or producing music, or of the nature of or resembling music, melodious, or fond of or skilled in music (*a musical instrument. The sound of the wheels was musical*).

Musicale is a noun meaning a program of music that forms part of a social evening. It is standard in the United States but not used in England. The word is simply a taking over into English of the last word of the French phrase *soirée* (or *matinée*) *musicale,* an evening (or afternoon) musical party.

muslin. See **calico**.

must is a present subjunctive developed from an obsolete verb form *mot,* meaning "may." It has no corresponding past subjunctive form. See **subjunctive mode**.

The verb *must* has no imperative, no infinitive, no past participle, and no *-ing* form. Grammatically it is treated as a past tense form, just as *went* is. It cannot follow (that is, it cannot be dependent on) another verb. We can no more say *will must, had must, used to must,* than we can say *will went, had went, used to went*. To express these ideas we use some form of *have to*. Since we cannot use auxiliary verbs, such as *do, be, have,* before *must,* we form negative statements and ask questions in the old direct way that is now obsolete for most verbs, as in *I must not stay* and *must you leave?*

Must itself is always used as an auxiliary and requires another verb to complete its meaning. It may be followed by the simple form of a verb, as in *I must leave,* or by *have* and a past participle, as in *he must have left*. In the first case, the statement refers indefinitely to the present or the future. In the second case, it refers to a past event. As a rule, the complementary verb must be actually stated or easily understood from a preceding sentence, as in *you must speak to her* and *I suppose I must*. But at one time verbs of motion were omitted after verbs of willing and this construction may still be found in poetry, as in *the sun is up and up must I* and *I must down to the seas again*.

must needs. See **need**.

mutatis mutandis, "with the necessary changes," is a cliché. Latin clichés, now that Latin plays a very small part in the learning of even the best educated, are particularly offensive. They show the speaker to be affectedly unoriginal. He has gone out of his way to be tedious. He has labored to be dull.

mutual; common; reciprocal. That is *mutual* which is possessed, experienced, performed, etc., by each of two or more with respect to the other or others. A mutual dislike, for example, would be a dislike of A for B and a dislike of B for A. When two men hold each other in mutual esteem each thinks well of the other. A mutual admiration society is a society in which each member thinks well of the others and is thought well of by them. *Common,* in the sense that it is sometimes confused with *mutual,* has to do with the relation of two or more people not to each other but in reference to some other person or thing. Thus two men who share the same hobby have a common interest. If A and B both regard C as a friend, then C is their common friend. He is often called their mutual friend and **this** usage, greatly strengthened by Dickens's **famous**

title, *Our Mutual Friend,* has been singled out, among popular errors, for particular disapproval by the purists. But usage is against them. The word was so used for centuries before Dickens lent it the authority of his name and it has the advantage of avoiding the ambiguity latent in *common* in this context. *A mutual friend,* though improper, is clearly understood; *a common friend* may be either a friend two men have in common or a vulgar or commonplace friend. *A mutual friend,* therefore, is now accepted as standard by all but a few die-hards.

Reciprocal means complementary or balancing. In some situations things that are complementary are equivalent and in such cases *reciprocal* may be synonymous with *mutual.* But even here *reciprocal* has uses that *mutual* does not. A *mutual* act or feeling must take place between two persons at the same time. A *reciprocal* act or thought can take place later than the one which it reciprocates (*In the spring he was able to pay him back with a reciprocal favor*). Then *mutual* is not applied to physical acts or material things. People exchange reciprocal gifts or blows, not mutual ones.

mutual cooperation. Since cooperation means working together, each assisting the other, *mutual cooperation* is redundant. *The cooperation of capital and labor,* for example, implies a mutual assistance and nothing is gained by adding the extra word.

muzzle. See **nozzle.**

my; mine. At one time the difference between these words was that *my* was used before a consonant and *mine* before a vowel, as in *my friends and mine enemies.* This usage had already become irregular in the time of Shakespeare and Milton. *Mine* continued to be used before *eyes,* as in *mine eyes have seen the glory,* long after it was obsolete before any other word. But this construction too is now archaic. In current English we say *my eyes are tired.*

Today, the form *my* is used to qualify a following noun and the form *mine* is used in any other construction, as in *you are my all and all mine* and *oh my Amy, mine no more. Mine* may be used immediately after a noun, as in *mistress mine, brother mine,* but this construction verges on the archaic and is not heard in natural speech. Because *my* cannot stand alone, the exclamation *my!* means *my goodness!* or something stronger.

The form *mine,* and not *my,* is used in a double possessive where the word is separated from its following noun by *and,* as in *mine and love's prisoner, mine and her child.* Today this construction is generally avoided. We say instead *my child and hers* or *my own and her child.* Neither word order shows clearly whether we are talking about one thing or two. As a rule, we use the word *our* when we are talking about one thing possessed in common, that is, we say *our child.* The constructions just described will generally be understood to mean separate things possessed by separate individuals unless the con-

text makes it clear that this is not what is intended.

myself is a reflexive pronoun. Its normal use is in a sentence that has *I* as the subject of the verb, as in *I taught myself.* (For a discussion of this, see **reflexive pronouns.**) But *myself* is also used in place of *I* or *me* in sentences where it does not reflect the subject of the verb. Some of these uses are more acceptable than others.

Myself may always be used where the formal rules of grammar require *I* but *me* is the traditionally preferred form. That is, *myself* may be used after a linking verb, as in *the guests were myself and Alyse;* after *than, as* or *but,* as in *no man was ever better disposed, or worse qualified, for such an undertaking than myself;* and in an absolute construction, as in *Miss Wordsworth and myself being in the rear.* (See **subjective pronouns.**) This use of *myself* is established beyond question, in speech and in literature.

Myself may also be used in place of *me* when it is part of a compound object, as in *he saw neither myself nor any other object in the street.* When *myself* is placed first, as it is in this example, the construction has an old-fashioned tone, but when it is the last element, as in *they invited my sister and myself,* it is normal spoken English today. It is literary English in either position.

Formerly, *myself* was often used as the simple object of a verb or preposition, as in *when we had placed him in his coach with myself at his left hand.* This construction is still heard in the speech of educated people, but it is no longer used in written English.

At one time *myself* could be used as part of the subject of a verb, as in *Mrs. Washington and myself adopted the two youngest children.* This construction is now old fashioned and is condemned by many grammarians.

Occasionally *myself* is used as the whole subject of a verb, as in *myself when young did eagerly frequent doctor and saint.* This construction is extremely rare, in speech and in literature, and therefore has an artificial tone. See **personally.**

mysterious, inscrutable, mystical, and **obscure** all designate something which is not understood.

That which is *mysterious* is unknown but puzzling. It arouses our curiosity or awe (*Who is this mysterious man who seems to have access to the mayor at any hour? God moves in a mysterious way/His wonders to perform*). That which is *inscrutable* is incapable of being searched into or investigated. It defies investigation (*God's inscrutable purposes, the Sphinx's inscrutable smile*). It arouses more awe than curiosity; while that which is mysterious arouses more curiosity than awe. That which is *mystical* has a secret significance. It is presumably incomprehensible to the uninitiated, but the initiate perceives the meaning which is attached to certain rites, words, and signs (*The swastika has served as a mystical symbol at many times and in many places. The mystical symbol of the fish that represented Christ*). That which is *obscure* is comprehended dimly or with great difficulty (*These obscure passages have lent themselves to divers interpretations among divers sects*). Since there is a possibility of a meaning under obscurity, *obscure* is often used by the modest and the polite as a euphemism for unintelligible (*The obscure wording of the note left me in doubt as to whether he would come to me or expected me to go to him*).

mystery. Except when used attributively in such established phrases as *mystery novel* or *mystery story*, *mystery* should be used sparingly as an adjective. *A man of mystery* is, actually, more effective, more mysterious, than *mystery man*.

The *mystery* of the old mystery plays is an entirely different word, now obsolete except in this phrase and historical references. It meant a craft or a trade and later one of the guilds that sponsored these little religious plays.

mystic; mystical. Although *mystic* and *mystical* are synonymous, *mystic*, perhaps because it is less commonly used, is a little more formal, especially in designating something comprehensible only to the initiated or to those more finely endowed. It is more likely now to be used in religious contexts than *mystical*, though *mystical* is definitely established in many liturgical phrases. *Mystical*, perhaps because of its frequent misuse as a mere synonym of *mysterious*, suggests less awful obscurities, at least in many passages (*'Tis the sunset of life gives me mystical lore,/ And coming events cast their shadows before*).

myth; legend; fable. A *myth* is one of a class of stories, usually concerning some superhuman being or great hero, which attempt to explain some belief or natural phenomenon (*The myth of the gorgon may be a poetical attempt to portray the combined beauty and horror of reality*). The word has come in popular usage to mean any invented story (*The election results destroyed the myth of his popularity which his followers had so assiduously cultivated*). In sociology and anthropology a myth is a collective belief that is built up in response to the wishes of the group instead of a rational analysis of the situation to which it pertains (*The myth of its own moral superiority is probably necessary to the self-preservation of any nation*).

Originally something to be read (from the Latin *legere,* to read), *legends* were written stories of admirable persons. In the *Legends of the Saints* there is no implication of the nonhistorical or the unverifiable that the word *legend* now carries (*The story of the cherry tree is only a legend*). A legend is now thought of as an unverifiable, and probably untrue or at least inaccurate, story concerning some real person or place, which has been handed down for several generations.

A *fable* is a fictitious story (often with animals or even inanimate objects as the actors or speakers and hence, plainly, not intended to be taken as factual history) which is designed to teach a moral (*Aesop's fable of the ass and the lapdog shows that a man will suffer from acting out of his station even if he has the best of intentions*). A fable differs from a parable in that the lessons suggested by fables are usually more practical and earthly than those conveyed by parables which usually concern themselves with ethical and religious concepts. See also **allegory.**

N

naïf; naïve; naive. *Naïve* is the acceptable adjective, whether masculine or feminine, to describe having or showing natural simplicity of nature, being unsophisticated, ingenuous. The shade of meaning that it has that these other words, and such words as artless and innocent, lack is a touch of amusement in the observer. The naïve person is not himself amused. He may be, indeed he probably is, most earnest, but his simplicity is amusing to the sophisticated onlooker (*It is naïve to assume that power won by struggle will be surrendered without a struggle*).

Though the French masculine *naïf* is sometimes used, and is certainly not improper, it is unnecessary and a little ostentatious with a suggestion of rebuke for the less knowing. A spelling, however, which is acceptable and deserves to replace *naïve* is *naive*, without the dieresis. *Naïvete,* however, always has the dieresis and usually with an accent mark on the final *e* (*naïveté*). See also **unsophisticated.**

nail one's flag to the mast. To prevent the shooting down of a flag being mistaken for its being lowered in surrender, doughty captains on going into combat often had the flag nailed to the mast. Nelson sometimes had several nailed to separate masts. It was a gallant gesture, but the use of the phrase *to nail one's flag to the mast* as a term for taking an unyielding position is now a cliché.

name; denominate; nominate. For giving a name to or specifically indicating by name, *name* is the everyday word (*They named the baby Abner. He was named in the suit*) and there is little need for seeking another. To *denominate* (*They of the papal faction were denominated Guelphs*) means to name, especially to call by a specific name, but it is a ponderous and literary word. To *nominate* used to mean to name or stipulate expressly (*Is it so nominated in the bond?*) but it has come, in American usage at least, to mean almost exclusively to propose as a proper person for appointment or election to an office (*Jackson was nominated for the presidency*).

name is legion. When Jesus demanded of the unclean spirit that infested the unhappy Gadarene that it reveal its name, the spirit answered *My name is Legion: for we are many.* The name *legion*, as the *New Standard Bible Dictionary* points out, had come to be used "in Greek, Rabbinical Hebrew, and probably in Palestinian Aramaic for any great number" and is used in this passage "with perhaps the thought of obedience to a superior will." But to say today of any great number of persons that *their name is legion* is to employ a cliché. That this phrase is almost always used to designate those of whom the speaker disapproves or is contemptuous, even though few speakers could tell whence the phrase derives, is an interesting illustration of the manner in which many words acquire a connotation in one context which they carry over into others. For there is a suggestion in the cliché that those spoken of are possessed with devils—with a faintly blasphemous suggestion (to the more knowing) concerning the speaker who would free them from their errors.

name of. *By the name of* and *of the name of* are wordy and pompous ways of saying *called* or *named*.

names identifying state origin. Only inhabitants of Montana and North Dakota seem to have escaped nicknames identifying them with the states in which they live. H. L. Mencken, G. E. Shankle, and David Shulman have called to general attention the following names for residents of each of the other forty-six states. Some of them were plainly not invented by the residents to describe themselves and many have now fallen into disuse.

Alabama—*Lizards, Yellowhammers*
Arizona—*Sandcutters*
Arkansas—*Toothpicks, Yahoos*
California—*Gold Diggers, Gold Hunters*
Colorado—*Silverines, Rovers, Centennials*
Connecticut—*Nutmegs, Wooden Nutmegs*
Delaware—*Muskrats, Blue Hen's Chickens*
Florida—*Alligators, Fly-up-the-Creeks, Evergladers, Gulfers*
Georgia—*Crackers, Buzzards, Goobergrabbers, Sand-Hillers*
Idaho—*Fortune-seekers, Cutthroats*
Illinois—*Suckers, Egyptians, Sand-Hillers*
Indiana—*Hoosiers*
Iowa—*Hawkeyes*
Kansas—*Sunflowers, Grasshoppers, Jayhawkers*
Kentucky—*Bears, Corn-crackers, Red Horses, Blue Grassers*
Louisiana—*Creoles, Pelicans*
Maine—*Foxes, Lumbermen, Pine-trees*

Maryland—*Clam-humpers, Craw-thumpers, Oysters*
Massachusetts—*Bay Staters, Baked Beans, Puritans*
Michigan—*Michiganders, Wolverines*
Minnesota—*Gophers*
Mississippi—*Mudcats, Mudwaddlers, Sharpshooters, Swelled Heads, Tadpoles*
Missouri—*Pukes, Pukers*
Nebraska—*Bug-eaters, Corn Huskers, Treeplanters*
Nevada—*Diggers, Miners, Sagehens*
New Hampshire—*Granite Boys*
New Jersey—*Clams, Clam-catchers, Foreigners, Jersey Blues*
New Mexico—*Spaniards, Spanish Indians*
New York—*Cockneys, Excelsiors, Knickerbockers*
North Carolina—*Tar-boilers, Tarheels, Tuckoes*
Ohio—*Buckeyes*
Oklahoma—*Okies, Sooners*
Oregon—*Beavers, Hard Cases, Webfeet, Webfoots*
Pennsylvania—*Broad-brims, Flying Dutch, Leatherheads, Pennamites, Quakers*
Rhode Island—*Gun-flints*
South Carolina—*Clay-eaters, Nullifiers, Palmettoes, Rice-birds, Sand-hillers, Sand-lappers, Weasels*
South Dakota—*Coyotes*
Tennessee—*Big-benders, Butternuts, Buckskins, Corn-crackers, Mud-heads, Volunteers*
Texas—*Beef-heads, Blizzards, Cowboys, Longhorns, Rangers*
Utah—*Brighamites, Mormons, Polygamists, Saints*
Vermont—*Green Mountain Boys*
Virginia—*Beagles, Cavaliers, F.F.V.'s, Sorebacks, Tuckahoes*
Washington—*Clam-grabbers, Evergreeners*
West Virginia—*Pan-handleites, Mountain Men*
Wisconsin—*Badgers*
Wyoming—*Sheep Herders*

name to conjure with. Names have had a magic importance in all cultures. Jehovah's name is, plainly, one of the awful mysteries of the Old Testament. When Jacob wrestled with the "man" at the ford (Jabbok) his chief desire was to know the spirit's name and after the event he changed his own name. Many American Indians kept their actual names secret, going through life under another name. In imperial China it was a crime to use the name of a reigning emperor, even when that name was the same as some word in common use. In diabolism the uttering of the name of an evil spirit put the spirit temporarily under the power of the necromancer, although when the demon was a particularly dreadful one (*Orcus and Ades, and the dreaded name/ Of Demogorgon*) his power might so far transcend that of the wizard who had invoked him as to entail disastrous consequences for his summoner.

All of this was once implied in the phrase

a name to conjure with, but it has now faded from it and the words are merely a hackneyed expression to designate one who is influential.

napkin. See **serviette.**

narcissus. The plural is *narcissuses* or *narcissi.*

narrate. See **describe.**

narrative. See **relation.**

nasty in American usage still means, primarily, physically filthy or disgustingly unclean, nauseous, or obscene (*The ill-kept barn was in a nasty condition. The famous elixir was a nasty-tasting stuff of a brownish-green color. When we used nasty words Aunt Susan used to make us wash our mouths out with soap and water. Nasty little boys*). Eighty years ago, Schele De Vere tells us in his *Americanisms,* the word itself was a nasty word in America, not to be spoken in the hearing of ladies. The meanings of the word now more common in England, of unpleasant or disagreeable (*He's in a nasty mood; I wouldn't ask him just now. I say, that's a nasty-looking bump you've got on your head. We were two hours in a nasty traffic jam on the Headington road*), would be recognized in America and even used—though probably with a slightly humorous intent—but the older meanings are far more common.

native. See **African.**

natural. See **normal.**

nature is used unnecessarily in such phrases as *the dangerous nature of the assignment* where *the danger of the assignment* would be more effective. It is a great favorite of those who like to make a short story long.

naught. See **aught.**

nautilus. The plural is *nautiluses* or *nautili.*

naval; navel. *Naval* is an adjective meaning of or pertaining to ships, especially, and now only, ships of war, or belonging to, or pertaining to, or connected with, a navy (*Trafalgar remains the greatest of all naval engagements. Naval regulations do not permit . . .*).

Navel is a noun. It designates the umbilicus or, in Sir Thomas Browne's words, "that tortuosity or complicated nodosity" that is empitted in the middle of the surface of the belly (*This ingenious theory, that the real "use or office" of Adam's navel was to tempt men into the sin of being sensible, was revived in 1857 by Philip Henry Gosse*); and, by extension, the central point or middle of any thing or place (*Within the navel of this hideous wood/ Immur'd in cypress shades a sorcerer dwells*).

The *navel orange* is so called because it has at its apex a navellike formation containing a small secondary fruit, but one often sees them marked, through ignorance or false delicacy, as *naval* oranges.

n.b. This is an abbreviation of the Latin words *nota bene* and means "note well."

near; nearly. *Near* was once the comparative form of *nigh* but it is now felt as a positive and given a regular comparison, *nearer, nearest. Near* may be used as an adjective to qualify a noun, as in *the nearest house, the near future.* Both *near* and *nearly* may be used as adverbs.

Nearly is ordinarily used as an adverb of degree meaning approximately or almost. In current English it is preferred to *near* in this sense, as in *it nearly broke her heart* and *it is not nearly as late as I thought.* Traditionally, *near* may also be used in this sense but sentences such as *it near broke her heart* and *it is not near as late as I thought* are now considered old fashioned. The construction is more acceptable today if *near* itself is qualified by an adverb of degree, as in *it very near broke her heart* and *it is nowhere near as late as I thought. Nearly* cannot be used as an adverb of place. For this we must use *near,* as in *I was standing near.*

The word *near* may be followed immediately by an object, as in *the atmosphere near the earth* and *it came near him;* or the preposition *to* may be used, as in *the atmosphere near to the earth* and *it came near to him.* Both constructions are acceptable. *Near* may be combined with some form of *come* or *go* to mean almost succeed. In this sense, forms of the verb *come* may be followed by *near* or *near to* and the *-ing* form of a verb, as in *this came near convincing him.* Forms of the verb *go* may be followed by *near to* and an *-ing* form, as in *this went near to proving it,* or by *near to* and the simple form of a verb, as in *this went near to prove it.* The idiom involving *go* is not often heard in the United States. See also **almost** and **practically.**

nearby. This word or compound is not standard in Great Britain. In the United States, it may be used as an adjective, as in *a nearby town,* or as an adverb, as in *there was a stream nearby,* but is not standard when used as a preposition with an object, as in *he stood nearby me.*

neat but not gaudy. Originally serious, with *neat* having the meaning of clear, bright, or fine, *neat but not gaudy* became ironical in the nineteenth century and in this use has become a cliché. It was made a part of several sayings whose humor now seems forced to us: *Neat but not gaudy, as the devil said when he painted his tail green* or *as the monkey said when he painted his tail blue, etc.*

nebula. The plural is *nebulas* or *nebulae.*

necessary; essential; indispensable; requisite. That is *necessary* which cannot be dispensed with or is the inevitable consequence of certain causes (*It is necessary to see him first. Must that necessarily follow?*). *Essential* means of the very essence of being (*Air is essential to the maintenance of human life*). Although it is a synonym of *necessary,* usage has made it—or, perhaps, lack of use has left it—a stronger word than *necessary.* If a man is told that it is necessary for him to attend a certain meeting, there is the implication of a strong compulsion. But if he is told that it is essential for him to go, there is an implication that the meeting or his own affairs, or both, simply will not continue in their present state of being if he does not go. *Indispensable* designates that which cannot be done without or removed from the rest of a unitary condition (*There is no indispensable man*). That is *requisite* which is judged necessary from the nature of things or of circumstances (*The first requisite is a room and a desk*). It is the weakest of the four words.

necessities; necessaries. Although *necessities* and *necessaries* are synonymous as words for things that are indispensable, *necessities* is by far the more popular word of the two in contemporary American usage, though some English writers insist that *necessaries* is to be preferred. The American preference may have been influenced by the fact that until recently a *necessary* was a euphemism in many rural areas for a privy or a chamberpot.

neck. The *crop* of *neck and crop* is the craw or pouchlike enlargement of the gullet of many birds. Why the phrase should be a term for completely, altogether (*Throw them out, neck and crop. We're going in for the new mode here, neck and crop*), is not clear. It is now a meaningless cliché. *Neck or nothing*, as an expression denoting a determination to take all risks, is also a cliché whose original meaning is now uncertain. It would seem to be a term from hard riding (*Away went Gilpin, neck or nought*) and may, perhaps, have had something to do with a willingness to risk breaking the horse's or the rider's neck in a fall. *Neck and neck* is clearly from horse racing and is not a cliché when used of horses that are abreast of each other in a race. In figurative uses, however, it is a cliché.

necropolis. The plural is *necropolises* or *necropoles*.

need. This is a regular verb with a past tense and participle *needed*. It may be followed by a *to*-infinitive which has an active meaning, as in *he needs to talk to us*, or by the *-ing* form which has a passive meaning, as in *he needs talking to.*

In negative statements and in questions, the word *need* may be used like the word *must*. That is, it may be used without an auxiliary verb such as *do, be, have*, may be followed by the simple form of a verb instead of the *to*-infinitive, and may not have the final *s* in the third person singular, as in *he need not go* and *why need he go?* Like *must*, the word *need* may also be followed by *have* to refer to a past event, as in *who knows whether I need have fled?* These forms are standard English. They exist in the language side by side with the regular forms which are also standard, such as *he does not need to go* and *who knows whether I needed to flee?* The verb *dare* also has both forms. But while *need* is a regular verb that is coming to be used as an auxiliary, *dare* is an old auxiliary that has developed regular forms. See **dare**.

The new constructions, following the pattern of *must*, cannot be used when *need* is not followed by another verb but has a noun or pronoun object, as in *he needs money*. We cannot say *need he money?* The new forms cannot be used in a truly positive statement, such as *that is what he need know*, but may be used when the statement is positive in form only and negative in meaning, as in *that is all he need know*. The words *needed* and *needs* always require the old, regular constructions. We cannot say *he needed go* or *needs he go?* Verbal phrases, such as *will need, did need*, also require regular constructions. They may be followed by a *to*-infinitive, as in *he will need to go*, but not by the simple form of a verb, as in *he will need go*. Constructions of this kind, without the *to*, are sometimes heard but are not literary English.

The words *need* and *needs* may also be used, principally in combination with *must*, as adverbs meaning necessarily, as in *he need must go* and *he must needs go*. The first form is now archaic and the second extremely artificial.

need; necessity; want. *Need* and *necessity* are nouns which designate a lack or a demand which must be filled. *Need*, a word of Old English origin, has connotations which give it a strong emotional appeal (*A friend in need is a friend in deed. I had most need of blessing, and "Amen"/ Stuck in my throat. O, reason not the need! Our basest beggars/ Are in the poorest thing superfluous*). *Necessity*, a word of Latin origin, is more formal and impersonal or objective. Though much stronger than *need* in expressing urgency or imperative demand, it is less effective in appealing to the emotions (*Necessity is the mother of invention. The art of our necessities is strange,/ That can make vile things precious*). *Want*, as a noun, is synonymous with *need* (*His wants were few and little would suffice*). It, too, is an Old English word and has strong emotional connotations and often great dignity (*For want of a nail a shoe was lost. They are wet with the showers of the mountains, and embrace the rock for want of a shelter*). It is used, especially, in dignified contexts, as a term for poverty (*So shall thy poverty come as one that travelleth, and thy want as an armed man. In Misery's darkest cavern known,/ His useful care was ever nigh,/ Where hopeless anguish pour'd his groan,/ And lonely want retir'd to die*). As a verb, *want* means to wish for, and is therefore weaker than *need* which means to lack something indispensable (*Buy not what you want, but what you need*). There are many contexts in which *want* as a noun is colored by its meaning as a verb or made ambiguous. Its literary associations have also made it a little too stately for common use.

needle in a haystack was originally *needle in a bottle of hay*, a *bottle* being an old word for a bundle of hay. As this meaning of *bottle* faded, the term was often changed to *needle in a bundle of hay*. In America, however, one hears only the phrase *needle in a haystack*, and one hears it all too often. Some years ago Mr. Jim Moran searched for and found a needle in a haystack on a street corner in Washington, D.C.

needs must. See **need**.

needs no introduction. How the hearts of audiences sink when the chairman assures them that the speaker *needs no introduction,* for the hackneyed phrase is usually the prelude to a long and dreary recitation of the feeble accomplishments and obscure honors of some unknown mediocrity palmed off on the listeners by a desperate program committee.

negatives. See the individual negative words.

neglect. This verb may be followed by an infinitive, as in *he neglected to wrap it.* It may also be followed by the *-ing* form of a verb, as in *he neglected wrapping it,* but the infinitive is generally preferred.

neglect and **negligence** imply carelessness, failure, or some important omission in the performance of one's duty. *Neglect* commonly refers to the act (*This slight neglect led to the tragedy*), *negligence* to the habit or trait of failing to attend to or perform what is expected or required. When Goneril, in *King Lear,* orders her servants to assume a *weary negligence* in carrying out her father's orders, it was the insolence of habitual disregard which she hoped would provoke the old tyrant to an outburst of which she could take advantage.

In contexts where *neglect* and *negligence* are interchangeable, *neglect* is the stronger word. *His death was the result of negligence* is not quite as strongly condemnatory as *His death was the result of neglect.*

negligent; negligible. The adjectives *negligent* and *negligible* present, respectively, active and passive aspects of neglect. *Negligent* means neglecting, guilty of or characterized by neglect (*He was habitually negligent of his personal appearance*). *Negligible* means deserving of or capable of being neglected or disregarded (*The saving from the long tax form is negligible*).

Negress. Although *-ess* is the regular suffix for forming distinctly feminine nouns (*hostess, lioness*) with no connotation of contempt, *Negress* is often used derogatorily and hence is likely to be offensive. So also is *Jewess.*

Negro; nigger; nigra; darky. *Negro* (the plural is *Negroes*) is the proper and, in formal writing, now the only permissible name for a member of the Negro race. Even when used as an adjective it is capitalized, although *white,* when used as an adjective to designate a member of or that which pertains to the white race, is not. *Nigger,* although originally merely a slurred pronunciation of *Negro,* is, and has been for centuries, a contemptuous and offensive term. Fowler's statement that the word when "applied to others than full or partial Negroes, is felt as an insult by the person described" is puzzling, though his further assurance that its use "betrays in the speaker, if not deliberate insolence, at least a very arrogant inhumanity" is unexceptionable.

Nigra is claimed by many who use it to be a fully respectful word, merely a pronunciation of *Negro.* It is not accepted as such by those to whom it is applied, who are inclined to regard it, rather, as an evasive pronunciation of *nigger* or at the best a reluctant compromise.

Darky, originally a euphemism and perhaps kindly intended (*All de darkeys am a-weeping,/ Massa's in de cold, cold ground*), has today the double opprobrium of sentimentality and condescension. It is particularly connected with the comic stereotype of the American Negro developed in the minstrel shows and passed on to vaudeville.

It is plain that it is not the word but the feeling behind it. There is no word which if spoken in contempt will not in time express that contempt and hence give offense. The supreme illustration—one by which many sociologists who feel that a new set of euphemisms would ease many tensions in the world ought to ponder—is the word *slave.* Derived from *Slav,* of which people many were enslaved by the conquering Romans, the word has acquired connotations of servility, timidity, and cowardice (*The doggerel that was produced by the third-rate poets who slavishly imitated Pope. This slavish flattery is disgusting. The coward slave, we pass him by,/ We dare be poor for a' that*). Yet *slav* in Slavic means glory. (See also **African, colored, Caucasian, Creole, European, mulatto.**)

neighborhood. Those British lions, Fowler, Horwill, and Partridge, unite in roaring at the American use of *in the neighborhood of* (*The work will cost in the neighborhood of two million dollars*) for about or nearly. Fowler calls it "a repulsive combination of polysyllabic humor and periphrasis." Partridge feels it to be "a bad and wholly unnecessary substitute." And Horwill notes with alarm that the expression has caught on in England. In the United States it is certainly standard, though it does seem awkward, vague, and unnecessary. See also **vicinage.**

neither. This word introduces alternatives and makes the statement in which it occurs negative for each of them. It may be used as an adjective, as in *neither man had arrived,* or independently as a pronoun, as in *neither had arrived;* or it may be used as a conjunction, as in *these neither laughed nor sang.* There may be more than two alternatives, as in *heat, light, electricity, magnetism . . . are all correlative . . . neither, taken abstractedly, can be said to be the essential cause of the others.*

When *neither* is used as an adjective it qualifies a singular noun and requires a singular verb, as in *neither box has arrived.* In any other construction a singular verb is permissible but a plural is preferred, as in *Thersites' body is as good as Ajax, when neither are alive* and *without that labor neither reason, art, nor peace, are possible to man.* A singular verb is particularly objectionable when the last alternative is *you* or *I,* as in *neither my dog nor I is for sale.* A plural pronoun may be used to refer to *neither,* as in *neither of them had their tickets.*

At one time *neither* might be followed by *or* or *nor.* In current English only the form *nor* is used after *neither.* Formerly *neither* might follow another negative, as in *these will not move her neither* and *not sparing neither man, woman, nor child.* This form of the double negative is generally condemned today and the word *either* is preferred in sentences of this kind. The construction with two negatives is more acceptable when the second negative is semi-independent, as in *there was no respite, neither by day nor by night,* but this too is condemned by many grammarians. However, when *neither* is used as the equivalent of *nor* to introduce a full clause, it must follow a negative statement, as in *if there are no teachers, neither are there disciples* and *they toil not, neither do they spin.* Here *neither* qualifies the second clause and so does not form a double negative.

   Neither is the negative form of the word *either.* Like *either,* the pronoun has a genitive form, as in *neither's house.* The adjective can be used to qualify a genitive noun, as in *neither man's house,* but cannot follow a genitive, as in *the man's neither house.* To express this idea we must use the pronoun form and say *neither of the man's houses.* See also **double genitives.**

neither fish, flesh, nor good red herring. The older form of the proverb—*neither flesh nor fish*—made a certain sense but the addition of the *good red herring* (as early as Heywood's *Proverbs,* 1546) reduces the whole thing to nonsense. Some have attempted to improve it by substituting *fowl* for *fish* and some have put in the *fowl* and still left in the *herring.* But all have used it much too much. The distinction between fish and flesh is not the universal thing it was. And the phrase, as a term for something's being neither one thing nor the other is now a cliché.

neither rhyme nor reason. As a way of saying that something is utter nonsense, *neither rhyme nor reason* is now a cliché. In various forms it has been in the language for more than four hundred years but overuse has exhausted it.

nemesis. When used in its classical sense, this word does not have a plural. It is the name of the goddess of retribution, or means retribution in the abstract. Anyone, therefore, who feels the need for a plural should use the English form *nemesises* rather than the pseudo-classical *nemeses.*

neophyte; beginner. The use of *neophyte* as a substitute for *beginner* seems to be especially dear to sports writers among whom has grown up a tradition of employing esoteric words flippantly. Basically *neophyte,* from a Greek word meaning newly planted, means a converted heathen or heretic. In the Primitive Church it meant one newly baptized; in the Roman Catholic Church it means a novice. From such specialized senses to that of *beginner* is a long leap, and only writers who habitually leap before they look take it.

ne plus ultra. As a term for the acme (*The ne plus ultra of fashion*) or in its more literal meaning of no further, *ne plus ultra* is now a cliché.

nether. This is the comparative form of an adjective meaning lower. It has a superlative form *nethermost.* The positive form of this word is no longer in use but a related form can be seen in the adverb and preposition *beneath.*

neurasthenic; neurotic. A person is *neurasthenic* who is suffering from a nervous debility or exhaustion, as from overwork or prolonged mental strain, characterized by vague complaints of a physical nature in the absence of objectively present causes or lesions (*This type of headache is commonly assumed to be neurasthenic in origin*). A person is *neurotic* who is suffering from an emotional disorder in which feelings of anxiety, obsessional thoughts, compulsive acts and physical complaints without objective evidence of disease, in various patterns, dominate the personality. *Neurasthenic* is not now used as much as it was a generation ago. *Neurotic,* however, has become a vogue word to designate almost everything from serious mental illness to little deviations from normal behavior that were formerly regarded as merely eccentric or cranky or moody or crotchety. The modest, who know the limitations of their own knowledge, will leave both words to the physicians. The exact will sometimes be puzzled which of the two words to use and will do well, when in doubt, to use neither. The courteous will certainly use neither within the hearing of the person or persons alluded to.

neurosis. The plural is *neurosises* or *neuroses.*

new; newly. The form *new* may be used as an adjective to qualify a noun. Either form may be used to qualify a participle. *New* is preferred with short, familiar words, as in *new laid eggs, new born child, new baked bread, new found pride; newly* is preferred with longer, less familiar words, *newly discovered pride, newly furnished rooms.* Neither form can be used to qualify a verb.

new and **novel** derive from a common Latin root but although they are often interchanged they are not properly interchangeable. *New* refers to position in time, to that which has not been long in existence, or to an original state or condition. *Novel* refers to kind and is opposed to that which is common or familiar, as *new* is opposed to that which is old or worn. *Novel* suggests newness which has an unexpected quality or is strange or striking but generally pleasing (*His coat was the novel part of his new suit, for it had no lapels*). When Ring Lardner said that Scott Fitzgerald was a novelist and his wife a novelty, he meant that Mrs. Fitzgerald was odd and strange in a delightful way.

new broom. Until recently a broom was brush or twigs or plant stems bound on a handle, the besom that witches are conventionally pictured as riding on. A number of proverbs and quotations indicate that when the twigs were green the broom swept clean but after a very little while (an Italian proverb says three days) the twigs lost their resilience and became brittle and often made more litter than they swept up. With changing times the proverb has lost some of its force and with repetition most of its freshness. To refer to anyone who assumes an office with vigor and bustle and good intentions as *a new broom* is to employ a cliché.

new lease on life. As a term for renewed hope and effort or an increment of vitality or interest, *a new lease on life* is a hackneyed expression.

news. In current English this word is always treated as a singular. We say *this news is good* and *where did you hear it?*.

Originally, the word was an adjective used as a noun and meant that which is new. Until about a hundred years ago it was often felt as a plural and used with a plural verb, as in *There are bad news from Palermo* and *ill news fly fast.* It could also be treated as a true singular, as in *a news so new,* and could be given a regular plural, as in *two important newses.* None of these constructions are standard today.

The form *news* is used as the first element in a compound, as in *newspaper* and *news broadcast.*

newsdealer; news agent; newsstand; news stall. One who deals in newspapers and magazines is in America called a *newsdealer,* in England a *news agent.* The place where newspapers and magazines are sold, especially if it is at a street corner or in a railroad or bus station or airlines terminal, is in America called a *newsstand,* in England a *news stall.*

newsroom; news-room. In England a *news-room* is a room, usually connected with a public library, in which various newspapers are available for reading. In America such a room is usually called a periodical room. In America a *newsroom* is that department of a newspaper office which deals with the news section of the paper (*Hemingway kept the newsroom of the old Toronto Star in stitches with his reportorial antics*).

newt; eft. In some parts of the United States the common *newt* in its land stage is still called by its ancient name of *eft.*

new wine in old bottles. The observation in Matthew 9:17 that men do not *put new wine into old bottles: else the bottles break, and the wine runneth out, and the bottles perish* has reference, of course, to wineskins which when dried out with age would burst under the pressures of fermentation of new wine. The age of a modern glass bottle has nothing to do with the age of the wine it can contain. For most people the meaning of the parable is lost and the phrase should be used as infrequently as possible.

New Year; new year; New Year's; New Year's Day. The phrase which unequivocally describes January 1 is *New Year's Day.* Though some English writers object to it, *New Year* and *New Year's* are acceptable in America. For the sake of absolute clarity, one may best use *New Year's Day* or *New Year's* to describe the first day of January and reserve *new year,* uncapitalized, to describe the year approaching or newly begun.

next. This word was once the superlative of *nigh* and may still be used in the sense of nearest, as in *the next of kin, the chair next the fire.* But as a rule in current English *next* is not a superlative. It ordinarily refers to a series and indicates the item immediately following. For example, *the next house* usually means the first house in the direction one is moving or facing and not the nearest house in any direction.

Next to may be used to mean nearly, as in *it was next to impossible. Next most* usually means just short of being most, as in *the next most desirable solution.*

nexus. The plural is *nexuses* or *nexus,* not *nexi.*

nexus; focus; cynosure. *Nexus* is sometimes used as if it were a synonym for *focus.* A nexus is a tie or link, a means of connection (*Cash Payment . . . the universal sole nexus of man to man*). *Focus,* the Latin word for hearth, was adopted by Kepler, in 1604, as a term in optics to designate the point at which rays of light that originally diverged from one point meet again. The figurative use of the word (influenced, perhaps, by its Latin meaning) is a gathering point, a center of attraction or interest, the point about which anything is concentrated (*More and more the school has replaced the church as the focus of community interest. As Augusta entered the room on her brother's arm she was the focus of all attention*).

A *cynosure* differs from a *focus* in that it is something which by its brilliance attracts attention (*Where perhaps some beauty lies,/ The Cynosure of neighboring eyes*). Attention is focused on something; it is attracted by a cynosure.

nice. Those who believe that a word has its "proper" meaning and should be used in no other sense should consider the wanderings of *nice.* Beginning as the Latin *nescius,* ignorant (from *ne,* not + *scire,* to know), it may have been influenced by Middle English *nesh,* delicate, but this is not absolutely certain. By the sixteenth century it had come to mean (among other meanings) fastidious, difficult to please (*Your nice critic will, of course, find no good in anything*). The reasons for this development are not clear. Perhaps the ignorant are finicky or, hesitating to choose because of ignorance, seemed hard to please. At any rate among those who are hard to please some are hard to please because they have high standards and make fine distinctions (*He has a nice eye for these delicate differences*) and the word was extended to designate the objects or situations which such people can perceive. For a time it was not altogether favorable; it could designate things which were poised in such delicate equilibrium that the nicest or finest impetus could incline them either way. *The nice hazard of one doubtful hour* upon which Hotspur felt it were not good to "set so rich a main" as all his fortunes was not a desirable or pleasant hour but one too dangerously poised between success and ruin. The Duke of Wellington's famous observation that Waterloo was for a while *a damn nice thing* did not mean that he had enjoyed it but that the issue of the battle had been uncertain and turned eventually in England's favor by a narrow margin of advantage or good fortune. Today, however, the word is almost entirely favorable. A nice apple is the sort of apple that a nice or discriminating person, a connoisseur of apples, would select, or just a good apple. And so with a nice day or anything else said to be nice. When someone says that someone else has said *the nicest things* about us, we do not assume that the compliments were fastidious or finely discriminating. We just know that something agreeable has been said.

From agreeable *nice* has also developed the meaning of decorous, proper, though this sense is expressed negatively in conjunction with *not* (*That's not a nice song. It's not nice of little boys to do such things*). From this, the word is now taking on the meaning of "kind," as in *be nice to him.*

nice; choice; dainty; fine. Unless it is to be reduced to a mere synonym of *pleasant*, as it so often is, *nice* should keep something of its older meaning of subtle or precise. *Choice* means worthy of being chosen, carefully selected; hence excellent, superior (*choice apples, choice phrases*). Where there is no selection the word might be absurd and it is so much overworked as an adjective of commendation (perhaps to suggest that the user is himself a judge of fitting selections) that it is well to use another word if possible. *Fine* (probably a back formation from *finish*), like *nice,* designates the sort of thing that would be selected by those capable of delicate or fine discrimination, hence of striking merit (*a fine-looking boy*). Feeling for this meaning has been largely lost and the word has become a vague synonym for *good* (*You're looking fine. We had a fine time*). An echo of the older meaning is heard in the common ironic use of the word. When someone says *A fine mess you made of it!* there is a suggestion that the mess is so bad that it could be selected from among other messes for its particular badness.

Dainty, akin afar off to *dignity,* first meant honor and then the sort of thing suitable to a person who is honored. Hence excellent, fine, choice (*Wasn't that a dainty dish to set before a king?*). But the preferences of such people seemed to the common man, apparently, to run to the delicate, the fragile, the exquisite (*Such dainty china was not for everyday use*). It's a point-of-view word and from the robust point of view, daintiness merges into squeamishness (*You can't be dainty about the boss's cigar, my girl.* See also **fastidious.**

nicknames. A nickname is a name given instead of or in addition to the actual name. It is usually descriptive, or a familiar form of the proper name. The word *nickname* is in itself a sort of nickname, since it is a corruption of *an eke name,* or an additional name, folk-etymologized, it would seem, under the influence of the common nickname *Nick.*

Sobriquet is given in most dictionaries as a synonym for *nickname,* and so it may now be used. But it is slightly pompous and there are differences in the meanings of the two words which the discriminating speaker or writer may wish to preserve. First, a nickname is likely to be an adjunct of the name itself and not peculiar to the individual (as *Tom* for *Thomas*), while a sobriquet is usually applied to a person because of some special association with a quality, achievement or incident (*Old Curmudgeon, Wizard of Menlo Park, Swedish Nightingale, Great Commoner, Last of the Red Hot Mamas*). In other words, a sobriquet is unique. Second, a nickname could generally be used in addressing a person. A sobriquet very often would not, or could not, be. One who knew Abraham Lincoln might have called him *Abe* in talking to him. But he would not have addressed him as *Great Emancipator* or *Rail Splitter.* Thus a nickname, while not necessarily more individual, is more personal.

Nicknames are usually derived from some adaptation of the regular name or from some individual characteristic, though this need not be unique. In the first instance it might be the result of a simple shortening—as *Dave* for *David;* a slight change in the form of the name or a part of it—as *Jim* for *James, Ned* for *Edward* or *Betty* for *Elizabeth. Dick* for *Richard* is hard to explain, though it is one of the commonest and oldest of all nicknames. It was a shortened form of the once common name *Dickon* and may simply have been transferred. Many nicknames are diminutives—*Johnnie* for *John.* Some are a combination of initials—*Casey* for *K.C., Ma Ferguson* for *Miriam A. Ferguson.* In the second instance, the nickname might develop from appearance—*Red, Slim, Shorty;* from a quality—*Speed, Happy, Gabby;* from place of origin—*Tex, Frenchy.* The line between nickname and sobriquet becomes blurred in such appellations as *Dizzy* Dean, *Hot Lips* Paige and *Pretty Boy* Floyd.

On the whole nicknames have friendly, pleasant connotations. Those with negative associations are comparatively rare. And nicknames are not as a rule taken. They are given. There is some recognition of a personality in the bestowing of a nickname. Perhaps that is why people in public life are so often referred to by their nicknames. It establishes an identification as a personality, something more than the mere bearer of a name. *Ike* Eisenhower, *Yogi* Berra, *Liz* Taylor, *Rocky* Graziano, *Danny* Kaye—all derive an intangible benefit from their nicknames.

The negative nicknames are those given to unpopular figures, such as criminals (*Scarface, Cherry Nose*) or those who have in some way offended the public (or perhaps a columnist). *Baby Face* Nelson was, apparently, so named by his criminal associates and the public (which, on the whole, is fond of its criminals) relished the irony. *Golf Bag Sam* Hunt, one of Chicago's more resourceful hoodlums, gained his nickname by carrying his sawed-off shotgun in a golf bag, a symbol of solid respectability that deceived the police and lured his victims into fatal inattention.

Nicknames are usually bestowed on people by those close to them, family or friends. But those in the public eye are often given sobriquets by journalists who may invent or record a striking appellation. Sometimes history pins a name on someone already dead—in the light of later events or appraisal. Thus Richard, whom we know as *The Lion-hearted,* was known to his contemporaries as *Richard Yea-and-Nay* because he so rarely kept his word.

A peculiar trend in nicknames in contemporary America is the giving of boys' nicknames to girls as their regular names. *Billie* Burke was one of the first. But now *Jackie, Tommy, Bobbie, Frankie, Gussie* and a dozen other nicknames that a generation ago were thought of as purely masculine are more used by girls than boys.

Sobriquets are sometimes invented for or assumed by people who wish to benefit from a trademark, usually entertainers. Frank Sinatra is *The Voice;* Bing Crosby is *The Groaner* or *Mr. Music;* Clara Bow is *The It Girl;* Marie MacDonald is *The Body.*

nick of time. As a term for opportunely, at the critical moment, or for the very last moment that would be useful, *in the nick of time* is a cliché. It is usually spoken with great intenseness, seeking to lend emphasis to the dramatic event it is always employed to depict. But intenseness exhausts itself as well as its audience and such phrases seem to be in continual need of additional emphasis. For centuries this phrase was *in the nick.* Then in the late seventeenth century it became *in the nick of time.* And there is now a tendency to make it *in the very nick of time.* It is best to avoid it altogether.

nigh. The comparative form is *nigher* or *near;* the superlative is *nighest* or *next.* The regular forms *nigher* and *nighest* have been in general use for only a few hundred years and are already archaic. See **near; next.**

As an adverb *nigh* means near in space, time, or relation. It is archaic in prose and has not been used effectively by a good poet since Thomas Hardy (*And all mankind that haunted nigh/ Had sought their household fires*). In the sense of nearly or almost, *nigh* is archaic or dialectal (*It's nigh sundown. He's nigh on to ninety*). As an adjective it means being near, not distant, near in relationship. With reference to animals or vehicles it means left or near (*the nigh horse*). One use of *nigh,* now chiefly dialectal or archaic, means parsimonious (*He may not be a miser, but he's mighty nigh*). *Close* in this sense remains standard. *Well nigh* is a cliché.

Night Riders, when capitalized, designates the members of a secret organization of Kentucky and Tennessee tobacco farmers which in 1908-09 tried to organize against a monopoly of tobacco buyers. The Night Riders burned the barns of those who refused to join their organization and dynamited some of the tobacco warehouses. See Robert Penn Warren's novel *Night Rider.*

night stick; truncheon. American *night stick* is English *truncheon.* In England the truncheon is carried at all hours. The night stick, a heavy stick or long club, is carried by policemen at night and sometimes in the daytime (*The police . . . charged the marchers and bystanders alike, swinging their nightsticks*).

nimbus. The plural is *nimbuses* or *nimbi.*

nine days' wonder. The Romans seem to have fixed nine days as the life span of a minor marvel or gossip sensation. Chaucer said that wonders last only nine nights "in toune," implying perhaps that country folk cherish them a bit longer. Shakespeare used the proverb several times and Robert Burton gave it an amusing addition: *A wonder lasts but nine days, and then the puppy's eyes are open.* In recent times it has come to be applied especially to sensational stories in the newspapers which are kept alive more by the papers than by their own intrinsic interest. The phrase is now worn out with overuse. (During World War II the term **ninety-day wonder** was applied derisively to graduates of the Officer Candidate Schools, who had been transformed from civilians to officers in three months.)

ninepins. When referring to the game, the plural word *ninepins* takes a singular verb, as in *ninepins was being played.* One piece is called *a ninepin* and *ninepins* used with a plural verb means several of these, as in *the ninepins were set up.* Only the singular form is used as the first element in a compound, as in *a ninepin alley.* See also **ten pins.**

nip. The English and the Americans have various special meanings for *nip* in addition to its common, standard meanings of to compress sharply between two surfaces or points, to pinch, bite, and so forth.

An English colloquial meaning is to move or go suddenly (*Well, I'll just be nipping along now*). Although *a nipping frost* would be standard American, the adjective *nippy,* to describe a sharply cold day, is English, used in America only for humorous effect.

Nip and tuck is an American expression. It describes the relation of competitors in a race or other contest in which the outcome is continually in doubt as one slightly gains over and then loses to the other. The nearest English equivalent is the phrase, also standard in America, *neck and neck.* However, they are not quite the same: *neck and neck* suggests a sustained equality; *nip and tuck* suggests fluctuating chances.

nip it in the bud. As a term for stopping something in the early stages before it can become a menace or even a serious threat, to *nip it in the bud* is hackneyed.

no. This word is primarily an adjective. It may qualify either a singular or a plural noun, as in *no man* and *no men.* A singular noun qualified by *no* requires a singular verb, as in *no man knows,* and a plural noun a plural verb, as in *no birds sing.* The adjective *no* cannot be used alone as a noun or pronoun; the form for this is *none.*

As a rule, the adjective *no* makes an entire statement negative. That is, *no great man would say that* is equivalent to *a great man would not say that.* For this reason, a noun can often be qualified by *no* when what is meant is the verb qualified by *not,* as in *I was troubled by no doubt* and *you need have no fear.* But this is not always true. *No little* usually means *much* and *no few, many,* as in *it added no little to his happiness* and *tender dreams, no few of which have since been realized.*

No may be used as an adverb to qualify *other, different,* and the comparative forms of adjectives and adverbs, as in *it is no different* and *I will wait no longer.* (The rest of this paragraph involves some hair-splitting. It should not be read except by those who enjoy this sort of thing.) Some grammarians feel that *no* is also used as an adverb with the positive form of certain adjectives, as in *at no inconsiderable yearly loss.* Here, if *no* qualifies only the word that immediately follows, that is, *inconsiderable,* it is an adverb. If it qualifies all the words that follow, including the noun, that is, if it qualifies *inconsiderable yearly loss,* it is an adjective. To say which of these interpretations is the better one requires a subtle feeling for the meaning of words. But anyone who can see the problem has a right to his own conclusions. If *no* is an adverb here it may be preceded by a definitive word, as in *at the no inconsiderable* or *at my no inconsiderable.* If it is an adjective it cannot be used after a word of this kind because *no* is itself a definitive. Some grammarians say that *no* is here an adjective and that therefore the construction with *the, my,* or any other definitive word, is ungrammatical. Others say that the fact that this construction is used proves that *no* is here an adverb.

No may be used to answer a question, as in *Did you hear that? No.;* or to introduce a negative statement, as in *No, I don't.* In these uses of the word, *no* is interpreted as an adverb qualifying a verb. This adverbial *no* may be used as a noun and has the plural form *noes,* as in *the noes have it. No* may also qualify a verb in the phrase *or no,* as in *shall I be saved or no?* and *tell me whether he is to be trusted or no.* In present-day English *or not* is generally preferred to *or no* in sentences of this kind. Except in these three constructions, *no* cannot be used to qualify a verb. The regular adverbial form of the word is *not.*

no expense has been spared. As a way of saying that plenty of money has been spent, usually in preparation for something, *no expense has been spared* is hackneyed.

no love lost. As a way of saying that two people do not like each other or (often) are enemies, to say there is *no love lost between them* is to employ a wornout understatement.

no object. When something is said to be *no object* (*There's no use shaving down expenses this way; money's no object to them*), *object* is used in the sense of the end toward which effort is directed (as in *the object of our visit*). In the example given *money* serves for "the saving of money." *No object* is sometimes used, however, as if it meant no objection or no impediment. This is a misuse of the phrase.

no respecter of persons is a cliché for one who makes no distinction in his treatment of people on account of their wealth or social position (from Acts 10:34, where God is said to be *no respecter of persons*).

no sinecure. To say of a difficult task that it is *no sinecure* is to employ a cliché. The word once had a definite meaning. A priest without a church was said to have *beneficium sine cura,* that is a benefice without cure (of souls). The word then came to be applied to any position (of which formerly there were many) that paid well but had no duties attached. Such positions are now almost unknown and the word has lost its specific meaning.

no thinking man; no man in his right mind. These expressions, the former largely English, the latter largely American, are bluffing or bullying formulas. The speaker uses them in an attempt to label anyone who disagrees with him as thoughtless or insane. Though they are often spoken as if they were terms of moderation, they are just downright name calling and serve notice that there can be no discussion but only subservience or quarreling.

noble. This word is always an adjective. When used to qualify a verb, as in *you did noble,* it is not standard.

noblesse oblige which means "nobility constrains" or "noble birth imposes the obligation of behaving nobly" is now a cliché and a rather dangerous one. It is spoken always in acknowledgment of an obligation but it carries with it an assumption of superiority and it sometimes seems to the listener that the obligation is acknowledged only for the opportunity of calling attention to the nobility.

nobody; no one. These words are singular and require a singular verb. They may be referred to by the singular pronouns *he, his, him,* or by forms of the pronoun *they,* as in *nobody's stopping you, are they?; nobody was hurt, were they?*

nodding acquaintance, as a term to describe someone whom we know only well enough to nod a greeting to, is a cliché.

nohow. This is a standard English word when it is used correctly, as in *we could nohow bring ourselves to do it.* But the word is seldom heard in the United States except in a double negative, as in *we couldn't bring ourselves to do it nohow.* Here it is not the word that is unacceptable, but the whole sentence. The form *nohows* is not standard.

noisome. This word, the first syllable of which is related to *annoy* and not to *noise,* means offensive or disgusting, often as to odor (*The noisome alleys and backways, teeming and* squalid, dark and fetid). It also means harmful, injurious, noxious (*The noisome pestilence*). It is sometimes misused for *noisy*. A good corrective for this error is supplied by a quotation from the poems of Henry Hirst in the *Oxford English Dictionary*: *Begirt with noisome ivy vines/ That shroud me like a pall.*

nom de plume; nom de guerre; pen name; pseudonym. Finding a name for a writer's assumed name seems to be difficult in English. *Nom de plume* is a French phrase coined in English from French words to mean pen name. *Pen name* means what it says, but it sounds artificial and is, for it developed after *nom de plume* as a translation of it. *Nom de guerre* (war name) is the French term for assumed name but can be used unself-consciously only by the French. The Greeks had a word for it, *pseudonym*, and if *assumed name* seems to have too strong criminal connotations, *pseudonym* is probably the least objectionable of the lot.

nominal means being such in name only (*The peace was nominal, for border clashes continued. He was the nominal ruler, but he was nothing but a figurehead, the actual functions of government being controlled entirely by the Chief Minister*). When it is used to describe a price or consideration, it means named as a mere matter of form, being trifling in comparison with the actual value. A nominal fee is not a low fee but one so low that it is not a fee at all but merely a token payment. The business men who served in Washington during World War I for a dollar a year received a nominal wage. When *nominal* is used with some such limiting word as *merely*, it designates complete contrast to something substantial.

nominate. See name.

nominative absolute. See participles.

nominative case. The nominative is a Latin case used to mark the subject of a verb. In modern English this relationship is shown by position. See **subject of a verb** and **subjective pronouns.**

nonce word. A *nonce word* is a word coined and used only for the particular occasion, not adopted into use (Coleridge's *mammonolatry* —mammon worship). Since in making such a coinage the author implies that he finds the immense vocabulary of the English language insufficient, there is always the danger in its use of being charged with vanity, affectation, or ignorance of the language. There is also the danger of not being understood or of annoying the reader by compelling him to stop and puzzle out the meaning of the strange word. If the author and the reader are clever there may be the surprise of a fine excess. But it's risky. Fowler says don't try it unless you're sure you're good.

none. At one time the words *no* and *none* had the same relation to each other that *my* and *mine* had. That is, only the form *none* could be used alone without a noun; either form could stand before a noun, and *no* was used before a consonant and *none* before a vowel, as in *no good* and *none evil*. This usage had become irregular by the end of the sixteenth century. In the King

James Bible we find in Deuteronomy 5:7 *thou shalt have none other gods before me*, but in Exodus 20:3 *thou shalt have no other gods before me*. In current English *none* is used chiefly as a pronoun and *no* is the regular adjective form. *None* may still function as an adjective provided it is separated from the noun it qualifies, as in *but answer there came none* and *better be jocund with the fruitful grape than sadden after none, or bitter, fruit*, but it cannot stand in the normal adjective position. We would now say *no other gods*.

The pronoun *none* may have a preceding noun as antecedent, such as *cause* in *men will fight for any cause, or for none;* or the antecedent may not be expressed, as in *none can now say*. The pronoun may be qualified by a following adjective, such as *living* in *none living can remember the day* and *stranger* in *This glass had seen some strange things. And surely none stranger than itself.* In *they cause none such to die,* *such* is an adjective qualifying the pronoun *none*. This construction is condemned by some grammarians, but it is traditional, literary English. *None* may be followed by an *of* phrase. Here *none of* may mean no part of, as in *none of it is his,* but it is more often an emphatic negative equivalent to *not at all* as in *it's none of your business* and *it's your misfortune and none of my own.* This too is standard, literary English. For genitive problems, see **double genitives.**

The pronoun *none* is ordinarily used to make a negative statement about all the members of a certain group. A statement of this kind is essentially plural. But grammar is not logic, and grammatically the word may be either singular or plural. It has been used in both ways for as long as we have any records of the language. An analysis of English literature shows that from the time of Malory (1450) to the time of Milton (1650), *none* was treated as a plural once for every three times it was treated as a singular; and from the time of Milton to 1917, it was treated as a plural seven times for every four times that it was treated as a singular. Its use as a plural has increased noticeably in the last forty years. In current English, *none* is always treated as a plural when it refers to persons. If we want to have the verb singular we must now use *no one* or *nobody* as the subject. The modern usage is seen in *no one thinks he is clever, but none except his family know how stupid he really is.* In speaking of things, *none* may still be treated as a singular, but it is more often treated as a plural.

None may also be used as an adverb in some constructions. It may qualify the comparative form of an adjective (or adverb) preceded by *the,* as in *none the worse for it, none the wiser, none the less surely;* or a positive form preceded by *too,* as in *none too soon, none too sure.* In Great Britain it may be used before a positive form qualified by *so,* as in *it's none so pleasant,* but this construction is not often heard in the United States. *None* may also be used alone with a verb to mean not at all, as in *I slept none that night.* The word is used in this way in the United States and Scotland and the construction is standard in those countries, but not in England. This has been true for at least 150 years. Boswell, using the speech that was natural to him, wrote: *we spoke none.* But he apparently considered this an inferior form of English, for he later corrected the sentence to *we had no conversation.*

noplace. The use of *noplace* as a substitute for *nowhere,* as in *I could find it noplace,* is condemned by many grammarians because the noun *place* is here being used instead of the adverb *where.* This usage is not acceptable in Great Britain but it occurs too often in the United States, in written as well as in spoken English, to be called anything but standard. It is acceptable English in this country.

nor. See **or.**

normal; regular; ordinary; natural. That is *normal* which conforms to the established standards for its sort of thing (*The normal response to such a statement would be derision. Anybody with normal intelligence would have known better*). That is *regular* which conforms to prescribed rule, accepted principle, recognized pattern (*The regular thing is to have dinner first. It's best to do it the regular way; it will cause less comment*). To say of someone that he is *a regular scoundrel* is to say that he conforms, in every respect, to the recognized pattern of scoundrelism. The slang commendation, that so-and-so is *a regular guy,* carries an interesting suggestion of the importance of conformity in achieving popular approbation. That is *ordinary* which is opposed to the uncommon, of the usual kind (*The ordinary driver seems to feel that traffic regulations are meant only for the other fellow*). That is *natural* which conforms to the principles of its own nature and since most normal and ordinary people and things do, there are many contexts in which the words are interchangeable. See **average, common.**

normalcy; normalism; normality; the normal; Normal. It was in Boston, in 1920, that Senator Warren G. Harding, moved by alliteration and the spirit of the times, declared that what America then needed was *not heroics but healing; not nostrums but normalcy; not revolution but restoration; . . . not surgery but serenity.* The idea seemed sound to the voters who elected him president. But the wits, who were just starting a brilliant decade in the opposition, seized on the word *normalcy* and made it a banner of derision. Without bothering to consult their dictionaries, they simply assumed that the Senator meant *normality* and had blundered. As late as 1953 even so astute and literate a man as Frederick Lewis Allen (in *The Big Change,* N.Y., Harper) could say of Harding: *He preferred to talk about what he called "normalcy," meaning normality.*

But *normalcy,* although until that moment a rare word, is a perfectly legitimate word, meaning the character or state of being normal. It is a complete and acceptable synonym for *normality,* and had been in use for at least seventy years before Mr. Harding's or his ghost writer's lust for alliteration led him to it.

Normality, however, the normal state or quality, is the common and most readily understood word, though it is being displaced by *the normal,* the standard or type.

Normalism is so rare a word that most standard dictionaries do not recognize its existence. Those that do identify it as a theological term designating an early Buddhistic belief in a cosmic order, opposed to animism, which is not subject to the will of a personal deity.

Normal schools (after the French *école normale*) are so called because they teach the norms or rules of teaching.

north; northern. These words have one comparative form, *more northern,* and two superlatives, *northmost* and *northernmost.*

nostalgia, derived from Greek words meaning "return home" and "pain," originally meant an aching longing for home, homesickness. Now a vogue word, *nostalgia* has come to mean any vague yearning, especially for the past and especially—as most yearning for the past is—when tinged with tenderness and sadness. It is so vague and yet so popular that it has become slightly comic (as in *The Night the Old Nostalgia Burned Down,* by Frank Sullivan, Boston, 1953). *Homesickness, yearning,* and *longing* should all be carefully considered whenever the impulse to use *nostalgia* comes upon us.

not. This word, which is an abbreviated form of *nought,* is now the simple adverb of negation. Until about six hundred years ago, the simple negative adverb was *ne.* It stood before the verb, as in *twenty thousand infants that ne wot the right hand from the left,* but could be strengthened by a following negative, as in *ne doubt ye nought.* This gave English a compound negative *ne . . . nought* somewhat like the French *ne . . . pas.* In time *nought* became *not* and *ne* disappeared. Although the old construction was forgotten, *not* kept its position after the verb, as in *pomp that fades not* and *this body dropt not down.*

In a normal English sentence a negative adverb stands immediately before the verb. A post-placed negative, as in *fades not* and *dropt not* is permissible but unusual. One would therefore expect to see *not* brought forward, and this was occasionally done, as in *I not doubt he came alive to land* and *they possessed the island but not enjoyed it.* This is the reasonable way to handle *not* and if grammar was controlled by reason this is the way we would now use the word. But we all feel that this word order is wrong or "impossible." That is because language is much too big a thing to be altered at will, even by school teachers or textbook writers. It is the speech habits of all the people who use the language, and these in turn depend upon speech habits handed down from the past. Language changes as the needs of people change. But it changes as a living creature does and cannot be manipulated mechanically. We, today, cannot place *not* in the normal position for an adverb because seven hundred years ago it was the object of the verb and has come down to us in the object position.

In present-day English we solve the problem of *not* by never using the word except in a verbal phrase, such as *he will not doubt*. Here it follows a verb form, as tradition requires, but stands before the meaningful verb, as the normal word order requires. In the simple past and present tenses, where we do not ordinarily have an auxiliary verb, we deliberately create a verbal phrase by using some form of *do*, as in *he did not doubt, he does not doubt*.

There is one exception to this rule. *Do* is never used with forms of the verb *to be*. Here we keep the old word order, as in *he is not here, I am not sure*. Fifty years ago it was considered better not to use *do* with the simple forms of *have*, and to say *he hasn't a pencil, he hadn't a pencil*. In America today *do* is used with *have* more often than not and most people would say *he doesn't have a pencil, he didn't have a pencil*. The old word order without *do* is still possible with any verb. We may still say *I doubt not your word*. It is still natural English with *have*, especially in the present tense, as in *he hasn't a nickel*. But it is required only after the verb *to be*.

When *not* follows *be, have,* or an auxiliary verb, we ordinarily do not pronounce the *o*. We say *isn't, doesn't, can't*. But in writing it is customary to use the full form. We write *I cannot come* when we would say *I can't come*. This is unfortunate because it makes the written sentences stiff and over-emphatic. But many people are offended when they see contractions in print. A writer must therefore decide whether it is better for him to use the full forms and be considered didactic by some people, or to use the contractions and be considered undignified by a great many others.

Not may be used to qualify one element in a sentence, an adjective, adverb, phrase, or clause. When it is, it is placed immediately before that element, as in *he told a not very convincing story* and *he said it not to me but to you*. But in most cases *not* is a sentence adverb and negates the entire statement. This is always true when it stands before the subject. The lines *not a drum was heard, not a funeral note, . . . not a soldier discharged his farewell shot* mean simply it is not true that a drum was heard, or a funeral note, or that a soldier discharged his farewell shot. When *not* stands in or immediately after the verb form, it has exactly the same force unless the subject of the verb is *some*.

These points may seem too obvious to be worth mentioning, but they are often overlooked in discussing negative statements that have *all* as subject. The sentence *all the invitations have not been mailed* says nothing about how many have been mailed. It merely denies that all have. If we want to say that none

have been mailed we must either use the word *none* or make an affirmative statement such as *all the invitations are still to be mailed. Not all have been mailed* is exactly the same statement as *all have not been mailed*. The fact that sentences of this kind say very little may be a reason for not using them. But it is no justification for trying to force a distinction on them which they do not have, logically or grammatically.

not un-. There are occasions when the *not un-* construction is justified, as where a situation or something said seems to have a negative import but actually does not. To say of some speaker that he was *not unkind* in his remarks is to imply that the remarks might very well sound unkind or it might be expected of this particular speaker on this particular occasion that he would be unkind, but that the context or the intonation or the exact choice of words or some other circumstance made it clear that in fact there was no unkindness in his utterance.

But for the most part the *not un-* construction is simply a bad habit, a circumlocution of timidity, a desire not to give offense that can be more annoying than the offense it seeks to avoid.

not wisely but too well. It was Othello who *lov'd not wisely, but too well*. Recognition of the original context, which once may have given this quotation a touch of wit, has now been lost, so far as the common user is concerned—if ever there was anything in it that made it particularly witty to apply to other situations.

not worth the paper it's written on. To say of some agreement, promise, or assurance that it is *not worth the paper it's written on*, as a way of saying that it is worthless and unreliable, is to employ a phrase that has been debilitated by overuse.

notable; noted; noticeable; notorious; famous. *Noted* means conspicuous, celebrated, famous (*A number of noted actresses attended the premiere*). That which or he who is *notable* is worthy of note or notice (*Only a few friends recognized Hopkins as a notable poet in his lifetime*). *Noticeable* means such as to attract notice (*The contents of the bottle were noticeably diminished. There was a noticeable sabre scar on his left cheek*). Many a noticeable person is not notable and few of the notable are noted and many who are noted are really *notorious*, that is, widely but unfavorably known (*Charles James Fox, the noted statesman, was a notorious gambler*). *Notorious* is the antithesis of *famous*, which means renowned or well-known in a favored sense; yet *infamous* is a far stronger word than *notorious*, expressing detestation where *notorious* expresses merely ill repute. Then, of course, the same person may be regarded as notorious and famous by different groups at the same time or by the same group at different times. Hitler was a famous statesman to many Germans, a notorious madman to his nation's enemies. Lola Montez, was, as a girl, a famous beauty; as a woman, a notorious adventuress. Then, if one is exceedingly notorious he may after his death become famous. We speak of famous, not notorious, criminals of the past. See also **celebrity**.

notary; notary public. The second form is preferred to describe a public officer authorized to authenticate contracts, acknowledge deeds, take affidavits, protest bills of exchange, take depositions, etc. The plural form is *notaries public*.

note and **notice** are interchangeable in the sense of to become aware of, to pay attention to, to observe, perceive (*The world will little note nor long remember what we say here, but it can never forget what they did here. Notice Neptune, though,/ Taming a sea-horse*). *Note*, however, often conveys the additional sense of mark down, as in writing, make a memorandum or notation of.

notice. When this verb is used in an active form it may be followed by an object and the simple form of a verb, as in *he noticed her hesitate*, by an object and the *-ing* form of a verb, as in *he noticed her hesitating*, or by a clause, as in *he noticed that she hesitated*, but not by a *to*-infinitive. We do not say *he noticed her to hesitate*. When *notice* is used in a passive form it may be followed by a *to*-infinitive, as in *she was noticed to hesitate*, or by the *-ing* form of a verb, as in *she was noticed hesitating*. See also **descry**.

notion. See **idea**.

notoriety. See **celebrity**.

notwithstanding. This word is ordinarily an adverb or a preposition, but it may also be used as a conjunction. That is, it may introduce a full clause without the aid of the word *that*, as in *John Hunter, notwithstanding he had a bee in his bonnet, was really a great man*.

nought. See **aught**.

nouns. It is very difficult to define a noun purely in terms of English grammar. If one can refer to Latin, the definition is easy. In Latin, nouns are words that have gender, number, and case and determine the gender, number, and case of other words in the sentence. As a rule, teachers of English mean by a noun, any word that would be a noun in Latin. But they can hardly offer this as a definition to American students.

The definition usually given, that a noun is "the name of a person, place, or thing," is unsatisfactory in two ways. In the first place, it is misleading to beginning students because it involves an unfamiliar meaning of the word *thing*. For example, in the lines:

> They are not long, the weeping and the
>   laughter,
> Love and desire and hate:
> I think they have no portion in us after
>   We pass the gate.

the words *weeping, laughter, love, desire, hate, portion*, and *gate* are all nouns. It is unlikely that anyone who did not already know that these words were nouns would think of calling *weeping* or *desire* a thing. In the second place,

it is illogical to try to distinguish the various parts of speech by classifying their meanings. A noun is not what it refers to, but simply a certain kind of word that needs to be distinguished from other words in some intelligible manner.

A noun might be defined functionally, according to the role that a word plays in a sentence. But such a definition would make nonsense of the question: When can a noun be used as an adverb? And some of the most interesting questions in grammar come in just this form. For this reason, a different type of definition, and one that may at first seem unnecessarily complicated, is more useful in the long run.

Most nouns have a singular and a plural form, such as *boy* and *boys*. Some, such as *mud*, have only a singular and some, such as *trousers*, have only a plural form. A few, such as *deer*, have the same form in the singular and in the plural. But whenever a noun is used, it must be used as a singular or as a plural. The question of number cannot be disregarded, as it is in words such as *green, quickly, toward*. Verbs are also said to have number, but in an entirely different sense. A plural verb, such as *they walk*, does not mean that they walk more than once. In languages that do not have a rigid sentence order, verbs take on special forms to show which word in the sentence they are attached to and a verb is said to "agree with its subject in number." A little of this survives in English and a few verb forms show number. But this is merely a reflection, or a matching, of the number which properly belongs to some noun. A noun, therefore, can be defined as "a word that has number," that is, a word that must be either singular or plural.

This definition is not completely satisfactory. Pronouns, which are words that are used in place of nouns, also have number. In addition, adjectives are sometimes used as nouns and when they are, they too have number, as in *the injured were removed*. One can distinguish nouns from pronouns by the fact that a pronoun is a word used instead of a noun, to designate something without naming it. That is, a pronoun is a function word and has no true meaning until we know what noun it is standing for. It is much harder to say whether a word is actually a noun or merely an adjective functioning as a noun. But since adjectives may be qualified by adverbs and nouns may not, most grammarians say that the word is an adjective as long as it is possible to use an adverb before it, as in *the seriously injured*. Recognizing these problems, we may define a noun more accurately as "a word that has number but that does not have an antecedent and cannot be qualified by an adverb."

(For problems having to do with number in nouns, see **singular nouns, plural nouns, generic nouns, group names, mass nouns,** and **adjectives as nouns.** For questions of number in verbs and pronouns, see **agreement: verbs** and the individual words.)

In addition to a singular and a plural, nouns also have a genitive or possessive case which enables them to function very much as an adjective does. (See **genitive case** and **nouns as adjectives.** The other functions of a noun are discussed under **subject of a verb, object of a verb, object of a preposition, indirect object, linking verbs,** and **nouns as adverbs.**)

Nouns are sometimes classified as *collective, common, proper, abstract,* and *concrete.* These terms are defined in this dictionary but are not used in discussions of noun problems.

(For questions regarding hyphens, see **compound words.**)

nouns as adjectives. It is sometimes impossible to say whether the first element in a compound is a noun or an adjective. For example, a nineteenth century English schoolmaster failed some children for saying that *cannon* was a noun in the compound *cannon ball.* During the 1880's the greatest English grammarians argued this question at length. Those who held that *cannon* was a noun seem to have had the best of it, but not to everybody's satisfaction. They pointed out that we use an adjective and not an adverb before *cannon ball.* But this proves nothing. Other compounds, such as *old age,* that obviously have an adjective for the first element, are qualified by adjectives. We say *extreme old age.* They pointed out that *cannon* cannot be compared. That is, we cannot speak of *a cannoner ball.* But some undoubted adjectives, such as *previous, several, yearly,* cannot be compared. They also showed that in the twelfth century, when English was an inflected language and it was easy to see the difference between a noun and an adjective, the first element in similar compounds, such as *sea water,* was a noun in the genitive and not an adjective. The answer to this is that such words "might have used the intervening seven or eight hundred years to become adjectives." A few nouns, such as *square,* have been used as qualifiers so consistently that they have even developed comparative and superlative forms, as in *he who can sit squarest on a three-legged stool.*

Those of us who are neither grammarians nor school children do not have to answer such difficult questions. Almost any English noun can be used in the singular form as if it were an adjective. That is, almost any English noun can be used to qualify another noun. It makes no difference whether we call this an adjective, a form of the genitive, or a noun used as an adjective. (See **singular nouns, compound words,** and **genitive case.** For the difference between a noun and an adjective in *-ing,* see **-ing.**)

Almost any prepositional phrase that limits the meaning of a noun can be dropped and the qualifying noun placed immediately before the principal one. In this way *research in sociology* becomes *sociology research* and *opportunities for outdoor recreation, outdoor recreation opportunities.* The construction is as old as the English language, but before 1900 it was pretty much restricted to short words and names of material things, such as *river bank, cotton dress, sea water.* Since then its use has been enormously extended. At first many people objected to the new forms. They objected particularly to compounds expressing abstract ideas, such as *word order, death threat, child management, thought relationships.* But the construction was too useful to be given up. It makes for a terse, compact style, very much in keeping with our modern temper. If too many syllables are involved, that is, if the individual words are too long—as they certainly are in the first examples given above—terseness loses most of its advantages. For this reason, good writers do not often combine nouns of more than two syllables each. And even when the words are short, there may be such a thing as too much terseness. Most people would find a sequence of eight nouns fatiguing, as in *he absconded with the River Street fire house Christmas Eve party funds.* But this is a question of style, not grammar.

As a rule, prepositional phrases that are evaluative or imply a judgment cannot be handled in this way. For example, in *an ornament of value, a man of honor, a work of distinction,* we cannot simply place the second noun before the first. We have to use an adjective form such as *a valuable ornament, an honorable man, a distinguished work.* The fact that in most cases an adjective form must be used for a phrase that is evaluative, while a noun form may be used when the phrase is defining or limiting, leads to the feeling that the adjective form is always evaluative. For this reason, although *educational* is not evaluative in the following example, many people would rather say *the education committee* than *the educational committee* in speaking of a committee that is to consider questions of education. Traditionally, both forms mean the same thing and can be used interchangeably. But the movement away from the distinctive adjective form is strong.

The noun in a descriptive phrase may itself be qualified by a definitive adjective (such as *the, this, that, my, any, no, some*), as it is in *a box of this size, a car of that color.* In phrases of this kind, the preposition may simply be dropped and the remaining words, such as *this size,* then function as adjectives. They may stand immediately after the principal noun, as in *a child that age,* or they may be separated from it by a linking verb, as in *the child was that age.* A prepositional phrase cannot be treated in this way unless the phrase noun is qualified by a definitive adjective. We cannot drop the *of* from *is it of use?* although we may say *is it any use?.* The preposition cannot be dropped from a phrase that is not purely descriptive. For example, the *of* cannot be dropped from a phrase that shows the whole of which something is a part, as in *one of these men.* But within the limitations just described, the construction is standard literary English and can be used on the most solemn occasions, as in *we are not now that strength which in old days moved heaven and earth.*

Today, words of this kind are sometimes placed before the noun they qualify instead of after it, as in *do you like this color car?.* This has been true of *age* and *size,* as in *what age child* and *any size box,* for almost two hundred years. But the free use of this construction, as seen in *this type engine, any style dress,* is very recent. It is heard too often in the speech of well educated people to be condemned. But it is not yet used in literary English. And it makes some older people very unhappy.

nouns as adverbs. Any adverbial idea can be expressed by a prepositional phrase, as manner is in *he worked with a will* and place in *he worked in the basement.* But a noun can often function as an adverb without first being made part of a prepositional phrase. If the common form of a noun is used, it is called an adverbial accusative. This may be either singular or plural. If the noun is clearly singular but nevertheless takes a final *s,* it is called an adverbial genitive.

1. A noun can be used as an adverb of extent, that is, as a word which shows "how much," as *bit* in *wait a bit* and *lot* in *he is a lot better. Five dollars* is an adverb of extent in *it cost five dollars.* In expressions such as *five dollars a lesson, twice a year, ten cents a piece,* the final noun is also called an adverb of extent. Actually, the *a* used here once meant *in* and these are remnants of prepositional phrases similar to the words *alive, asleep, awake, afloat.* (See **adjectives.**) *The* is sometimes used instead of *a* in expressions of this kind, as in *six dollars the pair.* This is a late development, influenced by French. It is acceptable, but *a* is preferred.

A noun used as an adverb of extent is ordinarily an adverbial accusative, as *way* is in *a long way off.* In *it is a long ways off,* the form *ways* is an adverbial genitive. This construction is no longer used in Great Britain and some grammarians say that it is no longer standard anywhere. But it was once literary English in England and is still standard in the United States. It is used by many well educated people and by some of our best writers. There is no feeling today that this is a genitive form and an apostrophe is never used here.

2. A noun can be used as an adverb of manner, that is, as a word which shows "how." We may say *send it air mail, travel pullman, don't act that way.* Nouns are used in this way more freely in the United States than they are in Great Britain, but the construction is natural English and needs no apology.

3. Nouns are not ordinarily used to show "place." They may be used to show distance, as *miles* in *five miles . . . the sacred river ran,* but this is considered an adverb of extent rather than of place. The verb *leave* takes an object which means "place from which," as in *leave town, leave school,* but this is not truly an adverb construction.

Words which represent the points of the compass, and the single word *home* can be used adverbially in the sense of "place to which," as in *swift hoofs thundering south* and *home they brought her warrior dead.* But we cannot say *office they go* or *they run school.* Nouns are used to show "place at or in which" in a few expressions, such as *he smote them hip and thigh* and *we painted it top and bottom.* But in general, nouns cannot be used in this way. We cannot say *I am staying office.*

In the United States the word *home* is used to show "place at which" as well as "place to which," as in *we stayed home all day.* This is not acceptable in Great Britain where an *at* is required, but it is standard English in this country. The noun *place* is also used in the United States to show "place to which," as in *we are going some place tonight,* and "place at or in which," as in *I have looked every place.* These constructions too are standard in the United States.

4. Nouns are used freely to show "extent of time," as *night* in *and trains all night groan on the rails,* and *years* in *wedded we have been these twice ten tedious years.* These may be classed as adverbs of extent or as adverbs of time. Nouns may also be used to show "time at which," as in *I dreamed I saw Joe Hill last night* and *tomorrow I shall miss you less.*

An adverbial genitive is used to show "repeated time," as in *he works nights.* This construction is condemned by some grammarians and is no longer standard in Great Britain, where it is replaced by a prepositional phrase, as in *he works at night.* But it is still acceptable, and widely used, in the United States.

nouns of multitude. See **group names** and **collective nouns.**

novel. See **new.**

novice. See **amateur.**

now. This word is primarily an adverb of time but it may also be used as an adverbial conjunction, as in *but, oh! the heavy change, now thou art gone.* Some grammarians claim that this is improper. That is, they insist that the conjunction *that* is required in a sentence of this kind. But *now* has been used to introduce a clause from the earliest times and by most of the great writers of English.

noway; noways; nowise. Both *-way* forms are standard English in such constructions as *he was noway* (or *noways*) *to blame.* In the United States *noway* is preferred to *noways.* The form *nowise* is also standard but it is not often used in this country.

nowhere; nowheres. *Nowhere* is the only acceptable form in written English. In the United States *nowheres* is often heard in the speech of well educated people, but it does not appear in print.

Nowhere is sometimes used with an unnecessary *that,* as in *nowhere that I have been.* This is not as well established as the similar use of *anywhere,* but it is acceptable to many educated people in the United States.

noxious and **obnoxious** both derive from the same Latin root meaning harm. Indeed *obnoxious* simply is, or was, the word *noxious* with the prefix *ob-* meaning towards or in the direction of. In modern usage, however, *noxious* is the stronger term, for it means injurious to health or physical well-being (*The chemical plant filled the air with noxious fumes. The strong smell of sulphur, and a choking sensation in the lungs, indicated the presence of noxious gases*). *Obnoxious* means objectionable, offensive, odious (*Many a pleasant man becomes obnoxious on becoming famous*). A thing may be both noxious and obnoxious, as mustard gas; obnoxious but not noxious, as a bugle call at dawn; noxious but not obnoxious, as a pipe of opium.

nozzle; nuzzle; nose; muzzle; snout. *Nozzle* is perhaps most familiar as the term to describe a projecting spout, terminal, discharge pipe, or the like, as of a bellows or hose. Among its other meanings is the slang one of "nose." *Nuzzle* is a verb only. Intransitive, it means to burrow or root with the nose, as an animal does, or to thrust the nose against (*The puppy nuzzled up close to the little boy and both fell asleep*). Transitive, it means to root up with the nose or to touch with the nose.

Nose is a noun or a verb. As a noun it describes the part of the face or head which contains the nostrils or anything which resembles the nose of a person or an animal, as a spout or nozzle, or the prow of a ship (*I'll hold her nose agin' the bank/ Till the last galoot's ashore*), or a projecting part of anything. As a verb it can mean to thrust with or as with the nose (*It looked as though she had made a safe landing but as soon as the propellers were reversed the airship nosed over, crumpling the right wing*). It has the special meaning (not shared by *nozzle* or *nuzzle*) of to smell out (*But indeed, if you find him not within this month, you shall nose him as you go up the stairs into the lobby*). The slang adjective *nosy*, prying, inquisitive, has a suggestion of both of these meanings of the verb *nose*—to thrust into and to smell out other people's affairs.

Muzzle, most familiar as describing the mouth, or end for discharge, of the barrel of a gun or pistol, also describes the projecting part of the head of an animal, including jaws, mouth, and nose, or a device placed over this part to prevent the animal from biting. As a verb it means to put a muzzle on or, by extension, to silence, to gag.

Snout, like *muzzle*, refers to animals. Unlike *muzzle*, it may be used in humorous or contemptuous reference to a person's nose when it is large or prominent.

nth degree. Although the idea of largeness is not inherent in *to the nth degree*, popular usage has made the phrase mean to the utmost extent, and exasperated mathematicians must console themselves with the reflections that language is not exact and that more sciences than their own have been so plundered.

nub is a variant of knob. It means a protuberance, a lump, or a small piece. In American slang it may also mean the point or gist of anything

(*The nub of his argument was that we were licked and had better make the best of it*).

nucleus. The plural is *nucleuses* or *nuclei*.

number. When used as a grammatical term, *number* means the distinction between singular and plural. Number exists in all nouns and some pronouns, such as *he, they,* and is reflected in a few adjectives, such as *this, these* and *much, many,* and in the present tense of most verbs, as in *he walks, they walk.* Problems of number are discussed in this dictionary under **agreement: verbs, dual words, plural nouns, singular nouns,** and the individual nouns, pronouns, and adjectives.

The word *number* itself is plural, that is, it requires a plural verb, when it is used with the article *a,* as in *a number of boxes were sent,* and is singular when it is used with the article *the,* as in *the number of boxes is small.* See **amount** and **numerals.**

number (song, tune). In the plural *number* can mean metrical feet or verse (*Tell me not in mournful numbers/ Life is but an empty dream*) or musical periods, measures, groups of notes (*Perhaps the plaintive numbers flow/ For old, unhappy, far-off things,/ And battles long ago*). In the singular it can mean a distinct part of an extended musical work, or one in a sequence of compositions. The word is being used with increasing frequency by band leaders, disc jockeys, and even publishers of music, to mean a song or dance tune (*Ginny Simms in a popular number. The next number is a waltz*). But this use is certainly not standard, being chiefly a piece of jargon.

number terms. In this book the expression *number terms* means: (1) the ordinal numerals such as *third, fifth,* and the related words *first, last, next, other;* (2) the cardinal numerals such as *three, five,* and the indefinite number words *few, many, several;* (3) the fractions and the words that represent a definite number but that are not part of the number system, such as *couple, dozen, gross;* and (4) under some circumstances, the degree words *more, most, less, least.* (See **numerals; fractions;** and the individual words.)

Most of the number terms can be used as adjectives. When they form part of a series qualifying the same noun, the number terms precede all other kinds of adjectives except the definitives (such as *the, this, my, some*), as in *my three beautiful big brown dogs.*

Sometimes several number terms are used together in the same series. When this happens, the individual words follow approximately the order in which they are listed above. The ordinals precede the cardinals, as in *the second three men. First, last,* and *other* are exceptions and may stand before or after a cardinal number or an indefinite number word, as in *the last two men* and *the two last men.* The cardinals and the indefinite number words precede the words in group three, as in *the first few dozen eggs.* The degree words are ordinarily last in a series of number adjectives, as in *bring two dozen more glasses.*

numerals.

CARDINAL NUMBERS

The cardinal numbers larger than *one*, such as *three, five, ninety-nine,* are primarily adjectives and qualify plural nouns, as in *the two men.* But when they refer to part of a specified group they must be treated as nouns and followed by the preposition *of,* as in *two of the men.*

A hyphen is always used in a compound cardinal, such as *twenty-one, fifty-four.*

The large numbers, such as *hundred, thousand,* the fractions, and a few other number words such as *couple, dozen, score,* are primarily nouns that have taken on some of the adjective functions of the cardinal numbers. Some of these changes are now standard English, such as *a dozen eggs,* and some, such as *a couple dollars,* are not. (For more specific information, see the individual words.)

Expressions involving cardinals greater than *one* are usually treated as plurals, as in *these ten men were ready.* But they may also be treated as singulars when the individual elements are thought of as a unit, as in *this three days was wasted* and *there was two hundred dollars in the purse.* When the numbers themselves are thought of, as in arithmetic, the words are being treated as nouns, not adjectives, and are usually considered singular, as in *twenty is greater than fifteen* and *two times three is six.* But this is not followed consistently and in multiplication and addition a plural verb is sometimes used, as in *two times three are six.*

In written material that contains a great many numbers, figures are better than words and should be used as much as possible. As a rule a figure is not used at the beginning of a sentence. But when a number is very large, as in *3,982 questionnaires were returned,* some writers begin the sentence with a figure rather than write out such a difficult number or recast the sentence into a less direct statement. Figures are also preferred to numbers in footnotes, where space should be saved. When all numbers are being expressed in figures, it is important to remember that the word *one* is not always a number. It is not a number in *one would think* and it usually is not a number in *one day we saw a bird.* See **one.**

In writing that is not primarily statistical the first word in a sentence is never a figure. Otherwise, figures are always used for dates, addresses, page numbers, decimals, and any number that cannot be expressed in two words. That is, we write out *ninety-nine* and *fifteen thousand* but not *102* or *350.* Generally, when one number in a sentence must be expressed in figures any others in the same sentence are also expressed in figures as in *between 90 and 120.*

ORDINAL NUMBERS

The ordinal numbers, such as *third, fifth, ninety-ninth,* name positions in a series. They are primarily adjectives and qualify singular nouns, as in *the second man.* Occasionally an ordinal is followed by *of* and a plural noun, as in *the second of the men.* This is an awkward expression and seldom means anything different from *the second man.*

Theoretically, expressions involving ordinals are singular and should be followed by a singular verb, as in *the second ten boxes is ready to go.* Here the word *second* qualifies the noun *ten,* which is understood as a unit. But the group may also be thought of as a plural, and we may say *the second ten boxes are ready to go.* Both forms are acceptable.

A hyphen is always used in compound ordinals, as in *twenty-first, fifty-fourth.* An ordinal is sometimes written in figures in a date, as in *January 12th.* This is now slightly old fashioned and *January 12* is generally preferred. In any other context, ordinals are written out in words.

Adverbs are formed from the ordinals by adding *-ly,* as in *thirdly, fifthly, ninety-ninthly.* These are used chiefly in numbering the steps in an argument or sermon. Simple ordinals would serve the purpose just as well.

(The words *first* and *last* are not pure ordinals; see **first** and **last.**)

POSITION

In a series of adjectives, cardinal and ordinal numbers both follow the definitive adjectives, such as *the, this, my, any.*

A cardinal number is sometimes treated as a name to distinguish one object from other similar ones, as in *page 10, chapter 3, room 20.* In such cases the numeral follows the common noun. The names of monarchs are sometimes followed by a numeral, as *Louis XIV, George III.* In such cases the number is written in Roman numerals and is read as an ordinal, as *Louis the Fourteenth, George the Third.* With these two exceptions, a numeral regularly precedes the noun it qualifies. Any reversal of this, such as *Soldiers Three,* is an unnatural order and should only be used when the strange effect is what is wanted.

When the two are standing together, an ordinal number always precedes a cardinal, as in *the second two dozen eggs.* This order is never reversed unless the ordinal is being used in a peculiar sense, as when a bridge club offers *ten second prizes.*

MULTIPLICATIVES

The words *once, twice, thrice, four times,* and so on, are called multiplicatives. They are adverbs and may qualify a verb or a cardinal number. They cannot qualify a noun, but they may stand before a definitive adjective and have the effect of qualifying the noun, as in *it has twice the population of Canada.* The words *single, double, triple, quadruple, five-fold,* and so on, are primarily descriptive adjectives and qualify nouns. But they may also be placed before a definitive adjective, as in *double the population of Canada.* They are then being used as multiplicative adverbs.

A cardinal numeral followed by *of* may also be used as a multiplicative in a comparison, as in *he is worth two of his son* and *you are a match for three of him*. Here *two of* means *twice*. This idiom is at least as old as Shakespeare. But it is used only in statements of this kind.

numerous, numberless and **many** describe the presence of a large number of units. *Many* is the commonest word to express this idea and still the best when there is any doubt as to which one to use. *Numerous* is more formal. It usually refers to a great number, very many units. *Numberless* suggests such a large number of units that they cannot be counted, that no exact number can be affixed to them.

nuptial. See **matrimonial.**

nuptials. See **wedding.**

O

O; oh. Both words are interjections. *O* is the word to be used before the name in address, especially in solemn or poetic language, to lend earnestness to an appeal (*O God our help in ages past*, "*O Pioneers!*," *O Wind,/ If Winter comes, can Spring be far behind?*); or with a word, phrase, or clause that makes up a unit of exclamation (*O dear! what can the matter be?*). Notice that no punctuation immediately follows *O*. On the other hand, *oh* is used independently, and is always followed by a comma or an exclamation point. It may express surprise, joy, pain, approval, disapproval (*Oh, what a man!*). Both *O* and *oh* may be used alone as exclamations, though *oh* is preferable. When it is used alone as an exclamation *O* is, of course, followed by an exclamation point. *O* is always a capital letter. *Oh* is capitalized only when it begins a sentence.

oaf. The plural is *oafs*, not *oaves*.

oarlock; rowlock. *Oarlock*, the older word for the contrivance on a boat's gunwale in or on which the oar rests and swings, is still the common and correct term in America (*Clinker-built boats, one pair ash oars and oarlocks*—ad in N. Y. *Evening Post*, 1904). In England it has been generally replaced by *rowlock*, a variant of *oarlock* by association with *row* (*He . . . surveyed the cushions, the oars, the rowlocks, and all the fascinating fittings*—Kenneth Grahame, *The Wind in the Willows*, 1908).

oasis. The plural is *oasises* or *oases*.

oats is a mass word with plural form. It is usually treated as a plural, as in *these oats are good* and *we will cook them*. But it may also be treated as a singular, as in *this oats is good* and *we will cook it*. We may also speak of *many oats* and of *much oats*.

The true singular form *oat* is rare. It is used by botanists to mean an individual plant or a species, and in this sense has a true plural, as in *I have found three oats*. The singular is also used for the grain in order to make an emphatic negative, as in *the horses would not touch an oat* and *he had not sown a single wild oat*.

The singular *oat* is preferred as the first element in a compound, as in *oatmeal* and *oat grass*.

When vegetables are spoken of in mass the plural form is used, as in *peas, beans, potatoes*. But the mass words for cereals, *wheat, barley, corn, rice*, and so on, are grammatical singulars. The only exceptions are *oats* and *groats* or *grits*, both of which originally meant *oats*. This has led some people to believe that our forefathers ate oats whole, like a vegetable, and did not grind it into meal like the other cereals.

oaves. See **oaf.**

object and **demur** mean to oppose, to disagree with. To *object* is to oppose or disagree with in thought or speech; whereas to *demur* always implies speech (*If you don't object, I'd like to think this over. Before you demur, let me explain my position*). To object may imply violent opposition; whereas demur implies quieter, more dignified opposition, or perhaps less certainty in the opposition (*I object to this procedure and will withdraw my support* / *I must demur at this unnecessary haste*).

The special meaning of *demur* is an interesting illustration of the way in which an older meaning of a word may lie concealed within it, as it were, unperceived but shaping its use. To demur originally meant to delay (*They dare not demur nor abide*), a meaning that survives in the technical word *demurrage*, the charge made for the detention of ships or railroad cars. Then it came to mean to pause in uncertainty, to delay by suggesting scruples or difficulties, by objecting irresolutely or taking exceptions (*My process was always very simple—in their younger days, 'twas "Jack, do this"; if he demurred, I knocked him down; and if he grumbled at that, I always sent him out of the room*—Sheridan, *The Rivals*, 1775). From that it was a short distance to the contemporary meaning.

In law *to demur* has the special meaning of to interpose a demurrer (*The plaintiff demurred, that is to say, admitted* [the] *plea to be true in fact, but denied that it was a sufficient answer*).

Object may be followed by the preposition *to* and the *-ing* form of a verb, as in *I object to saying anything which may compromise that lady*. It is occasionally followed by an infinitive, as in *we object to pass Sundays in a state of coma*.

The noun *objection* is also heard in both constructions, as in *I have no objection to doing it* and *you understand my objection to go through with it.* The infinitive construction is condemned by many grammarians but it is used by Shaw and other modern writers and is therefore acceptable English. However, the *-ing* form is generally preferred.

objective. See **target.**

objective pronouns. There are six objective pronouns, *me, us, him, her, them,* and *whom.*

The formal rules of grammar require these objective forms (and not their subjective counterparts) whenever the word is used as: (1) the object of a verb (*We saw them*); (2) the object of a preposition (*We talked to them*); (3) an indirect object (*We gave them some apples*).

In standard English practice the objective forms can always be used except when the word is standing in a subject position.

With one exception, an object never stands in a subject position. Therefore, with this one exception, the objective forms are always used where the rules call for them. The exception is the word *whom* which usually precedes the verb, as in *whom do you like best?* and *whom are you looking for?*. The subjective form *who* is preferred in sentences of this kind. See **who** and **whom.**

But in standard practice the objective forms are also used where the rules do not call for them. In general, objective pronouns which break the rules can be justified on the grounds of good usage. Again, the word *whom* is an exception. When this word is not required by the formal rules of grammar, it is also contrary to good usage and therefore cannot be defended. *Whom* is wrong, theoretically and practically, in sentences such as *whom is it?*.

object of a preposition. The noun or noun equivalent that unites with a preposition to form a qualifying or descriptive phrase is called the object of the preposition. *Wings* and *wind* are the objects of the prepositions *on* and *of* in *hang weights on the wings of the wind.*

A preposition is said to "govern" its object because the preposition determines the case of the object in languages that show case. This has practically no meaning in English. At most it would mean that the six subjective pronouns cannot be used as the object of a preposition. Many grammarians claim that this is true. In practice, educated people do not use a subjective pronoun as an object following a preposition. Since the pronouns that show case usually follow the preposition, the two rules amount to the same thing most of the time. But occasionally a pronoun that shows case precedes the preposition. Then the subjective rather than the objective form is preferred, despite the protests of the grammarians. See **who** and **whom.**

The relation between a preposition and its object has nothing in common with the relation between a verb and its object. Some grammarians do not like to use the term *object* for two such different relations and prefer to speak of the *regimen* of a preposition.

object of a verb.

MEANING

Some verbs, such as *swim, laugh, sleep,* express a complete idea and may occur as the last word in a normal declarative sentence, such as *he is sleeping.* But there are some verbs, such as *make, like, take,* which require additional words in order to express a complete idea. A word or group of words without which the meaning of a verb is incomplete is called the object of the verb, such as *noise* in *he is making a noise.*

An adverb, such as *suddenly* in *he suddenly made a noise,* also affects the meaning of the verb, but not to the same extent that the object does. The object completes the meaning of the verb; the adverb qualifies it. Without the object, the statement would have no meaning; without the adverb, it would be too broad or too crude.

A verb which has an object is called a transitive verb, and the action of the verb is said to "pass over" to the object. A verb which does not have an object is called intransitive. In English a great many verbs may be either transitive or intransitive, as in *he is playing ball* and *he is playing; he is reading the newspaper* and *he is reading.*

A linking verb—that is, a verb meaning *be, seem,* or *become*—does not express a complete idea without some additional words. But, unlike a transitive verb, it does not name an action. The words which follow a linking verb, such as *captain* in *he has become a captain,* are more closely related to the subject than they are to the verb itself. Traditionally, such words are called the complement of the verb but not its object. This distinction has no meaning in English except when the complement is a personal pronoun. The rules of Latin grammar require an objective pronoun for the object of a transitive verb and a subjective pronoun for the complement of a linking verb. Many grammarians claim that these rules should also be observed in English. But the practice in English is to use a subjective pronoun before a verb and an objective pronoun after a verb, regardless of whether the verb is transitive or linking.

KINDS

Sometimes the object of a verb merely repeats an idea already expressed by the verb, as *song* in *we will sing a song.* These are called cognate objects. Sometimes the full verb idea requires two objects, such as *him* and *prisoner* in *they took him prisoner.* In this case, the second object may be called an objective complement. In *sing us a song* we have an entirely different situation. Here the word *us* is not the object of *sing* in the sense in which we are using the word *object.* It is called an indirect object, and for this reason the true object of a verb is sometimes called a direct object. See **indirect object.**

As a rule, the object of a verb is more than a single word. It may be a noun and all the qualifying words that go with it, as in *she shot her man who was doing her wrong.* Here, all except the first two words are the object of *shot.*

In a case like this we say that the word *man* is "the simple object." Some verbs may be followed by a noun and the simple form of a verb, as in *let the lady pass*. Some may take the *-ing* form of a verb as object, as in *I enjoy dancing*; some may take a *to*-infinitive, as in *I want to dance;* and some may take a full clause, as in *I believe I will dance.* Very often a verb that is standard English with one kind of object is not standard with another. For example, *I enjoy to dance* is unnatural English. *I want that you should dance* is heard but is not standard. Infinitives are often used in the United States where an *-ing* form is required in Great Britain. The verbs that people are most likely to be uncertain about in this respect are listed in this dictionary. (See the individual verb.)

POSITION

The object of a verb usually follows after the verb without a break of any kind except for an indirect object, such as *us* in *sing us a song*. No other element in a sentence can be placed between the verb and its object without creating a break which may be fatal to the sense.

In *Job cursed the day that he was born* the word *day* is the simple object of *cursed*. But in *Job cursed, the day that he was born* the comma break destroys the verb-object relation and *day* becomes an adverb of time. To some extent, the same result would follow if an adverb such as *bitterly* had separated the verb and object, instead of a comma. Usually two meanings aren't possible for the same sentence and a break of this kind is not actually misleading. But it is always undesirable and should be avoided.

A direct object may also stand as the first element in a sentence or clause. An interrogative pronoun or a noun qualified by an interrogative adjective must always have this position, regardless of its relation to the verb, as in *what do you want?* and *which book did you read?*. When the object is not an interrogative, this front position is unusual and extremely emphatic, as in *talent, Mr. Micawber has; capital, Mr. Micawber has not.*

obligate. As an adjective, *obligate* means bound or constrained. It is used chiefly as a biological term to mean restricted to a particular condition of life, as certain parasites which must live in close association with their usual hosts in order to survive (*An obligate parasite is one that is of necessity parasitical*).

oblige may be followed by an infinitive, as in *he obliged us to go,* but not by the *-ing* form of a verb or by a clause.

oblige; obligate. To *obligate* is to bind morally or legally (*The treaty of peace obligates the United States to undertake the release of all Spanish prisoners. You are obligated to pay the tax, whether you like it or not*). In former times it was used as a synonym for *oblige* (*I am much obligated by the trouble you have taken* —1810) but this is no longer standard usage.

Oblige is a broader and more inclusive term than *obligate*. Basically, it means to require or constrain, as the law, a command, duty, or necessity does. When one of the Duke of Queensberry's servants who had answered the bell and had then been ignored, timidly asked His Grace if he wanted anything, the irascible duke shouted, *G-d d-m you, am I obliged to tell you what I want?* Among other senses, *oblige* conveys the idea of conferring a favor (*You will greatly oblige me if you return the book promptly*).

Much obliged, though often spoken with sincere gratitude, is a sort of democratic evasion of the acknowledgment of the even temporary inferiority thought to be implicit in an open statement of thanks. Visitors to America in the early days of the republic were struck by the unwillingness of the Americans to say "Thank you." The people were often friendly and obliging in the extreme, yet their sense of independence made them far more willing to confer than to accept favors and reluctant to acknowledge the acceptance when one had to be accepted. *Much obliged* is a sort of halfway thanks; it acknowledges an obligation and feels that sufficient gratitude is displayed in the acknowledgment. See also **appreciate, thank you.**

oblique; obliqueness; obliquity. *Oblique* is an adjective meaning neither perpendicular nor parallel to a given line or surface, but slanting or sloping (*Since he set a course oblique to the convoy, he was soon far behind it*). By extension it acquired the figurative meanings of indirectly stated or expressed (*These oblique accusations were the more galling because they could not be answered directly*), or deviating, especially morally or mentally, from the straight course of rectitude (*He prospered by oblique means*).

Obliqueness is the noun commonly used to characterize the literal sense of *oblique* (*The obliqueness of the intersection had been the cause of many accidents*). *Obliquity* suggests the figurative senses of *oblique,* that is, divergence from moral rectitude, mental perversity, or deviation from directness in action or speech (*The perverseness and obliquity of my will. The insolence of benefaction terminates not in negative rudeness or obliquities of insult. The obliquities of diplomatic negotiation make it a process particularly unsuited to the blunt, the direct, and the impatient*).

oblique case. This term is used variously to mean any case except the nominative, any case except the nominative and vocative, or any case except the nominative, vocative and accusative. So far as English nouns are concerned, the oblique case is the genitive. The word may or may not include the six objective pronouns, depending on who is using the term.

oblivious; forgetful; unmindful. The basic sense of *oblivious* is forgetful, without remembrance (*Faust, under the influence of Mephistopheles, was oblivious of his life as a scholar*). American usage permits the sense of unmindful, heedless (*He was oblivious of his responsibilities*), while British usage permits only the more carefully restricted sense of no longer mindful, forgotten. Furthermore American usage countenances the meaning of unconscious and, despite the indignant protests of Fowler, Partridge, and Sir A. P. Herbert, permits *oblivious* in this sense to be followed by either *of* or *to* (*She was oblivious of his infatuation. She was oblivious to his attentions*). In sum, *oblivious* can be synonymous with *forgetful* and *unmindful*. Like *forgetful* and *unmindful,* it may be followed by a clause without a preposition, as in *he was oblivious how closely his humanitarianism bordered on sentimentality.*

obloquy. See **abuse.**

obnoxious. See **noxious.**

obscenity. See **blasphemy.**

obscure. See **mysterious.**

obsequies. An *obsequy* is a funeral rite or ceremony. It is almost always used in the plural. *Funeral obsequies* is redundant. *Obsequies* is a word of high solemnity and rather pretentious and a little consciously elegant when applied to the ordinary funeral service. Since funerals are, however, commonly times when elegance and splendor are thought fitting, the very faults of the word may make it harmonious with the occasions to which it is applied.

One of the finest scenes in American literature is when the duke, in *Huckleberry Finn,* tries to persuade the king to substitute *obsequies* for the more original term *orgies.* But the king is too skilful a master of hokum and false etymology to have to admit a fault.

> *I say orgies* [he blandly observes], *not because it's the common term, because it ain't —obsequies bein' the common term—but because orgies is the right term. Obsequies ain't used in England no more now—it's gone out. We say orgies now in England. Orgies is better, because it means the thing you're after more exact. It's a word that's made up out'n the Greek orgo, outside, open, abroad; and the Hebrew jeesum, to plant, cover up; hence inter. So, you see, funeral orgies is an open or public funeral.*

As Huck says, "He was the *worst* I ever struck."

observance; observation. *Observance* describes the action of conforming to or following (*A wise coach insists on the observance of training rules*), the keeping or celebrating by appropriate procedure, ceremonies, etc. (*The observance of Easter* . . .).

Observation describes the act of noticing or perceiving, of regarding attentively (*The observation of the habits of birds has brought to light some very curious facts*), or the faculty or habit of noticing or observing (*His powers of observation were highly developed*), or an utterance or remark presumably based upon observing (*These unfriendly observations were not well received by the sullen crowd*). See also **remark.**

observe. When this verb is used in an active form it may be followed by an object and the simple form of a verb, as in *I observed him stop,* by an object and the *-ing* form of a verb, as in *I observed him stopping,* or by a clause, as in

I observed he stopped. When it is used in a passive form it may be followed by a *to*-infinitive, as in *he was observed to stop* or by the *-ing* form of a verb, as in *he was observed stopping.*

obsolete; obsolescent. That is *obsolete* which is no longer used, has been discarded, is out of date. That is *obsolescent* which is becoming out of use, is in the process of being discarded, is to all appearances going out of date. If a word is obsolete it is not used any more or is not used in a certain sense any more. There is very little dispute about whether or not a certain word is obsolete. *Obsolescent,* however, often reflects merely an opinion, an estimate, an assumption. It is nowhere near so certain a word as *obsolete.* There can be wide differences of opinion as to whether or not a word is obsolescent. It may, for instance, be going out of use in one part of the country, or in one social group, but flourishing in others.

obstacle, meaning something that stands in the way or obstructs progress, is properly followed by the preposition *to* (*His reluctance to compromise is an obstacle to his political success*).

obstacle; obstruction; hindrance; impediment. An *obstacle* is something material or non-material which stands in the way of literal or figurative progress (*The great obstacle to progress is prejudice. A roadblock was the first obstacle to the tank column's advance*). An *obstruction* is something that more or less completely blocks a passage (*An obstruction of the bowels precipitated his death*). When used figuratively, it often carries the suggestion of something that has been put in the way intentionally (*These delays seem a deliberate obstruction of justice*). A *hindrance* is something which hinders or holds back (*It is a question whether language has been an aid or a hindrance to knowledge. The fetters, which he had been unable to break off, proved a hindrance to his escape*). An *impediment* is derived from the Latin for a burden which by its weight shackles the feet. *Impedimenta* was the Latin word for the baggage of an army and the word is still occasionally used in this special sense (*The general decided to go ahead of his impedimenta*). In the sense of an obstacle, therefore, an *impediment* does not so much obstruct as hinder by being a burden (*Those impediments provided for my hindrance* . . .). In the sense of something that impedes the functions or health of the body, *impediment* is marked obsolete in the *Oxford English Dictionary* which, however, admits it in the special sense of stuttering as an impediment in the speech. In the United States *impediment* in this sense (*His defective hearing proved a severe impediment in his college work*) is standard.

obtain. See **get** and **secure.**

obtrude. See **intrude.**

obvious. See **apparent.**

occurrence. See **event, happening.**

octopus. The plural is *octopuses* or *octopodes* or *octopi. Octopuses* is good English, *Octopodes* is good Greek. *Octopi* is an incorrectly formed plural that has been in use so long that it has now become standard.

octoroon. See **mulatto.**

oculist; ophthalmologist; optician; optometrist. An *oculist* is a doctor of medicine skilled in the examination and treatment of the eye. The term is synonymous with *ophthalmologist,* a doctor of medicine skilled in ophthalmology, which is the science dealing with the anatomy, functions, and diseases of the eye.

An *optician* is one who makes glasses for remedying defects of vision, in accordance with the prescriptions of oculists and optometrists. He may also be a seller of optical glasses and instruments. An *optometrist* is one skilled in optometry, the practice or art of testing the eyes, by means of suitable instruments or appliances (usually without the use of drugs), for defects of vision.

odd; strange; peculiar; queer. All of these adjectives describe something which is not ordinary. That which is *odd* is irregular or unconventional, and sometimes approaches the bizarre (*His odd hat and bulbous nose made him an object of amusement*). *Strange* implies that the thing or its cause is unknown or unexplained. It is unfamiliar and unusual and since the unfamiliar and the unusual are often frightening, the word, in many contexts, has connotations of alarm (*It was a strange object, about three by five inches and very heavy. Strange, that he shouldn't be home by now; he's always here by six*). *Peculiar* emphasizes the existence of qualities not shared by others (*It was his peculiar virtue never to be afraid. He had a peculiar grin on his face that boded no good*). *Queer* sometimes adds to *odd* the suggestion of something abnormal or eccentric (*He's a queer duck. There are some queer things going on around here*). In American today *queer* carries connotations of sexual deviation and therefore should be used of persons, particularly males, seldom and with discretion. See also **funny, quaint.**

odd has as one of its meanings "additional to a whole mentioned in round numbers; being a surplus over a definite quantity." To convey the idea that there are 100 and a few more people, write *100-odd people* or *100 and odd people.* The phrase *100 odd people* is ambiguous and therefore to be avoided, for it may indicate a number in excess of 100 or merely 100 eccentric people. See also **suffixes.**

odds, as a term used in comparing probabilities, has no singular form. It is ordinarily treated as a plural today, as in *the odds are good.* Formerly it was sometimes treated as a singular. This is heard today only in the expression *what's the odds?*—meaning "is there any difference?"

odds and ends. The phrase used to be *odd ends,* or remnants of cloth, fragments, pieces cut off or things broken off, extraneous or additional to what is taken into account. *Odds and ends* seems to have been an improvement, a result probably of euphony, of the eighteenth century. When used of miscellaneous articles of no great value it is now so established as to be practically a

word in itself and it is hard to see how it could be avoided without circumlocution. But in its figurative extensions (*Having picked up several odds and ends/ Of free thoughts*) it is hackneyed.

odor; odour; odorous. The American spelling is *odor,* with *odour* admitted as a variant. The British spelling is *odour.* In both countries the adjective is *odorous.*

An *odor* is usually a fragrant odor. An unpleasant odor is usually designated by an adjective (*a rank odor, a foul odor*). *Odorous* is even more strictly confined to pleasant fragrances, since it has its opposite *malodorous.*

of. Until a few hundred years ago *of* and *off* were merely different pronunciations of the same word. Beginning with the physical meaning of "out from," the word was used to indicate origin or source. It was later used to translate the Latin genitive case and so acquired all the meanings expressed in Latin by the genitive. Today the form *of* is the principal word for showing a relation between nouns, as in *a hair of the dog,* or between adjectives and nouns, as in *full of, sick of.* It sometimes expresses one of its original meanings, such as origin or cause, as in *ashamed of,* or separation, as in *free of,* but it is used most often to express one of the genitive relations. See **genitive case.**

Of is also used with some verbs and may show any of the types of relations that it does between nouns. Frequently it means "concerning," as in *I have not heard the Eroica but I have heard of it.* It was once used with certain verbs to mean "some but not all," as in *taste of the soup* and *accept of my hospitality.* Such precise, or cautious, statements are now out of style and these compounds have a decidedly old-fashioned tone. But it is still used in a related sense to weaken the meaning of a verb. What verbs are conventionally weakened in this way varies with time. A century ago people said *I approve him* and *I disapprove your choice,* where we now use *of.* But we now say *remember* and *consider* where they said *remember of* and *consider of.* Until recently *repent* was followed by *of* but today the *of* is frequently dropped.

Of performs too many functions to be a meaningful word. Some of these functions are being taken over by more specialized prepositions. At one time *of* was commonly used to indicate the agent with a passive verb, as in *that face of all men feared.* It may still be used in this way but *by* is now preferred. In many expressions *of* competes with *for,* as in *love of, covetous of,* or with *from,* as in *purchase of, borrow of.* Where both sound right, the more specialized word is probably better.

of course. It is always well to avoid the obvious. People do not like to be informed of what they already know. When it is necessary to state some fact that is likely to be known to the reader or listener, the assumption of pompousness or condescension may be mitigated or removed by the interposition of *of course,* but the phrase can easily become a bad habit. In such a sentence as *It may have been a coin-cidence, of course, but if it were it was certainly an extraordinary one,* it is hard to see what purpose *of course* serves more than a rhythmic pause or a pompous clearing of the throat.

off. Originally *off* was the word *of* pronounced emphatically. The same difference between a *v* and an *f* sound can be heard today in the auxiliary verb *have,* which we sometimes pro-nounce *haff.* Speaking matter-of-factly, we might say *I have to leave,* but when we are insisting we say *I haff to leave.* For many centuries this was the only difference between *of* and *off.* (See **of.**) But eventually the words became inde-pendent. *Of* kept the vaguer genitive meanings and is now used only as a preposition, that is, it is used only with an object. *Off* kept the older meaning of separation or removal from contact with, and can be used as a preposition, as in *lift it off the shelf;* an adverb, as in *I can't get it off;* or an adjective, as in *an off season.*

In *he bought it off a peddler, off* expresses the genitive idea of source. This use of the word is still acceptable in Great Britain but not in the United States. In *we can make a meal off sandwiches, off* expresses the genitive idea of material. This is acceptable only in statements about eating. All other meanings of *off* are derived from the idea of separation and imply a discontinuity of some kind.

Off is related by its meaning to *from* and by its history to *of.* Formerly *off* was often fol-lowed by *of,* as in *lift it off of the shelf, make a meal off of sandwiches.* This construction is still used by educated people in the United States but is not so used in Great Britain. *Off* can always be followed by *from* when the idea of separation is involved, as in *we got off from work.* The combination *off from* is heard in Great Britain more often than it is in the United States. Actually neither *of* nor *from* is ever necessary after *off.* We can say simply *off the shelf, off sandwiches, off work.* This is the pre-ferred construction in the United States, but the compounds are also acceptable.

offensive. See **insidious.**

offer. This verb may be followed by an infinitive, as in *I offered to go in his place.* It is also heard with the *-ing* form of a verb, as in *I offered going in his place,* but the infinitive is pre-ferred.

office (in the sense of position). See **assignment.**

officer, in the commonest contemporary sense of the word, is one who holds a position of rank or authority in the army, navy, or any similar organization, especially one who holds a com-mission (*The unit consisted of three officers and thirty men. Every time an enlisted man sees an officer get an extra privilege, it breaks him down a little more*), though there are also petty offi-cers, warrant officers, and noncommissioned officers. In its broadest sense, *officer* designates one who is invested with an office. There are corporation officers and municipal officers, offi-cers on a ship (these are more like army and navy officers) and peace officers. It is in this last category that policemen fall and the addressing of a policeman as *officer* is more a slight archaism than the compliment it is often thought to be. Every policeman is an officer of the law and may be addressed as *officer,* but with the introduction into most police forces now of a gradation of rank similar to and modeled after that of the army, the word is coming to be applied to those in the force who hold ranks equal to those that would cause their holders in the army to be considered officers. The chances are that this tendency will increase with the increasing gradation of the police forces. If so, a new polite form of address for the common policeman will have to be found.

official; officious. *Official* means of or pertaining to an office or position of duty, trust, or au-thority (*His official powers were quite limited*), authorized or issued authoritatively (*The offi-cial report was eagerly awaited*), holding office (*He had no official capacity*), appointed or au-thorized to act in a special capacity (*He was at the convention as an official delegate*).

Officious formerly meant ready to serve, ready to exercise one's appointed function. When Dr. Johnson in his elegy on his friend Robert Levett (1782) referred to Levett as *officious, innocent, sincere,* he did not mean that Levett (who was a sort of amateur doctor) was meddlesome or intrusive but simply that he was always willing to help. It is a sad com-mentary on human nature, on either the vanity of many who give or the ingratitude of many who receive aid, that the word now connotes forwardness in offering help, a fussy obtrusion of unwanted assistance (*This officious bustling about, with here a nod and there a gesture of encouragement, was vastly annoying to most of those present*).

Generalizing on current usage, one can say that *official* is a general descriptive term, *offi-cious* an emotionally charged term imputing blame. In diplomatic usage, however, *officious* has a distinctly different meaning. *Official* in diplomatic usage retains its usual sense of for-mal, authorized; but *officious,* with no con-notation of meddlesomeness, means informal, unauthorized, not binding—the very antithesis of *official.*

offspring is properly plural (*The offspring of this union were five boys and three girls*). It has been used so much as a singular, however (*Have you ever met our offspring, Jimmy, girls?*), that this usage is accepted as standard, though it usually has a touch of the labored or facetious about it. The word is used of a child or animal in relation to its parent or parents or to designate a descendant or descendants collectively. By extension the word may mean the product, result or effect of something (*Xanadu was supposedly the offspring of an opium dream*).

often and **frequently** may be used interchangeably in most contexts but, where they differ, *often* is simpler and stronger. It suggests numerous repetitions and, sometimes, regularity of recur-rence (*I often visit my uncle who lives there*). *Frequently* suggests repetition at short intervals (*It happens frequently and I have warned him of the consequences*). Though *frequently* is the longer word, it has the advantage of having the adjective *frequent*. *Often* used to appear as an adjective (as in *By often use we accustom ourselves to hardship*), but this use is now obsolete.

oftentime; oftentimes. Today the only acceptable form is *oftentimes*. Formerly, *oftentime* was also used, but it is now obsolete.

O. Henry. William Sydney Porter published his famous stories under the pseudonym of *O. Henry* —not, as it is sometimes erroneously written, *O'Henry* (as in *A breathless story with an O'Henry ending was enacted in the streets today*). The *O. Henry ending*, which came to be widely imitated, was a surprise ending, a statement, usually in the last sentence or two, that gave a wholly unexpected interpretation to what had gone before or a wholly unexpected twist to the action. Wholly unexpected, that is, until you had read several of O. Henry's stories.

O.K. There are several spellings: *O.K., OK, okay.* The term is used as an adjective (*Is it O.K.?*), an adverb (*They're doing O.K. up there, I hear*), a verb (*The boss O.K.'d it*), and a noun (*Sure, I got his O.K. or I wouldn't have started. Here, you guys, put your O.K.'s on this page*).

Originating in the United States, *O.K.* has spread to almost every country on earth. There is something about the phrase as a term of assent or agreement that gives it universal appeal. It is probably today the most widely used single term in human speech. Yet it remains a colloquialism. Used a billion times a day in informal speech and business notes and letters, it has not yet been adopted into formal, written usage and may not be. *Approve, endorse, agree, assent to, confirm,* and a host of other words express shades of meaning in relation to agreement and giving consent so that the serious writer is not willing to give them up for so loose a blanket term.

Experts disagree on the origin of this remarkable term. Some think it is the Choctaw Indian *okeh,* "it is so." Others would trace it to the initial letters of a humorous or illiterate spelling of "all correct," *Oll Korrect,* or to a misreading of *O.R.,* meaning order recorded. It has been variously ascribed to Andrew Jackson, John Jacob Astor and one Obadiah Kelly, a mythical railroad clerk who initialed all the parcels he accepted for shipment. The explanation that has the most authoritative backing is that it derives from the *O.K. Club,* formed in 1840 by partisans of Martin Van Buren who allegedly named their organization in allusion to *Old Kinderhook,* Van Buren having been born at Kinderhook, N. Y.

O.K. must be accepted in informal speech and writing. Such slang extensions and derivatives as *oke* and *okeydoke* have not yet achieved this acceptance.

old. The comparative form is *older* or *elder*. The superlative form is *oldest* or *eldest*. The forms *older* and *oldest* have come into the language more recently than *elder* and *eldest* but are now the only forms that can be used for most purposes.

Older and *oldest* may be used of persons or things and usually refer to actual age. *Elder* and *eldest* are now used only in speaking of persons and indicate seniority, or relative date of birth, rather than age. That is, we would say *the eldest son died in infancy* and *the oldest child now living was her third*.

The form *elder* cannot be used with *than*. We cannot say *he is elder than she*. But when used with the article *the* it may be followed by an *of* phrase, as in *he is the elder of the two*. *Older* may be used with *than* or in the construction with *of*. *Elder* may be used as if it were a noun, as in *she is my elder* and *the village elders*. *Older* is never used in this way.

The eldest may be used with *of*, as in *the eldest of the children*, but *the oldest* is preferred in this construction. Both *eldest* and *oldest* may be used as singular nouns, as in *the eldest, I think, is seven*. (For the use of *old* with measures of time, such as *a child of one year old*, see **measures**.)

old; advanced; ancient; senile; senescent; veteran. The everyday, serviceable word for one who or that which is advanced in age is *old*. It is idiomatic to say of one who died when he was old that *He died in his old age* or *He died at an advanced age*. To say that he died *at an old age* is unidiomatic.

Ancient means of or in times long past, especially before the end of the Western Roman Empire (476 A.D.). Applied to persons, the word is archaic; it is now restricted to things. Coleridge's *Ancient Mariner* was deliberately archaic. (There is another word *ancient,* now obsolete, in English which sometimes puzzles the student. It is a corruption, actually, of *ensign*. So the *ancient Pistol* in Shakespeare's *Henry IV* and Iago, Othello's *ancient*.)

Senile means characteristic of old age, especially the feebleness of old age, its mental and physical weakness and degeneration. It has become one of the cruelest words in the language and, with the increasing life expectancy that is prolonging the lives of ever increasing millions, will become increasingly so. *Senescent* means growing old, aging. It does not have the full offensiveness of *senile,* though of necessity it has for the aging an unpleasant sound.

A *veteran* is one who is aged in experience. A man may be a veteran of love, for example, at twenty. In the United States it has the special meaning of one who has fought in a war, regardless of his age or the amount of his experience.

old Adam. As a term for the worse aspects of human nature, especially its carnality, *the old Adam* is a cliché.

old head on young shoulders. To say of some youth who has shown a gravity or wisdom beyond his years that he has *an old head on young shoulders* is to employ a cliché. It is falling somewhat into disuse as the wisdom of age, once assumed as axiomatic, is called into question and might not seem as much a compliment today as it was always intended to be in former times.

old school tie. Preparatory schools do not play as large a part in American life as in English and the distinctive tie as a symbol of loyalty to the old school and all that it stands for in the way of social position, good form, and so on, is not commonly known here. However the sophisticated among the educated picked up the term, with all its implications of derision, from the brighter young English set of the 1920's and wore it out. As a serious term it is practically never heard or seen. As a term of amused contempt it is now a cliché.

oldster. There is condescension in the word *old-ster*. Formed in ignorant good intentions on the analogy of *youngster*, it overlooks the fact that the *-ster* suffix usually implies contempt (*gangster, punster, whipster*), being, originally, a feminine suffix (*spinster*). Now a certain condescension to children is all right. They are used to it and it is commonly mitigated by affection. But *oldster* has the condescension without the love, and condescension without love is contempt. *The old* and *the aged* are sad terms, but at least they have dignity.

Olympian and **Olympic,** though interchangeable in former times, are restricted in contemporary usage to special and distinct meanings. *Olympian* means pertaining to or dwelling on Mount Olympus, as the greater gods of Greece (*the Olympian eagle's vision*), or in bearing or manner like these gods, grand, imposing, dignified above ordinary human dignity and hence, sometimes, pompous and condescending in a lofty way (*What . . . Max Müller . . . calls his* Olympian manners *never repelled me*). *Olympic* now means pertaining to the games held at Olympia in ancient Greece to honor Zeus (*Before Plato became a philosopher, he had won acclaim at the Olympic games*) or to the modern international contests that have adopted this name (*He captained the British team at the Olympic games that year*). *Olympic* can mean pertaining to Olympia, but when so used it can be ambiguous as it may also mean pertaining to Mount Olympus.

omission. See **oversight.**

omit may be followed by the *-ing* form of a verb, as in *he omitted reading the second page,* or by an infinitive, as in *he omitted to read the second page.* These forms are equally acceptable.

omnibus. The only plural is *omnibuses,* never *omnibi.* See also **bus.**

on; onto. The primary, physical, meaning of *on* was "in contact with the surface," and, later, usually the upper surface. It was also used to express motion toward such a position. From the first meaning, *on* has developed various uses relating to the idea of support, as in *rely on,* and also of "time when," as in *on that day.* From the second meaning it has come to express vaguer ideas, such as towards, as in *smile on;* continued motion, as in *roll on;* and against, as in *knock on.*

Today *on* is often used with an independent verb to emphasize the fact that an action was continuing and not completed, as in *she was darning on a sock, he was working on a poem. Begin on, improve on, refine on,* all suggest an unending process. It is also used with the meaning of "against" in speaking of something injurious or undesirable, as in *they played a trick on me, they shut the door on me.* Here *on* is used in contrast to *for* which carries the meaning of "in favor of," as in *they played a trick for me, they shut the door for me.* This is sometimes called the *on* of disadvantage.

As *on* lost its old meaning of direction toward "on-ness," this had to be supplied by the preposition *to,* as in *climb on to the box.* Keats is thought to have been the first person to write these as a single word *onto,* and the practice did not become general until this century. This is now customary when the two prepositions *on* and *to* have a single object, as in *climb onto the box.* When *on* is simply a qualifying word attached to the verb and not part of a prepositional phrase, as in *they went on to victory,* it must not be joined with *to.*

once and for all. The "and" in *once and for all* seems to have been added solely for rhetorical emphasis. The phrase used to be *once for all.*

once; oncet. *Oncet* is formed on the same pattern as *against, amidst, amongst,* but it has never been standard English. *Once* is the only acceptable form.

Ordinarily *once* is an adverb. It qualifies a verb and means one time. But in current English it is often used as a conjunction, to introduce a clause, and means when. Yeats uses it in this sense in *once out of nature I shall never take my bodily form from any natural thing.* This use of the word is condemned by some grammarians, but it is acceptable in the United States. Most conjunctions were originally adverbs and no one should be surprised to see a new one developing.

one is sometimes a numeral, but it is sometimes an indefinite adjective and sometimes a pronoun.

One is used as an indefinite pronoun meaning "a man, a person," as in *one may smile and smile and be a villain.* In Great Britain *one* in this sense is now considered a bookish word and *a man* is preferred in speech and informal writing. But in Great Britain today this *one,* when it is used, can only be referred back to by another form of the same pronoun, as in *one has to take care of oneself and one's family if one can.* In the United States this *one* is used in speech as well as in writing, and is regularly referred to by a form of the pronoun *he.* Using a form of *he* after *one* was standard practice in England from the time of Queen Elizabeth to the time of Victoria and is still standard in the United States. John Dewey in discussing automatic responses writes: *one notes, for example, a motor car bearing down on him.* An English editor would have changed this *him* to *one.* An American editor would be more likely to change a *one* in this position to *him.*

Except when it refers indefinitely to a human being, the pronoun *one* is anaphoric, that is, it is always used in place of a noun that has been mentioned a short time before. In this use, *one* has the plural *ones* and the genitive *one's*. It may be qualified by *the*, *a*, or any other adjective, as in *the good ones, the other ones, a ripe one*. It may even be qualified by the number *one*, as in *one good one*. *A one* is an emphatic form of *one*. The phrase is considered redundant by some people but it has been used at least since Elizabethan times, as in *there's not a one of them but in his house I keep a servant fee'd*, and is standard in the United States today.

One is often used after an adjective that is parallel to a preceding adjective and noun, as in *the big bear and the little one, this book and that one*. This construction is possible when we are speaking of individual, countable things, but not when we are using a mass word, such as *butter* in *this butter and that*. Modern grammarians say that in this construction *one* is a "prop word." It is logically unnecessary but required by our feeling for words which demands some noun equivalent after these adjectives. Fifty or seventy years ago the construction was considered pleonastic. (See **pleonasm.**) It is now standard English.

The pronoun *one* is always singular and the adjective *one* always qualifies a singular noun. *One* is usually followed by a singular verb. Although the subject is logically plural we ordinarily use a singular verb after *more than one*, as in *more than one is broken*. Theoretically, a singular verb is required because the subject is the word *one* and *more than* is merely a qualifying phrase. And practically, the singular verb feels right because the word *one* is standing immediately before it. With a phrase such as *one out of ten* we have a different situation and either a singular or a plural may be used. We may say *one out of ten is* or *one out of ten are*. In speaking of people the plural form is preferred.

One of must be followed by a plural noun, and this may be followed by a descriptive clause. When it is, the clause verb should, logically, be plural, as in *one of the best books that have appeared*. Actually, a singular is often used here, as in *one of the best books that has appeared*. This construction is condemned by many grammarians on the grounds of logic. But it is found in the earliest English and has been used by some of the greatest writers. It shows that the writer still has *one* in mind. Shelley wrote: *I am one of those who am unable to refuse my assent*. Here the word *I* has overridden *one* and *those*. This is unusual. But in the United States the more familiar construction, using a third person singular verb, does not offend anyone except grammarians.

When numerals are being written in figures the symbol *1* must not be used for the word *one* unless it actually represents a numeral. The pronoun *one* is almost never a numeral, although occasionally it may be, as in *somewhere*

among those hundreds of letters was my one. The adjective *one* is often a numeral, but not always. It may be no more than a particularizing adjective, as in *one man's meat is another man's poison*. The numeral *one* always means "one and one only." It usually stands in contrast to some other number word, such as *three, several, many*. In speech the numeral *one* has a particular stress that the word does not have when it is not a number.

The one . . . the other is an ambiguous form of speech. In *a man and a woman were coming down the road; the one was about twenty years old and the other, twice that age*, we cannot be sure whether it is the woman or the man who is twenty years old. On theoretical grounds, *the one* should mean the first and *the other* should mean the second, but we can't be sure that the writer knew this. And what is more to the point, if we are doing the writing, we can't assume that the reader will know this. The words are sometimes used to mean *the first . . . the second*, and sometimes to mean the reverse, *this one . . . that one*. They should therefore be avoided except where the context makes the meaning clear.

one another. See **each other.**

one foot in the grave. To say of someone feeble with age or mortally stricken with a serious sickness that he *has one foot in the grave* is to employ a worn expression.

one touch of nature makes the whole world kin is usually spoken as if it meant that any appeal to the simple, basic emotions will, by the immensity of the response, show the basic kinship of all men, their common humanity, the power of sympathy. The expression, however, is a line from Shakespeare's *Troilus and Cressida* (III, iii, 175), spoken by the cynical Ulysses. It is there a part of a passage which says that one natural trait shows the kinship of all men and this natural trait is inconstancy and a continued preference for anything new and gaudy, however worthless, over anything older of more solid worth.

oneself. This word was formerly written *one's self*. The old spelling is still acceptable, but the newer *oneself* is preferred. (For the ways in which *oneself* may be used, see **reflexive pronouns.**)

only. This word may be an adjective, an adverb, or a conjunction. The adjective *only* means sole or single of its kind and always stands before the noun it qualifies, as in *his only friend*. In current English the word has no comparative or superlative form although it was once possible to say *the onliest method*.

The adverb *only* is a negative and means "not anything except" or "nothing except." When it qualifies an individual element in a sentence it may stand before or after that element, as in *only here* and *here only*. It may seem to qualify the subject of the verb, as in *only children believe this*. But the word is not an adjective here because it in no way limits the meaning of the word *children*. On the contrary, the sentence says "no adults believe this." (The adjective *only* in this sentence would refer to children who have no brothers or sisters and would not be used except after a definitive adjective such as *these, some, such.*)

In most cases *only* is a sentence adverb and qualifies the entire statement. When used in this way its natural position is before the verb, as in *but now I only hear its melancholy, long, withdrawing roar.* This word order is standard literary English and should be followed unless there is a very good reason for placing *only* somewhere else in the sentence.

It is not true that when *only* stands between the subject and the verb it qualifies the verb alone. One might as well argue that *never* qualifies *saw* rather than the full statement in *I never saw a purple cow.* It is no more necessary to place *only* after *hear* and say *I hear only its roar* than it is to place *never* after *saw* and say *I saw never a cow. Only* may be placed later. But when it is, it puts special emphasis on a subordinate part of the sentence, and this is often undesirable. The original sentence quoted above, which is by Matthew Arnold, says that at the moment there is nothing in the world for him except this melancholy sound. It does not say that he only hears and does not see. And if *only* is placed after *hear* to avoid this imaginary ambiguity, *roar* is given undue importance. We may be left feeling that he heard the roar but not the other sounds that went with it.

Nor is it true that *only* standing in this position may be understood as qualifying the subject. If it is intended to qualify the subject, something must be done to make that clear. It may be placed ahead, as in *only I hear,* or it may be followed by a comma, as in *I only, hear.* Or the word *alone* may be used instead, as in *I alone hear.*

Like other negative adverbs, *only* must be placed ahead of its natural position if it is to be made emphatic. When *only* brings an adverb into the first position in a sentence, it also brings the verb ahead of its subject, as in *only then did he realize.* In *only less,* as used in *only less free than thou,* we also have a pre-placed *only.* What is meant is *less free than only* (nothing except) *thou.*

Only may also be used as a conjunction (or preposition). It cannot be used in place of the word *except,* as it is in *do not cross the railroad tracks only by the bridge.* But it may be used in place of *but,* as in *many a man would have become wise, only he thought he was so already* and *we would have come, only the car broke down.* Some grammarians condemn this construction. It has been literary English for six hundred years and so cannot be considered an innovation. Perhaps it is falling into disuse in some parts of the country. If so, it should be classed as old fashioned in those areas. But in many places the construction is used freely by all kinds of people and is therefore still standard English.

only too; more than. Whether one is *only too glad* to be of assistance or *only too willing* to

help or *only too ready* to give advice when it is asked for, he betrays in the confused excess of the phrase a certain doubt or reluctance inconsistent with the warmth of the assurance. Literally *only too glad* must mean that there are degrees of gladness beyond this excessive gladness which we recognize but to which we do not propose to yield ourselves. The whole phrase is rather silly. It is better simply to say *I am glad* or, if one is not glad, *I am willing.*

To say that one is *more than pleased* or *more than happy* to do something is a part of the same sort of excessive talk but in these phrases there is at least a sort of sense. One says, in effect, "I shall pass beyond a state of happiness or pleasure into one of rapture or ecstasy." Few listeners would take such an assurance literally and it is, as we say, "merely a manner of speaking." But it is not a good manner of speaking because like all excesses it tends to defeat its own purpose. The only possible aim of such a protestation could be to assure the listener of the warmth of our feelings towards him, but the exaggeration is likely to lead him to doubt our sincerity and hence our warmth altogether.

onomatopoeia is the technical name for the formation of a name or a word by imitating some sound associated with the thing designated. *Cuckoo* and *whippoorwill* are probable examples. *Bang, fizz, burp, rattle, smack, flop, sneeze* are others. There are hundreds of such words in the language.

As a device, onomatopoeia often appeals to poets and their use of it ranges from Vachel Lindsay's

Beat an empty barrel with the handle of a
*   broom*
Hard as they were able,
Boom, boom, BOOM.
With a silk umbrella and the handle of a
*   broom,*
Boomlay, boomlay, boomlay, BOOM.

to Swinburne's *With lisp of leaves and ripple of rain,* in which the sound of the wind and the rain is suggested in an appropriate combination of standard words.

In its wider application, onomatopoeia is a fitting of the sound to the meaning. Alexander Pope in his *Essay on Criticism* gave a famous pronouncement on this subject with a series of brilliant illustrations:

'Tis not enough no harshness gives offence,
The sound must seem an echo of the sense:
Soft is the strain when Zephyr gently blows,
And the smooth stream in smoother numbers
*   flows;*
But when loud surges lash the sounding shore,
The hoarse, rough verse should like the tor-
*   rent roar.*
When Ajax strives some rock's vast weight to
*   throw,*
The line too labours, and the words move slow:
Not so, when swift Camilla scours the plain,
Flies o'er th'unbending corn, and skims
*   along the main.*

This, of course, is obvious, as a good example should be. But Pope was able, when he chose, to achieve the effect with great subtlety, as in his description of a sneeze in *The Rape of the Lock:*

> *Sudden, with starting tears each eye o'erflows,*
> *And the high dome re-echoes to his nose.*

Milton is a great master of onomatopoeia. His skill in using the device contributes to the grandeur of many of his finest passages—as, for instance, the ominous reverberation in his description of the opening of the gates of Hell:

> *. . . on a sudden open flie*
> *With impetuous recoile and jarring sound*
> *Th'infernal dores, and on their hinges grate*
> *Harsh thunder. . . .*

But onomatopoeia in itself has little merit. The mere doing of it is a sort of trick or at best a skilful exercise, as in Poe's *The Bells.* It is only when it enhances the meaning, by creating a mood or contributing by the suggestion of its sound to the main thought, that it has value. No one should be encouraged to use it deliberately and in serious prose it should probably be avoided.

The adjective is *onomatopoeiac* or *onomatopoetic,* the first being the preferred form.

onset means basically an assault or an attack, the act of setting upon (*The onset at Omaha Beach was especially bloody*), a beginning or a start (*The onset of winter, with its lowering skies and dreary winds, was especially depressing*). Only in medical usage (*The onset of the disease was obvious on cursory examination*) may *onset* be used to designate initial symptoms or first signs.

onus; gravamen. An *onus* is a moral burden, a responsibility (*He shouldered the onus for the whole adventure*). The *gravamen* is that part of an accusation which weighs most heavily against the accused (*The gravamen of the charge was that the revolver which fired the fatal shot was found in the trunk of his car*). By extension *gravamen* means grievance. This meaning is obsolescent in England but standard in the United States (*The real gravamen of the charges* [against Democracy] *lies in the habit it has of . . . asking the powers that be whether they are the powers that ought to be*). The plural of *gravamen* is *gravamina.*

onward; onwards. *Onward* is the only form that can be used to qualify a following noun, as in *the onward course.* It is the preferred form in giving a command, as in *Onward, Christian soldiers.* Either form may be used in any other construction, as in *the road led onwards* and *he went onward.* In the United States the form *onward* is generally preferred.

op. cit. is an abbreviation of the Latin words *opere citato* and means *in the work cited.*

opera. See **opus.**

operative; operator. *Operative* is used chiefly as an adjective, meaning active, exerting force, efficacious, effective (*The original rules are still operative*). When used as a noun, *operative*

means a worker, one skilled in some branch of work, especially productive or industrial work; a workman, artisan, factory hand, especially one who tends a machine (*The cotton operatives, being unorganized, had no remedy for their miseries*). This use is now largely American, the English preferring *mill-hand* or *workman.* American also is the use of *operative* for a detective, a euphemism adopted by the Pinkertons at the turn of the century which passed into common usage (*I had pawned the pistol for twenty dollars . . ., and in its place I was carrying a small pistol belonging to another operative*).

Operator, in various combinations, is more specific than *operative* (*linotype operator, punch press operator, telephone operator*). Used alone —particularly in America—it applies to those conducting large-scale operations (*mine operators, mill operators*) and, especially, to those who operate in stocks in a large or speculative way (*Wall Street operators began jumping out of windows in the fall of 1929*). Big *operator* is a slang term, often with sarcastic overtones, for one who bustles about in self-importance, manipulating and maneuvering with great to-do.

ophthalmologist; optician; optometrist. See **oculist.**

opinion, in my. An opinion is a judgment or belief resting on grounds insufficient to produce certainty. When, therefore, one adds *in my opinion* to some statement, one is modestly or tactfully seeking to avoid the appearance of being dogmatic. This is admirable, but it may also be tedious and sometimes timid. Then the emphasis, somehow, seems to fall on *my* rather than on *opinion* and the phrase, meant to be disarming, is often pontifical and irritating. It is usually better to say *I think.*

opinionated; opinionative. *Opinionated* is an adjective describing one who is obstinate or conceited with regard to his opinions, conceitedly dogmatic (*At the risk of sounding opinionated, I say that Yeats is our best poet since Milton*). Since an opinion is a judgment not sufficiently grounded in fact to be a certainty and since conceit is an exaggerated estimate of one's own abilities, *opinionated* is necessarily a vague word. It is highly charged emotionally and usually conveys a wholly subjective estimate made by the user. It is now completely derogatory and comes, like *bigoted,* close to being a term of vulgar abuse. That does not mean, of course, that it is not useful. But in using it these things should be borne in mind.

Opinionative is a word faultily formed from its Latin root and seldom understood by writer or reader. Basically it means of, pertaining to, or of the nature of opinion (*That's a purely opinionative conclusion*). In a secondary sense it means *opinionated,* though in the interests of clarity one might better use *opinionated* when that is what one means.

opponent. See **antagonist.**

oppose. See **antagonize.**

opposite. As an adjective, *opposite* is followed by *to* (*His store is opposite to mine*); as a noun, it is followed by *of* (*My view is the very opposite of his*). See also **contrary**.

optimism was the name given by the Jesuits to Leibnitz's doctrine (propounded in his *Théodicée, 1710*) that our world is the "best of all possible worlds." The word gained currency from the attack on the doctrine by Voltaire in *Candide ou l'Optimisme*, 1759.

From this philosophical beginning the word has spread out to include many meanings which might otherwise be better conveyed. Among the more general senses of *optimism* are the belief that good ultimately predominates over evil, that good pervades reality, and (the loose, popular sense) the disposition to hope for the best, the tendency to look on the brighter side of things, to be hopeful in adversity. In this last sense *optimism* may, indeed often does, have no philosophical basis whatever. It is simply a loose synonym for *cheerfulness*, a term to express a function of sound health, the reflection of good luck or limited powers of observation.

optimist; pessimist; meliorist. Philosophically, an *optimist* is one who believes that because the Creator is infinitely good and infinitely powerful this is the best of all possible worlds. In the popular use of the term, he is simply a cheerful, hopeful person who, when faced with a number of possible happenings or consequences, assumes that the one most favorable to himself will occur.

Philosophically, a *pessimist* is one who believes that evil is dominant in the world, that life's unhappiness is not compensated for by its happiness. In popular use the word is applied to anyone who takes an unusually or consistently gloomy view of things and since the modern world, especially in its economic aspects, is wedded to optimism, the word is usually disparaging.

Really an optimist, though usually considered a "middle-of-the-roader," is the *meliorist*, one who believes that the world is not perfect but that it can be made better by human action. Most people are probably meliorists, but the word is not widely used or even known, the extremes being more suitable for popular discussion.

optimistic; hopeful; sanguine. All three of these words suggest a favorable view of things. The difference between *optimistic* and the other two is one of kind. Between *hopeful* and *sanguine* it is one of degree.

Optimistic, in its proper sense, describes a habit of mind, a disposition to take a favorable view of things. It is correct to say *He was optimistic* or even *He was optimistic about the future of mankind* or *about world government*. But the word which designates a habit of mind is not applicable to a small matter or a particular thing and it is improper to say *He was optimistic about his chance of getting a ticket*. Here *hopeful* or *sanguine* would be a better word. Of the two, *hopeful*, which means having hope or being full of hope, would be better in this context. *Sanguine*, which means naturally

cheerful and hopeful, confident, having a high degree of hope, is a stronger word than *hopeful*, but it is little used in England (except in the now slightly archaic expression *of a sanguine complexion* meaning "of a cheerful disposition") and almost never in America except in such stock phrases as *beyond our most sanguine expectations* and *not sanguine about the outcome*. *Optimistic*, however loosely it may convey the desired sense, seems to have crowded out its more accurate rivals.

optimum, as an adjective, is not merely a synonym for *best*. It means, rather, the best under the (usually conflicting) circumstances, the most favorable, that is, towards attaining some desired end. The best speed of a car might be its utmost. The optimum, if the desired end were economy of fuel, would be a great deal less than that. The optimum number of students that a college might seek to enroll would not be the largest number that could be accommodated in the dormitories or the classrooms but the largest number consistent with a number of conditions, such as the energies of the teaching staff, the facilities of the library, and so on, with a view to giving each student the best education possible under the circumstances.

option means the power or liberty of choosing, the right or freedom of choice (*It is his option, whether he will fight or run away*), something which may be or is chosen (*The town was dry by local option*), or—a special legal and commercial use—a privilege acquired, as by the payment of a premium or consideration, of demanding, within a specified time, the carrying out of a transaction upon stipulated terms (*If he does not take up his option within six months, the money in escrow will be forfeited*). A *choice* is simply the act of choosing, that which is chosen, or an alternative. It implies the opportunity to choose; where *option* stresses, rather, the free right or privilege of choosing. Where there is any doubt, *choice* is to be preferred to *option*, if only as the more common, less pretentious word. And certainly *option* is not to be used where the broader equivalent, *choice*, is superfluous. To say *I had no option but to sign* is a pompous, wordy way of saying "I had to sign."

opulent. See **rich**.

opus. The plural is *opera*, not *opi*. The English plural *opuses* is used only facetiously.

or; nor. These words are conjunctions and join elements that are grammatically alike. A personal pronoun following *or* or *nor* must have the form that it would have if it were being used in the sentence itself instead of after *or*. That is, the form *him* is required in *no one saw you or him* because *him* is required in *no one saw him;* and the form *he* is required in *either you must do it or he* because *he* is required in *he must do it*. In present-day English the verb is usually repeated after a subjective pronoun such as *he*, as in *either you must do it or he must*.

Nor makes the words that follow it negative.

Used with a negative statement, *nor* introduces an alternative and negates it, as in *he shall not fail nor be discouraged.* Since *nor* affects only the words that it adds to an already complete sentence it never forms a double negative with what has gone before. It can be used wherever the words *and not* could be used. When the words following *nor* include a verb and its subject, the verb stands before the subject. If written out fully, the sentence just quoted would read: *he shall not fail nor shall he be discouraged.*

After an affirmative statement *nor* adds a contrasting or contradictory negative and not an alternative. This construction is rare in present-day speech but it is standard English and is used in poetry and solemn prose, as in: *he will watch from dawn to gloom . . . the honey-bees in the ivy bloom, nor heed nor see what things they be.*

Or is used with an affirmative statement to introduce an alternative, as in *you told me or I read it somewhere.* The alternative must be affirmative or the simple negative of what has just been said, as in *he may come or he may not. Or* may be used in a negative statement to introduce an alternative to one of the negative elements, as in *I want no notes or promises; I want money* and *I will not agree to that, or even consider it.* In every case, the words following *or* must be parallel with some previous word or group of words that has been made negative. *Nor* can also be used in these same constructions and makes a more emphatic negative. We can say *I want no notes nor promises* and *I will not agree to that, nor even consider it. Or* cannot be used with a negative statement to introduce an alternative that is grammatically independent. We cannot say *he did not come or will not.* For this we must use *and* or *nor,* as in *he did not come nor will he.*

Or does not always introduce a simple alternative. It sometimes has the sense of *if so* or *if not* and gives the preceding clause the force of a conditional. This is the case whenever it joins an independent statement to a preceding negative, as in *I can't stay longer or I will be late,* or an independent negative statement to a preceding affirmative, as in *he told me himself or I would not believe it.*

In present-day English, *neither* is followed by *nor* and *either* by *or.*

Theoretically, when the subject of a verb is a compound joined by *or* or *nor,* the verb has the number and person of the element standing nearest to it. But in the best modern prose this rule is not strictly observed. If the element nearest the verb is plural the verb too is always plural, in practice as well as in theory, as in *either he or his neighbors are mistaken.* In practice, the verb is usually plural in a negative statement, as in *neither Eric nor Regina are there now,* and often plural in a question, as in *what are honor or dishonor to her?* In an affirmative statement the verb is usually singular if the part of the subject nearest it is singular, as in *either Eric or Regina is there now,* although even here a plural verb may be used, as in *marble, bronze, or clay are the materials of sculpture.* Questions of person, as distinct from number, only arise in connection with the pronouns *I* and *you.* The rule requires *either he or you are mistaken, either you or I am mistaken.* Most people avoid compounds of this kind and say *either he is mistaken or you are, either you are mistaken or I am.* See **agreement: verbs.**

oral. See **aural.**

oral and **verbal** are not synonymous, though *verbal* is misused for *oral* quite often, perhaps by persons encouraged to take as precedent the very special case of *verbal agreement* which means oral agreement, agreement in speech only. Actually *oral* means uttered by the mouth, spoken (*He teaches oral interpretation of literature*), as opposed to what is conveyed in writing. Though *verbal* is used for *oral* in *verbal agreement,* it normally applies to the words, spoken or written, in which thought or feeling is conveyed. When we refer to *a verbal account* of an event, we mean an account conveyed in words instead of one conveyed by gestures, pictures, or other means. Thus *verbal* is the more inclusive term, emphasizing words themselves as distinguished from ideas, emotions, actions, images.

orate. There was an old English verb *to orate,* meaning to pray, and we still have an *oratory,* a place of prayer. But this meaning of *orate* is now obsolete and the modern verb is actually a new coinage, a back formation from *oration.* It is used humorously and sarcastically to mean make an oration, hold forth in a lofty style (*I should hate exceedingly to have the present speeches of the gentleman from Pennsylvania orated around over the country as mine*—Congressional Record). If the giving of a public address is referred to seriously, the correct term is *deliver an oration* or, if one wishes to be less formal, *deliver* (or *make*) *a speech, speak in public.*

orchestra; stalls; pit. As used with reference to floor space in a modern theater, the word *orchestra* in America describes the space reserved for the musicians, usually the front part of the main floor, the orchestra pit, or, more often, it describes the entire main-floor space for spectators. The *stalls* in an English theater are the seats in the front division of the main floor or in the front of the lower balcony. The *pit* is a term used in England for a section of the main floor of a theater behind the orchestra and in front of the parquet, parterre, or orchestra stalls, usually of unreserved seats. In former times, when ladies and gentlemen of fashion frequented only the boxes, the pit was the station of the common man in the theater, the cheapest space available. The term *the pit* was applied to persons occupying this section and *playing to the pit* has much the same meaning in England as *playing to the gallery* has in America.

orchis. The plural is *orchides,* not *orches.* A new singular *orchid,* with a regular plural *orchids,* was coined by a botanist in 1854. It is now the usual name for these plants.

order. This verb may be followed by an infinitive, as in *he ordered her to go.* It may also be followed by a *that* clause with the clause verb a subjunctive or a subjunctive equivalent, as in *he ordered that she go.* The infinitive construction is generally preferred. When *order* is followed by a passive infinitive, as in *he ordered them to be sent,* the *to be* may be omitted, as in *he ordered them sent.* This construction is not often used in Great Britain but is standard practice in the United States.

order; command; instruction; direction; directive; injunction. All of these terms have the meaning of an authoritative mandate. *Order* is the most inclusive. In law it means the command of a court or judge (*He paid alimony by court order*). The military term (usually in the plural) describes commands or notices issued by military authorities. It may also describe assignments to duty stations.

In former times the wishes of the sovereign were *commands,* a meaning that survives in Britain in *command performance,* a theatrical performance in response to a royal invitation. The commands of the sovereign were often expressed as wishes (*Le Roi le veult*). Today *command* usually refers to the military. It is used in a number of senses, such as an order in prescribed words, usually given in a loud voice to troops at close-order drill; or it may designate a body of troops or an area or a station under a commander. It may also mean the possession or exercise of controlling authority (*I'm in command here*).

In one of its senses *instruction,* usually plural, means an order or direction (*Please read the instructions before assembling the antenna*). *Direction* in one of its senses means much the same as *instruction* and always appears in the plural. It is the usual word to describe instructions concerning the route to be taken to arrive at a desired destination (*If he follows my directions, he can't miss Rockefeller Center*).

Directive is a new noun. It means an authoritative instruction or direction (*A directive was issued by the Secretary of State on conduct of Foreign Affairs Officers*).

An *injunction* is usually thought of in its legal sense, which describes a judicial process or order requiring the person or persons to whom it is directed to do (or, more commonly, not to do) a particular thing. However, it can be more generally applied to mean a command, an order, or an admonition (*In spite of all injunctions of secrecy, the news had spread*).

order. The use of *order* in idiomatic expressions varies sufficiently in British and American usage to require comment. A speaker is *called to order* in England when the chairman finds it necessary to rebuke him for violating rules of procedure. A meeting is *called to order* in America by the chairman as he formally opens its proceedings.

In England *in order* means in accordance with rules of parliamentary procedure. In America it may also mean permissible, fitting, appropriate (*I hear that congratulations are in order*). *In short order* is an American phrase meaning immediately, in no time. A *short-order* cook is one who in lunch wagons, small restaurants, and so on, fries eggs, hamburgers, and griddle cakes, heats canned soup, makes coffee, and prepares other dishes that can be made ready quickly. From restaurant usage *order* has also come to mean, in the United States, a portion of food. When a waitress says *I had those two orders of potatoes right here on my tray* she does not mean a written order for the potatoes but the potatoes themselves.

ordinance; ordnance; ordonnance. *Ordinance* in America means an authoritative rule or law, a decree or command, a public injunction or regulation, usually municipal (*It is an ordinance in our city that residents must wrap their garbage*). The English equivalent is *by-law.* According to Horwill, *ordinance* is rarely used in England except historically (as the *Self-Denying Ordinance,* an Act passed by the Long Parliament in 1644, by which the members of Parliament bound themselves not to accept commands in the army) and in the phrase *religious ordinances* (religious rites).

Ordnance, a variant of *ordinance,* has become established in a series of special meanings. From an ordering, supplies, it has come to mean military supplies, primarily cannon or artillery, but also military weapons of all kinds with their equipments, ammunition (*At three o'clock the heavy ordnance was brought into position. During the war he got a job in an ordnance plant filling cartridges*).

Ordonnance is also an ordering, but not of political or religious affairs or of military equipment. It designates the ordering, disposition, arrangement of parts, as of a building, a picture, or a literary composition. Coleridge speaks of the difference *between the ordonnance of poetic composition and that of prose.*

In older English writing one often finds *ordonnance* used for *ordinance,* especially in reference to foreign decrees and promulgations.

ordinary. See **average, common, normal.**

ordure. Save in a few grim humorous contexts (such as *the natural ordure of things*) *ordure* as a term for filth or excrement is a literary euphemism.

Orient. See **East.**

orient: orientate. Both *orient* and *orientate* mean to place so as to face the east and, by extension, to adjust in relation to, or to bring into due relation to, surrounding circumstances, facts, and so on. In the United States *orient* is the preferred form for all meanings. In England *orientate* is still used for placing so as to face in some specific direction, particularly to the east but *orient* is used there in all figurative senses (*The whole village was oriented to gain the maximum sunlight. As soon as the Commandos were orientated, they began their advance along the quay.*

He was quick to orient himself to the community).

Many American colleges have what they call *orientation courses,* broad general introductory courses, usually in the social sciences, intended for the beginning student. Their professed purpose is to enable the student to "place" himself in history or the social structure of the world—or whatever the subject of the course may be. Since it is assumed that any introductory course serves this vague purpose to some extent, the term is unnecessary and pompous.

ornamental; ornate; decorative. Anything is *ornamental* which is used for ornament (*The plaid cape was more ornamental than useful*). There is perhaps an echo of our Puritan background, a suggestion in the word of something unnecessary and often a further suggestion of something insubstantial or tinselly. That is *ornate* which is elaborately or sumptuously adorned, showily splendid. Since modern taste disapproves of the sumptuous and since there is far more show of splendor than actual splendor, the word often carries a connotation of disparagement, especially in reference to speech. *Decorative* is a more favorable word, suggesting a becoming ornamentation, something which fittingly adds to an appearance of festivity.

The Englishman, Collins, holds that *ornamental* is an active term and that *ornate* and *decorative* are synonymous passive terms but American usage does not make these distinctions.

ostensible; ostensive; ostentatious. Although the dictionaries recognize *ostensible* and *ostensive* as synonyms, there are distinctions in their use which can be ambiguous and it is better not to use them interchangeably. *Ostensible* is a well known adjective, suitable for general use. *Ostensive* is a little-known, usually specialized term which should be used with discrimination.

That is *ostensible* which is given out or outwardly appears to be, is professed or pretended (*His ostensible motive was charity; his actual motive was self-glorification*). *Ostensive* means showing, but its primary meaning is showing in logic, setting forth a general principle by virtue of which a proposition must be true. An *ostensive demonstration* (in mathematics) is a demonstration which plainly and directly demonstrates the truth of a proposition, as distinct, say, from a *reductio ad absurdum.*

If that is *ostensible* which shows on the surface and that is *ostensive* which shows logically beyond cavil, that is *ostentatious* which is overly showy, pretentious, demonstrative beyond need in order to impress others. It is now a disparaging word, though in the days when public demonstrations of even affection were staged for political purposes it was not always so. When Octavius, in Shakespeare's *Antony and Cleopatra,* told his sister that her quiet and unexpected return to Rome had *prevented the ostentation* of his love, he merely meant that she had made it impossible for him to have her received with the pageantry and splendor which, as his loved sister, was her due. She had prevented him from making a public demonstration of his regard for her and this he felt was, under the circumstances, a political error.

O tempora! O mores! When the contemplation of Catiline's wickedness moved Cicero in 63 B.C. to exclaim in horror at the times and the manners that could produce such a monster, he so expressed the indignation of all who view with alarm that his phrase has been repeated ever since. Of late it has been so often repeated that it has become a cliché, the more meaningless because finally even our orators prefer (like Cicero) to speak in their own language.

other; otherwise. *Other* was once the ordinal form for the cardinal number *two* and meant what we now mean by *second.* It now has the vaguer meaning of additional or different from, but it is still used occasionally in its earlier sense, as in *we bake every other day.* Because it was once an ordinal number *other* may stand before a cardinal, as in *the other two men,* and because it no longer is an ordinal, it may stand after a cardinal, as in *the two other men.*

Other is primarily an adjective and may qualify either a singular or a plural noun, as in *the other man* and *the other men.* It may also be treated as a noun and given singular, plural, and genitive forms, as *other, others, other's, others'.* (When used in this way it is sometimes called a pronoun.) The adjective form *other* may be used alone as a noun in speaking of more than one person, as in *like other of the world's great men* and *two other among that handful of young soldiers.* This construction is acceptable before the word *of;* otherwise, the plural form *others* is preferred.

Other, in any of its forms, may be used in a comparison with *than,* as in *another world than ours. Other* followed by *from,* as in *another world from this,* is not standard English.

Other is sometimes used as an adverb before *than,* as in *it was impossible for her to speak other than kindly.* This construction is acceptable in the United States, but the regular adverbial form *otherwise* is generally preferred in any position that would call for an adverb. The form *otherwise* may be used to qualify a preceding noun, as in *the workers, industrial or otherwise.* Very often this is an elaborate way of saying something that could be said more simply. But there is nothing wrong with the construction grammatically. A noun may always be followed by an adjective or an adverb, or by both, as the noun is in *angel visits, few and far between.*

ought is an old past subjunctive form of the verb *owe.* It has no corresponding present subjunctive form. See **subjunctive mode.**

Grammatically, *ought* is a past tense form, just as *went* is. The verb has no imperative, no infinitive, no past participle, no *-ing* form, and therefore cannot follow (that is, cannot be dependent on) another verb. We can no more say *had ought, did ought, used to ought,* than we can say *had went, did went, used to went.*

This was not always true. At one time *ought* could also be used as a participle, corresponding to *gone*, and *had ought* was literary English. Today these forms are obsolete or dialectal. Since we cannot use auxiliaries, such as *do, be, have*, we form negative statements and ask questions in the old direct way that is now obsolete for most verbs, as in *he ought not to say it* and *ought I to tell you?*

Ought itself is always used as an auxiliary and requires another verb to complete its meaning. Usually this is a *to*-infinitive. It may be the infinitive of the meaningful verb, as in *I ought to tell her*, or it may be *to have* and a past participle, as in *I ought to have told her*. In the first case, the statement refers indefinitely to the present or the future. In the second case, it refers to a past event. The infinitive must be actually stated or easily supplied from the context. When it is to be supplied, we usually keep the word *to*, as in *I think you ought to*, although this is not required and we may also say *I think you ought*. In the United States the simple form of the verb is sometimes used instead of the *to*-infinitive after *ought not*, as in *you ought not stay*. The construction with *to* is generally preferred.

Some people claim that the word *ought* always means obligation or duty and that we cannot say *he ought to be hanged* because "that is the duty of others." There is no justification for this. The word is also used to mean befitting, advisable, expected, and so on, as in *you ought to take a nap* and *they ought to be here soon*.

ought. See **aught**.

our; ours. The form *our* is used to qualify a following noun, as in *our country, our all*. The form *ours* is used in any other construction, as in *this country of ours* and *all ours*. *Ours* is also the form used in a double possessive where it is separated from its following noun by *and*, as in *ours and Jacob's God*. Today this construction is generally avoided and *our God and Jacob's* or *our own and Jacob's God* is used instead. Neither word order shows clearly whether we are talking about one thing or two, but the old-fashioned form, *ours and Jacob's*, suggests one thing possessed in common more strongly than the forms which use *our*.

The plural word *our* is frequently used after a grammatically singular word such as *neither* or *each*, in order to avoid using *his* when the reference may be to either a man or a woman, as in *neither of us had broken our vow* and *each in our own way*.

In current English, the word *ours* is never written with an apostrophe.

ourn. This word was once acceptable English, but it has not been used in the literary language for three hundred years. The only acceptable form today is *ours*.

ourself; ourselves. Originally, the word *self* could be used as a plural or as a singular and the plural of *myself* was *ourself*. The form *ourselves* did not appear until the sixteenth century, but it has since driven *ourself* from natural speech. During the nineteenth century, the form

ourself was the preferred reflexive for a *we* that actually represented only one person, as in *we found ourself running among the first*. But this obviously defeated whatever purpose there was in using *we*. Today, *ourself* is recognized as the traditionally correct form to use with a "royal we," as in *which ourself have granted*. But in any other context it is felt to be a slip, and evidence that the user has not taken his *we* seriously but has been thinking *I* all along. The plural form *ourselves* is always used when more than one person is actually involved, as in *we ourselves have agreed*. (For the ways in which *ourselves* may be used, see **reflexive pronouns**.)

out; outer; outmost; outermost; utter; utmost; uttermost. The primary meaning of *out* is "away from within." It is used chiefly as an adverb to qualify a verb, as in *he is going out*, but it may also be used as an adjective to qualify a noun, as in *the out side* and *the out man*. When *out* forms part of a compound verb it frequently has the meaning of "going forth," as in *think out, write out*, or of "going beyond," as in *out-bid, outgush*.

In Great Britain *out* is never used as a preposition but must be combined with *of* before it can have an object, as in *he went out of the room, he jumped out of the window*. In the United States *out* requires *of* when it is used in the sense of *away from*, as in *he went out of the house, he went out of her life*, but it is used as a preposition without *of* when it means *through*, as in *he jumped out the window, he ran out the door*.

Outer and *outmost* or *outermost* are comparative and superlative forms of *out* and mean farther and farthest from the center. They are relatively new words that have been in general use less than three hundred years. *Utter, utmost, uttermost*, are older ways of expressing the same ideas. *Utter* was used in the sense of "exterior" until late in the seventeenth century, but this meaning is now obsolete. Today *outer* is used in this sense and *utter* always means "in a high degree" or "absolute." As a result, *outer darkness* and *utter darkness* mean different things. The superlative forms *utmost* and *uttermost* can still be used in both senses and may mean remote, extreme, or last in a series.

The words *outer* and *utter*, like the words *elder* and *former*, have comparative forms but are felt as positive descriptive adjectives and not as comparatives, and therefore cannot be used in a comparison with *than*.

out of one's depth. As a metaphor, signifying that anything from a social situation to an idea is too much for one, *out of one's depth* is hackneyed.

out of the woods. As a way of saying that a danger has not completely abated, *we are not yet out of the woods* is a cliché.

outdoor; outdoors. *Outdoor* is the preferred form when the word is used to qualify a following noun, as in *an outdoor fire place*. *Outdoors* is the preferred form when the word is used to qualify anything except a noun, as in *they lived outdoors*. But this distinction is not strictly observed. The same is true of *out-of-door* and *out-of-doors*. There is no difference between the forms with *of* and those without, in either meaning or use.

Both of the forms ending in *s* may be used as nouns, as in *the great outdoors, the great out-of-doors*.

outfit. As a standard noun *outfit* means an assemblage of articles for fitting out or equipping (*The explorer's outfit must include a few yards of mosquito netting*) or a set of articles for any purpose (*His grandmother gave him a carpenter's outfit when he was only twelve*). In American slang it has the further senses of a group associated in any undertaking, as a military body (*There was entirely too much coddling going on in the outfit*—Norman Mailer), a party, company, or set, especially men in charge of cattle (*The outfit consisted of three covered wagons, four tents, eighty saddle horses, three cooks, and about twenty riders*), and, by extension, a number of people combined for any purpose (*The Tammany outfit had supported him in the gubernatorial campaign*).

The basic sense of the word, as listed in the *Oxford English Dictionary*, the act of fitting out or furnishing with requisites (as in *If you secure the commissions, I'll make the outfit easy*), is seldom used in the United States.

out-Herod Herod. King Herod was represented in the old mystery plays as a bellowing, ranting, raging ruffian or a tyrant. He was obviously very dear to the audiences and successive generations of anonymous hams must have labored mightily to outdo each other in the role. By Shakespeare's time to *out-Herod Herod* was proverbial for tearing a passion to tatters, outrageous blustering, and violent denunciation. Shakespeare's use of the phrase kept it in the language long after its original meaning had faded. It is now a cliché.

outlandish. See **exotic.**

outline; summary; brief; synopsis. An *outline* is a rough draft or first general sketch, account, or report, in which the main features only of some book, subject, or project are set forth. It is a plan showing the parts of a discourse in some sort of skeletal form (*He submitted an outline of his speech to his superior for approval*). A *summary* is a brief statement or restatement of the main points, especially as the conclusion to a work (*The last chapter contained an excellent summary of the whole book*). As an adjective, *summary* means concise, brief and comprehensive, and, by extension, unceremoniously fast (*This summary dismissal of his plea was infuriating*). In relation to trials and courts-martial it means a proceeding which is conducted without or is exempt from the various steps and delays of a formal trial.

A *brief* is a detailed outline, by heads and subheads, of a discourse (usually legal) to be completed. It is an outline, the form of which is determined by set rules, of all the possible arguments and information on one side of a

controversy. Its contemporary use is confined almost entirely to law and debating.

A *synopsis* is a condensed statement giving a general view of some subject. In modern English it is most commonly used to designate a compressed statement of the plot of a novel or a play (*Such synopses have little value for the student, because the mere events of the action are not the most important part of the plays*).

outlook. See **lookout.**

outside. The single word *outside* may be used in place of the phrase *outside of,* and is generally preferred in the United States. It may be used literally of space, as in *outside the city limits,* or it may be used figuratively, as in *that is outside his interests*. The word means exterior to and fixes the mind on what is exterior. The statement *this is not done outside the South* is a statement about New York and Oregon. The speaker may have been thinking of what was interior and may have used *outside* as the equivalent of "except in." This is acceptable because it is still possible to hear the sentence with the conventional meaning of *outside*. But this is not possible when the word is used in place of "except for," as in *I have seen no one outside the milkman*. The fact that we can't hear the word with its usual meaning in a sentence of this kind calls our attention to its meaning, and the sentence becomes ridiculous.

outskirts once had a singular form *outskirt,* but this is now obsolete. The form *outskirts* is used with a plural verb as in *the outskirts were a few miles away,* but it cannot be qualified by a word implying number. We cannot speak of *a few outskirts,* for example.

outspoken. See **frank.**

outward; outwards. *Outward* is the only form that can be used to qualify a following noun, as in *the outward voyage*. Either form may be used in any other construction, as in *outwards bound* and *outward bound*. The form *outward* is generally preferred in the United States.

outworn; worn-out. One may use either *outworn* or *worn-out* to describe that which has been consumed by use, wear, or the action of time, whether the thing described is physical or figurative or that which is exhausted in strength or endurance. *Worn-out* has come, however, to be used more often in the sense of being so injured by wear as to be no longer serviceable or to be wearied or exhausted, as with toil; and *outworn* has acquired the peculiar senses of outgrown (as of clothes which are still serviceable but no longer large enough for a child) and obsolete, out of date (*I'd rather be/ A Pagan suckled in a creed outworn*). As a general rule, when either *outworn* or *worn-out* will serve, it is better to use *worn-out*. It is more idiomatic and straightforward.

over is primarily a preposition, as in *jump over the wall,* or an adverb, as in *think the matter over;* but adjective forms of the word survive in compound nouns, such as *overcoat* and *overlord*. From the earliest times the word has carried the meanings of in excess, as in *overeat;* above, as in *overhead;* beyond, as in *overseas;*

across, as in *come over;* and completion, as in *he thought it was over.*

Over with the idea of completely was often used with a numeral, as in *you shall have gold to pay the petty debt twenty times over,* or with *again,* as in *we will do it over again.* From this, it came to be used alone with the idea of repetition, as in *he plans to do it over.* But *over again* is better established historically than *over* in this sense, and is still preferred by most people. The idea of "complete" in *over again* has not been entirely lost. Today we say *again* when all we mean is "once more," as in *I'll see you again. Over again* still carries the idea of "start at the beginning again," and usually suggests that this is a tiresome thing to do.

over and above is a cliché as a term for "in excess of."

over and done with, as a term for finished or passed, is a cliché.

overall. As a noun, *overall* offers no difficulty. In Britain it designates a smock or loose housedress. The plural, *overalls,* designates in Britain a man's trousers, leggings, outer suit for dirty work or bad weather. In America it describes loose, stout trousers, most commonly of blue denim, often extending up over the breast, worn over the clothing to protect it, as by workmen and others.

The plural form refers to one garment but is always treated as a plural, as in *these overalls are dirty.* In order to use the word with a singular verb or to speak of more than one such garment, it is necessary to say *this pair of overalls is dirty* or *several pairs of overalls.* The form *overalls* is also used as the first element in a compound, as in *his overalls pocket.*

The trouble comes with the adjective, written *over-all* in Britain, *overall* in America. Properly speaking, it is used attributively to mean including everything between the extreme points (*The mine sweeper had an overall length of 120 feet*). In an extension of this use, *overall* has come to mean covering or including everything. As Sir Ernest Gowers has said, the wide use of this extension is "an egregious example of the process . . . (of) boring out a weapon of precision into a blunderbuss." It is commonly misused as a synonym for any number of more precise words, such as *aggregate, total, average, comprehensive, complete,* or *whole.* As Collins has observed, in most uses *overall* is at best an inelegant variation, a mere manifestation, that is, of a desire for variety even at the cost of precision and clarity. If *overall* can be justified in any sense beyond its literal one, it is in its power to combine in a single word the idea of "supreme" with the idea of "complete" or "comprehensive" (*The overall direction of the battle came from corps headquarters*).

overly is a double adverb, but so are many other forms ending in *-ly. The Oxford English Dictionary* lists it as found in Old English, and as being used in Scotland and the United States. It is not used in England but is acceptable in this country, especially before an adjective, as in *overly cautious.*

oversight; omission. An *omission* is an act of omitting. It may be deliberate or accidental. An *oversight* is a failure to notice or consider. When it is used to mean omission, it means one due to inadvertence, an unintentional omission (*Not inviting Joe to the party was an oversight*).

Occasionally one comes across *oversight* in its slightly obsolescent sense of supervision, watchful care, the function of an overseer (*Legree had general oversight of the plantation*).

overweening; overweaning. *Ween* is an archaic verb meaning to think or hope. It survives only in *overweening.* One who is overweening has expectations beyond merit or likelihood and hence is arrogant, egotistical. One occasionally sees the word misspelled *overweaning.* But this is simply a blunder or sheer ignorance. There is no such word as *overweaning.* If it existed it could only denote a mother who in some way weaned her children excessively, prematurely perhaps or was too eager to get the process done with.

overwhelming is most likely to be used correctly when one bears in mind that it derives from the transitive verb *to overwhelm* which means to come, rest, or weigh upon overpoweringly, to crush, to overcome completely in mind or feeling. *Overwhelming* means, then, that which overwhelms, that which, moving against us and overspreading us, is so great as to render opposition useless (*The demands of his admirers were not merely great; they were overwhelming*). *Overwhelming* is not to be used as a synonym of *vast* or *preponderant.*

Overwhelming odds and *an overwhelming majority* are clichés.

owe. When this word is used in speaking of something which we have already received in the past, the preposition *to* must be used in naming what we received it from, as in *we owe the discovery of the prismatic spectrum to Sir Isaac Newton.* When it is used in speaking of something which we must pay in the future, the *to* may be used, as in *I owe five dollars to the grocer,* or it may be omitted and the name treated as an indirect object, as in *I owe the grocer five dollars. Owe* in this second sense may be used in a passive construction, as in *five dollars is owed to the grocer,* but this is not possible when the word is used in the first sense. Instead, we must say *the discovery is due to Sir Isaac Newton.* (For the difference between *owing to* and *due to,* see **due to.**)

own. This verb may be followed by the *-ing* form of a verb with the preposition *to,* as in *she owns to knowing about it* and *she owned to having known about it.* It may also be followed by a perfect infinitive with *have,* as in *she owned to have known about it.* Both forms are acceptable, but the *-ing* construction is heard more often.

The adjective *own* does not ordinarily have a comparative or superlative form, but Tennyson wrote: *my ownest own.*

own flesh and blood, close relatives, usually spoken by parents about their children, is a hackneyed expression.

own worst enemy. To say of someone that he is *his own worst enemy,* meaning that he does himself more harm than anyone else does him, that, indeed, most others are well disposed towards him but that some unfortunate trait of character, such as drunkenness, stands in his way, is to employ a cliché.

ox. The plural is *oxen.* Very few Americans use the word *ox* except to call some one *a dumb ox.* Two such people would probably be called *dumb oxes,* and not *dumb oxen.* And where the animals themselves are actually used the plural *oxes* is often heard. *Oxes* is considered uneducated, but it is possible that it is used more than the literary *oxen.*

When *ox* is the second element in a compound the plural is *ox,* as in *three musk ox.*

oxymoron is a rhetorical term for a figure of speech which produces an effect by seeming contradiction. In general it brings together two words which would appear to be opposed to each other but which in the context of their juxtaposition have a pointed meaning. Thus the King of France, in *King Lear,* describes Cordelia, after her father has disowned her, as *this unpriz'd precious maid.* Common oxymorons are the proverbial injunction to the rash to *make haste slowly* and the sentimental sympathy for the *poor little rich girl* that the tabloids expend on unhappy heiresses.

ozone. The use of *ozone* for clear, invigorating, fresh air (*Among the pines, away from the haunts of men, he breathed deep of God's ozone and felt himself a better man*) is a vulgar elegancy. It is also an error. Although ozone is a form of oxygen, it does not possess oxygen's invigorating power; in anything but minute quantities it is poisonous.

P

pack. This verb may be followed by an adjective describing what is packed, as in *the place was packed tight,* or by an adverb describing the packing, as in *she packed it tightly.* As a rule there is no difference in meaning between these two constructions.

pack; packer; packing; package. *Pack* as a verb meaning to prepare food for preservation seems to be one of those words which survived in America but dropped out of English speech. It was used in this sense in England as early as 1494 and has been so used in America since colonial times but is not now so used in England. As a noun meaning the quantity of anything, as food, packed or put up at one time or in one season, *pack* is standard in America (*The salmon pack in 1952 was surprisingly large*) and acceptable in England.

Packer in America has the specialized meaning of one whose business is packing food, especially meat, for the market. This meaning was known in England up until the last century but seems to have fallen into disuse there except, as a sort of borrowing, in reference to the American packers. The term in America is particularly applied to the heads of the great meat-packing businesses (*The great packers— the Swifts, the Armours, the Wilsons—built gothic castles beside the lake*). *Packing* is the American term to describe the preparing and packaging of foodstuffs. This meaning is known in England but, again, it is now used there chiefly in reference to the American industry and its processes.

The noun *package* is in America equivalent to the British terms *packet* and *parcel;* it describes a bundle of things packed and wrapped (*He came home from the store with a large package under his arm*). In America a *packet* is a small package or bundle. A *parcel* is that which when wrapped up forms a single, small bundle (*parcel post*).

pact; compact. In the sense of an agreement, *pact* and *compact* are practically synonymous. A *compact* is a *pact,* an agreement between parties, a covenant, a contract. Some English authorities maintain that as a rule *pact* is used for an agreement between nations or large bodies of people (*North Atlantic Pact*) and *compact* for an arrangement between private persons (*The brothers acted together as if by compact*), and this may be the present tendency in English usage, though it is not supported by the *Oxford English Dictionary.* But in America *pact* may be used for an arrangement between private persons (*I make a pact with you, Walt Whitman*—Ezra Pound) and *compact* for an agreement between nations or large groups (*The Federal constitution has been styled a compact between the States . . .*—Wharton).

In America there is little distinction between the words, although *pact* for this sense is more frequently used.

paddle. The normal sense of the transitive verb *to paddle* is to propel, as a canoe, with a paddle. This sense has begotten, in America at least, a figurative slang term *paddle your own canoe,* meaning "mind your own business." Since a short paddle is used sometimes on young children and pledges of high-school and college secret societies, the verb is also used colloquially in America to mean to beat with or as with a paddle, to spank (*If you don't keep quiet and go to sleep, I'll paddle you*).

pagan. See **agnostic.**

page. Although the older meanings of *page* are known in America today through their preservation in romantic and historical novels, the commonest meaning, when the word is used to refer to a person, is a young male attendant, usually in uniform, in a legislative hall or a hotel (*A page took the message from the Clerk to the Speaker*). As a verb, *page* means to wait on or to follow like a page. In America it has the additional meaning of seeking a person by calling out his name, as a hotel page does (*I'll have him paged over the loudspeaker at the railroad station*).

paid. See **pay.**

pail. In its traditional sense a *pail* is a container of wood or metal with a bail or handle, for holding liquids (*The full-fed beast shall kick the empty pail*). In America only, *pail* may mean a vessel for carrying solids also. Hence the term *dinner pail* to describe the container once commonly used by schoolchildren and now by laborers and college professors to hold their noonday meal. Early in the twentieth century in America *The Full Dinner Pail* was a slogan of prosperity which Mark Hanna publicized in support of the claims of the Republican Party.

pains. When this means considerable care or trouble, as in *take pains with it,* it is a mass word and not a true plural. It is followed by a plural verb, as in *these pains were of no avail* and *no pains were taken,* but we cannot speak of *many pains.* Formerly the word was often used with a singular verb, as in *much pains was taken* and *all this pains was for nothing.* Today the singular construction is not used before a verb, but we can say *he didn't take much pains* or speak about *a great deal of pains.*

The singular form, *a pain,* and the true plural, *three pains* or *many pains,* always refer to sensations of pain, physical or mental.

pair. The plural is *pair* or *pairs. Six pair of gloves* is the older form. *Six pairs of gloves* is newer. Both are acceptable.

Pair, meaning "two," is a noun. It cannot stand immediately before another noun, as the word *two* can, but must be joined to it by *of.* The singular *pair* is regularly followed by a singular verb, as in *a pair of gloves is a nice present.* But when the meaning of a sentence is unambiguously plural, as it is in *a pair of thieves is conspiring to rob us,* it is better English to recognize this fact and use a plural verb, as in *a pair of thieves are conspiring to rob us.*

pair of twins; twins. A *pair of twins* is redundant, since *twins* itself implies two, forming a couple or pair. Yet custom sanctions the term and there is certainly no great harm in it. Twins are, after all, a living redundancy.

pajamas. The plural form refers to one garment, or set of garments, but is always treated as a plural, as in *these pajamas are new.* In order to use the word with a singular verb or to speak of more than one set, it is necessary to say *this pair of pajamas is new* or *several pairs of pajamas.* A singular form *pajama* is used as the first element in a compound, as in *pajama top* and *pajama pocket.*

palate; palette; pallet; pallette. *Palate,* now the best known of the four, describes, roughly, the roof of the mouth (*A cleft palate made it difficult for her to speak*). This part of the mouth is considered (popularly but erroneously) as the organ of taste and, by extension, the word is used for the sense of taste or discrimination in taste (*Though seen of none save him whose strenuous tongue/ Can burst Joy's grape against his palate fine*). The adjective *palatable,* by the way, is restricted to things of an agreeable taste.

Palette is a French word, now anglicized. It meant a flat-bladed instrument, but in its commonest English and American use it now means a thin, usually oval or long, board or tablet with a thumb hole at one end, used by painters to lay and mix colors on. By transference from this meaning, it may also mean the range of colors used by a particular artist.

There are two completely separate words spelled *pallet.* One derives from an Old French word for *straw* and means a bed or mattress of straw, a small or poor bed (*On your midnight pallet lying,/ Listen, and undo the door. The sick man was found in a wretched garret on a miserable pallet*). A second word, derived from the French *palette,* a flat-bladed instrument, has many technical applications. It is applied to special instruments in ceramics, horology, and gilding, none of which are in common use.

A *pallette,* derived from the same French word, is a term in armory describing a small armpit plate or a piece of armor for the head. And even here, just to add to the confusion, *palette* is the preferred spelling and *pallet* is an acceptable variant.

pales into insignificance. To say of something that loses much of its seeming importance in the light of certain circumstances that it *pales into insignificance* is to employ a phrase worn smooth by repetition.

palladium. The plural is *palladiums* or *palladia.*

pall mall; Pall Mall. See **mall.**

palmy days. The original sense of *palm* is the palm of the hand. The tree is so called because of the shape of its fronds, resembling the palm of the hand with the fingers expanded. A leaf of the palm tree was in ancient times carried or worn as a symbol of victory or triumph on festal occasions. Hence the word *palm* came of itself to stand for victory or triumph. *To receive the palm* was to be acknowledged as supreme and victorious, *to yield the palm* was to concede another's superiority, *to dispute the palm* was to question another's claim to superiority, and so on. One's *palmy days* were the time of one's glory and acknowledged excellence, unchallenged superiority. But *palmy state* and *palmy days* are now hackneyed, worn out and meaningless.

palpable lie. That is properly palpable which can be felt by touch. When a doctor palpates a patient's abdomen he presses down upon it with his fingers to see if he can feel anything abnormal in its contents. A *palpable lie* is, therefore, a lie so gross that you can actually *feel* it. Whoever first made this figurative extension was a bold and fortunate man. The violence of its exaggeration no doubt paralleled the violent exaggeration of the lie that moved him to the coinage. But centuries of use have worn it bare. Its meaning and glory have departed.

paltry. See **petty.**

panacea derives from a Greek word meaning "all-healing" and means a remedy for all diseases, a cure-all (*At first penicillin was hailed by the lay press as a panacea*). It is, therefore, incorrect to speak of a panacea for any particular disease (as *a panacea for polio, a panacea for cancer,* etc.). The same holds for figurative uses of the word. *A panacea for our social ills* is correct. *A panacea for the stock market* is not.

pandemic. See **epidemic.**

panegyric; praise. *Panegyric* is not synonymous with *praise.* It describes an oration, discourse, or formal writing in praise of a person or a thing, a eulogy (*I profess to write, not his panegyric, which must be all praise, but his Life*—James Boswell, of his *Life of Johnson*). The emphasis in *panegyric* is on public, formal praise, whether in speech or writing. See also **elegy; eulogy.**

panhandle. In America and England *panhandle* has the simple, basic meaning of the handle of a pan. In the United States there are two figurative extensions of this meaning. As a standard noun *panhandle* may describe a narrow projecting strip of land, especially part of a state extending between two others. West Virginia, Texas, Oklahoma, Idaho and Alaska have panhandles. There is a slang verb, *panhandle,* which suggests figuratively holding out a pan or cup for alms, hence begging, especially begging on the street (*Men in Skid Row are quick to panhandle each other*). From this verb there is a further slang noun, *panhandler,* one who panhandles (*You can't go a block on Michigan Avenue without having to claw off half a dozen panhandlers*).

panic. As an intransitive and a transitive verb, *panic* has the present participle, *panicking,* and the past and past participle, *panicked.*

In its transitive sense, *panic* means to affect with panic, a demoralizing terror with or without clear cause, often as affecting a group of persons or animals (*Word of the German breakthrough panicked civilians clogging the roads from Paris*). To *panic* also has, in theatrical slang, the meaning of to amuse an audience to the point of rendering it hysterical and disorganized (*Will Rogers panicked them with his Oklahoma drawl and his rope tricks*). In its intransitive sense, *panic* means to be affected with panic (*At the first shot the whole herd panicked*).

pants, a familiar abbreviation of *pantaloons,* in American use means men's trousers (*Sam, you made the pants too long. She wears the pants in that family*). In England *pants* is the colloquial term for *drawers* (what Americans would call *underpants*), garments for the lower part of the body and legs, to be worn next to the skin. This British sense is in America applied only to women's lower undergarments, though the more usual term is *panties* (*Ten students were suspended today after having entered the women's dormitory last night and taken several pairs of panties*).

The word refers to one garment but is treated as a plural, as in *these pants are new.* In order to use the word with a singular verb or to speak of more than one garment, it is necessary to say *this pair of pants is new* or *several pairs of pants.* The form *pants* is also used as the first element in a compound, as in *a pants pocket.*

papyrus. The plural is *papyruses* or *papyri.*

parable. See **allegory, myth.**

paradise; paradisal; heavenly. Whatever its perfections as a place, *paradise* has a peculiar imperfection as an English noun: it is extraordinarily difficult to base a satisfactory adjective on it. *Paradisaic, paradisaical, paradisiac, paradisiacal, paradisean, paradisal, paradisic, paradisical*—though correctly formed all sound awkward. Of them, in Fowler's opinion at least, *paradisal* is the least intolerable because it retains the sound of the last syllable of *paradise. Paradisaic, paradisaical, paradisial* and *paradisian* are ill formed on the substantive root, though this is not a matter of much concern to the common speaker or writer. Fowler's concluding suggestion, no doubt at least semi-humorous, that the wise man abandon the search and "take refuge" in *heavenly* is not wholly satisfactory because heaven and paradise are not the same places and have wholly different atmospheres, rights, privileges, and conditions. Then *heavenly* has become an enfeebled gushword. *Paradise* has a much stronger connotation of sensual delights, probably from its oriental associations, and, at the same time, a wistfulness or ominousness, from the Biblical associations, at the evanescence of its pleasures and the imminence of separation and expulsion.

paradox. A *paradox* is a statement which seems absurd, obviously untrue, self-contradictory, yet which upon investigation or explanation will be seen to be well founded. Many riddles are paradoxes (*These are old fond paradoxes to make fools laugh i' the alehouse*), but so also are many profound statements. Paradoxes are much used in rhetoric because of the force of their seeming self-contradiction. A good example is supplied by the 9th and 10th verses of the 6th chapter of Second Corinthians: *As unknown, and yet well known; as dying, and, behold, we live; as chastened, and not killed; as sorrowful, yet always rejoicing; as poor, yet making many rich; as having nothing, and yet possessing all things.*

The adjective is *paradoxical.* He who indulges in paradoxes is a *paradoxer.* And the holding and defending of paradoxes is *paradoxology.*

paraffin. See **kerosene.**

paragraphs. The break made by a new paragraph has two purposes. It causes the reader to make a fresh start and it breaks the monotony of the printed page. How long a paragraph should be depends a great deal on such mechanical matters as the size of the page, the width of the columns, the kind of type used. Breaks should be made where there is also some break in thought, where making a fresh start will not be disrupting. But as a rule, almost any paragraph could be broken into more than one or merged with the preceding or the following paragraph.

In general, paragraphs are longer in technical or intellectual material than in material that appeals to the emotions or is intended as entertainment. Paragraphs that are too long are fatiguing because they are difficult to follow. Paragraphs that are too short give the material an excited, hurried tone that may also be exhausting.

parallel constructions. Correlative conjunctions, such as *either . . . or, not only . . . but, both . . . and,* are used to connect statements or phrases that have the same importance in the sentence. It is sometimes claimed that the words which follow one member of the pair must be grammatically identical with the words which follow the other. This is called the rule of parallel construction. The sentence *they not only tell lies but bad lies* violates the rule, which requires either *they tell not only lies but bad lies* or *they not only tell lies but tell bad lies.* The original sentence is said to be faulty because the first conjunction is followed by a verb and the second is not.

This sentence was written by Jowett, and all the great writers of English, including Burke, De Quincey, Macaulay, have used correlatives more freely than the rule allows. Sometimes the difference is that they fail to repeat a word, such as *tell* in the example just given, and sometimes they do repeat a word unnecessarily, such as the second *he* in *he not only tells lies but he tells bad ones.* Constructions of this kind are standard literary English. The groups of words joined by a pair of conjunctions should not be so different that the feeling of similarity is lost. But so long as the intention is clear, there is no reason why one should use a stiff, unnatural English. Sentence rhythm and the spacing of significant words are very important factors in effective writing. They should not be sacrificed for mathematical precision, which has no value at all where it is not needed.

Whether and *or* are also correlative conjunctions. But the *or* is so often followed by the single word *not* that no one claims a parallel construction is necessary here.

paralysis. The plural is *paralyses.*

paramount is an adjective meaning above others in rank or authority, superior in power or jurisdiction (*In the eighteenth century England became the paramount power in India*), chief in importance, supreme, preëminent (*Matters of paramount importance are rarely discussed on the floor of the conference*). *Paramount* must not be used as a mere synonym of *important.* When a thing is said to be paramount, it can only mean that it is more important than all other things concerned.

paramount and **tantamount** look deceptively alike but they mean very different things. *Paramount* means supreme in rank, preëminent. *Tantamount* means equivalent, as in value, force, effect, or significance. It is usually followed by *to* (*Your statement is tantamount to a confession*).

Tantamount is properly applied to acts and statements but not to material things.

paramour. As a term for an illicit lover, especially of a married person, *paramour* is now slightly archaic and poetic. Yet there does not appear to be any modern substitute. Current usage seems to prefer that certain things shall be nameless.

paraphrase is a statement of the meaning of a text or passage in other words, for clearness, often to reveal some hidden meaning in the original. It is a free rendering or translation. Or it can even be a mere re-ordering of the language of the original (*Shakespeare's* Antony and Cleopatra *is a brilliant paraphrase of a section of North's* Plutarch).

paraphysis. The plural is *paraphyses.*

parasol; umbrella; sunshade. A *parasol* has always meant in English a light, portable protection against the sun, a carried sunshade. It is now restricted to such a device as carried by women (*What he saw was . . . a lady, at the stern, with a pink parasol*). *Umbrella* was at first used as a synonym for *parasol* but by the beginning of the eighteenth century it had become fixed in its modern meaning of a protection against both sun and rain, but especially against rain, carried by men and women. Swift, in his *Description of a City Shower* (1710) wrote of *The tuck'd up semstress* who walked with hasty strides *While streams run down her oil'd umbrella's sides.* Obviously the thing and the name were in common use by that time although there is a persistent legend, supported by almost every standard work of reference, that the umbrella was "invented," "introduced," or "pioneered" by Jonas Hanway (1712-1786).

A *sunshade* in its most general sense is something that protects from the rays of the sun. It thus includes visor, parasol, and any kind of an umbrella whether portable or stationary, lattice or awning. In contemporary American usage it refers often to a kind of awning in front of a store.

pardon me; excuse me. See **apology.**

parenthesis. The plural is *parentheses.* Parentheses are used chiefly to enclose explanatory material that is not to be considered part of the actual sentence. Specifically, they are used:

1. To illustrate, define or add information, as in *With so many new suburbs* (*now 14*) *springing up, the city public health program must be expanded* and *The Lexington* (*Kentucky*) *parade float won the prize.*

2. To set off comments or describe actions not intended to be included in the main statement, especially in dialogue written without quotation marks, as in *Erica* (*laughing*): *Well, that's what he said!* and *Q: Do you recognize this man* (*handing photograph to the witness*). *A:* (*examining photograph*) *No, I don't think I have ever seen him.*

3. To enclose letters or numbers in a series, as in *The reasons are as follows:* (*1*)................; (*2*) ....; *and* (*3*)...................

4. To eliminate any confusion in numbers

spelled out, the corresponding figure is inserted, enclosed in parentheses, as in *Please send seven (7) mongooses immediately.*

When a complete sentence is in parentheses, the period comes before the final parenthesis. Punctuation belonging to an including sentence comes after the parenthesis. A reference in parentheses at the end of a sentence comes before the period, as in *The new statistics reveal substantial changes (see fig. 1).*

When more than one paragraph is to be put in parentheses, each paragraph should begin with a parenthesis but only the last paragraph should end with a parenthesis.

Sometimes the parenthesis and the dash are used together. This is not necessary; in such a case the two marks are serving approximately the same purpose, and one should be dropped.

par excellence. The use of the French phrase *par excellence,* "by excellence or superiority," to mean preëminently or superior to others of its kind (*Of course the illustration par excellence is . . .*) is a cliché. The word *good* is usually preferable and usually more effective (*A good example is . . .*). Where the idea of supremacy is to be expressed it is better to say *the best example* or *the supreme example* or *a most illuminating* or *a most fitting example.* There are dozens of words and phrases that will do the job better than *par excellence.*

parish; parochial. Only in England is there an ecclesiastical division known as a *parish,* a subdivision of a county, originally a township or cluster of townships having its own Established Church and clergyman. In the United States the term, in its ecclesiastical sense, is more restrictive, since it describes a local church with its field of activity (*American parishes overlap, since there is no state church, and local churches draw their membership from a common area*). In both England and America *parish* may describe a non-ecclesiastical district. In England it is a civil district or administrative division of a county. In America (in Louisiana only) it is a county. In both countries *parish* may describe the people of a parish, ecclesiastical or civil (*The parish was resolved to have its bingo*).

The adjective is *parochial.* Americans often use *parochial* in a sense corresponding to the English *denominational.* A parochial school, to an American, means a school administered by a religious body, especially Roman Catholic or Lutheran, as distinct from one administered by the government. *Parochial* also implies a narrow quality of mind or a limited range of interest, a mind or point of view confined to or interested only in one's own parish or some small field (*Despite his cosmopolitan environment, the average New Yorker is parochial in outlook*).

park (noun). The commonest American meaning of *park,* a meaning also familiar in England, is a tract of land set apart, as by a city or a nation, for the benefit of the public (*London's Regent Park compares with New York's Central Park . . . but there are no such extensive parks in England as the Yellowstone or the Yosemite*).

Park is also commonly used in America to describe a tract of land set apart for recreation or sports, as an *amusement park* or a *ball park.* In a sense mainly British, *park* describes a considerable extent of land forming the grounds of a country house, used for ornament, recreation, and often for pasturing deer or cattle (*The deer park at Magdalen is one of Oxford's many unexpected beauties*). So important was the park to a great country house that it often formed a part of the name (*After the death of his only son Sir William retired to Moor Park, his country seat*). The British alone use *park* to describe an enclosed tract of land for wild beasts. The Americans alone use *park* to describe a high, plateaulike valley, as in Colorado and Wyoming, shut in by high hills or mountains (*The Indian name for these parks signified "cow-lodge" or "bull-pen" on account of the immense herds of buffalo with which they abounded*).

In two more senses, one popular and one semitechnical, *park* means enclosure. A *park,* or more commonly a *parking lot,* is a place where vehicles, especially automobiles, may be assembled or stationed. In military usage a *park* is the space occupied by the assembled guns, tanks, vehicles, stores, etc., of a body of soldiers, the assemblage so formed, or a complete equipment.

park (verb). As a verb *park* means to put or leave an automobile, etc. for a time in a particular place, as on the street. More and more the word is coming to mean leaving an automobile at some designated spot, either at the curb or in a parking lot, for the use of which a charge is made or the occupancy of which is limited by law as to time. This is not an absolutely clear distinction yet, but it is becoming one. If an American says *I parked the car* at such and such a place there is usually implied a sense of urgency or expense or limited time. If he says *I left the car* there is a suggestion that it is somewhere outside of the municipal parking lots or zones and not subject to these pressures.

The sense of merely putting or leaving the car, though American in origin, has been adopted in England.

In informal speech and writing, *park* has come to mean to place or leave in a suitable place or, rather, in a slightly unsuitable place (*He parked himself in Joe's office and has been there all day. Park your hat on the table here and join us*). The inseparableness of the automobile and social life in America has led *park,* in journalistic euphemism and slang, to be used as a delicate synonym for love making (*Many couples who have been parking at nights by the old water tower have been annoyed by young hoodlums*).

parlay. Unknown in British usage, *parlay* is a standard verb in the United States, transitive and intransitive, meaning to bet an original amount and its winnings on the same card or another race or contest and, from this, to build up with a gambler's boldness from a small beginning to a large fortune (*He parlayed his bet and won a fabulous sum. H. J. Heinz . . . par-*

layed a pickle into one of the most valuable fam-
ily heirlooms in America).

The word was formerly sometimes spelled
parley and sometimes *parlee*.

parley. In England the word *parley* is usually restricted to a discussion of terms between representatives of contending forces. This sense is
common in America where, however, the word
may also mean a discussion or a conference, as
it formerly did in British usage.

parlous, simply a variant in spelling and pronunciation of *perilous,* is archaic and its use a mild
and minor affectation. It survives chiefly in such
tired phrases as *in a parlous state, a parlous condition.*

parochial. See **parish.**

parody. See **burlesque.**

parole. In America and England *parole* means the
promise of a prisoner of war to refrain from trying to escape, or, if released, to return to custody
or to forbear taking up arms against his captors
(*Since the colonel refused to give his parole
there was nothing for it but to keep him under
close guard*).

In the United States, but not in England, the
commonest use of the word is an extension of
this to penology. *Parole* in America means the
liberation of a person from prison, conditional
upon good behavior, prior to the end of the maximum sentence imposed upon that person, or
such a release or its duration (*He had not been
out on parole a week before he committed another robbery*). Such persons must have a sponsor who will accept responsibility for them, and
they are said to be *paroled* into the custody of
or *paroled to* the sponsor. They must report at
regular intervals to a parole officer.

The English equivalent of *parole* in the peno-
logical sense is *ticket-of-leave* and the *parolee*
(as he is called in the United States) is on *ticket-
of-leave* or a *ticket-of-leave* man. Violation of
parole is regarded in America as a serious offense. The English public—whatever the attitude
of the law—seems to take a lighter or more merciful view of a former convict's lapses. For generations one of their most popular comic-strip
characters was Tom the Ticket-of-leave Man
whose burglarious adventures delighted the
young. Despite the dreadful nature of so many
American comics, it is inconceivable that one
could be based on eternal violations of parole.
But, then, American crimes are too often lethal
to be funny.

paronamasia is the technical term for punning.
See **pun.**

parricide; patricide. A *parricide* is one who kills
either of his parents or anyone else to whom he
owes reverence. It is also the act of so killing,
and especially the act or crime of killing one's
father. *Patricide* is specifically the killing of one's
father or one who has killed his father. Thus
parricide may be a synonym for *patricide,* when
the victim is a father, but *patricide* cannot always be used as a synonym for *parricide* which
can include the killing of a mother, of a sovereign to whom allegiance has been sworn or of

others who stand in a parental relationship to the
killer. The killing of a mother or one who kills
his (or her) mother is a *matricide.*

parson. From its traditional sense of the holder or
incumbent of a parochial benefice, *parson* has
come, even in British usage, to mean any clergyman, minister, or preacher, not solely an Anglican. In England today the term is slightly depreciatory. In America it is rarely used except
for humorous or archaic effect. *Minister, pastor,*
and *preacher* are the common words, though
the last, unless referring specifically to one who
preaches, is rustic. *Parsonage,* however, is in
use for the residence of a minister of religion.
See also **clergyman.**

part; parts. Either of these words may be treated
as singular or plural, depending on the meaning.
When referring to something inanimate, *part*
should be followed by a singular verb, as in *the
greatest part of these years was spent in work.*
When referring to a large number of human
beings, it should be followed by a plural verb,
as in *the greatest part of the population were
illiterate.* Similarly, the word *parts* must be used
with a singular verb when it refers to a single
unit or a portion, as in *three parts of him is ours
already.* If the plural verb *are* is used here, the
three parts become separate bits or pieces.

Only the plural form *parts* can be used to
mean "talents," as in *a man of parts*; or geographical areas, as in *foreign parts.*

part; portion; share; proportion; percentage. *Part*
is the general word to describe that which is less
than the whole (*All Gaul is divided into three
parts*). A *portion* is a specific part allotted or
assigned to a person or purpose (*Father, give me
the portion of goods that falleth to me*). A *share*
is a portion, rather as seen from the point of
view of the receiver than from that of the as-
signer (*That's less than my fair share. It was
agreed that because of the extra risks I ran I was
to have a larger portion than the others*). *Share*
also has about it, possibly for no better reason
than the rime involved, a suggestion of a fair or
due portion (*Share and share alike. Just relax and wait your turn; everybody will get his
share*). In a special sense, a *share* is one of equal
fractional parts into which the capital stock of a
joint-stock company or a corporation is divided.

Proportion should not be substituted loosely
for *part.* It should refer to ratio, to a comparative relation between things, or magnitude as to
size or quantity (*The proportion of organisms
that reach maturity is small compared to all that
start as fertile seeds or eggs*). *Percentage,* like
proportion, is derived from mathematics and is
often misused in general senses by the pretentious. It is best used in describing a rate or proportion per hundred, an allowance, duty, commission, or rate of interest on a hundred. In
looser use, *percentage* can mean a proportion in
general (*We hope for a lower percentage of casualties in the next landing*) and, in slang, it is
used to mean gain or advantage (*What's the percentage in working hard only to pay higher
taxes?*).

part; some. *Part* is not an exact synonym of *some.* *Part* means something less than the whole. *Some* means a certain unspecified number, amount, degree—something less than the total. *Part of our aircraft is missing* means that a part of an aircraft is missing. *Some of our aircraft are missing* means a certain number from the total number of aircraft are missing.

part and parcel. A *part* is a portion of the whole. The word emphasizes the separateness of the portion from the whole. *Parcel,* in the original meaning of this phrase, also meant a portion of the whole, but it emphasized the portion's inclusion in the whole rather than its separateness. The phrase *part and parcel* was a legal phrase until the end of the eighteenth century. It is now almost meaningless.

partake is not simply a fancy variant of *take.* It means to take or have a part or share in common with others. It always connotes sharing with others. One should not, for example, *partake of* a meal alone. As a matter of fact, one should not now *partake of* a meal under any circumstances, for the phrase, as a term for eating especially, is considered affected, genteel, stilted. *Share in* usually conveys the desired idea more effectively.

partiality. See **prejudice.**

partially; partly. Both *partially* and *partly* mean "in part, in some measure, not wholly." The difference between them (as Fowler has pointed out) may be made clear by their opposites: *wholly* is the opposite of *partly* and *completely* the opposite of *partially. Partly,* that is, emphasizes the part, and *partially* emphasizes the whole of which the action or condition is a part *(It was partly my fault. He was partially disabled).* If either word will give the required sense equally well, it is better to use *partly,* since *partially,* which looks more elegant, tends to be overused.

On the other hand, *partially* also means with a prejudice or bias in favor of a person, group, or side as in a controversy, unjustly *(Since he views everything partially, one cannot hope for a fair verdict).*

participles are verbal adjectives. They are sometimes used as adjectives and sometimes to form verbal phrases. See **-ing.**

The English verb has two participles. The first is made by adding *-ing* to the simple form of the verb, as in *breaking* and *mending.* This is sometimes called the present participle and sometimes the active participle. Neither name is satisfactory. The form does not show time and is used in past tense phrases as well as in present, as in *they were mending the wall.* Until recently it was indifferently active or passive and may still be understood in a passive sense, as in *it will bear telling, it is worth seeing, use every man after his deserts and who should escape whipping?.* It is essentially the form of the verb that refers to an action thought of as in progress (whether at the time of speaking or at some other time) and is used with forms of the verb *to be* to make the progressive tenses, as in *the box is breaking.* See **progressive tenses.**

The second participle is the third form given in the principal parts of a verb, such as *broken* and *mended.* (See **principal parts of a verb.**) It is sometimes called the past participle and sometimes the passive participle. It is used with forms of the verb *to have* to make the completed action tenses, as in *he has broken the box* (see **perfect tenses**), and with forms of the verb *to be* to make the passive voice, as in *the cup was broken* (see **passive voice**). But the form itself does not express time and may be used in speaking of the present, as in *glorious things of thee are spoken.* And it is used in the completed action tenses with an active meaning, as in *he has broken it.* Essentially, the second participle is the form of the verb that names an action as completed.

The participle *having* followed by the second participle of the meaningful verb, as in *having mended,* is sometimes called the third participle or the perfect participle. The word *perfect* may be confusing here since older grammarians called the second participle the perfect, because it represented completed action. *Being* followed by the second participle, as in *being mended,* might equally well be called the passive participle, but as a rule it is not given a name.

Besides being used to form the compound tenses, both participles may be used as adjectives. The *-ing* participles are adjectives in *a squeezing, wrenching, grasping, scraping, clutching, covetous, old sinner.* When they stand before the noun, as here, participles are classifying words. These, for example, tell us the kind of old sinner he was. A participle following a noun is descriptive, as in *a covetous old sinner, squeezing, wrenching, grasping,* and so on. See **position of adjectives.**

It is sometimes difficult to say whether a present participle is being used as an adjective or as part of a progressive verb form. If the preposition *to* is used to connect a participle following a form of *to be* with an object, as in *this was distressing to her,* the participle is certainly an adjective. If an object follows immediately, as in *this was distressing her,* it is part of the verb. If no object follows at all, either interpretation is possible. There is very little difference, so far as meaning goes, between these two uses of the word.

With the second participle there is a greater difference in meaning between the adjective and the verb form. The words *cut, grown, burned, learned,* are all second participles in *cut is the branch that might have grown full straight/ And burnéd is Apollo's laurel-bough/ That sometime grew within this learnéd man. Learned* is clearly an adjective and *grown* part of a verb form, but *cut* and *burned* might be adjectives or might be part of a passive verb. Most people today would take them as adjectives. When no form of the verb *to be* occurs in a verbal phrase, there is no question of how the participle is to be interpreted. It is part of the verb unless it is placed immediately after the object of the verb, and if it is placed after the object it is an adjective.

Written is part of the verb in *he had written a letter* and an adjective qualifying *letter* in *he had a letter written.*

When a participle is an adjective it may be qualified by the words *very* and *too,* as in *this had been very distressing to her.* When it is part of a verb form these words cannot be used. We cannot say *this was very distressing her.* Whether or not one can say *she had been very distressed* depends upon how the participle is interpreted. See **very.**

THE "NOMINATIVE ABSOLUTE"

The word *absolute* as used in grammar means "free" or "independent." The expression "nominative absolute" means a participial phrase that is not grammatically connected with the rest of the sentence and that contains the noun or noun equivalent that the participle qualifies, as in *that done, we started home,* where *done* is the participle and *that* the word qualified. A phrase of this kind has the force of a condensed clause showing time, cause, condition, or descriptive circumstance, and can always be replaced by a clause, such as *when that was done* or *since that was done.*

Both the present and the past participle are used in this way, as in *I having few friends, my business began to fail* and *the money spent, we went to work again.* The construction is unquestionably literary English. Some grammarians claim that "it is good Latin but not good English," meaning, presumably, that it is not natural English. But this is no longer true. The form was taken over from Latin and did not become popular in English until the seventeenth century, but it is now thoroughly naturalized. There is nothing over-bookish about *the river being high, we were afraid to go on* and phrases such as *that settled, everything considered, that being the case,* are in constant use.

When the word qualified by the participle in this construction is a personal pronoun, the rules say that the subjective form must be used. (*Nominative* means "subjective" and is applied to nouns as well as pronouns. The construction is called the *nominative absolute* because the nominative form is required here.)

The rule is observed in practice whenever an *-ing* participle is used, as in *she having finished the work, there was nothing for us to do.* An objective pronoun before an *-ing* in an absolute phrase, as in *maybe he can help, him being a scholar,* is considered incorrect. This is also true when no participle is used and the word *being* is implied, as in *it's very sad, and him so fond of children.*

The rule is not observed with a simple past participle. Milton, who uses the subjective pronoun before an *-ing* in this construction, uses the objective form before the past participle, as in *us dispossessed, me overthrown.* This is also used in contemporary speech where *him taken care of, we could go on* is more natural than *he taken care of.* Some people would begin a phrase like this with a preposition to justify the objective form, as in *with him taken care of.* Others would insert *having been* to justify a subjective form, as

in *he having been taken care of.* All three constructions are acceptable.

An independent phrase beginning with a preposition and containing an *-ing* form is called an absolute gerund phrase. Everything said so far and in what follows about the absolute participial phrase applies also to the gerund phrase, except that in a gerund phrase a personal pronoun is always objective, as in *with him being sick, she had a great deal to do.*

THE "DANGLING PARTICIPLE"

Very often a participial phrase does not contain a noun or pronoun that the participle can qualify. The word may be somewhere else in the sentence, as in *the children ran into the house calling for her,* where the phrase *calling for her* qualifies *children.* But sometimes there is no such word, as in *it rained hard coming back.* This is called the dangling participle by those who do not like it. It too is an absolute construction, but not the nominative absolute—because there is no nominative. It is a native English construction, not one borrowed from Latin, and is used by Chaucer and all our great writers before and since. But it is commonly condemned in textbooks. J. Lesslie Hall suggests that it should be called "the persecuted participle."

Children are usually taught that a participial phrase must either be a nominative absolute or qualify an easily identifiable word in the sentence. In order to persuade them that a sentence such as *knowing as much as you do, the situation is easily explained* is a grammatical mistake, they are shown sentences such as *having eaten our lunch, the bus went on to Chicago.*

The rule against the "dangling participle" is pernicious and no one who takes it as inviolable can write good English. In the first place, there are two types of participial phrase which must immediately be recognized as exceptions. (1) There are a great many participles that are used independently so much of the time that they might be classed as prepositions (or as conjunctions if they are followed by a clause). These include such words as *concerning, regarding, providing, owing to, excepting, failing.* (2) Frequently, an unattached participle is meant to apply indefinitely to anyone or everyone, as in *facing north, there is a large mountain on the right* and *looking at the subject dispassionately, what evidence is there?.* This is the idiomatic way of making statements of this kind and any other construction would be unnatural and cumbersome.

And the rule is still bad, even if these exceptions are recognized. There is no need to twist a sentence out of its natural form merely in order to make the subject of the participle also the subject of the principal verb. Good writers do not hesitate to use exactly the construction the rule forbids, as in *lying in my bed, everything seemed so different; taking up, by the merest chance, a finely bound book, it proved to be . . . ; thus loaded, our progress was slower; bred up from boyhood in the Custom House, it was his proper field of activity.*

The sentence in which the bus eats the lunch

is a mistake, not because the participle is dangling but because it isn't dangling, because it is firmly attached to *bus*. The rule should say that a participial phrase having the force of an adverb of time, manner, circumstance, should never be attached to a noun element in the sentence. To disregard this rule is indeed a grammatical blunder. And it might be added that the mistake is likely to occur when one is using *having* followed by a past participle. With any other form it is extremely rare, and occurs chiefly in made-up examples.

particular. See **special.**

parting of the ways. As a metaphor for the point at which a decision must be made and one of two different courses followed, or even for a personal separation, *the parting of the ways* (whether one "comes to it" or "reaches it") is hackneyed.

parting shot. As a term for a witty retort or an effective jibe or remark made as one is leaving, a *parting shot* is a cliché. It is a corruption, by the way, or folk-etymologizing of a *Parthian shot*, from the custom of the soldiers of Parthia, in western Asia, of shooting backwards from their horses as they ran away.

partly. See **partially.**

parts of speech. Words are traditionally divided into eight classes which may be defined, roughly, as follows.

1. *Nouns* name things. In this definition *space, time, whooping cough* and *earthquakes* are all considered things. In a given sentence a noun is either singular or plural. That is, an important characteristic of nouns is number.

2. *Verbs* show what happens to things. In a given sentence a true verb form must refer to either the past, the present, or the future. That is, an important characteristic of verbs is tense.

3. *Prepositions* show relations between things or events. These may be spatial, temporal, or logical.

4. *Adjectives* are words that qualify nouns, that is, they make the meaning of a noun more specific.

5. *Adverbs* qualify other words, but not nouns. It should be noticed that these five classes appear to be a break-down, or an analysis, of experience. They reflect distinctions which have seemed important to men in what they talk about. This is not true of the next two classes. These are purely grammatical devices and have no counterpart in what we call reality.

6. *Pronouns* are words that are used in place of nouns.

7. *Conjunctions* are words that show relations between other words, not between things.

8. *Interjections* are sounds that interrupt a sentence. They are put in a class by themselves because no rules apply to them.

The distinction between things and actions, or between things and qualities, does not seem as clear cut to us as it did to men a few centuries ago, and in modern English this classification of words is hard to defend. Nouns are freely made from verbs and verbs from nouns. Nouns and adjectives, adjectives and adverbs, adverbs and prepositions, merge into one another. Adjectives may be used as nouns, pronouns as adjectives, nouns as adverbs, and adverbs as conjunctions. In fact, most of the words in common use cannot be put into any one of the traditional classes exclusively. What part of speech a word is depends to a great extent on how it is used in a particular sentence. And even when we have the word in a sentence, it is sometimes impossible to say how it is being used. Of course, when it is impossible to say, it is also unnecessary to say.

The distinctions between the eight parts of speech, therefore, are not very helpful. But they do account for some of the preferences, and requirements, of modern English. They block out, in a rough way, the problems of language. And the old names are familiar to most people. All of this makes them as good a starting place as any for an analysis of English grammar.

In this book there is a general article on each of the parts of speech. These describe more exactly what is meant by *nouns, verbs, prepositions,* and so on, and list the problems that are involved in using words of each type. The problems, in turn, are discussed individually, in separate entries, and are cross-referenced to related problems. When he reaches this point, the reader will be face to face with the practical questions of grammar. The theoretical, or academic, distinctions will be behind him and he will probably find that the reality is not as strange as he had feared.

party; person. *Person* refers to one. *Party* refers to more than one constituting a group, whether social (*a dinner party*), political (*the Democratic Party*), or other (*A scouting party was sent forward*).

Party may be used with a singular verb, as in *the party was just setting out,* or with a plural verb, as in *the party were just setting out.*

When *party* seems to refer to one, it is in the special senses of one of the litigants in a legal proceeding or a signer of a legal instrument. And even here *party* means not so much one as a side (one or more persons) in a contract or action. Though *party* is not be to used in formal speech or writing for *person,* it is often humorously so used. Some authorities regard this usage as an Americanism, but Mr. Somerset Maugham, no American, referred to himself on his seventieth birthday as "a very old party."

Party also survives in telephone usage to designate a line shared by others and the person whom one calls (*Here's your party. To call another party on your line, dial "Operator," give her the number you want, and tell her it's on your line*).

pass. The past tense is *passed* or *past.* The participle is also *passed* or *past.*

Passed is the preferred form for the past tense and participle, but *past* may also be used here, as in *we past it an hour ago. Past* is now the only form used for other parts of speech, such as adjective, adverb, preposition. But this is a relatively new development. A gentleman wrote in 1773: *I received them handsomely at half past seven, as the modern English now is.*

Pass may be followed by an adjective describing the subject of the verb, as in *they pass unseen.* It may also be followed by an adverb describing the act of passing, as in *they pass quickly.*

Of the numerous senses of the verb *to pass* (the American College Dictionary lists 46), a few require comment. There is the transitive sense of omitting the payment of a dividend (*I dreamed that A.T.&T. passed a dividend*). This originated in America but is being accepted in England. Partridge believes it is an error to say that two trains *pass* when moving in opposite directions. He feels that one train can pass another only when, proceeding in the same direction, it overtakes it and goes beyond it, and that the proper word for trains going in the opposite directions should be *meet.* But *meet* to an American would suggest a head-on collision and *pass* is the accepted word under these conditions (*The eastbound and westbound limiteds pass between Erie and Buffalo*).

Among the intransitive senses, two are worth being mentioned. When followed by *for* or *as,* *pass* in the United States can mean to be accepted or received (*He made a grimace that passed for a smile*). Then there is a meaning of *pass* peculiar to America: a person with an inconspicuous strain of Negro blood who chooses to represent himself as a white is said to *pass* (*Possibly as many as 5,000,000 people with a "determinable part" of Negro blood are now "passing" as whites. Nettie went up to Cincinnati and passed; they don't write to her any more*). This may be an extension of the meaning of being accepted, or it may be a shortening of *passing over the line.*

pass away. See **die.**

pass up. The American expression *pass up* is the equivalent of the English (and American) decline, refuse, disregard (*Well, I guess I'll pass up the whole thing*).

pass, make a. Whether because of the frequency of the act or of the phrase, *make a pass* (usually followed by *at*), as a term for making an amorous overture or gesture, is now standard in American usage.

passable; passible. That is *passable* which may be passed (*That car's not passable here; wait till the road broadens at the foot of the hill*); which may be proceeded through or over, or traversed, penetrated, or crossed (*The roads became passable in early April*); which is tolerable, fair, or moderate (*The weather was passable, but I've seen it better*); which may be circulated or has valid currency (*Gold certificates are no longer passable; they must be redeemed at the bank*); which may be ratified or enacted (*I doubt if the bill is passable in its present form*).

Passible is a little-used and rather specialized term meaning capable of suffering or feeling; susceptible of sensation or emotion (*The Paradise Saints have bodies of flesh, passible, and such as must have food*—Baxter. *And as he [God] is the Head of that body, he is passible, so he may suffer....*—Donne).

passion; Passion. The sense of the Latin word *passio,* suffering. is preserved in the capitalized form *Passion* which describes the sufferings of Jesus Christ on the cross or his sufferings subsequent to the Last Supper, the gospel narrative of his sufferings, as in Mark 14–15 and parallel passages in the other gospels, a musical setting of this narrative, or a pictorial representation of these sufferings. The use of the word to designate the sufferings of a martyr is archaic.

The uncapitalized form, *passion,* has developed from the Latin sense to mean any kind of feeling or emotion, as hope, fear, joy, grief, anger, love, desire, especially when it is of compelling force. In popular usage *passion* specifically connotes strong amorous feelings (*He had felt tenderness before, but never passion*). And by extension it may describe any extravagant fondness, enthusiasm, or desire for anything (*She had a passion for fresh strawberries*). Its other specific popular sense is violent anger (*News of the defeat put the general in a passion*).

passivals. See **transitive verbs.**

passive voice. The form of the verb which shows that the subject is the recipient of the action named by the verb and not the agent, is called the passive voice, as seen in *the thief was robbed.* Only transitive verbs, that is verbs which imply both an object and an agent, can have a passive form.

FORMS

In English the passive voice is made by adding the past participle of the verb in question to any form of the verb *to be.* This may be a simple tense, as in *he was robbed*; a perfect (completed action) tense, as in *he had been robbed*; or a progressive (continued action) tense, as in *he was being robbed.* It may be an infinitive, as in *to be robbed,* or an imperative, as in *be hanged!* But the passive made with forms of the verb *to be* cannot be used in emphatic statements requiring the auxiliary *do.* We cannot say *he does be robbed* or *he did be robbed.*

The use of the passive in a progressive (or continued action) tense, as in *he was being robbed,* is a recent development. Until about a hundred years ago, the *-ing* form of a verb could be used with either an active or a passive meaning. Where we would now say *was being prepared,* George Washington wrote: *the entertainment which was preparing.* The new, specifically passive form with *being* and the past participle became popular around the middle of the nineteenth century. It offended conservative people, who claimed that it was pedantic, clumsy, unidiomatic, and not found in the Bible—all of which is undoubtedly true. One gentleman, writing in 1837, called it "philological coxcombry" and "an outrage upon English idiom, to be detested, abhorred, execrated and given over to six thousand penny-paper editors." But it was useful and it survived. It has spread rapidly since 1900. A grammarian writing twenty-five years ago said that the passive progressive forms could not be used in the completed action or future tenses. He claimed that one had to say *the house has been building* and *the house will be building* rather than *the house has been being built* or *will be being built.* This is no longer true. Today, very few people would say *the house has been build-ing*. Some people still object to *been being* and *be being*, but they have found new ways of avoiding the construction.

In present-day English, forms of the verb *to get* are often used instead of the corresponding form of the verb *to be* to make a passive voice, as in *he got robbed*. This is particularly true in the progressive tenses. People who object to *been being* or *be being* are likely to substitute *getting* for *being*, as in *he has been getting robbed* and *he will be getting robbed some day*. The verb *to get* can be used as a passive after *do*, as the verb *to be* cannot, and we therefore say *if he does get robbed*. A passive meaning can also be expressed by the verb *become* and a past participle, as in *they became known*. These three forms of the passive, *they became known, they got known, they were known*, are different in tone or emphasis. *Become* suggests a process; *get*, the simple act; and *be*, the resulting condition or state. This allows us a great deal of variety in our passive statements.

SUBJECT AND OBJECT

What would be the object of an active verb, as in *they gave a reward*, becomes the subject when the verb is in the passive voice, as in *a reward was given by them*. The subject of the active verb may be omitted entirely in the passive construction or may be introduced by a preposition. In current English the preposition is usually *by*. Formerly, *of* was often used in this way, as in *this dreaded sight, twice seen of us* and *possessed of the Devil*.

Theoretically, a passive verb cannot have an object. But in current English may also be made the subject of the passive form and this sometimes leaves a passive verb with an object, which is called the "retained object" by grammarians. In *they gave him a reward*, the word *him* is the indirect object of *gave* and the theoretically correct passive construction would be *a reward was given him*. But we may also say *he was given a reward*. This construction has been in use for several centuries but it is regarded by foreigners, and by some grammarians, as a monstrosity—chiefly because it cannot be translated into the other European languages. In Great Britain the construction is still considered objectionable when used with certain verbs, as in *he was written a letter, was sent a note, was telegraphed an answer, was done an injustice*. In the United States it is thoroughly acceptable, without restrictions of any kind.

In *they took no notice of him*, the object of *took* is *notice* and *him* is the object of the preposition *of*. Nevertheless, we can say *he was taken no notice of*. Here the whole compound *take-no-notice-of* is being treated as if it was a simple verb. Similarly, in *they hoped for something*, *hoped* is an intransitive verb without an object and *something* is the object of *for*. But we can say *something was hoped for*. Here again, we may say that what we actually have is a compound verb *hope for*, which is transitive. But however we explain them, constructions like

these represent an enormous extension of the passive voice as found in other European languages.

In English a great many verbs may also be used in a passive sense without being put in the passive voice. What is logically the object of a transitive verb may sometimes be made the grammatical subject without changing the form of the verb, as in *the pies sold quickly, the car drove easily, the fields flooded*. These forms are called "passivals." A passive voice, as in *the pies were sold quickly, the car was driven easily, the fields were flooded*, always suggests the agent. The passivals present the action as an independent fact. They are simple and vivid, and are generally preferred to a passive form when the agent is considered irrelevant. See **transitive verbs.**

USE AND MISUSE

The English passive is a powerful verb form. It is applied widely to constructions that traditionally could not have a passive voice, and it has a variety of forms which provide subtle shades of meaning. It can be used when one does not want to name the agent of an action, either because this should be concealed, as in *unkind things were said*, or because it is irrelevant, as in *the letter was mailed*. It can also be used to emphasize, or call attention to, the agent. For example, *a woman drove the car* has no special emphasis in written English, although it may be given an emphasis in speech. But there is a definite emphasis on *woman* in *the car was driven by a woman*. When the agent is mentioned in a passive construction it has more emphasis than it would have with an active verb.

The passive voice is a sophisticated device. It is used by educated people much more than it is by uneducated people. It is likely to be out of place in a narrative but is almost indispensable in presenting ideas and generalizations. One of the most conspicuous traits of current English is the large number of passive verb forms used. This increased use of the passive disturbs some people, simply because it is new. But a great many more find it very satisfactory. The claim that a passive construction is inherently "weak" or "clumsy" should not be taken too seriously. It may be based on nothing more than a love for the old ways.

However, there are three situations in which a passive voice may be undesirable. (1) The passive is not an effective form to use in a description or in a narrative. (2) When someone wants to know who was responsible for a given act, and a passive voice is used to keep this information from him, he is naturally annoyed. But he should blame the person who is not being candid, and not the grammatical form that makes this possible. (3) Finally, there is the passive of modesty. Some people seem to feel that *I said, I think*, and so on, are fighting words, and retreat into the passive in order not to inflict themselves on other people. Some think they know exactly how often *I* can appear per thousand words without giving offense. There is not a word of truth in any of these theories. Anyone who is only interested in himself is a bore, and he does not become less of a bore by using passive verbs. Anyone who is interested in the person he is speaking or writing to may use the word *I* as often as he likes. No one will ever see anything egotistical in *I like what you did and I wish you would tell me how I can pay you for it.*

past. See **pass.**

past history; history. *Past history* is redundant. *History* by itself conveys the idea of knowledge dealing with past events or the record of past events.

past master; passed master. The proper form in American usage of the term designating an adept, one who has ripe experience in any profession or art, is *past master* (*He was a past master of the art of prevarication*). In this sense it is always used humorously and in disparaging contexts.

Since this is the settled spelling, it doesn't make much difference whether it means one who was formerly the "master" of a lodge or club or guild and hence, assumedly, proficient in its secrets or one who by demonstrated proficiency had "passed" the necessary training or examination to qualify as a master—though, certainly, there is a difference between *a passed Master of Arts* and *a past master of arts.*

pastor; minister. *Pastor,* the Latin word for shepherd, was applied in the New Testament to Christ (John 10:11; 1 Peter 2:25) and thence transferred to the bishops and other clergy of the Christian church. It was applied to a minister or clergyman chiefly in reference to the care of his flock, as in visiting the sick, and so on. Bishop Simpson, in his *Lectures on Preaching,* made the distinction clear: *The minister* [he wrote] *is a pastor as well as a preacher. . . . As a preacher he speaks to the people collectively; but as a pastor he watches over them individually.*

Modern American usage confines both *pastor* and *minister* to Protestant sects and varies with different sects and even with the same sect in different localities and social groups. In Chicago, for example, *pastor* is used by Baptists, Congregationalists, Lutherans (Evangelical, Immanuel Evangelical, and Norwegian), Methodists, Methodist Episcopals, and the Church of Christ; *pastor* or *minister* is used by Presbyterians; *minister* is used by Evangelicals and the United Brethren; and *rector* is used by Episcopalians [reference: The Red Book, Chicago Classified Directory, December, 1951]. Yet in Evanston, a well-to-do suburb adjoining Chicago, there seems to be a preference for *minister.* The Lutherans and Baptists there retain *pastor,* but the Church of Christ, Congregationalists, and Methodists have changed to *minister.* And whereas the Presbyterian clergymen in Chicago are either *pastors* or *ministers,* in Evanston they are all *ministers* [reference: Classified Section of the Evanston, Illinois, Telephone Directory, April, 1954]. See also **preacher, rector.**

pastoral; pastorale; pastourelle; pastural; pasturable. *Pastoral* is both an adjective and a noun. Its first meaning as an adjective, in point of time,

is of or pertaining to shepherds (*Or sound of pastoral reed with oaten stops*). It can also mean used for pasture, as land (*The valleys of the Lake District are chiefly pastoral; they are unsuited to crops*). For this sense *pastural* is an obsolete variant. *Pasturable* means capable of affording pasture (*Though the field seemed pasturable, the profusion of wild onion made it useless for dairy cattle*). *Pastoral,* as an adjective, has many other meanings. It can mean having the simplicity or charm of pasture lands (*The landscape of the South Coast is pastoral*), pertaining to the country or life in the country (*Ours was a pastoral existence*), portraying the life of shepherds or of the country, as a work of literature, art, or music (*Pastoral poetry goes back at least as far as the Greek poets Theocritus, Bion, and Moschus. The Sixth, or Pastoral, symphony was written in 1808*). It also refers to a minister or clergyman or to his duties (*Chaucer believed that the good parson would devote himself chiefly to pastoral duties, leaving the pursuit of sinecures to others*).

As a noun, *pastoral* describes a poem, play, or the like, dealing with the life of shepherds (*The Bard whom pilfer'd Pastorals renown, / Who turns a Persian tale for half-a-crown. Though in form a pastoral, The Scholar Gipsy is one of the most modern of all nineteenth-century poems*). It is commonly conventional and artificial in manner. It may deal with simple rural life generally, and it was this meaning that Keats had in mind when he apostrophized the Grecian urn as *Cold Pastoral!* The noun *pastoral* may also stand for a literary work, usually of a hortatory nature, directed by a spiritual pastor to his people. Or it can mean a pastoral staff or crozier.

Pastorale is a noun. It is taken over from the Italian and applies only to music. It describes an opera, cantata, or the like, with a pastoral subject, or a piece of music suggestive of pastoral life. *Pastourelle* is also a noun. It is taken over from the French and applies primarily to dancing. It describes the fourth figure in the quadrille, a figure resembling the dance of shepherds and shepherdesses.

past tense. English has two basic tense forms. One, called the present, refers primarily to a period of time that includes the time of speaking. The other, called the past, refers primarily to a period of time that has passed away, as in *the Spartans on the sea-wet rock sat down and combed their hair.* The form of the verb which excludes the time of speaking is called the past tense.

The simple past tense is the second form given in the principal parts of an English verb. For most verbs it is made by adding *-ed* to the present tense form. There are approximately two hundred verbs which do not make the past tense in this way. These have all been listed in this book. (See the individual words and **irregular verbs.**) However it is made, the simple past tense of any verb has only one form. This is used in the singular and the plural in all persons. The only exception to this is the verb *to* *be,* which has the past singular *was* and the past plural *were.*

The simple past tense is used chiefly in speaking of a particular, individual action in the past, as in *he walked home.* It may be used of actions already completed at some time in the past, such as *finished* in *after he finished the work he walked home.* As a rule, we express habitual or customary action in the past by *used* followed by a *to*-infinitive, as in *he used to walk home.* See **used to.**

Did (the past tense of *to do*) followed by the simple form of a verb is used in place of a simple past tense in questions and in negative statements, as in *did Scott enjoy the concerts?* and *Lee did not say so.* The same form is used to make a simple past statement emphatic, as in *Ken did enjoy them.*

Had (the past tense of *to have*) followed by a past participle is used to show that an action occurred or was completed before some time which is also in the past, as in *he had told his story* and *they had walked home.* This is called the past perfect tense. Certain kinds of actions, such as thinking, hoping, believing, normally continue once they have begun. When a verb of this kind is put in the past perfect tense, as in *I had thought, I had believed,* the important thing about the statement is that the thinking or believing is completely in the past, no longer a thing of the present.

PROGRESSIVE FORMS

Was or *were* (the past tense of *to be*) followed by the *-ing* form of a verb is used in speaking of an action as in progress at some time in the past, as in *he was telling his story* and *they were walking home.* This is called the progressive past tense. It is also possible to speak of an action that was completed before some time in the past as in progress. For this we use the word *had* followed by *been* (the past participle of *to be*) and the *-ing* form of the significant verb, as in *they had been walking home.* This is called the progressive past perfect. The same form can be used in speaking of an habitual or repeated action in the past, as in *he had been getting up at five.* What is seen in progress here is the custom of getting up at five. In some contexts it may be impossible to say whether it was the act or the repetition that the speaker had in mind.

Until recently the progressive form was not used with verbs that naturally express a continuing action. This is no longer true. We may now say, for example, *I was believing every word of it* and *I was trusting him.*

In many European languages the present perfect is used as a past tense and the functions of the past tense are divided between the present perfect and the true past, which is often called the imperfect. Some European grammarians transfer these distinctions to English and say that the English simple past is equivalent to their present perfect and the progressive past to their imperfect. Statements of this kind often appear in foreign language textbooks in this country. It is true that the English progressive past can

never be used to translate their present perfect, but otherwise the distinction is misleading. The simple past tense is used in speaking of any kind of action in the past. It is used in speaking of completed action, as in *after he wrote the letter,* and of action that is in progress, as in *as he walked home.* The perfect and progressive tenses are merely refinements of the past tense and express these ideas without the help of additional words such as *after* and *as.* They are generally preferred to the simple past because they express these ideas more efficiently. The progressive form is more immediate and more vivid than the other forms. It is used to call attention to a particular act and has the effect of slowing down a narrative. The simple form is used to get on with the story.

Each of the past tense forms that have been discussed may also be expressed in the passive voice. (See **passive voice.**) When the principal verb in a sentence is in the past tense, the verb in a subordinate clause must usually be shifted to the simple past or past perfect. See **tense shifts.**

PAST SUBJUNCTIVE

The simple past tense can be used in conditional statements to refer indefinitely to the present or the future, as in *if he walked in tomorrow.* When a past tense is used with this meaning it is a past subjunctive and not a past indicative. (See **subjunctive mode.**) For all verbs except *to be* the past subjunctive and the past indicative have the same form and differ only in meaning. In the past subjunctive of the verb *to be,* the form *were* may be used as a plural or as a singular, as in *if I were you.* See **was; were.**

In a conditional clause the subjunctive *was* or *were* followed by a *to*-infinitive refers indefinitely to the present or the future, as in *if he were to walk in.* When not followed by a *to*-infinitive it refers to the present only, as in *if he were here.* A statement about the actual present that must be expressed conditionally is obviously contrary to the facts and the subjunctive forms *were* and *had* are often used to show this. That what is being spoken about is an imaginary condition and not an existing state of affairs can be shown without using the word *if,* by placing *were* or *had* before the subject, as in *were I you* and *had I the wings of a dove.* See also **can; could** and **shall; should.**

A past tense verb may be used in an *if* clause and still refer to the past, as in *if he came yesterday.* This is a simple indicative statement about a past fact. The *if* merely shows that the speaker does not know what the fact was. If we want to show that we are setting up a purely imaginary condition we use the past perfect, as in *if he had come.* Anything that is purely imaginary about the past is, of course, contrary to the facts and clauses of this kind are usually called "contrary-to-fact" conditions.

patent. See **apparent.**

pathetic fallacy. The *pathetic fallacy* is a phrase coined by John Ruskin to describe the tendency of writers, especially poets, to attribute feelings to things. *Pathetic* in the phrase is used in its original meaning of pertaining to emotion, not in the modern attenuated meaning of exciting pity or sadness.

The ascription of human feelings to inanimate objects had been overdone in the poetry of the eighteenth and early nineteenth centuries. Mountains mourned, winds sighed, fields smiled and trees rejoiced. Hawthorne says of a stream, in *The Old Manse,* that "it slumbers between broad prairies, kissing the long meadow grass, and bathes the overhanging boughs."

Ruskin, in deploring the use, reflected the new objectivity, greatly influenced by scientific thought, toward inanimate objects. He stressed the importance of seeing a thing as it is and rejected emotional attributions to nature of false appearances "unconnected with any real power or character in the object."

The present attitude of competent poets and critics is opposed to such attribution. As Professor George Boas says, in *Philosophy and Poetry,* ". . . our trees do not dance in the wind, our sunbeams do not smile. We struggle to avoid the pathetic fallacy."

However, most twentieth century versifiers disregard Ruskin and Boas and strive to emulate Joyce Kilmer, whose "Trees," one of the hymns of pantheism, mingles mixed metaphors and the pathetic fallacy in equal proportions. The tree, mouth on earth, robins in hair and snow on bosom, "lifts her leafy arms to pray." As Oscar Wilde said of the death of Little Nell, one has to have a heart of stone not to laugh.

pathos. See **bathos.**

patience; endurance; fortitude; resignation; stoicism. All of these words imply calmness and courage under trying circumstances. *Patience* may be active or passive. In enduring suffering with calm or, indeed, enduring anything with quiet acceptance and uncomplaining waiting (*He had not the patience to wait until it was given to him; he had to spoil it all by asking for it. Sad patience, too near neighbor to despair*), it is a passive virtue. But it can be an active one in the sense of endless assiduity with no indication of discontent (*With what patience the spider mended her web, day after day. It takes patience to learn anything so intricate as that*). *Endurance* denotes the ability to bear exertion or labor or pain or disgrace, without any implication concerning the moral qualities involved (*A winter campaign requires great endurance. There must be an endurance of evil, but one need not condone it. Endurance in quiet desperation is the lot of millions*). *Fortitude* is endurance of which we approve, patience coupled with noble courage (*The Duchess of Queensbury bears her calamity with great fortitude. Indifference, clad in Wisdom's guise,/ All fortitude of mind supplies/ . . . / When we are lash'd, they kiss the rod,/ Resigning to the will of God*). As its first syllable makes plain, *fortitude* connotes strength. It is one of the cardinal virtues. *Resignation* implies a voluntary submission of the will to the

purposes of some higher power, a deliberate restraining of complaint or reproach in the belief that our personal suffering is ordained in some obscure way for our own good and that it is impious to protest or even to cry out. *Stoicism,* conduct conforming to the precepts of the Stoics, who taught the repression of emotion and indifference to pleasure or pain, implies a calm fortitude, especially in the endurance of pain, without any of the usual external indications of suffering (*The Indians prided themselves upon their stoicism and felt the least murmur of anguish to be disgraceful. Only the stoical and the cynical can preserve a measure of stability; yet stoicism is the wisdom of madness and cynicism the madness of wisdom*).

patience of Job. In referring to the calm and uncomplaining endurance of the much tried man of Uz, the *patience of Job* (even though the Biblical narrative does not itself contain the word *patience*) will always be proper. But as a simile for the endurance of others, or a term for the utmost conceivable calmness in the face of provocation, it is hackneyed and to be used sparingly.

patients. See **inmates.**

patois. The plural is *patois.*

patrol; patrolman; patrol wagon. From its earlier sense of the act of going the rounds of a garrison or town for the purpose of watching, preventing or checking disorder, *patrol* has acquired certain transferred senses. In English and American military terminology it describes a detachment of troops sent out in advance of the main body to reconnoiter (*General Allen sent out three patrols; none returned*). In the American Boy Scout organization a *patrol* consists of eight boys; in the English organization it consists of six boys.

In the United States a *patrolman* is a member of a police force patrolling a certain district. The English equivalent is called a *police constable* or just a *constable.* However the constable is a constable at all times; whereas an American policeman is thought of as a patrolman only while on patrol duty. In both countries the district traversed is called the policeman's *beat.* The vehicle used by American police for the conveyance of prisoners is called a *patrol wagon* (more familiarly *paddy wagon* or *Black Maria*), that used by the English police is called a *prison van* (more familiarly also *Black Maria*).

patron; customer. A *patron* (the word is derived, ultimately, from the Latin *pater,* father) was originally a guardian, proprietor, or supporter. This meaning remains. Every charitable organization enlists the support of at least the names of the socially distinguished as *patrons.* To say *The Fords have become great patrons of higher education* is to use the word properly in its original sense.

As a term for a customer, a buyer, or one who attends a night club, a movie, or a theater, or buys a meal in a restaurant (or, more often, these in the plural, collectively) *patron* may be "commercial cant" and certainly is a little pretentious (*Notice to our patrons: We are not responsible for lost articles*), but it is definitely established in American usage. It may be base of merchants to flatter those who buy from them but usage is not concerned with motives: if enough people use a word often enough in a certain sense, that sense will become established and standard. And that is what has happened to *patron*. It is interesting to observe, however, that it is used less by shops than by theaters, night clubs, racetracks, and restaurants.

Stores prefer *customer*, and while this should mean one who customarily makes his purchases at a certain store (and so did mean in England, at least until recently, and in America at some of the more exclusive and expensive stores), it has come to mean merely a *buyer* [*q. v.*] and those who were formerly called *customers* are now often called *regular customers*.

patronize. Although most British authorities reject this usage as pretentious, *patronize* is accepted in the United States in its commercial sense of trading with or favoring a shop or restaurant, etc., with one's patronage (*We believe in patronizing our local stores*). To treat in a condescending way, an accepted standard meaning in England also, is in America now a secondary meaning (*Harvard men are thought to have a way of patronizing their less fortunate fellow collegians*). The least common sense in America is the basic sense in England: to act as a patron toward, to support (*He patronized several philanthropic causes*).

pause. See **stop.**

pavement; sidewalk. A *sidewalk* in American terminology is a walk, especially a paved one, at the side of a street or road (*On winter mornings he usually had to shovel snow from the sidewalk in front of his house*). The English term for such a paved walk is *pavement*. In America *pavement* means the paved part of a paved road, what the English call the *roadway* (*After the collision there was glass all over the pavement*).

pay. The past tense is *paid*. The participle is also *paid*. *Pay* may also mean to let out rope (followed by *out* or *away*). In this sense it is quite regular and has the past tense and participle *payed*.

pay (noun). See **honorarium.**

peak. See **top.**

peanut. American *peanut* is English *monkey nut* or, more soberly, *ground nut*, though the English understand and sometimes use the American term. The slang terms of *peanut* for someone who is petty or insignificant and *peanuts* for a trifling reward or remuneration (*Pauley estimated that altogether they involved less than $1,000,000—just "peanuts" in the whole scheme of things*) are not used in England.

pearls before swine. Urging someone *not to cast pearls before swine*, as a warning against offering art, literature, wit, or whatever it is, to the unappreciative, has become a cliché, to be used with care. Unless it is received with the same lack of thought that it is commonly spoken with, it is highly offensive. It is not merely that some-

one is called a swine. In this age of general abusiveness that might easily be forgiven. It is that one's own tastes, artistic productions, witticisms, or impulses, are considered as pearls. And that, in this democratic age, will not be forgiven.

peculiar. See **odd.**

peculiarly should not be used loosely as an intensive, in the place of such words as *especially, particularly,* or *very. Peculiar* derives from a Latin word meaning "pertaining to one's own" and it means that which exhibits qualities not shared by others or that which mystifies because it is so individual that we cannot understand it. So a memory, for example, which is *peculiarly* dear is not necessarily very dear; it is dear, rather, because it involves something not to be found in other memories or so closely pertaining to one's own experiences that a sense of its dearness could not easily be communicated to another.

pedantry is the undue display of learning, the presentation of material in a didactic fashion, or a finicking adherence to rules and technicalities. The pedant has been a stock comic character in literature because of his pompousness and lack of humor, his parade of knowledge without sense, and his remoteness from the everyday world.

Pedantic writing is characterized by polysyllabic words and circumlocution. It is most likely to be found in specialized fields of knowledge—where the necessary technical words seem to attract unnecessarily long and obscure companions. Authority and official position also seem to stimulate pedantry.

Grammar is a favorite haunt of the pedant. He is equipped with rules, which he is convinced came before practice, and effectiveness and lucidity, charm, wit, grace and the fine excesses that surprise us with delight are nothing to him. His sole delight is to pounce upon the violation of one of his rules.

peek; peep; peer. As verbs, *peek* and *peep* are synonymous, meaning to take a quick look through a narrow aperture or small opening, usually furtively or pryingly (*I can see his pride peep through each part of him. You shouldn't peek; you're expected to keep your eyes shut till we tell you to open them*). *Peek* is more often associated with children's games and usually has a connotation of childishness about it. It has almost been lost in England, where *peep* is much more frequently used. To *peer* is to look continuously and narrowly for some time in order to penetrate obscurity. (*And I peer into the shadows,/ Till they seem to pass away*).

peer, a noun, derives from the Latin *par*, equal, and means a person of the same civil rank or standing, an equal before the law, or one who ranks with another in respect to endowments or other qualifications (*He will be tried by a jury of his peers. He is the peer of any student in the college*). The word is frequently misused, however, to mean superior (as in *He is the equal, if not the peer, of anyone here* or *There may be a* *few others as good, but he never met his peer*). The error stems from the fact that *peer* in English usage describes a nobleman—a duke, a marquis, an earl, a viscount, or a baron. The holders of such titles are each other's peers. When they are tried by a jury of their peers, they are tried not by a jury of commoners but by the House of Lords or, as it is sometimes called, the House of Peers, or the Peers. Though they are each other's peers, they are not, legally, on a level with common citizens. Very few distinctions are now made, though formerly there were many and they were important, and it is only natural (linguistically) that the word which signified equality in the higher rank should signify superiority in the lower rank. But it is ironic that the error should be so persistent in the country which abrogated all distinctions of rank and reduced (or exalted) all to a peerage.

peevish. See **petulant.**

pejorative means depreciative, having a disparaging force. In grammar it is used of words which through certain uses and associations have come to have a worse meaning than the one they originally had and convey contempt or condemnation of that to which they are applied. Thus *knave* once meant a boy, a *boor* was only a farmer, and a *villain* a serf or peasant. Certain suffixes have a pejorative effect; *-ster* is one of these, though it does not invariably suggest disparagement. A *poetaster* is not a true poet but a mere versifier or dabbler in rime. In *punster* there is a suggestion of contempt for one who is addicted to punning.

pence; penny. *Pence* is a peculiarly British term to denote the collective plural of *penny*. The distributive plural of *penny* is *pennies;* that is, the word which describes the number of coins, in distinction from the sum indicating value (*I gave him three pennies to pay my threepence fare*). Since it is used collectively, *pence* is treated as singular (*Fourpence is the usual fee*). *Pence* is not used of American sums. *Penny* and *pennies* are used loosely, for *cent* and *cents,* a folk memory, perhaps, of the days before and the generation or so after the Revolution when the penny was a part of our currency.

penetrate; pervade. To *penetrate* is to pierce into or through, to enter the interior of (*Only heavy slugs will penetrate the armor. No one seems able to penetrate his reserve*). To *pervade* is to diffuse throughout, to extend activities and influence throughout (*Goodwill pervaded the conference*). If we say, for example, *The smell of ether penetrated the doctor's office,* we mean that the smell reached that far and entered. If we say *The smell of ether pervaded the doctor's office,* we mean that it was everywhere throughout the office. The difficulty lies in the fact that the two effects are not always clearly distinguishable. Oils and heat, liniments, and even ideas, can penetrate and pervade. This has led to the meaning of *pervading* often being expressed as *penetrating,* and where the two actions are inseparable the usage must be acceptable. But

where they are distinguishable it is well to use the proper verb. See also **pervade.**

penmanship. Pride in handwriting as expression of character is no longer cultivated. In fact, it seems to have been replaced by the notion that illegibility in itself reflects certain admired traits —such as dash, authority and savoir-faire. Perhaps our great-grandfathers spent too much time on penmanship, as they did on spelling, learning more to form attractive, readable characters than to express themselves in meaningful language.

In the late nineteenth century the approved style of penmanship was the Spencerian, recognizable by its light upstrokes, heavy downstrokes and elaborate curlicues. The twentieth century saw this superseded by the Palmer method, whose watchword was "free arm-movement." The decorative style of the Spencerian method was replaced by a simpler, more graceful script which sought only to be legible.

In most moderately progressive schools today, cursive writing is not taught until the third grade —and typing is usually offered as an elective in the eighth grade. It is claimed that small muscles are not sufficiently coordinated to make the fine movements necessary for handwriting; whereas printing is much less demanding. Many children continue to print as long as it is acceptable at school, or develop a combination of printing and cursive styles. If legibility is the aim there can be no objection to this, for it serves that end very well, and it may be that we have now waded so far into illegibility of script that the easiest way out is to go ahead with printing.

Certainly something will have to be done, unless we become complete artifacts and have typewriters built into us, for most handwritings now are almost entirely illegible. Much of everyday business still depends on written communications and memoranda and these must be legible. The Illinois Bell Telephone Company has stated that it loses $50,000 a year because operators can't write call tickets plainly, and probably every other large business suffers a similar loss, a loss which in the aggregate must run into many millions. Post offices across the country are full of dead letters, most of which are dead because they are illegible, illegible even to the staff of experts in illegibility which the Post Office has to maintain.

pen name. See **nom de plume.**

penniless. See **poor.**

penult, penultimate; antepenult, antepenultimate. *Penult* and *penultimate* are the short and long forms of a noun meaning the last syllable but one of a word. Of the two, *penult* is preferable (*The penult in* American *is i*). Similarly, both *antepenult* and *antepenultimate* are forms of a noun meaning the last syllable but two in a word (*The antepenult of* American *is er*). Again, the shorter form is preferable in the noun. In the adjective, *penultimate* and *antepenultimate* are preferred.

penurious. See **poor.**

people. In current English *people* is a true plural. It means more than one person and can be used with a numeral. This use of the word is now standard but it was considered unacceptable fifty years ago.

Originally *people* meant a tribe or nation. The word was commonly followed by a plural verb, as in *a people who have little in common with us*. The plural form was also *people* and two nations were usually called *two people*. When the word is revived for its literary or archaic effect, a plural with *s*, as in *two peoples,* occurs more often. This is seen in Tennyson's description of Armageddon, where he speaks of *the standards of the peoples plunging thro' the thunder storm.*

By extension, *people* came to mean any group of persons. Here too it was followed by a plural verb. But it was still felt to be a group name, like *family* or *jury,* and could not be used with a numeral, which would have meant more than one group. A grammarian writing in 1765 claimed that one could no more say *two or three people* than one could say *two or three cattle* or *two or three company. Company* is still a group name, but most people today have no difficulty at all in saying *two or three people* or *two or three cattle*. In its modern sense, the plural with *s,* as in *you peoples,* is not standard.

The use of *people* with a numeral was condemned by many grammarians in the early part of this century, but it is now standard English and is generally preferred to the word *persons*. We may now say *three people were present* or *three persons were present,* as we please. Most people prefer the first form, and *persons* now sounds pedantic or bookish. This may be because it is sometimes used to mean bodies, in contrast to spirits. Or perhaps *persons,* because of its association with *personage,* offends the popular sense of equality.

In its modern sense of "persons," *people* has the genitive form *people's,* as in *the people's opinions*. Some publishers omit the apostrophe and write *the peoples opinions*. This is unusual, but accepted. If the word is being used in its old sense of "nation," and if more than one nation is meant, the form *peoples'* might be defended, as in *two peoples' borders*. But even here *two people's borders* would be more literary.

pep (short for *pepper*), meaning vigor, spirit, energy, animation, drive, and so on, is classified as slang by most dictionaries (as in *I put in a new set of plugs and she's had lots of pep since then*). But in its use as an attributive adjective, describing college rallies and talks designed to stimulate enthusiasm before a football game, it is surely standard. No terms other than *pep talk* and *pep meeting* have been employed for thirty years and it would be hard to think of any other way of saying what these terms say without being tedious and pompous.

perceive. When used in an active form, this verb may be followed by an object and the simple form of a verb, as in *I perceived them stop*; by an object and the *-ing* form of a verb, as in *I*

perceived them stopping; or by a clause, as in *I perceive they have stopped*. When *perceive* is used in a passive form it may be followed by a *to*-infinitive, as in *they were perceived to stop,* or by the *-ing* form of a verb, as in *they were perceived stopping*. See **descry.**

percent; percentage. *Percentage* means a proportion reckoned in terms of one hundred. Thirty years ago *percent* was considered an abbreviation for *per centum* and was written *per cent.,* with a period. It was a prepositional phrase and meant "to the hundred." Today it is usually treated as a single word. Some publishers still print it as two words, as *per cent,* but the period has been dropped.

The word now means just what *percentage* means and is used in just the same ways. Perhaps *percentage* will disappear as other unnecessary words, such as *domestical,* have done. In the meantime, anyone who likes to make distinctions can do so. Some editors use one of these words as a noun and the other as an adjective, but there is difference of opinion as to which is which. The United States Bureau of the Census does not distinguish here between nouns and adjectives. They use *percent* in table headings and wherever it is important to save space. In the text of an article, they prefer *percentage* when the word is used without a numeral, as in *the high percentage,* and *percent* when it is used with a numeral, as in *three percent.*

perceptible; perceptive; perceptual. *Perceptible* means capable of being perceived (*Within ten minutes of the shifting of the wind there was a perceptible coolness in the air*). *Perceptive* means capable of perceiving (*Any perceptive judge would see the difference at once*). *Perceptual* is a specialized term meaning pertaining to perception (*In thinking we tend to move from perceptual images to concepts*).

perception; apperception. *Perception* designates the action or faculty of perceiving, cognition, taking cognizance of some object of which the senses can be aware, or an immediate or intuitive recognition, as of a moral or aesthetic quality. It may also mean the result or product of perceiving, as distinguished from the act of perceiving. In its specialized psychological sense, *perception* refers to a single unified meaning obtained from sensory processes while a stimulus is present. *Apperception* is used exclusively in a specialized psychological sense. It means conscious perception, perception clearly conceived, a full awareness that we have perceived.

perdurable, meaning permanent, everlasting, long enduring, eternal, was used chiefly in theological writings, and fell into disuse, even among the learned, about the middle of the seventeenth century. It was revived in the nineteenth century but remains largely a show word, a little artificial and forced. There are half a dozen better known synonyms which are to be preferred.

peremptory; preëmptory. *Peremptory* means imperative, dictatorial, leaving no opportunity for denial or refusal (*The peremptory nature of the demand angered the men but cowed them and they sullenly complied*). In legal terminology *peremptory* means that which precludes or does not admit of debate (*a peremptory edict*).

Preëmptory, formed from *preëmpt* and *preëmption*, is a much rarer word, referring to a special privilege to buy land resulting from its prior occupancy (*Since he had squatted on the land for five years, he claimed preëmptory rights*).

perennial, adjective, and **perennially,** adverb, mean enduring, lasting for an indefinitely long time. They do not mean recurring year after year (as in *You can perennially expect a cold spell in May in these parts*).

perfect; complete. That is *complete* which has all its parts, is fully developed, or carried to its fulfillment (*The toy ship was complete to the smallest detail. The plan has been a complete failure*). That is *perfect* which is not only complete but is also of high quality and free from defects or blemishes. A complete day, for example, would be either twenty-four hours or the full hours of daylight, depending on how the word *day* was meant. A perfect day would be a full day but also a delightful or successful one or one that in some way had fulfilled the highest expectations. It must have no blemishes. It must be unqualified in its excellence. And it is this last meaning that is conveyed in what seems a negative use of the word, as *a perfect fool* or *a perfect stranger*. Neither of these terms suggests excellence in the person referred to, but the adjective is not, strictly, applied to the person but to his folly or his strangeness.

For the use of the comparative and superlative forms of these words, see **comparison of adjectives and adverbs.**

perfectly is better restricted, at least in formal speech or writing, to its strict meaning of in a perfect manner or degree. In its common use as an intensive, to mean entirely or wholly or merely (*It's perfectly all right to go ahead. It's perfectly horrible of her to act this way*), the word is overworked. Usually it is a meaningless filler and the sentences in which it occurs would be more effective without it.

perfect tenses. Forms of the verb *to have* followed by the past participle of a verb make what are called the perfect tenses of that verb. For example, the present tense form *he has* followed by the past participle of *speak,* as in *he has spoken,* makes a present perfect form of the verb *to speak;* and the past tense *he had* makes the past perfect *he had spoken.* All forms of the verb can be given a perfect tense form. There is a perfect participle *having spoken* and a perfect infinitive *to have spoken.* These forms are called "perfect" because they refer to an action that is completed.

The forms have developed from the basic meaning of *have,* which is to possess. From a simple statement in which *have* is a full verb and *caught* an adjective, such as *I have a fish caught* or *I have a caught fish,* men came to use the form *I have caught a fish* to express the subtle notion of a present completed action. These are the perfect tenses. They are present tense forms if the present tense of *have* is used and past, if the past.

For a long time these forms with *have* could be used only with transitive verbs, that is, with verbs that have an object. With certain other verbs the same distinction, of completed action, could be expressed by forms of the verb *to be.* In some European languages *to be* is still used in this way and was used in English with verbs of motion until a few hundred years ago. These constructions can still be heard, as in *the hour is come* and *he was recently returned from abroad,* but they are now archaic or affected. For special problems in the use of perfect tenses, see **past tense, present tense,** and **infinitives.**

performance. See **rendition.**

perhaps. See **possibly.**

period. The period is used:

1. To indicate the end of any sentence, except one requiring an exclamation point or a question mark, as in *He went to town yesterday*. But a question which is actually a request can take a period, as in *Will you please return the book by next weekend.*

2. To indicate an ellipsis. See **ellipsis.**

3. For various typographical purposes:

a. It is used to indicate an abbreviation, as in A.B., Mr., Mrs. But it is not used with nicknames, such as *Al;* or with letters representing government agencies or some other organizations, such as *FHA, CIO, YMCA,* or compound terms, such as *mph.*

b. It is used to indicate a decimal point, as in *$12.35, 2.5 inches.*

c. It is used after identifying numbers or letters in a list, as in the numerals introducing the items in this article. If the number is enclosed in parentheses, the period is not necessary.

When a sentence ends with a quoted word or phrase, the sentence period always comes inside the quotation marks, as in *He said he would come "soon."*

perish. See **die.**

permission; consent; leave; permit. *Permission* describes formal or express allowance or consent (*Since she was only twenty, she had to get her parents' permission to marry*). *Consent* is a fairly restricted term; it refers to a definite decision to comply with an expressed request (*Silence gives consent*). A *permit* is something in writing, a written order granting leave to do something, an authoritative or official certificate of permission, a license (*He had to get a building permit from the city zoning commission*). *Leave* is restricted in modern American usage largely to the specific meaning of permission to be absent from duty (*He was on leave from the air base at the time*) or the time such permission lasts (*He got the usual two weeks' leave before going overseas*). It used, however, to be the most general of all the terms implying license or liberty granted to do something and is still understood in this sense (*May I have leave to speak? You have good leave to leave us*), but it is slightly archaic and hence now seems formal. Thus the old phrase *By your leave,* which not too long ago meant no more than "please," now seems stiffly formal and is used chiefly, because of this seeming excess of formality, ironically.

permit as a verb may be followed by an infinitive, as in *he permitted me to leave.* When the permission is impersonal, *permit* may be followed by the *-ing* form of a verb, as in *circumstances do not permit my leaving,* but even here the infinitive is more usual, as in *circumstances do not permit me to leave.* See also **allow.** For *permit* as a noun, see **permission.**

perpetrate; commit. *Perpetrate* is a transitive verb which conveys one meaning only: to perform, execute or commit something bad (*A skillful detective writer keeps even his most acute readers wondering who has perpetrated the crime*). *Commit* is a transitive verb which can be used in at least eight senses. Its basic sense is to give in trust or charge, to consign (*Into thine hand I commit my spirit*). In its commonest sense, however, it means to do, perform, perpetrate (*I committed an error in addition. We must find the man who committed the crime*). In their parallel senses, *commit* and *perpetrate* can refer only to the enactment of crimes or blunders and, unless one wants to use melodramatic language, *commit* is to be preferred. *Perpetrate* is often used humorously to imply that something which has been done is of the nature of a crime, as in *perpetrating* a joke or a plan. But in this sense it has been worn out and should be avoided.

perpetual. See **eternal.**

perpetually. See **constantly.**

persecute; prosecute. *Persecute,* used transitively only, means to pursue with harassing or oppressive treatment, to harass persistently, to oppress with injury or punishment for adherence to principles or religious faith (*Nero's evil reputation stems largely from the fact that he persecuted the early Christians*), to annoy by persistent attentions, importunities, or the like (*Most Americans have become reconciled to being persecuted by representatives of worthy causes in their communities*).

Prosecute, used transitively, is chiefly a legal term meaning to institute proceedings against a person, to seek to enforce or obtain by legal process, to conduct criminal proceedings in court against (*Violators of traffic rules will be prosecuted*), to follow or go on with something undertaken or begun (*He was prosecuting a course of studies begun nearly a decade ago*), to carry on or practice. Used intransitively, *prosecute* has the legal sense of instituting and carrying on a legal prosecution, of acting as prosecutor (*If you continue this trespassing, I'll prosecute*).

persiflage means, literally, whistle talk. It is light banter in which seriousness and frivolity are so mixed that the speaker may evade responsibility for what he wants the listener to infer. Since it assumes a superiority in the speaker and requires a skill and adroitness that few have, it usually degenerates quickly into sneering and scoffing. Except where one does not wish to be drawn into a serious conversation or wishes to annoy a pompous bore, persiflage is well avoided. It can be extremely tedious.

An unusually dreary form of persiflage is in America called *doubletalk,* a process in which the speaker deliberately uses confusing nonsense in order to triumph at the listener's bewilderment. The victim, after he has been bored and insulted, is expected to applaud the speaker's wit.

persistently. See **consistently.**

person. For the use of this word as a grammatical term, see **personal pronouns** and **agreement: verbs.** See also **people, individual,** and **party.**

personage; person; personality. *Personage* should not be used as a synonym for *person.* It means a person of distinction or importance (*When Lindbergh took off he was just another flyer; when he landed at Paris he was a personage*). The word was formerly used a great deal in England to designate a member of the Royal Family when a use of a proper name would have been indiscreet. (*A Certain Great Personage has lately been much seen in Mrs. Langtry's company*). In American slang the word has largely been replaced in recent years by the military term *V.I.P.* (*Very Important Person*), usually employed ironically.

Personage is also used sometimes to designate a character in a story or a play (*Othello is a personage the nobility of whose character many modern critics have questioned*).

Though not yet recognized as standard, *personality* is used widely in the United States today as a synonym for *personage,* especially to describe notables of the screen or radio or television. So-and-so is said to be a *television personality,* particularly when he is known to the public but cannot easily be classified as an actor or a newscaster. In this sense it is useful. *Personage* would be better, but the public has fixed on *personality* and shows every sign of adhering to it. See also **personality.**

persona grata, persona non grata. Except in the language of diplomacy, where it is too firmly established to be regarded as even a cliché, to refer to someone whose company is desirable as *persona grata* or to someone whose company is undesirable as *persona non grata* is pompous. It implies that the speaker sees trivial dislikes as matters of international protocol and veils the obvious in the dead language of dead learning.

personal; personnel. *Personal* is an adjective meaning of or pertaining to a particular person, individual, private (*This is a personal matter; I see no need to discuss it with a bunch of reporters*). It also means in person. A few purists object to this, insisting that if one is someplace he is, of necessity, there in person. But the moving pictures have changed this. An appearance may be merely on celluloid. A personal appearance implies presence in bodily form. Many film actors and actresses appear bodily in front of the screens that are to show their images. The public has to have a name for such appearances and *personal appearance* has been chosen. It's here to stay and all the philologists in the world can't change it.

Personnel (a French word, coined to distinguish the human element of the process of manufacture from the *matériel*) first appeared in English about a hundred years ago. In this sense, it was a mass word and was always treated as a singular. One might say *a large personnel* or *the personnel has been increased,* but not *many personnel* or *three personnel have been added.*

However, *personnel* is used today as synonymous with *employees,* and treated as a plural, as in *all personnel were asked to participate.* This use of the word as a plural is offensive to some people, but it is now established in business, sociology, and government and is not likely to be dislodged.

personal friend is an attempt to recover the value of *friend* which has been weakened, in general democratic and commercial bonhomie, till it means little more than *acquaintance.* None the less, *personal friend* is a cliché and a redundancy.

personality; character. *Personality* has taken the place in the twentieth century that *character* occupied in the nineteenth. It is now used chiefly to connote distinctive or notable personal character (*He has more personality than the other officers*). It may also mean a person as an assemblage of qualities (*These capacities constitute personality, for they imply consciousness and thought*). As a psychological term, *personality* means all the constitutional, mental, emotional and social characteristics of an individual, an organized pattern of all such characteristics, or a pattern of characteristics consisting of two or more, usually opposing, types of behavior (*"Dr. Jekyll and Mr. Hyde" is a classic story about a split personality*).

Nearer to the basic sense of the term is its application to describe the quality of being a person, personal identity (*The age of Homer is surrounded with darkness, his very personality with doubt*). It properly designates the essential character of a person as distinguished from a thing (*Man has personality as a tree has not*).

Personality is often misused for *person* or *people* (*The personalities involved in the struggle for control of the company are equally unlikeable*). Again, it is often used when *character* would be more suitable; for while *personality* describes the combination of outer and inner characteristics that determine the impression one makes upon others (*He has a pleasing personality*), *character* describes moral qualities, ethical standards, principles. *He was a man of weak character* is not synonymous with *He was a man of weak personality. Personality* may similarly be confused with such words as *disposition, manner, temperament.*

personality; personalty. Though both of these words refer to that proper to a person, the former describes those qualities which make a person what he is, while the latter, a legal term, denotes personal estate or property as distinguished from real property (*His personalty consisted of money and goods worth $10,000.00, his realty of a house and grounds worth $50,000.00*).

personality; pleasing personality. In common usage *personality* suggests distinctive or notable personal character, but there is no implication in the word itself of the nature of the distinctiveness. Therefore, the word frequently requires modification in the interests of clarity (*She has a friendly personality. He had a disagreeable personality*).

personally; myself. *Personally* is used by many to lessen the opprobrium that is commonly felt to be attached to the use of *I.* When a man says *I personally am of the opinion that . . . ,* he usually means to disavow any intention of speaking for mankind, or being universal, oracular, infallible. Such modesty is commendable, but the expression of an opinion carries certain risks and responsibilities that cannot be avoided by a mere redundancy. It is better to say *I* and accept the consequences unflinchingly. Some say *I myself,* but that is equally redundant and, to the ears of many, doubles the offensiveness of the first person singular.

Personally is justified when one wishes to say that so-and-so did something himself that normally would have been done by a deputy. Thus if one says *The president personally acknowledged the little girl's letter,* one stresses the fact that the acknowledgment was not, as would otherwise be assumed, the act of a subordinate using the president's name. If, however, one says, *The president personally shook hands with twelve hundred visitors,* the use of *personally* is redundant because he couldn't have done it any other way.

personal pronouns. When used as a grammatical term, *person* means the distinction between the person speaking (first person), the person spoken to (second person), and the person or thing spoken about (third person). In English there are four pronouns (*I, me, we, us*) which are first person, and one (*you*) which is second person. The seven pronouns *he, him, she, her, it, they,* and *them,* are third person, but so are all the nouns and all the other pronouns in the language. The form of a verb sometimes depends upon the person of its subject. For a discussion of this, see **agreement: verbs.**

The pronouns just mentioned, together with their possessive forms (see **possessive pronouns**), are called the personal pronouns. Formerly, English also had three other personal pronouns, *thee, thou, ye,* and the possessives *thine* and *thy.* (See the individual words.) Some personal pronouns are singular and some plural, but this is determined by the meaning of the word and gives no trouble. Some of these, such as *I, we, they,* are required when the word is standing before a verb. And some, such as *me, us, them,* cannot be used in this position. These problems are discussed under **subjective pronouns** and **objective pronouns.**

For some of the old uses of the personal pronouns that are now considered questionable, such as *I will build me a house* and *old Meg she was a gipsy,* see **reflexive pronouns** and **intensive pronouns.**

When words of more than one person are used together, it is considered courteous to place the first person word last, as in *let Sam and me know,* and the second person *you* first, as in *I will let you and Sam know.* But this convention is not strictly observed. A thoroughly polite person might say *let me and Sam know* or *I will let Sam and you know.*

personification is the attribution of personal nature or character to inanimate objects or abstract notions, especially as a rhetorical figure in poetry or high-styled prose. It differs from the pathetic fallacy (*q. v.*) in that it is done deliberately with no assumption that anyone will take it literally. When Carl Sandburg speaks of Chicago as the "City of the Big Shoulders" or John Crowe Ransom says that death is "a gentleman in a dustcoat trying/ To make you hear," neither expects the figure to be accepted as anything but a figure.

In contemporary poetry there is much less personification than in the poetry of earlier periods, possibly because the modern poet has less confidence in or use for his myth-making powers.

personnel. See **personal.**

persons. See **people.**

perspective; prospective. *Perspective* is chiefly used as a noun to convey specialized meanings in optics, architecture, and painting. It sometimes means the art of depicting on a flat surface various objects, architecture, landscape, etc., in such a way as to express dimensions and spatial relations (*Rossetti had a fine feeling for color, but he never mastered perspective*), the relation of parts to one another and to the whole, in a mental view or prospect (*Only after several years and much reflection could he regard the event in the proper perspective*), a visible scene, especially one extending to a distance, a vista (*Berchtesgaden affords a magnificent perspective*), or the appearance of objects with reference to relative position, distance (*In perspective, railroad tracks seem to converge as they disappear in the distance*).

Prospective is chiefly an adjective meaning in prospect or expectation, expected, future (*I liked my prospective father-in-law from the moment I met him*).

perspicacious; perspicuous. *Perspicacious* describes a quality in a person. It means having keen mental perception, being discerning, acute, penetrating, quick-witted (*Even a perspicacious reader may have trouble with Eliot's poetry*). *Perspicuous* describes a quality in the thing or person perceived. It means clear to the understanding, lucid, unambiguous, clear in expression and hence easily understood (*The report was uniformly perspicuous. So perspicuous a fool could only provoke a smile where a more cunning rascal might have stirred up anger*). *Perspicuous* has been used for *perspicacious* so long

and so often that those who insist it is now established as a synonym have considerable justification, but the *Oxford English Dictionary* labels the use "improper" and it does seem a loss to the language if so important a distinction is to be confounded merely because of a similarity of sound. The nouns are *perspicacity* and *perspicuity.*

perspire. Our great-grandfathers who sweat more than we do and bathed less, never heard of dry-cleaning and passed on their thick, heavy clothing from generation to generation, regarded the word *sweat* as indelicate and often expressed its meaning in euphemisms. Dr. John Armstrong, an eighteenth century physician, referred to it as *roscid balm. Perspiration* and *perspire* became the established terms of the fastidious. There was a Victorian joke that *Horses sweat, men perspire, ladies glow.* But *sweat,* like many coarse words, has a dignity and strength lacking in genteel substitutes (*In the sweat of thy face shalt thou eat bread, till thou return unto the ground*), and, of course, where one wants to emphasize the *sweatiness* of sweat (*Nay, but to live/ In the rank sweat of an enseamed bed,/ Stew'd in corruption, honeying and making love/ Over the nasty sty!*), *perspiration* would be ridiculous. It is not always as ridiculous, however, as the call-a-spade-a-spade school would make it out to be. Even euphemisms gain freehold rights through usage and the light sweat of fastidious people, a dewy glistening of the brow, is now more properly *perspiration* than *sweat.*

Sweat, however, is always the right word in reference to animals or to condensation on objects (*Iced glasses sweat in hot weather*). See also **sweat.**

persuade. This verb may be followed by an infinitive, as in *she persuaded him to go.* It is also used with the *-ing* form of a verb introduced by the preposition *into,* as in *she persuaded him into going,* but the infinitive construction is preferred. *Persuade* may also be followed by a clause. When the word means prevail on, the clause verb must be a subjunctive or a subjunctive equivalent, as in *she persuaded him he should go.* When it means merely cause to believe, the clause verb may be an indicative, as in *she persuaded him she was going.*

pert. See **impertinent.**

peruse; read. To *peruse* is to read through, to read with great care and thoroughness. One reads a billboard in passing. One should peruse an insurance policy, a deed, or a will. *Peruse* is often used loosely for *read* but such use is ostentatious and improper.

pervade; permeate. To *pervade* is to extend a presence, activities, influence, etc., throughout, to go everywhere (of a person), to pass or spread through (*Though he is rarely there, his influence pervades the entire department*). To *permeate* is to pass through the substance or mass of, to penetrate through the pores or interstices, to be diffused throughout, to saturate (*The spilled ink had permeated the manuscript, necessitating its complete retyping*). The words are, plainly, closely synonymous and in many contexts are interchangeable, but *pervade* is now found chiefly in figurative uses (*A vast discontent pervaded the populace*), whereas *permeate* is found in both concrete and figurative senses (*The oil had permeated the rug. The idea of progress permeates almost all social thinking*). See also **penetrate; pervade.**

pessimist. See **optimist.**

pessimistic. See **gloomy.**

petit; petite. The English adjective *petit* is now obsolete in the general sense of small or insignificant—though there are occasional literary echoes of it in such things as Edgar Lee Masters's poem *Petit the Poet.* In place of *petit* in this general sense we now use *petty.* In legal phrases *petit* hangs on (*petit jury, petit larceny*), though even here *petty* is taking over. On the other hand *petite,* the eternal feminine, is doing well. The French pronunciation and spelling have been preserved. The word means little, small, tiny. A *petite* woman is small and, it is implied, dainty.

pet peeve, a common slangy term for a particular aversion, is a dreary cliché kept feebly alive by its alliteration. In *pet,* with its suggestion of an aversion that is cherished and fondled, a hatred that we love, there was once a penetrating thought arrestingly conveyed in paradox. But all of this has been worn out by too much use.

petrol; petroleum. *Petrol* is the word used in England for what in the United States is called *gasoline.* The word was once used in the United States to designate what is now called *petroleum,* but this use is obsolete.

Petroleum is an oily, usually dark-colored, liquid which occurs naturally in various parts of the world and is obtained by boring. It is often called *crude oil.* It is used in its natural state, or after certain treatment, as a fuel, or it is separated by distillation into gasoline, naphtha, benzine, kerosene, paraffin, etc.

petty, paltry, trivial all apply to something so small as to be unworthy of serious attention. *Petty* connotes a good deal of contempt (*A petty quarrel. His fall was destined to a foreign strand,/ A petty fortress, and a dubious hand*). *Paltry* is even stronger. It derives from a word meaning a rag and suggests something so mean and worthless as to be despicable (*What a paltry fool, to delay forty people because he was two cents short in change*). *Trivial* means slight and insignificant. It is used especially to mark the incongruity of the trifling when compared with the serious and important. It is not as scornful a word as the other two (*I divert myself with these trivial things until I know for sure that I will be allowed to work on my great project*).

petulant; peevish; pettish. He is *petulant* who is moved to or shows some sudden, impatient irritation, especially over a trifling annoyance (*This petulant display over so slight and unavoidable a delay did his reputation a great deal of harm*). *Peevishness* is an expression of a more inveterate discontent than *petulance.* A *peevish* man's irritations are more ingrained. They manifest themselves consistently (whereas petulance may be sporadic) and evince a deep weakness of character. *Pettish* (meaning originally "like a small child") is a word not now much in general use. But it is none the less a useful word, suggesting one who, like a spoiled child, manifests irritation over matters so small as to be beneath the dignity of a normal adult's notice (*This pettish concern with who is or who is not served first is ludicrous*).

phalanx. The plural is *phalanxes* or *phalanges.* In speaking of military formations or other groups of persons, either plural may be used. *Phalanxes* is generally preferred. In botany and zoölogy the plural *phalanges* is preferred and this has a new singular *phalange* which can be used interchangeably with *phalanx.* In zoölogy the plural *phalanges* is used to mean one group, not several groups, and the singular *phalange* means one of the units of such a group.

phantasma. The plural is *phantasmas* or *phantasmata,* not *phantasmae.*

phantasy. See **fancy.**

phase; aspect. In an age such as ours which is strongly conscious of the difference between appearances and reality and sharply aware of the limitations of an individual's perceptions, terms such as *vision, point of view,* and *phase* have a strong appeal and have been greatly overworked. All one can say, in caution, is that *phase* should not be used merely as a synonym for *appearance* and that it should at least be alternated, for variety, with *aspect,* especially in contexts where ambiguity might arise from confusion with the special meaning of *phase* in science as one of the recurring appearances or states of something which, like the moon and the planets, continually goes through a cycle of regular changes in appearance.

Like *aspect, phase* is a complement of *point of view* (*q. v.*), and since point of view can be a very vague thing, so can *phase* and *aspect* and their vagueness is sometimes an attraction to those who wish to avoid the effort of being precise.

phase and **faze,** though pronounced alike, are totally different words and should not be confused. *Phase* is a standard noun meaning any of the appearances or aspects in which a thing of varying modes or conditions manifests itself to the eye or mind, a stage of change or development. It is synonymous with *aspect.* To *faze* in American slang means to disturb, discomfit, daunt, put out of countenance. *Phase* is almost never misspelled *faze,* but *faze* is often misspelled *phase.*

phasis. The plural is *phases,* from which etymologically the more common singular *phase* has developed. *Phasis* is now used only in the most learned writing, as a synonym for *phase.*

phenomena. See **phenomenon.**

phenomenal. In its original, strict, philosophical sense, *phenomenal* means that which is cognizable by the senses (*The wave moves onward, but the water of which it is comprised does not. The same particle does not rise from the valley* *to the ridge. Its unity is only phenomenal*—Emerson). It was applied, however (as in the illustration), to things which seemed so to the senses but of the reality of which there was a question. From this it came to be used to describe something which is perceived but cannot be accounted for—and this led to its being used, as it now is, to mean prodigious, unusual, remarkable, extraordinary, etc. (*Her first book was a phenomenal success. The rain has been phenomenal this season*). Fowler foresaw this loose extension of the word's meaning and sternly condemned it as "a sin against the English language." But his condemnation, though reiterated by a host of lesser authorities, could not stay the word's efflorescence or degradation. Its primary meaning now is certainly "extraordinary" or "prodigious" (*The new models have a phenomenal pick-up*). Where it will end, nobody knows. There are stars that after billions of years of stability suddenly explode and then subside. *Phenomenal* seems to be a similar phenomenon.

phenomenon. The plural is *phenomenons* or *phenomena.*

   Phenomena is also used as a singular with a regular plural *phenomenas.* These forms are offensive to some people but are used by too many competent writers to be frowned upon. Of the three plurals, *phenomenons* probably rouses less antagonism than *phenomena* or *phenomenas.*

phrases. Any group of words that does not contain a true verb and its subject (or an imperative) is called a phrase. A group of words that does contain these specified elements is called a clause. (See **clauses.**) Any part of a sentence may be a phrase. In *but to see her was to love her,* the verb *was* has a phrase as its subject and a phrase as its complement. In *it might have been,* the verb itself is a phrase. Phrases are sometimes named for the function they have in a particular sentence, such as an adverbial phrase, an adjective phrase. Sometimes they are named for the type of word that unites the phrase with the rest of the sentence, such as an infinitive phrase, a participial phrase, a prepositional phrase. The words *a prepositional phrase* always mean a phrase formed with a preposition, rather than a phrase functioning as a preposition, which is called a compound preposition.

phylum. The plural is *phyla.*

physical. See **corporal.**

physically, mentally, and morally is a cliché of the feebly eloquent and the sententiously vapid. Uttered usually with oracular gravity and measured emphasis, its bombination proceeds not from weight but hollowness.

physics. When this word means the science of matter or energy, it is always used with a singular verb, as in *physics is not what it was fifty years ago.* When used with a plural verb the word will be understood to mean purges, as in *physics are not what they were fifty years ago.* The only adjective form is *physical,* and this means material.

physiognomy. See **face.**

piazza. See **porch.**

pick and choose, as a term for fastidiousness in selection, is hackneyed.

Pickwickian sense. When Mr. Pickwick referred to certain of Mr. Blotton's actions as "vile and calumnious" and Mr. Blotton referred to Mr. Pickwick as "a humbug," the chairman of the distinguished club felt it imperative to demand whether these opprobrious terms were to be received in their commonly understood senses. It appeared that they were not, that the disputants held each other in the highest esteem, and that the terms were used solely in their "Pickwickian sense." The term has become a cliché of the literary and therefore should not be used in their company. It is totally meaningless to the unliterary and therefore should not be used in their hearing either.

   Like all clichés, however, it lends itself to wit because it is a cliché. Thus when Mr. Clifton Fadiman says of the cool reception that the first number of *Pickwick* received that "The book's reception was successful only in a Pickwickian sense," he is employing a cliché, but wittily, not as a cliché.

picture of health. To say of someone who seems in excellent health that he or she is *the picture of health* or *the very picture of health* is to employ a phrase worn smooth by repetition.

pidgin; pigeon. The proper word for the lingua franca composed mainly of debased English words following Chinese idiomatic usage is *pidgin,* a Chinese corruption of *business. Pigeon* is a still further corruption—an English pidginization, one might say—of *pidgin* and, though established, less common.

pie; tart. In English usage a *pie* is usually a meat pie (*steak and kidney pie, four-and-twenty blackbirds baked in a pie*). In American usage, it may be a meat pie or a sweet pie or even a layer cake with a filling of cream, jelly, or the like (*Boston cream pie*) or, if one includes the trade name *Eskimo Pie,* ice cream within a shell of chocolate frozen on a stick.

   Sweet pies are and long have been an important part of the diet of Americans and figurative extensions of the word (*as sweet as pie, as easy as pie, pie in the sky. The mayor certainly cut himself a mighty big piece of pie*) are favorable even if ironic.

   The American *tart* is a small, saucer-shaped shell of pastry, filled with cooked fruit or other sweetened preparation, and having (unlike the English *tart,* which in many ways corresponds to the American sweet *pie*) no top crust.

   It is a minor curiosity of language that *sweetie pie* is a term of vulgar and luscious endearment for a woman while *tart* (borrowed by the Americans from the English) is a term of gross disparagement.

pig; hog. *Pig* in America retains its original meaning of a young swine of either sex weighing less than one hundred and twenty pounds. In England the word is used broadly to mean any swine or hog, a secondary meaning in America. In both countries *pig* is used in a figurative sense to designate a person or animal of piggish character or habits, that is, gluttonous and filthy (*He made a pig of himself at the smorgasbord*). *Hog* is also so used in America, but it is a stronger, coarser word. As a term for one who takes more than his share (of most things other than food) or pushes in ahead of others, it is used in America far more than *pig* (*roadhog; that hog, did you see him cut in there? Come on, don't hog it all; leave some for the rest of us*). Indeed, *pig* is a mildly humorous word, conveying only a slight rebuke. *Hog* is strongly condemnatory. The English use *pig* as a verb, the Americans *hog*.

In metallurgy, a *pig* is an oblong mass of metal that has been run, while still molten, into a mold of sand or the like. *Hog*, too, has its special meanings, usually expressed in combination, such as *sandhog, groundhog*, and so on.

pigeon; dove. Although any bird of the pigeon family (*Columbidae*) is a *dove*, there are distinctions in popular usage between the words *pigeon* and *dove*. Despite the use of *dovecote* for the structure which houses them, domesticated doves are, by and large, called *pigeons* and wild ones are, in America, called *doves*. The wild passenger-pigeon is a marked exception, but its name seems to have become fixed and the species extinct before the modern distinction (which is by no means absolute) became established.

In poetry and literature *dove* is a term of innocence, gentleness and love. It was formerly much applied to women. In contemporary American slang *pigeon* is also applied to women but, while still a term of affection, it is slightly coarser, conveying more of the amatory nature of the dove than its assumed innocence and gentleness. In the lingo of the underworld *a dead pigeon* is anyone faced with imminent disaster.

In sacred literature and art the dove is a symbol of the Holy Ghost. So fixed is the word *dove* in this particular application that the use of the word *pigeon* in its place would be blasphemous.

pile Pelion on Ossa. It was the giants—so Homer tells us—who in their war against the gods sought to scale Olympus by piling Mount Ossa on Mount Pelion. As a term for heaping one difficulty on another until the whole thing becomes an outrage, the phrase is now a cliché. The giants and their war are known only to the learned. Pelion is now called Zagora and Ossa is now called Kissovo. It is, for most people, a meaningless phrase.

pilfer. See **steal.**

pillar of the church. To refer to one of conspicuous rectitude who is particularly active in his support of some church as a *pillar of the church* is to employ a hackneyed phrase.

pilot in nautical terminology describes one duly qualified to steer ships into or out of a harbor or through certain difficult waters (*The pilot is usually taken aboard off Sandy Hook*). A less common nautical meaning is steersman. In aviation, a pilot is one duly qualified to operate an airplane, balloon or other aircraft. This is probably the sense in which the word *pilot* is now

most often understood by the laity (*Pilot claims runway approaches unsafe*).

In a figurative sense, a *pilot* is any guide or leader (*When Guilford good/ Our pilot stood. I hope to see my Pilot face to face/ When I have crossed the bar*). *Sky pilot*, which to most young moderns would seem redundant, was a slang term much used a generation or two ago for a clergyman or chaplain.

In machinery, a *pilot* is a smaller element acting in advance of another or principal element and causing the latter to come into play (*Since the pilot on the gas range was out, he had to light the burner with a match*). A *pilot plant*, an extension of this sense, is a small plant built to test out processes of manufacture so that a larger plant or plants may thereafter be built and operated more efficiently.

pincers; pinchers. *Pincers* is the correct term to describe a gripping tool consisting of two pivoted limbs forming a pair of jaws and a pair of handles. The word is frequently replaced in America by *pinchers*, though this is dialectal, nonstandard. In recent years both terms have been replaced to a large extent by *pliers* and *nippers*.

The form *pincers* refers to one instrument but is usually treated as a plural, as in *these pincers are too small*. A singular construction, such as *here is a pincers*, is unusual but acceptable. In using a singular verb we more often say *here is a pair of pincers*, and the construction with *pair* must be used after a numeral, as in *three pairs of pincers*. The singular *pincer* is not used as an independent word but is the preferred form for the first element of a compound, such as *a pincer grip*.

pinch-hitter, as a term for a substitute, is a cliché. Except when used of baseball, the term is often misused. When a manager sends out a pinch-hitter, he assumes that the pinch-hitter will do better than the man at bat. But in other activities, when sickness or some other circumstance makes it impossible for the principal to appear and a substitute or understudy is rushed in to fill the place, he is not expected to do better than the principal would have done. It is a triumph if he or she does what is required in any acceptable fashion.

pins and needles. *On pins and needles*, as a term for being uneasy, impatient with overtones of anxiety, is a cliché.

pint. The British *pint* and the American *pint* are different quantities. In America the *standard pint* contains 16 U.S. fluid ounces and has a capacity of 473.6 cubic centimeters. In England the *imperial pint* contains 20 British fluid ounces and has a capacity of 568 cubic centimeters. The American pint, therefore, is just a little more than 83% of the British pint.

pious fraud. Originally a translation of the French *fraude pieuse*, referring to a deception practiced to serve what the practicer regarded as a good end, often for the furtherance of his religion, the term has come in common American usage to mean a hypocrite. It is applied far more often to persons than to acts or misrepresentations. **In** either sense, however, it is trite.

pit (of a theater). See **orchestra.**

pitcher, the word to describe a container, usually with a handle and spout or lip, for holding or pouring liquids (*Or ever the silver cord be loosed, or the golden bowl be broken, or the pitcher be broken at the fountain . . .*), is considered poetic or archaic in England but is the everyday word in America. The usual English equivalent is *jug.*

Pitcher has another meaning in American sports, where it describes the player in baseball who delivers or throws the ball to the batter (*Few pitchers manage to hold an opposing team to no hits in a whole game*).

piteous; pitiable; pitiful. *Piteous* is now restricted to that which exhibits suffering and misery and is therefore heart-rending (*He could hear the piteous cries of the injured children*). *Pitiable* means that which is deserving of pity or excites compassion (*Such a pitiable plea could not be ignored*), but it may also mean lamentable, wretched, or paltry (*They were in a pitiable condition, all ragged and dirty with no knowledge of the wrong that had been done them*). That is *pitiful* which touches our compassion or excites us to pity (*Tony Last's pitiful fate was to spend the rest of his life reading Dickens to an insane illiterate*). But the contempt which is so often allied to compassion has colored this word more than the others and one of its meanings is contemptible, despicable (*Your behavior was a pitiful exhibition of cowardice*).

place. The noun *place* is often used in compounds with *some, any, every, no,* instead of the adverb *where,* as in *they are living some place in Ohio.* This is standard English in the United States. But many grammarians object to it and hold that *place* must be made part of a prepositional phrase, such as *in some place* or *at some place.*

The word *place* is sometimes used as an adverb without one of the four qualifying words mentioned above, as in *we are going places tonight* and *what place are you going?.* This does not have the same standing as *some place, any place,* etc., but it is acceptable to many well educated Americans. (For *place* meaning "position," see **job.**)

place; put. The essential difference between placing and putting is that when something or someone is placed, it or he is put in a proper or assigned position or order. Something that is *put* on a shelf is simply picked up and set down there. Something that is *placed* on a shelf is something that belongs on that shelf. That is its proper place. No hard and fast rules can be laid down because no one can decide what is the proper place for another's things. To *place* something is also usually to *put* it with care and precision (*He put his car in the parking lot. He placed his car next to mine. He put the papers on his desk. He placed one sheet carefully on top of the other*). But the use of *place* as a straight synonym for *put* is vague and loose.

Place has some definite idiomatic meanings.

One can only *place* a person in one's memory when one recollects where and under what circumstances one knew him before. A horse is *placed* or, better, *places* when it crosses the finishing line of a race among the (usually first three) leading competitors.

placeable; placable; placatory. *Placeable* means capable of being placed. Except for a similarity of spelling which often leads to confusion, it has no connection with *placable,* which means capable of being placated or appeased, forgiving (*Since Hades was not placable, the Greeks offered him no sacrifices*). *Placatory* means tending or intended to placate (*Even the most placatory assurances failed to mollify the Queen*).

plague, avoid like the. To say of someone or something that he or it is to be *avoided* (or *shunned*) *like the plague* is to employ a cliché. It may be used, but should be used sparingly.

That all knowledge of, mention of, or reference to the bubonic plague in almost half the world is now confined to an outworn phrase is such an extraordinary indication of the alleviation of human misery that the phrase might deserve to be retained as a sort of monument.

plain as a pikestaff now means obvious, clearly visible. It originally meant unadorned, bare. But in whatever sense used, it is now a cliché. *Plain as the nose on your face* is also a cliché, with the additional disadvantage of being ambiguous and perhaps disparaging.

plain sailing is probably (*The Oxford English Dictionary* tells us) a corruption of *plane sailing,* that is, navigating by a plane chart or the art of determining a ship's position on the assumption that the surface of the earth is flat. In its figurative uses the term is a cliché.

plan. The verb *plan* may be followed by an infinitive, as in *they plan to come,* or by *on* and the *-ing* form of a verb, as in *they plan on coming.* The noun *plan* is followed by an infinitive in *I was thinking of a plan/ To dye one's whiskers green.* This is the standard idiom in the United States, but some British grammarians claim that *of* and the *-ing* form are required here. See **prepositions.**

planetarium. The plural is *planetariums* or *planetaria.*

plank, basically, means a long, flat piece of timber, thicker than a board. More loosely, it means something to stand on or cling to for support (*A floating plank saved him from drowning*). In a figurative sense, originally and chiefly American, a *plank* is an article of a platform of political or other principles (*The civil rights plank of the party platform was highly controversial*). This *plank,* a natural development of the idea of a *platform* as the body of principles upon which a party takes its stand to appeal to the voters (which, in turn, of course, is a figurative extension of the actual platform upon which a candidate would stand), has become so separated from the idea of an actual physical plank, being two metaphors removed, that most Americans would see nothing incongruous in being

plate 372

told that a certain plank has been "watered down" to appease a protesting group within the party.

To *plank,* meaning to bake, broil, and serve on a board (*Planked whitefish our specialty*), is a special American usage. In the sense of producing or putting down (usually money) readily (*He planked down a hundred dollars right then and there*), *plank* is slang.

plate. Certain uses of *plate* are exclusively American. In American restaurants one may choose a *plate lunch,* a *plate dinner,* a *vegetable plate,* *blue plate* special, or any of various other plates, meals in which an entire course is on a single plate. In journalism, *plate matter* or *boiler plate* describes a sheet of metal for printing from, formed by stereotyping or electrotyping a page of type, or metal or plastic formed by molding, etching, or photographic development (*Many a country weekly consists almost entirely of boiler plate sent out by a syndicate*). In baseball, the *plate* or the *home plate* is the home base.

In a sense chiefly British, *plate* means domestic dishes, utensils, etc., of gold or silver (*a salt-cellar of silver . . . one of the neatest pieces of plate that ever I saw*). See also **silver; silverware.**

plateau. The plural is *plateaus* or *plateaux.*

platitude. See **commonplace.**

play (as in *play the fool*). See **act.**

play fast and loose with. As a term for breaking one's word, making promises without intending to keep them, and being generally completely unscrupulous and unreliable in one's dealings with another, *to play fast and loose with* is hackneyed.

play the game. As a term for acting honorably, *play the game* is not as worn a cliché in America as it is in England. It is known and is used somewhat by those who admire the English and their ways, but, despite pious public pronouncements by coaches, a game is still, to the average American, a contest and winning more important than displaying good form and delicate consideration. An admonition to *play the game* would, by many Americans, be regarded as a request to stop bickering about the rules and get on with the struggle.

play with fire. As a term for trifling with something dangerous, especially in amatory matters, *play with fire* is worn smooth by repetition.

plead. The past tense is *pleaded* or *pled.* The participle is also *pleaded* or *pled.*

Pled may also be spelled *plead,* following the pattern of the past tense of the verb *read.* In the United States *pleaded* and *pled* are both acceptable for the past tense and for the participle. In Great Britain only the form *pleaded* is used and *pled* is considered an Americanism.

The *-ing* form of a verb after *plead guilty* requires the preposition *to,* as in *he pleaded guilty to stealing the watch.* When used after *guilty* alone it requires *of,* as in *he was guilty of stealing the watch.*

please. When *please* is used in a full verb form it may be followed by an infinitive, as in *he will be pleased to see you* and *I do not please to go.*

When it is used merely as a softener it is followed by the simple form of the verb, as in *please come. Come* in this construction is an imperative and the use of an infinitive, as in *please to come,* is not standard. See also **kindly.**

pleasure. See **happiness.**

plectrum. The plural is *plectrums* or *plectra.*

pled. See **plead.**

plenitude, for fullness, abundance, completeness (*The moon in her plenitude. The plenitude of the power of a king*), is now chiefly a literary word.

plenteous; plentiful. These words are synonyms meaning copious, abundant, existing in great plenty. Of the two, *plentiful* is to be preferred in ordinary use. *Plenteous* is chiefly literary.

plenty. In standard English *plenty* is a noun and is joined to other nouns by *of,* as in *we have plenty of time.* It may stand alone without a following noun, as in *I have plenty.* At one time *a plenty* was literary English, but this is now out of fashion. *Plenty* may be used with a singular or a plural verb, depending on whether it refers to something that is thought of as a unit or to a collection of individuals, as in *there is plenty of sugar* and *there are plenty of glasses.*

Plenty may be followed by *more,* with or without a noun. We may say *there is plenty more* or *there is plenty more sugar.*

Plenty is sometimes used immediately before a noun, as if it were an adjective, as in *we have plenty time* and *plenty money.* This is following a Scottish idiom which drops *of* after vague measurements, as in *a bit paper, a drap whisky.* The construction is not thoroughly established in the United States, but it is used by Scottish writers, such as Robert Louis Stevenson, and is acceptable to many well educated people.

Plenty is also used before adjectives, as in *plenty long, plenty high.* When *plenty* means enough, this construction has the same standing as the one just discussed, where *plenty* is used before a noun. But when *plenty* means extremely, as in *plenty tired, plenty angry,* the construction is not standard.

pleonasms. A redundant or unnecessary word that merely repeats what has already been said is called a *pleonasm.* In 1589, a grammarian wrote: "The first surplusage the Greeks call pleonasmus (I call him too full speech) and is no great fault." Since then, some grammarians have taken the stand that any unnecessary word is a grammatical mistake. Two natural English constructions have suffered, perhaps fatally, under this attack. See **double negatives** and **intensive pronouns.**

In general, pleonasms are a question of style or taste, not grammar. One may say *the reason* or *the reason why, gather* or *gather together.* Before anyone decides never to use a pleonastic word, he should ask himself how many of his sentences are necessary. A man who never said an unnecessary word would say very little during a long life and would not be pleasant company. Similarly, inside a sentence the mere sound, the mere number of syllables used, is sometimes more important than the bare meaning of the words. In writing, as in conversation, an economical use of words is not always what we want. See also **redundancy.**

plethora is properly a medical term, meaning an overfullness of blood. The word was much used to describe the condition that required bleeding, when bleeding was a common treatment. Today it is used to describe a morbid condition due to an excess of blood in the body.

The use of the word to mean any superabundance (*We have a plethora of wit but very little factual information*) is a little affected and bookish. If so used, it must not mean abundance, but a harmful excess over abundance.

plexus. The plural is *plexuses* or *plexus,* not *plexi.*

pliers. When referring to the instrument, the word means a single instrument but is usually treated as a plural, as in *these pliers are too large.* It may also be treated as a singular, as in *try a different pliers,* but the construction *try a different pair of pliers* is generally preferred. The construction with *pair* must be used after a numeral, as in *three pairs of pliers.* The form *pliers* is used as the first element in a compound, as in *a pliers case.*

The singular *plier* means one who plies and is never used in referring to the instrument.

plight. See **predicament.**

plight one's troth. As a term for becoming engaged, *plighting a troth* is a stale elegancy of the feebler society columns. Neither *plight* (in this sense) nor *troth* has been in common use for well over a hundred years.

plot thickens. As a serious comment on the increasing complexity of the action of a play or novel or even of things in general, *the plot thickens* has been a cliché for almost a century. As a humorous remark it is now also a cliché.

plough the sands. As a term for an effort which by its very nature is doomed to sterility, *plough the sands* is hackneyed. It is a cliché of the learned, one of those pseudo-earthy sayings by means of which bookish men attempt to disguise themselves as men of practical affairs.

pluck. See **guts.**

plump. See **fat.**

plurality. See **majority.**

plural nouns

USES

A plural noun means more than one of a certain kind of thing, as do *books, crowds, people.* In this work a noun is called a true plural when it can be used with a numeral or a word implying more than one, as *three books, several crowds, many people.* True plurals are qualified by *these* and *those,* used with plural verbs, and referred to by plural pronouns. (For words that refer to two things only, see **dual words.**)

Not every noun that is followed by a plural verb is plural. Singular nouns are sometimes used with plural meaning and are sometimes followed by plural verbs. (See **singular nouns, group names, generic nouns.**) Not every noun that ends in *s* is a plural. Sometimes it is a genitive. And sometimes it is impossible to say whether it is a genitive or a plural. (See **genitive case, measures, adverbial genitive.**) Some nouns ending in *s,* such as *gallows, hydraulics, news,* are treated as if they were singulars. Some, such as *clothes, dregs, munitions,* are treated sometimes as singulars and sometimes as plurals. See **mass nouns.**

Nouns may be made from the *-ing* form of a verb and from adjectives by adding *s,* as in *surroundings, flannels, shorts, heroics, economics.* These words do not have a singular and a plural form. Sometimes they are treated entirely as singulars but more often they are treated in certain respects as plurals. As a rule such words are qualified by *these* or *those* and not by *this* or *that,* are used with a plural verb, and referred to as *they,* as in *these surroundings are depressing but I don't know how to change them.* But because they do not have singular forms they are not qualified by words implying number. We do not speak of *several surroundings.* Adjective nouns that are the names of garments are sometimes used with a numeral, as in *I have three slacks.* This is a shortening of *three pairs of slacks* and is acceptable to some people but not to others. The names of most branches of science, such as *physics, optics, economics,* are also nouns made from adjectives. These words are regularly treated as singular when they refer to a system of thought, as in *his ethics is not based on religion.* But otherwise they are defective plurals like the other adjective nouns in *s* and are used with a plural verb, as in *his ethics are admirable.*

Some true plural nouns that can be used with numerals, such as *people, clergy, police,* do not have a singular. As a rule, these have developed from singular group names. Words of this kind are listed individually in this dictionary. Many singular nouns, such as *knowledge* and *mankind,* do not have plural forms. This is the case as long as we feel that the word means just one thing. As soon as someone believes that it refers to more than one thing, he coins a plural form. For example, astronomers and philosophers talk about *universes,* and social workers talk about *strengths,* although most people use these words only in the singular. New plurals of this kind are quite legitimate provided the word actually has two distinguishable meanings, that is, provided it refers to at least two things that are definably different. This is not true, for example, of the word *butter.* For this reason the singular form is used, even in such a plural statement as *good and bad butter are very different.* Goodness and badness are not essential qualities in what we mean by *butter.* (Of course a plural form might be used by someone who considered dairy butter, apple butter, and peanut butter different *kinds* of butter.) Meaningless plurals, such as *wisdoms* and *wealths,* should not be used. The hearer, who does not see the reason for the plural form, is first bewildered and then irritated.

Most English nouns, however, have a singular and a plural form. The plural is made from the singular according to certain rather simple rules.

FORMATION

Almost all English plurals are made by adding *s* to the singular form. If the singular ends in *y* following a consonant, the *y* is changed to *ie* before adding *s*, as in *skies, armies, studies.* But the *y* is not changed after a vowel, as in *toys,* nor in a proper name, as in *the four Marys.* If the singular ends in *ch, sh, s, x,* or *z,* so that an extra syllable must be used in pronouncing the plural, *es* is added to the singular and not simply *s,* as in *churches, fishes, masses, foxes, buzzes.*

All plural nouns in general use that are not formed according to this pattern are listed individually in this dictionary. These fall into four groups.

1. There are a few plural forms in modern English that are survivals from a time when the language had more than one way of making the plural. Some of these, such as *deer,* have the same form in the singular and in the plural. Some, such as *mouse* and *mice,* change the vowel. Some, such as *leaf* and *leaves,* change an *f* to *v.* And a few are even more irregular. All such nouns have been listed.

2. A few words that end in *o* following a consonant form the plural by adding *es,* as in *tomato* and *tomatoes.* But many more words of exactly this kind may have either *s* or *es* in the plural, as in *buffalos* or *buffaloes.* (A plural in *es* is permitted, but not required, for some nouns ending in *i,* as in *alkalis* or *alkalies.*) Nouns that may have either *s* or *es* in the plural are not shown in this dictionary, but nouns that are used frequently and require *es* are listed. To use an *s* instead of *es* in an unfamiliar word that does not often appear in print, such as *bilbo, bubo, gingo,* is not a serious mistake.

3. Figures and letters used as words may form the plural with an apostrophe and *s,* as in *the 1920's* and *three N's.* But the apostrophe is not necessary. Some publishers prefer the *1920s* and *three Ns.*

4. There are a great many words in English that have foreign plural forms, such as *alumni* and *alumnae.* In some cases the foreign plural is the only standard form, and it must therefore be used. More often, there is also an English plural which is equally acceptable, and one may use whichever form suits his purpose. Any noun in general use that has only an irregular or un-English plural can be found in this dictionary. Several hundred others which have a regular as well as an irregular plural are also listed. See **foreign plurals.**

COMPOUNDS

Most compound nouns, whether they are written as one word or two, have a regular plural formed by adding *s* to the final element, as in *forget-me-nots, good-bys, homecomings.* In a very few, the first element and not the last is made plural. There are five kinds of words in which this may be the case.

1. In literary English, agent nouns in *er* that are made from a verb and an adverb add the plural *s* to the *er* and not to the adverb, as in *lookers-on* and *onlookers.* Forms such as *looker-ons* are heard but are not standard. The same rule holds for the *-ing* form of compound verbs. That is, *comings-in* and *goings-out* are preferred to *coming-ins* and *going-outs* in literary English. However, nouns made from the simple verb plus an adverb have regular plurals, with *s* added to the final element, as in *upsets, set-ups, shakedowns.*

2. Compounds made up of a noun, a preposition, and a second noun, traditionally form the plural by making the first noun, which is the principal word, plural, as in *sons-in-law* and *coats of mail.* This rule is usually observed with words that are not often used, or not often used in the plural, such as *coats of mail* and *Commanders in Chief.* But in the United States the familiar *in-law* terms are often given a regular plural, as in *son-in-laws.* This offends many people, but it is widely used and is likely to become the standard form. The objection, that this makes the plural indistinguishable from the genitive, is irrelevant since most English plurals are indistinguishable from the genitive. When the first word in a prepositional compound is an adjective and not a noun, the plural is always formed regularly, as in *good-for-nothings.*

3. In some compounds a noun is followed by an adjective, in the French manner. Formerly, words of this kind always formed the plural by changing the first element, the noun, as in *attorneys general, courts martial, knights errant.* This is still the practice in Great Britain. But in the United States such words are more often treated as a unit and given a regular plural, as in *attorney generals, court martials, knight errants.*

4. Compounds with *and,* such as *whiskey and soda, brace and bit,* form plurals in all the possible ways—*whiskey and sodas, whiskeys and sodas, whiskeys and soda.* The regular form, *whiskey and sodas,* is preferred.

5. Some compounds with *man* or *woman* as the first element change both elements in the plural, as in *menservants, men dancers.* (See **man** and **woman.**) For all other words this "double plural" is contrary to the traditional rules of English. See **singular nouns.**

Questions of whether to write a compound as one word or two words or to use a hyphen are discussed under **compound words.**

P.M., p.m. See **A.M., a.m.**

pocketbook; purse. To an Englishman a *pocketbook* is a small book, usually a notebook, to be carried in the pocket, or a booklike case for papers, bank notes, bills. To an American a *pocketbook* is a small bag or case for papers, money, etc., usually carried by a handle or in the pocket. In America only is *pocketbook* used in the figurative sense of pecuniary resources (*Our prices are designed for the light pocketbook*). *Pocketbook* to describe a small book was once chiefly British, but with the increasing sale in recent years of small paper-backed books called *Pocket Books* on newsstands and in bookstores in America, the term is well understood to mean any small paper-backed book, even though many such books would never conform to the dimensions implied.

A *purse* is a small bag, pouch, or case for

carrying money on the person. The word is more used in America than in England in its literal sense but serves figuratively in England, as *pocketbook* does in America, to denote money, resources, or wealth (*During the war many English people grew accustomed to living on a very slim purse*). *Purse* has the special senses, in both countries, of a sum of money collected as a present or offered as a prize (*A purse was quickly raised to pay for the operation. The purse for the final race was the largest of the afternoon*).

poet; poetess. *Poet* is the correct word to describe one who composes poetry, regardless of sex. *Poetess*, a female poet, emphasizes the sex of the writer when the sex is largely irrelevant, unlike that of an *actress* whose femininity is essential to her art. *Poetess*, then, though not incorrect, seems unnecessary. Both *poet* and *poetess* are used of women who write poetry, but *poet* is the better term. For instance, the writer of the fly-leaf blurb to Edmund Wilson's *I Thought of Daisy* (1953) says, "The hero is in love with two women: one is the highly emotional and unpredictable poetess, Rita . . ."; yet in the text (p. 1) Mr. Wilson writes, "Rita Cavanagh, the poet, was to be there . . ." and in his Foreword he refers to "Rita, the romantic poet."

poetic diction may mean the language used in verse, or a particular choice of words fashionable for the poetry of a given literary period. Just as there are certain fashionable words in conversation, so there are vogue words in poetry. Out of these words each age constructs a poetic diction which second-rate poets, consciously or unconsciously, adopt. Thus contemporary verse is spattered heavily with such words as *lonely, horrible, uncomplaining* and *improbable*, words authorized by the usage of such first-rate poets as Yeats, Eliot and Auden.

Yet while bad poetic diction results from such selection of language at random according to current fashion, there is also a good poetic diction, a selection of language on supportable principles and for a reasonable purpose. At least since Aristotle composed his *Poetics*, critics have urged poets to employ a dignified, noble vocabulary.

The history of poetry has been the history of the hardening of poetic language into a certain sort of diction followed by a revolt which has led to a different sort of diction which in its turn has hardened and been rejected.

The last great revolutionary to whom poetry in English is indebted was William Wordsworth, who, in his Preface to *Lyrical Ballads* (1800), proposed that poetry be written "in a selection of language really used by men," since there was no "essential difference between the language of prose and metrical composition."

Wordsworth was protesting particularly against the elegant, archaic, circumlocutory diction which had almost frozen the stream of poetry in the eighteenth century. It is heard in Gray's *Elegy*, in such phrases as *the lowing herd* for cows, *the stubborn glebe* for fallow land, and so on. But it is not offensive there because

Gray's genius was great enough to infuse life into even such husks of verbiage. To see more clearly what Wordsworth was objecting to (and Johnson, by the way, in the 77th *Idler*, "Easy Writing"), one has to read the now mercifully forgotten minor poets of the day, or our own society and sport pages, where the tradition lingers in unspeakably repulsive moldiness. One finds it in those who, moved perhaps by "ambition of ornament and luxuriance of imagery," insist on calling bananas *elongated yellow fruit*.

In a far-off way they are being Miltonic. They are living—if people who speak that way can be said to live—in the dim afterglow of a once-great light. Shakespeare, a notorious barbarian, had used such vulgar phrases as *the blanket of the dark* and *to grunt and sweat under the weary load*. But Milton, over-educated, aloof, fastidious and, above all, "organ-voiced," had set a new style. To him a telescope was an *optic glass* and Galileo *the Tuscan artist*. Hell is *bottomless perdition* and the denizens thereof *the Stygian throng*.

This was not entirely a love of resonance and circumlocution. The immense vagueness of his language served to suggest the indescribable:

Things unattempted yet in Prose or Rhime.

And in many great combinations (such as *darkness visible* and *the vast abrupt* and *horror plum'd*) Milton did indeed soar above the Aeonian mount.

But one man's idiom can be another's idiocy and Milton's mighty harmonies, applied by lesser men to lesser themes, produced the stilted absurdity of the eighteenth century's poetic diction, the language of whose inebriations *elongated yellow fruit* is a dying hiccup.

There had been some of it before Milton. Spenser had called cows *milky mothers* and Lyly had shown that ten syllables could often do the work of one; but there is little doubt that the language against which Wordsworth protested was, to a considerable extent, a bad imitation of Milton. Fish became *the finny tribe* or *the fruitful spawn of ocean*. Flowers appeared as *the vernal bloom*. When applied externally, water was *the crystal element* and it *laved the corporeal frame* after strenuous exertion to remove that *roscid balm* of which our best friends are reluctant to tell us. Furs were *Muscovy's warm spoils;* bed, *th' enfeebling down*. And so on.

Long forgotten now as a poet but deserving some remembrance as the supreme perpetrator of this particular kind of polysyllabic poppycock is Dr. John Armstrong whose *The Art of Preserving Health* (1744) (which discusses "How best the fickle fabric to support/ Of Mortal man") ran through many editions. From this treasury of tripe it is hard to make a fitting selection; there is such an alluring wealth of bad writing in it. One seizes upon a description of appetite as *the grinding stomach's hungry rage* only to desert it for a reference to an egg as *the sleeping Embryo*. Perhaps full justice can only be done by quotation from a longer passage, such as his statement that the air is bad in cities and would be fatal were it not, fortunately, disinfected by the sulphur in coal smoke. Even so, however, it is unhealthy, and he urges his readers to live in the country:

Fly the rank city, shun its turbid air:
Breathe not the chaos of eternal smoke
And volatile corruption . . .
. . . and (tho' the lungs abhor
To drink the dun fuliginous abyss)
Did not the acid vigor of the mine,
Roll'd from so many thundring chimneys,
*   tame*
The putrid salts that overswarm the sky;
This caustic venom would perhaps corrode
Those tender cells that draw the vital air,
In vain with all their unctuous rills bedew'd;
Or by the drunken venous tubes, that yawn
In countless pores o'er all the pervious skin.
Imbib'd, would poison the balsamic blood,
And rouse the heart to every fever's rage.
While yet you breathe, away! the rural wilds
Invite.

Though Wordsworth's own verse, in general, illustrated his protest, he did not succeed in persuading most of the major nineteenth century poets who followed him to use the common language of common nineteenth century men. Coleridge, Rossetti and Morris drew heavily on the language of medieval ballads. Keats and Tennyson contrived a diction indebted to Spenser, Shakespeare and Milton. Landor, Arnold and Swinburne drew a great deal from the vocabulary of Greek tragedy.

The Wordsworthian revolution was not really carried out until the twentieth century, when the Americans, Ezra Pound and T. S. Eliot, made it clear that *any* word might be allowable in poetry if it were appropriate to the genre, tone and aim of a poem. One is surprised no longer to find in poetry the "language of men." Modern poets have gone beyond Wordsworth—who felt that such language should first be "purified"— to use slang, profanity and obscenity and even foreign words in their work. The last seven lines of *The Waste Land*, for instance, contain words in English, Italian, French and Sanskrit and the meaning of Ezra Pound's *Cantos*—if there is a meaning—is hidden in Chinese ideographs.

Thus while the term *poetic diction* may be (and usually is) a fault-finding one, since it tends to be used of the language of derivative poets, it need not be so. Poetic diction may describe the language really used by real poets, a language drawn from the whole range of our vocabulary but used more economically, more suggestively, more musically than is possible for versifiers and other ordinary men.

poetic license is the liberty taken by a poet in deviating from rule, conventional form, logic, or fact, in order to produce a desired effect. This may involve departure from prose word order or the selection of diction, rhyme or pronunciation appropriate to the requirements of a chosen metrical pattern.

A bad poet may think he is being poetic when he writes such lines as:

He did adore her eyes divine
Which seemed to say, "Swain, I am thine
Because thou art so masculine."

Here the license is obvious: the expletive use of *did* in "did adore" for the simple past *adored;* the inversion of order of adjective and noun in *eyes divine* in the interests of rhyme; the use of an archaic diction in such words as *swain, thine, art;* the forced mispronunciation of *masculine* in the interest of rhyme.

Because bad poetry may contain a good deal of this sort of thing, one cannot assume that good poetry will contain none of it. In the achievement of the desired effect any poet is free to depart from the norms imposed by prose. Thus Frost gains force by an inversion of normal word order in the opening line of "Mending Wall": *Something there is that doesn't love a wall.*

point, as a noun, may be used in about fifty distinct senses. Some of these are peculiar to either England or the United States. In relation to travel, *point* is used in the United States as *place* or *station* would be in England (*Milwaukee, Minneapolis, and points west*). In American schools, especially in the colleges, *point* often signifies a single credit, usually corresponding to an hour's class work per week for one semester (*He needs several more points before he can be regarded as an upperclassman*). Where an American says *point* or *pen-point*, an Englishman says *nib*. Where an American says *exclamation point* or *exclamation mark,* an Englishman says *point of exclamation* or *mark of exclamation*. The English use *point* in railroading to describe a tapering movable rail, as in a switch.

point-blank is a term, now largely outmoded, from gunnery. A shot was said to be *point-blank* when the barrel of the gun was aimed directly at its object and the ball moved towards the target without describing any appreciable curve. *Point-blank range* is the distance a missile will travel, from a horizontal barrel, before falling below the level from which it is fired.

The conditions that permitted point-blank firing were those that led to the most dreadful carnage and the term became a trope for blunt and uncompromising rejection or repulse, brutal frankness. But *point-blank refusal* and *point-blank denial* are now clichés, their meaning generally forgotten and their force spent.

point of view. Jeremy Bentham once made a list of motives, naming each motive in three columns, according as it was approved by the speaker, tolerated, or disapproved of. Thus "love of the social board" appeared in one column and "gluttony" in its opposite.

This is an interesting exercise for the writer because he must be aware of the manner in which our values, prejudices and passions reveal themselves in our choice of words. He must be aware, for example, that the woman whom others regard as "skinny" may regard herself as "slender," that one who considers himself "broad-minded" may be considered "unprincipled" by others, that "tact" and "hypocrisy," "fluency" and "glibness," and "frankness" and "brutality" may describe the same actions to different people. It may be that the only difference between a man's having "initiative" and being "a trouble maker" is whether or not we happen to approve of his ends. The proverb of the early bird is strictly for the birds; it offers no incentive for early rising to worms.

Point of view is inherent in almost every statement that passes a judgment and is often found in words and phrases that seem, superficially, to be purely descriptive. Thus in our references to China and Japan as "the East" we unconsciously reveal the fact that our world-outlook is European. And, still more striking, Japan, in her emblem of the Rising Sun, may reveal the same point of view. What an extraordinary comment on the insincerity of some of our democratic pretensions lies in our use of the word "exclusive" as a term of the highest commendation!

The writer must not only "see people as they are"—that is, as they seem to him—but he must see them as other people see them as they are! And he must accept the fact that under different circumstances different points of view can all be valid. To Hamlet Polonius is a "wretched, rash, intruding fool," a pompous, subservient dotard with weak hams and a weaker wit. To Ophelia he is a stern but loving father. To King Claudius he is a trusted counselor and to Queen Gertrude "the good old man." So completely does Shakespeare lead us to sympathize with Macbeth that we are startled, and almost offended, when after Macbeth and Lady Macbeth are dead Malcolm refers to them as "this dead butcher and his fiend-like Queen." We don't believe in "anthropophagi and men whose heads do grow beneath their shoulders," but we are shocked when Iago says that Othello won Desdemona's love "by bragging and telling her fantastical lies."

The ability to imagine a wholly different point of view is one of the surest indications of high intelligence and often serves in itself to make a book. The secret of H. G. Wells's *The War of the Worlds* is not that he had the power to create, in his Martians, something before unconceived, but that under disguise of the Martians he presented the white man much as he must have seemed to savages on their first disastrous contact with him. Virginia Woolf in *Flush* makes a much more successful attempt, one feels, to present life as a dog would experience it than does, say, Jack London in *White Fang* or *The Call of the Wild*.

One of the advantages of wit and paradox is that by shifting the viewpoint they force us to look at life from unaccustomed points of view and so enlarge the boundaries of truth.

A new point of view always comes as a shock to us. We don't regard our own point of view as a point of view at all; rather it seems to us the obvious, the only way of looking at the situation. We rarely say "This is the way it seems to one with my limitations and predilections," but rather "This is the way it is," "Anyone with an ounce of sense can see," etc. And when someone does *not* see it that way, we are taken aback. Ivor Brown says that he once asked an attendant at Highgate Cemetery how to find Karl Marx's grave. The attendant gave him the necessary instructions and then, to make sure, added, "Look for the name of Scrimmage. It's behind that."

point of view; viewpoint; standpoint. While all these terms have their legitimate uses, all are overworked and abused. *Point of view* (and, to a lesser extent, *viewpoint* and *standpoint*—with its annoying elaboration *from where I stand*) is often used merely to make a clumsy paraphrase of an adverb. Nothing is gained, for example, by saying *from the political point of view. Politically* would serve better. What does *from the point of view of maintenance plastic tile has many advantages* say that is not said as well in such a sentence as *plastic tile is easier to maintain* or *more economical to maintain?* The more abstract the point of view alluded to, the further removed from the possibility of a physical viewpoint (as in *from the point of view of regional planning* or *the point of view of resources development*), the greater the likelihood of ambiguity and confusion. It is not a fault that can be remedied by merely substituting one word for another. The whole sentence has to be rewritten and the thought behind it clarified. Perhaps the concept of "vision," which plays so large a part in business jargon and advertising rhetoric and spawns *angles, outlooks, phases, aspects,* and other such metaphors of augury and prognostication, is at bottom to blame. See **view, angle.**

poise. See pose.

poison. See venom.

police. When this word means the police force, and this is the only sense in which the word is used in the United States today, it is always treated as a plural. It is followed by a plural verb, as in *the police are looking for him,* and may be used with a numeral, as in *twenty police were on the scene.* But the word has no singular. One member of the force is *a policeman.* In order to speak of the force as a unit it is necessary to use the word *force* (*The police force is efficient*).

policy and **polity** derive from the same Latin word meaning government. But their meanings are now clearly distinguishable. *Polity* is the more reputable and dignified term, for it conveys an idea of permanence. It describes a particular form of government, civil, ecclesiastical, or other. Richard Hooker's famous defense of the Church of England was entitled *The Laws of Ecclesiastical Polity. Policy* refers not to permanent principles but to courses of action. Primarily it means a definite course of action adopted as expedient or from other considerations (*Our policy is to give the customer what he wants*), a course or line of action adopted and pursued by a government, ruler, political party, or the like (*Our foreign policy often bears little intelligible relation to the national polity*), action or procedure conforming to, or considered with reference to, prudence or expediency (*It is a good policy for a man with a knife at his throat to stand still. Honesty is the best policy*).

There are really two words *policy* in our language that have coalesced. One, as above, derives from the Latin word for government. But the other derives from a Greek word meaning a showing or a setting forth. In both England and America a *policy* may be a document setting forth the terms of a contract of insurance (*I took out my first policy when I was fifteen*). In the United States only, *policy* is also a method of gambling in which bets are made on numbers to be drawn by lottery.

polish and **burnish** both mean to make smooth and glossy, especially by friction, but in general use *polish* is to be preferred. One may polish floors, shoes, furniture, and so on. *Burnish* is used only with reference to metals (*His face shone like burnished copper*).

polite; courteous; civil; urbane. A *civil* man is, basically, one who fulfills his duties as a citizen, especially in the observance of those forms and ceremonies which serve to preserve the peace. He may be cold and distant, but he abstains from rough or abusive language, gives to every man his due, and observes all common forms of general respect for others. A *polite* man has a somewhat greater measure of kindness in his good manners. He is refined and sensitive and observes the forms of civility out of a desire to please. *Courteous,* derived originally from the conduct one found and practiced in the courts of princes, is a slightly stronger word than *polite.* The courteous man is polite and kind, but is also graceful, dignified, and complaisant. The word formerly had a sense of coldness about it, the practice of elaborate manners for their own sake as a social ritual, but in contemporary usage it connotes more of the warmth of sincere kindness. *Urbane* means cityish and denotes manners which are polished to an especial suavity and agreeableness, especially in the not giving or taking of offense, but are not necessarily moved by any great inner kindness or affection.

politic and **expedient** are both adjectives meaning prudent and sagacious, but *expedient* (from Latin words meaning to free a man who is caught by the foot) is more practical in its connotations than *politic. Expedient* is concerned with means, *politic* with ends. *Politic* means wise and prudent, with far-reaching consequences held in a long-term view (*Pillage and devastation are seldom politic, even when they are supposed to be just*), though it has also a baser meaning of crafty, cunning, and artful (*Cromwell's fanaticism seems to have been in a measure politic*). *Expedient,* emphasizing a tendency to promote some proposed or desired object, is often used disparagingly, in the sense that it represents a falling away from an ideal course of action (*It was expedient to promise a quick end to the war in the interest of a successful campaign*).

politician; statesman. In Elizabethan English a *politician* might be one versed in the science of government, but he was more likely to be a sinister schemer, a crafty, self-seeking, dangerous man (*I am whipped and scourged with rods,/ Nettled and stung with pismires, when I hear/ Of this vile politician Bolingbroke*). In contemporary American usage this disparagement lingers, but it has been softened a little. A *politician* is considered by many of us to be one who resorts to various schemes and devices, who engages in petty political maneuvers for purely partisan or personal ends (*The Governor is merely a politician*). Among those who accept politics as a necessity or a profession, there is no such contempt and the term, though freely granting many of the implications that make it pejorative to idealists and non-politicians, is even used in admiration (*Say what you want about Truman, the man was a consummate politician*).

Statesman in contemporary American usage is wholly laudatory. It suggests eminent ability, foresight, and unselfish devotion to the interests of the country (*Mr. Baruch is among the most distinguished of our elder statesmen*).

In England *politician* and *statesman* are both wholly laudatory, but there is a distinction in their meanings. *Politician* is still used in the traditional sense of one versed in the science of government. The London *Daily Mirror,* for example, on December 15, 1954, named Sir Anthony Eden *the politician* of the year for his work at the Geneva Conference and the London Conference on German Rearmament. Such a term would never have been bestowed in commendation in the United States for such distinguished service. In England all members of Parliament are, by courtesy, termed *politicians.* A *statesman* in England is an M.P. or a Cabinet Minister who has great influence and exercises it wisely. The difference between the terms in England, then, is not based on virtue but on power.

politicly and **politically** are not variant spellings but adverbs with separate meanings. *Politicly* refers to action characterized by policy, sagacious, prudent, expedient, or judicious. *Politically* means pertaining to or dealing with politics or a political party.

politics. Formerly this word was regularly used with a plural verb, as in *politics have been defined as the art of governing mankind by deceiving them.* Today it is more often used with a singular verb, as in *politics makes strange bedfellows.* Either form is acceptable.

The adjectives *politic* and *political* come from the same source and once meant pertaining to the state. Today *politic* means prudent, except in the expression *body politic* where it has its old sense. *Political,* which now means having to do with politics, has remained closer to the original meaning.

polypus. The plural is *polypuses* or *polypi.*

pommel; pummel. In England *pommel* is the usual spelling for the noun, *pummel* for the verb. In America *pommel* is the preferred spelling for both noun and verb. As a noun, *pommel* means a knob, as on the hilt of a sword, or the protuberant part at the front and top of a saddle. As a verb, *pommel* means to strike or beat with or as with the pommel or with the fist.

pond in English usage means an artificial pool. In American usage it can also mean a small natural lake (*The ducks seek these lonely ponds and marshes in the breeding season*).

pony. From its basic meaning of a horse of a small type, not over fourteen hands high, *pony* has acquired several specialized meanings in the United States. In American slang a *pony* may be a translation or other illicit aid used by a student to avoid doing his own work. This, in its turn, has led to another word, a synonym, *trot*. The English slang for an illicit translation is *crib*. In U. S. speech *pony* is used for a small glass of liquor (*He always downed a pony of brandy before he stepped out on the stage*). It has also been adopted to describe a book or magazine of small size (*In 1942 Time began publishing a "pony edition," a miniature magazine for overseas distribution*).

The British have a curious slang use of *pony* that can have nothing to do with *smallness*: it means twenty-five pounds sterling. Among English stockbrokers (says Partridge in his *Dictionary of Slang and Unconventional English*) a *pony* is twenty-five one-thousand-pound shares!

poor; impecunious; indigent; impoverished; penniless; penurious. *Poor* is the simple, everyday term for the condition of lacking the means to obtain the comforts of life (*And cold the poor man lies at night*). *Impecunious* is formal. It has a Micawberish quality to it that gives it a tinge of jocosity (*The alcoholic richness of the gentleman's breath made it plain that anything given to relieve his impecunious state would soon be disbursed in the nearest tavern*). If used seriously, it is a little over-elegant (*The solicitations of the impecunious children are profoundly moving*). *Indigent* is also a formal word, but a cold one, used in economic reports and the like (*an almshouse for the reception of the indigent*). The poor we have with us always; the indigent we encounter only in learned treatises. *Impoverished* usually implies a former state of plenty from which one has been reduced (*an impoverished nobleman, living in fierce isolation*). A poor soil is a soil lacking in the substances necessary for proper plant growth. An impoverished soil is one that once had such substances but has been deprived of them by leaching, erosion, windstorms, improper management, and so on. *Penniless* can mean destitute (*Left penniless with three small children, she cast about for some means of subsistence*), though it is sometimes used more lightly to designate a temporary lack of funds. Though *penury* still means poverty (as it did in Gray's *Chill penury repressed their noble rage*) and *penurious* used to mean poverty-stricken (*Dives, rich in this world, became exceedingly penurious in the other—1614*), it now means only niggardly, stingy (*Though he is rich, he is penurious, begrudging every penny spent*).

poor as a church mouse. Some modern churches, with their social halls, cafeterias, ladies' guild teas, receptions, box-suppers, father-and-son banquets, and the like, may offer opportunities for many a mouse to grow sleek and fat. But in the bare, unheated churches of our forefathers, restricted to exhortation, prayer and meditation, and where there fell only crumbs of grace, a mouse would have been poor (lean and emaciated, sickly and feeble) indeed. The phrase is now enfeebled by repetition and devoid of much of its meaning.

poor but honest, used humorously, is a cliché, stemming, Partridge believes, from its use in a humorous ballad which was popular about 1910. It is interesting that in the ballad *honest* had the Elizabethan meaning of chaste.

poor thing, but mine own. Touchstone did not refer to Audrey as *a poor thing, but mine own,* but as *a poor virgin, sir, an ill-favour'd* [ugly] *thing, sir, but mine own.* The corrupted (and weakened) form is now a cliché.

poppycock is evidence of the power of usage to sanction anything. An exclamation of annoyance and ridicule at something regarded as pretentious nonsense, it parallels a vulgar and unprintable expletive. *Poppycock* is particularly favored, as an expression of disgust, by the prim; yet it is merely a colloquial Dutch word, taken over by Americans, meaning a cake of semi-liquid (paplike) dung.

populace and **population** refer to a large group of people collectively, but the first connotes a degree of condescension or contempt and the second is an objective, descriptive term. *Populace* means the common people of a community, as distinguished from the higher classes. Matthew Arnold, in his book *Culture and Anarchy,* entitled a chapter on upper, middle, and lower classes "Barbarians, Philistines, Populace." *Population* means the total number of persons inhabiting a country, city, or any district or area (*The rise in the population is sure to overburden the schools*).

populace and **populous** both refer to people, but the first is a noun and the second is an adjective. *Populace* carries a derogatory connotation, for it means common people not simply as a class label but in the contemptuous sense of the mob, the great unwashed. *Populous,* the adjective, means full of people or inhabitants, well populated. It conveys no moral comment on the people as people but emphasizes their numerical size (*Belgium is one of the most populous countries in the world*).

porch; piazza; veranda. For the open portico or gallery, usually roofed and sometimes partly enclosed, attached to the exterior of a house, *porch* is now the everyday word. *Piazza,* borrowed apparently from the colonnaded Piazza San Marco in Venice, is now distinctly old-fashioned, rustic-elegant, and, even so, limited to a few localities. *Veranda* (also *verandah*) is more widely used than *piazza,* but it too is fading from general use and *porch* holds sway. (*When the evening papers were distributed he hurried home to sit on the porch before the house*).

In British usage *porch* is primarily an architectural term describing an exterior structure forming a covered approach to the entrance of a building, especially of a church or cathedral.

pore; pour. *Pore* is to meditate or ponder intently, gaze earnestly or steadily, read or study with steady attention or application. To *pour* is to send a liquid or fluid or anything in loose particles, flowing or falling, as from a container, or into, over, or on something, or to emit or discharge in a stream or to send forth words as in a stream or flood. *Pore* is often misspelled *pour* (as in this sentence from one of our leading intellectual journals: *Attorney General Herbert Brownell, Jr., and his deputy, William P. Rogers, have spent much of the past two years pouring through the files they inherited, hoping to find enough "mess" documentation to bring indictments against many a prominent Democrat*). But such spelling is incorrect.

pornography. See **blasphemy.**

port, harbor and **haven** all indicate a shelter for ships. A *haven* is usually a natural shelter which can be utilized by ships (*Milford Haven is well named, since its headlands provide natural protection against storms. And the stately ships go on,/ To their haven under the hill*). It is popular in a figurative sense to mean any safe place (*He found the club a haven of refuge from domestic confusion*). *Harbor* may describe a natural or an artificially constructed or improved shelter (*When steamships began to replace sailing vessels, harbors had to be found or built which would accommodate ships of deeper draft*). A *port* is a harbor viewed especially in its commercial aspect (*New York does more business than any other two American ports*).

port and **larboard** both mean the left side of a ship, facing toward the bow (opposed to *starboard*). *Larboard,* the more ancient term, has been largely replaced by *port* because it sounds too much like *starboard* in shouted orders.

portend is now used correctly only in the sense of to indicate beforehand, to presage, as an omen (*Such dark skies portend rain. What does this angry introduction portend?*). In the sense of to signify, as in Bardolph's assertion that his red nose *portended choler, portend* is obsolete.

portent retains meanings *portend* has lost. Basically, it means an indication or omen of something about to happen, especially something momentous (*A prodigy of fear and a portent/ Of broached mischief to the unborn times*). It may also mean ominous significance (*The dropping of the first atom bomb was an event of evil portent*) or a prodigy or marvel (*The Loch Ness monster is a portent, doubtless*), though to this last meaning there still clings some of the earlier belief that the appearance of monsters and prodigies was not an accident but a warning of events to come.

portion. See **part.**

portmanteau. The plural is *portmanteaus* or *portmanteaux*. It was Humpty Dumpty in his exegesis of *Jabberwocky* who applied *portmanteau* to those words in which "there are two meanings packed up into one word." In linguistics it is called *blending* and many words now quite legitimate came into existence this way, such as *dandle* which is a blend of *dance* and *handle*. The tendency, stimulated by some brilliant creations in *Time* (of which *cinemactress* is an example), is popular in contemporary America and England and often useful as well. *Brunch* serves a need as a name for an in-between meal, partaking of the nature of both breakfast and lunch, and is accepted as standard, though the ordinary American male would certainly feel a little self-conscious in using it. Certainly conscious blendings are the work of wits (such as Mr. Clifton Fadiman's reference to the *hullabalunacy* of so much of the puffing praise on book jackets) and deserve to be admired, but our admiration can be given only on the first hearing. After that the word must stand (like *squadrol*) on its usefulness or become tedious.

Portuguese. The singular and the plural are both *Portuguese*. In the seventeenth century this word had a plural form, *Portugueses*. This is now obsolete and *Portuguese* is the only acceptable form in the singular and in the plural, as in *one Portuguese* and *three Portuguese*. A new singular, *Portuguee,* is in use among fishermen and sailors, but it has not made its way into standard English.

pose; poise. *Pose* suggests something fairly temporary, an assumed or artificial posture or attitude (*Please hold that pose while the photographer takes one more picture. His heartiness is just a pose; actually, he's timid and frightened*). *Poise* suggests something more basic, a state of balance or equilibrium, as from equality or equal distribution of weight (*It takes great poise to walk a tightrope. The rock's poise was such that the least push would have moved it in either direction*). In figurative use it means composure, self-possession (*One needs poise on a witness stand to endure the attack of an unscrupulous cross-questioner*), steadiness, stability (*I could tell she had poise from the way she walked onto the stage*).

position. See **job.**

position of adjectives. 1. The primary position for an adjective is before the noun it qualifies, as *gray* in *gray goose*. An adjective standing in this position is called an adherent adjective, or sometimes an attributive adjective.

Any qualifying word that can be used in this position is an adjective. When a word that is ordinarily classed as an adverb is used immediately before a noun it arouses a great deal of opposition. This is what is wrong with the *there* in *that there house*. If the child who is determined to use all these words would only say *that house there* the teacher would be satisfied. Very few adverbs have been accepted in this position, and when one is, it is immediately recognized as an adjective, as *then* in *the then king of France, after* in *in after years,* and *down* in *a down stroke.* Ten or twenty years ago many editors would not accept *above* as an adjective, as in *the above remarks* and insisted on making this *the remarks above. Above* is now established in the adjective position. But we cannot today say *the below remarks.* This is a battle that each adverb must win for itself.

One might set up a system of English grammar in which an adjective was defined as a qualifying word that can stand immediately before a noun. One could then go on to discuss other positions in which either an adjective or an adverb could be used, sometimes with exactly the same meaning and sometimes with a difference in meaning. In this way the whole problem of adjectives and adverbs would be made much simpler. But this is not the definition now used in dictionaries or in teaching foreign languages, and it would be confusing to those who are already familiar with the accepted concepts. In this book we are, therefore, following the standard definition of an adjective. But this involves us in a certain amount of hair splitting and sometimes presents us with problems that simply can't be solved.

2. The second position in which an adjective may stand is immediately after a linking verb or a verb of motion, as in *the baby is asleep, he came here young and confident.* An adjective in this position is called a predicate adjective. But with any kind of intransitive verb, this is also the secondary position for an adverb (see **sentence adverbs**) and if an adjective is used predicatively often enough it develops an adverbial force. Sometimes it is impossible to say whether a certain word, such as *slow,* is an adjective or an adverb when it is used in this position.

There are a number of adjectives that begin with *a-,* such as *asleep, awake, afire, alive, aware,* which are used in this position but not ordinarily before the noun they qualify. For example, we say *the man is alive* but not *the alive man.* This *a* once meant *in* and these words were once prepositional phrases. They have come to be felt as single words but they are still used as a phrase would be used. An adjective phrase may occasionally precede its noun and these words, too, if they are qualified and form part of a group, may be used in this position, as in *the very much alive man.* But constructions of this kind are always felt to be exceptional and not according to the natural order of words.

These peculiar *a-* adjectives can be used alone in any position that an adjective can be used in, except before the noun they qualify. But there are a number of adverbs that begin with *a-,* such as *away, abroad, astray,* and that also can only be used in exactly the same positions. It is sometimes difficult to say whether a certain word, such as *adrift,* is an adjective or an adverb. For this reason some grammarians call all these words, including *afraid* and *alive,* adverbs. Those who recognize some as adjectives and some as adverbs have to depend on the meaning of the word to establish the difference. If the word names a quality which a thing might possess it is an adjective. If it names the time, place, or manner of an action it is an adverb.

Adjectives may be used after linking verbs and after verbs of motion. A linking verb is any verb that is used to mean *be, become,* or *seem.* For example, *grown* means *become* and is a linking verb followed by adjectives in *an elderly mother spider grown gaunt and fierce and gray.* Most linking verbs cannot be qualified by adverbs and there is usually no doubt that a following adjective really is an adjective and qualifies the subject of the verb rather than the verb itself, as in *the fudge turned hard.* See **linking verbs.**

This is not true of verbs which name motions. After a verb of motion, a word that is both an adjective and an adverb will usually be felt as an adverb qualifying the verb, as in *he moved slow.* But there are many words that are used only as adjectives and never as adverbs. These may be used after a verb of motion to qualify the subject. For example, *trembling* describes the hare and not the limping in *the hare limped trembling through the frozen grass.* Similarly, in *do not go gentle into that good-night* the adjective *gentle* necessarily attaches itself to the unexpressed subject *you,* and the sentence takes the meaning "do not be gentle when you go." The verb *appear* may be followed by an adjective because it is being used as a linking verb meaning "seem," as in *he appears happy.* Or it may be followed by adjectives because it is being used as a verb of motion meaning "come into sight," as in *Mont Blanc appears, still, snowy, and serene.*

The verbs *to be born* and *to die* are treated in English, and in many other languages, as verbs of motion. We say *he was born lucky* and *he died rich.*

3. An adjective may also stand immediately after a noun which is the object of a verb, as in *empty* in *we found the cage empty* and *clean* in *she swept the room clean.* An adjective standing in this position is called a factitive adjective or an object complement and has a very different function from an adherent adjective. These sentences do not mean *we found the empty cage* or *she swept the clean room.* This adjective is actually closely related to the verb, as if we had said *we found-empty the cage* and *she swept-clean the room,* and so approaches the function of an adverb. It is perhaps more closely related to the verb than an adverb would be. Adverbs too may stand in this position. They show when or how an action takes place but do not affect the verb idea itself. Whether a word in this position is an adjective or an adverb always affects the meaning of the sentence, but it is sometimes impossible to say which function a particular word is supposed to have, as *wrong* and *hard* in *he made the clock wrong* and *she boiled the eggs hard.*

4. Finally, an adjective may stand after the noun it qualifies, as in *geraniums (red) and delphiniums (blue).* An adjective in this position is called an appositive adjective.

The adjective follows the noun in certain phrases that have been taken over from French or Latin, such as *heir apparent, attorney general, court martial, proof positive, battle royal, devil incarnate.* Words of this kind that are in common use are generally felt as compound nouns and are sometimes printed with a hyphen. Those that are used less often have a strange flavor, even for people who do not know an adjective from a noun.

In current English the *-ing* form of a verb is frequently placed here, as in *for the time being, no man living, three days running.* But with other adjectives the construction is likely to sound pretentious, or ridiculous, as in *a babe unborn, a place divine, things mortal, darkness visible.* Old expressions and old names are allowed to keep this order but we do not form new ones in this way. We say *Pliny the elder* and *Asia Minor,* but *the elder J. P. Morgan* and *Greater New York.*

In English a descriptive clause stands immediately after the noun it qualifies and adjectives are acceptable here when they can be thought of as part of a clause, as in *a voice perfectly calm, a person new to the business, a gentleman turned eighty.* Here the mind can insert a *which is* or *who is.* The construction is most suitable for long, complex adjective phrases that resemble clauses, but it can also be used with a single word, provided the word implies a clause, as *forty* in *men forty do not say such things.* Adverbs may also be thought of as fragments of a clause and in this position adverbs may qualify nouns, as in *the people below, the first day out, the book there on the table.*

5. Adjectives may be limiting or descriptive. That is, they may limit or restrict the meaning of the noun or they may simply add a descriptive detail. For example, in *the industrious Japanese will solve this problem* the adjective *industrious* is descriptive if the sentence means that the Japanese, being industrious, will solve the problem. It is limiting if the sentence means that only the industrious ones will solve it.

In English an adjective standing before the noun is presumably limiting. An adjective that stands after the noun will usually be understood as descriptive. The difference can be seen in *the fighting cocks* and *the cocks fighting.* If the sentence about the Japanese had read, *the Japanese, industrious and frugal, will solve this problem,* the words would have been accepted as descriptive. This is also the intention of the original sentence which means *those industrious people, the Japanese.* The adjective limits the understood word *people* and is meant to distinguish the Japanese from some others. Because we feel this, we understand the sentence when it is read in its context. But because an adherent adjective is used primarily to limit the meaning of a noun, the other interpretation can also occur to us. (For the order that is followed when several adjectives qualify the same noun, see **adjectives.**)

position of adverbs. See **adverbs** and **sentence adverbs.**

positive and **positively** are sometimes used to mean downright, out-and-out, thoroughgoing (*The man's a positive jackass. He told a positive lie to protect his friends. That's positively not so*). In this use it is an intensive; therefore it is wrongly used to mean sure or certain (*I'm positive I saw it*) unless one is insisting on the certainty. It can be ambiguous when used loosely. The context should make it clear whether *a positive answer* is an emphatic answer or an affirmative or non-negative answer. Such common expressions as *he positively won't come* or *he positively said no* are confusing and surely a more suitable intensive could be found.

positively. See **absolutely.**

possess one's soul in patience. As a way of saying "be patient," to tell someone to *possess his soul in patience* is to use a worn-out phrase. The expression is a hackneyed misunderstanding of Luke 21:19 which in the Authorized Version reads *In your patience possess ye your souls. Possess* here, however, means not merely to have but to gain possession of, as is shown by the translation in the Revised Standard Version: *By your endurance you will gain your lives.*

possession; advantage; asset. A *possession* is something possessed, had as a property, belonging to one. An *advantage* is any state or circumstance, opportunity, or means especially favorable to success, interest, or any desired end. Possessions often confer an advantage, but all possessions are not advantages and advantage can lie in many things other than possession.

Asset and *assets* should not be used loosely as synonyms of *possession* and *advantage.* They are specific and limiting terms. *Asset* means a useful thing or quality (*Cleanliness is itself an asset*). *Assets,* more frequently used than *asset,* is a plural noun used in commerce to describe the resources of a person or business consisting of such items as real property, machinery, inventory, notes, securities, and cash. *Assets* is also used for property in general, as opposed to liabilities (*His assets did not equal his liabilities until after his death*). In accounting, *assets* means the detailed listing of property owned by a firm and money owing to it. In law, it refers to property in the hands of an executor or administrator sufficient to pay the debts or legacies of the testator or intestate. It is incorrect to say *Diamonds are a girl's best asset* when one means *possession* or to say *Membership in the University Club is an asset to an ambitious lawyer* when *advantage* is the exact word.

possessive adjectives. See **possessive pronouns.**

possessive case. See **genitive case** and **possessive pronouns.**

possessive pronouns and adjectives. The personal pronouns and the word *who* each have three forms, such as *he, him, his,* which in Latin grammar would be called the nominative, the accusative, and the genitive form of that pronoun. Because no other words in English have these three forms most grammarians treat these as different types of words rather than as forms of the same word and speak of the subjective pronouns, the objective pronouns, and the possessive pronouns. Very often, the possessive forms that can be used before a noun (*my, our, your, his, her, its, their, whose*) are called possessive adjectives, and only the forms that can be used without a noun (*mine, ours, yours, his, hers, its, theirs, whose*) are called possessive pronouns. In this book the term "possessive pronoun" refers to both groups indiscriminately.

One must be careful not to use an apostrophe with the forms that seem to have an added *s, ours, yours, hers, its, theirs, whose.* An apostrophe in any of these words is considered evidence of illiteracy. This was not always true. The most influential grammar book of the eighteenth century, published in 1762, required an apostrophe in these possessive pronouns. Forms such as *your's, her's,* occur in the writings of Benjamin Franklin and Thomas Jefferson. There they are not illiteracies. On the contrary, they show that the writers knew and carefully observed the correct forms. When the "Charge of the Light Brigade" is published in anthologies today, the famous line is sometimes printed as *Their's not to reason why.* This was conservative punctuation when the poem was written and has not been standard for seventy-five years. (For special problems, see the individual pronouns and **double genitive.**)

possible. That is *possible* which may or can be, exist, happen, or be done (*O that 'twere possible/ After long grief and pain/ To find the arms of my true love/ Round me once again!*). As such, it is an absolute term and may not be qualified. An event may be highly probable but not highly possible. One may say *It is possible that it may rain* but not *it is very possible.*

Not only is *possible* not to be qualified, it is also not to be used as if it meant necessary or unavoidable. It is correct to say *We will finish as quickly as possible.* It is incorrect to get swamped in negatives and say *We won't delay any longer than possible.*

possibly; perhaps. *Possibly* means not only "perhaps" or "maybe" but also "in a possible manner" and "by any possibility." In writing, one should indicate the "perhaps" sense, when there is any likelihood of ambiguity, by setting off the word with commas. Thus *He can't, possibly, stand up to his wife* means "perhaps he can't stand up to his wife"; whereas *He can't possibly stand up to his wife* means that there is no possibility of his standing up to his wife.

possum is still listed as colloquial by the dictionaries but *opossum,* the standard form of the word, would seem a little stilted in all but the most formal writing.

To *play possum* is a colloquial American idiom for feigning ignorance or disinterest or pretending to be asleep or doing anything that in any way suggests the opossum's habit (shared by many other animals) of falling into a cataleptic state when attacked (*When the police began to look for witnesses, he played possum*).

post. See **mail.**

postal card; post card. In the United States a *postal card* is a card with a printed governmental stamp, printed and sold by the government. A *post card* may describe such a postal card, but it more properly describes an unofficial card, often pictorial, mailable when bearing an adhesive postage stamp. In England *post card* is used to describe a card used for correspondence whether it bears a printed governmental stamp or must have a stamp affixed.

posted in the sense of informed, supplied with up-to-date facts (*When you are on your travels, be sure to keep us posted*), is a colloquialism, originally American.

postpone. This word may be followed by the *-ing* form of a verb, as in *he postponed leaving.* It is also heard with an infinitive, as in *he postponed to leave,* but this is not standard English.

post-prandial is a heavy and strained elegancy for *after-dinner.*

potato. The plural is *potatoes.*

potent; potential. *Potent* means full of power, powerful, mighty. It may describe a person or a thing. There are potent reasons, potent drugs, potent influences, potent leaders, potent charms, and so on. In reference to men it has a special meaning of sexual competency. *Potential* means possible as opposed to actual, capable of being or becoming, latent (*His record as prosecuting attorney makes him a potential candidate for the governorship*). *Potent* means being powerful; *potential* means capable of being powerful.

pother, as an equivalent for *bother,* is a literary word. It used to rime with *other* and *brother* but changed to its present pronunciation, apparently to make it resemble *bother,* in the nineteenth century. In the sixteenth and early seventeenth centuries it was a stronger word and was then pronounced, as it still is in some dialects, *pudder* (*Let the great gods,/ That keep this dreadful pudder o'er our heads,/ Find out their enemies now*).

potluck, take. To invite a guest home to dinner on a sudden impulse, with the phrase *take potluck with us,* is hackneyed. But, like many trite expressions, it is useful. To say, "if you are willing to eat whatever happens to be prepared for supper, knowing that since you are not expected it may be plain fare" would be tedious and a little pompous. None the less, the triteness of *take potluck* may belie the heartiness with which the invitation is usually extended, and since the recipient of such invitations usually suspects the sincerity of this sudden desire for his company (though he has little doubt of the plainness of the fare), the cliché works slightly against its own intention. This may seem the veriest trifle, but nuances of meaning are not in themselves trifling.

potter. See **putter.**

poultry. This word now means all the domestic fowls in a given lot considered as a group. It may be used with a singular verb, as in *the poultry is selling well,* or with a plural verb, as in *the poultry are selling well.* It may be qualified by the singular adjective *much,* as in *much poultry,* but not by a numeral.

At one time *poultry* could be used as a true plural with a numeral, as in *I have seen them bring twenty or thirty poultry to the market.* This construction survives to some extent in the United States, where people speak of *few poultry* and *many poultry,* as well as of *much poultry.*

pound (the unit of weight). Only the singular form *pound* can be used to qualify a following noun, as in *a five-pound baby.* We do not say *a five-pounds baby.* In the United States the plural form *pounds* is preferred in any other construction, when speaking of more than one. But in Great Britain the singular form is always used with a number word, as in *five pound of tobacco.*

pound of flesh. As a term for the full amount of something due, especially in reference to its being exacted by the one to whom it is due, a *pound of flesh* is a cliché. The reference is to Shylock's insistence, in Shakespeare's *The Merchant of Venice,* on having that pound of Antonio's flesh which had been nominated in their bond as a forfeit.

pour. See **pore.**

powers that be. As a term for those in authority in a particular situation, *the powers that be* is a cliché. It is an echo of Romans 13:1.

practical; practicable; possible. *Practical,* when applied to persons, means sensible, realistic, businesslike. When applied to things, it means efficient and workable. It is contrasted to the theoretical and the visionary. *Practicable* means capable of being put into practice or of being used (*He rode north along the river, looking for a practicable crossing*). *Practicable* differs from *possible* in that *possible* indicates something that may be performed if the necessary means can be obtained; whereas *practicable* indicates only those things that may be performed by the means at one's disposal.

The confusion in the use of the words is often rooted in the situations to which they are applied. Something may be both *practical* and *practicable* or one or the other exclusively. It may, for example, be both practical and practicable to drive with chains on an icy road; that is, one can drive with them and it is sensible to do so. A practical foreign policy may be devised by a government, however, which is rendered impracticable by the sudden emergence of some emotional storm or religious fury or patriotic excitement in the people of one of the nations that must be dealt with.

practical; virtual. Though some English authorities cry out against the use of *practical* for *virtual,* which has developed on the analogy of the accepted synonymity of *practically* and *virtually,* American usage sanctions it. Thus one may say *It is a practical certainty* and mean *a virtual certainty.*

practically; virtually; almost; nearly. In the strict sense, *practically* means "in effect, in practice," as opposed to "in theory" (*Though the theory of pacifism is persuasive, practically, pacifism won't do*). *Virtually* is very close to *practically,* for it means "in effect," though not actually or expressly so (*After George III relapsed into permanent insanity, the Prince of Wales was virtually king*).

It is not in its strict sense, however, that *prac-*

tically tends to be used. Rather it is employed loosely in place of the more precise *nearly* or *almost* where, as Sir Alan Herbert has cogently remarked, it often means "not practically." To say *We are practically there* when you mean *We are nearly there* is to abuse the word; you are not there in effect until you are there. But you can say that from 1810 on the Prince of Wales was *practically king of England,* because, although designated Prince Regent, he was, because of his father's incompetence, in practice and effect the king. Or (the example is Herbert's) you may say that a family is *practically extinct* when its sole survivor is a childless old man who is dying. If it were a childless old woman, *practically* would be even more justified.

practice (in the sense of *habit*). See **custom.**

practice; practise. In England the noun is spelled *practice,* the verb *practise.* In America *practice* is preferred for both noun and verb, though *practise* may be used for the verb.

praise. See **panegyric, elegy.**

preacher. When applied to one who preaches in specific reference to his preaching, *preacher* is still a word of some dignity in American usage (*Dr. Peale is one of the great preachers of our day. As a preacher Graham combines boyish charm with studied eloquence*). But as a synonym for *pastor* or *minister,* it is now slightly quaint (*Resolved, that . . . all licensed preachers . . . [be exempted] from working on public roads . . . when on their professional duties*) or humorously disparaging (*A preacher went a-hunting/ Upon a Sunday morn*). Its use as a part of a name is distinctly backwoodsy (*Preacher Jones was here about the money he says you owe him*). See also **pastor, parson, clergyman.**

precede; proceed. *Precede,* which is usually transitive, means to go before, as in place, order, rank, importance, or time (*A flash of lightning preceded the thunder. The ambassador preceded the other guests into the dining hall. A major precedes a captain in the military organization*). *Proceed,* which is invariably intransitive, means to move or go forward or onward, especially after stopping (*Upon receipt of these orders, you will proceed without delay to the nearest port of embarkation. If you are clear on the work so far, let us proceed to the next step*).

precedence and **precedent** both mean a going before, but in different senses. *Precedence* means the act or fact of preceding; priority in order, rank, importance (*A major has precedence of a captain*); priority in time (*Yalta has precedence of Potsdam*); the right to precede others in ceremonies or social formalities (*The Papal Nuncio was accorded the precedence. At state banquets the Premier had precedence*); the order to be observed ceremonially by persons of different ranks (*As a Washington hostess she had made a careful study of precedence*). *Precedent* means a preceding instance or case which may serve as an example for or a justification in subsequent cases (*The ambassador established an admirable precedent when he sent his children to the local school*). In law, *precedent* means a legal decision or form of proceeding serving as an authoritative rule or pattern in future similar or analogous cases (*In Marbury v. Madison a precedent for the Supreme Court's judicial authority was established.... They take special care to record all the decisions formerly made against common justice and the general reason of mankind. These, under the name of* precedents, *they produce as authorities, to justify the most iniquitous opinions . . .*—Jonathan Swift).

precession; procession. *Precession* is an astronomical term describing a change in the direction of the axis of a rotating body (*precession of the equinoxes; axis of precession*). *Procession* is the familiar word to describe the proceeding or moving along in orderly succession, in a formal or ceremonious manner, of a line or body of persons, animals, vehicles, or other things (*The commencement procession moved across the meadow toward the auditorium*).

precipitate and **precipitous** both derive from a Latin word meaning cast headlong, but they fulfill separate functions. *Precipitate* applies to actions and means rushing headlong or rapidly onward (*The Light Brigade engaged in a precipitate charge on the heights*); acting or done or made in sudden haste or without due deliberation, overhasty, rash (*His precipitate decision to abandon rocket research may have cost Hitler the war*). *Precipitous,* applied mainly to physical objects, means of the nature of a precipice, or characterized by precipices (*Mont Saint Michel is a precipitous island*); extremely or impassably steep (*There is a trail, scarcely perceptible, that winds down the precipitous side of the canyon*). *Precipitous* is also sometimes used in place of *precipitate* in the senses of that word illustrated above.

precipitately; precipitously. *Precipitously* refers to the steepness and *precipitately* to the suddenness of a descent. If the stairway descends precipitously, one may fall down it precipitately; indeed, the more precipitous, the more precipitate.

precisely; actually. *Precisely* means definitely, exactly (*Precisely at the first stroke of eight, the trap was sprung. It is precisely that objection which I hope to satisfy*). *Actually* means as an actual or existing fact, really (*There were actually three men of that name who applied for the position. You do not actually need to be there; you can appoint a deputy*). One may tell what actually happened by describing precisely how it happened.

preciseness; precision. Though synonymous in some uses, *preciseness* and *precision* are distinguishable in others. Where the exactness of limitation concerns moral or religious matters, punctiliousness, scrupulousness, squeamishness, *preciseness* is employed (*Among their preciseness was a qualm at baptism; the water was to be taken from a basin, and not from a font. My grandmother, in her preciseness, regarded the introduction of the hymnal into church services as profane and frivolous*). It is, perhaps, this association that makes *preciseness* preferred when the exactness of the act is a little ostentatious or

more than necessary and where the performer seems to pride himself on his exactness and wish to call attention to his own meticulousness (*He spoke French with an exaggerated preciseness.* To say that *He spoke French with precision* would be a more neutral statement, less colored by the speaker's feeling that the other person's French was unnecessarily exact and perfect). A tailor who takes measurements with precision is one who proceeds with deliberation to have the measurements exact; one who takes them with preciseness rather makes a show of it or calls attention to his exactitude.

Precision today is almost invariably the word for mechanical operations as opposed to human acts. Parts are machined *with great precision.* A camera is *an instrument of precision.* Tools for exactingly delicate work are *precision tools.*

predicament; dilemma; plight; quandary. A *predicament* is an unpleasant, trying, or dangerous situation with an element of the puzzling in it (*If he continues he will find himself in a predicament from which it will not be easy to extricate himself*). *Plight* originally meant peril or danger (*Blaming thy treason, the cause of all our plight*), but it is now a synonym for *predicament,* except that *plight* is most often used lightly and humorously (*What plight to be in, three dinner invitations for the same night!*).

In popular use a *dilemma* is a situation which requires a choice between equally undesirable alternatives. The element of puzzlement is somewhat stronger in *dilemma* than in *predicament* or *plight* and that of peril less. A man is *on the horns of a dilemma* when he must choose one of several possible courses of action, each of which may have unfavorable consequences for him. *Quandary* is also the state of perplexity of one faced with a difficult situation. One rarely hears the word any more except in the phrase *to be in a quandary.*

predicate. As a grammatical term, the predicate of a sentence means the verb, its complements and its qualifiers, or everything in the sentence that is not part of the subject. The verb is called the simple predicate. The complement may include an indirect object, a direct object, and an object complement, or in the case of a linking verb, a predicate nominative. The qualifiers may be words, phrases, or clauses. See **sentences.**

predicate. The use of *predicate* to mean to found or base a statement or action on something (*My plan is predicated on the assumption that their greed will blind them to their danger*) is standard in the United States, though condemned by some authorities in England. *Predicate* does not, however, mean to predict.

predicate adjectives. See **position of adjectives.**

predicate nominative. This is a term used by some grammarians for the noun or pronoun that a linking verb joins to its subject. *A box,* in the sentence *this is a box,* would be called a predicate nominative. See **linking verbs.**

preface. See **foreword.**

prefer. This word may be followed by an infinitive, as in *I prefer to read,* or by the *-ing* form of a verb, as in *I prefer reading.* It may also be followed by a *that* clause with the clause verb a subjunctive or a subjunctive equivalent, as in *I prefer that he leave,* but an infinitive construction, such as *I prefer to have him leave,* is generally preferred.

When *prefer* is used to compare two things, the second is traditionally introduced by the preposition *to,* as in *I prefer skating to swimming.* This would be impossible with two infinitives. We cannot say *I prefer to skate to to swim,* and a *than* is often used here, as in *he preferred to live with a native woman rather than to work for a living.* This construction is condemned by many grammarians, but in the United States it is accepted and used by well educated people.

prefer. See **favor.**

preferable. This word means more desirable and is not compared in present-day English. We say that one thing is preferable to another and not that it is more preferable.

preferred. In this dictionary, the word *preferred* indicates only that a particular term is used more frequently and by more people than another. It is not meant as a statement of what is more correct or what ought to be used.

prefixes are usually joined directly to the following word, but are separated by a hyphen in a few cases. There is general agreement that a hyphen should be used:

1. When a prefix is joined to a word that begins with a capital letter, such as *non-European.*

2. When a prefix requires special stress to prevent misunderstanding or mispronunciation. For example, *co-op* is not the same as *coop,* and *re-creation* is not *recreation.* The prefix *ex-,* meaning "former," always takes this stress, as in *ex-president, ex-wife.* The prefix *co-* always takes this stress when it refers to a person. *Co-worker* and *co-author* are always hyphenated, even by those who write *cooperation* and *coexisting.* Newly coined words, double prefixes, and unusual or difficult forms come under this rule, such as *pre-preparation, un-un-American, non-negative numbers.* This rule also allows a writer to stress a prefix when he needs to, as for example in contrasting *pre-war* and *post-war* attitudes.

3. To avoid doubling a vowel, as in *semi-independent,* except with one-syllable prefixes ending in *e* or *o* (*reenact*). Many publishers use the hyphen to avoid doubling any vowel except after *co-,* and write *pre-election, pro-optic,* but *cooperate;* and to avoid any two vowels coming together when the prefix is more than one syllable, as in *semi-educated, extra-official.* (But everyone writes *extraordinary.*) A few extremely conservative publishers go still further and use the hyphen to prevent any two vowels coming together, as in *co-operate;* and to prevent double consonants in relatively new words, such as *sub-basement, over-refined.* (But everyone writes *address, ennoble.*) Still another method used by many publishers to avoid mispronunciation when a vowel, especially *e* or *o,* is doubled, is to place a dieresis over the second vowel, as in *preëmp-*

tory, coördinate. The present trend, however, is away from the use of either the hyphen or dieresis, especially in very common words like *cooperate.* The hyphen is reserved for cases where it is considered necessary, not by arbitrary rule, but to insure ease of reading and clarity of understanding.

prejudice; partiality. Though in its strictest sense *prejudice* means any preconceived opinion or feeling, favorable or unfavorable (*The prejudice I had conceived in his favor proved to be fully justified. These base prejudices so often blind their possessors to the evidence that lies before them*), it is usually now interpreted as an unfavorable opinion or feeling formed beforehand or without knowledge (*The current prejudice against rationalism manifests itself in a thousand ways*).

Two senses which have grown out of the idea of unfavorable opinion are disadvantage resulting from such an opinion (*Such a decision is to the prejudice of the Balkan nationals*) and resulting injury or detriment (*The attack worked to the prejudice of his reputation*). In these two senses *prejudice* is being overworked. More appropriate words, such as *disadvantage, damage,* and *harm* are being neglected.

Perhaps the prevailing pejorative use of *prejudice* grows out of a misunderstanding of the legal sense of the phrase *without prejudice* which means without dismissing, damaging, or otherwise affecting a legal interest or demand.

Partiality has achieved currency to indicate a favorable prejudice (*The partiality of parents for their own children is often indefensible*). *Prejudice* is always either *against* or *in favor of. Partiality* is always *for.*

prelate is sometimes used in America, either carelessly or humorously, as if it were synonymous with *priest* or *parson.* It applies to an ecclesiastic of a higher order, as an archbishop, bishop, or church dignitary.

premature. See **immature.**

premeditate. See **contemplate.**

premise; premises. The singular word *premise* means a statement that is accepted as a basis for further reasoning. It has a regular plural and we may speak of *these three premises.* Only the plural form *premises* is used in speaking of a building and its grounds. In this sense, the word is treated as a plural, as in *these premises are closed to the public,* but it cannot be used with a numeral or a word implying number.

The English sometimes make a distinction in the spelling of the noun plural, using *premisses* to describe, in logic, parts of a syllogism, and *premises* to serve other uses. Americans use only *premises* to designate the plural.

prepared to admit. Such expressions as *I am prepared to admit* are verbose beyond the call of duty or the lure of pleasure. Admit or deny.

prepositions. A preposition is a word that connects a noun or noun equivalent with some other word in a sentence by naming a relation between the things, qualities, or actions, which these words represent. The noun equivalent which is added to the sentence is called the object of the preposition and together with the preposition forms a prepositional phrase. (In this dictionary other kinds of words have been defined without reference to their meaning. To carry out this principle, we might define a preposition as a word that is not functioning as one of the other parts of speech.) In *Jeanie with the light brown hair*, the preposition *with* forms a phrase with the noun *hair* and qualifies the noun *Jeanie*. A preposition may be a simple, adverb-like word, such as *before, after, in, on, to*, or it may resemble a verb form, such as *during, past, except*. Prepositions may be compound words, such as *into, upon*, or they may be phrases, such as *apart from, in regard to*. But in every case the preposition has only one form. It is never altered, as nouns are to show number, verbs to show tense, and some adjectives and adverbs to make a comparison.

According to the formal rules of grammar, a subjective pronoun cannot be the object of a preposition. This rule is observed in practice when the object follows the preposition, as in *this is for him*. The subjective form *he* cannot be used in this position. When the object precedes the preposition a subjective form may be used, as in *who is it for?*. (See **who; whom.**) With this exception, any kind of word may be used as the object of a preposition provided it has the force or the sense of a noun, as in *until now, from here, in short, at best*. (For the *to*-infinitive and the use of prepositions with the *-ing* form of a verb, see **verbal nouns.**)

Some words that are used as prepositions may also be used as conjunctions. A word of this kind is a conjunction whenever it is followed by a full statement that contains a true verb, as in *before the cock crowed*, and a preposition when it is followed by a noun or noun equivalent without a verb, as in *before the paling of the stars*. A personal pronoun following a word of this kind is considered the object of a preposition if no verb follows, and an objective form is used rather than a subjective, as in *you were here before me*. That is, a word of this kind is interpreted as a preposition wherever possible. (Other words that are treated in the same way, such as *than, as*, and *but*, are said by some grammarians to be conjunctions only and not prepositions. This means that a personal pronoun following one of these words would have to be subjective or objective depending upon its function in the sentence. For a discussion of this, see **conjunctions** and the individual words.)

Some words that are used as prepositions are also used as adverbs. A word of this kind is an adverb when it stands alone without an object, as *through* in *we have come through*. When the word is followed by an object it may be a preposition, as in *it came through the window*, or it may be an adverb forming part of a compound verb, as in *he read through the letter*. The noun object of a preposition can never stand immediately before the preposition, but the normal position for the object of a compound verb is between the two elements of the compound. Therefore, a word of this kind is an adverb if it is possible to place the object between it and the verb, as in *he read the letter through*. If the object cannot be placed between the verb and the word in question, as in *it came the window through*, the word is probably a preposition.

CHOICE OF PREPOSITION

Prepositions represent, primarily, spatial or temporal relations, which are the only kinds of relations that exist between physical things. When used for this purpose, the meanings of the words are clear enough and it is not hard to choose the appropriate one. But as English ceased to be an inflected language the old prepositions were also used to express logical or conceptual relations which were once expressed by case. In these senses, it is sometimes difficult to say which is the right preposition to use. For example, it is easy enough to decide whether we want to say *the note was with the book* or *the note was in the book*. But whether we should say *the man spoke with anger* or *the man spoke in anger* is not as clear cut. This is partly because the conceptual relations themselves are not clear cut, and partly because there is a large element of metaphor in expressing them in terms of physical relations.

Sometimes we have no choice in the matter because custom has already established certain words in certain phrases and these must be observed. For example, we may say *agree to* but not *agree at* and *decide on* but not *decide in*. English is less rigid in this respect than most languages. But when one preposition sounds more familiar than another in a given combination of words, it is probably the best one to use. When one sounds no better than another, it is time to examine the relation and choose the preposition that expresses it best. For help in this, see the individual prepositions.

POSITION OF A PREPOSITION

Etymologically, the word *preposition* means "placed before." But to argue from this that a preposition must be placed before its object is like arguing that a butterfly must be a fly. Even in Latin a preposition sometimes follows its object. In English there are some constructions in which the preposition must precede the object and some in which it must follow. And there are others in which either word order is acceptable.

In a normal declarative sentence a preposition must stand before its object unless the object is a relative pronoun. Most sentences are of this kind and most prepositions stand before their objects. But we have a different situation when (1) the sentence is interrogative, (2) the normal word order is disturbed for the sake of emphasis, and (3) the object of the preposition is a relative pronoun. (When the object of a preposition is made the subject of a passive verb the preposition remains in its original position, as in *I was made a fool of;* but this is not ordinarily thought of as an object preceding the preposition.)

1. In a question, a preposition that governs the interrogative word may follow its object, as in *what are you looking for?*, or may precede it,

as in *for what are you looking?* The first is the preferred word order. The second is permitted, but it is unnatural English and is seldom used by a native speaker of the language.

When children were taught that it was wrong to end a sentence with a preposition, they were sometimes given *where are you staying at?* as an example of what not to do. This was sleight of hand on the part of the textbook writers. The sentence is wrong because we do not use *at* with *where* and *at where are you staying?* is no improvement. On the other hand, *what hotel are you staying at?* is standard, literary English.

2. In a declarative sentence, the object of a preposition may be placed before the subject of the principal verb for the sake of emphasis, as in *these you must believe in* and *this I want to hear about.* The preposition may also be brought forward here, as in *in these you must believe;* but when it is, the advantage of the inverted word order is greatly reduced.

3. A relative pronoun is sometimes the object of a preposition. If the pronoun is *as* or *that,* the preposition must follow the verb, as in *such things as we are sure of* and *the things that we are sure of.* When a clause of this kind has no relative pronoun, it is treated as if the word *that* had been used and a preposition follows the verb, as in *the things we are sure of.* If the relative pronoun is *which* or some form of *who,* a governing preposition may follow the verb, as in *the things which we are sure of,* or it may precede the pronoun, as in *the things of which we are sure.*

There are certain prepositions which, until recently, always preceded their object in literary English. These include: (1) prepositions that resemble verb forms rather than adverbs, such as *except, during, concerning;* (2) compound prepositions involving some other part of speech, such as *by means of, as to;* (3) the word *of* when it represents possession or introduces the whole of which something is a part; and (4) prepositions used in a purely figurative or literary sense. Today these words are often placed after their object, as in (1) *the report which I wrote to you concerning;* (2) *the report which I wrote to you in regard to;* (3) *the house which he is the owner of, the book which I had read some of;* (4) *the dignity which he spoke with.* Expressions of this kind are heard too often to be called anything but standard. But they are offensive to many people and do not have the literary standing of other "post-placed" prepositions.

Where both word orders are acceptable, a preposition standing before a relative pronoun has a decidedly bookish tone. The construction may be used in written material for variety. And in an involved or inverted sentence it may be necessary to place the preposition first in order to make the relationship immediately clear. But where it is not required and nothing is to be gained by it, this word order is unnatural English and should be avoided.

An infinitive followed by a preposition sometimes has the force of a relative clause. Here too, most prepositions follow the object, as in *something to think about, someone to talk to.* The adjective *worth* and the *-ing* form of a verb followed by a preposition may also be used in the same way, as in *something worth thinking about, someone worth talking to.*

PREPOSITIONAL PHRASES

A prepositional phrase may function as a noun. It may be the subject or the object of a verb or it may be the object of a preposition, as in *from behind the tree.* In each case, it stands wherever a noun performing the same function would stand.

But more often a prepositional phrase has the function of an adjective or an adverb. The primary position for an adjective phrase is immediately after the noun it qualifies, as in *a hive for the honey bee.* But it may also follow a linking verb, as in *the bird is on the wing.* An adverbial phrase may show time, place, manner, cause, purpose, means, direction, or any other adverbial idea. Its primary position is immediately after an intransitive verb or immediately after the object of a transitive verb, as in *he finished on time* and *he finished the work on time.* An adverbial phrase may also stand before the subject of the verb, as in *by this time he had finished the work.* In this position it may be set off by a comma, but this is not required if the phrase is short.

These rules of position are very important. To disregard them may be disastrous, as in *the cow fell into a hole on her back* and *he wrote the poem while riding to town on a piece of scratch paper.*

presage. The noun means a presentiment or foreboding (*He had a clear presage that the conference would fail*). The transitive verb means to foreshadow (*Those black clouds presage rain*). The intransitive verb means to have a presentiment (*I presage that everything will end badly*). Usage has colored the word slightly towards a prophecy of ill rather than of good.

prescience; presentiment. *Prescience* means knowledge of things before they exist or happen, foreknowledge, foresight. It is a neutral term. *Presentiment* means an uneasy anticipation of something unpleasant, not exactly foreknowledge but a discouraging certainty of trouble to come. God has prescience. Men have presentiments.

prescribe; proscribe. *Prescribe,* the more innocent and familiar term, means to lay down, in writing or otherwise, a rule or course to be followed (*Prescribe not us our duties. I prescribe an hour's conversation in French every day*). In medicine the word has the special meaning of designating a remedy or treatment (*The doctor prescribed only aspirin for my headaches*). In law it means to render invalid, to outlaw through negative prescription; an action that has been prescribed cannot be taken up again.

To *proscribe* is to denounce or condemn a thing as dangerous, to prohibit (*Under Hitler the works of Heine were proscribed. We children knew that our father's study was proscribed territory*); to put out of the protection of the law, to banish or exile; to announce the name of a person as condemned to death and his property to confiscation, to doom (*The king told Rochester to choose any ministers of the Established Church, with two exceptions. The proscribed persons were Tillotson and Stillingfleet*).

Prescribe has a positive connotation, *proscribe* a negative (*The doctor prescribed exercise and proscribed smoking*).

prescriptive right is sometimes used as if it meant an absolute right, one which cannot be annulled. This is a mistake. *Prescriptive right* is simply a right based on established usage or opinion or custom (*Yon tall Tower,/ Whose cawing occupants with joy proclaim / Prescriptive title to the shattered pile*), a long or immemorial use of some right with respect to a thing so as to give a right to continue such use (*The American Indians may have had a prescriptive right to the Great Plains, but the frontiersmen opposed the rights of conquest and greater agricultural efficiency*). Actually a prescriptive right is a dubious right.

present. This adjective may mean now or here, depending upon its position in the sentence. When it stands before the noun it qualifies it means now, as in *the present king, the present plan*. When it follows the noun, or noun equivalent, it means here, as in *those present* and *we were present*. The word is not compared, in either sense.

presentiment; presentment. A *presentiment* is a feeling or impression of something about to happen, especially something evil, a foreboding (*He had a presentiment of disaster*). See **prescience**.

Presentment is a wholly unrelated word meaning the act of presenting (*I attended the presentment of the new ambassador*); a representation, picture, or likeness (*That presentment may be faithful, but it is certainly unflattering*). In commerce, *presentment* means the presenting of a bill, note, or the like, as for acceptance or payment (*No check, bank draft, or money order shall be considered payment of any premium unless it is actually paid to the company on presentment*). In law, it means the written statement of an offense by a grand jury, of their own knowledge or observation, when no indictment has been laid before them.

presently; currently. *Currently* means belonging to the time actually passing (*They are currently engaged in stocking the store for the winter's business*). *Presently* used to mean immediately, in the present, at the time spoken of (*a reward to be rendered hereafter, not presently*). This meaning had been regarded as obsolete since the 17th century but has recently been revived as a vogue word. Used emphatically in commands and assurances of obedience, suggesting that the act required or agreed to was to take place in the instant of speaking, the word came to mean at once, forthwith, without delay (*Go presently, and take this ring*). But power demands and subservience promises more alacrity than is usually forthcoming and the word has become blunted into meaning soon, in a little

while, by and by (*I can't come right away; I'll be there presently*). See also **immediately**.

present tense. English uses the simple form of the verb, such as *talk* or *do*, for the present tense except in the third person singular where a final *s* or *es* is added, as in *he talks, he does*. The only exceptions to this rule are: (1) the verb *to be* which has the first person singular *am*, the third person singular *is*, and *are* in the other forms; (2) the verb *to have* which has the third person singular *has;* and (3) a few defective verbs, such as *will, shall, must*, which do not end in *s* in the third person singular. All irregular verbs have been listed in this book.

The form of the present tense just described is called the simple present. It indicates that an event takes place, or a state of affairs exists, in a period of time that includes the time of speaking. It puts no other limitations on the period, which may be momentary or may extend "from everlasting to everlasting." This tense form is used in statements that are essentially timeless, such as *that is no country for old men*, and to express customary or habitual action, which need not be actually in process at the time of speaking, as in *I read, much of the night, and go south in the winter*.

Do or *does* (the present tense of *to do*) followed by the simple form of a verb is used in place of a simple present in questions and in negative statements, as in *why do you read at night?* and *you do not go south every winter*. The same form is used to make a simple present statement emphatic, as in *I do read* and *I do go south*. (See **do**.)

To show that an action is a single event taking place at the time of speaking, and not merely something customary or to be expected, we use the progressive present form of the verb, which is made up of the appropriate present tense form of *to be* followed by the *-ing* form of the meaningful verb, as in *I am old and day is ending*. The simple present can also be used in speaking of an event in progress, as in *the darkness deepens*. But this form is ambiguous and the progressive present is preferred. The progressive present is sometimes called the definite present. Until recently, verbs such as *see, hear, believe, doubt*, which naturally express a continued action, were not used in the progressive form. But they are occasionally used in this way today. Within the last fifty years a progressive form of the verb *to be* has become very popular. It is used to limit a general statement to the immediate present. For example, *you are being unreasonable* might be used in preference to *you are unreasonable*, because it suggests that the unreasonableness is temporary.

In order to speak of a completed action as a present fact, we use *have* or *has* (the present tense of *to have*) followed by the past participle of the meaningful verb, as in *I have sailed the seas and come to the holy city of Byzantium*. This form is called the present perfect tense. In Latin, and in many European languages today, the present perfect is felt as a past tense form and can be used in narrative. This is not true in English. The English present perfect is a retrospective present. It makes a statement about a present situation which is seen as the result of past events. We may say *I have been to New York* because we see this as a present fact. We cannot say *George Washington has been to New York* because his actions do not extend to the present. Similarly, we may say *England has had able rulers* but we cannot say *Assyria has had able rulers.*

Languages which use the present perfect as a past tense form frequently use the simple present to express completed action. In German, for example, it is possible to say *we are here two hours already.* This construction is also heard in English in the United States but it is not considered standard. The English simple present or progressive present cannot be used in speaking of a period of time that is closed in the present. This requires a present perfect form and we must say, for example, *we have been here two hours already.*

The present perfect also has a progressive form. Here *have* or *has* is followed by *been* (the past participle of *to be*), which in turn is followed by the *-ing* form of the meaningful verb, as in *he has been studying for years.* This form has the same time meaning as the present perfect, *he has studied for years,* but speaks of the completed action as continued over a time. It is sometimes more vivid than the present perfect and suggests more strongly that the action may be continuing into the future. This form of the verb is often used in speaking of a completed action that is repeated or habitual, as in *he has been going to New York for years.* Here what is continuing, possibly into the future, is the custom of going to New York. When the simple present is used to express habitual action, the action is treated abstractly, almost as a theoretical matter. When the progressive present perfect is used, the action is concrete, a solid, established fact.

Each of the forms that have been discussed may also be expressed in the passive voice. (See **passive voice.**) In addition, there is a present subjunctive form that is like the simple present but does not add *s* in the third person singular. (See **subjunctive mode.**) An idea that would normally be expressed by a present tense verb is expressed as a past tense in a subordinate clause that is dependent on a past tense verb. (See **tense shifts.**)

The present tenses are often used in speaking of the future. With verbs of motion this may be the simple present, as in *the boat sails tomorrow, he arrives Wednesday.* With other verbs it is more likely to be the progressive form, as in *we are having guests next Friday* and *he is speaking on the radio tomorrow evening.* This use of the present tense is standard English and always has been. In fact, English has no way of expressing the future that is not based on a present tense verb. In current English a simple present (or a present perfect) verb is required in conditional clauses and in clauses of time that are part of a statement about the future, as in *I will let you know if he comes* and *I will let you know as soon as he comes.* See **future tense.**

The present tense may be used in speaking about the past, but only with a sort of literary license. We often treat important contributions to knowledge made in the past as timeless and belonging to the present, and say *Plato teaches* or *Herodotus says.* This is always acceptable. Occasionally we use a present tense in describing a past event in order to make the action more vivid. This is called the historical present, or the dramatic present. It is acceptable when what is being told is really extraordinary, as in *I opened the bathroom door, and what do I see but a camel!* It is not acceptable when used to dramatize a conversation that is not dramatic, as in *He looked at her and he says, "Why not?" "Why not, indeed!" says she.* As in the examples given, the historic present is frequently used in sentences that also contain a past tense verb. This mixing of tenses is not a characteristic of nonstandard speech. It is also found in the works of great writers who have used the historic present.

present writer is a mock-modest variation on *I.* It might be called a symptom of the John Alden syndrome. If one is speaking for himself, he should speak for himself.

preserve in American usage describes a tract of public land set apart for any one of a number of special purposes. The forest preserves around Chicago, for example, are public pleasure grounds, with trails for hiking, bridle paths for horseback riding, and many picnic grounds and camping sites. In England *preserve* especially means a place set apart for the protection and propagation of game or fish for sport (*There are huge game preserves in Kenya*).

president; presidency. A *president* is a presiding officer. He may be elected or appointed. The office is the *presidency.* Hence a man is, properly, a candidate for the presidency, not "for president." In the United States *the* President is the chief executive officer of the republic, the holder of the highest office in the land and, when it refers to him, the word is always capitalized.

Most American universities designate their chief officer *president,* but there has been a tendency among some of these great ones to exalt themselves to loftier heights as chancellors and regents and to hand down the presidency to their next in command. In nothing does the principle of Gresham's Law work more vigorously than in titles, as *consul, captain, duke,* and a host of other faded splendors can attest, and we may live to see the term *president* bestowed in our universities upon janitors or professors.

press. When this verb means urge it may be followed by an infinitive, as in *we pressed him to come,* but not by the *-ing* form of a verb or by a clause.

presume. See **assume.**

presumption. See **assumption.**

presumptive; presumptuous. *Presumption* is the act of presuming, taking for granted. *Presumptive* and *presumptuous,* formerly synonymous, now reflect different aspects of presumption. *Presumptive,* restricted today almost exclusively to legal terminology, means affording grounds for presumption, based on presumption (*His title was presumptive rather than conferred*), presumed, or regarded as such by presumption (*The king's brother is heir presumptive to the throne until the heir apparent is born*). *Presumptuous* reflects our attitude towards those whose presumptions seem to us unwarranted, forward, impertinent, pushing. The word is derogatory, meaning brazen, brash (*His adoption of the titles of the office before he was elected was presumptuous, to say the least*).

pretend and **profess,** in their most familiar senses, both now carry the connotation of deception—a sad reflection on the value of human professions and pretensions.

Pretend, as a transitive verb, now means to put forward a false appearance of, to feign (*If I pretend illness, I won't have to go to the party*); to venture or attempt falsely to do something. As an intransitive verb, *pretend* means to make believe (*He pretended he was Donald Duck*); to lay claim to (*He pretended to the throne*); to make pretensions (*He pretended to great skill as a musician, though he hardly knew a piano from a drum*); to aspire as a suitor or candidate (*Don Cesare pretended to the Infanta's hand*). In its least common sense as a transitive verb, *pretend* may mean to allege or profess, especially insincerely or falsely (*He pretended deep sorrow at the news of his uncle's death*). The idea of feigning, apparent here, is now the commonest sense of *profess,* which, as a transitive verb, means to lay claim to a feeling, often insincerely, to pretend something that one does not feel. Actually, one can choose between *pretend* and *profess* in this sense only on the basis of whether the claim is voiced or not. One may *pretend* sorrow with a doleful face, *profess* it with doleful words. In senses clearly distinguishable from those of *pretend, profess* may mean to declare openly, announce or affirm, avow or acknowledge (*I profess myself unworthy of the honor you intend me. He never tired of professing allegiance to the flag*), to declare oneself skilled or expert in, or to claim to have knowledge of (*The wise professor professes only ignorance*).

pretend; affect; purport; claim. *Pretend* and *affect* are derogatory. *Purport* and *claim* are neutral.

Pretend and *affect* imply an attempt to create a false appearance. *Pretend,* specifically, means to create an imaginary characteristic or to play a part (*He pretended that he came from an old Virginia family*). *Affect* means to make a consciously artificial show of having qualities which one thinks would look well and impress others (*He affected a Harvard accent after two months Army training in Cambridge*).

Purport and *claim* carry no overtones of insincerity. *Purport* means to profess or claim, as by the thought or meaning which runs through something (*This text purports to be authentic; certainly the grammar, the spelling, and the local references are what one would expect*). To purport is to imply, to convey to the mind as the meaning or thing intended (*This purports to be an official declaration of foreign policy*). *Claim,* the less formal word, means to assert or maintain as a fact (*He claimed that there had been violations of election procedure*).

pretender; Pretender. A *pretender* in current usage is definitely one whose pretensions are without foundation, a claimant to a throne or office who has no just title to support his claim. In the application of the term to the son and grandson of James II of England, however, the term is neutral, and the word is always capitalized. The *Old Pretender* (which title has the further unfortunate connotation of long-practiced feigning) was James Francis Edward Stuart (1688-1766). The *Young Pretender* (also known as *the Chevalier* and *Bonnie Prince Charlie*) was Charles Edward Stuart (1720-1788).

preternatural. See **unnatural.**

pretty. The adjective *pretty* has had a great many meanings, including deceitful, tricky, cunning, clever, skillful, admirable, pleasing. In present-day English it means pleasing to the eye. In this sense, it has an adverb form *prettily,* as in *the child was prettily dressed.*

The form *pretty* is also used as an adverb meaning moderately, in some degree, as in *we are pretty sure* and *he gave a pretty full account. Pretty* does not work successfully as a synonym for *very.* It is not an intensive, but weakens the word it qualifies. *Pretty sure* means not completely sure, and *pretty well* in *I'm feeling pretty well* is equivalent to the old-fashioned *tolerable.*

pretty kettle of fish. As an ironical term for some irritating situation, some embarrassing predicament, *pretty kettle of fish* is now a cliché. The origin of the phrase is uncertain. It came into use in the middle of the eighteenth century. Thomas Newte in his *A tour in England and Scotland in 1785* (1788) says that it was customary for gentlemen who lived near the Tweed "to entertain their neighbours and friends with a Fete Champetre, which they call giving 'a kettle of fish' " in the course of which "a fire is kindled and live salmon thrown into boiling kettles." Whether these merrymakings degenerated into brawls or whether the figurative application of the term derived from the agonized thrashing of the salmon in the boiling water is not known.

prevaricate, which derives from a Latin word meaning to walk crookedly, to deviate, is a slightly affected term for *equivocate.* It is often used as a euphemism for *lie,* it being felt, apparently, that an elegant word covers up an inelegant act.

prevent; hinder. To *prevent* something is to stop it by forestalling action and hence rendering it impossible (*He prevented my escape by taking away my clothes*). To *hinder* something is to keep it back by delaying or stopping progress of an action (*The advance of the army was hindered by the weather and the condition of the roads*). *Prevent* has more the sense of complete stoppage, *hinder* more the sense of a clogging delay.

Prevent means, etymologically, to go before, and the student of English literature will often come upon obsolete meanings of the word that will puzzle him unless he bears its etymology in mind (such as: *Prevent us, Lord, in all our ways. It will be the study of my life to prevent your every wish. He had prevented the hour, because we might have the whole day before us, for our business*).

The *-ing* form of a verb following *prevent* is usually introduced by *from,* as in *he prevented me from going,* but it may also be used without *from,* as in *he prevented me going.*

preventive; preventative; preventitive. *Preventative* has been superseded by the briefer *preventive* which, as an adjective, means warding off disease (*Preventive medicine is largely responsible for the low death rate*), serving to prevent or hinder. As a noun, *preventive* is primarily a medical term meaning a drug for preventing disease, and, more broadly, a preventive agent or measure. *Preventitive* is a misspelling of *preventative* and cannot be justified at all.

previous. The adjective form *previous* is used with the preposition *to* to form a compound preposition which may introduce an adverbial phrase, as in *previous to this, he had been out of the room.* Otherwise, *previous* cannot be used as an adverb. We do not say *I had been there previous.* The adverbial form *previously* may also be used with *to,* but *previous to* is preferred to *previously to.*

The expression *a little previous* (or *too previous*) means "jumping the gun" and is intended as humor. When used in any other way, the construction is not standard.

prey on one's mind. To say of something that worries someone to the extent of impairing his spirits and even his health that it *preys on his mind* is to employ a worn phrase. The figure was once a strong one, suggesting the ravening of a beast of prey, but overuse has weakened it.

priceless. See **invaluable.**

prick up one's ears. In its figurative sense of suddenly paying attention and listening intently, *prick up one's ears,* a term taken from a characteristic action of horses and dogs, is now hackneyed.

pride; haughtiness; arrogance; vanity; conceit. Although *pride* in Christian theology is regarded as the deadliest of the Seven Deadly Sins, the word has, in common usage, a favorable as well as an unfavorable connotation. It can mean a becoming or dignified sense of what is due to oneself or one's position, self-respect, self-esteem of a proper kind (*He took great pride in his work. Civic pride has made many a town a better place to live in. He was his father's pride, his mother's joy*).

In its unfavorable connotation it means a lofty and arrogant assumption of superiority in some respect (*He had too much pride to accept manual labor. Pride goeth before destruction, and an haughty spirit before a fall*). *Haughtiness* means disdainful pride, superciliousness, and usually refers to a manner (*From the haughtiness of her bearing I concluded that she was at least a marchioness*). *Arrogance* consists of an offensive exhibition of real or assumed superiority, insolent pride (*His recent successes increased his arrogance*). *Haughtiness* tends to describe someone taking advantage of an established position, *arrogance* to characterize one newly arrived at a position of authority or power.

Pride, even in its unfavorable meaning, has often a justification in fact, but *vanity* implies a self-admiration and a desire to be admired by others that is groundless. The word used to mean emptiness, worthlessness, and this meaning lingers in moral and religious uses (*Vanity of vanities, all is vanity. The vanity of earthly wishes*) and colors the particular sort of pride that the word in its most common use now describes. When we say *It was vanity which prevented her from wearing glasses even when she read,* we imply that her pride in her appearance was carried, in this instance, to the point of folly and was a baseless pride. We may hate pride; we despise vanity.

Conceit, which originally meant a fancy, a whim, or a fanciful thought, idea or expression of a strained and far-fetched nature, when used as a synonym of *pride,* as it now most commonly is, is an even more contemptuous word than vanity. It implies an exaggerated estimate of very slight abilities or attainments, naïvely expressed, wholly lacking in dignity (*The conceit of that whelp in saying to Professor Ellison that one man's opinion was as good as another's*).

prima facie. See **a priori.**

primary; prime; premier; chief; primal. These words all mean highly important. In many contexts they are synonymous (*The primary/ prime/ premier/ chief/ first/ primal consideration should be the national security*). *Primary* means first or highest in rank or importance, chief (*Domestic policy was of primary importance during the Depression*). *Prime* means first in importance, excellence, rank (*He ordered prime ribs of beef*). *Premier* means first in rank, chief, leading, earliest (*The premier performance was held in Miss Bankhead's native city*). *Chief* means highest in rank or authority, most important (*The chief end of man is to glorify God and enjoy him forever*). *Primal,* a word now seldom used, means first, original, primeval, of first importance, fundamental (*We will grieve not, rather find/ Strength in what remains behind;/ In the primal sympathy/ Which having been must ever be . . .*).

prime of life. To say of someone of mature years in vigorous health that he is in the *prime of life* is to employ a phrase that has been weakened by overuse.

primeval; primitive; primordial. *Primeval* means of or pertaining to the first age or ages, especially of the world (*This is the forest primeval. Miss Kilman stood there . . . with the power and taciturnity of some prehistoric monster armored for primeval warfare*).

Primitive is used much more frequently and in a variety of senses. It primarily means being the first or earliest of the kind or in existence (*In South Africa have been discovered primitive weapons made from the bones of animals*), early in the history of the world or of mankind (*Primitive social organization tends to be authoritarian*). It can also mean characteristic of early ages or of an early state of human development (*African art is relatively primitive*), unaffected or little affected by civilizing influences, rough (*His manners were primitive and his morals nonexistent*).

Primitive has special learned senses. In anthropology it means of or pertaining to a race, group, etc., having cultural or physical similarities with their early ancestors. In biology it means rudimentary, primordial, denoting species only slightly evolved from early antecedent types.

Primordial means original, elementary, that from which something else derived, that which constitutes a beginning (*I should infer . . . that probably all the organic beings . . . on earth have descended from some one primordial form*—Darwin).

primrose path. As a trope for a gay but wicked course of conduct, especially in sexual matters, *primrose path* is now a cliché. The phrase is an echo of two passages in Shakespeare's plays: the *primrose path of dalliance* which the *puff'd and reckless libertine* treads in *Hamlet* and the *primrose way to th' everlasting bonfire* of which the porter speaks in *Macbeth*.

principal; principle. These words, pronounced alike and spelled so nearly alike, are unlikely to be confused if one remembers that *principal* is used as an adjective and also as a noun, while *principle* is a noun only. It is over the nouns that confusion usually arises, a confusion implied in the old joke, "I don't really hate the high school; it's just the principal of the thing."

As an adjective *principal* means first or highest in rank, importance, or value, chief, foremost (*Our principal allies are the British Commonwealth and France*). As a noun *principal* usually means a chief or governing head (*The principal of the high school handed a diploma to each of the graduating seniors*).

Principle refers not to a person but to an accepted or professed rule of action or conduct (*He is a man of high principle*), a fundamental, primary, or general truth, on which other truths depend (*The principles of political economy are not what they were in Adam Smith's day*), a fundamental doctrine or tenet (*Plato's philosophy rests on the principle of dual reality*).

principal parts of the verb. The forms of a verb usually given in a dictionary are:

1. The infinitive, such as *talk* or *speak*. In English, this form is also the imperative, the present subjunctive, and the present indicative, except for the third person singular which normally adds an *s* or *es*, as in *he talks, he speaks,* and for the verb *to be* which has a completely irregular present indicative.

2. The past tense, such as *talked* or *spoke*.

3. The past participle, such as *talked* or *spoken*. This form is used with the auxiliary verb *be* to make the passive voice, as in *he was spoken to,* and with the auxiliary verb *have* to express completed action, as in *he had spoken*. It may also be used as an adjective, as in *a well-spoken man was he*. In a regular English verb the past tense and past participle are made by adding *-ed* to the basic form of the word (the infinitive). Many

dictionaries do not list these forms of the verb unless they are made irregularly.

4. The present participle. This is always made by adding *-ing* to the basic form, and for this reason may not be listed. The *-ing* form is used with the auxiliary verb *be* to express continuing action, as in *he was speaking*. It may also be used as an adjective, as in *a speaking acquaintance,* or as a noun, as in *to study public speaking*. A few verbs, such as *can* and *ought,* do not have an *-ing* form.

These four forms are not only the "principal" parts of an English verb; they are all the parts there are except the third person singular in the present tense. (Again, the one exception is the verb *to be*.)

probe. In its historic and literal sense, *probe* means to explore a wound or cavity in the body with a surgical instrument (*He probed the wound until he found the bullet*). In America *probe* has come to be used widely, in a figurative extension of this sense, to mean to examine thoroughly, to question closely. There is also, in America, a noun *probe,* meaning an investigation, especially by a legislative committee, of suspected illegal activity. Both of these uses are now standard, though the verb is often used when a milder word, such as *question* or *investigate,* would be more suitable. Nonetheless, where *probe* is suitable, where the condition being searched is morbid, the searching accompanied by pain, and the purpose to restore health to the body politic, the term is vivid and useful.

proboscis. The plural is *proboscises* or *proboscides,* not *probosces*.

proceed is not to be used as a pretentious synonym for *go* or *come*. It is stilted to say *Let us proceed to the fountain for a drink* or *That information proceeds from a most unreliable source*. To *proceed* is to move forward, especially after stopping (*After a short recess, they proceeded with the hearing*). Some claim that in military language *proceed* is a recognized synonym for *go,* but this may be challenged. In military terminology, *proceed* does not so much mean *go* as *go on;* for it is assumed in military service that any given assignment will be followed by another to which one proceeds (*Upon receipt of these orders, you will proceed . . .*). See also **precede.**

procession. See **precession.**

proclaim. See **declare.**

proclaim from the housetops. As a term for making something public knowledge, *proclaim from the housetops* is a cliché. It is from Matthew, 10:27. The Authorized Version has *what ye hear in the ear, that preach ye upon the housetops*. The Revised Standard Version has *what you hear whispered, proclaim upon the housetops*.

prodigal. See **lavish.**

product; produce; proceeds. *Produce* refers especially to agricultural or natural products collectively (*The farmers brought their produce to town early each Saturday morning*). *Product* tends to mean something resulting from manufacture (*Our products include textiles, plastics, and dyes. Even if you have a good product, you* still have to find a market for it). *Product* may also be used figuratively to mean effect or result (*My book is the product of several years of research*). *Proceeds* is that which results or accrues, especially the sum derived from a sale or other transaction (*The entire proceeds of the bazaar will go to the Fund for Crippled Children*).

profanity. See **blasphemy.**

profess. This word may be followed by an infinitive, as in *he professed to have studied Sanskrit.* It is sometimes heard with the *-ing* form of a verb, as in *he professed having studied Sanskrit,* but this is not standard English.

profession; trade. The word *profession* was formerly confined to the vocations of theology, law, and medicine, but modern usage has extended it to include almost any vocation requiring knowledge of some department of learning or science. Today we speak of the *professions* of teaching, acting, architecture, and a dozen other activities. Indeed, were anyone engaged in any activity that plainly was not wholly manual to refer to his occupation as *my profession,* the phrase would probably be accepted without any resentment or amusement or sense of incongruity. In part this is due to the working of the principle of Gresham's Law in titles and honorifics, but in part it is also due to the fact that more and more occupations today require considerable knowledge and preparation.

A *trade* still suggests an occupation involving manual training and skill (*In his youth he had learned a good trade; he was a carpenter. The building trades . . .*). *Trade* by itself refers to the exchange of commodities, for other commodities or money. *The trade* refers collectively to those in the same line of business (*In the trade we call it a gimmick*). *In trade* is an English expression equivalent to the American *engaged in business,* though the English phrase often has a slight connotation of contempt wholly absent from the American expression. See also **avocation, calling, business, job.**

professor. The commonest meaning of *professor* in current usage is a teacher of the highest rank, usually in a particular branch of learning, in a university or college. Including associate professors and assistant professors (a gradation now almost universal in American colleges), more than half of any faculty is made up of professors. In England the term *professor* is reserved for a very few teachers in colleges and universities who hold chairs and are of the highest rank. Formerly the term *professor* was used humorously in America to designate piano players in taverns, bootblacks, wandering minstrels, and assorted mountebanks. More recently it has incurred odium from the reproaches of those who regard all intellectuals as subversives. And at all times it has suffered from the pretentiousness of many who have claimed it as their proper title of respect. Abashed by all this, most professors prefer to be called *Mister.*

The title *Professor* may be abbreviated as *Prof.* when it stands before a full name or a last name and initials, as in *Prof. Mary Calkins, Prof. M. W. Calkins.* When used immediately before a last name it is always spelled out, as in *Professor Calkins.*

Professor or *Prof.* is not used with other titles or with letters showing academic degrees, such as *Ph.D., D. Litt., LL.D.*

The word *Professor* may be used without a proper name as a form of address, as in *thank you, Professor.* It may also be used in speaking about the person, as in *the professor lives on Elm Street.*

proffer, tender and **offer** all mean to present for acceptance or refusal. *Offer* is the general word, the best of the lot, and the one most suitable for nearly all contexts. *Proffer* is now chiefly a literary substitute for *offer* in a figurative sense (*He proffered his heart in verses of his own composition*). *Tender,* no longer used in reference to concrete objects, is a ceremonious term for a more or less formal or conventional act (*He tendered his resignation when his party fell from power. Both bids were tendered on the same day*).

profuse. See **lavish; prolific.**

progressive tenses. Forms of the verb which refer to an action as in progress are called the progressive tenses. They are made by adding the *-ing* form of the verb to the appropriate form of *to be,* as in *he is laughing* and *they had been laughing.* The action can be presented as in progress in the present, the past, or the future.

Until a little over a hundred years ago the progressive forms were not used in the passive voice. Instead, they were understood as having either an active or a passive meaning, depending upon the sense of the statement. That is, *selling* would be understood as passive in *the books are now selling.* A New England grammarian, writing in 1855, said that this usage "is unquestionably of far better authority, and (according to my apprehension) in far better taste, than the more complex phraseology which some late writers adopt in its stead; as, 'The books are now being sold.'" Today, we may still say *the books are selling* but we do not feel that the progressive passive form is a complex phraseology. Some contemporary grammarians say that the progressive passive cannot be used in the perfect tenses or in the future tense. But it is used in these forms and in speech more often than in writing. See **passive voice** and **future tense.**

Contemporary grammarians also say that the progressive forms should not be used in the simple tenses for verbs of perception or attitude, such as *see, hear, believe, doubt,* since these naturally express a continuing state of affairs. But the progressive forms often are used with these verbs. We say *I am hearing every word* and *he was doubting it.* (For other questions about the use of these tenses, see **past tense** and **present tense.**)

prohibit. See **inhibit.**

prolific and **profuse** both suggest abundance, but they are not to be confused. *Prolific* means fruitful, producing offspring abundantly (*Americans were never more prolific than in the last half of the nineteenth century. Urban families used formerly to be much less prolific than rural families*), producing much or abundantly (*Upton Sinclair is among our most prolific writers. This act may be prolific of evil consequences*). *Profuse* is a passive term meaning poured forth, extravagant (*He was profuse in his outlays*), made or done freely and abundantly (*He made profuse apologies for his tardiness*), abundant (*Such a profuse rain of invective came as a surprise. Profuse strains of unpremeditated art*). See also **lavish.**

promenade. The basic meaning of *promenade* is a walk taken at a leisurely pace for exercise, amusement, or display, or as a part of a social ceremony (*On the day before the bullfights began, highborn señoritas took their promenade in the square*). By transference, *promenade* means a place for promenading (*a leisurely walk along the promenade*). In the United States only, *promenade* may also be used to describe a ball or dance in a school or college. The colloquial and commoner term is *prom* (*He desperately wanted to go to the Junior Prom, but didn't have the money*). *Promenade* may also, in America, describe a march of guests into a ballroom, constituting the opening of a formal ball, or a march of dancers in folk or square dancing. *Promenade deck* is the name for a space on an upper deck of a passenger ship for the use of passengers.

promote, from a Latin word meaning moved forward, advanced, means to further the growth, development, or progress of something (*The welfare of the school was promoted by the P.T.A. in a dozen different ways*). The word is used a great deal in America today as a synonym for *advertise* (*The new product was promoted on every billboard for forty miles around* [a subtle form of promotion for advertising]). Of course advertising does promote business and there is a considerable area in which the two words are synonymous. But where it plainly means merely to make a public announcement or give information to the public concerning something with the intention of increasing sales, *promote* is pompous and a little tricky. It suggests that the advertising has already accomplished what it hopes to accomplish, an idea which advertising men are, of course, eager to have their clients believe but which the client may resent having palmed off on him in this way.

To *promote* also means to advance in rank, dignity, or position (*Within a year he was promoted from teller to assistant cashier*). In education it means to put ahead to the next higher stage or grade of a course or series of classes (*Despite his inability to read, he was promoted to the fourth grade*). It has a special use in reference to the organizing of financial and other undertakings (*He promoted a dozen oil companies and two railroads*).

Promote is always to be used in the sense of furthering, making better. It does not mean simply to cause.

prompt. See **impel.**

prone, supine, and **prostrate** are all used to describe actual physical position as well as figurative condition.

Prone and *prostrate* mean lying face downwards on one's stomach; they also mean lying flat, at full length, without specifying the direction faced. *Supine* means lying face upwards on one's back.

The commonest meaning of *prone* is the figurative one of having a natural inclination or tendency to something, disposed, liable (*He is prone to these outbursts of temper. Dostoevsky was prone to attacks of epilepsy*). It is used as well, however, in its literal physical senses of lying face downwards (*One can fire a rifle most accurately from a prone position*), prostrate, as opposed to erect (*On the Acropolis is to be found many an ancient column, broken and prone*), or having a downward direction or slope (*From high Olympus prone her flight she bends*). Of the hand, it means with the palm downward.

Prostrate, although describing the same physical position of the body as *prone,* carries with it more of the sense of weakness, helplessness, submission. One may fall prone on purpose to escape a hail of bullets; one falls prostrate under the attack of a maddened dog. Figuratively, therefore, *prostrate* means overthrown, overcome, helpless (*Poland was prostrate before the advancing panzer columns*).

Supine is most commonly used in its literal, physical sense of lying on the back with the face upwards (*They buried their dead on their backs, or in a supine position*). Of the hand, it means with the palm upward. In a figurative sense, *supine* means inactive, passive, inert, especially from indolence or indifference (*Alberto Moravia's novel* The Indifferent Ones *is about supine Italians under Mussolini*).

In their figurative uses, *prone* suggests an active desire, *supine* a passive acceptance. Thus when William Faulkner speaks of barbers *above their prone clients* (*These 13*, 1931), he is misusing the word literally and figuratively.

pronominal adjectives. Words such as *all, any, both,* which are used as adjectives and as pronouns, are called pronominal adjectives when they qualify nouns or noun equivalents. The possessive personal pronouns are also regarded as pronominal adjectives by many grammarians. As a rule, these words stand before other qualifying words, as *any* in *any such outrageous, unheard of, not-to-be-put-up-with, nonsense.*

pronouns. Pronouns are defined as "words that are used in place of nouns." They are function words, or grammatical devices, and are used to indicate something that would be named by a noun, without naming it. For example, *such* is a pronoun in *of such is the kingdom of heaven.* We do not know what this sentence means until we know that *such* is here being used in place of *little children.* The word which a pronoun is used in place of is called its antecedent. The antecedent of a pronoun may not be mentioned, as is the case with *someone* in *someone told* *me;* and it may even be unknown, as is the case with *who* in *who can say?*. See **antecedent.**

The difference between a pronoun and a noun is not always clear. Some pronouns, such as *both,* were originally adjectives, and most pronouns can be used as adjectives to qualify nouns, as can most nouns. Most pronouns do not have the three forms (singular, plural, and genitive) that are characteristic of nouns. But some do have a genitive, such as *either's,* and a few have both a singular and a plural form, such as *other* and *others.* As a rule, a pronoun cannot be qualified by an adjective, but there are exceptions even to this. In any case, wherever it is impossible to say whether a given word is a pronoun or not, it makes no difference what one calls it.

Pronouns may be singular or plural. Some, such as *this,* are singular; some, such as *we,* are plural; and some, such as *who,* may be either singular or plural. According to the formal rules of grammar, a pronoun always has the same number as the word it represents. That is, it is singular if the word is singular and plural if the word is plural. But in English, from the earliest times, the number of a pronoun has been determined by the meaning or intention of the speaker rather than by the grammatical form of the antecedent. The number of a verb also depends upon the intention of the speaker, but not as completely as the number of a pronoun. Dr. Johnson, for example, said that he knew no instance of *a nation that has preserved their words and phrases from mutability.* Here the singular noun *nation* is followed by a singular verb *has,* but is referred to by the plural pronoun *their* because the writer was thinking of a large number of people, and not of a political unit.

A pronoun is also said to "agree with its antecedent in person." In present-day English, most of the problems of "person" are taken care of under "number." All that remains of this rule is the claim that whenever one of the three words *who, which,* or *that,* has *I, me,* or *you,* as an antecedent, it must be used with the same form of the verb that would be used with the antecedent. (For a fuller discussion of this, see **agreement: verbs.**)

A few pronouns have case. That is, a few pronouns are either subjective or objective. Although the number and person of a pronoun are determined by its antecedent, the case depends upon how the pronoun itself is being used. (See **subjective pronouns** and **objective pronouns.**)

Pronouns are classified partly by form, partly by meaning, and partly by use. These classes overlap to some extent and the same word may be found in more than one group. But the traditional classification does separate out problems that arise in connection with some words and not with others. (For a discussion of these problems, see **personal, possessive, objective, subjective, relative, interrogative, reflexive, intensive,** and **indefinite pronouns.**) Two other classes of pronouns, *demonstrative* and *reciprocal,* are defined in this book but present no problems.

proof. See **evidence.**

Proofreader's marks

⌃	Insert comma
⌄	Insert apostrophe
⌄⌄	Insert quotation marks
⊙	Insert period
⊙	Insert colon
;/	Insert semicolon
?/	Insert question mark
=/	Insert hyphen
1/M	One-em dash
2/M	Two-em dash
en	En dash
|·|·|	Ellipsis (If preceded by a period there will be 4 dots.)
⌇	Delete
⌢	Close up
⌣	Delete and close up
℈	Reverse; upside-down
⋀	Insert (caret)
¶	Paragraph
no ¶	No paragraph; run in
tr	Transpose (their, only is)
＝	Align
⌄	Superscript (number specified)
⌃	Subscript (number specified)
#	Insert space
hr#	Hair space between letters
↧	Push down space
[	Move to left
]	Move to right
⊔	Lower
⊓	Elevate
✗	Broken letter
⌒	Ligature (Æsop)
sp	Spell out (U. S.)
stet	Let it stand (some day)
wf	Wrong font
bf	Set in boldface type
rom	Set in roman type
ital	Set in italic type
sc	Small capitals
caps	Capitals
lc	Set in lower case
ld	Insert lead between lines

propaganda; publicity. *Propaganda* is the right word for the particular doctrines or principles propagated by an organization or concerted movement. The term takes its origin from the College of Propaganda, a committee of cardinals, established in 1622 by Pope Gregory XV, having supervision of the foreign missions of the Roman Catholic Church and of the training of priests for these missions.

Though in origin and history and in its special Roman Catholic sense, *propaganda* has no unfavorable connotations, in popular usage today it is a derogatory term. It is used to describe the efforts of those whom we regard as enemies to make their creed or policy known and accepted (*Communist propaganda. That's just a lot of propaganda*). Our own attempts to win acceptance for our creed or policy are termed a crusade, a campaign of enlightenment, or, more simply and more commonly, the truth.

Publicity, a more neutral term than *propaganda* and a more dignified one than the slang *ballyhoo,* describes the measures, process, or business of securing public notice, the state of being brought to public notice by announcements (aside from advertisements), by mention in the press, on radio or television, or any means serving to effect the purpose (*You can't even give money away today without a publicity campaign first*).

propellant; propellent. *Propellant* is a noun only. It means a propelling agent. In military usage it designates the charge of explosive used in a cannon to make the shell travel to the target (*Gunpowder is a propellant*). *Propellent* may be used as an adjective or a noun. As an adjective it means propelling, driving forward (*Gunpowder is a propellent force*). As a noun *propellent* means, like *propellant,* a propelling agent.

proper. When this word means "itself" or "strictly so-called," it stands after the noun it qualifies, as in *Prussia proper* and *the fishes proper.* When the word is used in any other sense it stands before its noun, as in *the proper study of mankind,* or after a form of the verb *to be,* either expressed or felt, as in *do you think it is proper?*

proper nouns. *Proper* here has its archaic meaning of "belonging to oneself." A proper noun is the identifying name of a particular person, place, or thing, such as *Rice Kemper, Mt. Vernon, the Wayside Inn.* Other nouns, such as *man, farm, barn, esth,* are called common nouns. They name a class of things and identify individuals only as members of that class. Proper nouns, and the adjectives made from them, are always capitalized in English. When a common noun is used as a proper noun, it too may be capitalized, as in *I will ask Father.* When a word that was originally a proper noun is no longer thought of in that sense, it loses its capital letter, as in *watt, ampere, brussels sprouts, paris green.* How soon this happens varies with different writers.

Except for its capital letter, a proper noun is treated like any other noun. It may be used in the plural, as in *the four Marys.* But here the plural does not mean four individuals who can be classified as *Mary,* in the sense in which that is what is meant when we speak of *the four girls.* It means four persons, each of whom is individually identified as *Mary*—namely, Mary Seaton, Mary Beaton, Mary Carmichael, and Mary Hamilton. By extension, and speaking figuratively, we may also say *a dozen Shakespeares,* meaning a dozen men who are equal to Shakespeare.

A proper noun may be qualified by adjectives. We may speak of *the younger Pitt.* The use of *a* with a proper name may be felt as derogatory when applied to a human being, as in *a Mr. Adams is waiting to see you. The* is sometimes necessary. It is always necessary when an identifying clause is to follow, as in *the Paris I am talking about is in Kentucky.*

Some proper names cannot be used without *the.* This is always true when some common noun, such as *river, ocean, city,* is part of the true name, whether this common noun is actually used or merely understood, as in *the Hudson, the Mediterranean, the Capital.* In such cases *the* is qualifying the common noun and performing its normal grammatical function. It is not a part of the proper name and is not capitalized. *The* (without a capital letter) is also required before plural proper names, such as *the United States, the Indies, the Alps, the Smiths.*

Sometimes *the* is made part of a title, as in *The Way of All Flesh* and *The New York Times.* When names of this sort are used in a construction that does not ordinarily allow the article *the,* the title *The* is dropped, as in *Butler's Way of All Flesh* and *a New York Times report.* When such names are used in constructions that ordinarily require the article *the,* only one *the* is used, as in *have you seen the New York Times?* Here the word *the* is sometimes capitalized and sometimes not. It is more logical not to capitalize it, on the grounds that the grammatical *the* has driven out the title *The,* just as *Butler's* and *a* did in the examples above. But practice varies. At present neither form can be considered wrong.

prophecy and **prophesy** were formerly merely variant spellings but they are now fixed as different parts of speech. *Prophecy* (with a *c*) is a noun. It means a foretelling or prediction, originally by divine inspiration, of what is to come, a revelation, or the action, function, or faculty of a prophet (*He had the gift of prophecy. And is this all your prophecy, that things will get either better or worse?*). *Prophesy* (with an *s*) is the verb. As a transitive verb it means to foretell or predict (*I prophesy that no good will come of this*), to indicate beforehand, to declare or foretell as by divine inspiration. As an intransitive verb it means to make predictions (*Cassandra was one of the most unfortunate women who ever prophesied*), to speak as a mediator between God and man or in God's stead (*In the reign of Saul, it was Samuel who prophesied*).

proponent; supporter. *Proponent,* the opposite of *opponent,* means one who puts forward a proposition or proposal (*Thomas Jefferson was the chief proponent of the Declaration of Independence*). In law a *proponent* is one who argues in favor of, especially one who seeks to obtain probate of a will. By extension, and by ignorant or willful misconstruction of the strict sense of the term, *proponent* has come to mean one who supports a cause or doctrine, a supporter. This extension is regrettable because it blurs the distinction between *proponent*, an author or prime mover, and *supporter*, one who merely upholds, endorses, or allies himself with that which the proponent has advanced.

proportion is a word which seems to invite misuse. Strictly speaking, it describes a comparative relation between things or magnitudes as to size, quantity, number, ratio (*His arms were long in proportion to the rest of his body. Though he has a quarter of the votes, this is not a large enough proportion to permit him to have things his own way*). By an understandable extension, *proportion* in the plural has come to mean dimensions (*It was a canvas of large proportions*). The real damage comes with the further extension to mean a portion or part without indication of its relation to a whole. If we say *The picnic was attended by a proportion of the higher officers of the company,* we have really said nothing. *Number* would have been a better word. See also **part; portion; share; etc.**

propose; purpose. These verbs, though variant forms of the same word, mean distinctly separate things. One *purposes* for oneself; one *proposes* to others. *Purpose* means to put before oneself as something to be done or accomplished (*I purpose to finish this book within three months*). *Propose* means to put forward a matter, subject, case for consideration, acceptance, or action (*I propose that we refer the matter to a committee for study and recommended action*).

Propose may be followed by an infinitive, as in *he proposes to go tomorrow,* or by the *-ing* form of a verb, as in *he proposes going tomorrow.* The two forms are equally acceptable. *Propose* may also be followed by a clause, but the clause verb must be a subjunctive or a subjunctive equivalent, as in *he proposes he go at once.*

Purpose may be followed by an infinitive, but not by an *-ing* form or a clause.

proposition; proposal; plan. Of these three words, *proposition* is the most specific, *plan* the most general. A *plan* is any method of thinking out acts and purposes beforehand (*What are your plans for Saturday night?*). A *proposal* is a plan, a scheme, an offer to be accepted or rejected (*The proposal of the union, to establish a retirement fund to which the company was to contribute half, was received coldly by the management. The enemy soon made proposals of peace*). The word has also a special meaning in the sense of an offer of marriage.

A *proposition* is a proposal in which the terms are clearly stated and their advantageous nature emphasized. A business proposition is a much more specific, immediate, and detailed thing than a business proposal. The trouble with *proposition* is that it is overused and often misused. It is frequently substituted for the more accurate *plan*

or *proposal* (*It looks like a paying proposition*), or for such words as *task, affair,* or *matter* (*That's a wholly different proposition!*).

In nonstandard American usage a *proposition,* in some contexts, means a suggestion, from a man to a woman, of illicit sexual relations. In this sense, and in this sense chiefly, the word is used as a verb (*You proposition a dame like that and she'll throw you out of the house*).

proprietrix is affected and **proprietress** unnecessary unless one wants to insist on the fact that a certain proprietor is a woman.

propriety. See **decorum.**

prosaic and **prosy** are closely related in meaning. Indeed, the primary sense of one is the secondary sense of the other, and vice versa.

Prosaic, in its commonest contemporary sense, means commonplace or dull, matter-of-fact, unimaginative (*Life in a small industrial town seems very prosaic to the sons and daughters who have been away to college*). In its now less used sense, though this was its original sense, it means having the character or spirit of prose as opposed to poetry, as verse or writing (*Wordsworth's later poetry is often prosaic*). *Prosy,* a word heard nowhere near so often, means, in its commonest contemporary sense, of the nature of or resembling prose (*That was a pretty prosy speech for so poetic an occasion*). In its less often used sense, it means prosaic, commonplace, dull or wearisome (*Daniel Deronda is an amiable monomaniac and occasionally a very prosy moralist*). Some pundits would have *prosaic* mean commonplace and *prosy* mean tediously commonplace; but although the distinction might be valuable, usage does not support it.

proscribe. See **prescribe.**

prosecute. See **persecute.**

proselyte; proselytize. The English use *proselyte* as a noun only, meaning one who has come over or changed from one opinion, religious belief, sect, or the like, to another; a convert. As a verb, meaning to induce someone to make such a change, the English use *proselytize*. Americans prefer to use *proselyte* as a verb also (*The older proselyting worked more slowly, perhaps more surely, but never so inclusively* — Walter Lippmann).

prospect, to signify what the English would call *a prospective customer,* must now be accepted as standard in American usage (*During the Florida land boom free buses took prospects about the major cities. We start off by sending form letters to several thousand prospects*).

prospective. See **perspective.**

prospective; putative. *Prospective* means expected, in prospect, future (*My prospective mother-in-law arrives tomorrow*). *Putative* means that which is supposed, reputed, or commonly regarded as such (*There are some who insist that Thomas Lincoln was only Abraham Lincoln's putative father and that his real father was John C. Calhoun*).

prospectus. The plural is *prospectuses* or *prospectus*, not *prospecti*.

prostrate. See **prone.**

protagonist and **antagonist** are to be used neither as synonyms nor as antonyms.

Protagonist means the leading character in a play (*Mio is the protagonist in Maxwell Anderson's* Winterset) or, by extension, any leading character or personage (*Communist China appears to be the protagonist in Asian politics. Amos is the protagonist of the older prophets*). The important thing to recognize about *protagonist* is that the prefix is *proto-* (first), not *pro-* (for). A protagonist, by definition, plays the leading part in something; it is not implied that he is in favor of what he is doing.

Antagonist means one who is opposed to or strives with another in any kind of contest, an opponent, an adversary (*Antagonists of the superintendent soon found that their friends and relatives were being dropped from the payroll*).

pro tem. This is an abbreviation of the Latin words *pro tempore* and means temporarily.

protest. Americans say *protest against* but they also say *protest* in many contexts where the English would say *protest against* (*A committee of clergymen called on him to protest his policy on vice*—Lincoln Steffens).

Protestant; protestant. The word *protestant,* one who protests, is now almost obsolete; when anyone hears the word he assumes it to mean *Protestant,* one who protests specifically against Roman Catholicism. And even this meaning must be modified, for the idea of *protest* in Protestantism is fading and the word is generally understood to mean any Western Christian not an adherent of the Roman Catholic Church, or an adherent of any of those Christian bodies which separated from the Church of Rome at the Reformation or of any group descended from them. The term seems to have been applied at first by their enemies to those German Princes who protested against the decision of the Diet of Spires, in 1529, which had denounced the Reformation.

prototype means the original or first model after which something is formed, the archetype (*The Iliad is the prototype of all epic poems*). A *prototype* is unique. Therefore it is not to be misused to mean any predecessor or model (as in *Auden's elegy on Yeats has as prototypes Arnold's* Thyrsis, *Shelley's* Adonais, *and Milton's* Lycidas).

protozoa. This word is plural and is always used as a plural. The singular is *protozoön,* or *protozoum,* or *protozoan.* All three forms are acceptable. The plural form *protozoans* is also acceptable, but the double plural *protozoae* is not.

protrude. See **intrude.**

proud parents, as a term for a wedded male and female who have begotten and delivered a child, is a cliché.

prove. The past tense is *proved.* The participle is *proven* or *proved.* The participle *proven* is respectable literary English. In the United States it is used more often than the form *proved.* In Great Britain *proved* is used more often and *proven* sounds affected to many people.

Prove may be followed by an adjective describing the subject of the verb, as in *it proved true.* It may also be qualified by an adverb describing the proving, as in *he quickly proved that it was true.*

provided; providing. Both of these words may be used as conjunctions to introduce a clause, as in *he will do the work providing you pay him.* Some people feel that *provided* is the only correct form, but the two words have been used as conjunctions for the same length of time and by equally good writers.

Provided and *providing* can only be used to introduce a stipulation or demand which, presumably, somebody would like to see met, as in the example given above. The conjunction *if,* on the other hand, merely indicates that the following clause states a condition; it is immaterial whether anyone would like to see the condition fulfilled or not, as in *my parents will worry if they don't hear from me. Provided* or *providing* should not be used loosely in place of *if* in a sentence of this kind.

provoke. This word may be followed by an infinitive, as in *do not provoke him to steal.* It may also be followed by the *-ing* form of a verb with the preposition *to,* as in *do not provoke him to stealing,* but the infinitive is generally preferred. See also **aggravate.**

proximity. Since *proximity* means nearness in place, time, or relation, *close proximity* is redundant.

proximo; prox. See **instant.**

prudent; prudential. *Prudent* is the word having general currency, as applied to persons or actions. He who or that which is *prudent* is thoughtful, sagacious, provident, careful of his own self-interest, worldly wise, discreet, decorous (*It is not prudent for us to meet thus openly where we may be seen. The prudent man looketh well to his going. The prudent students used to prepare to be teachers because teaching offered a secure living*). *Prudential* is a restricted term meaning of, pertaining to, or characterized by, prudence. It describes motives or considerations leading to action rather than the action itself or the person performing the action (*Prudential considerations dictate that I secure a second signature to your note*). Thus a prudent genius would be a genius who exercised prudence in the management of his affairs, a prudential genius would be one whose genius lay solely in the art of prudence.

pseudonym. See **nom de plume.**

psychological moment. The phrase when first coined in a German newspaper in 1870 meant *the psychological momentum* and referred to the psychological considerations that impelled or deferred the bombardment of the then-besieged city of Paris. But the German *moment* (equivalent to English *momentum*) was mistaken in an English translation of the article for the *moment of time* and the phrase, which for some reason had a jocular vogue, passed into our language as meaning "in the nick of time" or "at the critical moment." Oscar Wilde said that he knew *the precise psychological moment when to say nothing.*

The phrase was woolly in its inception, confused in its translation, affected in its adoption, and misunderstood in its application. It is pompous, meaningless, and tedious.

psychology. In an age which James Joyce has described as "jung and easily freudened," *psychology* is a word thrown about knowingly by about everyone capable of articulating a four-syllabled word, though not necessarily of spelling it. Basically it means the science of mind, or of mental states or processes, the science of human nature (*Burton's observations, though shrewd, remained fruitless for lack of a coördinating psychology; he saw human nature clearly, but he had no system to which to relate the disparate facts he so assiduously collected*). More generally, it means the science of human and animal behavior.

In common parlance *psychology* means the mental states and processes of a person or of a number of persons, especially as determining action (*To understand Hemingway's* The Sun Also Rises, *one must have some understanding of the psychology of the postwar expatriate*).

The word is used a great deal in everyday American speech to mean shrewdness, cleverness, or an understanding of human nature (*She certainly shows psychology in dealing with those children, making them think they want to do their lessons. That was real psychology, taking out all the dimes and leaving only quarters in the saucer*). This is often merely an ellipsis for *a knowledge of psychology*, but it is pretentious and usually vague.

psychosis. The plural is *psychoses* or *psychosises*.

publicity. See **propaganda.**

publish. Although the commonest contemporary meaning of *publish* is to issue, or to cause to be issued, in copies made by printing or other processes, for sale or distribution, as a book, periodical, or the like, the word has a different, or at least a severely restricted meaning in legal terminology. In the law of defamation, to *publish* a defamatory statement is to communicate it, in some form, to a person or persons other than the person defamed. A libel is *published* if it is merely repeated or written in a letter. In England, where the laws of libel are very severe, librarians are subject to prosecution for libel if they even permit a book which has been the subject of conviction for obscene libel to be consulted. The law has held that the mere showing of a book, by one individual to another, constitutes *publishing*. See also **allege.**

puerile. See **infantile.**

pugnacious. See **bellicose.**

pull, in the figurative sense of influence, as with persons able to grant favors (*You got to have pull to get those jobs*), is not standard.

pull chestnuts out of the fire. To say of those who take risks from which other men profit that they are *pulling the chestnuts out of the fire* is to employ a worn-out metaphor.

The phrase derives from an old story of a monkey that persuaded a cat to pull a chestnut out of the fire for him. The cat got a burned paw and the monkey enjoyed the chestnut. From the same story comes also the word *catspaw* as a term for one who is used by another to serve his purposes. In the older versions of the fable it was a puppy that was persuaded to take the fruitless risk and this is so much more suitable that it is believed that *cat* is simply a misunderstanding or mistranslation of the Latin *catellus*, puppy.

pull one's weight, a term from rowing, is a cliché. One hears it more often in the negative, as a reproach, than in the positive. It is said of so-and-so that he is *not pulling his weight*, that is, not doing a fair share of work in return for whatever pay or reward he is receiving.

pull the strings. As a term from puppetry, meaning to control affairs by moving others as if they were marionettes, *pull the strings* is now hackneyed.

Sometimes it was *pull the wires,* but a *wirepuller* in America today is not so much a master behind the scenes, manipulating others, as one who uses political influence or the like to win an advantage. The original metaphor from puppetry may have gotten confused with the idea of mechanical bell wires or other wires that transmit physical power and control machinery.

pummel. See **pommel.**

pun; paronomasia; assonance. A *pun* is a play on words, the use of a word in two different applications, or the use of two different words which are pronounced alike, in such a way as to present an incongruous idea and excite our sense of the ludicrous. A good pun can be very witty. That is, under the incongruity there can be a suggestion of some deeper truth that usually goes unspoken; or that which is absurd by itself may have great wisdom, often bitter wisdom, when juxtaposed to the original statement. Puns were formerly used seriously, often to give a wry touch of bitterness or irony. Thus when the mad Lear says to the blinded Gloucester, *you see how this world goes,* Gloucester answers *I see it feelingly* and the word play heightens the horror. Mercutio's dying *Ask for me tomorrow and you shall find me a grave man* is in keeping with his character and its gaiety intensifies the tragedy of his death. With us, however, puns are now used solely for humor and hence they are excluded, by contemporary taste, from serious expression. This is a loss, but custom in such matters must be heeded. The witty will always take their chances, but they are dangerous chances, for there is a widespread vulgar belief that a pun is "the lowest form of humor" and the successful *punster* (the very term is pejorative) runs the risk of being thought not only inept but laboredly dull.

Paronomasia is used so often as a synonym for punning that it must be so accepted. In its strictest sense, however, it means the use of words that are not quite alike, though very near it, in sound. The intention is not humor but emphasis (*To begirt the almighty throne/ Beseeching or besieging*) or antithesis.

Assonance is merely resemblance in sound. The careful writer will avoid accidental assonances, since they compel the reader to look for a contrast or an antithesis (or call special attention where no emphasis is intended) and hence distort the thought and annoy the reader. Thus one might say *Before delivering his address the governor ate a peach.* But to say, *Before his speech he ate a peach* is to introduce an unintended levity and to mar the passage with an unwanted jingle.

punch in both England and America has the basic meaning of a thrusting blow, especially with the fist (*I'll give you a punch in the jaw if you don't shut up*). In a figurative sense, *punch* is a slang term, originating in the United States and used chiefly here, meaning a vigorous, telling effect or force (*He speaks well, is informed, lucid, and reasonable, but his delivery lacks punch*). As a transitive verb, *punch* has the special sense in the western United States of to drive cattle (*As soon as the ranchers began to string fences, fewer cowhands were needed to punch cattle*).

The drink *punch* is, by the way, a wholly different word.

punctilious. See **meticulous.**

punctuation. In a publishing house, a great many people work on the same book and some of them work on a great many books at the same time. This would not be possible if certain details had not been worked out in advance and accepted by everybody. Punctuation is one of these details.

Every publisher must have a system of punctuation, but no publisher thinks that his system is the only right one. He knows, for example, that people in the writing trades disagree fiercely over the use of the comma in a series. But there is no way to compromise. One can't use half a comma. And one can't have half of the staff putting it in and the other half taking it out. So rules are laid down. No two publishers lay down exactly the same rules. This is partly because different rules are applicable to different kinds of material, and a style manual is likely to reflect the kind of material on hand at the time it was set up. The style manual of the Government Printing Office, for example, was designed for governmentese and would be inapplicable in a literary publication.

The information on punctuation given in this dictionary is satisfactory for any type of writing. However, in anything that is published, the punctuation will certainly be changed in some details by the publisher. A writer should not feel apologetic about this. (For detailed information on punctuation, see **apostrophe, asterisk, brackets, capitalization, colon, commas, dash, ellipsis marks, exclamation point, hyphens, parenthesis, period, question mark, quotation marks, semicolon.**)

punctuation at the beginning of a line. Except for quotation marks, brackets or parentheses, *no* mark of punctuation ever appears at the beginning of a line.

pupil; student; scholar. A *pupil* is one who is under the close supervision of a teacher, either because of his youth or because of specialization in some branch of study. In England *pupil* is used to describe one in school, which means up through public schools such as Eton or Harrow, or through the secondary schools, equivalent to the American high schools. In America *pupil* is now usually restricted to one who is in an elementary school. Those called *pupils* regardless of age because of their specialization in some branch of study are designated by the subject they are studying, as art pupils, music pupils, etc. *Student* describes one attending a higher institution of learning (*He was a student at Oxford, where he was a pupil of Professor David Nichol Smith*). In America *student* also describes one who devotes much attention to a particular problem (*I have been a student of Western European politics ever since I visited France in 1944*).

Scholar in former times was a synonym of *pupil* (*A diller, a dollar, a ten o'clock scholar*), but it also meant one devoted to learning, a man of learning and erudition (*He was a scholar, and a ripe and good one;/ Exceeding wise, fair-spoken, and persuading*) and this is the word's commonest contemporary meaning. It has also the meaning of one who through merit is granted money or other aid to pursue his studies (*One of the scholars always spoke the responses to the grace*), though this meaning is more often used in England than in America, where the word is rarely used in this sense unless preceded by a particularizing designation, as *Rhodes Scholar, Lowell Scholar,* etc.

puppet; marionette. *Puppet* is the more inclusive term. It describes a doll, or an artificial figure with jointed limbs moved by wires as on a miniature stage, or a person whose actions are prompted and controlled by another as a puppet is controlled by a showman. A *marionette* is a puppet in the second of these three senses only, a puppet moved by strings or the hands, as on a mimic stage.

purchase and **buy** both mean to obtain or acquire property or goods for a price. *Buy* is the common and informal word applying to any such transaction (*On the way to work he stopped to buy a paper at the corner newsstand*). *Purchase,* which formerly meant to take by violence, to seize by force or bold fraud, to capture, is now simply a formal synonym for *buy.* It may connote buying on a larger scale or in a more expensive store (*He purchased the estate from the last member of the old family. I purchase my hats in Bond Street*). *Buy* is usually the better word; *purchase* as a synonym in most contexts is a genteelism.

pure; mere. In one of its senses, *pure* means "mere," that is, being that and nothing else (*It is pure nonsense to talk of compromise under such circumstances*). However, one has to be careful not to introduce an ambiguity by such use. One may mean mere politics when he says *pure* politics, but there may also be the interpretation that the politics is free of corruption. In such cases, *mere* is the preferable word.

pure and simple. As a way of saying that something is plain and obvious, unadulterated, that which it is and clearly nothing else, *pure and simple* is a cliché.

purebred. See **thoroughbred.**

purist. By a purist we mean a person who is more concerned about the formal rules of grammar than most people are, a person who has an exaggerated respect for grammatical niceties. He is usually also concerned with the "proper" pronunciation of words and holds rather rigidly to the conviction that where there are variants one is of necessity the best and that to employ any of the others is wrong.

As in moral matters—to which his attitude is remarkably akin—there is in the purist who seeks (and usually thinks he has found) excellence a touch of the pharisaical. He thanks God and the lexicographers that he does not speak as other men and is continually moved with militant zeal to ask others why they do not speak as he does. This has led lesser men to use the term *purist* as a reproach. But this is unjustified, for the careful craftsman should be admired, whether he is formulating grammar-school English or building a ship in a bottle.

To be a purist one must have a thorough understanding of English grammar—and it is curious that of those who have a thorough knowledge of English grammar few if any are purists. Most of those who pose as purists have very little knowledge of English or any other grammar. They seem to think that "pure" English consists of avoiding a dozen or so phrases or pronunciations which they consider wrong. In other words, they are merely opinionated.

The true purist is informed. He follows general principles and is consistent in his criticism. If he objects to *who are you looking for?* he will also object to *whom shall I say is calling?* since both sentences violate the Latin rules of case. If he objects to *a more unique situation,* he will not accept *a more equal distribution,* since *equal* is just as much an absolute as *unique.*

It would be refreshing to meet a true purist.

Puritan; puritan. *Puritan* is an ecclesiastical term to describe one of a class of Protestants which arose in the sixteenth century within the Church of England, demanding further reforms in doctrine and worship, and greater strictness in religious discipline, and during part of the seventeenth century constituting a powerful political party (*In Cromwell's day England had to choose between Puritan and Cavalier*). A *puritan* is one who affects great purity or strictness of life and religious principles. In worldly circles it tends to be a derogatory term (*If she weren't such a puritan she would get a lot more fun out of sorority life*).

purloin. See **steal.**

purport. As a verb *purport* means to profess or claim, as by the tenor (*This letter purports to be from Edgar*), to convey to the mind as the meaning or thing intended, to express, or to imply. *Purport* cannot be used in the passive, since its significance is already passive—standing for, "is supposed, is represented to be." Also the subject of *purport* may not be a person; it must be a

thing or a person considered as a phenomenon (*This invasion purports to be a diversion, but there is reason to believe that it may be the real thing*).

Either as a verb or a noun, *purport* in the sense of *purpose* is rare, though the noun is used in England, more often than in the United States. See also **pretend; affect;** etc.

purpose (verb). See **propose.**

purse. See **pocketbook.**

pushcart. An American *pushcart,* a light cart to be pushed by hand, would be called in England a *barrow,* a word which Americans keep, in common use, only in the combination *wheelbarrow.* To the English *pushcart* means a perambulator or baby carriage.

put. The past tense is *put.* The participle is also *put. Put off* may be followed by the *-ing* form of a verb, as in *he put off going,* but not by an infinitive. *He put off to go* is not standard English.

put all one's eggs in one basket. As a warning against concentrating all one's efforts on an uncertain hope, or risking all on one venture, the adjuration not to *put all one's eggs in one basket* is threadbare. The expression has been in use for almost three centuries and its original homely force has been weakened by repetition. Like many clichés, however, it provides a solid assurance of common knowledge off of which one may bounce an epigram or stroke of wit, such as Pudd'nhead Wilson's *Put all your eggs in one basket and WATCH THAT BASKET* or a slogan of many Community Chest drives: *Put all your begs in one ask it.*

put a spoke in someone's wheel. As a term for thwarting someone, definitely checking his progress, *to put a spoke in his wheel* is now worn out.

The origin of the expression is obscure. Since the only known English meaning of *spoke* that is at all relevant is one of the bars, rods, or rungs, radiating from the hub or nave of a wheel and supporting the rim or felloe, and since this belongs in a wheel, the phrase has at least a certain ambiguity. The *Oxford English Dictionary* suggests that it is a mistranslation of a Dutch phrase in which *spaak* (a bar or stave) is used. Burton Stevenson, in his *The Home Book of Proverbs, Maxims and Familiar Phrases,* quotes two instances from nineteenth century books about the sea that show that among sailors the phrase meant to say something to a man's advantage, almost the opposite of what it meant to a landsman.

put back the clock. Used figuratively, especially of one who would rescind some reform and revert to a former practice, to *put back the clock* is now a cliché.

put one's foot down. In the figurative sense (presumably) of stamping to emphasize a determined opposition to someone else's actions or plans, *put one's foot down* is hackneyed.

put one's shoulder to the wheel. Used figuratively, from the strenuous assistance men often formerly had to give to a mired vehicle or one unable to move up a steep gradient, the term *put* one's shoulder to the wheel has now become a cliché.

putative. See **prospective.**

putter and **potter** both mean to busy or occupy oneself in an ineffective manner, to move or go about with ineffective action or little energy or purpose, to move or go slowly or aimlessly (*Oh,* *I'm up, yes; but all I can do is putter around the house. He liked to putter around the garden, though he hardly knew a dahlia from a daisy*). The English use *potter* and regard *putter* as dialectal. Americans use *putter* and regard *potter* as literary or elegant.

puzzle. See **riddle.**

Q

---

quadroon. See **mulatto.**

quaint; queer. That is *quaint* which is strange or odd in an interesting, pleasing, amusing, or picturesque way (*It was a quaint place, with its main street, no more than a pathway or a series of steps, leading down to the sea*), or having an old-fashioned attractiveness (*"God keep you!" It was a quaint farewell and moved us unexpectedly. . . . then worms shall try/ That long preserved virginity,/ And your quaint honor turn to dust,/ And into ashes all my lust*). That is *queer* which is odd in a strange or singular way, that makes us uneasy, that is at least slightly repellent (*"Good night. I hope we never meet again!" That was a queer thing to have said!*).

Quaint should not be used, however, when *odd* alone or *amusing* alone will suffice. See also **funny; odd.**

qualify. The basic meaning of *qualify* is to give or attribute qualities to. It is used as a grammatical term in the sense of to limit the meaning of. That is, a qualifying word names a quality which must be present before a particular statement is applicable, and so reduces or limits the number of things in the universe that the statement applies to. The "meaning" of a word, in this sense, is "what the word signifies," that is, all that it can be applied to or all that it names. For example, *blue* limits the meaning of *dress* in *a blue dress*, since there are more dresses in the world than there are blue dresses. Similarly, *dark* limits the meaning of *blue* in *a dark blue dress*, since there are more blues than there are dark blues. And *yesterday* limits the meaning of *I thought so* in *I thought so yesterday*. A word that qualifies a noun or pronoun is called an adjective. A word that qualifies any other part of speech, such as a verb, an adjective, or an adverb, is an adverb. A group of words may also function as an adjective or as an adverb and so qualify other words.

The word *modify* is used by grammarians in the same sense as *qualify*. Some prefer one term and some the other.

In general English, the word *qualify* may be followed by an infinitive, as in *the studies qualified him to teach*, or by the *-ing* form of a verb introduced by the preposition *for*, as in *they* *qualify him for teaching*. The *-ing* form is generally preferred when *qualify* is used in an active sense, and the infinitive when *qualify* is used as a passive, as in *he is qualified to teach*.

quandary. See **predicament.**

quantity; number. A *quantity* of something is a particular, indefinite, or considerable amount of it (*A small quantity of water lay in depressions in the rock*). A *number* designates separable units that could be counted (*My grandfather bought such a quantity of lead and powder that even yet a number of his homemade cartridges lie in our attic*). *Quantity* applies to bulk, extent, and size; *number* applies to individual units. See also **amount.**

quantum. The plural is *quanta*.

quarrelsome. See **bellicose.**

quarter. The fraction *one quarter* is treated like the regular fraction words. (See **fractions**.) Unlike the word *half*, the word *quarter* cannot be used without a preceding *one* or *a*. We say *a quarter of the men* or *one quarter of the men* but not *quarter of the men*. The only exception is in expressions of time, as in *at quarter past five*. Some grammarians claim that this is not permissible and that *a quarter* must be used even here. But in the United States *quarter* is treated like *half* in expressions of time and the form without *a* is generally acceptable.

quarters. Only the plural form is used to mean a place to live. It is treated as a plural and used with a plural verb, as in *these quarters are comfortable*, but the word cannot be used in this sense with a word implying number.

quay; key; cay. *Quay* designates an artificial landing place built along navigable water for vessels loading or unloading cargo (*See there she stands and waves her hand upon the quay,/ And every day when I'm away, she'll wait for me.*)

Key or *cay* designate a low island near the coast (*Columbus discovered no isle or key so lonely as himself*), especially any one of an extensive chain of low islands which, starting from north of Cape Florida, form an immense crescent as far west as the Tortugas, the Florida Keys.

queen; quean. See **housewife.**

queer. See **odd, funny, quaint.**

queer fish. From our anthropocentric point of view, fish are queer indeed, and the more one thinks of them the queerer they and all other things become. But, nonetheless, to call a strange or peculiar or puzzling man *a queer fish* is to employ a cliché. Fish remain queer but the phrase does not.

query; inquiry. A *query* is a question, but it is a specific and limited question (*I had a query today about those cedar posts*). It is sometimes synonymous with *doubt,* but here, again, it is a doubt that questions some specific point (*It seemed plausible, but there remained a query in the sheriff's mind: three shots had been fired but there were only two bullets missing from the gun*). *Inquiry* or *enquiry* may also be a synonym for *question* (*Address your inquiry to the young lady at the desk, please*), but it can also mean, as *query* cannot, an extensive investigation (*The inquiry dragged on for two weeks*). See also **enquiry; inquiry.**

question. See **inquire.**

question mark. The main uses of the question mark are:

1. To indicate the end of a direct question, as in *Do you think it will rain?* It is not used after an indirect question, as in *He wondered if it would rain.*

2. To show that a statement is approximate or in question, especially with dates, as in *Robert Southwell 1561?-1595* or *Robert Southwell 1561 (?)-1595.*

3. After a request, but only if a formal style is desired, as in *Will you please let me know immediately if this is agreeable to you?* If an informal style is desired, the request should end with a period.

4. To express more than one question in the same sentence, as in *Can John make it? or Joe? or anyone here?*

5. To show a direct question as part of a sentence, as in *Are you a man or a mouse? is the question.*

6. To show humor or sarcasm, as in *The report said that the average weight for women of that height is 915 (?) pounds.* This use should be avoided, except when the urge is irresistible.

A question mark is placed inside or after the final quotation mark, depending on whether it belongs to the quoted words or to the larger sentence, as in *He asked, "Which way did they go?"* and *Why do you think she said, "Tea is more esthetic"?*

When a question ends with a quoted question, only the first question mark is used, as in *Why did he ask "Why?"*

questions. A question is a sentence that calls for a verbal response. The fact that a sentence is a question is shown in speech by a special pitch pattern and in writing by a question mark. In addition, most questions have a characteristic word order.

At one time the fact that a sentence was a question and not a statement could be shown by placing the verb before the subject, as in *saw you my horses?* But in modern English the subject of a verb is distinguished from the complement principally by its position before the verb. We resolve this conflict by keeping the subject before the meaningful part of the verb and placing an auxiliary verb first, as in *can you see?, would you have seen?* For the simple tenses, which normally have no auxiliary, we create a verb phrase by using some form of *do,* as in *did you see?* Here the auxiliary *do* adds nothing to the meaning of the sentence. It simply allows us to begin a question with a verb without placing the subject after the verb.

The verb *to be* is not treated in this way. It is never used with the auxiliary *do* and the simple tenses stand before the subject in a question, as in *were you there?, is he ready?* The verb *have* may also be used in this way, as in *have you a match?* and *had you a match?;* or with the auxiliary verb *do,* as in *do you have a match?* and *did you have a match?* Thirty years ago the form without *do* was considered more elegant. Today the two forms are equally acceptable in the present tense, and the form with *do* is preferred in the past. The old word order is also heard in *how goes it?* and in sentences beginning with *how come.* (See **come.**) But with these exceptions a simple tense form placed before the subject is now archaic or artificial.

In a negative question, the word *not* usually stands before the subject, as in *don't you see?, weren't you there?*

Questions may also be formed by interrogative words, such as *who, which, what, when, where, how.* The interrogative word is always the first word in the sentence or clause. If it is the subject of the verb or if it is an adjective qualifying the subject, the subject precedes the verb, as in *who is there?* and *what child is this?* Otherwise, the subject and verb stand in the order described above, as in *what did he say?* and *where is he now?*

A short question may have the form of a declarative sentence, such as *you were there?,* or the form of an imperative, such as *go now?* A question may also be formed by adding an interrogative to a declarative sentence, as in *you were there, weren't you?* and *you weren't there, were you?* In questions of this kind, the declarative clause expresses what the speaker believes to be true and the interrogative is negative if an affirmative answer is expected and affirmative if a negative is expected. When both parts of the sentence are affirmative, as in *you were there, were you?,* it carries an implication of surprise or disbelief.

When a question is reported indirectly (that is, when the substance is given but not the exact words) the subject precedes the verb as in a declarative sentence, the clause is introduced by an interrogative word, and is not followed by a question mark, as in *I wonder whether she will come* and *I asked him what he was doing.* In current English, statements of this kind sometimes use the interrogative word order and omit the interrogative word, as in *I wonder will she come* and *I asked him what was he doing.* This construction is not traditional literary English, but it is acceptable to most people today. See **clauses.**

An indirect question may also follow verbs of saying or knowing, as in *he told me when he would come* and *I know what he is doing.* After verbs of this kind the interrogative word order is never used. (For the tense of the verb in a subordinate clause, see **tense shifts.**)

quick as a flash (of lightning) is a cliché.

quick; living. Rapid motion and vitality seem inseparable in our minds—as evinced by *step lively, please; a lively jig,* and so on. *Quick* formerly meant living (*My quick child thou hast stolen, and this dead bairn laid by me*) and this meaning survives in the archaic phrase *the quick and the dead* and is current to designate the tender flesh beneath the nails (*He pared his nails to the quick*) and in the description of a hedge composed of live plants as a *quick hedge.* But aside from these vestiges, it is now obsolete in its older sense and any attempt to revive it is something of an affectation.

quiet; quiescent. Although *quiet* and *quiescent* are in most uses synonymous, meaning being in a state of rest or inactivity, usage often gives *quiescent* a suggestion of only temporary inactivity (*Quiescent as he now sat, there was something about his nostril, his mouth, his brow, which, to my perceptions, indicated elements within either restless, or hard, or eager*).

Then *quiet* has a number of meanings, such as silent, free from bustle, not glaring or showy, for which *quiescent* is not a synonym (*sounds that break the quiet of the night, a quiet cup of tea, quiet draperies and light blue walls*).

quiet; quietness; quietude. *Quiet* is a state of being (*The holy time is quiet as a Nun/ Breathless with adoration. Quiet is requested for the benefit of those who have retired*). *Quietness* is the state of being quiet but it is also an exhibited quality (*the quietness of his manners. There was a quietness to the house and the whole surrounding valley that endeared it to us*). *Quietude* is a habit of quiet; repose, tranquility, and rest that have long endured (*There broods upon this charming hamlet an old-time quietude and privacy. The quietude of our forefathers' lives can scarcely be imagined by this restless and twitching generation*).

quit. The past tense is *quit* or *quitted.* The participle is also *quit* or *quitted.*

Quit is the preferred form for the past tense and the participle in the United States, where the word usually means cease or stop, as in *he quit smoking.* This meaning of the word, and also the form *quit,* are survivals from older English but are no longer heard in Great Britain, where they are considered Americanisms. In Great Britain *quitted* is the only form used in the past tense or the participle, and the word commonly means leave or depart from, as in *he quitted Paris after a week.*

The verb *acquit* has the regular form *acquitted* for the past tense and the participle. When *quit* is used to mean acquit, as it sometimes is in legal or archaic English (*Now, quit yourselves like men!*), it too is regular and takes the past form *quitted.* See also **stop.**

quite means completely, wholly, entirely (*She has not been quite the same since Andrew died*), actually, really, or truly (*Payment yes, but payment in gold, that's quite another matter*).

The use of *quite* as a monosyllable of assent (*You understand the instructions? Quite!*) is common in England but little used in America except in humorous imitation of English speech. The addicted would do well to consult Fowler and make sure when they mean *quite* and when *quite so.*

quite all right. Since *quite* means wholly or entirely and *all* means the whole of, *quite all right* is redundant. And it is the more absurd when we reflect that it is commonly used when things are not all right, when we wish to minimize something that is wrong. It cannot be too often repeated, however, that grammar is not logical. Words and expressions are what usage makes them and *quite all right* has become an accepted way of saying "Things are really pretty bad with me, but I am brave and can endure, and will not gratify the malice that shows plainly under the veneer of the assumed interest of your inquiry as to my welfare, by admitting the grievous nature of my plight."

qui vive. As a term for being on the alert, *on the qui vive* is a cliché. Though authorities agree that the French part of the phrase is a sentry's challenge, and the phrase as a whole means to be on the lookout like a watchful sentry, there is a difference of opinion as to the exact meaning of *qui vive.* Some think it is a corruption of *qui va là?* "Who goes there?" Others think it is *qui vive?* "Live who?"—a question to be answered by *Vive le roi!* or some other assertion of loyalty.

quiz. In American usage *to quiz* is to question, to interrogate. A *quiz* is an informal examination. A *quiz* section, in American colleges, is a small group, usually drawn from a large class, that meets with an instructor to discuss the work of the class more informally than the lecture meetings permit. In English usage *to quiz* is to banter or make fun of by asking ludicrous questions or to look inquisitively at. This last meaning is retained in *quizzical* in American usage, but lost in *quiz* itself. A *quiz* in English usage (according to Horwill) is a person given to such banter.

quoits. When referring to the game, the plural word *quoits* takes a singular verb, as in *quoits is being played.* The object thrown is a *quoit* and *quoits* used with a plural verb means several of these, as in *the quoits are heavy.*

Only the singular form is used as the first element in a compound, as in *quoit playing.*

quotation marks are used:

1. To set off quoted words from any comments or additions made by the person who is doing the quoting. This is one occasion when a writer should pay scrupulous attention to punctuation. Material enclosed in quotation marks must show precisely what was said and if there is any doubt about it, quotation marks should

not be used at all. A misquotation is unfair to both the quoted source and the reader. We may write: *He said, "I will not under any circumstances run for office!"* or *He said he would not run for office.* If the quotation runs into several paragraphs, the quotation marks should be placed at the beginning of each paragraph but at the end of only the last paragraph. If the quotation is indented and blocked off, or is to be put into smaller type, quotation marks can be dispensed with.

2. To indicate in dialogue when one character stops speaking and another begins. This may be additionally indicated by beginning a new indented line with each new speaker, as in

"What do you think could be the matter?" he asked, frowning severely.

"I don't know, but it's probably something simple."

Sometimes dialogue is written so that each paragraph begins with the identifying name of the person speaking, usually followed by a dash; in these cases, quotation marks are not needed. Also, some novelists dislike quotation marks and do not use them or any other identifying device.

3. To indicate that a word or phrase is being used ironically or with a special meaning, as in *Then this "lady" took a poke at him with her umbrella.* When the words *so-called* perform this same function, quotation marks should not be used.

4. To set off names of books (except the Bible), dramas, operas, statuary, music, paintings, which in more formal usage would be set off in italics, as in *Have you read "Effie Briest"?* Quotation marks are not used with names of ships, trains, airplanes, homes of famous people, or characters in plays or novels, as in *Have you been to Mount Vernon?*.

There is considerable difference of opinion about the ways in which quotation marks should be combined with other punctuation marks. But, in general:

1. The period and the comma are placed inside the quotation marks, as in *He said, "I'm ready to go now."* and *Although he said, "I'm ready to go now," it was not true.*

2. The question mark and exclamation point can come either inside or after the quotation marks, depending upon the sense of the sentence, as in *He exclaimed "There she is!" He asked, "Where is she?" What a pity he said "No"!; Who are these "liberal friends"?*

3. A colon or semicolon after a quotation will always be outside the quotation marks, as in *"The world is too much with us": This sentiment seems to grow truer with the years* and *She said, "Why, of course"; anything they desired was immediately theirs.*

4. Introductory words or phrases are usually set off from the quotation by a comma, as in *He said, "Let's get going."* However, if the phrase is short the comma can be dropped, as in *He said "Let's get going."* Two commas are used if a phrase interrupts the quotation or if the quotation is in the middle of a sentence, as in *"What made me say that," he explained, "is that I never have liked that color"* and *He said, "I never have liked that color," but everyone looked at him blankly.*

5. A quotation within a quotation is indicated by single quotation marks within regular double quotation marks, as in *Mary cried, "But then he said, 'Why do I have to?'"* If a writer uses single quotation marks as his regular identifying device, he must put his inside quotations within double marks. If a further level of quotation is introduced into the sentence, the double and single marks must alternate. In general, sentences of this kind should be avoided.

6. Quotation marks may be omitted when a single word is being used, as in *What will you do if she says No?* and *Suddenly a blur whizzed by, shouting Hello! as it passed.*

quote. See **cite.**

quoth. This one word is all that remains of a former verb. It has no past tense, no future tense, no *-ing* form, or anything else that a verb requires. It appears only in poetry, or humorous speech, and always in the inverted order, as in *quoth he.* It is not included in this dictionary because we think that some one might need to know these facts but simply in order to make the list of irregular verbs now found in English complete.

q.v. This is an abbreviation of the Latin words *quod vide* and means "which see."

R

rabbit; rarebit. See **Welsh rabbit.**

Rabelaisian. The designation of wild, coarse, satiric humor, characterized by an exuberance of vocabulary and extravagance of imagery, as *Rabelaisian* is fully justified. But to call any piece of indecency *Rabelaisian* is to utter a critical cliché and display an ignorance of Rabelais. *Freudian* is often similarly misused (by Sinclair Lewis, among others) as a sort of intellectual synonym for *dirty.* Such words are pretentious, and if one pretends to be familiar with Rabelais or Freud one ought not, in the very use of their names, to expose the fact that one has only a remote and confused idea of what they have written.

rabid. See **frantic.**

rack. See **wrack.**

rack and ruin. The *rack* of *rack and ruin* is a variant of *wrack,* wreck, and the entire phrase is a cliché kept feebly alive, as so many clichés are, by alliteration.

rack one's brains. The rack upon which one *racks one's brains* in an effort to remember something or to find a solution for some pressing problem was the old instrument of torture which compelled an answer by tearing the victim's limbs from their sockets. Whoever first applied this to the agony of desperate thought created a powerful image. But its power has faded as the rack has been forgotten, and overuse has reduced a once vivid figure to pallid feebleness.

racket; racketeer. *Racket* has acquired two slang senses in America. In the first, it means an organized illegal activity such as bootlegging or the extorting of money by threats or violence from legitimate businessmen (*Al Capone was believed to be behind many Chicago rackets*). The word is also a slang term in America for a dishonest scheme or trick (*During the war his racket was blackmarketeering in butter*). It is often used jocularly for legitimate business enterprises, with however a would-be worldly and cynical suggestion that there is an element of dishonesty in them (*I've been in the advertising racket for thirty years now*). Such a use is usually tedious and can be offensive.

A *racketeer* is one engaged in a racket. The implications are sinister, for a racketeer regulates competitive business by illegal and violent pressures (*The trouble with the New York waterfront was that racketeers had gained control of most of the hiring*). *Racketeer* is always strongly derogatory. A man who would join in the laugh when his business was referred to as a racket might yet be strongly offended if he himself were referred to as a racketeer.

Racket in this sense, by the way, derives from *racket* in the sense of a loud noise, especially one of a disturbing nature. English pickpockets used to make a racket of some kind (by the sudden throwing of firecrackers sometimes) in order to draw an excited crowd whose members, in their curiosity, would be heedless of the pickpockets' activities. The word had acquired its slang meaning in England as early as 1812 where, however, it seems to have been forgotten until reimported from America.

The agent suffix *-er,* when spelled *-eer,* is usually pejorative, as in *profiteer.*

racket; raquet. The word for a light bat having a network of cord or catgut stretched on a more or less elliptical frame, used in such games as squash and tennis, and for a snowshoe made in the manner of such a tennis bat, is *racket.* The plural *rackets,* construed as singular, describes a game of ball, played in a walled court, in which such bats are used. *Racquet,* a variation formed after the French word *raquette,* is unacceptable to the British but is accepted as a variant by Americans. The word for illegal activity and the word for noise is invariably *racket.*

racy. Deriving from a word meaning root, *racy* in both England and America means highly individual in an attractive way, lively, spirited, piquant, pungent (*H. L. Mencken's racy style . . .*). In America only, it has the additional sense of suggestive, risqué (*At bachelor dinners he would regale them with racy stories*). The nearest English equivalent is, perhaps, *salacious,* but *salacious* carries a connotation of stronger condemnation than *racy.*

radiantly happy, so happy that one sends out happiness from one like glowing heat or the splendor of the sun, is threadbare.

radical; Radical; revolutionary; radicle. Used as an adjective, *radical* (derived from the Latin *radix,* root) means basic, fundamental, going to the root or origin (*There will have to be radical changes in the plan before it will be accepted*), thoroughgoing or extreme, especially in the way of reform (*Only radical measures are likely to save the nation*). It also means existing inherently in a thing or person, rooted (*He had radical personality difficulties which tea and sympathy alone could not eliminate*).

Used as a noun, *radical* or *Radical* has specifically political connotations. It means one who advocates fundamental and drastic political reforms, one who would make basic changes in the social order by direct and uncompromising methods. In England the term *Radical* was applied toward the end of the nineteenth century to the left wing of the Liberal Party. In the early part of that century such Utilitarian Liberals as Bentham and James Mill called themselves Philosophical Radicals. In America, after the Civil War, *Radical* was the designation of that wing of the Republican party which desired the complete prostration of the Southern planters and their replacement by elements faithful to the Republican Party. These radicals were what today would be called rightwing conservatives. Since World War I, especially, *radical* (seldom capitalized) has been used to designate one who advocates political changes intended to produce economic equality. From the standpoint of an American conservative, a *radical* is a disorderly, if not necessarily subversive, individual. He is seldom, or never, referred to as a revolutionary (as he would be in other countries), for *revolution* has in America respectable and even conservative connotations. The Daughters of the American Revolution, for example, is a strongly conservative organization and eminently respectable.

Radicle is a specialized word. In botany, it means the lower part of the axis of an embryo, the primary root. In chemistry, it means an atom or group of atoms regarded as an important constituent of a molecule, which remains unchanged and behaves as a unit in many reactions. In anatomy, it means a small rootlike part, as the beginning of a nerve fiber. Except in these specialized senses, *radicle* is simply a misspelling of *radical.* And even in these senses, *radical* is replacing *radicle* as the preferred spelling (especially in chemistry).

radius. The plural is *radii* or *radiuses.*

radix. The plural is *radixes* or *radices*.

raft, as a colloquial term for a great quantity or a lot, especially of people (*There was a raft of folks crowding into town for the grand opening*), is now rustic and a little archaic.

rail, as short for railroad or railway, is standard American usage (*Ship by rail, I find it more convenient to go by air than by rail*). The objection of some English authorities to this usage is curious, since the English themselves are masters of the art of reducing syllables and often hold up their *tram* and *lift* in triumphant comparison to the American *streetcar* and *elevator*.

railroad; railway. In England *railroad* is seldom used. Since the beginning of the twentieth century *railway* has been the usual term there. In the United States *railroad* is the more common term, though *railway* also has its uses. In general, *railroad* is the term for a line for heavy traffic (*The Pennsylvania Railroad*), while *railway* describes a rail line with lighter weight equipment and roadbed (*The elevated railways are being replaced by buses and subways*).

As a verb, *railroad* has certain special American senses. It may mean to transport by means of a railroad, though this is now rarely heard, being replaced almost entirely by *ship* in relation to goods and *travel* or *go* in relation to persons. It may also mean to work on a railroad (*My husband and my two boys railroaded out in Kansas City for three years*), though this, too, is now rare. Colloquially, to *railroad* is to send or push forward with great or undue speed (*Jacksonians tried to railroad the Indian bill through Congress while Davy Crockett was off on a speaking tour*). As slang, but slang which is so old and so widespread that it might well be accepted as standard, *railroad* is to imprison on a false charge in order to be rid of (*Many people believe that Tom Mooney was railroaded*).

raining cats and dogs. Swift listed the phrase *rain cats and dogs* as a cliché in 1738 (in his *A complete collection of genteel and ingenious conversations*) but it remains in full use among those who seek to be original in an unoriginal way. Whoever first thought of the expression to describe a torrential downpour, with its suggestion of snarling and yelping tumult heard in the gurgle and drumming rush and splatter of the rain, had something so felicitous in its absurdity, so consonant in the violence of its own exaggeration with the violence it described, that he immediately captured all imaginations. But it is time to seek a fresher, newer image.

rain or shine, as a term for in any event, under any circumstance, positively, is hackneyed.

raise. This verb means "cause to rise." Historically, it does not mean *rise* even in speaking of dough, where we say *it is raising* and *set it to raise*. These are old passive uses of the *-ing* form and the infinitive, comparable to *supper is cooking* and *wait for it to cook*. Some people also say *the drawbridge raised*, rather than *the drawbridge rose*, because they are conscious of the fact that this is a passive act, something that is being done to the drawbridge. This use

of an active form with passive meaning is frequent in English and is seen in such familiar sentences as *the boat upset, the cup broke, the color washes well*. See **passive voice** and **transitive verbs**.

The same distinction holds between the nouns *raise* and *rise*. A salary increase is called *a pay raise* by those who feel that someone is responsible for the size of their salary. *A pay rise* carries the implication that these things happen of themselves, like a rise in the temperature. *Pay raise* is the preferred form in the United States, where *pay rise* was unknown before the 1930's. *Pay rise* is the preferred form in Great Britain. (For the difference between *raise* and *rear*, see **rear**.)

raise one's sights. One of the commonest metaphors of college presidents and others in charge of large funds or large hopes when they seek to arouse those who beg for them to even wilder frenzies of solicitation is to say that *we must raise our sights*. The metaphor, drawn from artillery, would be most unfortunate were it not that those who analyze metaphors form an inconsiderable portion of those upon whom the fund-raiser has his eye. Its naïve admission that the donor is something to be shot down and the fund-raiser one who carefully adjusts his weapon is so alien to the general tenor of the language of solicitation that one assumes it would be avoided if it were understood.

raison d'être, a French expression meaning the reason for being or existence, is an affectation when employed in English speech or writing for *reason* and an error when employed for *explanation*.

rake-off is an exclusively American slang term to describe a share or portion, as of a sum involved or of profits. Often the implication is that it is a share or amount taken or received illicitly, as in connection with a public enterprise (*Are you a man of business or a philanthropic distributor of rake-offs? Some estimate the alderman's rake-off at ten percent*).

rally has the special meaning in America of a coming together of persons, as for common action, political or religious or—in the colleges —sporting, which the British would call a mass meeting or a demonstration (*When they attended Montana political rallies, Mrs. Wheeler knitted with calm absorption. There will be a football rally for freshmen in the meadow tomorrow afternoon at five*).

ran. See **run**.

rancor. See **malice**.

rang. See **ring**.

rank and file. In the strictest sense a *rank* of soldiers is a number drawn up in line abreast. (*When the ranks are broken you have to fight singly*) and the *file* is the number of men constituting the depth from front to rear of a formation in line. Taken together, the two mean the body of an army, apart from officers or leaders. Used figuratively for ordinary people, the expression is a cliché.

rap. Formerly a slang term meaning to censure or criticize, *rap* is used so consistently in the headlines (*Trial Delays Rapped by Judge*) that it must, however reluctantly, be recognized as an established word. The English would say *rap on the knuckles,* the expression from which the American *rap* is derived. Still slang is the use of *rap* as a noun meaning punishment, usually unmerited punishment or punishment erroneously applied to the wrong person (*He carried the banner and took the rap for Roosevelt in the Senate for many years*).

Rap in the expression *I don't care a rap* is a standard word meaning the least bit. A rap was a counterfeit coin, worth about half a farthing, which formerly passed current in Ireland for a halfpenny. It must have been the most inconsiderable counterfeit coin ever made.

rapt. The adjective *rapt* derives from a Latin word meaning seized, transported, raped, snatched away. This sense is now obsolete. The word today means deeply engrossed or absorbed (*He was rapt in thought and did not hear my question*), transported with emotion, enraptured (*The bride was rapt with happiness*), or showing or proceeding from rapture (*She gave him a rapt smile*). See also **wrapt.**

rare and **scarce** both characterize that which is hard to find, exists in small quantities, or is uncommon. A thing is *rare* which is seldom to be met with and is therefore often sought after. The word usually implies exceptional quality or value (*O rare Ben Jonson! If it is really a rare book, you can expect a high price for it*). *Scarce* is applied to that of which there is an insufficient supply. It usually implies a previous or usual condition of greater abundance (*During the war certain food items were scarce*). *Scarce* usually applies to ordinary things. Its occasional application to persons (*Make yourself scarce. After they organized the vigilantes, robbers were mighty scarce for a while*) is intended as humor. *Rare* is applied to men and things of superior quality.

rare (of meat). Though as recently as the first part of the nineteenth century Englishmen used *rare* in reference to cooked meat in the sense that Americans now use it (*The same flesh, rotten-roasted or rare . . .*—Charles Lamb), the word is now regarded in England as an Americanism, though it may still be heard in some English dialects. No more trenchant comment could be made on English cooking than the fact that their word for what Americans call *rare* meat is *underdone.* Mrs. Rorer in her *New Cook Book* characterizes *the American fashion of serving meat rare* as "certainly objectionable," though most Americans regard a rare steak as a rare delicacy.

rates to the English mean what Americans would describe as local taxes.

rather. This is the comparative form of *rathe,* a word no longer heard in the positive or superlative. It is used with *than* in a comparison, as in *this is blue rather than green* and *she felt rather than saw,* and alone to mean "in a slight degree," as in *rather warm* and *I rather think so.*

The combination *had rather* means "would find more desirable," as in *I had rather be a dog and bay the moon, than such a Roman* and *I had rather be a doorkeeper in the house of my God than to dwell in the tents of wickedness.* The construction is similar to *had better* which means "would find more advantageous." In both cases *had* is used in its original sense of "hold" and is a subjunctive meaning "would hold." During the nineteenth century *would rather* was felt to be "purer" English than *had rather,* chiefly because the grammarians did not recognize the subjunctive *had* and so could not parse the phrase. Many writers, whose ear required *had,* took refuge in *'d,* as in *I'd rather be a pagan.* Some even said *had better* in place of *had rather.* But this was a mistake and has not survived. *Had rather* was justified on theoretical grounds around 1900. Today both forms, *had rather* and *would rather,* are standard English. *Had rather* is felt to be the more literary of the two.

In current English these forms are not followed by a *to*-infinitive. They may be followed by the simple form of a verb, as in *I would rather go,* or by a subjunctive clause with a past tense verb, as in *I would rather he went.* In literary English *rather* is never separated from the *had* or the *would* by another word. *I would rather have gone* is preferable to *I would have rather gone.* This broken construction is never heard with *had.*

rational; rationale. *Rational* is an adjective meaning agreeable to reason, reasonable, sensible (*That seems to me a perfectly rational explanation*), being in or characterized by full possession of one's reason, sane, lucid (*After several shock treatments he appeared quite rational*), or endowed with the faculty of reason (*Man is sometimes defined as a rational animal!*). *Rationale* is a noun meaning a statement of reasons, a reasoned exposition of principles, the fundamental reasons serving to account for something (*It is not difficult to discover the rationale for his attack on the President*).

rationalize. A word was needed for the process of finding rational-seeming reasons for our irrational behavior, socially acceptable explanations of actions which have their origins, at least in part, in our unconscious urges. Coleridge had used the term *motive mongering,* but he was ahead of his times and it was not until the 1920's that James Harvey Robinson supplied the general public with *rationalize.* The word has been violently attacked, especially by many purists in England. But it is a useful word and its use by the common man, in that it calls his attention to the process it designates and makes him aware of it, marks an immense step forward in human betterment which must, ultimately, depend on man's knowledge of himself. The thing that is wrong with the word is that it is used too often. The public is—though understandably—too fond of its new psychological insight and too pleased with itself for having it and we hear the word too much and are exasperated by it.

Rationalize is a dangerous word, too, and

should be used with great circumspection. Its use implies that the speaker understands the motives of another better than the other himself. This, when speaking of a third person, may seem only vanity, but to tell someone to his face that he is *only rationalizing* is to accuse him of obtusity, of lack of awareness, of being the blind instrument of his animal impulses, with sundry other smug assumptions, all uncomplimentary. Moreover, the speaker, while making these insulting assumptions, has exalted himself into the chair of omniscience and blandly taken upon himself to read the secrets of another's heart. There is no field in which angels more fear to tread than the judging of motives or into which our friends rush with more assurance. To question a man's professed motives is, in his eyes, to call him a liar and to elicit a great deal of good, healthy hostility. *Rationalize* should not be discarded, as some would have it; but it should be used with great care, after considerable meditation upon our own motives in using it.

raze. See **destroy.**

re; in re. *Re* is the ablative of the Latin *res,* thing, matter. It is used in legal documents to mean in reference to or in the case of. The layman, however, would do well to let the lawyer have his ablatives to him reserved and use the good English *about* or *concerning* or *in regard to*. *In re* is a hybrid monster, possibly, piling ignorance upon presumption, thought to be an abbreviation of *in regard to*.

reaction; response. Though *reaction* is unequivocal as a technical term in chemistry, biology, and mechanics, it needs to be used with some care in general contexts. One may define it as action in response to some influence or event, if one understands that the response is a more or less automatic rather than an intellectual and reflective one (*My reaction to his proposal was one of despair*). *Reaction* should not be used, however, as it so commonly is, as a technical-sounding synonym for the general terms *response, reply* or even *opinion* (*When you have had time to think it over, I would be grateful for your reaction*). It probably came to be so abused because it absolves one from the fuller responsibility entailed in using *opinion*. If a man states an opinion, he may be called upon to support or justify it. A reaction may be more easily abandoned as a mere impulse.

reactionary. Except for its technical scientific senses, to which it would be a mercy if it were confined, *reactionary* is a word so emotionally charged as to be little more than a term of abuse. It refers to one who favors political measures that seem to the speaker to react against the general good, especially measures that would rescind or nullify beneficial social legislation. It seems as easy for a liberal to call a conservative a reactionary as for a conservative to call a liberal a radical, a pink, a fellow-traveler, or a red. About the only American who calls himself a reactionary is the poet and critic Allen Tate (*Reactionary Essays,* 1936).

Mr. Tate is not sneering at himself, nor is his position one to be sneered at.

read. The past tense is *read*. The participle is also *read*. Although this looks like one of those very simple verbs, such as *cut, cut, cut,* the appearance is deceptive. The past tense and the participle *read* are pronounced like *red*. See also **peruse.**

read between the lines. As a term for perceiving a hidden or implied meaning in something said or written, *reading between the lines* is a hackneyed expression.

read the riot act. The Riot Act of 1714 empowered a justice, sheriff, mayor, or other person in authority to read a proclamation calling upon such persons as he deemed to be unlawfully, riotously and tumultuously assembled to disperse themselves and peaceably to depart to their habitations or to their lawful businesses. After the reading of the proclamation (or the hindering of the reading of the proclamation), continued assembly constituted a felony. The reading of this proclamation (not the Act itself) thus constituted a serious procedure and usually served to quell most tumults and disperse most unlawful assemblies, for felony was punishable by death. The modern expression *read the riot act* means no more than to state emphatically that a certain course of action must cease. It has become a cliché. It is particularly illogical to use it—as it so often is used—when applied to one person (*He read me the riot act!*).

real; really. Traditionally, the adjective *real* means true and the adverb *really* means truly, as in *a real friend* and *were you really there? Really* may qualify a verb, an adjective, or an adverb.

Today the form *real* is often used as an adverb meaning very, as in *I will write real soon*. In this sense it may qualify an adjective or an adverb but not a verb. This use of *real* is accepted spoken English in most parts of the United States but does not appear in formal, or impersonal, writing. The adverb *really* does not have this meaning. *I will write really soon* is neither natural nor literary English. (The use of *real* before a participle, as in *I was real amazed,* is acceptable in some Southern states, but not in other parts of the country.)

When used to qualify a noun, the form *real* refers to facts rooted in nature, actual things with objective existence, rather than imaginary. *Real trouble* means actual trouble, not imaginary trouble, it does not mean serious trouble. *Real* has definite, useful meanings of its own and it would be a loss if the word became a mere intensive.

reality; realty. *Reality* means the state or fact of being real, true to life or fact (*The reality of the situation is in no way affected by our illusions or wishes*). It is obsolete in the specialized sense of real property or real estate; in this sense the correct word is *realty* (*He left a large fortune in bonds and realty*).

realize. Though *realize* describes primarily a mental act, a grasping by the mind or an understanding (*I suddenly realized what he meant*), it may also mean to make real, or to give reality to, a hope, a fear, or a plan (*In securing a television set, the boy realized one of his greatest desires*), or to bring vividly before the mind.

In a specialized sense, *realize* is to convert into cash or money (*He realized a large sum by the sale of the plantation*). Loose application of this sense has led to such meanings as to obtain as a profit or income for oneself by trade, labor, or investment (*He realized huge profits from the Berlin black market*), to bring as proceeds, as from a sale (*The paintings realized $15,000. You won't realize much on that old chiffonier*). The use of *realize* in these last two senses is condemned by English authorities, accepted by American.

realize; know. *Realize* may suggest "know thoroughly." *Know* basically means to perceive or understand as a fact or truth, to apprehend with clearness and certainty. *Realize* means to apprehend fully, to understand clearly. It is often used for emphasis in a warning when the one speaking wishes to allow the one spoken to no chance of later pleading ignorance (*You realize that if you leave under these circumstances, you cannot hope to return? I hope you realize the gravity of what you are doing*).

really. See **actually, real.**

really and truly is redundant and hackneyed. Like so many expressions that seek a double emphasis, it defeats its own purpose and suggests either a childishness that is not wholly to be relied on or a suspicious excess of protestation.

rear. Originally this verb meant cause to stand up. It was already in the language when the verb *raise* appeared with exactly the same meaning. Through the centuries, *raise* has followed *rear* from meaning to meaning, gradually driving out the older word. Where both are used in the same sense, *rear* is frequently felt to be more bookish or more elegant.

In the fifteenth and sixteenth century *rear* came to mean foster, nourish, bring to maturity. It could be used of children, livestock, and plants, and one could speak of *rearing wheat*. About two hundred years later *raise* also acquired this meaning and could be used of plants or livestock. In the United States *rear* is no longer used in speaking about plants and *raise* is now used of plants, animals, and children. Some people believe that it is vulgar to talk about *raising* children and that we should always say *rear*. They claim that the verb *raise* puts the children in a class with the hogs. This is not very reasonable. *Raise* may put the children in a class with corn, and flowers, but they can't escape being classed with the hogs, since we certainly do use *rear* as well as *raise* in speaking of livestock. More people in the United States were *raised* than were *reared*. To many, *reared* seems an unnatural and pretentious word to use about their childhood. If they are afraid that *raise* will put their parents in a bad light, they are likely to shift to *was brought up* or *grew up*.

Rear may still be used in the sense of lift or cause to rise. But it is likely to be associated with literary words, such as *rear an imposing structure* and *rear a monument*. In ordinary speech, *raise* is preferred.

Unlike *raise*, which always means cause to rise, or cause to grow, *rear* may be used in a direct sense, similar to *rise*, as in *the horse reared, the baby suddenly reared back, the specter reared up before his eyes*.

The noun *rear* is often used as an adjective and has produced a superlative adjective form, *rearmost*, but no comparative form.

reason. *It stands to reason* is an exasperating expression which no intelligent man uses unless he is seeking to goad an antagonist into a self-betraying explosion. Spoken, as it so often is, with condescending assurance, it is stupid and unfair. Invoking reason's name, it is usually the prelude to an unreasonable dogmatism. If something stands to reason, it has only to be exposed to the light of examination and the processes of reasonable thought and it will stand. But to preface its presentation with the statement that it does stand to reason compels assent by implying that dissent is unreasonable. Or, rather, attempts to so compel assent but always fails, for reason cannot be compelled. If its implications are fully understood, it is an arrogant statement. If they are not, it is a stupid one.

reason why. See **why.** For **the reason is because,** see **because.**

reave. The past tense is *reft* or *reaved*. The participle is also *reft* or *reaved*.

recall. See **recollect, remember.**

recapitulate. See **repeat.**

receipt and recipe both once described a formula or prescription for the preparing of a food or a medicine, but *receipt* is now largely understood to mean a written acknowledgment of having received money, goods, or information specified. It is still sometimes used of cookery in America, less often in England. *Recipe*, on the other hand, has retained its traditional meaning. Primarily, it describes any formula, especially one for preparing a dish in cookery. But it may also describe a medical prescription (though *prescription* itself has almost entirely displaced it in this sense) and a method to obtain a desired end (*What is your recipe for success as a writer?*).

receptacle and **recipient** both designate a receiver, but a receptacle is a thing and a recipient a person (*The recipient of the letter read it hastily and then tossed it into the nearest receptacle, an empty nail keg*).

reciprocal. See **mutual.**

reciprocal pronouns. *Each other* and *one another* are sometimes called reciprocal pronouns.

reckon. This word is supposed to be the Southern equivalent of the Yankee *guess*. *Reckon*, used to mean "suppose," is in the great literary tradition and Southerners have been too modest in allowing the word to be classed with *calculate*, which is not used with this meaning outside rural America. By apologizing for it themselves, they have brought it into disrepute. A grammarian, writing a generation ago in defense of *reckon*, quotes Romans 8:18, *I reckon that the sufferings of this present time are not worthy to be compared with the glory which shall be revealed in us*, and then asks, rhetorically, "What hand will change that *reckon* to any one of its supposed equivalents!" In a recent translation of the Bible this *reckon* has been changed to *consider*.

re-collect; recollect; remember; recall. *Re-collect* (distinguished always by the hyphen) means to collect or gather together something which had formerly been gathered together but since scattered (*At the end of the game he re-collected the cards and prepared to shuffle them once more*). *Recollect* means to recall to mind, to recover knowledge of by an act or effort of memory (*Try hard to recollect what you saw just before the accident*). In the act of recollecting there is always a considerable effort. *Recall* also implies an effort, but not a very severe one (*He recalled the words of an old music hall song*). *Remember* implies that a thing exists in the memory, though not actually present in the thoughts at the moment, and that it can be called up without effort (*I remember, I remember, the house where I was born. You remember John Doe, don't you?*). See also **remember**.

recommend; recommendation. *Recommend* is a verb. Its use as a noun to mean *recommendation*, the act of recommending, a letter or the like recommending a person, or a representation in favor of a person or thing (as in *Will you give me a recommend for a job?*), is slang in America and inappropriate and incorrect in England.

reconcile. The word may be followed by the *-ing* form of a verb with the preposition *to*, as in *she reconciled herself to living there*. It is also heard with an infinitive, as in *she reconciled herself to live there*, but the *-ing* form is preferred.

recondition; renovate. Authorities in England will have nothing to do with *recondition*. They condemn it as etymologically unjustifiable, ugly, and unnecessary. *Renovate*, they affirm, is established, adequate, and available.

In America *recondition* is a standard word to describe the restoring to good or satisfactory condition of machines or equipment, and it deserves its acceptance because it implies more than *renovate* or any of its synonyms, such as *refit* or *reconstruct*. It implies a process of detailed alterations in the interest of more efficient operation. One may *renovate* a hat; but he ought to *recondition* an old car before starting on a transcontinental tour in it.

recopy; copy. There is little that *recopy* can do that *copy* can't do. *To copy* is to reproduce, duplicate, transcribe or imitate an original or any copy based on that original. *Recopy* cannot be used as a synonym of *reproduce*. And though it is correct in describing later duplicating steps, it is no more explicit than *copy*.

About the only time that *recopy* would be justified would be when a copy had been badly made and one wished to emphasize that fact in requesting that another copy be made.

recourse, resort, and **resource** are all nouns that suggest help in a situation of difficulty and though each has a special meaning they are often unintentionally interchanged.

Perhaps an explanation of their basic senses will make their proper use clear. *Recourse* derives from a Latin word meaning a running back and it means a turning back to a person or thing for help or protection, as when in difficulty (*The Prodigal Son had no recourse but to go unto his father*). *Resort*, which is an acceptable but not preferable alternative to *recourse* in many contexts (such as *He managed to make a halting translation but only by frequent recourse/ resort to the vocabulary in the back of the book*), derives from a Latin word meaning to go out. A pleasure resort or a summer resort was a place to which one went out. In the common phrase *the last resort* it is the last place to which one can go in a time of necessity or danger. *Resource*, from a Latin word meaning to rise again, means a source of supply, support, or aid (*My only resource in the emergency was a dull sheath knife*). *Resort* and *resource* are often used interchangeably and indiscriminately; yet *in the last resort* emphasizes the direction of a final attempt, while *as a last resource* emphasizes the basis of a final attempt. The fact that one can say *As a last resort he had recourse to his hidden resources* shows that the words do have different meanings.

recover; re-cover. The unhyphenated word goes back to a Latin word meaning recuperate. It means to obtain again what one has lost possession of (*The Germans recovered from the French the provinces of Alsace and Lorraine*). *Re-cover* means to cover again or anew (*How much material is needed to re-cover our sofa?*). See also **retrieve**.

recreation; re-creation. A *recreation* is an agreeable pastime or diversion which affords relaxation and enjoyment. A *re-creation* is an act of creating anew or a thing created anew.

recriminations; accusations; charges. *Recriminations* denote a more advanced stage in a controversy than do *accusations* or *charges*, for recriminations are countercharges brought against an accuser, accusations in return (*You must realize that if you bring charges against him, there will be recriminations*).

recrudescence meant the breaking out again of a wound or a disease or a pestilence (*If the brown rat returns, we may expect a recrudescence of the bubonic plague*). Authorities in England, following Fowler who regards any other use as "disgusting," will admit *recrudescence* in a figurative sense to mean a renewal or return only if the renewal is regarded as evil or objectionable (*After World War I there was a recrudescence of Klan activity*). In America, however, no such limitation prevails. *Recrudes-*

cence in the United States is taken to describe a breaking out afresh or into renewed activity, or the revival or reappearance in active existence of anything, good or bad. Such a distinction of meaning is one of the real pitfalls of understanding between Americans and British, for the surface meaning is the same although the attitude towards the act described might be diametrically opposite. Thus if an American said *During the Second World War there was a recrudescence of interest in religion,* he might regard this renewal of interest as a laudable thing but an Englishman, hearing him, would assume that he disapproved of it, regarding it as some sort of disease or pestilence.

rector; vicar; curate. In the Church of England a *rector* is a parson or incumbent of a parish whose tithes are not inappropriate, that is, the tithes are held by him rather than a layman. A *vicar* is one who acts in the place of a rector, a substitute (cf. the word *vicarious*). In England, then, whether the incumbent of a parish is a vicar or a rector depends chiefly on the disposition of tithes. In America, in the Protestant Episcopal Church, a *rector* is a clergyman in charge of a parish and a *vicar* is a clergyman whose sole or chief charge is a chapel dependent on the church of a parish, or a bishop's assistant in charge of a church or mission. *Curate* is chiefly a British term to designate a clergyman employed as assistant or deputy of a rector or a vicar. In both England and America the Roman Catholic Church employs *rector* to designate an ecclesiastic in charge of a college, religious house or congregation, and *vicar* to designate an ecclesiastic representing a bishop or the Pope. The Roman Catholic Church also employs *vicar* to designate the Pope as representative on earth of God. See also **pastor.**

recumbent, incumbent, superincumbent and **decumbent** all suggest lying or reclining.

The most familiar, and the one with the most varied uses, is *incumbent.* Though it conveys the literal sense of lying, leaning, or pressing on something, it more often conveys a figurative sense of resting on one as a duty or an obligation, obligatory (*The welfare of his people is incumbent on a good prince. Having sought the office, it is incumbent upon him to assume its responsibilities*). *Incumbent* is also used as a noun, in general terms meaning the holder of an office (*The first incumbent of the presidency was George Washington*), and in British use only, one who holds an ecclesiastical benefice (*The incumbent at Upper Tooting held startlingly advanced theological notions*).

Recumbent means lying down, reclining, leaning (*The beach was dotted with recumbent forms*), inactive, idle. In botany and zoology the word describes a part that leans or reposes on anything.

Superincumbent means lying or resting on something else (*He struggled to extricate himself from the superincumbent debris*), situated above, overhanging (*The Aar Gorge is practically bridged by superincumbent rock formations*). Figuratively it means exerted from above, as pressure, burdensome (*He felt acutely the superincumbent responsibilities of the mission*).

Decumbent may mean recumbent, but its chief use is a botanical one, to describe stems, branches and so on, lying or trailing on the ground with the extremity tending to ascend.

recurrence. See **reoccurrence.**

recurring and **frequent** are not synonymous. That is *recurring* which occurs again. There is no limitation, however, upon the interval between occurrences. *Frequent,* on the other hand, means happening or occurring at short intervals (*During the day he made frequent trips to the drinking fountain*).

red rag to a bull. To say of something that particularly infuriates a certain person that it is to him *like a red rag to a bull* is to employ a hackneyed metaphor based on zoological error, for bulls seem to be color-blind.

reduce. This word may be followed by the *-ing* form of a verb with the preposition *to,* as in *he was reduced to selling his car.* It is also heard with an infinitive, as in *he was reduced to beg or to starve,* but the *-ing* construction is generally preferred.

reduced. See **depleted.**

redundancy; tautology; pleonasm. *Redundant* means being in excess, exceeding what is usual or natural. A redundant humor, in the old theory of the four humors, was the one whose excess determined the patient's complexion. In grammar *redundancy* means the use of too many words to express an idea, such as *combine together, audible to the ear,* or *invisible to the eye.* A charming example is furnished by Miss Julia Moore, "The Sweet Singer of Michigan," in her plea, at the end of her collected poems, for leniency from her readers:

> *And now, kind friends, what I have wrote,*
>   *I hope you will pass o'er,*
> *And not criticise as some have done*
>   *Hitherto herebefore.*

Tautology is a form of redundancy, consisting of the needless repetition of an idea, especially in other words in the immediate context, without imparting additional force or clearness. President Coolidge's statement that *when more and more people are thrown out of work unemployment results* is a fine illustration, though the prize must be reserved for the enterprising Milwaukee optometrist who advertised EYES EXAMINED WHILE YOU WAIT.

Except where the redundancy is hidden in technical or obsolete terminology (such as the landlubber's *so many knots per hour*), tautology is one of the surest marks of militant dullness. The editors of a California weekly who gave thanks in their first number *for being blessed with the gratification of seeing the materialization of our dreams come to the fulfillment of our realization* could not hope to enlist many literate subscribers. And the New York firm which assured television producers, in its advertising brochure, that *it is impossible to produce any type of audience show without an audience* simply assured the discerning producers that they had nothing original to offer. The repeating of words (see **repetition**), so strenuously and often absurdly avoided, is not a very serious fault; but the repetition of ideas in immediate context is fatal.

Pleonasm is a synonym for *redundancy*. See **pleonasm.**

redundant; superfluous; unnecessary. Of these words *redundant* has the most specialized meaning, *unnecessary* the most general. *Redundant* applies primarily to the use of too many words to express ideas in speech or writing. *Superfluous* describes anything over and above what is sufficient or required (*Your acknowledgment is superfluous. It seems superfluous for me to add anything to what the previous speaker has said*). *Unnecessary* means not needed. This is a sweeping term, for it includes not only what is beyond that required (superfluous) but also qualifies the nature of the requirement itself.

reduplication is the immediate repetition of a sound, as in *the red red robin came bob-bob-bobbin' along*. It is used in all languages and delights children and adults alike.

It may occur in almost any pattern, but a few of these are overwhelmingly more popular than all the others. Almost all reduplications belong to one of the three following types:

1. A syllable or word may simply be repeated, as in *bonbon, can-can, frou-frou, goody-goody, girlie-girlie, pompom, beriberi* and *well! well!* Repetitions of this kind are often emphatic.

2. The vowel of the first element may be changed to form the second element. When this happens the first vowel is almost always an *i* sound which is changed to an *a* or an *o*. That is, the change is from the shrill to the more open sound, as in *dilly-dally, fiddle-faddle, riff-raff, wig-wag, clip-clop, ping-pong, hippity-hoppity*. In English the sound of a bell is represented by *ding-dong*, in German by *bim-bam*. Words in this class commonly represent indecision, vacillation, or something contemptible.

3. The initial consonant of the first element may be changed to form the second element. Here, more often than not, the second element begins with one of three consonants: (1) a *d,* as in *fuddy-duddy, handy-dandy, Humpty Dumpty, razzle-dazzle, super-duper;* (2) a *p,* as in *namby-pamby, higgledy-piggledy, hocus-pocus, Georgie Porgie, roly-poly;* or (3) a *w,* as in *nit-wit, pow-wow, boogie-woogie, teeny-weeny, tootsy-wootsy*. Words in this class are usually frivolous or playful.

reënforce; re-enforce; reinforce. In both England and America *reinforce* is the common and preferred word meaning to strengthen with something additional (*He reinforced the picture with a cardboard backing*). The other two forms are still often used in America, rarely in England.

reeve. The past tense is *rove* or *reeved*. The participle is *rove* or *reeved* or *roven*. This is a nautical word, meaning to pass a rope through something, and is not heard in general English.

refer. See **allude.**

referendum. The plural is *referendums* or *referenda*.

reflective; reflexive. Both these adjectives basically mean reflecting. But *reflexive* is now used only in grammatical senses, as of a verb which has identical subject and object (*He shook himself*), or of a pronoun which indicates identity of object with subject (as in the same example, *himself* being the reflexive).

Reflective has retained all the general senses. It means that reflects, reflecting (*When glass becomes warped it is not satisfactorily reflective*), of or pertaining to reflection, cast by reflection. Actually, however, the functions of *reflective* as regards light are being taken over by *reflecting* and *reflected* (*Reflected sunlight glimmered on the reflecting surface of the indoor pool*). In current usage *reflective* is chiefly used to describe not a physical but a mental characteristic. It is roughly synonymous with *meditative* (*Wordsworth's* Intimations of Immortality *is a classic example of reflective poetry*).

reflexive pronouns. The -*self* words, *myself, himself,* and so on, are called reflexive pronouns. Three of these words, *myself, yourself, ourselves,* are combinations of a possessive pronoun and the word *self*. An objective pronoun used here, as in *me-self, us-selves,* is not standard. Two of the words, *himself* and *themselves,* are combinations of an objective pronoun and the word *self*. A possessive pronoun is often heard here, as in *hisself* and *theirselves*. These were once acceptable forms but they have not been standard for more than five hundred years. In *herself, itself, oneself,* it is impossible to say whether a possessive or an objective pronoun is being used to make the combination.

The reflexive pronouns are used primarily when the subject of a verb must be repeated as an object, as in *she hurt herself, she laughed at herself, she made herself a cup of tea*. When a reflexive pronoun is not standing immediately after a verb or a preposition, it simply repeats the subject and makes it emphatic, as in *she herself made a cup of tea* and *she made a cup of tea herself*. Some grammarians call the -*self* words reflexive pronouns when they are used as objects and intensive pronouns when they are not. In literary English an intensive pronoun stands immediately after the subject, as in *she herself made it*. In present-day speech it usually stands at the end of the sentence, as in *she made it herself,* and is considered additionally emphatic when it immediately follows the subject. When there is no cause for this added emphasis, the reflexive in this position is likely to sound pretentious. An intensive pronoun may follow the word *who,* as in *a man who himself had seen it,* but not the word *that*. In literary English an intensive pronoun in a *that* clause is always placed at the end, as in *a man that had seen it himself*. *A man that himself had* is contrary to the literary tradition and contrary to present-day speech habits.

In current English, a reflexive pronoun is often omitted where formerly it would have been expressed. In *the population doubled* and *the fog lifted* a reflexive *itself* is understood. Similarly, a *yourself* is understood in *prepare to die* and *don't bother*. We say *the child behaved well* although a reflexive was required here until recently. A reflexive is still required after some verbs, including *perjure*. We must say *he perjured himself* although with the present-day meaning of this word he could not possibly perjure anyone else.

At one time the *-self* words and the personal pronouns could be used interchangeably. Today, the *-self* words are preferred in some constructions and the personal pronouns in others.

In older English, personal pronouns were often used as reflexives, as in *let every soldier hew him down a bough, I could accuse me of such things*, and *arm you*. This is still standard English after prepositions showing direction, as in *we looked at the stars above us* and *she drew it toward her*. There is still a tendency to use personal pronouns as reflexives when the word is an indirect object, as in *I will get me one*. This construction is condemned by many grammarians and seldom appears in print, but it is heard frequently in the speech of educated people. A personal pronoun may still be used reflexively as the object of the verb *lay*, as in *I lay me down at night to dream*, but in general a *self* word is required for the true object of a verb. We no longer say *I will wash me* or *I will dress me*. A personal pronoun is still very effective when used as an intensive, as in *the bells they sound so clear*. This construction is condemned by most grammarians on the grounds that the pronoun is redundant, but the device is too forceful to be given up, either in speech or in fine writing.

Formerly, the *-self* words were often used non-reflexively, that is, in sentences where they did not reflect the subject of the verb, as *yourself* in *I am inviting yourself and your wife*. In current English these words have an old fashioned tone and the personal pronouns, in this case *you*, are generally preferred. *Myself* is an exception and is still often used in place of *I* or *me*. See **myself**.

reflexive verbs. A verb is said to be reflexive when its subject and object represent the same thing, usually a person, as *feed* in *the baby can feed himself now*. See **transitive verbs**.

reft. See **reave**.

refuse. This word may be followed by an infinitive, as in *he refused to see me*. It is also heard with the *-ing* form of a verb, as in *he refused seeing me*, but this is not standard.

refute; confute; deny. *To refute* is to prove, by argument or countervailing evidence, that

something asserted as true is false or erroneous, to overcome in argument, to prove to be in error, to show that allegations or charges are groundless (*An insinuation is difficult to refute, for it rarely makes a specific charge that can be closely examined*). *To confute* is to prove to be false, to overthrow by evidence or stronger argument (*Ten yards of string and a stone were sufficient to confute the local belief that the well was bottomless*). *Confute* is confined to arguments, theories, reasoning, sophistries. *Refute* applies to arguments and charges. Both words, by the way, convey the suggestion of a quick as well as a thorough answer.

Deny is a much weaker term. It simply means that one asserts that an opinion or a charge is false or erroneous (*He denied the allegation and defied the alligator*). A denial does not necessarily carry any supporting argument or evidence; a refutation or a confutation carries overwhelming proof.

regal. See **kingly**.

regard; regards. The singular noun *regard* is used in the compound prepositions *with regard to, in regard to, in regard of*. These all mean "with reference to" and they are all standard English, although the last is not used as much today as formerly. The plural noun *regards* should never be used in these phrases.

As regards is a verbal phrase meaning "as far as it relates to" and the third person singular form ending in *s, regards,* should always be used.

The verb *regard* cannot be followed by an infinitive. We cannot say *I regard it to be an honor;* nor can we use an objective complement and say *I regard it an honor*. Idiom requires the use of *as here*, as in *I regard it as an honor*.

The noun *regard* is properly a mass noun and does not have a plural form. The plural *regards*, like the plural noun *respects*, is used only in formal expressions of good will, as in *give my regards to your mother*.

regarding; respecting; relating; concerning; with regard to; etc. Many writers will go to great lengths to avoid using the prepositions *about* and *on*. If all the memoranda beginning *Let me have your comments regarding/ respecting/ relating to/ with regard to* . . . were laid end to end they would reach to a wastebasket on the moon. See also **re; in re**.

regimen of a preposition. See **object of a preposition**.

register. In its broadest and earliest sense *register* is to enter formally in a register (*The spaniel's pedigree was fully registered*). Usage has established as standard the more specialized sense of "record," that is to indicate by record or to indicate as records do. From this it was only a step to "show," to indicate, as on a scale. And from this has come the popular figurative meaning of showing emotion as by facial expression or by action (*She registered all pleasant emotions by smirking and all unpleasant ones by frowning or pouting*). This is a vague use, which the careful writer will eschew in favor of a more explicit word, and has led to even vaguer uses in which *register* can mean to feel, to notice, or to be aware of (as in *I couldn't tell whether he heard me or not; he just didn't seem to register*). These last uses are not standard.

regret. This verb may be followed by an infinitive when speaking of the present or the future, as in *I regret to say I cannot come.* It may be followed by the *-ing* form of a verb when referring to something that is past, as in *I regret saying I could not come.* In the United States, *regret* may also be followed by a clause, as in *I regret I did not go.* British grammarians condemn this and say that a direct object, such as *it* or *the fact*, must be placed between *regret* and a clause, as in *I regret it that I did not go,* or an infinitive construction substituted, as in *I regret to say I did not go.*

regret; be sorry; deplore; lament. *Regret* is the formal term meaning to feel sorry about (*Mr. Stuyvesant Silver regrets that he will be unable to accept the kind invitation of Mr. Joab Johnson for the sixteenth*). It is used as often as the informal *sorry,* which tends to be used in set constructions (*Sorry! Sorry, to hear it*) and has acquired, especially in popular songs, a sentimental tinge (*I'm sorry I made you cry*).

Deplore means to regret deeply, and implies disapproval (*He deplored the conduct of compatriots in European cities*). It is a favorite more-in-sorrow-than-anger word and has acquired more than a tinge of condescension and hypocrisy in many contexts. *Lament* means to feel or express sorrow or regret for. Unlike *deplore, lament* implies an outward and vocal manifestation of sorrow (*He paused to lament the brave men who were not there to hear him speak*). Used for merely an inner feeling, as it often is (*I lament that your conduct has made it necessary for me to speak to your father*), it is stilted. See also **repent.**

regretful; regrettable. *Regretful* means full of regret, sorrowful because of what is lost, gone, done (*And love, grown faint and fretful,/ With lips but half regretful/ Sighs, and with eyes forgetful/ Weeps that no loves endure*). *Regrettable* means admitting of or calling for regret (*They were sullen and in no way regretful for their regrettable performance*). It is often used as a term of mild condemnation.

regular. See **normal.**

rehearse. See **repeat.**

reindeer. The plural is *reindeers* or *reindeer.*

reiterate. See **repeat.**

rejoinder. See **answer.**

relation; narrative. *Narrative* is now the general term for a story of an event or events told for any purpose and with or without much detail. *Relation,* which properly means the act of narrating or telling (*The relation of these events took up the better part of the night*), is now used as a synonym for *narrative,* though it has a faintly archaic flavor. It is used particularly to describe that type of narrative known as an account—a factual story of the past told in-

formally, often for entertainment, with emphasis on details of action (*I was amused by his relation of the exploits of Davy Crockett*).

relation; relative. Both *relation* and *relative* are used to describe a kinsman. Though there is little to choose between them, *relative* is preferred. *Relation* is slightly rustic, slightly old-fashioned, qualities which give it an added force of homeliness in certain contexts.

relatively. See **comparatively.**

relative pronouns. The words *who, whose, whom, which,* and *that,* are relative pronouns when they represent a noun or pronoun appearing earlier in the sentence and also form part of a subordinate clause, as *who* in *those who know him speak well of him.* See the individual words, and also **what** and **as.**

As a rule the relative pronoun is the first word in the subordinate clause. There are three recognized situations in which a relative may be the second or third word in the clause: (1) it may follow an *-ing* form, as in *saying which;* (2) it may follow a preposition, as in *to whom;* (3) it may be part of an *of* phrase, as in *all of whom.* Expressions such as these may open a relative clause. Most grammarians claim that with these exceptions the relative must be the opening word. Many great writers, including Defoe, Swift, Shelley, have used *and* to introduce a relative clause, as in *a man of low rank, heavily built, and who kept his face muffled,* and *an excellent house indeed, and which I do most seriously recommend.* Textbook rules of composition call for some word such as *one* before the relative in both of these sentences in order to make the relative the first word in its clause. Or they require a preceding relative clause which the *and who* or *and which* will be parallel to, as in *a man who was of low rank and heavily built and who kept his face muffled,* and *a house which is excellent indeed, and which I do most seriously recommend.*

Dickens often disregards the rules completely, as in *my father, the many reasons for not insulting whom you are old enough to understand* and *I might take leave of Mr. Wickfield, my old room in whose house I had not yet relinquished.* These are successful sentences, but dangerous to imitate.

A relative clause follows the word it qualifies. When two clauses qualify the same word, the second applies to the word as already qualified or limited by the first, as in *they murdered all they met whom they thought gentlemen.* This is similar to a series of adjectives standing before the noun, in that each element qualifies the noun as qualified by all the intervening elements. See **adjectives.**

The number and person of a relative pronoun is determined by its antecedent. (See **agreement: verbs.**) The case of a relative pronoun depends on its function in the subordinate clause. In English, *who* is the only relative pronoun that shows case. See **who; whom.**

A relative pronoun that is the subject of a verb must usually be expressed, as in *the book that fell on the floor,* but once it has been expressed it can serve as the subject of more than one verb, as in *the book that fell on the floor and was forgotten.* A relative pronoun that is the object of a verb or preposition may usually be omitted, as in *the book I bought yesterday.* (See **that; which** and **who; whom.**) Ordinarily a pronoun may function as the object of more than one verb or preposition. But a relative pronoun that follows a preposition cannot also function as the object of another preposition. We may say *a school which they sent their children to and thought highly of,* but not *a school to which they sent their children and thought highly of.*

relic; relict. A *relic* is a surviving memorial of something past (*The hitching post is a relic of horse and buggy days*), an object having interest by reason of its age or its association with the past (*The Museum contains a fine collection of Indian relics*), or a surviving trace of something (*Funeral processions are a relic of barbarism*). In ecclesiastical usage, especially in the Roman Catholic and Greek Orthodox Churches, a *relic* designates the body or part of the body or some personal belonging or memorial of a saint, martyr, or other sacred person, preserved as worthy of veneration (*Chaucer makes it plain that, in his opinion, the Pardoner's relics were spurious*). The plural, *relics,* has the special additional meaning of the remains of a deceased person (*By law his relics must be disposed of by an undertaker*).

Relict is no longer used as a synonym for *relic.* It now means the surviving member of a married pair, a widow or a widower, especially a widow, who, when the word is used at all, is spoken of usually as the relict of so-and-so (*He took to wife the virtuous Lady Emma, relict of King Ethelred*). The word is now archaic and rare.

religiosity. Although the primary meaning of *religiosity,* as given in the dictionaries, is piety, devoutness, the quality of being religious, its secondary meaning of an affected or excessive devotion to religion is, in current usage, its chief meaning. Religiosity is a sort of religious sentimentality, great enjoyment of religious feelings with very little awareness of any corresponding ethical feelings. Religiosity insists that there is something called religion wholly apart from any specific religion, something that has no creed nor dogma, no theology or scriptures, something which may be felt and need not be understood. There is much of it abroad and a name for it is needed.

remain may be followed by an adjective describing the subject of the verb, as in *remain silent, remain calm.* It may also be followed by an adverb describing *remain,* as in *remain quietly in the corner.*

remainder. See **balance.**

remains. This noun has no singular form. It is usually treated as a plural, as in *the remains of the meal are in the refrigerator.* But it may also be treated as a singular, as in *the remains of the*

meal is in the refrigerator. It cannot be used with a word implying number. We do not speak of *several remains.*

remark; comment; observation. A *remark* is usually a casual and passing expression of thought or opinion (*Except for a few remarks, she had nothing to say about the play*). A *comment* expresses a judgment or explains a particular point (*If I might be permitted to make a comment, I would say that the interpretation of Lear's madness is wholly at variance with what is made plain in the text*). An *observation* suggests a basis of judgment and experience. Like *comment,* it implies a considered statement (*After five years in Moscow, he was ready to set down his observations on the Soviet scene*).

remediable; remedial. *Remediable* means capable of being remedied (*The faults in the political system are clearly remediable. Not until we have corrected our remediable ills dare we upbraid Providence*). *Remedial* means affording remedy, tending to remedy something (*If you take a remedial reading course, you will soon be able to read rapidly and to understand better what you have read*).

remember. When speaking of a past event, *remember* may be followed by the *-ing* form of a verb, as in *I remember mailing the letter,* or, if *remember* itself is in the past, by an infinitive, as in *I remembered to mail it.* When speaking of a future event, *remember* may be followed by an infinitive, as in *remember to mail it,* but not by the *-ing* form. *Remember* may always be followed by a clause, as in *remember I will be there.*

remember; recollect; recall; reminisce. All of these words refer to bringing back before the conscious mind things which exist in the memory.

Remember implies that a thing exists in the memory, though not actually present in the thoughts at the moment, and that it can be called up without effort (*I will remember the raid as long as I live*). *Recall,* a rather conversational word, implies a voluntary effort, but not a great one (*I recognized his face but couldn't recall his name*). *Recollect* implies an earnest voluntary effort to remember some definite, desired fact (*Try to recollect where you were on the night of June 17*). *Reminisce* means to indulge in reminiscence, the act of remembering one's past. It often implies a narration of what is remembered (*When old college classmates get together they begin by reminiscing over old times*). In this sense it is almost a vogue word and greatly overused. See also **re-collect; recollect.**

remembrance; recollection; reminiscence; memory. In one of its senses, *memory* means a mental impression retained (*My earliest memory is of getting lost in a strange town*). *Remembrance* is basically synonymous with *memory* in this sense, though it tends to be used only in rather solemn references (*In remembrance of their sacrifice*). *Recollection* implies a deliberate effort in bringing back to mind (*How dear* *to my heart are the scenes of my childhood/ When fond recollection presents them to view*). *Reminiscence*, generally plural, means recollections narrated or told. *Recollections* and *reminiscences* are the staple of writers of memoirs and autobiography (*My Recollections of Lord Byron, Men and Memories: Recollections of William Rothenstein*, Carlyle's *Reminiscences*, and so on).

remembrance; reminder. A *reminder* is something which causes one to remember, usually at some fitting or necessary time (*Tie this string on your finger as a reminder*). A *remembrance* is something which serves to hold something or, more often, someone continually in the memory, usually with fondness or affection (*Keep this ring as a remembrance*).

remit; send. In America *remit* means primarily to transmit or send money to a person or place (*Please remit*). This meaning is known in England but is not common. This is the only sense in which *remit* means *send*. In some of its less common senses, *remit* may mean to send back, or give back (*He remitted the fine*) or, in law, to send back a case to an inferior court.

remittance; money. *Remittance* is a commercial term to describe money or its equivalent sent from one place to another (*Enclosed find my remittance in the amount of $25.00*). It is not to be used as a term for money, however, in social, as opposed to business, relations. When so used, it is affected, a sort of euphemism to avoid so coarse a word as *money*. A *remittance man* (the term is dying out, though not the practice upon which it is based) is one living abroad who depends for support on money sent from home, money which is sent on condition that he remain abroad and not come home to disgrace by his presence the respectable members of his family.

remove is one of those words that now seem slightly pompous, with an archaic flavor, to the English but are in everyday use in America where *Remove your hats* or *Let us remove your garbage* and similar public notices strike no one as incongruous.

remuneration is a rather lofty and affected word for *pay*. It is an apologetic word. It implies that the money is a base and inadequate recompense for the service offered or the loss endured. But it is quite unnecessary. Most people today are quite willing to accept pay—if there's enough of it.

Renaissance; renaissance; renascence. As a synonym for *rebirth*, *renascence* is the correct word (*The phoenix, the great poetic image of renascence, fascinated the old poets*). For a revival in art or literature, either *renaissance* or *renascence* will do, although *renascence* is preferred (Theodore Watts-Dunton, *Poetry and the Renascence of Wonder*). *The Renaissance* is the word to describe the activity, spirit, or time of the great revival of art, letters, and learning in Europe during the fourteenth, fifteenth, and sixteenth centuries, marking the transition from the medieval to the modern

world (Walter Pater, *The Renaissance*), or the forms and treatments in art used during this period.

rend. The past tense is *rent*. The participle is also *rent*.

render; make. English and American authorities do not agree on permissible uses of *render*. The English will not accept *render* in the sense of cause to be (*The blow rendered him helpless*) but this meaning is standard in American usage. In the context of making a decision, *render* is felt, in American usage, to be somewhat more formal than *make;* ordinary people make decisions, judges render them when they deliver them officially as judgments.

As a synonym for sing or play (*Miss Biffle will now render a charming lullaby of her own composition*), *render* is stilted since it means more than these—to bring out the meaning of by performance, execution, or interpretation. Such highfalutin words, by promising much, place the performer at a disadvantage.

render service. See **service.**

rendezvous. The plural is *rendezvous*.

rendition; performance. *Rendition* means primarily the act of rendering, the action of restoring, surrendering, yielding. In America, especially, it is used to mean the translation of a text (*I will not omit mention of Calverley's complete rendition of Theocritus*) and performance, as of a role or a piece of music (*The festivities were enlivened by the rendition of a few instrumental selections*). British usage prefers *rendering* to *rendition* in the senses of translation and performance.

Unless some unusual interpretation is attempted or accomplished, *performance* is definitely the word to be preferred as the term for singing or acting. *Rendition* implies the bringing out of a full or special meaning and while a good performance does this a bad performance does not and in either case the performer suffers from great claims being made for him.

renown. See **celebrity.**

rent. See **hire;** and **rend.**

reoccurrence; recurrence. *Reoccurrence*, a coinage of the late nineteenth century and still, happily, exceedingly rare, is really no more than a blunder for *recurrence*, an established and useful word, euphonious and satisfactory. There is no need for the more awkward form and most dictionaries do not recognize its existence.

repairable; reparable. *Reparable* is the general term to describe that which is capable of being repaired or remedied (*The mistake is easily reparable*). *Repairable* is preferred by authorities in England to describe material objects which are reparable (*A survey is needed to determine to what extent the buildings damaged by bombs are repairable*). In American usage, *reparable* is preferred in all circumstances. The negatives are *irreparable* and *unrepairable*.

repartee. See **answer.**

repast; collation; meal; banquet. *Repast* for *meal* is straining a little to be elegant and *sumptuous repast* and *rich repast* are journalistic clichés.

If a general term is wanted, *meal* is best and if a specific meal is referred to it is better to call it breakfast, lunch, or dinner. *Collation* is a very elegant word, now restricted to a very elegant light meal, and usually one served at some other time than a regular meal time. In the monasteries a collation was an unusually light meal permitted on days of general fast. It derives its name from the practice in the monasteries of reading the *Collations*, the lives of the Church Fathers, during such meals. A *banquet* is a ceremonious public dinner. In former times ceremonious public dinners were occasions for huge gormandizing and much prestige display of vast quantities of food, so that a *banquet* was a feast, far more sumptuous than a mere *meal* such as would be eaten at home. The fare at most banquets today, however, is inferior to what those who attend them would require of a good meal at home and the meaning of the word is shifting, emphasizing rather the ceremoniousness, the boredom, and the forced attendance.

repeat; recapitulate; rehearse; reiterate; iterate. *To repeat* is to do or say something over again (*If you will only repeat the order. He repeated the gesture with an air of defiance*). It is the common, everyday working word.

Recapitulate is a formal word, designating the exact naming of points that have been made before, the summing up of the principal heads of a previous discussion (*When they met, Sir William began by recapitulating what had been said at the last meeting*).

Though the primary meaning of *rehearse* is now to recite or act a play or a part in private by way of practice before a public performance, its basic meaning was to repeat, and this meaning is still to be met with in literature and, occasionally, in speech. When, for example, it is said in Judges that the governors of Israel shall *rehearse the righteous acts of the Lord*, it is plain that the common modern meaning could not pertain.

To reiterate is to do—or especially to say—something repeatedly over and over again (*He reiterated his complaints until the company was moved from pity to boredom. He reiterated his visits to the flagon so often that at length his senses were overpowered*). *Iterate* means to repeat over and over, but *reiterate* (which would seem a redundancy except that it describes a redundancy) has replaced it and *iterate* is now solely literary.

repeat the same is redundant. Repetition is the recurrence of the same thing. To say *He repeats the same stories over and over* is to be doubly redundant, though it may be argued that the redundance of the complaint merely echoes, for effect, the redundance of its provocation.

repel; repulse. *To repel* is to drive or force back, to excite feelings of distaste or aversion (*This insolence shall be repelled, and quickly. The company, which had come to admire, found themselves repelled by the poet's insufferable egotism*). *To repulse* is to drive back or repel in a stronger sense, to reject (*The attack was repulsed with heavy loss of life. She repulsed every suitor who proposed marriage*).

Repulse is sometimes used as if it were a back formation from *repulsive*. But this is an error. One who feels repulsion is repelled not repulsed.

repellent and **repulsive** both mean causing aversion. *Repellent* is the milder term. It means distasteful (*I found his effusiveness repellent*). *Repulsive* indicates that a much stronger aversion has been caused, that the person or thing alluded to is grossly or coarsely offensive to one's taste or feelings and is regarded with the strongest aversion and disgust (*Burns's world of Scotch drink, Scotch religion, and Scotch manners, is often a harsh, a sordid, a repulsive world*).

Repellent is sometimes used in America as a shortening of *water-repellent* in the advertising of certain outer garments which are not waterproof but will withstand a light drizzle. This is linguistically sound but psychologically unfortunate since it is certain to evoke the more common meaning of the word.

repent and **regret** are not synonyms. One regrets that of which one repents, but one does not always repent of that which one regrets.

That action is regretted which is looked back on with sorrow or grief or causes mental distress and makes us wish that we had not committed it. But bad men often suffer such feelings when they have inadvertently done good or have neglected an opportunity to do ill. If one repents he feels sorrow for some bad action. He feels regret but in addition contrition, compunction, a desire to amend his ways and to make amends to those who may have been injured by his action.

One regrets something. One repents *for* or *of* something. See also **regret; be sorry.**

repertoire; repertory. Both of these words may be used to describe the list of dramas, operas, parts or pieces which a company, actor, singer, or the like, is prepared to perform (*She had a large repertoire of folk songs*). *Repertoire* is the preferred term. *Repertory* alone may be used to describe a type of theatrical producing organization wherein one company prepares several plays or operas and produces them alternately (*Most good young actors learn their profession in repertory*). It is also the word for a store or stock of things available, a storehouse. The adjective is *repertory* (*Shakespeare's was a repertory company*).

repetition. The recurrence of a word or even of a sound in a sentence or a paragraph can be annoying to the reader and a careful writer will avoid this fault where such a recurrence is not essential to the expression of his thought or where the avoidance of it is not too obvious.

Of the two faults, the obvious avoidance of repetition is probably greater and more widespread than repetition. It accounts for a great deal of that sort of writing (of which Mr. Charles Morton of the *Atlantic Monthly* has made such a delightful and instructive collection) which having once mentioned a banana refers to it on the next occasion as "an elongated yellow fruit." For some reason—possibly because it's a fault which teachers find easy to identify—grade- and high-school pupils are taught that repetition is one of the gravest of all faults in writing and that no expression can be too stilted, pompous, polysyllabic or ludicrous so long as it enables one to avoid using a word twice in the same sentence. The writing of Thomas Wolfe should serve as a pleasant corrective to this illusion.

replace and **supplant** both refer to putting one thing or person in the place of another, but they convey different senses. *Replace* means to take the place of, to succeed (*John was elected to replace Joe on the board when Joe was made general director*). *Replace* may also mean to restore, to return (*Please replace all divots*). *Supplant* implies that that which takes the other's place has ousted the former holder, and usurped the position or function, especially by art or fraud (*Jacob supplanted his brother, Esau*).

replete means abundantly supplied or provided (*His lectures were replete with vivid illustrations and witty asides*), stuffed or gorged with food and drink (*After such a feast who would not be replete?*). *Replete* does not mean complete or furnished with, for neither of these terms conveys the sense of filled to overflowing. It would be inaccurate, for example, to describe a tool chest as *replete with the latest equipment* unless it was not only adequate and complete but also crowded.

replica; copy. Strictly speaking, a *replica* is a copy or reproduction of a work of art by the maker of the original (*Some authorities prefer his replicas to his originals*). A replica differs from a copy in that it is held to have the same right as the first made to be considered an original work. Authorities in England reject, while advanced American authorities accept, *replica* in the loose sense of a copy or reproduction (*The replica of Gainsborough's Blue Boy, done by a local craftsman in bits of colored glass, was much admired*). The careful writer, nonetheless, will prefer *copy* in such contexts.

reply. See **answer.**

report. When used in an active form, *report* may be followed by a clause, as in *he reports he has seen her,* or by the *-ing* form of a verb, as in *he reports seeing her.* When *report* is used in a passive form it may be followed by an infinitive, as in *he is reported to have seen her.*

repress. See **check.**

reprisal. See **retaliation.**

repudiate. See **deny.**

repulse. See **repel.**

repulsive. See **repellent.**

reputation. See **character.**

reputed; reported. That is *reputed* which is accounted or commonly supposed to be such, so held in general estimation or opinion (*The reputed owner of the place is a respectable*

suburbanite). That is *reported* which is communicated. But *reputed* implies an evaluation, estimate or opinion; whereas *reported* is merely communicated. The reputed owner may, of course, be reported as the owner; but that is not the same thing, for an admitted owner might also be reported as owner.

requests. See **imperative mode.**

require. This word may be followed by an infinitive, as in *I require him to help me,* or by a *that* clause with the clause verb a subjunctive or a subjunctive equivalent, as in *I require that he help me.* The *-ing* form of a verb following *require* always has a passive meaning, as in *he requires helping.* See **demand.**

required; compulsory; prescribed. In American schools and colleges those courses which are obligatory are called *required* courses (*One year of English composition is required in nearly all our colleges*). In England the equivalent term is *compulsory* or *prescribed* (*To the amazement of his tutor, he finished the prescribed reading for the degree in a year*).

requirement; requisite. A *requirement* is something demanded of a person in accordance with certain fixed regulations (*A knowledge of Latin is no longer a requirement for entering the state university*) or something demanded by a person as essential to the accomplishment of some task (*His first requirement was a long piece of copper wire. The army regards discipline as a fundamental requirement*). A *requisite* is something required by the nature of the case, some factor which is judged necessary under the circumstances (*The knave is handsome, young, and hath all those requisites in him that folly and green minds look after*). (For *requisite* as an adjective, see **necessary.**)

re-search; research. *Re-search,* usable as noun and verb, means to search again, explore something already explored (*I have searched the attic thoroughly but will re-search it if you insist on it*). *Research,* used chiefly as a noun, means diligent and systematic inquiry or investigation into a subject in order to discover facts or principles (*Research into causes of the common cold has so far been remarkably unfruitful*).

Research has become very popular in the United States since the outbreak of World War II. As Henry D. Smyth has observed, the idea that the object of research is new knowledge does not seem to be widely understood and "a schoolboy looking up the meaning of a word in the dictionary is now said to be doing research." Indeed, it has been debased even further. *Research* is frequently used to describe reading by those to whom reading, apparently, is a recherché activity, and for many a graduate student it is a euphemism for wholesale plagiarism. The word needs a rest or at least less promiscuous handling.

resent may be followed by the *-ing* form of a verb, as in *I resent being told that,* but not by an infinitive. *I resent to be told that* is unacceptable. *Resent* may also be followed by a *that* clause, as in *I resent that he is here,* but the -*ing* construction, as in *I resent his being here* is preferred.

reside; live; dwell. *Live* is the word to describe the act of occupying a permanent home (*There was a jolly miller/ And he lived by the Dee*). *Dwell* is old-fashioned (*the father of such as dwell in tents*), journalese (*Mrs. Merryweather-Smythe is dwelling at the country club while her Larchwood home is being completely redecorated*), or poetic (*I dreamt that I dwelt in marble halls*). *Reside* is pretentious, unless it describes the act of living in an important or pretentious residence (*The governor resides at Albany*) or is used, as of a quality, to mean to inhere or to be inherent in (*There often resides a deep stubbornness in these quiet natures*).

residence. The house in which one resides is legally one's residence, regardless of its size or condition. Otherwise, however, *residence* implies size and elegance of structure and surroundings (*Blenheim Palace, the residence of the dukes of Marlborough*). To use it as a synonym for house (*Ah, here we are, my modest residence*) is pretentious or forcedly humorous. See also **house; home.**

residue. See **balance.**

residuum. The plural is *residua.*

resign may be followed by the -*ing* form of a verb with the preposition *to,* as in *I have resigned myself to going,* or by an infinitive, as in *I have resigned myself to go.* Both forms are acceptable in the United States but the -*ing* construction is generally preferred.

resignation. See **patience.**

resin; rosin. *Resin* is the general name to describe any of a class of nonvolatile, solid or semisolid organic substances, such as copal and mastic, obtained directly from certain plants as exudations or derived from various products by special processes, and used in such things as medicine and varnish. *Resin* properly describes a substance in its natural state. *Rosin,* on the other hand, describes the result of a process. It is the hard brittle resin left after distilling off the oil of turpentine from the crude oleoresin of the pine, used in making varnish, for rubbing on violin bows, billiard cue tips, the canvas floor of boxing rings, and the like.

resist may be followed by the -*ing* form of a verb, as in *he resisted going.* It is also heard with the infinitive, as in *he resisted to go,* but this is not standard.

resolve. This verb may be followed by an infinitive, as in *he resolved to go.* If the -*ing* form of a verb is used it must be introduced by the preposition *on,* as in *he resolved on going.* The two forms are equally acceptable and there is no difference in meaning between them. See **decide.**

resolve; resolution. These nouns are distinguishable. A *resolve* is a conclusion, a determination made, as to follow some course of action (*That's an admirable resolve; I hope you'll stick to it*). In certain contexts *resolution* is used in the same sense, as in *a New Year's resolu-* tion. Primarily, however, *resolution* means a formal determination or expression of opinion of a deliberative assembly or other body of persons (*Resolutions as used in the practice of the Ohio General Assembly are of two kinds: House or Senate and Joint Resolution*). *Resolution* also means a solution or explanation, as of a problem or a doubtful point, and is to be preferred to *resolve* as the word for the mental state or quality of being resolved, resolute, and firm of purpose.

resort; resource. See **recourse.**

respectable; respectful. *Respectable* means worthy of respect or esteem, estimable, worthy (*No respectable girl would associate with a man of his reputation*), of good social standing and reputation (*Her main consideration in renting was to find a respectable neighborhood*), pertaining to or appropriate to such standing (*He had a quite respectable command of French*). It also means of moderate excellence, fairly good (*Though he was not brilliant, his lecture was a respectable performance*). *Respectful,* a word with fewer uses, means full of, characterized by, or showing respect (*His very look drew respectful attention from the company*).

respective; respectively. The use of *respective* and *respectively* can become a habit in speech. It is one to be on the lookout for and to check in time.

Respective is an adjective which means pertaining individually or severally to each of a number of persons or things. *Respectively* is an adverb formed on this adjective. In certain situations the words are desirable, even necessary, as in *Kit and Nick were given a pistol and a teddy bear respectively.* Here we must be informed that it was Kit who got the pistol and Nick who got the teddy bear. Without "respectively" either one might have received either gift or each might have received two gifts. There are many circumstances, however, under which *respective* and *respectively* are unnecessary. For instance, *respective* is not needed in the statement *He gave each organization its respective share of the total collection.* It would be just as effective to say *He gave each organization its share of the total collection.* If the shares were of different amounts and he saw to it that each organization received the amount it was entitled to (and that is often the sort of idea that is intended to be conveyed by *respective* in such contexts), the correct word would be *proper* or *due* or *agreed* or something like that. Even where *respective* and *respectively* are used correctly they might be omitted and the sentence rewritten more concisely and clearly (*Kit was given a pistol, Nick a teddy bear*).

response. See **answer.**

responsible. British authorities insist that *responsible* be restricted to human beings. American and English usage alike consider as basic senses of *responsible*: answerable or accountable, as for something within one's power or control or management—followed by *to* or *for* (*The* *business manager is responsible to the trustees for all the financial affairs of the university*); involving accountability or responsibility (*He held a responsible position*). Only American usage permits *responsible* in the much looser sense of the cause of, chargeable with being the author of, the cause or occasion of something —followed by *for* (*Heavy rains were responsible for the deplorable condition of the country roads*).

rest. This verb may be followed by an adjective describing what rests, as in *you must rest content.* It may also be followed by an adverb describing the resting, as in *rest quietly.* There is often no difference in meaning between the two constructions.

rest (in the sense of remainder). See **balance.**

rest upon one's laurels. Whoever first thought of a triumphant victor taking off his laurel wreath and making a mattress of it had a happy figure of speech to describe those who, having once accomplished something notable, have since given up all exertion and live solely on their reputations. But the expression is now worn out.

restive; restless. *Restive* means impatient of control, restraint, or delay, refractory, refusing to go forward, as a horse (*He became restive under the harsh discipline of the lieutenant*). Yet the word *impatient* connotes restlessness, and perhaps one can only say that restiveness is restlessness traceable to certain causes, such as restraint. *Restless* is a general term meaning characterized by or showing inability to remain at rest. A sick man might be restless with fever. He would be restive at the restrictions imposed on him by his physician, particularly as he grew well and found the restrictions increasingly annoying.

restrain. See **check, constrain.**

restrictive clauses. A defining clause that is essential to the meaning of a statement, such as *I told you about* in *the man I told you about is here now,* is called a restrictive clause. Clauses of this kind must not be separated from the noun they qualify by a comma or any other form of punctuation. (For the use of *that* or *which* in a defining clause, see **that; which.**)

resume; continue. *Continue* is the more inclusive term. It means either to go on with a course of action (*We will continue with our experiments until we find a solution*) or to go on after a suspension or interruption (*If you have had enough rest, we will continue with the lesson*). *Resume* may be substituted for the second of these two senses of *continue* (*After a brief stop, he resumed his ride*). Indeed, because it is specific, it is usually preferable to *continue* in this sense.

resume; résumé. *Resume* is a verb, meaning to take up or go on with again after an interruption (*The debate was resumed as soon as the guards had ejected the heckler*).

Résumé is taken from a French noun formed on the past participle of *résumer.* It means a summary, a summing up, that which has been taken up again (*In his notebooks he wrote résumés of the various arguments*).

retaliation; reprisal. Both of these words mean the return of like for like, the repayment of injury in kind, "an eye for an eye and a tooth for a tooth," so that the injury done back *tallies* exactly with that done.

Reprisal is the more ferocious term. It describes the infliction of similar or severer injury on the enemy in warfare, in retaliation for some injury, as by the punishment or execution of hostages or prisoners (*In reprisal for the murder of a German soldier, the Germans wiped out one whole French town*). *Retaliation* has milder connotations and is used in other circumstances (*In retaliation for inconsiderate treatment by certain English people when he was a boy, he was, as an editor, consistently anti-British and his influence was tremendous*).

reticent; secretive; taciturn; laconic. One is *reticent* who is disposed to be silent, who has an inclination to keep his own counsel, is reserved, not inclined to speak freely (*Like most tight-fisted men, he was exceedingly reticent about his will*). It may describe habitual behavior or special behavior on a particular occasion (*That evening he was surprisingly reticent about his war experiences*).

Secretive means extremely reticent, having a disposition to secrecy. It is a stronger word than *reticent* and carries a slightly pejorative connotation. Reticence is often admirable; secrecy suggests furtiveness and implies there is something improper to be hidden (*These secretive natures delight in trifling stratagems*).

Taciturn describes one who is habitually inclined to silence, reserved in speech, reticent in an uncheerful manner (*The rural New Englander is reputed to be taciturn*). *Laconic,* unlike *taciturn,* is a rather laudatory term. It means using few words, expressing much in a few words, being concise (*His political opponents considered Coolidge taciturn; his friends praised him for being laconic*). *Laconic* and *taciturn* are often point-of-view words, the choice often revealing more about the writer or speaker than about the one written or spoken about.

retire is now a little over-elegant and slightly affected when used to mean to go to bed. To retire is, strictly, to withdraw. And one retires from something or to something. The continuance of its use in America may have been due to prudery, for when legs were referred to as "limbs" the word *bed* was unmentionable. Charles Dickens on his first American visit had considerable trouble with two Misses Smith who were singing in an operetta of his, *The Village Coquettes.* They objected to the "immodesty" of certain lines and definitely refused to sing one quatrain:

> *A winter's night has its delight,*
> * Well-warmed to bed they go:*
> *A winter's day we're blithe and gay,*
> * Snipe-shooting in the snow.*

They were "horrified," Dickens wrote, "at the bare notion of anyone going to bed." So for the objectionable line he substituted:

Around old stories go.

But all has changed. In literature, at least, the bed is now the most frequently mentioned of all articles of furniture and we may go there without shame or circumlocution.

retort. See **answer.**

retort courteous. Touchstone in *As You Like It* (V, iv) names for Jaques the "degrees of the lie," the steps by which timid gallants who would seem, for honor's sake, to be quarrelsome might bluster and threaten without finally reaching the dreadful point at which they would have to draw their swords. The degrees were the Retort Courteous, the Quip Modest, the Reply Churlish, the Reproof Valiant, the Countercheck Quarrelsome, the Lie with Circumstance and, finally, the Lie Direct which, if not prefaced with a saving "if," required a man to demand satisfaction. It is all very delightful and witty, but it is best to let Shakespeare and Touchstone have full credit for any part of it. Used by itself, *the retort courteous* is now hackneyed.

retraction; retractation. In America the usual word to describe the withdrawal of a promise, statement, or opinion is *retraction* (*It was embarrassing to order the retraction of a commitment which should never have been made*). In England the word is *retractation* (*There are perhaps no contracts or engagements of which one can venture to say that there ought to be no liberty whatever of retractation*).

retreat; retire; withdraw. *Retreat* describes especially the act of drawing back in military operations (*They had to retreat all the way from Moscow to the Prussian border*). *Retire* may mean to draw away, as from battle or danger (*The Mexicans retired and regrouped for a fresh attack*), but it is more commonly a civilian term to describe withdrawal from office, business, or active life (*Most men hope to be able to afford to retire at sixty-five*). *Withdraw*, aside from its literal senses, means to go apart or away, especially after a formal or ceremonial visit (*He withdrew from the royal presence*). It is also the term in parliamentary procedure for removing a motion or an amendment from consideration (*I withdraw my motion*).

retrieve from its specific hunting sense of to search for and fetch wounded game (of dogs), has come to mean generally to recover or regain, especially to bring back to a former state of well-being or prosperity (*The war gave him an opportunity to retrieve the family fortunes*). Except in this last sense, however, or in the rare instances where it avoids ambiguity (such as *retrieving* an umbrella, where *recovering* would be open to another interpretation), *retrieve* is usually just a fancy word for saying what *recover*, *find*, *get*, or *restore* might express better.

retrospection. See **hindsight.**

reveal. See **disclose.**

revelation; disclosure. A *disclosure* is a making known, a revealing, an exhibition. It is a neutral word. The making known may be timely or untimely, advantageous or disadvantageous, honorable or shameful or neither one nor the other (*The disclosure of the stores of Greek literature had wrought the revolution of the Renaissance. An unseasonable disclosure of flashes of wit may do a man much harm. His reputation did not long survive these disclosures*). A *revelation* is a striking disclosure, as of something not before realized. It is especially applied to the disclosure of great truths by divine or other supernatural means (*When God declares any truth to us, this is a revelation. 'Tis Revelation satisfies all doubts/ Explains all mysteries except her own,/ And so illuminates the path of life*). Literally the word means an unveiling and its use in such sentences as *The revelation of her beauty left him speechless* is not improper, but because of the strong theological connotations of *revelation* it is usually better to use *disclosure* in most contexts.

Revelation(s). Strictly speaking, the last book of the New Testament is *Revelation*. The Authorized or King James Version of the Bible calls it *The Revelation of St. John the Divine*. The Revised Standard Version calls it *The Revelation to John. Revelations*, however, is so widely used and has been used by so many distinguished scholars for so long that it may as well be accepted, at least in speech. *The Revelations* (a confusion of the correct *The Revelation* with the colloquial *Revelations*) is unacceptable.

revenge. See **avenge.**

reverence; revere; worship; venerate; adore. *Reverence*, when used as a verb, means to manifest a feeling or attitude of deep respect tinged with awe (*In prayer the soul reverences the majesty of God*). *Venerate* connotes a little less awe, full respect but less fear (*We should venerate those who have become old without becoming selfish or peevish, who, knowing much, still have faith in and respect for their fellow men*). *Revere* also suggests less awe than *reverence* (*We often laugh in public at what we revere in private*).

To *worship* is to pay homage to a deity by outward forms, usually in places established or recognized by custom for that sole purpose (*A man of Ethiopia . . . had come to Jerusalem for to worship*—Acts). To *adore* is to pay divine honors to, to pay homage to a deity. It is usually an internal act or experience, not necessarily connected with any specific place or expressed in any prescribed form or manner. When applied to anything but a god, *worship* and *adore* are plainly hyperbolical, though even in the Bible *worship* is used to designate extreme deference to men (*As Peter was coming in, Cornelius met him and fell down at his feet, and worshipped him*—Acts 10:25). *Worship* has been greatly weakened by this hyperbolical use, so that it often means no more than "be fond of" (*For I loved that cook as a brother, I did,/ And the cook he worshipped me*) and *adore,* once one of the sublimest words in the language, is, as a pale synonym for *like,* a staple of school-girl gabble (*Oh, I adore fudge sundaes!*).

reverend is a title of respect given to clergymen. In the seventeenth century it was used as we now use *doctor* and *professor.* That is, it was used without the article *the* and could stand immediately before a surname, as in *Reverend Calvin.* It could also be used with other titles, as in *Reverend Bishop Hooper.* Today in Great Britain, *Reverend* is used as we use *Honorable.* That is, the article *the* is required and the title cannot stand immediately before a surname. Either the given name or initials must be used, or some title of respect must take their place, as in *the Reverend Edward Pusey* or *the Reverend Mr. Pusey.*

Both of these forms are standard in the United States today. The older form, in which the word is treated like the word *professor,* is preferred in the evangelical churches and wherever the New England influence is dominant. Where the contemporary British form is followed, the article *the* is sometimes omitted when the title is abbreviated, as in *Rev. George Ellison.*

People who feel that the article *the* is required before *Reverend* cannot use the title as a form of address. But other people do use the title with a proper name in speaking to a clergyman, as in *good morning Reverend Ellison.* To use the title *Reverend* without a proper name is generally considered undignified. But it is so used occasionally by well-educated people, as in *those who had not attained to military honors were either doctors, professors, or reverends* and *we are not so meddlesome as you reverends are.*

Reverence, as an ecclesiastical title used in mentioning or addressing a clergyman, is preceded by *your* or *his* (*His Reverence will not appear today. Your Reverence does me great honor in consenting to visit me*). Such locutions are seldom used in America.

reverend; reverent. *Reverend* means deserving reverence, worthy to be revered (*Reverend fathers, the respect due to your age and authority . . .*). *Reverent* means feeling, exhibiting, or characterized by reverence. *Reverend* is usually applied to the clergy. *Reverent* has more general application (*He was a reverent student of nature*).

reversal and **reversion** refer to the act of turning something the reverse way. *Reversal* designates the act of reversing or an instance of reversing (*This was a reversal of his previous position on the subject*) or the state of being reversed (*The demotion was a reversal in his career*). In law a *reversal* is the revocation of a lower court's decision by an appellate court.

Reversion is perhaps best known as a legal term, to describe the returning of an estate to the grantor or his heirs after the interest granted expires, or an estate which so returns or the right of succeeding to an estate. It is also a term in biology to denote the reappearance of ancestral characters that have been absent in intervening generations, an atavism or return to an earlier or primitive type (*Evolution ever climbing after some ideal good,/ And Reversion ever dragging Evolution in the mud*—Tennyson). *Reversion* may also be used in such general senses as the act of turning something the reverse way or the state of being so turned. In these senses it is synonymous with *reversal,* though *reversal* is to be preferred. It has the distinctive general sense of the act of reverting, the returning to a former practice, belief, condition (*The acceptance of Fort's assumptions constitutes a reversion to the Dark Ages*).

reverse. See **contrary.**

review and **revue** both derive from a French word meaning to see again.

Of the two, *review* is used most frequently and in a variety of senses. It may describe a critical article or report, as in a periodical, on some literary work, commonly some work of recent appearance (*He wrote perceptive reviews for a well known periodical*); a periodical publication containing articles on current events or affairs, books, art (*The* Quarterly Review *and the* Edinburgh Review *dictated public opinion in early nineteenth century Britain*); a viewing again, a second or repeated view of something (*I'd appreciate a review of the last step you demonstrated*); the process of going over a subject again in study or recitation in order to fix it in the memory or to summarize the facts, or an exercise of this kind (*I won't have much time for a review before the examination*); an inspection, or examination by viewing, especially a formal inspection of any military or naval force, parade, or the like (*At Midshipman School there was a review every Saturday morning*); a viewing of the past, contemplation or consideration of past events, circumstances, or facts (*Toynbee has arrived at his philosophy of history after a review of historical events*); a general survey of something, especially in words, a report or account of something (*He gave a review of the experiences which led to his decision*); a judicial re-examination, as by a higher court, of the decision or proceedings in a case (*His decision in the County Court is, of course, subject to review*).

Though *review* may also describe a form of theatrical entertainment in which recent events, popular fads, etc., are parodied, or any group of skits, dances, and songs, the better word is *revue* (*There are always a few revues on Broadway which are seen under unfortunate circumstances: the curtain is up*).

revolutionist; revolutionary. The English recognize only *revolutionary* and use it both as a noun and an adjective. Americans use *revolutionary* largely as an adjective meaning pertaining to, characterized by, or of the nature of a revolution, or complete or marked change (*He introduced revolutionary techniques in the teaching of languages*). It also means subversive to established procedure or principles (*Dostoevsky was arrested on charges of having plotted revolutionary activity*) and has the still further meaning, not often used in common speech or writing, of revolving (*His eyes glittered as they followed the revolutionary course of the roulette wheel*).

Though *revolutionary* may be used in America as a noun to describe one who advocates or takes part in a revolution, the more common term is *revolutionist*. This term is almost always reserved, however, for those engaged in or advocating political revolutions in other countries (*The Mexican revolutionists were soon brought under control by the government forces*). Those who advocate any such changes in America are most commonly referred to now as *subversives*, for any word deriving from the word *revolution* suggests to Americans the American Revolutionary War and hence creates considerable moral confusion. See also **radical.**

rhetoric in the United States still means primarily the art or science of the specially literary uses of language, in prose or verse, or the art of prose as opposed to verse. In England it is a disparaging term (*Rhetoric is the harlot of the arts*—Stanley Baldwin) meaning the use of exaggeration or display, in an unfavorable sense. This meaning is known and employed in America, but it is a secondary meaning.

rhinoceros. The plural is *rhinoceroses* or *rhinoceros* or *rhinocerotes*, but not *rhinoceri.*

rhyme and **rime** may both be used as nouns and verbs to describe agreement in terminal sounds of lines or verse, or of words. Of the two, *rime* is the older, but since the seventeenth century *rhyme* has been more common. *Rime*, however, has never been dropped out of use (Coleridge, *The Rime of the Ancient Mariner*) and recently it has been used in the title of an important discussion of modern prosody (Karl Shapiro, *An Essay on Rime*).

rhyme; rhythm. *Rhythm* is a pattern of recurrence. *Rhyme* is often an element in the rhythm of English poetry, but there can be rhythm without rhyme and there is often rhyme with imperfect or no perceptible rhythm.

Rhyme means agreement in the terminal sounds of lines in verse, or of words (*In the heroic couplet the rhymes are paired: "The hungry judges soon the sentence sign,/ And wretches hang that jurymen may dine"*). It may also mean verse or poetry having such correspondence in the terminal sounds of the lines (*Sometimes he expressed his thoughts in prose, at other times in rhyme*) or a poem or a piece of verse having such correspondence (*The children were very fond of one particular nursery rhyme*).

Rhythm is a much broader term. It may be used of more types of literature and may be applied to forms of art other than verse. Basically it means movement or procedure with uniform recurrence of a beat, accent, or the like (*In the human body there is rhythm in breathing, in the pulse, and in other subtler vital processes*). It can describe any measured movement, as in dancing (*A highly developed sense of rhythm is essential to a tennis player*). In music, *rhythm* means the pattern of regular or irregular pulses caused by the occurrence of strong and weak melodic and harmonic beats (*It was written in an ordinary ⁴⁄₄ rhythm*). In prosody, *rhythm* means metrical or rhythmical form, meter (*The basic rhythm in English poetry is iambic; that is, an unstressed syllable is followed by a stressed syllable*). In art, *rhythm* means a proper relation and interdependence of parts with reference to one another and to an artistic whole (*The paintings of Piero della Francesca have rhythm, while the imitative work of Kenyon Cox does not*).

rich; wealthy; opulent; affluent. All of these words indicate abundance in possessions. *Rich* is the general word, a word having many senses in addition to the primary one (as a rich tone or a rich color or a rich dessert). Often *rich* carries the implication of newly acquired possession (*Texas is not as full of rich oil men as the newsmagazines and television jokes assume*). *Wealthy* suggests permanence, stability, and appropriate surroundings (*The DuPonts are a powerful and wealthy family*). Both *rich* and *wealthy* may apply to a person, a family, a society, or a nation. *Opulent* and *affluent* are largely applicable to persons. *Opulent* suggests display of luxuriousness, outward signs of being rich (*Gatsby was opulent in his lavish villa, his yellow car, his pink suits*). *Affluent*, now slightly archaic, connotes a handsome income and a free expenditure of resources.

rich as Croesus, as. *Croesus*, king of Lydia (560 —c.540 B.C.), was famed among the Greeks for almost incredible wealth. His name became a proverb for riches, but few who use the hackneyed simile have now any knowledge of him.

rich beyond the dreams of avarice. When Dr. Johnson, bustling about in his capacity as an executor at the sale of Thrale's brewery in 1781, said *We are not here to sell a parcel of boilers and vats, but the potentiality of growing rich beyond the dreams of avarice,* he was quoting from *The Gamester,* a tragedy by Edward Moore (1753). Moore's phrase was imaginative and Johnson's use of it felicitous. But it is now exhausted by repetition and those who use it show neither imagination nor felicity.

Richard Roe. See **John Doe.**

riches was originally a singular word ending in an *s* sound, similar to *finesse,* and meant wealth. It is now treated as a plural, as in *your riches are corrupted and your garments are moth-eaten,* but there is no singular form *a rich* and the plural form cannot be used with a word implying number.

rickets. This word is plural in form but is regularly treated as a singular, as in *rickets is not contagious* and *it affects the bones.* We do not say *rickets are* or refer to the disease as *them.*

The medical name for this disease is *rachitis* and a child who has rickets is said to be *rachitic.* The older English adjective *rickety,* which is derived from *rickets,* is now used chiefly of inanimate objects, such as chairs.

rid. The past tense is *rid* or *ridded.* The participle is also *rid* or *ridded.* In the United States *rid* is the preferred form for the past tense and for the participle. In Great Britain *ridded* is preferred when the verb is active, as in *we ridded the cellar of rats,* and *rid* is preferred when the verb is passive, as in *we are well rid of them.*

ridden. See **ride.**

riddle; enigma; puzzle. These nouns all refer to something baffling or confusing which is to be solved. A *puzzle* is a question or problem intricate enough to be perplexing to the mind. It is sometimes a contrivance made purposely to test one's ingenuity. It tends to refer to non-verbal problems. Though a great many of the puzzle games have to do with the construction of words, they are not much concerned with obscure meanings (*His whole attitude is a puzzle to me. He spent his youth on jigsaw puzzles and his manhood on crossword puzzles*). Possibly because of its close association with games, the word *puzzle* is not often used to designate a serious perplexity. An American would be more inclined, for example, to say that the disposition of radioactive waste materials was a *problem* than to say it was a *puzzle.*

Riddle, on the other hand, applies to verbal problems. A *riddle* is an intentionally obscure statement or question, the meaning of or answer to which is to be arrived at only by guessing (*Oedipus won his throne by solving the riddle of the Sphinx*). The word has a connotation of children's games that requires some care in its use, but it is still capable of carrying great weight and solemnity (*Although a subtler Sphinx renew/ Riddles of death Thebes never knew*).

Enigma, originally meaning "riddle," now refers to some baffling problem with connotations of mysteriousness (*To many sincere persons the nature of the will of God is an enigma*).

ride. The past tense is *rode.* The participle is *ridden. Rid* was used as a past tense and as a participle in literary English well into the nineteenth century, but is no longer considered standard.

Though Englishmen and Americans understand *ride* in roughly the same senses, *ride* seems to be used in more contexts in America than in England. For instance, when Americans speak of a *boat ride,* English speak of *excursions* or *outings.* In England a trip on a train is a *railway journey;* in America it is a *train ride.* The American underworld has contributed the sinister expression *to take for a ride* to describe the process of luring an enemy into a car, killing him, and disposing of his remains in some unfrequented place.

ridiculous. See **funny.**

right; rightly. The form *right* may be used as an adjective, as in *the right answer.* Both forms may be used as adverbs to qualify a verb, as in *he answered right.* Only the form *rightly* is used in the sense of "properly" or "justifiably," as in *he rightly refused to answer;* either form may be used in the sense of "correctly." In any other sense, only the form *right* is used.

Rightly cannot qualify an adjective or adverb. *Right* was used in this way, as in *right glad, right soon,* from the time of Chaucer until the close of the nineteenth century. In Great Britain this construction is now considered archaic, or Biblical, except in titles such as *Right Reverend, Right Honorable.* In the United States it is still natural English but has an old-fashioned tone.

right away. See **immediately.**

right of way is most commonly used in America to describe a common-law or statutory right to proceed ahead of another (*If two vehicles are approaching an intersection at roughly the same time, the one to the right is said to have the right of way*). In both England and America *right of way* describes a path or route which may lawfully be used, or the right of passage, as over another's land (*The claim of the people at the trailer camp to have a right of way through the woodlot infuriated him*). A specifically American sense is that of the strip of land acquired for use by a railroad's tracks, what in England is called the *permanent way* (*Some of the most valuable western land was that immediately adjacent to a railroad right of way*). By extension of this sense, *right of way* describes land covered by a public road or land over which a power line passes.

rime. See **rhyme.**

ring. The past tense is *rang.* The participle is *rung.*

Rung was formerly used as a past tense, as in *heaven rung with jubilee,* but this is no longer standard.

Ring may be followed by an adjective describing the sound, as in *it rang hollow.* It may also be followed by an adverb describing the ringing, as in *it rang loudly.* There is usually no difference in meaning between the two constructions.

riot originally meant loose or wasteful living, debauchery (*The lamb thy riot dooms to bleed today*). *To run riot* meant to act without control or restraint (*They ran riot, would not be kept in bounds by their leaders*). The term died out of general use in the nineteenth century except for *letting one's imagination run riot,* and that is now a cliché.

riotous living. The Prodigal Son *wasted his substance with riotous living.* But though the expression may in 1611 have still retained some of its original vigor, as a description of extravagant and dissolute wantonness, it is now a cliché.

riposte. See **answer.**

rise. The past tense is *rose*. The participle is *risen*. *Rise* may be followed by an adjective describing what rises, as in *the sun rose hot* and *he rose victorious*. It may also be followed by an adverb describing the rising, as in *he rose wearily*.

Raise means "cause to rise." For the difference between these two verbs, see **raise**. See also **arise**.

risen. See **rise**.

risible. See **funny**.

risk life and limb. As a term for being willing to take dangerous chances, *risk life and limb* is a cliché, kept in use, as so many clichés are, by its alliteration.

risky; risqué. *Risky* is the general term, meaning attended with or involving risk, hazardous (*Underwater demolition is a risky business*). *Risky* may also mean daringly close to indelicacy or impropriety, running the risk of being indecorous. But *risqué* is the preferable term for this limited sense (*The natural habitat of the risqué story is the bachelors' smoker*). The word has been so often used as a synonym for *indecent* that it has practically come to mean that.

rive. The past tense is *rived*. The participle is *riven* or *rived*. *Riven* is the preferred form for the participle and the only form used immediately before a noun, as in *my riven heart*.

river. The position of the word *river* in relation to the proper name differs in English and American usage. In England the word, whether capitalized or uncapitalized, precedes the proper name (*The river Thames is a tidal river. William Browne wrote of the river Tavy*). In America the word follows the proper name and is always capitalized (*Liza crossed the Ohio River, clutching her child and leaping from one cake of ice to another, the bloodhounds in pursuit*).

roast. Though Hogarth immortalized the *Roast Beef of Old England* and English schoolchildren still sing songs in its honor, the term is now more current in America than in England where a piece of meat intended for roasting is now called a *joint*. In both England and America, *roast* is the verb to describe the process of making flesh or other food ready for eating by prolonged exposure to heat at or before a fire. Only in America is *roast* much used in the figurative and slang sense of ridiculing or criticizing severely or mercilessly (*They roasted him in Wyoming because of his Harvard accent*).

rob. See **steal**.

rob; robber; robbery. See **thief; robber; burglar** and **steal; purloin; pilfer**.

rob Peter to pay Paul. As a term for incurring one debt in order to pay another or take something, usually money, that is needed for one thing and use it for another, *robbing Peter to pay Paul* is hackneyed. The phrase has been in use since 1400, but its origin is unknown.

robe is a word more popular in America than in England, or at least there are more compounds based on it. For American *lap robe* the English

say *carriage rug*. Both Americans and English say *dressing gown*, but Americans, especially less elegant ones, say *bathrobe*.

rock. In both England and America, *rock* means primarily a large mass of stone forming an eminence, cliff, or the like (*The Rock of Gibraltar, the shadow of a great rock in a weary land, The Rock—Alcatraz*). While in England *rock* is taken more loosely to mean a large stone or boulder (*Come one, come all! this rock shall fly/ From its firm base as soon as I!*), in America it is taken more loosely still (colloquially) to mean a stone of any size, especially one used as a missile (*The boys threw rocks through the window and then ran up the alley*).

rode. See **ride**.

role. This word to describe the part or character which an actor presents in a play is best spelled role (without accent or italics). It is permissibly written *rôle* (with accent and italics), though in England, at least, this form is obsolescent.

romance; romantic. Derived from a word describing the Romance languages, that is, any of the group of languages which have developed out of Latin, *romance* and *romantic* applied originally to popular medieval tales written in these languages, as distinct from more sober writings which would have been in Latin. These tales were full of wonders, crude violence and strong passions and *romance* acquired a permanent coloring from that fact. The *Romantic Movement* invited attention to wonder. When applied to love affairs, *romance* and *romantic* suggest a conception of love as involving wonder, strong passions, and extravagance. That *romance* is a synonym for love today is not without its significance. The use of *romance* as a verb (*I wonder who's romancing her now*) is not standard.

roof. The plural is *roofs*, not *rooves*.

rooster; cock. *Cock* is the proper term for the male of any bird, especially of the gallinaceous kind. As a designation of the male of the domesticated breeds, commonly known as chickens, it is time-honored and dignified (*My tale is of a cock and a hen. Before the cock crow, thou shalt deny me thrice. The cock's shrill clarion, or the echoing horn,/ No more shall rouse them from their lowly bed*). *Rooster* was substituted in America in a period of ridiculous prudery and while it is too well established in usage now to be dismissed as absurd or infantile, it is not a dignified word. The English still say *cock*. In fact, as H. Allen Smith observed, they "get slightly apoplectic when we say 'rooster' instead of 'cock,' insisting that a cock is no more giving to roosting than a hen."

Prudery moves on prurience as a snail in its own slime and leaves the trail of this slime over all that it touches. The gallant cock and the patient ass are forever banished from our speech and we have only the nursery equivalents of *rooster* and *donkey*.

root of all evil. A reference to money as *the root of all evil* is a threadbare expression based on a misquotation of I Timothy, 6:10—*The love* *of money is the root of all evil.* However, since money in itself has no value and it is only the desire for it that makes it function as a medium of exchange, the whole thing may be a quibble.

rooves. See **roof.**

rose. See **rise.**

rosin. See **resin.**

rostrum. The plural is *rostrums* or *rostra.*

rotten. This is an old form of the participle *rotted* that is used now only as an adjective. We say *the wood had rotted and was now rotten.* There is a growing tendency to use *rotted* as the adjective also, in speaking about desirable forms of decay, such as *rotted leaves,* and to reserve *rotten* for what is undesirable, whether it has decayed or not, as in *rotten eggs* and *rotten politicians.*

roughneck; rowdy. American *roughneck* equals English *rowdy.* It is a slang term to describe a rough, coarse person. It may also suggest a tough (*Don't get mixed up with those roughnecks down at the poolroom, Jim.*)

round. See **around.**

route should be used only in a literal sense, to describe a way or road for passage or travel (*Route 66 is a famous American highway*), a customary or regular line of passage or travel (*The route led through the Cumberland Gap*). *Route* is not to be used figuratively as a loose synonym for method, manner, or procedure (as in *He uses every available route to achieve political power*).

rove; roven. See **reeve.**

row, as a word for a noisy dispute or quarrel, was for a century or more a slang word, and is only just beginning to be accepted by the dictionaries as standard. That being so, it certainly should not be used in contexts where the seriousness of the dispute requires that it be treated with dignity. The frequent reference in headlines to *boundary row* or *international row* often has an offensive flippancy about it, though the word when so used is probably chosen more for its size than its connotations.

royal. See **kingly.**

ruby. See **agate.**

rudimentary. See **vestigial.**

ruination is derived from *ruinate,* a verb form in common use up until 1700. It describes the act of ruining, a state of being ruined, or something that ruins (*That boy will be the ruination of me yet!*). But it has a slightly humorous, rustic tinge, as though (like *botheration*) it were a facetious lengthening of *ruin.* It is not, but since there are very few non-humorous contexts in which *ruin* will not serve as well or better, it is a word to be avoided.

rule the roost. As a term for being plainly the boss, especially at home, *rule the roost* is a cliché. The metaphor would seem to be drawn from the dominance of the cock over his hens, but there are those among the learned who insist that *to rule the roost* is a corruption of *to rule the roast* and their insistence is supported by the spelling *roast* in many old English uses of the expression. But the American form has always been *roost* and the more learned are

of the opinion that this is the proper form and *roast* is the corruption.

rumple. See **crumble.**

run. The past tense is *ran.* The participle is *run. Run* was also used as a past tense in literary English well into the nineteenth century, but this is no longer standard.

A verb following *run* that tells the purpose of the running may be a *to*-infinitive, as in *he ran to open the door,* or it may be joined to *run* with an *and,* as in *he ran and opened the door.* Under certain circumstances *run* may also be followed by the simple form of a verb without *to* or *and,* as in *run help your grandmother* and *you can run get me a spoon.* This construction is used chiefly in speaking to children. We don't often tell adults to move fast. For this reason it is not found in literature as often as the similar construction with *come* and *go.* It must therefore be classed as a colloquialism. But it is used freely by the same people who say *come look at it* and *go tell her* and is standard in the United States. (For information on when this form may be used and when it may not, see **come.**)

Run may be followed by an adjective describing what runs, as in *still waters run deep* and *the course of true love never did run smooth.* It may also be followed by an adverb describing the running, as in *run quickly.*

run one's head against a stone wall. As a figure for attempting the impossible, assailing an impregnable position, opposing forces which can defeat without effort our utmost effort, *to run* (or often *to butt*) *one's head against a stone wall* is a hackneyed expression.

rung. See **ring.**

run-on sentences. Some textbooks on English grammar claim (1) that when two or more independent clauses are joined by a coordinating conjunction (*and, or, nor, but,* or *for*), a comma must be placed before the conjunction, as in *knowledge comes, but wisdom lingers;* and (2) that when one independent clause follows another without a conjunction, a comma is not sufficient punctuation and a semicolon must be used, as in *I cannot rest from travel; I will drink life to the lees.*

Sentences which violate these rules, such as (1) *I am old and day is ending and the wildering night comes on* and (2) *white in the moon the long road lies, the moon stands blank above,* are called run-on sentences by those who accept the rule.

But our best writers do not observe any such rule of thumb. They sometimes use one form of punctuation and sometimes another, depending upon which suits their purpose best. See **commas** and **semicolon.**

runs may read, he who. The Lord instructed the prophet Habakkuk to *Write the vision, and make it plain upon tables, that he may run that readeth it.* Prophetic utterances are notably obscure but this would seem to be an injunction to record a certain vision so clearly that whoever reads and thus learns of it will be moved to run. Whether he will run out of fear or out of zeal to accomplish some end suggested by the vision is not certain.

What is certain, however, is that the passage has been misread and misquoted for centuries as *that he who runs may read.* That is, it is commonly assumed that the injunction was to write so plainly that even a running man could read it. Francis Bacon so interprets it in his *Advancement of Learning* (. . . *yet at some time it pleaseth God, for our better establishment and the confuting of those which are as without God in the world, to write it in such text and Capital letters, that, as the Prophet saith,* He that runneth may read it). And the pious Keble made the misreading the basis of one of his hymns (*There is a book, who runs may read,/ Which heavenly truth imparts*).

The corrupted form, used as an adjuration to write clearly and effectively, is now a cliché.

rush. In this century of speed and violent haste, *rush* seems to be the normal verb of motion. It is greatly overworked. For instance, it is the rather imprecise term frequently used to describe carrying or conveying with haste (*He was rushed to the hospital*), imprecise because *rush* properly implies the exercise of force, an exercise which is rarely necessary in getting the sick or injured to the hospital.

In American slang *rush* means to heap attentions on. One rushes a girl by courting her favor with numerous and insistent attentions. College and high-school secret societies rush prospective members; that is, they cultivate them assiduously with the view of getting them to join their organizations. The slang expression *the bum's rush* is a proper use of *rush,* for one treated to the bum's rush is violently propelled from one place to another.

S

Sabbath; Sunday. The *Sabbath,* the day on which the Commandment bids us to abstain from work, is the seventh day of the Jewish week. *Sunday,* kept as a day of special worship and rest from business, is the first day of the week. The word *Sabbath* has been applied to Sunday by Protestant religious bodies (*My father was a stern puritanical clergyman, who considered a smile on the Sabbath to be a sin*). This application should be restricted to the day as a day of religious observance.

sabotage, though sometimes used in contexts where *wreck, destroy,* or *damage* would serve better, is definitely established as a word to describe malicious injury to work, machinery or tools, or any underhand interference with production or business, by enemy agents during wartime or by hostile employees (*The continual breakdown of the new assembly lines suggested sabotage*). Sabotage is a new word that has come in with the machine to describe a certain situation, attitude, and activity peculiar to the use of the machine, especially in mass production. It carries a suggestion of malevolence and secrecy that *wreck* and *destroy* do not necessarily have and it is nonsense to complain about it. Figuratively, *sabotage* describes any malicious attack or undermining of a cause (*Certain Congressmen were quite successful in sabotaging the President's civil rights program*) and in figurative uses it is often abused. He who would use it correctly as a figure should be certain that the opposition he is describing is malicious and sly and that that which is wrecked has in some way the characteristics of a machine.

sacred; sacrosanct. That is *sacred* which is appropriated or dedicated to a deity or to some religious purpose, entitled to veneration or religious respect because of its association with divinity or divine things, pertaining to or connected with religion as opposed to the secular and profane (*He enjoyed both sacred and profane love*). That is *sacred* which is reverently dedicated to some person or object (*Sacred to the memory of our mother*) or regarded with reverence (*The sacred memory of George Washington*) and hence secure against violation (*The sacred rights embodied in the first Amendments to the Constitution*).

Sacrosanct means especially or superlatively sacred or inviolable. Its use is restricted to those things that are rendered particularly inviolable by religious sanction. That is, one may refer to our sacred political rights or our sacred heritage, and so on, but *sacrosanct* should be applied only to such highly sacred religious articles as the vessels used at the altar, the relics of a saint, or the person of an ecclesiastic.

sacrilegious is the proper spelling of the adjective of *sacrilege,* the violation or profanation of anything held sacred. It is often misspelled *sacreligious* under the mistaken opinion, apparently, that the word *religious* is in it. But there is no such word as *sacreligious.*

sadder and a wiser man. It was the luckless wedding guest in Coleridge's *The Rime of the Ancient Mariner* who first *rose the morrow morn . . . a sadder and a wiser man.* The term is now a cliché of the jocular.

safe and sane, especially when applied to a celebration of the Fourth of July unmarred by the use of dangerous explosives, is a peculiarly American term, and now a hackneyed one.

safe and sound, as a term to describe persons (and sometimes, loosely, objects) which having been lost have been found or returned secure and uninjured, is a cliché.

Sahara Desert. It is true that the word *desert* is implicit in *Sahara* and that, therefore, the term *Sahara Desert* is redundant. But its use is only a venial sin. There is a strong tendency to re-duplication in place names that are known in several languages. A hill or a river or a desert will be called simply *hill, river,* or *desert* in the original language. This word will then be taken by a new group that speaks another language to be the name of the particular hill, river, or desert and the new group's word for hill, river, or desert added. In countries which have been overrun and settled by different groups each with its own language, as England, the process may be repeated several times.

The Sahara is an immense tract of land which includes oases, mountains, and vast areas of wind-driven sand and desolate rocks. If by the term *Sahara Desert* it is intended to designate this last, to the exclusion of the oases and moun-tains, it might be better to say *the desert regions of the Sahara.* On the whole, though, it's a fine distinction and *Sahara Desert* is no great fault.

said. See **say.**

sailer; sailor. *Sailer* describes a vessel propelled by sail or sails or a vessel with reference to its powers or manner of sailing (*I can tell by that ship's lines that she is a fast sailer*). A *sailor* is a seaman or mariner (*He was a woebegone sailor when they haled him into court*). As an adjective, *sailor* describes things pertaining to a sailor (*Janice, wear your sailor hat today*).

Saint James. See **Court of St. James** and see **King James Version** (of the Bible).

sake. When a word preceding *sake* ends in an *s* sound, an additional *'s* is not added to form the genitive, as in *for conscience sake, for goodness sake, for righteousness sake.* An apostrophe alone may be used, as in *for conscience' sake,* but it is not required. When the preceding word is plural, the plural form *sakes* may be used. That is, we may say *for our sake* or *for our sakes.*

The exclamations *sakes!* and *sakes alive!* are Americanisms and are considered unacceptable in Great Britain. But in the United States a gen-eration ago, honored and beloved old ladies said *sakes alive!* In this country, therefore, the words have a certain charm and are considered old-fashioned rather than uneducated.

salad days. When twitted by Charmian about her former love for Julius Caesar, Cleopatra (in Shakespeare's *Antony and Cleopatra*) excused herself by saying that those ardors took place in her *salad days* when she was *green in judg-ment, cold in blood* and were in no way com-parable to the passion that she now felt for Antony. As a term for youth, especially naïve and inexperienced youth, green and fresh, *salad days* is now wilted.

salary. See **honorarium.**

salon; saloon. *Salon,* as used in England and America, means pretty much what the same word means in French. It describes a drawing room or reception room in a large house; an assembly of guests in such a room especially when such an assembly consists of leaders in fashion, art, or politics; or a hall or place used for the exhibition of works of art. In America the word is used to describe beauty shops (*Albert's Beauty Salon*). This term is not in-variable in this use, however; *shop, shoppe,* and *studio* are more often employed.

Saloon means a different thing to English and Americans. In America *saloon* designates a place for the sale of intoxicating liquors to be drunk on the premises. A man who runs such a place is a *saloonkeeper.* Introduced as a eu-phemism for *bar* or *tavern,* the word enjoyed a brief period of elegance and then, like so many euphemisms, sank into semi-disreputability. The word was strongly emphasized in temperance attacks (*The Anti-Saloon League*) and became so opprobrious that when prohibition was re-pealed in the United States, the liquor dealers, chastened and timid, chose to reopen their places of business under the older name of *taverns. Tavern* had once also been a disrep-utable name and *saloon* had been appropriated largely to cover *tavern*'s disrepute, but *saloon* had grown so much more disreputable that *tavern* (which had in the interim acquired a certain quaintness) seemed comparatively in-nocuous.

In England the word *saloon* describes that part of a public house which has a higher social status, though more frequently one hears it designated as a *saloon-bar.* A man who runs a public house is a *publican* (not to be con-fused, as many English schoolchildren do, with the publicans referred to in the New Testament, who are tax collectors). *Saloon* retains in Eng-land some of the elegance it once had in Amer-ica and is used to lend a touch of refinement (or to conceal the total lack of it) in *billiard saloons, boxing saloons,* and *hairdressing sa-loons.* The word is also used in England to describe that type of automobile which Amer-icans call a *sedan* (*He rode around in a Morris saloon*).

salt; salts. A chemist uses these words as a true singular and a true plural, respectively. He may speak of *a salt* or of *three salts.* But in the gen-eral vocabulary, both forms are mass nouns. The singular, *salt,* means table salt and cannot be used with the article *a.* In this sense we speak of *a saltcellar* or *a salt shaker.* The plural, *salts,* means smelling salts or Epsom salts and cannot be used with a numeral. In this sense we speak of *a salts bottle.*

salt of the earth. As a term for those who are essentially good, kind, modest and generous, *the salt of the earth* is now a cliché. Taken from Matthew 5:13, where the meek, the poor in spirit, the merciful, and those persecuted for righteousness' sake are assured that they are the salt of the earth, that which gives life its savor and preserves it from corruption, this great phrase has simply been exhausted by overuse. All it needs is rest.

salt, take with a grain of. The idea is plain enough: salt makes food more palatable and a grain of it will make some improbability more easy to "swallow." To this extent, the recommendation that an account of some unlikely event be *taken with a grain of salt* is merely a hackneyed metaphor. But those who insist on being doubly dull, on being trite in a dead language, and say *cum grano salis*, have made a double exposure of their insufficiencies because the proper Latin phrase is *addito salis grano*. And, what's more, no one knows exactly what it means in its original context. Pliny (of all people to whom to trace back a metaphor advising skepticism!) says that when Pompey seized Mithridates' palace he found the prescription for Mithridates' famous antidote against poison, the last line of which read *to be taken fasting, plus a grain of salt*. But there is no evidence that Pliny was tipping anyone the wink. Pliny never tipped a wink or took a grain of salt in his life.

salutary. See **healthy.**

salvation; salvage. *Salvage,* the more specialized and technical term, describes the act of saving a ship or its cargo from the perils of the sea, the property so saved, or compensation given to those who voluntarily save a ship or its cargo. By extension the word is used to describe the saving of anything from fire, danger, etc., the property so saved, or the value or proceeds upon sale of goods recovered from a fire. (See also **flotsam.**)

Salvation describes the act of saving or delivering (*The salvation of troops at Dunkirk was accomplished by the labors of the crews of hundreds of small boats*), the state of being saved or delivered, or the source, cause, or means of deliverance (*The military band was the salvation of many a soldier chafing under army discipline. The C.C.C. camps were the salvation of hundreds of thousands of boys during the depression years*). Theologically, *salvation* means the delivery from the power and penalty of sin, redemption (*Wherefore, my beloved, as ye have always obeyed, not as in my presence only, but now much more in my absence, work out your own salvation with fear and trembling*).

same may be used as an adjective or alone as a noun or pronoun. In present-day English the pronoun *same* means "exactly similar," as in *I paid him five dollars and I will pay you the same.* Formerly it could be used to mean the identical thing mentioned before, as in *our manifold sins and wickedness . . . that we may obtain forgiveness of the same.* This use of the word is now archaic and out of place in everyday speech. In literary English *same* is always preceded by the article *the* (or by *this* or *that*). Sentences such as *we are sending same today* are not archaic, but unliterary businessese.

Same means "identical with" and may refer to words that have preceded it or to words that are to follow. When the words follow and are less than a complete clause, that is, when they do not contain a true verb, they must be introduced by *as*, as in *he gave the same answer as before.* When what follows is a clause, it may

be introduced by *that, as, when, where,* or *who,* as in *he gave the same answer that I did, the same answer as I did, at the same time when I was, at the same place where I was, he is the same man who was here yesterday. That* can be used in place of *as, when, where, who,* as in *at the same time that I was, he is the same man that was here,* and is preferred to these words. When it would have any function except subject of the verb, *that* may be omitted, as in *at the same time I was, he is the same man I saw yesterday.*

Which is sometimes used to introduce a clause which explains the meaning of *same,* as in *it has the same effect which good breeding has* and *the same relation to them which the others have.* This is technically permissible, but it is unnatural English.

sample. See **example, section.**

sanatorium. See **sanitarium.**

sanatory; sanitary. *Sanatory* means healing, conducive to health, therapeutic (*the sanatory art, Fielding's voyage to Lisbon was not, alas, the sanatory journey his friends had hoped it would be*). *Sanitary* means pertaining to health or the conditions affecting health, with especial reference to cleanliness and precautions against disease (*An electric dishwasher is more likely to leave dishes sanitary than a dishrag*). *Sanitary* is often misused for *sanatory.*

sanction has acquired a number of popular meanings which are somewhat removed from its original meaning. The word is now commonly understood to mean authoritative permission, countenance or support given to an action, solemn ratification (*Have you the sanction of the board of governors for this action? The military government refused to give its sanction to fraternization between conquerors and conquered*). It also means something serving to support an action, binding force given, or something which gives binding force, as to an oath, a rule of conduct (*There is sanction for this in the Beatitudes*).

Sanction is used more strictly in law and international law. In law it means a provision of a law enacting a penalty for disobedience or a reward for obedience, or the penalty or reward so enacted. In international law it means action, short of war, usually a boycott, by one or more states toward another state calculated to force it to comply with legal obligations (*The English and the French failed to apply sanctions to the Germans when they marched into the Rhineland. The cruel farce of the sanctions applied against Italy when she invaded Ethiopia was interpreted by the fascist nations as an admission of weakness*).

sanctity of the home. In ancient Rome, where every paterfamilias was a priest and performed sacrifices within the house, where every house had its household gods and where ancestors were worshipped, the sanctity of the home was a real thing. But in crowded tenements, hotels and mass-produced suburbs among a migratory population, with the performance of religious observances restricted to a special class and certain places, the term *sanctity of the home* has little significance. It is true that the right of search and entry is limited, in theory at least, by definite laws and the home remains in certain senses inviolable. But this privilege, certainly one of the most valuable that we have, is more safely protected in clear and specific terms.

sanctum; sanctum sanctorum; den. A *sanctum* is properly a sacred or holy place. *Sanctum sanctorum,* "the holy of holies," is a term of such awful reverence that nothing but habitude prevents its use from being blasphemous. The use of *sanctum* for a man's study reflects the idea that, as head of the house, he is a god. *Sanctum sanctorum* is journalistic jocosity for the editor's office. Neither term is now used seriously and repetition has long since drained the last molecule of humor out of both. *Den,* a more recent term for a room in the house presumably reserved for the male head and inviolate, reflects the thought that he is not a god but a beast. The ordinary head of the house justifies neither assumption. His room is far from inviolate. And both names for it are flaccid clichés.

sand; grit. As a figurative expression, *sand* is used chiefly in America to convey colloquially the idea of pluck or firmness of purpose (*There don't seem to be anybody around here that's got the sand to take her away from Mr. Branford*), an idea for which the equivalent British colloquial term is *grit.* In older American speech, still heard in country places, there was a fuller expression, *to have sand in one's craw,* that meant the same thing (*When I got to camp . . . there wasn't much sand in my craw—Huckleberry Finn*). See also **guts.**

sand; sands. These words mean exactly the same thing. *Sand* is grammatically singular and *sands* grammatically plural, but both are mass nouns. *Sands* does not mean any more of the stuff than *sand* does. It is simply a poetic form of the word. An hour glass contains *sand,* if it is used for boiling eggs, and children play in the *sand,* but we leave behind us footprints on the *sands* of time.

sang. See **sing.**

sanguine. See **optimistic.**

sanitarium; sanatorium. A *sanitarium* is an establishment for the treatment of invalids. It is primarily a hospital but usually has patients needing special treatment (*He spent some time in a tuberculosis sanitarium at Saranac Lake*). *Sanatorium* is often used interchangeably with *sanitarium* and this synonymity is recognized by most dictionaries. But those who direct and inhabit them insist there is a distinction, that a *sanatorium* is less of a hospital and more of a health resort, usually located in pleasant surroundings and intended more for persons needing rest and recuperation than for those needing medical treatment.

The preferred plurals are *sanitariums* and *sanatoriums,* though *sanitaria* and *sanatoria* are permissible.

sank. See **sink.**

sarcasm. See **humor.**

sarcastic; sardonic. A remark is *sarcastic* that is derisive, sneering, bitterly ironic, taunting, gibing or cutting, and the adjective may be transferred to a look or a smile that is intended to convey the meaning of such a remark. *Sardonic* is often used as a synonym and the two words overlap in their meanings. *Sardonic* is more often restricted to a laugh or a smile which does not proceed from true gaiety but is forced, bitter, or derisive (*the sardonic grin of a bloody ruffian*). See also **humor.**

sarcoma. The plural is *sarcomas* or *sarcomata,* not *sarcomae.*

sarcophagus. The plural is *sarcophaguses* or *sarcophagi.*

sat. See **sit.**

sateen; satin. *Satin,* originally describing a silk fabric, now describes a fabric made in a warp face satin weave, which produces a glossy surface. It is usually of rayon or silk, but sometimes cotton or linen. *Sateen,* a word formed on *satin* by association with *velveteen,* describes a cotton fabric woven in satin weave and resembling satin in gloss.

satellite is properly an astronomical term for a small body which revolves around a planet, held in its position by the gravitational pull of the planet and deriving its light by reflection. The application of the word to an attendant upon a person of importance is a forced elegancy. Its application to the countries contiguous to Russia whose governments are merely puppet governments carrying out Russian policies is so apt and has become so established that it must be accepted as standard.

satire. See **humor.**

satiric; satirical; satyric. *Satiric* and *satirical* mean of, pertaining to, or of the nature of satire (*He gave the little wealth he had/ To build a house for fools and mad;/ To show by one satiric touch/ No nation wanted it so much*).

Satyric is a word used only by the learned and literary to describe one who is like a satyr, that is half-man and half-goat and lasciviously inclined. It is also used to describe a form of Greek drama having a burlesque character, the chorus representing satyrs.

satisfied; convinced. He who is *satisfied* has had his desires, expectations, needs, or demands fulfilled and is content. He who is *convinced* has been persuaded by argument or proof that something which has been alleged is true. There is in the word, or in human nature, a suggestion of a reluctance to believe overcome.

He who is convinced is satisfied with the validity and sufficiency of the proof or the soundness of the argument. But *satisfied* and *convinced* are not synonymous and there are many contexts in which the implications of *satisfied* are ludicrous when *convinced* is the proper word. Thus, reading in the newspaper, of a prominent citizen who had been found dead, that "Despite the doubts of the police, his family was satisfied that he had been murdered," a wit observed "Well, they may have been; but *convinced* would certainly have sounded better."

saturnalia. This word is a Latin plural and is still treated as a plural when speaking of the Roman feast, as in *the Saturnalia were held on the seventeenth and eighteenth of December*. When used to mean simply unrestrained license the word may still be treated as a plural, as in *these saturnalia*, but in the United States it is more often treated as a singular, as in *this saturnalia must stop*.

saucy. See **impertinent.**

Saul among the prophets. *Is Saul also among the prophets?* is often asked, in humorous amazement, of one of dissolute life or reputation when he is mentioned in connection with some religious or nobly disinterested activity. The quotation is correct, but its application usually shows a misunderstanding of its meaning. The term *prophet* in the Old Testament includes many kinds of men, from the great ethical teachers such as Micah and Isaiah to crazed and violent figures little better than madmen; and *prophesying* includes actions as diverse as foretelling the future and making homicidal attacks. Saul, the great leader of Israel, was subject to some form of seizures in the course of which he could be extremely violent and dangerous. Encountering a wandering company of prophets, one of his seizures came upon him and he "prophesied among them" (I Samuel 10:10-13). But the context makes it plain that the question *Is Saul also among the prophets?* was not spoken so much in admiration of his unexpected holiness (as it is now used) as in consternation that so great a man should be subject to these seizures.

save. The word *save* is sometimes used to mean "except." When this was natural English, *save* was followed by a subjective, not an objective, pronoun, as in *then were they all slain save I* and *where nothing save the waves and I may hear*. Today, *save* in this sense is sometimes followed by an objective pronoun, as in *whom wilt thou find to love ignoble thee save me, save only me?* But today this use of the word is so thoroughly artificial that it is meaningless to ask which form of the pronoun is preferred by the best writers and speakers. The word in this sense is unnatural English in any construction.

saving grace. A grace is a virtue or excellence of divine origin. A *saving grace* is such a virtue of sufficient merit to effect a man's salvation, to redeem him from otherwise certain damnation. The use of the term to describe some minor virtue or, more often, charm in an otherwise bad or unpleasant person is a cliché.

savings. When this word means money that has been set aside it is always followed by a plural verb. We say *his savings are small*, not *is small*. But it is a mass word and not a true plural. We cannot speak of *many savings* or *few savings*. When the word is not followed by a verb, it may be treated as a singular and we may speak of *much savings* or *little savings*. In this sense of the word, *savings* keeps its *s* when used as the first element in a compound, as in *a savings bank, a savings account*

saw. The past tense is *sawed*. The participle is *sawed* or *sawn*. *Sawed* is the preferred form for the participle in the United States. *Sawn* is preferred in Great Britain, as in *he had sawn the wood*. See also **see.**

say. The past tense is *said*. The participle is also *said*.

When *say* is used in a passive form it may be followed by an infinitive, as in *he is said to leave early*. When it has an active form it is followed by a clause, as in *he says he leaves early*. When what was said was a command, such as *hurry* or *tell him to hurry*, the clause verb is a subjunctive equivalent, as in *he said we should hurry* or *he said I should tell you to hurry*. These constructions are literary English. In the United States today an infinitive is often used in place of this subjunctive clause, as in *he said to hurry, he said to tell you to hurry, he said for you to hurry*. These constructions are condemned by some grammarians, especially the form using *for you*. But they can be heard in the speech of the best educated people and may well become the preferred forms.

Say may be used in speaking of written material, as in *the Bible says*. This is literary English and has been since at least the year 1000. But the impersonal construction, such as *it says in the paper*, does not have the same standing. It is acceptable spoken English but in writing would ordinarily be changed to *I read in the paper*.

Say is often used in the United States as an exclamation or to introduce a question, as in *say, can this be right?* Thirty or forty years ago this use of the word was objected to violently, on the grounds that "*say* as a form of address is an impertinence." Since then, the Star Spangled Banner with its *oh say, can you see* has been declared the national anthem. The expression is now acceptable but is not used as much as formerly. It is not often seen in written material. In Great Britain *I say* is used in much the same way. It is thoroughly acceptable in speech but is not often used in writing.

There is a theory in literary English that *he said* is the correct form to use when only the substance of what was said is being reported but that "when the quotation purports to be exact, the order of verb and subject is often inverted," as in *said he*. In written material an exact quotation is put between quotation marks but in the United States the form *he said* is generally preferred to *said he*, though either may be used in either situation. Among intelligent people, it is only necessary to say once that a speech is being reported. The constant repetition of *said* suggests that either the speaker or his audience does not have a very long attention span, except where it is used for humor, as in *I'll work on a new and original plan, said I to myself, said I*. The use of *says* for *said*, as in *says I*, is not standard. See also **state.**

say the least, to. Introduced immediately before or after some condemnation (or, more rarely, commendation), as a way of saying that one has been temperate where severity or superlative would have been justified, *to say the least* is a cliché. Since there is no virtue in being temperate in commendation, the phrase when used after some expression of praise is intended as a hyperbole, as a way of saying "No matter how effusive I have been in my praises I have been moderate and restrained compared to what might have been said."

sc. This is an abbreviation of the Latin word *scilicet* and means *namely*.

scab; blackleg. The term for a workman who refuses to join or act with a labor union, who takes a striker's place, or the like, is in the United States *scab,* in England *blackleg.* Both *scab* and *blackleg* may also be used as intransitive verbs, meaning to act as a scab or blackleg.

scabrous, which properly means rough with minute points or projections, is a somewhat affected literary word when used to mean bordering on the indecent (*These scabrous stories keep turning up; they've been attached to every great man for centuries*).

scales. In speaking of an apparatus for weighing, the singular *scale* originally meant one of the pans. The instrument itself, requiring two pans, was usually thought of as a plural, as in *the scales are false,* or called *a pair of scales.* Occasionally the instrument itself was called a *scale,* as in *to tip the scale* and *long time in even scale the battle hung.*

Most scales today do not have pans. The instrument may be referred to as *a scale* (*She gave me a scale at my shower*) or with the plural form *scales,* as in *the doctor's scales are more accurate* and *he tipped the scales at two hundred.* Instruments of this kind are not usually called *a pair.* The plural form *scales* may be treated as a singular, as in *a bathroom scales,* or may follow directly after a numeral, as in *the grocer has three scales.*

The singular *scale* is preferred as the first element in a compound, such as *scale tray* and *scale base.*

scan, in its original sense, meant and means to analyze verse as to its prosodic or metrical structure, to read or recite so as to test the metrical form (*When one scans neoclassical poetry, he discovers that a great deal of it is written in iambic pentameter*). The broader sense is to examine minutely, to scrutinize (*A careful scholar will scan his proofs for printer's errors*). Though the English will not permit it, and more conservative American authorities object to it, the use of *scan* in the sense of to glance at or to run through hastily (*He scanned the daily paper, then turned on his radio*) is generally acceptable in the United States. As a technical television term, *scan* means to traverse a surface with a beam of light or electrons in order to reproduce or transmit a picture.

scandal. See **libel.**

scarce; scarcely. The adjective *scarce* usually stands later in the sentence than the noun or noun equivalent it qualifies, as in *they are scarce as hen's teeth.* It may stand before the noun, as in *a scarce book,* but in present-day English *rare* is preferred here.

Scarce and *scarcely* can both be used as adverbs. As a rule, when we have a pair of adverbs like this some people avoid the form without *-ly* under the impression that it is uneducated or "ungrammatical." In this case the form without *-ly* frequently ought to be avoided —not because it is ungrammatical, but because it is over-refined in some situations. *He was scarce more than a child* is too bookish for a straightforward statement of this fact.

Scarcely is a restrictive, or negative, adverb. That is, *he had scarcely gone* is equivalent to *he had no more than gone.* It therefore forms a double negative when used in a sentence that has already been made negative, as in *there's not a yard of it, scarcely, that hasn't some defect.* The double negative can be avoided by writing *there's scarcely a yard of it that hasn't. . . .* A word is negative if its meaning is negative, regardless of its form, and *he left without scarcely hearing a word* also contains two negative words, *without* and *scarcely.* See **double negatives.** See also **hardly.**

scarf. The plural is *scarfs* or *scarves. Scarves* is a recent formation and is used in Great Britain more than it is in the United States. The old plural *scarfs* is the preferred form in this country.

scatheless, meaning unharmed, is one of the many archaic words which Sir Walter Scott brought back into literary use. *The Oxford English Dictionary* records no instance of its use between 1563 and 1818, when Scott used it in *The Heart of Midlothian.* Some modern scholars have been much exercised to distinguish between *scatheless* and *unscathed,* insisting that the distinction though fine was clear. But the common writer need not strain to follow their explanation; *scatheless* may still be considered archaic or dialectal and not used. *Unscathed* is now the word.

scavenger; scavenge. *Scavenger,* once both noun and verb, is now chiefly used as a noun. It describes an organism, object, or person that scavenges, especially any of various animals feeding on dead organic matter (*Vultures are among the most repulsive of scavengers*). It is also a term for a street cleaner (*Dick, the scavenger, with equal grace,/ Flirts from his cart the mud in Walpole's face*).

The related verb now commonly used is *scavenge.* Transitive, it means to cleanse from filth (*. . . sea anemones and corals and madrepores, who scavenged the water all day long, and kept it nice and pure*). It has also the technical senses of expelling burnt gases from the cylinder of an internal-combustion engine or, in metallurgy, the cleaning of molten metal by the introduction of another substance which will combine chemically with the impurities in it. Intransitive (the commoner use), *scavenge* means to act as a scavenger (*Bears often scav-*

cnge around North Woods camps), to become scavenged of burnt gases, or to search for food.

schedule. Americans work the word a good deal harder than the Britons do. Something in America goes *according to schedule;* in England it would go *as arranged.* A train, plane, or bus arrives in America *on schedule.* In England they arrive *punctually.* An American is *scheduled* to speak. An Englishman is *on the program* to speak.

schema. The plural is *schemata,* not *schemae.*

scholar. See **pupil.**

scholium. The plural is *scholiums* or *scholia.*

science; art. *Science* is knowledge and *art* is action. *Science* suggests a systematized knowledge (*Boy, he's got that down to a science!*). *Art* suggests a performance with a skill that defies analysis. The *science of cooking,* in modern usage, would imply the basic, systematized knowledge necessary to cooking. The *art of cooking* would imply a skill, acquired usually by one with a strong natural ability after long practice, that transcends all that can be communicated by the science.

scientific English. When a scientist is writing for specialists in his own field, he naturally uses a special vocabulary. Sometimes he uses words that are not found in general English. More often he uses familiar words in unfamiliar senses. This is inevitable, since he is writing about concepts that are unknown to the general public. If the reader knows nothing about this particular science he will find what is written unintelligible. But it does not follow that a paper is scientific merely because it uses words in peculiar senses and is difficult to read.

For example, Max Born writes: "The state of a mechanical system can be represented by a point in the 6N-dimensional phase space, *p,q,* and its motion by a single orbit on a 'surface' of constant energy in this space." If the reader has had no training in physics he will see at once that he cannot understand this sentence. He has no idea what a 6N-dimensional space is and will not attempt to guess what aspect of it might imaginatively be called a "surface." But he can see that this is a straightforward English sentence and has no reason to doubt that something has been said in the simplest way possible.

The situation is quite different in sentences such as the following: "Because of the complexity of the constellation of eye conditions which contribute to blindness or severe visual incapacity, it became essential for us in formulating our program to examine the various sight-threatening conditions in terms of their amenability to control." Here the reader finds no unfamiliar concepts. He understands thoroughly what is being said and sees that it is pathetically simple. He sees that the only unfamiliar or difficult thing about the statement is its vocabulary and sentence structure, and he quite rightly resents having been put to so much trouble for so little gain.

A great deal of bad scientific writing, especially in the social sciences, is due to the notion that ostentation and obscurantism give a scientific tone to one's writing, that they are expected of a learned man. But this is not so. Mystification belongs to magic, not to science. It is the illiterate, not the learned, who love long words for their own sake. The man who has something important to say should do everything in his power to say it clearly.

scientist. This word was coined by an Englishman in 1840, and was not well received. For many years it was condemned as "an American vulgarism," and as late as 1885 some people believed that *scientician* was a finer word.

scissors. The plural form refers to one instrument but is usually treated as a plural, as in *these scissors are sharp.* It may also be treated as a singular, as in *this scissors is sharp.* This is acceptable English but an unusual construction today. In using a singular verb we more often say *this pair of scissors is sharp.* The construction with *pair* must always be used after a numeral, as in *three pairs of scissors.*

The singular *scissor* is the preferred form for the first element of a compound, such as *scissor blade, scissor sharpener.* But the form *scissors* is also acceptable in compounds, as in *scissors blade,* and is preferred when the word means "scissor-like" and does not actually refer to a pair of scissors, as in *the scissors kick.*

scleroma. The plural is *scleromata,* not *scleromae.*

score. When used without a numeral, the word *score,* meaning twenty, is a noun and has the plural *scores.* These words are followed by *of,* as in *a score of years, scores of men,* except before such degree words as *more, less, too many,* where the *of* is dropped, as in *a score more men, scores more horses.*

When preceded by a numeral, *score* is treated as a cardinal number. That is, it is treated as an adjective and used without *of,* as in *threescore years and ten* and *sixscore thousand persons,* except when referring to part of a specified group, as in *two score of them.* The plural form *scores* is never used with a numeral.

scorn. This verb may be followed by an infinitive, as in *he scorned to beg,* or by the *-ing* form of a verb, as in *he scorned begging.* The infinitive is more forceful but both forms are acceptable.

Scotch; Scottish; Scots. Of these adjectives to refer to Scotland and its natives, *Scotch* is the form used in America, in Southern England and the English Midlands. In Northern England and in Scotland itself the word is *Scottish,* though *Scots* is enjoying an increase in popularity today. When these words are used as nouns to describe the dialect, *Scotch* is the British noun, *Scottish* the American, and *Scots* the one used in Scotland.

Scotchman; Scotsman; Scot. The basic name for a native of Scotland is *Scot.* The ancient Gaelic people who came from Northern Ireland about the 6th century and settled in the northwestern part of Great Britain called themselves *Scots.* The country was called Scotland. The **proper**

title of their most romantic queen is Mary, Queen of Scots. Natives of Scotland insist that the proper word for one of them is *Scotsman,* and *Scotsman* is the name of one of their leading newspapers. To their disgust and annoyance, Americans and Englishmen insist on calling them *Scotchmen.*

scratch pad is the American term for a pad of inexpensive writing paper. In England it is called a *scribbling-block.*

scream; screech; shriek. All of these words mean to cry out in a loud, piercing way. *Scream* is the most general. It may mean to utter a loud, piercing cry, especially of pain, fear or anger (*I heard the owl scream and the crickets cry. "You can't arrest me," he screamed; "my papers are in order"*), and it may mean to utter a little, barely audible, cry by one who is startled. *Shriek* suggests a pitch more intense than that of *scream,* and when due to fear or pain indicates more distress (*Not louder shrieks to pitying heaven are cast/ When husbands or when lapdogs breathe their last*). Both men and women scream; it is mainly women who shriek. *Screech* emphasizes not so much the emotion as the disagreeable shrillness and harshness of an outcry or a noise. It is used of animals (*screech owl*) and inanimate things (*the screech of a dry axle, the screech of his chair as he drew it along the stone floor*). When applied to the sound of the human voice there is a connotation of lack of dignity (*The screech of the old woman's voice could be heard above the babble of the children*).

screw up your courage is a shortening of the longer admonition to *screw your courage to the sticking-point* which is a misquotation of Shakespeare's *But screw your courage to the sticking-place,/ And we'll not fail* (*Macbeth,* I, vii, 60-61). Some scholars believe that Lady Macbeth's metaphor was drawn from the operation of an arbalest, wherein the string which would launch the missile was made taut by the slow action of a ratchet. Others are of the opinion that the metaphor was drawn from the screwing up of the cords of stringed instruments to their proper degree of tension, when the peg remains fast in its sticking-place. In either case, the phrase is now a cliché.

script; scrip. *Script* basically means handwriting, or the characters used in handwriting, or, in printing, a type imitating handwriting. In America *script* is a sort of general-purpose word in the entertainment world. In the theater and television it describes the manuscript of a play or role. In motion pictures, it describes the manuscript of a motion picture containing a synopsis of the plot, the scenario, the cast (*. . . he took up the first of two scripts that were his evening stint, that presently he would visualize line by line on the screen . . .*).

Scrip, a variant form of *script,* is the more specialized form. It means a writing, especially a receipt or certificate. In finance it means a certificate representing a fraction of a share of stock, a certificate to represent a dividend not paid in cash but a promise to pay at a later date. Since such promises are not always kept, *scrip* has a connotation of insecurity and risk. In American usage the word also describes paper currency, a certificate of indebtedness in place of government currency (*During the depression the unhappy teachers were often paid in scrip. The miners were paid in scrip which was redeemable, at a discount, at the company store*).

scripture; scriptures. These words are different grammatically but have the same meaning. Both mean the entire Bible. *Scrtptures* is followed by a plural verb and *Scripture* by a singular verb, but *Scriptures* does not mean more than one *Scripture.* The singular form *Scripture* is not ordinarily used with *the* or *a.* We say *the devil can quote Scripture.* (*The* may be used with *Scripture* only when what is meant is a Scripture selection, as in *the Scripture for today.*) The plural form *Scriptures* requires the article *the* but cannot be used with a numeral or a word implying number. We say *he has studied the Scriptures.*

These words are always capitalized when they mean the Bible. They are not capitalized when used in speaking of other sacred writings. In this second sense, the plural form *scriptures* may be qualified by *these* or *those* but not by a numeral.

scruple. This verb may be followed by an infinitive, as in *he did not scruple to repeat it.* It may also be followed by the *-ing* form of a verb with the preposition *at,* as in *he did not scruple at repeating it,* but the infinitive construction is generally preferred.

scrupulous. See **meticulous.**

scull; skull. *Scull,* in its narrowest sense, means an oar worked from side to side over the stern of a boat as a means of propulsion. More broadly, it means one of a pair of oars operated, one on each side, by one person (*. . . two men emerged, carrying a shell. They set it in the water and a moment later Bland came out, with the sculls*). Still more broadly, it is a boat propelled by a scull or sculls and, in its most general sense, a light racing boat propelled by one rower with a pair of oars (*On a bright afternoon the Charles was gay with sculls, whisking their sharp prows through the choppy water*).

Skull means the bony framework of the head, enclosing the brain and supporting the face, the skeleton of the head. The word may be used figuratively, usually in a disparaging sense, to describe the head as the seat of intelligence or knowledge (*Try to get this into your skull*). In the United States a meeting of football players at which they are lectured to on plays and general strategy is known as *skull practice.*

Scull was so named from the dishlike shape of the spoon-bladed oar. *Skull* may be derived from the same French word (*escueile,* dish, from Latin *scutella*). Related words are *scullion* (but not *scullery*) and *skillet.*

scurfy; scurvy. *Scurfy* means characteristic of, marked by, or pertaining to scurf. And *scurf* is the name for the scales or small shreds of epidermis that are continually exfoliated from the skin; or for any scaly matter or incrustation on a surface. In England today *scurf* especially means dandruff.

Scurvy, used as an adjective, means low, mean, contemptible. Except in the worn phrases *a scurvy trick, a scurvy knave, a scurvy remark* or *answer,* it is archaic and bookish.

Of course, a man may be both scurfy and scurvy.

The noun *scurvy,* the disease, is from the French *scorbut.* Its form was assimilated to that of the adjective.

scurrility. See **abuse.**

Scylla and Charybdis, between. *Scylla,* in Homer, was a rock opposite the whirlpool Charybdis and on this rock dwelt a monster of the same name. She had twelve feet and six heads, each on a long neck and each equipped with three rows of pointed teeth. Odysseus had to pass between the monster and the whirlpool and was warned that, for all that she would kill some of his men, the monster Scylla was the lesser of the two perils.

As a term for being between two equal dangers, *between Scylla and Charybdis* is now a cliché.

s.d. This is an abbreviation of the Latin words *sine die* and means *without date.*

seamy side of life. Before dry-cleaning, when the glittering state garments of the gallants were made to do for many years, their underside, the seamy side, must have contrasted strikingly with their external splendors. Emilia, in Shakespeare's *Othello* (Act IV, sc. ii, 1. 146), said that someone had turned her husband Iago's wit *the seamy side without* and made him suspect her of adultery with the Moor. From this remark our present use of the phrase appears to have come. But the original thought has been forgotten and the term is now simply a cliché.

seasonable; seasonal. *Seasonal* means pertaining to or dependent on the seasons of the year or some particular season, periodical (The Grapes of Wrath *recounts the ordeal of seasonal laborers during the Depression. Hay fever is a seasonal complaint*). *Seasonable* means suitable to the season (*They sailed west with the seasonable winds. Rain at this time of year is seasonable with us*), or suitable to the circumstances (*It is not seasonable to call a man a traitor that has an army at his heels*), or opportune (*Your arrival was seasonable, for we needed help*). American usage also permits *seasonable* to mean early (*They were stirring seasonable to mean early at a seasonable hour*).

second. See **minute.**

second to none. As a way of saying that something or someone is one of the best, *second to none* is hackneyed.

secret languages are essentially devices to bind together an in-group and exclude the outsider. They are used by children all over the world. In this country the best known and the easiest

to learn is Pig, or Hog, Latin. But there are also others, such as Tuttin, Arp and Ob. All of them depend on adding syllables and shifting initial letters.

Secret languages may also be used by adults for prestige purposes. Lucien Lévy-Bruhl, in discussing "undeveloped" or "savage" societies, says: "Frequently, too, the members of the secret societies which are so common a feature in social groups of a primitive type, are initiated into a language spoken and understood by themselves alone; their introduction to the society, or their promotion to a sufficiently exalted rank therein, gives them the privilege of using this mystic language. . . . They generally use the same words, but so transformed by the interposition or addition of other letters, that they appear to belong to a different language. Moreover, they have some words peculiar to themselves, by which they supersede those in general use."

Traces of this may be found in the language of many present-day savants. (See **argot.**) And among those "social groups of a primitive type" in our own country who furnish the members for high school and college Greek-letter organizations, great importance is attached to secret words. So secret are these, for the most part, that not one brother or sister out of a hundred could repeat them ten seconds after they were mumbled in his or her ear at the initiation. Yet so prestigious is even this fleeting knowledge of them felt to be that thousands of families have been plunged into gloom and shame because their child was permitted to hear one set of these words instead of another.

secrete. See **hide.**

secretion; concealment. *Secretion* is a term to be used exclusively to describe a physiological phenomenon. It means the process or function of an animal body, executed in the glands, by which various substances, such as bile or milk, are separated and elaborated from the blood (*The secretion of milk is in some way stimulated by changes that take place in the woman's body during pregnancy*). Or it may describe the product secreted (*This secretion is a sticky substance of the consistency of mucilage*). But although the verb *to secrete* can mean (in addition to producing by the process of secretion), making secret, hiding, concealing from observation or the knowledge of others, *secretion* is not to be used as a loose synonym for *concealment* (as in *The secretion of government property in personal belongings was one of the commoner crimes of the war*). This use, though common, is objectionable to many people in England and America.

secretive. See **reticent.**

section; cross-section; sample. A *section* of a community means a part of that community isolated geographically, by age, or by some other standard. A *cross-section* cuts across section lines and describes a typical selection, a sample showing all representative parts in accurate proportion. Thus a *section* of a community could be the aged, those who live to the north or to the south, and so on. But a *cross-section* of a town made up of five percent industrial managers, five percent professional men, fifteen percent merchants, fifteen percent clerks, and sixty percent manual workers would have to include, as a minimum, one manager, one professional man, three merchants, three clerks, and twenty workers. A *sample* is simply a small part of something intended to represent the whole (. . . *like the foolish man in the Greek story who, wanting to sell his house, carried about with him a brick as a sample*). A sample may be a cross-section if it is accurately representative. Yet it will still be a sample even if it is not, for there are many things of which a cross-section may not be made.

sector; section. Of these two nouns referring to cutting, *sector* has largely technical uses, while *section* has both general and technical uses.

In geometry, *sector* describes a plane figure bounded by two radii and the included arc of a circle, ellipse, or the like. A *sector* is also a mathematical instrument consisting of two flat rulers hinged together at one end and bearing various scales. In military phraseology, a *sector* is one of the sections of a forward combat area as divided for military operations (*Many of the American soldiers who were in the Anzio sector of the Italian Front still feel resentful*).

Section, in general, describes a part cut off or separated from a whole. More specifically, it may describe a distinct portion of a book, writing, or the like, or a subdivision, as of a chapter (*I didn't like those sections devoted to his philosophy of life*). It may also mean one of a number of parts that can be fitted together to make a whole (*Sections of the vacuum cleaner lay scattered over the rug*), or a distinct part of a country, community, or class (*The well-to-do live in the northwest section of town. One section of the community was implacably opposed to admitting all children to the public schools*). In most of the United States west of Ohio, each township is divided into *sections,* tracts of land each one mile square. *Section* can also mean the act of cutting, separation by cutting (*The baby was delivered by Caesarean section*). In military phraseology a *section* is a small unit which may consist of two or more squads. In railroad terminology a section may be a division of a division (*a section hand*), or it may be a division of a sleeping car containing both an upper and a lower berth (*You can reserve the whole section for little more than the cost of the lower*) or a train scheduled jointly with another or others (*The second section was due in ten minutes and the brakeman knew that he must flag it down*).

secundus; second. *Secundus* is a term used in England to describe the second male bearing the same name in a family (*John Monroe, secundus, is the nephew of John Monroe*). In America, *second* is used instead, though in recent years there has been a tendency to write

it in roman numerals (*Henry Mosby Cabot II*). See also **junior.**

secure. This verb may be used to mean procure or obtain and has been so used for more than two hundred years, as in *we took care to secure some powder, ball, and a little bread.* In most cases *get* would be better than *secure, procure,* or *obtain.*

sedan. In England *sedan* describes the now obsolete sedan chair, a closed vehicle to seat one person, borne on poles by bearers. In America *sedan* describes a closed automobile body seating four or more persons (including the driver) on two full-width seats, both in one compartment. The English equivalent of *sedan* in this sense is *saloon* or *saloon-car.*

sedulous ape. It was Robert Louis Stevenson (in the fourth chapter of his *Memories and Portraits,* 1887) who first used the phrase to *play the sedulous ape.* He said that he had *played the sedulous ape to Hazlitt, to Lamb, to Wordsworth, to Sir Thomas Browne, to Defoe, to Hawthorne, to Montaigne, to Baudelaire and to Obermann.* The wry charm of the phrase, its attractive paradox, and affectionate self-depreciation made it immediately popular. It was "taken up," overworked, and is already worn out.

Sedulous means diligent in application, persistently and carefully maintained, persevering in effort.

see. The past tense is *saw.* The participle is *seen.*

When used in an active form, *see* may be followed by an object and the simple form of a verb, as in *I saw him leave,* or by an object and the *-ing* form of a verb, as in *I saw him leaving.* When followed by an object and a to-infinitive, the word means "infer" and not "perceive with the eyes," as in *I saw it to be impossible.* In either sense, it may be followed by a clause, as in *I saw he was leaving* and *I saw it was impossible. See* may also be followed by an object and a past participle with passive meaning (that is, the *be* of a passive infinitive is usually suppressed), as in *I saw him stopped.* When *see* itself is used in a passive form it may be followed by a to-infinitive, as in *he was seen to leave,* or by the *-ing* form of a verb, as in *he was seen leaving.* See also **look.**

see; bishopric; diocese. Of these terms, *bishopric* is the broadest, being defined as the see, diocese, or office of a bishop. Perhaps it should be used mainly to describe the office or rank belonging to a bishop, for *see* is the more specific ecclesiastical term to describe the seat, center of authority, or the chair that symbolizes a bishop's authority over a particular diocese. *Diocese* is to be preferred to *bishopric* as the word to describe the district, with its population, falling under the pastoral care of a bishop (*Since Bishop Proudie came to this diocese I have exerted myself here a good deal*).

see eye to eye. As a term for harmony, agreement, unanimity or, in the negative, the lack of such harmony, especially in regard to a course of action to be pursued, to *see eye to eye* is a hackneyed expression. It is one of several phrases in common use drawn from the Bible but distorted in the process. It is taken from Isaiah 52:8 where, however (according to the *Westminster Commentaries* and the notes to the *Cambridge Bible*) it means to see (each other) face to face.

see how the land lies. In its figurative sense, meaning to make a preliminary investigation, to find out whether or not those with whom we must deal are favorably inclined or not, *to see how the land lies* is a cliché.

see with half an eye. To say of something obvious, particularly approaching trouble, that you can *see it with half an eye* is to employ a cliché.

seek. The past tense is *sought*. The participle is also *sought*. A verb following *seek* is always an infinitive, as in *he sought to persuade me.*

seek; search. *Seek* is an old-fashioned word which survives in such expressions as the game hide-and-seek and the Biblical *Seek and ye shall find.* *Search* or *search for* or, more colloquially, *look for* are better familiar usage.

As a synonym for *attempt,* however, where there is a suggestion that the attempt has included a search for the ideal or proper way or a searching among alternatives, *seek* is still standard (*Those who seek to prove . . .*).

seem. This verb may be followed by an infinitive, as in *he seemed to laugh at us.* It may also be followed by the *-ing* form of a verb, as in *the old man seemed gradually blending into the chair.* It could once be followed by a clause as in *she seemed she would speak.* This is no longer natural English unless the subject of *seem* is *it* or the clause is introduced by *as if* or *as though.*

Like other verbs, *seem* may be combined with the regular auxiliary verbs, as in *it would seem, he might seem.* But *I can't seem to do this,* meaning "I seem to be unable to do it," is an Americanism. It is acceptable in the United States but is not often heard in England, where *I don't seem able to* is the usual way of expressing this idea.

Seem is always used as a linking verb. It may therefore be followed by an adjective but not by an adverb, as in *it seemed good, it seemed different, he seemed happy.* See **linking verbs.**

seen. See **see.**

select (adjective). See **exclusive.**

self. The regular plural is *selves*. A new plural *selfs* is sometimes used in philosophic writing.

-self words. See **reflexive pronouns.**

sell. The past tense is *sold*. The participle is also *sold*. (See also **dispose of.**)

sell like hot cakes. Hot cakes, if they are to sell at all, must obviously sell fast. But just why they, of all comestibles, became proverbial is uncertain. The phrase is now drained by overuse of its once homely humor and flavor.

selvedge; selvage. Though *selvedge* is etymologically closer to the late Middle English word on which it is based (*self edge*), *selvage*, a cor-

ruption, is the form now commonly used to describe the edge of woven fabric finished to prevent raveling, often in a narrow tape effect, different from the body of the fabric, or any similar strip or part of surplus material, as at the side of wallpaper (*The trees have ample room to expand on the water side, and each sends forth its most vigorous branch in that direction. There Nature has woven a natural selvage*).

selves. See **self.**

semantics. In grammar *semantics* means the study of the meanings of words, in contrast to *syntax* which deals with the ways in which words may be combined to express more complicated thoughts. Since 1900 the grammarian's term *semantics* has been taken over and given new meanings, first by the philosophers and later by the general public.

In philosophy *semantics* meant, first, the study of the relation of signs (including words) to the objects they stand for and the conditions under which signs may be significant. It was an attempt to apply mathematical methods to philosophical problems and was stimulated by the publication in 1910 of Whitehead and Russell's *Principia Mathematica*. It can easily be shown that some of our intellectual, or scientific, problems grow out of the nature of the real world, the world of experience, and are to be solved by investigation, and that others are created by the structure of language, by the ways in which we must report our experience—and that it is often difficult to see which kind of problem we are dealing with. The mathematical philosophers were interested in clearing away "verbal" problems so that they could come to grips with "real" ones.

From this beginning, semantics has developed in a number of different ways. The word came into general English from the writings of Count Alfred Korzybski, who believed that language problems were the cause of most of our mental and social ills and developed a therapy which he claimed would "help any individual to solve his problem by himself, to his own and others' satisfaction." This position has a great deal in common with the work of the early Greek Sophists who also believed that language was significant in itself, independently of what it referred to.

To certain thinkers of a less hopeful cast than Korzybski, men so unstrung that they are not certain that any problem will ever be solved by anyone to his own *and* others' satisfaction, the claims of the semanticists are more touching than convincing. If we are to go to extremes, we might follow Swift's suggestion and abandon words altogether, each man carrying on his back the actual objects to which he wishes to refer. Though there is a happier middle ground, where most intelligent men meet, on which it is agreed that a more careful and precise use of language would avoid a great deal of confusion.

To the unphilosophical such claims as Korzybski's are ludicrous, if not immoral, and the word *semanticist* has suffered the same fate that the word *sophist* did. Harry Truman uses the word in its currently accepted sense in his description of an imaginary Cabinet: "I have appointed a Secretary of Semantics—a most important post. He is to furnish me $50 words, and tell me how to say yes and no in the same sentence without a contradiction. He is to tell me the combination of words that will put me against inflation in San Francisco and for it in New York."

semicolon. The *semicolon* is used principally in formal writing. Its uses are:

1. To separate statements too closely related for a period to intervene, but not closely enough related for a comma to serve the purpose, as in *the powerful are always right; the weak, always wrong.* This can be a powerful device to show a relation in the meaning of apparently independent statements.

2. To separate phrases which contain commas, either for clarity or for emphasis, as in *these are my favorite flowers: violets, for their sentimentality; roses, for their color; and buttercups, for their cheerfulness.*

3. To separate lengthy statements following a colon, as in *the requirements might be as follows: (1) the applicant must be an American citizen; (2) he must have a bachelor's degree or its equivalent; (3) he must have had at least two years experience in working in this or related fields.*

If a writer wishes to use an informal narrative style he should avoid semicolons as much as possible. Semicolons denote a longer break in the sentence than commas and they may slow down the reader unnecessarily.

seminar; seminary. *Seminar* applies to a group, *seminary* to an institution. A *seminar* is a small group of students, as in a university, engaged in advanced study and original research under a member of the faculty or the gathering place for such a group (*To be accepted as a member of Kittredge's seminar was a coveted honor. Graduate English students will meet in Seminar 8*). The word is also used to designate a course or subject of study for advanced graduate students (*Candidates for the Ph.D. degree in English are required to participate in three seminars*).

Seminary describes a school, especially one of higher grade. (In England it means broadly any place of secondary education.) It also means (and this is the sense in which it is most frequently understood in America) a school for the education of men for the priesthood or ministry (*I took my meals in Cambridge at the Episcopal Theological Seminary*). Formerly, more so than now although the meaning persists, it was used a great deal to designate a school of secondary or higher level for young women. *Seminary* may also mean a seminar, though *seminar* is to be preferred since it is unequivocal.

Semite. See **Hebrew.**

semi-yearly; semiannual; half-yearly. *Semi-yearly* is not acceptable in England. In America it is acceptable but *semiannual* is preferred as the adjective meaning occurring every half year (*I pay my insurance in semiannual premiums*) or lasting for half a year (*That plant is a semiannual*). In England *half-yearly* is used as the less favored alternative to *semiannual*. See also **biannual; biennial.**

sempstress; seamstress; needlewoman. In America *seamstress* is preferred to *sempstress* to describe a woman whose occupation is sewing. The English regard *sempstress* as obsolescent and prefer the downright *needlewoman* to *seamstress*.

send. The past tense is *sent*. The participle is also *sent*. See also **remit.**

send about his business. To say of someone who was dismissed with humiliating curtness that he was *sent about his business* is to employ a worn and stilted phrase.

senile; senescent. See **old.**

sensational, a word of fairly recent (late nineteenth century) coinage, meant originally that which could be perceived through the senses (*With sensational pleasures and pains there go, in the infant, little else but vague feelings of delight and anger and fear*). However, it soon came to mean that which excites intense interest and emotion, that which startles or provokes a thrilling response. And since in addition to the many truly startling events of our time, attempts at startling and thrilling people in order to gain attention for commercial purposes have become an immense industry, it is not astonishing that the word *sensational* has become one of the most overworked in our vocabularies. It needs a rest and we need a rest (which we are not likely to get) from it and the forces that exploit it and the facts that seek to justify it.

sense; feel. *Sense* as a verb is relatively young. It first appeared in the seventeenth century, meaning then to perceive by or as by one of the senses. Less than a century ago it was broadened to mean *feel*, to become aware of (*As soon as he saw her he sensed that something had happened*). American usage has taken up *sense* in still looser terms as a colloquialism meaning to comprehend or understand (*You can sense what great changes the new organizational plan will make in our objectives*). Philosophically, this is an almost complete reversal of meaning from the original idea of sense perception, but language is not logical or consistent and many such reversals have become accepted as standard through usage.

sensibility. See **sensitiveness.**

sensible; sensitive. Though *sensible* could once be used as a synonym for *sensitive* (the French *sensible* means sensitive), it is rarely and inadvisably so used today. *Sensible* now means having, using, or showing good sense or sound judgment (*He can usually be relied on for sensible advice*). In more specialized senses it means cognizant, keenly aware (usually followed by *of,* as in *He was sensible of his intellectual limitations*); appreciable, considerable (*There has been a sensible increase in the warmth of our winters in the past thirty years* or *There has been a quite sensible reduction in the price of coffee during the past six months*). It can also mean capable of being perceived by the senses (*Plato regarded the sensible universe as an imperfect imitation of the real universe*) or perceptible to the mind; conscious; or capable of feeling or perceiving, as organs or parts of the body (though for this meaning the negative, *insensible,* is more often used since, in many contexts—such as *The stomach is a sensible organ*—there might be a ludicrous ambiguity).

Sensitive means endowed with sensation (*Despite the local anaesthetic, his jaw was still sensitive*); readily affected by external agencies or influences (*Most politicians are sensitive to public opinion*); having acute mental or emotional sensibility, easily affected, pained or annoyed (*A favorite theme of the modern novel is the education of the sensitive young man*); pertaining to or connected with the senses or sensation. The word also has certain specialized scientific meanings. In physiology it means having a low threshold of sensation, responding easily to stimulation (*Some plants are highly sensitive; their leaves draw back when touched*). In chemistry and biochemistry it means highly susceptible to certain agents (*Photographic films and plates are sensitive to light*). In physics and mechanical matters it means constructed to indicate, measure, or be affected by, small amounts or changes, as a balance or thermometer. In radio it means easily affected by external influences, especially radio waves.

sensible; sensitive; susceptible. *Sensible of* expresses emotional consciousness (*I am sensible of the suffering you are undergoing. I am sensible of the many kindnesses that you have shown me*). *Sensitive to* expresses acute feeling (*His pallid skin was sensitive to the glaring sunlight*). *Susceptible to* or *of* expresses quick reaction to stimulus (*In his weakened condition he was very susceptible to colds*). Used by itself and of a young man *susceptible* usually means easily affected by female charms. In this sense it is almost a cliché.

sensitiveness; sensitivity; sensibility. *Sensitiveness* is the general term to describe the state or quality of being sensitive in both physiological and psychological contexts, having a capacity of sensation and of responding to external stimuli (*Parts of the body which lose all sensitiveness are likely to be seriously injured*). *Sensitivity* is the especially physiological version of *sensitiveness*. It describes the ability of an organism or part of an organism to react to stimuli; degree of susceptibility to stimulation (*If the sensitivity of women were really, as so often claimed, superior to that of men, they would be universally employed as piano-tuners,*

tea-tasters, and wool-sorters). *Sensitivity* is often used where *sensitiveness* would be more appropriate (as in *It was generally felt that his sensitivity over the scandal was excessive*).

Sensibility does not refer to being sensible but to being sensitive, in a special way. It now means the capacity to respond to aesthetic or emotional stimuli, delicacy of emotional or intellectual perception. William Elton (*A guide to the New Criticism,* Chicago, 1953, p. 39) limits the word to define "an innate sensitivity of the poet which permits him to absorb the appropriate experience, and to create, out of that experience, the substance and feeling of art."

sensual; sensuous; sensory. *Sensory* means pertaining to sensation; noting a structure that conveys an impulse that results or tends to result in sensation, as a nerve. The word *sensory* is easily distinguishable from *sensual* and *sensuous* which are sometimes confused.

Sensuous means of or pertaining to the senses, as opposed to the intellect. It was apparently invented by Milton who wanted to avoid certain connotations of *sensual.* He referred to poetry as being *simple, sensuous, and passionate.* Coleridge picked the word up in 1814, attributing it correctly to Milton but adding vaguely that it had also been used "by many other of our elder writers." Thus *sensuous* refers favorably to what is experienced through the senses. *Sensual,* meanwhile, has rather strengthened the taint that Milton wished to avoid and now refers entirely to those enjoyments derived from the senses with a connotation of grossness or lewdness (*sensual excesses, the sensual pleasures of the glutton*).

sent. See send.

sentence adverbs. An adverb may qualify one word in a sentence or it may qualify the entire statement. When it qualifies a single word it normally stands immediately before that word. (See **adverbs**.) When it qualifies the entire statement it may stand in any of several positions, but as a rule there is very little choice as to which of these it must occupy. A misplaced adverb simply does not say what the speaker intended it to.

1. In a declarative sentence, that is, in a sentence that makes an assertion, the primary position for a sentence adverb is immediately before or actually inside the verb form. In a simple tense where there is no auxiliary verb, the adverb stands between the subject and the verb, as in *he soon forgot.* (Simple tenses of the verb *to be* are an exception and are discussed below under the second position for sentence adverbs.) In the other tenses the adverb normally follows the first auxiliary, as in *he will never forget* and *he has never been forgotten.*

If an adverb is placed between the subject and the first auxiliary verb, it puts a heavy stress on the auxiliary. This is sometimes appropriate in an emphatic or contradictory statement, such as *he soon did forget* and *he already has been forgotten.* But the adverb cannot be used in this front position without having just this effect. Dickens's Mrs. Micawber often says, *I never will desert Mr. Micawber.* By placing the adverb first, she makes what was intended to be a reassuring statement seem like part of an undecided argument.

When an adverb is placed later, after the last auxiliary and before the meaningful verb, it qualifies the verb itself and not the sentence. For example, we place *heartily* after *be* in *they must be heartily congratulated.* But we could not use *surely* in this position. We would have to say *they must surely be congratulated.* The difference is that *heartily* qualifies *congratulate* and *surely* qualifies the sentence as a whole. H. W. Fowler sums this up by saying that an adverb may stand after the last auxiliary whenever the adverb and verb suggest a familiar adjective and noun combination, such as *hearty congratulations,* but not otherwise. We do not at present say *sure congratulations.*

As a rule, if an adverb has two forms, one resembling an adjective and the other ending in *-ly,* such as *slow* and *slowly,* the form that resembles the adjective cannot be used in the primary adverb position. This is not because it is not a true adverb. There is no question but that *hard* refers to the action, not the subject, and is therefore an adverb, in *he struck hard.* Moreover, the adverb *hardly* has an entirely different meaning and *hard* is in no way a "corrupt" form of *hardly.* But *hard* is also an adjective, as in *a hard blow.* Therefore we cannot say *he hard struck* or *he will hard strike.* We may use *hardly* in this position and say *he hardly struck,* but the word still means "scarcely" and not "hard-like."

In current English we form a question either by using a special interrogative word or by taking the first auxiliary verb out of its normal position in an assertion and placing it before the subject. (See **questions.**) The other words in the sentence keep the order they would have in an assertion. For example, *he has always known this* becomes *has he always known this?* and *he once did forget* becomes *did he once forget?* In a command, the adverb normally follows the verb, as in *go now, run quickly.* But it may be placed first for emphasis, as in *now go.* The words *always* and *never* usually have this front position, as in *always remember, never forget.* Exclamations sometimes have the word order of an assertion and sometimes the word order of a question, as in *he never did it!* and *how could he ever do it!*

The adverb *not* can never stand before the first element of a verb. We cannot say *he not goes.* In current English *not* cannot stand after the principal element of a verb, except a form of the verb *to be,* or occasionally a form of *to have.* We may say *he is not* but we no longer say *he goes not.* This was once a standard construction but it is now archaic. Today we introduce some form of the verb *do,* when no other

auxiliary is required, in order to place *not* before the principal verb without placing it before the entire verb, as in *he does not go.* When a negative sentence is given the form of a question, the auxiliary verb frequently carries the *not* forward with it, as in *didn't he go?,* *can't you say?.*

2. The second position for a sentence adverb is after the full verbal idea has been expressed. In the case of a transitive verb, this means after the object. We may say *he slowly ate the food* or *he ate the food slowly.* The second position calls attention to the adverb and makes it emphatic. It should not be used when the word does not justify this extra attention, as in *he told me the story soon.* On the other hand, a word that has special significance should not be left in the primary position, as in *I yesterday told him.*

An adverb should not be placed between a verb and its object, as in *the children ate slowly the food.* In English the fact that a word or group of words is the object of a verb is shown by their position immediately after the verb. To insert anything except an indirect object between these two parts of a sentence is always undesirable, and is sometimes fatal to the sense. (See **object of a verb.**) Conceivably, in some very intricate sentence the object itself may be so involved and require so many words that the adverb cannot be held over till the end. But sentences of this kind are very rare in modern speech.

This question does not arise with an intransitive verb, which has no object. Here the adverb may stand immediately after the verb. We may say *he slowly walked home* or *he walked slowly home.* We may also say *he walked home slowly.* In these sentences we do not have an object but two adverbs, *home* an adverb of place, and *slowly* an adverb of manner.

When several adverbs or adverbial phrases follow a verb, adverbs of manner usually stand first, adverbs of place second, and adverbs of time last, as in *she met him clandestinely in the garden every evening.* But this rule is not rigid and is set aside for the sake of emphasis. With both transitive and intransitive verbs, the further the adverb is removed from the verb, the more emphatic it becomes.

A verb that is used to mean "be," "seem," or "become," is called a linking verb and the words which immediately follow it are called its "complement." *My friend* and *cheerful* are complements in *he has always been my friend* and *he quickly became cheerful.* (See **linking verbs.**) Verbs of this kind are classed as intransitives but a complement is treated like the object of a transitive verb. An adverb used with any linking verb except a simple tense of the verb *to be,* may stand in the primary position, as in the examples given, or it may follow the complement, as in *he has been my friend always* and *he became cheerful quickly.* But it should not stand between the verb and the complement, as in *he has been always my friend* and *he* *became quickly cheerful.* In the last example, *quickly* ceases to be a sentence adverb and qualifies the isolated word *cheerful.* This would be the proper place for the word if that was what was intended, as in *he became obnoxiously cheerful.*

An adverb may stand between a simple tense of the verb *to be* and its complement, as in *he was always my friend, he is always cheerful.* Perhaps these words are used so often as first auxiliaries that they are always felt as auxiliaries. In any case, the adverb usually follows *am, is, are, was,* and *were,* whether the word is being used as an auxiliary or as the principal verb. An adverb placed before one of these forms gives the verb the same extra emphasis that it gives to a first auxiliary, as in *it was certainly a mermaid* and *it certainly was a mermaid.*

Adverbs that have the same form as adjectives may stand in this secondary position. But adjectives too may stand after the object of a transitive verb and after certain intransitive verbs. In these positions it is sometimes impossible to say which function a particular word is supposed to have. Sometimes it makes no difference how we interpret it. (See **position of adjectives.**)

3. A sentence adverb may also stand before the subject of the verb, as in *slowly he ate the food.* This is a normal position for certain kinds of adverbs, which are discussed below. But for most adverbs, such as *slowly,* this position is extremely emphatic and should not be used unless the circumstances justify it. It is appropriate in statements that are charged with emotion, as in *always, night and day, I hear lake water lapping.* And it can be used to express excitement, as in *away went Gilpin, away went hat and wig.* But it should not be used merely for variety.

An interrogative word always stands first in a sentence or clause. We therefore have no choice about the word order in *when will he come?, how will he do it?.* This is also true for a relative adverb, such as *when* in *call me when he comes.* In a negative statement an adverb that follows the negative qualifies the verb only and not the entire sentence, as *twice* in *you did not call me twice.* In order to qualify the sentence as a whole it must stand earlier, as in *twice you did not call me.* It may stand here or immediately after the subject, as in *you twice did not.* The position before the subject is more usual.

Negative adverbs normally stand in the primary position. If they come after the verb they are weakened, but they may be placed earlier for emphasis, as in *little he'll reck, if they let him sleep on.* When they stand before the subject they usually, but not always, bring the first element of the verb forward with them, as in *scarcely had he spoken, least of all could he believe,* and *never blows so red the rose.* A word that is negative in meaning cannot be used as a sentence adverb except in the first or third

position. If it follows the verb form, as in the second position, it qualifies the following word or words and not the statement as a whole. The difference can be seen in *I have never told him to go* and *I have told him never to go.*

A few adverbs, such as *therefore, nevertheless, moreover, still, then,* and a great many adverbial phrases such as *in the first place, on the other hand,* are used as connectives between sentences. They show the relation between what is to follow and what has gone before; for example, that it is a conclusion (*therefore*), or a contradiction (*nevertheless*), or more of the same (*moreover*). Some grammarians consider these words conjunctions and some do not. They are handled like adverbs and not like conjunctions.

A word of this kind, or a phrase with a similar but more subtle meaning, can stand in any position that an adverb can. But the sooner it occurs, the more effective it is. It is not true that these words must be buried inside the sentence. They should stand first unless some other part of the sentence needs special emphasis, or unless they are being used so often that the sentence pattern has become monotonous. When they are placed inside the sentence they are usually set off by commas, but this is not necessary for a single word or a short phrase. If they are placed too late in the sentence they lose their value and have the effect of an afterthought.

sentences. A sentence may be defined as "a meaningful group of words that is grammatically independent, that is, that is not part of any larger grammatical construction."

A sentence which calls for a verbal response is called a question, or an interrogative. A sentence which calls for action is called an imperative. A sentence which primarily expresses an emotion is called an exclamation. A sentence which primarily conveys information is called a declarative. In speech, questions, exclamations, and declarative sentences are distinguished by characteristic pitch patterns. In writing, this is indicated by a question mark, an exclamation point, or a period at the end of the sentence. An imperative is also followed by a period. It is distinguished from a declarative sentence by a special stress on the verb and, in most cases, by the fact that the verb has no subject. Any type of sentence may be either negative or affirmative. See **questions, exclamations, imperative mode,** and **not.**

The definition of a sentence given above includes such expressions as *Dear me!, Please don't, Where?.* Sentences of this kind are very common in speech. In written English, however, most sentences have a more complex structure and can be divided into a subject and a predicate. The subject may be defined roughly as the group of words that shows what is being spoken about; and the predicate, as the rest of the sentence, or the words that "predicate" something about the subject. The subject is always a **noun** or noun equivalent and its qualifiers. The **predicate** is a verb with its objects and **qualifiers.**

In the best written English more than ninety percent of the sentences have the word order: subject, verb, objects. If more than one noun equivalent follows the verb, the order is indirect object, direct object, objective complement. (For a more detailed discussion of these points, see **subject of a verb, indirect object, object of a verb.**) Adverbial qualifiers may stand in any of several positions. (See **sentence adverbs.**)

Any part of a sentence may be a single word or a group of words. (See **phrases.**) When a group of words contains a true verb and its subject (or an imperative) it is called a clause. Any part of a sentence, except the verb itself, may be a clause. In *when I was one-and-twenty I heard a wise man say, "Give crowns and pounds and guineas but not your heart away,"* the words inside the quotation marks form a clause that is functioning as a noun and the object of the verb *say;* and the words *when I was one-and-twenty* form a clause that functions as an adverb of time. (See **clauses** and **conjunctions.**)

A sentence that does not contain a dependent or subordinate clause and that contains only one independent clause is called a simple sentence. A simple sentence is not necessarily short and ideas expressed in it are not necessarily simple. For example, *the cliffs of England stand, glimmering and vast, out in the tranquil bay* is a simple sentence. A sentence that contains a clause as one of its subordinate elements is called a complex sentence, such as *I think we are in rats' alley where the dead men lost their bones.* A sentence that contains two or more independent clauses but no subordinate clause is said to be compound, as in *Don John's hunting and his hounds have bayed.* A compound sentence that also contains one or more subordinate clauses is said to be compound-complex, as in *she liked whate'er she looked on, and her looks went everywhere.* Some grammarians like to make distinctions of this kind, but they have very little practical value.

sentinel; sentry. *Sentry,* derived from an obsolete variant of *sentinel,* is now the more usual term, in England and America, to describe a soldier or other military person stationed at a place to keep guard and prevent the passage of unauthorized persons, etc. (*The sentry cocked his gun and demanded the password*). *Sentinel* may describe such a person, or anyone or that which watches, or stands as if watching (*Mont St. Michel stands like a sentinel above the tidal flats of Normandy and Brittany. And the sentinel stars set their watch in the sky*). *Sentinel* is used largely in metaphorical and literary contexts. It is sometimes, *sentry* never, used as a verb (*All the powers/ That sentinel just thrones double their guards/ About your sacred excellence*).

separate; divide. To *separate* is to disunite, to remove from each other, with a space or body intervening, things that had previously been joined or associated (*In the darkness the two platoons became separated*). To *divide* is to split or break up carefully, according to measurement, rule, or plan (*The property was divided equally between the two sons. The gold was divided into six unequal piles, each separated from the other by about a foot's distance*).

sequence of tenses. See **tense shifts.**

seraglio. The plural is *seraglios* or *seragli.*

seraph. The plural is *seraphs* or *seraphim* or *seraphims.* Seraphs are mentioned only twice in the Bible, each time in the plural. The form used in the King James Version is *seraphims,* but most modern scholars prefer the correct Hebrew plural *seraphim.* The singular form *seraph* was apparently created by Milton. This in turn produced the natural English plural *seraphs.* All three plural forms are acceptable today and there is no difference in meaning between them.

So far as the Biblical record goes, all that can be said about seraphs is that they have six wings and continually praise the Lord. Later tradition identified them as angels of the highest rank, who excel in love. In *Paradise Lost,* Satan is represented as a fallen seraph.

sere and yellow leaf. As a poetical figure for advancing years, especially for old age, *the sere and yellow leaf* is a cliché. It is taken from a speech of Macbeth's (*Macbeth,* V, iii, 23) and like many clichés is slightly distorted in both form and meaning. When Macbeth, despondent, says that his way *Is fall'n into the sere, the yellow leaf,* the text makes it plain that he does not thereby mean old age but middle age, not the winter of life but its autumn. For the things "which should accompany old age" he "must not look to have" but in their stead only servility and hatred.

sergeant; serjeant. In America, *sergeant* is the only term used as a military, police, or courtroom title. A sergeant is a noncommissioned army or marine corps officer of the rank immediately above that of corporal; or a police officer of rank higher than a common policeman or constable; or an officer of a court who is charged with the arrest of offenders, the summoning of defendants, and the enforcement of the decrees of the court or of its presiding official. A *sergeant at arms,* an executive officer of a legislative or other body, whose duty it is to enforce the commands of the body, preserve order, etc., is also often called a sergeant.

In England today the word *sergeant* means what it does in the United States. There was formerly, however, a special order of barristers, abolished in 1880, called *serjeants,* from which the common law judges were chosen. More explicitly, these barristers were called *Serjeants at law.* They are encountered today only in literature (*A Serjeant of the Law, wary and wise—* Chaucer. *Mr. Serjeant Buzfuz, who was counsel for the opposite party . . . —*Dickens).

series. The plural is *series.*

serum. The plural is *serums* or *sera.*

servant. See **help.**

serve my turn. As an expression for something that will do, though usually with a suggestion that it is not quite what is wanted or needed.

to say that *it will serve my turn* is to employ a cliché.

service; duty. *Service,* an act of helpful activity, is one of the great cant words of the twentieth century (*Why don't you stop in at our gentswear department and let us be of service to you*). *Duty* is that which one is bound to do by moral or legal obligation (*To do my duty in that state of life unto which it shall please God to call me*). It was a cant word of our grandfather's generation, and whereas *service,* when abused, is often simply fatuous, the greed showing innocently through the thin plating of altruism, *duty,* when abused, was often sinister, masking cruelties and tyrannies of the most dreadful kind.

Though it properly describes work or duty performed in the interest of another, obviously much *service* in its general usage is either duty without altruistic intent or self-regarding action hypocritically advertised as something else. *Service with a Smile* may mean cheerful robbery.

service; render service; serve. Though some authorities in England are reluctant to accept it, *service* as a transitive verb is well established in American usage. It means to give such service to as is necessary to maintain in working order, to make fit for service, to restore to condition for service, and is usually used with reference to mechanical things (*Let us service your automobile, television set, refrigerator,* etc.). In colloquial usage it has also pretty well ousted *serve* and *render service* (*Three transportation lines will service the Fair*).

A *service man* is one who comes to a house to service the various mechanical devices that need expert repair or maintenance. He is in no sense a *servant,* but one whose services must be sought with solicitude, who must be treated with obsequious respect, and whose shortcomings, even in his professed skills, must be delicately ignored. (A *serviceman* is a member of the army or navy.)

serviette; napkin. When Americans say *napkin,* they mean a rectangular piece of paper or linen or cotton cloth used at table to wipe the lips and hands and to protect the clothes (*Fold your napkins, children; don't leave them wadded in heaps on the table that way!*). In England, however, where diapers (once a euphemism) have come widely to be called napkins, napkins, to avoid the unsavory connotation, are often called *serviettes.* The word *serviette* is also employed in America, but not very widely and more as a touch of elegance than of modesty, though with the increasing use of *napkin* in "feminine hygiene" *serviette* may gain wider currency in the United States. At the moment, however, *napkin,* both the word and the thing, is in itself sufficiently elegant for the millions to need no substitute.

An interesting illustration of the importance of connotation in meaning is supplied, in connection with the word *napkin,* by the airlines. Some of the lines have been attempting to persuade their passengers to tuck their napkins, at mealtimes, in their collars so that they will protect the whole front instead of merely, as when more elegantly placed across the knees, the lap. On an airliner this is sensible and if followed would prevent a great deal of annoyance and complaint. The difficulty is that this generation of Americans, particularly those of the social groups from which a large portion of airline passengers is drawn, has been taught that tucking the napkin into the neck instead of laying it across the lap is, if not downright bad manners, at least rustic and inelegant. Some genius in the service of the airlines has, therefore, struck upon the happy idea of putting the instructions in French, the language above all languages of prandial elegance, and upon each tray is placed a small card suggesting *serviette au cou.* A simple drawing, above the inscription, of a clean and happy gourmand with his napkin in the proper place removes all possible doubt and, at the same time, leaves the passenger with the flattering realization that he can read French.

session. See **cession.**

set. The past tense is *set.* The participle is also *set.*

Originally this verb meant "cause to sit" and, by extension, "put." Unlike the verb *sit,* which could not be used with an object, *set* implied an object that was acted upon as well as an agent. But both object and agent did not have to be mentioned every time the verb appeared. There were two constructions in which *set* was used apparently without an object.

1. When the object was the agent's own body, as in *set yourself down,* the pronoun was sometimes omitted, as in *set down and rest your bones.* This construction is still heard but is not now accepted as standard. It was condemned by grammarians, who claimed that *sit* was required in sentences of this kind that did not have an expressed object. For generations, school children were told not to use *set* without an object. It seems that they finally learned not to use *set* at all in the sense of "cause to sit." As *set down* became unacceptable, people began to say *sit the baby down.* This must have distressed the purists even more than *set down,* but apparently no one had the heart to struggle against it. *Sit* is now acceptable English for "cause to sit." *Set* may also be used in this sense, provided the object is mentioned. But most people today avoid *set* unless it is quite clear that they do not mean "sit." They say *set the baby on his feet* but *sit him in the chair.*

2. When the verb in a sentence is passive, the thing acted on, the logical object, becomes the grammatical subject and is always mentioned, but the agent may be ignored. In many English verbs, the active form may be used with a passive sense, as in *the boat upset, tile washes well, the car drives easily.* (See **passive voice** and **transitive verbs.**) This was true for the verb *set.* People said *the jar sets on the shelf* and *the hen is setting,* just as we say *apples cook quickly* and *dinner is cooking.* This use of *set* was also

attacked by the people who objected to *set down,* but not with the same success. Generations of school teachers tried to turn *a setting hen* into *a sitting hen* and failed. *A setting hen* is still the preferred form. Perhaps rural people are naturally conservative. And perhaps they had other things to think about. The farmer is supposed to have said: "I don't care whether she's setting or sitting. I want to know when she cackles whether she's laying or lying." The teachers also tried to substitute *sit* for *set* in sentences such as *the jar sets on the shelf.* They partly succeeded. This use of *set* is now felt to be questionable English, although it can be justified historically. The solution seems to be to avoid the problem entirely and say *stand,* which can be used with or without an object, as in *I stood it on the shelf and there it stands.* A garment may either *set* or *sit,* as in *the coat sets well* and *it sits well.* Tailors usually prefer *set.*

Set is also used without an object when it means "descend," as in *the setting sun, the sun sets in the west;* and in many derived senses that no longer suggest "seated" or "put," as in *the plaster set, the blossoms set.*

When used before another verb, *set* calls attention to the beginning of an activity rather than the activity itself, as in *she set to work* in contrast to *she worked.* The second verb may be an infinitive, *she set him to work,* or the *-ing* form introduced by *to,* as in *she set him to chopping wood. Set out,* in this construction, suggests that the action had barely begun and probably did not continue, as in *she set out to walk. Set in* suggests that the action that is beginning is going to continue for a long time, as in *it set in to rain* and *she set in to talk.*

set (a social group). See **clique.**

set by the ears, a term from the causing of dogs to fight, is, when used metaphorically as a term for inciting a quarrel among persons or stirring up contentiousness in a group, hackneyed.

set one's face against. As a term for being determinedly opposed to some person or measure, especially some proposed but not yet executed plan, *to set one's face against it* is a cliché.

set one's hand to the plow. As an expression for having undertaken some project, usually of high purpose and importance, with the firm resolve of not wavering but carrying it through to a successful conclusion, to *set one's hand to the plow* is a worn-out expression. It is a slight misquotation of Luke 9:62: *And Jesus said unto him, No man, having put his hand to the plough, and looking back, is fit for the kingdom of God.* No impiety is commonly intended in the use of the phrase. It simply has the touch, felt in so many agrarian metaphors in our mechanical, urban civilization, of old-fashioned, earthy simplicity and, hence, sincerity.

set one's heart on. As a term for establishing a fixed determination to have something or to do something, *set one's heart on it* is a cliché. A point can be made, of course, that such expressions, in use for at least five hundred years, should be accepted as though they were single words, but they are hackneyed and there are usually single words that could be used in their places.

set one's teeth on edge. In its metaphorical sense of occasioning disgust or strong distaste, the phrase *it sets my teeth on edge* is a cliché. The exact meaning of the phrase is obscure. Ezekiel **18:2,** whence it is taken, says *The fathers have eaten sour grapes, and the children's teeth are set on edge.* The sensation to which it alludes is known to everyone but it is hard to attach any known meaning of *edge* to a description of it. The Vulgate has *obstupescere,* to be benumbed. The earlier expression (says the *Oxford English Dictionary*) was *to edge the teeth* and this, if it meant putting a (sense of) sharpness on the teeth, or making them feel as if their edges were grating together, conveys a more comprehensible meaning.

The expression, by the way, is described in Ezekiel (18:3) as a proverb and, at least in the Revised Standard Version, God commands that its use be discontinued.

set the world on fire. As a way of saying that someone is not likely to do anything startlingly brilliant in life, to say that he won't *set the world on fire* is a cliché. This is the American version. In England they say that he won't set the Thames on fire and other nations use other rivers. In these days of atomic fission and fusion the phrase has lost some of its assurance; there's no telling what a violently inclined lad, especially if he has a bent for physics, might not do.

seventh heaven (of delight). As an expression of extreme pleasure, ecstasy, *the seventh heaven,* especially *the seventh heaven of delight,* is a cliché. The term is taken from the Babylonian, later Jewish, and Mohammedan belief that there were seven heavens, the seventh being God's own dwelling.

several may be used as an adjective or alone as if it were a noun or pronoun, as in *several men agreed with him* and *several left early.* The word is always plural and requires a plural verb. When used in a series of adjectives it is treated as a numeral and placed before descriptive adjectives, as in *several large brown dogs.* See **few.**

sew. The past tense is *sewed.* The participle is *sewed* or *sewn. Sewed* is the preferred form for the participle. *Sewn* is heard in Great Britain more than it is in the United States, and is said to be used by women more than by men.

sewage; sewerage. *Sewage* is the word for the waste matter or refuse that passes through a sewer. *Sewerage* is the word for the removal of waste water and refuse by means of sewers. It is also the word for a system of sewers (*The sewerage of rainwater in heavy downpours is a serious problem in the lower parts of the city. The removal of sewage through the sewerage*). Usage permits also the use of *sewerage* as a substitute term for *sewage.* But of the two, *sewage* is preferable since it is unequivocal.

sewn. See **sew.**

sex. See **gender.**

shad. The plural is *shad,* occasionally *shads.*

shade; window blind. What Americans sometimes call a *shade* (*We'll be needing new shades in the kitchen soon. The old ones are worn out and the afternoon sunlight is unbearable*), the English, in correct and general speech, call only a *window blind*.

shade and **shadow** both designate a partial darkness, an area in which the brightness and heat of the sun or some other source of light does not fall. *Shade* differs from *shadow* in that it implies no definite form or limit (*Within the forest there was a cool and refreshing shade. In the shade of the old apple tree*); while *shadow* represents in form, though often distorted, the object which has intercepted the light (*He would quarrel with a man for stepping on the shadow of his dog*). Although *shadow* is often used in literature as a loose synonym for *shade* (*In the deep shadows of the narrow courts*), it usually has a sinister or eerie connotation, suggesting that the darkness is projected by objects or living things, even though imperfectly apprehended. *Shade* is almost always a word of pleasing connotations. *Shadow* can be, and used to be more so than now (*the shadow of a great rock in a weary land*), but it is becoming increasingly suggestive of something threatening or mysterious.

As a synonym for *ghost, shade* is gently poetic (*Nor e'er was to the bowers of bliss conveyed/ A fairer spirit or more welcome shade*).

shadow of one's former self. To say of someone wasted by sickness or fallen from greatness or faded in reputation that he is *but a shadow of his former self* is to employ a cliché.

shake. The past tense is *shook*. The participle is *shaken*.

Stand once had the same pattern as *shake*, with a past tense *stood* and a participle *standen*, as in *I have standen here an hour*. New participles, *stood* and *shook*, as in *I have shook his hand*, appeared in the language about the same time but have had very different histories. *Stood* has succeeded in driving out *standen* and is now the only form of the participle used. *Have shook*, on the other hand, was still a competing literary form in the nineteenth century but is now definitely considered incorrect. Words like these show us how completely grammar depends on usage and how unwise it would be to generalize or legislate about what "ought" to be standard English.

shake off the dust from one's feet. As a way of expressing one's determination to leave a place for which one has a fixed dislike, with a firm resolution not to return, and to make, in leaving, a clear gesture of aversion, *to shake off the dust from one's feet* is now hackneyed. It is from the Bible, from Christ's instructions to his disciples regarding their behavior when men shall not receive them nor hear their words. In Luke 9:5 it is *shake off the very dust from your feet*. In Mark 6:11 it is *shake off the dust under your feet*. And in Matthew 10:14, *shake off the dust of your feet*. Partridge says that this last was the original form

shall; should. In American English *shall* is always a present subjunctive, and *should* a past subjunctive, auxiliary.

These words are forms of a verb which originally meant "owe." There is no corresponding infinitive, no imperative, no -*ing* form, and no past participle. *Shall* is a present tense form but it does not have the characteristic final *s* in the third person singular. This is because it is an old past tense that has come to be felt as a present tense. *Should* is a newer past tense created for it, but it too is now used in speaking about the present and the future. In the United States *should* is not felt as a past tense form of *shall*, but as an independent verb similar to *must* and *ought*.

Since *shall* and *should* are both grammatically past tense forms, just as the word *went* is, neither of these words can follow (that is, be dependent on) another verb. We can no more say *can shall* or *did should* than we can say *can went* or *did went*. Since we cannot use auxiliaries, such as *do, be, have*, we form negative statements and ask questions in the old direct way that is now obsolete for most verbs, as in *he shall not* and *why shouldn't he?*.

Shall and *should* are themselves auxiliaries and require another verb to complete their meaning. They are followed by the simple form of the verb, as in *he shall leave, he should leave*, or by *have* and the past participle to express completed action, as in *he shall have left, he should have left*. The complementary verb must be actually stated or easily supplied from the context, as in *shall we start?* and *do you think we should?*.

In American English *shall* always implies compulsion. It is used chiefly in questions where it asks about the wishes or commands of the person spoken to, as in *shall I wait?, shall we dance?*. *Shall* is not used in negative questions and it is not used in second person questions. To most Americans *shall you?* sounds like a ridiculous affectation.

When used in a statement, *shall* in the second or third person, as in *you shall listen to me* and *he shall stay in bed*, implies that the speaker has the power to compel. It is used in the negative more often than in the affirmative and to children more often than to adults. The English negative form *shan't* is understood but is seldom used. Many Americans believe that it is an illiteracy. *Must, have to, have got to,* also express necessity but do not attribute it to the speaker's will. It is therefore considered more polite to say *you must listen* or *you have got to listen* than to say *you shall listen*. Forms of the verb *to be* followed by a *to*-infinitive express a milder and vaguer form of compulsion and are considered even more polite, as in *you are to stay in bed*.

Shall is sometimes heard in a first person statement, as in *I shall be there*. Here the speaker may be using the word in the English manner, but most Americans will hear it as an expression of determination, a self-imposed coercion,

I will be there is heard as a simple statement about the future. *I shall be there* is heard as a promise or a reassurance. When this is inappropriate, as in *I shall be late,* it is heard as "an un-American way of talking." (For the British use of *shall* and *should* as simple future tense auxiliaries, see **shall; will.**)

In the United States *should* usually carries the meaning of "ought to." It is used in this sense in all persons and in all types of sentences. Like "ought to," it may express what is morally binding, what is expedient, or what is merely expected, as in *he should return the money, a liar should have a good memory, they should be here any minute.* In these senses *should* may be followed by *have* and the past participle of the meaningful verb and refer to a past event, as in *he should have started earlier.*

Should is not used in America as a past tense form of *shall.* The statement *he shall not go* repeated in a past tense form would be *I said he could not go* or *I said he wasn't to go,* and not *I said he should not go.*

Should is sometimes used simply as a sign of the present subjunctive, without any meaning of its own. This is particularly true when a speaker wants to suggest uncertainty or soften a statement in a construction that no longer requires the subjunctive, as in *I'm sorry it should be this way* and *It's strange that they should be so powerful.* Here a statement about matters of fact calling for *is* or *are* has been softened by *should* into a statement about opinions. In *who should I see but Mr. Jones?,* should has the effect of making the question equivalent to *who do you think I saw?.*

In England *should* is used after verbs of requiring, suggesting, desiring, where Americans still use a present subjunctive. That is, an Englishman would say *it is necessary that he should come to the office* where an American would be more likely to say *it is necessary that he come to the office. Should* is used in place of a present subjunctive in hypothetical clauses in both England and America, as in *if he should come, I will tell you. Should* used in a conditional clause is treated as a present subjunctive and does not require a past tense subjunctive auxiliary in the conclusion. It can be placed before its subject to indicate a condition without the use of the word *if,* as in *should he come.* See **subjunctive mode.**

shall; will. The two verbs *shall* and *will* are used to express three ideas. *Will* expresses volition or willingness. *Shall* expresses obligation or compulsion. In these primary senses both verbs refer to the future. But we often want to speak about a future event without saying whether it is to come to pass by or against anyone's will. To do this, one of these verbs must be accepted as a mere sign of futurity. When it is so accepted, it loses its original meaning of volition or obligation.

An American grammarian writing in 1784 said: "*Will,* as an auxiliary term, is a mere sign of futurity . . . *shall,* even as an auxiliary sign, always denotes something more than mere fu-

turity, and constantly implies either obligation, possibility, contingency, or something conditional, and very often several of these together." This is the way *will* and *shall* were used in Old English. And it is the way they are used in American English today. In this country *will* is the empty auxiliary that can be used to indicate mere futurity, in all persons and in all types of sentences.

There was a period in English literature when this was not true. During the sixteenth century and earlier, in literary English at least, *shall* indicated simple futurity and *will* kept its meaning of volition. In the King James Bible *shall* is used as we would now use *will,* as in *the Lord shall preserve thee from all evil* and *goodness and mercy shall follow me all the days of my life.* Similarly, Macbeth is using *should* as we now use *would* when he says of his wife *she should have died hereafter.*

Some, but not all, of these sixteenth century *shall*'s and *should*'s are used by educated Englishmen today. According to the *Oxford English Dictionary,* "since the middle of the seventeenth century the general rule (subject to various exceptions) has been that mere futurity is expressed in the first person by *shall,* in the second and third by *will.* In indirectly reported speech, usage permits either the retention of the auxiliary used by the original speaker or the substitution of that which is appropriate to the point of view of the person reporting." The "various exceptions" are important and numerous. Nothing is said here about the forms used in a question. Anyone who wants to know more about this should consult *The King's English* by H. W. and F. G. Fowler. In this delightful book fifty pages are devoted to the problems of verbs and twenty of these are taken up with the difference between *shall* and *will.*

No American should attempt to use the British *shall* and *should* until he has studied the subject thoroughly. If he does, he will certainly misuse them and speak an English that is offensive on both sides of the Atlantic. Americans should, however, remember that an Englishman is likely to say *I should* or *we should* where an American would use *would.* For example, an Englishman sees nothing outrageous in the sentence, *the doctor thought I should die.* Again, the Englishman who wrote: *never in our hours of temptation should we sacrifice to the mere need for logical consistency our interest, our passion, our vanity,* did not mean that we ought not to be guided by reason but simply that, in a crisis, we wouldn't be.

In the United States a few people use the British *shall* and *will.* A few more consider *I shall* a decorative expression but do not use *we shall* or *should* as an Englishman does. But for most Americans, *shall* always means an order and *should* usually means an obligation. In this country *will* is used as the future auxiliary in all persons and in all types of sentences. The British *I shall* is recognized as something unfamiliar and "foreign." The British *I should* is simply misunderstood. No American sees anything ridiculous in such sentences as: *will you be late?, I'm afraid I will, will we regret it?, would you be able to recognize him?, I will not be able to finish it today.* (To understand how these sentences sound to an Englishman, an American should substitute the appropriate form of "be willing to" for *will* or *would*.)

An American grammarian writing in 1868, who must have spent more time reading his Bible than he spent talking with his neighbors, considered the American use of these auxiliaries a sin and a menace to the public safety. "To disregard obligation in the laying out of future action," he cried, "making arbitrary resolve the sole guide, is a lesson which the community ought not to learn from any section or class, in language any more than in political and social conduct." But this warning seems to have made no impression on his countrymen. In current American speech *will* occurs 217 times for every *shall;* and *would* occurs nine times for every *should.* Etymologically speaking, we are a very *will*ful people. (See also **shall; should** and **will; would** and **future tense.**)

shambles were originally benches or stalls in the market, especially those benches or stalls on which butchers exposed their meat for sale (*Whatsoever is sold in the shambles, that eat*). Where the market was large and the stalls fixed, the shambles came to indicate the section of the market reserved for the butchers (*The shambles remain one of the most picturesque parts of the old town of York*). This meaning is still retained in some parts of England.

More broadly, *shambles* is used to describe any place of carnage that in its bloody horror would suggest the butchers' stalls (*The afterdeck of the PC 565 was a shambles; thirteen dead men lay under light navy blankets*). Today *shambles* is used even more loosely, especially by journalists in search of the more lurid word, to describe a scene of material wreckage, though there may have been no loss of life or blood (*The robber, in his haste to find the money and get away before Delancey returned, had turned the place into a shambles*). This meaning is not yet standard, however, and the careful writer will avoid it—as he will all excessive terms.

share. See **part; portion.**

shares. See **stock.**

shark, as a word for a person who preys greedily on others (*Since his expenses exceeded his income, he soon fell into the hands of the loan sharks*), is a standard word in English and American usage. It would seem, at first thought, to be a figurative use of *shark,* the ferocious, elasmobranch fish; but there is more likelihood that the fish was named after the man than that the man was named after the fish. In America *shark* has the additional slang meaning of one who has unusual ability in a particular field (*He was a shark at mathematics*). The English slang equivalent is *whale,* in the sense of being a big fish among little ones.

shave. The past tense is *shaved.* The participle is *shaved* or *shaven. Shaved* is the preferred form for the participle. One may still say *he has already shaven,* but this is now rare. *Shaven* is preferred to *shaved* when used as an adjective, as in *a well shaven face.*

she. See **subjective pronouns.**

sheaf. The plural is *sheaves.*

shear. The past tense is *sheared.* The participle is *sheared* or *shorn.* Only the old form of the participle, *shorn,* can be used when speaking of a tonsure. Otherwise, in the United States the participle *sheared* is preferred when the word is meant literally, as in *the sheep have been sheared of their fleece,* and the participle *shorn* when the word is meant figuratively, as in *the men have been shorn of their power.* In Great Britain *shorn* is still used in a literal sense and one may say *the sheep have been shorn.*

shears. The plural form refers to one instrument but is usually treated as a plural, as in *these shears are sharp.* It may also be treated as a singular, especially after a qualifying word, as in *here is a pruning shears.* But the form *here is a pair of shears* is more usual. The construction with *pair* must be used after a numeral, as *three pairs of shears.* The singular form *shear* is preferred as the first element in a compound, such as *shear handles* and *shear manufacturers.*

sheaves. This is the plural of *sheaf.*

shed. The past tense is *shed.* The participle is also *shed.*

sheep. The plural is *sheep.*

sheer. One of the meanings of *sheer* is "unqualified" (*A conviction of inward defilement so sheer took possession of me that death seemed better than life*). In this sense the word is greatly overworked, especially in such semi-clichés as *sheer folly, sheer ignorance, sheer physical exhaustion,* and *sheer nonsense.* The word need not be avoided, but it should be used sparingly. There are many good substitutes, some of them more effective in some contexts. Among these may be listed: *utter, absolute, downright, unmixed, simple, mere, bare,* and *unqualified.*

shelf. The plural is *shelves.*

shell game; thimblerig. *Shell game* is the American term for a swindling game in which a small object, such as a pea or a pebble, is concealed under one of a number of walnut shells in such a way as to make it seem to have been placed under another and the unwary persuaded to bet on what they believe to be the evidence of their senses. The English term is *thimblerig,* their swindlers employing small thimblelike cups instead of shells. In both America and England the verb *to rig* means to manipulate fraudulently (*Small investors certainly believe the market is rigged*).

shelves. This is the plural of *shelf.*

shibboleth is sometimes used as if it meant slogan. It does not. It means a peculiarity of pronunciation, or a habit, or a mode of dress, or something of that sort, which distinguishes a particular class or set of persons. It is a Hebrew word meaning (it is generally believed) a stream in flood. Jephthah's men used it (Judges, 12:4-6) as a test word to distinguish the fleeing Ephraimites (who could not "frame to pronounce" the sound *sh* but pronounced it *s* instead) from their own men, many of the Ephraimites claiming to be Gileadites.

shine. The past tense is *shone.* The participle is also *shone.*

The verb meaning "cause to shine" is formed regularly with the past tense and participle *shined,* as in *he shined the light on the water* and *he shined his shoes.* This is literary English. In current speech the form *shone* is often used in the sense of "make a light shine," as in *he shone the light on the water.* This is condemned by some grammarians but is acceptable to many educated people. Only the form *shined* is used in the sense of "make shiny," as in *he shined his shoes.*

Shine may be followed by an adjective describing what shines, as in *the light shone red.* It may also be followed by an adverb describing the shining, as in *the light shone redly.* There is usually no difference in meaning between the two forms.

shingle. The basic sense of *shingle,* in America and England, is a thin piece of wood (or asbestos or asphalt-impregnated paper made to resemble wood shingles), usually oblong and with one end thicker than the other, used in overlapping rows to cover the roofs and sides of houses (*The wind ripped off most of the shingles on the north side*). It also described a type of hair cut (a *shingle-bob*) in which the hair being cut short and unevenly gave the back of the head the appearance of having been covered with shingles. It was popular in the 1920's.

The word has other meanings connected with this basic meaning. In America *shingle* is also a colloquial term to describe a small signboard, especially that of a professional man (*Soon after he passed his state bar examination, Johnson hung out his shingle in the town of Waterman*). To hang out one's shingle is often used figuratively for commencing one's professional career. In England *shingle* (perhaps onomatopoeic and not connected with *shingle* except by coincidence of sound) is used a great deal to describe small, waterworn stones or pebbles lying in loose sheets or beds on the seashore, or an extent of such stones or pebbles (*The sea of faith . . . Retreating . . . down the vast edges drear/ And naked shingles of the world*).

Shingle, usually plural *shingles,* the disease *herpes zoster,* is a wholly different word.

When *shingle* means a wedge-shaped piece of wood, it is a true singular and has a plural in *s,* as in *one shingle* and *three shingles.*

When *shingles* means a disease, it has no singular form *shingle.* But the plural form *shingles* may be treated as a plural or as a singular. We may say *shingles are serious; how long has he had them?* or *shingles is serious; how long has he had it?*

Either *shingle* or *shingles* may be used in speaking of the pebbles covering a beach. Both forms mean exactly the same thing. Both are mass nouns. *Shingles* does not mean any more of the stuff than *shingle* does. *Shingles* in this sense cannot be used with a numeral and *shingle* cannot be used with the article *a.*

ship as a verb means in England to put or take on board a ship or the like, for transportation. In America *ship* means this and in addition may mean to send or transport by rail, road, or air (*I shipped my trunk to New York by rail; so it was at the pier when I embarked*).

ship; boat; vessel. *Vessel* is the general term to describe a craft for traveling on water, now especially any craft larger than an ordinary rowboat. *Boat* is the term for a small craft, propelled by oars, sails, or other means, which is not seagoing. Byron, experienced in these matters, made the proper distinction more than a century ago: *My boat is on the shore,/ And my bark is on the sea. Boat* also describes a small craft carried for use on the deck of a large vessel (*lifeboat, whaleboat*) and is retained in a number of combinations (such as *ferryboat, gunboat,* and *Cross-Channel boat*). Then there are some boats with long cruising radiuses, such as the German WWII *E-boats* and Allied *motor torpedo boats.* But with such exceptions, it is a mark of ignorance to call any ship a *boat. A ship* is a large vessel or an airplane.

Ship of State. One of the most hackneyed of metaphors, the Ship of State has now for over twenty-five hundred years weathered storms, remained on an even keel, been threatened with shipwreck, been becalmed, kept on her course, been clogged with and cleared of barnacles, impeded by the remora, shivered her timbers, been brought or not brought to her desired haven in safety, and otherwise figuratively driven by the winds of rhetoric. She is the Flying Dutchman of political oratory and has had more bilge pumped out of her than all the actual vessels afloat. But as a trope she is now waterlogged and should be scuttled.

shipment. See **freight.**

ships that pass in the night. As a term for people who meet by chance, find each other interesting or attractive, but are compelled to part and go their ways and are not likely to meet again, *ships that pass in the night* (taken from Longfellow) is a good thing overworked.

shirk. This verb may be followed by the *-ing* form of a verb, as in *she shirks washing the dishes,* but not by an infinitive or by a clause.

shoe. The past tense is *shod.* The participle is also *shod.* A new past tense and participle *shoed* is sometimes heard but it is still rare.

shoe. See **boot.**

shone. See **shine.**

shook. See **shake.**

shoot. The past tense is *shot.* The participle is also *shot.*

shoot one's bolt. A *bolt* is an arrow, especially a short, thick arrow, usually called a quarrel, shot from a crossbow. The crossbow was more deadly than the longbow but it took longer—

particularly in the arbalest, where the ejecting string was wound up with a ratchet—to prepare a quarrel for shooting than it did to adjust the older type of arrow and draw back the bow-string. A crossbowman was more to be feared in battle than a longbowman—until he had shot his bolt. And then he was less to be feared and, indeed, until he had reloaded his crossbow, quite vulnerable. He had, therefore, to hold his bolt until it could be used most effectively and, above all, he had to resist excited urges to shoot the bolt before it would be most effective. Hence there was a proverb, *A fool's bolt is soon shot.*

Swift listed *You have shot your bolt* as a hackneyed phrase in 1738.

shop; store. Etymologically, a *shop* is a place in which things are made or *shaped*, a *store* is a place in which they are stored. Both words are used in England and America, but often with different applications.

As a noun, *shop* is preferred to *store* in England to describe a place for selling goods. In America *store* (in modern times usually the more accurate word) is preferred to *shop*, though exclusive and high-priced stores, especially those that restrict their sales to some specialty, tend to call themselves *shops*, perhaps to exploit the prestige often associated with British merchandise. Many of the great department stores maintain special departments known as *The College Shop* or *The Misses' Shop* or some such thing.

Shop is retained in America in its older sense of the place where things are shaped or made in such phrases as *machine shop* or *railroad shops*. We speak of a shoe repair shop, a barber shop, a cabinet shop, and so on. In America a *shopman* is a worker in a workshop. In England a *shopman* is one who sells things over the counter. In America a *closed shop* is a shop in which union membership is a condition of hiring as well as of employment, or one in which the employer must call on the union to furnish employees. An *open shop* is a nonunion shop which may or may not employ union members together with nonmembers, but which does not recognize or deal with a union as the representative of the employees; or, an anti-union shop in which union members are not knowingly employed; or, a shop in which a union, because chosen by a majority of the employees, acts as representative of all the employees in making agreements with the employer, but in which union membership is not a condition of employment. See also **store.**

shop, as a verb, has a somewhat looser definition in America than in England. Though in both countries as an intransitive verb it means to visit shops for the purpose of purchasing or examining goods, in America *shop* (especially among American women) often means little more than to go on a tour of inspection with no thought of buying at present. Hence the expression *window shop.* The English are as great shoppers in this sense as Americans but

they put the matter more obliquely, in expressions such as *go around the shops.*

shorn. See **shear.**

short; shortly. *Short* may be used as an adjective, as in *a short distance.* Either form may be used as an adverb, as in *he stopped short* and *they will be here shortly.* Either form may mean "curtly"; otherwise, the form *shortly* means "in a short time," and the form *short* is used for all the other senses of the word. See also **brief.**

short and sweet, as a term for something brief but enjoyable, is hackneyed. So is *a short life but a merry one* for a gay, adventurous career that may be cut short. It is far more often spoken of lives that *may* be short than of those that actually are or were.

short shrift, give. Though *shrift* originally meant penance, especially a penance prescribed in writing, it came to mean auricular confession and the sacrament of penance. Criminals, when execution often followed almost immediately upon judgment, were usually allowed a brief interval for confession, so that their souls would not suffer. Hence *short shrift* came to mean a brief respite and *to give short shrift* to make short work of, usually, as of a summary dismissal, in dealing unfavorably with someone in one's power. *Shrift* is now an archaic or historical word and the phrase *to give short shrift* a cliché.

shot. When *shot* means the ammunition, it has the plural *shot,* as in *piles of shot and shells.* It may be treated as a mass word and used with a singular verb, as in *much shot was wasted,* or as a true plural, as in *two shot have fallen to the leeward.*

In all other senses the word has a regular plural *shots,* as in *I've taken three shots at it* and *they were both good shots.* See **shoot.**

should. See **shall.**

show. The past tense is *showed.* The participle is *shown* or *showed. Shown* is used more often than *showed* as a participle, as in *I have shown you how to do it.*

show a clean pair of heels. Why the heels displayed by those who depart suddenly in fear or escape should be clean is not clear. Perhaps it simply means disencumbered. It used to be *a fair pair of heels* and *a light pair of heels.* Perhaps in the humorous suggestion of not waiting for shoes or stockings there is a suggestion that the naked heels would look white and clean. But whatever it may mean or have meant, the phrase is now exhausted.

show the white feather. As a figure of speech for manifesting cowardice, *to show the white feather,* a metaphor drawn from gamecocks, a white feather in whose tails (it is said) is a mark of inferior breeding, is a cliché.

showdown is drawn from the game of poker. It describes the laying down of one's cards, face up, as a player declares his hand. More generally, it means any forced disclosure of actual resources or power. It is now used colloquially to mean any trial of strength or even a personal quarrel. *When it comes to a showdown* is a pretty hackneyed phrase.

shower. As a verb, *shower* has different idiomatic uses in England and America. In America one showers a person *with* objects or words; in England one showers objects or words *on* a person.

As a noun, *shower* has the special meaning in America of a social gathering in which the guests (almost always women) bestow presents on a prospective bride or mother.

showy. See **loud.**

shrank. See **shrink.**

shred. The past tense is *shredded* or *shred.* The participle is also *shredded* or *shred. Shredded* is generally preferred for the past tense and for the participle, but both forms are acceptable.

shriek. See **scream.**

shrink. The past tense is *shrank* or *shrunk.* The participle is *shrunk* or *shrunken.* In Great Britain the past tense *shrunk* is no longer used and the participle *shrunken* is seldom heard except as an adjective. In the United States we may still say *it shrunk* and *it has shrunken.*

shrive. The past tense is *shrived* or *shrove.* The participle is *shriven* or *shrived.*

shrunk. See **shrink.**

shuffle off this mortal coil. As a term for dying, commonly used with an arch jocosity, *shuffle off this mortal coil* is a cliché. A punishment to fit the crime of using it would be to require the user to explain exactly what it means. The habitual offender should be compelled to read all of the explanations of its meanings offered by the various commentators. That *mortal coil* means the turmoil of this mortal life is generally agreed, though there are those who insist that it means noise and others who think it may mean something which coils about us. To *shuffle off* may mean to go with clumsy steps or a shambling gait, but the best opinion is that in this context it means to get rid of evasively, to dispose of in a perfunctory and unsatisfactory manner.

shut. The past tense is *shut.* The participle is also *shut.* In the United States we say that the door swung, blew, banged, etc., *shut.* This is a Scottish idiom not used in England, where they say the door swung, blew, banged, etc., *to.*

shut; close. These verbs both mean to cause something not to be open. *Close* is somewhat more refined than *shut* and more suitable in figurative contexts (*The library is closed on weekends*). *Shut* is the informal word referring especially to blocking or barring openings intended for literal or figurative ingress and egress. It is less refined than *close* but more vigorous and where vigor and vernacular strength are wanted, more effective (*I'll show him he can't shut the door in my face!*). See also **close.**

shut up, as a suggestion to someone that he stop talking, though rude, is not ungrammatical. It is an idiom long in use and did not always have the ill nature and hostility now generally associated with it. King Duncan in *Macbeth,* going to bed in Macbeth's castle, sent gifts and greetings to his *most kind hostess* and then, having said his gracious goodnight, *shut up in measureless content.*

Even where the worst construction may be put on the phrase, it is often suitable and almost always effective. Its terseness avoids the imputation of the very fault it seeks to check and often, with the gabby, two words, and they edgewise, are all an unwilling auditor can get in. And it fulfills the highest purposes of language in that it conveys to the one spoken to, with unequivocal clarity and irreducible brevity, the speaker's meaning, mood, and attitude towards him.

shy. See **modest.**

sic is a Latin word meaning *thus.* It is not an abbreviation and is not followed by a period.

sick. See **ill.**

sickness; illness; disease; malady; ailment; indisposition. *Sickness* is the common, everyday word (*Such a sickness leaves you weak for months afterwards. We've had a lot of sickness this winter*). *Illness* is a more formal word and is often attached to more serious sicknesses (*He's never been the same since that long illness. The President's illness made it necessary to postpone the Cabinet meeting*). Though in its origin, *disease* meant any deviation from a state of ease (Alexander Pope spoke of *this long disease, my life*), it now designates an organic deviation involving structural change, serious, active, prolonged and deep-rooted (*Tuberculosis, one of the most dreaded of human diseases . . .*). A *malady* is a lingering, chronic disease, usually painful and often fatal (*Sleeping sickness, a malady which ravaged the entire region and made it almost uninhabitable . . . There's no cure for the malady of age*). *Ailment* is often used lightly to describe some minor affliction, but it may also be used of something more serious, especially when the exact nature of the sickness is not known to the speaker (*He had some ailment, I don't know what; but it seemed to keep him away from work a great deal*). *Indisposition* is a rather ponderous euphemism for sickness. It is often preceded by *slight* and is never used of a serious sickness.

side may be used with or without *of* in phrases that begin with *on* and indicate a place, as in *on this side the grave* and *on both sides the river.* The construction without *of* is not used today as much as formerly but is still acceptable English.

In its literal sense *side* is clear enough. But its figurative and compound uses need some discussion. The English, for instance, use *side* to mean pretentious airs, or pretension itself. If a person is unpretentious in a praiseworthy sense, they say he has *"No swank, no side."* Americans call one who puts on side "a stuffed shirt" or else get downright abusive. The American expression *on the side* is roughly equivalent to such English terms as "an extra," "by the way," or "into the bargain" (*He worked for the Post Office as a mail carrier and drove a dry cleaning truck on the side).*

In American cities *side* is used to describe regions with reference to a central space. New York, for example, has its East Side, Chicago its Near North Side, West Side, South Side, and so on. This practice is not universal and unvarying, however, though in many smaller towns, until quite recently, the railroad tracks served as a line of social demarcation and *to come from the wrong side of the tracks* meant to have had an unfortunate and undesirable social background. In London, *end* is the equivalent term; the West End refers to the fashionable section, the East End to a working-class area.

Sideburns, a name for a special arrangement of the whiskers worn with an unbearded chin, is an exclusively American term. The fashion was named after General Ambrose Burnside, a Union general in the Civil War. The English word for whiskers so worn is *dundrearies,* named after a comic character, Lord Dundreary, in Tom Taylor's *Our American Cousin.* In American equestrian circles, a *side-check* is what the English call a *bearing-rein,* a checkrein carried at the side of a horse's head. Both English and Americans use the term *side-step* meaning to step, or avoid by stepping, to one side. In England the term is most often used in accounts of Rugby football. In America the term is most often used figuratively, meaning to evade, as decisions, problems (*Each party sidestepped certain issues in the interest of unity*). *Sideswipe* is an American term meaning to strike with a sweeping stroke or blow with or along the side. In its commonest use it describes a malpractice of reckless motorists. American *sidewalk* designates a walk, especially a paved one, at the side of a street or road. The equivalent English term is *pavement.* American *side-wheeler,* describing a vessel with a paddle wheel on each side, is in England a *paddle-boat.*

side of the angels. It was Disraeli, in a speech at the Oxford Diocesan Conference in 1864, who first announced that he was *on the side of the angels.* By this he meant, as he said, that in the controversy then raging over organic evolution he was with those who believed that man was not related to the apes but to the angels. The phrase became immediately and immensely popular and passed into use as a way of saying that one took a spiritual view of matters. In modern use it frequently means nothing more than that the person spoken of is on our side in some controversy.

sideways; sidewise. These forms are equally acceptable.

sight; spectacle. A *spectacle* is, in its basic senses, anything presented to the sight or view, especially something of striking kind; a public show or display, especially on a large scale (*The fireworks provided a magnificent spectacle*). A *sight* may be anything seen or to be seen. It is often derogatory, in a light humorous way (*That child was a sight! You never saw so much*

mud on a human being! She was a sight in that new hat). Where *spectacle* is used in this sense, there is a subtle difference; one who is a *sight,* is usually ludicrous and to be pitied; one who is a *spectacle* or, more often, *makes a spectacle of himself,* is obnoxiously showy and to be resented. When one sees the *sights* of a town he may be seeing *spectacles,* but more often he is only seeing the most interesting things that particular town can present to his sight.

sight for sore eyes. As a hearty hyperbole of delight at seeing someone, the assurance that they are *a sight for sore eyes* is a cliché, forgiveable, however, in its homely exuberance and genuine good nature. The meaning is "the sight of you is so pleasant that it would heal sore eyes."

sight unseen is used in America and in some English dialects of things which are bought without previous inspection, without, indeed, even being seen (*Many people lost money in the Florida boom because they bought lots sight unseen and found that they had to remain unseen because they were under several feet of brackish water*).

signal; single. These words sound nearly alike, and sometimes seem to mean the same thing; yet they must be differentiated. One *singles* someone out of a group when one pays or wishes to pay him some special attention, an attention due to this one, single person. It is conceivable that one could *signal* someone out of a group by making signals to him that would induce him to leave the group, but this use of *signal* is very rare and would almost have to be contrived. The confusion caused by the similarity of the two words' sound is heightened by the fact that *signal* as an adjective can mean conspicuous or notable, and one singled out is almost always conspicuous and if singled out by the right person under the right circumstances can be notable.

signature; autograph. A *signature* is a person's name, or a mark representing it, as signed or written by himself or deputy, as in subscribing a letter or other document (*An illegible signature seems the mark of a great executive*). A man's signature may be written by himself or may be reproduced by engraving or by a mechanical device that makes it possible for him in writing his signature once to affix it at the same time to many similar documents, checks, or the like. An *autograph* is a person's own signature in his own handwriting, but with the growing custom of seeking the autographs of celebrities, the growth of fan clubs, press agents, autograph books, and so on, the word is coming to mean chiefly the signature of someone of distinction (or someone thought to be of distinction or who hopes to be of distinction or was of distinction) for an admirer. And among those who write autographs there is a distinction between an *autograph* and a *signature.* Many of those who are asked for autographs are known to the public by a professional name, wholly different from their actual name. These people invariably write their professional names as an autograph and their actual names as a signature. And most of those who appear before the public under their actual names have, as a protective measure, a way of writing their name for "autographs" distinct from what they would consider their signature.

signed, sealed, and delivered. As an expression for something's being brought to a full and satisfactory conclusion, *signed, sealed, and delivered,* a jocular echo of legal terminology, is a cliché.

silent partner; sleeping partner. To describe a partner who takes no active part in the conduct of a business, or is not openly announced as a partner, Americans usually say *silent partner,* sometimes *sleeping partner.* The English always say *sleeping partner.*

silver; silverware; plate. *Silver* and *silverware* seem to be used interchangeably in America to describe table utensils, whether made of solid silver or merely plated (*The thieves took a fur coat and a set of silverware. If you're going on a vacation, you'd better put the silver in your safe-deposit vault*). Utensils of solid silver are a little more likely, especially among the upper middle classes, to be called *silver* and *the silver.* Domestic dishes, utensils, etc., of gold or silver are in England often referred to collectively as *plate* (*His lordship's plate alone was valued at five thousand pounds*). The term is not used in this sense in America.

silver lining. As a term for a bright aspect of an otherwise dark situation, an element of hope where things seem hopeless, an assurance that things cannot be as bad as they appear to be at the moment, a reference to the *silver lining* is hackneyed. It is drawn from the proverb *Every cloud has a silver lining* which is based on the common phenomenon of a bright ring encircling or partly encircling a storm cloud. The actual phrase is highly poetical and would be splendid had it not been tarnished by overuse. It seems to have originated from Milton's lines in *Comus* (*Was I deceiv'd, or did a sable cloud/ Turn forth her silver lining on the night?*).

similar; analogous. *Similar* means having likeness or resemblance, especially in a general way (*His war experiences were similar to mine*). *Analogous* means having analogy—that is, having a partial similarity, corresponding in some particular (*He regarded the resurrection of man as analogous to the resurrection of nature in the spring. The effect of historical reading is analogous, in many respects, to that produced by foreign travel*). In geometry, figures that are similar have the same shape: their corresponding sides are proportional and their corresponding angles are equal. In biology, *analogous* means corresponding in function but not evolved from corresponding organs, as the wings of a bee and those of a bird.

simile; metaphor. A *simile* is a direct comparison of things, proclaiming itself as such by *as* or *like,* often introduced for its own sake and usually elaborated to display many resemblances in its comparison:

Falstaff frets like gummed velvet

> *As when the potent rod*
> *Of Amram's son in Egypt's evil day*
> *Wav'd round the Coast, up call'd a pitchy cloud*
> *Of Locusts, warping on the Eastern Wind,*
> *That o'er the Realm of impious Pharaoh hung*
> *Like Night, and darken'd all the Land of Nile:*
> *So numberless were those bad Angels seen*
> *Hovering on wing under the Cope of Hell*
> *'Twixt upper, nether, and surrounding Fires;*

> *Like some bold seer in a trance,*
> *Seeing all his own mischance—*
> *With a glassy countenance*
> *Did she look to Camelot.*

A *metaphor* is an implied comparison, expressed often in a single word, introduced usually in order to make a meaning clearer. It almost always confines itself to the one principal resemblance of the comparison it establishes:

> *. . . but I tell you, my lord fool, out of this nettle, danger, we pluck this flower, safety*

> *The hounds of Spring are on Winter's traces*

> *The wind came down from heaven*
> *And smoked in the fields*

In every metaphor there is latent a simile. Every metaphor could be expanded into a simile and almost every simile could be compressed into a metaphor.

simple sentence. A sentence which contains only one clause is called a simple sentence. That is, a sentence is grammatically simple if it is impossible to lift a second sentence out of it. The idea expressed in a simple sentence is not necessarily simple. For example, *all the king's horses and all the king's men couldn't put Humpty Dumpty together again* is a simple sentence. See **sentences.**

simple verb form. The expression "the simple form of the verb" is used in this dictionary to mean the uninflected form, such as *talk.* In English this form is the infinitive, the imperative, the present subjunctive, and the present indicative except for the third person singular (which normally has an additional *s,* as in *he talks*); the verb *to be* is the only exception. Here the simple form *be* is the infinitive, the imperative, and the present subjunctive, but not the present indicative, which has the three forms *am, is, are.*

These various forms do not make a reasonable group and the expression "the simple form of the verb" is sometimes extremely awkward. In most cases it is used to avoid the word *infinitive.* More people seem to have heard of "the split infinitive" than ever heard of an infinitive and to use the term *infinitive* for something obviously unsplittable is to run the risk of making oneself incomprehensible. For this reason, in the discussion of specific words, where the reader is not expected to have any theoretical understanding of grammar, the infinitive with *to* is called simply an infinitive. It is called a *to*-infinitive when it is being contrasted to the simple infinitive, which in turn is called the simple form of the verb.

A few verbs, such as *ought, can, must,* do not have an infinitive or an imperative. These verbs are easily recognized by the fact that the third person singular in the present tense does not end in *s*. For example, we say *they must* and also *he must, they can* and also *he can*. Verbs for which this is true are considered not to have a "simple form" and are not included in any statements made about "the simple form of the verb."

simply conveys several ideas and needs to be used carefully to avoid ambiguity. Basically it means in a simple manner (*He spoke simply, yet his ideas were not superficial*), plainly, unaffectedly (*With such restricted means, he was forced to live simply*), artlessly (*Others had presented these thoughts simply; Pope presented them artfully*).

Three further uses need to be handled with care. *Simply* may mean merely, only (*I was simply trying to keep you out of trouble*), but it may also mean unwisely, foolishly (*Simple Simon has become a symbol of men who behave simply*). This last use is now obsolete. Or *simply* can, and in colloquial use as a vague intensive all too often does, mean absolutely (*She looked simply lovely*). This is one of those terms which may seem trivial in writing but which, its meaning indicated by the proper emphasis, can be quite meaningful.

simulacrum. The plural is *simulacra*.

simulate. See **dissimulate.**

simultaneous. See **synchronous.**

sin. See **crime.**

since may be used alone as an adverb, as in *I haven't seen him since,* or it may be used as a preposition with a simple object, as in *I haven't seen him since yesterday,* or as a conjunction introducing a clause, as in *I haven't seen him since he left.* In these cases *since* indicates a period of time beginning at the point mentioned and extending to and including the time of speaking. In a positive statement the word *ever* may be added to make *since* more emphatic.

Since is also used to introduce a clause showing cause or reason, as in *he must have taken it, since it isn't here.* This is standard, literary English. The conjunction *because* always indicates a cause, as in *it isn't here because he took it.* But *since,* like the conjunction *for,* may also be used to indicate a result from which one may deduce the cause, as in the example given.

In current English, when *since* introduces a temporal clause, the clause verb must be in the simple past tense, and the principal verb in the statement must be in the present perfect or past perfect tense, as in *we have* (or *had*) *seen him since he left.* If a simple past tense is used in the principal statement the conjunction *after* is required, as in *we saw him after he left.* When *since* introduces a statement of cause or reason, either verb may have any tense form, but the present perfect and past perfect are generally avoided in the principal clause.

sincerely; truly; faithfully. American and English practice with regard to the complimentary close in letters differ notably. The American business letter usually ends *Yours truly, Yours very truly,* or *Very truly yours.* Formal personal letters end *Sincerely yours, Yours sincerely, Cordially yours, Yours very truly,* or *Yours truly.* Intimate personal letters end *Yours* or with various expressions of sentiment. In England *Yours faithfully* or *Faithfully yours* is used at the close of all but intimate personal correspondence. It has pretty well ousted *Yours truly,* which was long used in informal communications. In personal communications *Yours sincerely* is the conventional term. For some reason the English are perturbed at the custom of many Americans of using the single word *sincerely* at the close of an informal letter. They seem to feel that *Yours sincerely* is an accepted formula that conveys no specific meaning other than a courteous leave-taking but that *sincerely* alone is insincere. Sometimes, apparently, the English slip and use *Yours sincerely* when they should use the more formal *Yours faithfully.* Collins warns his readers against this, telling them, in accents redolent of the Victorian moralists Smiles and Tupper, "When one is in doubt it is safer to be 'faithful' than 'sincere.' "

sine qua non. As a term for something essential, an indispensable condition, *sine qua non* (or *a sine qua non* or *the sine qua non*), a Latin phrase meaning "without which nothing," is a cliché.

sing. The past tense is *sang* or *sung.* The participle is *sung. Sang* is heard more often than *sung* for the past tense today. But seventy-five years ago *sung* was the preferred form. Both forms are acceptable in the United States.

single blessedness. Once a serious expression, meaning (according to the *Oxford English Dictionary*), "divine blessing accorded to a life of celibacy," *single blessedness,* as a term for the unmarried state, is now a jocular cliché.

singular. See **unique.**

singular nouns. The singular is the simple, basic form of the noun. When it is used to represent just one object, a singular noun is qualified by singular adjectives, such as *one, this, that, much, each;* is referred to by singular pronouns, such as *it, he, her;* and followed by a singular verb. But the singular form of the noun is also used in other ways.

1. Traditionally, the singular form is required for the first element in a compound, such as *tooth ache, child laborers, parcel post, brain*

trust, a five-dollar bill. But in current English, especially in the United States, a good many plural forms are appearing in this construction, as in *communicable diseases control, welfare services funds, correctional institutions specialist.* These expressions are poor English for many reasons, but the plural first element offends very few people when it is used in heavy, unfamiliar compounds made up of abstract ideas. In familiar names for physical things, a plural first element is still not considered standard, as in *teeth ache, geese feathers, a five-dollars bill.* (Compounds involving *man* or *woman* are not formed exactly like other compounds; see **man** and **woman.**)

The same question is involved in the choice between *a two-week vacation* and *a two-weeks vacation,* but here the form with *s* has a different status. See **measures.**

2. A singular noun may name a group or a class of individuals. Singulars used in this way cannot be qualified by plural adjectives, such as *many* and *few,* but in some cases they may be followed by a plural verb, as in *the sea-otter have disappeared* and *the jury were unable to agree.* See **generic nouns, group names,** and **adjectives as nouns.**

3. Many singulars, such as *butter, mud, childhood,* do not have a plural form. Words of this type are called mass nouns. They name a formless, undifferentiated whole rather than a kind of individual thing. In standard English such words are not made plural merely because we have several instances of the thing, all of which are essentially alike. That is, we say *I have three packages of butter,* not *I have three butters.* Similarly, we say *our reason tells us,* not *our reasons tell us,* and *they were together in their childhood,* not *in their childhoods.* When it is felt that two instances of a certain thing are essentially different, a plural form may be used. This is often the case with *life* and *death.* In certain states of mind the death of any one man seems to be a unique thing, and we might say *three men met their deaths.* In a more philosophic temper the difference between one man's death and another's seems unimportant and the singular form is used, as in *sad stories of the death of kings.* Meaningless plurals should be avoided. But if there is a real justification for the plural—either intellectual or emotional—it can always be used. The choice of a singular or a plural, with its implication of diversity or identity, can be a powerful device in the hands of a skillful writer, as it is in the lines: *we mutually pledge to each other our lives, our fortunes, and our sacred honor.* See **mass nouns.**

4. Some words which usually refer to specific individual things may be treated as mass nouns and used in the singular, as for example, *allusion* in *speeches full of classical allusion* and *detail* in *great attention to detail.* But this is only a literary mannerism. Here the difference between the singular and the plural does not have any particular force. *Classical allusions* and *attention to details* would mean exactly the same thing. Either form can be used, and nothing depends on the choice.

5. A true singular, which is not being used as a mass noun but names a well defined individual thing, may also be used when more than one of these things is meant. This is the case, for example, with *face* in *we are simple creatures and yearn to be loved for our face,* and *mouth* in *children put things in their mouth.* Here we are talking about a number of people and a number of things which each person has just one of. The same situation is seen in *singular nouns that have a plural form.* During the nineteenth century the use of a plural noun, such as *faces, mouths, forms,* in this construction was considered unliterary. But in the United States today, many people prefer to say *children put things in their mouths.* This plural form is also used in the King James Bible, as in *kings shall shut their mouths.* The singular form is still heard more often than the plural, but either construction is acceptable today. There is no difference, in meaning or in tone, between them.

6. The singular form is also used with plural meaning after adjectives joined by *and,* as in *the eighteenth and nineteenth century* and *the Old and New Testament.* When the adjectives are in the superlative, as in *the oldest and youngest child* and *the largest and smallest box,* the singular form is required—*The oldest and youngest children, the largest and smallest boxes,* would mean something quite different. When the adjectives are not in the superlative, the plural form of the noun may be used in current English, as in *the eighteenth and nineteenth centuries* and *the Old and New Testaments.* This is acceptable, but the singular form is usually considered more elegant.

It is possible for a word to change its number over a period of time. This is particularly true of singular group names which sometimes become true plurals, as has happened with *people* and *cattle.* (See **group names.**) Sometimes a true singular ending in *s* comes to be accepted as a plural. This has happened with *alms, eaves, riches.* As a rule, these words do not become true plurals. They do not develop new singular forms and cannot be used with qualifiers implying more than one, such as *several, many, few.* Occasionally a plural noun ending in *s* comes to be accepted as a singular. This has happened with *the United States, news, hydraulics,* and so on. Such words usually keep the plural form when used in a compound, such as *news letter, hydraulics engineer.*

sink. The past tense is *sank* or *sunk.* The participle is *sunk* or *sunken.* In Great Britain the participle *sunken* is not used except as an adjective, as in *the sunken cathedral.* In the United States *sunk* is the preferred form for the participle but *sunken* is still used, as in *it has sunken to the bottom.*

sink or swim. The earliest known use of *sink or swim,* in the metaphorical sense of succeed or fail, is 1538, where, however, it is preceded by "as hyt is commonly sayd." So the phrase was hackneyed four hundred years ago. And it has not grown fresher since.

sinus. The plural is *sinuses* or *sinus,* not *sini.*

Sioux. The singular and plural are both *Sioux.* Originally this word was plural, but it may now be used also as a singular, as in *one Sioux* or *three Sioux.*

sir; sire. Both of these words are now obsolete to describe a lord (as in *Sir Gawain and the Green Knight* or *The Sire de Maletroit's Door*). *Sir* today is a respectful or formal term of address to a man. Though formerly in almost universal use in the United States, it was being discontinued until World Wars I and II gave it renewed life. *Sir* was a mandatory term of address for all enlisted men to commissioned officers and for commissioned officers to their superior officers and the habit carried over, at least for some years, into civilian life.

In England *Sir,* capitalized, is still used as the title of a knight or a baronet (*Sir Winston Churchill, Sir John Falstaff*). Where the holder of this title is also a military man, the military title precedes the *Sir* and the honorific initials of any order the man may belong to succeed the full name (*General Sir Reginald Pinney, K.C.B.*). In America, as in England, *sir* is sometimes used as an ironic or humorous title of respect (*Sir Oracle, Sir critic*). The single word *Sir* is the most formal salutation in a letter addressed to one man.

Sir is sometimes used colloquially in America as nothing more than an intensive adverb, to make *Yes* or *No* more emphatic (*Yes sir, she's my baby. No sir! You don't catch me volunteering*). For further emphasis, it is sometimes enlarged to *sirree* (*No sirree, I'm not going around there tonight!*).

Sire is now restricted chiefly to the male parent of a quadruped (*Man of War was the sire of several famous race horses*). In poetic usage, it means a father or a forefather (*The sire his sword bequeathing to his son. Our sires died that we might live in freedom*). As a respectful term of address it is more restricted than *sir,* for it is now used only to a sovereign, and since sovereigns and opportunities of addressing them are rare, it is confined to poetry ("*You're wounded!*" "*Nay,*" *the soldier's pride/ Touched to the quick, he said:/ "I'm killed, Sire!*") and jokes (*Sire, a lady waits without*).

sistren. This is an old plural of *sister,* formed like *brethren* and *children.* It is now obsolete or dialectal.

sit. The past tense is *sat.* The participle is also *sat.* This verb does not necessarily mean assume a sitting posture. It may be used for inanimate and abstract things that do not have legs, as in *one of the low on whom assurance sits as a silk hat on a Bradford millionaire.* It may be used with an object, as in *he sits his horse well* and *he sat the meeting out.* It may also be used to mean cause to sit, as in *sit the baby up.* At one time *set* would have been preferred in this sentence, but in current English *set* has come to mean place rather than cause to sit. See **set.**

situate; situated. *Situate* as an adjective is archaic except in a legal sense (*The house is situate immediately adjacent to Christ Church*). In all general uses *situated* is the right word for located or placed (*Knoxville is situated downstream from the confluence of the Holston and French Broad rivers*). It may also mean fixed (*He is well situated financially*).

situation. See **job.**

six of one and half a dozen of the other, as a way of saying that there is little to choose between alternatives because they are so evenly matched, is a cliché.

skate on thin ice. Up until a generation ago when play became supervised, every boy who lived near a pond or a river knew the excitement and the voluptuous sensation of skating on thin ice and knew, as Emerson had said, that in such skating safety lay in speed. The experience was common and the metaphor drawn from it was immediately and universally understood. But it has been overworked and must now be classed as worn and weakened.

skeleton at the feast. It was Herodotus, in the fifth century B.C., who told us that the Egyptians used to produce "the image of a corpse" at their feasts to remind the feasters of their mortality. The gruesomeness of the procedure has fascinated the world for twenty-five hundred years and there are many references to the custom. It survives today chiefly as a humorous term for one who by his presence dampens the general gaiety, and as such it is hackneyed.

skeleton in the closet. As a term for a hidden shame, known to the members of a family but concealed from the outer world, *a skeleton in the closet* (the English say *cupboard*) is a cliché. The expression seems to have been invented by Thackeray.

skeptic; skeptical; sceptic; sceptical. For the adjective the English use *sc-,* the Americans *sk-.* The pronunciation is *sk-* in both spellings. *Skeptical* and *sceptical* are preferred to *skeptic* and *sceptic.*

The adjective means inclined to skepticism, having doubt (*Many people were skeptical about the long-range value of the project*), showing doubt (*That sudden, skeptical glance shook her confidence in her ability to carry off the story*), questioning the tenets of religion (*Many late Victorians were skeptical about the doctrine of special creation*), or of or pertaining to skeptics or skepticism (*He was instinctively drawn to a skeptical world view*).

skeptic; sceptic; disbeliever. American *skeptic* (English *sceptic*) is not to be confused with *disbeliever.* Actually a skeptic is one who questions the validity or authenticity of something purporting to be knowledge, one who maintains a doubting attitude (*There are some surly skeptics who don't think the new vaccine has yet justified the popular faith in it*). As applied to religion, a skeptic is one who doubts the truth of the Christian religion or of important elements of it. He does not deny absolutely the truth of Christianity, as does the *disbeliever.* In philosophy, the *Skeptic* (capitalized) is one who doubts or questions the possibility of real knowledge of any kind. See also **agnostic**.

ski. The plural is **skis** or **ski**.

skin of one's teeth. It was *with* the skin of his teeth that Job (chapter 19, verse 20) escaped, that is, with nothing at all. Or at least he so escaped up until the Revised Standard Version which accepts the common change, which has become a cliché, *by the skin of my teeth*.

skittles takes a singular verb, as in *skittles was played*. *Skittles* and *ninepins* are two names for the same game and both words have been in the language for several hundred years. *Ninepins* is the word used most often in the United States today and *skittles* is seldom heard except in the expression *beer and skittles*.

skull. See **scull**.

sky and **skies** can be used interchangeably.

The word *sky* once meant a cloud. This is no longer true but it has resulted in our being able to use either the singular or the plural form in speaking of the vault above us—whether it contains clouds or not. Both forms may also be used figuratively for the regions of the blest, as in *the eternal mansions of the sky* and *he raised a mortal to the skies, she drew an angel down*.

sky light; skylight. *Sky light* is the light or color of the sky. A *skylight* is an opening in the roof or ceiling, fitted with glass, for admitting daylight, or the frame set with glass fitted to such an opening.

slack; slake. *Slack* is primarily an adjective meaning not tense or taut (*The hawsers hung slack*); indolent, negligent (*He was slack about his duties*); lacking in activity, not brisk (*Business is always slack right after Christmas*); sluggish, as of the water, tide, or wind; slow in tacking, as of a sailing vessel. As a noun *slack* means a slack condition, interval, or part; part of a rope, sail or the like that hangs loose without strain upon it (*Pull the cable in there. Take up the slack*); a decrease in activity, as in business or work; or the state of the tide when there is no horizontal motion. As a verb *slack* may be used to mean to be remiss in some respect in some matter; to make or to allow to become less active, vigorous; to make loose or less tense; in nautical terminology, to ease off.

Slake is used exclusively as a verb. It may mean to make less active, vigorous, intense (like *slack*), yet *slacken* is a better verb than either one. *Slake* means primarily to allay thirst, desire, wrath, by satisfying (*They slaked their thirst in the muddy water*); to cool or refresh. It may also mean to disintegrate or treat lime with water or moist air, causing it to change into calcium hydroxide (*We used to slake lime with which to line the tennis courts*).

slain. See **slay**.

slander. See **libel**.

slang is language regarded as unsuitable for standard, cultivated speech and especially for formal writing. In slang the creative forces that shape language are often exceedingly active and much slang is vivid and clever and forceful.

Much more of it, however, is merely faddish and infantile and its consistent use does not display the fullness of expression that the user thinks it does but rather a triteness and a staleness that the user is apparently unaware of. Slang ages quickly and nothing so stamps a total lack of force or originality upon a man or woman as the steady use of outmoded slang. Slang is not as bold as many of its users believe it to be; it shares the taboos of ordinary speech and is rich in euphemisms. It often defiantly substitutes violence for elegance and the gruesome for the dainty, and sometimes this is a good corrective, but it is no more bold than standard speech. *Kick the bucket* may be a scornful jibe at the evasion of *pass away* but *die* maintains a cold dignity that neither dare approach. The vitality of slang, the manner in which it gives renewed expression to old thoughts that have become dimmed through usage and lost, as it were, in the very words that once expressed them, is shown in the fact that much slang merely repeats unknowingly the basic meaning of a standard word or phrase. *Know-how,* though used differently, is an English parallel of *savoir faire.* Even such a forced absurdity as *off his rocker* has its parallel in *delirious,* which means, etymologically, "out of his furrow." And there are hundreds more.

slant, as a noun, means literally a slanting or oblique direction, slope (*There was a steep slant from the back door down to the barn*). In America the word is also used figuratively to mean a mental tendency or leaning, a bias, or a point of view (*From his reading and travels he got a new slant on his native society*).

slash means literally to cut with a violent sweep or by striking violently and at random. In America it also means figuratively to reduce or to cut down. In this sense it is greatly overworked in newspaper advertisements announcing a reduction in prices (*Prices slashed!*).

Used as a noun, usually in the plural, *slashes* in the United States describes a tract of wet or swampy ground overgrown by bushes and trees.

slate in America is used figuratively to describe a tentative list of candidates, officers for acceptance by a nominating convention or the like. The actual list of candidates nominated or put forward by a political party or faction to be voted for is called a *ticket*.

slattern. See **sloven**.

slaughter. See **massacre**.

slay. The past tense is slew. The participle is *slain*. The form *slayed* is not standard English and is heard only in humorous exaggeration, as in *it slayed me!*

Though in England *slay* is a poetical or rhetorical word only (. . . *in thy book record their groans/ Who were thy sheep and in their ancient fold/ Slain by the bloody Piedmontese*), it is a standard everyday word in America, used as an alternative to *kill,* especially to kill by violent means (*Socially prominent couple slain in love nest. Slayer to get the chair*). It is a great favorite of newspapermen with **impoverished** vocabularies.

sled; sledge; sleigh. These nouns all describe a vehicle that is drawn by runners on snow or ice. *Sledge* is the usual term in England (*The Muscovites make use of sledges, made very low*) though *sleigh* is becoming more common. *Sleigh* is the American word to describe a light, usually open vehicle on runners, generally horse-drawn, used for pleasure driving (*Oh what fun it is to ride/ In a one-horse open sleigh*). In England *sleigh* is a military term to describe a sledge used for the transport of artillery.

Sled is used in America in two ways. It may describe a vehicle mounted on runners for conveying loads over snow, ice, or rough ground. That is, it suggests a freight vehicle as *sleigh* suggests a passenger vehicle (*In heavy winter weather my father used a bob-sled and horses to get through the drifts that lay between our farm and the town*). *Sled* is also used of a small light vehicle with runners used by children for coasting. *Bobsled* or *bob-sled* is an American term that formerly described a sled formed of two short sleds coupled one behind the other. And this is still likely to be its meaning on some farms. The modern *bobsled* (used in sled racing) couples the runners only, the seat portion being continuous.

sleep. The past tense is *slept*. The participle is also *slept*.

Sleep sound is standard idiom in the United States and Scotland, but not in England where they say *sleep soundly*. However, *sound asleep* is the accepted idiom even in England and no one wanting to pass for an Englishman should go so far as to say *soundly asleep*. See **slumber**.

sleep like a top. Some ingenious etymologists have sought to derive the "top" of the expression *to sleep like a top* from the French *taupe*, mole. But there is no need of it. Sleeping moles are rarely seen and sleeping tops, humming in seeming immobility as they spin, are common and were much more common. Then the French expression is *dormir comme un sabot* (shoe), not *comme une taupe*. But, however derived, the phrase is now worn out. It is more in use in England than in the United States.

sleep the sleep of the just. Now used almost entirely in a jocular way, *to sleep the sleep of the just,* as a term for sleeping soundly, is a cliché.

sleeper. In American railroad terminology a *sleeper* is what the English call a *sleeping car* (*I took the sleeper as far as Buffalo; it cost more, but I just couldn't bear to sit up all night in the coach*). By *sleeper* the English mean what the Americans call a *tie*, a timber or beam laid in a railroad track to serve as a foundation or support for the rails—a cross tie, bridge tie, or switch tie.

In American slang a *sleeper* may mean a racehorse which usually runs below its top stride or, by derivation from this, a cheaply made movie that enjoys enormous success, or anything or anyone that greatly exceeds what was expected of it.

sleeping partner. See **silent partner.**

slept. See **sleep.**

slew. See **slay.**

slick up is a colloquial expression of American origin meaning to make smart or fine (*They always slicked up the place before the governor paid them a visit*). *Slick* is simply a variant pronunciation of *sleek,* as *crick* is of *creek*. The English equivalents are *tidy up* and *brighten up.*

slide. The past tense is *slid*. The participle is *slid* or *slidden*.

slim. In figurative senses the adjective *slim* is obsolete in England. But it is frequently used in America as it formerly was in England, to mean poor (*He had a very slim chance of surviving the operation*), or small, inconsiderable, or scanty (*He won the election, it is true; but by a slim majority*).

sling. The past tense is *slung*. The participle is also *slung*.

slink. The past tense is *slunk*. The participle is also *slunk*.

slit. The past tense is *slit*. The participle is also *slit*.

slog. See **slug.**

slogan; watchword; motto; catchword. These words all mean a saying adopted as a guiding principle. *Watchword* was originally, and still means basically, a word or short phrase to be communicated, on challenge, to a sentinel on guard (*Jephthah used the watchword* Shibboleth *to distinguish enemy Ephraimites from his own men*). More loosely, *watchword* may mean a word or phrase expressive of a principle or rule of action, a rallying cry of a party, or a slogan. A *slogan*—though originally it meant a war cry or gathering cry—now more commonly means a distinctive cry or phrase of any party, class, body, or person. Since these phrases, especially as used in advertising and politics, are intended to be more inspirational than factual, the word is acquiring a connotation of mistrust (*Oh, that's just a slogan*). A *motto* is a maxim adopted as expressing one's guiding principle (*The motto on the coin reads "In God we Trust"*). A *catchword* is a word or phrase caught up and repeated for effect, as by a political party. One who uses the term uses it rather contemptuously, as if he considered it misleading and insincere (*"To make the world safe for democracy" seemed merely a catchword to soldiers bogged down on the Western Front*).

slogans. A slogan is a distinctive cry or phrase associated with a person, group or thing, usually invented for favorable identification. It was formerly a war cry or a gathering cry among the Scottish clans. The Gaelic *sluagh-ghairm*, host cry, appeared in an early form as *slughorn* and it was this which, misunderstanding, Browning had Childe Roland blow before the Dark Tower.

The word now describes any catchy phrase which will induce people to support a cause (*Liberty, Equality, Fraternity*), a candidate (*He kept us out of war*) or a product (*Ask the man who owns one*).

A good slogan must be brief, pointed, rhythmic or startling, and must be able to stand repetition. A strange or even repugnant idea may be made acceptable by a slogan heard often enough (*Votes for Women!*).

Although the high priests of the advertising world insist on "the positive approach," negative slogans have been used against opposing groups with devastating success (*Let 'em eat cake. Turn the rascals out. Kind regards to Mrs. Fisher*). Sometimes a phrase may be meaningless in itself and yet by its associations take on the character of a slogan (*Martin, Barton and Fish*). And every once in a while a slogan is turned back on its subject with ironic implication: *Back to normalcy, A chicken in every pot, We planned it that way.*

It seems to be a sign of the times that advertising slogans are not as long-lived as they used to be. Many slogans used to be almost institutional (*He won't be happy till he gets it. Eventually—Why not Now? 99.44% Pure*) but few products retain such slogans any more. Most of them change from season to season. Perhaps they pall more quickly with the greater repetition they now get. Perhaps copy writers must live. Or perhaps the public is more sophisticated. Slogans used to assume something of the character of pronouncements and people were expected to believe them; nowadays they are more generally accepted as simply devices for gaining attention.

slothful. See **lazy.**

slough of despond. As a term for a state of dejection or despondency, *the* or *a slough of despond,* taken from the dismal bog into which Christian, the hero of Bunyan's *Pilgrim's Progress,* falls, is now hackneyed.

sloven and **slattern** are closely related in their meanings. A *sloven* may be either male or female. It is one who is habitually negligent of neatness or cleanliness, one who is through negligence dirty and untidy (*General Patton, something of a dandy himself, tolerated no slovens in his army*). The word also means one who works, or does anything, in a negligent, slipshod manner (*What damned sloven left the mop lying there on the stairs, to break a body's neck!*). *Slattern* is narrower in reference. It means a slovenly, untidy woman or girl (*Her mother was a partial, ill-judging parent, a dawdle, a slattern . . . whose house was the scene of mismanagement and discomfort from beginning to end.* Come Back Little Sheba *is a moving treatment of a slattern*). See also **slut.**

slow; slowly. The form *slow* may be used as an adjective, as in *a slow train.* Either form may be used as an adverb.

The form *slow* has been used to qualify a verb, as in *how slow this old moon wanes,* for at least four hundred years. Even if this were not the case, road signs everywhere reading *drive slow* indicate that the word *slow* is standard English in this construction. This is because "standard English" means the English spoken by the responsible people in the community or nation. No other standard can be set up for a language. *Drive slowly* may also be

used, but anyone who claims that this is "better grammar" misunderstands the nature of language. And in this particular case, he is also unfamiliar with English literature over the past four hundred years.

slug is used in more senses in the United States than in England. In both countries it designates the shell-less, snail-like creature or anything that moves sluggishly, or a piece of lead or other metal for firing from a gun. As a noun *slug* was used in America, colloquially, to designate a coin. At the time of the California gold rush (1859) a slug was a $50 gold coin and these coins, with the same popular name, were made again in 1915 for the Panama-Pacific Exposition. In recent contemporary American usage, the most common meaning of the noun *slug* was a piece of metal shaped like a nickel used in place of a nickel in public telephones and mechanical vending devices. Since Congress outlawed the use of these slugs in 1944, however, the word in this sense has fallen into disuse.

Slug may also mean a drink or dram of liquor. This sense has died out in England, but it is common in America (*He always took a slug of whiskey just before he went onstage*). In the vocabulary of printers, in America and England, *slug* means a thick strip of type metal less than type-high, such a strip containing a type-high number, etc. for temporary use, or a line of type in one piece, as produced by a linotype machine.

Americans also use *slug* colloquially as a verb meaning to strike heavily, to hit hard, especially with a heavy club or blunt instrument (*Somebody slugged him from behind just as he went to turn on the light*). The verb may have derived from hitting with a slug, a piece of lead, but this etymology is conjectural. The English prefer *slog,* a variant of *slug,* to convey this idea. Both English and Americans use *slog* to mean to walk or plod heavily, as with burdened feet through mire.

slumber is not simply an elegant variation of *sleep.* It characterizes the sleep as light or fitful (*Behold, he that keepeth Israel shall neither slumber nor sleep. From carelessness it shall fall into slumber, and from a slumber it shall settle into a deep and long sleep*). By extension, *slumber* may describe a state of inactivity, quiescence (*Most German consciences lay in a slumber from 1933 until 1945*).

slung. See **sling.**

slunk. See **slink.**

slur, as a verb, means to pass over lightly, or without due mention or consideration. In this use it is often followed by *over* (*He slurred over his own responsibility for the failure of the venture*). It also means to pronounce a syllable or a word indistinctly, as in hurried or careless utterance (*They slur their consonants so! It's just a slack-mouthed drooling of pale vowels!*). In music, to *slur* is to sing to a single syllable, without a break, two tones of different pitch, or to mark with a slur. In the United States *slur* is also still used, in a sense archaic in England, to mean calumniate, disparage, or depreciate (*Like many great man, he has been slurred by the very people he helped*). The American idiomatic expression, *to cast* or *throw slurs at*, is the equivalent of the English *to put a slur on*.

slut is a dirty, slovenly woman. It is a much stronger and more offensive word than *slattern* (*q.v.*). Though in its ordinary use conveying the strongest disapprobation, it is—or more often was—like many terms of derogation, sometimes employed affectionately (*Our little girl Susan is a most admirable slut, and pleases us mightily*). In America in the nineteenth century, when dogs were much in evidence but the word *bitch* considered unspeakable in mixed company, the term was applied to the female dog. *Dog* was the word for the male and *slut* for the female (*The dog-pup and the slut-pup. The dog was of a dingy red color and the slut was black*). This usage was adopted in England but never became as fixed there as in the United States. And it may be this association that gives the word *slut* today a more derogatory sense in America than in England. In England it is simply a strong term for a slattern. In American use it means now primarily a woman of loose character, being almost as condemnatory as *whore*.

sly. American and English spelling differ in regard to the comparative and superlative forms of *sly*. American usage prefers *slyer* and *slyest* but permits *slier* and *sliest*. English usage permits *slyer* and *slyest* only.

small. See **limited.**

small fry. *Fry* are properly seed or offspring, especially with reference to human beings. The murderer in *Macbeth* calls Macduff's son a *young fry of treachery* as he stabs him. The word is usually employed in a collective sense to designate a swarm, as of children or any small animals, especially now of fish. In this sense it is plural (*What a fry of fools are here*). It is heard today chiefly in the expression *small fry*, which means young or small fish or unimportant objects or young and unimportant persons. For the most part this is plural, as in Steig's cartoons, so named, which depict the doings of young persons collectively. However, especially humorously in direct address, it is used in the singular; and with such precedent as the quotation from Shakespeare given above (if it applies solely to the one child, for several others were killed) it cannot be very severely condemned.

smallpox. This word has a plural form. The singular would be *pock*. But today it is regularly treated as a singular. We say *it is contagious*, not *they are contagious*. The use of the article, as in *the smallpox*, is countrified or old-fashioned. The form *smallpox* is used as the first element in a compound, as in *a smallpox vaccine*.

It is a grim reminder of the former ravages of syphilis, the *pox* or *great pox*, that this dread disease was only the *small* pox.

smart is a word more often used, and used in more ways, by Americans than by the English. It has been long established in American usage in the sense of shrewd or sharp, as of a person dealing with others, with a distinct connotation of admiration for such shrewdness (*He's a mighty smart business man, Henry is!*). As a synonym for *sensible* it has become a vogue word (*The smart thing would be to take the ferry; you can't rely on the planes in this weather*) that the discriminating will eschew.

Both English and Americans use *smart* to mean dashingly or effectively neat or trim in appearance, as persons in their dress, or to mean the socially elegant or fashionable (*That's really smart, worn that way! All the smart set left the city for the summer*). Americans more often than English use *smart* to mean impudent (*Don't get smart with me, young man, or I'll slap your face*), especially in speaking to children. *Smart aleck*, an American term for an obnoxiously conceited and impudent person, especially in situations where his conceitedness (for the term is applied almost exclusively to males) leads him to make unwelcome amatory overtures, is now a little old-fashioned. It is replaced by the humorous, less disparaging, slang term *smarty pants* which is applied to young people of either sex.

smell. The past tense is *smelled* or *smelt*. The participle is also *smelled* or *smelt*. In the United States *smelled* is the preferred form for the past tense and the participle. In Great Britain *smelt* is preferred.

Smell may be followed by an adjective describing the source of the smell, as in *it smelt so faint and it smelt so sweet* and in *supper smells good*. When used in this way *smell* is not followed by the adverb *well*. We do not say *it smells well*. But it is frequently used with other adverbs, as in *it smelled faintly, it smelled sweetly*. Many people find these constructions objectionable but others, equally well educated, do not. When used with a personal subject, *smell* may be qualified by any adverb, as in *I can smell it well*.

smell; stink. *Stink*, the good old-fashioned, established word for a foul, disgusting, or offensive smell, has, apparently, absorbed something of the quality it describes and is no longer considered a polite word. The euphemism (for stinks remain whether *stink* is polite or not) is *smell*, formerly a neutral word. But *smell*, like most euphemisms, has suffered contagion and unless qualified by a favorable adjective definitely means an unpleasant smell, though not so unpleasant a smell as a stink. The facetious figurative use of *stink* to mean a row or a protest, especially one following on the disclosure of something disgraceful that has been hidden, is not standard. See also **odor.**

smell a rat. As a term for suspecting something to be wrong, especially something dangerous or disgraceful that has been concealed, to *smell a rat* is somewhat musty.

smelt. See **smell.**

smite. The past tense is *smote*. The participle is *smitten*. A past tense *smit* and a participle *smited* were once literary English but are now archaic or dialectal.

smooch, a facetious term in the brighter young set for kissing, is not the slang term they probably think it is but a good old English word, much used by the brighter young Elizabethans (*I had rather than a bend of leather/ She and I might smouch together*—1600). Philip Stubbes, in his *Anatomy of Abuses* (1583), condemned dancing around the maypole as merely offering opportunities for *clipping . . . culling . . . kissing . . . smouching and slabbering of one another . . . filthy groping and unclean handling. . . .*

smote. See **smite.**

snake in the grass. As a term for a treacherous person, especially a treacherous or ungrateful friend, *a snake in the grass,* even though used chiefly in humor, is a cliché.

snarl. In the sense of bringing into a tangled condition, the verb *snarl,* which survives in England only in dialect, is current in America. Literally it means to get something all tangled up, as thread or hair. Figuratively, it means to render complicated or confused (*He had his instructions all snarled up*). *Unsnarled* is more commonly heard than *snarled.* As a noun, *snarl* means a tangle or, figuratively, a confused condition (*There was a bad traffic snarl at Randolph and Michigan*). Both verb and noun are used so much in relation to bad traffic conditions that they may become specialized in that sense.

snicker; snigger. Americans use *snicker* to mean to laugh in a half-suppressed, often indecorous or disrespectful manner (*A few students snickered as he stumbled on the step*). The English regard *snicker* as obsolescent and in its stead use the variant *snigger.* Both words may be used also as nouns to describe a half-suppressed laugh.

snout. See **nozzle.**

snuffer. The object used for snuffing out candles was once called *a snuffer* and treated as a singular. But today it is usually spoken of in the plural, as in *these snuffers are very old.* To use the word with a singular verb or to speak of more than one of these things, we say *this pair of snuffers is very old* or *several pairs of snuffers.* The singular form is still preferred as the first element in a compound, as in *a snuffer tray.*

so may be used as an adverb or as a conjunction.

When used to qualify a verb, *so* may mean "in the manner described," as in *so I did, love, so I do.*

It may be used to qualify the positive form of an adverb or of an adjective that does not stand before a noun. It was once possible to say *the so heavy burden thou bearest,* but in current English the adjective must stand alone or be separated from the noun by the word *a,* as in *the message was so insulting* and *so insulting a message.*

When qualifying an adjective or an adverb, the primary meaning of *so* is "to this extent," as in *it wasn't so cold yesterday.* With this meaning the word can only be used in a question or in a negative statement. When used in an affirmative statement it becomes a mere intensive and means "to an unusually high degree," as in *it was so cold yesterday.* It may also have this meaning when it qualifies a verb, as in *I love you so.*

So may be used with *as* in making a comparison, as in *it is not so large as mine.* Here again, *so* is restricted to questions and negative statements. We cannot say *it is so large as mine.* The words *as . . . as,* on the other hand, have no such limitation. Most writers prefer *as . . . as* to *so . . . as* even in a negative statement and use *so* in a comparison only when they want to stress the idea of a very high degree. See **as.**

So may be followed by *that* introducing a clause of purpose or result, as in *they hurried so that they would be on time* and *they were so close that I heard every word.* In the United States the *that* may be omitted from a sentence of this kind, as in *they hurried so they would be on time* and *they were so close I heard every word.* Formerly *as* could be used in place of *that,* as in *they had guards so posted as they were not to be surprised,* and *many came unto them from diverse parts of England, so as they grew a great congregation,* but this construction is no longer considered standard. In current English an infinitive must be used with *so . . . as* in order to express purpose or result, as in *they hurried so as to be on time* and *be so kind as to shut the door.*

Formerly *so* could be used in the sense of "if only" or "provided that," as in *we forgive much ill treatment, so it is secret.* This use of *so* is now considered affected. The similar use of *so as* or *so that* is considered unacceptable, as in *I don't care, so as you get them off* and *she did not care what she did so that it made some changes in her life.* Today the proprieties demand *so long as* in these sentences.

So is often used to introduce a conclusion and then has the force of "therefore," as in *you advised me to go, and so I went.* This is standard English. It may also be used to indicate mere sequence in time, as in *and so to bed.* This use of the word as a loose connective is now rare among educated people.

so to speak. Unless one has employed some extraordinary figure or some justified but startling periphrasis or in some way deviated to such a degree from the accepted modes of expression that an apology or at least an expression of one's awareness of what one has done is felt to be desirable, *so to speak* should not be used. It is a hackneyed and usually pompous interjection. If a figure is employed, it should be so apt and comprehensible that no apology is needed, especially since the sole purpose of using a figure is to make the meaning clearer. If an expression is so obscure and confusing that it will require an apology, it is better not to use it.

soak in certain figurative senses is peculiar to American slang. It may mean to beat hard, to punish (*Don't you let any of 'em give you any lip. If they do, soak 'em*), though this is being generally replaced by *sock*. Its commonest use is as a slang word meaning to charge exorbitantly (*Thirty cents for a cup of coffee! Boy, they really soak you in that joint!*). *Soak* used also to mean to put in pawn (*I've often soaked my watch when I was hard up*), but this is now obsolescent even as slang.

sober as a judge. A judge should certainly be a pattern of sobriety, certainly in the literal sense and probably in the extended meaning of being grave and of solemn mien, but the phrase *sober as a judge* is a hackneyed comparison.

sobriquet. See **nickname.**

sociable; social. As adjectives these words agree in being concerned with the mutual relations of mankind living in an organized society. *Social* is the general word, meaning pertaining to, devoted to, or characterized by friendly companionship or relations (*There is a danger of interpreting the social life of animals in too human terms. Because he worked hard he had little time for social life. Does the scientist, as a scientist, have any social obligations?*). *Social* seldom applies to persons, but *sociable* usually does. It means fond of company and society, companionable, genial, and affable (*He couldn't be sociable until he'd had a couple of drinks*). A social evening is one spent enjoyably in the company of others at a more or less formal event; a sociable evening is one spent companionably with perhaps only one person or a few. A social obligation is something the individual owes to society as a whole. A sociable obligation would be something due to sociability.

As nouns *social* and *sociable* both designate an informal social gathering, especially one held under the auspices of a church (*a church social, a church sociable*). Of the two words *sociable,* in this meaning, is now obsolescent, being replaced by *social.*

social butterfly, as a term for a gay young creature (usually a young lady) who flutters excitedly without much serious thought from one party to another, is a cliché. As much a cliché as *social whirl* for the collective parties of a season, a place, or a set.

social position and language. Languages are made by groups of people, not by isolated individuals, and so it is inevitable that the language we speak and the way we speak will show what sort of people we habitually associate with.

The great differences in language are, of course, geographical. The people in France do not speak like the people in Germany and the people in Maine do not speak like the people in Louisiana. Inside a particular area there are also speech differences which reflect different social or economic groups. The speech of the most admired group is ordinarily called "standard."

Social groups may differ in their pronunciation. This is true in England where the children of the upper classes do not go to the same schools that other children go to, and so learn to speak very differently. For example, upper-class Englishmen slur their speech more than the lower classes do. They elide or drop many vowels which the lower classes pronounce. In the speech of the English upper classes *secretary,* for instance, has three syllables and not four, and *medicine* and *venison* have two syllables and not three.

In the United States, where children from all kinds of homes go to the same schools, pronunciation is almost entirely a matter of geographical difference; though it is probably true that these differences are more marked in the speech of the uneducated than in the speech of the educated.

In the United States there are certain forms of speech—certain grammatical constructions, such as *he don't* and *we ain't* and *yous*—that are used only by the uneducated. Such constructions are called "mistakes" or "unacceptable" English or (by linguists) "substandard" or "nonstandard." (See **Standard English.**) There are not as many of these, however, as most people imagine. Charles Fries, certainly one of the greatest students of American English, has made a scientific study of this problem (*American English Grammar: The grammatical structure of present-day American English with especial reference to social differences or class dialects*). He says: ". . . the differences between the language of the educated and that of those with little education did not lie primarily in the fact that the former used one set of forms and the latter an entirely different set. . . . The most striking difference between the language of the two groups lay in the fact that the Vulgar English seems essentially poverty stricken. It uses less of the resources of the language, and a few forms are used very frequently. *Get,* for example, in its many senses appears in both the Standard English and the Vulgar English materials, but it is employed ten times as frequently [by the uneducated as by the educated]. . . . In vocabulary and in grammar is the mark of the language of the uneducated is its poverty."

society; Society. The general word is *society.* It means a body of individuals living as members of a community; the body of human beings generally associated or viewed as members of a community; human beings collectively regarded as a body divided into classes according to worldly status (*He came from the middle class of society in a small town*); the condition of those living in companionship with others, or in a community, rather than in isolation (*Thomas Henry Huxley believed that society was man's gallant protest against nature*).

Capitalized, *Society* is a restricted term. It commonly suggests the social relations, activities, or life of the polite or fashionable world; the body of those associated in the polite or fashionable world; the rich upper class (*Edith Wharton and Thorstein Veblen agree that Society is a conspicuous display of wealth*). The capitalized form of the word may also appear as part of the name of an organization or persons associated together for religious, benevolent, literary, scientific, political, patriotic, or other purposes (*The Royal Society was formed for the purpose of encouraging the advancement of scientific learning*).

Socratic irony is the assumption of ignorance for the purpose of leading (or misleading) another into an untenable, absurd or embarrassing position in discussion. This kind of disingenuousness was practiced by Socrates in his arguments with the Sophists. The irony lies in the discrepancy between the stated ignorance and the true knowledge.

By assuming ignorance, Socrates was able to unmask pretentiousness in others and to indulge his own sense of humor while doing so.

Socratic irony is a device often employed in satire for the opportunity it provides of disarming an adversary and then ambushing him. From Chaucer to Aldous Huxley, it has been a favorite device of the English satirists.

There is no such term as *Socratic luck,* but there ought to be. For whereas his victims always gave him the exact answer that enabled him to proceed to the next step in his course of reasoning, anyone who has ever tried the Socratic method in the classroom knows that this rarely happens. If one feigns ignorance, the student eagerly and sincerely agrees. When his contradictions are pointed out to him, he is unable to perceive them. Most teachers soon abandon all attempts at such subtle teaching.

soft; softly. *Softly* is always used as an adverb, as in *I will lead on softly. Soft* is ordinarily used as an adjective, as in *a soft answer turneth away wrath.* But *soft* may also be used as an adverb if placed before the subject of the verb. *Soft* has both functions in *soft went the music the soft air along.*

soft place in one's heart. As a way of saying that one is inclined favorably towards someone, with overtones of affection, to say one has *a soft place in one's heart* for him is to employ a cliché.

sold. See **sell.**

solecism. A solecism is a violation of grammatical structure or idiom, the intrusion of an unaccepted form into standard speech.

solicitor in England is one properly qualified and formally admitted to practice as a law-agent. His services consist of advising clients, representing them before the lower courts, and preparing cases for barristers to try in the higher courts. The American equivalent for *solicitor* in this sense is *lawyer.* In America a *solicitor* is one who solicits trade or personal attention. The term may be applied loosely to a salesman, a peddler, canvasser, or beggar. It is so used to some extent in England also. In some American towns the officer who has charge of the town's legal business is called the solicitor. See also **attorney.**

solid; stolid. *Solid* means having three dimensions, with the interior completely filled up (*a* solid ivory ball), without openings or breaks (*The walls were solid, not a crack to be seen*), uniform in tone or shade (*The car was painted a solid black*). Figuratively, when applied to persons, *solid* may mean sober-minded, sensible (*a solid citizen*); when applied to groups, unanimous, united in opinion (*General Eisenhower was the first Republican to crack the solid South*). In American slang *solid* may mean "on a friendly, favorable, or advantageous footing," especially in the phrase *in solid* (*To win the daughter, he got in solid with the mother*). Applied to the playing of jazz music, as a slang word, *solid* means vigorous, exciting, hard-driving, fast.

Stolid has only one sense. It means not easily moved or stirred mentally; impassive, as from dullness or stupidity.

solidarity; solidity. *Solidarity* is primarily a social term. It means union or fellowship arising from common responsibilities and interests, as between members of a class or body of persons, or between classes (*The war reconciled all factions and gave us as a nation a solidarity we had not had during the depression*). *Solidity* is primarily a physical term, meaning the state, property, or quality of being solid, of possessing substantialness. In geometry it means the amount of space occupied by a solid body, or volume. In a figurative sense, applied to persons, it means strength of mind, character, or finances.

soliloquy. See **dialogue.**

solo. The plural is *solos* or *soli.*

some. This word is used in order to speak of particular quantities, persons, or things, without specifying what ones. It may be used as an adjective before a singular or a plural noun, as in *some man, some butter, some books.* When used before a number word it means "approximately," as in *some six or seven men, it was some thirty years ago.* It may also be used alone as a pronoun, as in *I have some here* and *some say.* The pronoun may refer indefinitely to human beings. When not used in this way it must represent a word mentioned previously. It may be treated as a singular when it represents a mass noun, as in *"Where is the butter?" "There is some in the kitchen";* otherwise, the pronoun is always plural. The phrase *some of us* requires the pronoun *our* and not *their,* as in *some of us lost our heads;* and the phrase *some of you* requires *your.*

Some may be used as an adverb of extent to qualify a verb, as in *"Do you play golf?" "Some."* This use of the word is standard in the United States but not in Great Britain. *Some* used with the same meaning before the comparative form of an adjective, as in *he is some better today,* is a Scottish idiom, and the word *somewhat* is preferred in this country and in England. *Some* used merely to indicate approval, as in *my dog is some dog!* and *that's going some!,* is slang. It has never been standard in the United States but is accepted in Great Britain as an interesting Americanism. See also **few; part.**

somebody; someone. These words are always treated as singulars and used with a singular verb, as in *somebody is coming.* When it isn't known whether "somebody" is a man or a woman, forms of the pronoun *they* can be used instead of forms of *he* in referring to this individual, as in *somebody left their umbrella.* This device is used less often with *someone,* but is also acceptable with this word.

somehow; somehows. The only acceptable form is *somehow. Somehows* is unacceptable.

someone. See **somebody.**

someplace. The use of *someplace* as a substitute for *somewhere,* as in *I left it someplace,* is condemned by many grammarians because the noun *place* is here being used instead of the adverb *where.* This usage is not acceptable in Great Britain but it occurs too often in the United States, in written as well as in spoken English, to be called anything but standard. It is acceptable English in this country.

somersault; somerset. *Somersault* is the best word to describe an acrobatic movement of the body in which it describes a complete revolution, heels over head, or, figuratively, a complete overturn or reversal, as of opinion. As an intransitive verb, *somersault* means to perform a somersault. *Somerset* is an obsolescent and dialectal British variant. *Summersault* is a variant American spelling, as is *summerset.*

something; somewhat. Originally these words meant the same thing and could be used interchangeably. Either could be used as an indefinite pronoun or as an adverb of degree.

Either form may still be used in a statement implying a comparison, as in *he is something* (or *somewhat*) *like his father* and *the house was built something* (or *somewhat*) *more than a century ago.* Either form may be used before *of a,* as in *it was something* (or *somewhat*) *of an adventure.*

In any other construction the form *somewhat* is required for an adverb of degree. That is, *something* is now obsolete or dialectal when used to qualify a verb, as in *it something surprises me,* or as a purely descriptive adjective, as in *it sounded something awful.* On the other hand, *something* is the required form for the indefinite pronoun, and *somewhat* is now obsolete or dialectal when used in this way, as in *you can do somewhat* (or *some'at*) *for me.*

something in the wind. As a way of saying that preparations, usually of a menacing kind, are being made, even though one is uncertain about their nature or purpose, *there is something in the wind* is a cliché. It is drawn from observation of an animal scenting danger.

something rotten in the State of Denmark. Marcellus' fear that something was rotten in the state of Denmark proved to be well founded: the king murdered, the queen seduced, the heir cheated, the courtiers drunk, the councillor senile, invasion threatened, spies planted, ghosts abroad, and even the visiting actors a little uncertain of their lines—rotten indeed! But the quotation itself (slightly misquoted usually—

the original is *Something is rotten in the state of Denmark* not *There's something rotten in the state of Denmark*) is now stale, flat, and unprofitable and gives off a faint odor of decay all its own.

sometime; sometimes. In current English the form *sometimes* is felt as a plural and is used to mean "at times" or "now and then," as in *he comes here sometimes.* The form *sometime,* on the other hand, is felt as a singular and is used to refer to one unspecified time, as in *he will come sometime.*

Historically, these words are adverbs and do not have a singular or a plural form, any more than the word *soon* does. The final *s* in *sometimes* was simply an adverbial sign similar to the *s* in *backwards* and *endways.* The form *sometime* once meant "formerly" and in this sense could be used before a noun, as in *our sometime sister, now our queen.* This use of the word survives in England, but only in a few set phrases, such as *sometime fellow.* In current English *one-time* is preferred in this sense.

someway; someways; somewise. In the United States *someway* is used as the equivalent of *somehow,* as in *I will get one someway.* This is standard English in this country. *Someways* is not heard so often and does not have the same standing. In England both forms are considered uneducated and *somehow* is required. (When *ways* is part of a prepositional phrase, such as *in some ways he is a fool,* it is not being used as the equivalent of *somehow* and is standard everywhere.) *Somewise* is acceptable English, but it is not often heard in the United States.

somewhat. See **something.**

somewhen, though unusual, is acceptable. It has been in use since at least 1297.

somewhere; somewheres. *Somewhere* is the only acceptable form in written English. In the United States *somewheres* is often heard in the speech of well educated people, but it does not appear in print.

Somewhere is sometimes used with an unnecessary *that,* as in *somewhere that I have been.* This is not as well established as the similar use of *anywhere,* but it is acceptable to many educated people in the United States.

sonata. The plural is *sonatas,* not *sonatae.*

soon. See **early.**

sop to Cerberus. Cerberus was the three-headed dog that guarded the entrance to the infernal regions in Greek mythology. In Vergil's *Aeneid* he was put to sleep by being flung "a morsel drowsy with honey and drugged meal" which he caught "in his triple throat in ravenous hunger." As a term for appeasing someone formidable, giving him a bribe or a promise as a means of persuading him to relax his vigilance and hostility, to keep him quiet if only for a moment, giving *a sop to Cerberus* is a cliché, sustained for centuries by its alliteration.

soprano. The plural is *sopranos* or *soprani.*

sorry; afraid; fear; regret. *I'm afraid* and *I fear* are often used as elegant expressions of regret. When a man says *I'm afraid I'll have to go now,* he does not intend to imply any element or even pretense of fear. If he is vain he may be saying, in an elliptical fashion, "I am afraid you will be disappointed when I tell you that I must leave." If he is realistic, he may be saying "I am afraid you will not be disappointed when I tell you that I must leave." The unambiguous statement, *I'm sorry that I must go* or *I regret that I must go* is better. If that seems too hypocritical, *I must go* will do.

sort of. This expression is exactly equivalent to *kind of*. It is used in exactly the same ways and open to the same objections. We may say *this sort of tree is* or *these sort of trees are* or, if we are speaking of more than one sort, *these sorts of trees are* or *these sorts of tree are*. *Sort of a* is frequently condemned but is used by some our best writers, including Henry Adams. *Sort of* before an adjective or a verb, as in *it is sort of chilly* and *he sort of stumbled*, is condemned even more strongly than *sort of a*, but can be heard in the speech of the most highly educated people. For a fuller treatment see **kind of.**

sot. See **drunkard** and **set.**

sotto voce is a pretty highfalutin term for "in a low tone of voice." It is an Italian expression meaning literally "under voice," that is, under the normal voice level. It is better to express the meaning in English.

sought. See **seek.**

soul of honor. To describe a just, honest, or honorable man as *the soul of honor* or *the very soul of honor* is to employ a hackneyed phrase.

sound. This verb, meaning to make a sound, may be followed by an adjective describing what it is that sounds, as in *it sounds good*. It may also be followed by an adverb, as in *it sounds well*. Often there is no difference in meaning between these two constructions, but many people feel that the adjective, *good,* stresses the *it* and that the adverb, *well,* stresses *sounds*. This is certainly the case with other adverbs, such as *nicely, faintly, sweetly,* and so on.

Out is acceptable but unnecessary in the phrase *sound out* since *to sound* here means measure or try the depth of, to examine or investigate, to seek to fathom (*They sounded the Governor's views on the matter*), to seek to elicit the views or sentiments of a person by indirect inquiries or suggestive allusions. (For *sleep sound,* see **sleep.**)

sour grapes, applied to someone who is belittling something which he once wanted but was unable to obtain, is hackneyed. The phrase is drawn from Aesop's fable of the fox which, unable to reach some grapes, said he did not want them anyway because they were sour.

source; cause. A *source* is a *cause,* but all causes are not sources, for *source* means origin, first cause (*Pride, ill-nature, and want of good sense are the three great sources of bad manners*).

south; southern. The comparative form is *more southern*. The superlative form is *southmost* or *southernmost*.

sow. The past tense is *sowed*. The participle is *sowed* or *sown*.

sow one's wild oats. As a term for youthful dissipation (usually with a suggestion that there will be or was a later reform) *sowing one's wild oats,* in use for at least four hundred years, is now a cliché.

sox is a variant spelling of *socks*. It is not the standard form in England or in the United States.

spa derives from Spa, or Spaa, a resort town in East Belgium. southeast of Liège, which has famous mineral springs. Hence *spa* means a mineral spring or a locality in which such springs exist, especially when sanatoriums and resort hotels have been built in the vicinity (*Tunbridge Wells was a fashionable spa. Mr. Dombey and the Major visited Leamington Spa*). The name is widely used in England and has been adopted to some extent in the United States where it is, as in England, sometimes incorporated into a place name (*At Ballston Spa in upstate New York atomic power has just provided the first electricity for domestic uses*). Usually, however, a mineral spring is called simply a *spring* in the United States and this, too, is incorporated into some place names (*Warm Springs, Georgia; White Sulphur Springs*). In New England, *spa* may designate a drug store or other place where soft drinks are served.

spake. See **speak.**

span. See **spin.**

Spaniards; Spanish. Perhaps because of England's long struggle with Spain, the standard name for these people, a *Spaniard* or *the Spaniards,* has the derogatory formation seen in *coward, sluggard, drunkard,* and so on. This formation is no longer active in English and no derogatory tone is now felt in *Spaniard* or *Spaniards*. These are the only terms used in speaking of one or more individuals. But in speaking of the people of Spain as a whole, *the Spanish* seems to be replacing *the Spaniards*. At present both forms are acceptable.

spare no pains. As a phrase urging unstinted effort, or as an assurance that something has been carefully executed, *spare no pains* and *no pains have been spared* are clichés.

spark plug. The device inserted in the cylinder of an internal-combustion engine, containing the two terminals between which passes the electric spark for igniting the explosive gases, is called in the United States a *spark plug,* in England a *sparking-plug*. *Spark plug* is also used colloquially in America in a figurative sense to mean one who leads the activities or maintains the morale of a group (*Every ball team needs a spark plug or two to play its best ball*). *Spark plug* in this sense is also sometimes used as a verb, and abbreviated to *spark* (*There always has to be some one energetic man to spark these drives*).

spat. See **spit.**

spate, originally a Scotch word, is, strictly, a sudden flood or freshet, as in a river after heavy rains (*The Avon, in spate with heavy rains, was a muddy yellow. Whole spawning beds are swept away by spates*). In this, its literal sense, the word is more in use in England than in America. But in a figurative sense, of something excessive—and usually undesirable—that has come in a rush, sweeping all before it, the word has become a vogue word in America in the past few years and is often used where *rush* would be more suitable or even so mild a term as *many* or *several*. In such a phrase as *a spate of vituperation*, the idea of a suddenly overwhelming flood, as of muddy water, furiously sweeping all before it, is good. But in *It* ["White Christmas"] *includes a spate of Irving Berlin tunes, number* would have been more accurate and more appropriate.

speak. The past tense is *spoke*. The participle is *spoken*. An old form of the past tense, *spake*, is now archaic and found only in poetry.

speak of the Devil! The English say *talk of the Devil*. As an exclamation, usually uttered in boisterous jocularity, to hail the sudden appearance of someone who has just been the topic of talk, *speak* (or *talk*) *of the Devil* is a cliché. It is a fragment of the old proverb, *speak of the Devil and he's sure to appear*. In some versions it was *speak of the wolf and he's sure to appear*.

speaking terms. Whether used positively to indicate a slight acquaintance or negatively to indicate a coldness so extreme as to prevent the exchange of even simple civilities, *on speaking terms* is hackneyed.

special; especial; specially; especially. The adverbs *specially* and *especially* are equally acceptable today. *Specially* is the better word when what is meant is "specifically, particularly" and *especially* when what is meant is "chiefly, outstandingly." But this distinction is not followed strictly. There is the same difference in meaning between *special* and *especial*, but in the United States *special* is natural English in both meanings and *especial* is rarely heard.

special; particular; specific. That is *special* which receives, or which in someone's estimation ought to receive, unusual attention or treatment because it is uncommon (*He is a special friend of mine*). That is *particular* which has been selected from others of its kind for attention (*May I show you the particular paragraph to which I object?*). When we say of someone, however, that he is "not particular," we do not mean that he is unworthy of attention but that he does not single out details or small points as objects of concern or criticism. *Specific* implies the clear, unambiguous indication of a particular instance or example (*In the charge of disloyalty it was specifically alleged that on July 21, 1944, he had passed a confidential document to the agent of a foreign power*).

special delivery. That form of delivering mail which in the United States is called *special delivery* is in England called *express delivery*.

speciality; specialty. As the word to describe a special or particular character, or a special or distinctive quality or characteristic, a peculiarity, a special point or item, or a special subject of study, special line of work, or the like, the English prefer *speciality*, the Americans *specialty* (*Elegance was not then a specialty of pugilists but Gentleman Jim was suave. We make a specialty of hard-to-clean garments. Although Samuel Johnson was his specialty, he found himself teaching Chaucer*).

specie; species. *Specie* is a collective noun meaning coin or coined money (*The earliest coinage of specie is attributed to the Lydians. Checks and paper money were not accepted; payment had to be made in specie*). The word has no plural and cannot be used with the definite article, *a* or a numeral. If in some strange context it should be necessary to refer to the different specie of different countries, or to use a plural in some other way, the form would still be *specie*.

Species, which is also the form for both singular and plural, means a class of individuals having some common characteristics or qualities. It is the basic category of biological classification, intended to designate a single kind of animal or plant, any variations existing among the individuals being regarded as not affecting the essential sameness which distinguishes them from all other organisms (*College professors, on the whole, form a pretty poor species of speaker. The most important scientific publication of the nineteenth century was Darwin's great work on the origin of species*).

These words are often confused and the confusion is increased by the fact that in the eighteenth century *species* was used for *specie* (*Necker affirmed that . . . there was coined at the mint of France, in the species of gold and silver . . .—Burke. Species . . . is of easier conveyance—Garrick*) and the fact that there is a Latin phrase, *in specie*, meaning "in kind," sometimes used by English writers (*You must pay him* in specie, *Madam; give him love for his wit. These things must be exactly proportioned, as well in* specie *as in degree*).

specimen. See **example.**

specious originally meant fair, beautiful, pleasing to the sight, resplendent (*There is thy Savior . . . looking like a specious bridegroom—1675*) and this meaning, now obsolete, persisted down into the nineteenth century. A modification of this meaning—that is, having a fair appearance but actually being devoid of the qualities apparently possessed—which arose in the seventeenth century gained currency and displaced the earlier meaning. And this is now the meaning of the word. A specious appearance is something fair-seeming but in reality not at all what it appears to be. A specious statement is plausible and pleasant, but insincere. A specious argument sounds convincing, but it is in reality sophistical or fallacious. A specious person is one whose conduct, words, and actions all seem good but are not.

The cynicism or sad experience that led to this change continues its work and the word is often used now as if it meant evil or wicked or wrong. It is rarely applied to physical appearances any more but almost always to words, intentions, moral matters, etc. But this usage (which would completely reverse the older meaning) is, at the present stage of the word's development, erroneous. It has to designate something that at least seems convincing, desirable, good in some way. It cannot mean patently false, obviously evil, plainly insincere or dishonest.

spectacle. See **sight.**

spectacles. When this word means eyeglasses, the plural form refers to one object but is always treated as a plural, as in *these spectacles are weak.* In order to use the word with a singular verb or to speak of more than one of them, it is necessary to say *this pair of spectacles is weak* or *several pairs of spectacles.* At one time the singular *spectacle* was used in speaking of the pair, as in *he wore a spectacle.* This is now obsolete, but the singular is still the preferred form for the first element of a compound, as in *a spectacle case.*

Nancy Mitford tells us that in England the use of *spectacles* is a distinct shibboleth of upper-class speech. This is not so in the United States.

spectrum. The plural is *spectrums* or *spectra.*

speed. The past tense is *sped* or *speeded.* The participle is also *sped* or *speeded.* In older English *sped* and *speeded* were used interchangeably. Today there is a tendency to use *speeded* when we mean "caused to speed." That is, we say *her glance sped from face to face, the bullet sped across the field,* but *the work was speeded up.* If we hear that a man sped through the town we only know that he passed through quickly. But if we are told that he speeded through, we assume that he was not traveling under his own power but was driving a car and that he was driving it faster than the law allowed.

speed the parting guest. The phrase *to speed the parting guest* meant originally to wish him Godspeed on his journey, to express the wish that God would watch over him on his journey and bring him speedily to his desired destination. The modern use of the phrase to mean to hasten the (de)parting (of the) guest is an amusing distortion—and a cliché.

spell. The past tense is *spelled* or *spelt.* The participle is also *spelled* or *spelt.* In the United States *spelled* is the preferred form for the past tense and the participle. In Great Britain *spelt* is preferred.

We may say *the word is spelled wrong* or *it is spelled right.* An *-ly* form is sometimes heard here, as in *it is spelled wrongly, it is spelled rightly.* This is considered unacceptable by some people. The form without *-ly* is generally preferred.

spell has several colloquial uses in the sense of "period." It means a continuous course or period of work or other activity (*When seas were heavy he used to take a spell at the wheel*); a turn, bout, fit, or period of anything experienced or occurring (*Just before he was to speak he had a sneezing spell*); a period of weather of a specified kind (*We can expect a spell of hot weather in early August*); an interval or space

of time, usually indefinite and short (*After you've rested a spell, we'll continue the climb*).

Spell is peculiarly American in a sense of a fit of some personal ailment, disturbance of the temper, or the like (*Addie has spells, you know. When she's having a bad spell, all you can do is to keep quiet*). *Spell* is also used, chiefly in the United States, as a transitive verb meaning to take the place of or to relieve a person for a time (*They spelled one another off through the night, one steering while the other got what sleep he could*).

spelt. See **spell.**

spend. The past tense is *spent.* The participle is also *spent.*

spend money like water. As a description of prodigal recklessness, *to spend money like water* is a worn-out comparison. So is to let money *run through your fingers.* So also is the saying, of one who is eager to spend his money, that it *burns a hole in his pocket.*

spent. See **spend.**

sperm. The plural is *sperm* or *sperms.* Before 1900 *sperm* was used only as a singular mass noun, as in *when sperm is developed.* An individual cell was called *a spermatozoön* and several of them, *spermatozoa.* Today *sperm* may also be used in speaking of an individual cell, as in *every sperm counts, and, in samples, is counted,* and as a true plural, as in *more than two million sperm were produced.* The plural *sperms* is also acceptable.

spermatozoa. This is a plural word and is always treated as a plural, as in *a hundred thousand spermatozoa.* The double plural *spermatozoae* is wrong. The learned singular is *spermatozoön,* but the singular *spermatozoan* is also acceptable, as is its English plural *spermatozoans.*

sphinx. The plural is *sphinxes* or *sphinges.*

spick and span, as a way of saying "neat and clean," is hackneyed. Until very recently the expression was *spick and span new* and *spick and span,* when used, was only a shortening of the longer expression which, in its turn, was an enlargement of a very old expression *span-new. Span* in this phrase meant chip, and the expression meant "as new as a chip of wood." It is cognate with *spoon,* for spoons were originally chips of wood, or, more likely, chips of wood were used for spoons and the name transferred. *Spick* (the same word as *spike*) meant a splinter. It was added to the expression *span-new* late in the sixteenth century, for no better reason, apparently, than alliteration. However, in matters of language formation that is one of the most compelling reasons there is.

spike someone's guns. A spike driven into the touchhole of a cannon, in the days when cannon were fired by being ignited at the touchhole, rendered it harmless and removed its threat. In its modern, figurative sense of depriving someone of his power or of blocking his way or of rendering his plans ineffectual, *to spike someone's guns* is a cliché.

spill. The past tense is *spilled* or *spilt.* The participle is also *spilled* or *spilt.* In the United States *spilled* is preferred for the past tense and the participle. In Great Britain *spilt* is preferred.

spin. The past tense is *spun*. The participle is also *spun*. An old past tense form *span,* known in the famous couplet *when Adam delved and Eve span, who was then the gentleman?* is no longer heard but was retained in common use in England as late as the nineteenth century.

spiritual and **spirituous,** though derived from a common source, mean different things. *Spiritual* means of, pertaining to, consisting of spirit or incorporeal being; of or pertaining to the spirit or soul as distinguished from the physical nature (*His agony was spiritual, not physical*); characterized by or suggesting predominance of the spirit (*His was a highly spiritual nature*); or ecclesiastical (*He was spiritual adviser to a large congregation*). *Spirituous* means containing, of the nature of, or pertaining to, alcohol; alcoholic (*At the reception spirituous beverages were served*). In reference to liquors, it means distilled as opposed to fermented.

spit. The past tense is *spit* or *spat*. The participle is also *spit* or *spat*. In the United States *spit* is the preferred form for the past tense and the participle, but *spat* is being used increasingly. In Great Britain *spat* is the only form heard.

The verb meaning "pierce with a spit" is quite regular and has the past tense and participle *spitted*.

spit and image. The common expression for one who closely resembles another is variously given as *spit and image, spitting image, spit 'n image* or *spitten image*. Many origins have been suggested. Some believe it to be a slurring of *spirit and image*. Some point out that there was formerly an expression "to be as much like someone as the spit out of his mouth." But the best explanation seems to be that it is the old word *spit,* meaning a likeness, usually a family likeness (*You're a queer fellow—the very spit of your father*) with "and image" added in America sometime in the nineteenth century. The term is a cliché.

splendid; excellent. *Splendid* ought to suggest splendor, magnificence, sumptuousness. Its use in the sense of excellent or very good (*A quiet little place, no show, no fuss, but a splendid meal!*) is regarded by most authorities as acceptable but overused.

split. The past tense is *split*. The participle is also *split*.

split infinitives. The notion that it is a grammatical mistake to place a word between *to* and the simple form of a verb, as in *to quietly walk away,* is responsible for a great deal of bad writing by people who are trying to write well. Actually the rule against "splitting an infinitive" contradicts the principles of English grammar and the practice of our best writers. The construction is a relatively new one, but it is found in the writings of Sir Philip Sidney, Sir Thomas Browne, Donne, Pepys, Defoe, Samuel Johnson, Burns, Wordsworth, Coleridge, Lamb, Byron, De Quincey, Macaulay, Holmes, Whittier, George Eliot, Carlyle, Browning, Arnold, Pater, Ruskin, Henry James, Hardy, Meredith,

Galsworthy, Conan Doyle, Kipling, Shaw—and Benjamin Franklin, Abraham Lincoln, Theodore Roosevelt, Woodrow Wilson, and Herbert Hoover.

The *to*-infinitive is actually the preposition *to* with the simple form of the verb as its object, as in *a need to investigate the matter*. Grammatically it is comparable to a preposition with an *-ing* form of the verb as object, as in *a need for investigating the matter*. (See **infinitives**.) In the case of the *-ing* form a qualifying word preferably stands between the preposition and the *-ing,* as in *a need for secretly investigating the matter*. When we have a composite verbal phrase the normal position for a qualifying word is between the first auxiliary and the meaningful form, as in *he decided he would secretly investigate the matter*. In either case, the qualifying word may be placed after the complete verbal statement, as in *for investigating the matter secretly* and *he would investigate the matter secretly*. But when it is placed late, it acquires a special emphasis. It would follow that the normal position for a word qualifying an infinitive would be before the verb form but after any auxiliary element, as in *he decided to secretly investigate the matter*.

The notion that the *to*-infinitive was an exception to the general rules of word order and could not be handled in this way dates from the latter part of the nineteenth century—the period when the split infinitive first came into general use. The construction can be found as early as the fourteenth century but it is rare before 1850. This is because the type of sentence in which one would have any occasion to split an infinitive was rare before that time. One of the outstanding characteristics of current English is the enormous increase in the use of the infinitive where previously an *-ing* form or a clause was preferred. That is, formerly men said *he decided that he would investigate* where today we would be more likely to say *he decided to investigate*.

In the clause construction we may qualify the verb and say *he decided that he would secretly investigate*. If the infinitive is to be used in place of the clause it must be capable of expressing the same distinctions. This requires the freedom to place a qualifying word or phrase immediately before the verb form. In *he decided to secretly investigate,* the word *secretly* qualifies the word *investigate*. If *secretly* is placed before *he* or before *decided* it qualifies *decided*. If it is placed before *to,* as in *he decided secretly to investigate,* it is ambiguous. It probably applies to *decided,* although it may apply to *investigate*. If it is placed later than *investigate* it becomes emphatic. Therefore, if we cannot place *secretly* between *to* and *investigate* we cannot use the infinitive to say what is said in the clause.

In English the negative adverbs, such as *not* and *never,* and the restrictive adverbs, such as *only* and *scarcely,* are characteristically moved forward in a sentence. Words of this kind may therefore stand before the *to* and still qualify the infinitive, as in *he decided never to investigate.* The writer who is determined never to split an infinitive must remember that, with the exception of negative or restrictive adverbs, the qualifying word cannot be placed earlier than the *to* or it will qualify the principal verb instead of the infinitive; and, if it is placed later than the infinitive, it acquires a special emphasis which may not be intended. Frequently the only way to avoid a split infinitive and still write good English is to avoid the infinitive—and, with the increasing use of the infinitive, avoiding the infinitive may lead to wordy paraphrases that are not good English.

Those who have no objection to splitting an infinitive should remember two things. (1) In a composite infinitive involving the auxiliary *be* or *have* and a participle, the normal position for the adverb is after the auxiliary and not before it. That is, *to have always thought* is the normal word order and *to always have thought* is a variation that adds special emphasis. (See **sentence adverbs.**) (2) Any number of words may stand between *to* and the verb form. Browning wrote: *a scheme to quietly next day at crow of cock cut my own throat.* This is exactly comparable to placing a large number of words between a preposition and its noun object, as Macaulay does in *principles independent of, and indeed almost incompatible with, the sentiment of devoted loyalty.* Such constructions may be used occasionally but are decidedly tiresome when they become a mannerism.

splutter; sputter. These words mean pretty much the same thing, except that *sputter* suggests more immediately the idea of spitting. The word means to emit particles of anything in an explosive manner; to eject particles of saliva or food from the mouth in an explosive manner. *Splutter* suggests most immediately to talk hastily and confusedly or incoherently, as in excitement or embarrassment (*He had turned purple in the face when McDonald's thumping on his back finally produced a great sputtering roar. The old colonel spluttered with rage as the soldiers dragged him from the room*). This distinction, however, is not hard and fast.

spoil. The past tense is *spoiled* or *spoilt.* The participle is also *spoiled* or *spoilt.* In the United States the form *spoiled* is preferred for the past tense and the participle. In Great Britain *spoiled* is also the preferred form in written English.

spoilage; spoliation; spoilation. *Spoilage* is the act of spoiling or that which is spoiled (*Failure to ice the refrigerator cars resulted in heavy spoilage*). In printing *spoilage* has the special meaning of paper spoiled or wasted in presswork.

Spoilation is not listed in most dictionaries, though it would seem to be a natural formation.

Spoliation is the act of spoiling, but properly and strictly of *de*spoiling—that is of plundering, pillaging (*This pillaging and spoliation of their ships and goods was furiously resented*). In law it means the intentional destruction of or

tampering with a document in such a way as to impair its value as evidence. William Allen White's use of *spoilation* (*An era of gorgeous spoilation, a time when bombast concealed larceny*) would seem, plainly, to be an erroneous substitution for *spoliation.* But since the acts to which he is referring took place under the system known as The Spoils System and since *spoliation* is not in the common reader's vocabulary and *spoils,* in this sense, is well known, it would be pedantic to say that he was not justified.

spoilt. See **spoil.**

spoke; spoken. See **speak.**

sport; sports. Both forms of this word are used in speaking of sport in general, and both forms are used as the first element in a compound, as in *a sport shirt* and *a sports shirt.* The form with a final *s* is required in a word referring to human beings, such as *sportsman, sports writer,* and is generally preferred in other compounds, such as *sports car.*

sports English. Many terms drawn from sports have entered into our speech and become so common that one is not always aware of their origin. From cockfighting come *well-heeled, crestfallen, yellow-streak* and *show the white feather.* From archery, *to hit the bull's eye, second string,* and many other terms. From billiards, *behind the eight ball.* From boxing, *to throw in the towel, hitting below the belt,* and so on. From horseracing, *to have the whip hand, the inside track, neck and neck, dark horse,* and so on. From baseball, *to throw a curve, to catch off base, windup, two strikes against him,* etc. Thousands of words have come into the language from sports, and where they have come naturally and filled a need, they have enriched our speech.

The language of sports writers, however, is another matter. Their daily effusions are peculiarly circumscribed, much more so than the language of almost any other specialized field. In the arts, in the social sciences, in business, in science and in everyday relationships, there is a constant growth and change in language because of the development of new concepts, new methods and new associations. But in sports there are basically only two things to talk about —contests and records. Interest in sports is one of the lower common denominators among various groups throughout our society. Desirable as this may be from a democratic viewpoint, it compels sports writers to use simple words and a limited vocabulary.

Because it deals with struggle, sports writing is required to be vigorous, and because it scorns formality it must be slangy and colloquial. But slang is particularly unfitted for frequent repetition and sports writing is, above any other type of contemporary writing, repetitious, laden with clichés. The wretched sports writer, with slight material and often (one suspects) even slighter interest, is compelled to assume concern he does not feel and to conceal his yawns under forced shouts of simulated excitement. A tyrannical convention of his dreary craft prevents him from repeating his verbs; yet there are only a certain number of synonyms for *win* and *lose*. He has done what he can with *win, top, upset, pace, defeat, trounce, decision* (verb), *crush, sock, blitz, spank, clobber, whip, wallop, down, spill,* and the like, but the demand far exceeds the capacity of the language. No one apparently, using only the normal resources of the richest language known, can make sports interesting.

The strained variation is interspersed with the strained periphrasis. An injured thumb is *the dislocated digit* and the backfield is *a bevy of backs*. Alliteration is freely employed. Not since *Widsith* has its artful aid been so assiduously sought.

A legend has grown up that the sports pages have produced an immense number of writers who have gone on to literary triumphs. But as Nunnally Johnson asked, after Lardner, Broun, Kieran, Pegler, Gallico, Reynolds and Considine, who is there? Johnson's characterization of sports writing is not flattering: "Bad writing, grammar-school humor, foolish styles, threadbare phrases, spurious enthusiasm and heavy-footed comedy . . . nauseating sentimentality and agonized slang . . . [and] above all, breeziness, breeziness, breeziness!"

spouse is now a literary word. It has special religious and legal uses but in everyday speech it is an affectation either of elegance or of jocularity aping elegance. Christopher Morley's statement that the plural of *spouse* is *spice* deserves to be recorded.

sprain and **strain** imply a wrenching, twisting and stretching of the muscles and tendons. *Strain* is the more comprehensive term. It can mean merely to stretch to the utmost, to exert strenuously, with no implication of injury (*Strain to the utmost, to win the goal*). But it also means to stretch beyond measure, to exert beyond the proper limit, so that injury results (*I strained my shoulder and it hurts. He strained his eyes reading the fine print*). In this sense it is also used figuratively (*He strained his credit to buy the property*). To *strain a point* is to stretch a principle beyond its limit so that there is a deformity.

Sprain is limited to excessive strains of certain parts of the human body. It means to strain excessively but without dislocation, by a sudden twist or wrench, the tendons and muscles connected with a joint, especially those of the ankle or wrist (*He sprained his ankle when he slipped on the loose gravel*).

sprang. See **spring.**

spread. The past tense is *spread*. The participle is also *spread*.

spring. The past tense is *sprang* or *sprung*. The participle is *sprung*.

sprint; spurt. Both of these verbs convey the idea of going at great speed for a short distance. *Sprint*, the newer term, is now the usual one to describe racing at full speed for a short distance, as in running or rowing (*the harassed commuter, sprinting for the train, brief case and topcoat flying*). *Spurt* suggests a quickening of pace, or a sudden gushing or issuing as in a stream. It is more often used figuratively than *sprint* (*He'll dawdle until three o'clock and then spurt ahead and try to get done in time to leave early. Blood spurted from the wound in his shoulder*).

sprung. See **spring.**

spun. See **spin.**

spurious. See **synthetic.**

square in American slang has generally meant fair, upright, honest, open, just, and so on. The term seems to have originated from the carpenter's square—something that "drew a hard and fast line," made you go straight, had nothing crooked about it. One of the earliest slang phrases, now obsolete, to incorporate the idea was *to run on the square*. A *square shooter* was one who shot fairly, presumably in self-defense only, and gave his opponent a fair warning and chance. A *square deal* was a plain, open, and honest dealing of the cards. All of these expressions are, however, now a trifle musty. In the cynical terminology of bebop, *square*—perhaps in defiance of the older morality—is a word of contempt. A *square*, to the zoot-suit cognoscenti, is one who is not *hep*. He is stupid, out of fashion, not in the groove. But definitely.

square (division of a city). See **block.**

square meal. A square meal would seem, taken literally, to be uncomfortable and undesirable. It must originally have had a figurative meaning—perhaps such a meal as one who was treated squarely or got a square deal would be fed. It suggests a hearty meal, more substantial if less wholesome than a well-rounded meal. It is now fading from use a little. There's a suggestion of rusticity in it, a small townishness.

square peg in a round hole. As a term for a misfit, for one (usually a man of abilities) in a position unsuited to him, *a square peg in a round hole* is hackneyed.

Attempts to trace the origin of this expression have not been successful. *Punch* attributed it to Bishop Berkeley, and even furnished a quotation, but no one else has ever found the quotation in his works. Sydney Smith stated the idea in some detail in his *Sketches of Moral Philosophy* (1806) and has the best claim to be considered its originator.

squeamish. See **fastidious.**

stab in the back, as a term for an act of treachery, is a cliché.

staff. The plural is *staffs* or *staves*. When this word means a stick or pole, the modern plural *staffs* is preferred. The old plural *staves* has produced another singular *stave*, which now means one of the pieces of wood that form the sides of a vessel. The lines and spaces on which music is written is usually called *a staff* and a verse or stanza is usually called *a stave*, but either form can be used for either meaning.

Staff may also mean a body of assistants. In this sense it is a group noun and the plural *staffs* means several such groups. The singular form may be used with a singular verb or with a plural verb, depending on whether the staff is thought of as a unit or as individuals, as in *the staff was well trained* or *the staff were well trained*. In either case, it is the whole body of assistants that is referred to. Sometimes the word *staff* is used as if it were a true plural meaning more than one staff member, as in *a few staff were invited*. This is not at present standard English.

staff of life. The description of bread as *the staff of life* goes back to the early seventeenth century where it came into use as an adaptation or echo of several passages in the Bible in which bread is called *the stay and staff* and the cutting off of the food supply is described poetically as *breaking the staff of bread*. The phrase is now, in general use, hackneyed and stilted.

stag. See **hart.**

stage; arrange; perform. From its basic sense as a transitive verb, to put, represent, or exhibit on or as on a stage, *stage* has come rather loosely to mean arrange or, even more loosely, perform. In military usage it is quite proper to refer to the High Command as having staged the Normandy invasion, for the underlying meaning here seems to be "to erect a stage for" or "to travel by stages." It is not advisable, however, to say that a country is *staging an economic comeback* (unless it is meant that the country is coming back by stages) when *accomplishing, performing,* or *making* would be more accurate.

stage whisper. For a whisper on the stage, as a necessary part of the action of the play, loud enough for the entire audience to hear and yet, by dramatic convention, accepted as unheard by such members of the cast on the stage as are not supposed to have heard it, *a stage whisper* is the established term. But applied to any whisper elsewhere that is loud enough to be heard by all present, it is a cliché.

stagger. The use of *stagger* to mean to arrange in some other order or manner than the regular or uniform or usual one, especially at such intervals that there is a continuous overlapping (*By staggering office hours for employees, managers of large downtown concerns help solve morning and evening traffic problems. Divorce seems to be a form of staggered polygamy*) is now standard American usage and is becoming accepted in England.

This meaning would appear to be a figurative extension of a special use of the verb *to stagger* by wheelwrights, who *staggered* spokes into the hub when they set them alternately inside and outside (or more or less to one side of) a line drawn round the hub. A wheel made in this manner (for increased strength) was said to be a *staggered wheel*.

staggers. This word, meaning a disease of certain animals, is always treated as a singular, as in *staggers is hard to treat*.

staid. See **stay.**

stair; stairs. In Scotland a flight of steps is called *a stair* and treated as a singular, as in *a winding stair* and *the stair was dark*. In England a flight of steps is treated as a plural, as in *the stairs were dark,* or called *a flight of stairs,* or sometimes *a pair of stairs*. Both constructions are familiar in the United States and are equally acceptable.

In England one of the steps in a flight is called *a stair* and *three stairs* means three steps. This usage is rare in the United States. Here *three stairs* will usually be understood in the Scottish sense, as three flights.

When used as the first element in a compound, the singular form *stair* is preferred, as in *stair door, stair well, stair carpet*. This does not apply to the two words *upstairs* and *downstairs*. Here the form with *s* is always used, as in *an upstairs room*.

stalactite; stalagmite. These geological terms confuse the layman. He can never keep in mind which hangs down like an icicle and which rises up from the floor. Both are deposits of calcium carbonate formed by the dripping of percolating calcareous water in caves and sometimes they meet to form a column. The one that hangs down is a *stalactite*. The one that builds up from the floor is a *stalagmite*. Perhaps it would help if *icicle* were fixed in the mind and it was remembered that the one that resembles an icicle is the one that contains a *c*.

stall, in the sense of bringing to a standstill, checking the motion of, is obsolete or dialectal in England but is standard and common in America (*Korean truce talks were stalled over the issue of prisoner exchanges*). In the sense of acting evasively or deceptively and in its use as a noun to designate anything used as a pretext, pretense, or trick, *stall* is slang.

stalls. See **orchestra.**

stamen. The plural is *stamens* or *stamina*. Either plural may be used in botany. In general English the form *stamina* is also used to mean vigor or endurance. In this sense the word is always treated as a singular, as in *his stamina is amazing,* and does not have a plural.

stanch; staunch. Though both forms are acceptable as adjectives and verbs, *stanch* is the usual verb, *staunch* the usual adjective. The verbal sense is to stop the flow of a liquid, especially blood (*He stanched the bleeding with a cold compress*). The adjectival sense is steadfast or firm in principle, adherence, or loyalty (*He had only a few friends, but they were staunch ones and could be relied on*).

stand. The past tense is *stood*. The participle is also *stood*.

Stand, meaning "endure," may be followed by an infinitive, as in *I cannot stand to hear it,* or by the *-ing* form of a verb, as in *I cannot stand hearing it. Stand* may also be followed by a clause, with the clause verb a subjunctive equivalent, as in *I cannot stand that he should hear it,* but an infinitive construction, such as *I cannot stand to have him hear it,* is generally preferred. *Stand for* is frequently used in the United States when determination rather than endurance is being expressed, as in *I will not stand for such treatment*.

Stand may be used in literary English to mean "remain," as in *the milk had stood too long* and *still stands Thine ancient sacrifice, an humble and a contrite heart.* But this is permissible only when there is no possibility of a literal interpretation of the word. In speech centering around New York City, *stand* is used with this meaning—unacceptably—in contexts that are not sufficiently abstract. This usage has passed into sophisticated speech as a joke, especially in *I should've stood in bed.*

In legal language *stand* is often used as a mere form of the passive, equivalent to some form of the verb *to be,* as in *he stands condemned.*

Stand may be followed by an adjective describing the subject of the verb, as in *he stands firm.* It may also be followed by an adverb describing the standing, as in *he stands firmly.* Very often there is no difference in meaning between the two constructions.

Stand has several special meanings in America that are not accepted in England and at least one in England that is not in general use in America. In English usage a man *stands* for office when he is a candidate. In American usage *stand* in the sense of tolerate or endure is standard (*I can't stand people who give lectures on Europe after a week in Paris*), but the British can't stand this use of the word. In American slang *stand* also means to bear the expense of (*Come on, I'll stand all of you to a drink*).

As a noun *stand* has certain uses peculiar to the United States. In America the place where a witness sits or stands to testify in court is called a *stand* or *witness stand* (*As the witness took the stand a hum of excitement arose in the courtroom*). In England it is called the *witness-box* (*Sir John Aylesbury was now placed in the witness-box*). In America an open framework of pine wood to support cases of type is called a *stand,* in England a *frame.* A booth, table, or the like where articles are displayed for sale or some business is carried on in America is called a *stand* (*if you've got to follow the rodeos, why don't you get a stand and sell peanuts?*). In England it is called a *stall.*

standard English is the English used by educated people when they are speaking in public or writing to strangers. It is not very different from the English such people use in speaking or writing to their friends. It is also the English found in our best literary works.

The difference between spoken and written English is not as great as some people think it is, and it is not as great today as it was twenty-five or fifty years ago. Spoken English relies on gestures and intonation to fill out the meaning and therefore uses many loose sentences that might not be intelligible in print. But there are very few grammatical constructions that are acceptable in educated speech that are not also acceptable in literature and public addresses.

Standard English is not a set of rules learned in school and conscientiously applied throughout life. It is rather a set of language habits formed by reading English literature and talking chiefly with people who also read a great deal. It is an unconscious summing up of English usage over the past two or three hundred years, as modified and adapted to present-day needs. It is constantly changing, and it varies slightly from one locality to another.

At one time these local variations were what made up dialectal English. A grammarian writing in 1589 had no difficulty in saying what he meant by "good English." It was "that of London and the shires lying about London within LX miles, and not much above." But today we live in a much larger world, thanks to printing, radio, and travel, and we cannot be so precise. Regional differences should be recognized for what they are, but there is no need, and no way, to decide that the speech in one area is "better" than the speech in another.

For example, the sentence *she stayed home all evening* is standard English in the United States but not in Great Britain where an *at* is required, as in *she stayed at home all evening.* On the other hand, English people say *she is in hospital.* American usage requires a *the* here, as in *she is in the hospital,* although it allows *in jail, in school,* and so on. There are also differences inside the United States. For example, *they think like I do* is standard in the South but not in New England. Expressions of this kind show where a person comes from. But so long as one is not ashamed of being an American or an Englishman, or of coming from Boston or Charleston or San Francisco, there is no reason to change a speech form that is standard in one's own area.

This does not mean that any expression is standard if it is used by a great many people. Besides the literary tradition in English there is also an aural tradition, passed down from generation to generation among people who read very little and do not mingle with people who read. This is what is properly meant by "nonstandard" English. It has developed constructions that are not found in literary English, such as *you and me must wait,* and it contains many old forms that were once standard but that have not been used by educated people for many generations, such as *was you ever in Baltimore?* Speech of this kind shows that one's friends aren't bookish people. One may, or may not, want to conceal that fact.

But there is another kind of English that no one wants to be guilty of. These are the pretentious errors, the mistakes people make who are trying to speak according to the rules without understanding the rules. Anyone who wants to speak "better" English than most people use must be very sure of what he is doing. For example, *whom do you want?* is not idiomatic English. It suggests that the speaker has learned the language from a textbook and not from association with educated people. But it is technically correct. *Whom is it?,* on the other hand, is incorrect as well as unidiomatic. It suggests that the speaker has tried to learn English from a textbook and failed. The natural spoken English of educated people is always correct. English according to the textbooks may sometimes be inappropriate but it too is always correct, provided the rules are properly applied. But to reject natural English and misapply the rules is fatal. Mistakes of this kind will always be taken as evidence of "vaulting ambition, which o'erleaps itself and falls."

In this book, examples of how words may be used are often taken from poetry. This is because the poet is a master of language. He understands language better than most people do and he uses it to express ideas that are too vital to be put into a mathematical formula. Anyone who wants to use language more skillfully and more powerfully can learn from the poets. Sometimes a grammarian dismisses a great poet's use of words by saying "he did it for the sake of rhyme." This is a sad commentary on the grammarian. He is confusing a poet with a man who writes mottoes. Poets do frequently use archaic or unusual forms of speech, when they think this serves their purpose. But the poet is less likely than any other man to abuse language or to sacrifice its vital qualities for any reason whatever. See also **grammar** and the *Preface* to this book.

stand on one's own (two) feet. To say of someone who manifests independence that he can *stand on his own feet,* or, more often, for added emphasis, *on his own two feet* is to employ a cliché. The expression was formerly much employed by fathers in hortatory addresses to their sons.

standpoint. See **point of view, angle.**

stank. See **stink.**

stanza. See **verse.**

starlight; starlit. *Starlight* is chiefly a noun. It means the light proceeding from the stars or the time when the stars shine. It may also be used as an adjective, meaning of or pertaining to starlight, as in Gerard Manley Hopkins's poem *The Starlight Night.* But *starlit* is preferable as an adjective because it is used as an adjective only (*Michael walked down the spit-covered steps of the PX onto the worn soil of New Jersey, under the calm, starlit summer sky*).

start. This verb may be followed by an infinitive, as in *he started to read,* or by the *-ing* form of a verb, as in *he started reading.* The two constructions are equally acceptable. See **begin.**

startle. See **amaze.**

state, in a colloquial sense common to England and the United States, may mean an excited condition (*He was in quite a state by the time it came his turn to speak*).

state; say. *State* should not be used loosely as an alternative to *say.* It means to declare definitely or specifically (*I should like to state the assumptions upon which my argument rests*), to set forth formally in speech or writing (*In his funeral oration Mark Antony stated the claims that Caesar had on the Romans*).

stated as an adjective may mean fixed or settled (*He worked for a stated fee*); explicitly set forth (*These were the stated terms*); declared as a fact (*It is stated in the village that the bank cannot reopen*); recognized or official (*This is the stated policy*). All of these meanings are current in the United States but archaic and little used in England any more.

The word had another, peculiarly American, meaning in the nineteenth century: when applied to a minister or preacher, it meant one settled or established in a particular pastorate (*There were neither churches nor stated preachers in town*). There were also men called *Stated Supplies* who were employed to perform the duties of a pastor but were not inducted, in any formal way, into the pastoral office. Both of these meanings are now obsolete.

statesman. See **politician.**

station. See **depot.**

stationary; stationery. *Stationary* is an adjective meaning standing still, not moving, having a fixed position, not movable (*a stationary engine*). *Stationery* is a noun meaning writing materials, such as pens and pencils and, especially, paper (*Oh, I'm out of stationery, and I did so want to get that letter off!*). In America a place where such things are sold is called a *stationery store.* In England it is usually called a *stationer's.*

The two words are, actually, one and the same and *stationery* is the older spelling. Certain stands or stalls set up near St. Paul's Cathedral in London were granted permanent licenses and hence were stationary (as we now spell it) and those who occupied them were *stationers,* as opposed to itinerant peddlers who set up temporary booths and stands. These men, dependent upon the goodwill and business of the cathedral clergy as well as on that of the printers whose business was also established near the cathedral (a sensible—indeed necessary—location when the clergy made up a large portion of the literate), came to specialize in writing materials and in time were licensed to sell books.

statistics. Except when it means a course of study, this word is treated as a plural, as in *these statistics are impressive.* The word now means an arrangement of numerical data. Historically it is a plural word only in the sense in which the word *politics* is a plural. But a singular form of the word, *a statistic,* is now in use in the United States. This means to a statistician one of the elements in a statistical arrangement. It apparently means to the general public any piece of information involving numbers. The only adjective form in use in the United States is *statistical.*

status. The plural is *statuses* or *status,* not *stati.*

status quo. As a term for preserving the present state of things, especially of the economic order, *maintaining the status quo* is a cliché. The phrase means literally "the state which," or the existing state of affairs.

statute; statue; statutary; statuesque; statutory; statutable. A *statue* is a representation of a person or of an animal, carved in stone or wood, molded in a plastic material, or cast in bronze or the like, especially one of some size, in the round (*The Statue of Liberty beckons the op-pressed from the Old World*). A *statute*, in legal terms, is an enactment made by a legislature and expressed in a formal document (. . . *When the statute gleans the refuse of the sword*). A *statute* is also the document in which such an enactment is expressed. In international law, a *statute* is an instrument annexed to or subsidiary to an international agreement, as a treaty.

Statuary may be an adjective meaning of, pertaining to, or suitable for statues (*statuary drapery, this great quarry of statuary marble*). *Statuesque* means like or suggesting a statue, as in formal dignity, grace, or beauty (*His statuesque poses were sometimes assumed to conceal the indignity of his lameness*). The adjective meaning of or pertaining to a statute, prescribed or authorized by statute (*a statutory offense*), or legally punishable, is *statutory*. *Statutable* also means prescribed, authorized, or permitted by statute. Of an offense, it means recognized by statute, legally punishable. But it has the special meaning, not shared by *statutory*, of conformed or conforming to statutes.

stave. The past tense is *staved* or *stove*. The participle is also *staved* or *stove*. *Staved* is the usual form for the past tense and the participle in general English, and *stove* is pretty much confined to nautical matters. That is, we say *the boat was stove in* but *a bad cold was staved off*.

staves. See **staff.**

stay. The past tense is *stayed* or *staid*. The participle is also *stayed* or *staid*. These are merely alternate spellings for the same form.

Stay may be followed by an adjective describing the subject of the verb, as in *stay calm*. It may also be followed by an adverb describing the staying, as in *stay quietly*. There is often no difference in meaning between the two forms.

steady improvement, as a term for consistent and regular improvement, is hackneyed. There's nothing wrong with the phrase. It's really quite a good way of putting it. It simply is that the two words have been coupled so long and so remorselessly that the reader no longer recognizes them as individual words with meaning. Overuse has effaced them beyond recognition.

steal. The past tense is *stole*. The participle is *stolen*.

A participle *stole*, as in *had stole*, was once literary English but is no longer considered standard.

steal; purloin; pilfer; filch; thieve; rob; hold up. *Steal* is the general word meaning to take or take away dishonestly or wrongfully, especially secretly (*Who stole my heart away? The second-hand yards lose thousands every month from stealing*). It has also the acquired meaning of moving softly and unobtrusively, as a thief. Sometimes a connotation of evil-doing lingers in the word (*This stealing away doesn't look like innocence to me*), but it is often completely divorced from any such suggestion (*Steal away, steal away to Jesus. . . . Shall fold their tents, like the Arabs,/ And as silently steal away*).

To *purloin* was originally merely to remove far off, to set to one side. In the York Plays there is mention of one who having received good moral precepts *pertly purloined them,* that is, disregarded them, set them to one side. Apparently things taken far off offered a temptation to theft and the word has come to be associated with theft. It has a connotation of subtlety and is now largely a literary word (*The Purloined Letter. A certain document of the last importance has been purloined from the royal apartments*).

To *pilfer* is to steal in small quantities, to practice petty theft (*This pilfering cannot be taken lightly; it adds up in a year's time to a considerable sum*). Dampier said that he found the Malayans honest, not addicted to robbery, *but only the pilfering, poorer sort. Pilfer* carries a considerable connotation of contempt (*The Bard whom pilfered pastorals renown,/ Who turns a Persian tale for half-a-crown*).

To *filch* is to steal small things in a sly way. As with *steal*, the slyness often predominates in its meaning. Iago's *Who steals my purse, steals trash . . ./ But he that filches from me my good name/ Robs me of that which not enriches him,/ And leaves me poor indeed* plainly cannot intend *filch* to mean the stealing of a trifle, but, rather, the ruining of a reputation by sly insinuation.

Thieve is usually intransitive. It means to act as a thief, to commit theft. It is stronger than *filch* or *purloin* and much stronger than *pilfer*, but not as strong as *steal* or *rob. Thievery* is often preceded by *petty*.

Rob is a strong word. It carries a suggestion of violence and the theft of things of value. *Robbers* are dangerous men (*The First National Bank was robbed today by two masked gunmen. The police pursued the robbers, exchanging more than a dozen shots, several of which, they are sure, found their mark*). *Rob* takes as its object the person or institution from whom stolen. *Steal* takes as its object the thing stolen. Something is stolen; one is robbed *of* it. In America the armed robbery of persons is more and more being called a *hold-up* and the perpetrators *hold-up men, robbers* being restricted more to those who steal goods. The distinction is not yet definitely established as standard, however. See also **thief; robber; burglar.**

steal a march on. Derived from the military expression for moving troops, usually under cover of night, without the enemy's knowledge, *to steal a march on* in the figurative sense of secretly gaining an advantage is worn out with overuse.

steal someone's thunder. To say of someone who has used someone else's own methods or accomplishments in such a way as to deprive the originator of his due credit or authority that *he has stolen his thunder* is to employ a cliché.

The phrase was first uttered by the irascible critic and playwright John Dennis (1657-1734) when the "thunder" which he had devised (shaking a sheet of tin) for his play *Appius and Virginia* (1709), which failed, was used a few nights later in a production of *Macbeth*. Since the origin of so many phrases is quickly lost and since it is rare to have an accurate account of the origin of a phrase, it is worth quoting a paragraph from the *Biographia Britannica:*

> *Our author, for the advantage of this play* [Appius and Virginia], *had invented a new species of thunder, . . . the very sort that at present is used in the theatre. The tragedy itself was coldly received, notwithstanding such assistance, and was acted but a short time. Some nights after, Mr. Dennis, being in the pit at the representation of* Macbeth, *heard his own thunder made use of; upon which he rose in a violent passion and exclaimed,* See how the rascals use me! They will not let my play run, and yet they steal my thunder.

steer clear of. Used figuratively, the nautical expression to *steer clear of* is hackneyed.

stem. Where Americans say that something *stems from* this or that (*His talkativeness stems from an embarrassed self-consciousness*), the English say *springs from* or *originates in.*

stem-winder. Americans used to call a watch which is wound by turning a knob at the stem a *stem-winder.* The English call it a *keyless watch.* The tendency of the English to define negatively, to identify new things by saying what they are *not,* a reflection probably of their conservatism, of their facing of their great and successful past, is gradually changing. *Wireless* is the traditional form, but the American *radio* is making headway; though as H. Allen Smith, that keen observer of language and folkways, has remarked (*Smith's London Journal,* 1952, p. 77), a radio tube is still known in England as a wireless valve.

The use of *stem-winder* as a slang term of approbation, applied to one who has energy, ability, and initiative, is something of an affectation. It implies that the speaker is so venerable or comes from some place so quaintly old-fashioned that a stem-winding watch constitutes an admirable novelty. It may once have been a genuine expression but, like *cooking with gas,* it now sounds artificial and forced, an affectation of rustic simplicity.

step in the right direction. To say of some act that conduces to the achievement of a desired end, especially an initial act and above all of one that marks a change of course, that it is a *step in the right direction* is to employ a cliché.

step up; increase. *Step up,* an American engineering term applied to the process of gradually increasing the electric power applied by a switch with graduated steps, is now used in America and England to mean to raise or increase something that can in some figurative way be considered as being a form of power. Thus one would not say that he stepped up the amount of sugar in his coffee if he added some, but he might well say that he stepped up the dosage of a drug or medicine, especially if the increase was regarded as permanent.

Some authors insist that unless *step up* is clearly understood to mean to make greater by stages, it is merely a substitute for *increase* and hence a superfluous addition to the language. But even as a mere synonym for *increase*—which it is not exactly, because it has connotations that *increase* lacks—it is a dynamic, concrete locution.

stereotyped. See **commonplace.**

sterling worth, as a term of approbation for one of admirable qualities, is a cliché.

stern reality, as a term for the facts of a situation, especially when unfavorable, is worn out. So also is *hard facts* or *the grim facts.*

stew in one's own juice, as a term for allowing someone to suffer the consequences of his own actions, especially with a slightly spiteful or vindictive satisfaction, is a cliché.

stick. The past tense is *stuck.* The participle is also *stuck.*

stick in one's craw. To say of something that one is loath to accept but must that it *sticks in one's craw* (or *gizzard*) is to employ a phrase worn out by overuse.

stick to one's guns, as a term for tenacity, for a refusal to give up, and especially for a refusal to cede a point in an argument, is stale and worn.

sticker; stickler. A *sticker* is a person who (or sometimes a thing or animal that) is persistent. A *stickler* is a person who insists on something unyieldingly. The word is followed by *for* if mention is made of that upon which the insistence is laid (*He is a stickler for propriety*). *Sticker* is generally a term of approval, while *stickler* is generally a term of disapproval, especially if the one using the term is not himself inclined to admire niceties or regards that on which the stickler insists as unworthy of insistence.

stigma; stigmata. *Stigma* derives from a Greek word meaning mark. In common usage it is used figuratively to mean a mark of disgrace or infamy, a stain or reproach, as on one's reputation (*There should be no stigma attached to his failure to get through college; the financial difficulties were simply too great*). In its literal sense, *stigma* means a characteristic mark or sign of defect, degeneration, or disease. It may mean a birthmark or a naevus. In pathology a *stigma* is a spot or mark on the skin, especially a place or point on the skin which bleeds, or is alleged to bleed, during certain mental states, as in hysteria. In zoology it means a small mark, spot, pore, or the like, on an animal or organ. In botany it means that part of a pistil which receives the pollen. In the Roman Catholic Church *stigmata* (the plural of *stigma* in all except the figurative sense of disgrace, when the plural is *stigmas*) means marks said to have been supernaturally impressed upon certain persons in the semblance of the wounds on the crucified body of Christ.

The distinction between *stigmas* and *stigmata* is less than fifty years old. The verb *stigmatize* still carries both meanings.

still; stilly. The form *still* may be used as an adjective meaning quiet, as in *over the still stream,* and it may be used in other ways. The form *stilly* has only the one meaning of quietness and is now artificial English. It could once be used as an adjective, as in *oft in the stilly night,* or as an adverb, as in *stilly she glides in.* Today, *still* is preferred as the adjective and *quietly* as the adverb in this sense.

Still may also be used as an adverb. When it qualifies the comparative form of an adjective or adverb, it means "to a high degree" or "increasingly," as in *louder still and still more loud.* Otherwise it indicates that something remains unchanged up to a given moment, usually the time of speaking, as in *still is the story told.* Here the meaning of the word requires a continuing action. It cannot be used with a perfect tense verb form or with a simple past, present, or future tense unless the action is understood as continuing or habitual. In a negative statement it is better to place *still* before the meaningful element of the verb rather than after, as in *he is not still working.* See also **yet; already.**

Still may also be used as a connective meaning notwithstanding or nevertheless, as in *still, you must admit.* With this meaning, it may be used with a verb in any tense.

In many parts of the United States people use the expression *still and all,* meaning "just the same." This is undoubtedly derived from the Scottish phrase *still and on,* which in turn comes from the older English phrase *still and anon*— both of which mean nevertheless.

still small voice. The prophet Elijah, lodging in a cave on Mount Horeb, heard a voice that told him to go forth and stand upon the mount before the Lord. *And, behold,* it says in I Kings 19:11-13, *the Lord passed by, and a great and strong wind rent the mountains, and brake in pieces the rocks before the Lord; but the Lord was not in the wind: and after the wind an earthquake; but the Lord was not in the earthquake. And after the earthquake a fire; but the Lord was not in the fire: and after the fire a still small voice. And it was so, when Elijah heard it, that he wrapped his face in his mantle, and went out, and stood in the entering in of the cave. And, behold, there came a voice unto him, and said, What doest thou here, Elijah?*

The use of the phrase *still small voice* from this great passage as a term for the conscience, the voice of God speaking quietly within us, was finely conceived and it is a pity that overuse has deadened it.

stimulant; stimulus. *Stimulus* is the general word meaning something that incites to action or exertion, or quickens actions, feeling, or thought, or serves as a goad or an incentive. In ordinary usage *stimulus* is taken to be commendable, something which arouses to useful or desirable activity (*The love of fame is a powerful stimulus in high-minded young people. The infinitely complex organizations of commerce have grown up under the stimulus of certain desires existing in each of us*). The plural is *stimuluses* or *stimuli.*

Stimulant is a more restricted term. It is used to describe something which temporarily quickens some vital process or the functional activity of some organ or part (*Alcohol, nicotine, and coffee are all stimulants, and are all harmful if taken in excess*). *Stimulant* sometimes tends to be a deprecatory term.

sting. The past tense is *stung.* The participle is also *stung.*

stingy. See **economical.**

stink. The past tense is *stank* or *stunk.* The participle is *stunk.*

stink (noun). See **smell.**

stitch in time, as a term for some act or provision which will prevent the need for much greater action later or which, if omitted, would involve disastrous consequences, is a cliché.

stock. *Take stock of* and *take stock in* convey different ideas. *To take stock of* means to take an inventory of, to make an appraisal of (*As soon as they took stock of their situation, they saw that things were not so bad as they had feared*). *To take stock in* literally means to purchase shares of stock in a corporation, but its figurative, colloquial use means to take an interest in, attach importance to, or repose confidence in (*I don't take much stock in the patriotism of such bodies, however loudly they protest it*).

stock; shares. *Stock* is the normal term in American finance to describe the shares of a particular company or corporation. The English say *shares,* though an American will speak of so many *shares of stock.* The American terms *common stock* and *preferred stock* are paralleled by the English *ordinary stock, ordinary shares,* and *preference stock, preference shares.* An American *stockholder* is the equivalent of an English *share holder.*

stoic and **stoical** both mean resembling the school of philosophy founded by Zeno, who taught that men should be free from passion, unmoved by joy or grief, and should submit without complaint to unavoidable necessity. *Stoic* is the word most commonly used to describe one who maintains or affects the mental attitude required by the Stoics (*The stoic detachment is more to be admired than attained*). *Stoical* is used more loosely (and more frequently) to describe one who is impassive, characterized by a calm or austere fortitude, whether that fortitude has a philosophical basis or not (*Many who would not have thought they could have endured the terror of them learned to be stoical about the bombings and slept soundly between raids*).

stoicism. See **patience.**

stole; stolen. See **steal.**

stolid. See **solid.**

stomach. See **belly.**

stone is a British term for a measure of weight. Their *imperial standard stone* is fourteen pounds avoirdupois. There were formerly many different *stones*—that of meat or fish was eight pounds, that of cheese sixteen pounds, that of hemp thirty-two pounds, that of glass five pounds, that of lead twelve pounds, and so on. The term is now largely restricted to giving the weight of a man, where *stone* means fourteen pounds avoirdupois (*He was a small man, of not over ten stone or ten stone five at the most*).

This unit of weight is not used in America, though the word is known to most educated Americans and was, apparently, formerly used, at least in New England (*He was not a ghost, my visitor, but solid flesh and bone;/ He wore a Palo Alto hat, his weight was twenty stone—* Oliver Wendell Holmes).

In discussing the term as a unit, the plural is *stones* (*The many stones formerly in use in England were a cause of great confusion*), but the plural as the term of measurement of a man's weight is *stone* (*fourteen stone, stripped*).

stood. See **stand.**

stoop, as an architectural term, is a word to be found only in New World English. Derived from the Dutch *stoep,* it means a raised entrance platform with steps leading up to it, or a small verandah or porch to a house (*They sat out on the stoop in the cool of the evening, fanning themselves with palm-leaf fans and chatting with friends who chanced to stroll by*).

stooped. As an adjective describing a posture in which the head and shoulders are bent, or the body generally is bent, forward and downward from an erect position, Americans use the past participle *stooped* where the English use the present participle *stooping* (*She was startled to find him so stooped and gray*).

stop. This verb may be followed by the *-ing* form of a verb, as in *he stopped reading.* An infinitive following *stop* does not show what was stopped but only the purpose of the stopping, as in *he stopped to read.*

Stop may be used to mean "stay for a short time," as in *we stopped there for three days.* It has been used in this way in literary English for several centuries.

stop; cease; pause; quit. *Stop* is the everyday working word, pertaining to actions or to objects in motion (*The car ahead stopped suddenly. Oh, do stop talking that way!*). *Cease* is more literary and formal and suggests the coming to an end of something that has been going on for a while (*Cease this way of life and turn to better things. Cease and desist, in the name of the law*). *Stop* also, perhaps merely because of the abruptness of its sound, suggests a more abrupt cessation. If a violinist, for example, at a formal concert concluded a long and difficult piece, it might be said that he *ceased* playing. If there were some sudden interruption that compelled him to discontinue, it would most likely be said that he *stopped* playing.

Pause implies that the action or motion will continue after an interval. *The pause that refreshes* implies that the pauser, refreshed, will resume his activities with renewed vigor.

Quit in the sense of stop or discontinue is now standard usage in America though not used in England. It formerly meant to set free, to release (*Let's call it quits,* that is, let us release each other from our obligations and agreement), and in its sense of stop there is often a suggestion of release. A man *quits* a job he doesn't like; he would probably *leave* a position he liked. See also **end.**

store has different implications and uses in America and England. In the United States a *store* is a place where goods are kept for sale, what in England is called a *shop.* As J. B. Greenough and G. L. Kittredge explain in *Words and their Ways* (1901, p. 134), "This is not mere provincial grandiloquence, as is often supposed, but results from the fact that, when the use grew up, the places in question were really storehouses, as every 'shop' in a new country must necessarily be." The English reserve the word *store* largely for a storehouse or warehouse, though there are *cooperative stores* in England and a large shop divided into several departments, which Americans would call a department store, is in England called *the stores* (*James Ramsey, sitting on the floor cutting out pictures from the illustrated catalogue of the Army and Navy Stores, endowed the picture of a refrigerator . . . with heavenly bliss—* Virginia Woolf).

In America one says *drugstore,* in England *chemist's shop,* or simply *chemist's.* American *chain stores* are English *multiple stores.* An American *storekeeper* is an English *shopkeeper.* When the English use *storekeeper,* they refer to an officer or official in charge of naval or military stores; in America such a term may be used of a naval petty officer or warrant officer whose duties involve stores. In America *store* is often used colloquially in combination with other words to suggest that the object referred to was bought at a store instead of being made at home. Thus *store clothes* are clothes that have been bought, that are not homemade. *Store teeth* is a humorous (and hackneyed) term for false teeth (*You must have paid plenty for those store teeth, Pop*). Since it has now been several generations since any large number of Americans have been awe-struck at the superiority and splendor of "boughten" things, this use of *store* is now either an affectation of rusticity or a dreary whimsy. See also **shop.**

storey; story. Where Americans use only *story,* the English may use either *story* or *storey* to describe a complete horizontal section of a building, having one continuous or approximately continuous floor; the set of rooms on the same floor or level of a building; each of the stages, separated by floors, one above the other, of which a building consists (*a twenty-story skyscraper. He lived on the fifth story*).

Story may mean, in England and America, a narrative, either true or fictitious, in prose or verse, designed to interest or amuse the hearer or reader; a tale (*Tell me the old, old story*). In colloquial usage, cynicism has made the word synonymous for a lie (*That's a story, and you know it; I wasn't there at all*). It is used in this sense chiefly by children—or was so used; it's now a little archaic—as a euphemism for *lie.* In American journalism *story* has the loose sense of an account of some event or situation, especially as it appears in the paper (*The Philadelphia Story. It was when we were in New Orleans, working on the Mardi Gras story. The story broke in the afternoon editions*). The common journalistic phrase *the story broke* does not mean that the narrative collapsed but, on the contrary, that the news became public in a sensational manner.

storm brewing. Even when used of an impending meteorological disturbance, *there's a storm brewing* is a cliché. It is as much one, and more, when used figuratively of some trouble that is working itself up.

stout. See **fat.**

stove. See **stave.**

straight; straightly. The form *straight* may be used as an adjective, as in *keep a straight face,* or as an adverb, as in *come straight home.* Very often it is impossible to say whether the word is an adjective or an adverb (and unnecessary to say), as in *stand straight.* The form *straightly* is always an adverb, as in *of stature tall and straightly fashioned.* It is seldom used in the United States.

straight; strait. *Straight,* a commonly used term meaning unswerving, direct, is not to be confused with the archaic word *strait* which means narrow, affording little room, strict in requirements or principles. The expression to describe one (usually a woman) who is excessively strict in conduct or morality is *strait-laced,* not *straight-laced. Strait-laced* is archaic in the literal sense of being tightly laced or wearing tightly laced garments.

straight and narrow path. As a term for the path of virtue, now generally employed with a tedious jocularity, *the straight and narrow path* is a cliché. It is a shortening and a corruption of Matthew 7:14, *strait is the gate and narrow is the way, which leadeth unto life,* in which *strait means narrow, not straight.*

straight as a die. The die that is the standard of straightness in the hackneyed comparison is that which is known best in its plural, *dice.* Dice, of course, had to be made with utmost precision if their falling was to be wholly a matter of chance and their smoothness and exactness formed the basis of several comparisons—*as smooth as a die, as true as a die, as straight as a die.* All are now clichés.

straight from the horse's mouth is a colloquial jocularity as an assurance that something stated is on good authority. It is doubly hackneyed. It derives from estimating the age of a horse by examining its teeth. No matter what the horse trader declared the animal's age to be, the condition of its teeth furnished an accurate guide for the knowing.

straight from the shoulder. As a way of saying that some comment (usually of an unpleasant nature) was blunt, to say that it *came straight from the shoulder* (*He let him have it straight from the shoulder*) is a cliché. The expression is drawn from pugilism and shares the brutality of its origin. It is usually uttered with smug satisfaction, the utterer feeling that this particular manner of delivering his advice or criticism was admirable and would be wholesome for the one to whom it was delivered.

straightway; straightaway. See **immediately.**

strain. See **sprain.**

strain at a gnat. As a term for those who make a difficulty of accepting or "swallowing" some trifle (usually in the matter of opinion, or unlikely assertion, or relation of an unusual happening) when they have already accepted a much greater improbability without scruple, *to strain at a gnat and swallow a camel* is worn out by overuse.

The expression is often used with the assumption that "strain at" in this context means to make a great effort to swallow, to choke over, as it were, to retch or to vomit with revulsion and effort. Actually, however, it is another meaning of the word *to strain:* to filter. The expression comes from Matthew 23:23-24, which in the King James version reads: *Woe unto you, scribes and Pharisees, hypocrites! for ye pay tithe of mint and anise and cummin, and have omitted the weightier matters of the law, judgment, mercy, and faith: these ought ye to have done, and not to leave the other undone. Ye blind guides, which strain at a gnat, and swallow a camel.* This reading is not, as has been claimed, a mistranslation but it adopted a rendering already current which even then had proved misleading. The passage means "which strain the liquor if they find a gnat in it." The Revised Standard Version gives the proper meaning by having it read *which strain out a gnat.*

strain every nerve. The older meaning of *nerve* was sinew or tendon (*Awake, my soul, stretch every nerve,/ And press with vigor on*—1755). In modern usage, however, the use of the adjuration to *strain every nerve* to mean to make the utmost physical effort is a cliché.

straits. The word *strait* means narrow or tight, as in *strait is the gate, a strait jacket, in straitened circumstances.* The plural form *straits* may be used in speaking of a narrow water way or, figuratively, of a difficult situation, as in *the Straits of Gibraltar, the Straits of Magellan,* and *what brought you to these straits?* Before the sixteenth century the singular form *strait* was used more often than the plural in both these senses. This is now obsolete in England where only the plural form has survived. In the United States the singular *strait* is still standard and both forms are acceptable. Maps made in America usually show *the Strait of Gibraltar, the Strait of Magellan,* and people sometimes say *I was never in such a strait before.* In this last sense, the word is often misspelled *straight.*

strange. See **funny, odd.**

stratagem. See **trick.**

strategy; tactics. Primarily these words refer to military operations. *Strategy* refers to the planning and directing of projects which involve the movements of forces, etc., and *tactics* refers to the actual processes of moving or handling forces (*The generals work out the strategy, but it is often up to regimental officers to handle tactics. That Cromwell was a great tactical commander is beyond question, but the wisdom* of his strategy is a matter of dispute). More loosely, *strategy* describes skillful management in getting the better of an adversary or attaining a large end. It describes the method of conducting operations, especially by the aid of maneuvering or stratagem. *Tactics*, more loosely, is pretty close to the loose sense of *strategy*, though *tactics* is perhaps better for maneuvers themselves and *strategy* for the planning of those maneuvers.

The United States Air Force maintains a Strategic Air Command and a Tactical Air Command. The strategic forces are in time of war applied directly against the enemy nation itself as distinct from its deployed military forces. Tactical forces are concentrated against those elements of the enemy's military forces which constitute the greatest menace to the successful accomplishment of the theater mission.

stratum. The plural is *stratums* or *strata*. *Strata* is also used as a singular, with a regular plural *stratas*. These forms are objected to by many people but are used by competent writers.

stress; emphasize. In England *stress* means chiefly severe pressure, force or anguished concern. This meaning is known in America (*Men Under Stress. The stress of the past few weeks has been almost unendurable*), but the more common meaning of the word in the United States today is to lay emphasis on, to *emphasize* (*I want to stress three things*). British authorities discourage the use of *stress* in this sense, insisting that *emphasize* is more correct; but the usage is standard in America.

strew. The past tense is *strewed*. The participle is *strewed* or *strewn*. *Strewed* is preferred to *strewn* in purely verbal uses, and *strewn* is preferred as an adjective. But both forms may be used in either way.

stria. The plural is *striae*.

stricken. See **strike.**

stride. The past tense is *strode*. The participle is *stridden, strid, strided,* or *strode*. *Stridden* is the usual form of the participle in literary English. But Robert Louis Stevenson uses *strode,* as in *the captain who had so often strode along the beach,* and this form is acceptable in many parts of the United States. *Strid* is not heard in the United States but is a recognized form in Great Britain, where *strided* is also used and accepted.

strike. The past tense is *struck*. The participle is *struck* or *stricken*. *Stricken* is not used in Great Britain except as an adjective, but may still be heard in verb forms in the United States, as in *the clause was stricken out*.

When used as an adjective, *stricken* is more old-fashioned and bookish than *struck*. It occurs most often in set phrases such as *stricken with a disease, stricken in years, the stricken deer*. Only the form *struck* can be used when the word is meant in its literal sense, as in *struck with a cane*, and even when used in a figurative sense, *struck* is generally preferred to *stricken,* as in *struck with terror, moon-struck,* and so on.

strike while the iron is hot, as an adjuration to seize the propitious moment, to act while circumstances are favorable, is now a cliché.

string. The past tense is *strung*. The participle is also *strung*. A form *stringed* is used as a pure adjective with no verbal force. That is, we speak of *a well strung bow* but of *a stringed instrument*.

stripe is used figuratively in America to designate a distinctive style, variety, sort, or kind (*No Democrat of the Bryan-Hearst stripe could make headway in such an enterprise*). The equivalent English term is *kidney*. (See also **ilk.**)

strive. The past tense is *strove* or *strived*. The participle is *striven* or *strived*. *Strived* is no longer heard in Great Britain but is still acceptable in the United States for the past tense and the participle.

Strive may be followed by an infinitive, as in *with steps that strove to be, and were not, fast*. It cannot be followed by the *-ing* form of a verb. See **endeavor.**

strode. See **stride.**

strong as a horse. This simile is worn out and outworn. Even its appositeness may be questioned. Oxen, mules, donkeys, goats, and many other mammals are, pound for pound, stronger than horses, and the insects have strength, for their weight, which no vertebrate can remotely match. *As strong as an ant*—there's a real simile!

strong, silent man. The *strong, silent man* was a highly popular character, especially in novels by and for women, around the beginning of the twentieth century. By the 1920's he had been taken over as a figure of fun by the wits. But by now the term is utterly worn out, no longer appealing or amusing.

strong verbs. In Old English there were about four hundred verbs that changed the vowel in forming the past tense, as in *speak* and *spoke*. These are called strong verbs, in contrast to the weak verbs that formed the past tense by adding a *d* or *t* sound, as in *talk* and *talked*. Most of the old strong verbs have dropped out of the language or have developed weak forms. On the other hand, some verbs that were originally weak have developed strong forms.

In present-day English, all verbs that form the past tense and participle by adding *ed* to the present tense form are called regular verbs and all that do not, are called irregular, regardless of the history of the word. See **irregular verbs.**

strove. See **strive.**

struck. See **strike.**

strung. See **string.**

stuck. See **stick.**

student. See **pupil.**

studio; study. Among its many meanings as a noun, *study* means a room, in a house or other building, set apart for private study, reading, writing, or the like (*A scholar should have a study and a writer must have one*). *Studio* has as its basic meaning the workroom or atelier of an artist, as a painter or sculptor. More loosely used, it describes a room or place in which some form of art is pursued (*The music studio is on the fifth floor*). Since motion pictures, radio and television, *studio* has come to describe a room or a set of rooms or a building especially equipped for the characteristic activities of those enterprises. In common American usage *studio* has come to designate just about any service establishment: beauty shops are called *hair-do studios,* perfume shops *cosmetic studios,* dancing schools *studios of the dance.* A photographer's place of business is almost always just a plain *studio.*

stuff. See **matter; material.**

stung. See **sting.**

stung to the quick. *Quick* in this phrase means the living, sensitive tissue (as in *He pared his nails to the quick*). As a figurative expression for being suddenly and deeply hurt, as by an unkind remark or an insult, especially with the sort of smarting, burning pain that, like the pain of a sting, often stimulates a flash of aggressive anger, the metaphor was once a good one. For unexpected slights and insults do give sudden and intense pain, just like stings, and, like stings, they inflame and ache for a long time after and breed caution and resentment. Furthermore the metaphor has the satisfying implication that the inflicter of the pain is a subhuman, poisonous creature. But the aptness of the expression has led to its being overworked.

stunk. See **stink.**

stunt; stint. These words are confusingly close as nouns and as verbs. As a verb *stint* means to limit to a certain amount, number, share, or allowance, often unduly (*Because he had stinted on provisions, the hunting party soon had to forage for food*). *Stunt,* as a transitive verb, means to check the growth or development of (*All boys used to be told that smoking cigarettes would stunt their growth*). As an intransitive verb it means to display, often recklessly, strength and skill (*The Air Force does not encourage cadets to stunt*). As a noun it may mean a creature or plant hindered from attaining its proper growth, but this meaning is now so rare as to be obsolete. The commonest, almost the only meaning attached to the word as a noun in America today is a performance, usually one of no great significance, which serves to display strength or skill of a superficial kind (*He used to do stunts on the roof top just to impress the kids*). *Stint,* as a noun, means a limitation or restriction, especially as to amount (*He gave without stint to the campaign*); a limited or prescribed quantity, share, rate (*He did only his stint in the common enterprise*); an allotted amount or piece of work (*Interviewing students was a part of his daily stint*).

stylish. See **high-toned.**

stylus. The plural is *styluses* or *styli.*

subconscious. See **unconscious.**

subject of a verb. In a given sentence the subject of the verb is the word or group of words that answers the question *who* (or *what*) followed by the verb in the form used in the sentence. It may be a single word or it may be a group of words. In *he came yesterday,* the subject is *he;* in *reading such books frightens me,* it is *reading such books;* in *what you say has been said before,* it is *what you say.* The subject is always a noun or noun equivalent together with its qualifiers.

If the verb is in the active voice, as it is in the first two examples given above, the subject names the agent of the action. If the verb is in the passive voice, that is, if it is a form of the verb *to be* followed by the past participle of the meaningful verb, as it is in the third example, the subject names the person or thing affected by the action. A linking verb does not name an action and so its subject is neither an agent nor a person or thing affected. These verbs present special problems which are discussed below.

In a Latin sentence the subject of the verb is a noun in the nominative case, together with its qualifiers. In contemporary English, word order has taken over many of the functions of case and the subject of the verb is recognized by its position in the sentence. The rules for position are slightly different in declarative and in non-declarative sentences.

In questions that do not have an interrogative word for subject, and in wishes, the subject stands immediately after the element of the verb that shows tense, as in *did you see it?* and *may you never regret it.* A simple past or present tense form of the verb *to be,* or of the verb *to have,* may stand before the subject in a question, as in *were you there?* and *have you a match?.* With these exceptions, a question requires a verbal phrase, as does a wish, and the subject stands after the auxiliary and before the meaningful verb. A verbal phrase can also be used with *have,* as in *do you have a match?.* See **questions** and **subjunctive mode.**

In an imperative sentence the subject is usually omitted. Formerly, if it was expressed it followed the verb, as in *go ye into all the world.* Today, if it is used at all it precedes the verb, as in *you go first.* In an exclamation the subject normally precedes the verb, but sentences of this kind may also have the form of a question. See **exclamations** and **imperative mode.**

In a declarative sentence the subject normally precedes the verb and can be separated from it only by an adverb. In the best modern prose more than ninety percent of the sentences have the word order: subject, verb, object. The object may be placed first without disturbing the order of subject, verb. This order—subject, verb—is therefore a basic characteristic of English sentences. There are exceptions to the rule, and when the exceptions are listed there seem to be a great many of them. But this is deceptive. The exceptions are either limited to a few individual words or are rare constructions not often found in natural speech or writing.

1. The word *there* can be used without any real meaning in order to place the subject after the verb, as in *there is a pleasure in the pathless woods*. Today this construction is archaic except with the verb *to be* and a few other linking verbs such as *come, seem, appear;* but it was once used freely with verbs of any kind, as in *there lived a wife at Usher's well.* (See **there.**) The word *it* is also used in order to place a true subject later in the sentence. But *it* is a pronoun, or substitute subject, and sentences of this kind therefore still have the normal word order of subject, verb. (See **it.**)

2. In a clause introduced by *nor* an auxiliary verb must precede the subject, as in *you do not know, nor do I.* This is also true for the word *neither* when it is used in place of *nor,* as in *they toil not, neither do they spin.*

3. Ordinarily the word *so* does not affect the order of subject and verb; but it can be used in the sense of *also* with *to be* or an auxiliary verb standing alone, and in that case the verb must precede the subject, as in the final statement in: *He can tell you. So he can. But so can you.*

4. When a negative adverb, or an adverb that is restrictive, is placed before the subject for emphasis, it usually brings the verb forward with it, as in *never will I forget, scarcely had he spoken, only now do I realize.*

5. The words *here* and *there,* used with their full meaning, when placed before the subject may bring the verb forward too, as in *here are the letters, there goes an ambulance.* This construction is not obligatory even when the subject is a noun and is never used with the pronouns *he, she, it, they.* We say *here they are* and *there it goes.*

6. Verbs such as *say, reply, think,* when interpolated into a narrative may stand before their subject, as in *said he, thought I.* There is a theory that the normal word order, *he said,* should be used when only the substance of what was said is being reported and that the inverted order, *said he,* indicates that the exact words have been repeated. This distinction is not observed in the United States, where the normal order, *he said, I thought,* and so on, is generally preferred.

7. The words *had, were, could,* and *should,* may be placed before the subject in a conditional clause in order to avoid using the word *if,* as in *had he known, were I you.* This construction is extremely bookish. In ordinary speech we are more likely to use *if* and the normal word order of subject, verb.

8. In Old English the normal position for the verb in a declarative sentence was immediately after the first significant element, rather than immediately after the subject. This meant that the object of the verb, or any adverb, standing in the first position might bring the verb ahead of the subject. The old word order, as seen in *the boar's head in hand bear I* and *up jumped the swagman,* is still understood by us. But except in the seven cases listed above, it is no longer normal English. It is used in poetry and in stylized prose but is uncommon in matter-of-fact speech. If one wants the old-fashioned quality of a yarn one might say *in 1603 died good Queen Bess* but a serious historian would be more likely to say *in 1603 Queen Elizabeth died.*

9. In Old English the verb was sometimes made the first element in a declarative sentence in order to emphasize the action and add a sense of speed to the narrative. Chaucer uses this device in *ran cow and calf and eek the verray hogges,* but the construction was archaic even in his time. Today it is no longer archaic; it is simply unnatural English. And when it is used where no sense of speed is intended, as in *came the dawn,* it is ridiculous.

10. The verb *to be* is more likely to be brought ahead of its subject than other verbs are and when it is standing between its complement and its subject, as in *a strange bird is the owl,* it is sometimes difficult to say which is which. Logically, the subject is the less inclusive of the two terms. That is, a statement of this kind says that the subject belongs in the class of things named in the complement, and this must therefore be the larger class. *Owl* is a less inclusive term than *strange bird* and it is therefore the subject of the verb *is* in the sentence just given. But today there is a strong tendency to treat any noun or noun equivalent standing before a verb as the subject of the verb. We say *his greatest worry is taxes* and *taxes are his greatest worry.* Obviously, in these sentences we are treating whatever precedes the verb as the subject, without going into the question of which class of things includes the other. Some grammarians believe that this tendency is decisive in contemporary English and define the subject of a verb as any noun or noun equivalent standing in the subject position.

However it is defined, the subject determines the form of a present tense verb. For example, *worry* requires the singular *is,* and *taxes* the plural *are.* (See **agreement: verbs.**) An objective pronoun cannot be used in a subject position. (See **objective pronouns** and **subjective pronouns.**) The subject of the verb includes the noun or noun equivalent and all its qualifiers. As a rule, these have the order: adjective qualifiers, noun or noun equivalent, qualifying phrase or clause. (See **adjectives, position of adjectives, phrases,** and **clauses.**)

subjective pronouns. There are six subjective pronouns, *I, we, he, she, they,* and *who.*

The formal rules of grammar require these subjective forms (and not their objective counterparts) whenever the word is:

(1) The subject of a verb. (*He was there.*)
(2) Joined to the subject by a linking verb. (*That is he.*)
(3) Joined to the subject by *and, or, nor, but, than,* or *as.* (*I work harder than he.*)
(4) In an independent or "absolute" construction. (*He having no coat, we gave him one.*)

These rules do not represent standard English practice. In the speech of well educated people,

each of the above points is modified in one way
or another.

(1) The subjective pronouns are always used
when the word is standing in a position
appropriate to the subject of a verb. *Him
and me were there* is accordingly unacceptable. But in unusual constructions,
where the subject is out of its natural
place, an objective form is acceptable,
as *him* in *damn'd be him that first cries
Hold, enough!* and in *there will only be
him left.*

(2) Standard English uses a subjective pronoun after a linking verb in a simple
identity, such as *I am I*, and before the
-*self* words, as in *it was she herself I saw.*
The objective form is acceptable in all
other constructions, such as *that is him.*
In more complex sentences, such as *the
first person he recognized was me* and
is it us they are talking about?, a subjective pronoun is never used, except in
the most artificial prose. See **linking
verbs.**

(3) Standard English uses a subjective pronoun when the word is joined to the
subject of a verb by *and, or,* or *nor.*
After *but, than,* or *as,* a subjective pronoun is not often used unless it also
stands before a verb, as in *I work harder
than he does.* (See the individual words.)

(4) The "absolute" construction with a subjective pronoun is rare in current
English. It is usually replaced by a
clause, such as *since he had no coat, we
gave him one.* See **participles.**

To sum up, standard English requires the
subjective form of the pronoun whenever the
word is standing in a subject position. In most
other situations, the objective form is preferred.

In current English an objective pronoun can
often be used where the rules would require a
subjective form. But, with two exceptions, a
subjective pronoun that is not required by the
formal rules of grammar, such as the *I* in *life is
hard for a girl like I*, is also contrary to good
usage.

The subjective pronoun *who* is one exception.
When the word *whom* precedes the verb, as in
whom are you looking for?, the form *who* is
generally preferred. In this case, therefore,
either form is acceptable and the speaker may
follow his own taste. See **who; whom.**

The other exception is the form of the pronoun used after *let's* or *let us.* When the word
let is used alone, without the *'s* or *us*, an objective pronoun is required, as in *let him first
cast a stone.* For this reason, *I* should be *me*
in *let Dick and I do it* because what is meant is
let Dick do it and *let me do it.* By the same
reasoning, *I* should be *me* in *let's you and I
wait here.* It must be *me* according to the formal
rules of grammar, and a great many people,
including most grammarians, always use an objective pronoun after *let's.* But a great many
other equally well educated people prefer a
subjective pronoun. Both constructions must
therefore be recognized as acceptable today.

With these exceptions, a subjective pronoun
that is not required by the rules is a mistake.
Sometimes it is a pretentious mistake. That is,
the speaker realizes that he is not speaking
natural English but believes that what is unnatural must be superior. An honest confusion
about which form of the pronoun to use occurs
most often after the word *and*, as in *they invited
father and I.* People who would not make this
mistake in a simple statement sometimes do
when the same situation occurs in a more complicated sentence. In any kind of sentence, a
pronoun following *and* should have the same
form that it would have if it stood in place of
the word it is joined to. For example, *she* should
be *her* in *I would have both you and she know
the truth* because we would say *I would have
her know.* Similarly, *I* should be *me* in *there is
nothing for it but for you and I to go alone*
because we would say *for me to go alone.*

Using a subjective pronoun where an objective form is required is the most conspicuous
grammatical mistake in American speech today.
Textbook writers and school teachers are undoubtedly responsible for this. In their attack
on such expressions as *it is me* they have been
inconsistent and unreasonable. They have condemned this use of the objective pronoun in
half a dozen sentences and overlooked it in a
hundred others. (See **linking verbs.**) And they
have said that a construction which runs through
English literature, and which is used by respectable people everywhere, is nevertheless reprehensible. Under the circumstances, it is not
surprising that some children lose all feeling for
ease. What could an over conscientious child do
but avoid the offending words entirely?

No one who has had a high-school education
is likely to misuse an objective pronoun. But
the very people who are most anxious to speak
"correctly" often use subjective pronouns in the
wrong place. If there is any doubt at all about
which form is right, it is safer to use the objective.

subject to; addicted to. *Subject to* is the more inclusive term. It may mean open or exposed to
(*If we live very long we are subject to all kinds
of temptation*) or under domination, control, or
influence; liable to (*The severe headaches to
which he was subject gradually abated after his
fiftieth year. Subject to change without notice*).

Addicted to is the more limiting term. One
may be subject to temptation yet not yield to it,
but when one is addicted to a particular habit
he is devoted or given up to it (*A man may be
a heavy drinker and yet not be addicted to
alcohol*). *Addicted to* carries an implication of
moral disapproval. *Addiction* is the term to describe the state of being given up to some habit,
practice or pursuit, especially to the taking of
narcotics.

subjunctive mode. Many languages have special
forms of the verb, called subjunctive forms,
which must be used when one is speaking about
what is conceivable rather than about what

actually is or has been, about ideas rather than about events. The forms of the verb used in speaking about actual facts are called indicatives. English frequently uses an indicative where other languages would use a subjunctive. But the indicative cannot be used everywhere, even in English. Under certain circumstances, we must use a subjunctive form of the verb or else one of the auxiliary verbs that have a subjunctive meaning.

FORMS

The English verb has three forms that are used in a subjunctive sense. These are illustrated below. The first, called the present subjunctive, merely shows that what is being talked about is an idea and not a fact. The second, called the past subjunctive, stresses the uncertainty or improbability of a statement. The names *present subjunctive* and *past subjunctive* are misleading, because in modern English there is no time difference between these forms. Instead, they express different degrees of certainty. Both refer indefinitely to the present or the future. The third form, the *past perfect,* refers to the past.

1. The present subjunctive uses only the simple form of the verb, no matter what its subject may be. This means that the verb *be* is used instead of *am, is, are.* In other verbs, the present subjunctive is like the present indicative except that the third person singular does not have the characteristic *s* ending, as in *he say, he stop.* We have a present subjunctive whenever the word *be* is used directly with a subject, as in *we asked that the meeting be postponed.* We also have a present subjunctive whenever the third person singular does not have its *s,* as *he stop* in *the doctor insisted that he stop smoking.* In every case, the present subjunctive form shows that we are talking about an idea which someone has and not an actual event.

2. Except for the verb *to be,* the past subjunctive is exactly like the past indicative. The difference between the two modes does not lie in the form of the word but in its meaning. Whenever a past tense form is used in speaking of a present or future event, as in *if he walked in here tomorrow,* it has subjunctive force and shows that the event is thought of as unlikely. The past subjunctive of the verb *to be* is *were.* This is used for the singular as well as for the plural, as in *were he to go.* In most cases, the indicative singular *was* may also be used as a past subjunctive. (For a full discussion of this, see **was; were.**)

3. The past perfect is the tense formed by the word *had* and the past participle of a verb, such as *had known, had gone.* This is ordinarily an indicative tense. But when it is used in a conditional statement it implies that the condition is actually contrary to the facts. To show that a statement is conditional we either use a special word, such as *if, though, unless,* as in *if he had known,* or we place the auxiliary verb before the subject, as in *had he known.*

4. In addition to these subjunctive forms, English has a number of auxiliary verbs, such as *ought, must, may,* which have subjunctive meaning; that is, they express what is desirable or conceivable rather than what actually is. These verbs do not have the *s* ending in the third person singular because they are old past tense forms with a present or future tense meaning. *Will* and *can* are now used as present indicatives. *May* and *must* are always used as present subjunctives, and so is *shall* in American English. *Would* and *could* are sometimes used as the past indicatives of *will* and *can,* and sometimes as past subjunctives. *Ought* and *might,* and in the United States *should,* are always past subjunctives.

These auxiliary verbs have certain obvious advantages over the regular subjunctive forms. In the first place, each verb has its own special meaning and this allows us to make our subjunctive statements clearer and more precise. In the second place, these verbs can keep their subjunctive tense meanings and still refer to events in the past. We can say *he may have met her here* meaning "it may be true that he met her here," or *he might have met her here,* meaning "it might be true that he met her here." (The use of these auxiliaries in speaking of what did not occur, as *you might have let us know you were coming!,* is discussed below.)

The verbs *be* and *have* also have subjunctive force when they are followed by an infinitive, as in *he was to come this afternoon* and *he has to leave early.* The verb *have* can be used in this way in all tenses.

USES OF THE SIMPLE FORMS

The subjunctive is used in current English for two purposes: (1) to express a requirement, suggestion, or desire, and (2) to state a supposition, condition, or concession.

1. Statements of requiring or suggesting cannot be followed by a simple indicative verb form. We cannot say *I suggest that he goes now.* In the United States the present subjunctive is almost always used here, as in *I suggested he take it with him, we insisted that she get to work on time, it is imperative that he know the truth.* In Great Britain this use of the present subjunctive is considered "pedantic." Englishmen prefer to use the auxiliary *should,* as in *I suggested he should take it with him.* In the United States the simple subjunctive is the form used most often in natural speech. The construction with *should* appears too, but is felt to be "bookish" or "British."

A request or suggestion expressed in the main verb in a sentence is an imperative, as in *go at once* and *look at it again, why don't you.* A future tense can also be used to make what is clearly a command more courteous, as in *you will go at once.* A past subjunctive auxiliary softens a statement of this kind still further until it is little more than a comment, as in *you should go at once.*

The verb *wish* is followed by the past tense form of a verb, implying (whether sincerely or not) that the speaker does not expect to see the wish realized, as in *I wish you liked me* and *I wish you could come.* To express a wish which we expect to see realized we use the verb *hope*, which may be followed by a present indicative, as in *I hope you like it* and *I hope you can come*. (It may also be followed by a past indicative referring to a past event, as in *I hope you liked it*.) Other verbs of wishing or desiring may be followed by a clause containing a subjunctive or subjunctive auxiliary verb, or by an infinitive, as in *I long to have him come* and *I want him to go*. The infinitive construction is preferred.

Formerly a wish could be expressed in the main verb of a sentence by means of a present subjunctive. As this is identical in form with the imperative, these old expressions of wish are now felt as imperatives, however unreasonable that may be, as in *heaven forbid, perish the thought, long live America*. In present-day English the subjunctive auxiliary *may* is used to distinguish a wish from a command. It must stand immediately before the grammatical subject, as in *long may it wave* and *may she live to be a hundred*. The auxiliary *would* introduces a wish that seems to the speaker unlikely to be fulfilled, as in *would I knew what to do*. This construction is now archaic except in the combination *would to God*.

2. From the earliest times English has had three ways of making a hypothetical statement, indicating varying degrees of confidence in what is said. In addition, we may also show that what we are saying is known to be contrary to the facts. In what follows, everything that is said applies equally to suppositions, concessions, and conditions. Each of the examples given might equally well have begun with *suppose* (a supposition), *though* (a concession), or *if* (a condition).

If an event is thought of as probable, we may treat it as a fact and speak of it in the indicative, as in *suppose it is true* and *suppose he comes tomorrow*. These indicative statements may also appear in the past tense when that is appropriate, as in *I suppose it was true* and *I suppose he came yesterday*.

In the United States up to thirty or forty years ago, an event that was not thought of as a probable fact, but as an idea or theory, was expressed by a present subjunctive, as in *even though it be true* and *even though he come tomorrow*. This use of the subjunctive can still be heard but it is no longer as popular as it used to be. Today we are more likely to express this idea by means of *should*, as in *even though it should be true* and *even though he should come tomorrow*.

If an event is thought of as unlikely or doubtful, we use a past tense form, which is here a past subjunctive since it does not refer to a past event but to something vaguely in the present or the future, as in *even though they were right* and *even though he came tomorrow*.

In making a hypothetical statement about the past which we know to be contrary to the facts, we may use the auxiliary *had* or *could have*, as in *if he had come yesterday* and *if he could have come yesterday*. Any other statement about the past, such as *if he was here yesterday*, is now

felt to be a statement about the facts, about what happened yesterday, and an indicative form of the verb is therefore required. That we do not know what the facts are, is beside the point. The subjunctive *were* should not be used in speaking about a past event, as it is in *if he were here yesterday*. If we do not know what actually happened, the indicative *was* is required. If we know that he was not here, the past perfect form, *if he had been here yesterday*, is preferred.

A conditional statement is usually accompanied by another statement, called the conclusion, which tells what will happen if the condition is fulfilled or what would have happened if the condition had been fulfilled. If an indicative form of the verb is used in stating the condition, any form may be used in stating the conclusion, as in *if this is true, I might see him* and *if he was home yesterday, I will hear about it*. Similarly, if a present subjunctive is used in the condition, any form may be used in the conclusion, as in *though he slay me, yet will I trust in him*. But if a past subjunctive is used in the condition, a past subjunctive auxiliary is required in the conclusion, as in *if he came tomorrow, I might see him*. And if a past perfect tense or *could have* is used in the condition, one of these auxiliaries followed by *have* is required in the conclusion, as in *if he had come yesterday, I would have seen him*.

In literary English the fact that a statement is a conditional clause can sometimes be shown without a conjunction by simply placing the first element of the verb before the subject. For a simple condition, this is possible with the auxiliary verbs *could* and *should* and with *were* followed by a to-infinitive, as in *could I see him, I would . . .; should he go, I would . . .;* and *were I to go, I would. . . .* For a contrary to fact condition, this is possible with the auxiliary *could have*, the word *had* used in any manner, and *were* when it is not followed by an infinitive, as in *had I gone, I would have . . .; could I have gone, I would have . . .;* and *were I going, I would. . . .*

3. The subjunctive once had many other uses which are now expressed by the indicative, but which are similar to the uses of the subjunctive in some of the other European languages. Verbs of dreading and fearing still require a subjunctive when they are used with *lest*, as in *each fearing lest the other suspect it*. But this is now extremely literary. In ordinary speech we use *that* and an indicative, as in *each fearing that the other suspects it*. Formerly, the subjunctive was used to express result, as *die* in *he that smiteth a man so that he die*. And well into this century a few Americans used the subjunctive in expressions of time, as *fall* in *the tree will wither before it fall* and *send* in *I will wait till he send for me*. Just before World War I, these forms had crossed the Atlantic and were appearing in British newspapers, to the great distress of educated Englishmen. They are now obsolete in this country as well as in England. But a form of the temporal subjunctive is still

coming to us in British mystery stories, which are fond of such quaint expressions as *two weeks come Michaelmas.*

USES OF THE AUXILIARIES

The subjunctive auxiliaries are used to express obligation, uncertainty, unreality, and purpose. They are our only means of expressing obligation or of expressing uncertainty in the principal clause in a statement, as in *I may be late.* These uses depend entirely on the meaning of the individual words and give no trouble grammatically.

Certain other uses of the auxiliaries have already been discussed. To summarize: (1) *Should* is sometimes used in place of a present subjunctive. This is heard in England more often than in the United States. (2) *Could* and *would* may be used in conditional clauses as past-tense forms of *can* and *will.* (3) One of the past-tense auxiliaries must be used in the conclusion when a past subjunctive form has been used in a conditional clause; and one of these same auxiliaries followed by *have* is required when a past perfect tense is used in the condition.

In the United States until very recently, a present subjunctive was used in subordinate clauses expressing doubt or uncertainty, as in *I wonder whether it be wise* and *however hard he work.* Previously, this subjunctive had included everything one was not absolutely certain about, as in *I think the king be stirring.* Today, we use an indicative unless we want to emphasize the doubt. And if we want to emphasize it, we use one of the auxiliaries, such as *may be.*

The words *could, would,* and *might,* are often used with *have* to speak about what did not occur, as in *you might have let us know.* This is probably related to the use of these forms after a contrary-to-fact condition. That is, the form probably implies a conditional clause such as "if you had wanted to." *Could* may be used with *have* in a conditional clause that is contrary to fact, as in *if I could have found him, I would have told him.* This construction cannot be used with any word except *could.* The similarity between *if I could have found him, I would have* . . . and *if I had found him, I would have* . . . leads some people to use *have* after *had,* as in *if I had 've seen him.* This is generally condemned. In literary English the auxiliary *had* is never followed by *have.* One also hears *would have* in a contrary-to-fact condition, as in *if you would have told me, I could have helped you.* This too is generally condemned and the simple auxiliary *had* should be used, as in *if you had told me.* . . .

Sometimes a verbal phrase of the kind just discussed is followed by an infinitive containing a second *have,* as in *it would have been wiser to have left us* and *Rousseau would have been charmed to have seen me so occupied.* These sentences could have read *wiser to leave us* and *charmed to see me,* and some grammarians claim that the second *have* is redundant and therefore improper. But this particular construc-

tion containing two *have*'s has been used by all the great writers of English from Malory to Chesterton. It is the standard, literary idiom whenever the phrase following *to have* can be replaced by a contrary-to-fact clause, such as *if you had left us, if he had seen me.* This is possible in the examples just given. It is not possible in *I would have been willing to have gone back,* and sentences of this kind do not have the same standing. They are heard frequently and there is nothing wrong with them beyond being too wordy, but *I would have been willing to go back* is more literary.

The present-tense auxiliaries *will, may, can,* and the past-tense forms *would, might, could,* are used in clauses of purpose. A present-tense auxiliary is required after a present-tense verb, and a past-tense auxiliary after a past-tense verb, as in *he is saving his money so he can buy a car* and *he saved his money so he could buy a car.* In the United States an infinitive construction is preferred to either of these clauses, as in *he is saving* (or *saved*) *his money to buy a car.*

sublime; sublimated; subliminal. *Sublime* has general applications. *Sublimated* and *subliminal* have scientific applications only. *Sublime* means elevated or lofty in thought, language (*If any poem deserves to be called sublime, it is* Paradise Lost); impressing the mind with a sense of grandeur or power, inspiring awe or veneration (*Mont St. Michel is a sublime sight*). It may also mean supreme or perfect (*For a sublime moment, just before Diestl fired, Noah was happy*).

Sublimated, the past participle of *sublimate,* is a psychological term. It means to deflect sexual and other biological energies into nonphysical or more acceptable channels (*Much of his passion was sublimated into a desire to help the unfortunate*). *Subliminal* is another psychological term. It means below the threshold of consciousness (. . . *the subliminal ego doubtless deals the cards, as the throng of sleeping images, at this call or that, move toward the light*).

submit may be followed by the *-ing* form of a verb with the preposition *to,* as in *he will not submit to being separated from her,* or by an infinitive, as in *people will not submit to have their throats cut.* The *-ing* form is generally preferred.

Although authorities in England consider such use obsolete, it is standard American usage to employ *submit* to mean to subject, especially oneself, to conditions imposed, to accept treatment (*You must submit to the regime of the hospital. He submitted himself to the policeman's suspicious scrutiny*).

subnormal. See **abnormal.**

subordinate clauses. See **clauses.**

subpoena. The plural is *subpoenas,* not *subpoenae.*

sub rosa. Whether in Latin *sub rosa* or English *under the rose,* as a term for strict confidence, absolute privacy, complete secrecy, the expression is stale and a little forced.

There are a number of explanations of its origin, of which the most widely accepted is that Cupid bribed Harpocrates (the god of silence) not to divulge the goings-on of Venus by giving him a rose, the first ever created. A rose was sometimes carved in the ceiling of medieval dining halls as a hint that that which was said under the influence of good cheer should not be repeated.

subscription. See **superscription.**

subsequent and **consequent** bear a confusing relationship to one another. A subsequent event is not necessarily a consequent event, but a consequent event is always a subsequent event. *Subsequent* means simply coming later or after (*Subsequent to his release from the Air Force he got a job with a commercial air line*). *Consequent* means following as an effect or result, resulting (*Consequent on his great reputation as a flyer of military transport, he easily got a job as a pilot for a commercial freight air line*).

subsequent; subsequently. The form *subsequent* is an adjective and is used to qualify a noun, as in *a subsequent investigation*. The form *subsequently* is an adverb and is used to qualify any other part of speech, as in *an investigation made subsequently*. But *subsequent to* may be used to introduce an adverbial phrase, as in *subsequent to this, an investigation was made*.

subsist; exist. Though both of these words describe being, *exist* is the broader term. It means to have actual being, to be (*It is hard to conceive of a time when the world did not exist*). *Subsist* applies almost always to persons now, though it was formerly applied to other things. It means to continue alive (*He subsisted on bread and water for three months*).

substantial; substantive. As adjectives these words are synonymous in the senses of belonging to the real nature or essential part of a thing, being real or actual, as opposed to the transitory or apparent. Each has, in addition, some exclusive senses. As a noun *substantive* may mean a noun or any other word functioning as a noun. Or as an adjective it may mean independent, not to be inferred but itself explicitly and formally expressed (*The Queen, by a substantive enactment, declared her governorship of the Church*). *Substantial,* as an adjective, has the exclusive meanings of strong, stout, or solid (*It was a good substantial rope and could be relied on*), moderately wealthy or well-to-do (*Substantial citizens did not look with favor upon these suggestions since they would necessarily mean an increase in taxes*), real or true in the main, or of considerable amount (*He found substantial happiness in work. There is a substantial profit to be made in these transactions but only if they are well managed*), or vital, important (*A substantial objection to the measure proposed is that it will offend the local clergy*).

substantially. See **essentially.**

substantive. This term is used by some grammarians to mean any word or group of words used as a noun.

substitute and **replace** are not to be confused. *Substitute* means to put in the place of another.

Replace (aside from its meaning of putting back into a place formerly occupied) means to take the place of another (*Jacob substituted Leah for Rachel. Rachel was replaced by Leah*).

subterfuge. See **trick.**

subtract and **deduct** both express diminution, taking away in sum or quantity. *Subtract* applies primarily to numbers and means to withdraw or take away (*After he subtracted fifty dollars for his room rent, he found that his pay would barely carry him through the month*). To *deduct* is to take away an amount or quantity from an aggregate or total (*Ten percent is deducted if one pays cash*).

subway. In the United States a *subway* is an electric railroad beneath the surface of the streets in a city (*Every morning he took the subway from Columbus Circle to Times Square*). In England the subway is called an *underground railway* or, more often, *the underground*, or, colloquially, *the tube. Subway* in England designates what Americans would call an *underpass,* an artificial underground way for pedestrians or vehicle traffic. See also **underground.**

succeed may be followed by the *-ing* form of a verb with the preposition *in,* as in *he succeeded in finishing the work*. It cannot be followed by an infinitive.

succeed; follow. Although *follow* and *succeed* (in those of its meanings that are similar to the meanings of *follow*) both imply coming after something else in a natural sequence, they are not synonyms and cannot be used interchangeably. *Follow* is a more general term, meaning to move behind in the same direction (*The sheep all followed the bellwether out of the pasture*) or to come after in order of time (*The sound of the explosion followed the flash of light almost immediately*) or to come after as a result or consequence (*And it must follow, as the night the day,/ Thou canst not then be false to any man*). *Succeed* may mean to follow or replace another by descent, election, or appointment (*He succeeded his father to the baronetcy. President Eisenhower succeeded President Truman*) or to come next after in an order or series and, having so come, to take the place of (*He succeeded his father, the fifth earl*).

successfully; successively. *Successfully* means in the manner desired, attended with success (*He landed his plane successfully in a pasture*). *Successively* means following in order or in an uninterrupted course (*Infuriated, he fought successively the ten biggest men in his company*).

successive. See **consecutive.**

succinct; concise. Both of these words suggest brevity in statement or expression. *Succinct* means, literally, held up as by a girdle or band, hence compressed (*A strict and succinct style is that where you can take away nothing without loss, and that loss to be manifest*—Ben Jonson). A succinct manner of speaking, then, is one in which a great deal is conveyed in a few words. *Concise* refers to style, while *succinct* usually refers to matter. We speak of a succinct narrative and a concise phrase. *Concise* means the expression of much in a few words. Its original meaning was to cut off or to cut short. A concise style, as Ben Jonson said, is one which expresses not enough "but leaves something to be understood." Thus a succinct style is one in which a great deal is pressed into a statement, a concise style is one in which everything except what is absolutely necessary has been eliminated. See also **compendious; reticent.**

succor. See **help.**

succubus. See **incubus.**

such. Some grammarians list *such* as a demonstrative pronoun or adjective. Like the words *this* and *that,* its meaning ordinarily depends on something that has just been said or is about to be said. When this is not the case it is used as a blank, to represent some specific word or phrase that is not being provided, as in *the record shows that on such a date he left early.*

The adjective *such* may qualify a mass noun, as in *such knowledge,* or a plural, as in *such men.* To qualify a true singular we use the phrase *such a,* as in *such a man.* The fact that *such* regularly stands before *a* rather than after it has led some grammarians to class *such* as an adverb. But it is better to consider this simply an idiom. It has been in use for more than seven hundred years and has now completely replaced the normal form seen in *to lead such dire attack.* But this does not apply following the word *no. No such thing,* for example, is standard English and *no such a thing* is questionable.

Such or *such a* may be used as a pure intensive, as in *such beautiful weather, such a terrible storm.* Some grammarians object to this on the grounds that *such* is here being treated as an adverb. But a great many adjective forms are used as intensives and this use of *such* is established in literature and accepted by well educated people today. See **adjectives as adverbs.**

Such is used as a pronoun, or without a following noun, in literary English. But in speech there is a strong tendency to replace *such* with *one,* or *it,* or some other word. *One* would probably be substituted for *such* in *he is a friend and I treat him as such;* and *it* in *the grounds for such being established; this* in *such was not the decision;* and *those who* in *such as need our help. Such a one* seems to be acceptable when there is a preceding noun to which it can refer, as in *I have had good teachers, but never such a one as you describe.* When used without a preceding noun and referring to a human being, it is usually replaced by *some one.*

Such can always be followed by *as* introducing an explanatory or defining clause, as in *such as know what they want.* Formerly it could be followed by *as* introducing a clause of result, as in *with such violence and speed as nothing was able to sustain its force.* This construction is no longer standard. In current English *that* is required before a clause of this kind, and an infinitive must be used after *such as* to express result, as in *don't be such a fool as to refuse.*

A cardinal number precedes the word *such,* as in *of two such lessons.* When not qualifying a noun, *such* may be preceded by *none,* as in *none*

such can have been made for hundreds of years. The phrase *none such* has the force of "none like that" or "none of that kind," and is literary English. The form *no such* is now used only as an adjective before a noun, as in *no such nonsense.*

such stuff as dreams are made on is the correct form of the quotation (*We are such stuff/ As dreams are made on, and our little life/ Is rounded with a sleep—The Tempest,* Act IV, Scene 1), but since *on* here means *of,* it is pedantic to correct those who speak it in the modern version—*we are such stuff as dreams are made of.* Detached from the full quotation, the phrase by itself is a cliché.

suds may be treated as a singular or as a plural. We may say *this suds is better than that* or *these suds are better than those.* But it is a mass word and not a true plural. We may say *much suds* or *a great deal of suds* but not *many suds* or *several suds.* There is no singular form *a sud.*

suffer. When this word means "allow" it may be followed by an infinitive, as in *suffer the little children to come unto me,* but not by the *-ing* form of a verb. When the word means "experience pain" it may be followed by the *-ing* form with the preposition *from,* as in *I suffer from knowing it,* or by an infinitive, as in *I suffer to think of it.* See also **sustain.**

suffer fools gladly. Usually employed in any one of several negative forms (*not to suffer fools gladly, one who doesn't suffer fools gladly,* etc.) as an expression to describe one who is markedly impatient with the stupid, the phrase (a quotation from II Corinthians 11:19) is now hackneyed.

suffering; sufferance. *Suffering* is the act of one who suffers or a particular instance of that act. *Sufferance* now means tolerance of a person or thing, a tacit allowance but no more. It is most commonly used in the phrase *on sufferance* (*He stayed in college only on sufferance of the dean*). It conveys the sense of passive permission, permission in default of strong objection.

sufficient; enough. Either of these adjectives can be used in most contexts, but not both. *Sufficient enough* is redundant. Both mean adequate for the want or need, though *enough* is more commonly used. *Sufficient* is often felt to be a little more elegant. See also **ample.**

sufficiently may be followed by an infinitive, as in *sufficiently large to satisfy us.* It is sometimes used with a clause, as in *sufficiently large that we were satisfied,* but this is not standard English.

suffixes are usually joined to the preceding word without a hyphen, as *clockwise, manhood, stainless, spoonful.* But there are a few exceptions.

1. *Elect, odd, wide,* when used as suffixes, are usually hyphenated, as in *president-elect, forty-odd, nation-wide.*

2. *Fold* is joined without a hyphen to words of one syllable; otherwise it is written as a separate word, as in *tenfold, twenty fold.* (Some publishers join *fold* to any single word and print it separately with compound numbers, as in *twentyfold* and *twenty-two fold.*)

3. *Like* is joined directly to one syllable words that do not end in *l; otherwise* it is hyphenated, as in *childlike, eel-like, business-like.* (Some publishers use a hyphen only to prevent a triple *l*, and write: *eellike, businesslike,* but *bell-like.*)

suffragette; suffragist. *Suffragette* is a colloquialism to describe a female supporter, usually militant, of a vote for women. A *suffragist* is one who advocates the grant or extension of political suffrage, especially to women. Since women have been granted the suffrage in most English-speaking countries, both words have fallen into disuse and *suffragette* has become definitely a historical term. Those who today advocate the granting of further rights or privileges to women are usually called *feminists.*

suggested; suggestive. *Suggested* is a neutral word, meaning placed or brought to mind for consideration or possible action (*The suggested topic involved work in the local library*). *Suggestive* primarily means that suggests or tends to suggest thoughts or ideas (*He made a number of suggestive comments on the essay I had summarized*). In common parlance *suggestive* is usually employed in its secondary meaning: such as to suggest something improper or indecent (*He was the sort of man who could make "Hello" sound suggestive*).

suit and **suite** have a common French derivation. *Suit* is used in most senses. It may mean a set of garments intended to be worn together; the act or process of suing in a court of law; in cards, one of the four sets or classes into which playing cards are divided; the wooing or courting of a woman, a solicitation in marriage; a petition, as to an exalted person (*Your majesty, hear my suit*).

Suite means a company of followers or attendants, a retinue; a connected series of rooms to be used together by one person or a number of persons (*The General had a suite at the Waldorf Towers*). In music *suite* means an ordered series of instrumental dances, in the same or related keys, commonly preceded by a prelude (*Grieg's Peer Gynt Suite was one of his favorite musical compositions*). When it means a set of furniture, *suite* is often pronounced the same as *suit.* Of late there has been a marked and sensible tendency to use the word *set* instead.

suitable. See **adapted.**

sulfureous, sulfuric, and **sulfurous** all refer to sulfur in somewhat distinct terms. *Sulfureous* means consisting of, containing, pertaining to, or resembling sulfur. *Sulfuric* is a more specialized term. It means of, pertaining to or containing sulfur, especially in the hexavalent stage. *Sulfurous* has also specialized meanings. It means relating to sulfur, but it also means having the yellow color of sulfur or containing tetravalent sulfur.

sulphur and molasses; brimstone and treacle. The medicinal dose *sulphur and molasses* (also spelled *sulfur and molasses*) which was forced down our retching grandfathers in their youth as a spring tonic is known in England as *brimstone and treacle* or *brimstone and molasses.*

Dickens uses both forms in *Oliver Twist.* The term lingers on (*"Bilious," they said and dosed him with sulphur and molasses . . .*—Maude Hutchins, *The Memoirs of Maisie,* 1955) but it is confined to social history and to those who wish to seem unusually old-fashioned and rustic.

summary. See **outline.**

summit. See **top.**

summon; summons. *Summon* is the verb. It means to call as with authority to some duty (*He was summoned by the President for consultation on trade agreements*), to call together (*The legislature was summoned on the second Tuesday of the month*), to call into action or arouse (*He summoned his courage, leaped out of his foxhole, and sprinted for the bridge*). Either *summon* or *summons* may be used as the verb meaning to serve with a legal summons.

Summons is the noun form. It is singular and is always used with a singular verb, as in *the summons was delivered.* It has a regular plural *summonses. Summons* may mean an authoritative command or a call to do something. In law it may mean a call or citation by authority to appear before a court or a judicial officer or the writ by which such a call is made (*The summons was served by a grinning bailiff*). It may also mean an authoritative call or notice to appear at a specified place, as for a particular purpose or duty, or a call issued for the meeting of parliament or an assembly.

sumptuous; sumptuary. *Sumptuous* means costly and hence splendid and magnificent (*This sumptuous way of living made him greatly admired and envied for a short while but soon brought him to ruin*). The expression *sumptuous repast* for an excellent or unusually costly meal is a cliché.

Sumptuary, a related but less common word, means pertaining to or dealing with expenses and especially the regulation of expenditure. In former times when differences in social position were not only recognized in law but regarded as the very basis of a wholesome commonweal, most countries had laws governing the style and quality of clothing proper for each estate and these laws were known as *sumptuary laws* (*Elizabethan sumptuary laws forbade the use of velvet, save as mere trimming, to women of less than noble rank, and the use of silk altogether to men and women of no higher status than middle class. The Romans regulated the dress of each class and each age with the utmost precision by the enforcement of the strictest sumptuary laws*).

sums is a colloquial British term for school arithmetic (*They haven't reached sums yet, ma'am. They don't start them till standard two. Have you done your sums today, Harry? They're very hard*). It was formerly used in America, in and out of school, for an arithmetical problem to be solved, or such a problem worked out and having the various steps shown, but has fallen largely into disuse.

Sunday. See **Sabbath.**

sundry. See **few.**

sung. See **sing.**

sunk; sunken. See **sink.**

sunlight; sunshine. *Sunlight* means simply the light of the sun (*They have sunlight there only half the year*). *Sunshine* is used in a number of senses. It may describe the shining of the sun, its direct light, or a place where its direct rays fall (*They lie in the sunshine for hours, getting a tan*). *Sunshine* is also used figuratively to describe brightness or radiance, cheerfulness, happiness (*the sunshine of your smile*) or a source of cheer or happiness (*You are my sunshine*).

sunshade. See **parasol.**

super-. It is an interesting reflection on our democratic and mass-produced times that the prefix *super-*, especially in America, should be so unreservedly a term of commendation. Anything which is above the ordinary or is excessive is, apparently, admirable. We have *supermarkets* and *superhighways* and *superservice* stations and, colloquially and among college humorists, the prefix itself, unprefixed to anything (*Boy, that was super!*), is the height of praise. It was not always so. Time was that men disliked the excessive. In many older words (*supercilious, supererogate, superannuated*) the prefix suggests something unpleasant and undesirable. The furious Kent when upbraiding the contemptible Oswald (*King Lear,* Act II, Scene ii, line 19) can think of nothing more despicable to call him than *superserviceable.* Oswald would be rather pleased today.

superfluous. See **redundant.**

superhuman effort. As a hyperbole for an extraordinary exertion, *a superhuman effort* is a cliché.

superincumbent. See **recumbent.**

superlative degree. See **comparison of adjectives and adverbs.**

superlative; excellent. *Superlative* means of the highest kind or order, surpassing all others, supreme. It should refer to qualities (*He played tennis with superlative skill*), while *excellent,* which means possessing excellent or superior merit, remarkably good, should refer to persons and things (*He is an excellent tennis player and is justified in insisting on excellent equipment*).

supernatural. See **unnatural.**

supernormal. See **abnormal.**

superscription; subscription; signature. A *superscription* is the act of superscribing (writing above or on top of something) or that which is superscribed, such as an address on a letter, or the like. Authorities in England say that *superscription* applies only to a heading of a letter, but American authorities will also allow it as the address on the envelope. *Subscription* (writing under) means the writing of one's name under a document or statement as an indication that the sentiments expressed have the writer's approval or that he agrees to be bound by terms set forth. By extension *subscription* has come to mean a sum of money, the payment of which is guaranteed by signing one's name under a statement or agreement. *Subscription* is often used as a synonym for *signature,* though *sig-*

nature is the better word in this sense, since it is unequivocal. *Subscription* also means assent, agreement, or approval, expressed by, or as by, signing one's name. See also **signature; autograph.**

supersede; surpass. These words are not interchangeable. *Supersede* means to replace, in power, authority, effectiveness, acceptance, or use (*The electric refrigerator has superseded the icebox*). *Surpass* means to go beyond in excellence or achievement, to outdo (*His work surpassed that of all his rivals*).

supine (noun). Some grammarians call an infinitive with *to,* such as *to talk,* a supine. In this book an infinitive with *to* is called simply an infinitive, and a true infinitive, such as *walk,* is called the simple form of the verb. See **simple verb form.**

supine (adjective). See **prone.**

supplant. See **replace.**

supple and **subtle** are not to be confused. A *supple* mind is an agile mind, a mind which readily adapts itself. A *subtle* mind is one characterized by acuteness or penetration, or one which is skillful, clever, or ingenious, especially in perceiving fine but significant distinctions.

supplement and **complement** both indicate an addition to something. *To complement* is to provide something felt to be lacking or needed. It is often applied to putting together two things, each of which supplies what is lacking in the other, to make a complete whole (*They complement one another as doubles players: Joe is excellent at the net, Tom on the base line*). Things that so fit together, each supplying a lack in the other, are called *complements* and are said to be *complementary* or *complementary to* each other. *Supplement* means to add to. No lack or deficiency is necessarily implied, nor is there an idea of a definite relation (*In season he supplemented his diet with fresh fruit but otherwise made little change in his austere regime*).

supplementary; complementary; additional. These words all imply increase in number or quantity. *Complementary* suggests an essential increase required to make something complete (*His writing was complementary to his teaching; his articles on education gained him an enviable reputation and his reputation procured him a professorship*). *Supplementary* emphasizes not so much essential increase as the addition of something which was previously lacking (*The money earned from his writings was supplementary to his salary as a teacher; it enabled him to enjoy many comforts and luxuries which he otherwise would not have been able to afford*). *Additional* means simply added (*Every month, every day indeed, produces its own novelties, with the additional zest that they are novelties*). It is the least restrictive of the three adjectives.

supplied. See **issued.**

supporter. See **proponent.**

suppose may be followed by an infinitive, as in *he supposed me to know all about it,* or by a clause, as in *he supposed I knew all about it.*

The clause is generally preferred. See **imagine; think; suspect.**

supposedly and **presumably** carry different meanings. *Supposedly* means assumed as true, yet perhaps erroneously so (*He is supposedly in London, but then you know how unreliable these rumors are*). *Presumably* means probably, capable of being taken for granted (*Presumably he knows what he's talking about. He's regarded as the best guide in these parts*).

suppositional; suppositious; supposititious. *Suppositional* has practically crowded out *suppositious* to convey the idea of supposed, hypothetical, conjectural (*Men and angels have a certain knowledge of future things; but it is not absolute, but only suppositional*). *Supposititious* means put by artifice in the place of another, counterfeit, spurious. A *supposititious* child (*Queen Philippa . . . upon her deathbed . . . told Wickham that John of Gaunt was not the lawful issue of King Edward, but a supposititious son*) is not an illegitimate child, or at least not merely an illegitimate child, but one by artifice put in the place of or assuming the character of another. Thus when the notorious impostor Arthur Orton convinced Henrietta, Lady Tichborne, that he was really her son Roger, supposedly lost at sea off Rio de Janeiro, he became her supposititious son but certainly not her illegitimate son.

supranatural. See unnatural.

surcease, meaning, as verb and noun, stop, end, is archaic (*If the assassination/ Could trammel up the consequence, and catch/ With his surcease success—Macbeth*, Act I, Scene 7). It survives only in poetry. Its use in prose or everyday speech would seem bookish and affected.

sure; surely. In current English *sure* is used as an adjective to qualify a noun, as in *this is a sure sign,* and *surely* as an adverb to qualify any other kind of word, as in *this is surely a sign.* Formerly *sure* could also be used as an adverb, as in *he is sure a prince of royal courage.* In "The Raven," Poe uses both forms as adverbs. He first writes: *"Surely," said I, "surely that is something at my window"* and then a little later: *"Though thy crest be shorn and shaven, thou," I said, "art sure no craven."* Since then, everybody who ever went to school has learned that *sure* is an adjective and not an adverb, and to use it as an adverb now is to be lacking in a decent respect for the opinions of mankind. There is one exception. *Sure* may still be used as an adverb in the phrase *sure enough,* as in *and sure enough, the palms are there. Sure good* is not in a class with *real good* or even *right good.* It is, in fact, in a class with *this here man.*

When *sure* is followed by *of* and the *-ing* form of a verb, it means that the person spoken about feels sure, as in *he is sure of winning.* When it is followed by an infinitive, it means that everybody else can feel sure, as in *he is sure to win.*

surmise. See guess; suspect.

surplice; surplus. A *surplice* is a garment. A *surplus* is an amount. *Surplice* describes a loose-fitting, broadsleeved, white vestment, properly of linen, worn over the cassock by clergymen and choristers; a garment in which the fronts cross each other diagonally. *Surplus,* in accounting terms, is the excess of assets over liabilities accumulated throughout the existence of a business, excepting assets against which stock certificates have been issued; or an amount of assets in excess of what is requisite to meet liabilities. In general, common usage, *surplus* designates anything which remains above what is used or needed.

surprise. See amaze.

surrender; capitulate. *Surrender* is the general word. It means to yield or give up and may be used transitively or intransitively. It may describe the end of physical resistance, as in military combat, or it may be applied more generally. One surrenders an insurance policy for a consideration, the amount receivable (surrender value) depending on the number of years elapsed from the commencement of the risk. One surrenders an office or a privilege. One surrenders hope, comfort, or other pleasurable emotions.

To *capitulate* was, originally, to draw up a writing under chapter headings or articles; hence to draw up the terms of an agreement. The haughty Coriolanus, in Shakespeare's play, could not bring himself to *capitulate* "with Rome's mechanics;" that is, he could not bring himself, as a candidate for office, to discuss under specific headings, his qualifications and obligations with common working men. The detailed items considered in a capitulation today are the terms of a military surrender, but they formerly could have been terms of federation (*The archbishop's Grace of York, Douglas, Mortimer,/ Capitulate against us—1 Henry IV,* Act III, Scene 2). Today the word means to surrender, sometimes on stipulated terms but more often unconditionally (*I am ashamed to think how easily we capitulate to badges and names, to large societies and dead institutions. On learning that enemy reinforcements were approaching, the garrison capitulated. I must be conquered; I will not capitulate*).

surroundings. In speaking of what physically surrounds something, the plural form *surroundings* is used, and is treated as a plural, as in *the surroundings are pleasant.* A singular form *surrounding* is sometimes used in speaking of human beings, as in *a surrounding of friends,* but this construction is rare. The word cannot be used with a numeral in either sense.

susceptible. See sensitive.

suspect. This verb may be followed by an infinitive, as in *I suspect him to have done it,* or by a clause, as in *I suspect he did it.* The clause is generally preferred.

suspect; surmise; suppose; suspicion. All of these verbs apply to assumptions. *Suspect* has a derogatory sense. It means to imagine to be guilty, false, counterfeit, undesirable, defective, bad, with insufficient proof or no proof at all (*They suspected him of cheating at cards, but there* *was nothing to justify an open accusation*). *Surmise* has no such sinister overtones. It simply means to think or infer without certain or strong evidence, to conjecture or guess (*I surmised that you were his son from your striking resemblance to him. Or perhaps we are only surmising/ Just like all other love-dreamers do*). Though *suspect* may mean *surmise,* the latter, since it is unambiguous, is preferable where there is no derogation intended.

Suppose means to assume, without reference to its being true or false, for the sake of argument or for the purpose of tracing the consequences (*All right, suppose we do give him the money? What will happen then?*), to infer hypothetically. To *suppose* is not merely to imagine, for many things may be supposed (in mathematics and abstract thought) which cannot be imagined. Imagining is the mere imaging forth; supposing is setting up a proposition in order to trace its consequences.

The use of *suspicion* as a verb (as in *I suspicioned he wasn't a real doctor from the very beginning*) is not standard and is often regarded as an indication of illiteracy.

suspenders. A *suspender* is one of a pair of straps used to hold up the trousers. Unlike most words that refer to one object that has two parts, such as *breeches* and *scissors, suspenders* is a regular English plural, and means more than one suspender. The singular form *suspender* is always used as the first element in a compound, as in *a suspender buckle.*

The American dialectal word for suspenders is *galluses.* The English call them *braces.* What the English call *suspenders,* attachments to the top of stockings or socks to hold them in place, Americans call *garters.* A *garter* in this sense in English usage, when used at all, means strictly a band that passes around the leg. When capitalized, in England, it means the Order of the Garter, the highest order of knighthood.

suspension; suspense. Both of these words derive from a Latin word which means to hang up between two points.

Suspension may be used literally with reference to physics where it may describe the state of something hanging from two points or the state in which particles of a solid are mixed with a fluid but undissolved. In physical chemistry it means a system consisting of small particles kept dispersed by agitation (in mechanical suspension) or by the molecular motion in the surrounding medium (in colloidal suspension). In vehicles it means the arrangement of springs, shock absorbers, hangers, etc., in automobiles and railroad cars, connecting the wheel suspension units or axles to the chassis frame. In electricity it means a wire or filament by which the moving part of an instrument or device is suspended; and in music, the prolongation of a tone in one chord into the following chord, usually producing a temporary dissonance.

The most common uses of *suspension,* however, are figurative, with reference to the mind,

to describe a state of being suspended in judgment, or held in equipoise between conclusions and certainties, being held in doubt (*Until we have conclusive evidence, suspension of judgment is the only honorable course*). *Suspension* may also mean interruption, cessation or stopping for a time (*a suspension of further payments pending the investigation*).

Suspense is used exclusively in figurative senses. It means a state of mental uncertainty, as in awaiting a decision or outcome, usually with more or less apprehension or anxiety (*Between the sound of the air raid siren and the explosion of the first bomb we waited in suspense. This suspense is killing me. I wish they'd do one thing or the other!*); a state of mental indecision (*He was in suspense as to the right course to follow*); or undecided or doubtful condition, as of affairs (*For a few hours after the landing matters were in suspense*).

sustain; suffer. *Sustain* means to hold or bear up from beneath, to be the support of (*Doric columns sustained the roof*), to hold suspended or to keep from sinking into despair (*The rope sustained a greater weight than one would have thought it capable of bearing. These hopes sustain us*), to maintain, keep up, nourish (*This is insufficient to sustain life in so cold a climate. Foraging sustained the army throughout the summer*). It also means to bear, to endure without giving way or yielding (*He cannot hope to sustain the comparison which he has invited. To sustain one's dignity in the face of scorn is difficult*).

Sustain has been taken up by journalists, especially in reference to injury, loss, or other unpleasant experiences (*The injury to his arm which Ruth sustained ... The army sustained a heavy defeat*). In such contexts *suffer* is more precise. Indeed, it is insisted on by English grammarians, recommended by American grammarians.

swallow a camel. See **strain at a gnat.**

swam. See **swim.**

swan song is a hackneyed term for a last outburst of energy, especially when it expresses itself in rhetoric or poetry and produces something better than anything the individual has done before. It is based on the ancient—and fabulous—belief that just before its death the swan, unable all its life to sing, utters one melodious song.

swang. See **swing.**

swear. The past tense is *swore.* The participle is *sworn.* A past tense *sware* was once literary English but is no longer heard. A participle *swore,* as in *he has swore,* is heard but is considered illiterate.

swearing. See **blasphemy.**

swear like a trooper. The soldier, the fourth of Shakespeare's seven ages of man, is "Full of strange oaths and bearded like the pard" (*As You Like It,* Act II, Scene 7). Soldiers seem at all times to have been proverbial for their profanity, but they are not alone: one who swears excessively or with unusual vigor or imaginative blasphemy has been said, at different times, to swear like a tinker, a ruffian, an abbot, a gentleman, and a lord. In the eighteenth century the English milord was so famed throughout Europe for his profanity that he was known as *a goddam*. There must have been more to it, however, than this one expletive. "A footman," Swift said, "may swear, but he cannot swear like a lord. He may swear as often, but can he swear with equal delicacy, propriety and judgment?" A trooper's swearing was, presumably, more marked by vigor than by delicacy, propriety, or judgment. The phrase *to swear like a trooper* is now a cliché.

sweat. The past tense is *sweat* or *sweated*. The participle is also *sweat* or *sweated*. In the United States *sweat* is the preferred form for the past tense and the participle, as in *he sweat during the night* and *he has sweat a great deal*. This is no longer heard in Great Britain, where they would say *he sweated during the night*. In both Great Britain and the United States, *sweated* is the required form when the verb means "caused to sweat," as in *the doctor sweated him* and *sweated labor*. *Sweated* is also the preferred form for the past tense or participle in the expression *sweat it out,* meaning "pass through a period of anxiety."

Some people feel that *sweat* is not a delicate word to use in its literal sense when speaking of people, but they have no objection to its being used figuratively of people or literally of things. That is, ladies who insist that human beings merely "perspire," do not hesitate to say *they made him sweat for it* and *the walls are sweating*. See also **perspire**.

sweat of one's brow. Those who speak of earning (or, better still, of others earning) their bread *by the sweat of their brow* usually speak the phrase with a solemnity that implies they are under the impression that they are quoting Holy Writ. They are misquoting it. Genesis 3:19 reads: *In the sweat of thy face shalt thou eat bread*.

sweep. The past tense is *swept*. The participle is also *swept*.

sweeping statement. As a term, with connotations of mild disapproval, for an unjustified generalization, a *sweeping statement* is hackneyed. A *sweeping statement* differs from a *glittering generality* in that it is more dogmatic and aggressive and argumentative, less rhetorical.

sweepstakes has a singular form *sweepstake* but it is seldom used in the United States. Instead, the plural *sweepstakes* is used as both a singular and a plural, as in *he won a sweepstakes* and *he won three sweepstakes*. But the singular form is still preferred as the first element in a compound, as in *a sweepstake ticket*.

sweets. See **candy**.

swell. The past tense is *swelled*. The participle is *swelled* or *swollen*. In the United States *swelled* is preferred to *swollen* when used in a verb form, as in *the wood had swelled,* but *the wood had swollen* is also acceptable. In Great Britain *swollen* is used in this way more often than it is in the United States. In both countries *swollen*

is the preferred form after a form of the verb *be* or immediately before a noun, as in *the wood was swollen* and *a swollen river*.

swept. See **sweep**.

swerve. See **deviate**.

swift; swiftly. The form *swift* may be used as an adjective, as in *his terrible swift sword*. Either form may be used as an adverb, as in *Nor half so swift the trembling doves can fly . . . Not half so swiftly the fierce eagle moves*.

swim. The past tense is *swam*. The participle is *swum*. A past tense *swum,* as in *he swum the river,* and a participle *swam,* as in *he had swam it before* were both literary English a few generations ago, but they are no longer standard.

As a rule, the causative form of an irregular verb, meaning "make to do," is regular, as is the case with *shone* and *shined, sped* and *speeded*. But this is not true here. We say *he swam his horse across the river,* and not *he swimmed it*.

swine. The plural is *swine*. This is a purely literary word. We may speak of *a jewel in a swine's snout* or of *casting pearls before swine,* but the animals in the barnyard are hogs. *Swine* is used in England, both as a singular and a plural, as a term of strong contempt and moral disapprobation. It is much stronger than the American *hog*. See also **pig; hog**.

swing. The past tense is *swung*. The participle is also *swung*. A past tense *swang,* as in *they swang their partners,* was once literary English but is now archaic or dialectal.

Swiss. The singular and the plural are both *Swiss*. This word once had a distinct plural, as seen in *those Swisses fight on any side for pay*. This became obsolete about 1800 and *Swiss* is now the standard form for both singular and plural, as in *one Swiss* and *three Swiss*. But many people feel that *Swiss* is plural only. They hesitate to say *a Swiss* and prefer *a Switzer*. Both forms are acceptable. In England *Switzer* is considered archaic, but it is in general use and thoroughly established in the United States.

switch is a word which serves more purposes in America than in England. In railroad terminology, the movable rails which shift cars and trains from one track to another, known in America as *switches,* are known in England as *points*. As a verb, *switch,* in American railroad usage, means to shift or transfer a train or car, especially in a yard or terminal, or to drop or add cars or to make up a train. The equivalent English verb is *shunt*. Compounds referring to railroading are similarly differentiated. American *switchman* is English *pointsman*. An American *switchtower* is an English *signal-box*. An American *switchyard* or *marshalling-yard* is an English *shunting-yard*.

As an instrument of chastisement, a slender, flexible shoot or rod, used especially in whipping, an American *switch* finds its nearest equivalent in the English *cane,* though they are not exactly synonymous since a switch is usually cut fresh from a tree and is more limber and lashing than a cane. The old-fashioned English term *birch* would be a closer equivalent. Both *switch* and *cane* may be used as noun and verb. The American rustic exclamation, *I'll be switched,* has no equivalent in England, unless one accepts *I'll be damned* which is used in both countries but is somewhat stronger than *I'll be switched.*

Switch is used colloquially in the United States to mean a change of sides in controversy, especially in political opinions or allegiances (*Many on whom Taft had counted for support switched to Roosevelt and his Bull Moose Party. Shivers' switch to the Republican camp was a blow to Stevenson's hopes*). *Switch* has the further colloquial meaning in America of an interchanging or the making of a reciprocal exchange (*In the scuffle, Hamlet and Laertes switch rapiers*). In slang, especially in theatrical, movie, radio and television parlance, a *switch* is a reversal of an established, expected or stereotyped situation or action (*But here's the switch: it's the detective who goes to jail!*). In gayer moments this is also known as the *switcheroo.*

Though both Britons and Americans use *switchback* to describe a mountain railroad or highway having many hairpin curves, only the English also use *switchback* to describe what Americans call a *roller coaster.*

swollen. See **swell.**

swore; sworn. See **swear.**

swum. See **swim.**

swung. See **swing.**

syllabus. The plural is *syllabuses* or *syllabi.*

syllepsis; zeugma. *Syllepsis* is a term in rhetoric and grammar. It describes a figure of speech by which a word is used in the same passage to fulfill two syntactical functions, applying properly to one person or thing and improperly to another (as in *He fought with fury and a big blackjack* or *In his lectures he leaned heavily upon his desk and stale jokes*). *Zeugma,* which is really a form of syllepsis, is commonly used as the word for both figures. *Zeugma* is a figure in which a verb is associated with two subjects or objects, or an adjective with two nouns, although appropriate to but one of the two, yet suggests another verb or adjective suitable to the other noun. Although commonly merely a fault, zeugma may, once in a great while, be used intentionally by a skillful writer. One of the best-known examples is Pope's comment on Hampton Court:

> *Here thou, great ANNA! whom three realms obey,*
> *Dost sometimes counsel take—and sometimes Tea.*

The last line, however, is no blunder but one of the felicities of English poetry, not only because of the perfection of its humorous skill, but because of its touching suggestion that Queen Anne herself was a living zeugma, two unequal things yoked together: by the Grace of God, Defender of the Faith, Queen of England, Ireland, and Scotland and, at the same time, a pathetic, dumpy, dull, lonely, little woman, sad with her dead babies, bored with her stupid husband, and far more at home at the tea than at the council table.

symposium. The plural is *symposiums* or *symposia.*

synchronous; simultaneous; coincident. All of these adjectives mean existing, living, or occurring at the same time. *Coincident* means happening at the same time (*The attack on Pearl Harbor was coincident with the call of the Japanese envoys on the Secretary of State*). *Synchronous* means going on at the same rate and exactly together, recurring together (*The timers in the gun turrets and in the fire control room were synchronous*). *Simultaneous* means operating at the same time or in agreement in the same point or instant of time (*The salvoes from the two main turrets were simultaneous*).

Contemporary and *contemporaneous,* which also mean existing at the same time, differ from *synchronous* and *simultaneous* and *coincident* in that the time regarding which simultaneity or agreement is implied is indefinite. With regard to human beings, it may be a lifetime; with regard to events, it may be an age or an era. See also **contemporary; contemporaneous; coeval.**

synecdoche is a term in rhetoric for a figure of speech in which a part is named for the whole, as "sail" for "ship" in *a fleet of fifty sail* or "wheel" for "bicycle" in *he borrowed his wheel for a spin out to Iffley.* It may name the special for the general or vice versa, or the whole for the part. When Robert Frost, the poet, called himself a "synecdochist," he meant that in himself as an individual was figured the common experience of the race and vice versa.

synonym. A *synonym* is a word which has the same or nearly the same meaning as another word in the language (such as *happy* and *glad*) or a word or expression accepted as another name for something, as *Utopian* for *ideal.*

It is a great mistake, however, to assume that because words are synonymous at one point in their meaning they are synonymous at all points. In addition to their central or basic meaning, words acquire connotations, or secondary implied or associated meanings, and unless they agree in all of these—and few words do—they are not completely synonymous. Thus *house* and *home* are synonymous in indicating a dwelling, but their associations differ. *House* is the less emotionally weighted of the two words, suggesting usually no more than a structure, though it is sometimes used as an abbreviation of *house of ill fame,* or, in the combination *big house,* for a prison, in which usages it is strongly opposed to the commonest meaning of *home. Home* has commonly the associations of "a heap o' living" to make it a much warmer word than house, but used, as it often is, as a euphemism for a workhouse or old folks' home (*They put her in a home in Milwaukee*), it has sad and dismal connotations.

So with thousands of other synonyms. *Canine, dogged,* and *currish,* for example, are all synonymous in the sense of pertaining to or resembling a dog, but have little else in common. Synonyms must be chosen with care.

synopsis. The plural is *synopsises* or *synopses.* See **outline.**

synthesis. The plural is *syntheses.*

synthetic; artificial; imitation; ersatz; spurious. All of these adjectives describe something which is not natural in origin.

Synthetic is a chemical term to describe compounds formed by chemical reaction in a laboratory, as opposed to those of natural origin (*When the rubber plantations fell to the Japanese, America began seriously to manufacture synthetic rubber*). Though many synthetic products are superior to the natural substance in some ways, it was at first assumed that they were inferior and in extensions of the word it has a pejorative connotation, suggesting something manufactured which should have been natural (*The synthetic laughter at the boss's jokes was distressingly shrill*).

Artificial means made in imitation of, not genuine, whether its substance is synthetic or organic. It is to be used in describing something with a practical purpose (*In a remarkably short time after the operation, he was fitted with an artificial limb*). Though neutral in many technical applications, and becoming increasingly so as artificial products become equal or superior to those they are made in imitation of, in its figurative uses the word is still disparaging (*Her manners are so artificial, so awkward. These are artificial compliments, my friend. They creak*). See also **art; artifice.**

Imitation means made to imitate a genuine or superior article, or the act of so imitating, usually an article having aesthetic rather than practical value (*She wore imitation pearls on her long, slender neck*). In almost all uses the word is disparaging, though not as much so as it used to be.

Ersatz is a word taken over from the German.

It means serving as a substitute (*English sausages in 1943 were an ersatz delicacy, consisting largely of flour and potatoes*). The word was taken over from the Germans because in the period between World War I and World War II, faced with many scarcities, the Germans proved ingenious in manufacturing substitutes and their law required all ersatz products to be plainly so marked, so that the word *ersatz* was seen in every shop window and became a joke with them, half bitter and half proud.

Spurious means false, not genuine, counterfeited (*These spurious claims of heroism were soon exposed as a fraud*). It is a word of strong condemnation. A woman would know and, at least among her friends, freely admit that her pearls were artificial or imitation. They would not be called spurious unless she or someone else had stated that they were genuine and it had been shown that they were not. She would be humiliated and offended at the term.

systematic; systemic. *Systematic* is the general word; *systemic* has exclusively physiological implications.

Systematic means having, showing, or involving a system, method, or plan (*He drew up a systematic plan to teach himself French in three months*); characterized by system or method (*A systematic worker usually gets a great deal done, even though he is slow*); arranged in or comprising an ordered system (*systematic philosophy*).

Systemic is a physiological and pathological term. It means pertaining to or affecting the entire bodily system, or the body as a whole (*The systemic effects of shell shock are numerous and complicated*); pertaining to a particular system of parts or organs of the body.

systemize; systematize. *Systemize* is a variant, though one little used, in England or America, of the verb *systematize,* which means to arrange in or according to a system, reduce to a system, make systematic (*Darwin systematized the biological discoveries and insights of many researchers who had preceded him*).

T

tab. In general a *tab* is a small flap, strap, loop or similar appendage, as on a garment; a tag or label. In England a *red tab* is a staff officer, so called because of the red tab on his uniform, a *Tab* is a Cantab. or a Cantabrigian, a Cambridge University man.

In America *tab* is used in a number of colloquial and idiomatic expressions. As a noun *tab* may mean an account or check or memorandum of what is owed, especially a dinner check or the bill at a restaurant (*I got the tab for our party of*

eight) and, by extension of this meaning, to *pick up the tab* means to bear the expense (*Who's going to pick up the tab when the government is on relief?*—Chicago *Sun-Times,* Jan. 24, 1950, p. 27). *Keeping tab on* means keeping account of or a check on (*They were keeping tab on Clara's age, too, and began to think she would land on the Bargain Counter*—George Ade).

table (verb). *To table* a motion means, to an American, to stop talking about it, or at least to put it on the table of an assembly for future table   496

discussion, a procedure often used as a method of postponing or shelving it. *To table* a motion, to *lay it on the table* means, to an Englishman, to put it on the agenda. Sir Winston Churchill records that this confusion in meaning was the cause of a great deal of annoyance among the Allied leaders in World War II.

table d'hôte. This is a French term and the French plural is *tables d'hôte.* But the plural *table d'hôtes* is heard more often in the United States.

tableau. The plural is *tableaus* or *tableaux.*

taciturn. See **reticent.**

tactics. See **strategy.**

tactile; tactual. The precise writer will use *tactile* to mean endowed with the sense of touch and will apply it to organs and qualities (*The cat's whiskers are tactile and probably serve better than its eyes to guide the head through slender mazes*). *Tactual* is the more general word, meaning of or pertaining to touch (*Tactual tests still have great value in diagnosis*).

taffy. See **toffee.**

tag as a noun is used to describe a piece or strip of strong paper, leather, or the like, for attaching by one end to something as a mark or label. The English use *label. Tag* is also the American name for a game in which one player chases the others until he touches one of them. *To play tag* may be used figuratively to mean to touch upon, or come close to (*Thoroughly charged with special significance as it is, the drama plays tag with boredom none the less*). As a verb in this sense, *tag* means to touch in or as in the game of tag. By extension *tag* means in baseball to touch a base runner with the ball and thus put him out (*The pitcher whirled and threw to first base. The runner was taking too long a lead and was tagged out*).

American *tag day,* a day on which contributions to a fund are solicited, each contributor receiving a tag, is the equivalent of English *flag day.*

tag lines hold the same relation to wit that clichés do to style. To the innocent and the ignorant they seem to indicate one who is in the know. To the intelligent they indicate that the speaker is a poor, bleating thing, "a fellow of no mark or likelihood."

Tag lines may have been clever or pointed in their original application, but they become tag lines when used as a ready-made means of participating in conversation, especially when the speaker, who by their use demonstrates that he has no humorous invention of his own, intends them to show that he is bright and up to date.

The tag line is related to slang in that it is a novelty that secures immediate popularity. Its novelty, of course, fades as quickly as it bloomed, though the stale expressions often linger on and settle down among the trite phrases the language is heir to. The meaning—even the applicability —of a tag line may be lost *before* it has gained its full currency. And yet it will go on being repeated ten million times a day to the accompaniment of the idiot laughter of those who repeat

it without the faintest idea of its meaning. The extreme example of this was the phrase which shook the nation at the turn of the century— probably the most popular of all tag lines: *Twenty-three's your number!* At the very height of its raging popularity all attempts to discover its origin or meaning were futile. Unfortunates whose street address or office numbers happened to be 23, or who had arrived at the age of 23, were overwhelmed with gales of laughter whenever it was necessary for them to make the fact known in public. Yet no one knew why.

The tag line with the lowest common denominator is likely to have the greatest survival value, since its very lack of meaning makes it applicable to almost any situation. Thus *So what?* and *I know what you mean* are still with us, while *Applesauce* and *So is your old man* have lost the fascination they once had.

Tag lines most often originate in popular entertainment. Sometimes it is a line from a show or a recurring expression that is identified with a character or comedian: *Izzat so? You can't hardly get that kind no more. Here we go again! Toujours gai!* Sometimes it's a song title: *Life is just a bowl of cherries*—or an advertising slogan: *Eventually, why not now?*

To the feeble-minded they have their uses. They signify that the speaker is present and paying attention (*You tell 'em! Well, whaddya know? How about that? That's for sure!*). They permit him to make sage observations on the state of affairs (*That's a fact! Fifty million Frenchmen can't be wrong!*), to summarize the bitter wisdom of a full life (*I've had it!*), and to check the presumptuous with a devastating and unanswerable retort (*Get lost! Drop dead!*).

The wise find them useful too. There is no stronger incentive to humility than remembering our youthful pride in our wit and savoir-faire as we repeated *Yes, we have no bananas* and *Wanna buy a duck?*

take. The past tense is *took.* The participle is *taken.*

Took as a participle, as in *he had took it,* was literary English well into the nineteenth century but is not considered standard now.

Take may be followed by the *-ing* form of a verb with the preposition *to,* as in *he took to gambling,* but not by an infinitive when used in this sense. We cannot say *he took to gamble.* The sentence *he took to drink* is not an exception because *drink* is here a noun, and not a verb, and the sentence is comparable to *he took to cards.* When *take* means "understand" or "infer" it may be followed by an object and *to be,* as in *I take you to be an honest man,* or by a clause following the pronoun *it,* as in *I take it you are an honest man.*

Take is sometimes used to mean "caught," especially with the names of specific diseases, as in *he took pneumonia and died.* This now has an old-fashioned or countrified tone. But if the disease spoken about is something more general, this is still standard usage, as in *he took cold* and *I take everything that comes along.* The expression *take sick* is not used in Great Britain, where it is considered an Americanism, but it is acceptable spoken English in the United States. See **bring.**

take a leaf out of someone's book. As a term for imitating someone or following his example, *to take a leaf out of his book* is a cliché.

take by storm. As a term for overcoming resistance rapidly, making a favorable impression in an overwhelming manner, sweeping all hesitations and doubts aside, *to take by storm* is hackneyed. It is a metaphor based on a metaphor, since it is drawn from military action which, in turn, is named from the meteorological term.

take one's life in one's hands. To say of one who is starting on a dangerous enterprise that he is *taking his life in his hands* is to employ a cliché. It is no less a cliché if used humorously.

take the bit in one's teeth. As a term for obstinacy, for a rash determination to ignore all guiding control and proceed, usually with headlong violence, on one's own course, *to take the bit in one's teeth* is worn out. The expression seems to have been a proverb when Aeschylus employed it in *Prometheus Bound* (about 470 B.C.) A horse is guided by the pressure of the bit against the sensitive edges of its mouth. If it gets the bit in its teeth, as a young or intractable horse will do before it is fully broken in, the rider or driver no longer controls it and it usually runs away.

take the bread out of his mouth. As a way of saying that someone or something has destroyed a man's livelihood, to say that it has *taken the bread out of his mouth* is to employ a cliché.

take the bull by the horns. As a term for meeting a dangerous situation with courage, or a powerful person with resolution, especially when the one in danger advances to meet the danger, *to take the bull by the horns* is a cliché.

take the wind out of someone's sails. To come between an enemy's vessel and the wind, so that your ship was still maneuverable while his was suddenly becalmed and helpless, was one of the great objects of naval maneuvering in the days of sailing vessels. Used figuratively, to mean to nonplus someone, to abash him and by his sudden discomfiture to have him at a disadvantage, *to take the wind out of his sails* is stale and a little forced.

take the words out of one's mouth. As an expression for anticipating what someone else was about to say, *to take the words out of his mouth* or *to take the words right out of his mouth* or *to take the very words out of his mouth,* etc., is hackneyed.

take time by the forelock, as an expression for seizing an opportunity while it is favorable, is a cliché.

Several Greek fabulists represented opportunity or (the favorable) time as a man with a forelock which could be seized as he approached but bald behind, so that once he had passed nothing could be done. The figure of the old man with an hourglass and scythe, by which cartoonists represent time today, usually has an elongated forelock.

take to one's heels, as a term for running away, is hackneyed. Several other such expressions (such as *show a clean pair of heels*) that have to do with running away emphasize the heels, though the running is done on the sole or ball of the foot. Perhaps the heels are conspicuous to the one following or the one from whom the other runs away, the one who would be more likely to employ such phrases, all of which are good-humoredly contemptuous.

taken. See **take.**

talent. For talent in its meaning of a high order of natural ability, see **genius.**

In movie, radio, and television circles *talent* has the rather special group meaning of actors and performers of all kinds as distinguished from technicians or administrators (*The rule of no smoking on the set does not apply to talent during the course of a show*). There is no suggestion whatever in the use of the word that the talent are talented. There just has to be some word to mark the distinction and *talent* is it.

In the term *talent scout,* one who makes a business of searching out those possessed with talent in order that they may be tested on the stage or screen, there is something of the same meaning of *talent* but there is a shade more of expectation that the *talent* will be talented. These terms are both so thoroughly established that they must be accepted as standard.

talisman; talesman. *Talisman* (plural *talismans*) means a stone, ring, or other object, engraved with figures or characters under certain superstitious observances of the heavens, which is supposed to possess occult powers, and is worn as an amulet or charm (*Books are not seldom talismans and spells/ By which the magic art of shrewder wits/ Holds an unthinking multitude enthralled. By that dear talisman, a mother's name*).

Talesman (plural *talesmen*) means a person summoned as one of the *tales,* persons chosen from among the bystanders or those present in court to serve on the jury when the original panel has become deficient in number. It is a rare word, certainly very little used in contemporary America.

talk (as a noun). See **dialogue.**

talking through one's hat. As a term for talking nonsense, usually of a pompous sort, with a suggestion that the speaker knows that what he is saying is nonsense, *talking through one's hat* is a cliché. Although the expression seems to have originated in the early twentieth century, its origin is uncertain.

tall; high; lofty. *High* is a general term, and denotes either extension upward or position at a considerable height. It also carries a suggestion of bigness. A mountain is *high* and so is a wall (though the latter may be so because it sounds better to say *high wall* than *tall wall*). An airplane is spotted *high* in the sky. If it is directly above, especially above another plane, it is twelve o'clock high. *High* is the word applied to moral and intellectual matters (*a man of high courage*). In this sense, *lofty* is often used as a synonym. *Lofty* implies an impressive height (*a lofty room, lofty trees*). By itself, in figurative use, it is slightly disparaging, implying a cold aloofness or an assumption of unmerited superiority (*These lofty pretensions have very little support. She was very lofty this morning*).

Tall is a more limiting term than *high:* it is applied either to that which is high in proportion to its breadth (*I remember, I remember ... the fir trees, tall and high. Those are very tall glasses*) or to anything higher than the average of its kind (*A tall man with a high hat and whiskers on his chin/ Will soon be knocking at your door. London has few tall buildings*). *Tall* is used idiomatically and colloquially in America to mean extravagant, hard-to-believe (*He was full of tall tales about his life as a commando*); high-flown or grandiloquent (*That was mighty tall talk, but you notice that little came of it*). *Tall timber* to describe woods with high trees, is an American expression. So is the colloquial *tall drink*, a sort of pun on *highball*, another American term. *Highboy*, which in America describes a tall chest of drawers supported on legs, is generally in England a *tallboy*.

In its literal sense, *tall* seems confined by usage to that which lives and grows. Otherwise it is usually figurative. In general use, if one is in doubt which word to apply, use *high*.

tantalize; harass; irritate. *Tantalize* derives from Tantalus, a mythical Greek king who was punished by the gods by being stood up to his chin in water which receded as he stooped to drink, and placed under branches of fruit which always evaded his grasp. Thus to *tantalize* is to torment with, or as with, the sight of something desired but out of reach, to tease by arousing expectations that are repeatedly disappointed (*She knew how to tantalize men*). To be *tantalized* is to be *irritated*, to be excited to impatience or anger, but it is to be irritated in a particular way and the distinction of this particularity should be preserved. The verbs are not synonymous. *Harass*, a stronger word than *irritate*, describes torturing or tormenting by persistent disturbance or cares. *To harass* is to tire out by disturbing, to trouble with repeated attacks. It is often used in a military context (*German planes harassed the troops on the beach at Dunkirk*) or in the context of daily work (*He was harassed by the continual demands upon his time of trivial things that could not be dismissed but had to be dealt with even though they prevented him from accomplishing the important and urgent task that had been assigned to him*). *Continually harass* is redundant.

tantamount. See **paramount.**

tap. See **faucet.**

taps in America is the word to describe a signal on a drum, bugle, or trumpet at which all lights in soldiers' or sailors' quarters must be extinguished (*They lay in the darkness ... listening to Taps weep out over the public-address system,*

enormous and sorrowful over the herded shabby acres of men who were no longer civilians and not yet soldiers*). The English term is *lights out*. The signal is usually played at solemn military funerals and the word is used, figuratively and colloquially, to mean the end (*Taps for Private Tussie. It'll be taps for you, brother, if the boss catches you fooling around here in his office*).

tardy in America today means, primarily, late or behindhand (*He was tardy to school only once in his entire four years*). In England the principal meaning of *tardy* is moving or acting slowly, slow, sluggish, dilatory (*The finest timber is of tardy growth*). This sense in America is secondary and seldom used.

target; objective. Though a target is a form of objective, *target* and *objective* are not synonymous. Literally *target* designates a device, usually marked with concentric circles, to be aimed at in shooting practice or contests, or any object used for this purpose, or anything fired at (*An airplane at ten thousand feet is a very small target*). The extension of *target* to mean any goal or objective to be reached—a practice in which the English indulge even more than the Americans—has its dangers, particularly if the objective is one expressible in numerical terms, for no idea of numbers is implied in the basic meaning. If, for example, one is told that a fund drive has gone *beyond the target* one is being informed not that there has been a failure, as one would have to suppose if one kept the metaphor in mind, but that the drive has been more successful than anticipated.

tarred with the same brush. As a way of saying that someone shares, though perhaps to a lesser degree, the faults or sins of another, is defiled in the same way, *tarred with the same brush* is trite and worn.

The origin of the expression is disputed. Some think it has to do with tarring and feathering, once a legal punishment. Others connect it with the tarring of sheep, for identification and protection against ticks. In early American usage the phrase (along with *a touch of the tar brush*) was used to mean that the person spoken of had some Negro blood.

tart. See **pie.**

Tartar; Tatar. *Tatar*, the original term, is now used chiefly in an ethnological sense. The *Tatar Republic* is an autonomous republic in the Eastern Soviet Union in Europe, with a capital at Kazan.

Tartar (formed on *Tatar* by association with Tartarus, Hell, because to the Christians of Europe the Tatars seemed like fiends from Hell) is now usually the term to describe a member of any of a mingled host of Mongolian, Turkish, and other tribes who, under the leadership of Genghis Khan, overran Eastern Europe during the Middle Ages. It is also applied to a member of the descendants of this people, variously intermingled with other races and tribes, now inhabiting parts of the European and west and central Asiatic Soviet Union. *Tartar* may also describe any of several Turkic languages of west central

Asia, particularly Uzbeg. The uncapitalized form *tartar*, based on observed or imagined characteristics of *Tartars*, means a shrew or vixen, a savage, intractable person.

Catch a tartar, as an expression for getting hold of something you can't control, especially something which was ardently desired but which when obtained is found to be extremely unpleasant, is a cliché. The origin of the term is uncertain, though its meaning is fairly clear. There is what seems like a reference to the saying in Samuel Butler's *Hudibras* (1663), but the first clear statement of it occurs in Dryden's *The Kind Keeper* (1678). Francis Grose in his *Classical Dictionary of the Vulgar Tongue* (1785) attributes the origin to an Irishman who in a battle against the Turks called out excitedly that he had "caught a Tartar." When those on his side called back "Bring him here," he shouted "I can't; he won't let me." Whether historically true or not, the story certainly explains the idea of the expression.

taste. This verb may be followed by an adjective describing the source of the taste, as in *it tastes sour* and *it tastes good*. The use of an adverb here, as in *it tastes well*, is not technically correct and is considered unacceptable by many people. When *taste* is used with a personal subject it may be qualified by an adverb, as in *he tasted it quickly*.

tasteful(ly); tasty; tastily. *Tasteful* is the correct word for having, displaying, or being in accordance with good taste. *Tasty* is permitted in America but frowned on in England when used in this sense. In its sense of pleasing to the taste, savory, appetizing (*Freshly baked apple pie makes a tasty dessert*), the word is acceptable in speech.

As *tasteful* is to be preferred to *tasty*, so the adverb *tastefully* is to be preferred to *tastily*.

To say, especially of flowers on a table, that they are *tastefully arranged* is to employ a worn commendation.

taught. See **teach.**

tautology. See **redundancy.**

taxed to its utmost capacity as a way of saying that something can hold or do or stand no more, is trite.

teach. The past tense is *taught*. The participle is also *taught*. This verb may be followed by an infinitive, as in *teach your grandson to shoot a rifle*, or by a *that* clause, as in *they teach that the world is round*. *Teach* may be followed by a great many words ending in *-ing*, such as *reading, writing, swimming*, but only when these words are felt to be names of recognized courses of study. *Teach* cannot be followed by the *-ing* form of a verb in any other sense. That is, we may say he *taught me to struggle harder* but not he *taught me struggling harder*. See also **learn.**

teamwork; team spirit; the team; on our team; etc. The flippant, the scornful, the skeptical and the irreverent are always being reminded that their jokes may be offensive to those who do not share their disrespect of many established customs and values. Similarly however, and far less frequently, the solemn, the solid, and the conventional need to be reminded that the whole world does not share their outlook and that some of their expressions may have different connotations for some of their listeners than they have for them. Among these must be listed—not invariably, but more often than they have any idea of—unctuous clichés regarding *teamwork, the team, team spirit, our team,* and the like, especially in figurative extensions. One does not have to be too cynical to have at least some reservations about the educational, social, or even moral value of a great deal of organized athletics. Much of it is commercial and much is tainted with downright dishonesty and association with highly undesirable people. And *teamwork* is the keynote of its hucksters, barkers, and shills—a keynote which some do not find wholly inspiring.

tear. The past tense is *tore*. The participle is *torn*.

A participle *tore*, as in *had tore*, is heard but is not acceptable.

technic; technics; technique; technology. *Technic* and *technics* are seldom used. They would seem mispronunciations or affectations to the ordinary educated man.

As an adjective, *technic* is obsolescent for *technical*. As a noun, it has been largely replaced by *technique*. *Technics*, a noun, has been replaced by *technique* or, when it means the study or science of an art or of arts in general, especially of the mechanical or industrial arts, by *technology*. *Technique* is familiar as the description of method of performance, especially in artistic work. It is also used slangily in America to signify social adroitness, "smoothness" (*Your chin is weak,/ You lack technique,/ So what have you got/ That gets me?*). *Technology* is the branch of knowledge that deals with the industrial arts; the sciences of the industrial arts (*He studied at the Massachusetts Institute of Technology*). It may also describe the terminology of an art or science, technical nomenclature.

teeming with; rich in. There are in English three verbs *to teem*. One means to produce, to bring forth, to bear (*"What's the newest grief?" "Each minute teems a new one"*), or, intransitively, to be or become pregnant, to conceive, bear (*If she must teem,/ Create her child of spleen, that it may live/ And be a thwart disnatur'd torment to her*) or to be full, as a pregnant woman, or to be prolific, stocked to overflowing, abundantly fertile. Another, a rare meaning, is to be fit for, to be becoming, to think fit for. The third meaning, an entirely different word, is to pour, to empty and, intransitively, to come down in torrents. And it may be that the meaning of the third verb has colored the meaning of the first.

Teeming with is not so general as *rich in*. A stream may be teeming with, that is fertile with or prolific with or stocked to overflowing with, salmon and therefore be rich in salmon. Whereas a museum may be rich in Old Masters but not teeming with them.

teeth. See **tooth.**

telecast; televise. When these two words are used as verbs, *telecast* is the more limited in meaning.

It means to broadcast by television. *Televise,* on the other hand, means to record by means of television apparatus and to broadcast what is so recorded (*It was found that films could be telecast just as well as live shows. The news was televised on the spot*).

tell. The past tense is *told.* The participle is also *told.*

When *tell* means ask it may be followed by an infinitive, as in *tell her to come.* When it does not mean ask it may be followed by a clause, as in *tell her I have gone.*

tell; inform; advise; acquaint; apprise. *Tell* is the general word meaning to make known by speech or writing. *Inform* is a somewhat more formal word, meaning to impart knowledge of a fact or circumstance (*No Sir, a man has not a right to think as he pleases; he should inform himself and think justly*). In official circles *to inform* is not merely to impart a piece of knowledge but to put the recipient of the information on notice that he has been told (*Were you not informed of these things?*). If someone has been informed of something, we regard that something as more authoritative than if he had been informally told. *Informed sources* (though the term is often no more than a journalistic euphemism for rumor or gossip) are thought to be more reliable than someone who has simply been told something. In ordinary commercial correspondence *inform* is often pretentious (as in *We will inform you when your order is ready*).

Advise properly means to give counsel to, not merely to give information to (*I advise you to drive carefully over the holiday weekend*). To advise someone that an order has been shipped is preposterous, though one might advise him to have a care in dealing with those who used words with so little knowledge of their meaning. See **advice; advise.**

Acquaint in the sense of furnish with knowledge or inform is considered archaic in England but is standard in America (*I hope you will acquaint the public with what we have been doing*).

Apprise is a seldom used, formal word meaning to give notice to, inform (*He had not been apprised of the shift in foreign policy. Apprise my parents, make them rescue me*). It is often followed by *of.*

telling effect, with. To say of something that was forcible or vigorous that it was done or spoken or received or delivered, and so on, *with telling effect* is to employ a hackneyed term.

tell tales out of school. To say of someone who (often inadvertently) reveals information that may be hurtful to another that he is *telling tales out of school* is to employ a cliché. In addition to being tedious, it labors to be arch.

temperature. See **fever.**

tempers the wind to the shorn lamb, the Lord. As a pseudo-philosophic (and not wholly justified) comment on the fact that the tender and the helpless and the innocent are spared too severe affliction, the observation that *the Lord tempers the wind to the shorn lamb* is a cliché. Many who utter it are of the opinion that it is a quotation from the Bible. It is from Laurence Sterne's *A*

Sentimental Journey (1768) where it is a translation of a sentence in *Les Prémices* (1594) of Henri Estienne. Estienne refers to it as a proverb.

tempest in a teapot. As a term for making a great fuss over a trifle, *a tempest in a teapot* is now a cliché. The phrase has been traced back, in various forms, to 400 B.C. Cicero referred to one who "stirred up waves in a wine ladle" and added "as the saying goes."

tempo. The plural is *tempos* or *tempi.*

temporal; temporary. Though both of these adjectives refer to time, they do so in different senses. *Temporal* is opposed to *spiritual, temporary* to *permanent. Temporal* means of or concerned with the present life of this world, with things subject to the sway of time, worldly (*The king was the temporal authority, the Pope the spiritual authority*). Hence *temporal* is sometimes used in opposition to ecclesiastical, clerical, and sacred. *Temporary* means "for the time being." It implies an arrangement established with no thought of continuance but with the idea of being changed soon (*Joe got a temporary job driving a cab while he waited for his commission to come through*).

temporary compounds. A true compound word that is hyphenated, such as *secretary-treasurer* or *self-respect,* keeps its hyphen no matter where it appears in the sentence. (See **compound words.**) But there are other word combinations that are hyphenated under certain circumstances and not under others. Absolute consistency in the use of these hyphens cannot be maintained and it is questionable whether a ninety percent consistency is worth the time and trouble it requires. The following discussion is not offered as a guide to what ought to be done but merely as an explanation of the various hyphens one is likely to see in print.

1. *Oil-bearing shale.* These words mean "shale that is bearing oil." Inverted phrases of this kind, in which a present participle is preceded by its object and both qualify a following noun, are usually hyphenated, as in *habit-forming drugs, money-making ideas, life-giving water.* But the hyphen is not used when expressions of this kind follow the noun, as in *the drug became habit forming, the idea was money making.* (Present participle combinations do not come under this rule when the first word is not the object of the participle, as in *a slow moving train, a long suffering friend.*)

2. *A face-to-face encounter; under-water rocks.* Prepositional phrases are almost always hyphenated when they stand before the noun they qualify but not otherwise, as in *it was a face-to-face encounter, he met him face to face* and *there were under-water rocks, the rocks were under water.* (This rule does not apply to Latin phrases. We write *ante bellum days, per diem employees, an ex officio member.*)

3. *A light-yellow scarf; a rich-brown cake.* Occasionally a double adjective standing before a noun can be read in more than one way. *A light yellow scarf* might be a scarf that was light yellow or it might be a yellow scarf that didn't weigh much. *A rich brown cake* might be a cake

that was rich brown, or it might be a brown cake that was very fattening. The ambiguity depends on the fact that *light* and *rich* both have more than one meaning. There is no such difficulty with *a dark yellow scarf* or *a pale brown cake.* English has a great many punnable words of this kind and usually there is nothing to do about it. But in a case of this kind the hyphen can be used, and should be used, to link the first two words when that is what is intended.

4. *The man next door's radio.* Sometimes word combinations are hyphenated because the whole expression is a genitive. This is not necessary and a hyphen here is usually a mistake. We write *John Brown's body, the King of Spain's daughter,* and we should write *the man next door's radio.*

5. *A two story house.* Hyphens are helpful in some of the cases discussed above because the words themselves are being used in an unusual way and may therefore be ambiguous. Words are never ambiguous when they are standing in their proper position in a sentence, unless there is the possibility of a pun. *A two story house, a dark green dress, nineteenth century literature,* are all normal English and do not need hyphens in order to be understood.

Hyphens are often used in expressions of this kind, not for the sake of readability, but in order to avoid what some textbooks claim is a grammatical error. In the examples just given, the second word before the noun is qualifying the first word before the noun and not the noun itself. It is therefore functioning as an adverb. But these first words are all familiar as adjectives. Some people have the mistaken idea that if a word can be used as an adjective it cannot also lawfully be used as an adverb. Therefore, they argue, a construction of this kind must be wrong, although so far as sound goes it is obviously standard English. A hyphen is supposed to offer a way out of the difficulty by creating a new and respectable adjective form known as a "unit modifier." This is an artificial and rather silly device. No printer's mark that is not reflected in the spoken language can have any bearing on whether or not a construction is standard English.

6. *First-, second-, and third-grade children.* When more than one term is theoretically joined to the same word, each one may be given a hyphen, as in the example. But some editors prefer to omit the hyphens entirely in a series of this kind. They write *a third-grade child* but *first, second, and third grade children.* Either form is acceptable, but they should not be combined. That is, if the hyphen is dropped after *first* and *second,* it should also be dropped after *third.*

7. *New Jersey potatoes.* Proper nouns are never hyphenated merely because they are being used as adjectives. We write *New Jersey potatoes* and *New England clam chowder.*

8. *The New York-Pennsylvania highways; the Boy Scouts-Bears picnic. New York-Pennsylvania highways* means highways running through New York and Pennsylvania; *the Boy Scouts-Bears picnic* means a picnic arranged by some Boy Scouts and another group who call themselves *Bears.* No one who didn't already know what these terms meant would ever guess it from the punctuation. Actually, expressions of this kind are spoken with a comma break, but custom requires a hyphen and not a comma here. Some sensitive editors believe that they can relieve the situation by using a small dash instead of a hyphen. But since few people except printers can see the difference between a small dash and a hyphen, this solution doesn't accomplish much. Less sensitive editors sometimes ask a writer to recast the sentence—that is, to say something else that they know how to punctuate.

temporize; extemporize. *Temporize* applies primarily to actions, *extemporize* to words. *To temporize* means to act indecisively or evasively to gain time or delay matters; to comply with the time or occasion; to yield temporarily or ostensibly to the current of opinion or circumstances (*Queen Elizabeth was chiefly remarkable for her ability to temporize*). *To extemporize* is to speak extempore, without notes. It also means to sing or play on an instrument, composing the music as one proceeds, to improvise. See also **extemporaneous.**

tend may be followed by an infinitive, as in *it tends to bring them together.* It is also heard with the *-ing* form of a verb and the preposition *to,* as in *it tends to bringing them together.* The infinitive is generally preferred.

tend; attend. *Tend* as a shortened form of *attend* in the sense of pay attention to is now dialectal (*Why don't you tend to your own business?*). *Tend* still means to attend to by work or services (*Ab used to tend bar over at the Dutchman's place*) or to watch over (*Tending sheep is monotonous work*).

tend; trend. As verbs *tend* and *trend* are interchangeable in the sense of to be disposed or inclined to take a particular direction, to extend in some direction indicated (*The coast from there trends northeast*). Although *trend* in the sense of to have a general tendency is regarded as obsolescent in England, it is still acceptable in the United States. *Tend,* a verb only, is standard in the United States but regarded as poetic and old-fashioned in England. *Trend* is more used as a noun than as a verb. It means the general course, drift, or tendency (*The trend over the last one hundred years has been towards collectivism*).

tender (verb). Aside from its legal and commercial uses, *tender,* especially in the stereotyped phrases *tender condolences, tender regrets, tender sympathy, tender congratulations,* and the like, is slightly affected, over-elegant, a little pompous. It has been so, apparently, for centuries and must have been an elegant vogue word in Elizabethan times, if we may judge from Polonius's impatience at Ophelia's use of it (*Hamlet,* Act I, Scene 3).

tenpins; ninepins; ten-strike. *Tenpins* is a game, chiefly American, played with ten wooden pins at which a ball is bowled to knock them down. The word is also applied to the pins used in such a game. *Ninepins* is a game, chiefly English, played with nine wooden pins. Dickens, in his *American Notes,* described tenpins as "a game of mingled chance and skill, invented when the legislature passed an act forbidding Nine-pins." But although the high-mindedness and fervor with which the American people have passed laws governing moral conduct has been surpassed only by the ingenuity and celerity with which they have circumvented them, Dickens was wrong. *Loggets, nine-holes, or ten pinnes* are mentioned in an anonymous English pamphlet entitled *The Letting of humorous blood in the head vein,* published in 1600 and probably written by Samuel Rowlands.

A *ten-strike* is a stroke in tenpins which knocks down all the pins (the usual word is *strike*). By figurative extension, *tenstrike* is used in common speech to mean any stroke or act which is completely successful.

tense is the property of a verb, or the form of a verb, which shows the time at which an action occurred or a situation existed relative to the time of speaking. In a verbal phrase the tense is expressed by the first auxiliary, such as *has* in *Stanley has been living in Italy* and *was* in *Sam was expecting to see him.* See **verbs, past tense,** and **present tense.**

tense shifts. In literary English, when a verb in the past tense or past perfect tense has a clause as its object and the clause is in the indicative mode, the natural tense of the clause verb is shifted. A simple present tense, or a present tense auxiliary, is put in the past and a past tense form is put in the past perfect. Present tense forms are shifted to the past in the second of each of these examples: *he believes men are immortal, he believed men were immortal; he knows I will be there, he knew I would be there; he says he has seen you, he said he had seen you.* Past tense forms are shifted to the past perfect in: *this proves he was mistaken, this proved he had been mistaken.*

This sequence of tenses is observed in literary English, if only because it always has been observed and a violation of the rule makes a clause conspicuous, even to people who have never heard of the rule. It is also possible that the real purpose of the shift is to keep a subordinate verb from being more vivid, or more important, than the principal verb in the sentence. In any case, the shift has nothing to do with "real time." The subordinate verb is not put in the past tense because it represents a past event at the time of speaking. We say *how did you know I was here?* and *what did you say your name was?* when we are obviously speaking about the present. Tenses are shifted in timeless or universal statements, such as *it was a saying of his that no man was sure of his supper till he had eaten it.* This applies also to more solemn truths such as *Man ... who trusted God was love indeed and love Creation's final law.*

The tense shift can always be disregarded when one wants to make a subordinate clause conspicuous. This may happen when the only significant statement in the sentence is in the subordinate clause, as in *he told me the train leaves at three.* Or one may feel that a particular statement is too solemn to be subordinated under any circumstances, as in *he taught that God is love.* Neither of these reasons justify the use of the present tense in *Columbus believed the world is round,* where the significant statement is that Columbus believed this now commonplace truth. Sentences like this are written under the impression that what is still a fact should not be expressed in the past tense. Frequently the writer has been taught this in school. But that is regrettable, since the device sometimes spoils otherwise good writing by distorting the emphasis and putting trivia in a spotlight.

The rules just given for shifting tenses do not apply to subjunctive verbs. Where a present subjunctive form is required after a present tense verb it is also required after a past tense, as in *we insist that she get to work on time* and *we insisted that she get to work on time.* A past subjunctive does not become past perfect but keeps its original form. That is, *I wish I was dead* becomes *I wished I was dead* and not *I wished I had been dead.* Where either a present subjunctive or a past subjunctive may be used, the only difference being the degree of uncertainty, a shift may be made but it is not necessary. (For the rules governing tense in subjunctive clauses and in clauses of purpose, see **subjunctive mode.**)

tenterhooks were hooks from which cloth was suspended to be stretched free of wrinkles. The word was also applied to the hooks from which meat was suspended in front of butcher shops and it is likely that it was from this ghastly but common spectacle that the thought of tenterhooks as stretching instruments of painful torture was derived. *Tent* also meant the probing of a wound. To be *on tenterhooks,* to be in a state of painful suspense, is now a cliché, to be used sparingly.

terminal; terminus. These words are used differently in England and America. In England *terminals* (always the plural) is used to describe charges made by a railroad company for the use of a terminus or other station and for services rendered in loading and unloading goods. In America *terminal* means an originating or terminating point for trains, usually where important stations, yards, and shop facilities are located (*The cuts in rail service showed in lessened crowds at the Central, Union, LaSalle and Dearborn stations, which are terminals for the struck roads*). It is also used for a station or city at a terminus. For *terminal* in this sense, either end of a line, the English would use *terminus.* Americans may use either *terminal* or *terminus,* though *terminus* tends to mean a place, *terminal* a building. The plural of *terminus* is *terminuses* or *termini.*

terminate. See **end, expire.**

terra firma, as a term for solid earth, is affected if used seriously, dreary if used facetiously.

terrestrial. See **earthen.**

terrible; terrific. See **horrible.**

test (noun). See **trial.**

testimony. See **evidence.**

tetchy; techy; touchy. *Tetchy* and *techy* survive more vigorously in England than in America, but they are far less common in both countries, as adjectives meaning apt to take offense on slight provocation, irritable, than *touchy. Touchy* may also be used in senses not proper to *techy* and *tetchy:* precarious, risky, or ticklish (*It's a touchy business and must be handled with great tact*) or sensitive to touch (*Don't be so touchy; I've got to massage your side*).

than is used in making comparisons of inequality, or comparisons between things that are said to be dissimilar. It is used only in combination with the comparative form of an adjective or adverb or with one of the four words, *other, rather, different, else. Other* and *rather* are actually comparative forms and *different* is apparently felt as a comparative. (See these individual words.) *Else than* is still literary English but in current speech it is usually replaced by *but* or *except.*

In *we had no sooner finished our muffins than she said . . .,* the word *than* is standard English because it accompanies the comparative word *sooner.* In *scarcely had the reverberations died away than there came the sound of footsteps* there is no comparative form and *than* is being misused. Literary English requires *when* here. However, if a comparative form is used, *than* is required to complete the comparison and the word *when* is unliterary, as it is in *we had no sooner finished our muffins when she said. . . .*

Than is usually classed as a coordinating conjunction, which means that the words it joins in a comparison have the same function in the sentence. What are compared may be things, as in *the flesh will grieve on other bones than ours soon;* or actions, as in *he would have cut his hand off sooner than sign it.* But *than* is sometimes used in sentences where this interpretation is impossible, as in *he went no further than Philadelphia.* This sentence is standard English. But here *than* has a simple object, *Philadelphia,* and is therefore functioning as a preposition. When *than* stands before the relative pronoun *who,* the objective form *whom* is always used, as in *Mary Case, than whom there never was a wiser woman.* (See **who; whom.**) Here again one might say that *than* is functioning as a preposition, or one might say that this use of *whom* is an established but irregular idiom in English.

If *than* can be used as a preposition it would follow that a personal pronoun following *than,* that was not itself the subject of a following verb, would have an objective form. Most grammarians however claim that, with the exception of the two cases mentioned above, *than* must always be treated as a conjunction. This means that a personal pronoun following *than* must have a subjective or an objective form depending upon its function in the sentence, or depending upon the function of the word it is compared with. For example, according to these rules the subjective form *I* is required, and the objective form *me* must not be used, in *he understands this better than I,* because here the word is linked with *he* and is functioning as the subject of the verb *understand.* In current English we usually evade the problem by placing a dummy verb after the subjective pronoun, as in *better than I do.* On the other hand, the objective form *him* is required, and not the subjective form *he,* in *I have known better men than him to lie,* because here the word is linked with *men* and is functioning as the object of the verb *know.* That is, we use the objective form in this comparison because we would use the objective form in the simple statement *I have known him.* (Some grammarians claim that *than* is a subordinating conjunction in sentences of this kind, on the grounds that it is qualifying the word *better* rather than linking two independent elements.)

Textbooks sometimes say that a subjective pronoun should be used after *than* whenever it is possible to read a suppressed verb into the sentence, as in *I have known better men than he* (is) *to lie.* This is a mistake. It sometimes leads to ambiguous sentences, such as *I have known richer men than he* (is), where the hearer may suppose that the suppressed verb is *has.* And even where it is not ambiguous, this use of the subjective pronoun is contrary to the literary tradition and the practice of educated people, and is usually heard as a grammatical mistake.

When *than* is used after a form of the verb *to be* we have a different problem. Here it is a question of which form of the pronoun is to be used after a linking verb. If one says *it is me,* one would also say *is she taller than me?.* But if one says *it is I,* he should also say *is she taller than I?.* The objective form is generally preferred. See **linking verbs.**

thank. When *thank* is used as a polite word for ask it may be followed by an infinitive, as in *I'll thank you to hand me the salt.* The simple form of the verb here instead of the *to*-infinitive, as in *I'll thank you hand me the salt,* is considered an illiteracy in Great Britain. This form without *to* is not heard in the United States. When used in its ordinary sense of "express gratitude," *thank* is not followed by an infinitive but by *for* and the *-ing* form of a verb, as in *I thank you for handing me the salt.*

thanking you in advance. The quality of gratitude like that of mercy cannot be strained. To ask a favor and in the very act of asking it to state blandly that the person from whom the favor is begged need expect no thanks after it is done is so ludicrous that if it were not common, one would not believe that it had ever been done. There's a condescension in *thanking you in advance* that utterly denies any true sense of obligation. Some people object to the phrase because it is ungrammatical and illogical, but these are only minor faults: it is insolent.

thanks. Although the singular form *a thank* is no longer in use, *thanks* is a true plural. We say *many thanks, a thousand thanks,* and *these* *thanks are not deserved. Thanks* is used in *Hamlet* as a mass word in *for this relief much thanks.* This obsolete construction seems to catch the eye of teen-agers who continue to use the expression, facetiously, long after they have forgotten the origin of the joke.

Both forms, *thank* and *thanks,* are used as the first element in a compound, as in *thank-offerings* and *thanksgivings.*

thanks; thank you; I thank you. *Thanks* is the usual common elliptical expression used in America in acknowledging a favor, service, courtesy, or the like. *Thank you* is somewhat more formal and is insisted on by most English grammarians. *I thank you* is stiff and archaic, though it is sometimes used by orators in their perorations: *My friends, I thank you.*

As H. Allen Smith has observed, *Thank you* is an expression which the English can make go a long way, especially in the clipped form, "Kyuh." As he says, "They smile and even laugh when they hear us say, 'You're welcome.' This response to 'Thanks' or 'Kyuh' is never heard here and when a character in an American film says 'You're welcome,' the English audience laughs. The British response to 'Kyuh' is 'Kyuh,' the second 'Kyuh' being uttered in a higher tone than the first, and I assume it could go on forever" (*Smith's London Journal,* N. Y., 1952, p. 77). See also **oblige; obligate.**

Thanksgiving; Thanksgiving Day. Although *Thanksgiving Day* is the correct, formal name for the peculiarly American annual festival in acknowledgment of divine favor, usually held on the last Thursday of November, *Thanksgiving* (when capitalized) is sanctioned by usage (*They used to come over every Thanksgiving and bring the children*).

thank-you-ma'am is an exclusively American expression which began to disappear with the construction of modern highways. It was a hollow or ridge in a road, usually diagonal and especially on a hillside, to deflect water. These ridges or hollows were so called because when one drove over them the resulting bump made one's head bob and one's body seem to curtsy as if in the act of formally thanking a lady for some favor.

that. This word may be used as a demonstrative adjective, a demonstrative pronoun, a relative pronoun, or a conjunction.

When *that* qualifies a following noun, as in *that very small dog,* it is a demonstrative adjective. When it is used in place of a particular word or group of words (and does not introduce a qualifying clause), as in *I like that* and *that is what he said,* it is a demonstrative pronoun. The demonstrative *that* has the plural form *those* and is similar to the word *this.* See **this; that.**

When *that* stands for a word in the principal clause of a sentence and at the same time is an essential element in a qualifying, subordinate clause, as in *where is the dog that was here?,* it is called a relative pronoun. There is no difference in meaning between the demonstrative and the relative pronoun. But as a relative, *that*

is used in a more complicated construction, and in a way in which the other demonstrative pronouns cannot be used. As a relative pronoun, *that* competes with *which* and *who.* (For the use of *that* as a relative, see **that; which.**)

The word *that* is also used as a conjunction, as in *I know that the dog was here.* When it is used as a conjunction it does not represent any other word or refer to anything, and it is not grammatically a part of the clause that follows. It is merely a sign that the following clause is not an independent statement but a subordinate element in a larger sentence. This use of *that* has grown out of its use as a demonstrative pronoun. One may think of the conjunction *that* as the pronoun functioning as some element in a sentence and immediately followed by the clause that gives it meaning. In the example given, *that* functions as the object of the verb *know* and so makes the following clause the object of the verb. The relative pronoun *that* also introduces a clause but, unlike the conjunction, the pronoun represents a word appearing earlier and is itself a part of the subordinate clause. In speech, the conjunction *that* does not have the full vowel sound of the pronoun or the adjective. The difference can be heard in *I know that that is true,* where the first *that* is the conjunction and the second, the demonstrative pronoun.

A clause introduced by the conjunction *that* may be the object of a verb, as in the example given above, or it may be the subject of a verb, as in *that he denies it surprises me.* A clause represented by the dummy subject *it* is very often introduced by *that,* as in *it is true that he denies it.* (See **it.**) *That* is also used to introduce a purely adverbial clause of purpose or result, as in *I sent you to school that you might learn* and *what have I done that you should treat me so?* Clauses of this kind require a subjunctive auxiliary verb. The conjunction *that* sometimes occurs in exclamations where it introduces the object of an understood "I wish" or "I pray," as in *O that Ishmael might live forever!*

That may also be used after an adverb or a noun functioning as an adverb to show that the following clause is attached to, or is equivalent to, the preceding word, as in *we can start to work now that you are here* and *I knew it the first time that I saw him.* It is debatable whether *that* should be called a conjunction or a relative pronoun or adverb in a construction of this kind. If the word *that* is omitted from the sentence the adverb or noun itself becomes a conjunction introducing a clause. In current English we do not use *that* after a word that is thoroughly familiar as a conjunction, although this was once customary, as in *he could not live after that he was fallen.*

When there is no doubt that the clause following *that* is a subordinate element in the sentence, it is not necessary to use the conjunction. As a rule there is no doubt and the word *that* can be omitted. The conjunction is required when the clause stands before the principal verb, either as subject, as in *that he says so surprises me,* or as object, as in *that he said so I doubt*. Sentences of this kind are uncommon in current English, but if the construction is used, the conjunction must not be dropped. The conjunction is also required before a clause of purpose or result, but in current English an infinitive is generally preferred to a full clause here, as in *I sent you to school to learn* and *what have I done to have you treat me so?*. The conjunction *that* is sometimes needed after a coordinating conjunction (*and, or, nor, but*), as in *he wished he had gone and that he had taken Mary*. It is a convenience whenever there may be doubt about where a subordinate clause begins. For example, in *he said yesterday he had finished the work,* the word *yesterday* may belong with *he said* or with *he had finished*. The sentence would be clearer if a *that* was placed either before or after *yesterday*. In other cases, the word *that* can usually be omitted.

To omit unnecessary *that*'s is not careless or slovenly writing. It makes for better prose, for smoother and more natural English, to omit them than to use them when they are not necessary. Too many *that* conjunctions create an impression of laboring the obvious. This stylistic mistake is seen most often in technical writing, where the author is over-anxious to make his points clear. More confidence in the reader would ease the burden for both writer and reader.

that; which. The word *that* is primarily a demonstrative pronoun or adjective, but it is also used as a relative pronoun and as a conjunction. (For the use of *that* as a demonstrative, see **this; that;** for its use as a conjunction, see **that.**) It is a relative pronoun when it forms part of a subordinate clause and at the same time represents a noun or pronoun appearing in the principal clause of the same sentence. *Which* is primarily an interrogative pronoun or adjective, but it too can be used as a relative. It is more adaptable to Latin constructions than the word *that* and was first used as a relative in translations from Latin. From this it passed into general English and now competes with the relative *that*. (For all uses of *which* except as a relative pronoun, see **which.**)

That is the oldest and the most useful of the relatives. It may be used in speaking of persons, animals, or inanimate things, as in

This is the cock that crew in the morn,
Unto the farmer sowing his corn,
That met the priest with his pen and ink-horn,
That married the man so tattered and torn,
. . . and so on, to *the house that Jack built.*

During the sixteenth century *which* was used interchangeably with *that* as a relative. In the King James Bible (1611), Matthew 22:21 reads: *Render therefore unto Caesar the things which are Caesar's; and unto God the things that are God's.* The same verse occurs in Mark and Luke. In Mark *that* appears in both statements, and in Luke *which* appears in both. At that time *which,* like *that,* was used in speaking of persons as well as of things, and in this trans-

lation of the Bible we find *Our Father which art in heaven.* During the seventeenth century *that* almost disappeared from literary English and *who* replaced *which* as a relative referring to persons. (See **who; whom.**) But by 1700 *that* was coming into favor again. At first many educated people considered it a vulgar innovation. The *Spectator* of May 30, 1711, published a "Humble Petition of *Who* and *Which* against the upstart Jack Sprat *That,*" in which *Who* and *Which* say: "We are descended of ancient Families, and kept up our Dignity and Honor many Years till the Jacksprat *That* supplanted us." Actually, they were the intruders and eventually *that* regained its old position. In the Authorized Revision of the Bible (published in 1885) we find *Our Father that art in heaven,* the form that had been used in the Wycliffe translation of 1389. Today we make a distinction between *who* and *which,* and use *who* in speaking of persons and *which* in speaking of anything subhuman. *That* is generally preferred to *which* where both words are possible, but many people prefer *who* to *that* when the reference is to a person. Twentieth century translations of the Bible are likely to read, *Our Father who art in heaven.*

It is sometimes claimed that the relative pronoun *that* must be used in a defining clause that is essential to the meaning of a statement, as in *we use margarine that contains vitamin A* and *he was a bold man that first eat an oyster;* and that *who* or *which* is required in a clause that is merely descriptive, as in *we use butter, which contains vitamin A* and *he was a strange man, who cared for nothing.* Clauses of the first kind are called defining, restrictive, or explanatory. Clauses of the second kind are called descriptive, additive, or resumptive.

The distinction between restrictive *that* and descriptive *which* or *who* is an invention of the grammarians and a very recent one. Fowler, who recommends it, says, "it would be idle to pretend that it is the practice either of most or of the best writers." What is not the practice of most, or of the best, is not part of our common language. In actual practice, *which* is not often used in a defining clause today, but it may be. In the King James Bible, the woman who lost a silver piece and then found it, says: *I have found the piece which I had lost.* Twentieth century translators altered this sentence but felt no need to change the defining *which* to *that,* and wrote *I have found the coin which I had lost.* The relative *who,* on the other hand, is frequently used in defining clauses. No one today would see anything awkward in the sentence *he was a bold man who first ate an oyster.* The relative *that,* now as always, is used freely in descriptive clauses (as well as in defining ones), as in *those are Grecian ghosts, that in battle were slain* and *the last was Fear, that is akin to Death.* Very often *that* and *which* are used in the same sentence with identically the same function, as in *a circumstance that occurred, or which Shelley supposed did occur.*

Anyone who likes to do so may limit his own

that's to defining clauses. But he must not read this distinction into other men's writing, and he must not expect his readers to recognize it in his own. It is sometimes necessary to show that a clause is purely descriptive and not defining, but this cannot be accomplished by using the word *who* or *which*. In order to make this fact clear, the descriptive clause must be set off by a pair of commas, which have the effect of parenthesis marks, or the sentence must be recast.

In current English *which* is used in place of *that* chiefly for variety. The essential difference between these words today is described by a grammarian writing fifty years ago, who said: "In all ages of the English tongue *that* has been the standard relative of the body of the people, and to this day *which* is stiff and formal, suggestive of the student's lamp or the pedagogue's birch."

When the conjunction *that* is followed by the demonstrative pronoun *that,* there is a noticeable difference in the way the two words are pronounced, as can be heard in *I believe that that is true.* When a demonstrative *that* is followed by a relative *that* the two words are pronounced alike, as in *I have that that you gave me.* As a rule, *which* is preferred to *that* in this construction and we say *that which you gave me* or *what you gave me.* On the other hand, *that* is the only relative used after *who.* We say *who that has any pride* and not *who who* or *who which.* *That* is generally preferred to *who* or *which* following the word *same,* as in *it is the same man that was here yesterday.* The relative *that* cannot be preceded by a preposition, as *which* can. We say *the box that I spoke about* and not *the box about that I spoke.* Sometimes this determines which word is used. But with these exceptions, the words are pretty much interchangeable.

That and *which* are both singular or plural depending on the word they represent. Theoretically *that* may be first, second, or third person, but as a rule it is treated as a third person pronoun. (For special problems of person and number, see **agreement: verbs** and **one.**) In literary English *whose* is the possessive form for both *that* and *which,* as in *the house whose foundations are being laid, stars whose light has not yet reached us.* Thirty years ago the avoidance of *whose* in favor of *of which* was considered characteristic of the writing of people who had had very little education. Today it is seen too often in scientific work to be called anything but standard, but it is still un-literary.

In natural English a relative clause always follows the word it qualifies. It is sometimes said that a *that* clause must follow immediately and that *which* is required when there are intervening words. The lines quoted above from the *House that Jack Built* show that this is not true. Either pronoun is likely to attach itself to the nearest available word, which may not be the word that was intended, as in *the package on the table which I just wrapped up.* A comma before the relative pronoun will prevent its being attached to the immediately preceding word.

A clause that is distinctly descriptive and capable of being set off from the rest of the sentence by commas must be self-contained, and therefore must have its relative pronoun. In a defining clause, on the other hand, the relative pronoun can usually be omitted, as in *the people I stayed with.* A clause of this kind that does not have a relative pronoun is called a contact clause. The construction is as acceptable in written English as it is in speech, and is used frequently by Shakespeare, Swift, Fielding, Goldsmith, Sterne, Burke, Byron, Shelley, Carlyle, Dickens, Thackeray, Tennyson, Ruskin, R. L. Stevenson, and by all writers whose style is easy and natural.

Formerly the relative pronoun could be omitted even when it was clearly the subject of the following verb, as in *wilt thou ascribe that to merit now, was mere fortune* and *there arose a clatter might wake the dead.* This is no longer acceptable and a sentence of this kind is now either archaic or dialectal. But, except when used in a comparison, the relative may be omitted from any position in which the speech instinct calls for an objective rather than a subjective pronoun. It may be omitted when it is the object of a verb, as in *the songs we used to sing;* or the object of a preposition, as in *the boy we gave the apples to;* or the complement of some form of the verb *to be,* as in *he is not the man his father was,* or technically the subject of the verb *to be* but standing in the complement position, as in *we gave him all there was.* See **subjective pronouns.**

the. This word is a weakened form of *that* and its principal function is to distinguish one thing from others of the same kind.

In principle, *the* is not used before any word whose meaning is sufficiently definite without it, such as a proper name. Nor is it used in speaking of classes of things that have no individuality, where there is no need to distinguish one specimen from another, as in *sugar is sweet.* But no clear-cut rules are possible here. We may need to distinguish a proper name, as in *the John Adams I am talking about;* and we may need to speak of some particular lot of sugar, as in *the sugar is on the table.*

Because *the* individualizes one out of a class of things, it may be used to mark something non-human as unique or individual, even when it does not belong to a class of things, such as *the universe, the moon, the Creation.* Here *the* competes with the function of a proper name and we have such variation as *the Bible* and *Genesis, the Bronx* and *Manhattan.* (For the question of capitalizing *the* before a proper name, see **proper nouns.**)

When not used in speaking of a unique thing, *the* means "that particular one out of the lot of them." We may know what particular one is meant by what has been said before, or the identifying clause may follow immediately. *The man who lives next door* might be the opening words of some statement, but *the man said to me* requires something before it to give it meaning. When *the* does not refer back and is not followed by a defining clause, it indicates a typical specimen of the class, as in *the rat is larger than the mouse* Here the use of *the* approaches the use of *a*, which means "any." The words *man* and *woman* are never used with *the* to indicate the type, but any other word may be, as in *she was the perfect lady* and *he is always the artist.*

Formerly *the* was used with the names of diseases. Today we are likely to keep this *the* before names that we associate with the past, such as *the cholera, the grippe,* and to omit it before words that are current today, such as *rheumatism* and *asthma.* In the case of children's diseases we are more tolerant and may say either *the mumps, the measles* or simply *mumps* and *measles.*

The is dropped from certain prepositional phrases, such as *at church, on campus, in jail.* The rule is that the *the* is retained when one is thinking about the actual place, object, or institution, and omitted when what is uppermost in the mind is the thing's purpose or function. If so, Englishmen must be more function-minded than Americans, because they drop a great many *the*'s that we keep. They say *she is in hospital, we were at table, he looked out of window.* The last example particularly interested Mark Twain, who claimed that *out of the window* was one of the distinguishing marks of the American language.

The is primarily an adjective and qualifies a noun. But it may also be used to qualify the comparative form of an adjective or adverb, as in *I like him the better for it.* Here *the* is an adverb of extent and is equivalent to "that much." (See **comparison of adjectives and adverbs.**) The use of *the* before a measure term, as in *six dollars the bushel,* is an idiom borrowed from French. The natural, and preferred, form in English is with the word *a,* as in *six dollars a bushel.* (See **nouns as adverbs.**)

thee; thou. These words are no longer natural English, but they were once in everyday use as the singular of *you.* At that time *thee* was the objective pronoun and *thou* the subjective. The difference in the use of these two words can be seen in the lines: *Shall I compare thee to a summer's day? Thou art more lovely and more temperate.* By the end of the sixteenth century *thee* was often used in place of *thou,* very much as *me* is used in place of *I.* This can be seen in such phrases as *I would not be thee* and *not so blessed as thee.* But soon after this, the plural *you* replaced the singular altogether in natural speech and later poets have used *thee* and *thou* pretty much as they pleased. See also **you; ye.**

When *thou* was standard English, it had a distinctive verb form ending in *st,* as in *thou takest, thou hast, thou hadst, thou wast.* The *s* was omitted in the four words *art, wert, wilt, shalt.* Anyone wanting to write archaic English must recognize the difference between these forms, used with *thou,* and the old forms used with the third person singular, that is, used in speaking about a person or thing rather than to someone. The old third person ending was *th* and it was used just as we now use the ending *s,* as in *he*

taketh, he hath, he doeth. It was not used in the past tense. One did not say *he hadeth, he dideth.* Neither the *st* nor the *th* ending was used in a subjunctive verb form. That is, one said *though thou fall* and *though he fall.* (The form *is* has been preferred to *beeth* since before the time of Shakespeare.)

When *thee* and *thou* were becoming obsolete, the Society of Friends refused to accept the polite or flattering *you* and kept the old singulars, on the grounds that to use a plural word in speaking to one person was unnatural, unreasonable, and undemocratic. For a time the Friends used the words *thee* and *thou* conventionally. That is, *thou* was always the subject of a verb and *thee* the object; *thou* was followed by the old verb form ending in *st,* and was used only in speaking to one person, not in speaking to several people. But just as objective *you* drove out subjective *ye* in general English, objective *thee* drove out subjective *thou* in Quaker speech. Eventually *thee,* like *you,* was used as both the subjective and the objective pronoun. Unlike *you,* it was always used with a singular verb. For the last hundred years or so, it has been used with the form of the verb that normally follows *he* or *she,* as in *thee is a good woman, Dorothy.* It is now the only form of address and is used in speaking to any number of people.

their; theirs. The form *their* is used to qualify a following noun, as in *their home, their good friends.* The form *theirs* is used in any other construction, as in *friends of theirs, all theirs. Theirs* is also the form used in a double possessive where it is separated from its following noun by *and,* as in *theirs and your affectionate friend.* Today this construction is generally avoided and *their friend and yours* or *their own and your friend* is used instead. Neither word order shows clearly whether we are talking about one thing or two, but the old-fashioned form, *theirs and your friend,* suggests one thing possessed in common more strongly than the forms which use *their.*

The word *their* means "belonging to them." It must be distinguished from *they're,* which means "they are," and from *there,* which sometimes indicates a place and sometimes is simply a functional word with no meaning at all. These three words have the same sound, but they are written differently.

In current English, the word *theirs* is never written with an apostrophe. It must not be confused with *there's* which means "there is." See **possessive pronouns.** For the use of *their* in speaking of a single person, see **they.**

theirn is in use today but it has never been standard English, although it is formed on the pattern of *hisn, hern, ourn, yourn,* all of which were once standard. The only acceptable form is *theirs.*

theirselves. This word is not standard. The only acceptable form is *themselves.*

Theirselves is made with the possessive pronoun in the same way that *yourselves* and *ourselves* are. An older form, *theirself,* was once literary English but it dropped out of the standard language at least five hundred years ago. A grammarian writing in 1762 thought that *themselves* was a corruption and *theirselves* the logically correct form. But *themselves* was the acceptable form in 1762 and is the acceptable form today. However, the possessive form *their,* and not the objective form *them,* is required when another word stands between the pronoun and the word *selves,* as in *their very selves.*

theism. See **deism.**

them. The word *them* should not be used as an adjective. That is, it should not be used to qualify a noun, as in *them melons, them friends of yours.* Actually, it is used in this way and has been for about four hundred years, but the construction has always been considered uneducated usage. Even when standing alone, *them* cannot be used to point out anything inanimate, but only to refer back to something that has already been mentioned. In a grocery store we cannot say *I will take two of them melons.* Nor can we look hard at the melons and say *I will take two of them.* In both cases we must say either *these* or *those.* However, if the grocer says *these are very fine melons* we can then say *I will take two of them,* because at this point *them* refers to something already mentioned and is not being used as a demonstrative pronoun. This distinction does not apply when speaking about human beings. We can say *wait on them first* without anything having been said about "them" before. And the rule does not apply to *they.* This word is never used before a noun, but it can be used to point out something. We can look hard at another box of melons and say *they look nicer to me.* (For the use of *them* in speaking of a single person, see **they.** For when to use *them* rather than *they,* see **objective pronouns.**)

themself; themselves. Originally, the word *self* could be used as a singular or as a plural and, until about 1540, *themself* was the only form in use. Since then, the form *themselves* has driven *themself* from standard English. *Themself* is now archaic. (For the ways in which *themselves* may be used, see **reflexive pronouns.**)

then is primarily an adverb but it may also be used as an adjective before a noun, as in *the then president, the then Prince of Wales.* It has been used in this way for at least three hundred years.

there may be a demonstrative adverb meaning "in that place," as in *there nothing is wrong;* or it may be a function word without any meaning of its own, as in *there is nothing wrong.* The demonstrative adverb always has a heavy stress and the function word is always pronounced lightly. One may use both in the same sentence without seeming to have used the same word twice, as in *there there is nothing wrong.*

The only interesting thing about the demonstrative adverb is that it cannot stand before a noun. *That man there is my friend* is a dignified sentence. But *that there man is my friend* is at present unspeakable! Someone has said that *that there* is now "the most illiterate noise one can

make." The expression is not wrong because *there* repeats the demonstrative *that.* We have no objection at all to repeating an elemental notion, as in *the self-same song.* What we object to is the adverb standing before the noun, and when *there* follows *man,* all is well. The expression is grammatically comparable to *the above remarks, his then residence,* but it has been made a scapegoat, and a wise man will not associate with a scapegoat unnecessarily.

The second *there* (the function word) is much more interesting. It always stands where we expect to find the subject of a verb, and in this resembles the expletive *it.* (See **it.**) But the *there* type of sentence is different from the *it* type of sentence in structure and in meaning.

It may be used as a "dummy" subject with any verb, as in *it astonishes me that.* . . . In current English the empty *there* can only be used with a purely linking verb, principally *be, come, seem, appear.* The verb following *it* is always singular, even when the subject represented by *it* is plural, as in *it was his friends who told him.* The verb following *there* may be singular or plural. According to the rules, it is plural if the meaningful subject of the sentence is plural, and singular if it is not, as in *there were friends who told him* and *there was one in particular.* There is a strong tendency today to use only a singular verb after *there,* even with a plural subject. This is now acceptable English when the word closest to the verb is singular, as in *there was a man and two women.* A singular verb is often heard before a plural word, as in *there was two women,* but this offends many people and is condemned by most grammarians.

The subject represented by *it* may be a noun or pronoun but more often it is a *that* clause or an infinitive. The meaningful subject of a *there* sentence is never a clause or an infinitive.

The expletive *it* is used simply to fill the subject position, so that we may place the true subject somewhere else, either to make it emphatic or because it is too long to handle efficiently before the verb. If we replace *it* with the words it represents the sentence loses emphasis or becomes unwieldy. The *there* construction on the other hand makes a vague or indefinite statement. It is used chiefly with indefinite qualifying words such as *a, no, some, any, few, many,* as in *there are some who say, there is a man who says.* When particularizing words such as *the, this, that, my,* are used, the individual in most cases is being offered as a type or an example, as in *there is the man who says* and *there is the child next door, for example.* The principal statement in a *there* sentence is "this exists," or "this seems to be," and the meaningful statement is subordinated to this. The *there* construction detaches the statement from the speaker and makes it impersonal. If such a sentence is recast it does not lose emphasis but becomes more immediate, more concrete and more vivid.

thereabout; thereabouts. These words are used interchangeably today, and have been for several centuries. Some grammarians claim that *there-*

abouts ought to be the preferred form, because the word is used to qualify a verb and *s* is a formal adverbial ending. But there is no evidence that it actually is preferred. Both forms may be used figuratively, as *thereabouts* in *5000 inhabitants or thereabouts.*

there's the rub; ay, there's the rub. For those who choose to vary tedium with monotony the cliché *there's the rub* may at times be replaced by its fuller form *ay, there's the rub. Rub,* in this famous phrase (*Hamlet,* Act III, Scene 1), means an obstacle, impediment, or hindrance, of a nonmaterial nature. It is derived from a term used in the game of bowls, where a *rub* is some obstacle or impediment by which a bowl is hindered or diverted from its intended course.

thesaurus. The plural is *thesauruses* or *thesauri.*

these. See **this; that.**

thesis. The plural is *thesises* or *theses.*

they. The words *they, them, their,* are used in speaking of more than one individual. They may also be used in speaking of a single individual whose sex is unknown. For example, only the word *his* would be used in *every soldier carried his own pack,* but most people would say *their* rather than *his* in *everybody brought their own lunch.* And it would be a violation of English idiom to say *was he?* in *nobody was killed, were they?* The use of *they* in speaking of a single individual is not a modern deviation from classical English. It is found in the works of many great writers, including Malory, Shakespeare, Swift, Defoe, Shelley, Austen, Scott, Kingsley, Dickens, Ruskin, George Eliot.

They may be used generally or with a vague reference, as in *they say, what have they done to you?,* and *they had strikes even then.* This construction may be out of place when something more specific than *they* is wanted. But grammatically, this use of *they* is in a class with the similar use of *people* or *men* and is equally acceptable.

They may be used before a numeral, as in *they two will wed the morrow morn.* This is literary English, but archaic. To many people it sounds like the unacceptable use of *them* before a noun, as in *them books,* and the forms *these two, those two, the two,* are generally preferred. Traditionally, *they* and *them* may stand before a qualifying phrase or clause, as in *blessed are they that mourn* and *the third and fourth generation of them that hate me,* but in current English the words *those* or *these* are generally preferred in this position. (For when to use *they* rather than *them,* see **subjective pronouns.**)

thick as thieves. As a humorous simile for a close, and slightly conspiratorial, intimacy, *as thick as thieves,* although it seems to be a creation of the twentieth century, is already a cliché. For those who want to avoid it but still feel a need for some such comparison, there are many established metaphors waiting: as thick as hail, as thick as hops, as thick as huckleberries, for those who wish to emphasize profusion; as thick as porridge, for those who have specific density

in mind; and for chumminess, a fine old Scotch simile, as thick as three in a bed.

thief. The plural is *thieves.*

thief; robber; burglar; bandit; gangster. A *thief* is one who takes another's property by stealth, without the other's knowledge. It is a word of contempt (*Now does he feel his title/ Hang loose about him, like a giant's robe/ Upon a dwarfish thief*). A *robber* trespasses upon the house, property, or person of another, and makes away with things of value, even using violence (*The robbers seem to have made their escape through the trap door and over the roofs. Three masked robbers held up the First National Bank shortly after noon today*). Where the robbery is committed in the open, with the threat or use of a knife or gun, or with felonious assault, the more common term in America today is *hold-up man* or *men* and the robbery itself is termed a *hold-up.* Masked robbers or robbers whose depradations are accompanied by some dash or bravado are usually called, in the papers at least, *bandits.* It is a journalistic cliché, however, being little employed in ordinary speech or writing unless one is referring to Mexican outlaws. *Gangster,* a far-too-common word, is applied to members or assumed members of armed gangs, especially to those thought to be members of closely knit organizations controlled by some criminal mastermind, or to robbers or murderers whose violence is akin to that employed by the gangsters in their feuds or brushes with the law. *Burglar* is now a slightly old-fashioned term. It describes a felonious housebreaker, especially one who commits robbery by breaking into a house at night. See also **steal; purloin; pilfer;** etc.

thieve. See **steal.**

thieves. This is the plural of *thief.*

thimblerig. See **shell game.**

thine. See **thy; thine** and **my; mine.**

thing. In present-day English *thing* ordinarily means a material and inanimate thing, but the word is not limited to this meaning. Whatever can be talked about may be called a thing, as in *men who were engineers and business managers and a dozen other things.* Under some circumstances even a quality may be called a thing, as in *she was good, kind, honest, and everything a woman should be.*

think. The past tense is *thought.* The participle is also *thought.*

If *think* is used in a passive form it may be followed by an infinitive, as in *he is thought to have left.* When it is used in an active form it may be followed by a clause, as in *I think he has left.* If the *-ing* form of a verb is used it must be introduced by *of,* as in *he did not think of leaving. Think,* in an active form, is sometimes followed by an infinitive, as in *I did not think to tell him.* If in this sentence the word *think* means plan or expect, the construction is archaic. If it means remember, the construction is condemned by some grammarians, but is standard usage in the United States today.

Think for is the standard English idiom in comparisons with *than* or *as,* as in *more than you think for* and *as much as he thought for.* Today this *for* is often dropped, as in *more than you think,* perhaps out of fear of "ending a sentence with a preposition." This usage is so widespread that it cannot be called anything but standard, but it strikes the ears of anyone familiar with literary English as a clipped phrase that has been stopped before it was finished.

An old verb meaning "it seems" or "it appears" has become merged with the verb *think.* It is seen in such statements as *I think it's going to rain.* When used in this sense, the long form of the present tense with *thinking,* as in *you're a good woman, I'm thinking,* is a Scottish or Irish idiom and not standard English. In most cases it is impossible to say which verb the speaker intended. *I am thinking it is going to rain* may mean that he is turning this thought over in his mind, in which case the construction is thoroughly acceptable. In the United States, *guess, reckon,* and sometimes *calculate,* are used for this sense of the verb *think.*

The same old verb survives in *thinks I.* This is not in a class with *says I,* partly because it has a literary background but chiefly because it is not heard so constantly in the speech of uneducated people. *Methinks* is the same verb in its purest form, but this is now obsolete. It is used today only by people who believe they can create a Walter Scott atmosphere with half a dozen words.

think; deem; judge; suppose. *Think* is the general word for forming or having a thought or opinion (*I think; therefore I am. I think that I shall never see/ A poem lovely as a tree*). *Judge* suggests a careful balance of reason and evidence and a judicial detachment in arriving at a conclusion (*Do not judge me by my appearance*). It is used a little pompously as a synonym for *think* by those who believe, or would like to suggest, that their slightest opinions are reached in judicial detachment only after weighing evidence and consulting reason (*I judge it'll take us about half an hour to get these potatoes peeled*). *Deem* meant originally to pronounce judgment or to sit in judgment (*As ye deme, ye shall be demed*). It is cognate with *doom* and is the base of the family name *Dempster.* In modern use it is a formal synonym of *judge,* with a fine antique flavor suitable for commencement exercises, political orations, elegies, editorials, and other places and pronouncements where clarity and ease are to be avoided (*I deem it an honor to be asked to speak before so distinguished a group. We deem that in these troubled times . . .*). *To suppose* is to have an opinion that seems justified (*I suppose he knows what he's doing*) but which we are not willing to back up as a definite conviction. See also **calculate, consider, feel.**

third person singular. This is the form of the verb used whenever the subject is singular and is not either of the pronouns *you* or *I.* In the usual analysis of verb forms, the third person singular seems to be only one out of six forms. But in actual practice this is the form of the verb used most often. In a typical page of written material more than half the verbs are in the third person singular.

this; that. These words may be used as demonstrative adjectives which qualify a following noun, as in *this young child,* or without a following noun as demonstrative pronouns, as in *that tastes good.* In general, *this* indicates what is close, and *that* what is distant in relation to the speaker. *This* is always singular and has the plural form *these.* When used as a demonstrative, *that* too is always singular and has the plural form *those.* (For the use of *that* as a conjunction, see **that;** for its use as a relative pronoun, see **that; which.**)

All four words are used, primarily, in speaking about something that can be seen or pointed at, as in *this is my brother* and *is that you?* They are also used to represent something that has just been said. This may be a single word or it may be an idea that required several sentences to express. The word *that* is preferred when an exact repetition of what has just been said is intended, as in *I'll repent, and that suddenly.* The word *this* is preferred when the reference is less specific. It is often used as a summarizing word and means "all that has just been said."

This and *these* are also used to represent words that are to follow. In this construction the reference is usually specific, as in *this above all, to thine own self be true* and *we hold these truths to be self-evident: That all men are created equal; that. . . . That* and *those* may be used in speaking of something that is not immediately present and has not been mentioned before, but the reference is usually vague. As a rule, explanatory words follow immediately, as in *that which is hardest to bear* and *those who say such things. That* followed by a relative pronoun is frequently replaced by *what.* (See **what.**) In current English *those* is preferred to *they* or *them* when used with a defining word or phrase, as in *those present, those in the basket, those he sent.* The adjective *those* may also be used generically to indicate an entire class of things, as in *those large police dogs are very intelligent.*

The words *this* and *that* may be used in identifying a human being, as in *do you see that woman crossing the street* and *that child looks sick.* When there is no need, or no intention, of identifying, the words are derogatory, as in *that woman!, this son of yours. That* seems to be stronger than *this* as an expression of contempt; *those* can occasionally be used in this way, as in *those Joneses!,* but *these* never is.

This and *that* are sometimes used to show "how much." It is unquestionably standard English to use *this* or *that* before *much* or *many* when these words are standing alone, as in *I know this much* and *I did not think there were that many.* Here *much* and *many* are interpreted as nouns and *this* and *that* as adjectives. But when *much* or *many* is used before a noun it becomes an adjective and *this* and *that,* in turn, adverbs of degree, as in *to whom he owed this*

much courtesy and *to have that much science.*
Some grammarians claim that *this* and *that*
should not be used to qualify an adjective and
that these constructions are therefore wrong. In
practice, this use of the words is acceptable English so long as the meaning of *this* or *that* is defined. It may be defined in speech by a gesture
of the hands, as in *the box was this wide.* Or it
may be defined by what has just been said, as in
Can you come at six? I can't get there that early
and *so long as men continue to live in this competitive society . . . that long will the scab continue to exist.* When the word is not actually
defined, as in *we have never been this rich
before,* it is questionable. When the word is used
purely as an intensive, as in *I was that pleased!*
and *I am that sleepy!,* the construction is slang
or dialectal.

this world's goods. There may have been originally, in some deeply religious minds, a sincere
distinction between the goods of this world and
those of some other world, or the hereafter. But
in most mouths the term was a canting phrase
and is now a cliché, especially in the expression
rich in this world's goods. The modern attitude
is expressed in the hackneyed assurance that
"You can't take it with you."

thoroughbred; purebred. With reference to animals, these words are synonymous, but *thoroughbred* is preferred, especially in relation to horses,
there being a tendency among many farmers
and breeders to restrict *thoroughbred* to horses
and to use *purebred* in relation to other animals.
Both words, whether used as nouns or adjectives,
mean of pure or unmixed breed, stock, or race.
In reference to dogs, cats, cattle, and often swine,
there is an increasing tendency in America to use
the word *pedigreed* instead of either *thoroughbred* or *purebred* and *pedigreed* has the further
meaning that the animal is not only purebred
but that a valid document exists or can be procured to attest this fact.

There is a special breed of horses called the
Thoroughbred, an English breed of racehorses
developed by crossing domestic and Middle Eastern strains. Only *thoroughbred* may be applied
to persons and only figuratively. That is, the
reference must be not to genetics but to qualities
of behavior or character. In this it is parallel to
breeding. A *thoroughbred* is a well-bred person,
well-trained, polite (*She traveled with the thor-
oughbreds, and was always Among Those Present*—George Ade). The word was a vogue word
among the realists at the turn of the century
(*"By Jove," he cried, "You are a thoroughbred"*
—Frank Norris) but it has fortunately fallen
into disuse and would seem a little affected and
absurd today.

thoroughfare retains its original meaning in the
negative injunction: *No Thoroughfare.* It means
literally *a passage through,* hence a street open
at both ends, hence a main road or highway. It
also means various passages of other sorts, as a
strait, river or the like, allowing passage through.

those. See **this; that.**

thou. See **thee; thou.**

though; although. *Though* may be used as a simple adverb meaning nevertheless. When used in
this way it must stand at the end of its clause, as
in *I believe him though.*

Either word may be used as a conjunction to
introduce a clause that concedes a point. *If* may
be used in the same way, but it always suggests
that what is conceded is doubtful. *Though* and
although make light of the concession. They indicate that what follows may be true but that it
has no bearing on the point at issue, as in *though
he slay me, yet will I trust him.* There is very
little difference between *even if* and *even though,*
and none at all between *as if* and *as though.*

Although always stands first in its clause.
The conjunction *though* usually does. It always
stands before the subject and verb but may
sometimes stand after a word describing the
subject, as in *young though he is.* The verb in
a *though* clause may be in the subjunctive or in
the indicative mode. See **subjunctive mode.**

thought. See **think.**

thousand. This word was originally a noun and
was followed by *of,* as in *a thousand of sensible
men.* Today the singular form *thousand* is treated
as a cardinal number. That is, it is an adjective
and used without *of,* as in *twenty thousand Cornish bold* and *a thousand thousand slimy things,*
except when it refers to part of a specified group,
as in *two thousand of these men.* An expression
involving *thousand* is usually treated as a plural,
as in *three thousand cars were sold,* but it may
also be treated as a singular, especially when referring to money, as in *three thousand dollars
was set aside.*

The plural form *thousands* cannot be qualified
by a numeral. It is a noun and requires *of* when
followed by the name of anything countable, as
in *thousands of men;* the *of* is omitted only before a degree word such as *more, less, too many,*
as in *thousands more men.*

Few usually takes the adjective construction,
as in *a few thousand men; many* usually takes
the noun construction, as in *many thousands of
men.* But either form may be used with either
word.

thrash and **thresh** are, originally, two spellings of
the same word. Today *thresh* is generally preferred when the beating has some value, as in
thresh grain or *thresh out a problem,* and *thrash*
is reserved for a simple flogging, as in *thrash the
boy. Thrash* is also the preferred word at sea, as
in *the ships thrashed to windward.*

thrash, beat, beat up all refer to the giving of a
blow or blows. *Beat* implies the giving of repeated blows (*How we boys used to hate the business of hanging the carpets on the clothesline
and beating them*). The use of *beat* to describe
brutal attacks by hold-up men (*An unconscious
man, apparently the victim of a hold-up who
had resisted and been beaten, was found in an
alley early this morning*) has given the word a
more sinister and more violent meaning in
America than it has in England where such
felonious assaults seem to be fewer.

Thrash implies inflicting repeated blows as

punishment, to show superior strength (*Dr. Keate's admirers boasted that he had thrashed half the bishops, generals, and cabinet ministers of England*). By one of those associations of words that get fixed in languages, bullies always seem to get thrashed. The English apply *thrash* more than the Americans do to the infliction of punishment on children. In America *whip* and *spank* are the more common words and both (though *whip* only in that context) suggest lighter and less violent treatment than *thrash*.

Though some English authorities regard the *up* of *beat up* as unnecessary, it does mean something when one understands *beat up* to mean, as it does mean to most Americans, not merely to beat but to beat until the one beaten is in a state of physical collapse (*The hitchhikers beat up the driver and went off with his car*). In slang usage *beat up*, as an adjective, means battered, showing signs of excessive wear (*He wore a wonderful old beat-up hat, sloppy corduroy pants and dirty sneakers*) or utterly tired out. One who is beaten up is one who has sustained a severe beating. One who is beat up is tired, exhausted.

threadbare excuse is a threadbare phrase for an excuse made so often (usually by the same person) that it can no longer be accepted with even the pretense of credence.

threaten. This word may be followed by an infinitive, as in *he threatened to resign*. It is also heard with the *-ing* form of a verb, as in *he threatened resigning,* but the infinitive construction is preferred.

thresh. See **thrash.**

threw. See **throw.**

thrifty. See **economical.**

thrilled. See **bored to death.**

thrive. The past tense is *thrived* or *throve*. The participle is *thrived* or *thriven*.

In the United States *thrived* is now preferred for the past tense and the participle. In Great Britain the preferred forms are the older *throve* and *thriven* (*He that would thrive must rise at five;/ He that has thriven may lie till seven*).

through thick and thin. The "thick" of *thick and thin* is a thicket, that is, a dense growth of shrubs, undergrowth, and small trees, a brake. To go *through thick and thin* (*thicket* had been shortened to *thick* in this expression even by Chaucer's time) was to go relentlessly ahead, through thicket and open spaces. Hence to push on through everything in the way, disregarding all obstacles and impediments, or to adhere to some party or course under all circumstances, come what may. The phrase is now hackneyed and lacks specific meaning.

throve. See **thrive.**

throw. The past tense is *threw*. The participle is *thrown*.

Throwed was once literary English but is no longer standard, except in the nursery where *throwed up* is sometimes used as an idiot euphemism for *vomited*.

throw; cast. These two verbs mean to hurl or fling. *Cast* is the more formal, *throw* the one which serves everyday uses.

Cast is chiefly used in idiomatic expressions.

There are Biblical uses: *Cast not your pearls before swine. Let him first cast a stone at her.* There are everyday uses: cast a vote, cast lots, cast nets, cast a fishing line, cast off the bow line, castaways, cast-off clothing, and so on. Deer cast their antlers, snakes their skins. Men *cast off* evil habits and bad companions, the doing of which is felt to be noble, but *throw off* prosaic things like colds or headaches. We cast aspersions, cast an eye over a manuscript or an audience, cast aside scruples, caution, fear (*Cast a cold eye/ On life, on death,/ Horseman, pass by!*).

Throw, in addition to its literal and prosaic uses, also has idiomatic senses. We throw off disguises or illnesses. We throw a veil over a discreditable incident. In American slang we throw a party when we give one that we hope will be distinguished by unusual gaiety and verve. We throw a game when we deliberately, for a bribe or some other base motive, permit the opponent to win. To *throw the book* at someone is to make him suffer the severest penalties. The term is a cliché. To *throw a scene* is to put on an exhibition of temperament. To *throw up,* to vomit, is standard in America in relation to children. In England it is obsolescent. In speaking of adults, it is better to use *vomit*.

throw down the glove. It has been many centuries since any knight threw down his glove or gauntlet to another in defiance. As a term for challenging someone, *to throw down the glove to him* is now stilted and worn.

throw off the scent. Used figuratively to mean to divert attention, and especially to divert suspicion, *to throw off the scent* is a cliché.

thrown. See **throw.**

thrust. The past tense is *thrust*. The participle is also *thrust*.

thumbtack; drawing pin. American *thumbtack,* a tack with a large, flat head, designed to be thrust in by the thumb, is equivalent to English *drawing pin*.

thusly seems to have originated in the Boston *Journal* in 1889. Whether it was the product of illiteracy or exuberance is not known, but it is hard to see what purpose it serves. *Thus* is an adverb and nothing is gained by attaching the regular adverbial suffix *-ly* to it (as in *For many months, motivated thusly by his curiosity . . . etc.*).

thy; thine. These words are no longer natural English. When they are used, they follow exactly the pattern of *my* and *mine*. See **my; mine.**

ticket has a number of special senses in America. As a noun it can mean the list of candidates for election nominated or put forward by a political party. (See also **slate.**) To *vote a straight ticket* is to vote for all of the candidates nominated by one party. As a verb *ticket* in the United States can mean to furnish with a ticket or to issue a ticket to (*The little girl was ticketed through to Cincinnati*).

tickle means primarily to touch or stroke lightly with the fingers, a feather, etc., so as to excite a tingling or itching sensation in, to titillate (*Nothing tickles that does not pinch. Some chil-*

dren when tickled lose all control of themselves).
In America an older meaning of *tickle*, though
merely a figurative extension of its primary
meaning, is to gratify, to excite agreeably. This
is still standard, often intensified by the addition
of *to death* or *pink* (*Nellie was tickled to death
with that dress you sent her!*). This meaning
used to be common in English usage (*But, lord
Christ! when that it remembreth me/ Upon my
youth, and on my jollity,/ It tickleth me about
mine heart's root./ Unto this day it doth my
heart boot/ That I have had my world as in my
time*—Chaucer) but is now little used in England. *Tickle* may also mean to excite amusement
in (*That kid's comic; it tickles me every time I
see him*).

tidbit; titbit; delicacy; dainty. *Tidbit* only is used
in America. The English prefer *titbit* but allow
tidbit. The primary sense in both countries is
that of a delicate bit of food, and the secondary
sense is that of a choice or pleasing bit of anything, especially news. The secondary sense is
becoming the more common in America, with
the suggestion that the choice bit of news is
slightly scandalous.

In the primary sense, a *tidbit* is a particularly
choice or delicious morsel of food, a small
amount taken from a larger amount on account
of its excellence. A *delicacy* is something choice
(*His table was always furnished with delicacies*).
Overuse has weakened the word and it is usually
strengthened, in common use, by *rare*. *Dainty*, as
a noun, is a stronger word than *delicacy*. It is a
rare delicacy and likely to be slightly curious
and exotic.

tidy in standard usage means neat, trim, orderly.
But it has different colloquial uses in England
and America. In England, especially among the
lower class (according to Partridge), it may
mean moderately satisfactory (*He managed to
become a tidy fisherman*) or good of its kind (*A
tidy shot that, I flatter myself*). In America,
especially, it means considerable (*He made a
tidy fortune in cigarets when he was stationed in
Berlin*). The English know this meaning but do
not employ it as much as the Americans do.

tied to his mother's apron strings. To say of a
child who is deeply attached to his mother or of
a grown man who remains under his mother's
dominance that he is *tied to his mother's apron
strings* is to employ a hackneyed term.

tighten one's belt. As an expression for practicing
economy, bracing oneself to meet adversity, especially want, *to tighten one's belt* is a cliché.

tilde is the name of the diacritical mark ($\sim$)
placed over a letter, as over the letter *n* in Spanish, to indicate a palatal nasal sound. Thus Spanish *cañon* is pronounced like English *canyon*.

till; until. These words mean the same thing and
can be used interchangeably. *Till* is the older of
the two forms and should not be written as *'til*.

Both words are used in speaking of an interval
of time and are equivalent in meaning to the
more general word *to*. Either may be used as a
preposition with a simple object, as in *wait till
tomorrow*, or as a conjunction introducing a full
clause, as in *a son's a son till he takes a wife*.

They cannot be used without an object and so
are not adverbs, but they are like the adverbial
conjunctions *before, after, since*, rather than the
pure conjunctions, such as *if, unless, because*.

The words following *till* or *until* show the time
up to which an action or state of affairs continues. The verb in the principal clause may have
any tense. In the subordinate or time clause, a
present or present perfect tense verb is used in
speaking of the future, as in *wait till the rain
stops* or *wait till the rain has stopped*. In speaking of a past event a past perfect or a simple past
tense may be used without any difference in
meaning, as in *he waited till the rain stopped*
and *he waited till the rain had stopped*.

Till (or *until*) may be used to qualify a negative statement, as in *he did not learn of it till the
next day*. Here we may say that what continues
is the negative condition, namely that "he did
not learn." This explanation is not possible with
a sentence such as *it was not long till we realized*.
Here the principal clause *it was not long* makes a
statement which cannot be thought of as continuing. The same is true of *he wasn't in the
room five minutes till I realized*. . . . This loose
use of the word *till* (or *until*) is acceptable in the
United States but not in Great Britain, where the
word *before* or *when* is required.

tilt at windmills. As an expression, usually mildly
contemptuous, for attacking imaginary foes and
warding off nonexistent dangers, *to tilt at windmills* is a cliché. It is taken from Don Quixote's
attack on a windmill which he thought to be a
giant.

timber; timbre. Though these words are pronounced alike, their meanings and derivations
are quite different. In America *timber* retains an
older English meaning of the wood of growing
trees suitable for structural uses, or the growing
trees themselves, or wooded land (*There was
some fine timber in his woods. The company had
over two hundred thousand acres of good timber*). The cry of *Timber!* is American lumber-
jacks' warning that a tree which is being felled
is about to fall. A *timber*, in England and America, is a single beam or piece of wood forming
or capable of forming part of a structure (*They
support not only these sides, but also another
timber which upholds the roof. Though her timbers still held together, she was no longer a ship*).
Figuratively, especially in England, *timber* means
personal character or quality, the stuff of which
a person is made (*Men of that timber are not
satisfied with promises*). In English law *timber*
has, or formerly had, some special and curious
limitations. It means the trees growing upon
land and forming part of the freehold inheritance, but is commonly restricted to the oak, ash,
and elm, of the age of twenty years or more. In
some districts, by custom, other trees are included, such as birch in Yorkshire and beech
in Buckinghamshire. Such timber could not be
taken by a tenant-for-life.

Timbre is an acoustical and phonetic expression, common to England and America, meaning
that characteristic quality of a sound, independent of pitch and loudness, from which its source

or manner of production can be inferred. The trombone and the trumpet have different timbres and so do the vowels of *gate* and *goat*. In music, *timbre* is regarded as the characteristic quality of sound produced by a particular instrument or voice, its tone color.

time; times. When *time* means a period in the world's history, either the singular or the plural form may be used without any difference in meaning, as in *peace in our time* and *in these modern times*. When it means a point in time, the singular form means one point and the plural more than one, as in *at that time* and *at different times*. *Time* may also mean any one of the occasions on which something occurs, and in this sense too there is a difference between the singular and plural forms, as in *he came one time* and *he came several times*.

When the word *time* means occasion, it can be used as an adverb without a preposition, as in *he will come this time*. When it means a point in time, it is ordinarily introduced by a preposition, as in *I expect him at this time*. In the United States, *time* is used in this second sense without a preposition when it is combined with *some, any*, or *what*, as in *I will see him sometime, come anytime, what time are you leaving?* This use of *sometime* is standard, literary English. *Anytime* is not used this way in England but is standard in the United States. *What time* is a more recent development. It is acceptable to most Americans, but not to all. (It is generally condemned by grammarians.) *No time* used in this way still requires the preposition, as in *at no time*. *Every time* always refers to occasions, and to speak of points of time in this way, we must say *at all times*.

The phrase *all the time* is sometimes used to mean *at all times* or *always*, as in *he complains all the time*. This is acceptable in the United States but is condemned by some British grammarians as "slang."

When the word *time* is used with the genitive of some word that represents an interval of time, as in *a year's time, an hour's time*, it has a softening effect and makes the statement vague. *In an hour's time* is not as definite as *in an hour*.

The article *the* may be omitted before *last time* and *next time*, but not before *first time*. We may say *he said so last time he was here* and *do it next time you come*, but *tell him the first time you see him*.

The word *times* may be used in comparing a large thing with a small one, as in *it is three times as large* and *it is three times larger*. The first form is perfectly clear but the second is ambiguous. It means to some people *three times as large* and to others *four times as large*. For this reason, it should be avoided. When a small thing is compared with a large one the word *times* should not be used. The small thing is *one-third as large as* or *two-thirds smaller than* the other.

Time as a noun has many senses besides its primary one. In England, for example, there is the famous phrase *Hurry up, please, it's time* which

marks the closing of the pubs. In America, in athletics, *time* may mean the end of the game or time out, that is, time not to be counted among the limited moments allowed in a football game (*In the last minute of play Northwestern's captain called time*). *On time* in England simply means punctually; in America it means punctually but it also means by time or by installment payments (*They bought a car and a refrigerator and a television set, all on time*). An American *has a time* when he experiences difficulties (*I had quite a time with that washer. It got stuck somehow*). To *make time* is American slang meaning to ingratiate oneself with, usually spoken of a man in relation to a woman with the understanding that the ingratiation has sexual intimacy as its object. *Two-time*, a verb, is American slang for betraying, using duplicity in a relationship, especially in matters of love. To *do time* is to serve a sentence in jail.

time and time again is verbose for *repeatedly*.

time immemorial and **time out of mind** are hackneyed expressions for a period of time beyond human memory.

time was ripe. As a way of saying that circumstances were propitious, especially the circumstance of a project's being advanced to the proper point or public opinion being prepared for the unfolding of a plan or the statement of an idea or principle, *the time was ripe* is a cliché.

time words. Names for intervals of time, such as *minute, day, week, year*, are often used with a final *s* that would not be used in measures of distance. That is, we say *a three mile drive* but we might say *a three hours delay*. Historically, this is an old genitive ending which survives in a few adverbs, such as *always* and *backwards*, and in certain measures of time. See **adverbial genitive, measures,** and **nouns as adverbs.**

Time nouns often serve as conjunctions, or relative adverbs, and introduce a subordinate clause, as *minute* in *I remembered it the minute I saw him*. See **conjunctions.**

The article *the* is omitted before words or phrases used adverbially to show time "at which," as in *I saw him day before yesterday* and *I'll do it week after next*. In the United States the article *the* is also omitted after *all* in expressions that show time "during which," as in *all summer, all week, all year*. This is standard English in the United States. In Great Britain this *the* is omitted from *all day* and *all night* but is required with all other words, such as *summer, week, year*.

timid. See **cowardly.**

tirade. See **harangue.**

tired; fatigued; exhausted. These words all suggest a depletion of physical energy, in the order of severity in which they are arranged. *Tired*, unless strengthened by some adverb, does not suggest a very serious condition (*I'm tired for some reason this morning. I'll just sit down and rest my feet awhile*). In American usage it also means impatient, disgusted, annoyed (*You make me tired with all that big talk. I tell you frankly, the people in this town are tired of these street brawls and are going to do something about* *it*). *Fatigued* suggests a degree of tiredness so great that, at least for the moment, continued exertion seems impossible (*Lydia was too much fatigued to utter more than an occasional exclamation of "Lord, how tired I am!" accompanied by a violent yawn*). One who is *exhausted* is fatigued to the point of having no strength or energy at all left. Hyperbole has weakened the word, in relation to the physical condition of persons, by using it when *fatigued* or even *tired* would have been more suitable. But used in its proper meaning, it is a strong word (*The exhausted horse had abandoned the struggle and lay half-buried in the mire, its flanks quivering and its belly heaving pitifully in great, intermittent, sobbing breaths*). *Fatigued* and *tired* can be applied only to human beings and animals. *Exhausted,* meaning utterly emptied or completely used up, may be applied to almost anything (*By January the food supply was exhausted. After three hours of discussion the topic was exhausted; there was nothing more to be said*). See also **wearied; weary.**

title (for book). See **volume.**

tizzy. There was an English slang word for sixpence, a *tizzy,* but the current American slang term for a state of excited confusion must have some other origin. Perhaps in some obscure way it is connected with *phthisis,* a wasting away. Or perhaps it is a portmanteau combination of *terror* and *dizzy.* Or perhaps it is connected with the *tizwin* home brew that the Southwestern Indians crazed themselves with (*When officers learned that the Apaches were indulging in a "tizwin drunk" they knew that mischief was afoot*). But whatever its origin, it is certainly established in current informal use and shows signs of becoming accepted in formal usage. As a noun it means a state of trembling excitement and fear (*Word that the Germans were preparing to attack threw the captain into a tizzy*). Quite recently the word has appeared as an intransitive verb in a serious article in a highly respectable publication (*In some respects, Americans of middle-class mentality have repeated the pattern of their counterparts in these European countries. They have shown the same quick readiness to tizzy, the jealous sense of property and status.* . . . —Eric Goldman, *The Reporter,* September 14, 1954). It is interesting that this extension of *tizzy* was made not by a journalist but by a college professor.

to. The basic, physical meaning of this preposition is "in the direction of." Where it approaches the uses of *at* or *in,* it always carries the implication of motion or change, as in *he went to the office, he had been to New York,* but *he was at the office, he was in New York.*

To is used to indicate that a following verb form is an infinitive, as in *he wants to go.* (See **infinitives.**) It may be used to represent an infinitive that is not expressed, as in *he wants to.* This way of speaking began in the middle of the nineteenth century. At that time it was distressing to some people, who considered it improper. The claim that the simple word *to* should not be used

to represent the full infinitive sometimes appears in textbooks today, but it is no longer true. This use of the word has now become standard English.

To is also used to represent the relation of indirect object. (See **indirect object.**) As an extension of this, it is often used after nouns or adjectives to indicate the person or thing affected, as in *an injury to, injurious to, pleasing to.*

An apparently unnecessary *to* is added to many verbs meaning "assert," as in *admit to, attest to, certify to, testify to, swear to.* Here it has the effect of weakening the sense of the verb slightly, almost as if the verb meaning were being qualified by the basic meaning of *to,* "in the direction of."

toe the mark. As an expression for making someone live up rigorously to some prescribed course of conduct, to make him *toe the mark* is hackneyed.

toffee; toffy; taffy. *Taffy,* the oldest of these synonyms, is not now used in England, but it persists in the pronunciation of Northern England and is standard in Scotland and in the United States. It means a candy made of sugar or molasses boiled down, often with butter or nuts added. In the last two or three decades of the nineteenth century *taffy* was a widely used slang word in America, meaning crude flattery, blarney, soft soap. *Giving taffy* meant flattering, especially in love-making (*Taffy, just a little bit of taffy/ . . . You are giving taffy too*). The English use the word *toffee* (the spelling of which may have been affected by *coffee*) and, less often, *toffy.* The word has with them become a part of several vulgar expressions, such as *not for toffee* which means "not under any circumstances" and *not to be able to do a thing for toffee* which means to be incompetent at it.

In the United States *toffee* is used to describe imported English toffee or a form of taffy in which cream is used instead of butter. *Taffy* has a homely, rustic connotation, *toffee* the elegance of an importation. A *taffy pull* is a social gathering in which taffy is made and the making involves a drawing out of the substance as it is cooling. A *toffee pull* would be a linguistic and social monstrosity.

together. This word is often used where, theoretically, it is not needed, as in *we gather together to ask the Lord's blessing, we will meet together this evening,* and *they consulted together.* Usually, as in the examples given, it replaces a reflexive or reciprocal pronoun such as *ourselves* or *one another.* The verbs in these examples are all transitive verbs that normally require an object but are here used intransitively. The speech instinct apparently requires some word in the object position. Although *together* does not actually repeat the subject as *one another* would, it recalls the subject and rules out the possibility of any other object following the verb. The verb *join* normally requires a double object, as in *join this to that.* Here too *together* is often used in place of the second element and means "**to**

one another," as in *those whom God hath joined together*. This use of *together* is condemned by some grammarians as redundant. But the construction is standard literary English and the feeling for it is very strong. The word can always be omitted, and this may make for more precise English. But if it is omitted, many hearers or readers will have the uncomfortable feeling that they ought to ask *gather what?, consulted whom?*

token of esteem. To designate a gift a *token of esteem,* even when it is a token of esteem, is to employ a cliché. True esteem will find something, or should find something, more suited to the particular occasion than a hackneyed and pompous phrase that has been drained of meaning by endless repetition.

told. See **tell.**

tomato. The plural is *tomatoes.*

tome. See **volume.**

ton. Only the singular form *ton* can be used as an adjective to qualify a following noun, as in *a five ton truck*. We do not say *a five tons truck*. In the United States the plural form *tons* is preferred in any other construction, when speaking of more than one. But the singular form may be used in other constructions after a number word, as in *several ton of coal* and *he ordered several ton*. This is the usual practice in Great Britain and is acceptable in the United States.

The context in which the word *ton* is used must be clearly understood before its sense is clear. It is first of all a unit of weight, now usually 20 hundredweight, commonly equivalent to 2,000 pounds avoirdupois (*short ton*) in the United States, and 2,240 pounds avoirdupois (*long ton*) in Great Britain. It is also a unit of volume for freight, varying with the different kinds, as 40 cubic feet of oak timber, 20 bushels of wheat, etc. (*freight ton*); a metric ton (1,000 kilograms); a unit of displacement of ships, equal to 35 cubic feet of salt water (*displacement ton*); a unit of volume used in transporting by sea, commonly 40 cubic feet (*shipping ton*); a unit of internal capacity of ships, equal to 100 cubic feet. In all of these additional senses English and American use is the same.

Ton is also used in a loose sense to mean a great amount (*There are tons of pickles—everybody brought pickles. Her father's got tons of money*). A *ton of bricks* as a metaphor for something that comes down with a smashing roar (*He caught him sneaking out half an hour early again and came down on him like a ton of bricks*) is hackneyed.

tone; tune. *Tune* is a variant spelling of *tone* and originally had the same meaning. *Tone* retains the meaning of any sound considered with reference to its quality, pitch, strength, source; quality or character of sound; vocal sound. In reference to the human voice it often means an implication or meaning which a particular intonation may suggest even though the literal meaning of the words suggests something wholly different (*I know he said he didn't mind, but I didn't like the tone of his voice*). *Tune* now primarily means a succession of musical sounds,

a series of *tones,* forming an air or melody, with or without the harmony accompanying it. In a figurative sense, *tone* means style, distinction, elegance (*That hotel certainly has tone. There's a quiet distinction about it*). *Tony,* an adjective based on this meaning, is, however, slang (*He's a real tony guy, always in style*). *Tune* may also be used figuratively to mean accord (*In Tune With the Infinite. The world is too much with us; late and soon,/ Getting and spending, we lay waste our powers:/ . . . / For this, for everything, we are out of tune*).

tongs. The plural form refers to one instrument but is most often treated as a plural, as in *these tongs are hot*. In Scotland it is commonly treated as a singular. This is acceptable in the United States, especially when used with a qualifying word, as in *a fire tongs, a sugar tongs,* but *a pair of tongs* is more usual. The construction with *pair* must be used after a numeral, as in *three pairs of tongs*. The form *tongs* is preferred as the first element in a compound, such as *a tongs maker, a tongs man.*

tongue in cheek. To say of someone who is insincere or who has affirmed something with unspoken reservations, whose words belie his intent and go contrary to his true meaning, that he is speaking with his *tongue in his cheek* is to employ a hackneyed expression. The term is fairly recent, the first recorded instance being in *The Ingoldsby Legends* (1842). It would seem to refer to some gesture which, like a wink, informed the knowing that the statement was not to be taken at its seeming value. But although some people, guided chiefly by the phrase, do stick their tongues in their cheeks as such a humorous warning, it is certainly not a widespread custom nor, so far as is known, has it ever been.

too. When this word is used as a sentence adverb it means "also." It has the same meaning when it qualifies a preceding adjective or adverb, as in *he is young too*. When it qualifies a following adjective or adverb it means "beyond what is desirable or allowable," as in *he is too young*. In either case, it cannot be used with a comparative or superlative form. From meaning "in excess," *too* has come to be used as an intensive in combination with *only,* as in *only too anxious to leave*. Used as an intensive without *only,* as in *it was too wonderful!,* it has a false ring and suggests that the speaker is trying to conceal a lack of interest by overstatement.

When *too* means "in excess" it cannot qualify a verb. Participles, such as *discouraged* and *discouraging,* are verbs and adjectives at the same time and it is debatable whether or not one can say *he was too discouraged to go on*. Actually, this is acceptable English everywhere in the United States, but some grammarians claim that it ought not to be acceptable. The same arguments apply to the use of *very* before a participle. (For a fuller discussion of this question, see **very.**)

took. See **take.**

tooth. The plural is *teeth*. Traditionally, only the singular *tooth* can be used as the first element in a compound, as in *toothbrushes* and *tooth marks.* In some parts of the country people are said to complain of the *teethache.* This is painfully vivid, but it is not standard English. On the other hand, dentists sometimes speak of *the teeth roots.* This cannot be classed with *teethache.* Since it occurs in technical material it must be considered a new or unestablished form rather than an illiterate one.

tooth and nail, as a term for the utmost exertion, especially in contention or conflict, is a cliché.

top; summit; peak; apex. All these words describe the highest point of something. *Top* is the everyday, working word (*the top of a tree, the top of the house*). *Summit* literally describes the highest point, as of a hill (*Two members of the expedition reached the summit of Mt. Everest*). *Peak* is the pointed top of a mountain, a mountain with a pointed summit (*Most of all they enjoyed the ascent of Pike's Peak. The peaks were bathed in a rosy light*). *Apex* is primarily understood in its mathematical sense as the vertex of a triangle or cone; more broadly, the tip or highest point of something.

Each of these words also has its figurative uses. We say that a boy finished at the top of his class or that a certain goal was the summit of his aspiration. The highest-level political talks, in the summer of 1955, were called *talks at the summit. Peak* may be used to suggest a maximum in relation to other quantities during a specified time (*Peak traffic on the Drive was from 8:30 to 9:00 in the morning and 5:00 to 5:30 in the afternoon*). Used figuratively, *apex* means climax, acme (*That sixty-yard run was the apex of his college career*).

Top is used as an adjective more freely than the other three words. It has developed a superlative adjective form *topmost,* but no comparative form.

topnotch; top-hole; tip-top. *Topnotch* is an American slang term for first-rate, excellent (*He telegraphed last night for four topnotch people to join us. He did a topnotch job on that assignment*). *Top-hole* and *tip-top* are British slang equivalents.

tore; torn. See **tear.**

tornado. See **cyclone.**

torpedo. The plural is *torpedoes.*

tortuous; torturous; tortious. *Tortuous* means full of twists, turns, or bends; twisting; winding; crooked (*The driver must be alert as he drives along the tortuous road on the Tennessee-North Carolina border*). In figurative senses *tortuous* means not direct or straightforward, as in a course of procedure, thought, speech, writing; deceitfully indirect or morally crooked (*The inevitable result of this tortuous policy was the complete loss of the public's confidence*). *Torturous* means inflicting excruciating pain, especially from sheer cruelty or in hatred, revenge, or the like.

Tortious is a legal term, meaning of the nature of or pertaining to a tort, a civil wrong (*If a civil officer . . . have process against one individual and through mistake arrest another, this arrest is wholly tortious*).

tortures of the damned, suffer. If you believe in the damned and their tortures, the expression *to suffer the tortures of the damned* will seem, when applied to any discomforts of our earthly state, an impious exaggeration. If you don't believe in the damned and their tortures, the phrase is just mocking verbiage. In either case, it is hackneyed.

total. See **complete.**

tote is an American colloquialism, largely Southern, meaning to carry or bear, as on the back or in the arms, as a burden or load (*He toted a fifty-pound pack all over the state of Georgia*). The best known use of the word today, in the song "Old Man River" (*"Tote dat barge"/ "Lift dat bale"/ Get a little drunk,/ And you land in jail*), seems to be a misuse.

Tote can also mean to wear or carry about one (*Jed always toted a pistol*) or to haul in a vehicle (*The manure in the feed lots is scraped up by a bulldozer and toted away to the field in a spreader*), though this, too, may be an attempt to convey a rustic flavor without too clear a knowledge of the term. In New England logging roads are sometimes called *tote roads.*

touch and go. As a term for a narrow escape, for a precarious situation in which the outcome was for a moment delicately poised between success and failure, *touch and go* is hackneyed.

The expression seems to have been borrowed from pilotage where "touch and go" was said to be "good pilotage," but to take a ship through so narrow a channel or so close to the rocks that you felt her touch and yet go on must have been precarious. There was also a boys' game called *touch and go* which, from Austin Dobson's description of it, must have been something like hide and seek.

touch it with a ten-foot pole, I wouldn't. Although many clichés are pompous and stilted, there are slang clichés as well, for one can be just as stale informally as formally. To say of something one wants no part of or doesn't want to meddle in that one *wouldn't touch it with a ten-foot pole* is to employ a cliché. The English equivalent is *I wouldn't touch it with a pair of tongs* or *I wouldn't touch it with a barge pole.*

touchy. See **tetchy.**

tough, as an adjective, applied to people, conveys different meanings in England and America. In England it means stubborn, persistent. In America it carries the more sinister meaning of hardened, incorrigible, disorderly, rowdyish (*He got into a very tough gang*). In America *tough* may also mean hard to bear or endure (*He's had a tough time of it, what with the drouth one year and the hoof and mouth disease the next*). As a noun, *tough* in America means a ruffian, a rowdy. The English equivalent is *rough.*

toward; towards. These forms are both standard English. In Great Britain the form *towards* is heard more often and *toward* is considered archaic or Biblical. In the United States *toward* is the preferred form.

towering passion or **rage** is now a cliché. The adjective, in a now-forgotten meaning of mounting, is taken from falconry (*A falcon, tow'ring in her pride of place,/ Was by a mousing owl* *hawk'd at and kill'd*). It was originally a good adjective because it suggested that the mounting anger would be followed by a sudden, precipitous, murderous strike upon the victim, but this meaning is now unknown and the phrase empty.

tower of strength. To refer to someone upon whom others can rely in time of need as *a tower of strength* is to employ a worn and stale expression. Every city used to have its fortified tower (as *The Tower of London*) to which the besieged could resort for a last desperate stand if their walls were scaled or breached. Such a tower sometimes held out for months after the city itself had been taken and was the rallying point from which the invaders were sometimes driven out. So that so long as the tower was not taken, the city was not truly captured.

town. See **city.**

trace; vestige. A *trace* is a mark, token, or evidence of the former presence, existence, or action of something (*On the worn features of the weariest face/ Some youthful memory leaves its hidden trace*). *Trace* is the more general word. It may mean a last faint mark or sign, or it may mean a small amount of anything (*There was barely a trace of sugar in the tea*), or it may stand for the clue or track by which pursuit may be made (*They came on the trace of game in the late afternoon*). *Vestige* is more limited. It refers to some slight, though actual, remains of something that no longer exists (. . . *the stickpin, the malacca cane, and other vestiges of his former wealth . . . Scarce any trace remaining, vestige gray,/ Or nodding column on the desert shore,/ To point where Corinth, or where Athens stood*).

track is used more often and in more ways in America than in England. In America *track* or *tracks* describe a structure consisting of a pair of parallel lines or rails with their cross ties, to provide a road for railroad trains. The English say *the line* or *the rails*. *Tracks* in America is the word to describe footprints or other marks left by an animal or person; the English tend to use *trace*. American trains jump the track or leave the track; English trains run off the line. American *race track* is English *racecourse*. *Trackman* and *trackwalker* are exclusively American terms to describe a man who inspects, installs, or maintains railroad tracks. *Track* when used as a verb in America may mean to make a track of footprints on a floor (*They're always tracking mud into the kitchen*). *Track* is used in American sports to describe collectively those sports performed on a track. A *track meet* is a series of athletic contests such as running, jumping, vaulting. There are several idiomatic expressions in America such as *make tracks* (leave hurriedly), *lose track* (lose contact with), *right side of the tracks* (the more socially acceptable part of town).

trade, in trade, the trade. See **profession.**

trademarks. A trademark is the name, symbol, figure, letter, word or mark adopted and used by a manufacturer or merchant in order to designate the goods he manufactures or sells and to distinguish them from those manufactured or sold by others.

Trademarks are interesting in themselves and because they sometimes enter into general use as generic terms or catchwords.

There have been a number of patterns of trademarking. For instance, after the Spanish-American war the Spanish *-o* appeared in the names of many products, such as *Perfecto* cigars and *Eterno* lead pencils. In the 1920's there was an extension of such suffixes as *-teria* (*cafeteria, cattleteria*), *-burger* (*hamburger, cheeseburger, nutburger*), *-mat* (*Automat*) and *-matic*. Use of the medial connective *-a-* or *-o-* has been common more recently (*Stack-a-Door, Perma-lift, Ford-o-matic, Expand-o Sock*). Another favorite suffix is *-tex*, perhaps with an echo of *texture*: *Playtex, Plastex, Kotex*. One of the most popular devices is word-welding, as in *Nabisco* and *Quink*. Another is the substitution of *k* for *c*: *Kake Kover, Bread Kabinet*. Still another is manipulated spelling: *Ayds* (a reducing candy), *Styl-Eez* (shoes). Some trademarks rely on puns: *Taylor-Made* shoes, *Enna Jettick* shoes, *Vermont Maid* syrup.

Because of inadequate laws, many words which began as trademarks, words like *cellophane, escalator, linoleum* and *aspirin,* have fallen into the public domain and ended in the dictionaries as generic terms. The Lanham Act of 1946 has helped to insure more effective protective measures, but some very popular trademarks still tend, in popular consciousness, to be regarded as generic. *Kodak,* for example, is often employed as a general term, and so too are *Vaseline, Coke, Frigidaire, Jell-o* and *Victrola.*

trade with. See **patronize.**

traffic in American usage has a special pejorative connotation in such phrases as *The Opium traffic, The White Slave traffic*. This embodies an older use of the word *traffic,* meaning trade or business, especially a trade or business that required considerable going to and fro (*The passage and traffic of merchants was forbidden*). The word early acquired sinister connotations (*They make a traffic of honor. You make the most shameless traffic and barter of yourselves*), but since World War II many activities that had formerly been labeled *traffics* have become *Black Markets. Traffic* remains fixed, however, in *the White Slave traffic,* perhaps because a White Slave Black Market would sound ludicrous.

tragedy; disaster. *Tragedy* applies first of all to art; *disaster* to life. In its primary sense *tragedy* means a dramatic composition of a serious or somber character, with an unhappy ending. There must be a sense of greatness in the person to whom the tragedy befalls and the unhappy ending must, at least in part, be the consequence of some fault—even though that fault be an excess of virtue—in the person. The use of *tragedy* to describe some lamentable, dreadful, or fatal event, a common journalistic practice, is loose. *Disaster* or *calamity* is the right word when the event is of such magnitude as to involve many people, *misfortune* when it involves a single person.

tragic; tragical. *Tragic* is the only adjective current in America meaning characteristic or suggestive of tragedy; mournful; melancholy or pathetic in the extreme (*His was a tragic plight*); dreadful, calamitous, disastrous, or fatal (*The decision to attack was a tragic error*); pertaining to or having the nature of tragedy (*He made a careful study of the Elizabethan tragic drama*); acting in or composing tragedy (*Shakespeare may have been a minor tragic actor, but he was a major tragic playwright*). *Tragical* is a seldom used alternative that has an archaic flavor (*"The Tragical History of Dr. Faustus" has some farcical scenes*). In England *tragic* is the general word but some English grammarians argue that the meanings "sad" and "gloomy" should be conveyed by *tragical,* and only "of or pertaining to tragedy" by *tragic.*

train. This verb may be followed by an infinitive, as in *they trained him to recognize these things.* It is sometimes followed by the *-ing* form of a verb and the preposition *for,* as in *they trained him for recognizing these things.* The infinitive construction is very much preferred, except when the *-ing* word is felt to be the name of something some one would study, as in *they trained her for nursing, they trained him for flying.*

transcendent; transcendental. *Transcendent* is to be preferred as the term meaning surpassing, superior, or supreme (*The conference is of transcendent importance, since vital issues must be discussed now*). In theology (used of God), it means transcending the material universe, as opposed to *immanent,* residing in the material universe.

Transcendental, except as a term in metaphysics, means outside ordinary experience, thought or belief; extraordinary, supernatural; abstract, idealistic, lofty (*Such speculations are too transcendental for me*).

transitive verbs. A verb that requires an object to complete its meaning is called a transitive verb. The action named by the verb is said to "pass over" to the object. (See **object of a verb.**) A verb that does not require an object, because its meaning is complete in itself, is called intransitive. The verbs are intransitive in *a lonely cab horse steams and stamps.* They are transitive in *they bite their threads and shake their heads and gnaw my name like a bone.* Some verbs, such as *shall, may, must,* require another verb to complete their meaning. These may be thought of as a special kind of transitive verb or as being in a class by themselves. (See **auxiliary verbs.**)

A verb that is essentially transitive may sometimes be used intransitively, as in *I hoed and trenched and weeded.* Some grammarians say that in such cases the verb is a transitive "used absolutely," because they claim that an object, here *garden* or *farm,* is understood. Others consider any verb intransitive when the sentence does not contain an object. This is a question of terminology and makes no difference in practice.

Sometimes the object of a transitive verb is a pronoun referring back to the subject or agent. For example, people could once say *I will wash me and dress me and fix me up fine.* Today, the

-self words (*myself, himself,* and so on) may be used in this way, but they are omitted more often than not. We usually say *he shaved and dressed* rather than *he shaved himself and dressed himself.* In many cases, such as *he overate, he overslept, the population doubled,* the reflexive pronoun is no longer thought of. In others, such as *he hid, he behaved well, don't bother,* it may be used or omitted. In still others, such as *he prided himself on, he conducted himself well,* it is required. Practically all grammarians consider verbs of this kind transitive when the pronoun is used, and intransitive when it is not.

Verbs such as *tear, split, sell, cook,* are essentially transitive, but they are used intransitively in *the cloth tore, the wood split easily, the pies sold, the apples cooked quickly.* What is meant here is that somebody or something tore the cloth, split the wood, sold the pies, cooked the apples. What is logically the object of the verb has not been dropped but has been made its grammatical subject. This happens also when a verb is put in the passive voice and some grammarians call these forms "passivals." The verb is intransitive in form but passive in meaning. The construction is used widely—dust brushes off, foods spoil, boats upset, doors slam, hearts break, and the value of the dollar depreciates. A true passive, such as *the dust was brushed off, the boat was upset,* always suggests an agent. A passival, on the other hand, presents the action itself, as if it occurred spontaneously. They are simpler than the passive forms and are preferred whenever the fact that there was an agent is felt to be irrelevant.

This use of the transitive verbs *lay* and *set* has been severely attacked during the last hundred years. As a result of not being allowed to use these verbs naturally, many people are now afraid to use them at all. (See **lay** and **set.**) More recently, it has been claimed that *graduate* used as a passival, as in *he graduated last June,* is ungrammatical. In the case of *lay* and *set,* there were intransitive verbs *lie* and *sit* which the grammarians thought they were protecting. But in the case of *graduate,* it is hard to see why someone chose this word to attack rather than any of a thousand others.

transitory; transient; transitional. All of these adjectives suggest shortness of duration. *Transient* and *transitory* both mean passing away, not lasting, momentary, short-lived, ephemeral, temporary, impermanent. However, *transient* tends to be used with people, *transitory* with things (*Transient guests at the hotel were more likely to tip freely than the permanent dwellers in its musty corridors. One can hardly be expected to sacrifice solid advantages for these transitory delights*). *Transient* more frequently emphasizes the fact of brief duration, *transitory* the quality of brief duration.

Transitional means going from one thing to another (*We are living in a transitional period of history. Every period, however original and creative, has a transitional aspect in its relation to the years before and after*).

Transient may also be used as a noun, meaning one who is transient, a transient guest, boarder, or the like. *Transient* is a bookish term in England but in common use, both as a noun and an adjective, in the United States.

transmit. See **forward.**

transom means basically a crosspiece separating a door or the like from a window or fanlight above it. In America *transom* is also used to describe a window above such a crosspiece. In the famous ballad *Frankie and Johnnie,* Frankie *looked over the transom,* though *looked through the transom* would certainly be understood and perhaps more commonly used today. In England the window above the crosspiece is called a *transom window.* Publishers in America humorously refer to unsolicited manuscripts as coming in *over the transom.*

More broadly, a transom is a crossbar, as of wood or stone, dividing a window horizontally. In shipbuilding, a transom is a crossbeam in the frame of a ship, or any of several transverse beams or timbers fixed across the sternpost of a ship, to strengthen and give shape to the after part.

transpire; happen. *Transpire* originally meant to breathe out through the surface or to exhale (*The leaves transpire more fluid than the stem can take up. This, that, and ev'ry thicket doth transpire/ More sweet than storax from the hallowed fire*). Then it meant to pass out, as an exhalation. The brilliant Elizabethan eccentric, Sir John Harington, believed that "his thoughts transpired from him and took the shape of flies or bees." From such uses of the word it was natural for it to mean to escape from secrecy to notice, to become known where it was intended to keep secret (*This letter goes to you in confidence. You will not let one syllable of it transpire*). Dr. Johnson (in 1755) condemned this meaning as "lately innovated from France without necessity." Nonetheless, this was until fairly recently the word's standard meaning.

Its commonest meaning now is to happen, occur, take place. Perhaps this change arose from a misunderstanding of such sentences as *has anything transpired in my absence?* where the coming to light of some secret knowledge and the taking action might be closely related. However this may be, there is no doubt that *transpire* now has the meaning of "happen" for many people. But there is also no doubt that a great many other people regard this usage as wrong. Indeed, with some it has become a shibboleth, a touchstone of literacy and refinement; anyone who uses *transpire* to mean "happen" is, in their estimation, vulgar, illiterate, and contemptible. Yet many of the best grammarians recognize this meaning of the word.

Under these circumstances, what is the ordinary man to do? If he is timid, he can avoid using the word altogether: there are other ways of saying that something has escaped from secrecy to notice than saying it has transpired, and *happen* is always understood and acceptable. Or if the ordinary man is bold and self-confident he may defy the purists and use *transpire* to mean

"happen," stoutly insisting that what was good enough for the Adamses of Boston is good enough for him. But that won't save him from being regarded as a vulgar illiterate by the purists, and if he is in a position where their so regarding him will be harmful to him, he must expect to suffer.

Among the mass of people the use of *transpire* for "happen" will pass unnoticed. Among linguists it will be accepted as a word that has acquired a new meaning through usage, however erroneous that meaning may have been when first acquired. Among quite a few who regard themselves as linguists, however, its use in this way will arouse contempt. So that when one is among such people and does not want, or cannot afford, to arouse their contempt, and has not the opportunity, time, or ability to enlighten them, it is better to avoid using the word in this sense.

transportation; ticket. In one of its less prominent senses, *transportation* is used in the United States to mean the means by which transportation is obtained, that is, tickets or permits (*I got transportation on the Super Chief*).

trauma. The plural is *traumas* or *traumata,* not *traumae.*

travel; travail. *Travel* was originally merely a variant form of *travail,* labor, toil, strenuous exertion so severe as to cause suffering. The connection of the two words is at once a good, simple lesson in etymology and in social history, for it suggests what an arduous undertaking it once was to go from one place to another. *Travail,* which once meant to suffer in strenuous labor, has now narrowed to mean to suffer the pangs of childbirth, has become specialized, that is, in reference to one kind of labor. *To travel* is now simply to go from one place to another and would on the whole (especially by those who have not traveled much) be classified as a pleasure. In the United States *to travel* also means, in slang, to move with speed (*By the time he reaching the city limits he was really traveling*).

travesty. See **burlesque.**

treachery; treacherous; treason. Both *treachery* and *treason* imply betrayal of trust. *Treachery* may designate secret disloyalty to a friend, especially when the disloyalty is concealed beneath a seemingly friendly and loyal attitude (*He was a timid enemy and a treacherous friend*). In its personal application, *treachery* is a word of strong condemnation and contempt. *Treachery* may also apply to traitorous conduct towards one's country. *Treason* is, definitely and solely, wishing to harm one's country or government and performing overt, open acts to help its enemies (*The gradual steps by which Arnold progressed from loyalty to treason mark a path of personal resentment*). *Treason,* perhaps because of the enormity of the crime it designates, is a more dignified word than *treachery.* Every man has felt the treachery of friends and smarts at the recollection the word evokes. We suffer in common from the effects of treason and agree in universal detestation of it but it is too far removed from our immediate knowledge or experience to be viewed with much personal rancor.

tread. The past tense is *trod*. The participle is *trodden* or *trod*. When *tread* is used in the idiom *tread water* it is a regular verb and has the past tense and participle *treaded*.

treasonable and **treasonous** both mean involving treason, traitorous (*It was a treasonable/ treasonous libel*). In the extended sense of "of the nature of treason, perfidious," *treasonable* is preferred. Indeed, *treasonable* is now generally preferred to *treasonous* in all possible senses.

treble. See **triple.**

trek is not to be used loosely as a synonym for *travel* (as in *Now is the time to trek to the Wisconsin Dells*). It means to migrate, and refers specifically to the migrations of the Boers in South Africa (*Thus the early Cape Boers adopted the nomad habit of trekking, which simply meant enlarging the range of their occupation of new land and a further advance into the interior*). If it is to be applied to travel, it is properly applied, even humorously, only to the movement of masses of people and, presumably, a permanent removal (*The trek of retired Iowa farmers to California continues unabated*).

tremblor; temblor; tremor. *Tremblor* is a misspelling of the American word *temblor*, probably by association with *tremor*. *Temblor* is an American word (from the Spanish *temblar*, tremble) for a *tremor*, an earthquake. A *tremor* is any tremulous or vibratory movement, a vibration (*Modern research has shown a typical earthquake to consist of a series of small tremors succeeded by a shock, or series of shocks*). The English call a light disturbance similar to an earthquake an *earth tremor*.

tremendous. See horrible.

trend. See tend.

trepan; trephine. *Trepan* is the older term and the one still largely in use by laymen. As a noun it means a boring tool for sinking shafts or, in surgery, an obsolete form of the trephine, resembling a carpenter's bit and brace. As a verb it means to operate with a trepan. *Trephine* is the term for a surgical instrument resembling a small circular saw with a center pin mounted on a strong hollow metal shaft to which is attached a transverse handle and which is used to remove circular discs of bone from the skull. As a verb it means to operate upon with a trephine.

trial; experiment; test. All of these nouns imply an attempt to find out something or to find out about something. *Trial* is the general word for a trying of anything (*Two Weeks Free Trial! Knowing as little as we do, there is no course open to us but trial and error. A trial run*). *Experiment* looks to the future, and is a trial conducted to prove or illustrate the truth or validity of an assumption, or an attempt to discover something new (*As an experiment he and a companion lived on nothing but meat for more than a year*). *Test* is a stronger and more specific word, referring to a trial under approved and fixed conditions, or a final and decisive trial as a conclusion of past experiments (*After months*

of experiment and trial, he was ready for the final test).

trick; maneuver; stratagem; subterfuge. All of these words imply gaining one's ends by creating a false impression. *Trick* is always a pejorative term, in this sense, meaning to cheat (*Jacob tricked Esau out of their father's blessing*) or, as a noun, an underhanded act (*That was a dirty trick to play on a friend!*). *Maneuver* is also both a verb and a noun. It is primarily a military term. As a noun it means a planned and regulated movement or evolution of troops; an adroit move; an artful procedure (*It was only a maneuver to get defensive patrol vessels out of the way before the commandos landed*). As a verb, *maneuver* means to manipulate with skill or adroitness. The English spell the word *manoeuvre*.

Stratagem, in distinction to *maneuver*, means a plan, scheme, or trick for deceiving the enemy. It is the plan of action, literally, rather than the action itself. *Subterfuge*, like *trick*, is a pejorative term. It describes an artifice or expedient employed to escape the force of an argument or to evade unfavorable consequences (*His disguise as an expectant mother was a brazen subterfuge to insure a place in one of the lifeboats*).

trillion; billion. A *trillion* is, in America and France, a cardinal number represented by one (1) followed by 12 zeros (1,000,000,000,000). In England and Germany a *trillion* is a cardinal number represented by one (1) followed by 18 zeros (1,000,000,000,000,000,000). A *billion* in America is equal to a thousand millions (1,000,-000,000), in England to a million millions (1,000,000,000,000). Thus the American *trillion* is equal to the English *billion*. See also **million.**

trim his sails. The sailor who *trims his sails*, who adjusts them, that is, with reference to the direction of the wind and the course of the ship, so as to obtain the greatest advantage, is a good seaman and from the point of view of seamanship admirable. But in its figurative uses, the expression is disparaging, because the emphasis, in the figure, shifts from the skill in management to the purposes of management. One who trims his sails metaphorically shifts with shifting winds and has no fixed principle beyond the achievement of his own advantage. That he pursues his own advantage skillfully is not, in common estimation, grounds for admiration.

tri-monthly; quarterly. *Quarterly* means, quite unambiguously, once in a quarter of a year. *Tri-monthly*, in its conventional use, is a synonym of *quarterly*, since it means taking place once each three months. Yet *tri-monthly* is ambiguous, since it can mean, and is sometimes used to mean, three times a month. It would be useful to the language if it were fixed in this meaning and *quarterly* reserved to mean once in three months.

trip; voyage; journey; flight. These words all describe a course of travel made to a particular place, usually for some specific purpose. In England *trip* means a short journey or voyage. An English *tripper* is the equivalent of an American *excursionist;* he's on a short outing, of a few days or a week or two at the most. In America *trip* is the general word, indicating going any distance and returning, by walking or any means of locomotion, for either business or pleasure and in either a hurried or a leisurely manner (*We don't go to the end of the line this trip, lady. A trip to the moon is now thought an at-least-remote possibility*). A *voyage* is travel by air or water, usually for a long distance, and for business or pleasure. In reference to travel by air, *flight* is replacing all other words; although if one announced that he was making a trip to New York, he would not feel it inappropriate if someone asked if he were going by air. *Making* a trip, by the way, in American contemporary usage, suggests that it is a business trip or undertaken of necessity; *taking* a trip is more likely to suggest that it is a pleasure trip. If the journey is to be by water, *voyage* has a connotation of leisureliness, lacking from *trip* or *journey* (*For their honeymoon they took a voyage around the world*). Because of the emphasis on luxury in air travel, especially in the advertisements, and because it is still for most people a new, exciting, and slightly dangerous way of traveling, *flight*, in this context, is a glamorous word.

A *journey* is a trip of considerable length, wholly or mainly by land, for business or pleasure, and is now applied to travel which is more leisurely or more fatiguing than a trip. A return is not necessarily implied (*It was a sentimental journey into the past when he set out for the little village on the Mississippi in which he had spent his boyhood*).

triple and **treble** both convey the sense of threefold, but they may be distinguished. Except for its special musical sense of soprano, *treble* is pretty close in meaning to *triple*, though it is more often used as a verb and a noun, at least in England, and *triple* as an adjective and in combinations.

As a verb *treble* means to make or become three times as much or many (*You can treble your income if you buy the right stocks*). As a verb *triple* conveys roughly the same idea and is more often used in America than *treble*. Indeed, *treble* is now rarely used in the United States, *triple* being preferred in almost every sense. As an adjective *treble* means threefold, three times as much, as in: *There was a treble veneer on the table. Triple* may mean this too, but it may also mean a veneer of three kinds or anything else of three kinds (*The poem has triple implications— esthetic, ethical, and metaphysical*). *Triple* has certain peculiarly American uses when applied to baseball. As a noun, a *triple* is a three-base hit. As a verb, *to triple* is to hit a three-base hit. As an adjective, *triple,* in the expression *triple play,* means a play in which three "outs" are achieved, three men are retired, before the ball is again put into play.

Triple is used in many combinations; e.g., *triple-action, triple-time, triple-decker* (sandwiches), etc.

trite. See **commonplace.**

triumphal; triumphant. These adjectives both pertain to a triumph, but *triumphal* is the narrower term. It means pertaining to a triumph; celebrating or commemorating a triumph or victory (*A triumphal arch opens on the Champs Elysées*). *Triumphal* cannot be applied to persons, but only to objects and activities, such as processions or celebrations. *Triumphant* means chiefly having achieved victory or success, and may be applied to the successful person or the success itself (*The triumphant runner was carried out of the amphitheater on the shoulders of admiring freshmen. He would have done well to have suppressed that triumphant laugh. The administration of the polio vaccine was hardly triumphant*).

trivial. See **petty.**

triviality. See **commonplace.**

trod; trodden. See **tread.**

troop; troops; trooper; troupe; trouper. These words all stem from a Late Latin word meaning flock. Thus a *troop* means an assemblage of persons or things, a company or band (*A troop of Oxford hunters going home,/ As in old days, jovial and talking, ride!*); a great number or multitude (*. . . as honor, love, obedience, troops of friends*). In American military terminology a troop is an armored cavalry or cavalry unit consisting of two or more platoons and a headquarters group. In English military terminology, a troop is "that subdivision of cavalry which corresponds to a company of infantry and a battery of artillery" (Partridge). In the American Boy Scout organization, a troop is a unit of thirty-two scouts, equal to four patrols. In the English Boy Scout organization, a troop is simply a company of boy scouts. *Troops* (plural) describes a body of soldiers or police (*The troops were brought up during the night and the prison surrounded*). *Troop* is used as a verb in England in such an expression as *to troop the colour* or *colours* (to perform that portion of the ceremonial known as mounting guard in which the color, or flag, is received). A *trooper* is a horse cavalry soldier (*An obscure trooper who called himself Silas Tomkyn Comberback was actually Samuel Taylor Coleridge*); a mounted policeman; a horse ridden by a trooper; or, chiefly in England, a troopship (*The trooper lay at the dockside, grim with the significance of her camouflage*). In a number of American states the state police are officially called troopers.

The singular *troop* means a body of men and the plural *troops* means several bodies of men. However, when the word is used with an improbably large number, such as *two thousand troops,* it is understood to mean two thousand individual men. But two men in uniform could not be called *two troops,* or even *two of our troops.* We would have to say *two men from our troops.* Only the singular form *troop* is used as the first element in a compound, as in *troop movements.*

Troupe and *trouper* are very limiting terms. *Troupe* means a troop, company, or band, especially of players, singers or the like, or, as a verb, to travel as a member of a theatrical company, to barnstorm. *Trouper* means an actor in a theatrical company, especially a veteran actor. It is often used figuratively of one who, having experienced many vicissitudes and known many hardships, can be relied on to play his part with professional competence.

trope. See **figure of speech.**

troubled; troublesome; troublous. *Troubled* means worried or disturbed. It may apply to persons, atmosphere—as sea, sky—or to moods, thoughts, feelings (*His troubled look frightened her. They love to fish in troubled waters*). In the sense of disturbed, it may have social rather than physical implications. Irwin Shaw's book, *The Troubled Air* (N.Y., 1951), dealt with the problem of loyalty among radio artists. *Troublesome* means causing trouble, vexatious (*He preferred a troublesome cough to a troublesome doctor*). *Troublous* is an archaic word meaning characterized by trouble; disturbed; unsettled (*The Reconstruction Era was a troublous time*). Its use now would seem a little affected.

trouser; trousers. *Trousers,* a plural substantive, is the usual form to describe a loose fitting outer garment for men, covering the lower part of the trunk and each leg separately, and extending to the ankles; or a shorter garment of this kind, reaching to the knees, especially as worn by boys. In America *trousers* in this second sense is customarily qualified (*He wore short trousers until he was eleven*). It would be felt as a little stilted or, perhaps, a euphemism, the common term for boys' short trousers being *pants* or *short pants* (*My Mama done tol' me/ When I was in knee pants . . .*) and for men's short trousers, *shorts.*

A pair of trousers is the correct singular form. The English have a slang verb *to trouser,* meaning to put money into the trouser pocket, to pocket. Both Americans and English use the figurative idiom *she wears the trousers in that house* to mean that she (the wife) is the dominant person. Most Americans, however, say *she wears the pants.*

A singular form *trouser* is preferred as the first element in a compound, as in *trouser pockets,* but the form *trousers pockets* may also be used.

trousseau. The plural is *trousseaus* or *trousseaux.*

truck; truckle. *Truck* in the phrase *to have no truck with* is derived from the French *troquer,* to barter. The phrase is now a cliché, devoid of any specific meaning to most of those who use it.

To *truckle,* in the sense of yielding obsequiously, is derived from sleeping on a *truckle bed,* a pallet on casters or truckles which was rolled under the regular bed. Servants used to sleep on truckle beds, sometimes directly under their masters in the old, high-raised four-posters with their canopies (*If he that in the field is slain/ Be on the bed of honor lain,/ He that's beaten may be said/ To lie in honor's truckle bed*). Why of all the miseries and indignities which servants formerly had to endure this particular one was singled out as a symbol of servility is not clear. Housewives who wonder why it is so hard to get "help" might profit from setting down a list of words in English drawn from the living conditions of servants which express contempt for the servants on the part of the masters. It would be a long and instructive list.

truculent does not mean base, mercenary, though a truculent man may very well be base and mercenary. It means fierce and cruel; brutally harsh, savagely threatening or bullying (*One of my superiors was a truculent fellow who would have loved being a storm trooper under Hitler*).

true blue, as a term for one who is staunchly loyal, unshakable in admirable principles, is a cliché. It is a very old term, based on the fact that among the early dyes blue was one of the best, least likely to fade. The term today has the further disadvantage of suggesting high-minded schoolgirlish enthusiasm, the sort of term that the head of a summer camp might use in a pep talk.

true verb. In this dictionary, the term *a true verb* means any verb form that has tense, that is, that refers to either the past, the present, or the future. The infinitive, the *-ing* form, and the past participle, do not have tense when they are used as nouns or adjectives. Some grammarians call these forms that do not have tense verbals, verbids, or nonfinite verb forms.

truism. See **commonplace.**

truly. See **faithfully.**

trunk. English and American usage of *trunk* differ in some of its meanings. What the English call the *main line* of a railroad is in America often called a *trunk line, trunk road,* or simply *trunk* (*Chicago in 1871 served as the junction point for thirteen trunk-line railroads*). In the terminology of the telephone companies, *trunk* means a telephone line or channel between two central offices or switching devices, which is used in providing telephone connections between subscribers generally. The *trunk call* of the English system is the *long distance call* of the American. The English colloquially say *trunk,* the Americans *long distance.*

Trunks (plural) is used, especially in England, to describe short, tight-fitting breeches, as worn over tights in theatrical use. In the United States only, *trunks* may also mean short drawers worn by athletes such as runners, boxers, swimmers, basketball players. In this sense, *trunks* is always treated as a plural, as in *these trunks are new.* In order to use the word with a singular verb or to speak of more than one such garment, it is necessary to say *this pair of trunks is new* or *several pairs of trunks.* The form *trunks* is used as the first element in a compound, as in *the trunks pocket.*

trust. This verb may be followed by an infinitive, as in *trust her to tell him about it.* It is also heard with the *-ing* form of a verb, especially in an exclamation that is meant to be condemning, as in *trust her telling him about it,* but this is not standard English.

trustee; trusty. A *trustee* is a person, usually one of a body of persons, appointed to administer the affairs of a company or institution (*He became a trustee of his college ten years after gradu-*

ating); a person who holds the title to property for the benefit of another. *Trusty* is a specifically American term to describe a well-behaved and trustworthy convict to whom special privileges have been granted. Many trusties have been recruited from the second sort of trustee.

trustworthy; trusty. Both of these adjectives mean worthy of trust or confidence, reliable. *Trustworthy* is more often used, especially in reference to persons. *Trusty* is now slightly archaic (*I shot him with my trusty flintlock. And here's a hand, my trusty fiere,/ And gie's a hand o' thine*).

truth. See **veracity.**

truthful; true. See **veracious.**

truth is stranger than fiction. It seems to have been Byron who first observed that truth was stranger than fiction and the observation when first made, by whomever made, was an original and arresting comment on the incredibleness of reality and the feebleness of the human imagination. And the first million or so wits who repeated the observation earned thereby a reputation for profundity. But it is now exhausted, worn out, flat and banal.

Like many banalities, however, it can serve as the basis for a stroke of wit, as when Mark Twain observed drily that truth certainly seemed stranger than fiction to many people but, as for himself, he was quite familiar with it.

try. In literary English, the *-ing* form of a verb following *try,* as in *he tried shouting,* does not mean the same thing as the infinitive following *try,* as in *he tried to shout.* The infinitive names what he is attempting to do. The *-ing* form names something he is using as a means for whatever it is he is attempting to do.

Try and is standard English for *try to,* as in *try and come early.* The construction is used in Great Britain more often than it is in the United States but it is standard in both countries. It can be used only with the form *try,* and not with *tries, tried,* or *trying.* We do not say *he tried and came* or *he tries and comes.* See also **endeavor.**

try; try out; test; test out; tryout. *Try out* and *test out* are recent introductions as synonyms of *try* and *test. Try out* has much greater currency than *test out.* One may, for instance, *try* or *try out* a new invention. *Tryout* is an American informal expression meaning a trial or test to ascertain fitness for some purpose (*Sixteen Juniors attended the tryout for cheerleader last night*).

tube. What Americans refer to in radio and television sets as *tubes,* the English call *valves.* The English, however, make an exception in this: they, like the Americans, call the large glass bulb which is the "screen," the *picture tube.*

The English call the tubular tunnel in which an underground railroad runs a *tube* and, colloquially, the railroad itself. The American equivalent is *subway.*

tubercular; tuberculous. These adjectives tend to be used interchangeably as meaning affected with tuberculosis. Actually, *tubercular* should be used to mean pertaining to or having the nature of a tubercle or tubercles or characterized by tu-

bercules. But it is used so much to mean of or pertaining to the disease of tuberculosis (which is characterized by tubercules) that its use in this sense must be accepted as standard in the United States. Indeed, in popular usage, *tubercular* seems to be preferred to *tuberculous* in all contexts. *Tuberculous* is the pathological and medical term (*X-rays disclosed a tuberculous growth in the lower lobe of the left lung*) and, in strict usage, is the proper adjective to use when one means of or pertaining to the disease of tuberculosis.

tummy. See **belly.**

tune. As a phrase to introduce a sum of money owed or necessary to the accomplishment of some end, *to the tune of* (*You can do it, yes, but to the tune of five million!*), even though used only as slang, is a cliché. Perhaps it derived from the idea of "paying the piper." See **tone.**

turn, when used in the sense of "become," may be followed by an adjective describing what turns, as in *it turned white, it turned sour.* Even in this sense, it may also be qualified by an adverb describing the turning, as in *it quickly turned sour.*

The word *turn* occurs in a great many clichés: *give someone a turn* or *quite a turn* for to frighten them; *turn a deaf ear* for a refusal to hear a plea or a request; *not to turn a hair* for remaining calm and unruffled; *turn an honest penny,* now chiefly jocular, for earning some money; *turn in one's grave,* usually *it's enough to make so-and-so turn in his grave,* spoken when something is said or done that would have startled so-and-so or left him aghast; *turn over a new leaf,* for starting anew with good intentions; *turn tail* for retreating; *turn the other cheek,* to accept insults or injuries meekly, especially when the phrase is used jocularly; *turn the tables on someone,* for reversing a position in relation to one who up to that time had an advantage; *turn up like a bad penny,* for some undesirable person who makes an appearance when he is not expected and not wanted; *turn up one's nose at,* to scorn, especially when the scorn does not seem warranted to the speaker or at least when he feels that the person to whom he applies the phrase is not warranted in being disdainful.

turpitude is a stilted and literary word, the common equivalents being *indecency* and *depravity.* It is perhaps this pompous nature of the word that makes the legal term *moral turpitude* seem slightly ridiculous.

tweezers. The plural form refers to one instrument but is regularly treated as a plural, as in *these tweezers are too small.* In order to use the word with a singular verb or to speak of more than one of these instruments, it is necessary to say *this pair of tweezers is too small* or *three pairs of tweezers.* A singular form *tweezer* is preferred in compounds, such as *a tweezer case.*

twelve good men and true. A reference to a jury by the old phrase by which juries were formerly described in writs and other legal documents, *twelve good men and true* is now a piece of ponderous jocularity.

twice; twicet. *Twicet* is formed on the same pattern as *against, amidst, amongst,* but it has never been standard English. *Twice* is the only acceptable form.

twice over. Some authorities consider *twice over* as redundant, insisting that *twice* conveys the identical meaning. But *twice over* has acquired the suggestion that the repetition is immediate; whereas that which happens *twice* simply happens again, any time after the first time. Browning's wise thrush that *sings each song twice over,/ Lest you should think he never could recapture/ The first fine careless rapture* hardly expects the listener to stand around all day waiting for the demonstration of his virtuosity.

twinkling of an eye, in the. In addition to its present meaning of scintillating, *twinkling* used to mean nictitation or the act of winking. Philemon Holland, in his translation of Pliny (1601), speaks of an ague accompanied "with head-ache and much twinkling or inordinate palpitation of the eyes." The 1609 Douay Version of Isaiah 3:16 speaks of the daughters of Sion walking with "stretched out neck . . . and twinglings of eyes." The King James Version has "wanton eyes" and the Revised Standard Version has "glancing wantonly with their eyes." But, except for its lack of dignity, the informal "batting their eyes" would have been better.

At any rate, this meaning of *twinkling* is obsolete and the phrase *in the twinkling of an eye* is now a cliché.

twins. See **pair of twins.**

twist around one's little finger. To say of one who seems to have complete domination over another that he can *twist him around his little finger* is to employ a hackneyed expression.

tycoon is the transliteration into English of a Chinese term meaning "great prince." The term was employed in Japan, from 1603 to 1867, as a title to describe the shogun of Japan to foreigners. *Shogun* was a Japanese term, originating in the eighth century, describing the commander in chief in their wars against the Ainu. In later Japanese history tycoon was applied to a member of a quasi-dynasty, holding the real power though parallel to the imperial dynasty, which was theoretically and ceremonially supreme.

In the twentieth century, largely due to its use in the Luce publications, tycoon has become an American term (meant to be gay and informal) to describe a businessman having great wealth and power, an industrial magnate (*One tycoon on Robinson Street had paved the thoroughfare in front of his house with blocks of marble. There was something indecent about this new pose. It was a little too much like the tycoon who spends the first part of his life sucking and crushing and the last part giving away dimes and Benjamin Franklin's advice*).

type of. The singular form *type of* and the plural form *types of* may each be followed by either a singular or a plural noun. Bertrand Russell, for example, speaks of *a type of relation, a type of relations, the types of relation,* and *the types of relations. Type* is always followed by a singular verb, and *types* by a plural verb, regardless of the form of the noun used. In this respect *type of* does not follow the pattern of *kind of* and *sort of.*

In the United States *type* is sometimes used immediately before a noun, in the sense of *type of,* as in *this type car, that type person.* This construction does not appear in written English but is too widespread in speech to be called anything but standard. See **nouns as adjectives.**

typesetter; compositor. *Typesetter* is an exclusively American term to describe one who sets or composes type. The American alternative term, less common than *typesetter,* is *compositor,* which is the term used in England.

typhoon. See **cyclone.**

typical. See **average.**

typist is one who operates a typewriter. In England the word *typist* also carries the older sense of one who uses type, a printer, a compositor.

typographic; typographical. These adjectives are synonyms meaning pertaining to typography or printing. *Typographical* is more common (*The proofreader marked all of the typographical errors*). In common use they are often substituted for stenographic or typewriting (*Whenever he had been away from his typewriter for a few days he noticed that he made an unusual number of typographical errors when he began to type again*).

tyrannic; tyrannical. *Tyrannic* is rarely used and *tyrannical* is generally preferred as the adjective meaning arbitrary or despotic, despotically cruel or harsh, severely oppressive (*He liked to blame most of the faults and misfortunes of his life on a tyrannical father*).

U

ugly as sin. Though sin is repulsive to the virtuous, she is highly attractive to the wicked. But aside from any such argument, *ugly as sin* is a cliché.

ugly duckling. To refer to an unattractive or seemingly stupid child that turns out to be a handsome or talented adult as *an ugly duckling* is to employ a badly worn metaphor. The figure is drawn from Hans Christian Andersen's story of the duck that hatched a swan's egg among her own and regarded the cygnet, which eventually became a beautiful swan, with dislike because it was so ugly. The application is a natural one but it has been overdone.

The story, by the way, owes a great deal of its popularity in the nursery, as does *Cinderella,* to the unconscious appeal it makes to children's egotism and self-pity.

ultimately. See **finally.**

ultimatum. There is no question but that *ultimatum* means the final terms of one of the parties in a diplomatic relationship, the rejection of which by the other party may involve a rupture of relations or lead to a declaration of war. More loosely, it is used to mean any final proposal or statement of conditions (*Her ultimatum was that he must get rid of the Great Dane or she would leave their trailer home*).

The question is over the form of the plural. The conservative *Oxford English Dictionary* holds that *ultimata* is the plural, but more progressive English and American grammarians agree in preferring *ultimatums.*

ultimo; ult. See **instant.**

ultra, used as an adjective meaning going beyond what is usual or ordinary, excessive, extreme, is obsolescent in England but remains in standard use in America (*He was an ultra sophisticate. The ultra conservative viewpoint has few rational adherents . . .*). It is not as much used in the United States now as it was in the 1920's when the excessive was in vogue.

umbrage. As a term for being offended, *take umbrage* is a literary term and would seem a little strange or affected in ordinary speech. Yet it is a fine phrase, suggesting one shadowed in offended pride, retreating into the darkness of proud indignation, withdrawing into dark clouds of wrath whence will come the lightning of rebuke and retribution and a thunderclap of scorn.

umbrella. See **parasol.**

umlaut is a German word accepted in linguistics as the term to indicate an internal vowel change, usually caused by a following vowel or a semivowel. The term is also used to designate the diacritical mark (¨) placed over a vowel in German to indicate such a change, to show that the letter is to be pronounced with a different vowel than it would be pronounced with were the umlaut sign not there.

The principle of the umlaut survives in English in a number of what are now considered irregular plurals. As the Germans say *mann* for the singular and *männer* (rhyming with English *tenor*) for the plural of *mann,* so we have a normal umlaut in *goose, geese* and *tooth, teeth* and a development of what was a normal umlaut in *mouse, mice* and *cow, kine,* and so on. Umlaut also survives in some irregular verb forms: a tree *falls,* but it is *felled,* and so on.

unable. See **incapable.**

unalloyed pleasure, with its suggestion of "pure delight" or "golden hours," is a cliché.

unambiguous means not open to various interpretations, not having a double meaning, not equivocal. Yet even if there is only one meaning, one is not justified in equating *unambiguous* with *clear* or *perfectly clear;* for even a word or statement which has only a single meaning may be hard to comprehend.

unapt. See **inapt.**

unaware; unawares. At one time these words were used interchangeably. Today, *unaware* is the only form that can be used to qualify a noun or pronoun, as in *he was unaware of his danger.* Either form may be used to qualify any other part of speech, as in *I blessed them unaware* and *he came upon it unawares.* The form with *s* is generally preferred.

unbeknown; unbeknownst. Neither of these words occurs in natural speech today, and one is as good as the other if the purpose is to be quaint. But a hundred years ago, when the words were used to mean "unknown," the form *unbeknown* was standard English, and *unbeknownst* was condemned.

unbelievable. See **incredible.**

unbend as a transitive verb means to release from the strain of effort or close application or to relax by laying aside formality. In mechanical things it means to release from tension, as a bow in archery. It can also mean to straighten from a bent position (*He unbent the paper clip and used it to clean the stem of his pipe*). In nautical terminology, to *unbend* is to loose or untie, as a sail or a rope, or to unfasten from spars or stays, as sails (*As some grave Tyrian trader . . ./ . . . held on indignantly/ . . . To where the Atlantic raves/ Outside the Western Straits, and unbent sails/ There . . ."*). The intransitive form is more often used, and misused, of persons. It means to relax the strictness of formality or ceremony, to act in an easy, genial manner (*Doesn't he ever unbend? Is he always this stiff and formal? Sometimes he would unbend and spend a social evening with a few select friends*).

In using the ideas of bending and unbending in figures of speech, there is a danger that has to be watched for. As applied to physical objects, such as bows, bending involves increase in tension and unbending relaxation of tension. In regard to human beings, however, the situation is ambiguous. A state of tension may be conveyed by straightness, erectness, stiffness, which is *relaxed* by bending. Yet one may also be under tension when bending and relax by straightening up—as anyone knows who has ever picked berries or worked with a hoe. One has to be certain, therefore, when using *bending* and *unbending* in reference to human beings, especially in figurative uses, that one's meaning is clear.

uncomparable; incomparable. *Uncomparable* is more limited in meaning than *incomparable.* It means that cannot be compared (*Apples and automobiles are uncomparable*). *Incomparable* means matchless or unequaled, beyond comparison by reason of excellence rather than by reason of dissimilarity (*Venezia's beauty was incomparable*). *Incomparable* is also used to convey the sense of *uncomparable,* far more often indeed, in contemporary usage, than *uncomparable* itself.

unconscious; subconscious. In popular usage *subconscious* means imperfectly or not wholly conscious (*Some subconscious thought told me not to sell, attractive as the offer then seemed*). In psychological terminology, *the subconscious* means those processes of being and awareness which exist or operate beneath or beyond consciousness (*The subconscious self is the subject matter of many modern novelists*).

Unconscious in ordinary use means not conscious, temporarily without consciousness (*He was unconscious for five minutes after Johnson knocked him out*); not aware of something (*Mrs. Wiggs was apparently unconscious of the sensation she was causing*); not known to or perceived by oneself (*It was an unconscious slip of the tongue and he was plainly puzzled by the subdued laughter that greeted it*); unintentional (*He was the victim of an unconscious slight*). As a psychoanalytical term, *the unconscious* means an organization of the mind containing all psychic material not available in the immediate field of awareness.

uncontrollable. See **incontrollable.**

uncorrected. See **incorrect.**

uncouth. See **exotic.**

unctious; unctuous. *Unctious* is a common misspelling and mispronunciation of *unctuous*—though the misspeller and mispronouncer may unctuously insist, if he chooses, that he is merely employing an obsolete variant. *Unctuous* means of the nature of or characteristic of an unguent or ointment, oily, or greasy. Used figuratively, it is a term of disparagement, meaning complacently agreeable and self-satisfied, a little more than *smooth*, a little less than *greasy*. It is applied particularly to those who are characterized by religious unction or fervor, especially of an affected and insincere kind (*There was no really good unctuous violence to be had except by turning champion of religion*—Sinclair Lewis). Used of certain minerals, with no suggestion of disparagement, it means having an oily or soapy feel.

The English have a slang word *soapy* which is somewhat stronger than *unctuous* as a figurative term of disparagement, or at least more open in its contempt (*Bishop Wilberforce, colloquially known as "Soapy Sam," was brought up as the heavy artillery to demolish the godless theory of evolution once and for all*).

under is primarily an adverb or preposition. When combined with a verb it may carry the meaning "beneath," "short of," or "supporting." It may also be used as an adjective to qualify a noun, as in *the under portion, the under side*. As an adjective it has a superlative form, *undermost*, but no comparative.

under (in clichés). *Under* introduces many clichés. To be *under a cloud* is to be temporarily out of favor or in disgrace. To be *under the aegis of* is to be under the protection of someone powerful. The aegis was the storm-cloud and thunder-cloud of Zeus, imagined in Homer as a shield forged by Hephaestus, blazing brightly and fringed with tassels of gold, and in its center the dreadful head of Medusa, the sight of which turned men to stone. It was borne not only by Zeus but by his daughter, Pallas Athene, and sometimes in battle the god or goddess interposed it between a favorite and a threatened danger. *Under the sun* has passed almost beyond the stage of being a cliché

into being accepted as a phrase-word for *anywhere*. To be *under the thumb* of someone is to be completely controlled by that person, often with the suggestion that the controlled one has lost the very power of making decisions, or even wishes, for himself. To be *under the weather* is to be sick, not violently or desperately sick but vaguely unwell, usually with an accompanying dejection of spirits. The phrase is a nineteenth-century coinage of uncertain origin.

All of these expressions are now clichés. Each originally had an idea or a figurative application of some known fact that made it arresting and pungent. But overuse has deadened them.

under the circumstances. See **circumstances.**

under (over) one's signature. That which is written *over one's signature* is simply something to which one has signed his name. It could be a letter, a poem, anything. That which is written *under one's signature* (as, in the legal phrase, *under my hand and seal*) is by the use of this phrase indicated to be authorized, warranted, or attested by the signer. See also **superscription.**

under separate cover. See **enclosed herewith.**

under way. See **way; weigh.**

underground. For half a century *underground* has been the English term for underground railroad, what Americans call the *subway*. In United States history *underground railroad*, before the abolition of slavery, was the name of an arrangement among opponents of slavery for helping fugitive slaves to escape into Canada or some other place of safety. *Underground* has also a recent sense of a secret organization, fighting the established government or occupation forces, especially such an organization in the fascist-overrun nations of Europe before and during World War II. Since World War II *underground* has been applied to organized anti-Communists in Communist countries and to organized Communist sympathizers in Western countries.

undershirt; vest. What an American calls an *undershirt*—an inner shirt, worn next to the skin —an Englishman calls a *vest*. What most Americans call a *vest*, an Englishman calls a *waistcoat*. Americans know and use the word *waistcoat* but not so much as formerly. It is interesting that Oliver Wendell Holmes, an American, regarded *vest* as a "cockney" term.

understand. The past tense is *understood*. The participle is also *understood*. An old form of the participle, *understanded*, is sometimes used today for its archaic effect. It has not been normal English since about the year 1600. See **know.**

understand, I. So many meanings can be attached to the common phrase *I understand* that it must be used with caution if one wishes to be clear. It can mean, at one end of its scale, that one is not only fully aware of the meaning of something that has been said but comprehends all of its implications as well (*I comprehended all that he said, but I failed to understand why he was so upset*). At the other end of its scale of meanings it can mean "I do not understand at all and never will be able to." The English use it in this sense more than Americans do, interjecting it with humorous modesty into technical explanations (*These things work, I understand, on the principle of,* etc.). What the speaker means is "I have been told, but it's beyond my comprehension." In between these extremes, the expression can mean to believe, to suspect, to know, to have been informed, or, as Sir Alan Herbert adds, "There is a strong rumor at the club." Certainly there is a difference between saying *I understand that you are not satisfied* and saying *I know that you are not satisfied* and all the difference in the world in the signification of *I understand* in *I understand that you are not satisfied* and *I understand why you are not satisfied.* See also **know; comprehend; understand.**

understood. See **understand.**

undiscriminating; indiscriminating. *Undiscriminating* is the term strongly preferred in England and America to mean not discriminating and *indiscriminate* to mean not discriminated.

undoubtedly; doubtless; indubitably. *Undoubtedly* is the usual word, signifying beyond doubt, indisputably. *Doubtless* is not so strong a word. It means without doubt, unquestionably; but it also is concessive, suggesting probability or presumption. *Indubitably* is a pretentious substitute for either *undoubtedly* or *doubtless.*

undue, meaning not requisite, not necessary, excessive, too great, needs to be used with intelligent care. For instance, the statement *He didn't seem unduly concerned about his grades,* that is, "He didn't seem any more concerned than there was reason for concern," is a pretty loose statement by itself. One has to know how much concern would have been reasonable before the statement can convey a clear idea. Even more unfortunate is the use of *undue* in such a statement as *There was no undue drunkenness in town Saturday night.* One wonders how much drunkenness was due. *Undue,* in such a context, needs qualification. It has a meaning in: *There was no undue drunkenness in town, if we remember that this was the first liberty the crew had had in three months.*

undying, deathless, and **immortal** all mean not liable or subject to death, though they seem to express slightly different shades of conviction of perpetuity. *Undying* has often the sense of unceasing (*the undying worm, the undying baritone of the sea*), a sense not shared with the others. In the common phrase *undying affection* the ideas of unceasing and lasting forever are combined. *Deathless* and *immortal* are closer together in meaning not subject to death or destruction, unceasing or perpetual in time (*Ne'er shall oblivion's murky cloud/ Obscure his deathless praise*). While *deathless* stresses freedom from death, *immortal* emphasizes endurance through all time (*Unto the King eternal, immortal, invisible, the only wise God, be honor and glory for ever. Lap me in soft Lydian airs,/ Married to immortal verse*). *The immortals* are the classical divinities. *The Forty Immortals* are the members of the French Academy.

unelastic. See **inelastic.**

unestimable; inestimable. *Inestimable* is the only form now used in the United States (*His opinion was of inestimable value*). It is the preferred form in England, although *unestimable* is still accepted there in the sense of too great to be estimated.

unexplainable. See **inexplicable.**

unfertilized; infertile; unfertile. *Unfertilized* is the correct word meaning unimpregnated (as of animals or plants) or unenriched (as of soil). *Infertile* is the preferred word meaning not fertile, unfruitful, unproductive, barren. *Unfertile* is its less used synonym.

unfrequent; unfrequented; infrequent; infrequency. *Infrequent* is greatly preferred to *unfrequent* to convey the idea of happening or occurring at long intervals or not often (*These infrequent visits to the city became an increasing burden*); not constant, habitual, or regular (*He was an infrequent visitor to the city*). *Unfrequented* is correct, *infrequented* incorrect, in the sense of not frequented, little resorted to or visited, solitary (*Kidd was believed to have hidden his gold on an unfrequented island*). *Infrequency* is the preferred noun meaning the state of being infrequent (*Gradually she became accustomed to the infrequency of his visits*). The American alternative, *infrequence,* and the English alternatives, *infrequence* and *unfrequency,* are rarely used.

unharmonious. See **inharmonious.**

unheard-of. From its primary sense of that which was never heard of, *unheard-of* has come to mean such as was never known before, new, strange, unprecedented. In this changing meaning there is a likelihood of ambiguity that must be watched for. If a message, for instance, is described as *unheard-of,* the context must make it plain whether this means that the message was not received or heard of, or whether it was in some way, perhaps in its insolence, unprecedented.

unhuman; inhuman. *Inhuman* is the correct adjective meaning lacking natural human feeling or sympathy for others; brutal (*The inhuman treatment inflicted on the captives sowed the seeds of undying hatred*). In America *inhuman* also has the secondary sense of not human, unlike some human attribute or function. The English express this sense with the word *unhuman* (*It was an unhuman voice, more like a crow's*). Americans use *unhuman* as the less desirable alternative to both senses of *inhuman.*

unimportant. See **inconsequent.**

unintelligible. See **unthinkable.**

uninterested. See **disinterested.**

unique once meant "only," as in *his unique son.* It can no longer be used in this sense. Today *unique* may mean "in a class by itself," but it more often means "unparalleled" or simply "remarkable." In this, it is following the pattern of *singular.* In all its current senses *unique* may be used with words that imply degrees, such as *more unique* and *quite unique.* Some people believe that there is something about the meaning of *unique* that makes expressions of this kind "illogical" or improper, but these expressions are used freely by outstanding writers and educators today. One grammarian, commenting on the much condemned *quite unique* points out that the word here means "unparalleled" and that we certainly do say *quite unparalleled*. He then says of the word *unique* itself: "I don't see anything quite unique in it." See also **comparison of adjectives and adverbs**.

unique; singular; exceptional. *Unique* and *singular* may be used as synonyms, but *singular* is more often used in the sense of extraordinary, remarkable (*The child has a singular inability to comprehend the simplest instruction*). *Exceptional* also may be used as a synonym for *unique* in its sense of forming an exception, or forming an exceptional or unusual instance. However, it is more often used, like *singular,* to mean simply unusual or extraordinary.

United States. National or geographical names that have plural forms are usually treated as plurals, as in *the Netherlands are in Europe, the Hebrides are part of Scotland*. But *the United States* is usually treated as a singular in English. We say *the United States is in North America*. The plural construction *these United States* is used, but it is felt to be poetic and it is avoided before a verb. That is, we might say *in these United States we believe in elections* but we would not say *these United States are having an election*. See **America**.

unities. The *unities* are the three principles of dramatic plot construction: action, time and place. The only really important unity is that of action; that is, a logical connection between the incidents of a play. Aristotle called attention to the essential character of this unity when he defined tragedy as "an imitation of an action that is complete and whole."

The principle of unity of time was an outgrowth of Aristotle's observation that "tragedy endeavors, as far as possible, to confine itself to a single revolution of the sun, or but slightly to exceed this limit." It remained for sixteenth century Italian critics to convert this description into dogma. Once the rule was established it was interpreted variously: some followed Aristotle in judging a day to consist of a single revolution of the sun, or twenty-four hours; others limited the time to twelve hours (day, as distinguished from night); a fastidious few felt that the hours represented in the action should not exceed the hours actually consumed in the theatrical presentation.

The principle of unity of place is not Aristotelian at all, but is the innovation of Italian Renaissance critics. Interpretations of what constituted unity of place have been various: some critics insist that the action of a whole play must be played at a particular spot; others are content if it is confined to a given locality, as a city.

Ben Jonson's *The Alchemist* is an English play which observes the unities. But good plays that do so are rare. From Shakespeare on, play-

wrights in English have generally observed unity of action, but unity of action only—though some neoclassicals, such as Dryden and Congreve, have observed the other unities as well.

Actually the unities have interested critics more often than they have interested dramatists. Today the playwright is most concerned with unity of impression—which may or may not follow from a unified action.

unity is one of the three basic principles of rhetorical structure. The other two are coherence and emphasis. Unity means the relation of all the parts or elements of a work in such a way as to produce a harmonious whole with a single general effect.

A sentence, for example, becomes a sentence by virtue of having unity, of completing a thought.

Paragraphs lack unity if they include unrelated materials. They are likely to have unity if their material is appropriate to fulfilling a definite segment of the writer's larger purpose. A good way for the beginner to test his paragraphs for unity is for him to see whether or not the whole point of the paragraph can be summarized in a single sentence.

A piece of writing as a whole has unity if the fundamental interest, the subject, permeates the entire composition and makes it one thing. A unified piece of writing is the fruit of clear, systematic thinking.

university; college. In the United States a *university* is an institution of learning of the highest grade, having a college of liberal arts and a program of graduate studies, together with several professional schools, as of theology, law, medicine, engineering, and authorized to confer degrees. In England, the *university* is the whole body of teachers and students pursuing, at a particular place, the higher branches of learning. In the United States *college* means an institution of higher learning, especially one not divided, like a university, into distinct schools and faculties, and affording a general or liberal education rather than technical or professional training (*The College of William and Mary is one of our oldest institutions of higher learning*); a constituent unit of a university, furnishing courses of instruction in the liberal arts and sciences, usually leading to the degree of bachelor (*Harvard College is the undergraduate unit of Harvard University*); an institution for special or professional instruction as in medicine, pharmacy, agriculture, or music, often set up as a part of a university (*The College of Agriculture was some distance from the main university buildings*). In England, a college is an endowed, self-governing association of scholars incorporated within a university (*Pembroke College was in Johnson's affectionate phrase, "a nest of singing birds"*); a charitable foundation of the collegiate type; or other educational corporations which prepare students for the universities (*Eton College, Winchester College*).

In idiomatic usage, *university* and *college* are

differently referred to: one goes to college, one goes to *the* university.

unknown; unknownst. *Unknown* is standard English. *Unknownst* is considered incorrect.

unlawful. See **illegal.**

unless is usually a conjunction. It introduces a condition and is equivalent to *if not,* as in *how shall I know, unless I go to Cairo and Cathay?* But it may also be used as a preposition, that is, without introducing a full clause. In that case, it has the meaning of "except" or "but," as in *nor was he ever known to curse, unless against the government.*

unmaterial; immaterial. *Immaterial* is the word used in both England and America to mean of no essential consequence, unimportant (*It's immaterial to me whether you report it or not*); not material, incorporeal, spiritual (*The soul is immaterial, unfleshly*). If *unmaterial* is used, it may only be used as a less desirable substitute for *immaterial* in the second sense.

unmeasurable; immeasurable. The English prefer *unmeasurable* in the literal sense of incapable of being measured (*the unmeasurable depths of space*), whether because of size or insusceptibility to measurement. In transferred figurative senses they prefer *immeasurable* (*immeasurable courage, immeasurable gratitude*). In the United States *immeasurable* is preferred in all contexts and *unmeasurable* is becoming obsolete as an alternative.

unmindful. See **oblivious.**

unmoral. See **immoral.**

unnatural; supernatural; supranatural; preternatural. *Unnatural* means not natural, not proper to the natural constitution or character; having or showing a lack of natural or proper instincts or feeling (*Her composure at her mother's funeral appeared unnatural to many people*). It also means contrary to the nature of things; at variance with the ordinary course of nature, unusual, strange, abnormal; artificial or affected, forced or strained (*He will even speak well of the bishop, though I tell him it is unnatural in a beneficed clergyman*—George Eliot). One of the commonest meanings, a derivation from the first meaning, is more than usually cruel or evil (*No, you unnatural hags,/ I will have such revenges on you both. . . .*).

Supernatural means being above or beyond what is natural, something not being or done through the operation of merely physical laws, but by some agency above and separate from these (*Supernatural beings were taken for granted by the ordinary Greek. These supernatural explanations which come so readily to the uninformed and undisciplined mind entail a series of consequences which the same uninformed and undisciplined mind would be the first to reject if it could understand them*). *Supernatural* is also used loosely to mean extraordinary or abnormal (*It's just supernatural, the way that guy finds things out*). *Supranatural* is a synonym of *supernatural,* used occasionally in England but almost never in the United States.

Preternatural designates something out of the ordinary course of nature, abnormal, exceptional, unusual. It was formerly used to describe something which might have been a work of nature, but was not (*Dogs have a preternatural sense of smell. Bats have a preternatural sense of sight, for they can fly in total darkness and avoid objects placed in their way*), but with the extension of our knowledge of the natural—"The unnatural," said Goethe, "that also is natural"—it has come to be a slightly humorous hyperbole for abnormal, exceptional (*Mr. Pickering was a widower—a fact which seemed to produce in him a sort of preternatural concentration of parental dignity*—Henry James), or is used as an evasive synonym for *supernatural* by those who like to dabble in the occult but do not wish to accept the intellectual consequences of full immersion.

unnecessary. See **redundant.**

unorganized; disorganized. That is *unorganized* which is not organized, which lacks organic structure (*He could take an unorganized group of boys and mold them into a team*); not formed into an organized or systematized whole (*This is not a book but simply an unorganized mass of notes*). *Unorganized* has also the specific meaning, in contemporary American usage, when applied to labor, of not being organized into a labor union. *Disorganized* means having an existing organization destroyed or disrupted (*Enemy infiltration had left the Command Post disorganized*).

unpractical. See **impracticable.**

unqualified; disqualified. *Unqualified* means not qualified, not fitted, not having the requisite qualifications (*Many students are unqualified to do advanced work*). It also means not modified, not limited or restricted in any way (*He rarely gave unqualified approval. He always had doubts and reservations and was hesitant to commend*). *Disqualified* means deprived of qualification or fitness (*He was disqualified from running for office because of a criminal record*).

unreadable. See **illegible.**

unreligious; irreligious. In England *unreligious* is taken primarily to mean having no connection with or relation to religion. Only rarely does it have the secondary meaning of *irreligious.* In the United States, however, the primary meaning of *unreligious* is *irreligious,* and an ordinary secondary meaning is the neutral one of having no connection with religion (*A minister has many duties that may perhaps be called unreligious, such as the repair and maintenance of the church building, the care of the lawn, and so on*). In both England and America *irreligious* is a derogatory term, at least from the standpoint of the religious. It means not religious, impious, ungodly, showing a disregard of or hostility to religion.

unresponsible; irresponsible. The currently used word is *irresponsible,* meaning not responsible, not answerable or accountable, careless, reckless and indifferent to consequences (*He entrusted* *nis business to an irresponsible relative and soon found himself ruined*). It also means not capable of responsibility, done without a sense of responsibility (*A young child is naturally, in many respects, irresponsible*). *Unresponsible* is a synonym used seldom in England, almost never in the United States.

unsanitary; insanitary. Some authorities in England urge the use of *unsanitary* in the sense of not possessing sanitation—though not posing, necessarily, a health problem (*The unsanitary marshes, with their brackish smell . . .*), and *insanitary* to mean injurious to health, unhealthy (*insanitary slums. Open garbage cans and insanitary refuse lying in heaps showed all too plainly the city's indifference to the health of those who lived in this neighborhood*). In the United States, where the menace to human health of any non-sanitary condition has, perhaps, been more insistently dinned into the general consciousness (though that does not mean that more has been done about it than in England), *unsanitary* is the term in all senses and *insanitary* is a seldom-used synonym.

unsatisfied; dissatisfied; disgruntled. *Unsatisfied* and *dissatisfied* both mean not contented, but *dissatisfied* is the stronger term. *Unsatisfied* means not satisfied in the sense of falling short of satisfaction (*The one helping of porridge left his hunger unsatisfied and, to the consternation of Mr. Bumble, he asked for more*). *Dissatisfied* means positively discontented, not pleased, offended (*I was dissatisfied with his manners at the party*), showing dissatisfaction (*He had a dissatisfied expression on his face*). *Dissatisfied* is often a euphemism for *offended*, especially when spoken to one who has been remiss by one to whose satisfaction the other must perform a task. *Disgruntled* is a stronger word than *dissatisfied*, implying a sulky discontent, a feeling of resentment at the failure to be satisfied.

unsavory reputation is a journalistic cliché for a bad reputation or a bad name. How fine, by the way, the old term *bad name* sounds in contrast to this cumbrous substitute! (*Endow a canine with an unsavory reputation and you might as well immerse him in an aqueous solution until he expires*).

unsolvable. See **insoluble.**

unsophisticated; inexperienced; naïve; artless. *Unsophisticated* indicates an unfamiliarity with or an inexperience of the ideas, tastes or manners of a worldly society (*The unsophisticated are often charming in their innocence*). *Inexperienced* is a more restrictive term. It means not experienced, without knowledge or skill gained from experience, and is usually applied to a particular activity (*He was inexperienced at handling a large audience and gave way to panic at their laughter*). *Naïve* means having or showing natural simplicity, ingenuous. It tends to be used of those whose behavior is so simple as to be laughable or at least amusing (*One has to be pretty naïve to believe in the selflessness of the senator's patriotism*). *Artless* may be a neutral

term, describing one who is free from deceit, cunning or craftiness, guileless (*The artless manner in which the child revealed the secret, without being at all aware of what she was doing, would have been amusing had not the secret itself been so dreadful*). It may also be used, in a mildly deprecatory manner, to suggest a lack in art, knowledge, or skill (*The little artless Rosey thumped the piano and warbled her ditties. I can take only so much of her artless prattle*). See also **naïf; naïve; naive.**

unspeakable and **ineffable** both mean inexpressible, but in their common, everyday uses they show how strongly connotation can color a meaning. For *unspeakable*, in its generally accepted sense, means that which cannot be expressed because it is so vile (*His conduct in the presence of the ladies was unspeakable. He ought to be horsewhipped!*); while *ineffable* means that which cannot be expressed or uttered because it is too wonderful (*the ineffable joys of heaven*) or dare not be uttered because it is too sacred (*the ineffable name of God*).

unsufferable; insufferable. *Insufferable* is the usual word used to mean not to be endured, intolerable, unbearable (*The man is an insufferable jackass and I refuse to go if he will be there*). *Unsufferable* is dying out as an alternative, both in the United States and in England.

unthinkable; inconceivable; unintelligible. That is *unthinkable*, in the strictest sense, which cannot be thought or made an object of thought (*What is contradictory is unthinkable*). Except for infinity, the nature of God, and other metaphysical concepts, it is hard to think, indeed almost a contradiction in terms to try to think, of anything unthinkable. It is most commonly used, however, to mean something which will not be entertained in the mind or the imagination because it is highly improbable or because it is too base or degrading (*It is unthinkable that he should be this late and not call me, unless he has met with an accident. Such a compromise is unthinkable; we prefer to accept the consequences of refusing to agree to your terms*). *Unthinkable* should not be used to mean unlikely or impossible, for the mind is well able to think of the unlikely and the impossible.

Inconceivable means that which cannot be conceived or realized in the imagination (*It is inconceivable that two straight lines should enclose a space*). In common usage it means incredible or inexplicable (*It is inconceivable that Alda should have taken the money. I will not believe it without absolute proof and her own full confession*). In this sense it is a close synonym for *unthinkable*, but it does not carry as strong a condemnation as *unthinkable* does.

Unintelligible is sharply restrictive. It is confined almost exclusively to words which convey no conception whatever but are, for any reason, mere confused sounds or gibberish (*I could distinguish his voice shouting to me through the storm across the arroyo, but the words were unintelligible to me*).

until. See **till.**

untimely end as an expression for an early, particularly a premature, death, and especially in the phrase *to come to an untimely end,* is a hackneyed expression.

untold wealth does not mean income feloniously concealed from the Collector of Internal Revenue but wealth so great that it cannot be counted. (An amusing illustration of the ineffectualness of euphemisms (*which see*) is supplied by the fact that this unpopular official has been renamed the Director of Internal Revenue without, so far as can be ascertained, mitigating the misery of payment or decreasing its attendant resentment one iota.) *Told* in the expression is the past participle of the verb *tell* in the now obsolescent meaning "to count." The old meaning survives in the *teller* of a bank, *telling* one's beads, in the phrase *all told,* and various other fossilized forms such as the nursery rime *Young lambs to sell,/ Young lambs to sell./ If I'd as much money as I could tell,/ I never would cry, "Young lambs to sell!"* The shepherd who was telling his tale under the hawthorne in the dale was not relating a narrative but counting his *tally* of sheep. *Untold wealth* is now a cliché.

untruth. See **lie.**

unwanted; unwonted. These words must have their meanings carefully distinguished. *Unwanted* means not wanted, not needed, not desired (*They made little effort to conceal from the boy that he was an unwanted child. Unwilling, unwieldy, unwanted George*). *Unwonted* means unaccustomed, not customary, not habitual, not usual (*The unwonted exercise soon had the fat man puffing heavily*).

unwritten law. In England the expression *the unwritten law* means the general code of decency which by common understanding, outside of the specific injunction of statutes, governs the conduct of reasonable men. This meaning is recognized in America, but in common usage *the unwritten law* refers exclusively to the supposed principle of the right of the individual to avenge wrongs against personal or family honor, especially in cases involving relations between the sexes. It must be said, however, that except in Texas, an appeal to *the unwritten law* is not accepted (though frequently made) as an extenuation of murder.

up. This word is primarily an adverb meaning "toward a higher position," as in *look up;* but it may also be used as an adjective to qualify a noun, as in *the up stroke.* As an adjective it has the comparative form *upper* and the superlative forms *upmost* and *uppermost. Upper* is comparative only in form. It is felt as a positive, descriptive adjective and cannot be used in a comparison. *Up* is occasionally used as a preposition, as in *up the river,* and as a verb meaning raise, as in *he upped one end of the plank* and *he upped the price.* In the nursery it is sometimes used to mean vomit.

The adverb *up* has a variety of meanings. It may have its literal sense, as in *climb up, sit up,*

get up. The idea of "higher" is easily extended to what is superior, increased, or advanced, and *up* may be used with these implications, as in *up from slavery, heat up, speed up, grow up.* It carries the sense of "advanced in time" in *up to now* and *from his youth up.* It is also used in a great many ways that are not so obviously connected with its basic meaning. Two of these are worth noticing.

Up sometimes carries the idea of "completion," which may have grown out of the idea of "advanced in time." Both ideas can be seen in *the time is up.* In any case, many of the so-called meaningless *up's* actually have the force of "completely," as in *buy up, fill up, hush up, hurry up, wake up,* and should not be condemned as useless verbiage.

Up is also used to suggest commotion, or increased energy, as in *their sounds rouse up the astonished air, up in arms,* and the more homely expressions, *an up and coming town, he up and ran. Speak up* asks for more energy than *speak.* And the dialectal *he up and died* surprises us with its note of willfulness; *he lay down and died* seems a more natural way to act. A number of verbs can be used with either *up* or *down,* without any real difference in meaning. Often, but not always, *down* is the reasonable, descriptive adverb that one would expect to see used and *up* is substituted for it when a greater effort is required. Men drink down their beer but children are told to drink up their milk. We write down an address but we write up a report. *Slow up* is perhaps more abrupt than *slow down.* On the other hand, there is no such difference between *burn up* and *burn down, sober up* and *sober down.*

A number of verbs may be used with either *up* or *out,* but here there is usually a slight difference in meaning, as in *think up, think out; figure up, figure out; clean up, clean out; crop up, crop out; act up, act out.* The word *out* always adds something of the sense of "from within" or "from concealment" that is lacking in the compounds with *up.*

Up is also used in speaking of geographic directions. In Great Britain it may mean inland, or away from the coast, or it may mean toward a place of greater importance, such as London or a nearby city. In the United States we are more map-minded and *up* usually means "north," or toward the top of the map. If a city is neither up nor down from us on the map, we are likely to go *on* to it; and although we say *down on the farm,* we usually go *out* to rural areas.

up in arms, as a term for being aroused, especially with indignation, and ready to take action in defense or reprisal, is worn and stale.

up to scratch. This used to be *to come up to scratch* or *to come up to the scratch.* The *scratch* was a line drawn formerly across the boxing ring, up to which the boxers were brought to start a bout. One who came up to (the) scratch did what was expected of him, was prepared to go through with the encounter to which he was committed. The expression is used to mean this today but is also used loosely to mean up to normal, doing as well as could be expected. In either sense it is hackneyed.

up to the hilt. A dagger plunged into someone's body *up to the hilt* was, plainly, in as deep as it could go. But one may be deeply involved in many things of such a nature or in such a way that the phrase is ludicrous. And, in any event, it is a cliché.

upper; upmost. See **up.**

upset the applecart. The Romans had a saying *You've upset the cart,* meaning "You've ruined everything." What genius in the eighteenth century thought of making it an applecart will now never be known, but it was one of those additions to a homely phrase (like Shakespeare's "son and heir of a mongrel bitch") that surprised with a fine excess and caught the popular fancy at once. Unfortunately the humorous vigor and vividness of the amended expression had too wide an appeal. It was soon overworked and is now exhausted.

upward; upwards. *Upward* is the only form that can be used to qualify a following noun, as in *an upward movement.* Either form may be used in any other construction, as in *he looked upwards* and *he looked upward.* The form *upward* is generally preferred in the United States.

Both forms, *upwards* and *upward,* may be used to mean "more than," as in *upwards of five hundred people* and *upward of twenty years.*

urbane. See **polite.**

urge. This verb may be followed by an infinitive, as in *I urged him to go,* or by the *-ing* form of a verb, as in *I urged his going.* It may also be followed by a clause but the clause verb must be a subjunctive or a subjunctive equivalent, as in *I urged that he go.* The infinitive construction is generally preferred.

us. See **objective pronouns.**

use; utilize; exploit; work. *Use* is the everyday word for making something serve one's purposes (*Use your eyes, child! It's right there in front of you!*). When applied to persons, it has a selfish and even sinister connotation (*He's only using you*). It would be more tactful, for example, to say, *I could use your help this afternoon* than to say, *I could use you this afternoon;* though where the relationship is friendly the second wording would be accepted as a mere shortening of the first. The use of *used* as a commercial euphemism for second-hand or worn has given it a depreciatory meaning.

Utilize implies a practical or profitable use and, in its stricter sense, making a practical or profitable use of something when something else more desirable is not available (*Well, you'll just have to utilize what's there. Such slips of the tongue are often utilized by unscrupulous men when they lack anything definite to charge their opponents with*).

To *exploit* is to turn to practical account, to use for profit (*He exploited the concession to the last penny*). It often means—and when applied to persons invariably means—to use selfishly for one's own ends (*They have exploited that child mercilessly*).

To *work,* as a transitive verb, in its serious senses, is to expend labor upon (*He worked the soil. If the clay is worked in the hands it will soon become soft and malleable*). In loose speech it is often used as a synonym for *exploit* and *utilize* in their pejorative senses (*She's been working him for forty years*).

use; usage. *Use* is the act of employment or putting into service (*Have you any use for a good set of matched irons?*). *Usage* means either a manner of use—often, in a derogatory sense, rough and therefore somewhat damaging use (*These tools have had hard usage, friend; I can't give you much for them*), or a habitual practice which has served to create a standard, especially in matters of language and the meanings of words (*A Dictionary of Modern English Usage*). It is in this last sense that the word *usage* is employed in this volume.

used to. The verb *use,* meaning to make use of, is perfectly regular with a past tense and participle *used,* as in *I used it yesterday.* It is never followed by a verb form and presents no problems.

The expression *used to* means something quite different. When it is combined with a form of the verb *be* it is followed by the *-ing* form of a verb, as in *he was used to sleeping late,* and means accustomed to or familiar with. In any other construction *used to* is followed by the simple form of a verb (or we might say *used* is followed by a *to*-infinitive), as in *he used to sleep late.* Here it means "habitually did, at some unspecified time in the past." *Would* may also be used to express habitual action, but with *would* the time at which the action was habitual must be specified. We may say *I used to get up early,* but if *would* is used there must be some specifying clause, such as *when I was a child I would get up early. Would* in this construction suggests endless repetition more strongly than *used to* does and is a more literary form. When used in ordinary speech it gives the impression that the speaker is composing his memoirs rather than giving a factual account of the past. *Would* cannot be used in this sense with a verb that does not imply action. We can say *I used to like chocolate* but not *when I was a child I would like chocolate.*

In speech the *d* of *used* merges with the *t* of *to* and the two words are always pronounced *use to.* But in the United States the form *use to* never appears in print except after the verb *did,* and there it is required.

In the United States, questions and negative statements involving *used to* require the word *did,* as in *did there use to be owls here?, he didn't use to drink, didn't you use to like her?.* In Great Britain, the auxiliary *did* is never used and these American constructions are generally condemned. Englishmen say *used there to be owls* here?, he usen't to drink, and usen't you to like her?. The negative statement he used not to drink is acceptable in both countries.

Used to may follow had, as in where they had used to be, but this is an extremely literary construction. In everyday speech we say merely where they used to be. Used to cannot follow a subjunctive auxiliary. Sentences such as I couldn't used to are sometimes heard but are not considered acceptable.

usual; customary; habitual. That is usual which occurs more often than not, which is to be expected, is the normal state of affairs (Business as usual during alterations. The poor, there as elsewhere, live in their usual misery). That is customary which occurs in the larger part of all cases observed, which is consonant with the custom or use or practice of an individual or, especially, a community. (It was customary among country folk then to proportion the blessing to the food, and Sunday dinner, the heaviest and best meal of the week, was always prefaced with an unusually long grace. 'Tis not alone my inky cloak, good mother,/ Nor customary suits of solemn black). And as a habit is more deeply ingrained than a custom, so habitual goes beyond customary (as customary goes beyond usual) in indicating a uniform and unbroken

adherence to some act, or a response so deeply ingrained as to be beyond conscious control and a part of the character (The habitual frown that darkened his countenance had so come to be considered his ordinary expression that this unexpected smile, cracked grimace as it was, tended more to alarm than to warm the onlookers. The habitual tendency of all people to turn on their former idols . . .).

usual; usually. The form usually is required immediately before or after a verb, as in he spoke more than he usually does, he spoke more than he does usually, and immediately before an adjective, as in he is usually quiet, he was more than usually quiet. In any other position the form usual is required, as in he spoke more than usual and he was more quiet than usual. The form usual may be used to qualify a noun, as in his usual reticence.

utilize. See **use.**

utter. In addition to its common, everyday meaning of giving audible expression to, the verb to utter has several specialized legal meanings that sometimes startle the ordinary reader. To utter a libel is to publish it, to make it publicly known by any means. To utter forged documents or counterfeit money is to put them into circulation.

utter; utmost. See **out.**

V

vacant. See **empty.**

vacation; holiday. Although the English recognize vacation as a holiday, they no longer use the word much in this sense, confining it to those periods during which the activities of the law courts, universities, and schools are suspended. In the United States the word means any freedom from release of duty, business, or activity, a holiday period (Visitors to Oregon have a wide choice of attractions from which to supplement sight-seeing and other vacation activities in Oregon's cool, green vacationlands. I think I'll take a vacation this weekend; I'm fed up with always taking work home from the office). In this, as is often the case, the American usage is the older English usage.

For vacation the English would say holiday; for those on vacation, holiday-makers; and for the verb to vacation, to take a holiday (It took place about ten years ago when I was vacationing at Mackinac Island. I was taking my holiday at Margate when Ethel's husband died). Holiday, in American usage, is pretty much confined to some one specific day fixed by law or custom on which ordinary business is suspended or to a special day off from school (Washington's birthday has been declared a holiday. The teachers had their annual convention and the kids got a

holiday). In this second meaning, day off would probably be more common.

vacuity; vacuous; vacuousness. Vacuity and vacuousness are nouns referring to emptiness. Vacuous is the adjective. It means empty, without contents. Its connotation of "vacuum" makes it a stronger word than empty. Used figuratively, and it is commonly used only figuratively, it means empty of ideas or intelligence, completely empty—as empty as a vacuum is of air; stupidly vacant; showing mental vacancy (I could tell from the vacuous look on his face that we were wasting time asking him questions). Vacuity is the usual noun to describe the state of being vacuous or empty; absence of contents; emptiness; an empty space; a vacuum; absence or lack of something specified; vacancy of mind, thought; absence of idea or intelligence; inanity (The vacuity of these conversations is depressing); something inane or senselessly stupid. Vacuousness is the noun commonly used to describe a face or an expression which is vacuous (From the vacuousness of their expressions he could tell that he was not in the presence of intellectual giants).

vacuum. The plural is vacuums or vacua.

valise in England is now used only in a military context to describe a soldier's knapsack; specifically, a cylindrical cloth or leather case for carrying the kit or outfit of a soldier, especially of a cavalryman or artilleryman (*The officer commanding a piquet will decide if patrols are to wear valises or not*). In the United States the word continues to have its old meaning of a traveler's case for holding clothes and toilet articles, now especially one of leather, of moderate size, for carrying by hand, a traveling bag (*I usually carry my valise myself and leave the heavier suitcases for the porter*).

valuable; valued. *Valuable* applies to whatever has value, but especially to what has considerable value either in money or because of its usefulness or rarity (*He kept a valuable edition of* Comus *locked in his private safe*). That is *valued* which is highly regarded or esteemed, estimated or appraised, or has had its value specified (*His was a highly valued opinion. The car was valued at not more than fifty dollars*). Something which is valuable may not be valued, and, conversely, something which is valued may not be valuable.

valuable asset seems, on first thought, to be redundant, since *asset* itself, a useful thing or quality, a property, is regarded as valuable. Yet where there are many assets one may be valuable compared to the others or even a single asset may have a special value. It's illogical, but it is serviceable and standard usage to refer to a *valuable asset.* (*Moore is a valuable asset to the department; we wouldn't want to lose him*).

vanish into thin air. Since our ancestors knew very little about the varying density of air, *thin air* was simply an intensive for *air* which was thin compared to the other substances they knew. When Prospero in *The Tempest* said that the actors in his pageant *were all spirits and/ Are Melted into air, into thin air,* he was simply using (and, what's more, going back and repeating himself in order to do so) what was even then a hackneyed phrase, for ghosts invariably *melted* or *vanished* into *thin air*. The phrase, now not used of ghosts so much as, usually in a tone of irritation, lost articles, is hackneyed.

vanity. See **pride.**

vantage and **advantage** were once interchangeable but are now distinct. *Advantage* means any state, circumstance, opportunity, or means especially favorable to success, interest, or any desired end (*He had the advantage of familiarity with the terrain*); benefit, gain, profit (*It is to the advantage of any young man to learn to depend on himself*); superiority or ascendancy (*The fact that the one wrestler weighs thirty pounds more than the other gives him an unfair advantage*). It is an interesting reflection on the highly competitive nature of our society that the amenities and cultural pleasures of a well-to-do home are so frequently referred to as *advantages* or, often, *every advantage* (*The child's had all the advantages, coming from a nice home like that and in one of the best suburbs, too!*).

Vantage describes a particular sort of advantage. If *advantage* means opportunity, *vantage* means particular, special opportunity. It applies to a position or condition affording superiority, as for action (*He operated from the vantage of the New York publishing centers. Henry Tudor at Bosworth Field had the vantage of wind, sun, and ground*). It may also mean position likely to give superiority: literally this may be used to describe a man looking over the countryside from the vantage of a hill or tower; figuratively, it might describe, for example, a poet reading new poetry from the vantage of his own knowledge of the art.

vapid; insipid. *Vapid* means savorless and *insipid* means tasteless. Both words, that is, refer to something without or with very little taste, flat, without sharpness or distinction in savor. *Insipid* is more often used in the literal sense (*Those shiny red apples look fine but the taste is insipid*). In figurative terms, both words mean without animation or spirit, dull, uninteresting, tedious, as in talk, writing, or persons. *Vapid* has more of the suggestion of stupidity (*This vapid, meaningless talk. Ninety-nine percent of all that appears in newspapers is vapid stuff*). *Insipid* simply means without distinction, interest, or attractive qualities (*The verse in ladies' magazines is usually free from technical faults, but it rarely has any passion or even sensuousness and avoids any serious ideas. It's insipid*). In America *insipid* is used in all senses far more often than *vapid*.

varicolored and **variegated** mean practically the same thing in the United States. *Varicolored* means having various colors, variegated in color, motley; and, more loosely, varied, assorted. *Variegated* means varied in appearance or color, marked with patches or spots of different colors; and, more loosely, varied, diversified, diverse. The words are used similarly in England, though some recent authorities insist that *varicolored* must be used in reference to color and that *variegated* should be. This would leave only *varied* to designate assorted or diversified.

variety (in writing). See **repetition.**

various. See **different.**

varlet, for a low fellow or rascal, is now relegated to fraternity-house rodomontade.

varmint; varmit. See **vermin.**

vastly means to a great extent or in great proportions, especially when part of a comparison (*He spoke in a vastly larger hall and found it disconcerting*), but it may also be used to mean much, greatly, to a great degree (*The Dean was vastly annoyed at the committee's delay*). The English regard this last use as an affectation.

Vastly amused is almost a cliché.

venal and **venial** look and sound much alike but they are quite different. *Venal* has implications of corruption, while *venial*, a word of mild reproach, means excusable.

Venal, as applied to a person, means ready to sell one's services or influence unscrupulously, accessible to bribery, corruptly mercenary (*Many city politicians are not venal, but honest aldermen are in the minority*). As applied to a thing, it means purchasable like mere merchandise, but always with a suggestion that there is something sordid and improper in the transaction (*The temple itself is exposed to sale, and the holy rites, as well as the beasts of sacrifice, are made venal*). As applied to conduct, it means characterized by venality (*They managed to come to a venal understanding with the police*).

That is *venial* which may be forgiven or pardoned, which is not seriously wrong (*He committed the usual venial indiscretions of college boys*), excusable (*Those venial slips of the tongue, which are excusable and seem trivial, though often amusing in what they reveal, are not without considerable significance*). In the Roman Catholic Church, a *venial sin* is a voluntary transgression of God's law which, without destroying charity or union with God, retards man in attaining final union with Him.

venal; mercenary; hireling. All of these words, when applied to persons, mean willing to be employed for pay and each carries a different degree of derogation, a suggestion of a different degree of dishonor involved in the willingness.

Venal is the strongest in its condemnation. A venal man is willing to sell his honor, his individuality. He has no principle above "getting ahead" and acquiring wealth (*Venal and licentious scribblers, with just sufficient talents to clothe the thoughts of a pander in the style of a bellman . . .*). *Venal*, when so applied, also has a suggestion that the person referred to has sufficient intelligence to be aware of the moral problem involved and often has a high degree of intelligence and ability. *Mercenary* stresses the greed involved and the activity it incites, the fact that the sole motive for action is the desire for money (*Mercenary troops, perfectly acquainted with every part of their profession, irresistible in the field, powerful to defend or destroy, but defending without love and destroying without hatred. These mercenary considerations, at a time when the thoughts of the others were moved by pity, came as a shock. What should have been an art, he has made a mercenary trade*). When used as a noun, *mercenary* now refers exclusively to soldiers who fight solely for pay, and it is to the credit of human nature that the word in this sense does not carry quite as much opprobrium as it does when, as an adjective, it is applied to non-military matters. There may be something base about a man's offering to sell his life for money, but there is also something pitiful, especially when the money was so little; and there is something noble, mitigating the initial baseness, in the fact that mercenary soldiers so often lived up to their bargain and died for their pay. It was the Swiss mercenaries, for example, that died defending Louis XVI when the mob stormed the Tuileries (August 10, 1792).

Hireling as a noun, however (even though almost everybody today works for hire), is used only in contempt or reprobation, possibly because it has become fixed in scorn in the famous Biblical passage (*The hireling fleeth, because he is an hireling, and careth not for the sheep*). As an adjective, *hireling* stresses servility (*A hireling host and ruffian band/ Affright and desolate the land / While peace and liberty lie bleeding*).

It carries strong contempt but its effectiveness is weakened by the fact that it is now a literary word and if you are out to abuse someone it is well to avoid literary words.

venerate. See **reverence.**

venery. There are two *venery*'s. One means the gratification of sexual desire, the other the practice or sport of hunting (*A monk ther was, a fair for the maistrye,/ An outridere that lovede venerye*). The word in both senses is now archaic. A famous old English work, *The Boke of Venerye* [just to prevent undergraduates from putting library staffs to unnecessary trouble], is concerned with hunting.

vengeful. See **avenge.**

venom and **poison** both describe substances that injure the health or destroy life when absorbed into the system, especially of a higher animal.

Poison is now the general word. Literally, it means any substance which by reason of an inherent deleterious property tends to destroy life or impair health (*Prussic acid is one of the most powerful poisons known*). Figuratively *poison* means anything harmful, fatal, baneful, or highly pernicious, as to character, happiness or wellbeing (*The poison of totalitarian ideology is in almost everybody's veins*).

Venom is a more limited term, describing the poisonous fluid which some animals, as certain snakes, spiders, scorpions, bees, secrete (*Toad, that under cold stone/ Days and nights has thirty-one/ Sweltered venom sleeping got . . .*) and introduce into the bodies of their victims by biting or stinging (*The venom of a rattlesnake will make a man very sick but will not necessarily kill him*). Figuratively, *venom* means something resembling or suggesting poison in its effect; spite; malice (*There was considerable venom in his criticism*). The word carries the suggestion that the one who secretes or discharges the venom is reptilian.

venture; adventure. Both words convey the idea of a hazardous or risky undertaking or enterprise. *Venture* is used chiefly to describe a business enterprise or proceeding in which loss is risked in the hope of profit; a commercial or other speculation (*If the venture succeeds, they stand to make well over a million. If it fails, they will be wiped out, to a man!*).

Adventure means any exciting experience, often one in which there is an element of danger (*In the night's battle he had enough adventure to last a lifetime*). When commerce had its real physical dangers, *adventure* could be used of a business undertaking. The Merchant Adventurers was an incorporated group of London merchants (whose Governor, by the way, was Sebastian Cabot). Perhaps business has become safer or more prosaic or perhaps excitement and glamour are now romantically conceived of as lying wholly outside of any commercial activity.

In the phrase *at a venture* there is now no suggestion of danger or risk; it simply means "at random."

The adjective of *adventure* is *adventurous*. The adjective of *venture* is *venturesome*, with *venturous* less often preferred.

veracious; truthful; true. *True* is the general word. *Truthful* means conforming to the truth (*It was a truthful statement, not misrepresenting the event in any way*) or habitually telling the truth (*All through the valley he was known as a truthful person*) or corresponding with reality (*It was a truthful representation of their family life and all of them hung their heads in shame to hear it thus publicly stated*). *Veracious* is roughly synonymous with *truthful,* but it is rather formal and pretentious and therefore, by a subtle suggestion, unsuited to the very quality it designates. It is seldom used.

veracity; truth. *Veracity* is not a synonym for *truth.* Indeed, it is incorrectly used in the hackneyed statement *I doubt the veracity of that statement. Veracity* means not *truth* but truthfulness in speaking; habitual observance of truth (*He was a man of proven veracity*); or conformity to truth or fact.

veranda; verandah. See **porch.**

verbal. See **oral.**

verbal adjectives. See **participles.**

verbal nouns. The infinitive and the *-ing* form of a verb both express the meaning of the verb without any further limitations. That is, they refer to the action without giving the specific information that is shown by tense, number, person, voice, or mode. They can be handled in a sentence as if they were nouns and are therefore called *verbal nouns.*

Both forms can be used as the subject of a verb and as the complement of the verb *to be,* as in *but to see her was to love her* and *seeing is believing.* Both forms can be used in an unattached or independent phrase, as in *speaking frankly, I don't like it* and *to be candid with you, I don't like it.* And both forms can be used as the object of a verb, as in *Betty likes to travel* and *Betty likes traveling.* But as a rule, both forms cannot be used with the same verb. We say *John wants to hear the story* or *John enjoys hearing it,* but we cannot say *John wants hearing the story* or *John enjoys to hear it.*

When either form can be used, some people feel that the infinitive is more concrete, and more forceful, than the *-ing* form. But frequently there is no choice. *Avoid, postpone, stop, tolerate,* can be followed by an *-ing,* but not by an infinitive. *Agree, ask, desire, expect,* can be followed by an infinitive, but not by an *-ing.* There is no reason for this. The difference is entirely a matter of custom, but it is often obligatory.

Verbs that give the most trouble in this respect have been listed individually in this dictionary. The statements in these entries about what kind of object is acceptable with a particular verb represent American usage, not British. A construction that is acceptable in Great Britain is usually acceptable in the United States, but it may not be the preferred form. On the other hand, what is the preferred form in the United States may be unacceptable in Great Britain. In general, an American uses more infinitives than an Englishman does. In a book on language published in England recently, the author says in the preface that what the book *aims at doing is to show that there is no real reason for being discouraged.* These *-ings* have a curious, countrified tone to most Americans, who are more likely to use *aim to do* and *no reason to be.*

verbiage; verbosity. The distinctions between these two words are somewhat differently drawn in England and the United States. In the United States *verbiage* means an abundance of useless words, as in writing or speaking, wordiness (*One had to cut a swathe through verbiage to get his main ideas*). The word connotes contempt and there is often a suggestion of insincerity (*Oh that was all verbiage! You didn't expect a real promise to be hidden in that twaddle, did you?*). *Verbosity* means a quality of being verbose; wordiness; superfluity of words, prolixity. It may be used of the speaker or writer or of what is spoken or written (*He was a kind man, but his verbosity was exasperating. The verbosity of the statement could not conceal its real intent or soften the blow it dealt*). It is not quite so contemptuous a word as *verbiage* (which may, perhaps, have acquired something from the resemblance of its sound to *garbage*). *Verbiage* describes a result and *verbosity* either a quality or a result.

In England *verbiage* is applied mainly to writing, *verbosity* to speaking. Also, with the English, *verbosity* may mean wordiness, circumlocution; whereas *verbiage* suggests excessive wordiness.

verbosity is the use of too many words, and it is a serious fault. This does not mean that one should never use a word that one can get along without; the laconic have their own way of being tedious. Very often repetitions and extra syllables that are not strictly necessary to the sense add a great deal to the tone or rhythm of a sentence. (See **pleonasms.**) But when a superfluity of words dilutes or drowns out the meaning of a sentence, it is a different matter.

The fault is a common one. We find it among all kinds of people, from Shakespeare's simpleton who says: "The young gentleman according to fates and destinies, and such odd sayings, the sisters three, and such branches of learning, is indeed deceased, or as you would say in plain terms, gone to heaven" to the twentieth century pundit who writes: "As often with history, interesting questions may be forever closed to the adequate answers because the tattered evidence which has been left to us by the rats who have gnawed at the documents in the archives, and the loss of pertinent documents, and the undeveloped state of the social sciences at the time when the relevant data were not collected preclude us from making significant comparisons historically on some points."

These are not rich, colorful or luxurious outpourings. They are simply "an infinite deal of nothing . . . two grains of wheat hid in two bushels of chaff; you shall seek all day ere you find them, and when you have them, they are not worth the search."

verbs. In a normal sentence we say something about something. Usually we say that there has been a change of some kind, that something has happened, although we can also say that no change has taken place. Changes involve the idea of before and after, which is what we mean by time. Words that are grammatically constructed to express time are verbs. Words that refer to aspects of reality as if they were independent of time are nouns. In *the light flashes at eleven o'clock,* the word *flashes* is a verb and indicates an event or change that takes place in time. In *the flashes were seen at eleven o'clock,* the flashes are treated as things, which may change but which are not the change itself, and the word is therefore a noun. (Sometimes we want to make a statement involving time without saying that anything has changed. This is the principal function of the verb *to be* and of the other linking verbs. See **linking verbs.**)

A verb may be defined as "a word that has tense." Most verbs show tense, or relative time, by their form, as present or current time is shown in *I always walk to work,* and past time in *I walked to work today,* and future time in *I will walk today.* A few verbs have the same form in the present and the past, as *put* in *I always put it there* and *I put it there yesterday,* but in any given sentence the word refers to either the past or the present. It is never indifferent in respect to time as the noun *rug* is.

In English the verb has two simple tenses, the present and the past, as in *he walks* and *he walked.* We form a future tense by means of a compound verbal phrase, such as *he is going to walk, he will walk.* We may also use verbal phrases to express distinctions inside the tenses, as in *it flashed, it was flashing, it had flashed.* These forms are all past tense but they express different aspects of the past. They are sometimes called simple action, progressive or continued action, and perfect or completed action tenses. See **past tense, present tense, future tense,** and **tense shifts.**

In addition verbs have mode and voice, which also tell us something about the action being reported. Mode is the form of the verb that shows whether a sentence is to be understood as a statement about matters of fact, a supposition, or a call for action. The form of the verb used in talking about matters of fact is called the indicative mode. It is the form we use most often. In this dictionary, statements about verbs are always about the indicative form of the verb unless another form is specifically mentioned. For the other modes, see **subjunctive mode** and **imperative mode.**

Voice is the form of the verb that shows whether the thing spoken about (that is, the subject of the verb) is the agent or the recipient of the action. When the subject is the agent, as in *he jumped off,* the verb is said to be in the active voice. When the subject is the recipient, as in *he was pushed off,* the verb is said to be in the passive voice. See **passive voice.**

Verbs also have person and number. Person shows whether the subject of the verb is the person speaking, as in *I am, I have;* the person spoken to, as in *you are, you have;* or some person or thing spoken about, as in *it is, it has.* Number shows whether the subject of the verb is one person or thing, or more than one, as in *he is, they are; he has, they have.* These differences in the verb forms do not affect the meaning of the verb itself but are devices for relating it to its subject. The verb has the same person and number as its subject, and in some languages this is the only thing that shows which word in the sentence is the subject. In English the relation of subject and verb is shown by position, and person and number are a nuisance rather than a convenience. (For problems of person and number in present-day English, see **agreement: verbs.** For archaic forms, such as *wert thou* and *he hath,* see **thee; thou.**)

Throughout this dictionary, the forms of the verb that have tense are called true verb forms or true verbs. The infinitive, the *-ing* form, and the past participle do not have tense. They are actually nouns or adjectives with the same meaning as the verb. They are often used in combination with another verb, as in *he ought to step aside* and *I have heard it said.* In such cases the other verb provides the tense (and also person and number) and the whole phrase is a true verb form. But these parts of the verb may also be used alone, simply as a noun or an adjective, as in *to step aside is human* and *heard melodies are sweet.* It is these uses of the word that are excluded when we speak of "a true verb form." See **infinitives, participles, -ing.**

Verbs are classified according to what is needed to complete their meaning. For example, *he slept* is complete in itself, but *he must* and *he made* are not. *Must* requires some other verb, such as *go* or *speak,* to give it meaning; and *made* requires a noun or noun substitute, such as *a table* or *a mistake.* (For the different kinds of verbs, see **transitive verbs, intransitive verbs, auxiliary verbs,** and **linking verbs.**)

If one tries to distinguish a noun from a verb by saying that a noun represents a thing and a verb an action, one runs into trouble. Is a flash of lightning, or a war, or a man's life, a thing or an action? Some philosophers claim that even an oak tree is really a long, slow action when properly understood. The chances are that the difference between a thing and an action is not something in the real world that has forced itself on language, but a grammatical device that distorts the way we think about the real world. It is much better, therefore, to recognize that nouns and verbs are simply different kinds of words and to define nouns as words that have number as their distinguishing characteristic, and verbs as words that have tense.

In English we can always form a verb from a noun, as in *he carpeted the floor, he papered the wall, he pocketed the money.* We can form verbs from adjectives by adding the syllable *-en,* as in *he blackened his shoes, he sweetened his coffee,* or sometimes without adding *-en,* as in he *blacked his face.* In fact any part of speech can be used as a verb if the sense allows, as in *he upped the price* and *she oh'd and she ah'd.*

On the other hand, the essential meaning of a verb can always be expressed as a noun. We can always use a relatively empty verb, which does little more than show tense, person, and number, with a noun that carries the meaning of what we want to say, in place of a meaningful verb. This practice has become very popular in the last thirty or forty years. Many people would rather say *there was a heavy snow fall last night* than *it snowed heavily*. Some grammarians object to this. But in spoken English, constructions such as *he took a walk, we had a swim, she gave a sigh,* are heard more often than the direct forms *he walked, we swam, she sighed.* The same preference is seen in technical writing where we find *make an examination* and *reach a decision* more often than *examine* or *decide.* Obviously, the professional man sitting down to write an article and his friends and neighbors in their relaxed moments all feel that a noun is more forceful and more concrete than a verb. To call the construction pompous or stilted in one situation and careless or colloquial in another is foolish. It is simply a very powerful trend in present-day English. If carried through completely, we would need only the verb *to be* and the appropriate nouns to express all our verbal ideas.

For the primary forms of the verb, see **principal parts of a verb** and **irregular verbs.**

veritable, for being truly such, genuine, real (*It was a veritable fairyland, with all the Japanese lanterns and the colored lights playing on the fountain*), is a little affected. The emphasis that it hopes to lend is slightly shrill and forced.

vermin. Originally this word was a singular, as in *a savage vermin in a trap,* and had a regular plural, as in *full of maggots, vermins, and worms.* The singular could also be used, as all singulars can, to typify the class, as in *a vermin in our pillows which did bite far worse than fleas.* None of these constructions are in common use today. In *these vermin are driving us out,* the singular form *vermin* is being used as a plural. Sixty years ago this was condemned as ungrammatical. Today it is standard English, and is practically the only way in which the word *vermin* is used.

Varmit, or *varmint,* is a variant form of *vermin* heard in many parts of the United States. It has a regular plural *varmits* and presents no grammatical problems. It is not standard English, but it is a much more useful word than *vermin.*

vernacular; language; dialect; jargon. All of these words refer to patterns of vocabulary, syntax, and usage characteristic of communities of various sizes and types. *Language* is applied to the general pattern of a people or a race (*The English language is common to the United States and the United Kingdom*). *Dialect* is applied to certain forms or varieties of a language, often those which provincial communities or special groups retain or develop even after a standard has been established (*The East Tennessee dialect is almost impossible to imitate accurately*). One who has been reared to speak a certain dialect almost never loses it entirely. Slight variations in pronunciation, cadence, vocabulary, and so on, will mark his speech. Sir Walter Raleigh, though an accomplished courtier, spoke with a Somersetshire accent and Dr. Johnson, though he edited the greatest dictionary of his century and was the acknowledged dictator of letters in his time, kept "a slight Staffordshire burr" in his pronunciation. Where a dialect is native, there is nothing wrong in this; indeed, it often confers a pleasing distinction. But, unfortunately, snobbery sometimes attaches opprobrium to some dialects (such as the cockney or that of New York's lower East Side). Outside of the community where such dialects prevail, even a tincture of them may do a man harm. It's cruel, but that is the way of the as-yet-imperfect world.

A *jargon* is an artificial pattern used by a particular, usually occupational, group within a community; or a special pattern created for communication in business or trade between members of the groups speaking different languages (*The jargon of sports writers varies from nation to nation*). Special words, of course, must be used in each trade and profession and the use of these technical terms to each other by members of these trades or professions when engaged in their work or when talking about their work does not, in the common acceptance of the term, constitute jargon. It does not become jargon until it is used outside of the special field in contexts where standard English words and expressions are available and would make their meaning clearer to the ordinary man. Thus if a doctor says of a patient, after examining him, that rest "is indicated," meaning "is needed," or "is advisable" or "would do him good," the layman is not justified in accusing the physician of speaking jargon. Other words might do as well, but the members of the medical profession, in their inscrutable wisdom and Eleusinian ways, have decided on the term for the circumstances and they have the privilege of so deciding. But if the same physician at the corner filling station should, when the rod drawn from his engine shows him to be two quarts low, say that two quarts "is indicated," meaning "needed" or "is advisable," he would be guilty of speaking jargon; for the common acceptance of the phrase would lead the filling station attendant to assume that only two quarts were indicated on the rod and, therefore, the supply of oil in this particular crankcase was dangerously low. Most jargon does not mislead in this way, but it remains incomprehensible and therefore defeats the chief end of speech.

A *vernacular* is the authentic natural pattern of speech used by persons indigenous to a certain community, large or small (*South Boston vernacular is not, or at least in a happier age was not, the same as Back Bay vernacular*).

verse; stanza. These are terms for metrical groupings in poetic composition. *Verse* is often mistakenly used for *stanza* (as in *Now read the next verse, all eight lines, please*) but it is properly only a single metrical line ("*Something there is that doesn't love a wall*" is the opening verse of

Robert Frost's "Mending Wall"). A stanza is a succession of lines (verses) commonly bound together by a rhyme scheme, and usually forming one of a series of similar groups which constitute a poem (*A quatrain is a stanza consisting of four verses*).

The term *verse* is also used of metrical composition in general, as opposed to prose (*Verse that a virgin without blush may read*). In church music a *verse* is a passage or movement for a single voice or for soloists, as contrasted with chorus. *Verse* as a term for the divisions of the books and chapters of the Scriptures has a special meaning.

vertebra. The plural is *vertebras* or *vertebrae*.

vertex. The plural is *vertexes* or *vertices*.

vertigo. The plural is *vertigoes* or *vertigines*.

verve, a word for energy or enthusiasm, especially in literary or artistic work; spirit, liveliness or vigor, is a French word and slightly affected. There are plenty of English synonyms expressing many shades of meaning, some one of which will usually do better as far as the meaning goes and a great deal better as far as not annoying the reader or listener goes.

very was originally an adjective meaning true and is still used as an adjective. It may mean actual or identical, as in *the very man I was looking for*. It may be a pure intensive, as in *the very jaws of death*. Or it may have the force of "even," as in *lo! the very stars are gone*. *Very* once had a comparative form *verier* but this is now obsolete. It has a superlative form *veriest* which is used as an intensive, as in *the veriest rubbish*. It also has an adverbial form *verily*, which means "truly," as in *I verily believe*. The superlative and the adverbial forms are in use today but they are considered either old-fashioned or bookish.

About five hundred years ago *very* began to be used as an adverb before adjectives and adverbs. It has now completely replaced *full* as an intensive, as in *full high, full many, full well*, and is preferred to *right* in this role. It has also replaced *much* before the simple form of an adjective. We can no longer say *I am much happy, I am much sorry*, as was once normal English. When the past participle of a verb is used as an adjective before a noun, as in *a disappointed man, a worried man*, it may be qualified by either *very* or *much*. Today *very* is preferred here. *Very* is not used before adjectives or adverbs in the comparative form. We cannot say *it is very greener*. It is not used to qualify a verb. We cannot say *I very prefer* or *I very appreciate*. It cannot be used even in a passive verb form, which is composed of some form of the verb *to be* and a past participle. We cannot say *it was very praised* or *it was very remembered*. We can say *very much* in cases like this because *much* is a true adverb that can qualify a verb, and *very* here qualifies the word *much* and not the verb itself.

About a hundred years ago *very* began to be used with participles following forms of the verb *to be,* when these compounds were not actually felt as passive verbs, as in *he was very pleased, he was very amused, he was very worried*.

A philologist writing in 1861, and discussing the ways in which languages change and develop, chose *very* to illustrate his point. He wrote: "There is apparently a very small difference between *much* and *very*, but you can hardly ever put one in the place of the other. You can say *I am very happy* but not *I am much happy*. On the contrary, you can say *I am much misunderstood* but not *I am very misunderstood*. It is by no means impossible, however, that this distinction between *very*, which is now used with adjectives only, and *much*, which precedes participles, should disappear in time. But if that change takes place, it will not be by the will of any individual, nor by the common agreement of any large number of men, but rather in spite of the exertions of grammarians and academies."

Although the distinction between *very* and *much* has not disappeared, changes have indeed taken place in the use of these words. Anyone who now says that *very* cannot be used before a participle that follows a form of the verb *to be* is merely repeating what was true seventy-five years ago but is not true today. Some careful grammarians say that *very* may be used before the participle in a construction of this kind when what is being talked about is a mental state, such as *pleased, amused, worried*, but not when what is being talked about is a physical condition, as in *he is very changed, it is very scratched*.

In the United States today *very* is preferred to *much* before participles that name mental states. That is, most people consider *he was very pleased, he was very amused*, more natural English than *much pleased, much amused*. *Very* is also acceptable before participles that name physical conditions, such as *very changed, very scratched*, but *much* is not considered as unnatural with words of this kind as it is with the others. In all cases, the two words *very much* may be used with everybody's approval.

A prepositional phrase, such as *on his own, at a loss*, may be qualified by *much* but not by *very*. Certain peculiar adjectives that begin with *a-*, such as *afraid, aware, alive*, were originally prepositional phrases and are still treated in some respects as phrases. For example, they cannot be used before the noun they qualify as other adjectives can. Some grammarians claim that they cannot be qualified by *very*. But in the United States *very afraid, very aware*, are as acceptable as *very amused*.

vespers. This word has a singular form *vesper* which is still in use today, as in *a vesper well sung*, but the plural form *vespers* is heard more often. It is usually followed by a plural verb, as in *vespers were sung*, but may also be followed by a singular verb, as in *vespers was sung*. The singular form is preferred as the first element in a compound, as in *vesper bell* and *vesper book*.

vessel. See **ship**.

vest. See **undershirt**.

vestige. See **trace**.

vestigial; rudimentary. *Vestigial* means pertaining to or of the nature of a vestige, and a vestige is a mark or trace or a visible evidence of something which once was but no longer is present or in existence. It is incorrect to use *vestigial* as a synonym for *rudimentary* (as in *In Transjordan there is a council, recently established; but it is vestigial, it has no power, though some hope that in time it will acquire power*), because *rudimentary* means pertaining to or of the nature of a rudiment, and a rudiment is a mere beginning, the first slight appearance, the undeveloped or imperfect form of something. A *rudiment* and a *vestige* are the very opposites of each other.

veteran. See **old.**

veto. The plural is *vetoes.*

via, strictly used, means by way of, by a route that passes through (*She traveled from Boston to San Francisco via Chicago*). In American usage, however, *via* is often used also to describe the means of travel or the agency employed in shipping, and while the first of these uses (*You folks going via car or railroad?*) is still informal, the United States Post Office has given sanction to the second. On the front of the American airletter appears the phrase VIA AIR MAIL. The corresponding English airletter reads BY AIR MAIL. Almost all stickers and envelopes specially printed for airmail use in the United States have VIA AIR MAIL on them.

vicar. See **rector.**

vice. See **fault.**

vice; vise; visa; visé. The immoral and evil habit or practice is always spelled *vice.* The device with two jaws which may be brought together or separated by means of a screw, lever, or the like, used to hold an object firmly while work is being done upon it, may also be spelled *vice* but is preferably spelled *vise.* The endorsement made upon a passport of one country, testifying that it has been examined and found in order for passage to a country which so indicates, is called a *visa* but may be spelled *visé.*

vicegerent and **vice-regent** are uncommon words, especially the first, but the very fact that they are uncommon makes it necessary, if one is going to use them at all, to use them correctly. The use of a strange word is always accepted by the common reader or listener as an assumption of superiority on the part of the user—as it generally is—and superior people make easy targets.

Vicegerent has much the wider application. It describes an officer deputed by a ruler or supreme head to exercise the powers of the ruler or head (*These popes claimed that they were God's vicegerents upon earth, and that the kings ruled solely as their representatives*) or any deputy. *Vice-regent* (which should be spelled with the hyphen) means a deputy regent.

vice-queen; vicereine. These words have some use in England but are so little used in the United States that they do not even appear in some of the most recent authoritative American dictionaries. A *vicereine* is a viceroy's wife and, less usually, a woman ruling as the representative of a queen. *Vice-queen* takes this latter meaning only. A *vice-queen* in America would probably be assumed to be the head of a syndicate of prostitutes.

vicinage; vicinity; neighborhood. These words all may refer to the region near or about some place or thing. *Vicinage,* a holdover from early English law, is least used of the three. It is a legal term and is not current in American speech or ordinary American writing. *Vicinity* is a familiar term. It differs in meaning from *neighborhood* largely in emphasis: *vicinity* describes a larger, *neighborhood* a compact or smaller area (*When we began to see driftwood we realized we were in the vicinity of land. The nineteenth-century Unitarians are said to have believed in the fatherhood of God, the brotherhood of Man, and the neighborhood of Boston*). *Neighborhood* is sometimes used, as *vicinity* is not, to mean those dwelling in the neighborhood (*The whole neighborhood was aroused at the crime*). Perhaps because of its association with *neighbor,* in its sense of friend (*Which now of these three, thinkest thou, was neighbor unto him that fell among the thieves?*), and *neighborliness,* and perhaps because of the natural gregariousness of the American people, and perhaps because of the relentless reiteration of the word *neighborhood* in radio and television commercials, *neighborhood* has connotations of warmth and friendliness wholly lacking from *vicinity. Your neighborhood grocer* is a friendly member of the community, wholly different from the cold and mercenary fellow who merely happens to sell groceries in the vicinity.

vicious. See **abandoned.**

vicious and **viscous** are unrelated, though often confused, especially in college freshman themes. *Vicious* means addicted to or characterized by vice or immorality; depraved; profligate. *Viscous* means sticky, adhesive, glutinous or ropy. Warm tar is viscous.

vicious circle was originally a term in logic, and still is. *Vicious* in this context means impaired or spoiled by a fault. *Circle* means a mode of reasoning wherein a proposition is used to establish a conclusion and then this same conclusion used to prove the proposition. It is called a circle because it has no real starting place—and, one might add, because there's no end to this sort of thing. It is one of the most popular of all fallacies, the darling of the pompously ignorant.

The term *vicious circle* is commonly used to describe a situation in which solution of one problem creates other problems whose solution is incompatible with the original circumstances. Or, more loosely, some bad situation that, by its nature, seems to get worse and worse. In any use but as a term in logic the expression is now a cliché.

victim. See **martyr.**

Victrola. In the United States any phonograph is often called a *victrola.* Properly speaking, the word should be capitalized, *Victrola,* and used solely in reference to the phonograph made by the Victor Talking Machine Company. That it is not proves the superior wisdom of the Greek admonition "Nothing in excess" to the Yankee slogan "Nothing succeeds like success." Like many other names, *Victrola* "caught on" so successfully that the populace simply adopted it as a generic name, thereby lessening its advertising and identification value.

victuals; food; viands. *Food* is the plain, useful, everyday word for what is eaten or taken into the body for nourishment, at all stages from the furrow to ingestion. Like all basic, necessary words, it has strength and dignity. *Victuals* (rarely used in the singular and often spelled *vittles*) does not mean simply *food* but articles of food prepared for use. As a verb, especially in military contexts (*to victual an army. The garrison was well victualed and could hold out indefinitely*), it is standard. The noun use was introduced as an elegancy and, like many elegancies, has sunk below a vulgarism into a quaintness (*I shore like my vittles on time. Lan' sakes, the vittles that man eats!*) and its use is now an affectation not of elegance but of rusticity. *Wittles* was a favorite word of the Wellers. *Viands* is reserved for dishes of food, presumably of a choice and delicate kind. It is an elegancy, often coupled, with double vulgarity, with *costly*.

view; viewpoint. *View,* used figuratively, means a particular way of regarding something; a conception, notion, or idea of a thing; an opinion or theory. *View* and *opinion* are often, unfortunately, supplanted by more pretentious, longer, yet no more precise terms, like *viewpoint, point of view,* and *standpoint.* For a fuller discussion, see **point of view** and **angle.**

The phrase *in view of* must be followed by a noun or noun equivalent, as in *in view of what you have said.* The phrase *with a view to* may be followed by the *-ing* form of a verb, as in *with a view to preventing such a catastrophe,* or by the simple form of a verb, as in *with a view to prevent such a catastrophe.* The construction using the *-ing* form is preferred. Sometimes the preposition *toward* is used with the *-ing,* as in *with a view toward increasing our skills,* and sometimes the preposition *of,* as in *with a view of rousing his friends,* but *to* is generally preferred.

vigil, strictly speaking, means a keeping awake for any purpose during the natural hours of sleep, a watch kept by night. There are connotations of seriousness of purpose about it; an all-night carouse could only be called a *vigil* in humor. More loosely, a *vigil* means a watch kept by nights or at other times (*He put his hands in his coat pockets and turned back eagerly to his scrutiny of the house, as though my presence marred the sacredness of his vigil. So I walked away and left him standing there in the moonlight—watching over nothing*). *Vigil* also means a course or period of watchful attention, or a period of wakefulness because of inability to sleep. It may not be used as if it meant a wait, least of all a short wait.

vinculum. The plural is *vinculums* or *vincula.*

vindictive. The chief meaning of *vindictive* in America today is disposed or inclined to re-

venge, vengeful (*A vindictive man will often regard a position of power as primarily a means for "getting his own back"*), or proceeding from or showing a revengeful spirit (*The vindictive look she gave him was full warning of what she would do if she ever had the opportunity*). In England, but in England only, *vindictive* is still also used to mean involving retribution, retributive, requital according to merits. If an Englishman said that a certain attack was *solely vindictive* he might mean something entirely different from what an American listener would understand him to mean.

vine. In the United States *vine* means any plant with a long, slender stem that trails or creeps on the ground or climbs by winding itself about a support or holding fast with tendrils or claspers (*The mock-cranberry's red-berried creeping vine*). In England *vine* means plants bearing the grapes from which ordinary wine is made. Americans call these *grapevines.*

violin. See **fiddle.**

violincello; violoncello. *Violincello* is an incorrect spelling, based on the mistaken assumption that the word is related to *violin.* Actually it is related to *viol* and *violone* (the bass viol) and the correct spelling is *violoncello.*

V.I.P. See **personage.**

virile. See **male.**

virtual. See **practical; constructive.**

virtually. See **practically.**

virtue of necessity, make a. The phrase properly means the doing of what must be done, especially when it is something unpleasant or humiliating, with such a grace that the doing of it will be a virtue. The meaning is often lost or ignored and the expression is used to mean "Well, we've got to do it, so we might as well do it and get it over with." If so used, it is certainly a cliché.

virtuoso. The plural is *virtuosos* or *virtuosi.*

virus. The only plural is *viruses.*

visa; visé. *Visa* is the term preferred in the United States to describe a government endorsement on a passport of one country testifying that it has been examined and found in order, for passage to the country granting the visa. The British prefer *visé* and they italicize both forms. In the United States and England the words may be used as nouns or verbs.

visage. To use *visage* as a synonym for *face* is an affectation, a pomposity. The *visage* is the face as affected by the state of mind (*His visage was stern*). It is much the same as *countenance,* but it regards the face as seen by an observer. See also **face; countenance.**

viscera. This word is a plural. The singular, which is seldom used, is *viscus.*

vision literally means the act of seeing with the eye; the power, faculty, or sense of sight (*Your vision is excellent; you have no need of glasses*). It also means the act or power of perceiving what is not actually present to the eye, whether by some supernatural endowment or by natural intellectual means, or that which is so perceived (*your old men shall dream dreams, your young men shall see visions*). *Vision* also means an imaginative power to see the consequence in the future of present acts or trends, to look into the seeds of time (*Where there is no vision, the people perish*). This solemn term has been debased in current usage to refer, in effect, to facile optimists or promoters, especially in the hackneyed term *men of vision*. A true man of vision might be a very depressing fellow whose sighs would precipitate a financial crash. Most men of vision in Germany in the 1930's, who could, walked quickly to the nearest exit.

visit is largely an American term. The English say *call*, unless they mean to designate a stay of considerable duration. A very brief visit is informally called a *chat* in England. It's a pity that Dr. Johnson's "dawdle over a dish of tea" didn't catch on. Americans still use *visit* to describe the act of visiting, regardless of duration, or a call paid to a person, family, etc. (*Oh, do not ask, "What is it?" / Let us go and make our visit*). Yet—such are the ways of language—the small card bearing one's name, used on social occasions, is called in America a *calling card* and in England a *visiting card*. *Visiting card* was formerly used in America but has been out of fashion for well over a generation.

visit; visitation. *Visitation* is a more formal term than *visit*. It means a visit for the purpose of making an official inspection or examination. In Christian theology the *Visitation* was the visit of the Virgin Mary to her cousin, Elizabeth (Luke 1: 39-56), or a church festival, held on July 2, in commemoration of this visit. It may also mean, uncapitalized, a visiting with comfort or aid, or with affliction or punishment, as by God; a special dispensation from heaven, whether of favor or of affliction; any experience or event, especially an unpleasant one, regarded as occurring by divine dispensation (*He regarded his illness as a visitation, a plain mark of Divine disapproval of his recent utterances*).

vituperation. See **abuse.**

viz represents the Latin word *videlicet* and means *namely*. It need not be followed by a period.

vocation. See **avocation, business, calling, job.**

vocative case. The vocative is a Latin case that marks a word used in direct address. In some Latin names the vocative is not identical with the nominative and the distinction between the two cases has some meaning. But this is not true in English. All that can be said about the vocative in an English grammar is that we do not address people in the genitive. We do not say *Sarah's, how are you?*

Words of address may appear anywhere in a sentence except between the verb and its complement. They are always set off by commas, as in *these, Sarah, are very good* and *this, my dear, is wonderful.*

voice. The form of the verb which shows what relation the subject has to the action expressed by the verb is called its voice. The form of the verb which shows that the subject is the agent of the action, as in *he wrote the report,* is called the active voice. The form which shows that the subject is the recipient of the action, as in *the report was written by him,* is called the passive voice. See **passive voice.**

voice; express. *Voice* as a verb means to give voice, utterance, or expression to an emotion, opinion or idea. In the United States it is also acceptably used as a synonym for *express*. English grammarians insist that *voice* may not be substituted for *express* except in those circumstances where speech is involved. One may, therefore, *voice* an opinion in a letter to the *New York Times* but can only *express* an opinion in a letter to the London *Times*.

voice crying in the wilderness. Aside from the danger of blasphemy in any reckless or flippant use of this phrase, it is to be avoided because it is a cliché and, as such, is usually misused. It was the voice of John the Baptist that, crying in the wilderness, foretold the coming of Jesus Christ. The phrase, therefore, has some application to any great foretelling or, even, perhaps, warning. But it is often used to indicate that the foretelling will go unheeded because it is uttered where none can hear or, if hearing, cannot or will not understand. This is a distortion of the original meaning, affected probably by the general associations of *wilderness*.

volume; tome; title; book; work. These words all refer to a collection of printed sheets bound together. A *volume* is a collection of printed sheets bound together and constituting a *book,* or a book forming one of a related set or series (*He brought out the first volume of his history just before the war*). *Tome* is adopted from the French and is synonymous with *volume* in its second sense. It may also mean any volume, especially a ponderous one. The use of the word, however, is confined to the pretentious or the feebly witty. *Title,* though it properly describes the distinguishing name of a book, poem, picture, or the like, is now used in publishers' jargon as if it meant *book* (*We are bringing out six new titles in our paperbacked series*). A *work* is a product of exertion, labor, or activity, and a book has long been considered such. In the singular the word may sound a little pretentious (*It is a work of singular merit*) but the plural (*His works are the glory of our civilization. Collected works. The works of Charles Dickens in thirty-five volumes . . .*) is commonplace. *Book* is the basic term to describe a written or printed work of some length, as a treatise or other literary composition, especially on consecutive sheets fastened or bound together (*Of the making of books there is no end. Another damned, big thick book! Always scribble, scribble, eh, Mr. Gibbon?*).

vortex. The plural is *vortexes* or *vortices*.

vouchsafe does not mean merely to give. It means to condescend to give, to grant as a favor, to give as an act of grace. The word is a little pretentious, but this is often felicitously consonant with what it designates. In prayers to the deity it is straightforward. In almost all others uses it is tinged with irony.

voyage. See **trip.**

vs. is an abbreviation of the Latin word *versus* and means *against.*

vulgar. See **common.**

vulgarity. See **blasphemy.**

W

wad is generally taken to mean a small mass or lump of anything soft (*He always had a wad of gum in his mouth*); a small mass of cotton, wool, or other fibrous or soft material, used for stuffing, padding, packing; a ball or mass of something squeezed together (*The throwing of paper wads, or shooting them with rubber bands, is now an almost sacred tradition of American schoolchildren*). In American usage a *wad* is also a roll, as of paper money: American *wad of bills* is the equivalent of the English *sheaf of notes*. In American slang a *wad* is a large amount of money (*He's really got a wad, that guy; he could buy the whole town if he wanted to*). A stingy person, called in England *tightfisted* or *close-fisted,* is in America most commonly called a *tightwad* (*There's no use asking that tightwad for any money. He won't give a cent*).

Wad is also used to describe the plug of cloth, tow, paper, or the like, used to hold the powder or shot, or both, in place in a gun or cartridge. It is probably from this meaning that the slang phrase *shot his wad,* meaning having done all he can, expended his resources, derives.

wade is used colloquially in the United States to mean to make a sharp attack or energetic beginning. In this sense it is followed by *in* or *into* (*You waded single-handed into a man almost twice your size*). By figurative extension, it may also mean to criticize severely (*Father* [Theodore Roosevelt] *spoke in Chicago, wading into the New York and Indiana machine crowd*). In both uses it is now slightly outmoded.

wages. A few centuries ago this word meant recompense for services, regardless of the person being paid. But later it came to mean only money paid to "a workman or servant." Originally the two forms *wage* and *wages* were used indiscriminately, without any difference in meaning, and the plural form was often followed by a singular verb, as in *their daily wages is so little*.

In the United States today *wages* has lost most of its connotation of low-paid labor. It is always used with a plural verb, as in *his wages are good*. This is a mass word and cannot be used with *many, few,* or a numeral. But the singular form *wage* is used with the article *a,* as in *a better wage*. The singular form is preferred as the first element in a compound, as in *a wage increase*. See also **honorarium.**

wages of sin. Used jocularly, *the wages of sin* is a cliché. It is from Romans 6:23 (*For the wages of sin is death; but the gift of God is eternal life through Jesus Christ our Lord*) where *wages,* though plural in form, means a single payment and is construed as singular.

waist, for a garment or a part of a garment covering the body from the neck or shoulders to the waistline, especially in women's or children's dress, though occasionally heard, especially in relation to children's dress, is now almost obsolescent (*Handsome Flaxon finish, Checked white dimity, Desirable for waists*—Sears, Roebuck and Co., *Catalogue No. 135,* 1917). *Shirtwaist* is still in use, but *blouse* is now the preferred word and, with the trend towards mannishness in women's styles, *shirt* has also come to be used. A recent advertisement in *The New Yorker* shows a picture of a young woman in a woman's adaptation of a man's checked shirt. That the word is to be applied to a garment intended solely for women (though one is never certain in these days) is suggested by the text of the advertisement: "Notice the way Hathaway cuts and shapes their shirts to a girl's greatest advantage. Bosoms are such. Shoulders are natural. Waistlines go tiny."

Waist is now usually restricted to meaning the waistline or the actual, physical waist. *Pantywaist,* a slang and rather affected term for an effeminate and over-elegant young man, is borrowed from schoolboy derision of a generation or so ago for boys whose mothers dressed them in what the other boys regarded as feminine attire.

waistcoat. See **undershirt.**

wait on hand and foot. As a term for assiduous personal service, spoken usually in annoyance and resentment, *to wait on somebody hand and foot* is hackneyed.

waive; wave. *Waive,* a derivative of *waif,* meaning to make waif or to abandon, means basically to forbear to insist on, to relinquish, to forgo (*He waived the prize money awarded him*). In law it means to relinquish a known right intentionally (*He waived diplomatic immunity in order to contest the issue*). It can also mean to put aside for the time, to defer, to put aside or dismiss from consideration (*He waived these unpleasant thoughts from his mind, however, and turned to the pleasure at hand*).

Wave always involves motion. As an intransitive verb, it means to move with advancing swells and depressions of surface (*At last the American flag waved over Iwo Jima*) or to move the hands in greeting (*She waved to us from the train*). As a transitive verb, it means to cause to wave, to move (*The boys frantically waved their hands as we drove away*).

wake; waken. The past tense is *woke, waked,* or *wakened*. The participle is *waked, wakened, woke,* or *woken*. Each of these nine forms may have the prefix *a*, as in *awake, awaken, awoke,* and so on, or it may form a compound verb with *up*, as in *wake up, woke up, wakened up,* and so on. This gives us twenty-seven forms for the principal parts of this verb, where ordinarily two forms are enough, as in *talk, talked*. This is certainly more words than we need for such a simple act.

The participles that have the vowel *o*, as in *had woke, has awoken,* and so on, are not considered standard in the United States but are still acceptable in Great Britain. Aside from this, all the forms are equally acceptable and which one is used is entirely a matter of individual taste.

There is a tendency to prefer the forms with *en* when the verb is used in the passive, as in *he was wakened*. There is also a tendency to prefer the forms with the prefix *a* when the verb is used figuratively, as in *she awoke to the danger*. When the verb is both passive and figurative these tendencies combine and *awakened* is the preferred form, as in *she has been awakened to her danger*.

There is a theory that the past tense form *woke* is preferable for an actual waking up when the verb does not have an object, as in *he woke at six,* and the form *waked* when the verb does have an object, as in *she waked him at six,* but this is not borne out in practice.

There is one more form of this verb that has not been mentioned yet, making twenty-eight forms in all. This is an old participle *awake*. It is now used only as an adjective following a verb, as in *she is awake*.

wale; weal; wheal. *Wale* is the best word to describe a streak, stripe, or ridge produced on the skin by the stroke of a rod or whip, a welt (*A livid wale across his back testified to the force of the blow*). *Wheal* means a small, burning or itching swelling on the skin, as from a mosquito bite. Because *ea* was formerly in many words pronounced (as it now is in *great*) to rime with *say* (*Where thou, great Anna, whom three realms obey,/ Dost sometimes counsel take, and sometimes tea. Perhaps the pleasure is as great/ In being cheated as to cheat*), *wheal* and *wale* were easily confused. *Weal* (not the *weal* of *weal or woe*) in this sense seems to have no justification other than as a sort of variant spelling of *wale* or *wheal*.

walking encyclopedia, as a term for someone who has an astonishing fund of general information, is a cliché.

walking on air. As a way of saying that someone is ecstatic, usually with exultation at some good fortune, to say that he is *walking on air* is hackneyed.

wane; flag. To *wane* is to decline, to grow less, to decrease, in extent, quantity, importance, brilliance, splendor, or the like (*The long day wanes: the slow moon climbs: the deep / Moans round with many voices. His influence in the company had, actually, long been waning and his displacement was not the sudden reversal that it seemed to those who were unaware of this fact*). When applied to the moon, *wane* is to decrease in the periodical manner characteristic of the second half of the lunar period (*A savage place! as holy and enchanted/ As e'er beneath a waning moon was haunted/ By woman wailing for her demon-lover!*).

To *flag* is to fall off in vigor, energy, or activity, to droop (*He began with great bustle and effort but soon flagged*). *Flagging* differs from *waning* in that an effort that *flags* may revive. The slackening of exertion or interest may be only temporary and may revive to full force, but that which *wanes* (except for the moon) declines or decreases permanently.

want (noun). See **need.**

want. This verb may mean desire or will, or it may mean need or lack. It may have either meaning in the sentence *he wants the proper clothes*.

When *want* means need it may be followed by the *-ing* form of a verb, as in *it wanted saying, the coat wants mending*. In this sense, *want* may be followed by *for*, as in *he wants for nothing*.

When *want* means desire it may be followed by an infinitive, as in *she wants to mend the coat, I want you to come*. It cannot be followed by an *-ing* form of a verb or by a clause. *I want you should come* is not regarded as acceptable English. In this sense, *want* cannot be followed by *for. I want for you to come* is usually condemned.

At one time it was usual to omit verbs of motion after verbs of willing, as in *thou shalt to prison*. This custom survives in Scotland and in some parts of the United States, as in *I'll awa' up the glen* and *the cat wants out*. A similar contraction is seen in *let me in*. After *let* this old usage is standard everywhere. After *want* it is standard in some sections of the United States, principally the Middle West and South. In other sections it is unusual and is thought to be Pennsylvania Dutch.

Want may also be used as a very weak form of *ought*, as in *you want to go slow*. This is acceptable English, at least in the United States.

want; wish; desire. *Desire* is the most formal of these three words. It suggests a strong wish (*The people desire political reforms and will make their displeasure known at the polls*). In a specialized sense it means to desire in sexual intercourse. *Wish* is the familiar term meaning to feel an impulse toward attainment or possession of something (*I wish you were here*). The feeling it expresses may be of greater or less intensity (*I wish you would pay attention; I've had to ask you twice. I wish I were dead. I wish the wind may never cease,/Nor fashes in the flood,/Till my three sons come home to me,/In earthly flesh and blood!*). *Wish* has connotations of desiring the unattainable, or of an impulse but weakly connected with any energetic or disciplined will to accomplish. *Want* is the least formal of the three words. It suggests a feeling of lack or need which imperatively demands fulfillment (*I want my supper! Mr. Watson, come here. I want you*). *Wish* is sometimes misused, in vulgar elegance, for *want* in such demands as

Do you wish some more potatoes? The fault here is that the bodily wants (the satisfaction of which, presumably, is the sole reason for the potatoes being offered) are so basic and fundamental, so imperative in their demands, that only *want* will do. The various shades of meaning latent in *wish* are all inapplicable to the situation.

wapiti. See **elk.**

-ward; -wards. Originally, *-ward* was an adjective ending that meant "having the direction of." Words ending in *-ward* were used to qualify nouns, as in *the homeward journey*. The final *s* in *-wards* was a genitive ending which made adverbs of these adjectives, very much as the ending *-ly* is used today to make adverbs from adjectives. The *-s* forms were used to qualify words that were not nouns, as in *homewards bound*.

Today the *-ward* forms are still the only ones used to qualify a following noun. But either form may be used in any other construction. Some grammarians claim that either form may be used when the word describes direction, as in *look homeward, Angel,* but that the form with *s* is required when the word describes manner, as in *he does everything backwards*. This distinction is not observed in the United States, where the forms without *s* are generally preferred for both direction and manner.

Words may be freely coined on this pattern, as *stationward, dinnerward, usward*.

warden means one charged with the care or custody of something, a keeper. In the United States it has been specialized to mean the chief administrative officer in charge of a prison. (*The warden told them, over the loudspeaker, that they had one hour in which to surrender and evacuate the cell block*). Though the term is employed, or was, in one specialized instance in England in the same sense (*Warden* is the title of the man in charge of the Fleet prison), it is used today in England, in relation to prisons, to designate what in America is called a guard (*A prison has many advantages over a school. In prison, for example, the wardens protect you from attack by your fellow prisoners*). The American *warden* is the English *governor*.

Warden may also mean any of various public officials charged with superintendence, as *game warden, fish warden, fire warden*. These are chiefly American terms, but *fire warden* was taken over in England during World War II to designate those who watched for and attempted to control incendiary bombings. In England *warden* is also used as the name for the heads of certain colleges (*The Warden of All Souls, Dr. Pember, was that year Vice-chancellor*) and other educational and charitable institutions.

ward heeler is an exclusively American expression to describe a minor hanger-on of a political machine who canvasses voters and does party chores, a man who, like a dog, comes to heel when his master, the political boss, the Ward Boss, gives commands (*He said that the Census Bureau is violating the constitutional rights of the American people when it "sends 168,000 political hacks and ward heelers . . . to snoop into the people's finances"*).

Wardour Street English is an expression used in England but unknown in America, except to the learned, for the affected, and often erroneous, use of archaic words. *Ye Olde Radio Repaire Shoppe* would be a good example of Wardour Street English. Wardour Street was a street in London famed for its fake antiques.

warm as toast is a hackneyed comparison. In former days when houses were cold in winter, toast taken directly from before the fire was, apparently, strikingly warm, but today one does not think of it as particularly warm. In England where — by American standards — the toast is frigid, the phrase is meaningless.

warm the cockles of one's heart. To say of something pleasing that it *warms,* or *rejoices,* or *delights the cockles of the heart,* is to employ a cliché.

Cockle is the name of bivalve molluscs of the genus *Cardium*. The resemblance in shape between the shell of the mollusc and the heart has long been recognized and is, indeed, implicit in the name of the genus. But *the cockles of the heart* implies some special part or parts of the heart, though just what or why is unknown. Probably it is no more than an intensive, like *in my heart of hearts*.

warn may be followed by an infinitive, as in *I warned him to leave at once,* or by a clause, as in *I warn you I am leaving*. If the *-ing* form of a verb follows *warn,* it must be introduced by the preposition *against,* as in *I warned him against leaving*.

warp. See **woof.**

warrant; warranty; guarantee; guaranty. *Warrant* and *guarantee* are frequently interchangeable to indicate that something is safe or genuine. To *warrant* is to give a pledge or assurance that something is what it seems or claims to be (*I warrant he's telling the truth*). To *guarantee* is to make something sure or certain by binding oneself to replace it or refund its price if it is not as represented (*The watch is guaranteed for a year*). The word is thrown around recklessly in advertisements and only the most careful reading can ascertain just what is guaranteed, if anything. *Warrant* has the meaning, not shared by *guarantee,* of to justify (*This does not warrant such expenditures!*).

Warrant and *guarantee* may also be used as nouns. In the specialized sense of an authorization for arrest, *warrant* alone may be used. The prevalence of this use, with its unpleasant associations, tends to make *guarantee* the common word for all other uses.

Warranty, a noun only, and *guaranty,* noun or verb, are used in specialized senses. *Warranty* is chiefly a legal term meaning an engagement, express or implied, in assurance of some particular in connection with a contract, as of sale; or a covenant in a deed to land by which the party conveying assures the grantee that he will enjoy the premises free from interference by any person claiming under a superior title. A *warranty deed* is a deed containing such a covenant, as distinguished from a *quitclaim deed,* which conveys without any assurances only such title as the grantor may have. In the law of insurance, a *warranty* is a statement or promise, made by the party insured, and included as an essential part of the contract, falsity or nonfulfillment of which renders the policy void. *Warranty* may also mean a judicial document, as a warrant or writ. *Guaranty* means a warrant, pledge, or promise given by way of security. As a verb it means to guarantee. *Guaranty* is used in England in many contexts where Americans would use *guarantee* which, in the United States, is by far the commoner of the two forms in all uses.

was; were. These two words form the past tense of the verb *be. Was* is always singular and cannot be used with a plural subject. We cannot say *we was, they was,* or *you was. Were* is usually plural, but it may also be used, under some circumstances, with a singular subject.

Were is used with the pronoun *you,* even when *you* refers to only one person, as in *were you there, Charlie?* This has been standard English since about 1820. Before that, educated people said *you were* when speaking to more than one person and *you was* when speaking to only one, as in *you was mistaken, John.* This was a useful distinction that may someday come back into the language. At present we have no standard way of showing whether *you* is singular or plural and resort to makeshift plural forms such as *you people, you all,* and the unacceptable *yous.*

The other cases in which *were* may be used with a singular subject are not as clear-cut as this. It is not true that the singular *were* can always be used after the word *if.* Sentences such as *in my childhood I admired a man if he were rich,* where *were* is wrong and *was* is required, show that the writer is using *were* self-consciously, out of anxiety about his grammar, and not out of any feeling for the old literary forms.

Were is the singular, as well as the plural, in the old past subjunctive of *be.* It is therefore permissible to use it with a singular subject wherever a past subjunctive is appropriate, principally after the verb *wish* and in hypothetical statements that are indefinite as to time, as in *I wish I were wonderful, suppose it were true,* and *if I were living in a desert.* (See **subjunctive mode.**) But, with two exceptions which will be discussed later, the singular *was* may also be used in these same constructions, as in *I wish I was wonderful, suppose it was true,* and *if I was living in a desert.* This is not a recent development. *Was* has been used as a past subjunctive in literary English for more than three hundred years and is the preferred form today.

In current English there are two constructions in which *were* is preferred to the subjunctive *was.* One is the simple expression *if I were you. Was* is also used here, and is not wrong, but *were* is generally preferred. The other is a purely literary construction. The idea that is ordinarily expressed by an *if* clause may be expressed without the *if,* by placing the verb before the subject, as in *were I in a desert.* Formerly, *was* might be used in this way. Sterne, for example, wrote *was I in a desert.* But this is no longer standard. In present-day English *were* is required in this construction and *was* cannot be used. In any other construction where both forms are permissible, *was* is now felt to be more forceful, more vivid, than the singular *were.*

As a rule, the singular *were* cannot be used in a statement about the past. If we are uncertain about the facts, the indicative *was* is required, as in *if he was thirty when I met him.* Sometimes *if* introduces a statement which we know was true and this also calls for the indicative *was,* as in *she was sixty if she was a day.* If we know that what we are saying is contrary to the facts and we are speaking about a specific event, the past perfect with *had* is required, as in *if he had been there.* In speaking of the past, the singular *were* is used only in descriptive statements, which are relatively timeless, and only when these are known to be contrary to the facts, as in *he looked as grim as if he were made of stone* and *he treated her as tenderly as if he were her own mother.* Even here, *was* is permissible and *had been* is generally preferred.

To sum up, the singular *were* is used with the pronoun *you,* in the expression *if I were you,* and in hypothetical statements with inverted word order, such as *were he here.* It may be used, but need not be, to express what is imaginary or doubtful, provided the statement refers to the future or is indefinite as to time, as in *if he were given a chance.* In current English *was* is heard more often than *were* in such statements. Some grammarians claim that *were* is required in a contrary-to-fact statement that does not refer to a specific past event. But these same men also complain that *was* is now invading this "last stronghold" of the singular *were.* The invasion has been under way for several centuries and no one should be frightened into using *were* where *was* seems more natural. It is almost impossible for anyone who has a high school education to use *was* where *were* is required. But the writer who gets self-conscious about his subjunctives can very easily use *were* where literary English requires *was.* To be safe, one should write as one speaks.

wash is more frequently used in compounds in America than in England. *Washboard* is of American origin. American *washbowl* is English *washbasin.* American *washcloth* or *washrag* is English *face-cloth* or *face-flannel.* American *washroom* (often a synonym for *privy*) is English *lavatory,* which is often, to an American's annoyance, a mere washroom. American *washday* is English *washing day.* Both English and Americans say *washstand* and *washtub. Washhouse,* an English term for a small separate outbuilding used solely for washing clothes and containing the *coppers* (in America called *boilers* or *tubs*) is unknown in the United States. In both England and America the older word to describe a woman who washed clothes for hire was *washerwoman.* American usage only permits *washwoman* as well. The word is being largely replaced by the more elegant *laundress* and perhaps justifiably so, as the heavier, dirtier work that used to be a part of the week's or season's *washing* is now sent to the laundry and the dry cleaners, leaving only the lighter and finer things (which were properly handled by a laundress instead of a washerwoman) to be done at home. To say *washlady* is to speak vulgarly in England or America.

In America *washout* describes a washing out of earth by water, as from an embankment or a roadway by heavy rain or by a freshet, or the hole or break so produced. As a figurative slang term, *washout* in America means a failure or fiasco (*The whole dramatic production was a washout*). In England *washout* is a special term in mining engineering.

washing. See **ablution.**

washing dirty linen in public. As a term for those who in mutual recriminations reveal matters, especially family matters, discreditable to themselves and expose to public view things that in decency should be kept private, *washing their dirty linen in public* is now a cliché.

washing one's hands of something. As a term for a public disavowal of all further connection with some enterprise or the disowning of all association with some person, *washing one's hands of the matter or business* is a cliché. It is derived, in English, from Pilate's washing his hands in public as a sign of his refusal to accept responsibility for the crucifixion of Jesus Christ; yet from the very manner in which Pilate performed this ablution it is apparent that the term and the ritualistic nature of the act were established.

wastage; waste. *Wastage* is neutral, *waste* (except in a number of technical applications) deprecatory. *Wastage* means loss by use, wear, or decay (*A certain amount must be allowed for wastage*). *Waste,* in common everyday usage, means useless consumption or expenditure, or use without adequate return (*It is a waste of time to listen to him*).

waste your breath. Used commonly in some negative adjuration, as an assurance that speech, usually of persuasion or admonition, will be vain, to *waste your breath* is hackneyed.

wastebasket is now standard and almost universal in American usage, though the longer form, *wastepaper basket,* still used in England, is known and used occasionally in the United States.

watch. This verb may be followed by an object and the *-ing* form of a verb, as in *I watched them working,* or by an object and the simple form of a verb, as in *I watched them work.*

watchword. See **slogan.**

water; waters. *Water* is a mass noun and in everyday English does not have a plural form. But the plural *waters* was formerly used, and may still be used, in certain limited senses.

The plural form is always used in speaking of the seas belonging to a particular nation or in a particular part of the globe, as in *American*

waters and *southern waters.* It is also used in figurative expressions such as *deep waters* and *troubled waters.*

The plural form is still used occasionally in speaking of mineral water, as it is in *it is long, very long, Mr. Pickwick, since you drank the waters.* It may be used in poetry or dramatic prose in speaking of large bodies of flowing water, as in *like waters shot from some high crag* and *the waters of the Danube.*

Formerly, the plural form was used in speaking of a flood as in *the waters had risen.* This is now felt to be artificial or bookish. The amniotic fluid was also called *the waters.* We now speak of it as *the water,* and *waters* is considered old fashioned or dialectal.

water, of the first. Used figuratively, as a designation of the highest worth, the expression *of the first water,* drawn from a now outmoded classification of the quality of diamonds, is a cliché.

water under the bridge (and **over the dam**). As a way of saying that much has happened since a certain event took place, *much water has flowed under the bridge since then* is a cliché. The water seems to be the stream of time or life, the bridge, perhaps, the bridge of sighs. It's all very mystical and tedious. *Water under the bridge,* by the way, is not to be confused with *water over the dam* which is a term for something that has happened and cannot be recalled. It, too, is a cliché. Every now and then some luckless orator blends the two.

watershed; divide. *Watershed* is chiefly English in the sense of the ridge or crest line dividing two drainage areas, a water parting. Americans usually say *divide.* In both England and America *watershed* is also used to describe the region or area drained by a river, a drainage area (*A number of government dams have been built in the Tennessee River watershed*).

wave. See **waive.**

wave of optimism. As a term for an access of courage or a widespread renewal of hope, *a wave of optimism* is hackneyed. It always "sweeps through" the group referred to.

wax. When this is a verb meaning grow or become it may be followed by an adjective describing the subject, as in *it waxed late, it waxed cool.* It may also be followed by an adverb describing the waxing, as in *it waxed steadily worse.*

way. The noun *way* may be used as an adverb to show direction or manner, as in *step this way* and *do it your own way.* Shakespeare uses the form *ways* to show direction in *what cursed foot wanders this ways tonight?,* but this is no longer standard English.

The noun *way* may also be used as an adverb showing distance, as in *a long way from home* and *he had come quite a way.* In the United States the form *ways* is also used in this sense, as in *a long ways from home* and *quite a ways inland.* This construction has not been considered standard in England for more than fifty years, but it was used by most of the great writers of English and is still standard in this country.

The word *way* is sometimes used without the article *a* to mean "far off," as in *way down upon the Swanee river*. This is a Scottish idiom. It is acceptable in the United States but not in England, where *away* is required, as in *away down the river, a hundred miles or more*.

The suffix *-ways* (but not the suffix *-way*) may be added to a noun to show direction, as in *edgeways, endways, sideways*. Both forms, *-way* and *-ways*, are used in adverbs of manner, as in *anyway* and *anyways*. Some grammarians hold that words expressing manner should not have the *s* ending, but should be *anyway, someway,* and so on. This restriction is not observed in literary English, but the forms without *s* are generally preferred in the United States today.

way; weigh. *Under way* is the correct expression to mean in motion, or moving along, as a ship that has weighed anchor and is moving on her course (*We got under way at midnight and by sunrise were in position to bombard the coastal defenses*). *Weigh*, when applied to an anchor, has the highly specialized meaning of to lift or raise. Many people use *under weigh*, being apparently of the impression that it has something to do with weighing anchor. But while a ship cannot be under way until she has weighed anchor, she may weigh anchor and yet not get under way. The term is no less incorrect when used figuratively (as in *Now that he had a project under weigh his spirits rose*).

we. The word *I* does not actually have a plural. *We* means "I and others" rather than "more than one I." Who the others are is sometimes vague. When necessary we can make it specific by adding words, as in *we the people* or *we here present*.

We is sometimes used to mean a single individual. One form of this is called the modest *we*. Here a person uses a plural form in order not to call attention to himself as an individual. This device is sometimes silly, but it is very old and is found even in classical Latin.

There is also a royal *we*. At one period in history the Roman empire was governed by two or three men who ruled together and issued joint proclamations, using a plural form. Later, smaller rulers used the same form because they were speaking for themselves and a body of advisors. In this way the plural became associated with the highest authority and was eventually used by single, independent rulers as a sign of royalty. In English the old form *ourself*, and not the modern plural form *ourselves*, is used in referring to a royal *we*, as in *we will ourself take time to hear your cause*.

The editorial *we* is often a true plural. That is, a writer often uses *we* to mean himself and his associates or himself and his readers. When he does, he will also use the plural form *ourselves*, as in *we ourselves believe*. When the form *ourself* is used here, as in *we ourself believe*, the editorial *we* slides into the royal *we* and becomes pompous.

Finally, there is a *we* that is only used in speaking to very young children or adults who are sick. Here *we* actually means *you*, as in *how are we feeling today?* and *can't we open our mouth a little wider?* This might be called the patronizing *we*, or the humiliating *we*.

For when to use *we* rather than *us*, see **subjective pronouns.**

weak verbs. See **strong verbs.**

weaker sex. To refer to women as *the weaker sex* is to employ a tedious — and questionable — banality.

weakness. See **fault.**

weal. See **wale.**

wealthy. See **rich.**

wear. The past tense is *wore*. The participle is *worn*. A participle *wore*, as in *had wore*, is heard but is standard only as a term in sailing, where it means a particular way of bringing a ship about.

Wear may be followed by an adjective describing what wears, as in *it wore thin*. It may also be followed by an adverb describing the wearing, as in *it wore well*.

wear and tear, especially when used as a mere intensive for *wear,* is hackneyed.

wear one's heart upon one's sleeve. As a term for making an ingenuous display of one's feelings and hence, one's affections being known, to be vulnerable to slights and scorns, *to wear one's heart upon one's sleeve* is a cliché. The expression is taken from one of Iago's early speeches in *Othello* when, boasting to the gullible Roderigo, he says that he is not what for his own purposes he seems to be, *For when my outward action doth demonstrate/ The native act and figure of my heart/ In compliment extern, 'tis not long after/ But I will wear my heart upon my sleeve/ For daws to peck at.*

wearied; weary; wearisome. *Weary* is now simply a synonym for *tired*. It is slightly bookish. *Wearied* still retains a little of the older idea of being exhausted with exertion, worn out of strength or patience. *Wearisome* has now almost exclusively the sense of "tedious." See also **tired.**

weasel. Figurative uses of *weasel* are apparently an American phenomenon. A *weasel* is a cunning, sneaking fellow who models his behavior on the sinuous animal. *Weasel words* mean intentionally ambiguous statements. The image is not, as commonly assumed, of words that can glide, as a weasel glides, out of their seeming meaning. It is a better figure than that. It is based on the weasel's habit of sucking eggs. And a weasel word is one which, by equivocal qualification, sucks all the real meaning out of the word to which the hearer or reader has attached significance. The phrase seems to have been coined by Stewart Chaplin in an article in *Century Magazine* in 1900 and popularized by Theodore Roosevelt in a speech delivered at St. Louis in 1916. Roosevelt said, "One of our defects as a nation is a tendency to use what have been called 'weasel words.' When a weasel sucks an egg, the meat is sucked out of the egg; and if you use a 'weasel word' after another there is nothing left of the other."

Weasel is used colloquially as a verb, mean-

ing to make ambiguous. It is also used colloquially (perhaps a portmanteau combination of
wiggle and *greasy*, with a suggestion of the
weasel's cunning and ferocity) to mean to get
out of something by shady means (*He'll weasel
out of his promise; he never kept one yet unless
it was to his advantage to do so*).

weather, everybody talks about . . . It was
Charles Dudley Warner, not Mark Twain, who
first said, *Everybody talks about the weather,
but nobody does anything about it.* It was a fine
drollery on its first utterance, a profound criticism of the "let's-*do*-something-about-it" school
of moral zealots with which the country then
abounded, a pensive reminder that we are not
omnipotent and that at least some of the troubles
of our proud and angry dust are from eternity
and will not fail. As a witticism it merited the
first five or six hundred million repetitions it received. But now that it has been said countless
billions of times (and always ascribed to the
wrong man), it deserves a rest. This is something
we *can* do something about.

weather the storm. As a term for surviving some
period of stress and danger, *weathering the
storm* is a cliché.

weave. The past tense is *wove*. The participle is
woven or *wove*. A past tense and participle
weaved is heard but is not standard when applied
to actual weaving. However, this is the preferred
form when the word means "follow a winding
course," as in *the drunken man weaved his way
through the crowd.*

web. See **woof.**

wed. The past tense is *wed* or *wedded*. The participle is also *wed* or *wedded*. In the United
States *wed* is the preferred form for the past
tense and the participle. In Great Britain *wedded*
is preferred. *Wedded* is the preferred form in
both countries when the word is used as an adjective, as in *a wedded life* and *I am not wedded
to the idea.*

Actually, this verb is seldom used in contemporary American speech, except in the expression *the newly weds.* We ordinarily prefer the
word *marry.*

wedded bliss, as a term for ecstatic happiness in
marriage, is a cliché. It is now used almost entirely in heavy jocularity, but it is nonetheless a
cliché.

wedding; marriage; nuptials. *Marriage* is the
simple and usual term for the ceremony which
unites couples in wedlock. It has no implication
as to circumstances and is without emotional
connotations (*They announced the marriage of
their daughter. Marriage is a basic social institution*). *Wedding* has strong emotional, even
sentimental, connotations, and suggests the accompanying festivities, whether elaborate or
simple (*Will you dance at my wedding?*). *Marriage* may be used to describe the union of a
wedded couple throughout its entire duration;
wedding is restricted solely to the ceremony of
union and the immediate social events. *Nuptials*
is a formal and lofty word applied to the ceremony and attendant social events. It does not

have emotional connotations but strongly implies surroundings characteristic of wealth, rank,
pomp, and grandeur (*Millions of Britons bought
newspapers to read of the royal nuptials*). *Nuptials* is too elegant a word to be applied to the
ordinary wedding ceremony.

weep. The past tense is *wept*. The participle is
also *wept*. See **cry.**

weft. See **woof.**

weighty and **heavy** both mean weighing a great
deal, but *heavy* is the usual term. In figurative
senses their meanings differ. *Weighty* means
burdensome (*He had weighty cares of office*)
or important (*The weighty problems of the
office seemed to find their best solutions on the
golf course*). *Heavy* may also mean burdensome,
yet the sense is of very great burdens (*Heavy
taxes made the amassing of a competence almost
impossible*). It is sometimes used as a synonym
for *great* when the greatness has a figurative
sense of burdening, pressing down (*The whole
family sustained heavy losses in the stock market
crash*) and is frequently used to mean sorrowful
(*One can only view these ravages with a heavy
heart*).

welkin. It's been about five hundred years since
ordinary people in everyday speech referred to
the sky as the *welkin*. The word seemed to have
a fascination for poets, however, and remained
in their vocabularies up into the nineteenth century, though Shakespeare (*Twelfth Night,* III,
1, 65) was apparently amused at it as an elegant variation and Mark Twain (*Tom Sawyer
Abroad,* Chapter V) had Tom Sawyer use the
word and justify it as pure ornament, "like the
ruffles on a shirt." *To make the welkin ring* (or
howl, or *crack,* or *roar*), as a hyperbole for some
clamorous noise, is a venerable cliché.

well. This word is, first of all, the adverbial
equivalent of the adjective *good* and has the
comparative and superlative forms *better* and
best.

In standard English the word *good* cannot be
used to qualify a verb, as in *she sings good.* But
the word *well* may be used after verbs of appearing where the formal rules of grammar
require the adjective *good.* That is, we may say
it sounds good or *it sounds well* and *it looks
good on you* or *it looks well on you.* See **linking verbs.**

Well sometimes means in good health. Here
the word has the same comparative form that it
has when it means "good." We say *Rowan is better today* not *Rowan is weller.* But it does not
have the superlative form *best.* If a superlative is
used, it is *wellest,* as in *the wellest of them all,*
but this form is questionable. In literary English
we are compelled to say *healthiest.* In the United
States *well* meaning *healthy* is thoroughly established as an adjective and we speak of *a well
baby.* In Great Britain the word still has an
ambiguous status. It is not used immediately
before a noun, which is the primary position for
an adjective, but only after a verb, as in *the baby
is well,* in a position where both adjectives and
adverbs may appear. The comparative form is

not used immediately before a noun even in the United States. We do not say *a better baby,* meaning a healthier one.

well earned rest deserves one.

well nigh which, as a synonym for *almost,* Partridge lists as an elegancy or vogue word in England, is, in the United States, rustic or comic.

Welsh Rabbit; Welsh Rarebit. The proper name for the melted cheese dish is *Welsh Rabbit. Rarebit* is a corruption, due to highbrow folk-etymologizing. Any chef is, of course, free to call any concoction by any name he chooses. But he is not free, among the informed, to overawe others with his own ignorance.

wend one's way, an archaism revived by Scott, is affected.

went. See **go.**

wept. See **weep.**

were. See **be.**

west; western. The comparative form is *more western.* The superlative form is *westernmost.*

wet. The past tense is *wet* or *wetted.* The participle is also *wet* or *wetted.* In the United States *wet* is the preferred form for the past tense and the participle, as in *he wet his lips, he had wet the grass,* and *wetted* is seldom used except when speaking of something other than water, as in *the particles were wetted by the oil.* In Great Britain *wetted* is the preferred form in all contexts and *wet* is seldom heard.

wet to the skin is hackneyed.

wharf. The usual plural is *wharves,* but *wharfs* is also acceptable and has been standard English for several centuries.

what is primarily an interrogative pronoun or adjective, as in *what do you mean?* and *what kittens?* It is also used as a compound relative, equivalent to *that which,* as in *he did what he could* and *he spent what money he had.*

The interrogative *what* differs from the interrogative *which* in two ways. (1) *Which* asks about members of a limited group, as in *which do you want?* and *which books did you take?,* where the questions mean "which of the ones we are talking about." *What,* like *who,* is unlimited in range. *What do you want?* and *what books did you take?* ask about anything possible. (2) The interrogative *which* is used in speaking of persons as well as things. *What* on the other hand supplements *who,* which is used only as a pronoun and only in speaking of persons. As an adjective *what* may be used in speaking of human beings, as in *what child is this?* As a pronoun it may ask about a human characteristic, function, or office, as in *what is he?,* but not about the person himself. The interrogative *what* may be used in exclamations, as in *what strange men!, what nonsense!* When used in an exclamation before a singular concrete noun, *what* always precedes the article *a,* as in *what a tale!*

What may also be used as a compound word equivalent to the demonstrative pronoun *that* followed by the relative *which,* as in *I heard what he said.* It does not represent a preceding word in the sentence, but can be thought of as a relative that carries its own antecedent, or as a substitute for *that which.* At one time *what* could be used as a simple relative and represent a preceding word, as in *I had a horse what wouldn't go,* but this is no longer standard.

The *that* contained in the compound relative *what* always represents or is explained by a following group of words, as in *she was still what is called young.* In order to refer to what has already been said we use the word *which,* as in *he is a well-known man, which I am not, and, what is more, I am poor.* In current English *what* is usually preferred to the two words *that which* when the *that* is defined by the following clause, as in *believe what he tells you. What* cannot be used when the contained *that* represents something not defined by the following clause, as in *it was that which brought me here.*

The interrogative *what* may also be used in a subordinate clause, as in *I know what he said.* In a sentence of this kind the difference between the interrogative *what* and the compound relative lies in the intention of the speaker. If what is meant is "I know the answer to the question: what did he say?" the word is an interrogative. If, as in the sentence using the word *heard,* the meaning is "I heard the words which he said," we have the compound relative. Very often the distinction is meaningless.

What should not be used in referring to a person. Otherwise, the word is being properly used whenever it carries an implied question or can be replaced by *that which* or *those which. What* can be replaced by *that which* and is therefore standard English in *an easier yoke than what you put on me* and *Padua affords nothing but what is kind.* It cannot be replaced by *that which,* and is therefore not standard, in *I laughed heartier then than what I do now. What* is also not standard in *there's no one but what says . . . ,* because here it refers to a person. When it does not refer to a person, a technically improper *what* after *but,* as in *not but what you're right* and *who knows but what it's all true,* is acceptable English in the United States. But it is condemned by some grammarians and avoided in formal writing.

The adjective *what* may qualify either a singular or a plural noun, as in *to what green altar?* and *what men or gods are these?* The pronoun may be followed by either a singular or a plural verb, as in *what appears to be the important points* and *what appear to be the important points.* When the words represented by *what* are unknown, as in a true question, it is usually treated as a singular, as in *what is going on?*

Whatever means "anything, no matter what." It should not be used as an interrogative, as in *whatever have you done?* But otherwise, it may be used as a pronoun, as in *eat whatever you like,* or as an adjective, as in *for whatever reason.* The adjective is often placed after a noun qualified by *any,* for additional emphasis, as in *if for any reason whatever.* The word *whatsoever* is now archaic in Great Britain, but is still natural English in the United States, especially when used to make a negative statement emphatic, as in *for no reason whatsoever.*

At one time the word *what* could be used as an indefinite relative equivalent to *whatever,* as in *unmoved, I stand what wind may blow.* This is now archaic except in a few set phrases, such as *come what will, say what you please.* The same indefinite *what* could also be used as an adverb or conjunction. This is now obsolete except for the set phrase *what with,* as in *what with one thing and another.*

wheal. See **wale.**

wheels within wheels, as a term for bureaucratic complexity or the involvements of administrative responsibility in a power hierarchy of some kind, is a cliché. It may derive from Ezekiel's vision of *a wheel . . . in the midst of a wheel.* From this also—though more likely from the Negro spiritual based on it—may also derive the slang term of *big wheel* or just *wheel* for a man of power in an organization.

when is primarily an interrogative adverb meaning "at what time," as in *when will he come?* But it is also used in several senses as a conjunction.

When used to introduce a clause, *when* may still be an interrogative and mean "at what time," as in *he didn't tell me when he would be back.* But it may mean "at that time," as in *he didn't tell me when he was here.* In this case *when* approaches the meaning of *while* but suggests a particular point in time rather than a period of time. In speaking of a future event, *when* in this sense is used with a present tense, rather than a future tense, verb. We say *when the end comes, it will come quickly.*

When may mean no more than "considering that," as in *who shall decide, when doctors disagree?* Here the idea of "at that time" has paled to a mere logical connection. The word has almost the meaning of *if,* except that it does not carry any suggestion of doubt.

When may also be used to introduce a sharp contrast, as in *you rub the sore when you should bring the plaster.* Here again it approaches the meaning of *while.* But the contrast introduced by *when* is sharper than the contrast introduced by *while.* As a contrasting conjunction, *while* never entirely loses the sense of *although,* and none of this is carried by *when.*

These uses of *when* are all standard English, and have been for nine hundred or a thousand years.

When cannot be used to join a clause to a noun as children sometimes do in giving a definition, as in *intoxication is when you've had too much to drink.* There must be two full clauses, as in *a man is intoxicated when he has had too much to drink,* or *intoxication is the condition a man is in when,* and so on.

whence is a bookish word, not very much used in contemporary speech. It means "from what place" or "from which place," as in *look unto the rock whence ye are hewn.* It may also be used with the word *from,* as in *too proud to care from whence I came.*

whenever is used to introduce a clause and means "at any time" or "at whatever time," as in *come whenever you like.*

It is sometimes used to mean "as soon as," as in *we will start whenever you are ready.* This is a Scottish and Irish idiom. It is acceptable in the United States but not in England.

In Great Britain *whenever* is sometimes used as an interrogative adverb, as in *whenever will he come?* This is not considered a literary construction but it is accepted spoken English.

Whensoever is an archaic form of *whenever.*

where. This word is primarily an interrogative adverb meaning "in, at, or to what place," as in *I know where to go;* but it may also be used without the implication of a question and mean merely "in, at, or to which," as in *he is in heaven, where thou shalt never come.*

At one time the word *whither* was used to indicate "place to which," and the word *whence* to indicate "place from which." Both words are now archaic and in current English we express these ideas by means of *where.* The word *where* has not absorbed the meaning of *whence* and we have to add the word *from* to express this idea. We cannot say *where are you coming?* On the other hand, *where* has absorbed the meaning of *whither* and it is possible to say *where are you going?.* But we may emphasize this meaning by adding the word *to,* as in *where did it go to?* Some grammarians claim that this redundant *to* is improper, but it is used by educated people throughout the United States and can be found in the most formal writing. *Where* has always contained the meaning of "at" and sentences such as *where are you staying at?* are generally condemned. But they may become standard in time. It is as if the speech instinct argued: It was all very well not to say *at* when that was what *where* meant. But now that it means three things it should get a specifying word each time.

Where may be used in place of the phrase *in which* or *at which* to introduce a clause that qualifies a noun, as in *teas, where small talk dies in agonies.* Formerly it could also be used like the word *that* to introduce a clause that is the object of a verb, as in *I have heard where many of the best respect in Rome have wished that noble Brutus had his eyes.* This construction can still be heard today in the speech of educated people, as in *I read where a plane was lost,* but it is condemned by many grammarians and does not often appear in print. *Where* cannot be used, as the word *what* can, to introduce a definition, as in *perjury is where a man lies under oath.*

whereabout; whereabouts. These words mean the same thing and are used in the same ways. The form *whereabouts* is preferred, but *whereabout* is also acceptable. Either form may be used to qualify a verb, as in *whereabouts is it?* and *whereabout is it?* Either form may also be used as a noun. Both forms are considered singular and are followed by a singular verb, as in *her whereabouts is unknown.*

In current English the form *whereabouts* is sometimes followed by a plural verb, as in *her whereabouts are unknown*. This is heard too often to be called anything but standard, but it is distressing to some grammarians. Historically, the final *s* in *whereabouts* is an old adverbial ending, similar to the *s* sound in *once, twice, endways, towards,* and not a noun plural.

whether was once a pronoun or pronominal adjective and was used like the modern *which,* as in *whether thing is heavier, water or wine?*. Today it is always used as a conjunction and introduces an alternative. The choice may be between more than two alternatives, as in *for whether beauty, birth, or wealth, or wit, or any of these all, or all, or more.* Or only one may be mentioned, as in *I know not whether heaven will have it so.* Here one can say that the alternative *or not* is understood. Fifty years ago grammarians were insisting that this *or not* had to be expressed, on the grounds that if it was omitted *whether* ceased to introduce an alternative and became merely an adverb of doubt. But the struggle to tidy up the word was short-lived. It always had been used in just this way and still is. *Whether* is not used when there is no doubt. In literary English one does not say *I don't doubt whether you are right.* Here the conjunction *that* is required.

which. The word *which* is primarily an interrogative pronoun, as in *which do you like best?*, or adjective, as in *which boys did you send?* It may also be used as a relative to introduce a qualifying clause, as in *the books which I brought with me.*

When used as an interrogative, *which* may be singular or plural and may refer to persons, animals, or inanimate things. It always asks about some out of a definite, known group, in contrast to *what* or *who* which imply an undefined or unlimited group. That is, *which are you taking with you?* means which of these people or things we have been talking about. *Who are you taking with you* and *what are you taking with you* have no such limitation. The group implied by *which* is not necessarily limited to two members but may include any number greater than one, as in *I don't know which thought of it, John, Evelyn, or Sally.*

Theoretically the interrogative pronoun *which* is referred to by a third person pronoun such as *his* or *their* and we should say *which of you left his umbrella?* and *which of us have finished their work?* In practice we do use the third person form after *which of us* but are more likely to say *your* after *which of you.*

The interrogative *which* is often used in a subordinate clause, either as a pronoun, as in *I don't know which he took,* or as an adjective, as in *I don't know which road he took.* When used in this way it is sometimes confused with the relative *which.* There are important differences between these two uses of the word in contemporary English. (1) The relative *which* always represents a noun or pronoun that has

been mentioned previously. This is called its antecedent. The interrogative *which* asks about something unknown and cannot possibly represent a word already mentioned. (2) The interrogative clause always implies a question, while the relative clause gives information. (3) The interrogative *which* may refer to individual, adult human beings, but the relative *which* is no longer used in speaking of anything that is felt to have personality. (For the regular uses of the relative pronoun *which,* see **that; which.**)

Which may be used as a relative adjective, as in *we came to a cross roads, at which place we parted company.* Formerly, it might be used without an antecedent, as the equivalent of *that which* or *what,* as in *they interpret literally which the doctors did write figuratively,* but this construction is now obsolete. At one time the article *the* could be used before a relative *which,* as in (this world) *o'er the which we stride so fiercely* and *the which tokens of homage he received graciously,* but this is now obsolete.

Which can sometimes be used as the equivalent of *this* or *and this,* as in *if you had seen her, which I doubt.* Here *which* is not a relative because (1) it represents a clause and not a noun or pronoun, and (2) it introduces an independent or coordinate statement rather than a subordinate clause. This use of the word is standard English when it refers to something preceding. The construction is not standard when *which* is used in place of *what* to refer to something that follows, as in *which I wish to remark, and my language is plain—the heathen Chinee is peculiar.*

Whichever is an indefinite pronoun and can also be used as an adjective, as in *take whichever you like* and *take whichever piece you like.* It may be singular or plural. It does not refer to a preceding word in the sentence and should be thought of as a telescoped word containing a demonstrative and a relative pronoun, equivalent to *that* (or *those*) *which.* It is not an interrogative and should not be used in a question, as it is in *whichever did you take?* But it is like the interrogative *which* and unlike the relative *which* in its meaning. That is, it may be used in speaking of persons as well as of things, as in *ask whichever of the boys you see first,* and differs from *whatever* and *whoever* in that it implies a limited group. *Whichsoever* was once the preferred form, but this is now archaic.

while; whilst; whiles. These three words are conjunctions and are used to introduce a clause. The form *whiles* is now archaic, but *while* and *whilst* are both in regular use in Great Britain. In the United States *while* is the preferred form and many people consider *whilst* a would-be elegance.

The form *while* was originally a noun meaning "a space of time." It may still be used as a noun, either in a prepositional phrase, as in *once in a while,* or alone without a preposition to show "an extent of time," as in *stay a while* and *I've been waiting all this while. Wait a while* is grammatically comparable to *wait a minute,* but when used in this way, as an adverb of extent, custom allows the two words to be written together, as if they were a simple adverb, as in *wait awhile.* But when the same form is used after a preposition, as in *wait for awhile,* it is generally considered a mark of illiteracy. There is no justification for this distinction, since true adverbs sometimes follow a preposition, as in *away from here,* but many people feel very strongly about it.

When it is used as a conjunction, *while* may mean "at the same time," as in *it rained while Bill was at the theater.* Or it may be used to introduce a contrast. Used in this way *while* may have the force of *although,* as in *while Dave is good in mathematics, he is not good in English;* or it may have the force of *but,* as in *Mr. Chapman likes classical music while Jim likes modern jazz.* These three uses of *while* are all literary English and have been for centuries. Sometimes *while* is used where no contrast and no reference to time is intended, as in *Charlie comes from Michigan, Sandy comes from New Jersey, while Bill comes from New York.* Here it has only the force of *and.* This use of *while* is about a hundred years old and is usually condemned as "journalese."

whip. The past tense is *whipped* or *whipt.* The participle is also *whipped* or *whipt.*

whip hand. As a way of saying that one has a decided advantage over another, so decided that resistance would be useless, *to have the whip hand over* (formerly *of*) *him,* or just *to have the whip hand,* is a cliché.

whipped cream. Although the form *skim milk* is preferred to *skimmed milk,* the form *whipped cream* is preferred to *whip cream.* This may be because of the sound. Or it may be because thirty years ago a study of English usage chose *whip cream* to represent words of this kind and found that it was "illiterate." This may have kept students of domestic science from using the word. But nothing had been said about *skim milk* and so there they may have felt at liberty to do as they pleased. (This same study found that it was perfectly all right to speak of "driving" a car.)

whipsaw, literally, is a saw used for cutting curved kerfs, consisting essentially of a narrow blade stretched in a frame. Americans use the word figuratively in colloquial contexts to mean to win two bets from a person at one turn or play or, more loosely, to defeat or worst in two ways at once, or, even more loosely, simply to get the better of (*They were just hoodwinked and whipsawed by Michigan's slickers*). *Whipsaw* may be used figuratively as a noun to describe a double defeat, and as an adjective to mean violently opposing (*The Santa Vittoria reached Georges Banks with its whipsaw currents and dangerous shoal waters*).

whirl; whorl. Though their meanings are related, these words are not interchangeable. *Whirl* is both a verb and a noun; *whorl* is a noun only.

As an intransitive verb, *whirl* means to turn round, spin, or rotate rapidly (*In the ballroom the dancers wheeled and whirled*); to turn about or aside quickly; to move, travel, or be carried rapidly along on wheels or otherwise (*The stagecoach whirled merrily along*). As a transitive verb, *whirl* means to send, drive, or carry in a circular or curving course (*He whirled his hat across the room. Whirling a light malacca cane, he strolled along the avenue*). As a noun, *whirl* means the act of whirling, a rapid rotation or gyration, a whirling movement, a quick turn or swing (*The eddy and whirl of the whispering flood waters. He could see the whirl of the carousel in the distance*). In the United States *whirl* is also used in the slang expression *give it a whirl* meaning "have a try" (*I still think it won't hurt to give 'em a whirl and see*). This figurative use would seem to be drawn from the roulette wheel. To give a girl a whirl means to press attentions upon her, to hurry her from one pleasure to another, until she is, supposedly, giddy with delight.

Whorl is used only in special connections. In botany it means a circular arrangement of like parts, as leaves, flowers, round a point on an axis; a verticil. In zoology it describes one of the turns or volutions of a spiral shell. In anatomy it describes one of the turns in the cochlea of the ear. In general, it may describe anything shaped like a coil.

whiskers; moustache. *Whiskers* is not so inclusive a term as it once was. If used to describe the full beard now, the use is intended to be humorous and is confined to Santa Claus, hoboes, Russians, and other quaint folk. It is now used only dialectally to describe the hair growing on the upper lip; the more acceptable alternative is *moustache.* Yet the bristly hairs growing about the mouth of certain animals, such as cats and rats, are always *whiskers.* The slang expression of admiration, *It's the cat's whiskers!,* may simply be an elaboration of "outstanding." Sometimes *whiskers* describes the beard generally (*Admiral Blake was very fond of combing his whiskers*) but usually today the term describes the hair growing on the side of a man's face, especially when worn long and with the chin clean-shaven.

When people had more occasion to speak about whiskers than they have today, the hair on a man's face might be referred to generally as *whiskers,* or it might be called *a pair of whiskers,* or it might be treated as a singular, like the word *beard,* and called *a whisker,* as in *a tall gentleman with a carefully brushed whisker.*

white; whitened; whited. That is *white* which has the color of white, whether it has always had it or has acquired it some way. That is *whitened* which has become or been made white (*His hair whitened over night when he used up the last of his dye*). *Whited* has become fixed in a specialized pejorative sense by its use in Matthew 23:27: *Woe unto you, scribes and*

Pharisees, hypocrites! for ye are like unto whited sepulchres, which indeed appear beautiful outward, but are within full of dead men's bones, and of all uncleanness.

white as a sheet is a natural comparison. But to characterize pallor as *as white as a sheet* is to use a hackneyed expression.

white-collar is an American adjective which means belonging or pertaining to workers, professional men, and others who may wear conventional dress at work, especially clerical helpers and lesser executives (*D. H. Lawrence had a strong distaste for white-collar workers, men who lived by head rather than by hand*). The white-collar worker draws a salary rather than wages and is, for the most part, not organized into labor unions. The equivalent English term is *black coat*.

white elephant, as a term for a costly but useless possession, usually one that requires considerable maintenance and cannot be gotten rid of, is now a cliché. The term, once apt and simply worn out by overuse, is drawn, as is well known, from the fact that formerly in Siam immense importance was attached to an albino elephant. All that were born were the property of the King of Siam and none of them could be used for work or destroyed without his permission. It is said that he would sometimes bestow one of these beasts upon some courtier whom he disliked, the luckless recipient of this royal maleficent munificence being required to keep the creature in idleness at ruinous expense.

who; whom. The word *who* may be used as an interrogative pronoun or as a relative pronoun. In either case it may be singular or plural.

INTERROGATIVE

There are three interrogative pronouns, *which, what,* and *who.* The interrogative *which* asks about something belonging to a limited and known group. That is, *which do you want?* means "which, among those we are speaking about." It may refer to persons or to things and may be used as a pronoun or as an adjective, as in *which ones do you want?.* (See **which.**) *What* and *who* refer to an unlimited group. That is, *what do you want?* and *who do you want?* put no limits on what the answer may be.

Who is used only as a pronoun and only in reference to persons. *What* may be used as a pronoun or as an adjective and may refer to animals and inanimate things. The adjective *what* can be used in asking about a person's function, status, reputation, as in *who is Sylvia? what is she?* Three hundred years ago it could be used in asking about the person himself, as in *and what are you that live with Lucifer?,* but this is no longer customary. Today only the word *who* is used in a question of this kind and *what* suggests something subhuman or monstrous.

RELATIVE

Who is also used as a relative pronoun. That is, it may be used in a subordinate clause that qualifies a noun or pronoun which appears earlier in the sentence and which is represented in the clause by the word *who,* as in *I know the man who told you that.* Here *who told you that* qualifies the word *man,* which in turn is represented in the clause by *who.* The interrogative *who* may also be used in a dependent clause, as in *I know who told you that,* but it is unlike the relative in function and in meaning. The interrogative *who* never represents a preceding word, and always implies a question. That is, the sentence just given could be paraphrased as *I know the answer to the question: who told you that?* The relative does not imply a question and must refer back to another word.

As a relative pronoun *who* competes with *that* and *which,* and we do not have the clearcut distinctions that exist between the interrogative pronouns *which, what,* and *who. That* has been the standard relative pronoun for about eight hundred years and can be used in speaking of persons, animals, or things. Four hundred years ago *which* became popular as a substitute for the relative *that* and was used for persons, animals, and things. Three hundred years ago *who* also became popular as a relative. It was used in speaking of persons and animals but not of things.

This left English with more relative pronouns than it has any use for. Grammarians first tried to get rid of the relative *that* and failed. More recently they have tried to limit *that* to one kind of relative clause but they have not succeeded in this either. In the meantime, the users of English gradually restricted *who* until now it is used only in speaking of persons. In this specialized area it has driven out the relative *which,* and this is now used only in speaking of animals or things. *Who* may in time drive out *that* as a relative referring to persons, but it has not yet done so. For the difference between *that* and *which,* see **that; which.**

That may still be used in speaking of a person, as in *the child that has been subject to nagging is in perpetual terror.* It is required when the antecedent, that is, the word in the principal clause which the relative represents, is an interrogative pronoun, as in *who that has seen her can deny . . .* and *which of us that is over thirty would say. . . .* We apparently object to doubling these *wh-* words and saying *who who has* or *which of us who is.* On the other hand, the word *who* is required when the antecedent is the proper name of a familiar person, as in *Nathaniel Hawthorne who was born in 1804 entered Bowdoin College in 1821.* When the person is not familiar and is identified by the following clause, some grammarians claim that the relative *that* is required, as in *the Nathaniel Hawthorne that was born in 1776 was his father.* But *who* is also used here and is preferred by many people.

In current English *who* is preferred to *that* when the antecedent is a personal pronoun, as in *he who, we who.* Formerly it was customary to use *that* after a personal pronoun, as in *he that, we that*. This is still acceptable English but it now has a bookish tone. In speaking about more than one person the form *those who* is now preferred to *they* (or *them*) *who*.

The choice between *who* and *which* depends on what seems to have personality and what does not. We must use *which* and not *who* when we are speaking about a type, function, or role, and not about the actual person, as in *if I were his wife, which I thank goodness I am not* and *he is exactly the man which such a school would turn out. Which* must also be used in speaking about a group of people considered as a unit, as in *the family next door, which is large.* If we are thinking of the individual members of the group we use a plural verb and the pronoun *who,* as in *the family next door, who stay up till all hours.* Very young children are often spoken of as if they did not have personality. We might say *they had one child, which died in infancy* but we would certainly use *who* in *they had one child, who went away to college.*

When the relative refers to both a person and a thing, the rule is that we should use *that.* In actual fact we consider only the word that stands closest to the pronoun. We may say *anything or anyone who wasn't familiar to him* and *anyone or anything which had amused him.*

Theoretically a relative pronoun has the same person and number as its antecedent and these determine the form of the verb when the relative is the subject of the subordinate clause. But this rule is not strictly observed. (For exceptions, see **agreement: verbs** and **one.**)

INDEFINITE

At one time *who* could be used as the equivalent of a personal pronoun and a relative pronoun combined, such as *he who* or *they who,* as in *who was the Thane lives yet.* This is similar to the way in which we now use *what,* meaning "that which." The construction is no longer natural English when *who* refers to one or more specific individuals, as in the quotation just given. It may be used when *who* refers indefinitely to anyone or everyone, as in *who steals my purse steals trash,* but even here the form is archaic and *whoever* is preferred. See **whoever.**

WHOM

If English followed the rules of Latin grammar we would use the form *whom* whenever the word was the object of a verb or preposition and the form *who* (or *whose*) in all other situations. But this is not the way these words are used in English. The interrogative pronoun *who* is treated as an invariable form, similar to *what* and *which.* The relative pronoun has the two forms *who* and *whom,* but *whom* is used where the Latin rules would call for *who* more often than it is where they would call for *whom.*

Sentences such as *whom are you looking for?* and *whom do you mean?* are unnatural English and have been for at least five hundred years.

Eighteenth century grammarians claimed that this form ought to be the one used, but Noah Webster vigorously opposed this theory. He wrote: *"Whom did you speak to?* was never used in speaking, as I can find, and if so, is hardly English at all."* He goes on to say that this *whom* must be the invention of Latin students who had not given much thought to English, and concludes: "At any rate, *whom did you speak to?* is a corruption and all the grammars that can be found will not extend the use of the phrase beyond the walls of a college."

The literary tradition was with Webster and against the Latinists and this use of *whom* never became standard English. Today the form *who* is preferred when the word stands before a verb, as in *who did you see?* The form *whom* is required when the word follows a preposition, as in *to whom did you speak?,* but this is an unnatural interrogative word order. The form *whom* may be used, but is not required, when it follows the verb, as in *you saw whom?* A few people habitually observe the eighteenth century rules of grammar, but this is likely to be a disadvantage to them. To most of their countrymen, the unnatural *whom*'s sound priggish or pretentious.

In the case of the relative pronoun the situation is different and the form *whom* is required in certain constructions. Two of these however are purely literary. (1) The indefinite *who* is now archaic but if used, the Latin rules must be strictly observed, as in *whom the gods love die young.* (2) The form *whom* is required after *than,* as in *Beelzebub, than whom none higher sat* and *Dumas the Elder, than whom there never was a kinder heart.* Theoretically these sentences call for the subjective form *who,* but this irregular use of *whom* is so well established in our finest literature that all grammarians accept it as the standard idiom.

The form *whom* is also used as the subject of a verb when a parenthetical clause stands between the relative pronoun and the verb, such as *they say* in the lines from Shakespeare, *Arthur, whom they say is killed tonight,* and *I really think* in the sentence by Keats, *I have met with women whom I really think would like to be married to a poem.* This construction is used frequently in speech, as in *we are feeding children whom we know are hungry.* Many grammarians claim that it is a mistake and that *who* is required here. But this technically incorrect form represents the principal use of *whom* in natural English today. In sentences such as these either *who* or *whom* is acceptable to all except purists.

The form *whom* is required after a preposition, as in *the man to whom I spoke.* This construction can be avoided, as in *the man I spoke to,* but it is used more often, and is more acceptable, in a relative clause than it is in a question. When the relative is the object of a verb, *that* is generally preferred to *whom,* as in *a man that I respect,* or a contact clause containing no relative is used, as in *a man I respect.* Neither *that* nor a contact clause can be used after a proper name. Here *whom* is preferred to *who* when the word is the object of the verb; but *who* is also acceptable, as in *Fanny, who I hope you will see soon.*

whoever; whomever. *Whoever* is an indefinite pronoun and may be used as a singular or a plural. It can be thought of as a combined personal pronoun and relative pronoun, such as *he who* or *they who,* and is used in statements about everyone who fits the description that follows, as *whoever comes, whoever likes me.* It is not an interrogative and should not be used where no description can be given, as in *whoever do you mean?* and *I can't imagine whoever you are thinking of.* Sentences of this kind are not standard and nothing is saved by writing *whoever* as two words, as in *who ever do you mean?* However, a question such as *who ever heard of that?* is entirely different. Here *ever* is an adverb attached to *heard,* and is above reproach.

The form *whoever* is required whenever the word is the subject of a verb, as in *whoever told you that is mistaken.* It is also acceptable as the object of a verb or preposition, as in *ask whoever you see* and *ask whoever you speak to.* The form *whomever* is not required but may be used when the word is the object of the verb or of a preposition in the subordinate, descriptive clause. It should not be used when the word is the subject of the subordinate verb. For example, *whoever* is required and *whomever* would be a mistake in *he tells whoever comes along* and *he was angry with whoever opposed him,* because the form of the word is determined by the fact that it is the subject of the following verb, *comes* or *opposed,* and not by the fact that it is the object of a preceding verb, *tells,* or a preceding preposition, *with.* *Whomever* is an extremely literary word and should not be used unless it is used in the literary manner.

Whoever (and *whomever*) came into general use a little more than three hundred years ago. The King James Bible uses an older form *whosoever,* which is now archaic. A still older form, *whosomever,* was archaic in 1600 and does not appear in Biblical English, but it is still heard in rural areas in the United States.

In current English the possessive form of *whoever* is *whoever's,* as in *whoever's dog it is.* But an older form, *whosever,* is also used, especially when no noun follows, as in *whosever it is.* Since *whosoever* is a purely literary word, it has only the old possessive form *whosesoever.*

whole. See **complete.**

whorl. See **whirl.**

whose is a possessive pronoun. When used as the possessive form of an interrogative pronoun, it refers only to persons, as in *whose it is?* When used as the possessive form of a relative pronoun, it may refer to things as well as to

persons or animals, as in *a land whose stones are iron and out of whose hills thou mayest dig brass. A country whose rainfall is abundant* is better English than *a country, the rainfall of which is abundant.*

The form *who's* is a contraction of *who is* and should not be used in place of the possessive pronoun *whose.*

why. This word may be used at the beginning of a sentence to show surprise, as in *Why! This is a pleasure!* It may be used anywhere in a sentence so long as it means "the reason" or "for what reason," as in *I know why he didn't stay.*

The word *reason* is often followed by the word *why,* as in *I know the reason why he didn't stay.* This use of *why* is sometimes condemned as redundant or pleonastic, but the phrase *the reason why* is a standard English idiom, and has been for many centuries. Anyone who wants to can always omit words that are not strictly necessary to his meaning, but if this is done consistently the result is a stiff, unnatural English. As a rule, it is better to be natural than to be correct according to theories that other people have never heard of. (For *the reason is because,* see **because.**)

The use of *why* in the middle of a sentence, as a loose connective with no reference at all to a reason, does not have the same standing. Sentences such as *when I got there, why she was waiting for me* are heard only in careless or uneducated speech.

wide. See **broad.**

-wide. See **suffixes.**

wide awake; wide-awake; wideawake. *Wide awake* means fully awake, alert, keenly conscious and aware. In England *wideawake* and *wide-awake* may be used as adjectives meaning fully awake, with the eyes wide open (*He gave him a wide-awake stare*); alert, keen, or knowing (*only a wide-awake young man can fill the position*). As nouns, *wideawake* and *wide-awake* were used formerly to describe a soft, low-crowned felt hat. In the United States only *wide-awake* is now used as an adjective, though *wideawake* (especially in reference to the hat) once was.

wideness, width. See **breadth.**

wide open spaces. Used seriously in reference to the unsettled sections of the country, particularly the western desert and semi-desert, *the wide open spaces* is a cliché. Used facetiously, it is a bore.

wife. The plural is *wives.*

The expression *an old wives tale* contains an old form of the genitive and is equivalent to *an old wife's tale.* This is not an instance of a plural noun used as the first element in a compound. And *wife's* here means "woman's" not necessarily "married woman's."

wild horses could not drag it from me. As a hyperbolic affirmation of secrecy, the assurance that *wild horses couldn't drag it from me* is a cliché. The reference is to a form of torture and punishment in which each arm and each leg of the victim was attached to a horse and the horses were driven in different directions until the victim was dismembered.

will; would. *Will* is a present tense form. Its past tense is *would*.

He will does not have the *s* ending that we ordinarily expect in a present tense verb. This is because *will* is an ancient past tense form that had come to be felt as a present tense before English became a written language. *Would* is a new past tense that was created for it. Today *would* is sometimes used as the past tense of *will*, as in *he said he would come*, but it has also acquired a present tense meaning, as in *would you help me with this? Will* has a negative form *won't* which is less emphatic than the full form *will not*.

This verb has no infinitive, no imperative, no *-ing* form and no past participle. Because the words *will* and *would* are grammatically past tense forms, just as the word *went* is, they cannot follow (that is, they cannot be dependent on) another verb. We can no more say *might will* or *used to would* than we can say *might went* or *used to went*.

English also has a regular verb *to will* which has an infinitive, an imperative, an *-ing* form, and a past participle. It has a regular past tense *willed* and final *s* in the third person singular of the present tense, as in *what God wills*. This verb is used chiefly in the progressive (or continuing action) forms and is followed by a *to*-infinitive, as in *he is willing to go*. (When used without a following verb, the infinitive *to be* can always be supplied, as in *he willed it so*.)

The auxiliary verb *will*, with its past tense *would*, cannot be followed by a *to*-infinitive but requires the simple form of the verb, as in *he will go*. When followed by *have* and a past participle it expresses completed action, as in *he will have gone*. In present-day English the complementary verb must be actually stated or easily supplied from the context, as in *he won't go* and *why won't he?* But at one time verbs of motion could be omitted after verbs of willing and this construction is still heard occasionally, as in *murder will out*.

The auxiliary verb *will* originally meant to desire, wish, or choose. It is still used in this way, as in *will you come in?* and *who will have coffee?* It is also used to express determination. When used in this sense it is spoken with a heavy stress, as in *he WILL not see us* and *he WILL meddle in things that don't concern him.* But the principal use of the word *will* today is to indicate futurity. That is, it is used without any meaning of its own, simply to indicate that what is being said refers to the future. In a verbal phrase of this kind the principal stress falls on the meaningful verb and not on the auxiliary, as in *he will not SEE us* and *he will MEDDLE in everything.* In the United States *will* is used as a future auxiliary in all persons and in all types of sentences. (See **future tense.** For the English use of *shall* and *should* as future auxiliaries, see **shall; will.**) *Will* may also

be used to express what is customary or habitual, a timeless state of affairs, as in *a man will tire of carrying a baby before a nurse maid will* and *boys will be boys.*

The past tense form *would* is used in all the ways that the present tense form *will* is used. One of the principal uses of *would* is to show desire or determination. When used in this way it is a past subjunctive. (See **subjunctive mode.**) In this sense it does not refer to the past, but refers indefinitely to the present or the future, as in *would you help me?* and *he would come if he could.* When used in a conditional clause *would* always expresses volition or willingness, as in *if he would tell me.* To express a simple condition without the idea of willingness we must use a simple past subjunctive, as in *if he told me,* or the auxiliary *should,* as in *if he should tell me.*

Would is often used as a past subjunctive form of the simple future auxiliary. Here it always refers to the future. For example, the verb *hope* is followed by an indicative form of the verb and we say *I hope the snow will melt,* but the verb *wish* requires a past subjunctive form and we therefore say *I wish the snow would melt. Would* is used in place of the future *will* to indicate uncertainty or unreality. It usually has this meaning in the conclusion of a conditional statement, as in *what would you think if I told you . . . .* Sometimes this *would* is used apparently in place of a present tense verb, as in *I would think* and *it would seem.* Expressions of this kind represent the most extreme caution. The thinking or seeming is first placed in the future and then made conditional or uncertain. It is a very modest way of speaking.

Occasionally *would* is used in a future tense phrase that has been shifted to the past, as when *I know he will come* is changed to *I knew he would come.* Here *would* is a past indicative of the future auxiliary *will.*

Would is also used to express customary or repeated action. It may be used in speaking of the past but in that case the time when the repeated events occurred must be specified, as in *every morning he would get up at six.* If no time is specified *would* indicates that the action is customary or characteristic of the person spoken about and does not refer to the past, as in *what else would he do?, what would you expect him to do?,* and *that is what most men would do.*

Would is used with *have* in a conclusion following a contrary-to-fact condition, as in *I would have gone if I had known about it.* It cannot be used with *have* in a conditional clause. *If I would have known* is not standard. *Would* may be used in place of *had* in the expression *had rather.* (See **rather.**) It should not be used in place of *had* in the expression *had better.* (See **better.**)

Will and *would* may be contracted to *'ll* and *'d,* as in *he'll be here soon* and *he'd have come sooner if he could.* These contractions are standard spoken English and there is no reason why they should not be used in print.

win. The past tense is *won.* The participle is also *won.*

win hands down. As a term for winning easily, *to win hands down* is hackneyed. It is drawn, Partridge says, from a jockey's letting up on the reins and allowing his hands to fall when victory is certain.

wind. The past tense is *wound.* The participle is also *wound.*

This verb means twine or twist. Another verb, meaning blow a horn, has become confused with it. At one time the noun *wind,* meaning a moving current of air, was pronounced with the *i* as in *wine,* and there was a regular verb, *wind, winded,* meaning more or less "make a wind." One would say *he winded his horn.* But when *wind* came to be pronounced with the *i* as in *win,* the old verb seemed to have no connection with it and people began to say *he wound his horn.* Since horns of this kind do not play much part in our lives today, these words are now found chiefly in poetry and it is impossible to say which is the preferred form.

Since then, a new regular verb *wind, winded,* with the *i* as in *win,* has been formed from the noun *wind* with its modern pronunciation. This may either mean "exhaust the wind of," as in *the climb winded him,* or "get the wind of," as in *the hounds winded the fox.*

windshield; windscreen. American *windshield* equals English *windscreen.*

wire. During the nineteenth century *wire* used as a verb meaning to telegraph was considered an Americanism and people who used it were said to be "striving to debase the language." It is now thoroughly respectable (*It's wise to wire*). It may be followed by a clause, as in *she wired she was coming,* or by an infinitive, as in *she wired us to come.* The infinitive construction is also frequently used with the preposition *for,* as in *she wired for us to come.* This construction is condemned by some grammarians but is in respectable use in the United States.

wish. This verb may be followed by an infinitive, as in *I wish to see it.* It may also be followed by a clause, but the clause verb must have a past tense form, as in *I wish he was here.*

When *wish* expresses a desire that involves only the speaker it can no longer be followed by a direct noun object without the preposition *for,* as in *eagerly I wished the morrow.* This construction is now obsolete. But the form is still acceptable when the wish is for something or someone other than the speaker, as in *I wish the plan success* and *I wish them happiness.* See also **want.**

wishful thinking, although introduced only a generation ago, is already a cliché. It lent itself too facilely to a superficial explanation of other people's opinions.

wist. See **wot.**

wit. See **humor.**

with. Originally this word meant "against." This meaning survives in a few compound verbs,

such as *withstand, withhold.* But the usual meaning of the word today is "accompanying," as in *to go with.* By extension, it is used to indicate means or attendant circumstances, as in *cut it with the scissors* and *handle it with care.*

When *with,* meaning "accompanying," joins something to the singular subject of a verb, the rule is that the verb remains singular, as in *the sheriff with his men was at the door.* In practice, a plural verb is also acceptable here. See **agreement: verbs.**

With may be joined to a verb to indicate that the action is mutual, as in *talk with, agree with.* But occasionally it retains something of its old meaning of "against," as in *fight with, make way with, dispense with.*

with a vengeance, which meant originally with a curse or malediction thrown in for good measure, has been used as an intensive (even, formerly, of good things) for more than four hundred years. It is now worn out.

with bated breath, that is, with breathing reduced or subdued under the influence of awe or fright, is a cliché. *Bated,* now archaic, except in this phrase, is the participle of the verb to *bate,* to lower, reduce (*Yet I argue not/ Against Heaven's hand or will, nor bate a jot/ Of heart or hope*), an aphetic form of *abate.*

with might and main, usually *with all one's might and main,* is hackneyed. *Might* is the quality of being able and *main* is sheer brute force or violence.

withdraw. See **retreat.**

without may be used as an adverb with no object, as in *we must go without.* Or it may be used as a preposition with a simple noun or pronoun object, as in *without supper, without him.* The *-ing* form of a verb is treated as a noun and may be used after *without,* as in *they never met without quarreling.* But in current English *without* cannot be used as a conjunction to introduce a full clause. Formerly this use of the word was acceptable, as in *he may stay him; marry, not without the prince be willing.* The construction is still heard, as in *they never met without they quarreled,* but is no longer considered standard.

without let or hindrance, to mean unhampered, unimpeded, is a cliché. It is pompous and is often used as a jocular expression intended to ridicule pomposity but pompous in its jocularity. *Let* originally meant hindrance, impediment, obstruction. In 1649 it was possible to speak of one whose talents *recompensed his natural let in speech,* but the word is now archaic except in the phrase *let or hindrance.* Until quite recently, however, it survived in other combinations, such as *let and disturbance of the peace, doing as one pleases without let or inquiry, without let or stay.*

without rhyme or reason, unless used literally, as it might be in reference to some modern poetry, is a cliché.

withstand. The past tense is *withstood.* The participle is also *withstood.*

witness as a verb means to bear witness to, to testify to, to give or afford evidence of (*The* *fossils, in their own way, also witness to the glory of the Lord. The prisoner brought several persons of good credit to witness to her reputation*). As a synonym for *see* (*I witnessed an amusing incident yesterday*) it is now acceptable in American usage, but it is stilted and *see* is to be preferred where it is applicable. *Witness* is to be preferred where one's presence is formal or where one's seeing is likely to be the basis of subsequent testimony. One sees a new model automobile; one witnesses an accident.

witness stand; witness box. The place occupied by one giving testimony in court is called the *witness stand* in the United States, the *witness box* in England. These are usually shortened to *stand* and *box* respectively. The witness *takes the stand* and *enters the box.*

wives. See **wife.**

woke; woken. See **wake.**

wolf. The plural is *wolves.*

wolf in sheep's clothing. As a term for one whose inner evil nature or intention is concealed under an innocent-seeming exterior, *a wolf in sheep's clothing* is a cliché.

wolves. This is the plural of *wolf.*

woman. The plural is *women.* Compounds that have *woman* as a qualifying element have the form *women* in the plural, as in *women friends, women writers.* This is contrary to the usual practice in English, according to which the first element of a compound remains singular even when the whole is made plural, as in *lady friends, lady writers.*

When the first element of a compound is the object of the second element, and not a qualifier, only the singular form *woman* can be used, as in *woman haters.*

woman; female; lady; gentlewoman. *Woman* is the general term for the adult female of the human species (*Woman's place is in the home. Her voice was ever soft,/ Gentle and low—an excellent thing in woman*). It is a word of dignity (though the plural *women,* for some reason, does not have quite the same dignity) and is always to be preferred when in doubt. One of the finest touches in Shakespeare's delineation of Mistress Quickly's garrulous vulgarity is her indignation when, in the course of an argument, Falstaff calls her a woman (FALSTAFF: *Go to, you are a woman, go!* HOSTESS: *Who, I? No; I defy thee! God's light, I was never call'd so in mine own house before!*).

Female refers especially to sex. A woman is a female human being, and she is a female as a man is a male, but since the word is applicable to all females in all species in which there is a sexual differentiation, from philosophers to cockroaches (*The female of the species is more deadly than the male*), its application to a woman usually has a contemptuous implication (*She's a scheming female, my boy*). *Female* used to be used as an elegant euphemism for *woman* or *young woman* or *woman's* or *women's* (*A charming female, egad! Bolton's*

Female Academy for Accomplished Young Ladies. Recommended for All Female Complaints), but this usage is obsolescent and no longer even funny when used in mockery of its pretentiousness.

In England *lady* has a social connotation. Fowler calls it an "undress substitute" for *marchioness, countess, viscountess,* and *baroness.* It is also a courtesy title for the wife of a knight or baronet or the younger daughters of an earl. Such uses are unknown in America where *lady* carries implications of gentility (*She behaved like a lady*) but, in the proper democratic way, is used for almost any woman of whom one wishes to speak with some formality (*Is the lady of the house in?*). Well-meaning souls have carried it further until, in its excesses, it is almost a joke word (*"Who was that lady I seen you with?" "That wasn't no lady; that was my wife." The scrub lady called. Tables for ladies and gents*). It is sometimes used as a formal term in direct address (*Lady, you dropped your glove. I gave you the right change, lady! What are you arguin' about?*) but the proper form (and the more effective term if one wants to be disagreeable) is *madam.*

A *gentlewoman* is a woman of good family or breeding (*It has gotten so that you can't keep half a dozen young gentlewomen at their needlework but you are accused of running a bawdy house!*), but the word is now archaic and is used chiefly in hackneyed (*a decayed gentlewoman*) or facetious phrases. In America, except as a literary affectation, it is not used at all. See also **female.**

womanly. See **female.**

women. See **woman.**

won. See **win.**

wondrous is a bookish word, whether used as an adjective or an adverb. As an adjective it means wonderful, marvelous (*Some of serpent kind/ Wondrous in length and corpulence. When I survey the wondrous cross/ On which the Prince of glory died,/ My richest gain I count but loss,/ And pour contempt on all my pride*), though this use is archaic, surviving chiefly in humorous passages (*A saloon near a newspaper office is always a lovely institution, filling the nights with wondrous sights and sounds*). As an adverb it is archaic for *wondrously,* which is also a bookish term. As such, it means in a wonderful or surprising degree, remarkably (*There was a man in our town/ And he was wondrous wise./ He jumped into a bramble bush/ And scratched out both his eyes*).

wont. This is a present tense form. The verb does not have an infinitive or an imperative. The past tense is *wonted.* The participle is *wonted* or *wont.*

There was once a verb *won,* meaning "stay" or "be used to." It gradually disappeared from the language leaving only its two participles, *wonted* and *wont,* which came to be used as adjectives meaning "usual." This old construction survives today in such expressions as *his wonted energy* and *he is wont to act with energy,* where *wonted* is used only before a noun and *wont* only after a form of the verb *to be* and before an infinitive.

Out of this limited use of two words, some new verb forms have developed. There is a present tense, singular and plural, as in *he wonts to act with energy* and *they wont to act with energy,* and a past tense form, *in those days he wonted to act with energy.* The verb has no other forms, and these forms are very rare. Although they are standard, they are decidedly artificial.

This verb should not be confused with *want,* or with *won't,* which means "will not."

wood; forest; woods. A *forest* is an extensive wooded area, preserving some of its primitive wildness and usually having game or wild animals in it (*This is the forest primeval, the murmuring pines and the hemlocks. The National Forests are among our most valuable possessions*). In England *forest* is applied to an unenclosed tract, regardless of whether it has trees, used as a game preserve. The famous New Forest was not wholly wooded and there are deer forests in the Scottish Highland where there are few or no trees.

Wood or *woods* describes a wooded tract smaller than a forest and resembling one, but less wild in character and nearer to civilization.

Woods, when it means a grove of trees, usually takes a plural verb, as in *the woods are full of them* and *there are woods near the house.* But it is sometimes treated as a singular, as in *there is a woods near the house.* This is acceptable in the United States but not in Great Britain, where the singular form *a wood* is required, as in *there is a wood near the house.* In the United States the singular form, *a wood,* is a purely literary word. It suggests a romantic and poetic place utterly unlike any stand of trees in this country. The feeling that *woods* is singular is so strong in the United States that it has produced the adjective *woodsy,* as in *woodsy and wild and lonesome.* In Great Britain the adjective is always *woody,* as in *a woody glen.*

wood for the trees. As a figurative description of someone who is so taken up with details that he cannot see or loses sight of the whole, to say that he *can't see the wood for the trees* is to employ a cliché. It has been in use as a proverb for over four hundred years and it is more than two hundred years since Swift listed it as a cliché.

wooded; wooden; woodsy; woody. *Wooded* means covered with or abounding in woods or trees (*Heavily wooded banks were an important feature of flood control*). *Wooden* means consisting of or made of wood (*The wooden steps of the back porch had been painted battleship gray*). Used figuratively, *wooden* means stiff, ungainly, or awkward (*A wooden Indian is wooden in every sense of the word. The recruit gave the captain a wooden salute*). It may also mean without spirit or animation (*The only response to his encouragement was a wooden stare*), or dull and stupid (*These wooden-headed louts don't seem able to understand the simplest statements!*). There are several American idiomatic expressions containing *wooden,* such as the dreary, rustic jocularity, *don't take any wooden nickels. Woodsy* is an American word meaning of, like, suggestive of, or associated with the woods, sylvan (*Ship Island region was as woodsy and tenantless as ever*—Mark Twain). *Woody* has the special meanings of resembling wood (*The center of the stalk was a thick, woody substance*), or sounding as wood sounds when it is struck (*The piano had a dull, woody tone*). It shares with *wooded* the meaning of abounding in woods (*Between the hills and the river there was an extensive woody area*) but, unlike *wooded,* it is not qualified by an adverb (*a heavily wooded area, a woody area*).

woof; warp; web; weft. All of these words refer to weaving. The *warp* is a set of yarns placed lengthwise in the loom. The yarns which travel from selvage to selvage in a loom, interlacing with the warp, are called collectively the *woof* or *weft.* Sometimes *woof* is used more loosely in the sense of texture (*There was an awful rainbow once in heaven:/ We know her woof, her texture; she is given/ In the dull catalogue of common things*—Keats).

Something formed as by weaving or interweaving of warp and woof is a *web* (*Penelope's web was a means of delaying the acceptance of a proposal*).

woolen; woollen; woolly. *Woolen* (or especially in England, *woollen*) means made or consisting of wool (*The Western Isles of Scotland are famous for their woollen goods*). *Woolly* may also mean consisting of wool or having the property or feeling or appearance of wool, but even in this sense the wool is understood to be attached to its producer or what would seem to be its producer, unlike *woolen* which refers to a detached material (*My father gave me a woolly Shropshire lamb on my seventh birthday. In the most lucid brains we come upon nests of woolly caterpillars*). Keats's *and silent was the flock in woolly fold* is an exceptional use. Figuratively, *woolly* suggests blurred, imprecise (*This woolly, maggotty metaphysics . . . The third drink made his speech woolly*). In the United States the Old West was called, colloquially, *wild and woolly* because of its rough atmosphere. In England *woolly* is used colloquially as a noun to describe a sweater or other light outergarment of wool; in America it is used, or was when the object existed in the plural, to describe an undergarment of wool (*Ten below! Boy, you'd better put on your woollies*).

word of mouth. *By word of mouth* is a wordy way of saying "orally" or "verbally" or "he told me so." It is redundant and stilted, and to be avoided.

word's as good as his bond. To say, as an assurance that someone can be relied on, that he will keep his promises and fulfill his obligations, that *his word is as good as his bond* is to employ a wornout expression. *Bond* here means a written or signed agreement.

words cannot describe and **words fail** are hackneyed as hyperbolic phrases of introduction. If taken literally, the rest should be silence. If not to be taken literally, they should be omitted and the speaker or writer get on as best he can with what words he can command.

wore. See **wear.**

work. The past tense is *worked* or *wrought*. The participle is also *worked* or *wrought*. When this verb does not have an object, only the form *worked* may be used for the past tense or the participle, as in *he worked all day*. *Wrought* may be used when the verb has an object, as in *he wrought happiness for many* and *see what God hath wrought*, but even here it has a decidedly bookish tone. *Wrought* is preferred as an adjective in some expressions, such as *wrought iron*, but *worked* may also be used here.

   Work is sometimes used to mean "become," and in that case may be followed by an adjective describing what becomes, as in *the hinge worked loose*. When not used in this sense it may be followed by an adverb describing the working, as in *the hinge worked loosely*. See **use.**

work (for book). See **volume.**

worked to death has been worked to death. Let it rest in peace.

workingman; working-man; working man; workman; workmen. *Working man* is a general and vague term. It simply describes any man who works. English *working-man*, American *workingman* describe a man of the working class; more specifically, a man, skilled or unskilled, who earns his living at some manual or industrial work (*When Jurgis had first come to the stockyards he had been as clean as any workingman could well be*). *Workman* means specifically a man employed or skilled in some form of manual, mechanical or industrial work (*A workman's compensation law was passed late in the century*). Used in the plural, it differs from *workingmen* in plainly implying some skill (*I got me cunning workmen. The workmen always had their tools packed and were ready to quit on the stroke of four. We have had workmen in the house, papering, painting, plastering, tiling, sanding!*).

work one's fingers to the bone. As an expression for working very hard, used commonly in pitying or self-pitying reproaches, *to work one's fingers to the bone* is a cliché. Applied originally, in the nineteenth century, to seamstresses, it had a hyperbolic meaning that is now pretty well dissipated.

works. In Great Britain factories and industrial shops are sometimes called *works*, as in *the steelworks south of the town*, and opinion is divided as to whether the word takes a singular or a plural verb when used in this sense. The problem does not arise in the United States

where we use the word *plant* instead. *Plant* is clearly singular and takes a singular verb.

world. See **earth.**

world, the flesh, and the Devil. The *world* is the sum of worldly things, as opposed to spiritual matters. The *flesh* is human weakness with its susceptibility to the allure of worldly things. And the *Devil* is the tempter, always playing upon that susceptibility. The phrase is from *The Book of Common Prayer*. Used in any context but its original one, it is now a cliché, even when used humorously.

world of good, world of truth, world of trouble, etc. *World of* is used for "a great deal of" in a number of phrases. Most of them are now hackneyed.

world is mine oyster. When Ancient Pistol (in *The Merry Wives of Windsor*, Act II, scene 2, lines 3-4) said that *the world's mine oyster,/ Which I with sword will open,* he coined a metaphor so ludicrous and at the same time so apt that it caught the popular fancy and became a saying and in time a cliché. It's not quite so apt anymore. Artificial pearls are now superior to all but the very finest natural pearls and, as O. Henry observed, a sword is a far more suitable instrument than a typewriter for opening oysters.

worldly. See **earthen.**

worn. See **wear.**

worn-out. See **outworn.**

worse, worst. See **bad.**

worship. See **reverence.**

worth; worthy. These words are both adjectives and qualify nouns. *Worth* always follows the word it qualifies and is itself followed by an object. The object may be a noun, as in *the book is worth ten dollars,* or it may be the *-ing* form of a verb used with a passive meaning, as in *the book is worth reading*.

   The adjective *worthy* may stand before a noun, as in *a worthy cause*. It may be followed by an infinitive, as in *he is worthy to take his place*. The compound *worthy of* may be followed by a noun, as in *worthy of his position,* or by the *-ing* form of a verb, as in *worthy of taking his place*.

worth one's weight in gold. As a way of saying that something or someone is extremely valuable, usually spoken of someone who is not only efficient and industrious but exceedingly good-natured and willing as well, *it* or *he is worth its* or *his weight in gold* is a cliché. When spoken of persons, it loses some of its metaphorical value from the fact that quite a few persons (specifically anyone who owns more than $100,-000 and weighs less than two hundred pounds) are actually "worth," in the meaning of possessing that much wealth, their own weight in gold.

wot. The past tense is *wist*. The participle is also *wist*. There was once a verb *wit* meaning know. The infinitive survives in *to wit* and the *-ing* form in *witting* and *wittingly*. It had a past tense *wot*. Since there is very little difference between once knowing and still knowing, *wot* came to be felt as a present tense. Later a new past tense was made for it, *wist*. Exactly the same thing has happened with some other verbs, such as *can* and *ought*. Like these other verbs, *wot* did not have an *s* in the third person singular, as is seen in the expression *God wot*. Except in this expression, *wot* is no longer natural English. When it is revived for its archaic effect, a false *s* often appears, as in *he wots not of the danger*.

would. See **will.**

wound. See **wind.**

wove; woven. See **weave.**

wrack; rack. Both *wrack* and *rack* are correct in the sense of ruin or destruction, especially in the phrase *to go to wrack/rack and ruin*. Except for that phrase, however, *wrack,* a cognate of *wreck,* is more general than *rack,* a variant of *wrack.*

Rack, however, may be used in senses exclusively its own. It describes, for instance, a framework of bars, wires, or pegs, on which articles are arranged or deposited (*There was a clothes rack just inside the door*) or a spreading framework set on a wagon (*As a boy he rode the hayrack to and from the fields*). One of its best known meanings is an instrument formerly used for torturing persons by stretching the body. The terror of this particular instrument of torture caught the public imagination and the word, in consequence, appears in many figurative uses (*I am on the rack until I hear from him*). It is the figurative extension of this word as a verb that is used for a strain in mental effort (*I've racked my brains for a solution but haven't thought of a thing!*).

wrangle; wrangler. In England and America *wrangle* is to argue or dispute, especially in a noisy or angry manner (*The radio breakfast program has as its chief characters a married couple who wrangle*). However, in the idiom of the western United States, *wrangle* also means to herd, to tend horses. *Wrangler* has the general meaning of one who wrangles or disputes and the special western United States meaning of one who wrangles horses. *Little Joe, the wrangler,* hero of a pathetic Western ballad, was neither disputatious nor scholarly; he just took care of the horses. At Cambridge University, in England, up until 1909, *wrangler* was the name given to one of those in the first class of honors in mathematics. The man first on the list was called *senior wrangler,* and the other first classmen were numbered in decreasing order of merit, as *second wrangler, third wrangler.*

wrap. The past tense is *wrapped* or *wrapt*. The participle is also *wrapped* or *wrapt*. In the United States *wrapped* is generally preferred to *wrapt*. Both forms are used in Great Britain.

wrapt; rapt. *Wrapt* is a little-used variant spelling of *wrapped,* the past and past participle of *wrap,* to wind, fold, or bind about (*He carried an extra pair of shoes wrapt in a newspaper. The mother then brought a mantle down and wrapt her in it*). *Rapt* (etymologically akin to *rapture*) derives from a verb meaning to snatch or hurry away, to transport, ravish. It is now confined to ecstatic states of delight or contemplation in which we have been carried outside of ourselves (*Looks commercing with the skies/ Thy rapt soul sitting in thine eyes*), or, more loosely, engrossed or absorbed (*He found her in rapt contemplation of the necklace*).

wrath; wrathful; wrathy; wroth. *Wrath* is the noun meaning strong, stern, or fierce anger, deeply resentful indignation, ire (*The wrath of God descended upon them*); or vengeance or punishment, as the consequence of anger. *Wrath* is also used, though undesirably, as an archaic adjective meaning the same as *wroth.*

Wrathful is the attributive adjective meaning full of wrath, very angry, ireful (*Such wrathful words destroyed all hope of reconciliation*), or characterized by or showing wrath (*He shot him a wrathful glance*). *Wrathful,* by its very strength, its emphasis on an excess and impetuosity of anger, is a word to be used carefully. It should not be used where *angry* will do. *Wrathy,* originally early nineteenth century and chiefly American, is an informal expression meaning wrathful or angry. It is (fortunately) falling into disuse.

Wroth is a predicate adjective meaning angry, wrathful (*Cain was very wroth, and his countenance fell*). It is largely a literary word today.

wreck is often used colloquially in America to describe a person who is seriously disorganized in one way or another (*The ordeal made a physical and nervous wreck out of him*). *Wrecker* and *wrecking* also have special meanings in American usage. In America a *wrecker* or a *wrecking crew* tears down a building; in England it is a *housebreaking gang*. In America a *wrecking crew* removes wreckage from railroad tracks; in England it is a *breakdown gang*.

wrest; wrestle; wresting; wrestling. *Wrestle* and *wrestling* are related to, and derive from, *wrest* and *wresting,* yet their meanings must be distinguished.

Wrest means to twist or turn, pull, jerk or force by a violent twist (*He wrested the gun from him with a sudden motion*), or to take away by force (*England wrested much of eastern Canada from the French in the fighting that culminated with Montcalm's defeat at Quebec*), or to get by effort (*He wrested a bare living from a barren soil*). *Wresting* is the present participial form of *wrest,* meaning to extract or extort by twisting, pulling, turning.

Wrestle, as an intransitive verb, means to engage in wrestling, or to contend, as in a struggle for mastery; to grapple. As a transitive verb, it means to contend with in wrestling, to force by or as if by wrestling (*He wrestled the packing case to the corner of the storage room*). In the western United States *wrestle* also means to throw an animal for the purpose of branding. Though one wrestles with physical objects, the word is used figuratively where a struggle as fierce as a physical struggle takes place (*He wrestled with religious doubts all through the years at the seminary*). *Wrestling* is the act of one who wrestles. It commonly describes an exercise or sport, subject to special rules, in which two persons struggle hand to hand, each striving to throw or force the other to the ground.

wring. The past tense is *wrung.* The participle is also *wrung.*

write. The past tense is *wrote.* The participle is *written.* A past tense and participle *writ* were once literary English, as in *we are persuaded that he writ the truth* and *one whose name was writ in water.* This form is now archaic or dialectal.

Write may be followed by a clause, as in *she wrote she was coming,* or by an infinitive, as in *she wrote me to come.* The form *she wrote for me to come* is condemned by some grammarians but is in general use in the United States.

Write is frequently used without a true object, that is, without naming what is written, as in *write me soon.* This construction is standard usage in the United States but is considered illiterate by some British grammarians who claim that the preposition *to* must be used if the verb does not have a true object, as in *write to me soon.*

writer. See **man of letters.**

writer; the present writer; the author; I. Though these expressions are not downright incorrect, they are often superfluous. That is, an opinion which is obviously the author's opinion need not be introduced by *the present writer believes that . . .* or *it seems to the writer* or *the author maintains.* Though such expressions may seem less egocentric, more modest, than *I,* actually *I,* if any identifying word is needed, is the word to use. It is straightforward and brief and avoids the implication of over-solemnity that sometimes lies in the use of the third person when alluding to oneself.

written. See **write.**

wrong; wrongly. Only the form *wrong* can be used to qualify a noun, as in *the wrong answer.* Only the form *wrongly* can be used immediately before a verb, as in *the words were wrongly spelled.* Either form may be used

following a verb, as in *the words were spelled wrong* and *the words were spelled wrongly.* The form *wrong* is preferred to *wrongly* in this position.

wrong side of the tracks. In many American towns the railroad tracks did at one time make a clear social demarcation and whoever first observed this and used it as a symbol of social position coined a good phrase. It was meaningful, pungent, penetrating, and evocative. But like many good phrases it has been overworked and is now as tedious as the endless sniggering of the Restoration wits at those who had the misfortune to live in the city of London instead of in the West End. Furthermore with the proliferation of our cities and the decline of at least the social importance of the railroads the phrase has lost much of its meaning. It is now a hackneyed anachronism.

wrong tack. *On the wrong tack,* as a term for pursuing a wrong course of inquiry or conduct, is a jaded expression. In its original nautical use, the *tack* of a ship is her direction in relation to the position of her sails. When used of a progression on land, a *tack* is one of the movements of a zigzag course. In no sense is it merely a synonym for *direction.*

wrote. See **write.**

wrought. There is an amusing passage in one of Robert Benchley's essays in which he tells of his frenzied search for the present form of the verb of which *wrought* is the past participle. He thinks of *wrught, wrouft, wraft* and a few other strange combinations of letters and gives it up. And certainly anyone who tried to guess it from the analogy of other participles of the same sound would come to some queer conclusions. On the analogy of *caught,* it ought to be *wratch;* on that of *taught, wreach;* on *bought,* it should be *wruy;* on *thought, wrink;* on *fought, wright;* on *fraught, wreight.* Actually, as Mr. Benchley no doubt knew, it is the participle of the verb *work.* See **work.**

wrung. See **wring.**

X

X. There are very few words in English which begin with the letter *X.* In the great *Oxford English Dictionary* the entire section under *X* takes up less space than the single word *get.* The words that do begin with *X* are almost all scientific terms, consciously borrowed from Greek or made up to meet a special need. Two-thirds of them were coined in the nineteenth century. Because words beginning with *X* have been in the language such a short time and are used in such a restricted field, they are completely regular so far as usage goes and present no problems for the grammarian.

Xmas is an abbreviation of *Christmas.* Here *X* represents the syllable *Christ.* This is not a modern, commercial invention. *X* has been used in this way in English, as in *Xtianity* for *Christianity,* since at least the year 1100, and the form *Xmas* is found in print as early as 1551.

X-ray. In the United States this word is customarily written with a hyphen, probably because it became popular at a time when hyphens were popular. Similar scientific terms are usually written without the hyphen, as in *X chromosome.*

Y

y-clept; y-cleped. These are both participles and are the only surviving forms of an old verb *clepe* meaning call. One form is as good as the other and neither of them is good. The verb, already archaic, should be allowed to pass into oblivion and is included here only to complete the list of irregular verb forms found in English today.

ye. The word *ye* is a special form of the pronoun *you* that is no longer used in natural English. (For more about the history of this word, see **you; ye.**)

Many Americans believe that the word *the* was pronounced *ye* a few hundred years ago. This is based on a misunderstanding. Today, the letters *th* may represent either of two distinct sounds, both of which can be heard in the words *this thing.* At one time the first *th* sound, which is also heard in *the, that, they,* and so on, was represented in print by the letter *y.* Governor Bradford of Plymouth sometimes used this form in his writing and sometimes *th.* For example, in speaking of a renegade Mr. Blackwell, he wrote: *He declined from ye trueth wth Mr. Johnson & ye rest, and went with him when yey parted assunder in yt wofull maner.* Bradford was not usually so consistent, and he also wrote: *full litle did I thinke yt the downfall of ye Bishops . . . ,* and *they had done them no wrong, neither did yey fear them.* But regardless of which symbol he used to represent the sound, he pronounced these words as we do.

Current English, therefore, has a new adjective *ye,* which is pronounced like the old pronoun *ye.* It is used instead of *the* in the names of certain shops and restaurants, such as *ye olde gifte shoppe,* and should probably be called the "decorative *the*" or the "interesting *the.*"

year in and year out, as a term for continually, or for a very long time, is hackneyed.

yearn. This word may be followed by an infinitive, as in *I yearn to hear from you,* but not by the *-ing* form of a verb or by a clause.

yellow dog. In the United States *yellow dog* is used figuratively to describe a contemptible, worthless or cowardly fellow. *Yellow-dog contract* refers to a contract of employment which provides that the employee promises not to join a labor union under pain of dismissal if he does.

yellow journalism; yellow press. The use of sensational reporting and conspicuous displays as a means of attracting readers to a newspaper or journal is called in the United States *yellow journalism (The story she was playing up was a natural for yellow journalism: a messy divorce case involving some of Arizona's best people).*

The term is said to have originated in the New York *World* (1895) with a cartoon in which the central figure, a child, was in a yellow dress. The chief purpose of this color printing—then a novelty—was to attract attention. The expression was borrowed by the English but slightly adapted to the *yellow press.*

yeoman's service. To say of one who or something that has performed a task or fulfilled a function efficiently and usefully that he or it has *done yeoman's service* is to employ a cliché.

yes man is an an American slang expression to describe one who registers unequivocal agreement with his superior, without consideration; a man who never takes an independent stand *(A military staff conference is an excellent situation for the encouragement of yes men. In Wakeman's* The Hucksters *the hero is defeated when he realizes that he too has become a yes man).*

yet; already. These words are both adverbs of time. *Yet* may also be used as a conjunction. German-speaking people sometimes have difficulty distinguishing *yet* and *already.* Sometimes in desperation they use both words at once, as in *he's a sergeant already yet.* But the words are not interchangeable and one cannot be used where the other is needed.

Already shows that an action has occurred or was occurring at a particular time. It is used with verbs in the perfect or progressive tense forms, but in literary English it is not used with a verb in the simple past or future tense unless the verb itself names a continuing action. That is, one may say *he already knew about it* but not *he already looked at it.* A perfect or progressive form is required here, as in *he has* (or *had*) *already looked at it* or *he was already looking at it.* (In the United States this rule is frequently disregarded in speaking of something in the past. Many educated people would say *I already saw that movie.* Sentences of this kind are therefore acceptable spoken English in this country, but they do not appear in print. The rule is never disregarded in speaking of something in the future. One can say *tomorrow he will have seen it already* but a sentence such as *tomorrow he will see it already* is simply not English.)

Yet, used as an adverb of time, indicates that an action or condition (usually a negative condition) existed for an indefinite period preceding a particular moment. The word *yet* is usually a counterpart of *already,* but occasionally it encroaches on the meanings of *still.* Like these words, it cannot be used with a simple past or future tense verb unless this is understood in a continuing or progressive sense. (This rule is never disregarded in speaking of the past. We do **not** say *he looked at it yet.* The word may be **used** with a simple future tense, as in *he will look at it yet,* but then it takes on the peculiar meaning of "nevertheless" or "in spite of everything.")

Both words, *already* and *yet,* can be used in both affirmative and negative questions, as in *has* (or *hasn't*) *he seen it already?* and *has* (or *hasn't*) *he seen it yet?* The word *already* can also be used in an affirmative or a negative *if* clause and in an affirmative statement, as in *if he has* (or *hasn't*) *seen it already* and *he has seen it already.* It cannot be used in a negative statement. We do not say *he hasn't seen it already.* The word *yet,* in the sense in which it is a counterpart of *already,* can be used in both types of question, as illustrated above, and in a negative *if* clause, such as *if he hasn't seen it yet,* or a negative statement, such as *he hasn't seen it yet.* It cannot be used in an affirmative *if* clause or an affirmative statement. We do not say *if he has seen it yet* or *he has seen it yet.* (*Yet* may be used with a progressive verb form in an affirmative statement or *if* clause, where it is equivalent to *still,* as in *he is looking at it yet.* In this sense *yet* is a bookish word and *still* is generally preferred.)

Yet may be used to qualify the comparative form of an adjective or adverb, as in *louder yet.* Here it has the same meaning as *still.*

It may also be used as a connective or loose conjunction to introduce a contrast or contradiction. When used as a connective it stands immediately before the contrasting word or phrase, as in *he is old yet energetic.* This may be a full sentence, as in *yet I believe what he says.*

Yiddish; Hebrew. *Yiddish* is a language used by many Jews, but it is not linguistically related to the Hebrew language. *Yiddish* is actually a group of closely similar High German dialects, with vocabulary admixture from Hebrew and Slavic, written in Hebrew letters, spoken mainly by Jews in countries east of Germany and by Jewish emigrants from these regions, and now the official language of Biro-Bidjan, an autonomous Jewish region in the southeast part of the Soviet Union in Asia. *Hebrew* is the name of a Semitic language, the language of the ancient Hebrews, which although not a vernacular after 100 B.C. was retained as the scholarly and liturgical language of the Jews and now is used as the language of Israelis. See also **Hebrew; Israelite.**

yoke. When this word means a pair of draft animals, it has the same form in the singular and the plural, as in *a yoke of oxen, five hundred yoke of oxen. Yoke* cannot be treated as a numeral. It cannot be placed immediately before a noun but must be joined to it by *of.*

yonder may be used as an adjective, as in *on yonder hill there lives a maiden,* or as an adverb, as in *but, as I live, yonder comes Moses.* The word is archaic in either construction.

Yorick. See **Alas, poor Yorick!**

you; ye. At one time, normal everyday English had four related words, *thou, thee, ye,* and *you,* **which** corresponded to the four related words *I, me, we,* and *us.* Today, of the first group,

only the one form *you* is in general use.

In the thirteenth century the plurals *ye* and *you* were used in speaking to a single person, as a mark of respect. This is still the practice in many European languages. But in England this courtesy was gradually extended to everybody, even one's own children, and the singular forms *thee* and *thou* disappeared entirely. (See **thee; thou.**) We are paying for this excessive politeness today by not having any way to distinguish between a singular and a plural *you.* For a time a plural verb was used in speaking to several people, as in *you were there,* and a singular verb, in speaking to only one person, as in *you was there.* But this distinction is no longer standard and *you* is now always used with a plural verb. In Ireland the old *ye* is sometimes used to indicate a plural, but this is not standard English. In the Southern United States *you all* is an accepted and respectable plural of *you.* But in literary English the plural cannot be shown except by adding some other word, as in *you ladies, you people.*

Of the two plural forms, *ye* was the subjective pronoun comparable to *I* and *you* the objective pronoun comparable to *me.* The difference in use is seen in *ye shall know the truth and the truth shall make you free.* But by the year 1600, *you* was generally used for the subject as well as the object of a verb and *ye* disappeared from natural English. If grammar books had not become so popular a hundred years or so later, the same thing might have happened to the other subjective pronouns, *I, we, he,* and so on, and questions about case, such as when to use *I* and when to use *me,* would no longer exist.

The pronoun *you* may also be used indefinitely in the sense of "one" or "anyone," as in *at that time you had to have property to vote.* This is good, literary English. But the construction must be handled with care. If it is at all possible to apply the word *you* to oneself, somebody is going to do it, and general statements such as *when you think how insignificant you are* or *when you have had too much whiskey* are likely to be taken in the wrong way.

When used as a term of abuse *you* may appear after the principal word as well as before it, as in *you fool you, you traitor you.*

you took the (very) words (right) out of my mouth, as a way of saying that someone has anticipated you in expressing a thought or has said what you were about to say, is a cliché.

young; youthful. *Young* is the general word for that which is undeveloped, immature, and in the process of growth (*The young trees must be protected from the strong west winds. Bliss was it in that dawn to be alive,/ But to be young was very heaven!*). *Young* may be applied not only to persons but to things and institutions (*Young hares are called leverets. We're living in a young country, don't forget that!*). *Youthful* has connotations suggesting the favorable characteristics of youth, such as vigor, enthusiasm, hopefulness, and freshness and physical grace (*How do you keep your youthful figure?*). Only the young are young, but we all long to be youthful.

young in heart. Usually applied to those among the elderly who are hopeful and good-natured and are interested in the affairs of others in a helpful way, *young in heart* is hackneyed. It's really not very apt, for the hearts of the young are often tortured and timid and almost always self-concerned.

your; yours. The form *your* is used to qualify a following noun, as in *your uncle, your careful consideration.* The form *yours* is used in any other construction, as in *an uncle of yours, yours truly. Yours* is also the form used in a double possessive where it is separated from its following noun by *and,* as in *yours and your uncle's opinion.* Today this construction is generally avoided and *your opinion and your uncle's* or *your own and your uncle's opinion* is used instead. Neither word order shows clearly whether we are talking about one thing or two, but the old-fashioned form, *yours and your uncle's,* suggests one thing possessed in common more strongly than the forms which use *your.*

The word *your,* like the word *you,* may be used indefinitely in the sense of *anyone's* or *the,* as in *your gravest beast is the ass.*

Your means "pertaining to you." It must not be confused with *you're,* which means "you are."

In current English the word *yours* is never written with an apostrophe.

your earliest convenience. As a term for "soon" or "when you can" or "as quickly as possible," *at your earliest convenience* is hackneyed.

yourn. This word was once acceptable English but it has not been used in the literary language for three hundred years. The only acceptable form today is *yours.*

yourself; yourselves. Originally, the word *self* could be used as a singular or as a plural and *yourself* was the reflexive form of the plural pronoun *you.* The form *yourselves* did not appear until the sixteenth century. Since then, the word *you* has come to represent one person as well as more than one. Today we use the form *yourself* in speaking to one person and the form *yourselves* in speaking to more than one.

Yourself and *yourselves* are sometimes used in place of the personal pronoun *you,* as in *yourself and your friends are invited.* Thirty years ago this construction was frowned upon. But it provides a singular and a plural form for the word *you* and many people like it for this reason. It is in better standing today than it was thirty years ago, and, although it is not literary English, it can no longer be regarded as unacceptable.

For the regular uses of *yourself* and *yourselves,* see **reflexive pronouns.**

yous. Some grammarians feel that the word *yous* is an attempt to create a separate plural form for the word *you,* comparable to the Southerners' *you all.* Presumably the word *you* would be used in speaking to one person and the word *yous* in speaking to more than one. This is a distinction which the language needs. But in New York City, a single person is often addressed as *yous.* In any case, no matter what the word means, it is not standard today.

youth. When this word means a young person, it is a true singular and has a regular plural in *s,* as in *one youth* and *two youths.*

The singular form may also be used with the article *the* as a group name, to mean all the young people in a given area. In this sense it takes a plural verb, as in *the youth of this city are well behaved.* But this is not a true plural and the word cannot be used with a numeral or a word implying number. In standard English we may speak of *twenty youths* but not of *twenty youth* or *many youth.* When used in this sense the word is distinctly literary. In normal speech we say *young people* or *the young.* For this reason, anyone using *youth* in this way should use it correctly. Otherwise he is distinguishing himself by his mistakes.

When *youth* means the period in which one is young, it is a mass word and, traditionally, does not have a plural form. In literary English we say *they knew each other in their youth.* The plural form is sometimes heard, as in *they knew each other in their youths.* This is not literary English and is offensive to some people. But here the word *youth* is not being used pretentiously. In this sense it is part of normal speech. And the plural construction is heard too often not to be recognized as standard English.

Z

zany, for a fool, especially a rustic, exuberant fool, is archaic. It is all right to use it in historical contexts or where one deliberately seeks a rustic or antique flavor, or for humorous effect, or in any way at all so long as one is aware that it is out of fashion and bookish.

zeugma. See **syllepsis.**

zoom. To *zoom* is to drive an airplane suddenly and sharply upward at great speed for a short distance, as in regaining altitude, clearing an obstacle, signaling, and so on. It may be used transitively and intransitively (*He zoomed unexpectedly. He zoomed his plane unexpectedly*). It is incorrect to use it of a downward motion (as in *Albert zoomed down the incline in two minutes flat, seconds ahead of his nearest competitor*).